HARRIS, O'BOYLE & WARBRICK: LAW OF THE
EUROPEAN CONVENTION ON HUMAN RIGHTS

HARRIS, O'BOYLE & WARBRICK
LAW OF THE EUROPEAN CONVENTION ON HUMAN RIGHTS

Second edition

DAVID HARRIS LLM, PHD, CMG
*Emeritus Professor in Residence, and Co-Director, Human Rights Law
Centre, University of Nottingham*

MICHAEL O'BOYLE LLB, LLM
Deputy Registrar, The European Court of Human Rights

ED BATES, LLB, LLM PHD
Lecturer in Law, University of Southampton

CARLA BUCKLEY, LLB, LLM
Research Associate, Human Rights Law Centre, University of Nottingham

Chapter 8 by
COLIN WARBRICK MA, LLB, LLM
Honorary Professor, University of Birmingham

Chapter 9 by
URSULA KILKELLY BA, LLM, PHD
Senior Lecturer, Faculty of Law, University College Cork

Chapter 10 by
PETER CUMPER LLB, LLM
Senior Lecturer in Law, University of Leicester

Chapter 11 by
YUTAKA ARAI LLM, PHD
Senior Lecturer in International Law, University of Kent

Chapter 20 by
HEATHER LARDY LLB, PHD
Senior Lecturer, University of Aberdeen

OXFORD
UNIVERSITY PRESS

OXFORD
UNIVERSITY PRESS

Great Clarendon Street, Oxford OX2 6DP

Oxford University Press is a department of the University of Oxford.
It furthers the University's objective of excellence in research, scholarship,
and education by publishing worldwide in

Oxford New York

Auckland Cape Town Dar es Salaam Hong Kong Karachi
Kuala Lumpur Madrid Melbourne Mexico City Nairobi
New Delhi Shanghai Taipei Toronto

With offices in

Argentina Austria Brazil Chile Czech Republic France Greece
Guatemala Hungary Italy Japan Poland Portugal Singapore
South Korea Switzerland Thailand Turkey Ukraine Vietnam

Oxford is a registered trade mark of Oxford University Press
in the UK and in certain other countries

Published in the United States
by Oxford University Press Inc., New York

© Oxford University Press, 2009

The moral rights of the authors have been asserted

Crown copyright material is reproduced under Class Licence
Number C01P0000148 with the permission of OPSI
and the Queen's Printer for Scotland

Database right Oxford University Press (maker)

First published 1995
2nd edition 2009

British Library Cataloguing in Publication Data

Data available

Library of Congress Cataloging in Publication Data

Data available

Typeset by Newgen Imaging Systems (P) Ltd., Chennai, India
Printed in Great Britain
on acid-free paper by
Ashford Colour Press Ltd., Gosport, Hampshire

ISBN 978-0-40-690594-9

1 3 5 7 9 10 8 6 4 2

PREFACE

The European Convention on Human Rights has developed remarkably since the first edition of this book in 1995. The number of states subject to it has increased greatly, mainly as a result of the admission of post-communist states to the Council of Europe. For this and other reasons, the number of applications registered annually has grown astonishingly, causing a spectacular increase in Strasbourg's workload. In response, radical changes to the system of supervision were made by Protocol 11. Most notably, the two part-time bodies that used to rule upon applications—the European Commission on Human Rights and the European Court of Human Rights—were replaced by a single full-time Court which now operates a more streamlined procedure. The opportunity was also taken to improve the extent and quality of the Convention remedy by making the right of individual petition compulsory for all states parties and by providing for the final decision in all admitted cases to be taken by the Court, with the role of the Committee of Ministers to take some such decisions being eliminated. But Protocol 11 did not solve the workload problem, despite the huge army of lawyers recruited to the Court's Registry. More changes to speed proceedings were adopted in Protocol 14, but this is not yet in force, notoriously requiring one further and not immediately likely ratification—by Russia. In any event, Protocol 14 would not provide a complete answer; more reforms, yet to be agreed, are needed. Currently, the Court functions on the basis of a permanent emergency regime, with a huge backlog of cases that will not go away in the foreseeable future. The sad situation is that what was in 1995 unquestionably the most successful system for the international protection of human rights is, while still deserving of that description, now seriously at risk of a lowering of its reputation and effectiveness, unless further radical steps are taken.

One consequence of the great increase in the Court's workload is the overwhelming number of judgments that the Court now gives annually, with consequential problems for those, such as the authors of this book, who try to keep up with the Court's jurisprudence. The constant flood of judgments on the right to a fair trial under Article 6 is the most striking example. More positively, the mass of judgments has contributed considerably to the clarification and development of the Convention guarantee. Whereas in the first edition of this book there was not a single Court judgment under Article 2 (the *McCann* case was still pending), there is now a host of such judgments giving meaning to the right to life. Another positive feature has been the continued creativity and dynamism apparent in the Court's interpretation of the Convention. The development of positive obligations to protect life, the introduction of a 'right to the environment', supportive judgments on sexual orientation and gender identity, and the evolution of the right to property are examples. Another striking feature of post-1995 case law has been the high proportion of the Court's new jurisprudence that derives from cases coming from post-communist states. A further development has concerned the relationship between the Convention and the European Union, whose members are all Convention parties. At the same time as the Union has been articulating its own fundamental rights law and the Strasbourg Court has found a way in the *Bosphorus* case for the two regimes to co-exist, constitutional provision has been for the Union to adhere to the Convention and the European Court of Justice frequently relies upon the Convention in its own judgments.

At the national level, the most notable development for the United Kingdom has been the entry into force of the Human Rights Act, 'bringing home' the Convention. A consequence has been a substantial impact upon United Kingdom law in the area of human rights, with the Convention being relied upon and developed by the national courts to great effect.

Many of the above considerations have made the preparation of this second edition a daunting task. Updating the book on the scale of the first edition has required a larger team of contributors. Of the original authors, Michael O'Boyle and David Harris were available to participate substantially as before. In Michael's case, his chapters were prepared with the considerable assistance, both in research and in drafting, of Paul Harvey, a member of the registry of the Court. The authors would like to express their appreciation to Paul for his valuable contribution, in particular to Chapters 22 to 24. Colin Warbrick was not in a position to contribute as fully as before, but did update Chapter 8, for which we are very grateful. It is also important to record that much of the text of the other chapters which Colin wrote remains in place and that his influence on the character of the book as a whole is still fully apparent. Two new authors, Ed Bates and Carla Buckley, were brought in and have made large contributions. In addition, particular chapters have been updated by other contributors, namely, Yutaka Arai, Peter Cumper, and Ursula Kilkelly. Chapter 20 was updated by Heather Lardy and Ed Bates. Michael O'Boyle and David Harris would like to express their thanks and gratitude to all of the new members of the team, in some cases working under considerable time pressure, for taking part in what has been a most challenging endeavour. All of the contributors would like to express their sincere thanks to Dr Anne Lister, Research Fellow at the University of Nottingham Human Rights Law Centre, who was responsible for ensuring that the footnotes throughout the book were in style and consistent. We would also like to thank Genevieve Woods of the European Court of Human Rights Library for her kind assistance with the Note on Citations.

The views expressed in this book are personal to the authors and do not represent the views of any institution.

The publication of this edition is timely because it coincides with the 50th anniversary of the European Court of Human Rights. It is the hope that it will assist students, practitioners, and others in understanding and working with what, despite its difficulties, remains the most sophisticated international system of human rights protection and one providing a human rights remedy of the first importance for persons in Europe.

David Harris
Michael O'Boyle
Ed Bates
Carla Buckley
7 November 2008

TABLE OF CONTENTS

NOTE ON THE CITATION OF
STRASBOURG CASES

The footnote references to Strasbourg cases in this book cite (i) the official reports of the European Commission of Human Rights and the European Court of Human Rights, and (ii) the European Human Rights Reports

Official Reports

Before 1996, there were two series of publications of the judgments of the Court by way of official reports, in English and French: Series A (Judgments and Decisions) and Series B (Pleadings, Oral Arguments and Documents). Series B was incomplete, ceasing with volume 104, published in 1995. Series A reports are cited as follows: *Soering v UK* A 161 (1989).

As of 1996, the Series A volumes, which were for individual cases, were replaced by annual volumes of the *Reports of Judgments and Decisions*, containing Court judgments, or extracts from them, plus some decisions as to admissibility or extracts from them. Many judgments and most decisions as to admissibility are not published in the official reports.

From 1996 to 1998 these official reports covered both the Commission and the Court; from 1999 they cover only the Court, following the demise of the Commission. The annual volumes are published as separate parts. The judgments and decisions are published in English and French. Citations indicate the volume and part, but not the page number within the volume. Eg. *Khan v UK* 2000-V. There is no equivalent to the Series B reports.

Of great importance is the Court's HUDOC database, to be found on the Council of Europe website: http://www.echr.coe.int/echr/. HUDOC has all the recent Court judgments and admissibility decisions, whether they are printed later in the official reports or not. Judgments in HUDOC are cited as follows: *Ploski v Poland* hudoc (2002). Decisions as to admissibility are cited as follows: *Gonzalez v Spain No 43544/98* hudoc (1999) DA. DA is added to assist in finding the case in HUDOC. HUDOC judgments are in English and French or, in the case of less important cases, English *or* French.

Some report series are specific to the former European Commission of Human Rights:

Collection of Decisions of the European Commission of Human Rights.
This series (volumes 1–46, 1959–1974) was published by the Council of Europe in English and French. These are cited as follows: *X v Norway No 867/60* 6 CD 24 1961.

Decisions and Reports of the European Commission of Human Rights.
This series (volumes 1–94, 1975–1998) was published by the Council of Europe. It contains in English and French selected Commission decisions as to admissibility; Commission friendly settlement reports; and Commission reports on the merits under the former Article 31 of the Convention when the case was not referred to the Court. In the case of an Article 31 report, the Committee of Ministers resolution is also printed. As of volume 76, the volumes are published as volumes 76-A and 76-B, etc, with volume A containing the original language of the decision, etc, and volume B containing the translation.

Digest of Strasbourg Case-Law Relating to the European Convention on Human Rights, vols 1–5 and an index (vol 6), published 1984–1985, plus 11 looseleaf supplements published to 1997. Although linked to the Council of Europe, the Digest is not strictly an official source. It contains extracts from some Commission cases not reported elsewhere. These are cited as follows: *No 7126/75 (1977)* 1 Digest 87

European Court of Human Rights Reports

This commercial series publishes in English only the judgments of the European Court of Human Rights and certain Commission reports and decisions as to admissibility. Cases are cited as follows: *Soering v UK* A 161 (1989); 11 EHRR 439.

LIST OF EUROPEAN COURT OF HUMAN RIGHTS AND EUROPEAN COMMISSION OF HUMAN RIGHTS CASES

LIST OF NATIONAL COURT CASES

LIST OF HUMAN RIGHTS
COMMITTEE CASES

LIST OF EUROPEAN
COURT OF JUSTICE CASES

1

THE EUROPEAN CONVENTION
ON HUMAN RIGHTS
IN CONTEXT

1. BACKGROUND

The European Convention on Human Rights[1] was adopted in 1950. It was drafted within the Council of Europe, an international organization that was formed after the Second World War in the course of the first post-war attempt to unify Europe. The reason for the Convention was partly the need to elaborate upon the obligations of Council membership.[2] More generally, the Convention was a response to current and past events in Europe. It stemmed from the wish to provide a bulwark against communism, which had spread from the Soviet Union into European states behind the Iron Curtain after the Second World War. The Convention provided both a symbolic statement of the principles for which West European states stood and a remedy that might protect those states from communist subversion. It was also a reaction to the serious human rights violations that Europe had witnessed during the Second World War. It was believed that the Convention would serve as an alarm that would bring such large-scale violations of human rights to the attention of other West European states in time for action to be taken to suppress them. In practice, this last function of the Convention has remained largely dormant, playing a role so far in just a small number of inter-state applications and cases arising out of the state of emergency in

---

[1] 87 UNTS 103; ETS 5. See generally Frowein and Perkert, *Europaische Menschenrechts Konvention: EMRK-kommentar*, 2nd edn, 1996; Greer, *The European Convention on Human Rights*, 2006 (hereafter *European Convention*); Janis, Kay, and Bradley, *European Human Rights Law*, 3rd edn, 2008; Leach, *Taking a Case to the European Court of Human Rights*, 2nd edn, 2005; Macdonald, Matscher, and Petzold, eds, *The European System for the Protection of Human Rights*, 1993 (hereafter *European System*); Mahoney, Matscher, Petzold, and Wildhaber, eds, *Protecting Human Rights: the European Perspective: Studies in honour of Rolv Ryssdal*, 2000 (hereafter *Ryssdal Melanges*); Matscher and Petzold, eds, *Protecting Human Rights: the European Dimension: Studies in Honour of Gérard J Wiarda*, 1988 (hereafter *Wiarda Mélanges*); Pettiti, Decaux, and Imbert, *La Convention européene des droits de l'homme*, 2nd edn, 1999; Reid, *A Practitioner's Guide to the European Convention on Human Rights*, 3rd edn, 2008; Robertson and Merrills, *Human Rights in Europe*, 4th edn, 2001; Van Dijk and Van Hoof, *Theory and Practice of the European Convention on Human Rights*, 4th edn, 2006; White and Ovey, *Jacobs and White: The European Convention on Human Rights*, 4th edn, 2006. On the drafting of the Convention, see Marston, 42 ICLQ 796 (1993); Simpson, *Human Rights and the End of Empire: Britain and the Genesis of the European Convention*, 2001; Teitgen, *European Supervision*, Ch 1; and Wicks, 2000 PL 438.

[2] Under Article 3, Statute of the Council of Europe 1949, 87 UNTS 103; ETS 1, a member state 'must accept the principles of the rule of law and of the enjoyment by all persons within its jurisdiction of human rights and fundamental freedoms'. The importance of the Convention's role in giving meaning to these obligations has been highlighted in recent years by the fact that becoming a party to the Convention is now a political obligation of membership of the Council: Parliamentary Assembly Resolution 1031 (1994), para 9.

Turkey.[3] The Convention has instead been used primarily to raise questions of particular violations of human rights in states that basically conform to its requirements and are representative of the 'common heritage of political traditions, ideals, freedoms and the rule of law' to which the Convention Preamble refers, or, in the case of post-communist member states, that have committed themselves to move in this direction. Increasingly, it has evolved in the direction of being a European bill of rights, with the European Court of Human Rights having a role with some similarities to that of a constitutional court in a national legal system.

The Convention entered into force in 1953 and has been ratified by all forty-seven member states of the Council of Europe,[4] whose total population of over 800 million people is protected by it. The number of contracting parties increased greatly following the fall of the Berlin Wall in 1989 and the disintegration of the Socialist Federal Republic of Yugoslavia in the early 1990s. As a consequence largely of the policy of admitting Russia and other post-communist states to the Council of Europe in the period that followed these changes, the number of states parties rose from twenty-two in 1989 to forty-seven in 2008. As will be seen, this development, while in other ways welcome, has introduced new problems of interpretation and application of the Convention for the Court and greatly increased its workload.[5]

The substantive guarantee in the Convention has been supplemented by the addition of further rights by the First,[6] Fourth,[7] Sixth,[8] Seventh,[9] Twelfth,[10] and Thirteenth[11] Protocols to the Convention that are binding upon those states that have ratified them. There have also been other Protocols that have amended the enforcement machinery. The most recent Protocol of this second kind currently in force is the Eleventh Protocol,[12] which introduced fundamental reforms to the enforcement machinery of the Convention as of 1998. The Fourteenth Protocol[13] will take the process of reform significantly further when it enters into force.

---

[3] On the Convention and gross violations, see Kamminga, 12 NQHR 153 (1994); Reidy, Hampson, and Boyle, 15 NQHR 161 (1997) (Turkey); and Sardaro, 2003 EHRLR 601. On state applications, see Prebensen, 20 HRLJ 446 (1999) and below, p 821.

[4] These are Albania, Andorra, Armenia, Austria, Azerbaijan, Belgium, Bosnia and Herzegovina, Bulgaria, Croatia, Cyprus, Czech Republic, Denmark, Estonia, Finland, France, Georgia, Germany, Greece, Hungary, Iceland, Ireland, Italy, Latvia, Liechtenstein, Lithuania, Luxembourg, Malta, Moldova, Monaco, Montenegro, Netherlands, Norway, Poland, Portugal, Romania, Russia, San Marino, Serbia, Slovakia, Slovenia, Spain, Sweden, Switzerland, the former Yugoslav Republic of Macedonia (FYRM), Turkey, Ukraine, and the UK. The European states of Belarus and the Vatican City are not Council of Europe members.

[5] See Greer, *European Convention*, p 105 and Ch 3; Gross, 7 EJIL 89 (1996); Harmsen, 5 IJHR 18 (2001); Schokkenbroek and Zeimele, 75 NJB 1914 (2000); Skubiszewski, *Valticos Mélanges*, 521.

[6] 213 UNTS 262; ETS 9. Adopted 1952. In force 1954. Forty-five parties: all Convention parties except Monaco and Switzerland.

[7] 1469 UNTS 263; ETS 46. Adopted 1963. In force 1968. Forty parties: all Convention parties except Andorra, Greece, Spain, Switzerland, Turkey, and the UK.

[8] ETS 114. Adopted 1983. In force 1985. Forty-six parties: all Convention parties except Russia.

[9] ETS 117. Adopted 1984. In force 1988. Forty-one parties: all Convention parties except Belgium, Germany, Netherlands, Spain, Turkey, and the UK.

[10] ETS 177; 8 IHRR 300 (2000). Adopted 2000. In force 2005. Seventeen parties: Albania, Andorra, Armenia, Bosnia and Herzegovina, Croatia, Cyprus, Finland, Georgia, Luxembourg, Montenegro, Netherlands, Romania, San Marino, Serbia, Spain, FYRM, and Ukraine.

[11] ETS 187; 9 IHRR 884 (2002). Adopted 2002. In force 2003. Forty parties: all Convention parties except Armenia, Azerbaijan, Italy, Latvia, Poland, Russia, and Spain.

[12] ETS 155; 1–3 IHRR 206 (1994). Adopted 1994. In force 1998. Ratified by all Convention parties. See Caflisch, 6 HRLR 403 (2006).

[13] ETS 194; 9 IHRR 884 (2002). Adopted 2004. Ratified by all Convention parties, except Russia. For the reforms it will introduce, see below, p 863.

The Convention is a part of a network of international human rights treaties of universal or regional application. It is the regional counterpart to the International Covenant on Civil and Political Rights 1966 (ICCPR),[14] to which all Convention parties are parties.[15] At the regional level, it is comparable with the American Convention on Human Rights 1969[16] and the African Charter on Human and Peoples' Rights 1981.[17] As with these treaties, the Convention protects rights first spelt out in the Universal Declaration of Human Rights 1948.[18]

2. THE SUBSTANTIVE GUARANTEE

The human rights in the Universal Declaration are commonly divided into civil and political rights, on the one hand, and economic, social, and cultural rights, on the other. Civil and political rights are those that derive from the natural rights philosophy of the late eighteenth century in Europe. Economic, social, and cultural rights[19] appeared with the emergence of socialist governments in the early twentieth century. The European Convention protects predominantly civil and political rights.[20] This was a matter of priorities and tactics. While it was not disputed that economic, social, and cultural rights required protection too, the immediate need was for a short, non-controversial text which governments could accept at once, while the tide for human rights was strong. Given the values dominant within Western Europe, this meant limiting the Convention for the most part to the civil and political rights that were 'essential for a democratic way of life';[21] economic, social, and cultural rights were too problematic and were left for separate and later treatment.[22] The Convention, including its Protocols, protects most civil and political rights, but not all. It does not directly guarantee the rights of members

[14] 999 UNTS 171. See Joseph, Schultz, and Castan, *The International Covenant on Civil and Political Rights*, 2nd edn, 2004; McGoldrick, *The Human Rights Committee: its Role in the Development of the International Covenant on Civil and Political Rights*, 1991; and Nowak, *UN Covenant on Civil and Political Rights: CCPR Commentary*, 2nd edn, 2005.

[15] The ICCPR provides for an optional right of individual communication. All Convention parties have accepted the ICCPR right of communication except Monaco, Switzerland, and the UK. As to the inter-relationship between the ICCPR and Convention rights of petition, see below, p 784.

[16] 1144 UNTS 123. In force 1978. Twenty-four parties.

[17] 1520 UNTS 143; 21 ILM 59 (1981). In force 1986. Fifty-three parties. The African Charter is not limited to civil and political rights.

[18] GA Res 217A (III), GAOR, 3rd Sess, Part 1, resns, p 71.

[19] Examples are the rights to work, to health, and to take part in cultural life respectively.

[20] The Convention strays into the field of economic, social, and cultural rights with its guarantees of the rights to property and education (Articles 1 and 2, First Protocol) and of equality between the spouses (Article 5, Seventh Protocol). There are also certain overlaps between the two categories in the case of freedom from forced labour (Article 4, Convention), the right to respect for family life (Article 8, Convention), and freedom of association (Article 11, Convention). The non-discrimination guarantee in the Twelfth Protocol applies generally. In *Airey v Ireland* A 32 (1979); 2 EHRR 305 para 26 the Court stated that there is no 'watertight division' separating Convention rights from economic and social rights. See Pellonpää, *European System*, Ch 37 and Warbrick, in Baderin and McCorquodale, eds, *Economic, Social and Cultural Rights in Action*, 2007, Ch 10.

[21] M Teitgen, CE Consult.Ass, Debates, 1st Session, p 408, 19 August 1949.

[22] Economic and social rights are now protected by the 1961 European Social Charter, 529 UNTS 89; ETS 35 and the 1996 Revised European Social Charter, 2151 UNTS 279; ETS 163; 3 IHRR 726 (1996). See Harris, *The European Social Charter*, 2nd edn (by Harris and Darcy), 2001. Thirty-nine Council members are parties to the Charter or the Revised Charter or both. The missing members are Bosnia and Herzegovina, Liechtenstein, Montenegro, Monaco, Russia, Serbia, San Marino, and Switzerland.

of minority groups,[23] freedom from racist or other propaganda or the right to recognition as a person before the law. The above rights are protected by the ICCPR, which also contains fuller guarantees of the rights to be treated with 'humanity' and 'dignity' while in detention,[24] to a fair trial,[25] and to participate in public life.[26] The ICCPR also prohibits derogation from its obligations in time of war or public emergency in the case of more rights than does the European Convention.[27] In addition, some Convention guarantees are found only in Optional Protocols which not all parties have accepted.[28] However, the generally worded guarantees in the Convention text have been interpreted purposively so as to remedy some, at least, of these defects.[29]

3. THE STRASBOURG ENFORCEMENT MACHINERY

Compared to most other international human rights treaties, the Convention has very strong enforcement mechanisms. It provides for both state and individual applications.[30] Under Article 33, any party may bring an application alleging a breach by another party that has ratified the Convention. In addition, and considerably more important in practice, under Article 34 all parties accept the right of 'any person, non-governmental organisation or group of individuals', regardless of nationality,[31] claiming to be a victim of a breach of the Convention to bring an application against it.[32] Under Protocol 11, both state and individual applications go to the European Court of Human Rights,[33] which is a permanent court composed of full-time judges. The Court decides whether the application should be admitted for consideration on the merits.[34] If it is admitted, the Court decides in a judgment that is binding in international law whether there has been a breach

---

[23] These are the subject of the Council of Europe Framework Convention for the Protection of National Minorities 1995, 2151 UNTS 246; ETS 157; 2 IHRR 217 (1995). In force 1998. Thirty-nine parties, including the UK. See also the European Charter for Regional or Minority Languages 1992, 2044 UNTS 246; ETS 148. In force 1998. Twenty-two parties, including the UK. Neither of these Conventions has a right of petition. Some protection is indirectly afforded by the Convention to members of minority groups, through eg the non-discrimination guarantees in Article 14, Convention and the Twelfth Protocol to the Convention. See below, pp 602, 611.

[24] Article 3, Convention covers the more extreme cases.

[25] Some Article 6 'fair trial' omissions are made good by the Seventh Protocol for the parties to it. Even with the Seventh Protocol, the Convention contains a less extensive guarantee for juveniles and of the right to appeal in criminal cases.

[26] Article 3, First Protocol is narrower than Article 25, ICCPR.

[27] See Article 4, ICCPR. The Article 4, ICCPR prohibitions may, however, apply under the Convention by virtue of Article 15(1), Convention: see below, p 637.

[28] The most important of these is the free-standing non-discrimination guarantee in the Twelfth Protocol.

[29] Eg, freedom from self-incrimination (in Article 14(3)(g) ICCPR) has been read into Article 6 Convention, below, p 259.

[30] Article 52 also provides for occasional reports by states on their compliance with the Convention, as and when requested. This procedure has seldom been used, although in 2005 it provided the vehicle for requesting from parties information about rendition in torture cases: see <http://www.coe.int>. Before that, it had been used just five times: see Mahoney, *Wiarda Mélanges*, p 370.

[31] An application may be brought by both nationals and non-nationals of the respondent state.

[32] This right was made compulsory by the Eleventh Protocol as of 1998; before then, it was only applicable as against those parties that made a declaration accepting it.

[33] The Court has its seat at Strasbourg, France and operates within the framework of the Council of Europe, which has its headquarters there. The Court is totally distinct from the European Court of Justice which has its seat in Luxembourg and is the Court of the European Union.

[34] There is also provision for the friendly settlement of cases.

of the Convention.[35] The execution by parties of Court judgments against them is monitored by the Committee of Ministers of the Council of Europe, which is composed of government representatives of all of the member states.

4. THE INTERPRETATION OF THE CONVENTION[36]

I. THE GENERAL APPROACH

As a treaty, the Convention must be interpreted according to the international law rules on the interpretation of treaties.[37] These are to be found in the Vienna Convention on the Law of Treaties 1969.[38] The basic rule is that a treaty 'shall be interpreted in good faith in accordance with the ordinary meaning to be given to the terms of the treaty in their context and in the light of its object and purpose'.[39] A good example of the use of this rule is the case of *Luedicke, Belkacem, and Koç v FRG*.[40] There the Court adopted the 'ordinary meaning' of the words *'gratuitement'* and 'free' in the two authentic language texts[41] of Article 6(3)(e), which it found 'not contradicted by the context of the sub-paragraph' and 'confirmed by the object and purpose of Article 6'. The terms in the Convention have their 'ordinary' meaning. Accordingly, words such as 'degrading' (Article 3) have been understood in their dictionary sense.[42]

II. EMPHASIS UPON THE OBJECT AND PURPOSE OF THE CONVENTION

In accordance with the Vienna Convention, considerable emphasis has been placed in the interpretation of the Convention upon a teleological approach, ie one that seeks to realize its 'object and purpose'. This has been identified in general terms as 'the protection of individual human rights'[43] and the maintenance and promotion of 'the ideals

[35] Prior to the Eleventh Protocol, in force 1998, there was a second Strasbourg institution, the European Commission of Human Rights, composed of independent experts, which decided on the admissibility of state and individual applications and assisted with friendly settlements. It also adopted non-legally binding reports on the merits of admitted cases, which could, if the respondent state accepted the Court's jurisdiction, be referred to the Court by the Commission or a state with a recognized interest for a legally binding judgment, or—if the respondent state was a party to the Ninth Protocol—by the individual applicant. If no such reference was made, the case was decided by the Committee of Ministers of the Council of Europe. Both the Commission and the Court were part-time bodies before 1998.

[36] See Bernhardt, *Wiarda Mélanges*, p 95; Golsong, *European System*, Ch 8; Maatscher, id, Ch 5; Greer, *European Convention*, Ch 4; Van der Meersch, *Legros Mélanges*, 1986, p 207; Orakhelashvili, 14 EJIL 529 (2003).

[37] See eg, *Golder v UK* A 18 (1978); 1 EHRR 524 para 29 PC, and *Johnston v Ireland* A 112 (1986); 9 EHRR 203 para 51 PC. See Rosakis, in *Valticos Mélanges*, 487.   [38] 1155 UNTS 331. See Articles 31–3.

[39] Article 31, Vienna Convention. The 'context' of a treaty includes its preamble and any agreement or instrument relating to and made in connection with it: Article 31(2). The subsequent practice of the parties to a treaty and any relevant rules of international law shall be taken into account 'together with the context': Article 31(3). On the use of the *travaux préparatoires*, see below, p 16.   [40] A 29 (1978); 2 EHRR 149 para 46.

[41] Ie, the English and French texts. Where, as was not the case in the *Luedicke* case, the two authentic texts of the Convention differ in their meaning, they must be interpreted in such a way as to 'reconcile them as far as possible': Article 33(4), Vienna Convention. If they cannot be reconciled, the 'object and purpose' becomes decisive: see *Wemhoff v FRG* A 7 (1968); 1 EHRR 55 and *Brogan v UK* A 145-B (1988); 11 EHRR 117 PC.

[42] *Tyrer v UK* A 26 (1978); 2 EHRR 1.

[43] *Soering v UK* A 161 (1949); 11 EHRR 439 para 87 PC. Cf, the *'Belgian Linguistics' Case* A 6 (1968); 1 EHRR 241 PC.

and values of a democratic society'.[44] As to the latter, it has been recognized that 'democracy' supposes 'pluralism, tolerance and broadmindedness'.[45] The primary importance of the 'object and purpose' of the Convention was strikingly illustrated in *Golder v UK*.[46] There the Court read the right of access to a court into the fair trial guarantee in Article 6. It did so, in the absence of clear wording in the text to the contrary, mainly by reference to guidance as to the 'object and purpose' of the Convention to be found in its Preamble.[47] This indicated, *inter alia*, that the drafting states were resolved to 'take the first steps for the collective enforcement of certain of the rights stated in the Universal Declaration' in furtherance of the rule of law. As the Court stated, one could not suppose compliance with the rule of law without the possibility of taking legal disputes to court.

The Court also confirmed in the *Golder* case its earlier pronouncement in *Wemhoff v FRG*[48] that '[g]iven that it is a law-making treaty, it is also necessary to seek the interpretation that is most appropriate in order to realize the aim and achieve the object of the treaty, and not that which would restrict to the greatest possible degree the obligations undertaken by the parties'. This approach was forcefully opposed by Judge Fitzmaurice in his separate opinion in the *Golder* case. Judge Fitzmaurice argued, *inter alia*, that the 'heavy inroads' made by the Convention into an area previously within a state's domestic jurisdiction, namely the treatment of its own nationals, demanded 'a cautious and conservative interpretation'. Such an argument, which emphasizes the character of the Convention as a contract by which sovereign states agree to limitations upon their sovereignty, has now totally given way to an approach that focuses instead upon the Convention's law-making character and its role as a European human rights guarantee that must be interpreted so as to permit its development with time.

It is in this last connection that statements to the effect that the Convention represents 'the public order of Europe'[49] are relevant. They signify that in the interpretation and application of the Convention the overriding consideration is not that the Convention creates 'reciprocal engagements between contracting states', but that it imposes 'objective obligations' upon them for the protection of human rights in Europe,[50] with the Convention evolving in the direction of becoming Europe's constitutional bill of rights.[51]

---

[44] *Kjeldsen, Busk Madsen, and Pedersen v Denmark* A 23 (1976); 1 EHRR 711 para 53. Both of the considerations mentioned in the above sentence are confirmed by the Convention Preamble. The Preamble also identifies 'the achievement of greater unity between its Members' as the aim of the Council of Europe. See Gearty, 51 NILQ 381 (2000); Harvey, 29 ELR 407; Marks, 66 BYIL 209 (1995); Merrills, 29 Thes Acroasium 37 (2000); and Mowbray, 1999 PL 703. The commitment to democracy was crucial in *United Communist Party of Turkey v Turkey*, below, p 527.

[45] *Handyside v UK* A 24 (1976); 1 EHRR 737 para 49 PC. Cf, *Dudgeon v UK* A 45 (1981); 4 EHRR 149 para 53 PC.   [46] A 18 (1975); 1 EHRR 524 PC.

[47] The Court also referred to the emphasis on the rule of law in the Statute of the Council of Europe (Preamble, Article 3).

[48] A 7 (1968) p 23; 1 EHRR 55 at 75. Cf, *Delcourt v Belgium* A 11 (1970); 1 EHRR 355 para 25, concerning Article 6 in particular.

[49] *Austria v Italy* No 788/60, 4 YB 112 at 140 (1961). Cf, *Ireland v UK* A 25 (1978); 2 EHRR 25 para 239 PC; *Soering v UK* A 161 (1989); 11 EHRR 439 PC; *Chrysostomos, Papachrysostomou and Loizidou v Turkey* Nos 15299/89, 15300/89 and 15318/89, 68 DR 216 at 242 (1991) (the Convention is a 'constitutional instrument of European public order in the field of human rights'); and *Loizidou v Turkey* A 310 (1995); 20 EHRR 99 para 93. See generally Frowein, *2 Collected Courses of the Academy of European Law* 280 (1990) and Alkema, *Ryssdal Mélanges*, p 41.

[50] *Ireland v UK* A 25 (1978); 2 EHRR 25 para 239 PC. The 'objective' character of the obligations manifested itself in *Austria v Italy*, previous note, in that Austria was permitted to question Italian conduct that occurred before Austria became a party to the Convention.

[51] On the translation of the Convention from a purely international law instrument to a constitutional guarantee for Europe, see Alkema, *Ryssdal Mélanges*, p 50; Greer, *European Convention*, pp 165ff; and Warbrick, 10 MJIL 698 (1989).

III. DYNAMIC OR EVOLUTIVE INTERPRETATION

It follows from the emphasis placed upon the 'object and purpose' of the Convention that it must be given a dynamic or evolutive interpretation.[52] Thus, in *Tyrer v UK*,[53] the Court stated that the Convention is 'a living instrument which…must be interpreted in the light of present-day conditions'. Accordingly, the Court could not 'but be influenced by the developments and commonly accepted standards in the penal policy of the member states of the Council of Europe' when considering whether judicial corporal punishment was consistent with Article 3. What was determinative, the Court stated, were the standards currently accepted in European society, not those prevalent when the Convention was adopted. In terms of the intentions of the drafting states, the emphasis is therefore upon their general rather than their particular intentions in 1950.[54] Other decisions that follow the *Tyrer* approach have reflected changes in the policy of the law in European states resulting from changed social attitudes towards, for example, children born out of wedlock[55] and homosexuals[56] and from other policy developments.[57] However, the Convention may not be interpreted in response to 'present-day conditions' so as to introduce into it a right that it was not intended to include when the Convention was drafted. For this reason, Article 12, which guarantees the right to marry, could not be interpreted as including a right to divorce, even though such a right is now generally recognized in Europe.[58] In this way, a line is sought to be drawn between judicial interpretation, which is permissible, and judicial legislation, which is not. Mahoney[59] has suggested that, with this distinction in mind, the Court tends to emphasize incremental, rather than sudden change. The closed shop cases[60] are good examples of this gradualist approach. However, as in national law, the line between judicial interpretation and legislation can be a difficult one to draw, particularly in the case of generally worded provisions. Decisions can be seen either as instances of judicial creativity that move the Convention into distinct areas beyond its intended domain or as the elaboration of rights that are already protected. For example, the Court's finding of positive obligations for states throughout the Convention[61] and, more particularly, its application of Article 3 to cases of removal of individuals from a state's territory[62] and of Article 8 to environmental matters[63] can

---

[52] See Mosler, in *Van Panhyus Essays*, 1980, p 149 and Sorensen, *Proceedings of the Fourth International Colloquy on the European Convention on Human Rights*, 1976, p 86. The term 'evolutive', rather than 'dynamic', is sometimes used by the Court: see eg, *Johnston v Ireland* A 112 (1986); 9 EHRR 203 para 53 PC. On the interpretative and law-making role of the Court, and formerly the Commission, generally, see Gearty, 52 CLJ 89 (1993); Mahoney, 11 HRLJ 57 (1990); and Stavros, *The Guarantees for Accused Persons under Article 6 of the European Convention on Human Rights*, 1993, pp 340–50 (hereafter Stavros).

[53] A 26 (1978); 2 EHRR 1 para 31.

[54] Cf, Mahoney, 11 HRLJ 57 at 70 (1990). See also Nicol, 2000 PL 152.

[55] *Marckx v Belgium* A 31 (1979); 2 EHRR 330 PC.

[56] *Dudgeon v UK* A 45 (1981); 4 EHRR 149 PC. Cf, *L and V v Austria* 2003-I.

[57] See eg, *Soering v UK* A 161 (1989); 11 EHRR 439 PC (death penalty); *Sigurjonsson v Iceland* A 264 (1993); 16 EHRR 462 (closed shops); *Stafford v UK* 2002-IV; 35 EHRR 1121 GC (life sentences). The Convention enforcement machinery provisions are also to be interpreted dynamically: *Loizidou v Turkey* A 310 (1995); 20 EHRR 99 para 71.

[58] *Johnston v Ireland* A 112 (1986); 9 EHRR 203 PC. *Quaere* whether the sensitive nature of the divorce question in Ireland at the time was another factor in the *Johnston* case.

[59] 11 HRLJ 57 at 60 (1990). Mahoney draws an analogy with the judicial activism and judicial restraint distinction found in the jurisprudence of the US Supreme Court.

[60] See below, p 540. Cf, the gradual extension of Article 6(3) to pre-trial criminal proceedings: see below, p 306. See also the Court's approach to different retirement ages for men and women in *Stec v UK* 2006-VI GC.

[61] See generally Mowbray, *The Development of Positive Obligations under the European Convention on Human Rights by the European Court of Human Rights*, 2004.

[62] See *Soering v UK* A 161 (1989); 11 EHRR 439 PC.   [63] See below, p 390.

either be seen as the discovery of obligations that were always implicit in the guarantees concerned or as the addition of new obligations for states.

When deciding a case by reference to the dynamic character of the Convention, the Court must make a judgment as to the point at which a change in the policy of the law has achieved sufficiently wide acceptance in European states to affect the meaning of the Convention. In the course of doing so, the Court has generally been cautious, preferring to follow state practice rather than to precipitate a new approach. But the Court does not necessarily wait until only the defendant state remains out of line before it recognizes a new approach.[64] For example, in *Marckx v Belgium*[65] the Court relied upon a new approach to the status of children born out of wedlock that had been adopted in the law of the 'great majority', but not all, of Council of Europe states by 1979. The Court adopted a somewhat different and less demanding approach than this in the case of *Goodwin (Christine) v UK*.[66] In a series of transsexual cases from the mid-1980s onwards, the Court had indicated that it was not satisfied that a common new European standard requiring the full recognition in law of the new sexual identity of post-operative transsexuals had emerged; standards were still in transition with 'little common ground between the contracting states'.[67] However, in the *Goodwin* case, while recognizing that there remained no 'common European approach' on the matter, the Court was persuaded to overturn its earlier rulings by 'clear and uncontested evidence of a continuing international trend', both in Europe and elsewhere, in the direction of 'legal recognition of the new sexual identity of post-operative transsexuals'. It thus referred to national standards around the world, as well as European, and did not require that a 'great majority' of European states follow the new approach.[68]

IV. RELIANCE UPON EUROPEAN NATIONAL LAW STANDARDS

The question whether the Court should be influenced by the law in European states in its interpretation of the Convention is relevant not only in contexts in which the policy of the law has changed. The question may arise when the Court has to decide how rigorously to interpret the requirements of the Convention in other circumstances also. Here, too, any European consensus that exists has had a considerable impact upon the Court's jurisprudence.[69] For example, the Court's ringing pronouncements on the importance of freedom of speech and of the press in a democratic society[70] stem from a confident conviction as to longstanding values that generally underpin European society. Equally clearly, the easy incorporation into Article 1, First Protocol of a compensation requirement for the taking of the property of nationals followed from the 'legal systems of the contracting states'.[71] Former Judge Van der Meersch[72] has pointed to the paradox of

---

[64] A state that is entirely on its own is particularly at risk of an adverse judgment if its practice offends common European standards relevant to human rights: see eg, the *Tyrer* case, above (corporal punishment) and *Unal Tekeli v Turkey* 2004-X; 42 EHRR 1185 (married women's surnames). For an exception, see *EB v France* hudoc (2008) GC.

[65] A 31 (1979); 2 EHRR 330 para 41 PC. Cf, *Dudgeon v UK* A 45 (1981); 4 EHRR 149 PC and *Hirst v UK (No 2)* 2005-IX; 42 EHRR 849 GC.   [66] 2002-VI; 35 EHRR 447 para 85 GC.

[67] *Cossey v UK* A 184 (1990); 13 EHRR 622 para 40. For other cases, see below, p 385.

[68] A 'majority', but not the 'great majority', of member states provided for full legal recognition: *Sheffield and Horsham v UK* 1998-V; 27 EHRR 163 paras 35, 57 and *Goodwin (Christine) v UK*, above, n 66.

[69] See Heringa, 3 Maastricht JECL 108 (1996).

[70] See *Lingens v Austria* A 103 (1981); 8 EHRR 407 para 41 PC.

[71] *James v UK* A 98 (1986); 8 EHRR 123 para 54 PC. Other examples include *A v UK* 2002-X; 36 EHRR 917 (parliamentary immunity) and *Bryan v UK* A 335-A (1995); 21 EHRR 342 (judicial review of administrative action).

[72] 1 HRLJ 13 at 15 (1980).

taking standards in national law into account when interpreting an international treaty whose purpose is to control national law. The convincing justification that he provides is that there is a necessarily close relationship between the Convention standards and the European 'common law' by which they are inspired. Another reason may be that an interpretation of the Convention that deviated substantially from general European practice would undermine state confidence in the Convention system and thereby threaten its continued success or acceptance by states.[73] Generally, the Court's reliance upon any European consensus is acceptable in that it is likely to be in accordance with recognized human rights standards, as in the case of the emphasis placed upon freedom of speech. Even so, the Court needs to be aware that government and individual interests do not always coincide and that a practice may not be acceptable in human rights terms simply because it is generally followed.

In the absence of a European consensus, the Court has tended to reflect national law by applying a lowest common denominator approach or to accommodate variations in state practice through the margin of appreciation doctrine[74] when deciding upon the meaning of a Convention guarantee. The result is that a state's law or conduct may well escape condemnation if it reflects a practice followed in a number of European states or where practice is widely varied. For example, the fact that members of a linguistic minority may not be able to vote in an election for candidates whose language is theirs[75] or that civil servants may sit as expert members of a tribunal[76] does not present problems for the rights to free elections (Article 3, First Protocol) and an independent and impartial tribunal (Article 6) respectively, given that such situations are common in European states. Widespread differences in practice in European states can lead to a similar tolerance, as in the case of laws governing abortion[77] and artificial insemination.[78] Other examples can be found in connection with the right to a fair trial, where there is much diversity of practice resulting, most clearly, from the differences between civil and common law systems of criminal justice. Thus, when interpreting the Article 6(1) requirement that judgments be 'pronounced in public', the Court has taken account of the fact that courts of cassation in civil law jurisdictions commonly do not deliver their judgments in public.[79] Similarly, the Court has been influenced in its approach to the 'trial within a reasonable time' guarantee in Article 6(1) by the characteristics of civil law criminal justice systems.[80]

It is encouraging, however, that, faced with a diversity of practice, the Court has sometimes acted positively in the interests of protecting human rights. This is the case, for example, in the Court's application of Article 6(1) to administrative justice, its strict reading of the requirement of an impartial tribunal that is found in the same provision, and its expansive interpretation of the residual 'fair hearing' guarantee.[81] More controversial perhaps is the balance that the Court has struck between the rights of parents and their children. The policy of some states of permitting their child care authorities to intervene to protect children at the expense of parental rights more than most European states do so has led to findings of breaches of the Convention in several cases.[82]

---

[73] See Stavros, p 346.   [74] As to this doctrine, see below, p 11.

[75] *Mathieu-Mohin and Clerfayt v Belgium* A 113 (1987); 10 EHRR 1 para 57 PC ('a good many states').

[76] *Ettl v Austria* A 117 (1987); 10 EHRR 225 para 40 ('domestic legislation...of member states affords many examples').   [77] See *Vo v France* 2004-VIII; 40 EHRR 259 GC.

[78] See *Evans v UK* hudoc (2007); 46 EHRR 728 GC.   [79] See below, p 277.

[80] See below, p 283. Note also the absence of any need for jury trial in criminal cases, which is not found generally across Europe. For other examples of differing practice concerning the law of evidence and trial *in absentia*, resulting in a 'low common denominator', see Stavros, pp 238 and 265–266.

[81] See below, pp 228, 284, and 246 respectively.

[82] See eg, *Andersson (M & R) v Sweden* A 226-A (1992); 14 EHRR 615.

Finally, it is interesting to consider the evidence that the Court has available to it when it acts by reference to the standards in European national law or international law. After many years in which the Court lacked the time or resources to undertake research in relevant areas of law, it now has a small research division which is asked to carry out studies on questions of comparative or international law that arise in cases before the Grand Chamber. This is an important new development in the practice of the Court that has taken place over the last five years or so.[83]

Thus today Grand Chambers and occasionally Chambers will have at their disposal in-house documents that provide extremely useful and detailed comparative and international law information. Beyond such resources, the Court relies upon the collective knowledge of its members and its registry and upon the *amicus curiae* briefs of non-governmental organizations and others, which have been of great assistance on occasion.[84] The contribution of judges is obviously valuable but is curtailed by the Court's practice of hearing cases in chambers and the fact that judges are unlikely to claim expertise in all areas of their national law.

V. THE PRINCIPLE OF PROPORTIONALITY[85]

The principle of proportionality is a recurring theme in the interpretation of the Convention. As the Court stated in *Soering v UK*,[86] 'inherent in the whole of the Convention is a search for a fair balance between the demands of the general interest of the community and the requirements of the protection of the individual's fundamental rights'. The achievement of such a balance necessarily requires an approach based, *inter alia*, upon considerations of proportionality. Reliance on the principle of proportionality is most evident in areas in which the Convention expressly allows restrictions upon a right. Thus, under the second paragraphs of Articles 8–11, a state may restrict the protected right to the extent that this is 'necessary in a democratic society' for certain listed public interest purposes. This formula has been interpreted as meaning that the restriction must be 'proportionate to the legitimate aim pursued'.[87] Similarly, proportionality has been invoked when setting the limits to an implied restriction that has been read into a Convention guarantee[88] and in some cases in determining whether a positive obligation

---

[83] For earlier doubts as to whether the Court made a thorough investigation of the law of European states when relying on common standards, see eg, the dissenting opinion of Judge Matscher in *Öztürk v FRG* A 73 (1984); 6 EHRR 409 PC and, among writers, Bernhardt, *European System*, p 35; Helfer, 26 Corn ILJ 133 at 138–40 (1989); and Mahoney, 11 HRLJ 57 at 79 (1990).

[84] See eg, the reliance on a study by the NGO Liberty in *Goodwin (Christine) v UK* 2002-VI; 35 EHRR 447 GC. As to third party interventions, see below, p 853.

[85] See Van Drooghenbroeck, *La proportionalité dans le droit de la Convention européenne des droits de l'homme*, 2001. See also Eissen, *European System*, Ch 7; McBride, in Ellis, ed, *The Principle of Proportionality in the Laws of Europe*, 1999, p 23; and McHarg, 62 MLR 671 (1999).

[86] A 161 (1989); 11 EHRR 439 para 89 PC. Cf, *'Belgian Linguistics' Case (No 2)* A 6 (1968); 1 EHRR 252 PC; *Sporrong and Lönnroth v Sweden* A 52 (1982); 5 EHRR 35 PC; and *Fayed v UK* A 294-B (1994); 18 EHRR 393. More recently, see eg, *JA Pye (Oxford) Ltd v UK* hudoc (2007); 46 EHRR 1083 GC.

[87] *Handyside v UK* A 24 (1976) para 49; 1 EHRR 737 PC. See also the 'absolutely necessary' test in Article 2(2), where the test is one of 'strict proportionality'. As to this test and the proportionality principle's possible use in connection with the death penalty under Article 2, see below, pp 61 and 60 respectively. The principle has also been applied to differently formulated restrictions in other Articles, eg, Article 5 (*Winterwerp v Netherlands* A 33 (1979); 2 EHRR 387 para 39); Article 12 (F *v Switzerland* A 128 (1987); 10 EHRR 411 PC); and Article 1, First Protocol (*James v UK* A 98 (1986); 8 EHRR 123 para 50 PC).

[88] *Mathieu-Mohin and Clerfayt v Belgium* A 113 (1987); 10 EHRR 1 para 52 PC (Article 1, First Protocol) and *Fayed v UK* A 294-B (1994); 18 EHRR 393 para 71 (Article 6(1)). In the former case the Court also stated that a

has been satisfied.[89] The principle has also been introduced into the non-discrimination rule in Article 14, so that for its prohibition of discrimination to be infringed there must be 'no reasonable relationship of proportionality between the means employed and the aim sought to be pursued'.[90] Finally, the principle is relied upon when interpreting the requirement in Article 15 that measures taken in a public emergency in derogation of Convention rights must be 'strictly required by the exigencies of the situation'.[91] In general, the principle of proportionality is not applied under Article 3, which contains an absolute guarantee.[92] A limitation upon a right, or steps taken positively to protect or fulfil it, will not be proportionate, even allowing for a margin of appreciation (see below), where there is no evidence that the state institutions have balanced the competing individual and public interests when deciding on the limitation or steps, or where the requirements to be met to avoid or benefit from its application in a particular case are so high as not to permit a meaningful balancing process.[93]

VI. THE MARGIN OF APPRECIATION DOCTRINE[94]

A doctrine that plays a crucial role in the interpretation of the Convention and that has been extensively commented upon is that of the margin of appreciation. In general terms, it means that the state is allowed a certain measure of discretion, subject to European supervision, when it takes legislative, administrative, or judicial action in the area of a Convention right. The doctrine was first explained by the Court in *Handyside v UK*.[95] This was a case concerning a restriction upon a right within the Articles 8–11 group of rights. In the *Handyside* case, the Court had to consider whether a conviction

restriction must not impair the 'essence' of the right: *ibid*. Cf, *Ashingdane v UK* A 93 (1985); 7 EHRR 528 para 57 (Article 6(1)). The Court not uncommonly uses this last idea when vetting a restriction under any of the headings discussed above, whether as an element of 'proportionality' or as a separate requirement.

[89] See eg, the Article 8 cases of *Rees v UK* A 106 (1986); 9 EHRR 56 para 37 PC and *Gaskin v UK* A 160 (1989); 12 EHRR 36 para 49 PC.

[90] *'Belgian Linguistics' Case* A 6 (1968) p 34; 1 EHRR 241 at 284 PC. Cf, the recourse to proportionality when interpreting the term 'forced labour' in Article 4: *Van der Mussele v Belgium* A 70 (1983); 6 EHRR 163 para 37 PC.

[91] See *Lawless v Ireland* (Merits) A 3 (1961); 1 EHRR 15 and *Ireland v UK* A 25 (1978); 2 EHRR 25 PC. Although the term proportionality is not mentioned in these judgments, the principle is applied in fact.

[92] See *Saadi v Italy*, below, p 87. A 'fair balance' was relevant in the *Soering* case, above, p 10, in the sense that an individual may be extradited where the danger of ill-treatment contrary to Article 3 abroad subsides sufficiently.

[93] *Hirst v UK (No 2)* 2005-IX; 42 EHRR 849 GC (absolute ban on prisoners' right to vote) and *Dickson v UK* hudoc (2007); 46 EHRR 927 GC (strict limits on prisoners' artificial insemination). See, however, *Odièvre v France* 2003-III; 38 EHRR 871 GC (no right to know one's biological parent) where the Court majority gave little heed to such considerations.

[94] See further below, p 349. And see Arai-Takahashi, *The Margin of Appreciation Doctrine and the Principle of Proportionality in the Jurisprudence of the ECHR*, 2002; id, 13 ERPL 1161 (2001); Benvenisti, 31 NYJILP 843; Brauch, 11 Col JEL 113 (2004); Brems, 56 ZAORV 240 (1996); Greer, *The Margin of Appreciation: Interpretation and Discretion under the European Convention on Human Rights*, Council of Europe Human Rights File 17, 2000; Hutchinson, 48 ICLQ 638 (1999); Jones, 1995 PL 430; Kavanagh, 2006 EHRLR 422; Lavender, 1997 EHRLR 380; Letsas, 26 OJLS 705 (2006); Macdonald, in *European System*, Ch 6; articles by Mahoney, Callewaert, Ovey, Prebensen, Winisdoerffer, Schokkenbroek, and O'Boyle, 19 HRLJ 1–36 (1999); Merrills, *The Development of International Law by the European Court of Human Rights*, 2nd edn, 1993, Ch 7; Van der Meersch in *Wiarda Mélanges*, p 201; Sweeney, 54 ICLQ 459 (2005); and Yourow, *The Margin of Appreciation Doctrine in the Dynamics of European Human Rights Jurisprudence*, 1996.

[95] A 24 (1976); 1 EHRR 737 paras 48–9 PC. It had in effect been relied upon by the Court earlier, following the Commission, in *Lawless v Ireland* (Merits) A 3 (1961); 1 EHRR 15 para 28, in the context of public emergencies (Article 15). On the use of the doctrine in Articles 8–11, see further below, Ch 8.

for possessing an obscene article could be justified under Article 10(2) as a limitation upon freedom of expression that was necessary for the 'protection of morals'. The
Court stated:

> By reason of their direct and continuous contact with the vital forces of their countries,
> state authorities are in principle in a better position than the international judge to give an
> opinion on the exact content of those requirements [of morals] as well as on the 'necessity'
> of a 'restriction' or 'penalty' intended to meet them...
>
> Nevertheless, Article 10(2) does not give the contracting states an unlimited power of
> appreciation. The Court, which, with the Commission, is responsible for ensuring the
> observance of those states' engagements, is empowered to give the final ruling on whether
> a 'restriction' or 'penalty' is reconcilable with freedom of expression as protected by
> Article 10. The domestic margin of appreciation thus goes hand in hand with a European
> supervision.

The doctrine has since been applied in the above sense to other Convention articles. As
well as Article 10, it has been relied upon when determining whether an interference with
other rights in the Articles 8–11 group of rights is justifiable on any of the public interest
grounds permitted by paragraph (2) of the Article concerned. The doctrine is also used
when assessing whether a state has done enough to comply with any positive obligations
that it has under these[96] and other Articles[97] and when determining whether a state's
interference with the right to property protected by Article 1, First Protocol is justified in
the public interest.[98] A margin of appreciation is also allowed in the application of other
guarantees where an element of judgment by the national authorities is involved, as in
certain parts of Articles 5[99] and 6[100] and in Article 14.[101] It has been instrumental as well
in the application of Article 15 when deciding whether there is a 'public emergency' and,
if so, whether the measures taken in response to it are 'strictly required by the exigencies of the situation'.[102] As will be apparent, these Articles largely coincide with those to
which the principle of proportionality spelt out in the *Handyside* case applies, the point
being that in assessing the proportionality of the state's acts, a certain degree of deference
is given to the judgment of national authorities when they weigh competing public and
individual interests in view of their special knowledge and overall responsibility under
domestic law. Finally, it should be noted that national courts are allowed considerable
discretion, either under an implied margin of appreciation doctrine or under the fourth
instance doctrine (see below), in the conduct of trials in respect of such matters as the
admissibility or evaluation of evidence. Thus the Court has stated that Article 6(3)(d)
generally 'leaves it to the competent authorities to decide upon the relevance of proposed

---

[96] See eg, *Abdulaziz, Cabales, and Balkandali v UK* A 94 (1985); 7 EHRR 741 para 67 PC and *Keegan v Ireland*
A 290 (1994); 18 EHRR 342 para 49.

[97] See eg, *Mathieu-Mohin and Clerfayt v Belgium* A 113 (1987); 10 EHRR 1 PC (Article 3, First Protocol); and
Vo v France 2004-VIII; 40 EHRR 259 GC (Article 2).

[98] See eg, *James v UK* A 98 (1986); 8 EHRR 123 PC.

[99] See *Winterwerp v Netherlands* A 33 (1979); 2 EHRR 387 (person of unsound mind); *Weeks v UK* A 114
(1987); 10 EHRR 293 PC (release on parole); *Brogan v UK* A 145-B (1988); 11 EHRR 117 PC (terrorist suspects).
No margin of appreciation in Article 5(3): see below, p 174. As to a margin of appreciation in connection with
the 'absolutely necessary' test in Article 2: see below, p 62.

[100] See eg, *Osman v UK* 1998-VIII; 29 EHRR 245 (1998) (right of access), but no margin of appreciation on trial
within a reasonable time: see below, p 279.

[101] *'Belgian Linguistics' Case* A 6 (1968) p 35; 1 EHRR 24 at 284 PC and *Rasmussen v Denmark* A 87 (1984);
7 EHRR 371 para 40.

[102] *Ireland v UK* A 25 (1978); 2 EHRR 25 PC.

evidence'[103] and that 'it is for the national courts to assess the evidence before them'.[104] An interference with a right that has been ordered or approved by the objective decision of a national court following a full examination of the facts will also benefit from a margin of appreciation in its favour.[105]

The margin of appreciation doctrine is applied differentially, with the degree of discretion allowed to the state varying according to the context. A state is allowed a considerable discretion in cases of public emergency arising under Article 15,[106] in some national security cases,[107] and in the protection of public morals.[108] Similarly, the margin of appreciation 'available to the legislature in implementing social and economic policies should be a wide one.'[109] It will be wide too when 'there is a no consensus within the member states of the Council of Europe, either as to the relative importance of the interest at stake or as to the best means of protecting it, particularly where the case raises sensitive moral or ethical issues'.[110] A wide margin also usually applies 'if the state is required to strike a balance between competing interests or Convention rights'.[111] At the other extreme, the margin of appreciation is limited where 'a particularly important facet of an individual's identity or existence is at stake'[112] and is reduced almost to vanishing point in certain areas, as where the justification for a restriction is the protection of the authority of the judiciary.[113]

The margin of appreciation doctrine reflects the subsidiary role of the Convention in protecting human rights.[114] The overall scheme of the Convention is that the initial and primary responsibility for the protection of human rights lies with the contracting parties.[115] The Court is there to monitor their action, exercising a power of review that has some similarities with that of a federal constitutional court over conduct by democratically elected governments or legislatures within the federation.[116] The margin of appreciation doctrine serves as a mechanism by which a tight or slack rein is kept on state conduct, depending upon the context. The doctrine is nonetheless a controversial one. When it is applied widely, so as to appear to give a state a blank cheque or to tolerate questionable national practices or decisions,[117] it may be argued that the Court has abdicated its responsibilities. However, the doctrine

---

[103] *Engel v Netherlands* A 22 (1976); 1 EHRR 647 para 91 PC.

[104] *Isgro v Italy* A 194-A (1991) para 31. A state is also allowed a margin of appreciation under Article 6 in deciding whether an accused must be legally represented: *Croissant v Germany* A 237-B (1987); 16 EHRR 135 para 27.

[105] See eg, *Handyside v UK* A 24 (1976); 1 EHRR 737 PC.   [106] See below, p 626.

[107] See eg, *Leander v Sweden* A 116 (1987); 9 EHRR 433 para 67.

[108] See eg, the *Handyside* case, n 95 above.

[109] *Hatton v UK* 2003-VIII; 37 EHRR 611 para 97 GC (airport noise), citing *James v UK* A 98 (1986); 8 EHRR 123 PC (taking of property).

[110] *Evans v UK* hudoc (2007); 46 EHRR 728 para 77 GC. Cf, *Rasmussen v Denmark* A 87 (1984); 7 EHRR 371 (fathers' rights) and *Vo v France* 2004-III; 40 EHRR 259 (abortion). Even so, a state's discretion is not unlimited: *Dickson v UK* hudoc (2007); 46 EHRR 927 GC.   [111] *Evans v UK*, ibid.

[112] *Ibid.* Cf, *Dudgeon v UK* A 45 (1983); 4 EHRR 149 PC (homosexual acts).

[113] *Sunday Times v UK* A 30 (1979); 2 EHRR 245 PC. The Court may have been influenced by the disagreement within the relevant UK institutions as to the need for the restriction.

[114] See Matscher, *European System*, Ch 5 at p 76. On the principle of subsidiarity in the Convention generally, see Petzold, *European System*, Ch 4 and Rysdall, 1996 EHRLR 18 at 24ff. On the principle in the Court's jurisprudence, see eg, *Z v UK* 2001-V; 34 EHRR 97 GC and *Vilho Eskelinen v Finland* 2007-GC.

[115] *'Belgian Linguistics' Case* A 6 (1968) p 34; 1 EHRR 241 at 284 PC and *Handyside v UK* A 24 (1978); 1 EHRR 737 para 48 PC. Thus Article 1 requires the contracting parties to 'secure' the rights' in the Convention. See also Articles 13 and 53, Convention.

[116] See Mahoney, 11 HRLJ 57 at 65 (1990), who compares the roles of the European Court and the US Supreme Court.

[117] See eg, *Barfod v Denmark* A 149 (1989); 13 EHRR 493 paras 28–36.

has its counterpart in the context of judicial review in national systems of administrative law and serves as a lubricant at the interface between individual rights and public interest. It may also be essential to retain state confidence in the operation of the system. In its absence, Strasbourg might well be seen as imposing solutions from outside without paying proper regard to the expertise and responsibilities of local decision-makers. Underlying the doctrine is the understanding that the legislative, executive, and judicial organs of a state party to the Convention basically operate in conformity with the rule of law and human rights and that their assessment and presentation of the national situation in cases that go to Strasbourg can be relied upon. Given this premise, the doctrine can probably be justified. The difficulty lies not so much in allowing it as in deciding precisely when and how to apply it to the facts of particular cases.

VII. REFERENCE TO INTERNATIONAL STANDARDS

The Court increasingly refers to other sources of international human rights standards when interpreting the Convention in its judgments. Thus the Court refers to other human rights treaties and other relevant instruments—both of the Council of Europe itself[118] and of other international institutions[119]—and decisions by bodies applying them. A treaty may be referred to whether the respondent state is a party to it or not.[120] The Court also interprets the Convention, as a treaty, against the background of public international law generally.[121] This is all to be welcomed in ensuring a uniformity of approach where this is appropriate.

VIII. THE FOURTH INSTANCE DOCTRINE

The Court, and formerly the Commission, has made it clear that it does not constitute a further court of appeal, ie a fourth instance ('*quatrième instance*'), from the decisions of national courts applying national law. In the words of the Court, 'it is not its function to deal with errors of fact or law allegedly committed by a national court unless and insofar as they may have infringed rights and freedoms protected by the Convention.'[122] An application that merely claims without more that a national court has made an error of fact or law will be declared inadmissible *ratione materiae*.[123] A claim that that such an error is a breach of the right to a fair hearing in Article 6 will not succeed, as Article 6 provides a procedural guarantee only; it does not guarantee that the outcome of the proceedings is fair.[124] However, where the Court is called upon to determine the facts of a case in order to apply a Convention guarantee (eg whether there was inhuman treatment contrary to Article 3),

---

[118] See eg, *Sorensen and Rasmussen v Denmark*, below, p 541 (European Social Charter); *Dickson v UK*, below, p 408 (European Prison Rules); *Oneryildiz v Turkey*, below, p 42 (Committee of Ministers and Parliamentary Assembly recommendations).

[119] See eg, *Al Adsani v UK*, below, p 242 (UN Torture Convention); *Jersild v Denmark*, below, p 445 (UN Racial Discrimination Convention); *Siliadin v France*, below, p 113 (ILO Conventions); *Eskelinen v Finland*, below, p 221 (EU Charter on Fundamental Rights); and *Demir and Baykara v Turkey*, below p 545.

[120] See eg, *Marckx v Belgium*, below, p 392 (Children Born Out of Wedlock Convention).

[121] See eg, the *Bankovic* case, below, p 805 (jurisdiction), and *Waite and Kennedy v Germany*, below, p 242 (sovereign immunity). For references to non-human rights treaties, see *Glass v UK*, below, p 399 (Oviedo Convention on Bioethics) and *Taskin v Turkey*, below, p 377 (Aarhus Convention on Access to Information, etc, on Environmental Matters). See also *Al Adsani v UK*, below, p 242 (ICTY judgment).

[122] *Garcia Ruiz v Spain* 1999-I; 31 EHRR 589 para 28.

[123] See eg, *X v FRG No 254/57*, 1 YB 150 at 152 (1957).

[124] For this general position and possible exceptions, see below, p 202.

it is not bound by the finding of facts at the national level.[125] Where an application alleges that national law violates the Convention, the Strasbourg authorities will not in principle question the interpretation of that law by the national courts[126] However, it may do so where the interpretation by the national court is 'arbitrary',[127] or where it is a part of a Convention requirement that national law be complied with (eg that an arrest is 'lawful': Article 5(1)).[128] Even so, it is very exceptional for the Court to disagree with any decision by a national court on its interpretation and application of its own national law.[129]

IX. EFFECTIVE INTERPRETATION

An important consideration which lies at the heart of the Court's interpretation of the Convention, and which is key to realizing its 'object and purpose', is the need to ensure the effective protection of the rights guaranteed. In *Artico v Italy*,[130] the Court stated that 'the Convention is intended to guarantee not rights that are theoretical or illusory but rights that are practical and effective'. There the Court found a breach of the right to legal aid in Article 6(3)(c) because the legal aid lawyer appointed by the state proved totally ineffective. The Court has relied upon the principle of effectiveness in other cases also when interpreting positive obligations.[131] In other contexts, the Court has emphasized the need to ensure the effectiveness of the Convention when interpreting the term 'victim' in Article 25[132] and when giving the Convention extra-territorial reach under Article 3.[133]

X. CONSISTENCY OF INTERPRETATION OF THE CONVENTION AS A WHOLE

In *Stec v UK*,[134] the Court stated that the 'Convention must be read as a whole, and interpreted in such a way as to promote internal consistency and harmony between its various provisions'. Accordingly, in that case a crucial factor for the Court in ruling that the right to property in Article 1, First Protocol extended to non-contributory as well as contributory benefits was that it had been held that rights to both kinds of benefit were protected by the right to a fair trial in Article 6 of the Convention.

XI. LIMITS RESULTING FROM THE CLEAR MEANING OF THE TEXT

Although the Strasbourg authorities rely heavily upon the 'object and purpose' of the Convention, they have occasionally found that their freedom to do so is limited by the clear meaning of the text. Thus in *Wemhoff v FRG*,[135] it was held that Article 5(3) does not apply to appeal proceedings because of the wording of Article 5(1)(a). Remarkably, in

---

[125] See eg, *Ribitsch v Austria* A 336 (1995); 21 EHRR 573.

[126] *X and Y v Netherlands* A 91 (1985); 8 EHRR 235 para 29.

[127] See eg, *Van Kuck v Germany* 2003-VII; 37 EHRR 973. See also *Von Hannover v Germany* 2004-VI; 43 EHRR 139.

[128] See eg, *Lukanov v Bulgaria* 1997- II; 24 EHRR 121.

[129] *Winterwerp v Netherlands* A 33 (1979); 2 EHRR 387 para 46.

[130] A 37 (1980); 3 EHRR 1 para 33. Cf, *Airey v Ireland* A 32 (1979); 2 EHRR 305.

[131] See *Klass v FRG* A 28 (1978); 2 EHRR 214 para 34 PC.

[132] *Marckx v Belgium* A 31 (1979); 2 EHRR 330 PC.

[133] *Soering v UK* A 161 (1989); 11 EHRR 439 para 87 PC.

[134] 2006-V para 48 GC. Cf, *Klass v FRG* A 28 (1978); 2 EHRR 214 PC.

[135] A 7 (1968); 1 EHRR 55.

Pretto v Italy,[136] the Court went against the clear wording of the Convention text in order to achieve a *restrictive* result. There it held that the unqualified requirement in Article 6(1) that judgments be 'pronounced publicly' (*rendu publiquement*) does not apply to a Court of Cassation. The Court considered that it must have been the intention of the drafting states (although there was no clear evidence in the *travaux préparatoires*) to respect the 'long-standing tradition' in many Council of Europe states to this effect.[137] For this reason, the Court did not 'feel bound to adopt a literal interpretation' and preferred a more flexible approach that it felt was not inconsistent with the basic 'object and purpose' of Article 6.

In *Soering v UK*,[138] the Court raised the possibility of informal amendment of the text of the Convention. Faced with wording in Article 2 which expressly permits capital punishment, the Court stated that '[s]ubsequent practice in national penal policy, in the form of a generalized abolition of capital punishment, could be taken as establishing the agreement of the contracting states to abrogate the exception provided for under Article 2(1)'. In fact, it found that this had not happened as the Convention parties had recently seen the need to adopt the Sixth Protocol, which abolishes the death penalty for those parties that accept it.[139]

XII. THE AUTONOMOUS MEANING OF CONVENTION TERMS[140]

Legal terms that might be considered as referring back to the meaning that they have in the national law of the state concerned have not been so interpreted. Instead, they have been given an autonomous Convention meaning. They includes terms such as 'criminal charge', 'civil rights and obligations', 'tribunal', and 'witness' in Article 6.[141] The words 'law' and 'lawful', however, have a mixed national law and Convention meaning. They both require that there be a national law basis for what is done and are imbued with a Convention idea of the essential qualities of law. As to the latter, a 'law' must not be arbitrary; it must also be consistent with the general principles of the Convention, publicly available and have a reasonably predictable effect.[142]

XIII. RECOURSE TO THE *TRAVAUX PRÉPARATOIRES*

Recourse may be had to the *travaux préparatoires*, or preparatory work, of the Convention[143] in order to confirm its meaning as established in accordance with the rule in Article 31 of the Vienna Convention or where the application of that rule leaves its meaning 'ambiguous or obscure' or 'leads to a result which is manifestly absurd or

---

[136] A 71 (1983); 6 EHRR 182 para 26 PC. See further below, p 277.

[137] The Court's approach may have been influenced by the fact that the text of Article 6 was probably drafted with only trial proceedings in mind.

[138] A 161 (1989); 11 EHRR 439 para 103 PC. See also *Cruz Varas v Sweden* A 201 (1991); 14 EHRR 1 para 100 PC.

[139] This illustrates the risk that an optional protocol to the Convention may foreclose a broad interpretation of the original Convention, which is binding upon all parties. See, however, *Ekbatani v Sweden* A 134 (1988); 13 EHRR 504 para 26 PC in which the Court stated that the addition of a right in a protocol was not to be taken as limiting the scope of the meaning of the original Convention guarantee.

[140] See Letsas, 15 EJIL 279 (2004); Matscher, *European System*, Ch 5 at pp 70–3, and Van der Meersch, *Wiarda Mélanges*, p 201.

[141] See below, pp 205, 209, 212, 285 and 323. Cf, the autonomous meaning of the terms 'vagrant' and 'persons of unsound mind' in Article 5(1)(d), below, pp 154, 156.

[142] See below, pp 133 and 344, concerning Articles 5 and 8–10.

[143] For the *travaux préparatoires* of the Convention, see the *Collected Edition of the Travaux Préparatoires of the European Convention on Human Rights*, 8 vols, 1975–85 (hereafter *TP*).

unreasonable'.[144] In practice, the Court, and formerly the Commission, has made only occasional use of the *travaux préparatoires*.[145] This is partly because the *travaux* are not often helpful[146] and partly because of the emphasis upon a dynamic and generally teleological interpretation of the Convention that focuses where relevant upon current European standards rather than the particular intentions of the drafting states.[147]

XIV.   THE INTERPRETATIVE ROLE OF THE COURT

The interpretation of the Convention is the role of the Court. The Committee of Ministers makes no attempt to interpret the Convention when it monitors compliance with judgments under Article 46(2). Before its abolition in 1998, the Commission also played an important part in the interpretation of the Convention. The Commission gave reasoned decisions at the admissibility stage, particularly when it declared an application to be inadmissible.[148] In addition, the Commission's reports on the merits of admitted applications were fully reasoned.[149] However, it followed from the scheme of the Convention that in practice the 'last word'[150] as to its meaning rested with the Court. If the Court interpreted the Convention differently from the Commission, the Court's view prevailed and the Commission, if sometimes slowly, changed its mind.[151] Although the Court has since 1998 developed its own jurisprudence on admissibility and has filled in many of the gaps in its interpretation of the Convention's substantive guarantee, some pre-1998 Commission interpretations remain of authority in the absence of Court pronouncements.

There is no common law distinction between *ratio decidendi* and *obiter dicta* in the practice of the European Court of Human Rights. Any statement by way of interpretation of the Convention by the Court, and formerly the Commission, is significant, although inevitably the level of generality at which it is expressed or its centrality to the decision on the material facts of the case will affect the weight and influence of any pronouncement. Clearly, a Grand Chamber ruling is more authoritative generally than one by a Court Chamber.

There is no doctrine of binding precedent in the sense that the Court is bound by its previous interpretations of the Convention (or those of the former Commission).[152] The rules concerning precedent have to be read in the context of a Court that sits in five separate Chambers of equal standing and a Grand Chamber to which certain cases may be relinquished by the Chamber for an initial decision on the merits or to which a case that

---

144   Article 32, Vienna Convention.

145   See eg, *Johnston v Ireland* A 112 (1986); 9 EHRR 203 para 52 PC and *Lithgow v UK* A 102 (1986); 8 EHRR 329 para 117 PC.

146   See eg, *Cruz Varas v Sweden* A 201 (1991); 14 EHRR 1 para 95 PC (*travaux préparatoires* 'silent').

147   Remarkably, in *Young, James and Webster v UK* A 44 (1981); 4 EHRR 38 PC and *Sigurjonsson v Iceland* A 264 (1993); 16 EHRR 462 the Court resorted to the *travaux préparatoires* only to reject the evidence that it found: see below, p 540.

148   Applications are sometimes admitted (now by the Court) on the basis that they raise complex issues of fact and law that should be left to the merits; in such cases, there is no reasoning at the admissibility stage.

149   In contrast, Commission Reports (and now Court judgments) on friendly settlements contain little or no interpretation of the Convention.

150   Mosler, in *Van Panhuys Essays*, p 152. In theory, the contracting parties to the Convention have the 'last word' as to the meaning of their treaty and could, if they were all agreed (either when meeting within the Committee of Ministers or otherwise), adopt an interpretation that would prevail over that of the Court.

151   Eg, the Commission adopted (see eg, its Report, para 95 in *Buchholz v FRG* B 37 (1980)) the Court's approach to the interpretation of the reasonable time requirement in Article 5(3) following the Court's rejection of the Commission's approach in *Wemhoff v FRG* A 7 (1968); 1 EHRR 55.

152   On precedent in the Court, see Wildhaber, in *Ryssdal Mélanges*, p 1529.

has been decided initially by a Court Chamber may be referred for a re-hearing.[153] In *Cossey v UK*,[154] the Plenary Court stated that it 'is not bound by its previous judgments' but that 'it usually follows and applies its own precedents, such a course being in the interests of legal certainty and the orderly development of the Convention case-law'. However, the Court continued, it is free to depart from an earlier judgment if there are 'cogent reasons' for doing so, which might include the need to 'ensure that the interpretation of the Convention reflects societal changes and remains in line with present day conditions'. For example, in *Goodwin (Christine) v UK*,[155] the Grand Chamber reversed the ruling of the Plenary Court in the *Cossey* and other cases on the legal status of post-operative transsexuals in the light of changing trends. Reformulating the position taken by the Plenary Court in the *Cossey* case, in the *Christine Goodwin* case, the Grand Chamber stated that 'it is in the interests of legal certainty, foreseeability and equality before the law that it should not depart, without good reason, from precedents laid down in previous cases.' This 'cogent' or 'good reason' approach applies to Grand Chamber reversals of its own or Plenary Court decisions; it will feel much freer to reverse previous Chamber decisions.[156] As to Chambers, it follows from the above approach that a Chamber should follow an earlier decision of another Chamber unless there are 'cogent reasons' not to do so. All Chambers are expected to follow Grand Chamber judgments, regardless of 'cogent reasons', unless the case can be distinguished in some other manner.

5. NEGATIVE AND POSITIVE OBLIGATIONS AND *DRITTWIRKUNG*[157]

Article 1 of the Convention requires the contracting parties to 'secure' the rights and freedoms included in it. Together with the text of later articles dealing with particular rights, this wording in Article 1 has been interpreted as imposing both negative and positive obligations upon states. A negative obligation is one by which a state is required to abstain from interference with, and thereby respect, human rights. For example, it must refrain from torture (Article 3) and impermissible restrictions upon freedom of expression (Article 10). Since such obligations are typical of those that apply to civil and political rights, it is not surprising that most of the obligations that a state has under the Convention are of this character.

A positive obligation is one whereby a state must take action to secure human rights. Positive obligations are generally associated with economic, social, and cultural rights[158] and commonly have financial implications, as, for example, with an obligation to provide medical treatment in realisation of the right to health. However, positive obligations

---

[153] Articles 30, 43, Convention. See below, p 826.

[154] A 184 (1990); 13 EHRR 622 para 35 PC.

[155] 2002-VI; 35 EHRR 447 para 74 GC. As well as the need for a dynamic interpretation of the Convention, other 'cogent reasons' recognized by the Court are the needs to clarify the meaning of the Convention (*Vilho Eskelinen v Finland*, below p 221) and to tackle the rise in application numbers (*Kudla v Poland*, below p 570). See Mowbray, 9 HRLR (2009) (in press).

[156] The Grand Chamber is, of course, totally free to reverse a decision of a Chamber in the same case: see eg, *Dickson v UK* hudoc (2007); 46 EHRR 927 GC. Before 1998, the Plenary Court used to hear serious cases affecting the interpretation of the Convention and has been replaced in that role by the Grand Chamber.

[157] See Alkema, in *Wiarda Mélanges*, p 33; Clapham, *Human Rights in the Private Sphere*, 1993, Ch 7; Cherednychenko, 13 Maastricht JECL 195 (2006); Conforti, 13 ItYIL 3 (2003); Drzemczewski, *European Human Rights Convention in Domestic Law*, 1983, Ch 8; and Van Dyk, *Bahr Collection*.

[158] See Van Hoof, in Alston and Tomasevski, eds, *The Right to Food*, 1984, p 97.

can also be imposed in respect of civil and political rights and they are to be found the European Convention. Before considering those in the Convention, it should be noted that, although the Strasbourg Court keeps to the typology of negative and positive obligations, a different, tripartite typology of obligations to respect, protect and fulfil human rights is now well established[159] and might usefully be adopted by the Court in its judgments. In this typology, obligations to respect are negative obligations. Obligations to protect and to fulfil are positive obligations, requiring respectively state protection from the acts of other persons and other positive action within the power of the state to fulfil a human right.

A number of positive obligations are expressly present in, or necessarily follow from, the text of the Convention. There are, for example, obligations to protect the right to life by law (Article 2(1)); to provide prison conditions that are not 'inhuman' (Article 3); to provide courts, legal aid, and translators in connection with the right to a fair trial (Article 6); and to hold free elections (Article 3, First Protocol).

Other positive obligations have been read into the Convention by the Court.[160] This process finds its source in the Court's jurisprudence in *Marckx v Belgium*.[161] There the Court stated, in the context of the right to 'respect for family life' in Article 8, that 'it does not merely compel the state to abstain from such interferences: in addition to this primary negative undertaking, there may be positive obligations inherent in an "effective respect" for family life'. In that case, a positive obligation had been infringed, *inter alia*, because Belgian family law did not recognize a child born out of wedlock as a member of the mother's family, thus not allowing the mother and child 'to lead a normal family life'. In *Airey v Ireland*,[162] the same approach was used to establish a positive obligation, this time one involving public expenditure,[163] under the same Article 8 guarantee to provide for effective access to a court for an allegedly battered wife to obtain an order of judicial separation. Generally, the Court has justified its finding of positive obligations as being necessary to make a Convention right effective.[164]

In the *Marckx* and *Airey* cases, the state's positive obligations were to grant individuals the legal status, rights, and privileges needed to ensure that their Convention rights were 'secured' (Article 1). In terms of the tripartite typology referred to above, they were obligations to use the power of the state to fulfil Convention rights. Other obligations of this kind of great importance that have been read into the Convention by the Court are the obligations to investigate suspicious deaths (Article 2)[165] and allegations of torture (Article 3).[166]

In other cases, following the same typology, the Court has established that there are positive obligations upon contracting parties to 'protect' Convention rights, by protecting persons' rights from the acts of others. The first clear indication of this came in *X and*

---

[159] It was first formulated in UN Doc E/CN.4/Sub.2/1987/23 and is used by the UN Committee on Economic, Social, and Cultural Rights. See Koch, 5 HRLR 81 (2005).

[160] See generally Mowbray, *The Development of Positive Obligations under the European Convention on Human Rights by the European Court of Human Rights*, 2004.

[161] A 31 (1979); 2 EHRR 330 para 31 PC. Cf, *Abdulaziz, Cabales and Balkandali v UK* A 94 (1985); 7 EHRR 471 para 67 PC and *Goodwin (Christine) v UK* 2002-VI; 35 EHRR 447 GC. See also the *'National Union of Belgian Police' Case* A 19 (1975); 1 EHRR 518 para 39.

[162] A 32 (1979); 2 EHRR 305 para 32.

[163] For other cases involving public expenditure, see eg, *Bouamar v Belgium* A 129 (1988); 11 EHRR 1 and *Poltoratskiy v Ukraine* 2003-V; 39 EHRR 916 para 148.

[164] See Mowbray, above, n 160, p 221.

[165] See below, p 48. This obligation includes investigation of alleged killings by both state and private actors.

[166] See below, p 108.

Y v Netherlands,[167] where a state was held liable because its criminal law did not provide a means by which a sexual assault upon a mentally handicapped young woman could be the subject of a criminal prosecution. In the words of the Court, the Article 8 obligation to respect an individual's privacy imposed positive obligations that 'may involve the adoption of measures designed to secure respect for private life *even in the sphere of the relations of individuals themselves*'. The same formula was later used in *Plattform 'Ärzte für das Leben' v Austria*,[168] in which the Court held that a state must take reasonable and appropriate measures to protect demonstrators from interference by other private persons intent upon disrupting their demonstration in breach of the right to freedom of assembly protected by Article 11. More recently, the Court has found positive obligations to protect individuals from assault[169] and other ill-treatment[170] and from invasions of their privacy.[171] The full extent to which the Convention places states under positive obligations to protect individuals against infringements of their rights by other private persons has yet to be fully established, with the Court continuing to add to their number. Domestic violence (Article 3),[172] and deprivation of liberty by terrorists or other kidnappers (Article 5)[173] are obvious areas to which an obligation to protect individuals against interferences with their rights by other persons could extend.

The question of the protection under the Convention of individuals against other private persons is sometimes spoken of, misleadingly, in terms of the concept of *drittwirkung*. This concept, which is most developed in German legal thinking and law,[174] supposes that an individual may rely upon a national bill of rights to bring a claim against a private person who has violated his rights under that instrument.[175] Given that this involves the liability of private individuals, or the horizontal application of law, it can have no application under the Convention at the international level,[176] because the Convention is a treaty that imposes obligations only upon states.[177]

Insofar as the Convention touches the conduct of private persons, it does so only indirectly through such positive obligations as it imposes upon a state. As noted earlier, the basis for the state's responsibility under the Convention in the case of such obligations is that, contrary to Article 1, it has failed to 'secure' to individuals within its jurisdiction the rights guaranteed in the Convention by not rendering unlawful the acts of private persons that infringe them.

The position may be different, however, where the private conduct falls within the area of a Convention right or is the result of 'privatization'. The first of these situations

---

[167] A 91 (1985); 8 EHRR 235 para 23. Italics added. See also *Young, James and Webster v UK* A 44 (1981); 4 EHRR 38 PC.

[168] A 139 (1988); 13 EHRR 204 para 32.

[169] *Osman v UK* 1998-VIII; 29 EHRR 245 (death threat); *Özgür Gündem v Turkey* 2000-III, 31 EHRR 1082 (protection of journalists from attack); and *A v UK* 1998-VI; 27 EHRR 611 (parental corporal punishment).

[170] *Z v UK* 2001-V; 34 EHRR 97 GC.   [171] *Von Hannover v Germany* hudoc (2005); 43 EHRR 139.

[172] See below, p 78.

[173] See below, p 129. For the Strasbourg jurisprudence on racist speech and blasphemy by private persons, see below at pp 449 and 439.

[174] For its meaning in German law, see Lewan, 17 ICLQ 571 (1968).

[175] This is the concept of direct *drittwirkung*. For indirect *drittwirkung*, which likewise does not refer to positive obligations of the kind that exist under the Convention, see Lewan, *ibid*.

[176] What may happen, however, is that in a state in which the Convention is a part of national law, the Convention guarantee may be treated, like some national bills of rights, as generating rights vis-à-vis private persons: see Drzemczewski, *European Human Rights Convention in Domestic Law*, 1983, Ch 8, particularly concerning Germany (p 210).

[177] See Article 1. Accordingly, as explained below, p 787, an application may not be brought under Article 34 against a private person and Article 33 supposes only inter-state applications.

existed in *Costello-Roberts v UK*[178] which was a case concerning corporal punishment in a private school. The Court noted that the case fell within the ambit of a right—the right to education—that was protected by the First Protocol to the Convention.[179] It stated that 'the state cannot absolve itself from responsibility' to secure a Convention right 'by delegating its obligations to private bodies or individuals.'[180] Accordingly, the Court held that, although the act of a private person, the treatment complained of could engage the responsibility of the defendant state under Article 3. This approach was followed *mutatis mutandis* in *Woś v Poland*[181] in the situation where the defendant state had entrusted a private law foundation to administer a compensation scheme established under an international agreement that it had made with Germany. The Court held that the 'exercise of state powers which affects Convention rights and freedoms raises an issue of state responsibility regardless' of the fact that their exercise may have been delegated by the state to a private actor. Consequently, given the need to protect rights effectively, the defendant state was accountable under the Convention for the acts of the foundation. It would be consistent with this reasoning for the state to be directly responsible under the Convention for the acts of private companies and other persons to whom powers that are traditionally state powers have been transferred by privatization, as in the case of private prisons.

6. RESERVATIONS[182]

Article 57 (formerly Article 64) of the Convention allows a party on signature or ratification 'to make a reservation in respect of any particular provision of the Convention to the extent that any law then in force in its territory is not in conformity with the provision'. Reservations have been made by over twenty of the forty-seven parties to the Convention.[183] They have been invoked successfully in several cases to prevent a claim being heard,[184] although some reservations have been held to be invalid.[185] Article 57 requires that a reservation must not be 'of a general character'. In *Belilos v Switzerland*,[186] the Court stated that a reservation falls within this prohibition if it is 'couched in terms that are too vague or broad for it to be possible to determine their exact meaning and

---

[178] A 247-C (1993); 19 EHRR 112. For the Court's current, broader approach to private corporal punishment under Article 3, see below, p 105.

[179] The Court indicated that the right to education included school discipline and applied without discrimination to state and private schools.

[180] A 247-C (1993); 19 EHRR 112 para 27. The Court referred to *Van der Mussele v Belgium* A 70 (1983); 6 EHRR 163 PC, in which, in a case alleging 'forced labour' contrary to Article 4 of the Convention, it had rejected the defendant state's argument that it was not responsible for the conduct of a private professional body, the *ordre des avocats*, concerning legal aid, when the defendant state relied upon the arrangements for legal aid made by the *ordre* so as to comply with the obligation to provide legal aid in Article 6(3)(c).

[181] No 22860/02 hudoc (2005) para 72 DA.

[182] See Frowein, *Wiarda Mélanges*, p 193. The rules on reservations in Articles 2(1)(d) and 19–23 in the Vienna Convention on the Law of Treaties 1969 apply to the Convention as customary international law: *Temeltasch v Switzerland* 5 EHRR 417 at 432 (1983) Com Rep.

[183] For the text of reservations, see <http://www.coe.int>. Most current reservations concern Articles 5 and 6. A few reservations have been withdrawn (eg Finland: Article 6). Reservation may be for a limited time: see *Jecius v Lithuania* 2000-IX; 35 EHRR 400 (one year).

[184] See eg, *Chorherr v Austria* A 266-B (1993); 17 EHRR 358; *Helle v Finland* 1997-VIII; 26 EHRR 159; and *Shestjorkin v Estonia* No 49450/99 hudoc (2000) DA.

[185] See *Belilos v Switzerland* A 132 (1988); 10 EHRR 466; *Eisenstecken v Austria* 2000-X; 34 EHRR 860; and *Weber v Switzerland* A 177 (1990); 12 EHRR 508.

[186] A 132 (1988); 10 EHRR 466 para 55. See Bourguignon, 29 VJIL 347 (1989); Macdonald, 21 RBDI 429 (1988); and Marks, 39 ICLQ 300 (1990).

scope'. In that case, having confirmed its competence to rule on the validity of reservations, the Court held that a Swiss reservation concerning the scope of Article 6 was invalid, *inter alia*, on the basis of this test.[187] Reservations that 'do not specify the relevant provisions of the national law or fail to indicate the Convention articles that might be affected by the application of those provisions' are reservations of a 'general character' and hence invalid.[188] A reservation is limited in its scope to the articles and national law to which it refers.[189] Moreover, it may only concern the extent to which a national law in force in a state's territory at the time of signature or ratification is consistent with the Convention; it cannot provide a shield for laws or amendments to laws that come into force later.[190] The text of Article 57 suggests that reservations may only be made to the Articles of the Convention that contain its substantive guarantees. Accordingly, reservations limiting the territorial scope of the Convention are not permitted[191] and a reservation to the right under Article 34 to make an application to the Court is almost certainly invalid.[192] A question that remains to be decided is whether a reservation to a provision such as Article 15 is invalid, either on this basis or as being of a 'general character.'[193]

In the *Belilos* case, the Court also held that a further requirement of a valid reservation in (now) Article 57(2) had not been satisfied, namely, that any reservation 'made under this Article shall contain a brief statement of the law concerned'.[194] Since this is 'not a purely formal requirement but a condition of substance',[195] non-compliance with it renders a reservation invalid without more.

The outcome of the Court's decision in the *Belilos* case was that Switzerland was bound by (and found in breach of) Article 6 without the shield of the reservation that was held to be invalid. In holding that this was the case, the Court noted that it was 'beyond doubt that Switzerland is, and regards itself as, bound by the Convention irrespective of the validity of the declaration' and that it had recognized the Court's competence to rule on the question of validity.[196] In later cases in which the Court has held a reservation to be invalid, the Court has not referred to such matters,[197] seemingly taking the view that severance is always the outcome, the state remaining a party to the Convention without the benefit of the reservation regardless of its intention when making the reservation or the importance of the reservation to it.

---

[187] The reservation read: 'The Swiss Federal Council considers that...Article 6...is intended solely to ensure ultimate control by the judiciary over the acts or decisions of the public authorities'. A reservation must be interpreted in the language in which it is made, which need not be either the English or French authentic Convention languages: *X v Austria No 2432/65*, 22 CD 124 (1967).

[188] *Slivenko v Latvia No 48321/99* hudoc (2002) para 60. In that case the Court also rejected a government argument that its uncommunicated (and incorrect) 'assumption' that the requirements of an earlier Latvian-Russian treaty complied with the Convention amounted to a 'quasi-reservation': id, para 61.

[189] *Gradinger v Austria* A 328-C (1995).

[190] *Fischer v Austria* hudoc (1995); 20 EHRR 349 and *Shestjorkin v Estonia No 49450/99* hudoc (2000) DA.

[191] *Assanidze v Georgia* 2004-II; 39 EHRR 653 GC.

[192] Cf, *Loizidou v Turkey* A 310 (1995); 20 EHRR 99 (on restrictions to declarations accepting the former optional right of application). See Barratta, 11 EJIL 413 (2000).

[193] See the French reservation to Article 15 which restricts the competence of the Court to question the French government's judgment as to the need for emergency measures. See below, p 642.

[194] In *Belilos*, there was no statement of the law at all. The 'brief statement' need not include a summary of the law concerned; an indication of its subject matter and a reference to an official source in which the text may be found is sufficient: *Chorherr v Austria* A 266-B (1993); 17 EHRR 358 para 21.

[195] Id, para 59. The requirement was 'both an evidential factor' and contributed to 'legal certainty'; generally it was intended to ensure that a 'reservation does not go beyond the provisions expressly excluded by the state concerned': *ibid*. Cf, *Weber v Switzerland* A 177 para 38 (1990); 12 EHRR 508 in which another Swiss reservation was held to be invalid for non-compliance with Article 64(2). See also *Eisenstecken v Austria* 2000-X; 34 EHRR 860.   [196] *Belilos v Switzerland* A 132 (1988); 10 EHRR 466 para 59.

[197] See the *Eisensteken* and *Weber* cases, above, n 195. On the severance of reservations to treaties generally, see Aust, *The Modern Law of Treaties*, 2000, pp 117–23.

In the *Belilos* case, the Court also held that an instrument deposited on signature or ratification may qualify as a reservation even though it is not described as such; it is sufficient that the state intended it to be a reservation. In that case, Switzerland had deposited on ratification what it described as two 'interpretative declarations', including the instrument in issue, and two 'reservations'. The Court held that the 'interpretative declaration' concerned was a reservation for the purposes of (now) Article 57 (although it proved not to be a valid one) in the light of the evidence in the Swiss *travaux* as to Switzerland's intentions. The Court's approach can be criticized as not taking account of the need for certainty in this regard and the reasonable expectation that a state knows the distinction in international law between a reservation and an interpretative declaration, particularly when it uses both terms in the instrument that it deposits.[198]

7. THE CONVENTION IN NATIONAL LAW[199]

I. THE APPLICATION OF THE CONVENTION BY NATIONAL COURTS

International human rights guarantees are most valuable when they are enforceable in national law. Even in the case of as successful an international guarantee as the European Convention on Human Rights, a remedy in a national court will generally be more convenient and efficient than recourse to an international procedure. Accordingly, if the Convention can be relied upon in a party's national courts, an important extra dimension is added to its effectiveness, particularly in a state that lacks its own national bill of rights.[200] Application through national courts is also consistent with the principle of subsidiarity[201] which underlies the Convention, by which the primary responsibility to enforce the Convention falls upon the states parties.

Under Article 1 of the Convention, the parties undertake to 'secure' the rights and freedoms in the Convention to persons within their jurisdiction. This does not require a party to incorporate the Convention into its law.[202] While compliance with this obligation finds 'a particularly faithful reflection in those instances where the Convention has been incorporated into domestic law',[203] a party may satisfy Article 1 instead by ensuring, in whatever manner it chooses,[204] that its law and practice is such that Convention rights are guaranteed. In fact, the Convention has now been incorporated into the law of all the contracting parties.[205]

---

[198] Note, however, that Article 2(1)(d), Vienna Convention on the Law of Treaties defines a reservation as a 'unilateral statement, *however phrased or named*'. Italics added.

[199] See Bernhardt, *European System*, Ch 3; Blackburn and Polakiewicz, eds, *Fundamental Rights in Europe*, 2001; Drzemczewski, *European Human Rights Convention in Domestic Law*, 1983; Gardner, ed, *Aspects of Incorporation of the European Convention of Human Rights into Domestic Law*, 1993; Gearty, ed, *European Civil Liberties and the European Convention on Human Rights*, 1997; Greer, *European Convention*, Ch 2; Polakiewicz, 2 All-European Human Rights Yearbook (1992), 11, 147; *ibid*, 18 HRLJ 405 (1997); Ress, in Maier, ed, *Protection of Human Rights in Europe*, 1982, p 209; *ibid, European System*, Ch 36; id 40 Texas ILJ 359 (2005). See also the *European Convention on Human Rights and National Caselaw*, 2004; id, 2005; id, 2006, supplements to Council of Europe *Human Rights Information Bulletin*, Nos 65, 68, and 71.

[200] The UK is one such state.   [201] See above, p 13.

[202] See eg, *Observer and Guardian v UK* A 216 (1991); 14 EHRR 153 PC.

[203] *Ireland v UK* A 25 (1978); 2 EHRR 25 para 239 PC.

[204] *'Swedish Engine Drivers Union' Case* A 20 (1976); 1 EHRR 617.

[205] See the survey in Blackburn and Polakiewicz, *op cit* at n 199 above.

Although incorporation of the Convention into national law is desirable, it does not by itself ensure a remedy in a national court for a breach of the Convention. In states follow-ing the 'monist' approach to the relationship between international and national law,[206] the Convention will automatically be part of the national law as a result of its ratification. However, in the legal systems of such states, the Convention may only be relied upon in the national courts as the basis for a claim if the Convention guarantee as a whole, or the relevant article or part of it, is regarded by the court concerned as self-executing.[207] By this is meant that the court accepts that the relevant provision creates a right that can be relied upon directly before it without further steps being needed by way of legislative or other state action.[208] National courts following the monist approach have differed in their assessment of the self-executing character of Convention provisions.[209] For example, the Austrian and Swiss courts have generally applied Convention provisions as self-executing. In Belgium, whereas the negative obligation under Article 8 not to interfere with family life was held to be self-executing, the positive obligation to create an appropriate legal status for children born out of wedlock required legislation.[210] The Italian Court of Cassation regards the Convention as a whole as stating only programmatic rules for the guidance of the legislature. Even if a Convention provision is regarded as self-executing, it does not necessarily follow that national courts will actually make use of what is seen as 'foreign' law. Most noticeably, where a state, such as Germany, has its own well-established national bill of rights, the Convention has tended to be given only a limited role, with the local courts preferring to rely upon the bill of rights in the national constitution.[211] In contrast, courts in some states have emphasized the Convention because of its constitutional status (Austria) or the absence of a detailed national bill of rights (Switzerland).

In states following the dualist, not the monist, approach, further legislative action in all cases needs to be taken following ratification for the Convention to be enforceable in the national courts, with the precise way in which it is enforceable being dependent upon the terms of the legislation. Thus, in the case of the United Kingdom, the Human Rights Act 1998 provides for the indirect incorporation of the rights of the Convention into UK law as 'Convention rights'.[212] This has two main consequences. First, if, despite all efforts, primary UK legislation applicable in cases coming before the courts cannot be interpreted compatibly with the Convention, the competent court may make a 'declara-tion of incompatibility'. This does not affect the validity of the legislation, but alerts the government to the need to amend the law. Second, a victim has a public law right of action for damages or other relief against a public authority (not a private person) which acts inconsistently with a 'Convention right'. The Human Rights Act has greatly increased the powers of the UK courts to provide a remedy nationally for a breach of the Convention

---

[206] On the monist and dualist approaches, see Brownlie, *Principles of Public International Law*, 7th edn, 2008, pp 31–3.

[207] Another factor is the precise status that the Convention has in the legal system of the state concerned in relation to other national laws that contradict it. In the law of some parties, the Convention has only the status of an ordinary law. In most—including Central and East European states—it prevails over subsequent as well as prior inconsistent legislation but is subject to the constitution. In Austria, it has the status of constitutional law. See Poliakiewicz in Blackburn and Poliakiewicz, eds, *Fundamental Rights in Europe*, 2001, Ch 2. In the Netherlands, the Convention is superior to the constitution: see *Oerlemans v Netherlands* A 219 (1991); 15 EHRR 561. On Russia, see Koroteev and Golubok, 7 HRLR 619 (2007).

[208] On self-executing treaty provisions, see Brownlie, *Principles of Public International Law*, 7th edn, 2008, p 48.

[209] See Polakiewicz, in Blackburn and Poliakiewicz, eds, *Fundamental Rights in Europe*, 2001, Ch 2 and Polakiewicz and Jacob-Foltzer, 12 HRLJ 65, 136 (1991) from which the examples below are drawn.

[210] *Vermeire v Belgium* A 214-C (1991); 15 EHRR 488 para 11.

[211] See Ress, 40 Texas ILJ 359 at 360 (2005).

[212] Cf, the Irish European Convention on Human Rights Act 2003.

with the result that the numbers of both Strasbourg applications and adverse judgments against the United Kingdom has decreased.[213]

There has generally been a marked increase in reliance upon the Convention in national courts in recent years.[214] With the dramatic increase in the extent and impact of the European Court's jurisprudence, national courts have become all too aware that their decisions may find their way to Strasbourg to be scrutinized there by reference to Convention standards.[215] When the Convention is relied upon by a national court, the question arises whether, although not bound to do so, it will follow the interpretation of it that has been adopted at Strasbourg. In practice, national courts have usually done so, although there have been exceptions.[216] Where a point of interpretation has not been ruled upon in a Strasbourg case, the national courts will have no choice but to adopt their own interpretation. Insofar as they do so, it is possible that courts in different legal systems may interpret the Convention differently, particularly as there is no procedure for the reference of a case to Strasbourg for a definitive ruling.[217]

Whether a state incorporates the Convention into its law or not, it is required by Article 13 to provide an 'effective remedy' under its national law for a person who has an arguable claim under the Convention. Thus, for example, a wife whose husband has been excluded from a state's territory because of an immigration law that may infringe the Convention must have an effective remedy under national law by which to challenge the legality of the husband's exclusion.[218] The Court's jurisprudence suggests that a state that does not make the Convention enforceable in its national law is especially at risk of being in breach of Article 13.[219]

II. THE EXECUTION OF STRASBOURG JUDGMENTS[220]

A Court judgment is 'essentially declaratory'.[221] Article 41 of the Convention provides that the Court may award a victim 'just compensation'—a power which has been understood to permit the award of monetary compensation and legal costs.[222] Otherwise, 'in principle, it is not for the Court to determine what remedial measures may be appropriate

---

[213] On the impact the Human Rights Act generally, see UK Department of Constitutional Affairs, *Review of the Implementation of the Human Rights Act*, 2006.

[214] See Polakiewicz, in Blackburn and Polakiewicz, *Fundamental Rights in Europe*, 2001, pp 50–2. See also Costa, 38 Texas ILJ 455 at 458 (France). Many key UK human rights cases, eg *A (FC) v Secretary of State for the Home Department* [2004] UKHL 56 and *R (application of Al-Skeini) v Secretary of State for Defence* [2005] EWCA Civ 1609, would have lacked a legal basis without the Human Rights Act. But the Convention is far less known and used as yet by the courts in most post-communist states parties.

[215] Cf, Polakiewicz and Jacob-Folzer, 12 HRLJ 136 at 141.

[216] Polakiewicz and Jacob-Folzer, *ibid*, refer to rulings by Austrian, Belgian, and French courts on the scope of Article 6(1) as ones in which exceptionally the Court has been 'openly defied'.

[217] Contrast the provision made under Article 234, Treaty of Rome for the reference by national courts of cases to the European Court of Justice for the interpretation of European Union law. The Report of the Group of Wise Persons to the Committee of Ministers, CM (2006) 203, para 80, considered such a mechanism as 'unsuitable' for the Convention.

[218] *Abdulaziz, Cabales and Balkandali v UK* A 94 (1985); 7 EHRR 471 para 93 PC.

[219] The number of applications and adverse judgments against the UK under Article 13 has declined since the Human Rights Act.

[220] See Barkhuysen, van Emmerik, and van Kempen, *The Execution of Strasbourg and Geneva Human Rights Decisions in the National Legal Order*, 1999; Janis, 15 Conn JIL 39 (2000); and Lambert-Abdelgawad, *The Execution of Judgments of the European Court of Human Rights*, CoE Human Rights File 19, 2nd edn, 2008.

[221] *Marckx v Belgium* A 31 (1979); 2 EHRR 330 para 58 PC. A judgment 'cannot of itself annul or repeal' inconsistent national court judgments or national law: *ibid*.

[222] See below, p 856.

to satisfy the respondent state's obligations';[223] instead it is for that state 'to put an end to the breach and make reparation for its consequences in such a way as to restore as far as possible the situation existing before the breach.'[224] Whereas, in accordance with this approach, the Court used always to refrain from specifying action that should be taken to comply with its judgments, it has modified its position recently.[225] In some cases, although these remain the exception, it has indicated specific forms of restitution for the victim of a breach of the Convention. Thus it has required the return of the property concerned *as an alternative* to the payment of compensation for a breach of Article 1, Protocol 1.[226] In the case of the continued detention of an individual contrary to Article 5, the Court has found itself competent to specify, without in this context allowing any alternative, that the individual's release be secured, on the basis that the 'very nature' of the breach does not 'leave any real choice as to the measures required to remedy it.'[227] Finally, in cases in which a person has been convicted of a criminal offence in proceedings in breach of Article 6, the Court has stated that 'a retrial or reopening of the case, if requested, represents in principle an appropriate way of redressing the violation'.[228] However, the Court does not have jurisdiction to order a new trial or the quashing of a conviction.[229]

As well as specifying particular forms of restitution for the victim, the Court has also, but again exceptionally, moved in the direction of giving some indication in its judgments of the steps that a state found in breach of the Convention should take more generally to bring its law or practice into line with its Convention obligations. Whereas formerly the Court had left it entirely to the state concerned to decide what should be done, in *Broniowski v Poland*[230] the Court introduced the idea of 'pilot judgments'. These are appropriate where there is a breach of the Convention that results from a 'systematic defect' which may give rise to many claims. In such a case, the Court stated, some indication of the general measures that a state should adopt is in order 'so as not to overburden the Convention system with large numbers of applications deriving from the same cause'.

The judgments of the Court arising out of applications to Strasbourg are binding in international law upon the parties to them.[231] However, a national court is not obliged under the Convention to give them direct effect; this is a matter for the national law of the defendant state, which is free to implement Strasbourg judgments in accordance with the rules of its national legal system.[232] Assessments of the record of states in complying with

---

[223] *Broniowski v Poland* 2004-V; 43 EHRR 495 para 193 GC.

[224] *Brumărescu v Romania* (Article 41) 1999-VII; 35 EHRR 887 para 19.

[225] See Leach 2005 EHRLR 148.

[226] See eg, *Papamichalopoulos v Greece* (Article 50) A 330-B (1995); 21 EHRR 439 and *Brumărescu v Romania* (Article 41) 2001- I; 33 EHRR 887 GC.

[227] *Assanidze v Georgia* 2004-II; 39 EHRR 653 para 202 GC. See also *Ilaşcu and Others v Moldova and Russia* 2004-VII; 40 EHRR 1030 GC.

[228] *Sejdovic v Italy* 2006-II para 126 GC. See also *Öcalan v Turkey* 2005-IV; 41 EHRR 985 GC.

[229] *Lyons v UK* No 15227/03 2003- IX; 37 EHRR CD 183 and *Komanický v Slovakia*, No 13677/03 hudoc (2005) DA (civil case). It did not do so in *Sejdovic* or *Öcalan*.

[230] 2004-V; 33 EHRR para 193. See further below, p 851. A pilot judgment suspends the consideration by the Court of other applications deriving from the same defect pending measures being taken. In *Hirst v UK (No 2)* 2005-IX; 42 EHRR 849 GC the Court declined a government request to give guidance on what restrictions were permissible on the right to vote in the absence of a systematic defect.

[231] See Article 46(1), Convention.

[232] See eg, *Vermeire v Belgium* A 214-C (1991); 15 EHRR 488. Under Malta's European Convention Act 1987, its Constitutional Court is empowered to enforce judgments of the Strasbourg Court. In national legal systems generally, practice varies as to whether legislative or administrative action is required or whether the national courts are competent, where appropriate, to act, eg by quashing a national court decision, including a criminal conviction, found at Strasbourg to be in breach of the Convention. In Spain, the courts can so act; in

judgments has until recently been very positive. In 1996, the President of the Court stated that they had 'not only generally but always been complied with by the Contracting States concerned. There have been delays, perhaps even examples of minimal compliance, but no instances of non-compliance'.[233] This was true of the payment of compensation and costs awarded by the Court under (now) Article 41, the steps by way of restitution taken to remedy a wrong done to an individual applicant and the amendment of legislative and administrative practices found contrary to the Convention. In a number of cases, a Strasbourg judgment has provided a government with a lever to help overcome local opposition to law reform, as with the change in the law on homosexuality in Northern Ireland following *Dudgeon v UK*.[234] But sometimes it is uncertain whether the steps taken by the defendant state go far enough.[235] In other cases, a state may be slow in putting the necessary measures in place because of constitutional difficulties.[236] Thus it took fifteen years before the Isle of Man Tynwald enacted the Criminal Justice (Penalties, etc) Act 1993 to abolish judicial corporal punishment, thereby bringing the United Kingdom fully into line with its obligations under Article 3 following the *Tyrer* case.[237] Prior to the 1993 legislation, in the context of the special constitutional position of the Isle of Man,[238] the UK government had informed the Manx government after the *Tyrer* case that judicial corporal punishment would be contrary to the Convention and the case was brought to the attention of the local courts by the Manx authorities. Although this was considered sufficient by the Committee of Ministers, acting under what is now Article 46(2), to comply with the *Tyrer* judgment,[239] it would appear that the United Kingdom's obligation to 'secure' the rights and freedoms in the Convention required that it go further and for the relevant law to be amended.

While the record of state compliance with judgments remains generally good, recent reviews have been more critical.[240] Central and East European states have found particular difficulty in complying with some judgments against them, although they have

---

Germany, they cannot: see Bernhardt, *European System*, Ch 3, at p 38. See generally *The European Convention on Human Rights: Institution of Relevant Proceedings at the National Level to Facilitate Compliance with Strasbourg Decisions*, Council of Europe Committee of Experts Study, 13 HRLJ 71 (1992).

[233] Ryssdal, in Bulterman and Kuijers, eds, *Compliance with Judgments of International Courts: Schermers Symposium Proceedings*, 1996, 49 at 67. Cf, Leuprecht, *European System*, Ch 35 at p 798. For a case of minimal compliance, see the Contempt of Court Act 1981, below, p 473. A clear case in which a state refused point blank to change its (terrorism) law to comply with a judgment is *Brogan v UK*, below, p 170, in which the UK made an Article 15 declaration instead. This was considered sufficient by the Committee of Ministers: see *Brannigan and McBride v UK*, below p 170.

[234] A 45 (1981); 4 EHRR 149 PC.

[235] As Churchill and Young, 62 BYIL 283 at 346 (1992) point out, it may be unclear what steps are required by a judgment or whether the legislation read *in abstracto* is sufficient. Where possible, legislation intended to comply with a judgment should be interpreted by national courts as doing so.

[236] Delays in the payment of compensation or legislative or administrative change have many other causes, including the cost involved, political or public opposition, or the parliamentary timetable.

[237] A 26 (1978); 2 EHRR 1. There was much delay in complying with *Marckx v Belgium*, below, p 392. See also Mahoney and Prebensen, *European Supervision*, Ch 26 at p 636.

[238] The Isle of Man is a Crown possession that by convention is not subject to the legislative powers of Westminster on most internal matters.

[239] CM Res DH (78) 39. There was no case in which a sentence of judicial corporal punishment was executed prior to its abolition in 1993. In *Teare v O'Callaghan*, 4 EHRR 232 (1981) a post-*Tyrer* sentence of corporal punishment was quashed by the Isle of Man High Court on the ground that it was contrary to Isle of Man international obligations and should be imposed only if other forms of punishment are unsuitable.

[240] See Greer, *European Convention*, Ch 2; Lambert-Abdelgawad, *op cit* at n 220 above, pp 64-7; and Polakiewicz, in Blackburn and Polakiewicz, eds, *Fundamental Rights in Europe*, 2001, pp 69ff.

not been alone in this respect.[241] A result is that the role of the Committee of Ministers in supervising the execution of judgments has become more demanding and important.[242] Unfortunately, the Committee, being a political body composed of representatives of member states, is not the best equipped or motivated body to question whether the steps taken go far enough.[243]

8. THE CONVENTION AND THE EUROPEAN UNION[244]

The European Union (EU)[245] has legislative and executive jurisdiction by which it may act against member states[246] or private persons[247] in a way that impacts upon their Convention obligations and rights respectively. When exercising jurisdiction in these ways, it is possible that EU institutions may infringe Convention rights. The question therefore arises whether these institutions must comply with the Convention when they act. A related question is whether member states are responsible under the Convention for the effect on private persons of their national legislative or other public acts that are a consequence of EU membership.

As to the position of the EU, an application may not be made to Strasbourg against it under the Convention for any conduct on the part of its institutions because the EU is not a party thereto.[248] Following much debate and hesitation over many years, the Treaty on European Union (TEU), as amended by the Treaty of Lisbon, provides that the EU 'shall accede' to the Convention.[249] The Convention does, however, control EU conduct within its own legal order as the Convention has been incorporated into EU law. The TEU[250] states that the 'Union shall respect fundamental rights, as guaranteed by

---

[241] On Central and East European states and on the systemic problems in Italy, see Greer, *European Convention*, pp 103ff.

[242] On the role of the Committee of Ministers, see below, pp 871ff. See also Lambert-Abdelgawad, *op cit* at n 220, pp 32–9. For earlier literature, see Klerk, 45 NILR 65 (1998); MacDonald, *Valticos Mélanges*, 417; Tomkins, 1995 EHRLR 49. The Parliamentary Assembly has also assumed a role. The Assembly's Committee on Legal Affairs and Human Rights prepares excellent periodic reports on 'Implementation of Judgments of the European Court of Human Rights': see Lambert-Abdelgawad, *ibid*, pp 59–62.

[243] See Leuprecht, *European System*, Ch 35 at p 798. Former Judge Martens concludes that the Committee of Ministers exercises only a light or '*prima facie* control': Martens, in Bulterman and Kuijer, eds, *Compliance with Judgments of International Courts: Schermers Symposium*, 1996, p 77.

[244] See Craig and de Búrca, *EU Law*, 4th edn, 2003, Ch 11 and Gaja, in Alston, ed, *The EU and Human Rights*, 1999, Ch 24. For a comparison of the interpretation of the Convention by the Strasbourg and Luxembourg courts, see Spielmann, in Alston, id, Ch 23, and Turner, 5 EPL 453 (1999). See also Conforti, *Cassese Collection*, 221.

[245] The term European Union is used to refer to the European Union generally and to the European Community in particular.

[246] Eg, by requiring them to take certain action: see the *Bosphorus Airways* case, at n 257 below.

[247] Eg, to impose a fine: see the facts of *M and Co v FRG No 13258/87*, 64 DR 138 (1990).

[248] *Matthews v UK* 1999-I: 29 EHRR 361 GC. The same is true of other European institutions: *Heinz v Contracting States also Parties to the European Patent Convention No 21090/92*, 76A DR 125 (1994); 18 EHRR CD 168 (European Patent Office).

[249] Article 6(3) (Treaty of Lisbon amendments not yet in force). The ECJ had earlier opined that the EU was not competent to accede to the Convention without an EU treaty amendment empowering it to do so: Opinion 2/94 [1996] ECR I-1759. Article 17, Protocol 14, Convention amends Article 59, Convention to permit the EU to accede.

[250] Article 6(2). The same provision is repeated, with drafting changes, in Article 6(3), TEU, as amended by the Treaty of Lisbon (not yet in force). ECJ case law is to the same effect: see eg, *ERT v DEP and Sotirios Kouvelas*, Case C-260/89 [1991] ECR I-2925. See also the 2000 EU Charter of Fundamental Rights, Preamble and Article 52(3). See Peers and Ward, eds, *The EU Charter of Fundamental Rights*, 2004. The Charter is not legally

the European Convention…and as they result from the constitutional traditions common to the member states, as general principles of law'. Accordingly, claims may succeed before the European Court of Justice (ECJ) on the basis that the challenged EU action is inconsistent with the Convention.[251] This way of indirectly subjecting EU institutions to the Convention is comparable to its incorporation into the national law of a state and falls short in its impact of Union accession to the Convention. In particular, as noted, it does not allow an individual to make an application to Strasbourg against the EU. Moreover, insofar as the Convention is applied as a part of EU law, the Convention would not prevail over a conflicting provision of Union primary (ie, treaty) law[252] and the interpretation and application of the Convention remains a matter for the ECJ, not the Convention's own Court.[253] Generally, the present situation is not satisfactory and EU accession to the Convention is clearly desirable.

With regard to the position of individual EU member states,[254] the following general rules apply. The Convention does not prohibit states parties from transferring sovereign power to an international (including supranational) organization such as the EU, but this will not in itself take away from their responsibility under the Convention for acts done as members of the organization. However, there is a presumption that a state party is not in breach of its obligations under the Convention by virtue of acts that are necessarily undertaken by it in fulfilment of obligations as members of the organization so long as the organization concerned provides human rights protection that is 'equivalent' to that in the Convention 'as regards both the substantive guarantee offered and the mechanisms controlling their observance'.[255] But this presumption may be rebutted if the protection provided by the other organization is 'manifestly deficient' on the facts of the particular case.[256] These general rules were formulated by the Court in the leading case of *Bosphorus Airways v Ireland*.[257] There the Irish authorities impounded a civil aircraft leased by the applicant Turkish company from the Yugoslav national airline that had landed in Dublin. The authorities did this in compliance with a legal obligation imposed on EU member states by an EU regulation adopted in implementation of UN Security Council resolutions requiring economic sanctions against the Federal Republic of Yugoslavia in the context of the conflict in the Balkans. The Court rejected a claim that the impounding was a violation by Ireland of the right to property guarantee in Article 1, First Protocol to the Convention, for the reason that Ireland was carrying out an obligation of its membership of the EU and 'equivalent' human rights protection was provided for the applicant in the EU legal order on the facts of the case. The protection afforded by the EU was 'equivalent' substantively, because of the reliance on the Convention as a source of human rights protection in EU law, and, in terms of mechanisms, through the remedies provided to enforce the substantive guarantee before the European Court of

binding, but would become such under Article 6(1), TEU, as amended by the Treaty of Lisbon. See Craig, 2008 ELR 137 at 162.

[251] See eg, *P v S and Cornwall CC*, Case C-13/94 [1996] ECR I-2143.

[252] See the *Matthews* case, below, p 730. Secondary legislation (regulations, directives) must be read subject to the Convention.

[253] See Jacque, *European System*, Ch 39 at pp 894–5.

[254] All EU member states are parties to the Convention, though not to all of its Protocols.

[255] *Bosphorus Hava Yolları Turizm ve Ticaret Anonim Şirketi (Bosphorus Airways) v Ireland* 2005-VI; 42 EHRR 1 para 154 GC. Organizations other than the EU to which the general rule applies include the UN. See the *Behrami* and *Saramati* cases, below p 790. See also *Waite and Kennedy v Germany* 1999-I; 30 EHRR 261 GC (European Space Agency); and *Capital Bank AD v Bulgaria* 2005-XII (IMF). And see *Prince Hans-Adam II of Liechtenstein v Germany* 2001-VIII GC (Convention prevails over later inconsistent treaty obligation). 'Equivalent' means 'comparable', not 'identical': id, para 155.

[256] *'Bosphorus Airways' Case*, para 156.   [257] *Ibid.* See Costello, 6 HRLR 87 (2006).

Justice and national courts. The resulting presumption that Ireland had not infringed the Convention by impounding the aircraft was not rebutted as this protection was not 'manifestly deficient' on the facts: judicial review, through the national courts and a preliminary ruling at Luxembourg, had been available and had been used to challenge the interference with the Convention right to property.

The immunity allowed by the *Bosphorus* case does not apply where the state has some discretion in its application of EU law, in which case the state will be in breach of the Convention if it does not exercise its discretion consistently with it.[258] Nor does the immunity apply to an act of a member states that is in execution of a treaty or other EU primary law obligation that has, by definition, been freely entered into by the member state and that, as primary law, is not subject to judicial review within the EU legal order. This was the case in *Matthews v UK*[259] where the EC Act on Direct Elections governing elections to the European Parliament, which was a EC treaty by which the UK was bound, excluded persons in Gibraltar from voting even though EC law applied to Gibraltar. The UK was held to be responsible for the resulting breach of Article 3, Protocol 1 of the Convention on free elections because it had freely agreed to the Act, which as primary law could not be challenged in the European Court of Justice.

9. ACHIEVEMENTS AND PROSPECTS[260]

I. CONTRIBUTION TO THE INTERNATIONAL LAW OF HUMAN RIGHTS

The Convention was an important landmark in the development of the international law of human rights. For the first time, sovereign states accepted legal obligations to secure the classical human rights for all persons within their jurisdiction and to allow all individuals, including their nationals, to bring claims against them leading to a legally binding judgment by an international court finding them in breach. This was a revolutionary step in a law of nations that had been based for centuries on such deeply entrenched foundations as the ideas that the treatment of nationals was within the domestic jurisdiction of states and that individuals were not subjects of rights in international law. If it has since been joined by other regional and universal treaty-based guarantees of human rights, the Convention remains the most advanced instrument of this kind. It has generated the most sophisticated and detailed jurisprudence in international human rights law and its enforcement mechanisms are unrivalled in their effectiveness and achievements. The Court has made a large contribution to the jurisprudence of international human rights law concerning the meaning of the particular rights it protects, the development of key concepts of general application, such as the principle of proportionality, and its strongly teleological approach to the interpretation of human rights norms.[261]

---

[258] See eg, *Procola v Luxembourg* A 326 (1995); 22 EHRR 193 and *Cantoni v France* 1996-V. Costello, *id*, p 111, suggests that *Bosphorus Airways* was exceptional on its facts; there will normally be some discretion.

[259] 1999-I; 28 EHRR 361 GC. See Harmsen, 7 EPL 625 (2001) and Canor, 25 ELR 3 (2000).

[260] See Mowbray, 5 HRLR 57 (2005); O'Boyle, 2008 EHRLR 1; and Wildhaber, 40 CYIL 309 (2002).

[261] However, the Court's margin of appreciation doctrine has not been taken up by other bodies, such as the UN Human Rights Committee and the Inter-American Court of Human Rights. The Inter-American Court of Human Rights and the African Commission on Human and Peoples' Rights, but not the Human Rights Committee, commonly refer to the Court's jurisprudence.

In addition, it has contributed to other areas of international law,[262] particularly the law on state jurisdiction[263] and state immunity,[264] and on the functioning of international courts (eg the local remedies rule and interim measures).[265]

II. IMPACT ON THE PROTECTION OF HUMAN RIGHTS IN EUROPE

a. Influence upon national law

The Convention has had a considerable effect upon the national law of the contracting parties. It has served as a catalyst for legal change that has furthered the protection of human rights at the national level and has, in so doing, assisted indirectly in the process of harmonizing law in Europe.[266] Changes in the law have occurred mostly following judgments on the merits[267] in cases to which the state amending its law has been a party. Insofar as a judgment involves a determination that a national law or administrative practice is inconsistent with the Convention,[268] the respondent state is required by international law to change its law or practice in order to comply with its treaty obligation in Article 1 of the Convention to 'secure' the rights and freedoms guaranteed. In compliance with this obligation, the parties to the Convention as a whole have made many legislative or other changes following decisions or judgments against them.[269] At a more general level, Frowein[270] has pointed to the considerable impact that the European Court's judgments have had on the constitutional traditions of contracting parties, involving, for example, the strengthening of the role of national courts in reviewing legislation and the introduction or increased importance of the principle of proportionality as a basis for overturning restrictions upon human rights.

In a number of cases, states have acted to amend their law or practice to bring it into line with the Convention following judgments in cases to which they have not been a party.[271] For example, the Netherlands amended its legislation on children born out of wedlock as a consequence of *Marckx v Belgium*.[272] There have also been instances of a state changing its law in order to comply with the Convention or a Protocol before becoming a party.[273]

---

[262] See generally Merrills, *The Development of International Law by the European Court of Human Rights*, 2nd edn, 1993 and Wildhaber, 56 ICLQ 217 (2000).

[263] See below, p 805.   [264] See below, p 242.   [265] See below, pp 764 and 842.

[266] See Leonardo, 8 ERPL 1139 (1996).

[267] States have also undertaken to change their law or administrative practice in some friendly settlement cases: see the examples below, p 830.

[268] This will not always be the case. For example, the failure to try a person within a 'reasonable time' or to treat a prisoner humanely may result from inefficiency or ill-conduct respectively on the particular facts.

[269] See above, p 27. For further details, see Greer, *European Convention*, Ch 5; Ress, in *European System*, pp 812ff; id, 40 Texas ILJ 395 (2005); Polakiewicz and Jacob-Foltzer, 12 HRLJ 65, 125 (1991); Blackburn and Polakiewicz, *Fundamental Rights in Europe*, 2001, *passim*. As to the UK, see Churchill and Young, 62 BYIL 283 (1992).

[270] Lecture reprinted in *Dialogue between Judges*, published by the European Court of Human Rights, 2007, p 73.

[271] Although, as non-parties, they are not legally bound by the judgment, they are bound to 'secure' the rights guaranteed by the Convention.

[272] A 31 (1979); 2 EHRR 330 PC. The Netherlands also amended its law concerning the time limit within which a suspect must be brought before a court in the light of the *Brogan* case: see Myjer, NCJM-Bulletin 1989, p 459. The Danish law on the closed shop was amended following *Young, James, and Webster v UK* A 44 (1981); 4 EHRR 38 PC: see Bernhardt, *European System*, Ch 3 at p 39ff. France amended its law on interpretation costs because of *Luedicke, Belkacem, and Koç v FRG* A 29 (1978); 2 EHRR 149: see French Decree no 87–634 of 4 August 1987. For other examples, see Polakiewicz and Jacob-Foltzer, 12 HRLJ 125 (1991).

[273] See Polakiewicz and Jacob-Foltzer, *ibid* and Polakiewicz, in Blackburn and Polakiewicz, eds, *Fundamental Rights in Europe*, 2001, p 50.

The Convention's influence upon the law of states that are not parties to a case illustrates the following general point. The real achievement of the Convention system can be said to go beyond the statistical tally of cases and the provision of remedies for individuals. It resides in the deterrent effect of an operational system. States, confronted with a system that works, must keep their law and administrative practices under review. As happens in Whitehall, new legislation must, as far as foreseeable, be 'Strasbourg proofed'.[274] In this way the Convention radiates a constant pressure for the maintenance of human rights standards and for change throughout the new Europe. A judgment of the Court in a case brought by one person may have an impact on forty or more national jurisdictions.[275]

Finally, it may be noted that the Convention has also influenced national law outside of Europe. Its text is echoed in the bills of rights of a number of states that were formerly colonies of Convention parties[276] and the jurisprudence of the Court has been relied upon or cited in cases decided in the national courts of non-European states.[277]

b. A remedy for individuals

For individuals who claim to be victims of human rights violations, the primary effect of the Convention has been to provide a remedy before an international court of justice when all national remedies have failed. 'We will now take our case to Strasbourg' is a familiar refrain that may mean more than just 'blowing off steam'.

One measure of the undoubted value of the Convention remedy from the individual's point of view is the large number of admitted applications that have led to a favourable outcome for the applicant in a judgment of the Court or by way of a friendly settlement.[278] Another is the wide variety of cases in which breaches have been found. Most violations have concerned the right to a fair trial. Cases under Article 6 have brought to light many delays in the hearing of cases in breach of the right to 'trial within a reasonable time'. Other common infringements have concerned the right of access to a court and the requirements of an independent and impartial tribunal and of equality of arms. The next most problematic guarantee for states has been that of freedom of the person. Many breaches of Article 5 have been found concerning various aspects of defendants' rights, such as the right to pre-trial release, the length of detention on remand, and the need for a remedy to challenge detention. Other cases have involved the preventive detention of terrorists and the detention of the mentally disordered, vagrants, children, and deportees. In recent years, the right to property in Article 1, First Protocol has generated a large jurisprudence and many breaches. Claims relying upon the right to respect for family life, privacy, etc, in Article 8 have been almost equally successful. In this context, the Court has made great use of its 'dynamic' approach to the interpretation of the Convention in the light of changed social values and the idea that there may be positive obligations upon states, requiring them, for example, to legislate so as to respect the

274 See now the statement of compatability required by s 19, Human Rights Act 1998.
275 Cf, Judge Ryssdal, *European System*, p xxvii.
276 Eg, Nigeria: see Elias, *Nigeria: the Development of its Laws and Constitution*, 1967, p 142. Cf, *Minister of Home Affairs v Fisher* [1980] AC 319 at 328 PC (Caribbean states).
277 See eg, *State v Ncube* 90 ILR 580 (1992) (a Zimbabwean case referring to the *Tyrer* case). See also *Pratt v AG for Jamaica* [1993] 4 All ER 769, a Privy Council case which cites *Soering v UK* A 161 (1989); 11 EHRR 439 PC. For other examples, see Mahoney and Prebensen, *European Supervision*, Ch 26 at p 637.
278 A breach of at least one article of the Convention has been found by the Court in the great majority (90% in 2007) of the cases in which a judgment has been given on the merits. For friendly settlement figures, see below, p 831. However, only a tiny percentage of applications lodged are admitted.

rights of homosexuals, children born out of wedlock, and transsexuals.[279] Cases under Article 10 have confirmed the fundamental importance attached to freedom of expression, particularly freedom of the press. Violations of Article 3 have been found, in such diverse areas as the ill-treatment of persons in detention, judicial corporal punishment, and extradition to face the death row phenomenon, with the concepts of 'inhuman and degrading treatment' being given a broad interpretation. At the other extreme, the guarantees of freedom from slavery and forced labour (Article 4) and all of the rights in the Fourth and Seventh Protocols have so far led to few adverse rulings.

Analyzing the Strasbourg case-law from another perspective, the blind-spots revealed by the Convention have varied from one state to another. For example, in the United Kingdom the Convention has thrown a spotlight on prisons, causing an antiquated system of prison administration to be brought up to date. It has also provided checks upon state conduct in the same country in such diverse contexts as the Northern Ireland emergency, courts-martial, and discretionary life sentences. In the Netherlands and Sweden, the Convention has highlighted the absence of judicial control over executive action in such areas as the licensing of commercial activities. In Italy, it has uncovered repeated delays in the administration of justice. In Central and East European states it has revealed problems in the restitution of property and various weaknesses in the administration of justice left over from the former Soviet systems. The latter include the non-enforcement of judicial decisions in a number of such states and the re-opening of final judicial decisions by way of special supervisory procedures in Russia or as regard property decisions (Romania).

If the Convention may thus provide a valuable remedy in respect of human rights violations over a wide range of subject areas, the Strasbourg procedures nonetheless have certain limitations or disadvantages from the applicant's standpoint. Some of these are inherent in all international remedies. Recourse to Strasbourg is inevitably less convenient than to a local court for obvious reasons such as language, distance, and cost. Similarly, any international remedy will be less efficient because of procedural weaknesses, such as the absence of a power to subpoena witnesses or to enforce or execute properly interlocutory injunctions or judgments respectively.

Other limitations are particular to the Strasbourg system as it functions at present. By far the most serious of these is the length of proceedings at Strasbourg. Although this has always been a problem, the situation has been made worse by the huge backlog of cases that has developed in recent years (see below). As has often been pointed out, it is somewhat ironic that the Court could well be considered to infringe the trial within a reasonable time guarantee which it enforces against others.

Given the importance now attached to the Convention system as providing a remedy for individuals, it is interesting to note how matters have progressed in this regard beyond the intentions of the drafting states. The original purpose of the Convention was not primarily to offer a remedy for particular individuals who had suffered violations of the Convention but to provide a collective, inter-state guarantee that would benefit individuals generally by requiring the national law of the contracting parties to be kept within certain bounds. An individual (as well as a state) application was envisaged as a mechanism for bringing to light a breach of an obligation owed by one state to others, not to provide a remedy for an individual victim. In accordance with this conception of the Convention, no provision was made for individuals to refer their case to the Court

---

[279] The concept of a positive obligation to 'secure' the rights to life and freedom from torture has also led to findings of breaches of Articles 2 and 3 respectively.

or to take part in proceedings before it. This, however, is not how the Convention has evolved. The individual has been brought more to the centre of the stage by allowing him a right of audience before the Court and also by making the right of individual petition to the Court compulsory. The Court's, and formerly the Commission's, constructive use of the friendly settlement procedure, which usually leads to an immediate remedy for the applicant (compensation, pardon, etc), and the Court's application of Article 41 to award an applicant compensation and costs have also enhanced the value of the Convention remedy from the standpoint of the individual.[280] The situation that has thus developed by which Strasbourg provides an international remedy for all individual victims of violations of the Convention is, however, now under threat because of the great increase in the Court's workload (see below).

III. PROSPECTS

As to the substance of the Convention's guarantee, the Court's future lies in the consolidation and further development of its jurisprudence, particularly in cases coming from post-communist states. The momentum of the Court's work has increased rapidly in recent years, with the Court giving detailed meaning to many different parts of the Convention guarantee. Reassuring examples of the Court's continued willingness to read the Convention in a positive, teleological way are its ruling that the Convention imposes positive obligations to secure various rights, such as the rights to life and privacy,[281] and extends to protection from environmental pollution.[282] Jurisprudence interpreting and applying the free-standing non-discrimination guarantee in the Twelfth Protocol, which entered into force in 2005, will add a new dimension to the Convention guarantee. While it is to be hoped that the Court will continue to conceive of its function as the guardian of human rights in a dynamic and probing way, it must at the same time take care to respect the rich diversity of law in the legal systems of the contracting parties and not lose touch with common European values.

There is much that the contracting parties themselves could do to improve the Convention's impact. They could immediately increase its effect by withdrawing such reservations as they have made and by ratifying the Protocols that they have not yet accepted. A Protocol bringing appropriate economic and social rights within the Convention system of individual petitions would also be valuable.[283] Although member states constantly acknowledge that economic and social rights are indivisible from and just as important as civil and political rights,[284] states lack the necessary conviction to establish rights of individual petition for the former, even though they are familiar with judicial remedies for the breach of obligations concerning economic and social rights in EU law and their own national law.[285] A move in this direction is now even less likely than formerly in view of the pressure upon the Court in coping with its workload under the existing Convention guarantee.

The immense difficulties besetting the Convention's enforcement machinery resulting from the overloading of the system by the great increase in the number of applications

---

[280] See further, below, pp 830 and 856.   [281] See below, Chs 2 and 9.   [282] See below, p 367.

[283] On previously unsuccessful attempts to add a Convention protocol protecting economic, social, and cultural rights, see Berchtold, in Matscher, ed, *The Implementation of Economic and Social Rights*, 1991, p 355. There is a collective complaints mechanism under the European Social Charter: see references above, n 22.

[284] See eg, the Final Resolution of Council of Europe Ministerial Conference on the European Social Charter, Turin, 1991, para 2.

[285] See eg, the ECJ case law under Article 119 on sexual discrimination in employment and national law remedies before employment and social security courts or tribunals.

in recent years is by far *the* main problem facing the Court. These difficulties have now reached crisis point. Paradoxically, the large number of applications to the Court that are a testimony to the success of the Convention could also be its undoing. Reasons for the startling increase in applications include the greater awareness of the Convention on the part of individuals and non-governmental organizations, the adoption of more Convention protocols protecting rights,[286] and the fact that the individual right of petition became compulsory for all contracting parties in 1998. But by far the most important reason is the large increase since 1989 in the number of contracting parties (from twenty-two to forty-seven), including most significantly post-communist states.[287]

The number of applications, which was manageable in the early years, rose steadily in the 1980s and 90s[288] to the point where worries about the backlog of pending applications and the anticipated further growth in new applications led to the procedural reforms of the Eleventh Protocol, which came into effect in 1998. But, despite Protocol 11, the number of applications has continued to spiral upwards. At the beginning of 2008, there were over 100,000 cases pending before the Court.[289] This was despite a big increase in the Court's output in 2007[290] following the Eleventh Protocol and other reforms and increases in registry staff.[291] The Court's docket will continue to increase: the Court is already unable to dispose of all of the applications reaching it each year[292] and the annual number of new applications is expected to rise further for some years.[293] The consequence of the current situation for applicants is that cases generally take a very long time and are likely to take longer.[294]

Aware of an impending crisis, the Council took steps to streamline and otherwise reform the Court's procedure further by the adoption of the Fourteenth Protocol to the Convention.[295] The Protocol, which requires ratification by all Convention contracting parties, has been ratified by all but Russia. It would be a considerable setback for the Convention system if this were to prove a final decision by Russia, given the gross overloading of the Court and the estimation that the Fourteenth Protocol reforms would reduce the backlog of cases by at least 25 per cent.[296] But, as will be apparent, such a reduction would be far from solving the Court's problems. For this reason, further reforms are under consideration.[297]

---

[286] As yet, these have not generated many cases, but the Twelfth Protocol on discrimination may change this.

[287] Another factor is the large number of Turkish cases resulting mainly from the response to the threat posed by the PKK, some of which have involved fact-finding in Turkey. For other reasons, see Greer, *European Convention*, pp 38ff.

[288] Registered applications rose over tenfold, from 404 in 1981 to 4,750 in 1997.

[289] For details, see below, p 812.

[290] In 2007, there were 1,735 judgments (in 1998, when the new Court started, there were just 105). In addition, 25,802 applications were declared inadmissible or struck off: Survey of Activities 2007, Tables.

[291] For staff numbers, see below, p 818.

[292] In 2007, only 30,000 of the 40,000 applications that were allocated to a decision-making body were disposed of.

[293] More than half of the 100,000 were against just five states: Russia, Romania, Turkey, Ukraine, and Poland: see below, p 812. Whereas the number of applications against Turkey may fall, those against Central and East European states will continue to rise for some time.

[294] In 2004, 2000 applications (4%) had been pending for more than five years: Lord Woolf, Review of the Working Methods of the European Court of Human Rights, 2005, p 8 <htpp://www.coe.int>.

[295] For a full account of the reforms contained in the Fourteenth Protocol, see below, Chs 24 and 26. See also Caflisch, 6 HRLR 403. Among other reforms, the Protocol further streamlines the admissibility stage where much of the Court's difficulty lies: more than 95% of lodged applications are declared inadmissible or struck out: see the Explanatory Report to the Fourteenth Protocol, para 7.

[296] Speech by Court President Costa, 19 January 2007.

[297] See the proposals in the Report of the Group of Wise Persons, CM (2006) 203.

States may also do a great deal to reduce the Court's difficulties, consistently with the principle of subsidiarity. Above all, action to reduce the figure of over 60 per cent of judgments on the merits attributable to 'repetitive' violations resulting from structural problems that states have not rectified following judgments against them[298] would help greatly.

However, there is a growing belief that, whatever procedural reforms are put in place, it will not be possible for the Court to cope with the numbers of individual applications generated by more than 800 million individuals across Europe in the case by case way that it has done to date. The argument runs that the Court must convert itself into a constitutional court.[299] By this is meant that, while continuing to take jurisdiction through the medium of individual applications, as the Convention provides, the Court should focus more upon making general rulings as to what the Convention requires in a particular context, rather than providing individual justice. Thus it might in a selected case make a ruling that a national law or practice is contrary to the Convention, spelling out the Convention requirements in the subject area for the benefit of states parties generally.[300] It would then not take other cases on the same point at least from the same state, supposing that the state concerned will make the necessary changes to the benefit of others within its jurisdiction.[301] This approach might require a further amending protocol[302] and would pre-suppose the co-operation of states in reforming their law and practice in line with the Court's judgments and in providing effective judicial remedies for individuals at the national level.

The Convention's future is also bound up with that of the new Europe. Providing both a statement of European human rights values and machinery for their enforcement, it can continue to have a key role in the process of European integration. This is a role that has taken on an extra dimension as cases are arriving from the new Council of Europe member states in Central and Eastern Europe. The Convention's relationship with the European Union remains unresolved. The fact that the member states of the European Union are subject to the Convention, but that the supranational institutions to which they have transferred certain of their powers are not, is a weakness in the arrangements for securing human rights in Europe that should be remedied by the accession of the European Union to the Convention. While the current situation remains, and while the Strasbourg Court continues to have severe and increasing workload problems, the European Union's Court of Justice in Luxembourg will have a considerable opportunity to develop a larger human rights role for itself vis-à-vis the Union and its member states.

---

[298] Explanatory Report to the Fourteenth Protocol, para 7 (figure for 2003). A high proportion concern unreasonable delay in court proceedings: Mahoney, 21 Penn State ILR 101 at 110 (2002). State co-operation with the Court in the hearing of cases and the provision of effective local remedies also assists: *ibid.*

[299] See Greer, *European Convention*, pp 174ff; Harmsen, 5 IJHR 18 (2001); and former Court President Wildhaber, 23 HRLJ 161 (2002).

[300] Cf, the role of the US Supreme Court and the German Constitutional Court: see Greer, id, pp 181ff. However the 2006 Report of the Group of Wise Persons, CM (2006) 203, para 42, opposed giving the Court the power to take a case at its discretion (cf, the US Supreme Court's certiorari jurisdiction) as risking 'politicising the system'. But the Report stressed that the Court already had a constitutional role, viz to 'lay down common principles and standards of human rights', which it already exercises but could take further *ibid*, para 24.

[301] Cf, the Court's new pilot judgment approach, below, p 851.

[302] A broad interpretation of the admissibility criterion added by the Fourteenth Protocol would go some of the way.

2

ARTICLE 2: THE RIGHT TO LIFE

Article 2

1. Everyone's right to life shall be protected by law. No one shall be deprived of his life intentionally save in the execution of a sentence of a court following his conviction of a crime for which this penalty is provided by law.

2. Deprivation of life shall not be regarded as inflicted in contravention of this article when it results from the use of force which is no more than absolutely necessary:
   (a) in defence of any person from unlawful violence;
   (b) in order to effect a lawful arrest or to prevent the escape of a person lawfully detained;
   (c) in action lawfully taken for the purpose of quelling a riot or insurrection.

The first right guaranteed in the Convention, in Article 2, is the right to life, the most basic human right of all.[1] The fundamental nature of this right is recognized by the fact that Article 2 is one of the few Convention Articles that cannot be derogated from in time of war or other public emergency.[2] Together with the prohibition of torture, etc, in Article 3, it 'enshrines one of the basic values of the democratic societies making up the Council of Europe'.[3] For these reasons, the circumstances in which the deprivation of life may be justified under Article 2 (eg in self-defence) must be 'strictly construed'.[4] As well as a negative obligation not to take life, Article 2 places upon states a positive obligation to protect the right to life. This positive obligation must be interpreted and applied so that it is 'practical and effective'.[5] Where relevant, Article 2 applies to unintentional as well as intentional killings.[6]

1. THE OBLIGATION TO PROTECT THE RIGHT TO LIFE BY LAW

The first sentence of Article 2(1) states that 'everyone's right to life shall be protected by law'. In *LCB v UK*[7] the Court held that this establishes a positive obligation for states to take 'appropriate steps to safeguard the lives of those within their jurisdiction'. From this flows a 'primary duty on the state to secure the right to life by putting in place an

---

[1] On the right to life in Article 2, see Buckley, 1 HRLR 35 (2001); Korff, *The Right to Life: A Guide to the Implementation of Article 2 of the European Convention on Human Rights*, Council of Europe Human Rights Handbook No 8, 2006; Mathieu, *The Right to Life in European Constitutional Law and Conventional Caselaw*, 2006; Ni Aolain, 19 NQHR 21 (2001); and Opsahl, *European System*, Ch 11.

[2] See Article 15(2), Convention. Exceptionally, derogation may be made from Article 2 'in respect of deaths resulting from lawful acts of war': *ibid*.   [3] *McCann v UK* A 324 (1995); 21 EHRR 97 para 147 GC.

[4] *Ibid*.   [5] Id, para 146. Cf, *Oneryildiz v Turkey* 2004-XII; 41 EHRR 325 GC.

[6] *Ogur v Turkey* 1999-III; 31 EHRR 912 GC.

[7] 1998-III; 27 EHRR 212 para 36. For the first statement of this obligation, see *Association X v UK No 7154/75*, 14 DR 31 (1978).

appropriate legal and administrative framework to deter the commission of offences against the person, backed up by law enforcement machinery for the prevention, suppression and punishment of breaches of such provisions'.[8] The 'legal and administrative framework' referred to requires the adoption of (usually criminal) laws prohibiting the taking of life, and calls for the regulation of the use of force by the police and other state agents and of dangerous and other activities that might involve a risk to life. The 'law enforcement machinery' includes the police, the criminal prosecution services, and the courts.

I. LEGAL AND ADMINISTRATIVE FRAMEWORK

a. Laws prohibiting the taking of life

Effective criminal laws to deter the commission of offences against the person are generally required to protect life.[9] The principle of proportionality suggests that the degree of criminal liability (murder, manslaughter, etc) and the sentence may vary with the circumstances.[10] There must be criminal liability for gross negligence resulting in death in respect of dangerous activities.[11] Civil liability may be sufficient in some cases of unintentional killing.[12] In any case, the 'law' that protects the right to life should be 'formulated with sufficient precision to enable the citizen to regulate his conduct'.[13] Liability for the taking of life must extend under a state's law to the acts of private persons, as well as persons acting for the state.[14]

A state need not make every taking of life illegal. Certain permissible exceptions are indicated in or may be inferred from the text of Article 2. Capital punishment is expressly permitted by Article 2(1), as is the taking of life by the state in the cases listed in Article 2(2). There are other cases in which the taking of life does not usually give rise to liability under European national law and which, accordingly, are not required by Article 2 to be made illegal. Examples are killings in self-defence by private persons[15] and accidental deaths in sporting contests.

b. Euthanasia

A controversial case in national law is euthanasia. Article 2 does not require that passive euthanasia, by which a person is allowed to die by not being given treatment, is a crime.[16] There may be a different answer in the case of active euthanasia, where the person's death is brought about by the positive act of another. The consent of the patient will be relevant in such cases. Article 2 can be taken to require that euthanasia without the consent of the person concerned (involuntary euthanasia) is a crime, even in the case of the

---

[8] *Makaratzis v Greece* 2004-XI; 41 EHRR 1092 para 57 GC.

[9] *Osman v UK* 1998-VIII; 29 EHRR 245 para 115 GC.

[10] A system of prison leave in preparation for final release may comply with Article 2: *Mastromatteo v Italy* 2002-VIII GC.

[11] *Oneryildiz v Turkey* 2004-XII; 41 EHRR 325 GC.

[12] *Calvelli and Ciglio v Italy*, below, p 41 (medical negligence).

[13] *Sunday Times v UK* (No 1) A 30 (1979); 2 EHRR 245 para 49 PC, interpreting the word 'law' in Article 10, Convention.

[14] *Osman v UK* 1998-VIII; 29 EHRR 245 para 115 GC. *Quaere* whether members of the public must be obliged to assist in a medical emergency: see *Hughes v UK No 11590/85*, 48 DR 258 (1986).

[15] These do not fall within Article 2(2)(a).

[16] *Widmer v Switzerland No 20527/92* (1993), unreported. The turning off of a life support machine is not a positive act, but part of an act of omission by which steps are not taken to keep a person alive: cf, *Airedale v NHS Trust v Bland* [1993] AC 93, HL.

'mercy killing' of a person with an incurable or painful illness. Article 2 clearly requires that the involuntary killing of the mentally subnormal or physically disabled are criminal. Less clear is the case of voluntary active euthanasia, which is now permitted, subject to stringent safeguards, by the law of at least two European states.[17] Similarly, it is not clear whether Article 2 requires that assisted suicide, by which X assists Y to commit suicide him or herself by, for example, placing a drug by the bedside on request, be made a crime.[18] In the light of European practice generally, it can be supposed that Article 2 does not require that suicide itself be a crime. As yet, there has been almost no Strasbourg jurisprudence under Article 2 on these difficult legal and moral questions. As in the case of abortion (see below), it is likely that a wide margin of appreciation would be allowed if it could be shown that national practice varied greatly.

c. No right to die

In *Pretty v UK*,[19] it was held that Article 2 does not guarantee a 'right to die'. In that case, there was no breach of Article 2 because the husband of the applicant, who was terminally ill and not able to commit suicide by herself, would be subject to prosecution for a criminal offence under English law if he assisted her to die. The Court explained its position as follows:

> Article 2 is unconcerned with issues to do with the quality of living or what a person chooses to do with his or her life. To the extent that these aspects are recognised as so fundamental to the human condition that they require protection from state interference, they may be reflected in the rights guaranteed by other articles of the Convention, or in other international human rights instruments. Article 2 cannot, without a distortion of language, be interpreted as conferring the diametrically opposite right, namely a right to die; nor can it create a right to self-determination in the sense of conferring on an individual the entitlement to choose death rather than life.

Whereas the *Pretty* case concerned assisted suicide on its facts, it is clear from the above passage that Article 2 also does not guarantee a right to voluntary euthanasia[20] or to commit suicide by one's own hand. Nonetheless such rights may be guaranteed by another Convention right.[21]

d. Amnesties

In *Dujardin v France*,[22] the Commission stated that an amnesty for murder is not a breach of Article 2 'unless it can be seen to form part of a general practice aimed at the systematic prevention of prosecution of the perpetrators of such crimes'. In that case, an amnesty was provided for some fifty individuals who were being prosecuted for murdering gendarmes during a political disturbance. The Commission held that the amnesty, as a part

---

[17] Belgium and the Netherlands. See the survey in <http://www.coe.int/t/e/legal_affairs/legal_co-operation/bioethics/activities/euthanasia/INF(2003)8e_replies_euthanasia.pdf>. For Netherlands law, see Korff, *op cit* at n 1 above, p 16. The law has not been challenged at Strasbourg by any 'victim', eg a family member. In an early case in West Germany, it was held that a doctor did not infringe Article 2 by giving an overdose of drugs to the terminally ill: Decision of the Verwaltungsgericht, Bremen, 8 November 1959 NJW (1960) 400, cited in Fawcett, p 36.

[18] The question was left unanswered in *Pretty v UK* 2002-III; 35 EHRR 1; see below, which concerned the offence of assisted suicide under the UK Suicide Act 1961, s 2. On assisted suicide, see Morris, 2003 EHRLR 65.

[19] 2000-III; 35 EHRR 1 para 39. See also *Sanles Sanles v Spain No 48335/99* hudoc (2000) DA.

[20] As to whether, on the contrary, it must be prohibited, see above.

[21] On the position under Article 8, see below, p 367.

[22] *No 16734/90*, 72 DR 236 at 243–4 (1991). An amnesty that prevented civil (but not criminal) proceedings against the perpetrator might infringe the right of access to a court in Article 6: *ibid*.

of a process of resolving conflict between rival communities in a French overseas territory, was consistent with Article 2 because it maintained a proper 'balance between the
legitimate interests of the state and the interests of individual members of the public in
having the right to life protected by law'. Given the current move in public international
law towards bringing persons guilty of war crimes and crimes against humanity to justice
rather than approving amnesties in a post-conflict situation,[23] it may be that in some contexts the Court might adopt a more rigorous approach to the compatibility of amnesties
with Article 2 in a post-conflict situation than the *Dujardin* case might suggest. A general
legal immunity from criminal liability or prosecution for homicide for state agents that
was not a response to a particular situation of conflict could certainly not be justified
under Article 2.

e. Regulation of activities that may pose a risk to life

Article 2 requires that activities that may pose a threat to life be the subject of an appropriate regulatory regime to reduce the risk of a fatal injury as far as possible. Thus, given
that the police and other state agents may use deadly force in circumstances falling within
Article 2(2), the obligation to protect the right to life requires that 'a legal and administrative framework should define the limited circumstances in which law enforcement
officials may use force and firearms, in the light of international standards' and provide
for their proper training in accordance with those standards.[24] In *Nachova v Bulgaria*,[25]
it was held that the required 'framework' was missing, in breach of Article 2, when the
relevant regulations effectively permitted lethal force to be used by the military police
when arresting a member of the armed forces 'for even the most minor offence'; under
the regulations it was lawful to shoot any fugitive who ignored an oral warning and after
a shot had been fired over his head.

A regulatory regime must also be provided 'compelling hospitals, whether public or
private, to adopt measures for the protection of their patients' lives'.[26] Similarly dangerous industrial activities must be subject to regulations geared to the particular activity
and governing the licensing, operation, and monitoring of it.[27]

II. LAW ENFORCEMENT MACHINERY

The 'law enforcement machinery' needed to protect the right to life consists centrally of
'an effective judicial system' to enforce the criminal or other laws required by Article 2.[28]
This will entail criminal investigation and prosecution in criminal courts, or in some
cases the availability of civil and administrative courts to which victims have access; disciplinary procedures may also be relevant. Although criminal law remedies will normally
be required, where the taking of life is unintentional, a civil remedy may be sufficient. In

---

[23] See Cassese, Gaeta, and Jones, eds, *The Rome Statute of the International Criminal Court: A Commentary*,
2002, Vol 1, p 18.

[24] *Makaratzis v Greece* 2004-XI; 41 EHRR 1092 para 59 GC. The Court referred to the UN Basic Rules on the
Use of Force and Firearms by Law Enforcement Officials 1990 <http://www.unchr.ch/htm>. See also *Hamiyet
Kaplan v Turkey* hudoc (2005) and *Simsek v Turkey* hudoc (2005) (need for centralized command). And see
De Sanctis, 10 IJHR 31 (2006).

[25] 2005-VII; 42 EHRR 933 para 99 GC.

[26] *Calvelli and Ciglio v Italy* 2002-I para 49 GC. On the regulation of medical decisions to withdraw life support, see *Burke v UK No 1987/06* hudoc (2006) DA.

[27] *Oneryildiz v Turkey* 2004-XII; 41 EHRR 325 GC. See below, p 51.

[28] Id, para 92. On the Article 2 procedural obligation to investigate, see below, p 48.

Calvelli and Ciglio v Italy,[29] a baby had died shortly after birth in a private clinic, allegedly as a result of medical negligence. Criminal proceedings for involuntary manslaughter against the doctor were commenced but became time-barred because of delays during the police inquiry and the judicial investigation. The Court found it unnecessary to decide whether the failure of the criminal proceedings because of delays for which the state was responsible gave rise to a breach of Article 2. It did so because the applicants had the possibility of an action for damages in the civil courts, which could be followed by disciplinary proceedings. In its judgment, the Court confirmed that the positive obligation under Article 2 to 'take steps' to protect life applied to the 'public health sphere', requiring 'an effective independent judicial system to be set up so that the cause of death of patients in the care of the medical profession, whether in the public or the private sector, can be determined and those responsible made accountable'. As to the kind of 'accountability' required, the Court stated that in 'the specific sphere of medical negligence the obligation may...be satisfied if the legal system affords victims a remedy in the civil courts, either alone or in conjunction with a remedy in the criminal courts...Disciplinary measures may also be envisaged'. The same approach was followed in *Vo v France*,[30] in which an involuntary abortion had resulted from medical negligence. Criminal proceedings for two possible offences were brought against the doctor, but were unsuccessful because one offence did not apply to the 20 to 21 week-old foetus and an amnesty applied to the other. There was, however, no breach of Article 2 because the applicant could have brought a claim for damages in the administrative courts (but failed to do so).[31] This civil remedy was sufficient: no mention was made of disciplinary proceedings.[32]

The Court's approach in the *Calvelli and Ciglio* and *Vo* cases is open to criticism in respect of serious cases of medical negligence resulting in death in which criminal, as well as civil, liability would normally be present at the national level. The essential purpose of the positive obligation in Article 2 in this context is to discover the facts and to make those responsible accountable for the loss of life. Although civil proceedings may certainly assist in establishing the facts surrounding a death and civil damages may to an extent make those responsible accountable, criminal proceedings (and mechanisms such as inquests) are much better equipped to achieve both of these ends than civil ones. The Court's attempts at explaining the role of civil actions, which are centrally about compensation between private persons, within the theory of Article 2 are not convincing[33] and it is arguable that it might do better to consider civil actions exclusively as possible Article 13 remedies for breaches of Article 2.[34]

A different question is whether in some non-medical contexts the positive obligation in Article 2 requires that the applicant must have a civil remedy against the state for compensation *in addition to* a criminal one. The Court left this question open in the *McCann* and *Osman* cases on the ground that any claim to such a remedy was more appropriately considered under Articles 6 and 13. Later, in *Mastromatteo v Italy*,[35] on the basis that the

---

[29] 2002-I paras 49, 51. See also *Powell v UK No 45305/99* hudoc (2000) DA; and *Rowley v UK No 31914/03* hudoc (2005) DA.

[30] 2004-VIII; 40 EHRR 259 GC.

[31] The Court has stressed the need to pursue available remedies: *Calvelli and Ciglio* and *Powell* cases.

[32] It has been suggested that 'civil, administrative *or* even disciplinary' remedies may be sufficient: *Oneryildiz v Turkey* 2004-XII; 41 EHRR 325 para 92 GC. Italics added.

[33] See the doubts in the dissenting opinion of Judges Rozakis and Bonello in *Calvelli and Ciglio v Italy* 2002-I GC.

[34] On Article 13, see below, Ch 14. See also *Ergi v Turkey* 1998-IV; 32 EHRR 388.

[35] 2002-VIII GC. Those responsible had been convicted of murder.

applicant had not invoked Article 13,[36] the Court indicated, again with a view to ensuring the effectiveness of the law protecting the right to life and the accountability of those responsible, that Article 2 required a civil remedy against the state in a case of murder in which the state had been at fault.

2. PREVENTIVE MEASURES

The obligation in Article 2(1) to take 'appropriate steps' to protect life also requires the state, in some circumstances, to take preventive measures. In *LCB v UK*,[37] the applicant claimed that her leukaemia, which was life-threatening, had been caused by her father's exposure, as a member of the armed forces, to radiation from nuclear tests on Christmas Island before she was born. The Court rejected the applicant's claim under Article 2 that the authorities should have informed her parents of the possible risk to any child and have monitored her health from birth. It did so because the information available to the authorities at the time of the tests was such as to allow them to be reasonably confident that her father had not been exposed to radiation and, in any event, was not such as to lead them to believe that such exposure would cause a real risk to her health. The Court accepted, however, that Article 2 imposed an obligation upon the state to do 'all that could have been required of it to prevent the applicant's life being avoidably put at risk'.[38]

The *LCB* obligation applies to the unintentional loss to life resulting from dangerous activities. In *Oneryildiz v Turkey*,[39] the Court stated that 'this obligation must be construed as applying in the context of any activity, whether public or private, in which the right to life may be at stake, and *a fortiori* in the case of industrial activities, which by their very nature are dangerous, such as the operation of waste-collection sites'. In that case, a methane explosion occurred at a municipal refuse tip. A landslide of waste material engulfed ten slum dwellings, including that of the applicant, killing thirty-nine people, including nine of his close relatives. The public authorities had allowed the tip to operate in breach of health and environmental regulations despite an expert report highlighting the serious operational risks involved and had not prevented the unauthorized construction and occupation of slum dwellings adjacent to it. In addition, they had taken insufficient steps to inform the inhabitants of the risks they ran.[40] The Court found that the authorities knew or ought to have known that there was a real risk from explosion to the lives of the persons living near the tip. As a result, they had infringed their obligation under Article 2 to take such preventive measures as were necessary to protect them. The judgment has considerable importance for states, which must put in place and enforce satisfactory laws and regulations concerning dangerous industrial activities generally.[41]

---

[36] This was also the case in *McCann*.   [37] 1998-III; 27 EHRR 212.

[38] Id, para 36. In *R (Catherine Smith) v Deputy Coroner for Oxfordshire* [2008] EWHC 694 Collins J stated that it might be a breach of Article 2 to send troops on patrol or into battle without sufficient equipment.

[39] 2004-XII; 41 EHRR 325 para 71 GC. See also *Ledyayeva v Russia No 53157/99* hudoc (2004) DA.

[40] The public's right to information about the danger to life resulting from dangerous activities was held to fall within Article 2 as well as Article 8, as to which see *Guerra v Italy*, below, p 390.

[41] Cases of severe environmental pollution may also raise an issue under Article 8 concerning the right to respect for one's family life and home: see *Taskin v Turkey* 2004-X; 42 EHRR 1127 (dangerous gold mine). On the question whether nuclear testing and the disposal of radioactive waste could give rise to liability under Article 2, see also *No 715/60* (1960) id, cited in Fawcett, p 37.

The preventive obligation deriving from the *LCB* case can be seen to provide the basis for several Strasbourg rulings in other areas. Thus the former Commission held that the state is required to take preventive measures to protect individuals from the risk to life caused to an individual by smoking in public by other individuals.[42] However, there is a margin of appreciation left to the state in balancing the competing interest of smokers and non-smokers: a complete ban on smoking in public places to protect non-smokers is not required; a state that limits cigarette advertising, prohibits smoking in certain public areas, and campaigns to inform the public of the injurious effect of smoking complies with Article 2.

The *LCB* obligation applies more commonly to the situation where an individual's life is threatened by the criminal acts of another person. In *Osman v UK*[43] it was held that there is 'in certain well-defined circumstances a positive obligation on the authorities to take preventive operational measures to protect an individual whose life is at risk from the criminal acts of another individual'. The obligation arises where the following conditions are met:

> ... it must be established ... that the authorities knew or ought to have known at the time of the existence of a real and immediate risk to the life of an identified individual or individuals from the criminal acts of a third party and that they failed to take measures within the scope of their powers which, judged reasonably, might have been expected to avoid that risk....[44]

The Court acknowledged two further limitations upon the obligation. First, in view of 'the operational choices which must be made in terms of priorities and resources', it 'must be interpreted in a way which does not impose an impossible or disproportionate burden on the authorities'.[45] Second, the police have to respect due process and other human rights guarantees, such as those in Articles 5 and 8.[46] In *Osman*, a schoolteacher had developed an unhealthy attachment to a teenage schoolboy. After various incidents, the schoolteacher shot and injured the schoolboy and killed his father. A claim that the duty of protection under Article 2 had been infringed was rejected. Although the police had been alerted to general statements by the schoolteacher that he intended to commit a murder and to other indications of a disturbed mind, the Court held that it could not be said that they knew or ought to have known on the facts that the lives of the Osman family were at 'real and immediate risk'. Moreover, there were no measures which, 'judged reasonably', could have been taken to neutralize the threat from the schoolteacher or lead to his detention following court proceedings. The police could not 'be criticised for attaching weight to the presumption of innocence or failing to use powers of arrest, search and seizure having regard to their reasonably held view that they lacked at relevant times the required standard of suspicion to use those powers or that any action taken would in fact have produced concrete results.'[47] The Court did not respond in terms to the applicants' claim that the police should have kept a watch on the Osmans' home. It can be supposed

---

[42] *Wockel v Germany No 32165/96*, 93-A DR 82 (1998). The case was considered under Articles 2 and 8. See also *Barrett v UK No 30402/96*, 23 EHRR CD 185 (1997) (control of excessive alcoholism in army).

[43] 1998-VIII; 29 EHRR 245 para 115 GC. See also *Bromiley v UK No 33747/962* hudoc (1999); 29 EHRR CD 111 and *Danini v Italy No 22998/93*, 87-B DR 24 (1996). The *Osman* obligation does not apply to medical negligence cases: the procedural obligation to investigate, see below p 48, applies instead: *Powell v UK No 45305/99* hudoc (2000) DA.

[44] 1998-VIII; 29 EHRR 245 para 116 GC. See also *Denizci v Cyprus* 2001-V para 375.

[45] 1998-VIII; 29 EHRR 245 para 116 GC. See also *W v UK No 9348/81*, 32 DR 190 (1983).

[46] *Ibid.* Thus preventive detention is not permitted and there are limits on powers of surveillance.

[47] 1998-VIII; 29 EHRR 245 para 121.

however, that the *Osman* obligation might extend to such a requirement in extreme cases, within the limits of 'priorities and resources'.[48]

The *Osman* obligation to take preventive operational measures was infringed in *Gongadze v Ukraine*,[49] in which the decapitated body of a political journalist who had criticized the government was found a month or so after his disappearance. Some two months before his disappearance, at a time when eighteen other journalists had been killed in Ukraine, the journalist had informed the Prosecutor General, whose Office was responsible for supervising police conduct, that the police were questioning his relatives and had him under surveillance, and had requested both an investigation and protection. No such action was taken despite a newspaper article identifying the police officers responsible for the disappearance. The Court held that the authorities had been at best 'blatantly negligent', a conclusion underlined by the fact that the identified police officers were arrested and convicted of the journalist's murder shortly after a change of government.

The *Osman* obligation has also been applied by the Court in a number of Turkish cases in the different context of the protection of persons at risk in the Kurdish emergency situation. A series of cases have concerned the protection of persons allegedly associated with the Kurdish cause who were killed by persons unknown. In *Akkoc v Turkey*[50] the applicant's husband, of Kurdish extraction, had been shot dead by unknown perpetrators on his way to work as a schoolteacher in south-east Turkey. He had been involved with his wife in the activities of an unlawful trade union and in a teachers' demonstration protesting at assaults by the police, after which the applicant and her husband had received death threats by telephone. In these circumstances, the Court found, the husband was at 'real and immediate' risk of an unlawful attack of which the authorities were aware. The public prosecutor had been petitioned about the death threats and the authorities should have known of official reports that supported allegations that there were contraguerrilla groups, acting with the knowledge or connivance of elements in the security forces, targeting individuals viewed as acting contrary to the state's interest. As to the measures taken by the state, the Court focused not on the perfunctory examination of the petition by the public prosecutor, but on deficiencies in the criminal justice system in south-east Turkey which took away its effectiveness as a deterrent and generally sent the wrong signal to wrongdoers. The Court recalled its rulings in two earlier cases[51] that, in breach of the Article 2 obligation to investigate suspicious deaths, the system by which alleged offences by the security forces were investigated, not by the public prosecutor but by an administrative council composed of civil servants responsible to the Governor, did not provide an independent or effective procedure for investigating deaths allegedly involving those forces. The Court noted too that it had decided a series of cases in which it had held that the Article 2 procedural obligation to investigate suspicious deaths and the Article 13 obligation to provide an effective remedy for a killing had been infringed, in all of which cases complaints alleging killings by the security forces had not been seriously considered.[52] Finally, the Court recalled that it had previously held that the State

---

[48]   See *X v Ireland No 6040/73*, 16 YB 388, 392 (1973) (no duty to provide special protection for a person at risk from the IRA, 'at least not for an indefinite nature').

[49]   2005-XI; 43 EHRR 967. See also *Kontrova v Slovakia* hudoc (2007) in which there was a breach of Article 2 when the police took no action against a man who killed his children (and himself), despite emergency calls and knowledge of his prior record of physical and mental abuse and threats with a shotgun.

[50]   2000-X; 34 EHRR 1173. See also *Kaya (Mahmut) v Turkey* 2000-III; *Kilic v Turkey* 2000-III; 33 EHRR 1357; and *Koku v Turkey* hudoc (2005).

[51]   See the *Gulec* and *Ogur* cases, considered below, pp 65–6.

[52]   See the cases cited below, p 52.

Security Courts, which had jurisdiction over terrorist offences, were not independent under Article 6 ECHR because they had military judges.[53] The overall result in the *Akkoc* case was a breach of the Article 2 obligation to protect the applicant's husband:

> The Court finds that these defects undermined the effectiveness of criminal law protection in the south-east region during the period relevant to this case. It considers that this permitted or fostered a lack of accountability of members of the security forces for their actions which, as the Commission stated in its report, was not compatible with the rule of law in a democratic society respecting the fundamental rights and freedoms guaranteed under the Convention...Consequently, these defects removed the protection which Zubeyir Akkoc should have received by law.[54]

This is a strong condemnation of the Turkish criminal justice system as it operated at the time in south-east Turkey[55] and one that demonstrates the inter-relationship between the obligation to protect persons at risk and the obligation to investigate killings that occur.[56]

The *Osman* obligation applies to persons in detention. The state must take reasonable measures to protect detained persons in real and immediate danger of life-threatening attacks from other detainees of which the authorities knew or ought to have known. Given the vulnerable position of detainees and the special knowledge that the state will have of the circumstances, the state must account for the death of a detainee and is subject to a high burden of proof in doing so.[57] The obligation to protect detained persons from other detainees was infringed in *Edwards v UK*.[58] In that case, a vulnerable remand prisoner was killed by a dangerous, mentally ill remand prisoner with whom he was made to share a cell. A breach of Article 2 was found because of the failure of those acting earlier in the case (doctors, police, courts) to pass on to the prison authorities information relevant to the murderer's condition and of the inadequate nature of the screening process when he was admitted to prison.

In *Keenan v UK*,[59] the *Osman* obligation was extended in principle to cases of suicide in which state officials knew or ought to have known that the detainee posed 'a real and immediate risk' of suicide. However, there was no breach of Article 2 on the facts as the prison authorities had done all that could reasonably have been expected of them to counter the risk of suicide by placing him in hospital care and under watch when he showed suicidal tendencies.[60]

A failure to protect a detainee from other risks to his health by monitoring his condition or providing medical care resulting in death may be a breach of Article 2 also.[61] This obligation was applied to the use of police restraining techniques in the immediate post-arrest stage in *Saoud v France*.[62] In that case, police were called to the home of a mentally

---

[53] See *Incal v Turkey*, below, p 289.

[54] 2000-X; 34 EHRR 1173 paras 91–2.   [55] Cf, Mowbray, 1 HRLR 127, 129 (2001).

[56] The Court has sometimes not pursued a 'protection' claim if it has found a breach of the 'investigation' obligation: see eg, *Kaya v Turkey* 1998-I; 28 EHRR 1 and *Tanrikulu v Turkey* 1999 IV; 30 EHRR 950 GC.

[57] See *Salman v Turkey* 2000-VII; 34 EHRR 425 paras 99–100 GC.

[58] 2002-II; 35 EHRR 487. See also *Rebai v France No 26561/95* 88-A DR 72 (1997).

[59] 2001-III; 33 EHRR 913 (no Article 2 breach: reasonable measures taken, but a breach of Article 3: see below, p 97). See also *Tanribilir v Turkey* hudoc (2000); *Younger v UK No 57420/00* hudoc (2003) DA, and *Slimani v France* 2004-IX .

[60] There was a lack of appropriate medical treatment in breach of Article 3: see below, p 97.

[61] *Anguelova v Bulgaria* 2002-IV; 38 EHRR 659; *Douglas-Williams v UK No 56413/00* hudoc (2002) DA; *Slimani v France* 2004-IX; *Tais v France* hudoc (2006); and *Tarariyeva v Russia* 2006-XV. But see *Scavuzzo-Hager v Switzerland* hudoc (2006), Article 3 may also apply: see below, p 97.

[62] Hudoc (2007). See also *Douglas-Williams v UK No 56413/00* hudoc (2002) DA.

disabled young man who was holding his sister captive on a balcony. Following his arrest, he was pinioned to the ground for some thirty minutes or so, which caused his death by slow asphyxiation. Finding a breach of Article 2, the Court 'deplored' the fact that no medical examination of the deceased was conducted during the period of restraint, despite it being established that his mental state and the dangerous nature of the restraining technique that was used were known and that a doctor was available at the scene. A refusal to release a sick prisoner that results in a reduction of his or her life expectancy may similarly raise an issue under the obligation to protect life.[63]

A difficult question is whether a state must forcibly feed a prisoner on hunger strike to save his life. When deciding that the forced feeding of a prisoner on hunger strike was not a breach of Article 3,[64] the Commission noted that the obligation under Article 2 to secure the right to life 'should in certain circumstances call for positive action on the part of the contracting parties, in particular an active measure to save lives when the authorities have taken the person in question into their custody'. Although the Commission might be understood as taking the view that such action included forced feeding, it is submitted that a state should not be liable under Article 2 for an omission that respects the will and physical integrity of an individual who is capable of taking a decision as to matters of life and death. As Opsahl[65] suggests, there is a duty to make food and water available to persons in custody, but no more.

The *Osman* obligation extends in principle beyond the protection of particular individuals to the protection of the public at large from dangerous individuals. Thus, when operating a system of leave or relaxed custody for prisoners in preparation for their release at the end of their prison term, the state owes a duty of care to members of the public in respect of any risk to their lives that may be reasonably anticipated.[66]

3. HEALTH CARE AND OTHER SOCIAL SERVICES

The general Article 2 obligation in the *LCB* case to 'take appropriate steps' to protect life may have a further meaning relating to the provision of health care.[67] Its possible application in the context of health care was in issue in *Cyprus v Turkey*,[68] in which it was claimed that Greek Cypriots and Maronites in northern Cyprus had been denied access to available or adequate medical services in northern Cyprus or, because of restrictions on freedom of movement, in southern Cyprus. The Court appeared to accept that in principle Article 2 could extend to the provision of health care. It stated, first, that there may be liability under Article 2 where a state places an individual's life at risk by denying him or her medical care that is available to the general public, but rejected the claim on the facts. Second, in response to the applicant state's criticisms of the level of health care

---

[63] *Grice v UK* No 22564/93, 77-A DR 90 (1994) (no evidence of adverse effect on life expectancy of detention of AIDS prisoner). See also *WM v Germany* No 35638/97, 24 EHRR CD 79 (1997) and *Naddaf v FRG* No 11604/85, 50 DR 259 (1986) (suicide risks resulting from home eviction and husband's imprisonment respectively).

[64] *X v FRG* No 10565/83, 7 EHRR 152 at 153 (1984). Article 3 prohibits 'inhuman or degrading treatment'.

[65] *European System*, Ch 11 at p 221. See also the facts of *Marcella and Robert Sands v UK* No 9338/81, unreported, cited by Opsahl, *ibid*.

[66] *Mastromatteo v Italy* 2002-VIII GC (son killed by released prisoners; no breach of the duty of care on the facts).

[67] On the separate question of protection from medical negligence in particular cases, see above at n 45. On health care for detainees, see below, p 97.

[68] 2001-IV; 35 EHRR 731 GC.

provided to the general public in northern Cyprus, the Court stated that it did not 'consider it necessary to examine in this case the *extent* to which Article 2 of the Convention may impose an obligation on a Contracting State to make available a certain standard of health care.'[69] It is reasonable to infer from the word 'extent' that the Court accepts that such an obligation exists to some undefined degree. Confirmation of such an interpretation of Article 2 would extend the guarantee of the Article 2 obligation to protect life in a way that would be in accord with national health care standards in European states and indirectly provide a partial, but welcome guarantee of the right to health, which is an established human right[70] that is not otherwise protected by the Convention, except through the prohibition of inhuman or degrading treatment in Article 3, which has been applied to health care in a few situations.[71] As far as Article 2 is concerned, although European states—certainly those in Western Europe—are in a better position to comply with an obligation to make available life-saving health care for individuals, both nationals and non-nationals, within their jurisdiction than are most other states, the obligation must be one that is to some extent limited by financial considerations.[72] Although a European state may be expected to provide basic or emergency health care at public expense, any Article 2 obligation to ensure more extensive health care is likely to be held to be subject to 'available resources', as is commonly the case in European national law.[73] The role of the Court in such cases would be one of reviewing whether the failure to provide health care—for example, for an expensive drug or operation—needed to protect life was a reasonable use of limited financial resources, with the state being allowed a margin of appreciation in its allocation of resources, and did not infringe fundamental human rights norms, such as non-discrimination and due process.[74]

Social services other than health care which may have a bearing on the right to life in Article 2—as well as on freedom from inhuman or degrading treatment or punishment in Article 3—include social assistance and housing,[75] which are both the subject of recognized social rights.[76] However, it has been held that neither Article 2 nor any other Convention provision guarantees a right for a person in need to financial assistance from the state.[77] As to housing, there has scarcely been any Strasbourg jurisprudence on the question whether the failure to provide housing might raise an issue under Article 2.[78] The right to life has been interpreted in some national jurisdictions, most notably India, to cover the quality of life as well as mere physical existence. On this basis, rights such as

[69] Id, para 219. Italics added.
[70] See Article 11, Revised European Social Charter and Article 12, ICESCR.
[71] See below, p 91. Cf, Opsahl, *European Supervision*, Ch 11 at p 212.
[72] See *Nitecki v Poland No 65653/01* hudoc (2002) DA and *Pentiacova v Moldova No 14462/03* hudoc (2005) DA. The question whether medical care should be free was raised but not answered in *X v Ireland No 6839/74*, 7 DR 78 (1976) and *Scialacqua v Italy No 34151/96* hudoc (1998) DA.
[73] Cf *N v UK*, below, p 89, on the cost of medical care and Article 3.
[74] For national court cases that adopt such an approach, see *Soobramoney v Minister of Health*, Kwazulu-Natal (1997) 4 BHRC 308 South African Const Ct (no dialysis treatment to prolong life of man with irreversible renal failure: reasonable policy allocating scarce resources); *Minister of Health v Treatment Action Campaign* (2002) 13 BHRC 1, South African Const Ct; and the English cases discussed by McHale, in Burchill, Harris, and Owers, eds, *Economic, Social and Cultural Rights: Their Implementation in United Kingdom Law*, 1999, Ch 7.
[75] On the right to housing, see *Govt of the Republic of South Africa v Grootboom* (2000) 10 BHRC 84 South African Const Ct.
[76] See respectively Articles 13 and 31, Revised European Social Charter and Articles 9 and 11 ICESCR.
[77] *Wasilewski v Poland No 32734/96* hudoc (1999) DA.
[78] In *X v FRG No 5207/71*, 14 YB 698 (1971), a complaint that the forced eviction of an elderly woman endangered her life was admitted, but later rejected as an abuse of the right of petition on the facts.

the rights to health[79] and to a livelihood[80] have been made indirectly justiciable through the civil right to life. There is no reason in principle why states should not be obliged under Article 2 to 'take appropriate steps' to protect life in the context of such rights on the basis of the same approach as that suggested in respect of health care, ie taking into account 'available resources' where relevant. The interpretation of Article 2 along these lines would probably take the Convention further in the direction of protecting social rights than was intended in 1950.[81] However, other Convention guarantees have been interpreted dynamically[82] and even without regard to economic cost.[83] A reading of Article 2(1) that developed the positive obligation to protect life in its first sentence in the direction suggested and that respected standards in the national law of the contracting parties generally would be consistent with the object and purpose of the Convention and would be in step with the evolving interpretation of the equivalent 'right to life' guarantee.

4. THE PROCEDURAL OBLIGATION TO INVESTIGATE

The preceding paragraphs have concerned the substantive element of the obligation in Article 2(1) to take 'appropriate steps' to protect life. When read in conjunction with the general obligation in Article 1 to 'secure' Convention rights, the obligation in Article 2 to protect the right to life also imposes a procedural obligation upon the state[84] to investigate deaths, whether they occur at the hands of state agents,[85] private persons,[86] or persons unknown.[87] The obligation extends beyond violent deaths,[88] to all cases of death other than from natural causes.[89] But the nature of this procedural obligation will vary according to whether or not the substantive obligation to protect the right to life in Article 2 requires a criminal sanction.[90] This distinction was spelt out in *Oneryildiz v Turkey*.[91] In that case, in the context of deaths caused unintentionally by an explosion at a municipal refuse tip, it was held that an investigation leading to possible criminal proceedings is required in cases involving dangerous activities where it is established that there has been gross negligence by public authorities. This was so because, as evidenced by developments in European law, criminal sanctions in such cases—to which an investigation was a necessary prelude—are required by the substantive obligation in Article 2. In contrast, in cases in which the substantive obligation in Article 2 requires only that there be a civil or other non-criminal remedy of which the victims might avail

---

[79] See *Paramand Kataria v Union of India* (1989) 4 SCC 286

[80] *Olga Tellis v Bombay Municipal Corp* (1986) AIR 180.

[81] Social rights are guaranteed within the Council of Europe system by the European Social Charter, see above, p 3, which does not provide for individual petitions.

[82] On the dynamic interpretation of the Convention, see above, p 7.

[83] See *Airey v Ireland* A 32 (1979); 2 EHRR 305.

[84] A contracting party to which a suspect has fled must co-operate with the state conducting the inquiry: *Cummins v UK No 27306/05* hudoc (2005) DA.

[85] *McCann v UK* A324 (1995); 21 EHRR 97 GC.   [86] *Menson v UK No 47916/99* hudoc (2003) DA.

[87] *Togcu v Turkey* hudoc (2005); *Kaya v Turkey* hudoc (2006); and *Yasa v Turkey* 1998-VI; 28 EHRR 408. Deaths in or out of custody must be investigated: *Salman v Turkey* 2000-VII; 34 EHRR 425. On the obligation to investigate, see Mowbray, 51 ICLQ 437 (2002).

[88] *McCann v UK* A 324 (1995); 21 EHRR 97 GC and *Çakici v Turkey* 1999-IV; 31 EHRR 133 GC.

[89] *Calvelli and Ciglio v Italy*, above, p 41 (medical negligence) and *Ucar v Turkey* hudoc (2006) (suicide).

[90] As to which, see above, p 41.

[91] 2004-XII; 41 EHRR 325 para 93 GC. Cf, *Pereira Henriques v Luxembourg* hudoc (2006) (building site accident).

themselves,[92] the procedural obligation in Article 2 may be satisfied by the opportunities provided by these remedies to establish the cause of death and to make those responsible accountable in civil law. In cases in which Article 2 requires a criminal sanction, a criminal prosecution and trial that results in a conviction and an appropriate sentence may satisfy the procedural obligation, as may a trial that results in an acquittal although there are a number of acquittal cases in which the criminal proceedings have been considered not to satisfy the investigation obligation in Article 2.[93] Other procedures, such as an inquest in common law jurisdictions, may do so also when no case to take forward to prosecution is established.[94]

The procedural obligation in Article 2 may arise in some cases even though the victim of the attack has not died. These may include cases of disappeared persons whose fate is unknown. Thus in *Cyprus v Turkey*,[95] it was held that the obligation exists where there is 'an arguable claim that an individual, who was last seen in the custody of agents of the State, subsequently disappeared in a context which may be considered life-threatening', whether or not the individual may be presumed to be dead. On this basis, Turkey was held to be in breach of Article 2 when it failed to conduct an investigation into the whereabouts or fate of nearly 1,500 civilians in northern Cyprus who had disappeared following the 1974 Turkish military invasion.

The 'essential purpose' of the investigation is to 'secure the effective implementation of the domestic laws which protect the right to life' and to ensure the accountability of those responsible.[96] The obligation is for the state authorities to initiate an investigation once the matter has come to their attention; it is not dependent upon the lodging of a formal complaint by the next of kin or their suggesting a particular line of inquiry or investigative procedure.[97] The authorities are not relieved of their obligation to conduct an investigation by the difficult circumstances resulting from a state of emergency.[98] The precise form that the investigation takes may vary according to the circumstances and national practice, so long as it meets the requirement of effectiveness.[99]

This requirement contains a number of elements. First, the persons who are responsible for the investigation and who conduct it must be 'independent and impartial, in law and in practice'.[100] In the words of the Court, what 'is at stake here is nothing less than public confidence in the state's monopoly on the use of force'.[101] In *Ergi v Turkey*,[102] there was no independence in practice where the prosecutor relied totally on the evidence of gendarmes implicated in the death, without interviewing other persons. Nor is the

---

[92] See *Calvelli and Ciglio v Italy*, above, p 41 and *Powell v UK No 43505/99* hudoc (2000) DA. The investigation conducted in disciplinary proceedings would also be sufficient.

[93] See eg, *Akkum v Turkey* 2005-II 43 EHRR 526; *Fatma Kacar v Turkey* hudoc (2005); and *Erdogan v Turkey* hudoc (2006). Disciplinary proceedings as well as prosecution are not required: *McBride v UK No 1396/06* hudoc (2006) DA.

[94] *McCann v UK* A 324 (1995); 21 EHRR 97 GC. See also *Douglas-Williams v UK No 56413/00* hudoc (2002) DA and *Bubbins v UK* 2005-II; 41 EHRR 458. In *Bubbins*, remarkably, the Court held that an inquest complied with Article 2 on its facts, discounting UK judicial decisions to the contrary in other cases, eg *R (Amin) v Secretary of State for the Home Dept* [2003] UKHL 51, HL.

[95] 2001-IV; 35 EHRR 731 para 132 GC. Cf, *Kaya v Turkey* hudoc (2006). For a non-disappearance case, see *Yasa v Turkey*, below, p 53.

[96] *Nachova v Bulgaria* 2005-VII; 42 EHRR 933 para 110 GC. Cf *Ramsahai v Netherlands* hudoc (2007); 46 EHRR 983 GC. A related purpose is to enable 'the facts to become known to the public and in particular the relatives of any victims': *Sieminska v Poland No 37602/97* hudoc (2001) DA.

[97] *Nachova v Bulgaria* 2005-VII; 42 EHRR 933 GC.

[98] *Yasa v Turkey* 1998-VI; 28 EHRR 408. Derogation from Article 2 is not permitted: Article 15(2).

[99] *Hugh Jordan v UK* 2001-III; 37 EHRR 52 and *Velikova v Bulgaria* 2000-VI.

[100] *Nachova v Bulgaria* 2005-VII; 42 EHRR 933 para 112 GC. The obligation is both a subjective and objective one: *Jordan v UK* hudoc (2001); 37 EHRR 52.

[101] *Ramsahai v Netherlands* hudoc (2007); 46 EHRR 983 para 325 GC.

[102] 1998-IV; 32 EHRR 388.

investigation of a death by police officers who are colleagues of other implicated officers acceptable, even for a short period of time immediately after the death.[103] The fact that an investigation by police officers of a death implicating other police officers was supervised by an independent body did not satisfy the requirement of independence in the absence of other sufficient safeguards.[104] The investigation must be conducted with particular 'vigour and impartiality' where an attack is racially motivated.[105]

Second, the investigation must be adequate in the sense that it must be capable of leading to a decision as to the cause and circumstances of the death, as to whether any use of force was justified under Article 2 and as to the 'identification and punishment of those responsible'.[106] This element of the obligation was explained by the Court in *Jordan v UK*[107] as follows:

> This is not an obligation of result, but one of means. The authorities must have taken the reasonable steps available to them to secure the evidence concerning the incident, including *inter alia* eyewitness testimony, forensic evidence and, where appropriate, an autopsy which provides a complete and accurate record of injury and an objective analysis of clinical findings, including the cause of death (see concerning autopsies, eg *Salman v Turkey* ... para 106; concerning witnesses eg *Tannrikulu v Turkey*...ECHR 1999-IV para 109; concerning forensic evidence eg *Gul v Turkey*... para 89). Any deficiency in the investigation which undermines its ability to establish the cause of the death or the person or persons responsible will risk falling foul of this standard.

The absence of a power to compel testimony by eyewitnesses or other witnesses with material evidence may prevent an investigation from being effective,[108] as may a culture within which it is understood that police conduct may not be investigated.[109] Public interest immunity certificates which prevent the disclosure of official documents may also do so.[110] However, the grant of anonymity to prosecution witnesses or the non-disclosure of police documents is permissible if the rights of the defence are not prejudiced.[111] Generally, the 'investigation's conclusions must be based on a thorough, objective and impartial analysis of all the relevant elements and must apply a standard comparable to the "no more than absolutely necessary" standard required by Article 2(2)' when determining the facts and deciding a breach of Article 2 has occurred.[112]

The adequacy of an investigation was in issue in *Ramsahai v Netherlands*.[113] In that case, a suspected robber was shot dead by a policeman after pulling out a gun when confronted in the street. Following an investigation, the prosecutor decided not to prosecute

---

[103] *Ramsahai v Netherlands* hudoc (2007); 46 EHRR 983 GC.

[104] *Jordan v UK* hudoc (2001); 37 EHRR 52. Supervision by a public prosecutor who decided on prosecution and who was hierarchically independent of the police was sufficient: *Ramsahai v Netherlands* hudoc (2007); 46 EHRR 983 para 325 GC.

[105] *Menson v UK No 47916/99* hudoc (2003) DA.

[106] *Nachova v Bulgaria* 2005-VII; 42 EHRR 933 para 113 GC. Article 2 does not require an inquiry into broader policy issues that a case may raise: *Taylor et al v UK No 23412/94*, 79-A DR 127(1994).

[107] Para 107. Cf, *Nachova v Bulgaria* 2005-VII; 42 EHRR 933 para 113 GC. See also *Baysayeva v Russia* hudoc (2007). In *Finucane v UK* 2003-VIII; 37 EHRR 656 there was a failure to investigate sufficiently allegations of collusion by security personnel.

[108] *Jordan v UK* hudoc (2001); 37 EHRR 52 para 105; *Edwards v UK* 2002-II; 35 EHRR 487. No breach if requests to examine witnesses (or see documents) are allowed in fact: *Taylor v UK No 23412/94*, 79-A DR 127 (1994).

[109] *Bilgin (Irfan) v Turkey* 2001-VIII; 35 EHRR 1291.

[110] *McKerr v UK* 2001-III; 34 EHRR 553. Lack of public scrutiny of police reports and other investigative material may be justified on confidentiality grounds: *Hugh Jordan v UK* 2001-III; 37 EHRR 52.

[111] *Bubbins v UK* 2005-II; 41 EHRR 458.

[112] *Nachova v Bulgaria* 2005-VII; 42 EHRR 933 para 113 GC.   [113] Hudoc (2007); 46 EHRR 983 GC.

the policeman because he had acted in self-defence. Reversing the Chamber judgment, the Grand Chamber held, by thirteen votes to four, that the investigation had not been adequate because of various deficiencies, including the failure to conduct certain forensic tests, to conduct a reconstruction of the incident, and to follow good practice in the questioning of the two key police officers. In a joint dissenting opinion, Judges Rozakis, Bratza, Lorenzen, and Vajic argued that a deficiency or deficiencies in an investigation should only give rise to a breach of the procedural obligation if the result is to undermine the investigation as a whole and concluded, persuasively, that this was not the case on the facts.

Third, the investigation must be initiated promptly and conducted with 'reasonable expedition'.[114] A prompt response by the authorities is needed 'to ensure public confidence in their maintenance of the rule of law and in preventing any appearance of collusion in or tolerance of unlawful acts'.[115] Fourth, there must be a 'sufficient element of public scrutiny of the investigation or its results to secure accountability in practice as well as in theory' and, again, to maintain public confidence.[116] Although the degree of public scrutiny may vary with the facts, in all cases 'the next of kin of the victim must be involved in the procedure to the extent necessary to safeguard his or her legitimate interests'.[117] It may be sufficient in some cases that the investigation takes place in private, provided that the report is made public.[118] However, in other cases, the circumstances of the case may be such that the public interest in state accountability requires that the investigation be conducted in public.[119] Finally, legal aid may be required where this is necessary for the family's effective participation.[120]

Where more than one investigation procedure is used, the deficiencies of one procedure may be made good by the merits of another.[121] A failure to conduct an effective pre-trial investigation may be overcome by the establishment of the facts at the criminal trial of the murderer,[122] but this will not be the case where witnesses are not called because the accused pleads guilty[123] or not all of the relevant witnesses and material evidence is before the court.[124]

In *Oneryildiz v Turkey*,[125] the procedural obligation was extended beyond the investigation to the trial stage. The Court held both that the investigation must result in a prosecution where this is called for on the facts and that the national courts must treat the case with the appropriate seriousness, giving it the 'careful scrutiny' and imposing a sentence that will deter others. In that case, this last requirement was not met when the Turkish courts gave two local mayors, who were the only persons prosecuted, suspended sentences of the minimum possible statutory fine (about 9.70 euros) for the negligent performance of their duties resulting in the loss of many lives.

---

[114] *Jordan v UK* hudoc (2001); 37 EHRR 52 para 108 (inquest); *McKerr v UK* 2001-III; 34 EHRR 553 (police investigation): both breaches. See also *Tas v Turkey* 2000-XI; 33 EHRR 325; *Edwards v UK* 2002-II; 35 EHRR 487; *Byrzkykowski v Poland* hudoc (2007); 46 EHRR 675; and *Silih v Slovenia* hudoc (2007) (referred to Grand Chamber).

[115] *Akpinar and Altun v Turkey* hudoc (2007) para 58 and *McKerr v UK* 2001-III.

[116] *McKerr v UK, ibid.*

[117] *Hugh Jordan v UK* 2001-III; 37 EHRR 52 para 109. This will include sufficient participation in an inquiry in camera (*Edwards v UK* 2002-II; 35 EHRR 487) and the disclosure to them of documents (*Ogur v Turkey* 1999-III; 31 EHRR 912 and *Jordan v UK* hudoc (2001); 35 EHRR 52 para 133). See also *Gulec v Turkey* 1998-IV; 28 EHRR 121 (victim's father not informed of decision not to prosecute).

[118] *Taylor et al v UK* No 2341/94, 79-A DR 127 (1994).

[119] *Edwards v UK*; 2002-II; 35 EHRR 487 (issues involved in prison death required public hearing).

[120] *Jordan v UK* hudoc (2001); 37 EHRR 52.   [121] *Ibid*, and *Tanribilir v Turkey* hudoc (2000).

[122] *McKerr v UK* 2001-III; 34 EHRR 553.   [123] *Edwards v UK* 2002-II; 35 EHRR 487.

[124] *Gul v Turkey* hudoc (2000); 34 EHRR 719.   [125] 2004-XII; 41 EHRR 325 para 96 GC.

The obligation to conduct an effective investigation was infringed in several ways in a series of Northern Irish cases with similar facts, including *Jordan v UK*.[126] In that case, the applicant's son had been shot and killed by an RUC police officer after the son's car had been pursued by the police. The incident led to a police investigation by the RUC, in the light of which the Director of Public Prosecutions decided not to prosecute the policeman concerned. An inquest was opened, and was still pending when the case was decided at Strasbourg. The Court held that these procedures did not comply with Article 2, either individually or collectively. As far as the police investigation was concerned, it was not independent as it was conducted by other RUC officers. Although the DPP was independent in fact, his failure to give reasons for his decision not to prosecute infringed the requirements of 'objective independence' ('the appearance of independence') and of public scrutiny in a case in which the police investigation, upon which the DPP relied, had not been independent and the facts called for a reasoned decision, both 'to reassure a concerned public that the rule of law had been respected' and to assist the family in challenging the decision. With regard to the inquest, it was not effective on several counts. In contrast with the inquest in the *McCann* case, the police officer who had fired the shot was not required to give evidence, and did not do so, with the result that his reliability and credibility could not be assessed, thereby detracting from the inquest's capacity to determine the lawfulness of the use of force. Moreover, the inquest was unable to make a finding of unlawful death, which might have required the DPP to reconsider his decision not to prosecute.[127] In addition, although the inquest was held in public, the public scrutiny requirement had been infringed because the victim's family's ability to participate in the proceedings had been prejudiced by the non-disclosure to them of witness statements until the witnesses gave evidence.[128] Finally, the inquest had not been commenced promptly or completed within a reasonable time.[129]

The obligation to investigate was also infringed in a large number of Turkish cases arising out of the Kurdish situation.[130] The investigation by the public prosecutor in these cases was found deficient in various ways, including the failure to investigate the possibility of security force, as opposed to terrorist, involvement,[131] lack of thoroughness in other respects,[132] and delay in the conduct of the investigation.[133] There were also breaches because of lack of institutional or practical independence.[134]

In these Turkish and other cases, the procedural obligation to investigate has led to a finding of a breach of Article 2 when no breach of the substantive guarantee has been found because the Court has not been satisfied beyond a reasonable doubt that a death was attributable to state agents.[135]

---

[126] Hudoc (2001); 37 EHRR 52. See also *Kelly v UK* 2001-III; *McKerr v UK* 2001-III; 34 EHRR 553; *Shanaghan v UK* 2001-III; and *McShane v UK* hudoc (2002); 35 EHRR 593.

[127] The inquest could only identify the date, place, and cause of death. It could also not investigate the possibility of collusion with the security forces: *Shanaghan v UK* 2001-III.

[128] *Hugh Jordan v UK* 2001-III; 37 EHRR 52 para 133. The Court contrasted its approach in the *McCann* case, where the same limitation had not been considered problematic, stating that the Court now required more family involvement.

[129] The inquest was still pending eight years after the shooting.

[130] As to the inter-relation in some Turkish cases between the obligation to investigate and the obligation to protect lives, see above, p 44.

[131] *Kaya v Turkey* 1998-VI; 28 EHRR 1.   [132] *Kaya (Mahmut) v Turkey* 2000-III.

[133] *Tanrikulu v Turkey* 1999-IV; 30 EHRR 950.

[134] *Ergi v Turkey* 1998-IV; 32 EHRR 388 and *Orhan v Turkey* hudoc (2002).

[135] For cases, see below, n 176.

5. APPLICATION OF THE OBLIGATION TO PROTECT LIFE TO NON-FATAL CASES

Where relevant, both the substantive and procedural obligations in Article 2 to take steps to protect life may apply even though the person at risk, on the facts of the case taken to Strasbourg, does not die. Thus the substantive obligation was held to apply in the *LCB* case,[136] so as to require the state to do all that could be reasonably required of it to prevent the applicant's life being avoidably put at risk from her father's exposure to radiation. It also applied in the *Osman* case[137] to the obligation to protect both a son and his father from a real and immediate risk to their lives posed by a private person, even though only the father was killed. The procedural obligation to conduct an investigation was held to apply in *Yasa v Turkey*[138] where the applicant had survived an attack by an unknown gunman.

6. PROTECTION OF THE UNBORN CHILD?

The first sentence of Article 2 states that 'everyone's right to life must be protected. The question whether the word 'everyone' includes an unborn child—and if so from what point in its development and the extent to which protection is offered—has yet to be fully decided.[139] The question has arisen in the context of both voluntary and involuntary abortion.

I. VOLUNTARY ABORTION

The question has arisen mostly in the context of voluntary abortion.[140] In *X v UK*,[141] the Commission ruled that the abortion of a ten-week-old foetus under British law to protect the physical or mental health of a pregnant woman was not in breach of Article 2. In doing so, it stated that Article 2 does not recognize an *absolute* right to life of an unborn child. However, the Commission left open the controversial question whether Article 2 does not protect the unborn child at all[142] or whether the foetus has a right to life under it subject to certain implied limitations. It was able to do so because, even if the latter were the position, the facts of the case came within one such limitation, namely the protection of the pregnant woman's health. The Commission's position was further developed in *H v Norway*.[143] There a lawful abortion of a fourteen-week-old foetus on the statutory ground that the 'pregnancy, birth or care for the child may place the woman in a difficult

---

[136] Above, p 42. Non-lethal physical attacks will generally be considered under Article 3.

[137] Above, p 43.

[138] 1998-VI; 28 EHRR 408.

[139] See Peukert, in *Wiarda Mélanges*, p 115. The death of a child from premature birth caused by security forces may be a breach of Article 2: *Mentes v Turkey* 1997-VIII; 26 EHRR 595 GC.

[140] Other 'right to life' issues concerning the unborn child include those arising out of embryonic and foetal research and the taking of hazardous drugs by pregnant women. See Byk, *Medical and Biological Progress and the European Convention on Human Rights*, 1994.

[141] No 8416/78, 19 DR 244 (1980) (the *Paton* case).

[142] As the Commission noted, the textual evidence supports a negative interpretation. Thus the wording of Article 2 beyond the first sentence of Article 2(1) can only apply to persons already born and in most other Convention articles in which the word 'everyone' appears it has the same limited meaning.

[143] No 17004/90, 73 DR 155 (1992).

situation of life'[144] was held not to be contrary to Article 2. This goes beyond the *X* case in that the abortion was later in time and for social, rather than health, reasons. The key to the Commission's decision in *H v Norway* was its understanding that 'national laws on abortion differ considerably' within the states parties to the Convention.[145] In view of this, it considered that 'in such a delicate area the contracting states must have a certain discretion'. It then held that the defendant state's law, as it was applied to the facts of the case, did not exceed this 'discretion'. Whether the Commission would have reached the same conclusion if the case had involved that part of the defendant state's law that gave the pregnant woman an unlimited right to abortion during the first twelve weeks of pregnancy is not clear. In this connection it is interesting to note that, while again finding that it did not have to decide the question whether Article 2 protected the unborn child at all, in *H v Norway* the Commission did state that it did not exclude that 'in certain circumstances' it does offer such protection, without indicating what those 'circumstances' were.

The Commission's approach in the *X* and *H* cases was followed by the Court in *Boso v Italy*.[146] In that case, the Court held that an abortion that was performed under Italian law within the first twelve weeks of pregnancy because of a risk to the woman's physical or mental health was not a breach of Article 2. Such a law struck 'a fair balance between, on the one hand, the need to ensure protection of the foetus and, on the other, the women's interests'. The Grand Chamber reviewed, without criticizing, the *X*, *H*, and *Boso* cases in *Vo v France*. The *Vo* case was one of involuntary abortion and is considered separately under that heading below. It is of more general interest, and hence relevant to voluntary abortion cases also, in regard to the wide measure of discretion it leaves to states on the question whether or when an unborn child is a person ('everyone') whose right to life is protected by Article 2 in the context of voluntary as well as involuntary manslaughter.

The limitations upon any right to life that the unborn child may have that the jurisprudence of the Court and the former Commission allows are, as they have applied nationally, capable of covering most cases in which a voluntary abortion is sought and are likely to remain consistent with Article 2 so long as the present variation in European practice continues.

A claim alleging that a voluntary abortion is in breach of Article 2 may only be brought by a 'victim' in the sense of Article 34, who must be someone personally affected. The 'potential father' qualifies as a 'victim' for this purpose so that he can bring a claim where the woman seeks or obtains an abortion without his consent.[147] An ordinary member of the public who opposes legislation permitting abortion is not so affected.[148] Nor is a church minister, even though he loses his office for refusal to carry out his functions as a result of his opposition to abortion.[149] Cases involving voluntary abortion issues may well be brought not by someone seeking to prevent an abortion under Article 2, but by a pregnant woman arguing for an abortion as a part of her right to privacy under Article 8.[150] Insofar as such cases are successful, there are inevitable ramifications for Article 2, since

---

[144] English translation of the Norwegian abortion statute in the Commission's decision.

[145] See Plomer, 5 HRLR 311 at 335 (2005).

[146] *No 50490/99* hudoc (2002) DA. The question was not directly in issue and the Court found no need to consider it in *Open Door Counselling and Dublin Well Woman v Ireland* A 246-A (1993); 15 EHRR 244 para 63 PC.

[147] *H v Norway No 17004/90* hudoc (1992) (partner) and *Boso v Italy No 50490/99* hudoc (2002) DA.

[148] *X v Austria No 7045/75*, 7 DR 87 (1976). Cf, *X v Norway No 867/60*, 6 CD 34 (1961).

[149] *Knudsen v Norway No 11045/84*, 42 DR 247 (1985).

[150] See, in particular, *Bruggemann and Scheuten v FRG No 6959/75*, 10 DR 100 (1978). In that case, the Commission found it unnecessary to decide, in the context of an Article 8 claim, whether an unborn child is a person having a right to life for the purposes of Article 2. See Mr Fawcett's dissenting opinion.

an abortion that is protected by Article 8 cannot at the same time be contrary to Article 2. In contrast, an unsuccessful claim to a 'right to an abortion' under Article 8 on the basis of respect for private life[151] does not necessarily have consequences for Article 2.

II. INVOLUNTARY ABORTION

In *Vo v France*,[152] the applicant went to hospital for her regular pregnancy test, but, having been mistaken for another woman with the same name who was not pregnant but who was attending hospital to have a coil removed, was subjected without medical examination to a procedure that caused her to lose her baby. The question for the Grand Chamber was whether Article 2 required a criminal sanction for the medical negligence that had led to the involuntary abortion of the applicant's 20 to 21-week-old foetus against her wishes, or whether the civil remedy for damages that French law provided on the facts was sufficient. Deciding that the latter was the case, the Court, as in the voluntary abortion cases, found no need to decide whether an unborn child qualified for protection under Article 2 and, if so, at what stage in its development (eg, nidation, viability) this occurred. The Court did, however, state that, given the absence of a European legal, medical, ethical, or religious consensus as to when life begins, a margin of appreciation applies, even to the point where the Court doubted whether it was 'desirable, or even possible as matters stand, to answer in the abstract the question whether the unborn child is a person for the purposes of Article 2'.

In *Evans v UK*[153] the Court followed the same margin of appreciation approach to embryos created by *in vitro* fertilization (IVF). In that case, the applicant and her partner underwent IVF treatment, resulting in embryos that later could be implanted into the applicant's womb. But when the relationship broke down, the partner withdrew his consent to the use of the embryos in this way, which meant under English law that they had to be destroyed. The Grand Chamber rejected the applicant's claim that their destruction would be a breach of Article 2 on the basis that the position in English law, by which an embryo did not have a right to life, fell within the margin of appreciation that states had on this matter, given 'the absence of any European consensus on the scientific and legal definition of the beginning of life'.

A question that has not been considered directly is whether the state must provide adequate protection against acts (eg the pregnant woman's taking of drugs harmful to the foetus) that may reduce the 'quality of life' of a child once born without actually causing loss of life.[154] The Commission has in other contexts required that there be evidence of a danger to life, not just of ill-health, for Article 2 to apply.[155]

III. OTHER HARMFUL ACTS

In an early case[156] the Commission expressed the opinion that in certain circumstances a sterilization operation might be contrary to Article 2, presumably by denying a person

---

[151] In *X v UK*, the husband's claim to respect for family life under Article 8 failed because of the 'rights of others' restriction in Article 8(2) (the wife's rights).

[152] 2004-XIII; 40 EHRR 259 para 85 GC. See Plomer, 5 HRLR 311 (2005).

[153] Hudoc (2007); 46 EHRR 728 para 54 GC.

[154] The Convention does not require a 'wrongful life' remedy for being born disabled by medical negligence: *Reeve v UK No 24844/94*, 79 DR 146 (1994). But see *Maurice v France* 2005-IX; 42 EHRR 885 GC.

[155] *De Varga-Hirsch v France No 9559/81*, 33 DR 158 (1993) and *M v FRG No 10307/83*, 37 DR 113 (1984). Cf, *X v Austria No 8278/78*, 18 DR 154 (1979).

[156] *No 1287/61*, cited in Fawcett, p 36.

the possibility even of conception. The application was refused on its facts because the operation was for medical reasons and the sterilized person had given her consent.[157] The question has not arisen since under Article 2 and would seem to come more properly within Articles 3 and 8.

7. THE PROHIBITION OF THE TAKING OF LIFE BY THE USE OF FORCE

I. THE GENERAL RULE

Article 2 prohibits the taking of life where this is not justified by any of the four exceptions permitted by its text. The prohibition extends to the use of force resulting in the unintentional, as well as to the intentional taking of life.[158] It applies to the taking of life by the police,[159] soldiers,[160] and other state agents.[161] It does not make a state directly responsible for the taking of life by private individuals; a state's obligation in such cases is limited to the provision of protection in accordance with the first sentence of Article 2(1).

Physical assault by a state agent that does not result in death will 'almost always' be examined under Article 3, not Article 2.[162] But Article 2 may apply in the absence of death in 'exceptional circumstances': relevant factors are the 'degree and type of force used and the intention or aim' underlying it.[163] In *Makaratzis v Greece*[164] there were 'exceptional circumstances' that brought Article 2 into play when the applicant was seriously injured after thirty or so police fired sixteen or more bullets into his car during a chaotic car chase. Although there was no intention to kill the applicant, the use of force was 'potentially lethal' and it was only 'fortuitous' that he was not killed.

A state may be liable under Article 2 not only for the conduct of its agents who actually kill an individual, but also for those at a higher level if a life-threatening operation is not planned or managed by the authorities 'so as to minimise, to the greatest extent possible, recourse to lethal force'.[165] Killings will be in breach of Article 2 even though they are in accordance with national rules governing the use of firearms by the police and other state agents where those rules do not satisfy the Article 2 strict proportionality test.[166]

A state may be responsible under Article 2 for deporting or extraditing an individual to another state when there are substantial grounds for believing that this would involve a real risk there to his or her life from the acts of state agents or private individuals,[167] although in practice such cases are treated under Article 3.[168]

---

[157] The applicant was the husband who had not given his consent.

[158] *McCann v UK* A 324 (1995); 21 EHRR 97 GC.

[159] See eg, *Kakoulli v Finland* hudoc (2005); 45 EHRR 355.

[160] See eg, *Isayeva,Yusupova and Bazayeva v Russia* hudoc (2005); 41 EHRR 847.

[161] Village guards or security officers who hold themselves out as acting for the state are state agents: *Avsar v Turkey* hudoc (2001); 37 EHRR 1014.

[162] *Ilhan v Turkey* 2000-VII; 34 EHRR 869 para 76 GC.   [163] *Ibid.*

[164] 2004-XI; 41 EHRR 1092 paras 52, 54 GC. Cf, *Acar v Turkey* hudoc (2005) and *Green v UK No 28079/04* hudoc (2005) DA.

[165] *McCann v UK* A 324 (1995); 21 EHRR 97 para 194 GC. Cf, *Ergi v Turkey* 1998-IV; 32 EHRR 388; and *Isayeva v Russia* hudoc (2005); 41 EHRR 791.

[166] *Nachova v Bulgaria* 2005-VII; 42 EHRR 933 GC and *Makaratkis v Greece* 2004-XI; 41 EHRR 1092 GC.

[167] *Gonzalez v Spain No 43544/98* hudoc (1999) DA and *Headley v UK No 39642/03* hudoc (2005) DA.

[168] On death penalty cases, see below, p 61.

a. Killing by a state agent

For the state to be liable under Article 2 for the killing of any individual, it must first be shown beyond a reasonable doubt that the individual was killed by one of its agents.[169] This requirement has presented considerable problems of proof. These problems have been eased for the applicant where an individual dies in custody. In that situation, given the vulnerability of the detainee and the state's special access to information about what happened, the burden of proof shifts to the state to show that the death is not the responsibility of its agents. In *Salman v Turkey*,[170] the Court stated:

> Where the events in issue lie wholly, or in large part, within the exclusive knowledge of the authorities, as in the case of persons within their control in custody, strong presumptions of fact will arise in respect of injuries and death occurring during that detention. Indeed, the burden of proof may be regarded as resting on the authorities to provide a satisfactory and convincing explanation.

This burden of proof was not satisfied in cases in which the victim was in good health on being taken into detention and there was no post mortem or other evidence to confirm the state's claim that he had died from a heart attack[171] or to explain injuries to the body satisfactorily.[172] Nor was it met when a prisoner was killed by an explosion when the authorities were not able to explain why he had been put in a place where he was at risk.[173]

The difficulty of proving beyond a reasonable doubt that a state agent is responsible for a non-custodial killing is in some cases, eg, a killing on the street with no witnesses,[174] increased where the state fails to co-operate in establishing the facts. In this situation too, the Court is prepared to assist, again on the basis of the exclusive knowledge of the authorities. In particular, it has held that where the applicant has made out a *prima facie* case that the killing was by a state agent and the defendant state refuses to produce relevant evidence, the burden of proof shifts to that state to show that the refusal is for a good reason or to provide a satisfactory explanation of the killing.[175]

Although a breach of the state's substantive obligation not to take life by force may be impossible to establish in some cases, Article 2 has sometimes been found to have been infringed in them because the state has failed to comply with its procedural obligation to investigate the killing.[176] A breach of Article 2 may also be found in some cases on the basis that an unattributable death which results from a state operation, for example

---

[169] If the perpetrator is shown to be a state agent, it will then be for the state to show that the killing falls within one of the permitted exceptions in Article 2: see *McCann v UK*, below, p 63.

[170] 2000-VII; 34 EHRR 425 para 100 GC. Cf, *Musayeva v Russia* hudoc (2007). As to proof that an individual has been detained, see *Celikbilek v Turkey* hudoc (2005). The state must prove the release of a detained person: *Suheyla Aydin v Turkey* hudoc (2005). See further on the burden of proof, below, p 849.

[171] *Salman v Turkey* 2000-VII; 34 EHRR 425 GC and *Tanli v Turkey* 2001-III; 38 EHRR 31. Contrast *Ucar v Turkey* hudoc (2006).

[172] *Velikova v Bulgaria* 2000-VI and *Anguelova v Bulgaria* 2002-IV; 38 EHRR 659.

[173] *Demiray v Turkey* 2000-XII.

[174] See eg, *Akkoc v Turkey* 2000-X; 34 EHRR 1173; *Yasa v Turkey* 1998-I; 28 EHRR 408; and *Kaya (Mahmut) v Turkey* 2000-III. On the difficulty of satisfying the burden of proof, see Buckley, 1 HRLR 35, 36 (2001).

[175] *Estamirov v Russia* hudoc (2006); 46 EHRR 696; *Khashiyev and Akayeva v Russia* hudoc (2005); 42 EHRR 397 and *Luluyev v Russia* 2006-VIII. Failure to provide evidence may also involve a breach of the state's obligation to provide 'all necessary facilities' (Article 38(1)(a), Convention): *Akkum v Turkey* 2005-II; 43 EHRR 526. For a (now exceptional) case in which the Court held that inferences could not be drawn on the facts from a state's lack of co-operation, see *Tanrikulu v Turkey* 1999-IV; 30 EHRR 950 GC.

[176] See the *Akkoc, Yasa,* and *Kaya (Mahmut)* cases, above, n 174. On the procedural obligation, see above, p 48.

against terrorists, has not been planned or conducted by the authorities so as to minimize the risk of loss of life of innocent bystanders.[177]

b. Disappeared persons

There may be liability for a breach of the state's substantive obligation under Article 2 not to take life where a person has disappeared, but no body has been found. There may be a taking of life in breach of Article 2 in such a case (i) where it is established beyond reasonable doubt that the disappeared person has been detained by the state; and (ii) there is 'sufficient circumstantial evidence, based on concrete elements, on which it may be concluded beyond reasonable doubt' that the person is dead.[178] When these two requirements are met, the burden of proof is transferred to the state to account for the death of a person in its custody.[179] The question of liability under Article 2 for disappeared persons first arose in *Kurt v Turkey*.[180] There it was found the applicant's son had been detained by soldiers, the state's claim that the son had left his village with PKK terrorists being rejected. But, in the absence of any evidence as to where he had been taken or his fate in the intervening four and a half years, the Court disposed of the case under Article 5, concerning freedom of the person, not Article 2. The Court rejected the applicant's submission that her son could be presumed to be dead because of the life-threatening context of his arrest and a claimed administrative practice of disappearances in Turkey leading to death; in the absence of more concrete, post-arrest evidence, these claims were not by themselves sufficient to prove 'beyond reasonable doubt' that the applicant's son had died in state custody.

In contrast, breaches of the substantive obligation in Article 2 not to take life have been found in a series of post-*Kurt* cases involving disappeared persons in Turkey. In *Timurtas v Turkey*,[181] the Court found that the applicant's son had been arrested by gendarmes and taken to an identifiable place of detention. There was documentary evidence to this effect[182] and credible evidence that two fellow detainees had seen the son in a place of detention in the month or so after his arrest, but he had not otherwise been seen during the six and a half years following his arrest: further enquires had been discouraged by state officials. Finding that in this case there was sufficient concrete circumstantial evidence of death and no explanation of the son's fate by the defendant state (which claimed not to have detained him), the Court found a breach of Article 2. The *Kurt* case was distinguished on the basis that a longer period of time had passed since the son's disappearance;[183] that there was credible evidence of his presence in a place of detention after the arrest; and that there was much stronger evidence than in the *Kurt* case that the son was previously wanted by the state in connection with PKK activities, a fact that made his unacknowledged detention life-threatening in the context of south-east Turkey where, the Court had decided in other cases,[184] the security forces were not held accountable for their actions. Other post-*Kurt* cases from Turkey have followed a similar pattern. In some of these cases, which have generally involved

---

[177] *Ergi v Turkey* 1998-IV; 32 EHRR 388.   [178] *Çakici v Turkey* 1999-IV; 31 EHRR 133 para 85 GC.
[179] *Ibid.*   [180] 1998-III; 27 EHRR 373.   [181] 2000-VI; 33 EHRR 121.
[182] This was a photocopy of a post-operation report; the government challenged its authenticity, but the Court inferred otherwise when the government declined on security grounds to produce supporting evidence.
[183] The longer the period of disappearance the less other circumstantial evidence is needed: *Timurtas v Turkey* 2000-VI; 33 EHRR 121 para 83.
[184] See *Kilic v Turkey* 2000-III; 33 EHRR 1357 and *Kaya (Mahmut) v Turkey* 2000-III.

disappearances for five years or longer,[185] *Kurt* has been expressly distinguished;[186] in others it has not.[187]

Recent Russian cases confirm that the Court is now more ready to presume death. Thus, in *Baysayeva v Russia*,[188] the applicant's husband was, the Court found, arrested along with others by military servicemen when a security operation was being conducted in his village, since when there had been no news of him for some six years. The defendant state denied that he had been arrested by the state and had no custody records for him. The Court accepted the applicant's contention that when, in the context of the conflict in Chechnya, a person was arrested by unidentified servicemen without any subsequent acknowledgment of detention, the arrest could be considered life-threatening. In these circumstances, and noting also that the authorities had not taken the necessary early steps to open an investigation, the Court held that it could be presumed that the husband was dead.[189] While the period of disappearance was longer than in *Kurt*, the Court accepted an argument as to existence and relevance of a life-threatening situation which it had rejected in that case, and there was no post-arrest 'circumstantial evidence'.

II. PERMITTED EXCEPTIONS

a. Capital punishment

The first exception concerns the death penalty, which is expressly permitted by Article 2(1). The use of the death penalty had to be allowed when the Convention was drafted because it was then generally provided for in the law of West European states. Practice has changed radically since, to the point where provision for the death penalty is almost entirely absent in Council of Europe states or, where it is available, is not carried out.[190] Accordingly, the Sixth Protocol to the Convention[191] requires the abolition of the death penalty in peacetime for the parties to it. This partial prohibition was made total by the Thirteenth Protocol,[192] which requires the abolition of the death penalty in time of war also. Nonetheless, Article 2 remains the governing provision for the parties to the Convention insofar as they are not parties to the two Protocols. Article 2 does not in terms prevent a state that has abolished the death penalty from re-introducing it,[193] but acceptance of the Protocols does.

In *Soering v UK*,[194] the Court stated that it would have been possible for the parties to the Convention to have 'abrogated' the exception provided for in Article 2(1) by the 'generalised abolition of capital punishment' in their national law. However, given the adoption of the Sixth Protocol as recently as 1983, the Court considered that this had not

---

[185] But see *Tanis v Turkey* 2005-VIII; 46 EHRR 211 (four and a half years).

[186] See eg, *Cicek v Turkey* hudoc (2001); 37 EHRR 464; *Orhan v Turkey* hudoc (2002); and *Ertak v Turkey* 2000-V.

[187] See eg, *Bilgin v Turkey* hudoc (2000) 36 EHRR 879 and *Akdeniz v Turkey* hudoc (2001). See also *Cyprus v Turkey* hudoc (2001); 35 EHRR 731 GC (breach only of the procedural obligation).

[188] Hudoc (2007).

[189] *Ibid*. See also *Bazorkina v Russia* hudoc (2006); 46 EHRR 261; *Luluyev v Russia* 2006-VIII; and *Imakayeva v Russia* 2006-VIII.

[190] In 2008, Russia was the only Convention party that retained the death penalty in law in either peacetime or war; it operated a moratorium in practice.

[191] On the Sixth Protocol, see below, p 745. All Convention parties are parties to the Protocol except Russia.

[192] On the Thirteen Protocol, see below, p 746. 40 parties.

[193] Contrast Article 4, ACHR.   [194] A 161 (1989); 11 EHRR 439 PC.

occurred, despite the considerable move towards the abolition of the death penalty that had taken place by the time the case was decided in 1987. The position was, therefore, that the Article 2 exception continued in being, although the 'circumstances relating to a death penalty' might give rise to an issue under Article 3.[195] This position was reviewed again in *Öcalan v Turkey*[196] in which it was noted by the Court Chamber that there had been 'a considerable evolution' in state practice concerning the death penalty since the *Soering* case. When the *Öcalan* case was decided, the position was that all but one of the 44 Convention parties had abolished the death penalty in peacetime, with the remaining state, Russia, applying a moratorium, and new Council of Europe member states undertook to abolish the death penalty as a condition of membership. The result was that the territory of Council of Europe states constituted a 'zone free of capital punishment'. In consequence, it could 'be said that capital punishment in peacetime has come to be regarded as an unacceptable, if not inhuman, form of punishment which is no longer permissible under Article 2'. The Grand Chamber agreed with this conclusion.[197] No such conclusion was drawn in respect of the dealth penalty in time of war, given that a large number of states, now less in number, were not parties to the Thirteenth Protocol.[198]

Even though states may still not be required by Article 2 to abolish the death penalty or refrain from applying it, they may nonetheless infringe Article 2 if its provisions regulating the use of the death penalty are not complied with. Article 2 permits the death penalty where it is imposed as 'a sentence of a court following...conviction of a crime for which this penalty is provided by law'. On its face, Article 2 permits the death penalty for any 'crime'. However, the principle of proportionality must apply, so that it should be permissible only for 'the most serious crimes'.[199] It is likely that the word 'crime' has an autonomous meaning in Article 2, as it has in Article 6.[200] The death penalty must be 'provided by law'. This means not only that there is a basis for it in national law, but also that this basis is 'accessible' and 'foreseeable', as these requirements have been interpreted in other Convention articles.[201] A death sentence must be imposed by a 'court', which means an 'independent and impartial tribunal' in the sense of Article 6.[202] Beyond that, it has been held that Article 2 will be infringed unless 'the most rigorous standards of fairness' are observed in the criminal proceedings leading to a death sentence, both at first instance and on appeal.[203] Thus the imposition of the death penalty in breach of the fair trial guarantee in Article 6[204] is a breach of Article 2,

---

[195] Id, para 104.
[196] Hudoc (2003); 37 EHRR 238 paras 195–8: italics added. See also *Shamayev v Russia* 2005-III.
[197] 2005-IV; 41 EHRR 985 para 163.   [198] On Article 3, see below p 90.
[199] Cf, *Soering v UK* A 161 (1989); 11 EHRR 439 para 104 PC. And see *Meng v Portugal* No 25862/94, 83-B DR 88 (1995) (death penalty for multiple car thefts: case settled) and *MAR v UK* No 28038/95, 23 EHRR CD 120; (1997) Com Rep, F Sett (drugs possession offences). Article 6, International Covenant on Civil and Political Rights and Article 4, ACHR, permit the death penalty only for 'the most serious crimes'. In the ACHR, it is also prohibited for 'political offences or related common crimes'. In the ICCPR, the imposition of the death penalty must not be contrary to the Genocide Convention (ie, it must not be imposed so as to effect genocide). Proportionality may also govern the method of execution. But issues concerning proportionality generally may be considered by the Court under Article 3, not Article 2.
[200] See *Engel v Netherlands* A 22 (1976); 1 EHRR 647 PC.
[201] *Öcalan v Turkey* 2005-IV; 41 EHRR 985 para 166 GC.
[202] *Ibid*. On the Article 6 guarantee, see below, p 284.   [203] *Ibid*.
[204] *Öcalan v Turkey* 2005-IV; 41 EHRR 985 and *Bader and Kandor v Sweden* 2005-XI; 46 EHRR 197. Whereas *Bader and Kandor* refers to a 'fair trial' generally, *Öcalan*, paras 173–4, refers to Article 6.

as must be its imposition in breach of the prohibition of retroactive criminal punishment in Article 7 and for an offence involving conduct protected by the Convention.[205] Discrimination contrary to Article 14 in the imposition of the death penalty would be a breach of Articles 2 and 14 taken together.

There will also be a breach of Article 2 where the deportation or extradition of an individual occurs when there are substantial grounds for believing that there is a real risk that he or she will be subjected to the death penalty in circumstances in which the above provisions in Article 2 regulating the death penalty will not be complied with, as when there would not be a fair trial.[206] Whether deportation or extradition to face a real risk of the death penalty, in peacetime or in wartime, is *per se* a breach of Article 2 is subject to the same considerations as those indicated above when discussing the *Öcalan* case in connection with the use of the death penalty by a contracting party within its own jurisdiction.[207] Cases of deportation or extradition involving the death penalty are considered under either Article 2 or 3, or both.[208]

b. Deaths resulting from the use of force for permitted purposes

Article 2(2) lists three other situations in which the taking of life by the state is justified. These are when it results from the use of force which is no more than absolutely necessary:

(i)   in self-defence or the defence of another;

(ii)   to effect a lawful arrest or prevent an escape from lawful detention; and

(iii) to quell a riot or insurrection.

This list is exhaustive. At one stage in the drafting, a fourth exception was permitted:[209] where force is used to prohibit 'entry to a clearly defined place to which access is forbidden on grounds of national security'. This wording was finally omitted so that the taking of life on this basis was not intended to be allowed. The taking of life to prevent crime[210] or escape from a state's territory[211] is not permitted. Action against terrorists resulting in the loss of life has to be justified with Article 2(2)(a)–(c).[212] Article 2(2) regulates the unintentional as well as the intentional taking of life by the use of force.[213]

Article 2(2) permits the taking of life only when it results from the use of force which is 'no more than absolutely necessary' for one or more of the authorized purposes. The burden of proof is upon the state to show that the force used meets this requirement.[214] Force is 'absolutely necessary' only if it is 'strictly proportionate' to the achievement

---

[205] See *Sobhani v Sweden No 32999/06*, unreported (1998) DA (sexual orientation (Article 8): case settled).

[206] *Bader and Kandor v Sweden*, above n 205.

[207] See above, p 60. The Court has suggested that a real risk of the death penalty might in itself infringe Article 2 in some deportation or extradition cases: see eg, *F v UK No 17341/03* hudoc (2004) DA and *SR v Sweden No 62806/00* hudoc (2002) DA. Deportation or extradition by a party to the Sixth or Thirteenth Protocol to face a real risk of the death penalty would be a breach of those Protocols. As to the relevance of undertakings by the receiving state not to impose the death penalty, see eg, by analogy *Soering v UK*, below, p 80, and *Nivette v France No 44190/98* hudoc (2001) DA.

[208] See eg, *Shamayev v Russia* 2005-III.   [209] See 3 TP 282 and 4 TP 58.

[210] *Kelly v UK No 17579/90*, 74 DR 139 (1993).

[211] *Streletz, Kessler, and Krenz v Germany* 2001-II; 33 EHRR 751 GC.

[212] *McCann v UK* A324 (1995); 21 EHRR 97 GC; *Ergi v Turkey* 1998-IV; 32 EHRR 388; and *Isayeva v Russia* hudoc (2005); 41 EHRR 791.

[213] *Ogur v Turkey* 1999-III; 31 EHRR 912 GC.

[214] *McCann v UK* A 324 (1995); 21 EHRR 97 para 148 GC. Cf, dissenting opinion of Judge Bratza in *Agdas v Turkey* hudoc (2004).

of a permitted purpose.[215] In this respect, Article 2(2) imposes a more rigorous test of necessity than that which applies under paragraphs (2) of Articles 8–11 of the Convention where the requirement is simply one of proportionality.[216] Another crucial difference is that states are allowed no 'margin of appreciation' under Article 2(2); the Court makes its own objective assessment of the strict proportionality of the force used.[217] The requirement of strict proportionality applies not only to the 'actions of the agents of the state who actually administer the force, but also all the surrounding circumstances including such matters as the planning and control of the actions under examination'.[218] This is particularly so 'where deliberate lethal force is used'.[219] The requirement of 'strict proportionally' may require a verbal warning and a warning shot aimed in the air before potentially lethal force is used.[220]

While it must be permissible in some circumstances for the police and other state agents to use firearms when confronted with dangerous individuals who are honestly and reasonably believed to be armed, the 'absolutely necessary' test dictates caution. Questions and considerations that arise include the following:

> Is it proportionate to continue to fire even when the suspect has been wounded or appears to be neutralised in order to ensure that no residual threat remains? Under what circumstances may firearms be used to deal with persons armed with less dangerous weapons? The concept of proportionality must also take into account the possibility of reasonable error on the part of the actor. For example a policeman believes that he is confronted with a real weapon when, in fact the assailant is only armed with a toy gun or an unloaded weapon. The proportionality of his response must be judged in the light of the perceived facts as they occurred (against the background of the law concerning police use of firearms) as opposed to the facts established *ex post facto*.[221]

There may be liability for the actual disproportionate use of force or for the planning or control of an operation involving the use of force for a purpose permitted by Article 2(2) that does not minimize the risk to life as far as possible.[222]

For the taking of life to be justified under Article 2(2), the action taken must be 'lawful'. This is expressly stated in respect of Article 2(2)(b) and (c) and can be supposed to be the case in respect of Article 2(2)(a). This means that the action must be lawful under national law, so that the use of force in the particular circumstances must be authorized by national law.[223] It also means that it must be consistent with the requirements

---

[215] *McCann v UK*, id, para 149 GC. Force includes using a vehicle to clear barricades: *McShane v UK* hudoc (2002); 35 EHRR 593.

[216] *McCann v UK*, ibid. The requirement in national law need not be expressed in terms of 'absolute necessity', so long as it is essentially the same in substance, as applied in practice: id, paras 152–5.

[217] There is no reference to a margin of appreciation in *McCann* or later cases. On the margin of appreciation, see above, p 11.

[218] *McCann v UK*, ibid. For the facts, see below, p 63. See also *Huohvanainen v Finland* hudoc (2007) and the Russian cases, below, p 64.

[219] *McCann v UK*, ibid, para 148.

[220] Ibid. See also *Kakoulli v Turkey* hudoc (2005); 45 EHRR 355 and *Nachova v Bulgaria*, below, p 65.

[221] O'Boyle, *The Use of Lethal Force under Article 2 of the European Convention on Human Rights*, CE Doc DH-Ed-COLL (90), p 5. Other considerations are whether the lives of innocent bystanders are placed at risk and the time available to the actor to assess the situation. See *Stewart v UK No 10044/82*, 39 DR 162 (1984); *McCann v UK* below, p 63; and *Ergi v Turkey*, below, p 65. See also the UN Basic Rules on the Use of Force and Firearms by Law Enforcement Officials, n 24, above.

[222] See the *McCann* and *Ergi* cases, below, pp 63 and 65.

[223] See *Kelly v UK No 1759/90*, 74 DR 139 (1993); *Stewart v UK No 1004/82*, 39 DR 162 (1984); and *X v Belgium*, below, p 66.

of the Convention.[224] These include the rule of law requirement that the national law is 'formulated with sufficient precision to enable the citizen to regulate his conduct'[225] and, for the purposes of Article 2(2)(b), the prohibition of arbitrary arrest in Article 5.[226]

c. In self-defence or the defence of another

Article 2(2)(a) allows the use of force by state agents in self-defence or the defence of another; it does not permit it in defence of property. It justifies the use of force in self-defence only if it is 'absolutely necessary'. This test was found not to have been complied with in *McCann v UK*.[227] In that case, three members of the Provisional IRA were shot dead on the street by SAS soldiers in Gibraltar. The persons killed, whom the British authorities had allowed to cross the border from Spain, were suspected of having on them a remote control device to be used to explode a bomb that was believed to be in a car parked in a public place, the explosion of which would have caused a devastating loss of life. In fact, the suspects did not have such a device on them and there was no bomb in the car. Instead, they were on a reconnaissance visit to Gibraltar and the car had been left to save a parking space for a later bombing mission. The Court found unanimously that the actual killings were not in breach of Article 2, because the four soldiers had an honest and reasonable belief when they shot to kill that the suspects had made movements to activate remote control devices on them that would have exploded the bomb causing serious loss of life. However, the Court held, by ten votes to nine, that Article 2 had been infringed because the use of force had not been 'strictly proportionate' to the attainment of its objective, namely the saving of lives, as the operation could have been planned and controlled so as to achieve that objective without the need to kill the suspects. It based this decision on three considerations. First, the authorities could have stopped the suspects from entering Gibraltar at the border, thereby eliminating any risk of loss of innocent lives. The Court rejected the defendant state's argument that it was justified in not doing this because there would probably then not have been enough evidence to detain and try the suspects for any offence, leaving them or others free to try again later. Secondly, the authorities had made insufficient allowance for the possibility that their intelligence assessments might be incorrect. In particular, they had passed their possible, but mistaken, suspicions as to the device and the bomb to the soldiers as facts, so that the use of lethal force by the latter was made 'almost unavoidable'. Thirdly, in accordance with their training, the soldiers had shot to kill, not wound, the suspects on the basis that this was necessary to immobilize them to save the lives of others. In the view of the majority, this lacked 'the degree of caution in the use of firearms to be expected from law enforcement personnel in a democratic society, even when dealing with dangerous terrorist suspects'.[228] In their joint opinion, the dissenting judges disagreed with the Court's conclusions on each of these three points. More generally, they cautioned against 'the temptations offered by the benefit of hindsight'[229] and stressed the large number of innocent lives at risk.

The approach in the *McCann* case was followed shortly afterwards in *Andronicou and Constantinou v Cyprus*,[230] but in that case the Court found in favour of the defendant

---

[224] Cf, the interpretation of 'lawful' in Article 5: see eg, *Bozano v France* A 111 (1986); 9 EHRR 297.

[225] *Sunday Times v UK* (No 1) A 30 (1979); 2 EHRR 245 para 49 PC.

[226] See below, p 136.

[227] A 324 (1995); 21 EHRR 97 GC. See Joseph, 14 NHRQ 5 (1994).

[228] A 324 (1995); 21 EHRR 97 para 212 GC. However, the Court unanimously rejected a claim that there had from the outset been a plan to kill rather than arrest the suspects: *ibid.* para 178.

[229] *Ibid*, dissenting opinion para 8.

[230] 1997-VI; 25 EHRR 491. See also *Bubbins v UK* 2005-II; 41 EHRR 458; *Huohvanainen v Finland* hudoc (2007) (no breach); *Kakoulli v Turkey* hudoc (2005); 45 EHRR 355 (breach); and *Saoud v France* hudoc (2007).

state on the facts. There Cypriot police special forces were called in to deal with a situation in which a young man was holding his fiancée hostage with a gun in their flat. When the police stormed the flat to rescue the fiancée, they killed them both in the course of using lethal force in defence of themselves and the fiancée. The Court held that the actual killings were 'strictly proportionate' on the facts and, by five votes to four, that the planning and control of the operation was 'strictly proportionate' too. The *McCann* and *Andronicou and Constantinou* cases are both to be contrasted on the facts with *Gul v Turkey*,[231] in which the massive force used by the police as they stormed the flat of a suspected terrorist was held to be 'grossly disproportionate' to what was needed by the police in self-defence.

Article 2(2)(a) has been relied upon unsuccessfully in the context of measures taken by the state in response to armed insurrection in a number of other cases. In particular, cases in which civilian lives were lost in the course of the Russian military response to the emergency in Chechnya have led to findings of breaches of Article 2 because of planning inadequacies or of a disproportionate use of armed force. In *Isayeva v Russia*,[232] a large group of rebel fighters had entered the applicant's village, which had a population of about 20,000. In response, the Russian armed forces implemented a plan involving an air and artillery attack upon the village, using high explosion aviation bombs and missile strikes. A bomb which was dropped from a Russian military plane exploded near the applicant's family's mini-van while they were trying to leave the village, killing the applicant's son and three nieces and injuring the applicant. The Court considered that using the kinds of weapons that were deployed 'in a populated area, outside wartime and without prior evacuation of the civilians, is impossible to reconcile with the degree of caution expected from a law enforcement body in a democratic society'.[233] While accepting that Article 2(2)(a) allows the state to use force to protect lives when faced with a situation in which the population of a village is held hostage by well-equipped and trained fighters, 'the massive use of indiscriminate weapons stands in flagrant contrast with this aim and cannot be considered compatible with the standard of care prerequisite to an operation of this kind'.[234] Although accepting that the operation had a legitimate aim, the Court did not consider that it was 'planned and executed with the requisite care for the lives of the civilian population', and hence was in breach of Article 2.[235] A similar lack of planning and proportionality in execution was found in *Isayeva, Yusupova, and Bazayeva v Russia*,[236] in which Russian military planes, engaged in a counter-terrorism operation in the area, bombed a large convoy of civilian vehicles escaping the armed conflict in Grozny on an open stretch of road, killing, among others, two children of the applicant. The pilots claimed that, having obtained permission from their air controller, they were defending themselves against machine gun fire from two trucks carrying Chechen rebel fighters, and that they were not aware of the convoy. The Court, which did not accept that the pilots had not seen the convoy, found that the counter-terrorism operation had not been planned with sufficient attention to possible civilian casualties and that the use of extremely powerful air to ground missiles was disproportionate in the circumstances.[237]

[231] Hudoc (2000); 34 EHRR 719. Fifty or more shots were fired at the door as the suspect unlocked it, killing him. [232] Hudoc (2005); 41 EHRR 847.
[233] Id, para 190. Steps taken to inform the inhabitants of a safe passage out of the village were found inadequate.
[234] Id, para 191. The number of civilian deaths may have been 'significantly higher' than the forty-six identified by the state: id, para 197.
[235] Id, para 200. [236] Hudoc (2005); 41 EHRR 847.
[237] As noted in the argument in these cases, question of liability under international humanitarian law also arose.

d. To effect an arrest or prevent an escape

The use of force is justified under Article 2(2)(b) if it is 'absolutely necessary' to effect an arrest or to prevent an escape. In *Nachova v Bulgaria*[238] it was held that 'potentially deadly force cannot be considered absolutely necessary where it is known that the person to be arrested poses no threat to life or limb and is not suspected of having committed a violent offence', and that this is so even though 'a failure to use lethal force may result in the opportunity to arrest the fugitive being lost'. Thus, in the *Nachova* case there was a breach of Article 2 when the applicants, known to be unarmed and not dangerous, were shot and killed by the police when, despite being ordered by the police to stop or be fired upon, they ran away to avoid arrest in connection with an offence of unauthorized absence from work. The fact that it is the only way to stop an individual from avoiding arrest cannot justify the use of 'potentially deadly force', particularly by firearms, even where the individual to be arrested is honestly and reasonably thought to be a 'threat to life or limb'. A contrary view is inconsistent with the purpose of arrest under the Convention, which is to bring an arrested person before the appropriate authorities in accordance with Article 5, and ignores the possibility of a later arrest.[239] However, the use of firearms in such a case may be permissible, depending on the facts, on the ground of self-defence. The use of firearms in the context of an arrest may also be justified where warning shots are fired not directly at the individual to be arrested, but into the air.[240]

The above considerations also apply to the use of force against a person who is already under arrest or in detention to prevent his or her escape (Article 2(2)b)).

e. To quell a riot or insurrection

The terms 'riot' and 'insurrection' in Article 2(2)(c) have autonomous Convention meanings. This was held in *Stewart v UK*[241] in respect of the term 'riot' and can be taken to be true of 'insurrection' also. In the *Stewart* case, the Commission declined to define the term 'riot', deciding only on the facts of the case that 'an assembly of 150 persons throwing missiles at a patrol of soldiers to the point that they risked serious injury must be considered, by any standard, to constitute a riot'.[242] Similarly, without defining the term, in *Gulec v Turkey*,[243] the Commission found that 'a crowd of several thousand people, throwing projectiles at members of the security forces so that the latter were at risk of being injured, and breaking windows of public buildings' constituted a 'riot'.

In the *Stewart* case, the Commission established that there is no obligation to retreat when quelling a riot. But, as in the case of the other exceptions permitted by Article 2(2), the 'strict proportionality' interpretation of the 'absolutely necessary' requirement adopted in the *McCann* case is important in ensuring caution on the part of law enforcement officers when dealing with large crowds at public meetings and demonstrations that get out of control. In accordance with *McCann*, the requirement of 'strict proportionality' applies not only to the conduct of the state agents who use force to quell a riot or insurrection, but to the planning and control of an operation as well. Thus in *Ergi v Turkey*[244] there

---

[238] 2005-VII; 42 EHRR 933 paras 95, 107 GC. See also *Aytekin v Turkey* 1998-VII; 32 EHRR 501; *Kakoulli v Turkey* hudoc (2005); 45 EHRR 355, and *Ramsahai v Netherlands* hudoc (2007); 46 EHRR 983 GC.

[239] But see the different approach in *Kelly v UK No 1759/90*, 74 DR 139 (1993), as to which see Smith, 144 NLJ 354 (1994).

[240] See *Ogur v Turkey* 1999-III and *Kakoulli v Turkey* hudoc (2005); 45 EHRR 355. Cf, the *Gulec* case, below, p 66.

[241] *No 10044/82*, 39 DR 162 (1984).   [242] Id, at 172.

[243] 1998-IV; 28 EHRR 121 para 232. The Court accepted the Commission's findings. See also *Simsek v Turkey* hudoc (2005) on the need for proper police training and centralized command.

[244] 1998-IV; 32 EHRR 388.

was a breach of Article 2 when an innocent villager was killed in cross-fire in a security forces ambush of terrorists which had not been planned in such a way as to minimize the possible risk to the lives of third parties. The 'strict proportionality' requirement was also held to have been infringed on this basis in the *Güleç* case. There the applicant's son and another person were killed as security forces fired live bullets in order to disperse 3,000 villagers who had become very disorderly while demonstrating against the destruction of a neighbouring village in the fight against terrorism. The Court found that, contrary to the government's submission, the demonstrators were unarmed and the security forces had fired not above their heads but at the ground in front of them, with an obvious risk of ricocheting bullets. The Court held that the force used had not been 'absolutely neces-sary'. The Court reached its decision on the *McCann* basis that the operation had not been planned so as to minimize the risk of life, stressing that the security forces had resorted to live bullets because they had not been provided with other less powerful weapons, such as truncheons, riot shields, water cannon, rubber bullets, or tear gas—despite the fact that the area was one in which a state of emergency had been declared and disorder could be expected. It might be that the Court would have reached the same conclusion on the basis that live bullets should never be planned to be used to quell a riot, even by firing above the head of the crowd in view of the risk of accident or mistake.[245]

The use of force must be 'lawful'.[246] In *X v Belgium*,[247] the shooting of an innocent bystander by a policeman acting to quell a riot was not excused as being within Article 2(2)(e) because his use of firearms had not been 'lawful' under Belgian law for the reason that the required authorization had not been given.

8. CONCLUSION

It was not until 1995 that the European Court of Human Rights was called upon to take its first decision on the merits under Article 2, in the Northern Irish case of *McCann v UK*.[248] Since then, it has decided many more Article 2 cases, with the result that the meaning of Article 2 has become much clearer. The most striking consequence is the very extensive meaning that has been given to the obligation to take steps to protect the right to life. The state must have appropriate laws prohibiting the taking of life and judicial machinery to enforce them. This obligation requires the regulation of activities that may pose a threat to life, such as the use of firearms by the police and dangerous industrial activities. The state must also take preventive operational measures in some circumstances to protect an individual whose life is at risk. This includes police protection of members of the public and protection in places of detention. There may also be an obligation to provide health care and social services to safeguard life, although the Court has yet to explore the issue fully. In addition to these substantive obligations, there is also a procedural obligation to protect the right to life by investigating suspicious deaths in accordance with strict standards that have been spelt out by the Court, leading in appropriate cases to criminal proceedings. The development of this procedural obligation has seen it become a rigor-ous one that has utterly transformed Article 2, not infrequently providing the basis for a breach of Article 2 when no breach of the substantive obligation not to take life has been

---

[245] On the use of plastic bullets, see Jason-Lloyd, 140 NLJ 1492 (1990) and Robertson, 141 NLJ 340 (1991). On the use of CS gas, see *No 7126/75* (1977) 1 Digest 87.

[246] For the meaning of 'lawful', see above, p 62.

[247] *No 2758/66*, 12 YB 174 (1969). See also *Stewart v UK No 10044/82*, 32 DR 162 (1984).

[248] A 324 (1995); 21 EHRR 97 GC.

found. In a striking development, the obligation was extended to the fields of health and safety and environmental law in the *Oneryildiz* case.[249] The case law is extensive and is often the focus of national court decisions applying Article 2, as in the case of the United Kingdom.[250]

The meaning of the state's negative obligation not to take life arbitrarily has also been clarified. The capital punishment exception has become redundant in peacetime in what has become a European death penalty free zone. The parameters of the exceptions allowed by Article 2(2) have been set. Some of the cases have concerned the dispropor-tionate use of force by the police or security forces in safeguarding life or public order or in effecting arrests in non-emergency circumstances. But a high proportion of them have concerned the emergencies in Northern Ireland, south-east Turkey, and more recently in Chechnya. The cases arising out of the last two of these situations especially have raised issues previously more familiar to the Inter-American human rights system[251] than its European counterpart, involving responsibility for the disappearance of insurgents and other opponents of government and killings by unknown perpetrators, as well as the failure to investigate such incidents. These cases have presented considerable fact-finding problems. In the absence of reliable findings of fact in such cases by national courts, the Commission (now the Court) has made its own factual determinations, sometimes, in the case mainly of Turkey,[252] after time-consuming on-the-spot hearings of witnesses. They are also cases in which human rights law overlaps with international humanitarian law. After early hesitations, the Court has been prepared to draw inferences from the lack of state co-operation in generally life-threatening situations when determining whether state involvement in killings that do not by any stretch of the imagination fall within the exceptions allowed by Article 2(2) has been proved beyond a reasonable doubt.

Finally, some progress has been made in resolving the question whether the obligation to protect the right to life applies to the unborn child. Treading cautiously in the light of the different approaches across Europe as to when life begins, the Court has, in the absence of consensus and on such a contentious issue, allowed states a wide margin of appreciation, which would seem to accommodate the practice of most European states.

---

[249] Above, p 42.
[250] See eg, *R (Amin) v Secretary of State for the Home Department* [2003] UKHL 51; [2004] 1 AC 653.
[251] See Harris and Livingstone, eds, *The Inter-American System of Human Rights*, 1998, p 2.
[252] See below, p 847.

3

ARTICLE 3: FREEDOM FROM TORTURE OR INHUMAN OR DEGRADING TREATMENT OR PUNISHMENT

Article 3

No one shall be subjected to torture or to inhuman or degrading treatment or punishment.

1. INTRODUCTION[1]

Article 3, which applies to human beings but not to other legal persons,[2] contains an absolute guarantee of the rights it protects.[3] It does so in two senses.[4] First, it cannot be derogated from in time of war or other public emergency.[5] It is this, as well as the historical background to the Convention, that has led to the argument that Article 3 should not be trivialized, ie understood to prohibit other than the most serious forms of ill-treatment.[6] But, as Judge Fitzmaurice pointed out, the temptation to lower the threshold of Article 3 is great since 'the Convention contains no prohibition covering intermediate forms of maltreatment ... [so] that, if they are not actually caught by the strict language of the Convention, they deserve to be ... because ... they are nevertheless irreconcilable with the high ideal of human rights'.[7] In practice, the 'threshold' has been lowered to cover certain intermediate forms of maltreatment,[8] without any noticeable trivialization.

Secondly, Article 3, unlike most Convention articles, is expressed in unqualified terms. This can be understood as meaning that ill-treatment within the terms of Article 3 is never permitted, even for the highest reasons of public interest. On this basis, it has been held that the need to fight terrorism[9] or organized crime[10] cannot justify state conduct that would otherwise be in breach of Article 3. Nor does it permit the return of an individual

---

[1] On Article 3 generally, see Addo and Grief, 20 ELR 178 (1995) and Cassese, *European System*, Ch 11.

[2] *Kontakt-Information-Therapie and Hagen v Austria No 11921/86*, 57 DR 81 (1988).

[3] See Addo and Grief, 9 EJIL 510 (1998); id, 23 ELR 17 (1998); and McBride, 25 ELR 31 (2000).

[4] *Ireland v UK* A 25 (1978); 2 EHRR 25 para 163 PC.   [5] Article 15(2), Convention.

[6] See eg, the joint partially dissenting opinion of Messrs Schermers, Batliner, Vandenberghe, and Hall in *Warwick v UK No 9471/81*, 60 DR 5 at 20 (1986) Com Rep; CM Res DH (89) 5.

[7] *Ireland v UK* A 25 (1978); 2 EHRR 25 PC. Separate opinion.

[8] On the lowering of the threshold for prision conditions, see below, p 94. See also the lowering of the threshold, for torture, below, p 70.

[9] *Tomasi v France* A 241-A (1992); 15 EHRR 1 para 115.

[10] *Selmouni v France* 1999-V; 29 EHRR 403 GC. Generally the 'reprehensible nature' of the applicant's conduct is irrelevant: *D v UK* 1997-III; 23 EHRR 423 para 47.

to another state's territory on national security grounds, where the return would involve a real risk of ill-treatment contrary to Article 3 in the receiving state.[11] However, there are recognized exceptions to the absolute nature of Article 3 in this second sense. If the taking of life by the state is not contrary to Article 2 of the Convention in certain circumstances (eg, on grounds of self-defence), 'it must follow a fortiori that severe wounding is in such circumstances justifiable'.[12] Similarly, conditions of detention that might otherwise be in breach of Article 3 may be justified by reference to the need to prevent escape or suicide.[13] In addition, considerations of penal policy may lead to the different treatment of conduct causing the same or a greater level of suffering. For example, whereas judicial corporal punishment is degrading punishment contrary to Article 3,[14] imprisonment in normal prison conditions, which may be just as or more degrading, is not. More generally, the 'suffering or humiliation involved must in any event go beyond that inevitable element of suffering or humiliation connected with a given form of legitimate treatment or punishment'.[15] Finally, the absolute nature of the guarantee in Article 3 is qualified by the fact that consent may negate liability under Article 3, at least in some cases concerning medical treatment.[16]

As Article 3 provides an absolute guarantee, there is no room for a margin of appreciation doctrine in the way that there might be if the text allowed certain exceptions to the negative obligation that it contains,[17] although the Court has been influenced by the presence or absence of uniformity of practice in European states when deciding whether state conduct is consistent with Article 3.[18]

Ill-treatment 'must attain a minimum level of severity' if it is to fall within Article 3.[19] The threshold level is a relative one:

> it depends on all the circumstances of the case, such as the nature and context of the treatment, the manner and method of its execution, its duration, its physical or mental effects and, in some cases, the sex, age and state of health of the victim.[20]

These factors are relevant both when determining whether the suffering caused is sufficient to amount to inhuman or degrading treatment or punishment and when distinguishing between these lesser kinds of ill-treatment proscribed by Article 3 and torture. In an important ruling, in *Selmouni v France*[21] the Court established that the categorization of ill-treatment may change over time, so that 'acts which were classified in the past as "inhuman and degrading treatment" as opposed to "torture" could be classified differently in the future'. This followed from the dynamic character of the Convention

---

[11] *Chahal v UK* 1996-V; 23 EHRR 413 GC. See below, p 87.

[12] Mr Fawcett, separate opinion in *Ireland v UK* B 23-I, p 502 Com Rep (1976). Cf, *Stewart v UK No 10044/82*, 39 DR 162 (1984). See also *Hurtado v Switzerland* A 280-A (1994) (proportionate force).

[13] See *Kröcher and Müller v Switzerland No 8463/78*, 34 DR 24 (1982) Com Rep; CM Res DH (83) 15.

[14] *Tyrer v UK* A 26 (1978); 2 EHRR 1.

[15] *Kalashnikov v Russia* 2002-VI; 36 EHRR 587 para 95. Cf, *Ilascu v Moldova and Russia* 2004-VII; 40 EHRR 1030 GC.

[16] See below, pp 97ff. On self-inflicted conditions of detention, contrast *McFeeley v UK No 8317/78*, 20 DR 44 (1980) ('dirty protest'), below, pp 97ff, and *Soering v UK* (prolongation of time on death row by appeals), below, p 80.

[17] See Callewaert, 19 HRLJ 6 (1998). The positive obligation under Article 3, see below, p 107, is not subject to the margin of appreciation or proportionality either. See Palmer, 65 CLJ 438 (2006).

[18] See eg, *V v UK*, below, p 91; *MC v Bulgaria*, below, p 110; and *Jalloh v Germany*, below, p 100.

[19] *Kudla v Poland* 2000-IX; 35 EHRR 198 para 91 GC.

[20] *Ibid*. Cf, *Ireland v UK* A 25 (1978); 2 EHRR 25 para 162 PC. As to duration, see eg, *Kalashnikov v Russia*, below, p 93. As to age and sex, see eg, *Aydin v Turkey* 1997-VI; 25 EHRR 251 GC. As to health, see eg, *Keenan v UK*, below p 97 (mental health). As to other personal circumstances, see *Selcuk and Asker v Turkey*, below, p 75.

[21] 1999-V; 29 EHRR 403 para 101. See further, below, p 74.

and the Court's view that 'the increasingly high standard being required in the area of the protection of human rights and fundamental liberties correspondingly and inevitably requires greater firmness in assessing breaches of the fundamental values of democratic societies'. Similarly, the 'minimum level of severity' has been reduced by the Court in recent years, most notably concerning prison conditions and treatment, as the Court has become more demanding of states under Article 3.

Where the facts of a case warrant this, the Court may distinguish between the different categories of ill-treatment listed in Article 3. In some cases, the Court does not do this, simply finding a breach of Article 3 as a whole.[22] Although there is no need to draw such distinctions in the sense that Article 3 is infringed whatever the precise category of ill-treatment concerned, the boundary between torture and other forms of ill-treatment is relevant both to the question of compensation that may be awarded under Article 41 and to a state's reputation. With regard to the latter, the United Kingdom's concession before the Court in *Ireland v UK*[23] that the 'five techniques' were torture, not just inhuman or degrading treatment, proved to be ill-conceived when the Court held that only the latter had occurred. The text of Article 3 contrasts with the equivalent Article 7 of the ICCPR insofar as it omits any reference to 'cruel' treatment or punishment. This is not significant. The prohibition of 'cruel' treatment or punishment has been subsumed under the existing terms of Article 3.[24]

When considering whether there has been ill-treatment in breach of Article 3, the Court examines all the evidence presented to it, whether emanating from the applicant, the defendant state or from other sources,[25] or which it obtains *proprio motu*.[26] The rules concerning the burden of proof, applicable to Convention claims generally, are explained below.[27] When weighing the evidence before it, the Court applies a high standard of proof 'beyond a reasonable doubt'; 'such proof may follow from the coexistence of sufficiently strong, clear and concordant inferences or of similar unrebutted presumptions of fact'.[28]

A state may be responsible under Article 3 for the acts of its servants or agents that are *ultra vires*. In *Ireland v UK*,[29] the Court considered whether a state might claim not to be responsible on the basis of ignorance of the conduct of its servants of agents. It stated that where the conduct in breach of Article 3 amounted to a practice incompatible with the Convention, it was 'inconceivable that the higher authorities of a state should be, or at least be entitled to be, unaware of the existence of such a practice'. Moreover, 'under the Convention those authorities are strictly liable for the conduct of their subordinates; they are under a duty to impose their will on subordinates and cannot shelter behind their inability to ensure that it is respected'. In *Cyprus v Turkey*,[30] the Commission found the defendant state to be responsible for rapes committed by its soldiers on the 'positive obligation' basis that adequate measures had not been taken to prevent them or to effect disciplinary measures after the event.

---

[22] See eg, *Soering v UK* A 161 (1989); 11 EHRR 439 PC and *A v UK* 1998-VI; 27 EHRR 611.

[23] A 25 (1978); 2 EHRR 25 PC.   [24] *Ibid.*

[25] These include the European Committee for the Prevention of Torture and Inhuman or Degrading Treatment or Punishment (see below), UNHCR, and non-governmental organizations such as Amnesty International.

[26] *Ireland v UK* A 25 (1978); 2 EHRR 25 para 160 PC.

[27] P 849. On the state's burden of proof where Article 3 claims involve injuries suffered in detention or arrest, see below, p 77.

[28] *Ireland v UK* A 25 (1978); 2 EHRR 25 para 161 PC. The Court may draw inferences from the state's failure to produce evidence: *Aydin v Turkey* 1997-V; 25 EHRR 251 GC.

[29] A 25 (1978); 2 EHRR 25 para 159 PC.

[30] *Nos 6780/74 and 6950/75* (First and Second Applications) 4 EHRR 482 at 537 (1976) Com Rep; CM Res DH (79) 1.

A claim under Article 3 may raise an issue under another article of the Convention as well. In practice, this overlap has occurred mostly in the areas covered by Articles 3 and 8, particularly in connection with the rights to respect for family and private life. In such cases, the approach has been to concentrate primarily upon the claim under Article 8.[31] If Article 8 is not infringed, it is unlikely that there will be a breach of Article 3.[32]

Article 3 is supplemented by the European Convention for the Prevention of Torture and Inhuman and Degrading Treatment or Punishment 1987.[33] Whereas the European Convention on Human Rights provides a remedy for an individual victim of proscribed ill-treatment after it has occurred, the Torture Convention establishes a preventive system whereby an independent committee of experts—the European Committee for the Prevention of Torture and Inhuman or Degrading Treatment or Punishment (CPT)—is authorized to visit public places of detention in states parties to the Convention to examine the treatment of detained persons 'with a view to strengthening, if necessary, the protection of such persons from torture and from inhuman or degrading treatment or punishment' (Article 1). The CPT has visited places of detention (police stations, prisons, mental hospitals) of its choice in all of the states parties to the Convention. In contrast with the European Court, the CPT has no jurisdiction to adjudicate on applications. It adopts national reports on the basis of its visits in which it makes recommendations and suggestions as to improvements for the protection of detained persons generally[34]. If a state refuses to co-operate or to act upon the CPT's recommendations, it is empowered, as its only sanction, to issue a public statement.[35] The European Court has made use of evidence of ill-treatment contained in the CPT's reports in many cases.[36] There is, however no precise equivalence between the standards of Article 3 and those of the CPT, with the latter sometimes criticizing states in its reports about conditions of detention that would not necessarily give rise to a successful application under Article 3.[37]

2. TORTURE

In *Ireland v UK*,[38] the Court defined torture as 'deliberate inhuman treatment causing very serious and cruel suffering'. Applying this test, it held that neither the use in interrogation of the 'five techniques'[39] nor the physical assaults that had occurred in that case were torture. By 'deliberate' the Court meant that suffering must be inflicted intentionally. Suffering must also be inflicted for a purpose, such as obtaining evidence, punishment,

---

[31] See eg, *Marckx v Belgium* A 31 (1979); 2 EHRR 330 PC and *Mentes v Turkey* 1997-VII; 26 EHRR 595 GC.

[32] Eg, a decision to take a child into public care is unlikely to be a breach of Article 3 if consistent with Article 8: *Olsson v Sweden (No 1)* A 130 (1988); 11 EHRR 259 PC.

[33] ETS 126. The Torture Convention has been ratified by all Convention parties. On the Torture Convention, see Evans and Morgan, *Preventing Torture: A Study of the European Convention for the Prevention of Torture and Inhuman or Degrading Treatment or Punishment*, 1998.

[34] See the annual *Yearbook of the European Convention for the Prevention of Torture* and <http://www.coe.int> for the Committee's visit reports.

[35] See the 1992 and 1996 Statements on Turkey and the 2001, 2003, and 2007 Statements on the Chechen Republic of Russia <http://www.coe.int>.

[36] See below at p 93.

[37] See Murdoch, 5 EJIL 220 (1994), and Peukert, in Morgan and Evans, eds, *Protecting Prisoners*, 1999, Ch 3.

[38] A 25(1978); 2 EHRR 25 para 167 PC. On *Ireland v UK*, see Bonner, 27 ICLQ 897 (1978); Cohn 11 CWRJIL 159 (1979); Maftin, 83 RGDIP 104 (1979); Mertens, 13 RBDI 10 (1977); O'Boyle, 71 AJIL 674 (1977); Pelloux, 24 AFDL 379 (1978); and Spjut, 73 AJIL 267 (1979).

[39] For the 'five techniques', see below, p 78.

or intimidation.[40] In *Denizci v Cyprus*,[41] the applicants were Turkish Cypriots who were detained by the police in Cyprus pending being returned to northern Cyprus. The Court held that they had been subjected by the police to intentionally inflicted inhuman treatment contrary to Article 3, but had not been tortured, partly because it had not been established that there had been any particular aim underlying the assaults, such as obtaining information. Because of the absolute nature of Article 3, the causing of 'very serious and cruel suffering' cannot be saved from being torture on public interest grounds, such as that its purpose is to extract information from terrorists that will protect innocent lives.[42]

The first Strasbourg case in which torture was held to have occurred as a matter of final decision was the *Greek* case,[43] in which the Commission's finding was confirmed by the Committee of Ministers. In that case, the Commission concluded that political detainees had been subjected by the Athens security police to an administrative practice of 'torture and ill-treatment' contrary to Article 3. This had most often taken the form of *falaka*[44] or of severe beatings of all parts of the body with a view to extracting a confession or other information as to the political activities of subversive individuals.[45] In *Ireland v UK*, the Court held that torture had not occurred because the intensity of the suffering inflicted was insufficient. Remarkably, the unanimous opinion of the Commission in that case that the use in combination of the 'five techniques' of interrogation had amounted to torture was rejected by the Court by a large majority. The Court would appear to have applied a more rigorous test for suffering to amount to torture; it is also possible that it was less impressed than the Commission by the effects of psychological methods of interrogation.[46] Nonetheless, as has been pointed out, the Court's ruling was surprising 'given that the Commission had found convincing evidence of weight loss, mental disorientation and acute psychiatric symptoms during interrogation in some of the 14 suspects subjected to these techniques'.[47] Both the Commission and the Court considered that the physical assaults of detainees in the same case caused insufficient suffering to amount to torture, although, like the use of the 'five techniques', they did constitute inhuman treatment.

Since *Ireland v UK*, the Court has found that torture has occurred in a disturbing number of cases, all involving physical (and sometimes mental) ill-treatment by state agents. The first was *Aksoy v Turkey*.[48] In that case, the applicant's arms were paralyzed after he had been stripped naked and suspended by his arms, which were tied behind his

---

[40] *Ihlan v Turkey* 2000-VII; 34 EHRR 869 para 85 GC. Cf, *Akkoc v Turkey* 2000-X; 34 EHRR 1173 and *Ireland v UK* A 25(1978); 2 EHRR 25 para 167 PC. In *Ireland v UK*, Judge Matscher supposed that sadistic pleasure would be purposive. In the same case, Judge Sir Gerald Fitzmaurice opposed any purpose requirement.

[41] 2001-V. Cf, *Egmez v Cyprus* 2000-XII; 34 EHRR 753.

[42] *Selmouni v France* 1999-V; 29 EHRR 403 GC. Although the UK Parker Committee Report, Cmnd 4901, had justified the conduct of the security forces in Northern Ireland in terms of its anti-terrorist purpose, the UK made no such argument in *Ireland v UK*.

[43] 12 YB (the *Greek* case) 1 at 504 (1969) Com Rep; CM Res DH (70) 1.

[44] Beating of the feet causing excruciating pain and leaving no marks. See also *Corsacov v Moldova* hudoc (2006).

[45] The Commission also characterized as 'torture *or* ill-treatment' (italics added) certain other instances of ill-treatment: see below, p 76.

[46] Note Judge Evrigenis' concern in *Ireland v UK* A 25 (1978); 2 EHRR 25 PC, that the Court's judgment might be read as excluding from torture 'new forms of suffering which have little in common with the bodily pain caused by the conventional torments' and which aim 'at inducing even temporarily the disintegration of the human personality, the destruction of man's mental and psychological balance and the annihilation of his will'.

[47] Amnesty International, *Torture in the Eighties*, 1984, p 15.

[48] 1996-VI; 23 EHRR 553.

back ('Palestinian hanging'). A single act of rape by a state agent may constitute torture. In *Aydin v Turkey*,[49] a seventeen-year-old girl was detained at gendarmerie headquarters for three days. While there, she was raped by an unidentified person. She was also subjected to other 'terrifying and humiliating experiences' by the security forces, being kept blindfolded, beaten during questioning, spun in a tyre under water pressure, and paraded naked. The Court held that the 'accumulation of acts of physical and mental violence inflicted on the applicant and the especially cruel act of rape' gave rise to suffering amounting to torture. The Court stated that it would have reached this conclusion on the basis of just the rape (or of the other instances of ill-treatment taken together).[50] Torture has also been found in cases involving the ill-treatment of prisoners in a variety of other ways. Forced feeding of a prisoner on hunger strike amounted to torture because of the manner of its administration in *Nevmerzhitsky v Ukraine*,[51] as did an extreme regime of solitary confinement in *Ilascu et al v Moldova and Russia*.[52] The use of electric shock treatment to obtain a confession was torture in breach of Article 3 in *Mikheyev v Russia*.[53]

Of great importance was the ruling in *Selmouni v France*[54] that, as a result of the increasingly high standard being applied in the protection of human rights, ill-treatment that might previously have been regarded by the Court as causing suffering falling short of 'torture' (though still in breach of Article 3), could now be classified as 'torture'. In that case, the applicant had, in police custody, been beaten, called upon to perform oral sex with a police officer, urinated upon by the officer when he refused to do so, and threatened with a blow lamp and a syringe. The Court held that his treatment constituted torture, when, by inference, the Court would only have found 'inhuman' or 'degrading' ill-treatment if it had applied the standard of suffering that it had used earlier in *Ireland v UK*. The lower *Selmouni* threshold was relevant to the finding of torture in, for example, *Menesheva v Russia*[55], in which the applicant, who, as a young woman being questioned by several policemen was 'particularly vulnerable', was twice beaten up and subjected to other kinds of physical and mental pressure, including the threat of rape.

It is implicit in *Ireland v UK*[56] that mental suffering may constitute torture provided that it is sufficiently serious; suffering caused by bodily injury is not essential.[57] In the *Greek* case,[58] the Commission referred to 'non-physical torture', which it described as 'the infliction of mental suffering by creating a state of anguish and stress by means other than bodily assault'. Evidence which the Commission considered under this heading, without concluding that any amounted to torture on the facts, involved mock executions and threats of death, various humiliating acts, and threats of reprisal against a detainee's family. Mental suffering, when combined with physical suffering, has contributed to a finding by the Court of torture in a number of cases. It has included mental suffering

---

[49] 1997-VI; 25 EHRR 251 GC.

[50] In certain circumstances, rape is also a crime against humanity and a war crime contrary to international humanitarian law: see Schabas, *An Introduction to the International Criminal Court*, 3rd edn, 2007, pp 106, 116.

[51] 2005-II. See below, p 99.   [52] 2004-VII; 40 EHRR 1030 GC. See below, p 96.

[53] Hudoc (2006). See also *Abdulsamet Yaman v Turkey* hudoc (2004) (electric shocks, blindfolded, stripped naked, immersed in cold water, suspended by arms). Other torture cases include *Bursuc v Romania* hudoc (2004) and *Ilhan v Turkey* 2000-VII; 34 EHRR 869 GC.

[54] 1999-V; 29 EHRR 403. See further, above, p 70.

[55] 2006-III; 44 EHRR 1162. See also *Bati v Turkey* 2004-IV; 42 EHRR 736.

[56] See also *Tyrer v UK* A 26 (1978); 2 EHRR 1; *Campbell and Cosans v UK* A 48 (1982); 4 EHRR 293; and *Soering v UK* A 161 (1989); 11 EHRR 439 PC.

[57] Cf, the definition of torture in the UN Torture Convention 1984, Article 1.

[58] 12 YB (the *Greek* case) 1 at 461 (1969) Com Rep; CM Res DH (70) 1.

resulting from the psychological pressure imposed by incommunicado detention,[59] being kept blindfolded,[60] threats of harm to one's family,[61] the humiliation of being paraded naked,[62] mock executions,[63] and fear of execution while waiting on death row and of other physical ill-treatment.[64] As yet, there has been no case in which the Court has found that mental suffering by itself has constituted torture.

The fact that the suffering is inflicted only for 'a short period of heightened tension and emotions' may weigh against a finding of torture.[65] It may also be difficult to prove torture in the case of a person who dies in custody: any such allegation must be substantiated by medical evidence of traumatic injury to the deceased's body; eye-witness evidence of such injury is not sufficient.[66]

3. INHUMAN TREATMENT

Ill-treatment 'must attain a minimum level of severity' if it is to amount to inhuman treatment contrary to Article 3.[67] In particular, it must 'cause either actual bodily harm or intense physical or mental suffering'.[68] Where relevant the suffering caused must 'go beyond that inevitable element of suffering' that results from a 'given form of legitimate treatment or punishment'.[69] In contrast with torture, inhuman treatment need not be intended to cause suffering[70] and there is no need for the suffering to be inflicted for a purpose for it to be inhuman.[71] Otherwise, as the Court has emphasized,[72] the crucial distinction between torture and inhuman treatment lies in the degree of suffering caused. Clearly, less intense suffering is required than in the case of torture. A threat of torture, provided that it is 'sufficiently real and immediate', may generate enough mental suffering to be inhuman treatment.[73] Mental suffering by itself has been found sufficient in several contexts. For example, in *Selcuk and Asker v Turkey*,[74] there was inhuman treatment when, as a part of a security operation, the security forces destroyed the elderly applicants' home and property in a contemptuous manner in their presence, without regard to their safety or welfare and depriving them of their livelihood and shelter, causing them great distress. The mental suffering caused to an individual by the ill-treatment of a close family member may also be a breach of Article 3.[75] The anguish caused by being

---

[59] Eg, *Dikme v Turkey* 2000-VIII.

[60] Eg, *Aydin v Turkey* 1997-VI; 25 EHRR 251 GC and *Dikme v Turkey* 2000-VIII.

[61] Eg, *Akkoc v Turkey* 2000-X; 34 EHRR 1173. [62] Eg, *Aydin v Turkey* above, p 74.

[63] Eg, *Ilascu v Moldova and Russia* 2004-VII; 40 EHRR 1030 GC. [64] *Ibid.*

[65] *Egmez v Cyprus* 2000-XI; 34 EHRR 753 para 78 (assault during arrest and transportation to a police station: inhuman treatment, not torture).

[66] *Tanli v Turkey* 2001-II. See also *Salman v Turkey* 2000-VII; 34 EHRR 425 GC. Reliable eye-witness evidence may be sufficient to prove torture in the case of a disappeared person: *Cakici v Turkey* 1999-IV; 31 EHRR 133 GC.

[67] See above, p 70. [68] *Kudla v Poland* 2000-XI; 35 EHRR 198 para 92 GC. [69] *Ibid.*

[70] *Ireland v UK* A 25 (1978); 2 EHRR 25 para 167 PC. Premeditation is taken into account when deciding whether treatment is inhuman, *ibid*, but it is not required. But see Cassese, *European System*, Ch 11, at p 246.

[71] *Denizci v Cyprus* 2001-V and *Egmez v Cyprus* 2000-XII; 34 EHRR 753.

[72] *Ireland v UK* A 25 (1978); 2 EHRR para 167 PC.

[73] *Campbell and Cosans v UK* A 48 (1982) para 26.

[74] 1996-II; 26 EHRR 477. Cf, *Bilgin v Turkey* hudoc (2000); 36 EHRR 879 and *Dulas v Turkey* hudoc (2001). In the absence of 'distinctive elements' such as those in *Selcuk and Asker*, the destruction of homes in a security operation will not be a breach of Article 3, but may infringe Article 8: *Orhan v Turkey* hudoc (2002) para 362.

[75] *Mubilanzil Mayeka and Kaniki Mitunga v Belgium* 2006-XI. On disappeared persons cases, see below, p 90.

detained illegally may contribute to a finding that conditions of detention are inhuman treatment.[76]

Conduct giving rise to inhuman treatment may take a number of forms, which are considered in the following sections. These include physical assault, the use of psychological interrogation techniques, the subjection of a person in detention to inhuman conditions or treatment and the deportation or extradition of a person to face ill-treatment in another country.

I. ASSAULTS

Most cases of assault have occurred in detention or during arrest by police. Assaults that amounted to inhuman treatment were unanimously held to have occurred in *Ireland v UK*. In that case, four detainees were found by a prison doctor to have contusions and bruising which were caused by severe beatings by members of the security forces in Northern Ireland during interrogation at Palace Barracks.[77] In the *Greek* case,[78] assaults by Greek security police upon political detainees in the course of interrogation during the Regime of the Colonels were 'torture or ill-treatment' contrary to Article 3. In addition to *falaka* and severe beating of all parts of the body;[79] these included 'the application of electric shock, squeezing of the head in a vice, pulling out of hair from the head or pubic region, or kicking of the male genital organs, dripping water on the head, and intense noises to prevent sleep'.[80]

The level of suffering in the above cases was clearly high. More recent pronouncements by the Court suggest that the threshold level of suffering required for a violation of Article 3 may be lower in the case of assaults upon persons in detention. In *Ribitsch v Austria*,[81] the Court stated that 'any recourse to physical force which has not been made strictly necessary by his own conduct diminishes human dignity and is in principle an infringement' of Article 3. This suggests that any physical rough handling of a detained person by the police, prison warders, or other state agents may be a breach of Article 3, unless it is required, for example, to restore order or to prevent an escape: the loss of dignity involved generates sufficient suffering or humiliation to engage Article 3 as either inhuman or degrading treatment respectively.[82] However, in practice, when deciding whether Article 3 has been infringed, the Court would still appear to treat such cases in terms of inhuman, rather than degrading, treatment and look for evidence of bruises, etc, causing a degree of suffering beyond that which might result, for example, from a basis level of physical restraint.[83] Whether the early ruling by the Commission in the *Greek* case[84] that rough treatment consisting only of 'slaps or blows of the hand on the head or face' was not inhuman treatment remains good law is not clear.

---

[76] *Fedotov v Russia* hudoc (2005); 44 EHRR 544.

[77] The Court focused upon this group of cases to establish that there had been an administrative practice contrary to Article 3. It also drew attention to, but did not rule upon, other assaults during transit or interrogation that 'must have been individual violations of Article 3': A 25 (1978) para 182 PC.

[78] 12 YB (the *Greek* case) 1 (1969) Com Rep; CM Res DH (70) 1. The term 'ill-treatment' was used to refer generally to treatment in breach of Article 3 other than torture.

[79] These are described as 'torture *and* ill-treatment' (italics added) elsewhere in the report: see above, p 73.

[80] 12 YB (the *Greek* case) 1 at 501 (1969) Com Rep; CM Res DH (70) 1.

[81] A 336 (1995); 21 EHRR 573 para 38. Cf, *Caloc v France* 2000-IX; 35 EHRR 346. See also the dissenting opinion of Judge De Meyer in *Tomasi v France* A 241-A (1992); 15 EHRR 1.

[82] There was both inhuman and degrading treatment in the *Ribitsch* case.

[83] See eg, the facts of *Ribitsch v Austria* A 336 (1995); 21 EHRR 573 para 38. See also *Toteva v Bulgaria* hudoc (2004); *Balogh v Hungary* hudoc (2004); and *Rivas v France* hudoc (2004).

[84] 12 YB (the *Greek* case) 1 at 501 (1969) Com Rep; CM Res DH (70) 1.

In cases of assault, the applicant must first provide reliable medical or other[85] evidence as to the injuries claimed to have been sustained. For example, in *Tomasi v France*,[86] medical certificates and reports by four different doctors that attested to the 'large number of blows inflicted upon Mr Tomasi and their intensity' were found to be sufficient. The Court also noted that the applicant had at once drawn attention to the bruises on his body when he was brought before a judge following his release from police custody.

In the case of proven injuries that occur in police custody, it is for the state to show that no force was used by the police or that the force used by them was not excessive.[87] This runs counter to the normal rule, by which each party must prove what it alleges.[88] In *Selmouni v France*,[89] the Court stated that 'where an individual is taken into police custody in good health but is found to be injured at the time of release, it is incumbent upon the State to provide a plausible explanation of how these injuries were caused'. When deciding whether such an explanation has been provided, the Court takes into account whether the detained individual was medically examined (or allowed to see a lawyer or family member who might serve as a witness) at intervals during the detention, and not only upon being released.[90] The Court also pays great attention to any relevant findings of fact in national court proceedings, but these are not always conclusive. Thus in *Ribitsch v Austria*[91] the applicant had bruises on his arm on his release from police custody. According to the state, these had been caused not by police assaults, as the applicant alleged, but by the applicant falling against a car door. The conviction by an Austrian trial court of a policeman for assaulting the applicant was overturned on appeal by the Vienna Regional Criminal Court on the ground that the evidence before it did not allow it to choose between the two versions of events so as to prove the defendant's guilt to the required criminal standard of proof. The Strasbourg Court reached a different conclusion. It considered the 'car door' explanation to be 'unconvincing' and, in the absence of any other plausible explanation by the state, found that the injuries suffered by the applicant had been caused by the police.[92]

Similarly, where injuries are sustained not in police custody but in the course of an arrest by the police, 'the burden rests on the Government to demonstrate with convincing arguments that the use of force was not excessive'[93] and was 'indispensable'.[94] This burden was not met by the state in *Rehbock v Slovenia*.[95] There the applicant suffered a broken jaw and facial contusions when, with two others, he was arrested as a suspected drug dealer at a border crossing by a team of thirteen policemen. Given that the police had time to plan the arrest; that the applicant had not resisted arrest; that the government's claim that

---

[85] Eg, the evidence of witnesses at the time of release: *Ribitsch v Austria* A 336 (1995); 21 EHRR 573. For a case in which insufficient evidence was provided, see *Indelicato v Italy* hudoc (2001); 35 EHRR 1330.

[86] A 241-A (1992); 15 EHRR 1 para 115.

[87] The same applies to injuries that occur in prison: see eg, *Satik v Turkey* hudoc (2000).

[88] See below, p 849.

[89] 1999-V; 29 EHRR 403 para 87 GC. Where it is argued that the force occurred not in custody but earlier on arrest, it is for the state to provide medical evidence to prove this: *Altay v Turkey* hudoc (2001).

[90] *Algur v Turkey* hudoc (2002) (no examination at the beginning or during fifteen days' detention). See also *Akkoc v Turkey* 2000-X; 34 EHRR 1173 para 118, in which, in the context of an Article 3 complaint, the Court endorsed the CPT view that 'proper medical examinations are an essential safeguard against ill-treatment of persons in custody'.

[91] A 336 (1995); 21 EHRR 573. See also *Caloc v France* 2000-IX; 35 EHRR 346.

[92] Whereas, in effect, the burden of proof was on the applicant in the national court case, the reverse was true at Strasbourg.

[93] *Rehbock v Slovenia* 2000-XII para 72.   [94] *Ivan Vasilev v Bulgaria* hudoc (2007) para 63.

[95] *Ibid.* For cases in which the force used was not excessive, see *Berlinski v Poland* hudoc (2002); *Hurtado v Switzerland* A 280-A (1994) F Sett before Court; and *Douglas-Williams v UK No 56413/00* hudoc (2002) DA.

the applicant's injuries had been caused when he fell against a car was not credible; and that there had been no national court proceedings in which the force used might have been found to have been justified, the Strasbourg Court held that there was a breach of Article 3, the state having failed to furnish 'convincing and credible arguments which would provide a basis to explain or justify the degree of force used'.

Interestingly, in the first case concerning injuries sustained during an arrest, the Court had taken a different approach from that in *Rehbock*, with no mention of the burden falling on the state to show that excessive force has not been used. In *Klaas v Germany*,[96] a woman driver suffered injuries in the course of being arrested by the police for a blood alcohol test. Whereas the applicant argued that the injuries had been caused by excessive police force, the defendant state claimed that the applicant had injured herself while resisting a lawful arrest. Faced with this conflict of evidence, a German court had rejected a civil claim for compensation against the police because the applicant, who had the burden of proof under German law, had not satisfied it that excessive force had been used. Relying on the findings of fact by the German court, the Strasbourg Court held that Article 3 had not been infringed. In doing so, it seems to have supposed that, as in German civil law, it was for the applicant to prove excessive force. Such an approach, which contrasts with that followed in the Strasbourg cases concerning alleged assaults in police custody, can be justified on the basis that a distinction can be drawn between injuries which occur to an arrested person while out of sight in a police station and those which occur in an 'on the street' incident, where there may be non-police witnesses.[97] The argument for a more rigorous approach, which the Court has now adopted, is that it is always difficult to marshal evidence sufficient to convince a court of police misconduct. Such an argument, which applies whether the applicant is under arrest or not, is not supported by the law of European states, in which there is commonly no such general reversal of the burden of proof in civil proceedings for assault against the police.[98]

Cases of rape have been held to involve assaults that fall within Article 3. In *Cyprus v Turkey*,[99] incidents of rape by Turkish soldiers following the invasion of Cyprus by Turkey were considered to be inhuman treatment contrary to Article 3. A single act of rape may also involve inhuman and degrading treatment, if not torture.[100] There would be a breach of Article 3 in a case of rape both where the rapist was a state agent and where the act by a private individual was not a crime under national law or the law was nor properly enforced against that individual.[101]

II. USE OF PSYCHOLOGICAL INTERROGATION TECHNIQUES

Intense suffering not resulting from physical assaults of an old-fashioned 'beating up' kind was found to have been caused in *Ireland v UK*[102] by the use of 'five techniques' during the interrogation of persons placed in preventive detention in connection with

---

[96] A 269 (1993); 18 EHRR 305.   [97] But see the dissenting opinion of Judge Walsh in *Klaas*.

[98] As to English law, for example, see Clayton and Tomlinson, *Civil Actions against the Police*, 3rd edn, 2004, Ch 4.

[99] Nos 6780/74 and 6950/75 (First and Second Applications) 4 EHRR 482 at 537 (1976) Com Rep; CM Res DH (79) 1.

[100] See *Aydin v Turkey*, above, p 74, where an 'especially cruel act of rape' in police custody was torture.

[101] See *MC v Bulgaria*, below, p 110. On the positive obligation to protect, see below, p 107.

[102] A 25 (1978); 2 EHRR 25 para 96 PC. The techniques had previously been used by the UK authorities against terrorists in colonial situations.

acts of terrorism.[103] The techniques were described by the Court as follows:

(a) *wall standing:* forcing the detainees to remain for periods of some hours in a 'stress position', described by those who underwent it as being 'spreadeagled against the wall, with their fingers put high above the head against the wall, the legs spread apart and the feet back, causing them to stand on their toes with the weight of the body mainly on the fingers';

(b) *hooding:* putting a black or navy coloured bag over the detainees heads and, at least initially, keeping it there all the time except during interrogation;

(c) *subjection to noise:* pending their interrogations, holding the detainees in a room where there was a continuous loud and hissing noise;

(d) *deprivation of sleep:* pending their interrogations, depriving the detainees of sleep;

(e) *deprivation of food and drink:* subjecting the detainees to reduced diet during their stay at the centre and pending interrogations.

These methods 'were applied in combination, with premeditation and for hours at a stretch; they caused, if not actual bodily injury, at least intense physical and mental suffering to the persons subjected thereto and also led to acute psychiatric disturbances during interrogation'.[104] They were accordingly inhuman treatment contrary to Article 3.[105]

III. CONDITIONS OF DETENTION AND TREATMENT OF DETAINEES

In their early jurisprudence under Article 3, the Commission and the Court generally considered cases concerning the conditions of detention and the treatment of detainees under the heading of inhuman treatment, emphasizing the suffering caused to the detainee. Although some detention cases continue to be considered by the Court under that heading,[106] such cases are now more commonly decided by it as a matter of degrading treatment, emphasizing the humiliation involved.[107] For convenience, in this chapter the application of Article 3 to conditions of detention and the treatment of detainees is considered wholly in the section on degrading treatment.[108]

IV. EXTRADITION OR DEPORTATION[109]

A state's right in international law to refuse to admit an alien to its territory is not affected by the Convention.[110] Nor do aliens who have been admitted have a right under the Convention not to be extradited or deported or to political asylum.[111] With regard to extradition, it is not *per se* contrary to Article 3 to extradite a fugitive offender in breach of an extradition treaty or of national extradition law: it is not the function of the Strasbourg

---

[103] Several of the techniques did, however, involve illegal assault.   [104] Id, para 167.

[105] The ruling was by sixteen votes to one. For Judge Fitzmaurice, who dissented, the evidence of the effects of the use of the 'five techniques' did not prove suffering of the required severity.

[106] Eg, some cases of medical assistance or solitary confinement. See below, pp 95ff.

[107] In some cases the Court simply refers to Article 3 generally or, where the facts warrant this, to both inhuman and degrading treatment.

[108] Below, p 93.

[109] See Allweldt, 4 EJIL 360 (1993); Arai-Takahashi, 20 NQHR 5 (2003); Vogler, in *Wiarda Mélanges*, p 663.

[110] *Chahal v UK* 1996-V; 23 EHRR 413. But discriminatory exclusion may be degrading treatment: see below, p 101. See also *Fadele v UK No 13078/87*, 70 DR 159 (1991) F Sett.

[111] *Chahal v UK ibid.*

authorities in this context 'to supervise the correct application of extradition law'.[112] Nor is it contrary to Article 3 to extradite a person for a political offence.[113] As to deportation, the exercise of the state's sovereign power to deport aliens is not generally in breach of Article 3.[114]

Nonetheless, extradition or deportation may, if imminent,[115] be in breach of Article 3 in certain exceptional cases. In the leading case of *Soering v UK*,[116] the Court held that it would be a breach of Article 3 for a party to the Convention to send an individual to another state 'where substantial grounds have been shown for believing that the individual concerned, if extradited, faces a real risk of being subjected to torture or to inhuman or degrading treatment or punishment in the requesting country'.[117] Although the rule, which has since been extended to deportation (below), applies to a risk of all kinds of breaches of Article 3, it is considered for convenience here under the heading of inhuman treatment.[118]

In the *Soering* case, which is one of the most important cases that the Court has decided, the UK Home Secretary signed a warrant for the extradition of the applicant, a West German national, to face capital murder charges in the state of Virginia in the United States, where he was accused of killing the parents of his girlfriend. The Court held unanimously that the return of the applicant would be a breach of Article 3.[119] The Court first held that there was a real risk of the death penalty being imposed if the applicant were extradited. This was because there was a real risk that he would be convicted, having admitted the killings, and because the policy of the Virginia courts was such that the death penalty was likely in view of the vileness of the murders. This was so despite mitigating factors that the trial court might take into account[120] and the fact that, in satisfaction of the terms of the applicable UK-US extradition treaty, the United Kingdom had been given an undertaking that the prosecuting attorney in Virginia would make a representation to the trial court that the British government did not want the death penalty imposed. The Court gave little weight to this last point because the attorney had indicated that he would nonetheless press for the death penalty.

---

[112] *Altun v FRG No 10308/83*, 36 DR 209 at 231 (1983). This applies to treaty obligations to extradite nationals as well as aliens.

[113] *Ibid*.

[114] Exceptionally, Article 4, Fourth Protocol, below, p 744, prohibits the collective expulsion of aliens and Article 8 may apply, see below, p 371.

[115] *See Ghosh v Germany No 24017/03* hudoc (2007) DA (self-inflicted injury, so extradition not imminent). Article 3 ceases to apply if deportation order annulled (*Kalantari v Germany* 2001-X), but not if just suspended (*Ahmed v Austria* 1996-VI; 24 EHRR 278).

[116] A 161 (1989); 11 EHRR 439 PC. On the *Soering* case, see Breitenmoser and Wilms, 11 MJIL 845 (1990); Finnie, 1990 SLT 53; Gappa, 20 GJICL 463 (1990); Lillich, 85 AJIL 128 (1991); O'Boyle, in O'Reilly, ed, *Human Rights and Constitutional Law*, 1992, p 93; Quigley and Shank, 30 VJTL 241 (1989); Schabas, 43 ICLQ 913 (1994); Shea, 17 YJIL 85 (1992); Steinhardt, 11 HRLJ 453 (1990); Van Der Meersch, I RTDH 5 (1990); Warbrick, 11 MJIL 1073 (1990); Wyngaert, 39 ICLQ 757 (1990); Yorke, 29 ELR 546 (2004).

[117] A 161 (1989); 11 EHRR 439 para 91 PC. Cf, the prohibitions on return in the Refugee Convention 1951, Article 33 and the UN Torture Convention 1984, Article 3.

[118] In the *Soering* case, there was a finding of a breach of Article 3 generally. On the facts, there were probably elements of both inhuman treatment and punishment.

[119] Remarkably, the case was decided only twelve months after the application was lodged. After the Court's judgment, the UK refused extradition on the charges of capital murder but surrendered the applicant on charges of non-capital murder: see CM Res (90) 8. The applicant was then convicted in Virginia of the two murders and given two life terms. The applicant's girlfriend was already serving a long term of imprisonment for the murders when he was convicted.

[120] These included the applicant's youth, lack of criminal record, and mental state.

The Court's reasoning was not that the imposition of the death penalty *per se* would result in a breach of Article 3. The applicant did not claim this and it could not have been so because of the continued presence in Article 2 of the Convention of a provision permitting the death penalty.[121] However, the extradition of a fugitive offender to face the death penalty could involve a breach of Article 3 in the particular circumstances of a case. The Court stated that the 'manner in which it is imposed or executed, the personal circumstances of the condemned person and a disproportionality to the gravity of the crime committed, as well as the conditions of detention awaiting execution, are examples of factors capable of bringing the treatment or punishment received by the condemned person within the proscription under Article 3'.[122]

In terms of the factors set out in the above list, the Court's decision on the facts of the *Soering* case turned mainly on a combination of the 'conditions of detention' and the 'personal circumstances' of the applicant. As to the conditions of detention, the crucial consideration was the exposure to the 'death row phenomenon' that the applicant would face.[123] A condemned individual in Virginia spent six to eight years subject to a stringent security regime and severe mental stress awaiting execution. In this connection, the Court discounted the fact that much of this time resulted from the convicted individual's resort to the appeal procedures available because it was 'part of human nature that the person will cling to life by exploiting those safeguards to the full'.[124] The Court's approach on this point can also be supported on the basis that the conditions that a condemned man must suffer on death row while appealing the claim under Article 3, are the responsibility of the state. This distinguishes the situation from that of the 'trial within a reasonable time' guarantee in Article 6(1), concerning which the Court has always held that the state is not responsible for delay caused by the applicant.[125]

In terms of his 'personal circumstances', the applicant in the *Soering* case was only eighteen when the offence was committed[126] and there was psychiatric evidence supporting the view that he was not mentally responsible for his acts. Moreover, when assessing the United Kingdom's responsibility under Article 3, it was relevant that West Germany had also requested the return of its national to face trial there for the murder without the risk of the death penalty.[127]

With regard to the other factors listed in the *Soering* case, the 'flagrant denial' of a fair trial is relevant to the manner in which the death penalty is 'imposed'.[128] The form

[121] The question whether the death penalty might *per se* be a breach of Article 3 once all Convention parties have ratified the Sixth and Thirteenth Convention Protocols prohibiting the death penalty was left open in *Öcalan v Turkey* 2005-IV; 41 EHRR 985 para 165 GC. Removal to another state by a party to the Sixth or Thirteenth Protocols to face a real risk of the death penalty may be a breach of those Protocols: see *Aylor-Davis v France No 22742/93*, 76 DR-A 164 (1994).

[122] A 161 (1989); 11 EHRR 439 para 104 PC.

[123] Cf, *Poltoratskiy v Ukraine* 2003-V; 39 EHRR 916 and *GB v Bulgaria* hudoc (2004).

[124] Id, para 105.   [125] See below, p 279.

[126] The Court referred to the prohibition of the death penalty for individuals under eighteen (and hence less responsible for their acts than older persons) in Article 6, ICCPR and Article 4, ACHR. The standards in these later instruments 'at the very least' indicated that as a general principle the youth of the person concerned was a circumstance which was liable, with others, to put in question the compatibility with Article 3 of measures connected with the death penalty': id, para 108.

[127] This can be seen as a personal circumstance or as a separate factor additional to those listed by the Court that may be relevant. The UK gave the US request priority because it was made earlier and demonstrated a *prima facie* case, which the German request did not.

[128] *Soering v UK* A 161 (1989); 11 EHRR 439 para 113 PC. See *Bader v Sweden* hudoc (2006); 46 EHRR 197 (deportation case). See also the *Öcalan* case, below, p 90. In the *Soering* case itself a fair trial claim was argued, and for that reason decided, under Article 6, not Article 3: see below, p 205.

that the death penalty takes is relevant to the manner in which it is 'executed'.[129] As to proportionality, the kind of offence for which the death penalty is imposed and the facts of the particular case are considerations under both Articles 2 and 3.[130] In *Jabari v Turkey*,[131] the Court found a breach of Article 3 when it accepted that there was a real risk that if the applicant were returned to her national state of Iran she would be punished, seemingly after criminal proceedings, for adultery by stoning to death, a finding that goes both to the manner of execution and the proportionality requirement.

The rule in the *Soering* case applies to extradition not only in death penalty cases. Considerations such as the risk of an unfair trial and proportionality must be relevant under Article 3 where a person is returned for trial for a non-capital offence also. Similarly, it may be 'inhuman treatment' to extradite an individual for an offence where there is good reason to believe that the extradition process is being abused by the requesting state in order to prosecute him, contrary to the principle of speciality, for a political offence 'or even simply because of his political opinions'.[132] The 'inhuman treatment' in such cases would result from the risk that such proceedings would lead to an 'unjustified or disproportionate sentence'.[133] However, the mere fact that an individual extradited to another state may on his return face prosecution for a criminal offence that carries a severe sentence or one that is more severe than would apply in other European states does not in itself amount to a breach of Article 3.[134] Exceptionally, return to face a real risk of a sentence of life imprisonment without the possibility of release may be a breach of Article 3.[135]

The basis for liability under the rule in the *Soering* case is that the extraditing state has 'taken action which has as a direct consequence the exposure of an individual to proscribed ill-treatment'.[136] The returning state is 'not being held directly responsible for the acts of another state but for the facilitation, through the process of extradition, of a denial of the applicant's rights by that other state'.[137] On the basis of this approach, a state could be liable under the Convention if an individual's extradition presented a real risk of the infringement of any Convention Article, not just Article 3.[138] As the Court noted in the *Soering* case, the situation is an unusual one in that liability normally arises under the Convention only where a violation has in fact occurred; the prospect of a breach, however probable, is normally not sufficient. The Court explained its extension of liability to a case involving only the risk of a violation on the basis that 'where an applicant claims that a decision to extradite him would, if implemented, be contrary to Article 3 by reason of its foreseeable consequences in the requesting country, a departure from this principle is necessary in view of the serious and irreparable nature of the alleged suffering risked, in order to ensure the effectiveness of the safeguard provided by that Article'.[139] This reasoning carries most weight in a case where the receiving state is not a party to the Convention; in other cases, it is possible if necessary to bring a claim under the Convention against

---

[129] Under the ICCPR, Article 7, the form used must involve 'the least possible physical and mental suffering': *Ng v Canada* 1–2 IHRR 161 at 177 (1993) (gas asphyxiation 'cruel and inhuman treatment').

[130] As to Article 2, see above, p 60.   [131] 2000-VIII (deportation case).

[132] *Altun v FRG No 10308/83*, 36 DR 209 at 232–3 (1983).   [133] Id, at 233.

[134] *C v FRG No 11017/84*, 46 DR 176 (1986). See also *Pavlovic v Sweden No 45920/99* hudoc (1999) DA (five years' imprisonment for desertion not a breach). And see *Kilic v Switzerland No 12364/86*, 50 DR 280 (1986). Return to face military service is not inhuman treatment: *A and FBK v Turkey No 14401/88*, 68 DR 188 (1991).

[135] See eg, *Saoudi v Spain No 22871/06* hudoc (2006) DA (no breach: assurances given by the receiving state). As to whether such a sentence is a breach of Article 3, see the *Kafkaris* case, below, p 91.

[136] A 161 (1989); 11 EHRR 439 para 91 PC.   [137] O'Boyle, at n 116 above, p 97.

[138] Cf, the pre-*Soering* discussion by Vogler, *Wiarda Mélanges*, p 663.

[139] A 161 (1989); 11 EHRR 439 para 90 PC.

the receiving state itself.[140] As far as a receiving state is concerned, although it cannot be held liable under the Convention for infringing Article 3 in proceedings to which it is a party, there is no doubt, as the Court acknowledged in the *Soering* case,[141] that the Court's approach 'inevitably involves an element of assessment of conditions' in that state against the standards of the Convention, whether that state is a party to the Convention or not. But, as the Court also noted, 'there is no question of adjudicating on or establishing the responsibility of the receiving country, whether under general international law, under the Convention or otherwise.'[142]

A final point that emerges from a consideration of the *Soering* case is that insofar as Article 3 prohibits the extradition of a person when this is required by an extradition treaty, the requested state is placed in a position to which the rules as to inconsistent treaty obligations apply.[143]

The rule in the *Soering* case applies to deportation as well as extradition. In *Cruz Varas v Sweden*,[144] the applicants were a Chilean national who had been refused asylum in the respondent state, and his wife and child. The first applicant alleged that he had been ill-treated contrary to Article 3 by the Chilean police because of his political activities and that there was a real risk of this happening again if he were deported to Chile. The Court applied the rule in the *Soering* case but decided that it had not been shown that there was a real risk on the facts. In particular, the Court was not convinced by the applicant's story of previous ill-treatment by the government. The Court also noted that in any event the political situation in Chile had improved, leading to the voluntary return of refugees from Sweden and elsewhere. In addition, the Court was influenced by the fact that the defendant state had considerable experience of assessing Chilean asylum claims and had examined the facts of the case closely.

The *Cruz Varas* case addressed the question of the evidence to be taken into account when assessing liability in cases of extradition or deportation in which, as in the *Cruz Varas* case, the applicant has already been returned when the case is decided at Strasbourg. The Court stated that in such a case the presence of a real risk of ill-treatment is to be judged 'primarily' by reference to what the defendant state knew or ought to have known at the time of the return. The Court may take into account, however, information that comes to light subsequently when judging whether the risk to the applicant has been rightly or wrongly assessed by the respondent state. Thus in the *Cruz Varas* case account was taken of the fact that following his return the applicant had been unable to produce witnesses or other evidence in support of his claim of prior ill-treatment. The Court did not mention the fact that the applicant had not been ill-treated following his return. In later cases, the Court has increasingly placed reliance upon evidence of post-return treatment when judging whether the risk to the applicant has been rightly or wrongly assessed by the defendant state.[145] In cases in which the defendant state has not yet removed the applicant to another state, the Court decides whether his removal would infringe Article 3 by reference to the

---

[140] The Court does take into account that the receiving state is a Convention party when ruling on Article 3 cases: *Aronica v Germany No 72032/01* hudoc (2002) DA (extradition) and *Tomic v UK No 17837/03* hudoc (2003) DA (deportation).

[141] A 161 (1989); 11 EHRR 439 para 90 PC.   [142] *Ibid*.

[143] Article 30, Vienna Convention on the Law of Treaties 1969. The UK was not in this position in the *Soering* case: see s 11, Extradition Act 1870 and Articles IV and V(2), UK-US Extradition Treaty 1972.

[144] A 201 (1991); 14 EHRR 1.

[145] See eg, the *Shamayev, Al-Moayad,* and *Mamatkulov* cases, below, p 85.

facts as they are known to the Court at the time of the Court's decision.[146] In all cases, the Court assesses the situation 'in the light of the evidence put before it or, if necessary, material obtained proprio motu'.[147]

As indicated above, for there to be a breach of Article 3, the risk of ill-treatment must be a 'real risk', not just a 'mere possibility'. This point was clearly made on the facts of *Vilvarajah v UK*.[148] There the five applicants were Sri Lankan Tamils who claimed to be at risk of ill-treatment contrary to Article 3 by state security forces in the conflict between the Sri Lankan government and the Tamil liberation movement. The applicants were refused asylum by the respondent state and returned to their national state. The Court held that their return was not a breach of Article 3. Earlier there had been considerable government violence against the Tamil community as a whole, triggered by the activities of the liberation movement, so that it might then have been accepted that there would be a real risk that any member of the community would have been ill-treated upon his return. However, the position had improved to the point where large numbers of Tamils were returning to Sri Lanka of their own volition. Whereas there remained the 'possibility' that the applicants, as Tamils, might be detained and ill-treated, this was not sufficient to establish a breach of Article 3.[149] In the situation that prevailed, it was necessary to show that the applicants were especially at risk, which was not the case.[150] The Court was not influenced in its decision by the fact that three of the applicants were in fact subjected to ill-treatment on their return since 'there existed no special distinguishing features in their cases that could or ought to have enabled the Secretary of State to foresee that they would be treated in this way'.[151]

Assurances given by the receiving state to the returning state about the treatment that the applicant will receive in the receiving state on return are taken into account when assessing the risk of ill-treatment, but they have not in themselves proved decisive; they may be inadequate in themselves or outweighed by other contrary evidence. In *Chahal v UK*,[152] in which there were fears for the safety of the applicant if he were deported to India, the Indian government gave the United Kingdom a general assurance that the applicant 'would enjoy the same legal protection as any other Indian citizen' and 'would have no reason to expect to suffer mistreatment of any kind at the hands of the Indian authorities.' Nonetheless, in view of reliable evidence from Indian and international sources of extra-judicial killings by the Punjab police, who had a particular reason to seek out the applicant as a leading Sikh separatist, the assurance, although accepted by the Court as genuine, did not prevent there being a 'real risk' of ill-treatment in breach of Article 3. In *Saadi v Italy*,[153] the Grand Chamber reached a similar conclusion in respect of a more

---

[146] Eg, *Soering v UK* A 161(1989); 11 EHRR 439 PC and *Ismoilov v Russia* hudoc (2008). In some cases, the non-removal is in response to Court interim measures: see below, p 842.

[147] *Saadi v Italy* hudoc (2008) GC. The Court attaches importance to Amnesty International and similar country reports: id, para 131. In *N v Finland* hudoc (2005); 43 EHRR 195, a Court fact-finding mission interviewed the applicant and others in the sending state to assess the applicant's claims.

[148] A 215 (1991); 14 EHRR 238 para 111. Cf, *Said v Netherlands* 2005-VI (real risk that the applicant would be subjected to extra-judicial punishments amounting to inhuman treatment as a military deserter if expelled to Eritrea).

[149] In the *Salah Sheekh* case, below at p 861, it was sufficient to show that members of the applicant's clan, as opposed to the whole population or the applicant in particular, were generally at risk. Cf, *Saadi v Italy* hudoc (2008) para 132 GC. And see *Paez v Sweden* 1997-VIII (links to terrorist organization).

[150] Where the 'general situation' evidence before the Court is not sufficient, it is for the applicant to produce other evidence corroborating his allegations: *Saadi v Italy* hudoc (2008) GC.

[151] *Vilvarajah v UK* A 215 (1991); 14 EHRR 238 para 112.

[152] 1996-V; 23 EHRR 413 GC. See Lester and Beattie, 2005 EHRLR 565.

[153] Hudoc (2008) GC. The sources included Amnesty International and US Department of State reports.

limited government statement. Asked by the respondent government to give a diplomatic assurance that the applicant would not be ill-treated contrary to Article 3, the Tunisian government simply responded that Tunisian laws guaranteed prisoners' rights and that Tunisia had acceded to the relevant international treaties. The Court stated that such laws and accessions 'in principle are not in themselves sufficient to ensure adequate protection against the risk of ill-treatment where, as in the present case, reliable sources have reported practices resorted to or tolerated by the authorities which are manifestly contrary to the principles of the Convention', to which the applicant, as a convicted terrorist in the Tunisian courts, would be liable to be subjected.[154] Similarly, in *Ismoilov v Russia*,[155] a general assurance of 'human treatment' by the Uzbekistan government was not sufficient to counter the evidence from a number of objective sources (eg, the UN Special Rapporteur on Torture) that there was systematic torture of prisoners generally and that persons, such as the applicants, who were wanted in connection with a serious disturbance aimed at the government, would be particularly at risk of torture. In all of these cases, the assurances were very general or limited. Whether the Court would take the same negative view of assurances with more detailed substantive, procedural and monitoring safeguards has yet to be tested.[156] The likelihood that states that tolerate or engage in ill-treatment in breach of Article 3 would not respect their 'paper' undertakings suggests that the same negative view should prevail.

In all of the above assurance cases the Court has been called upon to make decisions before an individual is returned.[157] In other post-return cases in which assurances have been given, the Court, although still judging the respondent state by reference to what it knew or ought to have known at the time of return,[158] has had knowledge of the applicant's fate on his return—knowledge which would seem to have contributed to rulings that no breach of Article 3 has occurred. In *Shamayev v Georgia and Russia*,[159] Georgia extradited to Russia five Russian nationals who had escaped across the border from Chechnya on charges of mainly terrorist-related offences. It did so on the basis of letters of guarantee from the Russian Acting Procurator General that the applicants would not be sentenced to death or subjected to torture or treatment or punishment that was cruel, inhuman, or contrary to human dignity. The Court noted that these guarantees were given by the highest official responsible for criminal prosecutions and for the treatment of prisoners in Russia and that there was no evidence that could otherwise reasonably have given the Georgian authorities cause to doubt their credibility. In finding no breach of Article 3, the Court also attached importance to the fact that information and evidence obtained subsequent to the applicants' extradition did not indicate that the applicants had been treated contrary to Article 3. Similarly, in *Al-Moayad v Germany*,[160] the applicant Yemeni citizen was extradited to the United States to face charges in an ordinary criminal court of providing money and equipment to Al-Qaeda and Hamas. The United States Embassy gave assurances to the German authorities that the applicant would not

---

[154] Id, para 147.   [155] Hudoc (2008).

[156] See the UK memoranda of understanding with several states; for details, see Moeckli, 8 HRLR 534 (2008).

[157] In some pre-return cases, assurances that the death penalty or irreducible life imprisonment (as opposed to torture) would not be imposed have been held to be sufficient to permit return: see eg, *Saoudi v Spain* No 22871/06 hudoc (2006) DA.

[158] See the *Cruz Varas* case, above, p 83.

[159] 2005-III. See also *Mamatkulov and Askarov v Turkey* 2005-I; 41 EHRR 494 GC in which assurances by Uzbekistan that the applicant would not be subjected to torture or capital punishment contributed to a finding of no violation of Article 3, but in which the absence of evidence of post-extradition ill-treatment in medical reports and other sources was important.

[160] *No 35865/03* hudoc (2007) DA.

be prosecuted before a military or other extra-ordinary court. The German executive authorities and courts at the highest level understood these assurances to mean that the applicant would not be detained in Guantanamo Bay or a third state, places in respect of which the Court stated it was 'gravely concerned' by 'worrying reports' about the interrogation methods at variance with Article 3 used by the US authorities on individuals, such as the applicant, suspected of involvement in international terrorism. In assessing the effectiveness of the assurances, and finding no breach of Article 3, the Court noted that Germany had previously found that assurances given by the United States in the context of extradition had been fully respected and that the post-extradition evidence indicated that the assurances in the applicant's case, which were binding in international law, had been respected and that he had not been ill-treated.

Article 3 does permit the sending of an individual to a particular part of a state where he would not be at risk of ill-treatment, even though there is such a risk elsewhere in the state. But, as held in *Salah Sheekh v Netherlands*,[161] he must be able to 'travel to the area concerned, gain admittance and settle there.' Where this is not so, his return there will be a breach of Article 3 if there is a 'real chance of his being removed to, or his having no alternative but to go, to areas of the country' where there is a 'real risk' of ill-treatment.[162] In the *Salah Sheekh* case, the applicant was a Somali national whom the Dutch authorities sought to return to a safe area of Somalia after refusing him asylum. On the facts, the Court held that whereas there was good evidence from UNHCR that the area concerned was safe for members of the clans who resided there, it was unlikely that the applicant, as a member of a different clan, would be allowed to settle and that, as a member of his particular Ashraf clan, there was a 'real risk' that he would be ill-treated elsewhere in Somalia, so that his return would infringe Article 3.

Similarly, state A may be in breach of Article 3 if it removes an individual to state B where there is a real risk that he will be expelled by that state to state C in which there is a real risk that he will be subjected to proscribed ill-treatment. The Court stated this rule in *TI v UK*.[163] In that case, the United Kingdom had ordered the removal of the applicant to Germany. The applicant had entered the United Kingdom illegally after being refused asylum in Germany, whose authorities had issued an order to deport him to Sri Lanka, his national state. The Court considered there was a risk of his being ill-treated if he were returned to Sri Lanka, but declared the application inadmissible as there was no longer a 'real risk' that Germany would now return the applicant to Sri Lanka.

Where the authorities have information indicating that there is a real risk of ill-treatment, they must conduct a 'proper assessment' of the situation and must not return the person unless they have taken steps that are sufficient to counter the risk. This was stated in *Garabayev v Russia*,[164] in which the applicant had informed the respondent state of his fears of torture and persecution if extradited to Turkmenistan and, in the view of the Court, the respondent state had, in the light of the evidence available to it, been put on notice that there was a real risk of ill-treatment. Finding that the state had extradited the applicant without making a 'proper assessment' of the situation and without taking steps such as obtaining assurances from the requesting state's government or arranging for medical reports or visits by independent experts to counter the risk, the Court found a breach of Article 3.

Where there remains a real risk of ill-treatment in another state, the obligation not to send an individual to that state is an absolute one; it is not open to the respondent state to claim that its own public interest reasons for deporting or extraditing the individual

---

[161] Hudoc (2007) para 142. Cf, *Hihal v UK* 2001-II; 33 EHRR 31.   [162] Id, para 143.
[163] *No 43844/98* hudoc (2000) DA.   [164] Hudoc (2007).

outweigh the risk of ill-treatment on his return, regardless of his offence or conduct. Thus in *Chahal v UK* [165] there was a real risk that, as a well known supporter of Sikh separatism, the applicant Indian citizen would, wherever he was deported to in India, be sought and killed by the Punjab police, who were out of lawful control. Given this real risk of a breach of Article 3, the United Kingdom could not argue that, on balance, the applicant could nonetheless be deported to India because of the threat to its national security that his activities in the United Kingdom posed.

The absolute nature of the guarantee established in *Chahal* was confirmed by a unanimous Grand Chamber in *Saadi v Italy*.[166] In that case, the applicant was a Tunisian national against whom the respondent state had issued an order deporting him to Tunisia on the grounds that his conduct was disturbing public order and threatening national security in Italy because of his active role in supporting fundamentalist Islamist cells engaged in international terrorism. The order was made upon his release after serving a prison sentence resulting from his conviction in the Italian courts for offences the facts of which provided evidence of such a role. The applicant claimed that if he were returned to Tunisia he would be tortured, seemingly in connection with the investigation of terrorist activities which had led to charges against him in Italy.[167] Confirming the applicant's claims, the Court had before it reports, which it had no doubt were reliable, from Amnesty International, Human Rights Watch, and the US Department of State indicating that persons accused of terrorist offences were regularly tortured by the state in Tunisia to obtain confessions and other information. In these circumstances, the Court concluded that there was a 'real risk' of treatment contrary to Article 3 in Tunisia if the applicant were deported there.[168] A unanimous Grand Chamber was not prepared to accept that the values underlying the European Convention that were articulated in Article 3 were open to compromise, however compelling the public interest justification. While acknowledging that 'states face immense difficulties in modern times in protecting their communities from terrorist violence' and that the 'scale of the danger or terrorism today' and the threat it poses to the community cannot be underestimated, the Court nonetheless rejected arguments, presented by the United Kingdom, intervening, and supported by the respondent state, that there were reasons to qualify the absolute nature of the guarantee spelt out in the *Chahal* case. The United Kingdom first argued that, whereas a rule of absolute liability should apply under Article 3 in cases where the ill-treatment was inflicted by the respondent state itself, in cases in which the risk was of ill-treatment by the authorities of another state, it should be balanced against 'the dangerousness he or she represents to the community' in the respondent state. Essentially, the United Kingdom was arguing that the feared harm to the individual on the facts, which might range within Article 3 from torture to lesser forms of inhuman or degrading treatment, should be weighed against the danger to the community in the returning state, which might range from the most serious 'ticking bomb' scenario to lesser degrees or kinds of danger. The Court characterized this argument as 'misconceived', on the basis that the 'concepts of 'risk' and 'dangerousness' in this context do not lend themselves

[165] 1996-V; 23 EHRR 413 GC. See also *Ahmed v Austria* 1996-VI; 24 EHRR 278 (deportation because of criminal conviction). The fact that an individual is illegally present in the returning state's territory does not justify his return to face ill-treatment: *Amekrane v UK No 961/72*, 16 YB 356 (1973); F Sett Report of 19 July 1974.

[166] Hudoc (2008) GC. See Moeckli, 8 HRLR 534 (2008).

[167] While serving his sentence in Italy, the applicant had been convicted by a Tunisian military court *in absentia* of membership of an international terrorist organization and incitement to terrorism and sentenced to twenty years' imprisonment. Presumably the risk was of ill-treatment in connection with the investigation of other terrorist activities or links while in prison serving this sentence.

[168] As to the question of diplomatic assurances, see above, p 84.

to a balancing test because they are notions that can only be assessed independently of each other'.[169] The Court then rejected a second, related UK argument to the effect that stronger evidence of a risk of ill-treatment in the receiving state must be adduced where the applicant poses a threat to national security in the respondent state than in cases in which the public interest risk is of a less vital kind. In doing so, the Court stressed that it already requires 'substantial grounds' for believing that a real risk exists: that it 'applies rigorous criteria and exercises close scrutiny' when it decides upon the existence of a real risk of ill treatment, as evidenced by the fact that it had only 'rarely' decided that such a risk existed.

Although most decided cases concerning extradition or deportation involve claims that the applicant will be ill-treated at the hands of the public authorities of the receiving state, the responsibility of the sending state also may be engaged where the risk is of ill-treatment by private groups or individuals. For example, a state may be in breach of Article 3 if it sends an individual to another state where there is a real risk of that individual being subjected there to ill-treatment by private drug traffickers[170] or by warring clans in a civil war situation,[171] or that a woman would be subjected to female genital mutilation.[172] For the returning state to be liable in such cases on a *Soering* basis, it must be shown that the public authorities in the receiving state are unable to provide protection against the private actors concerned, whether this failure is the fault of the receiving state or not.[173]

In very exceptional cases of serious illness, humanitarian considerations may prohibit the return of an individual to another state. In *D v UK*,[174] the applicant, who had AIDS, was ordered to be returned to his national state of St Kitts after he had completed his prison sentence for drug smuggling. Pending his removal and the outcome of his case at Strasbourg, the applicant had been placed in a hospice and was in the terminal stages of his illness when the European Court ruled that his return would be in inhuman treatment in breach of Article 3. This was because the 'sophisticated treatment and medication' being given to him in the United Kingdom would not be available in St Kitts and he would not have family or other moral or social support there. Although the absence in St Kitts of the specialist treatment and medication available in London did not mean that his return would fall short of the standards in Article 3, the 'abrupt withdrawal' of his current treatment and medication, with the inevitable hastening of the applicant's death, would cause 'acute mental and physical suffering' and would 'expose him to a real risk of dying under most distressing circumstances'. In these 'very exceptional circumstances', involving 'compelling humanitarian considerations', the Court found a breach of Article 3. The Court stressed that Article 3 did not provide generally for an alien who is subject to expulsion any entitlement to remain in a Convention state in order to benefit from medical, social, or other forms of assistance that would not be available in the state to which he was to be sent and that in a case of this kind it would examine very carefully the circumstances of the case, *inter alia* comparing the applicant's medical and other conditions that would pertain if he were not removed with those that would apply if he was. The D case has been relied upon in a number of cases since it was decided, all cases involving physical or mental health, but in none has the Court found the humanitarian considerations to be sufficiently compelling to find a breach, underlining the point that

[169] 1996-V; 23 EHRR 413 para 139 GC.   [170] *HLR v France* 1997-III; 26 EHRR 29.
[171] *Ahmed v Austria* 1996-VI; 24 EHRR 278 (Somalia).
[172] *Collins and Akaziebie v Sweden No 23944/05* hudoc (2005) DA (no real risk on facts).
[173] *HLR v France* 1997-III; 26 EHRR 29.   [174] 1997-III; 24 EHRR 423 paras 51–4.

the combination of circumstances in the *D* case were very exceptional.[175] In these cases the Court has stressed that it is not sufficient to show that medical treatment will be less good in the receiving state and emphasized that in the *D* case the applicant was both near to death and would lack family as well as medical support.

The above approach and thereby 'very high threshold' established in the *D* case was confirmed by the Grand Chamber in *N v UK*.[176] In that case, the applicant was a Ugandan national who was to be returned to Uganda after her asylum claim had been rejected. She had been diagnosed with AIDS on her arrival in the United Kingdom, but, as a result of the free medication she had been given during the nine years of her asylum application, she was in a stable medical condition, with the prospect of many years of life. If she was deprived of this medication, she would die within a few years. The required medication was available, highly subsidized, in Uganda but the applicant claimed that she would not be able to afford it and that it would not be available in her home rural area. While accepting that the quality of the applicant's life and her life expectancy would be affected if she were returned to Uganda, the Grand Chamber, finding against the applicant by fourteen votes to three, noted that, in contrast with the *D* case, the applicant was not yet critically ill and that the 'rapidity of the deterioration which she would suffer and the extent to which she be able to obtain access to medical treatment, support and care, including help from relatives must involve a certain degree of speculation', particularly as AIDS treatment was evolving worldwide.[177] In doing so, it made the following important general comment:[178]

> Although many of the rights it contains have implications of a social or economic nature, the Convention is essentially directed at the protection of civil and political rights....Advances in medical science, together with social and economic differences between countries, entail that the level of treatment available in the contracting state and the country of origin may vary considerably....Article 3 does not place an obligation on the contracting state to alleviate such disparities through the provision of free and unlimited health care to all aliens without a right to stay within its jurisdiction. A finding to the contrary would place too great a burden on the contracting states.

Where deportation separates an individual from his family, or where children are deported from the state in which they have been brought up the mental suffering caused will probably not reach the threshold level required by Article 3; the case is more likely to fall with Article 8 instead.[179] In some early cases, the Commission held that the deportation of stateless or other individuals who are unlikely to be admitted to settle elsewhere may raise issues under Article 3.[180]

Where an individual physically resists deportation or extradition, reasonable force, including the use of sedatives, may be used to effect the return.[181] But an individual should not be returned where he or she is not medically fit to travel.[182] Moreover, considerations of humanity are relevant to the manner of return. In *Mubilanzila Mayeka and*

---

[175] See eg, *Bensaid v UK* 2001-I; 33 EHRR 205 (mental illness); *Arcila Henao v Netherlands No 13669/03* hudoc (2003) DA (AIDS); and *Hukic v Sweden No 17416/05* hudoc (2005) DA (Downs syndrome). But see *BB v France* 1998-VI F Sett.

[176] Hudoc (2008) GC. *N v UK* applies beyond AIDS to physical and mental illness generally: id, para 45.

[177] Id, para 50.

[178] Id, para 44. But see the strong joint dissenting opinion of Judges Tulkens, Bonello, and Spielmann.

[179] See eg, *PP v UK No 25297/94* hudoc (1996) DA. But see *Fadele v UK No 13078/87*, 70 DR 159 (1991) F Sett.

[180] *Harabi v Netherlands No 10798/84*, 46 DR 112 (1986) and *Giama v Belgium No 7612/76*, 21 DR 73 (1980).

[181] *Raidl v Austria No 25342/94*, 82-A DR 134 (1995).   [182] See *D v UK* 1997-III; 24 EHRR 423 para 53.

Kaniki Mitunga v Belgium[183] the return of an unaccompanied five-year-old girl without proper arrangements for her care in transit or on arrival caused her such 'extreme anxiety and demonstrated such a total lack of humanity' as to be inhuman treatment.

V. DISAPPEARED PERSONS

Claims have been made that Article 3 has been infringed in a number of cases involving disappeared persons. Insofar as a claim is brought on behalf of the disappeared person, in the absence of the required evidence of proscribed ill-treatment, the case falls to be considered under Article 5 (freedom of the person), not Article 3.[184] However, in *Cakici v Turkey*[185] it was held that there may be a breach of Article 3 in relation to a family member of the disappeared person, but only where there are 'special factors' which give the applicant's suffering 'a dimension and character distinct from the emotional distress which may be regarded as inevitably caused to relatives of a victim of a serious human rights violation'.[186] Relevant considerations include 'the proximity of the family tie—in that context, a certain weight will attach to the parent-child bond—, the particular circumstances of the relationship, the extent to which the family member witnessed the events in question, the involvement of the family member in the attempts to obtain information about the disappeared person and the way in which the authorities responded to those enquiries'.[187] The essence of the violation in respect of a family member lies not in the fact of the disappearance, but the 'reactions and attitudes' of the state authorities.[188] Taking this into account, in *Cakici* the Court held that a disappeared person's brother was not a victim of a breach of Article 3.[189] He had not been present at the arrest or played the leading role in complaining to the authorities, and there had been no 'aggravating features' in their response. In contrast, there was a breach in *Kurt v Turkey*[190] in relation to the disappeared person's mother, who had witnessed his detention, led the complaints against it, and suffered 'the authorities' complacency in the face of her anguish and distress'.[191]

VI. OTHER KINDS OF INHUMAN TREATMENT

Various other instances of inhuman treatment have been found or postulated, of which the following are examples. The destruction of a person's home may be inhuman treatment.[192] In *Ocalan v Turkey*,[193] the imposition of the death penalty 'following an unfair trial by a court whose independence and impartiality were open to doubt' was inhuman treatment in view of the anguish caused by the fear of execution over a lengthy period. The risk of ill-treatment for being a homosexual,[194] of child abuse,[195] or of female genital

---

[183] 2006-XI para 69. Cf, *Nsona v Netherlands* 1996-V.

[184] *Kurt v Turkey* 1998-III; 27 EHRR 373 para 115; *Cicek v Turkey* hudoc (2001); 37 EHRR 20 para 154; *Orhan v Turkey* hudoc (2002) para 354. As to Article 2, see above, p. 58.

[185] 1999-IV; 31 EHRR 133 GC.   [186] Id, para 98.   [187] *Ibid.*

[188] *Ibid.* Cf, *Tas v Turkey* hudoc (2000); 33 EHRR 325.   [189] Cf, *Ekinci v Turkey* hudoc (2002).

[190] 1998-III; 27 EHRR 373. For other breaches see eg, *Cyprus v Turkey* 2001-IV; 35 EHRR 731 para 157; *Tanis v Turkey* 2005-VIII; 46 EHRR 211. For Chechnya cases, see *Bazorkina v Russia* hudoc (2006); 46 EHRR 261 and *Luluyev v Russia* 2006-XIII.

[191] *Cakici v Turkey* 1999-IV; 31 EHRR 133 para 98, distinguishing *Kurt* from *Cakici.*

[192] See *Selcuk and Asker v Turkey*, above, p 75.

[193] 2005-IV GC para 165. For this reason it was found unnecessary to reach a 'firm conclusion' as to whether the implementation of the death penalty was *per se* inhuman and degrading treatment contrary to Article 3 while a large number (now less) of states were not parties to the Thirteenth Protocol.

[194] See *Fashkami v UK No 17341/03*, Court Information Note No 65 June 2004 DA .

[195] See *Giusto v Italy No 38972/06*, Court Information Note No 97 DA.

mutilation may also be inhuman treatment.[196] In *Tanko v Finland*[197] the Commission stated that it did 'not exclude that the lack of medical care in a case where someone is suffering from a serious illness could in certain circumstances amount to treatment contrary to Article 3'.

In contrast, in *V v UK*[198] it was held that the attribution of criminal responsibility at the age of ten years was not in breach of Article 3.[199] Crucial to the Court's decision was that there was no consensus as to the minimum age of responsibility among member states of the Council of Europe and that, although most of them set a higher limit, the age of ten was not so young as to differ 'disproportionately' from European states generally and some states[200] had a lower age limit. In the same case, it was also held that the trial of a juvenile in public in an adult court (though with some modifications) was not in breach of Article 3: the suffering caused did not go significantly beyond that which would inevitably be present in any procedure that the authorities might adopt.[201] The suffering resulting from injuries caused by the use of a pepper spray to control demonstrators was not inhuman treatment.[202]

4. INHUMAN PUNISHMENT

Although there has been very little jurisprudence specifically on inhuman punishment, its meaning may be gauged from cases concerning other elements of Article 3, as the same general considerations apply. There is no clear distinction between inhuman treatment and punishment in the Strasbourg jurisprudence. In cases involving punishment, the Court often does not distinguish between the two, finding both inhuman treatment and punishment.[203]

As a general proposition, a sentence imposed upon an individual convicted of a criminal offence will not be reviewed under Article 3. Instead the kind of sentence imposed for a particular offence or the length of a term of imprisonment is left to national courts. However, there are exceptions. In *Tyrer v UK*, the Court considered whether the suffering resulting from a sentence of corporal punishment reached the threshold level of inhuman punishment, but concluded that 'on the facts of the case' (three strokes of the birch) it did not.[204] Some more severe sentence of corporal punishment might be regarded differently, as might a death penalty imposed by some method that did not involve 'the least possible physical and mental suffering'.[205] As to length of sentence, a sentence of life imprisonment without the possibility of release may be inhuman punishment.[206] However, there is no breach of Article 3 where 'national law affords the possibility of review of a life sentence with a view to its commutation, remission, termination or the conditional release of

[196] See *Collins and Akaziebie v Sweden* No 23944/05 hudoc (2007) DA.

[197] No 23634/94 hudoc (1994) DA. See also *Pretty v UK* 2002-III; 35 EHRR 1 para 53. On the medical care of deportees, see *N v UK*, above, p 89. On the medical treatment of detainees, see below, p 97.

[198] 1999-IX; 30 EHRR 121 para 74.

[199] The Court's judgment is in terms of a breach of Article 3 as a whole.

[200] Eg, Cyprus, Ireland, and Switzerland.   [201] There was a breach of Article 6: see below, p 250.

[202] *Ciloglu v Turkey* hudoc (2007).   [203] See eg, *Keenan v UK* 2001-III; 33 EHRR 913.

[204] It was a degrading punishment: see below, p 104.

[205] See *Ng v Canada*, above, n 129. See also *Jabari v Turkey* (stoning to death for adultery), above, p 82.

[206] *Kafkaris v Cyprus* hudoc (2008) GC. See also *Léger v France* hudoc (2006) (referred to Grand Chamber). And see *R (on the application of Wellington) v Secretary of State for the Home Department* [2008] UKHL 72. On extradition to face unlimited life sentences, see above, p 182. As to the imprisonment of the very old or ill, see below, pp 98–9.

a prisoner'.[207] An indeterminate life sentence, by which a person may be detained beyond a punitive period for such time as he or she remains a danger to society, is not *per se* a breach of Article 3, but it may be such if account is not properly taken of the detained person's development when considering detention beyond the tariff period[208] or if there is an 'unjustifiable and persistent' delay in fixing the tariff period, leaving the detainee in uncertainty as to his or her future.[209] The principle of proportionality might indicate a breach of Article 3 in some extreme cases. For example, in *Weeks v UK*[210] an indeterminate life sentence for a seventeen-year-old for robbery of 35 pence, not surprisingly, 'raised doubts', but was held not to infringe Article 3 because of the very special circumstances of the case.

5. DEGRADING TREATMENT

Treatment is degrading if it 'is such as to arouse in the victims feelings of fear, anguish and inferiority capable of humiliating and debasing them'.[211] Or, in the language of an alternative formula that the Court sometimes adopts, treatment is degrading if it 'humiliates or debases an individual showing a lack of respect for, or diminishing, his or her human dignity or arouses feelings of fear, anguish or inferiority capable of breaking an individual's moral and physical resistance'.[212] In contrast with inhuman treatment, the emphasis is upon humiliation or debasement rather than physical or mental suffering, although clearly the two overlap. As with other kinds of ill-treatment proscribed by Article 3, the test is a relative one, depending upon all the circumstances of the case.[213] Moreover, the humiliation involved must be more than that which follows inevitably from accepted forms of treatment, such as that relating to conditions of imprisonment.[214] The public nature of any treatment is relevant to its degrading character, although it may be sufficient that a person is humiliated in his or her own eyes.[215]

It is not essential that there be an intention to humiliate or debase for treatment to be degrading. The presence of such an intention is one of the factors that the Court will take into account, 'but the absence of any such purpose cannot conclusively rule out' a finding of a breach of Article 3.[216] In *Price v UK*,[217] the treatment of a disabled person in prison was degrading despite the absence of any evidence of an intention to humiliate or debase.

The same treatment may be both degrading and inhuman, as in the case of resort to the 'five techniques' of interrogation used in *Ireland v UK*[218] and to physical assault in *Tomasi v France*.[219] In those cases, it was relevant that it is humiliating to oblige a person by force to answer questions (or otherwise act) against his will or to violate his physical integrity. In the *Greek* case,[220] the Commission supposed that 'all torture must be inhuman and

---

[207] *Kafkaris v Cyprus* hudoc (2008) para 98 GC. See *Stanford v UK No 73299/01* hudoc (2002) DA and *Wynne v UK No 67285/01* hudoc (2003) DA.

[208] *Hussain v UK* 1996-I; 22 EHRR 1.

[209] *V v UK* 1999-IX; 30 EHRR 121 PC. As to inadequate review in the post-tariff period, see *Curley v UK* 2000-V; 31 EHRR 14.

[210] A 114 (1987); 10 EHRR 293 para 47 PC. See the dissenting opinion of Judge De Mayer.

[211] *Kudla v Poland* 2000-IX; 35 EHRR 198 para 92 GC. On degrading treatment or punishment, see Arai-Yokoi, 21 NHRQ 385 (2003) and Vorhaus, 31 Common L World R 374 (2002) and 32 id 65 (2003).

[212] *Pretty v UK* 2002-III; 35 EHRR 1.   [213] See further, above p 70.

[214] *Kudla v Poland* 2000-IX; 35 EHRR 198 GC.   [215] See *Tyrer v UK*, below, p 104 (punishment case).

[216] *V v UK* 1999-IX; 30 EHRR 121 para 71 GC.

[217] 2001-VII; 34 EHRR 1285. Cf, *Yankov v Bulgaria* 2003-XII.   [218] A 25 (1978); 2 EHRR 25 PC.

[219] A 241-A (1992); 15 EHRR 1.   [220] 12 YB (the *Greek* case) 1 at 186 (1969).

degrading treatment, and inhuman treatment also degrading'. However, all degrading treatment or punishment is not necessarily inhuman as well.[221]

I. CONDITIONS OF DETENTION AND THE TREATMENT OF DETAINEES

a. Generally

The conditions of detention or treatment of individuals in a place of detention may amount to inhuman treatment or degrading treatment or both, depending upon the presence of the required suffering or humiliation or both on the part of the detainee. In recent years, the Court has tended to consider Article 3 issues arising out of detention under degrading, rather than inhuman, treatment, although some decisions are still based upon a finding of the latter.[222] For convenience, such issues are considered in this chapter wholly under the heading of degrading treatment.

b. Conditions of detention and treatment of detainees

Conditions of detention have been found to amount to inhuman or degrading treatment in a variety of contexts. These are mainly cases of detention on remand[223] or following criminal conviction,[224] but include cases of detention pending deportation,[225] for civil contempt,[226] or as a mentally disabled person.[227] When examining conditions in a place of detention, the Court gives weight to the conclusions of the CPT when the latter has reported on it.[228] When assessing the conditions, the Court takes into account their cumulative effect as well as particular allegations made by the applicant. It also looks to the length of time during which the conditions prevailed.[229] Both of these considerations were relevant in *Kalashnikov v Russia*[230] in which both the applicant's prison conditions and the cramped conditions in which he was transported from prison to the court were held to infringe Article 3. The applicant had been detained on remand for nearly five years in a detention facility that was recognized by the Russian government as falling short of European standards. He was one of normally at least fourteen prisoners in a cell that had a space per prisoner well below CPT guidelines even for the eight prisoners for whom it was designed. Because of the overcrowding, the applicant shared a bed with sometimes two other prisoners on an eight hour a day shift basis. The 'filthy, dilapidated cell' had one toilet, with no screen to ensure privacy, inadequate ventilation, and was infested with pests. The applicant contracted skin diseases and fungal infections while in detention. The Court found that the conditions, 'in particular the severely overcrowded and insanitary

[221] *Raninen v Finland* 1997-VIII.   [222] Cf, above, p 79.
[223] *Kalashnikov v Russia* 2002-VI; 36 EHRR 587. On the non-criminal detention of minors, see *DG v Ireland* 2002-III; 35 EHRR 1153.
[224] *Ilascu et al v Moldova and Russia* 2004-VII; 40 EHRR 1030 GC.
[225] *Dougoz v Greece* 2001-II; 34 EHRR 1480.   [226] *Price v UK* 2001-VII; 34 EHRR 1285.
[227] *B v UK* No 6870/75, 32 DR 5 (1981) Com Rep; CM Res DH (83). See also *A v UK* No 6840/74, 3 EHRR 131 (1980) F Sett and *Simon Herald v Austria* No 4340/69, 14 YB 352 (1971) F Sett.
[228] *Dougoz v Greece* 2001-II; 34 EHRR 1480. But see *Peers v Greece* 2001-III; 33 EHRR 1192. Compliance with the European Prison Rules 2006 is likely to mean compliance with Article 3: see *Ramirez Sanchez v France* 2006-IX; 43 EHRR 1161 para 130 GC. On non-compliance with the Rules, see *Eggs v Switzerland* No 7341/76, 6 DR 170 (1976).
[229] But it may be quite short: twenty-two hours' detention in terrible conditions in a police cell was inhuman treatment: *Fedotov v Russia* hudoc (2005); 44 EHRR 544. See also *Kaja v Greece* hudoc (2006).
[230] 2002-VI paras 101–2. For two of many other Russian cases, see *Khudoyorov v Russia* 2005-X and *Grishin v Russia* hudoc (2007) (referred to Grand Chamber).

environment and its detrimental effect on the applicant's health and well-being', combined with the length of the period of detention, amounted to degrading treatment. The
defendant government argued that the conditions, which it had taken steps to improve, as
the Court acknowledged, were no worse than those of most detainees in Russia and were
the result of financial constraints. The Court was not prepared to make any allowance
for such considerations, applying the European standard built into Article 3 for all states
that have become parties to the Convention, regardless of their economic and other local
circumstances.[231]

Prison conditions have been found to amount to inhuman or degrading treatment in
large numbers of other cases in the Court's recent jurisprudence. To take one of many
cases, in *Modarca v Moldova*,[232] there was a breach of Article 3 when the applicant was
detained for almost nine months 'in extremely overcrowded conditions with little access
to daylight, limited availability of running water, especially during the night and in the
presence of heavy smells from the toilet, while being given insufficient quantity and quality of food or bed linen'. In *Cyprus v Turkey*,[233] the withholding of food and water and
medical treatment from detainees was inhuman treatment. There was also a breach of the
obligation to provide proper nourishment in *Moisejevs v Latvia*[234] when, on days when
he attended court, a remand prisoner was given wholly inadequate amounts of food, particularly bearing in mind the stress of a courtroom appearance.

In *Poltoratskiy v Ukraine*,[235] the applicant had been sentenced to death and then subject
to a moratorium on the death penalty before it was abolished. The Court accepted that the
feelings of fear and anguish of those sentenced to death may contribute to a finding of a
breach of Article 3, although on the facts it was the conditions of his detention for several
years under the strict prison regime applicable to those sentenced to death that gave rise
to a breach of Article 3.

Strip searches of prisoners may amount to degrading treatment. They may be justified
on security or public order grounds, but must be conducted in an appropriate manner
with due respect for the individual's dignity. In *Iwanczuk v Poland*,[236] a remand prisoner
who sought to cast his vote in a parliamentary election and who posed no security or
other threat was forced to strip to his underclothes before prison guards and ridiculed
by them. When he refused a further order to strip naked and undergo a body search, he
was not allowed to vote. The Court found that there was degrading treatment, the search
not being justified or conducted in an appropriate manner. There was degrading treatment on the latter ground in *Valasinas v Lithuania*[237] when, in the course of a search for
illegal items after a visit, a male prisoner was forced to strip naked in the presence of a
female guard and his sexual organs and food brought by his visitor were examined by
guards who were not wearing gloves. In other more borderline cases, the Court may have
difficult decisions to make as it assesses the justification for strip searching. In *Wieser
v Netherlands*,[238] the Court held, by a majority of four to three, that the police were not

---

[231] Cf, *Poltoratskiy v Ukraine* 2003-V; 39 EHRR 916.

[232] Hudoc (2007) para 68. Cf, the *Greek Case*, 12 YB (the *Greek* case) 1 (1969) Com Rep; CM Res DH (70)
1. For other examples, see *II v Bulgaria* hudoc (2005); *Tekin v Turkey* 1998-IV; 31 EHRR 95. On toilet arrangements, see Foster, 2005 PL 35.

[233] *Nos 6780/74 and 6950/75* (First and Second Applications), 4 EHRR 482 at 541 (1976) Com Rep; CM Res
DH 79(1).

[234] Hudoc (2006).   [235] 2003-V 39 EHRR 916. Cf, *GB v Bulgaria* hudoc (2004).

[236] Hudoc (2001). See also *McFeeley v UK No 8317/78*, 20 DR 44 at 81 (1980) and the *Greek* case 12 YB (the
Greek case) 1 at 461, 463, 465 (1969) Com Rep; CM Res DH (70) 1.

[237] 2001-VIII. On the strip searching of visitors, see *Wainwright v UK* 2006-X; 44 EHRR 809 (breach of
Article 8, not Article 3).

[238] Hudoc (2007).

justified in strip searching a handcuffed and dangerous man for weapons in his home on arrest. Inhuman and degrading treatment were found in *Van Der Ven v Netherlands*[239] because of routine, weekly strip searches for over three years, for which insufficient justification was provided by the respondent government, coupled with other aspects of a strict security regime in a high security remand facility.

In *Yankov v Bulgaria*[240] the Court stated that the forced shaving off of a prisoner's hair may 'in principle' be degrading treatment. In that case, the applicant's hair was shaven off when he was placed in seven days' solitary confinement as a punishment for writing statements critical of the authorities. The Court held that this had an arbitrary punitive element that was likely to humiliate him, particularly in view of his age, fifty-five years, and the fact he was to appear in court nine days later. Insistence that a prisoner wear a prison uniform is not degrading treatment.[241]

In a different kind of case, in *Price v UK*[242] the applicant was a four-limb deficient thalidomide victim who was sent to prison for civil contempt. She was kept overnight in a police cell in which she was 'dangerously cold' and then moved to a prison for two nights where she was unable to use the toilet without the assistance of male officers and where conditions otherwise were unsuitable for a severely disabled individual. This was held to be degrading treatment.

c. Solitary confinement

Solitary confinement, or segregation, of persons in detention[243] is not in itself a breach of Article 3; it is permissible for reasons of security or discipline or to protect the segregated prisoner from other prisoners or *vice versa*.[244] It may also be justified in the interests of the administration of justice, eg to prevent collusion in respect of pending proceedings,[245] or to prevent a prisoner from making external criminal contacts.[246] In each case, 'regard must be had to the particular conditions, the stringency of the measure, its duration, the objective pursued and its effects on the person concerned'.[247] Generally, prolonged solitary confinement is undesirable, especially where the person is detained on remand.[248] As the Court has indicated, 'complete sensory isolation, coupled with total social isolation can destroy the personality and constitutes a form of inhuman treatment which cannot be justified by the requirements of security or for any other reason'.[249]

Applying this approach, the Court, and formerly the Commission, has found arrangements for the solitary confinement of prisoners of the kind typically found in European

---

[239] 2003-II. See also *Frerot v France* hudoc (2007).

[240] 2004-XII.   [241] *McFeeley v UK No 8317/78*, 20 DR 44 at 81 (1980).

[242] 2001-VII; 34 EHRR 1285. See also *Hurtado v Switzerland* A 280-A (1994) Com Rep F Sett (applicant defecated in trousers following grenade explosion on arrest; not allowed to change trousers until the next day and after questioning).

[243] Most of the case law on solitary confinement concerns remand or convicted prisoners. The following section also applies *mutandis mutandis* to other persons in detention, such as mental patients (see eg, *Dhoest v Belgium* 55 DR 5 (1987) Com Rep; CM Res DH (88) 1) and persons in preventive detention (see eg, the *Second Greek Case No 4448/70*, 34 CD 70 (1970)).

[244] *Ilascu et al v Moldova and Russia* 2004-VII; 40 EHRR 1030 para 432 GC.

[245] *Rohde v Denmark* hudoc (2005); 43 EHRR 325.   [246] *Messina v Italy* 1999-V.

[247] *Ensslin, Baader and Raspe v FRG No 7572/76*, 14 DR 64 at 109 (1978), cited by the Court in *Ramirez Sanchez v France* 2006-IX; 43 EHRR 1161 para 120 GC.

[248] *Ibid.* As to duration, excluding a prisoner from association with others by confinement to her cell for under two hours for bad behaviour was not degrading treatment: *Bollan v UK No 42117/98* hudoc (2000) DA.

[249] *Ilascu et al v Moldova and Russia* 2004-VII; 40 EHRR 1030 para 432 GC. Sensory isolation results from restrictions on access to natural light, sound, etc: *Ensslin, Baader and Raspe, loc cit* at n 247, p 110.

criminal justice systems not to be in breach of Article 3.[250] In some extreme cases, the Court has found a breach of Article 3, most notably in the *Ilascu* case[251] in which the Court found that the conditions amounted even to torture. There the applicant was detained for eight years 'in very strict isolation' before his conviction and sentence to death for terrorist-related offences was quashed. He 'had no contact with other prisoners, no news from the outside since he was not permitted to send or receive mail and no right to contact his lawyer, or receive regular visits from his family. His cell was unheated, even in severe winter conditions, and had no natural light source or ventilation'. He was also deprived of food as a punishment. These conditions and a lack of medical care caused his health to deteriorate. As a whole, they amounted to torture in breach of Article 3, a finding in which the stringency and length of the solitary confinement regime were prominent.

In several other extreme cases, involving prolonged segregation but lesser degrees of sensory or social isolation than in *Ilascu*, the Court has not found a breach of Article 3. For example, *Ramirez Sanchez v France*[252] concerned the detention of a notorious international terrorist ('Carlos the Jackal') in solitary confinement for eight years following his conviction for terrorist-related offences. Although segregated from other prisoners, he had access to television and newspapers and generally was detained in conditions that complied with the European Prison Rules. Arrangements for visits by his priest, lawyers and family were satisfactory, and the applicant was in good health. The Court was concerned, however, by the duration of the applicant's solitary confinement. While accepting that dangerous prisoners may, as is common in European prison systems, be segregated to prevent their escape or to preserve order and security within the prison, the Court stated that in cases of prolonged segregation the Court was required, under Article 3, to conduct a 'rigorous examination to determine whether the measures taken were necessary and proportionate compared to the available alternatives, what safeguards were afforded to the applicant and what measures were taken by the authorities to ensure that the applicant's physical and mental condition was compatible with his continued solitary confinement'. In this connection, the state must, following periodic review, give reasons for any decision to continue segregation and ensure regular monitoring of the detainee's physical and mental condition. Judicial review must be available to challenge continued prolonged segregation. The Court's approach was coloured by its awareness of the psychological dangers of prolonged segregation and that solitary confinement, 'even in cases entailing only relative isolation, cannot be imposed on a prisoner indefinitely'.[253] Applying its approach to the facts of the case, the Court held, by twelve votes to five, that Article 3 had not been infringed. In particular, the Court was responsive to the efforts made by the respondent state and the fact that, some months before the Court's

---

[250] See *Rohde v Denmark* hudoc (2005); 43 EHRR 325, in which the need for effective monitoring of mental health was in issue. For UK cases, see eg, *X v UK No 8158/78*, 21 DR 95 (1980); *X v UK No 8231/78*, 28 DR 5 (1982). See also *Yurttas v Turkey* hudoc (2004).

[251] 2004-VII; 40 EHRR 1030 para 438 GC. See also *Mathew v Netherlands* 2005-IX; 43 EHRR 444 (disruptive remand prisoner; lengthy segregation in ordinary prison in Aruba; inhuman treatment) and *Van der Ven v Netherlands* 2003-II; 38 EHRR 967 (limited contact with others).

[252] 2006-IX; 43 EHRR 1161 GC. Cf, *Öcalan v Turkey* (the notorious leader of an armed terrorist movement (the PKK) detained six years on remand as the only prisoner in an island prison, but in otherwise largely acceptable conditions: no breach of Article 3). For terrorist cases in which the Commission found no breach of Article 3 despite considerable sensory and social isolation, see *Ensslin, Baader and Raspe v FRG No 7572/76*, 14 DR 64 (1978); *McFeeley v UK No 8317/78*, 20 DR 44 (1980) (IRA hunger strikers; 760 days' solitary confinement); and *Kröcher and Müller v Switzerland No 8463/78*, 34 DR 2S (1982) Com Rep; CM Res DH (83) 15. See also *M v UK No 9907/82*, 35 DR 130 (1983) (convicted murderer who killed two prisoners segregated in specially adapted cell for six years: no breach).

[253] 2006-IX; 43 EHRR 1161 para 145 GC.

judgment, it had ended the applicant's solitary confinement—a position which the Court stated 'should not in principle be changed'.[254]

d. Medical assistance

Article 3 requires that detainees are provided with the 'requisite medical assistance.'[255] This follows from the obligation that Article 3 imposes upon states to 'protect the physical well being of persons deprived of their liberty'.[256] Where the lack of the 'requisite medical assistance' gives rise to a medical emergency or otherwise exposes the applicant to 'severe or prolonged pain', the breach of Article 3 takes the form of inhuman treatment.[257] Where it does not, a breach of Article 3 may nonetheless be found if the humiliation caused to the applicant by the stress and anxiety that he suffers because of the absence of medical assistance may reach the threshold level of 'degrading' treatment in the sense of Article 3.[258] In *Hummatov v Azerbaijan*,[259] the lack of medical treatment for the applicant's various illnesses, including tuberculosis contracted in prison, was 'degrading' because it caused considerable mental suffering diminishing his human dignity'.

In some cases, the required regime of assistance has been put in place, but has proved inadequate in particular circumstances. In *McGlinchey v UK*,[260] the prison authorities had not provided the requisite medical care in response to a convicted prisoner's heroin withdrawal symptoms, from which she died. Although there was a generally acceptable regime in place to monitor her medical condition, this did not provide for monitoring by a doctor over the weekend and not enough was done then in response to the serious deterioration of her medical condition. In other cases, little or no regime has been put in place at all. In *Khudobin v Russia*[261] a remand prisoner had epilepsy and other serious medical conditions that required regular medical care; he was also HIV positive and suffered from a serious mental disorder. Although he was treated in the prison hospital when he became ill, no regular monitoring of his condition and medication to prevent illnesses and emergencies was provided.

Ordinary medical negligence that does not cause the level of suffering or of anxiety or stress generating the necessary humiliation does not involve a breach of Article 3.[262] Breaches of Article 3 have sometimes been found because of the delay in providing assistance. In *Hurtado v Switzerland*,[263] a person who had been forcibly arrested was not given an X-ray, which revealed a fractured rib, until six days after he requested it.

A number of cases have concerned the provision of psychiatric care. In *Keenan v UK*,[264] a convicted prisoner committed suicide the day after he was awarded seven days' solitary

---

[254] Id, para 150.
[255] *Kudla v Poland* 2000-XI; 35 EHRR 198 para 94 GC. Cf, *Cyprus v Turkey* 2001-IV; 35 EHRR 731 GC. The required standard is adequacy, not the best available to the public outside prison: *Khudobin v Russia* 2006-XII.
[256] *Khudobin v Russia* 2006-XII para 93.
[257] *McGlinchey v UK* 2003-V; 37 EHRR 821. Cf, *Pilcic v Croatia* hudoc (2008) (failure to organize kidney stone operation inhuman and degrading) and *Popov v Ukraine* hudoc (2006) (no regular check-ups for cancer victim).
[258] *Sarban v Moldova* hudoc (2005); *Khudobin v Russia* 2006-XII; and *Paladi v Moldova* hudoc (2007).
[259] Hudoc (2007).
[260] 2003-V; 37 EHRR 821. See also *Melnik v Ukraine* hudoc (2007) (failure to diagnose and adequately treat tuberculosis).
[261] 2006-XII. See also *Gorodnitchev v Russia* hudoc (2007); *Boicenco v Moldova* hudoc (2006); and *Paladi v Moldova* hudoc (2007).
[262] See eg, *Filip v Romania* hudoc (2006). [263] A 280-A (1994) Com Rep F Sett before Court.
[264] 2001-III; 33 EHRR 913. See also *Kudla v Poland* 2000-XI GC; 35 EHRR 198; *Rivière v France* hudoc (2006); and *Petrea v Romania* hudoc (2008) (overcrowding and lack of mental treatment).

confinement and twenty-eight additional days of imprisonment for assault as a disciplinary punishment just nine days before his expected release. The Court found that the
imposition of this punishment in circumstances in which the prisoner, who was a known
suicide risk, had not been adequately monitored or, as the Court emphasized, given the
requisite psychiatric care, was inhuman and degrading treatment and punishment. In
the same case, the Court also stated that when assessing whether the treatment given to
mentally ill persons results in suffering in breach of Article 3 it is necessary to take into
account 'their vulnerability and their inability, in some cases, to complain coherently or
at all about how they are being affected by any particular treatment'.[265]

In *Dybeku v Albania*,[266] the Court held that certain categories of prisoners require
places of detention that offer conditions of detention and treatment suited to their particular medical and other needs, rather than a place that is aimed at 'ordinary' prisoners.
It identified the mentally disabled; persons with a serious physical illness;[267] the physically disabled;[268] the elderly;[269] and drug addicts suffering from withdrawal symptoms[270]
as falling within these categories. In the *Dybeku* case, the Court held that the regime in
the general prison in which the applicant was detained were 'entirely inappropriate' for a
person with mental health problems.[271]

The fact that imprisonment is not in the best interests of a prisoner's health is not of itself
sufficient to require his or her release to avoid liability under Article 3 since imprisonment
following, for example, conviction or on remand is obviously permissible.[272] Article 3 does
not contain a 'general obligation to release a detainee on health grounds or to place him
in a civil hospital to enable him to obtain a particular kind of medical treatment'.[273] In
most cases, while sometimes calling for humanitarian measures,[274] the Court has found
that adequate medical assistance has been available in prison[275] or made available by way
of visits from prison to outside hospitals for treatment.[276] As stated in *Wedler v Poland*,[277]
however, should a prisoner's state of health become such that adequate medical or nursing assistance cannot be provided in detention, the Court has held that Article 3 requires
that a prisoner be released, subject to conditions that the state reasonably imposes in the
public interest. Thus in *Mouisel v France*,[278] the applicant, who was serving a long sentence for armed robbery, had been diagnosed with cancer for which he needed frequent
chemotherapy treatment that was not available in prison. Ultimately, he was released
on parole in the custody of his family to facilitate his treatment. The Court held that his
detention before his release for the two year period after his illness had been diagnosed
amounted to inhuman and degrading treatment. In the same way, the detention over a
lengthy period of an elderly person with serious problems of health or infirmity may also
be in breach of Article 3, although cases in which this has been raised as an issue have

---

[265] Id, para 110.   [266] Hudoc (2007).
[267] Eg, *Mouisel v France*, below.   [268] Eg, *Price v UK*, above, p 95.
[269] Eg, *Papon v France*, below p 99.   [270] Eg, *McGlinchey v UK*, above, p 97.
[271] Cf, *Aerts v Belgium* 1998-V; 29 EHRR 50 and *Rivière v France* hudoc (2006).
[272] See Article 5(1)(a)(e).   [273] *Wedler v Poland* hudoc (2007) (remand case).
[274] *Chartier v Italy* No 9044/80, 33 DR 41(1982) Com Rep; CM Res DH 83 (12).
[275] See *ibid*. Cf, *Bonnechaux v Switzerland* No 8224/78, 18 DR 100 (1979) Com Rep; CM Res DH 83 (12) and
Kudla v Poland 2000-XI; 35 EHRR 198. Claims that prisoners with AIDS should be released have been rejected
in several cases: see eg, *Gelfmann v France* hudoc (2004); 42 EHRR 81.
[276] See *Henaf v France* 2003-XI; 40 EHRR 990. See also *Tarariyeva v Russia* 2006-XV (taken to hospital in
unsuitable van: inhuman treatment).
[277] Hudoc (2007).
[278] 2002-IX; 38 EHRR 735. See also *Tekin Yildiz v Turkey* hudoc (2005) (neurological syndrome: unfit for
prison) and *Khudobin v Russia* 2006-XII.

generally been unsuccessful on their facts.[279] If the state places a disabled individual in prison, it must ensure that the place of detention is suitable.[280]

The obligation to provide medical assistance includes a requirement to review arrangements for detention continuously in the interest of a prisoner's health and well-being.[281] When determining compliance with Article 3, account may be taken of the applicant's refusal of prison treatment[282] or to permit a medical examination,[283] but treatment may not be refused because of the prisoner's ill-conduct.[284]

e. Compulsory medical intervention

There is no obligation under Article 3 to provide medical assistance to a person in detention against that person's will. At the same time, the giving of such assistance, by force if necessary, will in principle not be in breach of Article 3 where it is 'of therapeutic necessity from the point of view of established principles of medicine' in the interests of the person's physical or mental health.[285] In such cases, the medical necessity must be 'convincingly shown' and appropriate procedural guarantees must apply. In addition, the manner in which the assistance is given must not exceed the minimum level of suffering or humiliation in order to avoid a breach of Article 3. In *Herczegfalvy v Austria*[286] the Court held that the forcible administration of food and drugs to a violent, mentally-ill patient on hunger strike, which was in accordance with established principles of medicine, was not in breach of Article 3. The Court stated that in such cases 'the position of inferiority and powerlessness which is typical of patients confined in psychiatric hospitals calls for increased vigilance' when reviewing compliance with the Convention. Nonetheless compulsion and force could be justified 'to preserve the physical and mental health of patients who are entirely incapable of deciding for themselves and for whom [the medical authorities] are therefore entirely responsible'. Despite hesitation, the Court found unanimously that the evidence before it was 'not sufficient to disprove the government's argument that, according to the psychiatric principles generally accepted at the time, medical necessity justified the treatment in issue'.[287] In contrast, in *Nevmerzhitsky v Ukraine*,[288] there was a breach of Article 3 where the applicant was subjected to forced feeding while on hunger strike. The Court found that the medical necessity to force feed the applicant in order to save his life had not been shown and that the applicable procedural safeguards had not been complied with. Beyond this, and most strikingly, the Court found that the manner of forced feeding—involving handcuffs, a mouth widener, and a special rubber tube inserted forcibly—gave rise to suffering at the level of torture, not just inhuman treatment.

---

[279] *Papon v France (No 1) No 64666/01*, 2001-VI DA and *Farbtuhs v Latvia* hudoc (2004) (imprisonment of a ninety-year-old with a heart problem not inhuman: medical treatment available and his general health good). See also *Sawoniuk v UK No 63716/00* hudoc (2001) DA.

[280] *Price v UK*, above, p 95.   [281] See the *McFeeley* case, above, p 96.

[282] *De Varga-Hirsch v France No 9559/81*, 33 DR 158 (1983).

[283] *RSA and C v Portugal Nos 9911/82 and 9945/82*, 36 DR 200 (1984).

[284] *Iorgov v Bulgaria* hudoc (2004); 40 EHRR 145.

[285] *Jalloh v Germany* 2006-IX; 44 EHRR 667 para 69 GC.

[286] A 244 (1992); 15 EHRR 437 para 82. Cf, *X v FRG No 8518/79*, 20 DR 193 (1980). See also *B v UK No 6870/75*, 32 DR 5 (1981), in which, despite 'certain reservations', the psychiatric treatment of a Broadmoor patient was held not to be in breach of Article 3. And see *Dhoest v Belgium No 10448/83*, 55 DR 5 (1987) Com Rep; CM Res DH (88) 1 and the *Winterwerp* case, below, p 158.

[287] A 244 (1992); 15 EHRR 437 para 83. Cf, *MB and GB v UK No 35724/97* hudoc (2001) DA. But see *Henaf v France*, below, p 300.

[288] 2005-II; 43 EHRR 32. Cf *Ciorap v Moldova* hudoc (2007).

The use of a medical procedure against a suspect's will to obtain evidence of a crime is not in breach of Article 3 if certain conditions or safeguards similar to those applicable to forced feeding are satisfied. The Court's approach was formulated in *Jalloh v Germany*[289] as follows:

> ... any interference with a person's physical integrity carried out with the aim of obtaining evidence must be the subject of rigorous scrutiny, with the following factors being of particular importance: the extent to which the forcible medical intervention was necessary to obtain the evidence, the health risks for the suspect, the manner in which the procedure was carried out and the physical pain and mental suffering it caused, the degree of medical supervision available and the effects on the suspect's health.... In the light of all the circumstances of the individual case, the intervention must not attain the minimum level of severity that would bring it within the scope of Article 3.

In the *Jalloh* case, an emetic was forcibly administered to the applicant, causing him to regurgitate a drug bubble which was then used as the main evidence against him in proceedings leading to his conviction and sentence to six months' imprisonment for a minor drug dealing offence. As to whether the medical intervention was necessary, the Court recognized the public interest in controlling drug trafficking, but noted that the applicant was not a major drug dealer and that anyway the police could have waited for nature to take its course, as was the approach in many other European states. The procedure also posed a health risk, two deaths having resulted in other German cases, and there had been no proper assessment of these risks in the applicant's case. Moreover, the emetic was administered forcibly by a tube which must have caused pain and anxiety. The Court held, by ten votes to seven, that the applicant had been subjected to inhuman and degrading treatment contrary to Article 3. A requirement that an accused person submit to a psychiatric examination in connection with the investigation of his case is not degrading.[290]

Experimental medical treatment[291] may be inhuman treatment, if not torture, in the absence of consent.[292] Compulsory sterilization was understood to be contrary to the Convention during its drafting.[293]

f. Handcuffing, transport, etc

The handcuffing of a prisoner is not degrading contrary to Article 3 provided that it is reasonably necessary in the circumstances.[294] Relevant considerations are the danger of escape or violence or the suppression of evidence, the degree of force used to effect the handcuffing and the extent of any exposure to the public.[295] In *Erdogan Yagiz v Turkey*,[296] the applicant, a doctor, was subjected to treatment that, in the absence of a good public interest reason, was degrading when he was placed in handcuffs on arrest

---

[289] 2006-IX; 44 EHRR 667 GC para 76. The Court noted that the taking of compulsory blood and saliva samples had been held not to violate Article 3: *X v Netherlands No 8239/78*, 16 DR 187 and *Schmidt v Germany No 32352/02* hudoc (2006) DA.

[290] *X v FRG No 8334/78*, 24 DR 103 (1981). Cf, *Skawinska v Poland No 42096/98* hudoc (2001) DA.

[291] Although this is a matter not limited to the ill-treatment of person in detention, experimental medical treatment is most likely to occur in detention and is considered here for convenience.

[292] See *X v Denmark No 9974/82*, 32 DR 282 (1983).   [293] 1 TP 116–7.

[294] *Raninen v Finland* 1997-VIII; 26 EHRR 563 and *Öcalan v Turkey* 2005-IV GC.

[295] *Ibid.* As to transportation in public in handcuffs or uniform, see also *X v Austria No 2291/64*, 24 CD 20 (1967) and *Campbell v UK No 12323/86*, 57 DR 148 at 156 (1988). On the transport of prisoners generally, see *Khudoyorov v Russia* 2005-X.

[296] Hudoc (2007).

in a public car parking area at his place of work and later taken in the course of the investigation to his place of work and home in handcuffs, all in the sight of his work colleagues, family, and neighbours. It is also degrading contrary to Article 3 for the accused to be required to appear in handcuffs[297] or to be kept in a cage[298] at public hearings in court when there is no good public interest reason to justify it. The handcuffing of a prisoner seriously ill with cancer while being taken to hospital outside of prison was degrading in *Mouisel v France*.[299] In *Henaf v France*[300] the shackling to his bed overnight of a seventy-five-year-old prisoner who had been taken to hospital for an operation, which made sleeping difficult, was inhuman treatment in breach of Article 3. In contrast, 'although worrying', the handcuffing and strapping of the applicant by his ankles for two weeks because of the 'danger of aggression and the death threats' that he was making did not lead to a breach of Article 3 in *Herczegfalvy v Austria*.[301]

II. DISCRIMINATION

Discrimination may constitute degrading treatment under Article 3.[302] Such an interpretation is consistent with the probability that the drafters of the Convention had anti-Semitism in mind when prohibiting degrading treatment. Racial discrimination was found to be degrading treatment contrary to Article 3 in the *East African Asians* cases.[303] In those cases, twenty-five East African Asians had retained their status as UK citizens when Kenya and Uganda became independent rather than take the local nationality. They did so on the understanding that this would allow them continued access to the United Kingdom free from immigration control.[304] Following the adoption of a policy of Africanization by the Kenyan and Ugandan governments and in order to control immigration from those states, legislation was enacted at Westminster terminating the right of entry of UK citizens lacking ancestral or 'place of birth' connections with the United Kingdom. The Commission considered in its opinion on the merits that this legislation was racially discriminatory and that applicants' subjection to it, with the attendant publicity and in the special circumstances of their cases, was an affront to their dignity to the point of being 'degrading treatment' in breach of Article 3.[305] Further to its opinion in the *East African Asians* cases, in *Abdulaziz, Cabales, and Balkandali v UK*[306] the Commission stated that, although a state has a sovereign power to admit persons to its territory, by virtue of Article 3 'the state's discretion in immigration matters is not of an unfettered character, for a state may not implement policies of a purely racist nature, such as a policy prohibiting the entry of any person of a particular skin colour'. Confirming the Commission's approach, in *Cyprus v Turkey*,[307] the Court found that there was discrimination by the government of the Turkish Republic of Northern Cyprus (TRNC)[308] against the Karpas Greek Cypriot minority living in northern Cyprus that amounted to degrading treatment in breach of Article 3. This discrimination was motivated by the different 'ethnic origin, race and religion' of the Greek Cypriot minority and

---

[297] *Gorodnitchev v Russia* hudoc (2007).   [298] *Sarban v Moldova* hudoc (2005).

[299] 2002-IX; 38 EHRR 735.   [300] 2003-XI; 40 EHRR 990. See also *Tarariyeva v Russia* 2006-XV.

[301] Above, p 99.   [302] *Cyprus v Turkey* 2001-IV; 35 EHRR 731 para 305 GC.

[303] *Nos 14116/88 and 14117/88*, 76A DR 5 (1993); 3 EHRR 76 Com Rep; CM DH (77) 2.

[304] The Commission did not find that there had, as argued, been an express undertaking to admit citizens who retained their nationality and left open the question whether there was an implied one.

[305] The Committee of Ministers did not rule on the question of a breach. After much delay and all of the applicants had been admitted to the UK, it decided that no further action was called for: CM Res DH (77) 2.

[306] A 94 (1985); 7 EHRR 471 para 113.   [307] 2001-IV; 35 EHRR 731 paras 307–11 GC.

[308] Turkey was responsible for the TRNC's acts: id, para 77.

was a consequence of the 'bi-zonal' policy of the TRNC government and would inevitably result in the community dying out. In particular, the members of the minority were not allowed to bequeath immovable property to relatives who did not live in the North; there were no secondary school facilities in the North; and Greek Cypriot children who went to school in the South were not allowed to reside in the North later as adults. There were also further freedom of movement and other limitations upon the Greek Cypriot minority that significantly restricted its members' rights to privacy and family life and to practise their religion. The result was that the 'conditions under which that population is condemned to live are debasing and violate the very notion of respect for the human dignity of its members'.

Racial discrimination also contributed to the finding by the Court of a breach of Article 3 in *Moldovan v Romania*.[309] That case arose out of the death of a non-Roma villager after a fight with three Roma. In reprisal, a non-Roma crowd, including two police officers, *inter alia* destroyed the applicants' homes, following which destruction they were forced to live in appalling living conditions in cellars, hen houses, and stables, etc. This, together with the generally hostile attitude of the judicial and executive authorities when considering the applicants' claims, generated mental suffering and degradation to the level of a breach of Article 3. An 'aggravating factor' were the gratuitous remarks made by the courts and the mayor about the applicants' 'honesty and way of life', which, in the absence of any substantiation, were 'purely discriminatory'.

It can be supposed that other individual cases of racial discrimination may raise issues under Article 3. This view is supported by *Hilton v UK*[310] in which the Commission stated in its decision as to admissibility that an allegation of racial discrimination by prison officers against a prisoner raised an issue under Article 3. If Article 3 did not apply to such cases of racial discrimination they would not be in breach of any part of the Convention unless Article 14 could be invoked.[311] Article 14, however, provides a remedy in just some cases because it applies only where there is racial discrimination in the protection of a right guaranteed by the Convention. Hence it has no application in important areas of life, such as employment and housing. In the case of discrimination by private persons in such contexts, state responsibility under Article 3 would be based upon a positive obligation upon the state to ensure that private individuals do not lawfully infringe other individuals' rights.[312]

A further question is whether discrimination on grounds other than race is subject to Article 3.[313] Although the Commission stated in the *East African Asians* cases that it is 'generally recognised' that 'a special importance should be attached to discrimination based on race',[314] this was not necessarily intended to suggest that there might not be other important categories. Legislation discriminating against illegitimate children and their parents was held in *Marckx v Belgium*[315] not to be degrading treatment contrary to Article 3. However, since the *Marckx* case, discrimination against children born out of wedlock has, like racial discrimination, been identified as a kind of discrimination

---

[309] 2005-VII; 44 EHRR 302 para 110.

[310] *No 5613/72*, 4 DR 177 (1976) (alleged racial abuse: no breach on the facts): 3 EHRR 104 Com Rep; CM Res (79) 3 (1979). See also *Glimmerveen and Hagenbeek v Netherlands Nos 8348/78 and 8406/78*, 18 DR 187 at 195 (1979) and *X v Switzerland No 9012/80*, 24 DR 205 (1980).

[311] Article 3 may apply in discrimination cases whether or not Article 14 applies: *Cyprus v Turkey* 2001-IV; 35 EHRR 731 GC.

[312] On the Article 3 obligation to protect against private action, see below, p 107.

[313] Racial discrimination is understood in the sense of discrimination by reference to 'race, descent or national or ethnic origin': Convention on the Elimination of Racial Discrimination 1965, Article 1.

[314] 3 EHRR 76 at 86 (1973) Com Rep; CM Res DH (77) 2.   [315] A 31 (1979); 2 EHRR 330 para 66.

given special protection by Article 14, as have discrimination on grounds of sex, religion, and sexual orientation.[316] It is arguable that discrimination on any of these grounds is degrading contrary to Article 3. The Court has moved in this direction in the case of sexual orientation. In *Smith and Grady v UK*,[317] the Court did 'not exclude that treatment which is grounded upon a predisposed bias on the part of a heterosexual majority against a homosexual minority... could, in principle, fall within the scope of Article 3'. However, on the facts, it found that, although distressing and humiliating, the investigation into the applicants' sexual orientation and their subsequent discharge from the navy solely in pursuance of a Ministry of Defence policy that excluded homosexuals from the armed forces did not, in all the circumstances, reach the minimum threshold of degrading treatment.[318]

III. OTHER KINDS OF DEGRADING TREATMENT

Claims of degrading treatment have been considered in various other diverse contexts. The mutilation of a son's body was degrading for a near relative,[319] and allegations of the smearing the lips of Kurdish villagers with human excrement by Turkish security forces were admitted for consideration on the merits under Article 3.[320] Although the Convention does not protect the right to a reputation, it has been stated that, in an exceptional case, the humiliation suffered by defamatory remarks made by a public authority might qualify as degrading treatment.[321] In principle, a wholly insufficient amount of pension and other social benefits may amount to inhuman and degrading treatment.[322] Constant surveillance by the police could also, exceptionally, be degrading.[323] However, a criminal investigation and imprisonment would not be degrading because it was politically motivated.[324] Nor is a state's failure to recognize a transsexual's new sex.[325] The treatment of disabled persons may also be degrading.[326]

As with the claims of inhuman treatment, claims concerning private or family life that involve allegations of degrading treatment are more likely to succeed under Article 8. For example, the omission by a state to provide adequate criminal sanctions in the case of a sexual assault by a private person was not considered under Article 3 in respect of the humiliation suffered by the victim because liability had been established under Article 8.[327] Similarly, in *Lopes Ostra v Spain*[328] the noise and smells from a waste treatment plant near the applicant's family home infringed Article 8, but did not give rise to degrading treatment.

---

[316] See below, pp 591ff.   [317] 1999-VI; 29 EHRR 493 para 121.

[318] It was in breach of Article 8.

[319] *Akkum v Turkey* 2005-II; 43 EHRR 526 (return of body to father with ears cut off). Cf, *Akpinar and Altun v Turkey* hudoc (2007).

[320] *Gurdogan et al v Turkey* Nos 15202–5/89, 76A DR 9 (1989) F Sett.

[321] See the *East African Asians* cases 3 EHRR 76 at 80 (1973) Com Rep; CM Res DH (77) 2. In *Stewart-Brady v UK* No 9 27436/95, 24 EHRR CD 38, defamatory statements about a notorious prisoner were not degrading. See also *Agee v UK* No 7729/76, 7 DR 164 (1976).

[322] *Larioshina v Russia* No 56869/00 hudoc (2002); 33 EHRR CD 36 (inadmissible on facts). On the application of Article 3 to socio-economic conditions generally see Cassese, 2 EJIL 141 (1991).

[323] See *Adali v Turkey* hudoc (2005). See also *D'Haese, Le Compte v Belgium* No 8930/80, 6 EHRR 114 (1983).

[324] *Gusinskiy v Russia* No 70276/01 hudoc (2002) DA.

[325] *B v France* A 232-C (1992) Com Rep.   [326] Lawson, 56 NILQ 462 (2005).

[327] *X and Y v Netherlands* A 91 (1985); 8 EHRR 235. *Hendricks v Netherlands* No 9427/78, 29 DR 5 (1982): Com Rep; CM Res DH (82) 4. As to cases of rape, see above, p 74, under torture.

[328] A 303-C (1994); 20 EHRR 227. Claim under Article 8 succeeded.

6. DEGRADING PUNISHMENT

'Degrading' here has the meaning that it has in connection with degrading treatment. In *Tyrer v UK*,[329] the Court characterized a degrading punishment as follows:

> In order for a punishment to be 'degrading' and in breach of Article 3, the humiliation or debasement involved must attain a particular level and must in any event be other than that usual element of humiliation referred to in the preceding sub-paragraph (ie that which follows from the very fact of being convicted and punished by a court). The assessment is, in the nature of things, relative: it depends on all the circumstances of the case and, in particular, on the nature and context of the punishment itself and the manner and method of its execution.

Applying this test to the facts of the case, the Court held that a judicial sentence of three strokes of the birch imposed by an Isle of Man juvenile court on a fifteen-year-old boy for assault and executed by a police constable at a police station was a degrading punishment contrary to Article 3. With regard to the 'manner and method of its execution', the Court noted that medical and other safeguards[330] had been applied and that the birching had occurred in private. As to the private character of the birching, the Court stated that whereas publicity 'may be a relevant factor' in assessing whether a punishment is degrading, it did not consider that 'the absence of publicity will necessarily prevent a given punishment from falling into that category: it may well suffice that the victim is humiliated in his own eyes, even if not in the eyes of others.[331] Also relevant was the three-week delay in administering the punishment pending an appeal and the fact that the birching was effected by a stranger. Finally, the 'indignity of having the punishment administered over the bare posterior aggravated to some extent the degrading character of the applicant's punishment', although 'it was not the only or determining factor'.[332]

What was crucial in deciding the case were considerations concerning the 'nature and context' of judicial corporal punishment generally. The Court emphasized that such punishment was 'institutionalised violence' imposed by one individual upon another in the name of the state, the individual being 'treated as an object in the power of the authorities'; it was 'an assault on precisely that which it is one of the main purposes of Article 3 to protect, namely a person's dignity and physical integrity'.[333] Moreover, it was irrelevant that Manx public opinion favoured the birch on grounds of deterrence; a punishment did not cease to be degrading because it was or was believed to be effective and Manx public opinion was in any event out of step with 'commonly accepted standards in the penal policy' in Council of Europe states.[334] Adopting its 'dynamic' approach to the interpretation of the Convention, by which the Convention is to be interpreted in 'the light of present day conditions,[335] the Court considered that such standards were to be taken into account.

Although the *Tyrer* case did not in terms declare judicial corporal punishment to be degrading *per se*, it is unlikely, given present day West European penal policy, to

---

[329] A 26 (1978); 2 EHRR 1. See Zellick, 27 ICLQ 665 (1978). On corporal punishment under Article 3 generally, see Phillips, 43 ICLQ 153 (1994). As to the steps taken to comply with the *Tyrer* decision, see above, p 27.

[330] There was a prior medical examination and a doctor and the boy's father were present.

[331] A 26 (1978); 2 EHRR 1 para 32.   [332] Id, para 35.

[333] Id, para 33. The Court added, somewhat inconclusively, that it could not 'be excluded that the punishment may have had adverse psychological effects': *ibid*.

[334] Id, para 31.   [335] Ibid. As to the Courts' 'dynamic' approach see above, p 7.

pass muster however administered. The case also makes the point that the Convention contains a distinction between acceptable and unacceptable *kinds*, as well as *degrees*, of degradation. In the case of imprisonment, which is obviously not in itself in breach of Article 3, the fact of incarceration and the conditions that necessarily go with it mean that the level of humiliation must be at least as high as that which accompanies the use of the birch on a single occasion in circumstances such as those in the *Tyrer* case.

There have also been several cases concerning disciplinary corporal punishment in schools.[336] In *Costello-Roberts v UK*[337] the Court held, by five votes to four, that a disciplinary measure at a private boarding school by which a seven-year-old boy was given three 'whacks' on the bottom with a gym shoe over his trousers by the headmaster with no one else present was not a degrading punishment. The Court distinguished the *Tyrer* case by reference to the fact that the applicant in the *Costello-Roberts* case was much younger; the punishment was less severe and resulted in no visible bruising; that it was not administered to the boy's bare bottom; and the delay in executing it (three days) was much shorter.[338] The Court also distinguished between the official state violence involved in the execution in a police station of a judicial sentence and the informal administration of a private school disciplinary code. The four dissenting judges[339] gave the following reasons for disagreeing: 'After a three-day gap, the headmaster of the school "whacked" a lonely and insecure seven-year old boy. A spanking on the spur of the moment might have been permissible, but, in our view, the official and formalized nature of the punishment meted out, without the adequate consent of the mother, was degrading.' In contrast with the *Costello-Roberts* case, in which neither the Court nor the Commission[340] considered that Article 3 had been infringed, in two other cases— *Warwick v UK*[341] and *Y v UK*[342]—the Commission was of the opinion that there had been a breach of Article 3. In the *Warwick* case, a sixteen-year-old girl at a state school who had been caught smoking a cigarette was given one stroke of the cane on the hand, causing bruising, by the headmaster in his office in the presence of the deputy headmaster and another similarly delinquent girl immediately after being reported. The Committee of Ministers could not decide whether Article 3 had been infringed, being unable to obtain a two-thirds majority either way.[343] In *Y v UK*, a fifteen-year-old schoolboy at a private school was given four strokes of the cane on his bottom through his trousers, resulting in heavy bruising. The caning was administered by the headmaster in private as soon as

---

[336] On the earlier cases, see Ghandi, 33 ICLQ 488 (1984). As to other, non-corporal forms of school disciplinary punishment, see *Valsamis v Greece* 1996-VI; 24 EHRR 294 (one day's suspension not degrading).

[337] A 247-C (1993); 19 EHRR 112. As to the basis on which Article 3 applies to private schools, see below, p 107.

[338] The Court noted further that in the *Tyrer* case the applicant was 'held by two policemen whilst a third administered the punishment, pieces of the birch breaking at the first stroke': id, para 31.

[339] Judges Ryssdal, Vilhsalmsson, Matscher, and Wildhaber. As to 'adequate consent', in *Costello-Roberts* the school prospectus stated that a high standard of discipline was maintained, but did not mention corporal punishment.

[340] The Commission did, however, find a breach of the right to respect for private life under Article 8. The Court found no breach of Article 8.

[341] No 9471 /81, 60 DR 5 (1986) Com Rep; CM Res DH (89) 5. There have been several other UK cases. See eg, *X v UK No 7907/77*, 24 YB 402 (1981), in which the UK made an ex gratia payment of £1,200 compensation and £1,000 costs where a fourteen-year-old girl at a state school had been caned.

[342] A 247-C (1993); 17 EHRR 238, Com Rep.

[343] It is likely that the voting was influenced in favour of the respondent state by changes in UK law of which the Committee was informed. The Committee did, however, recommend that the UK pay the applicants' costs.

the pupil was sent to him for defacing another boy's file. A county court claim in assault had been unsuccessful on the basis that the parents had agreed by contract to caning as a disciplinary punishment and the force used was reasonable. The case was not decided by the European Court, having been struck off its list following a friendly settlement.[344] It is noticeable that, like the majority of the Court in the *Costello-Roberts* case, the Commission did not discuss in these cases the question of parental consent, which would not appear to prevent liability under Article 3. In the one other case on school corporal punishment that has reached the Court, it was held in *Campbell and Cosans v UK*[345] that the *threat* of corporal punishment (resulting from its availability in a state school) did not cause sufficient suffering or degradation to be 'inhuman' or 'degrading' treatment.

Generally, the conclusion to be drawn from the jurisprudence of the Court and the Commission is that the imposition of disciplinary corporal punishment in state or private schools is suspect from the standpoint of Article 3, particularly where physical harm is inflicted or where the manner of its administration is humiliating. Bearing in mind that the problem would appear to be uniquely British, it should be noted that UK disciplinary corporal punishment cases should cease following legislative changes.[346]

Disciplinary corporal punishment by parents is also subject to Article 3. In *A v UK*,[347] it was held that English law failed to provide adequate protection for children against such punishment. In that case, a step-father had caned his 'difficult' nine-year-old step-son several times, causing bruising and suffering contrary to Article 3. He was prosecuted for assault occasioning actual bodily harm, but acquitted by a jury by a majority verdict. As the Strasbourg Court noted, under English law the step-father had a defence of lawful punishment, ie punishment that was moderate and reasonable in the circumstances, and the burden of proof was upon the prosecution to show beyond reasonable doubt that the assault had exceeding this limit. The Court held that, although the state had prosecuted the step-father, there was a breach of Article 3 because the law did not provide adequate protection, as the respondent government acknowledged in argument. It remains to be seen whether Article 3 will be interpreted as requiring the prohibition of all parental corporal punishment or as permitting some use of force within *stricter* limits than those that existed on the facts of *A v UK*.[348] It is submitted that the best approach would be one similar to that in *Costello-Roberts*, by which a law that permitted a modest and proportionate use of force—unlike that used in the *A* case—would not be in breach of Article 3, particularly when only a small minority of European states totally prohibit parental corporal punishment.[349] Presumably, disciplinary corporal punishment by child-minders is subject to the same rule as that applicable to parents, although there have been no cases as yet.[350]

---

[344] The UK government agreed to pay £8,000 compensation and £9,000 in costs.

[345] A 48 (1982); 4 EHRR 293. There was a breach of Article 2, First Protocol: see below, p 706.

[346] Corporal punishment is now prohibited in the UK in both state and independent schools: see the School Standards and Framework Act 1998, s 131.

[347] 1998-VI; 27 EHRR 611. See Ghandi and James, 3 IJHL 97 (1999).

[348] The defence of reasonable punishment of a child has been curtailed, but still permits smacking, etc, insufficient to cause cuts or bruises: see Children Act 2004, s 58.

[349] In 2002, nine states totally prohibited it: see the opening address by Ms de Boer-Buquicchio, Deputy Secretary General, Council of Europe, Council of Europe Seminar on Corporal Punishment of Children within the Family, Strasbourg, 2002.

[350] On the liability of child-minders in English law, see *Sutton LBC v Davis* [1994] 2 WLR 721 Fam.

7. THE OBLIGATION TO PROTECT INDIVIDUALS FROM TORTURE, ETC

In addition to the negative obligation not to subject an individual to torture or inhuman or degrading treatment or punishment, Article 3 contains a positive obligation to take appropriate steps to protect individuals from such ill-treatment or punishment. This implied obligation echoes that which the Court has read into Article 2 on the right to life.[351] The obligation has both a preventative and an investigative dimension.

I. THE OBLIGATION TO PREVENT ILL-TREATMENT

A state must have a 'framework of law' of a preventative kind that 'provides adequate protection' against ill-treatment by state agents or private persons.[352] As far as preventing ill-treatment by *private* persons is concerned, the obligation was first examined in *Costello-Roberts v UK*.[353] There the Court held that a state must provide appropriate legal protection against disciplinary corporal punishment in private schools. The Court reached this conclusion on very narrow grounds. It noted that there was an obligation in Article 2, First Protocol to the ECHR, which the respondent state had accepted, to secure for children the right to education—a right that included limits on school discipline and that supposed no distinction between state and private schools. In the Court's view, a state could not avoid liability under the Convention by delegating its obligation to 'secure' a right protected by it to private institutions or individuals. After this cautious first step, the Court extended the scope of the obligation to protect against private ill-treatment in the parental corporal punishment case of *A v UK*.[354] In that case, the Court ruled that the Article 1 obligation to 'secure' the rights in the Convention requires that states 'take measures designed to ensure that individuals within their jurisdiction are not subjected to' treatment proscribed by Article 3, 'including such treatment administered by private individuals'. 'Children and other vulnerable individuals', the Court said, 'are entitled to protection, in the form of effective deterrence, against such serious breaches of personal integrity.' Applying this approach, the Court held, in a judgment that makes no mention of any link with a Convention right,[355] that the United Kingdom had infringed Article 3 because its law did not adequately protect a child against the infliction by a parent of suffering that reached the threshold of Article 3. The same obligation of protection applies to other private acts that result in suffering at the level of Article 3, as in the case of some acts of racial discrimination.[356]

The preventative element of the obligation to protect also requires that a state take appropriate steps to protect an individual from ill-treatment in a particular case of which its authorities knew or ought to have known. For example, in *Kaya (Mahmut) v Turkey*[357] a doctor had been subjected to inhuman treatment by unidentified persons before being killed by them. There was a breach of Article 3 because the state knew that the doctor was at risk of being targeted by contra-guerrilla elements in the security forces on suspicion of giving medical assistance to wounded PKK members and had not taken specific

---

[351] See above, pp 37ff.
[352] *Kaya (Mahmut) v Turkey* 2000-III para 115 and *MC v Bulgaria* 2003-XII; 40 EHRR 459.
[353] A 247-C (1993); 19 EHRR 112. See also *X and Y v Netherlands*, below, p 384.
[354] 1998-VI; 27 EHRR 1 para 22.
[355] The right to education relied upon in the *Costello-Roberts* case was not available.
[356] See above, p 102.   [357] 2000-III para 115.

measures to protect him. Moreover, the general lack of effectiveness of the criminal law system in the region meant that, quite apart from special measures of protection, he was not adequately protected from ill-treatment contrary to Article 3.[358] The obligation to prevent ill-treatment by private person was infringed in *97 Members of the Gladani Congregation of Jehovah's Witnesses v Georgia*[359] when the police failed to act when Jehovah's Witnesses attending a religious meeting were physically attacked by members of the Orthodox Church.

In a different context, in *Z v UK*[360] the Court found a breach of Article 3 because there was a failure within the state's social services system to take reasonable steps to provide the applicant children with protection from 'serious long-term neglect and abuse' by their parents of which the services had or ought to have known. There was also a breach of the duty of protection in *Mubilanzil Mayeka and Kaniki Mitunga v Belgium*[361] when, in the absence of any other more suitable accommodation, an unaccompanied five-year-old girl was kept by the state for two months in a detention centre for *adult* illegal immigrants, with no one being assigned to her to provide counselling or educational assistance.

In *Pretty v UK*,[362] it was held that a state is not under an obligation under Article 3 to provide in its law or practice for a spouse of an individual in the final stages of an incurable illness to assist in the individual's suicide in order to avoid a distressing death. Although a state may be liable for acts or omissions on its part that exacerbate suffering or humiliation caused by a naturally occurring illness,[363] it has no obligation to protect an individual from a distressing death, involving suffering or humiliation, by authorizing or facilitating suicide in such a case: such an interpretation of Article 3 would require a state to sanction actions intended to end life, which would be inconsistent with the values underlying the right to life in Article 2.

Finally, in terms of protection, Article 3 does not require state A to provide a civil remedy for torture that has occurred in state B where state A has no causal connection, through its agents or otherwise, with the act in question.[364]

II. THE OBLIGATION TO INVESTIGATE AND TO ENFORCE THE LAW

Article 3 also imposes a procedural obligation to investigate and to provide an effective judicial or other remedy in response to an arguable claim of ill-treatment in breach of Article 3.[365] While the comparable Article 2 procedural obligation applies to all Article 2 cases, it is not clear whether the Article 3 obligation has the same general application. The Article 3 obligation was first identified in *Assenov v Bulgaria*,[366] in which a Chamber

---

[358] Cf, the *Akkoc* and other cases on the Article 2 procedural obligation, including *Kaya (Mahmut)* itself, above, p 44.

[359] Hudoc (2007); 46 EHRR 613. The obligation to investigate was also infringed.

[360] 2000-V; 34 EHRR 97 para 74. See also *E v UK* hudoc (2002) (failure to protect children from sexual abuse) and *Okkali v Turkey* 2006-XII (failure to assign lawyer to child accuded). And see *DP and JC v UK* hudoc (2002).

[361] 2006- XI. The Court also seemed to see the case as involving a breach of the negative obligation prohibiting inhuman treatment.   [362] 2002-III; 35 EHRR I para 52.

[363] Eg, deportation or failure to provide medical care: see above, pp 88 and 97. On the positive obligation to provide social assistance, see above, n 322.

[364] *Al-Adsani v UK* 2001-XI; 34 EHRR 273 GC.

[365] See generally, Mowbray, 51 ICLQ 437 (2001). If it finds a breach of the substantive obligation the Court may decide not to rule on the procedural obligation: see *Denizci v Cyprus* 2001-V.

[366] 1998-VIII; 28 EHRR 652. The *Assenov* approach was followed in the pre-*Ihlan* cases of *Labita v Italy* 2000-IV; 46 EHRR 1228 GC and *Veznedaroglu v Turkey* hudoc (2000); 33 EHRR 1412.

of the Court expressly derived it from the Article 2 obligation and supposed that it had the same scope. In *Assenov*, the Court justified the obligation on the basis that it was necessary to make the substantive obligation in Article 3 effective, by preventing the abuse of power by state agents with impunity. However, in *Ihlan v Turkey*[367] a Grand Chamber took a more restrictive approach. It stated that the requirement of an effective remedy in Article 13 was 'generally' sufficient for an individual with an arguable claim of a breach of Article 3,[368] and that the existence of a procedural obligation to investigate under Article 3 would 'depend on the circumstances of the particular case', which, by implication, would be exceptional. The Court explained the difference between Articles 2 and 3 in this respect partly on the textual ground that whereas Article 2 requires that the right to life be 'protected by law', thus providing a basis for inferring a positive procedural obligation to act by way of investigation, Article 3 is phrased purely in terms of a substantive obligation not to torture, etc.[369] In addition, noting that the purpose of a procedural obligation to investigate is to contribute to the effective protection of the Convention right concerned, the Court argued that this purpose can be realized through Article 13 in Article 3 cases more generally than is the case for Article 2. This was so because the individual whose right to life has allegedly been violated will in most cases be dead in Article 2 cases, thus reducing the likelihood of an Article 13 claim being brought and meaning that the knowledge of the facts of the case needed to establish a breach of the Convention right is more likely to be in the hands of the state alone than it is in Article 3 cases.[370] The Grand Chamber's restrictive approach in the *Ihlan* case finds support in the fact that the Court has recognized the importance of an Article 13 remedy in view of the 'fundamental importance' of the prohibition of torture and the 'vulnerable position' of a torture victim.[371] It has the disadvantage that Article 13 may be derogated from in time of public emergency, whereas Article 3 may not.

Following the *Ihlan* approach, two kinds of exceptional circumstances in which the procedural obligation exists have been established. First, in the *Ilhan* case itself the Court stated that it exists in cases in which the evidence before it is insufficient to show beyond a reasonable doubt that a breach of the substantive obligation not to ill-treat has occurred and this was the result 'at least in part'[372] of the failure of the state authorities to conduct an effective investigation, as was true on the facts, the Court noted, in the *Assenov* case.[373] Second, it exists if the applicant has not relied upon Article 13.[374] This second exception is a surprising one, since the Court may always *ex officio* examine a case under an Article not relied upon by the applicant.

However, despite the fact that the ruling in the *Ihlan* case was by a Grand Chamber, in later cases the Court has not always looked for exceptional circumstances. In *Satik v Turkey*,[375] a Chamber of the Court, referring to *Assenov* but not *Ihlan*, applied (and found a breach of) the obligation to investigate simply on the basis that there was an arguable breach of the substantive obligation not to ill-treat in Article 3. Since the Court also found a breach of the latter in the *Sadik* case, that case is also inconsistent with a reading of *Ihlan* by which its restrictive approach applies only where a breach of the substantive obligation

---

[367] 2000-VII; 34 EHRR 869 para 91.   [368] A breach of Article 13 was found in *Ihlan*.

[369] However, as the Court pointed out in *Assenov*, Article I of the Convention requires that parties 'secure' the right in Article 3, which supports an obligation to take positive action, eg by investigating alleged breaches.

[370] In some Article 3 cases also the individual will be dead, as in *Kaya (Mahmut) v Turkey* 2000-III.

[371] *Aksoy v Turkey* 1996-VI; 23 EHRR 553.   [372] *Ihlan v Turkey* 2000-VII 267; 34 EHRR 869 para 90.

[373] The *Labita* and *Veznedaroglu* cases, n 366 above, may also be explained on this basis.

[374] *Dikme v Turkey* 2000-VIII.

[375] Hudoc (2000). Curiously, three of the unanimous *Ihlan* Grand Chamber also sat in *Satik*.

has not been found. Other cases have similarly followed *Assenov* rather than *Ihlan*[376] and it would appear that the Court is moving towards giving the procedural obligation the same general scope that it has in Article 2.

As in the case of Article 2, the procedural obligation in Article 3 to investigate extends to allegations of ill-treatment by private persons as with as state officials. Thus in *MC v Bulgaria*[377] there was a breach of Article 3 when the authorities did not investigate all of the circumstances of the case in a prosecution for rape before deciding not to prosecute. The case was one of 'date rape' in which the authorities focused unduly on the lack of physical resistance, not checking other evidence indicating lack of consent. The Court had considerable evidence before it indicating that European states generally now made lack of consent, not lack of physical resistance, the constituent element of the crime of rape. Since it was not clear whether Bulgarian law followed this approach or not, the Court did not find a breach of Article 3 on the preventative basis that the proper frame-work of law had not been put in place. Instead, it did so on the basis that in any event the investigation had not focused on lack of consent, whether shown by resistance or in other ways, as European standards required.[378] *Macovei v Romania*[379] was another case of ill-treatment by private persons, in which the applicants were seriously injured following an altercation with neighbours. The Court held that there was a breach of Article 3 when there was no possibility of appealing against the prosecutor's decision to bring criminal proceedings.

The procedural obligation in Article 3 requires an 'effective official investigation' that will be thorough and 'capable of leading to the identification and punishment of those responsible'.[380] Such an investigation must be launched *ex officio*, in the absence of a complaint, if there are sufficiently clear indications indications that torture or other ill-treatment has occurred.[381] In *Boicenco v Moldova*[382] the Court stated that this meant that the person conducting the investigation must be independent of those implicated in the alleged ill-treatment, both institutionally and in practice.[383] There was a breach of the latter requirement in the *Boicenco* case on this ground because the investigation was conducted by the prosecutor who had filed criminal charges against the applicant and had applied for his remand in custody. In the same case it was stated that all reasonable steps must be taken to obtain relevant evidence, including forensic[384] and eye-witness evidence. The available witnesses[385] and possible suspects[386] must be questioned and the investigation must be conducted with reasonable expedition.[387] Reasons must be given

---

[376] See *Toteva v Bulgaria* hudoc (2004) and *Boicenco v Moldova* hudoc (2006) in which breaches were found of both the substantive and procedural obligations. In *Poltoratskiy v Ukraine* 2003-V; 39 EHRR 916, in which no substantive breach was found, Judge Bratza argued that *Ihlan* should be followed and that Article 13 was sufficient on the facts, perhaps even in all cases.

[377] 2003-XII; 40 EHRR 459. See Pitea, 3 JICL 447 (2005). On rape as a breach of Article 3, see above, pp 74 and 78.

[378] The Court also found a breach of Article 8. In the earlier case of *X and Y v Netherlands*, below, p 384, the Court had only found a breach of Article 8.

[379] Hudoc (2007).

[380] *Assenov v Bulgaria* 1998-VIII; 28 EHRR 652 para 102. Cf, *Veznedaroglu v Turkey* hudoc (2000); 33 EHRR 1412 (no investigation at all). A failure to investigate possible racial motives for ill-treatment may infringe Articles 3 and 14: *Bekos and Koutropoulos v Greece* 2005-XIII; 43 EHRR 22.

[381] *97 Members of the Gladani Congregation of Jehovah's Witnesses v Georgia* hudoc (2007); 46 EHRR 613.

[382] Hudoc (2006).   [383] *Ibid.*

[384] See also *Poltoratskiy v Ukraine* 2003-V; 39 EHRR 916 (medical examination unduly delayed).

[385] *Assenov v Bulgaria* 1998-VIII; 28 EHRR 652. See also *MC v Bulgaria* 2003-XII; 40 EHRR 459 (confrontation of witnesses required).

[386] *Satik v Turkey* hudoc (2000).   [387] *Labita v Italy* 2000-IV; 46 EHRR 1228 GC.

for rejecting a complaint.[388] All of these requirements feature in the procedural obligation under Article 2 and it is predictable that other elements of the Article 2 obligation will be established as a part of the obligation in Article 3.

The procedural obligation also requires that, where the facts warrant this, the investigation lead to effective criminal, or, where appropriate, civil, disciplinary, or other proceedings for the enforcement of the law against those responsible for the ill-treatment. This requirement was not met when criminal proceedings against police officers for serious physical ill-treatment of a child suspect resulted in the clearly inadequate imposition of only minimum sentences that would anyway not be enforced if no further offences were committed within five years.[389]

8. CONCLUSION

Article 3 has proved a difficult provision to interpret because of the generality of its text. The terms 'inhuman' and 'degrading' especially have no clear legal meaning and tend to be over-used in ordinary speech. As a result, Article 3 has led to an extraordinary variety of complaints. Correspondingly, it offers a considerable opportunity for judicial creativity and in some respects the Court, and formerly the Commission, has not disappointed.

Most striking has been the adoption of the *Soering* principle, so that Article 3 prohibits extradition or deportation to face ill-treatment abroad, whether at the hands of state agents or private individuals. After some early disappointing decisions, the principle has come to be of value in asylum as well as other kinds of cases.[390] Its humanitarian potential in other particular factual situations was graphically illustrated in the AIDS victim case of *D v UK*. Of great importance is the ruling in the *Chahal* and *Saadi* cases that the *Soering* principle is an absolute one, in the sense that a person may not be returned to face ill-treatment however compelling the public interest reason that the returning state may have to remove the person from its territory.

Another development that might also not have been anticipated is that Article 3 has been interpreted so as to impose a positive obligation upon the state to protect individuals from ill-treatment in breach of it. The obligation contains both preventative and investigatory elements. It follows the example of the positive obligation of protection in Article 2, although the preventative obligation is not so well developed as that in Article 2 and the obligation to investigate is not so extensive. The preventative obligation requires a state to take appropriate steps to protect individuals against other private persons, so that, most significantly, there is a duty to protect children from physical and sexual abuse by parents and others.

More predictably, though after a hesitant start, Article 3 has been interpreted as applying to conditions and treatment in prisons, on the basis that they are inhuman or degrading or both. In this connection, the Court is increasingly making use of the findings of the CPT in its reports on prison visits. In the *Kalashnikov* case, the Court confirmed that, in accordance with its general approach, lack of funds is not a defence to a claim of bad prison conditions.

On a related matter, the decision in the *Tomasi* and later cases reversing the burden of proof in cases of physical assault in police stations or in prisons is an important development that reflects evolving international human rights standards.

---

[388] *Poltoratskiy v Ukraine* 2003-V; 39 EHRR 916.
  [389] *Okkali v Turkey* 2006-XII.   [390] See Cruz, 72 Nederlands Juristenblad 672 (1997).

The continuing need for a human rights guarantee for Council of Europe states prohibiting torture has been confirmed by findings of torture by state agents in an increasing
number of cases at Strasbourg, not all of which have involved the ill-treatment of suspected terrorists in an emergency context. The Court signalled its concern in this regard
by its ruling in the *Selmouni* case that the threshold for torture should be lowered in order
to underline the firmness that is needed to protect the fundamental values of democratic
societies. Also of importance in the Court's interpretation of Article 3 is its ruling in the
Aydin case that rape may constitute torture.

Of potential importance for members of minority groups is the ruling by the Court in
Cyprus v Turkey (2002) that discrimination on grounds of ethnic origin, race, or religion
may be in breach of Article 3. Coupled with the positive obligation upon states to control
private conduct, this may cause Article 3 to become a valuable remedy for members of
such groups in discrimination cases.

Although the dynamic or broad interpretation of Article 3 adopted by the Court in
several of the above contexts would scarcely have been anticipated by its drafters, they are
nonetheless in tune with present day European standards.

4

ARTICLE 4: FREEDOM FROM SLAVERY, SERVITUDE, OR FORCED OR COMPULSORY LABOUR

Article 4

1. No one shall be held in slavery or servitude.

2. No one shall be required to perform forced or compulsory labour.

3. For the purpose of this Article the term 'forced or compulsory labour' shall not include:

   (a) any work required to be done in the ordinary course of detention imposed according to the provisions of Article 5 of the Convention or during conditional release from such detention;

   (b) any service of a military character or, in case of conscientious objectors in countries where they are recognised, service exacted instead of compulsory military service;

   (c) any service exacted in case of an emergency or calamity threatening the life or well-being of the community;

   (d) any work or service which forms part of normal civic obligations.

Article 4, which 'enshrines one of the fundamental values of democratic societies',[1] has generated very little case law. *Siliadin v France*[2] is the only case among the few that have been decided by the Court on their merits in which a breach of Article 4 has been found.

1. FREEDOM FROM SLAVERY AND SERVITUDE

Article 4(1) requires that no one 'shall be held in slavery or servitude'. Its importance is underlined by the fact that it contains an absolute guarantee and cannot be derogated from in time of war or public emergency.[3]

In the *Siliadin* case, the Court adopted the 'classic meaning' of slavery that is found in Article 1 of the Slavery Convention 1926.[4] There, slavery is defined as 'the status or condition of a person over whom any or all of the powers attaching to the right of ownership are exercised'. In the *Siliadin* case,[5] the applicant was found not to have been held in slavery as the couple who employed and exercised control over her did not have 'a genuine right of legal right ownership over her, thus reducing her to the status of an "object"'.

---

[1] *Siliadin v France* 2005-VII; 43 EHRR 287 para 112 GC. See Cullen, 6 HRLR 585 (2006).

[2] *Ibid.*   [3] See Article 15(2), Convention.   [4] 60 LNTS 253; UKTS 161 (1927), Cmd 2910.

[5] 2005-VII; 43 EHRR 287 para 122 GC.

In the same case,[6] the Court stated that servitude in Article 4 means 'an obligation to provide one's services that is imposed by the use of coercion'. Although distinct from slavery in that it does not involve legal ownership, servitude is linked to it in that servitude involves 'a particularly serious form of deprivation of liberty' and control over the person concerned. In distinguishing servitude from forced or compulsory labour, the Court adopted the statement by the Commission in the *Van Droogenbroeck* case[7] that the status of servitude includes:

> in addition to the obligation to provide certain services...the obligation on the 'serf' to live on another's property and the impossibility of changing his status.

In the *Van Droogenbroeck* case, the Commission was of the opinion that the applicant was not held in servitude when a court, having convicted him of a criminal offence, ordered that on completion of his prison sentence he should be placed at the disposal of the state for a number of years, during which time he could be recalled for detention. The Commission noted that the applicant was placed at the disposal of the state for only a limited period of time; that any recall decision would be subject to judicial review; and that the resulting detention would be compatible with Article 5 of the Convention. However, as the Court, which also found that the applicant was not held in servitude, stated in the same case, the compatibility of any detention with Article 5 does not by itself prevent it involving servitude contrary to Article 4(1).[8]

In contrast, in the *Siliadin* case, the Court found that the applicant had been held in servitude. In that case, the applicant was brought to France on a tourist visa from her home country, Togo, when a 15-year-old by a Mrs D, with the consent of the applicant's family. She was 'lent' by Mrs D to Mr and Mrs B, and required to work for them for several years as a general housemaid and to look after their four children fifteen hours a day, seven days a week and without pay. Her passport was confiscated, she was not allowed to leave the house without the children and she was encouraged by her employers to fear that she under threat of being arrested as an illegal immigrant. Thus she had no free time or freedom of movement and, as a vulnerable minor with no resources or friends, was completely dependent on Mr and Mrs B, with no prospect of regularizing her status.

The prohibitions of servitude and forced or compulsory labour in Article 4 overlap in that the 'work' or 'service' required of a person in servitude in breach of Article 4(1) may also be forced or compulsory labour contrary to Article 4(2) (see below). However, the degree of overlap is limited by the fact that certain kinds of work that might contribute towards servitude do not count as forced labour because of Article 4(3). Thus in the *Boy Soldiers* cases,[9] while considering that the applicants' military service could not be forced labour because it was excluded by Article 4(3), the Commission none the less assessed it on the merits before deciding that it did not amount to servitude in the sense of Article 4(1).

2. FREEDOM FROM FORCED OR COMPULSORY LABOUR

Under Article 4(2), no one 'shall be required to perform forced or compulsory labour'. In the *Siliadin* case, the Court adopted the meaning of 'forced or compulsory labour' found in the ILO Forced Labour Convention 1930,[10] Article 2 of which defines it as 'all work or

---

[6] Id, para 124.   [7] B 44 Com Rep para 79.   [8] A 50 (1982); 4 EHRR 443.
[9] *W, X, Y and Z v UK* Nos 3435/67–3438/67, 28 CD 109 (1968).
[10] 39 LNTS 55; 134 BFSP 449; Cmd 3693.

service which is exacted from any person under the menace of any penalty and for which the said person has not offered himself voluntarily'. On the facts, the Court found that the applicant was subjected to forced labour (as well as servitude). The fear of arrest, which was encouraged by Mr and Mrs B, amounted to the menace of a penalty, and the applicant's work was not voluntary as she had no choice but to work for them.

Forced or compulsory labour does not include a requirement that a lawyer give his services free to assist indigent defendants. In *Van der Mussele v Belgium*[11] the applicant, a pupil advocate, was called upon to provide such services. As the Court noted, this was part of a longstanding tradition in Belgium and certain other Convention parties by which legal aid was provided on a voluntary basis by the legal profession rather than through the publicly funded legal aid schemes which were now coming to replace such arrangements.[12] The Court held that the work required of the applicant was labour within Article 4(2). Labour ('*travail*' in the French text) extended beyond physical work to all kinds of 'work or service', as became clear from the wording of Article 4(3). The Court then held that the labour was forced or compulsory in the sense of the Forced Labour Convention 1930 definition. Although the applicant had committed no criminal offence by not participating, he would have run the risk of being struck off the roll of pupils. This was sufficient to amount to a 'penalty' for the purposes of Article 4(2). As to whether the applicant had 'offered himself voluntarily', the fact that he had given his prior consent when he became a pupil advocate was not conclusive. However, in a case of prior consent, it required a 'considerable and unreasonable imbalance between the aim pursued'[13]— here entry to the legal profession—and the obligations accepted as a condition of achieving that aim for there to be forced labour. In determining whether that imbalance existed, it was necessary to look at 'all the circumstances of the case'. In the present case, the question was whether the service imposed a 'burden which was so excessive or disproportionate to the advantages attached to the future exercise of [the legal] profession that the service could not be treated as having been voluntarily accepted'.[14] In answering this question in the negative, the Court took into account the fact that the required service was not unconnected with the profession in question; that, in return for it, advocates generally received certain advantages, including the exclusive right of audience in the courts; that the work contributed to a pupil advocate's professional training; that the requirement related to a right guaranteed in the Convention (the right to legal aid: Article 6(3)(c)) and was similar to the 'normal civic obligations' exception allowed by Article 4(3)(d); and that the burden imposed upon the applicant, involving in particular work without remuneration, was not such as to leave him without sufficient time for paid work.[15]

---

[11] A 70 (1983); 6 EHRR 163. Cf, *Gussenbauer v Austria No 5219/71*, 15 YB 558 (1972); F Sett Rep (1974). See also *X v FRG No 4653/70*, 46 CD 22 (1974) and *X v FRG No 8682/79*, 26 DR 97 (1981) (not forced or compulsory labour to pay low fees to lawyers for legal aid work). Free medical examinations required of doctors were not forced or compulsory labour: *Reitmayr v Austria No 23866/94*, 20 EHRR CD 89 (1995). But see *Enders v Germany No 25040/94* hudoc (1996) DA.

[12] The state was responsible under Article 4 for the profession's scheme as it had an obligation to provide legal aid under Article 6(3)(c) of the Convention which it could not delegate to others.

[13] A 70 (1983); 6 EHRR 163 para 40.

[14] Id, para 37. See also *Ackerl et al v Austria*, 78-A DR 116 (1994).

[15] The Court adopted a different, somewhat broader definition of forced labour from the following two part test used by the Commission in *Iversen v Norway No 1468/62*, 6 YB 278 (1963): '...the labour or service must be performed...against his will and...the obligation to perform this labour or service must be either unjust or oppressive or the service itself must constitute an avoidable hardship.' On the facts, the Commission had ruled inadmissible an application by a dentist who was required by Norwegian law on pain of criminal sanction to take paid work on qualifying in the public dental sector for a year and in a part of the country in which dentists

In the small number of other cases in which Article 4(2) has been applied, it has, *inter alia*, been held that it was not forced or compulsory labour to require a notary to charge less for work done for non-profit-making organizations (eg churches),[16] to require an employer to deduct social security payments or income tax from an employee's salary,[17] to require an unemployed person to accept suitable employment as a condition of receiving unemployment benefit,[18] or to move to another job.[19]

3. PERMITTED WORK OR SERVICES

Article 4(3) excludes certain kinds of work or service from the prohibition of forced or compulsory labour in Article 4(2). These kinds of work or service are not restrictions on the exercise of the right protected by Article 4(2), in which case they would be interpreted narrowly; instead they are part of the definition of forced or compulsory labour in Article 4(2) and so serve as an aid to interpretation of that paragraph.

I. WORK DURING DETENTION

Article 4(3)(a) excludes from the prohibition of forced or compulsory labour 'work required to be done in the ordinary course of detention imposed according to the provisions of Article 5' or 'during conditional release from such detention'. This exception includes work required in the course of any kind of detention that is permitted by Article 5(1) of the Convention. It includes, therefore, not only work during detention following conviction by a court of law,[20] which will be the most common case, but also work required of a detained minor[21] or vagrant.[22] The fact that a person whose detention is permitted by Article 5(1) is, in breach of Article 5(4), not provided with a remedy to challenge the legality of his detention does not render any work required of him in detention forced or compulsory labour.[23] Article 4(3)(a) refers to work required during 'the ordinary course of detention'. This wording refers not only to the work that the state concerned ordinarily requires of a detained person; it also incorporates a European standard by which a particular state's practice can be measured. Such scrutiny relates to the purpose of the work required, as well as its nature and extent. Thus in the *Vagrancy* cases,[24] work in a

---

were in short supply. Four members of the majority of the Commission found that the facts did not amount to forced labour. On the *Iversen* case, see Schermers, 11 NILR 366 (1964).

[16] *X v FRG No 8410/78*, 18 DR 216 (1979).

[17] *Four Companies v Austria No 7427/76*, 7 DR 148 (1976). The question whether Article 4 could protect a company was left open. See also *Puzinas v Lithuania No 63767/00* hudoc (2005) (deductions form prison wage to cover board).

[18] *Talmon v Netherlands No 30300/96* hudoc (1997) DA. Cf, *X v Netherlands No 7602/76*, 7 DR 161 (1976).

[19] *Antonov v Russia No 38020/03* hudoc (2005) (no coercion).

[20] See *Van Droogenbroeck v Belgium* A 50 (1982); 4 EHRR 443. This includes work done by a convicted prisoner for a private firm as well as work done in prison: *Twenty One Detained Persons v FRG No 3134/67 et al*, 11 YB 528 (1968).

[21] *X v Switzerland No 8500/79*, 18 DR 238 (1979).   [22] *X v FRG No 770/60*, 6 CD 1 (1960).

[23] *De Wilde, Ooms and Versyp v Belgium (Vagrancy cases)* A 12 (1971); 1 EHRR 373 para 89. Cf, *Van Droogenbroeck v Belgium* A 50 (1982); 4 EHRR 443.

[24] Id, para 90. See also *X v Switzerland No 8500/79*, 18 DR 238 (1979) (work not abnormally long or arduous for a juvenile). In the *Vagrancy cases*, the Court did not consider the size of the 'allowances' or 'wages' paid to detainees which, in common with normal European practice, were small. The Commission has consistently regarded the 'extremely small' amounts commonly paid to working prisoners as consistent with Article 4(3)(a): see eg, *Twenty One Detained Persons v FRG No 3134/67 et al*, 11 YB 528 (1968).

vagrancy centre had not exceeded the limits set by Article 4(3)(a) because it was aimed at the rehabilitation of vagrants and was comparable to that in several other Council of Europe member states.

II. MILITARY SERVICE OR SUBSTITUTE CIVILIAN SERVICE

Article 4(3)(b) excludes 'any service of a military character or, in case of conscientious objectors in countries where they are recognised, service exacted instead of compulsory military service'. There has been no case yet in which the length or conditions of compulsory military service, in those European states that retain it,[25] has been considered. 'Service of a military character' includes voluntary enlistment in the armed forces as well as compulsory military service. This was held in the *Boy Soldiers* cases[26] in the light of the drafting history of Article 4. In those cases, the four applicants had, at the age of fifteen or sixteen and with the consent of their parents, enlisted in the armed forces until the age of eighteen and for a nine-year term thereafter. They could apply for release from the armed forces in certain exceptional circumstances (eg compassionate grounds) and had a statutory right to buy themselves out in the first three months of service. Since voluntary as well as compulsory military service fell within Article 4(3)(b), the applicants were not able to argue that the terms of their service amounted to forced labour. Otherwise, the question whether there was a 'considerable and unreasonable imbalance', as required by the Court in the *Van der Mussele* case, on the facts of the *Boy Soldiers* cases would have been a difficult one to answer. Article 4(3)(b) also excludes from the definition of 'forced labour' compulsory civilian work in substitution for conscription. A conscientious objector who refuses to do such work may be kept in detention for the period of military service. Since the Convention recognizes in Article 4(3)(b) that a conscientious objector may be required to do substitute civilian work, a state may take measures to ensure that such work is done or impose sanctions for non-compliance.[27]

III. COMMUNITY SERVICE IN A PUBLIC EMERGENCY

Article 4(3)(c) excludes 'any service exacted in case of an emergency or calamity threatening the life or well-being of the community'. It was on this basis that two members of the majority of the Commission in the *Iversen* case[28] were of the opinion that the requirement that the applicant serve a year in the public dental service in northern Norway was not forced or compulsory labour. Noting that the Norwegian government had enacted the law imposing the requirement because, in the government's opinion, the shortage of volunteer dentists had created an emergency that threatened the well-being of the community in northern Norway, the two members, applying the margin of appreciation doctrine, accepted the government's assessment of the situation. In another case, the Commission decided that a requirement that a person holding shooting rights over land take part in the gassing of foxholes as a measure of control over rabies was within Article 4(3)(c).[29]

---

[25] At least fifteen Convention parties retain it. The number is declining.

[26] *W, X, Y and Z Nos 3435/67–3438/67*, 28 CD 109 (1968).

[27] *Johansen v Norway No 10600/83*, 44 DR 155 (1985). See also *Grandrath v FRG No 2299/64*, 10 YB 626 (1967) Com Rep; CM Res DH (67) 1 (Jehovah's Witness refusal to do military or substitute civilian service). See further on conscientious objection Article 9, p 432, below.

[28] *No 1468/62*, 6 YB 278 (1963).   [29] *S v FRG No 9686/82*, 39 DR 90 (1984).

IV. NORMAL CIVIC OBLIGATIONS

Finally, Article 4(3)(d) excludes from the prohibition in Article 4(2) 'any work or service which forms part of normal civil obligations'. This includes compulsory jury service[30] and fire service.[31] Having held that it did not amount to forced or compulsory labour, the Court found it unnecessary in the *Van der Mussele* case to decide whether unpaid legal aid work required of pupil advocates came within Article 4(3)(d). In other cases, the Commission has ruled the following to be 'normal civic obligations': obligations imposed by the state upon a lessor to arrange for the maintenance of his building,[32] upon a holder of shooting rights to participate in the gassing of foxholes[33] and upon an employer to deduct taxes from an employee's income.[34] Discrimination between men and women in the imposition of a civil obligation may be a breach of Article 4 and Article 14, as success- fully claimed by male applicants in the *Zarb Adami* and *Schmidt* cases for discrimination in respect of jury and fire service.[35]

4. POSITIVE OBLIGATIONS

As well as imposing upon states parties a negative obligation not to subject persons to slavery, servitude or forced or compulsory labour, Article 4 also contains a positive obli- gation requiring them to protect persons from subjection thereto at the hands of state officials or private persons. In particular, the Court established in the *Siliadin* case that states parties have a positive obligation 'to adopt criminal law provisions which penal- ise the practices referred to in Article 4 and to apply them in practice'.[36] In reaching this conclusion, the Court reasoned that limiting compliance with Article 4 only to a negative obligation would be inconsistent with contemporary international norms and trends[37] and would render Article 4 ineffective. In the *Siliadin* case, the applicant's employers had been convicted of offences of exploiting an individual's labour and submitting him or her to working conditions incompatible with human dignity, but the convictions had been quashed on appeal. However, a court order of compensation for the applicant had been made. The Court held that this civil remedy was insufficient. Given that a breach of Article 4 involved a breach of a fundamental value of democratic societies and the par- ticular vulnerability of children, the criminal law legislation in place, which had been interpreted and applied so as not to punish those responsible for subjecting the applicant to servitude and forced or compulsory labour, did not afford her the effective protection that Article 4 demanded.

5. CONCLUSION

For many years, Article 4 had little impact. This may change as a result of the *Siliadin* case, which has signalled the relevance of Article 4 to what are sometimes called modern forms of slavery. These currently present much more serious human rights issues in European

[30] *Zarb Adami v Malta* (2006)-VIII; 44 EHRR 49.
[31] *Schmidt v Germany* A 291-B (1994); 18 EHRR 513 para 22.
[32] *X v Austria* No 5593/72, 45 CD 113 (1973).   [33] *S v FRG* No 9686/82, 39 DR 90 (1984).
[34] *Four Companies v Austria* No 7427/76, 7 DR 148 (1976).   [35] See nn 30 and 31 above.
[36] 2005-VII; 43 EHRR 287 para 89.
[37] The Court referred, *inter alia*, to the ILO Forced Labour Convention 1930, Article 4 and the Convention on the Rights of the Child 1989, Article 32.

states than the traditional forms of ill-treatment that are associated with slavery, servitude and forced or compulsory labour in response to which Article 4 was drafted.[38] In the light of the *Siliadin* case, it is clear that, where the circumstances amount to forced labour, Article 4 can be applied beyond cases of the domestic labour kind present on its facts to human trafficking for sexual and other migrant labour and other purposes and to govern both adult (mainly women) and child labour. Equally important is the establishment of a positive obligation to protect persons from the abuse involved in such trafficking by the enactment and proper enforcement of appropriate criminal law offences.[39]

---

[38] See Salt, 38 Int Migration 31 (2000) and Kelly, 43 id 235.

[39] See also the Council of Europe Convention Against Trafficking in Human Beings 2005, ETS 197. In force 2008. Seventeen parties. And see the Protocol to Prevent, Suppress and Punish Trafficking in Persons, Especially Women and Children (the Palermo Protocol) to the UN Convention Against Transnational Organized Crime 2000.

5

ARTICLE 5: THE RIGHT TO LIBERTY AND SECURITY OF THE PERSON

Article 5

5(1) Everyone has the right to liberty and security of person. No one shall be deprived of his liberty save in the following cases and in accordance with a procedure prescribed by law:

(a) the lawful detention of a person after conviction by a competent court;

(b) the lawful arrest or detention of a person for non-compliance with the lawful order of a court or in order to secure the fulfilment of any obligation prescribed by law;

(c) the lawful arrest or detention of a person effected for the purpose of bringing him before the competent legal authority on reasonable suspicion of having committed an offence or when it is reasonably considered necessary to prevent his committing an offence or fleeing after having done so;

(d) the detention of a minor by lawful order for the purpose of educational supervision or his lawful detention for the purpose of bringing him before the competent legal authority;

(e) the lawful detention of persons for the prevention of the spreading of infectious diseases, of persons of unsound mind, alcoholics or drug addicts or vagrants;

(f) the lawful arrest or detention of a person to prevent his effecting an unauthorised entry into the country or of a person against whom action is being taken with a view to deportation or extradition.

(2) Everyone who is arrested shall be informed promptly, in a language which he understands, of the reasons for his arrest and of any charge against him.

(3) Everyone arrested or detained in accordance with the provisions of paragraph 1(c) of this article shall be brought promptly before a judge or other officer authorised by law to exercise judicial power and shall be entitled to trial within a reasonable time or to release pending trial. Release may be conditioned by guarantees to appear for trial.

(4) Everyone who is deprived of his liberty by arrest or detention shall be entitled to take proceedings by which the lawfulness of his detention shall be decided speedily by a court and his release ordered if the detention is not lawful.

(5) Everyone who has been the victim of arrest or detention in contravention of the provisions of this article shall have an enforceable right to compensation.

1. ARTICLE 5: GENERALLY[1]

Article 5(1) protects the 'right to liberty and security of person'. The notion of 'liberty' here covers the physical liberty of the person,[2] which the Court views alongside Articles 2, 3, and 4 as 'in the first rank of the fundamental rights that protect the physical security of an individual'.[3] The Court's jurisprudence contains several statements affirming the paramount importance of the right to liberty in a democratic society,[4] its relationship with the principle of legal certainty and the rule of law, and generally explaining that the overall purpose of Article 5 is to ensure that no one should be dispossessed of his liberty in an 'arbitrary fashion'.[5]

In keeping with those principles, any loss of liberty requires a legal basis in accordance with the grounds exhaustively set out in paragraphs (a) to (f) of Article 5(1). The restrictions found here are much narrower than those under Articles 8(2)–11(2) and are generally interpreted restrictively by the Court.[6] They repeatedly emphasize the procedural and substantive lawfulness of detention.

Article 5(2)–(5) guarantee 'a corpus of substantive rights which are intended to minimize the risks of arbitrariness by allowing the act of deprivation of liberty to be amenable to independent judicial scrutiny and by securing the accountability of the authorities for that act'.[7] In particular, Article 5(2) requires that reasons be given to a detainee for his arrest. Article 5(3) requires prompt judicial control over detainees facing criminal charges (Article 5(1)(c)) and the need for there to be a trial within a reasonable time. It requires the state to justify detention at all stages, and to release the detainee, on bail if necessary, unless there is a good reason to continue holding him. Article 5(4) applies to all categories of detainee and requires a remedy by which the detainee can challenge the legality of his detention (at reasonable intervals for some categories of detainee). By Article 5(5) an applicant should have an enforceable right to compensation in domestic law if there has been a breach of Article 5(1)–(4).

All kinds of detention by the state are controlled by Article 5 and the right applies to 'everyone', including for example personnel in the military who may be the subject of special legal regimes.[8] Most cases that have arisen have concerned arrest and detention in the context of criminal proceedings, but there have been many other important cases on such matters as the detention of minors, the mentally disordered, and persons being deported or extradited. In two relatively recent cases where there has been a clear violation of Article 5 the Court has taken the exceptional measure of ruling that the state concerned should take appropriate steps to secure the release of the individual concerned.[9]

---

[1] See Kohl, 108 JT 485 at 505 (1989); Macovei, *The right to liberty and security of the person*, 2002; Murdoch, 42 ICLQ 494 (1993); Trechsel, 1 HRLJ 88 (1980); id, *European System*, Ch 13 and id, *Human Rights in Criminal Proceedings*, 2005, Chs 17–19.

[2] *Engel v Netherlands* A 22 (1976); 1 EHRR 706 para 58 PC.

[3] *McKay v UK* 2006-X; 44 EHRR 827 para 30 GC.

[4] See eg, *Winterwerp v Netherlands* A 33 (1979); 2 EHRR 387 para 37; *Storck v Germany* 2005-V; 43 EHRR 96 para 102.

[5] See eg, *Engel v Netherlands* A 22 (1976); 1 EHRR 706 PC para 58; *Bozano v France* A 111 (1986); 9 EHRR 297 para 54; *Assanidze v Georgia* 2004-II; 39 EHRR 653 para 175 GC.

[6] Cf *McKay v UK* 2006-X; 44 EHRR 827 para 30 GC.

[7] *Kurt v Turkey* 1998-III; 27 EHRR 373 para 123.   [8] See below at p 125.

[9] *Assanidze v Georgia* 2004-II; 39 EHRR 653 para 203 GC (detention in defiance of domestic court order for release); *Ilaşcu v Moldova* 2004-VII; 40 EHRR 1030 para 490 GC (detention ordered by a court of a regime not recognized in international law).

2. THE MEANING OF ARREST OR DETENTION (IE LOSS OF 'LIBERTY')

The Court has stated that loss of liberty under Article 5 contains both an 'objective element' ('confinement in a particular restricted space for a not negligible length of time'),[10] and 'an additional subjective element' in that a detainee must not have validly consented to the confinement in question[11] (assuming the detainee has the capacity to provide such consent).

I. LOSS OF LIBERTY

As regards the 'objective' element just referred to, arrest or detention[12] in the sense of Article 5 is an extreme form of restriction upon freedom of movement, which is a separate right and generally protected by Article 2, Fourth Protocol to the Convention.[13] There have been several cases in different factual contexts in which the Strasbourg authorities have had to draw the line between these two provisions.

The classic case of detention in the sense of Article 5 occurs when a person is kept securely in a closed prison. However, Article 5 is not confined to this situation. As the Court has put it, '[d]eprivation of liberty may...take numerous other forms. Their variety is being increased by developments in legal standards and in attitudes; and the Convention is to be interpreted in the light of the notions currently prevailing in democratic States'.[14] This was demonstrated by *Guzzardi v Italy*.[15] There the applicant was required by a judicial compulsory residence order to live for sixteen months on a remote island off the coast of Sardinia on suspicion of illegal Mafia activities. He was restricted to a hamlet in an area of the island of some 2.5 sq kilometres that was occupied solely by persons subject to such orders, although the applicant's wife and child were allowed to live with him. While the applicant could move freely within the area and there was no perimeter fence, he could not visit other parts of the island. Islanders were allowed to enter the area, but seldom did so. The applicant had to report to officials twice daily and was subject to a curfew. Drawing an analogy with the conditions typically found in a modern-day open prison, the Court held, by eleven to seven, that the applicant's conditions involved a sufficient degree of deprivation of liberty to fall within Article 5. The ruling on this point was crucial as there was no sub-paragraph of Article 5(1) that could justify the applicant's detention and Italy was not at the relevant time a party to the Fourth Protocol.

In the *Guzzardi* case, the Court gave some general guidance as to the approach that should be followed when setting the parameters of Article 5. It stated that the distinction between restrictions upon freedom of movement serious enough to fall within it and others subject only to the Fourth Protocol is 'merely one of degree or intensity, and not one of nature or substance'.[16] When assessing whether the required 'degree or intensity' of restriction exists, regard must be had to 'a whole range of criteria such as the type, duration, effects and manner of implementation of the measure in question'.[17] As to the duration of detention, in other cases very short periods of detention fall within Article 5 in

---

[10] *Storck v Germany* 2005-V; 43 EHRR 96 para 74.   [11] *Ibid.*

[12] No legal consequence turns upon the distinction between these two terms.

[13] See below, Ch 21.   [14] *Guzzardi v Italy* A 39 (1980); 3 EHRR 333 para 95 PC.   [15] Id.

[16] Id, para 93.

[17] Id, para 92, adopting the language of *Engel v Netherlands* A 22 (1976); 1 EHRR 706 para 59 PC. Cf, *Ashingdane v UK* A 93 (1985); 7 EHRR 528.

typical cases of close arrest by the police and other public authorities.[18] As the *Guzzardi* case demonstrates, however, as the degree of physical constraint lessens (for example, from that in a prison cell to that in a hamlet), so considerations such as social isolation and the other circumstances of detention identified by the Court come into play.[19]

It is clear that house arrest for twenty-four hours a day is a deprivation of liberty.[20] However, in what circumstances might a home curfew, combined with other restrictions, amount to a deprivation of liberty within the meaning of Article 5?[21] In accordance with *Guzzardi*, one must look to the facts of the case and the concrete situation of the applicant in order to assess the degree of restriction upon freedom of movement applicable and the general extent to which the state regulates the day to day life of the individual. Whilst the period of confinement is clearly a key factor, the impact of other restrictions both during and outside the confinement period are critical too. For example, *Raimondo v Italy*[22] concerned special police supervision whereby the applicant was not allowed to leave his home without telling the police, had to report to them on such days, and had to stay at home between 9 pm and 7 am unless there were valid reasons for not doing so and the authorities were informed of his absence first. There was no deprivation of liberty, but a mere restriction on the liberty of movement to which Article 2, Fourth Protocol applied.[23] Article 5 did not apply either to an applicant's 'home arrest' which operated between 7 pm and 7 am weekdays and at all hours during the weekend, for the applicant was 'allowed to spend time at work as well as at home' during the (almost) sixteen-month period during which the regime operated.[24] So this admissibility decision looked to the extent of the control imposed by the state outside the curfew period and also took into account that the applicant was restricted to his own home, rather than another place. It would seem then that if the individual can maintain a (relatively) normal daily balance between work and home then there may not be a deprivation of liberty[25] It is implicit in this decision too that an individual may be required to stay at his home for up to twelve hours a day, and even the whole weekend, without this being a loss of liberty under Article 5. It may be noted, however, that the Court has stated generally that there is a loss of liberty for non-consensual 'confinement in a particular restricted space for a not negligible length of time'.[26] Perhaps when making this statement the Court principally had in mind physical, 'institutional' confinement of the individual by the state. If the statement is of general application it is hard to see why Article 5 does

---

[18] See below, p 125.

[19] See also *Guzzardi v Italy No 7960/77* (1977) unreported (Article 5 inapplicable when 'Guzzardi' transferred to mainland and restricted to an inhabited village where living conditions were the same as those for other residents, except reporting obligation). See also *Cyprus v Turkey (First and Second Applications)*, below at n 20.

[20] See *NC v Italy* 2002-X para 33 GC and *Nikolova v Bulgaria (No 2)* hudoc (2004) para 60. For older authorities see the *Greek case*: 12 YB (the *Greek case*) 1 at 134–5 Com Rep; CM Res DH (70) 1. Article 5 applied to compulsory confinement by Turkish troops of Greek Cypriots to detention centres/private houses/hotel: *Cyprus v Turkey (First and Second Applications) Nos 6780/74 and 6950/75*; 4 EHRR 482 at 529 (1976) Com Rep; CM Res DH (79) 1. There was a breach of Article 5(1). Cf, *Cyprus v Turkey (Third Application)*; 15 EHRR 509 (1983) Com Rep; CM Res DH (92) 12.

[21] This has been of great relevance to anti-terrorism 'control orders' in the UK see *Secretary of State for the Home Department v JJ & Others* [2007] UKHL 45.

[22] A 281-A (1994); 18 EHRR 237 para 39.

[23] In another application, the Commission took the view that some Greek Cypriots' confinement to a village by Turkish troops was subject to the Fourth Protocol, not Article 5, see *Cyprus v Turkey*, above n 20, 4 EHRR 482 at 524 (1976) Com Rep. Cf, *Aygun v Sweden No 14102/88*, 63 DR 195 (1989) (restriction to Stockholm not subject to Article 5) and *SF v Switzerland No 16360/90*, 76A DR 13 (1994) (restriction to Italian enclave surrounded by Switzerland not subject to Article 5).

[24] *Trijonis v Lithuania No 2333/02* hudoc (2005) DA (citing *Guzzardi* paras 90–5).

[25] See also *JJ & Others v SSHD* [2006] EWHC 1623 (Admin) *per* Sullivan J at para 77.

[26] *Storck v Germany* 2005-V; 43 EHRR 96 para 74.

not apply in some of the cases just mentioned, unless the fact of confinement in a home makes a difference (it is still, however, likely to be a 'restricted space'). A ruling from the Court clarifying such matters and the general scope of Article 5 in the context of 'control regimes' would be welcome.

In practice, most cases of arrest or detention occur at the hands of the police in connection with criminal proceedings. Detention for a period of fifty-five minutes has been held to qualify in a case where the applicant was deemed to be behaving suspiciously and taken to a police station for the purposes of verifying his identity.[27] In most circumstances it can be taken that where a policeman, by physical restraint or by words or conduct, indicates to a person that he is not free to leave, there is an arrest for the purposes of Article 5. So it is submitted that a person who is made to believe that he is obliged to remain when stopped on the street or elsewhere by the police for the purpose of being questioned, searched, or subjected to a test in the administration of the criminal law should be protected by Article 5.[28] That Article would clearly apply were the person led away and/or handcuffed.[29]

Cases concerning the detention of the mentally ill illustrate that for Article 5 what counts is not so much whether the person is held under 'locked' conditions, but the extent to which he or she is in fact subject to a regime of continuous supervision and control, plus whether in practice he or she would be free to leave were this to be an issue.[30] In *Ashingdane v UK*,[31] a person kept compulsorily in a mental hospital under a detention order was protected by Article 5, even though he was in an 'open' (ie unlocked) ward and was permitted to leave the hospital unaccompanied during the day and over the weekend. The position would have been different if, although still subject to a detention order, he had been provisionally released.[32] Article 5 also applied in the case of *HL v UK*,[33] which concerned a vulnerable incapacitated individual treated within a psychiatric institution as an 'informal patient' rather than one compulsorily detained under mental health legislation. Owing to his state of mental health he had been compliant and unable to express his consent or objection to his admission and continued residence in the psychiatric institution, which he had never attempted to leave. The evidence was not entirely clear whether he was or was not held in 'locked' conditions, however either way Article 5 applied as the reality of the 'concrete' situation facing the applicant was that the health care professionals had exercised 'complete and effective control over his care and movements'.[34]

As far as restrictions upon the freedom of movement of members of the armed forces are concerned, in *Engel v Netherlands*[35] the Court stated that restrictions that follow from 'normal conditions of life within the armed forces of the contracting states' do not

---

[27] *Novotka v Slovakia No 47244/99* hudoc (2003) DA (taken against will and held in a cell; 'the relatively short duration of the interference' did not change the fact that there had been a deprivation of liberty). See also *X v Austria No 8278/78*, 18 DR 154 (1979) (short period of restraint for the purpose of a blood test) and *X and Y v Sweden No 7376/76*, 7 DR 123 (1976) (detained less than two hours for the purpose of deportation). Although problems may arise in complying with the procedural guarantees in Article 5 if it applies to very short periods of detention (see Trechsel, *European System*, p 288), they are not insuperable.

[28] See, however, *R (on the application of Gillan) v Commissioner of Police of the Metropolis* [2006] UKHL 12 (Lord Bingham at para 25) and [2004] EWCA 1067 (Lord Woolf at paras 36–46). In fact, detention to conduct a normal stop and search is potentially covered by Article 5(1)(b): see below at p 142.

[29] Id, Lord Bingham para 25.   [30] Cf, *HL v UK* 2004-IX; 40 EHRR 761 paras 91–2.

[31] A 93 (1985); 7 EHRR 528 para 42. Contrast *Nielsen v Denmark*, below at p 127.

[32] *W v Sweden No 12778/87*, 59 DR 158 (1988) and *L v Sweden No 10801/84*, 61 DR 62 (1988). Cf, *Weeks v UK* A 114 (1987); 13 EHRR 435 PC (applicant out on licence, ie 'free', when recalled to hospital; Article 5 applied at that point (the recall) as 'liberty' was a question of fact).   [33] 2004-IX; 40 EHRR 761.

[34] Id, para 91 (despite powerful objections from the respondent government, para 80).

[35] A 22 (1976); 1 EHRR 706 para 59 PC.

involve a deprivation of liberty. However, further constraint, including that which results from a sentence imposed for a military disciplinary offence, may be such as to fall within Article 5. Thus in the *Engel* case it was held that the 'strict arrest' of soldiers, by which they were locked in a cell in army barracks and accordingly unable to carry out their normal duties, fell within Article 5. *A fortiori*, their committal to a military disciplinary unit was subject to Article 5. In contrast, their 'aggravated arrest', by which soldiers continued with their normal duties but were confined during off-duty hours to a specially designated building within army premises, but not locked up, did not. This ruling should be seen in the special context of military detention.[36]

In exceptional circumstances Article 5 may apply even though the authorities are not literally 'detaining' individuals as they are, technically, free to leave. *Amuur v France*[37] concerned individuals who were denied entry to France and spent twenty days in the international transit zone at Paris airport, this being the time it took for their asylum applications to be refused. They were then returned to Syria. Over the twenty days they had been closely monitored by the police but essentially left to their own devices. They had been free to exit France but in reality they were deprived of legal and social assistance and had nowhere else to go, indeed their return to Syria only became possible following Franco-Syrian negotiations which secured assurances that the applicants would not be shuttled back to Somalia (Syria was not bound by the Geneva Convention relating to the Status of Refugees).[38] Article 5 applied for the holding in the international zone of the airport was, on the facts, 'equivalent in practice, in view of the restrictions suffered, to a deprivation of liberty'.[39] Emphasis was placed upon the fact that the individuals concerned were asylum seekers and so likely to be in a vulnerable situation. In order to prevent Article 5 from applying, the 'restriction upon liberty' involved could only be brief, ie long enough to 'enable states to prevent unlawful immigration while complying with their international obligations [under the Refugee Convention and the ECHR]'.[40] In another case concerning asylum seekers in a transit zone, this time for over one month at Vienna airport, the Court considered that Article 5 did not apply.[41] Unlike in *Amuur*, the asylum applications were processed in three days and it was the applicants' choice to stay thereafter. Further the applicants had declined an offer to be lodged in a specially equipped zone, were not generally kept under special police surveillance, so they could 'go about their daily lives and ... correspond and make contact with third parties without interference or supervision by the Austrian authorities', and throughout legal and social assistance was provided by a humanitarian organization. The Court did not accept that the applicants' situation was 'in practice comparable with or equivalent to the situation of persons in detention'.

II. ABSENCE OF CONSENT

As noted above, Article 5 also has 'an additional subjective element'[42] in that a detainee must not have validly consented to the confinement in question. Evidently a person can only properly consent if he or she has the capacity to do so.[43] If a person has such capacity

---

[36] In a civilian context, house arrest will, and curfew may raise Article 5 issues, see text accompanying n 21 above.

[37] 1996-III; 22 EHRR 533. See also *Shamsa v Poland* hudoc (2003).   [38] Id, para 48.

[39] Id, para 49 (Court concluded violation of Article 5(1), unanimously; the Commission thought Article 5 inapplicable as applicants could leave by flying elsewhere. Cf, *S v Austria No 19066/91*, 74 DR 179 (1993)).

[40] Id, para 43.   [41] See *Mahdid and Haddar v Austria No 74762/01* hudoc (2006) DA.

[42] *Storck v Germany* 2005-V; 43 EHRR 96 para 74.

[43] Id, para 76.

it is assumed that they gave consent to the way they were treated if they did not raise objections at the time.[44] In *Storck* the facts were unclear as to whether the applicant's confinement in a psychiatric institution was consensual or not. The Court inferred from the fact that she had tried to escape on several occasions that it was non-consensual.[45] Of course, even if consent is given it can be withdrawn. As the Court has put it, 'the right to liberty is too important in a democratic society for a person to lose the benefit of Convention protection for the single reason that he may have given himself up to be taken into detention..., especially when it is not disputed that that person is legally incapable of consenting to, or disagreeing with, the proposed action'.[46]

Article 5 protects children as well as adults, and so the question arises as to the relationship between Article 5 and an exercise of parental rights leading to a child's detention. In *Nielsen v Denmark*,[47] a state hospital placed a twelve-year-old boy in a closed psychiatric ward at the request of his mother, who had sole parental rights, for treatment for his neurotic condition. The son, acting through his father, claimed that the resulting detention was a deprivation of his liberty against his will contrary to Article 5. The Court saw the case as one of the exercise of parental rights by the mother, not one involving a restriction upon freedom of movement by the state. It noted that the exercise of such rights was a fundamental element of family life, respect for which was recognized as a right in Article 8 of the Convention,[48] and that parental rights in the law of the contracting parties to the Convention included parental competence 'to decide where the child must reside and also impose, or authorise others to impose, various restrictions on the child's liberty'.[49] These restrictions, the Court stated, included rules with which a child must comply within 'a school or other educational or recreational institution'[50] and decisions as to hospitalization for medical treatment. They presumably also include disciplinary measures taken by parents involving detention at home. Although such parental restrictions might appear to fall within Article 5, the Court held that Article 5 was simply not intended to apply to them, provided that they were imposed for a 'proper purpose'.[51] This was the case on the facts of the *Nielsen* case as the mother had consented to her child's hospitalization for the protection of his health, not as a means of keeping him away from his father, as had been suggested. The Court concluded, therefore, that the hospitalization of the applicant did not bring Article 5 into play as it 'was a responsible exercise by his mother of her custodial rights in the interest of the child'.[52] It noted, however, that in principle 'the rights of the holder of parental authority cannot be unlimited and that it is incumbent on the state to

---

[44] *Ibid*; see also *HL v UK* 2004-IX; 40 EHRR 761 at para 93.

[45] Id, paras 77–8.

[46] *HL v UK* 2004-IX; 40 EHRR 761 para 90. See also *De Wilde, Ooms and Versyp v Belgium* A 12 (1971); 1 EHRR 373 para 65 PC and *Storck v Germany* 2005-V; 43 EHRR 96 para 75.

[47] A 144 (1988); 11 EHRR 175 PC.   [48] See below, Ch 9.

[49] *Nielsen v Denmark* A 144 (1988); 11 EHRR 175 para 61 PC.

[50] Usually the obligation to attend school and to accept disciplinary rules (including, perhaps, detention as punishment) are a state-imposed legal obligation (ie not a matter of parental consent). Taking of a child into public care/placing in a children's home does not automatically raise Article 5 issues (see *Family T v Austria No 14013/88*, 64 DR 176 (1989)), however, actual detention in such an environment may do so.

[51] Cf, the requirement of lack of 'arbitrariness' in respect of the exceptions to the 'right to liberty' permitted by Article 5(1)(a)–(f). The exercise of parental rights would also need to be lawful under municipal law.

[52] *Nielsen v Denmark* A 144 (1988); 11 EHRR 175 para 73 PC. The Court subsequently distinguished the factual scenario existing in *Nielsen* from that in *HL v UK* 2004-IX; 40 EHRR 761 (discussed above) on the basis that in the later case the hospital did not have legal authority to act on the applicant's behalf in the same way as the mother in *Nielsen* (see para 93).

provide safeguards against abuse'.[53] The judgment was by twelve votes to seven with the dissenting judges,[54] like the Commission, considering that there had been a sufficient restriction upon the son's freedom of movement to make the case one of detention within Article 5 and that, although the case involved parental consent, the state was responsible for the detention, having 'associated itself with it through the action and assistance of its organs and officials'.[55] The better and it is submitted, acceptable,[56] rationale for the Court's decision in *Nielsen* is that there is an implied limitation to the right to liberty in Article 5 that follows from the conjunction of Articles 5 and 8 as regards the 'responsible' exercise of parental rights in the interests of the child.

The Court drew a comparison with the *Nielsen* case in *HM v Switzerland*,[57] where a neglected pensioner, unable to perform the necessities of life such as nourishment and hygiene, and whose appalling living conditions and deteriorating state of health reflected this, had been placed in a nursing home against her will (initially at least). The precise reasons for the Court's conclusion that Article 5 did not apply are not entirely clear. It was intimated, for example, that the applicant did not ultimately truly object to what had occurred and pointed out that she was not placed in a secure ward, had freedom of movement and was able to maintain social contact with the outside world.[58] Taking the facts as a whole, in particular the fact that domestic authorities had concluded that the applicant's placement in the nursing home was in her own interests in order to provide her with the necessary medical care, satisfactory living conditions, and standards of hygiene, and also taking into consideration the comparable circumstances in *Nielsen*, the Court concluded that there had been no deprivation of liberty, rather what had occurred was 'a responsible measure taken by the competent authorities in the applicant's interests'.[59] Happily this phraseology has not been repeated in subsequent case law. Indeed, in his dissent in *HM*, Judge Loucaides warned, amongst other things, of the dangers of an approach to Article 5 which relied too much on whether the action was intended to serve the interests of the person concerned, and which might be abused by the state or 'scheming relatives'. Other separate opinions in the Court's jurisprudence have stressed the need for unremitting vigilance as regards psychiatric committal to avoid the abuse of legislative systems and hospital structures.[60] Certainly any trend whereby the scope or

---

[53] Id, para 72.

[54] Judges Thor Vilhjalmsson, Pettiti, Russo, Spielman, De Meyer, Carrillo Salcedo, and Valticos.

[55] See below p 129 (private detention) and cf, *Koniarska v UK No 33670/96* hudoc (2000) DA (local authority had care orders in respect of the seventeen-year-old child; Article 5 applied since order placing child in secure accommodation made by a court which did not have parental rights). See also *DG v Ireland* 2002-III; 35 EHRR 1153 para 72.

[56] For criticism see Murdoch, 42 ICLQ 494 at 498 (1993), Trechsel, *European System*, p 287 and Kilkenny, *The Child and the European Convention on Human Rights*, 1999, pp 34–8.

[57] 2002-II; 28 EHRR 17.

[58] In *Nielsen*, the Court also suggested, rather dubiously, that, in any event, the restriction involved in the applicant's placement in a 'closed' psychiatric ward, which 'did not, in principle, differ from those obtaining in many hospital wards where children with physical disorders are treated', was not a deprivation of liberty in the sense of Article 5 (para 72). Moreover, the reasoning on this point in both *Nielsen* and *HM* (freedom of movement and social contact) is inconsistent with the Court's decision concerning detention in a mental hospital in the *Ashingdane* case, above p 125. On this point see the dissenting opinion of Judge Loucaides in *HM*.

[59] Id, para 48. (Judges Jörundsson and Loucaides argued that Article 5 was applicable: Judge Jörundsson considered the detention justified under Article 5(1)(e) (unsound mind); Judge Loucaides thought Article 5(1)(b) could apply given appropriate national legislation). See *HL v UK* 2004-IX; 40 EHRR 761 para 93, where the Court argued that in *HM* Article 5 had been inapplicable as the applicant's situation in the nursing home was not of a '"degree" or "intensity" sufficiently serious to justify the conclusion that she was detained'. See also *Storck v Germany* 2005-V; 43 EHRR 96 para 77.

[60] See the separate opinion of Judge Pettiti in *Nielsen v Denmark* A 144 (1988); 11 EHRR 175 PC.

application of Article 5 is curtailed must be treated with great caution given the importance of the right to liberty.[61]

3. LOSS OF LIBERTY: FURTHER ISSUES

I. ENGAGING THE RESPONSIBILITY OF THE STATE AND
THE EXISTENCE OF POSITIVE OBLIGATIONS TO
CONTROL PRIVATE DETENTION

Article 5 may be of relevance to various situations where the person(s) directly responsible for detention are private individual(s), as opposed to public authorities. *Storck v
Germany*[62] concerned the detention, in confusing circumstances and against the background of family conflict, of an eighteen-year-old in a private psychiatric institution on
the instructions of her father. Over the next two years she tried to escape a number of
times and at least once was forcibly returned by the police. The Court stated that the first
sentence of Article 5(1) lays down a positive obligation on the state to protect the liberty
of its citizens. Such a conclusion, it noted, is in keeping with its case law on Articles 2,
3, and 8, reflects 'the importance of personal liberty in a democratic society', and plugs
what would otherwise be a 'sizeable gap in the protection from arbitrary detention'.[63]
Therefore, the state is 'obliged to take measures providing effective protection of vulnerable persons, including reasonable steps to prevent deprivation of liberty of which the
authorities have or ought to have knowledge'.[64] Hence, private psychiatric institutions
must not only be licensed but regularly supervised and controlled to check that confinement and medical treatment is justified.[65]

A deprivation of liberty effected by non-state authorities may be imputed to a respondent state in several ways.[66] First, the state might breach the positive obligation just identified. Secondly, the state authorities may become actively involved in private detention, as
when an applicant flees from a private psychiatric unit and, despite express objections,
the police forcefully return him or her. Such circumstances should prompt the police
or another state authority to review the lawfulness of the private detention.[67] In *Riera
Blume v Spain*[68] the adult applicants had been brainwashed by a religious sect. Although
initially detained, their release was ordered. However, contrary to judicial instruction
the police transported the unwilling applicants to a location where they were detained
by their relatives for a number of days for 'de-programming'. Subsequent visits by the
police confirmed that they were aware of the applicants' ongoing situation. The Court
considered that 'the national authorities at all times acquiesced in the applicants' loss

---

[61] The same may be said for an overly broad reading of the legitimate grounds for detention as listed under
Article 5(1)(a)–(f). See the discussion of the meaning of 'alcoholics' under Article 5(1)(e) in *Witold Litwa v
Poland* 2000-III; 33 EHRR 1267, below at p 154.

[62] 2005-V; 43 EHRR 96.   [63] Id, para 102.   [64] *Ibid.*

[65] Id, paras 103 and 108 (Article 5 breached as private detention would not have occurred if proper supervision had been in place).

[66] Cf, *Cyprus v Turkey* 2001-IV; 35 EHRR 731 para 81 GC and *Ilaşcu v Moldova* 2004-VII; 40 EHRR 1030 para
318 GC (state responsibility may be engaged via authorities' 'acquiescence or connivance... in the acts of private
individuals which violate the Convention rights of other individuals'). As regards the Convention's applicability
to possible secret detention facilities administered by a third state on the territory of a Convention state, eg at a
military base, see *Opinion on the International Legal Obligations of Council of Europe Member States in Respect
of Secret Detention Facilities and Inter-State Transport of Prisoners* adopted by the Venice Commission at its
66th Plenary Session (17–18 March 2006), CDL-AD(2006)009.

[67] *Storck v Germany* 2005-V; 43 EHRR 96 paras 91 and 106.   [68] 1999-VII; 30 EHRR 632.

of liberty'. Whilst others bore the direct and immediate responsibility for the supervision of the applicants, the detention needed the active co-operation of the authorities. Article 5(1) applied as 'the ultimate responsibility for the matters complained of…lay with the authorities in question'.[69]

Finally, state responsibility under the Convention for a private detention may occur when, in a subsequent legal action for compensation brought against the private 'detainer', the domestic courts fail to interpret domestic law 'in the spirit of Article 5'.[70]

II. CONDITIONS OF DETENTION AND ARTICLE 5

Article 5 is generally concerned only with the fact of detention, not the conditions in which a person is detained, which are a matter for Article 3.[71] Thus Article 5(1)(a) was not violated when a drug addict and smuggler was detained in an ordinary prison, not an appropriate centre to receive treatment for his addiction as stipulated by the convicting court. The dominant reason for detention was punishment for a crime under Article 5(1)(a). The detention was therefore 'lawful' even though an earlier release date might have been obtained if the applicant had benefited from medical treatment to aid his addiction.[72] However, 'lawfulness' under Article 5(1) requires that 'there must be some relationship between *the ground of permitted deprivation of liberty relied on* and the place and conditions of detention' (emphasis added).[73] So, in principle a mentally ill detainee must be held in an appropriate institution, not a regular prison.[74] Nonetheless, there was no breach of Article 5(1) in *Ashingdane* where there had been a nineteen-month-long failure to implement the applicant's transfer from the 'special' psychiatric hospital to an ordinary psychiatric hospital where there was in fact a different and more liberal regime of hospital detention. The Court determined that the place and conditions of detention that the applicant was subjected to remained capable of satisfying Article 5(1)(e) at all times.[75]

Disciplinary steps, imposed formally or informally, which have effects on conditions of detention within a prison (such as confining a prisoner to their cell), cannot generally be considered as constituting a deprivation of liberty.[76]

---

[69] Id, para 35.

[70] *Storck*, id, paras 89 and 93 (domestic court's failure to interpret civil law relevant to applicant's compensation claims in contract and tort in the spirit of Article 5 resulted in an 'interference imputable to the respondent state with the applicant's right to liberty as guaranteed by Article 5(1)', para 99).

[71] *Ashingdane v UK* A 93 (1985); 7 EHRR 528 para 44.

[72] *Bizzotto v Greece* 1996-V (it was conceded that suitable facilities did not exist; the Commission, concluding that Article 5(1)(a) had been violated, stated that it was incumbent on the Greek government to provide them).

[73] *Ashingdane*, above n 71 para 44.

[74] See p 158 below. See also *Mubilanzila Mayeka and Kaniki Mitunga v Belgium* hudoc (2006); 46 EHRR 449 paras 101–5 (violation as five-year-old detained under Article 5(1)(f) was held in adult detention centre) and *Riad and Idiab v Belgium* hudoc (2008) (detention in transit zone at airport; violation of Article 5(1)).

[75] See, however, *Mancini v Italy* 2001-IX (violation of Article 5, by four votes to three; applicant remained in prison for one week longer than required by a court order which required his transfer to house arrest; the latter promised 'a change in the nature of the place of detention from a public institution to a private home', id, para 19).

[76] However, see *Bollan v UK No 42117/98*, 2000-V DA. See also *X v Switzerland No 7754/77*, 11 DR 216 (1977) and *D v FRG No 11703/85*, 54 DR 116 (1987). Articles 3 and 8 may be relevant. An extension of the period of detention by virtue of a prison disciplinary sentence would raise a question under Article 5: see *Campbell and Fell v UK* A 80 (1984); 7 EHRR 165 (loss of remission).

III. TRANSFER ACROSS BORDERS

Extradition or deportation of fugitive offenders must not interfere with any specific rights recognized in the Convention.[77] In *Öcalan v Turkey*[78] the leader of a terrorist organization in Turkey had fled to Kenya and there was no extradition treaty in place between the two countries. The applicant was seized by Kenyan operatives who facilitated his handing over to Turkish operatives in the international zone of Nairobi Airport. The latter arrested him inside an aircraft under effective Turkish authority[79] and immediately flew him back to Turkey. The Court observed that the mere fact that a fugitive is handed over as a result of co-operation between states does not in itself make the arrest unlawful or, therefore, give rise to any problem under Article 5.[80] However Article 5 might apply if there was a lack of consent on the part of the refuge state for this would affect the person concerned's 'individual rights to security under Article 5(1)'.[81] The critical issue would be whether the 'seizing' state acted extra-territorially in a manner that was 'inconsistent with the sovereignty of the host state and therefore contrary to international law'.[82] As this was not the case, and as the arrest complied with Turkish domestic law and so fell within Article 5(1)(c), there was no violation of Article 5 in *Öcalan*.

If, on the facts of *Öcalan*, there had been an extradition treaty in place between Turkey and Kenya the rules established by it would have been a relevant factor to be taken into account for determining whether the arrest that led to the subsequent complaint to the Court was 'lawful'.[83] Otherwise the Convention contains no provisions concerning the circumstances in which extradition may be granted, or the procedure to be followed. The Court has stated: 'subject to its being the result of cooperation between the states concerned and provided that the legal basis for the order for the fugitive's arrest is an arrest warrant issued by the authorities of the fugitive's state of origin, even an extradition in disguise cannot as such be regarded as being contrary to the Convention'.[84]

Another scenario may be that a defendant state merely receives a detainee from a neighbouring state at its own border. Here, as regards transfer from a non-Convention state to a Convention state, an applicant will not succeed in a complaint that he was illegally detained prior to the hand over.[85] However, in terms of action that may be brought against the receiving Convention state, this is subject to what has just been stated as regard the applicability of an extradition treaty. Of course, transfer between two Convention states enables a case to be brought directly against the transferring state.[86]

---

[77] *Öcalan v Turkey* 2005-IV; 41 EHRR 985 para 86 GC.

[78] Id, see also *Öcalan v Turkey* hudoc (2003); 37 EHRR 238 (Chamber judgment).

[79] Hence Article 1 ('jurisdiction') applied, see para. 91. See also *Illich Sanchez Ramirez v France No 28780/95*, 86 DR 155 (1996) ('Carlos the Jackal' abducted in Sudan and taken to France by aircraft; Convention inapplicable as French authorities not in control of aircraft).

[80] Id, para 87. Indeed the element of co-operation may help establish the lawfulness.

[81] Id, para 85.   [82] Id, para 90. As to burden of proof see para 90.   [83] Id, para 87.

[84] *Öcalan v Turkey* hudoc (2003); 37 EHRR 238 para 91 (statement from the Chamber was not repeated by the Grand Chamber). See also *Al-Moayad v Germany No 35865/03* hudoc (2006) DA (applicant tricked into going to Germany from Yeman; subsequent extradition to USA).

[85] *Altmann v France No 10689/83*, 37 DR 225 (1984) (the *Klaus Barbie* case).

[86] See *Bozano v France* A 111 (1986); 9 EHRR 297, see below at p 160.

IV. THE RIGHT TO SECURITY OF PERSON, 'DISAPPEARANCES', AND IMPLIED PROCEDURAL SAFEGUARDS DERIVED FROM ARTICLE 5(1)

Article 5(1) guarantees the 'right to liberty *and security* of person' (emphasis added). The italicized words have received little elaboration by the Court. 'Security of person' must be understood in the context of physical liberty[87] so that it cannot be interpreted as referring to quite different matters such as a right to social security[88] or to submit a civil claim to a court.[89] It does not impose an obligation upon the state to give someone personal protection from an attack by others.[90] Instead, the Court indicated in *Bozano v France*[91] that the function of the wording 'security of person' is to require that an arrest or detention not be 'arbitrary'. Accordingly, the guarantee of 'security of person' serves merely to underline a requirement that the Strasbourg authorities have already developed when interpreting the 'right to liberty' in Article 5. In view of this, the fact that a person's 'security' is, unlike his 'liberty', not subject to any exceptions in the text of Article 5(1)[92] is not significant.

The notion of 'security of person' has been referred to in some relatively recent judgments where very serious violations of Article 5 have been in issue, such as cases of unacknowledged detention—'disappearances'—in which allegations under Articles 2 and 3 have also been raised.[93] Here the Court has recapitulated some key aspects of Article 5:[94] it protects against abuse of power and addresses 'both the protection of the physical liberty of individuals as well as their personal security in a context which, in the absence of safeguards, could result in a subversion of the rule of law and place detainees beyond the reach of the most rudimentary forms of legal protection'. In cases when it is established that an individual has been taken into detention,[95] Article 5 places an obligation on the state to provide a plausible explanation of the whereabouts and fate of that individual. Flowing from this is a positive obligation[96] to take certain procedural steps, which if not taken, may also entail a violation of Article 5. A state must conduct a prompt and effective investigation into an arguable claim that a person has been taken into custody and has not been seen since.[97] It must also take effective measures

---

[87] *East African Asians v UK* 3 EHRR 76 at 89 (1973) Com Rep; CM Res DH (77) 2.

[88] *X v FRG No 5287/71*, 1 Digest 288 (1972).

[89] *Dyer v UK No 10475/83*, 39 DR 246 (1984); 7 EHRR CD 469 (1985).

[90] *X v Ireland No 6040/73*, 16 YB 388 (1973). See, however, Article 2, above, Ch 2. As to the 'security' of stateless persons seeking immigration, see *X and Y v UK No 5302/71*, 44 CD 29 at 46 (1974). See also *Zilli and Bonardo v Italy No 40143/98* hudoc (2002) DA ('security of person' inapplicable to insecurity of an applicant's personal circumstances arising from the danger of landslides) and *Mentes v Turkey* 1997-VIII; 26 EHRR 595 paras 79–81 (Court declined to examine whether insecurity of applicant's personal circumstances arising from the loss of his home, following its destruction by security forces, fell within the notion of 'security of person').

[91] A 111 (1986); 9 EHRR 297 paras 54 and 60. See also the statement made by the Court in *Öcalan v Turkey*, in text accompanying n 81 above. Cf, *East African Asians* case *loc cit* at n 87 above and *Arrowsmith v UK No 7050/75*, 19 DR 5 at 18 (1978); 3 EHRR 218 para 64. See also *Dyer v UK No 10475/83*, 39 DR 246 (1984); 7 EHRR CD 469 and *Adler and Bivas v FRG Nos 5573/72 and 5670/72*, 20 YB 102 at 146 (1977).

[92] See *Kamma v Netherlands No 4771/71*, 18 YB 300 at 316 (1975) Com Rep; CM Res DH (1975) 1.

[93] See eg, *Kurt v Turkey* 1998-III; 27 EHRR 373; *Timurtas v Turkey* 2000-VI; 33 EHRR 121 and *Bazorkina v Russia* hudoc (2006); 46 EHRR 261.

[94] *Kurt v Turkey* 1998-III; 27 EHRR 373 paras 122–4.

[95] In 'disappearances' cases it may be very difficult for relatives to establish incontrovertible evidence of state detention. Here a government's failure to submit information to which only it could have access may give rise to inferences that the applicant's charges are well-founded, see *Timurtas v Turkey* 2000-VI; 33 EHRR 121 para 66.

[96] See Mowbray, *The Development of Positive Obligations*, 2004, pp 68–72.

[97] *Kurt v Turkey* 1998-III; 27 EHRR 373 para 124; *Taş v Turkey* 2000-XI; 33 EHRR 325; *Cyprus v Turkey* 2001-IV; 35 EHRR731 para 150 GC and *Varnava v Turkey* hudoc (2008) (referred to GC).

to safeguard against the risk of disappearances. Thus, 'the recording of accurate holding data concerning the date, time and location of detainees, as well as the grounds for the detention and the name of the persons effecting it, is necessary for the detention of an individual to be compatible with the requirements of lawfulness for the purposes of Article 5(1)'.[98]

4. 'IN ACCORDANCE WITH A PROCEDURE PRESCRIBED BY LAW' AND THE 'LAWFULNESS' REQUIREMENT

The introductory wording of Article 5(1) stipulates that any deprivation of liberty must be 'in accordance with a procedure prescribed by law';[99] and the wording of each sub-paragraph of Article 5(1) supposes that any detention is 'lawful'. The two requirements overlap and in practice the Court sometimes merges their consideration, treating procedural, as well as substantive regularity by reference to the single requirement that a deprivation of liberty be 'lawful'.[100] This requirement of 'lawfulness' entails that any detention must satisfy standards which can be summarized as follows:

(i) The detention has a basis in, and is in conformity with the applicable domestic law;[101] and

(ii) The application of that domestic law is in conformity with the Convention: the detention must properly be for one of the grounds covered by Article 5(1)(a)–(f), such that it is not 'arbitrary'.[102]

Furthermore, as regards the domestic law, the notion of 'lawfulness' requires that the tests of legal certainty and 'quality of law'[103] be satisfied, and that there be compliance with general principles expressed or implied in the Convention, 'particularly the principle of the rule of law'.[104]

I. REVIEW OF DOMESTIC LAW

With regard to (i) as just identified, it is in the first place for the national authorities, particularly the courts, to decide whether the relevant municipal law has been complied

---

[98] *Çakici v Turkey* 1999-IV; 31 EHRR 133 para 105 GC, also *Kurt v Turkey* 1998-III; 27 EHRR 373 para 124. Other 'custody records' cases include *Anguelova v Bulgaria* 2002-IV; 38 EHRR 659 and *Orhan v Turkey* hudoc (2002).

[99] The term 'procedure' includes the procedure followed by a court when ordering detention (*Van der Leer v Netherlands* A 170-A (1990); 12 EHRR 567) and rules governing the making of arrests (*Fox, Campbell and Hartley v UK* A 182 (1990); 13 EHRR 157 para 29).

[100] See eg, *Van der Leer v Netherlands* A 170-A (1990); 12 EHRR 567. In *Bouamar v Belgium* A 129 (1988); 11 EHRR 1, they were considered separately.

[101] Municipal law includes directly applicable EEC law: *Caprino v UK No 6871/75*, 12 DR 14 at 19 (1978). This Commission case has not yet been confirmed by the Court. Although argument was based on an EEC directive in *Bozano v France* A 111 (1986); 9 EHRR 297, the Court did not refer to it. As to whether Nazi law was 'law', see *X v FRG No 4324/69*, 14 YB 342 (1971).

[102] *Winterwerp v Netherlands* A 33 (1979); 2 EHRR 387 para 39.

[103] *HL v UK* 2004-IX; 40 EHRR 761 para 115, also stipulates the need in domestic law for 'adequate legal protections' and 'fair and proper procedures'.

[104] *Ilaşcu v Moldova* 2004-VII; 40 EHRR 1030 para 461 GC.

with.[105] If a national court rules,[106] or a defendant state concedes in argument[107] that
the procedures required by municipal law have not been complied with, the Court is
unlikely to disagree. In other cases it is likely to accept the interpretation and application
of municipal law suggested by the defendant state.[108] However, the Court will of necessity retain a supervisory role since, with Article 5(1), compliance with the national law is
inextricably linked with legal justification for detention. As the Court has stated, it must,
as a supervisory body, have this ultimate power to interpret and apply national law when,
as with Article 5, the Convention requires that a state comply with its national law.[109]
Hence where the national authorities can clearly be seen to have infringed municipal law,
a violation of Article 5 will be found.[110] The same applies if an applicant is detained in
defiance of a court order for his immediate release.[111] If the respondent state provides no
reasons for the applicant's detention the Court will find a violation of Article 5.[112]

II. 'QUALITY OF THE LAW'

The applicable national law must meet the standard of 'lawfulness' set by the Convention
('in accordance with the law'/'prescribed' by law', see Articles 8(2)–11(2)) as regard the
'quality of the law' in question,[113] although that test is 'not an end in itself' and is only
relevant if the applicant's substantive Convention rights have been 'tangibly prejudiced'
by the poor 'quality of the law' in issue.[114] As with Articles 8(2)–11(2), the test requires
that all law, whether written or unwritten, be public and sufficiently precise to allow the
citizen—if need be, with appropriate advice—to foresee, to a degree that is reasonable in
the circumstances, the consequences which a given action may entail[115] and so as to avoid
'all risk of arbitrariness'.[116]

A Code of Criminal Procedure might permit measures of restraint in 'exceptional circumstances', such as remanding the applicant in custody before being charged. However,
the 'quality of law' requirement of Article 5 will not be met if the Code does not provide
details of what constitutes 'exceptional circumstances' and the government cannot submit practice or case law which help to identify the same.[117] A deprivation of liberty will
not be prescribed by law within the meaning of Article 5(1) when the legal provision
used to justify it has been shown to be vague enough to cause confusion as to its practical

---

[105] *Winterwerp v Netherlands* A 33 (1979); 2 EHRR 387 para 46 and *Bozano v France* A 111 (1986); 9 EHRR
297 para 58.
[106] See eg, *Bonazzi v Italy No 7975/77*, 15 DR 169 (1978).
[107] See eg, *Naldi v Italy No 9920/82*, 37 DR 75 (1984). Cf, *Schuurs v Netherlands No 10518/83*, 41 DR 186 (1985)
F Sett.
[108] See *Winterwerp v Netherlands* A 33 (1979); 2 EHRR 387 and *Wassink v Netherlands* A 185-A (1990).
[109] *Winterwerp v Netherlands* A 33 (1979); 2 EHRR 387 para 46.
[110] See *Van der Leer v Netherlands* A 170-A (1990); 12 EHRR 567 and *Koendjbiharie v Netherlands* A 185-B
(1990); 13 EHRR 820 Com Rep.
[111] *Assanidze v Georgia* 2004-II; 39 EHRR 653 GC.   [112] *Denizci v Cyprus* 2001-V paras 392–3
[113] See above p 344.   [114] *Bordovskiy v Russia* hudoc (2005) para 49.
[115] *Steel v UK* 1998-VII; 29 EHRR 365 para 54; *HL v UK* 2004-IX; 40 EHRR 761 para 119 (doubts expressed
whether, even with legal advice, detention on the basis of necessity satisfied the forseeability aspects of the test
of 'lawfulness') and *Nasrulloyev v Russia* hudoc (2007) (Russian law governing detention of persons with a view
to extradition was neither precise nor foreseeable).
[116] *Hilda Hafsteinsdóttir v Iceland* hudoc (2004) para 56. See also *Amuur v France* 1996-III; 22 EHRR 533
paras 53–4 (unpublished circular was too brief and lacking in appropriate guarantees) and *Dougoz v Greece*
2001-II; 34 EHRR 1480.
[117] *Gusinskiy v Russia* 2004-IV; 41 EHRR 281 paras 63–4.

effects even amongst the competent state authorities.[118] However there is room for some flexibility as in *Steel v UK*[119] when the Court accepted that the concept of 'breach of the peace' was sufficiently clear, in principle, for Article 5 as it had been clarified by a series of domestic rulings. In the same case an order to be bound over to keep the peace and be of good behaviour—which the applicants had breached, leading to their detention—satisfied (on the facts) the notion of 'lawful order of a court' (Article 5(1)(b)).[120] Whilst the relevant order was vague and general, with the expression 'to be of good behaviour' being particularly imprecise, it followed a finding that the applicants had committed a breach of the peace. So the Court considered that in the circumstances the order would have been sufficiently clear to the applicants themselves in that they should refrain from causing further, similar, breaches of the peace during the ensuing twelve months.[121]

There is an obvious breach of Article 5 if no legal provision exists to justify detention,[122] if an applicant is held beyond the period of his sentence[123] or if domestic law is otherwise blatantly ignored.[124] However, a flaw in a detention order does not necessarily render the underlying period of detention unlawful within the meaning of Article 5(1),[125] especially when what has concerned is a 'slip-up' and the meaning of the order must have been clear to all concerned.[126] As the Court has put it, 'a period of detention will in principle be lawful if it is carried out pursuant to a court order... [a] subsequent finding that the court erred under domestic law in making the order will not necessarily retrospectively affect the validity of the intervening period of detention'.[127] A detention which, it transpires, has been ordered in violation of national law, remains 'lawful' for the purposes of Article 5 if under national law the deciding judge or magistrate acted inside his jurisdiction, if he did not act in bad faith, and if the order was not void *ab initio*.[128] Issues may

---

118 *Ječius v Lithuania* 2000-IX; 35 EHRR 400 para 59 (leading domestic authorities presenting differing views as to the practical effect of the legal provision insofar as it permitted detention of applicant).

119 1998-VII; 29 EHRR 365. See also *Lucas v UK No 39013/02* hudoc (2003) DA (Court rejecting as inadmissible a Scots law case regarding 'breach of the peace').

120 Id, para 76-8.

121 Id, para 76, note, however, the joint partly dissenting opinion of Judges Valticos and Makarczyk in which they strongly protested against the treatment of one of the applicants, Steel, who was committed to prison for twenty-eight days as she had refused to agree to an undertaking she considered to be too vague. Cf, *Hashman and Harrup v UK* 1999-VIII; 30 EHRR 241 GC (hunt saboteurs bound over to be 'of good behaviour'—an imprecise formulation which breached the 'prescribed by law' requirement of Article 10(2)).

122 *Baranowski v Poland* 2000-III (prosecutor's decision to continue detention once an indictment had been served as this was the habitual practice).

123 *Grava v Italy* hudoc (2003) (detention exceeded period applicable under domestic law as applicant served a longer sentence than the one which would have resulted had he been granted remission and the decision on this was taken at too late a stage).

124 Eg, *Tsirlis and Kouloumpas v Greece* 1997-III; 25 EHRR 198 (applicants were ministers of religion and so exempt from military service; military courts blatantly ignored this, detaining applicants for failure to perform military service).

125 *Benham v UK* 1996-III; 22 EHRR 293 paras 42-7. See also *Slivenko v Latvia* 2003-XI; 39 EHRR 490 para 149 GC (putative error immediately detected and redressed by release).

126 *Ječius v Lithuania* 2000-IX; 35 EHRR 400 para 69.

127 *Benham v UK* 1996-III; 22 EHRR 293 para 42. Hence the Court rejects applications from persons convicted of criminal offences who complain that their convictions or sentences were found by the appellate courts to have been based on errors of fact or law.

128 Id, paras 43-7, note, however, the partly dissenting opinions presented by four judges. See also *Perks v UK* hudoc (1999); 30 EHRR 33 (Court confirmed that magistrates had jurisdiction to order detention following refusal to pay poll tax; deprivation of liberty was 'lawful' even though the detention order was potentially 'Wednesbury' unreasonable and so capable of being quashed by a higher court (there was no arbitrariness on the facts). A fettered exercise of discretion or failure to have regard to a relevant piece of evidence could theoretically render arbitrary an otherwise formally lawful decision, para 70).

arise, however, if there is a significant delay in replacing the defective detention order with a valid one.[129] In the absence of a clear domestic legal authority resolving whether a first instance judge acted inside or outside his jurisdiction, the European Court examines 'whether it can be said, with a degree of certainty, that the applicant's detention was unlawful under domestic law'.[130]

III. ARBITRARY DETENTION—GENERAL AND SPECIFIC PRINCIPLES

As noted above, the requirement of lawfulness entails compliance with the substantive and procedural rules of national law. However, Article 5(1) additionally requires that 'any deprivation of liberty should be in keeping with the purpose of protecting the individual from arbitrariness'[131] and this notion 'extends beyond lack of conformity with national law'.[132]

Although the Court has not produced an all-encompassing definition of 'arbitrariness' for the purposes of Article 5(1), certain key principles have emerged from the case law.[133] First, even if there is compliance with the letter of national law, a detention will be arbitrary if there has been 'an element of bad faith or deception on the part of the authorities'.[134] Secondly, 'both the order to detain and the execution of the detention must genuinely conform with the purpose of the restrictions permitted by the relevant sub-paragraph of Article 5(1)'.[135] Thirdly, 'there must in addition be some relationship between the ground of permitted deprivation of liberty relied on and the place and conditions of detention'.[136] Finally, the principle of non-arbitrariness and 'lawfulness' also entails that certain general express and implied principles may be read into Article 5(1). For example, where deprivation of liberty is concerned, it is particularly important that the general principle of legal certainty be satisfied.[137] HL v UK[138] concerned an incapacitated but compliant person held in a mental health institution on what the Court considered to be an 'arbitrary' basis. He was detained under the common law doctrine of necessity, so there were no fixed legal rules as regards admission and detention, rather the applicant was held on the basis of his doctors' clinical assessments completed when necessary. There being no doubts as to the doctors' professionalism, the violation of Article 5(1) stemmed from the absence of procedural safeguards to protect individuals against any misjudgments and professional lapses.

---

[129] See *Mooren v Germany* hudoc (2008) (referred to GC).

[130] *Benham v UK* 1996-III; 22 EHRR 293 para 46.

[131] *Saadi v UK* hudoc (2008) para 67 GC (citing *Winterwerp v Netherlands* A 33 (1979); 2 EHRR 387 para 37; *Amuur v France* 1996-III; 22 EHRR 533 para 50; *Chahal v UK* 1996-V; 23 EHRR 413 para 118, and *Witold Litwa v Poland* 2000-III; 33 EHRR 1267 para 78).

[132] Id, para 68.   [133] See id, para 69.

[134] Id, para 69 (citing *Bozano v France* A 111 (1986); 9 EHRR 297 and *Conka v Belgium* 2002-I; 34 EHRR 1298). Eg, detention ostensibly for the purpose of deportation that is really aimed at illegal extradition would be 'arbitrary', see *Bozano, ibid*. Assuming detention can be justified under Article 5(1), a violation of Article 18 of the Convention read with Article 5 may still be found if there exist additional, impermissible reasons for the detention. See *Gusinskiy v Russia* 2004-IV; 41 EHRR 281 paras 73–8.

[135] Id, para 69 (citing *Winterwerp v Netherlands* A 33 (1979); 2 EHRR 387 para 39; *Bouamar v Belgium* A 129 (1988); 11 EHRR 1 para 50; and *O'Hara v UK* 2001-X; 34 EHRR 812 para 34).

[136] Id, para 69 (citing *Bouamar v Belgium* A 129 (1988); 11 EHRR 1 para 50; *Aerts v Belgium* 1996-V; 29 EHRR 50 para 46; and *Enhorn v Sweden* 2005-I; 41 EHRR 633).

[137] See eg, *Ječius v Lithuania* 2000-IX; 35 EHRR 400 para 56; *Baranowski v Poland* 2000-III; and *Riad and Idiab v Belgium* hudoc (2008).

[138] *HL v UK* 2004-IX; 40 EHRR 761 para 121.

The general principles just referred to apply to any detention under Article 5(1), but the Court's case law also reveals that additional, higher standards of non-'arbitrariness' may apply depending on the particular sub-paragraph of Article 5(1) that is in issue. For some categories of detention the Court will scrutinize whether it was actually necessary to detain the individual to achieve the aim stated within the sub-paragraph.[139] The individual approaches adopted for each sub-paragraph of Article 5(1) are discussed in detail below. By way of overview, the stricter approach (whether detention is necessary to achieve the stated aim)[140] is taken for sub-paragraphs (b), (d), and (e). The principle here is that 'detention of an individual is such a serious measure that it is justified only as a last resort where other, less severe measures have been considered and found to be insufficient to safeguard the individual or public interest which might require that the person concerned be detained'.[141] By contrast, no such approach is taken for Article 5(1)(f), which only requires good faith on the authorities' part: detention under this provision will not be arbitrary provided it can be said that it is for the immigration or deportation purpose identified in the Article. However, the importance of the right to liberty is reflected in the understanding that a detention may be rendered arbitrary under this heading if certain standards are not observed: the immigration detention might last an unreasonable time, for example, or deportation proceedings are not pursued with due diligence.[142] The least strict approach under Article 5(1) is taken for Article 5(1)(a).[143] Under this provision the Court will not question the length of a sentence or the decision to impose it; instead the safeguard against arbitrariness is reflected in the notion that there must at least be a sufficient 'causal connection' between conviction and the ensuing detention.[144]

5. ARTICLE 5(1)(A)–(F): GROUNDS FOR DETENTION

Article 5 recognizes that the 'right to liberty' cannot be absolute. Article 5(1), sub-paragraphs (a) to (f), provides an 'exhaustive' list of circumstances in which the state may detain an individual in the public interest.[145] The Court has stated that these grounds for detention must be given a 'narrow interpretation',[146] although this principle has not always prevailed.[147]

---

[139] Although the authorities may benefit from a certain discretion or 'margin of appreciation' in their assessment of the situation: see eg, *Winterwerp v Netherlands* A 33 (1979); 2 EHRR 387 para 40; *Weeks v UK* A 114 (1987); 10 EHRR 293 para 50 PC; *Zamir v UK No 9174/80*, 40 DR 42 (1983); 5 EHRR 242 (1983).

[140] *Saadi v UK* hudoc (2008) para 70 GC.

[141] *Ibid* (citing see *Witold Litwa v Poland* 2000-III; 33 EHRR 1267 para 78; *Hilda Hafsteinsdóttir v Iceland* hudoc (2004) para 51; and *Enhorn v Sweden* 2005-I; 41 EHRR 633 para 44). See also *Varbanov v Bulgaria* 2000-X para 46.

[142] For full details, see pp 159–63 below.

[143] Article 5(1)(c) is complex. A strict test applies for detention on remand, but less so for initial arrests. The Article should be read alongside the special guarantees afforded by Article 5(3), see below.

[144] See p 140 below.

[145] Article 9(1) ICCPR has no equivalent 'list', it simply reads: 'Everyone has the right to liberty and security of person. No one shall be subjected to arbitrary arrest or detention. No one shall be deprived of his liberty except on such grounds and in accordance with such procedure as are established by law.'

[146] *Winterwerp v Netherlands* A 33 (1979); 2 EHRR 387 para 37.

[147] See *Monnell and Morris v UK* A 115 (1987); 10 EHRR 205 and *Witold Litwa v Poland* 2000-III; 33 EHRR 1267 below, p 154.

It should also be noted that the exceptions listed in Article 5 are not mutually exclusive: the detention of a person in a mental hospital as a result of a conviction by a court may, for example, come within both Article 5(1)(a) and (e).

I. ARTICLE 5(1)(A): DETENTION FOLLOWING CONVICTION BY A COMPETENT COURT

Article 5(1)(a) permits 'the lawful detention of a person after conviction by a competent court'. The purpose of detention must therefore be the execution of the sentence of imprisonment imposed by a court judgment.

The provision refers to 'lawful detention', not 'lawful conviction', so there will be no review of the legality of a conviction[148] and Article 5(1)(a) cannot be relied upon to challenge the length or appropriateness of a sentence of imprisonment.[149] Conditions of detention are generally irrelevant.[150] Detention will not be rendered retroactively 'unlawful' for the purposes of Article 5(1)(a) because the conviction or sentence upon which it is based is overturned by a higher municipal court on appeal.[151] However, detention will no longer be 'lawful' if the authorities do not grant remission when they are bound to do so and as a result the applicant serves a sentence which was longer than that imposed, taking into account the remission.[152]

Several points may be made in connection with the word 'conviction' under Article 5(1)(a). It has an autonomous meaning[153] covering a 'finding of guilt' in respect of an offence that has been found to have been committed. Accordingly, it does not include detention as a prevention or security measure in anticipation of an offence being committed.[154] A 'conviction' is a conviction by a trial court, so detention pending appeal is justified by reference to Article 5(1)(a), not Article 5(1)(c)[155] (this permits the detention pending his appeal of an accused who is on bail before his conviction).[156] A 'conviction' exists so as to justify any detention based upon it even though the judgment, giving the reasons for the conviction, has not been delivered yet.[157] Article 5(1)(a) applies to 'convictions' for disciplinary, as well as criminal, offences under municipal law provided that the outcome of

[148] *Krzycki v FRG No 7629/76*, 13 DR 57 at 61 (1978).

[149] *Weeks v UK* A 114 (1987); 10 EHRR 293 para 50 PC (Court referred to Article 3, not to Article 5, when referring to the harsh life imprisonment in that case). See also *V v UK* 1999-IX; 30 EHRR 121 GC and *Hussain v UK* 1996-I; 22 EHRR 1 para 53 (lifelong detention of a juvenile might raise an issue under Article 3). Perhaps a better approach would be for the Court to claim the power to review the legality under municipal law of a conviction or sentence, but to acknowledge, as is the normal practice, that it will only be exercised in clear cases of illegality.

[150] However see above, p 130. See also *X v UK No 7977/77*, 1 Digest 305 (1981) (transfer from prison to Broadmoor raised no Article 5(1)(a) issue as was permitted by the court sentence).

[151] *Krzycki v FRG No 7629/76*, 13 DR 57 at 61 (1978). But see *Artico v Italy No 6694/74*, 8 DR 73 at 89 (1977).

[152] *Grava v Italy* hudoc (2003).

[153] *Engel v Netherlands* A 22 (1976); 1 EHRR 706 para 68 PC. Cf, *Ezeh and Connors v UK* ECHR 2003-X; 39 EHRR 1 para 124 GC (prison governor's award of additional days to person already lawfully in prison and after a finding of culpability constituted fresh deprivations of liberty imposed for punitive reasons. Note, however, the dissenting opinion of Judges Pellonpää, Wildhaber, Palm, and Caflisch).

[154] *Guzzardi v Italy* A 39 (1980); 3 EHRR 333 para 100 PC.

[155] *Wemhoff v FRG* A 7 (1968); 1 EHRR 55 para 9 (Article 5(1)(a) takes over from Article 5(1)(c) even in legal systems, such as that in Germany, where detention pending appeal is treated as a continuation of detention on remand). For criticism of the Court's decision, see Trechsel, *European System*, p 297.

[156] *Wemhoff v FRG* A 7 (1968); 1 EHRR 55 para 9. See also *B v Austria* A 175 (1990); 13 EHRR 20 para 39.

[157] *Crociani v Italy No 8603/79*, 22 DR 147 (1980).

the proceedings is the convicted person's detention.[158] It will cover cases in which a person is found guilty of an offence and, instead of being given a sentence of imprisonment by way of punishment, is ordered to be detained in a mental institution for treatment as mentally disordered.[159] Sub-paragraphs (a) and (e) overlap in applying to such cases,[160] at least initially.[161] Where, however, an accused is acquitted of an offence and then ordered to be detained in a mental institution, only Article 5(1)(e) applies.[162]

A 'competent' court is one with jurisdiction to try the case.[163] As with the same term in Article 5(4), 'court' in Article 5(1)(a) means a body that is independent of the executive and the parties and that provides 'adequate judicial guarantees'.[164] The 'adequate judicial guarantees' required by Article 5(1)(a) are 'not always co-extensive with those of Article 6'; account must be taken of the particular circumstances.[165] For example, whereas a 'public hearing' might be required in a criminal case,[166] the same might not be true in military disciplinary proceedings.[167]

To the extent that there is an overlap between Article 5(1)(a) and Article 6, a breach of Article 6 in the trial of a person sentenced to imprisonment following his conviction might also mean that the detention is not justified by Article 5(1)(a). In *Stoichkov v Bulgaria*[168] the applicant had been convicted *in absentia* and was imprisoned on his return to the country. Initially the detention, based on the original conviction, was lawful under Article 5(1)(a), but it became unlawful upon the denial of a request for the case to be re-opened.[169] The detention contravened Article 5(1) as it was 'manifestly contrary to the provisions of Article 6 or the principles embodied therein'.[170]

A similar test was employed in *Drozd and Janousek v France and Spain*[171] where the applicants were imprisoned in France after being convicted in Andorra (not a party to the Convention at the time)[172] following a trial which appeared contrary to Article 6. The Court determined that the detention in a French prison would be justified by

[158] *Engel v Netherlands* A 22 (1976); 1 EHRR 706 para 68 PC.

[159] *X v UK* A 46 (1981); 4 EHRR 188 para 39.

[160] The claim in *Ashingdane v UK* A 93 (1985); 7 EHRR 528 was made and considered under Article 5(1)(e). The particular basis for the claim may dictate the sub-paragraph that is most appropriate. See *M v FRG No 10272/83*, 38 DR 104 (1984).

[161] Cf, *X v UK* A 46 (1981); 4 EHRR 188 para 39 (Court supposed both paragraphs applied to initial detention, but expressed doubt if Article 5(1)(a) continues to apply if a person ordered to be detained in a mental institution is released and then recalled to the institution by an administrative decision). *Van Droogenbroeck v Belgium* A 50 (1982); 4 EHRR 443 PC, suggests Article 5(1)(a) continues to apply provided that there is a 'sufficient connection' between the recall and the initial court sentence.

[162] *Luberti v Italy* A 75 (1984); 6 EHRR 440 para 25. Cf, *Dhoest v Belgium No 10448/83*, 55 DR 5 (1987) (Com Rep; CM Res DH (88) 1); 12 EHRR CD 135.

[163] *X v Austria No 2645/65*, 11 YB 322 at 348 (1968) and *X v Austria No 4161/69*, 13 YB 798 at 804 (1970). Complex questions arise if the court belongs to an entity not recognised under international law, see *Cyprus v Turkey* 2001-IV; 35 EHRR 731 paras 231 and 236–7 GC (as a minimum the court in issue must form 'part of a judicial system operating on a "constitutional and legal basis" reflecting a judicial tradition compatible with the Convention') and *Ilaşcu v Moldova* 2004-VII; 40 EHRR 1030 para 460 GC.

[164] *De Wilde, Ooms and Versyp v Belgium* A 12 (1971); 1 EHRR 373 para 78 PC and *Engel v Netherlands* A 22 (1976); 1 EHRR 706 para 68 PC. As to the invariable need for 'independence', see *Eggs v Switzerland No 7341/76*, 15 DR 35 at 62 (1978) Com Rep; CM Res DH (79) 7 (chief military prosecutor not a 'court'). As to the meaning of 'court' in Article 5(4), see below, p 188.

[165] *Engel v Netherlands* A 22 (1976); 1 EHRR 706 para 68 PC.

[166] *Wemhoff v FRG* A 7 (1968); 1 EHRR 55.   [167] *Engel v Netherlands* A 22 (1976); 1 EHRR 706 PC.

[168] Hudoc (2005); 44 EHRR 276.   [169] Id, para 58.   [170] Id, para 56.

[171] A 240 (1992); 14 EHRR 745 para 110 PC. Cf, *Iribarne Perez v France No 16462/90*, 76A DR 18 (1994).

[172] Andorra ratified the Convention in 1996.

Article 5(1)(a)[173] unless the conviction in Andorra was 'the result of a flagrant denial of justice'.[174] On the facts this very high threshold was not satisfied, so there was no breach of Article 5(1) (twelve votes to eleven).[175]

Detention will not be 'arbitrary' because the period of time spent in detention awaiting extradition from another state to serve a sentence in prison following escape is not taken into account as a part of that sentence.[176] The transfer of a prisoner to a country likely to release him on parole later than the respondent state entails no violation of Article 5(1) provided that the sentence served does not exceed that imposed in the criminal proceedings.[177] However, it is possible that 'a flagrantly longer de facto sentence in the administering state could give rise to an issue under Article 5', so engaging the responsibility of the sentencing state under that Article. Here 'substantial grounds would have to be shown to exist for believing that the time to be served in the administering state would be flagrantly disproportionate to the time which would have had to be served in the sentencing state'.[178]

a. Detention 'after' conviction ('causal connection')

The reference to detention 'after' conviction entails the need for there to be a causative link between ongoing detention and a conviction for a particular offence, as opposed to merely a chronological requirement that detention follows conviction. In Van Droogenbroeck v Belgium[179] the applicant had been sentenced by a court to two years' imprisonment for theft and, on grounds of recidivism, 'placed at the Government's disposal' for ten years thereafter. Under Belgian law the two parts of the sentence constituted 'an inseparable whole'.[180] The two-year sentence was completed and the applicant released from prison but then detained by administrative decision for much of the next few years on the basis of the original court sentence. The Court held that these further periods of detention fell within Article 5(1)(a). Although they occurred several years after the sentence, they were authorized by it and were intended to achieve its purpose. The connection with the sentence would have been broken, so that Article 5(1)(a) would not have applied, if the decision to recall the applicant had been 'based upon grounds that had no connection with the objectives of the legislature and the court or on an assessment that was unreasonable in terms of those objectives'.[181] In that case, a detention that was lawful at the outset would have become 'arbitrary' and hence incompatible with Article 5. In these cases the Strasbourg authorities may review the merits of an administrative decision ordering detention in such a case, but will allow the national authorities a 'margin of appreciation' in assessing the factual situation when doing so.

---

[173] Hence the 'conviction' may be that of a foreign court, whether a party to the Convention or not. See X v FRG No 1322/62, 6 YB 494 at 516 (1963).

[174] See also Ilaşcu v Moldova 2004-VII; 40 EHRR 1030 para 461–4 GC (violation of Article 5: 'flagrant denial of justice' (para 461) and 'sentence had no legal basis or legitimacy for Convention purposes' (para 436). The conviction was by a court of a regime not recognized in international law, para 436). Cf, Pellegrini v Italy 2001-VIII; 35 EHRR 44 regarding judgments from a non-Convention state which may not have complied with Article 6.

[175] Whereas the majority stressed that it was not for the Convention parties to impose the standards of the Convention on non-parties, certain of the dissenting judges referred to the Explanatory Report on the 1970 European Convention on the International Validity of Criminal Judgments (ETS 70), which states that a condition of the enforcement of foreign criminal judgments is that the decision must have been rendered in accordance with Article 6, European Convention on Human Rights. See the joint dissenting opinion of Judges Pettiti, Valticos, Lopes Rocha, approved by Judges Walsh and Spielmann.

[176] C v UK No 10854/84, 43 DR 177 (1985).   [177] Veermäe v Finland No 38704/03 hudoc (2005) DA.

[178] Ibid.   [179] A 50 (1982); 4 EHRR 443 para 35 PC.   [180] Ibid.   [181] Id, para 40.

Van Droogenbroeck was applied in *Weeks v UK*[182] to the system of discretionary life sentences in English law. In that case, the applicant, aged 17, was given a life sentence for armed robbery. In fact, he had stolen 35 pence from a pet shop after threatening the owner with a starting pistol. As the European Court stated, on first impression the life sentence was extremely harsh and arguably an 'inhuman punishment' contrary to Article 3 of the Convention. However, it was given because the applicant, who was characterized by the trial court judge as a 'very dangerous young man', could be released on licence when no longer a threat to the community or himself, which might be much sooner than would be the case if he were sentenced to a particular term of imprisonment appropriate to the offence. In fact, the applicant's condition remained such that he was not released on licence for nearly ten years. He was then recalled by the Home Secretary a year after his release, following incidents involving minor offences. The Court considered that the case was comparable to the *Van Droogenbroeck* case in that here too the purpose of the recall, which was the act of detention in question, was the legitimate one of social protection and the rehabilitation of the offender. Moreover, despite the considerable time that had elapsed, the causal link between the recall and the original sentence had not been broken: the Home Secretary's intention in recalling the offender was consistent with the objectives of the sentencing court. As to the justification for recalling the applicant on the facts, the Court noted that there was evidence of unstable and aggressive behaviour such as to give the Home Secretary grounds to act and that national authorities were allowed a 'margin of appreciation' in assessing such evidence.[183]

For an individual already serving a sentence, there must be a sufficient causal connection between the purpose of the original detention and the reasons subsequently given by a body with responsibility for assessing whether the individual should be released. In *Stafford v UK*[184] the applicant was a mandatory life prisoner by virtue of his murder conviction in the 1960s. He had been let out on licence and, many years later, convicted and imprisoned for fraud. The Home Secretary, relying on the mandatory life status of the applicant, then prevented his release in 1997 citing perceived fears of future *non-violent* criminal conduct. This was contrary to 'the spirit of the Convention, with its emphasis on the rule of law and protection from arbitrariness'.[185] For the causative link with the life sentence to remain intact presumably the continued detention would not require fear of an identical offence to the original one (murder) being committed, but offences bearing a resemblance to it (violent crime).[186] Evidently fear of fraud did not suffice on the facts.

Finally, the Court has indicated that it is prepared to accept a flexible approach to the notion of causal connection when a conviction has expired and a legal process to obtain prolongation of detention on security grounds is underway, notably when the individual concerned has deviant tendencies and there is a serious danger that he will commit further criminal offences.[187]

---

[182] A 114 (1987); 10 EHRR 293 PC. For another causal connection case see *Monnell and Morris v UK* A 115 (1987); 10 EHRR 205 (no violation of Article 5(1) when Court of Appeal ordered that twenty-eight and fifty-six days respectively of the applicants' detention pending appeal would not count toward their sentence).

[183] On the application of Article 5(1)(a) to administrative recalls of mentally disordered offender patients, see *X v UK*. A 46 (1981); 4 EHRR 188.

[184] 2002-IV; 35 EHRR 32 GC.   [185] Id, para 82.

[186] See the separate opinion of Judge Rozakis. See also *Waite v UK* hudoc (2002); 36 EHRR 1001.

[187] *Eriksen v Norway* 1997-III; 29 EHRR 328. Note, however, the concurring opinion of Judge Repik arguing against the applicability of Article 5(1)(a).

II. ARTICLE 5(1)(B): DETENTION FOR NON-COMPLIANCE WITH A COURT ORDER OR AN OBLIGATION PRESCRIBED BY LAW

Article 5(1)(b) permits 'the lawful arrest or detention of a person for non-compliance with the lawful order of a court or in order to secure the fulfilment of any obligation prescribed by law'. This provision does not apply to the ordinary enforcement of the law after breaches have occurred. If a person is detained on reasonable suspicion of having committed a crime, Article 5(1)(c), with its attendant Article 5(3) safeguards, applies, not Article 5(1)(b).

The concept of 'lawfulness' in this context was relevant to *Steel v UK* which was discussed above.[188]

The first limb of Article 5(1)(b) authorizes the detention of a person who has failed to comply with a court order *already* made against him, as in cases of civil contempt. It includes failure to pay a court fine[189] or maintenance order and refusal to undergo a medical examination ordered by a court.[190] A wilful refusal to pay a local (poll) tax may lead to a detention under this provision.[191] Here the Court will not consider arguments to the effect that detention is unnecessary in the circumstances.[192] In *K v Austria*,[193] there was a breach of Article 5(1) when the applicant was imprisoned for failure to comply with a court order to give evidence in court, which itself breached Article 10 of the Convention.

The second limb of Article 5(1)(b) provides a means of justifying various powers of temporary detention exercisable by the police (eg, random breath tests, road blocks, powers of stopping and searching) to enforce obligations in connection with the administration of the criminal law to which Article 5(1)(c) would not extend. Examples of 'obligation[s]' under Article 5(1)(b), which must be consistent in their nature with the Convention,[194] include an obligation to do military, or substitute civilian, service;[195] to carry an identity card and submit to an identity check;[196] to make a customs or tax return;[197] or to live in a designated locality.[198]

A number of general principles apply to this second limb of Article 5(1)(b). They restrict its potentially very broad application[199] and confirm that detention in this context must be a last resort measure.[200] It covers the situation where a person is detained 'to compel him to *fulfil* a *specific and concrete* obligation which he has *until then* failed to satisfy' (emphasis added).[201] As the Court has stated 'there must be an unfulfilled obligation

---

[188] P 135.   [189] *Airey v Ireland No 6289/73*, 8 DR 42 (1977).

[190] *X v FRG No 6659/74*, 3 DR 92 (1975). See also *Paradis v France No 4065/04* hudoc (2007) DA and *No 6944/75*, 1 Digest 355 (1976) (failure to hand over property); *X v Austria No 8278/78*, 18 DR 154 (1979) (failure to take blood test); *Freda v Italy No 8916/80*, 21 DR 250 (1980) (failure to observe residence restriction); and *X v FRG No 9546/81*, 1 Digest Supp para 5.1.4.2. (1983) (failure to make a declaration of assets). Detention for non-compliance with a court order for the enforcement of a contractual obligation merely because the person has been unable to comply with the order (eg for lack of funds) would be a breach of Article 1, Fourth Protocol to the Convention, but not Article 5.

[191] *Perks v UK* hudoc (1999); 30 EHRR 33.   [192] Id, para 70.

[193] A 255-B (1993) Com Rep F Sett before Court.

[194] *McVeigh, O'Neill and Evans v UK Nos 8022/77, 8025/77 and 8027/77*, 25 DR 15 at 39 (1981); 5 EHRR 71 para 176 and *Johansen v Norway No 10600/83*, 44 DR 155 (1985); 9 EHRR CD 103. Eg, an obligation to complete a census return must be consistent with the right to respect for privacy in Article 8 of the Convention.

[195] *Johansen, ibid.* Any work or service listed in Article 4(3) of the Convention that is required of a person presumably qualifies.

[196] *Reyntjens v France No 16810/90* (1992) unreported and *B v France No 10179/82*, 52 DR 111 (1987).

[197] See *McVeigh*, above n 194, para 185.   [198] *Ciulla v Italy* A 148 (1989); 13 EHRR 346 para 36 PC.

[199] See also *Vasileva v Denmark* hudoc (2003); 40 EHRR 681 paras 36–7.

[200] See *Saadi v UK* hudoc (2008) para 70 GC.

[201] *Engel v Netherlands* A 22 (1976); 1 EHRR 706 para 69 PC.

incumbent on the person concerned and the arrest and detention must be for the purpose of securing its fulfilment and not punitive in character'.[202] So Article 5(1)(b) cannot justify detention that may be connected with an obligation, but that occurs before the obligation arises,[203] whilst an obligation imposed upon a Mafia suspect to 'change your behaviour' is not sufficiently 'specific or concrete'.[204] As soon as the relevant obligation has been fulfilled, the basis for detention under Article 5(1)(b) ceases to exist.[205] Further, a balance must be struck between the importance in a democratic society of securing the immediate fulfilment of the obligation in question, and the importance of the right to liberty.[206] The duration of detention is a relevant factor in striking such a balance.[207]

It follows from what has just been stated that Article 5(1)(b) does not justify preventive detention of the sort that a state might introduce in an emergency situation,[208] which would be clearly inconsistent with the rule of law.[209] Having said this, when it is 'specific and concrete' an obligation imposed in connection with the enforcement of the criminal law may come within Article 5(1)(b). In *McVeigh, O'Neill and Evans v UK*,[210] under anti-terrorism legislation persons entering Great Britain were potentially obliged to submit to 'further examination' at the point of entry. This was so for the three applicants who were stopped when travelling from Ireland. They were questioned, searched, photographed, and fingerprinted, and released after nearly two days (forty-five hours). No charges were ever brought. The Commission accepted that Article 5(1)(b) applied. It drew a distinction between the obligation in issue and that in Regulation 10, made under the Civil Authorities (Special Powers) Act (NI) 1922, that was relevant in *Ireland v UK*.[211] Under Regulation 10, any person could be detained at any time in Northern Ireland for interrogation 'for the preservation of the peace and maintenance of order'. This was held (*Ireland v UK*) not to impose an obligation in the sense of Article 5(1)(b) and viewed by the Commission in *McVeigh* as an example of 'a general obligation to submit to questioning or interrogation on any occasion, or for any purpose'. By contrast the obligation in issue in *McVeigh* was significantly more 'specific and concrete' in that it applied only upon entering and leaving Great Britain to check the particular matters set out in the relevant legislation. It aimed at controlling the well recognized problem of terrorism in Northern Ireland, in which context there was a 'legitimate need to obtain immediate fulfilment of the obligation to submit to such checks'.[212] Noting that examinations were made as far as possible without resort to detention and that, to be effective, it was necessary for any 'further examination'

[202] *Nowicka v Poland* hudoc (2002) para 60; *Vasileva v Denmark* hudoc (2003); 40 EHRR 681 paras 36–7. See also *Eggs v Switzerland No 7341/76*, 15 DR 35 (1978) Com Rep: CM Res DH (79) 7 and *Johansen v Norway No 10600/83*, 44 DR 155 (1985); 9 EHRR CD 103.

[203] *Ciulla v Italy* A 148 (1989); 13 EHRR 346 para 36 PC (detention prior to decision imposing an obligation restricting freedom of movement).

[204] *Ibid.*   [205] *Nowicka v Poland* hudoc (2002) para 60.

[206] See *Nowicka*, id, para 61 (psychiatric examination ordered by a court—violation of Article 5(1) for two separate reasons: the applicant was not released immediately following the examination, para 64; she was also held unnecessarily for several days prior to examination, so there was no balance between the importance of securing the immediate fulfilment of the obligation in question, and the importance of the right to liberty, para 63). See also *B v France No 10179/82*, 52 DR 111 (1987) and *Reyntjens v Belgium No 16810/90*, 73 DR 136 (1992). This balancing test also applies to the first limb of Article 5(1)(b): *Paradis v France No 4065/04* hudoc (2007) DA.

[207] *Vasileva v Denmark* hudoc (2003); 40 EHRR 681 paras 36–7. See also *Saadi v UK* hudoc (2008) para 70 GC.

[208] *Lawless v Ireland* A 3 (1961); 1 EHRR 15 and *Guzzardi v Italy* A 39 (1980); 3 EHRR 333 para 101PC.

[209] *Engel v Netherlands* A 22 (1976); 1 EHRR 706 para 69 PC.

[210] *Nos 8022/77, 8025/77 and 8027/77*, 25 DR 15 (1981); 5 EHRR 71. See Warbrick, 32 ICLQ 757 (1983). Followed in *Harkin v UK No 11539/85*, 48 DR 237 (1986) and *Lyttle v UK No 11650/85*, 9 EHRR 381 (1986).

[211] A 25 (1978); 2 EHRR 25 para 195 PC. Aricle 15 applied to this case.

[212] *McVeigh*, above n 210, para 192.

to take place subject to a limited period of detention, the Commission found that the applicants' detention was justified by Article 5(1)(b).[213]

McVeigh establishes that in certain 'limited circumstances of a pressing nature' Article 5(1)(b) extends not only to cases in which there has been a prior failure to comply with an obligation, but also to cases in which short-term detention is considered necessary to make the execution of an obligation effective at the time that it arises. The Commission spelt out the test to be applied as follows:[214]

> In considering whether such circumstances exist, account must be taken...of the nature of the obligation. It is necessary to consider whether its fulfilment is a matter of immediate necessity and whether the circumstances are such that no other means of securing fulfilment is reasonably practicable. A balance must be drawn between the importance in a democratic society of securing the immediate fulfilment of the obligation in question, and the importance of the right to liberty. The duration of the period of detention is also a relevant factor in drawing such a balance.[215]

Evidently the context will be all important to the issue of whether the balancing exercise noted above is met. *McVeigh* concerned the 'exceptional context'[216] of prevention of terrorism. There was an obvious violation in *Nowicka v Poland*,[217] which concerned an obligation under a court order to carry out a psychiatric examination which took an inordinate amount of time to carry out, the total period of detention being eighty-three days. In *Vasileva v Denmark*[218] the detention period was 13½ hours, but this too violated Article 5(1)(b) as it was unreasonable on the facts. The police detained the sixty-seven-year-old applicant for the statutory offence of refusing to reveal her identity after a dispute had evolved regarding whether she had a valid travel ticket. What was initially Article 5(1)(b)-compliant detention became unlawful as the deprivation of liberty exceeded a period proportionate to the cause of her detention: the offence (refusal to disclose identity) was minor (according to domestic law it only carried a fine); the applicant was not in possession of any documentation, which could have revealed her identity; it was not acceptable that no efforts were made to get the applicant to identify herself between 11 pm and 6.30 am upon the basis that the applicant needed sleep. As regards identity checks generally, the Court accepts that it is a fundamental condition for the police in order to carry out their tasks, and thus ensure law enforcement, that they can establish the identity of citizens.[219] Detention for a reasonable period of time in the circumstances to effect this is permitted.[220] However, the *Vasileva* case should send a powerful message to domestic authorities in the Convention States that they must constantly justify the reasonableness of maintaining detention under Article 5(1)(b).

---

[213] *Ibid.* The Commission considered that the detention did not fall within Article 5(1)(c) or any other part of Article 5. Cf, *B v France No 10179/82*, 52 DR 111 (1987).

[214] 25 DR 15 at 42 (1981).

[215] Cf, *Vasileva v Denmark* hudoc (2003); 40 EHRR 681 para 38 (importance of: 'the nature of the obligation arising from the relevant legislation including its underlying object and purpose; the person being detained [eg, their age and condition] and the particular circumstances leading to the detention; and the length of the detention').

[216] *Vasileva v Denmark* hudoc (2003); 40 EHRR 681 para 41.   [217] Hudoc (2002) para 61.

[218] *Vasileva v Denmark* hudoc (2003); 40 EHRR 681. See also *Epple v Germany* hudoc (2005) (applicant validly arrested under Article 5(1)(b) for disobeying police order to leave an area proximate to a folk festival; but nineteen-hour delay until brought before a court was disproportional).

[219] Id, para 39. See also *Reyntjens v Belgium No 16810/90*, 73 DR 136 (1992).

[220] See *Novotka v Slovakia No 47244/99* hudoc (2003) DA (detained for fifty-five minutes, no violation).

III. ARTICLE 5(1)(C): DETENTION ON SUSPICION OF HAVING COMMITTED A (CRIMINAL) OFFENCE, ETC

Article 5(1)(c) permits 'the lawful arrest or detention of a person effected *for the purpose of bringing him before the competent legal authority* on *reasonable suspicion* of having committed an *offence* or when it is reasonably considered necessary to prevent his committing an offence or fleeing after having done so' (emphasis added).

This sub-paragraph governs the arrest or detention of suspects in the administration of criminal justice.[221] It is the first of three provisions (see also Article 5(3) and Article 6) that trace the steps that are followed in the course of investigating and prosecuting a person for a criminal offence.[222] It should be said at the outset that these provisions, both separately and as inter-related, present considerable difficulties of interpretation. This results partly from curious drafting, especially of Article 5(1)(c) and (3). Although the Strasbourg authorities have done much, sometimes paying only limited respect to the text, to give these provisions a meaning that reflects the essentials of the administration of criminal justice in Europe, their task has been complicated by the fundamental differences between the systems of criminal procedure in civil and common law jurisdictions. Certain of the Court's judgments make more sense for one kind of criminal justice system than for another.[223] Moreover, the Court has sometimes found it difficult to strike a proper balance between insistence upon a common European standard in the interests of procedural justice and respect for diverse national traditions by which the same end is achieved in different ways.

As will be seen below, there are three main issues to be examined as regards Article 5(1)(c): firstly, the meaning of 'offence', secondly the issue of the *purpose* of detention permissible under the Article, and finally the question of what is 'reasonable suspicion'.

a. 'Offence'

An 'offence' for the purposes of Article 5(1)(c) obviously includes one under domestic criminal law,[224] but the reach of Article 5(1)(c) is wider than this. *Steel v UK*[225] concerned protesters at events such as a grouse shoot and an arms sales fair and who had committed a 'breach of the peace', which is not classed as a criminal offence under English law. However, the Court considered that an 'offence' within the meaning of Article 5(1)(c) was in issue, bearing in mind the nature of the proceedings in question (breach of the peace being a public duty and an arrestable offence) and the penalty at stake (imprisonment if an individual refused to be bound over the keep the peace).[226] Military *criminal* proceedings fall within Article 5(1)(c),[227] though probably not regular disciplinary or regulatory

---

[221] As to a private arrest of a suspected criminal, as permitted by municipal law, arguably Article 5(1)(c) should be interpreted as containing a positive obligation requiring that contracting parties ensure that this is permitted under its law only within the limits set by that sub-paragraph.

[222] Article 5(1)(c) itself does not regulate the questioning of suspects, either before or after arrest. However, Article 5(2) places certain positive obligations on the state, see below p 164. Moreover, the actions of the authorities at the initial stage of detention covered by Article 5(1)(c) can have an impact on the fairness of a subsequent criminal trial (Article 6), in terms of, eg, the right to remain silent, freedom from self-incrimination, and the right of a detainee to have full and free access to a lawyer, see Ch 6. As regards access to others, eg families, issues may arise under Article 8 see *McVeigh, O'Neill and Evans v UK Nos 8022/77, 8025/77 and 8027/77*, 25 DR 15 (1981); 5 EHRR 71 para 239. Questions of surveillance and search and seizure of the person or property come within Article 8 of the Convention.

[223] See eg, *Monnell and Morris v UK* A 115 (1987); 10 EHRR 205 and *B v Austria* A 175 (1990); 13 EHRR 20.

[224] See eg, *Ciulla v Italy* A 148 (1989); 13 EHRR 346 para 38 PC.   [225] 1998-VII; 29 EHRR 365.

[226] Id, para 49. See also *Hood v UK* 1999-I; 29 EHRR 365 para 51 GC.

[227] See *De Jong, Baljet and Van Den Brink v Netherlands* A 77 (1984); 8 EHRR 20.

offences as such proceedings do not normally commence with the arrest of the accused. However, military *disciplinary* proceedings may do so and may lead to 'convictions' in the sense of Article 5(1)(a),[228] so it is submitted that an arrest in connection with such proceedings should be subject to Article 5(1)(c) and (3).[229] At the very least, an autonomous Convention meaning of 'offence' in Article 5(1)(c) ought to include the more serious instances of military, and possibly other, disciplinary, offences as 'offences'.[230] Given that 'offence' must have an autonomous Convention meaning,[231] it could be interpreted as setting limits to the seriousness of the offence for which a state may authorize an arrest. It is submitted that Article 5(1)(c) should set such limits, either through an interpretation of 'offence' or of the word 'lawful'[232] in order to prevent arrest in connection with minor offences that do not justify detection.

The term 'offence' was interpreted in *Brogan v UK*.[233] The case concerned a statutory power to arrest any person 'concerned in the commission, preparation or instigation of acts of terrorism', where the definition of 'terrorism' was the 'use of violence for political ends'. Although such involvement was not itself a criminal offence, the power of arrest was held to be justified under Article 5(1)(c). The definition of 'acts of terrorism' was 'well in keeping with the idea of an offence'[234] and, following their arrest, the applicants had at once been questioned about specific offences of which they were suspected. Whereas the first consideration mentioned by the Court might suggest that it was applying an autonomous Article 5 meaning of 'offence', it would seem from the second that the Court decided the point on the basis that involvement in 'acts of terrorism' indirectly meant the commission of specific criminal offences under Northern Irish law, which would appear to be the better approach on the facts.

b. Purpose of detention

A person may be detained within the meaning of Article 5(1)(c) only in the context of criminal proceedings, for the purpose of bringing him before the competent legal authority on suspicion of his having committed an offence.[235] The meaning of 'competent legal authority' is the same as that of 'judge or other officer authorised to exercise judicial power' in Article 5(3).[236] In terms of English law, the 'competent legal authority' would be a magistrate.

The fact that a person who is detained is not eventually charged or taken before a 'competent legal authority' does not necessarily mean that the 'purpose' required by Article 5(1)(c) is not present when he is arrested; provided that 'reasonable suspicion' exists, a person may be arrested in good faith for questioning with a view to establishing the evidence needed to bring a charge without the arrest falling foul of Article 5(1)(c) because such evidence is not forthcoming.[237] More generally the scheme of Article 5(1)(c) and (3), which must be read together,[238] make it clear that Article 5(1)(c) is limited to the arrest or detention of persons for the purpose of enforcing the criminal law. Accordingly, the Court

---

[228] See above, p 126.

[229] Article 5(1)(c) is not relevant to the segregation of convicted prisoners in connection with prison disciplinary offences since they are detained under Article 5(1)(a).

[230] Cf, the inclusion of some disciplinary offences as 'criminal' charges in Article 6(1), below, p 208.

[231] See above, p 138.   [232] See above, p 133.   [233] A 145-B (1988); 11 EHRR 117 PC.

[234] Id, para 51. Cf *Ireland v UK* A 25 (1978); 2 EHRR 25 para 196 PC.

[235] See *Ječius v Lithuania* 2000-IX; 35 EHRR 400 paras 50–1.

[236] *Schiesser v Switzerland* A 34 (1979); 2 EHRR 417 para 29.

[237] *Brogan v UK* A 145-B (1988); 11 EHRR 117 para 53 PC; *Murray v UK* A 300-A (1994); 19 EHRR 193 para 67 GC; *Labita v Italy* 2000-IV 99; 46 EHRR 1228 para 155 GC.

[238] *Ciulla v Italy* A 148 (1989); 13 EHRR 346 PC.

has held that the detention of a person to bring him before a 'competent legal authority' in connection with court proceedings for a compulsory residence order (on suspicion of involvement in Mafia activities) is not justified by Article 5(1)(c) since the detention was not related to proceedings that could lead to conviction for a criminal offence.[239]

The fact that Article 5(1)(c) concerns only detention in the enforcement of the criminal law is relevant to the interpretation of the three grounds for arrest that it permits. Whereas the scope of the *first* of these grounds—suspicion of having committed an offence—is clear from its text, that of the second and third is less certain. In fact the *third* ground of Article 5(1)(c) appears redundant since a person who is 'fleeing after having' committed an offence can in any event be arrested under the first limb. As to the *second* (prevention of an offence), at first sight it could be read as authorizing a general power of preventive detention. However, this interpretation was rejected in *Lawless v Ireland*,[240] as 'leading to conclusions repugnant to the fundamental principles of the Convention'.[241] Ruling that the wording 'for the purpose of bringing him before the competent legal authority' applied to all three of the limbs of Article 5(1)(c), the Court rejected the defendant government's argument that the detention of the applicant, a suspected IRA activist, under a statute that permitted the internment of persons 'engaged in activities... prejudicial to the... security of the state', could be justified as being 'necessary to prevent his committing an offence'. This was because the detention of an interned person under the statute was not effected with the purpose of initiating a criminal prosecution.[242] The Court's stance here, which is in accordance with the rule of law and European standards concerning preventive detention, as well as with the criminal law context of Article 5(1)(c), makes it difficult to give any meaning to the second ground for detention set out under Article 5(1)(c). Conduct that amounts in municipal law to the offence of attempting to commit an offence is itself an 'offence', so that the first limb of Article 5(1)(c) applies.

As a rule the 'prevention of an offence' ground of Article 5(1)(c) does not justify re-detention or continued detention of a prisoner, even though there is a suspicion that he might commit a further similar offence when released. However, this can be the case in exceptional and narrowly defined circumstances, as in *Eriksen v Norway*[243] which involved a violent applicant detained under terms whereby the authorities were able to keep him in detention for an extra four weeks when his sentence expired, pending a decision by a court on whether or not detention should be extended. The exceptional, 'bridging' detention was Article 5(1)(c)-compliant for several reasons.[244] These included: the special scheme operating which ensured a close link between the original criminal proceedings and the resulting conviction and security measures; the violent past of the applicant and his mental state at the relevant time such that there were substantial grounds for believing that he would commit further similar offences (hence, the anticipated offences were sufficiently concrete and specific in accordance with Convention requirements); finally, the detention was of a short duration, imposed in order to bring the applicant before a

---

[239] *Ibid.*   [240] *Lawless v Ireland* A 3 (1961); 1 EHRR 15.

[241] Id, para 14. Cf, *Guzzardi v Italy* A 39 (1980); 3 EHRR 333 para 102 PC: '... the phrase under examination is not adapted to a policy of general prevention directed against an individual or a category of individuals who, like mafiosi, present a danger on account of their continuing propensity to crime; it does no more than afford the contracting parties a means of preventing a concrete and specified offence.' See also *Ječius v Lithuania* 2000-IX 235; 35 EHRR 400 paras 50–2.

[242] Cf, *Ireland v UK* A 25 (1978); 2 EHRR 25 PC and *Guzzardi v Italy* A 39 (1980); 3 EHRR 333 PC, also *Ciulla v Italy* A 148 (1989); 13 EHRR 346 paras 38–41 PC.

[243] 1997-III; 29 EHRR 328.

[244] The Commission considered Article 5(1)(c) inapplicable. The Court considered that both Articles 5(1)(a) and 5(1)(c) applied.

judicial authority, and required so that a mental health report could be obtained, plus the applicant had opposed efforts to secure a preventive supervision scheme outside prison.

c. Reasonable suspicion

Returning to the first ground for detention under Article 5(1)(c), it will be noticed that a person may be kept detained only when there is a 'reasonable suspicion' that he has committed an offence. The fact that a suspicion is merely held in good faith is insufficient.[245] However, it is not necessary that, ultimately at least, charges be brought against the detained individual, nor for the authorities to have obtained sufficient evidence to bring charges upon arrest or during detention.[246] Indeed the object of the detention before charge is 'to further a criminal investigation by confirming or discontinuing suspicions which provide the grounds for detention'.[247] Nonetheless the clear condition that suspicion be based on reasonable grounds 'forms an essential part of the safeguard against arbitrary arrest and detention'.[248] The constraint provided by this provision, as well as Article 5(2), may be of great importance since Article 5(1)(c) does not seem to set an absolute limit to the length of time that a person may be detained prior to being charged.

As the Court stated in *Fox, Campbell, and Hartley v UK*,[249] 'reasonable suspicion' supposes 'the existence of facts or information which would satisfy an objective observer that the person concerned may have committed the offence'. What may be regarded as 'reasonable' will 'depend upon all of the circumstances'.[250] In this connection, it is permissible to take into account the fact that a case concerns the investigation of terrorist activities, so that allowance may be made for the need the police have to act urgently (on reliable information) and not to place their informants at risk. On the one hand, the Court accepts that states 'cannot be required to establish the reasonableness of the suspicion grounding the arrest of a suspected terrorist by disclosing confidential sources of information'. On the other hand, the Court insists that 'the exigencies of dealing with terrorist crime cannot justify stretching the notion of "reasonableness" to the point where the safeguard secured by Article 5(1)(c) is impaired'.[251] In such a cases 'the respondent government has to furnish at least some facts or information capable of satisfying the Court that the arrested person was reasonably suspected of having committed the alleged offence'.[252]

In *Fox, Campbell and Hartley v UK*, the accused were arrested in Northern Ireland by a constable exercising a statutory power (since abolished) allowing him to arrest for up to seventy-two hours 'any person whom *he* suspects of being a terrorist' (emphasis added), ie if the individual policeman had an 'honestly held suspicion'. Although, therefore, the power of arrest was capable of permitting an arrest that did not comply with Article 5(1)(c), the question for the European Court was whether there had on the facts been a 'reasonable suspicion' in the sense of that sub-paragraph, not whether the statute

---

[245] *Gusinskiy v Russia* 2004-IV; 41 EHRR 281 para 53. As to arrest on the basis of information from an anonymous source see *O'Hara v UK* 2001-X; 34 EHRR 812 para 43.

[246] *Ibid.*   [247] *Ibid.*   [248] *Ibid.*

[249] *Fox, Campbell and Hartley v UK* A 182 (1990); 13 EHRR 157 para 32. There was a clear violation in *Stepuleac v Moldova* hudoc (2007).

[250] *Ibid.* The circumstances are those as they were known at the time of the arrest: *Nielsen v Denmark No 343/57*, 1 Digest 388 (1961). A confession is likely to give rise to a 'reasonable suspicion': *AV v Austria No 4465/70*, 38 CD 58 at 60 (1970).

[251] *O'Hara v UK* 2001-X; 34 EHRR 812 para 35.

[252] *Fox, Campbell and Hartley v UK* A 182 (1990); 13 EHRR 157 para 34. See also *O'Hara v UK* 2001-X; 34 EHRR 812 para 35.

concerned was invalid *in abstracto*. Here the only evidence produced by the defendant government was that the applicants had, some seven years previously, been convicted of terrorist offences and that they were, on arrest, questioned about specific terrorist acts, the government arguing that, as the information justifying the arrest had been from informants, it could provide no further information for fear of endangering the lives of others. While accepting that some allowance could be made for the difficulties faced by the police in the emergency situation, the Court concluded that the evidence that had been provided was insufficient to establish that there was a 'reasonable suspicion', objectively determined, as Article 5(1)(c) required. As a result, Article 5(1) had been infringed.[253]

The Court has acknowledged that there may be a 'fine line between those cases where the suspicion grounding the arrest is not sufficiently founded on objective facts and those which are'[254] and this is apparent from two further 'terrorist' cases from Northern Ireland when it was accepted that Article 5(1)(c) had not been breached: *Murray v UK*[255] and *O'Hara v UK*.[256] In the latter case the applicant had been detained for over six days before being released without charge. The Court was faced with one version of events from the respondent government (essentially it referred to the quality of intelligence information it had received from four informers) and a completely different one from the applicant (claiming there was no intention to charge him, rather that he was simply targeted by the authorities as a prominent member of a political party supporting the Republican movement). However, unlike the *Fox* and *Murray* cases the standard of suspicion set by domestic law for arrest was closer to Article 5(1)(c): honest suspicion on reasonable grounds. This was 'a significant safeguard against arbitrary arrest'[257] and, on the facts, the Court, was influenced by this together with the applicant's ensuing failure to pursue the issue of 'reasonable suspicion' before the domestic courts (where he had focused on claims of assault and ill-treatment) and where, on the limited materials before him, the judge had inferred the existence of reasonable grounds of suspicion. Overall the European Court stated that there was no basis in the material provided to it to reject the government's version of events that the arrest was a pre-planned operation, more akin to the earlier *Murray* case, and based on slightly more specific detail than *Fox, Campbell and Hartley*. As to whether reasonable suspicion had existed, it stated that the domestic courts' approach was not incompatible with the standard imposed by Article 5(1)(c), and that the domestic legal regime provided checks against arbitrary arrest plus did not confer any impunity with regard to arrests conducted on the basis of confidential information. In the Court's view (six votes to one), it could therefore be said that Article 5(1)(c) was satisfied.[258]

It will be appreciated from these cases that Article 5(1)(c) does not permit the detention of an individual for questioning merely as part of an intelligence gathering exercise (there must be an intention, in principle at least, to bring charges, otherwise the person must be released). In practical terms, however, it will be very hard for an international court to ensure that Article 5(1)(c) is always applied in good faith by the national authorities.

---

[253] See also *Berktay v Turkey* hudoc (2001) paras 199–201.

[254] *O'Hara v UK* 2001-X; 34 EHRR 812 para 41. See, however, *Smirnova v Russia* 2003-IX; 39 EHRR 450 for a clear violation.

[255] A 300-A (1994); 19 EHRR 193 paras 56, 61–2. There was evidence from national court proceedings in the case and corroborative evidence about terrorist activity by other family members. The fact that the maximum length of detention in this case was only four hours was also 'material to the level of suspicion required'.

[256] 34 EHRR 812.   [257] Id, para 38.

[258] See, however, the strong dissent of Judge Loucaides. One commentator (referring to Article 5(1)(c) generally) has suggested, '[t]here is a certain reluctance perhaps by the Court to find that authorities have acted in bad faith in carrying out arrests', Reid, *A Practitioner's Guide to the ECHR*, 3rd edn, p 234.

Cases such as *Fox, Campbell and Hartley* and the others considered immediately above concerned Article 5(1)(c) in the context of an 'arrest' and in the period immediately thereafter. However, this provision may provide the basis for detention for a significant period of time beyond arrest. During this time, the continuing need for detention may be subject to periodic review under Article 5(3).[259]

d. Lawfulness

Although the Court is competent to decide that the applicable municipal law concerning arrest has not been complied with, it will, in recognition of the primary competence of the national authorities, particularly the courts, intervene only in cases where there has been a clear breach of it.[260] For practical reasons too the Court will not be in a good position to decide whether, on the specific facts, an arrest for broad offences such as being drunk and disorderly was justified. However, the Court is prepared to find a violation of Article 5(1) when it is clear from the facts that the grounds for arrest simply did not exist. An example is *Steel v UK*,[261] where the Court found that, for certain of the applicants, their protest had been entirely peaceful such that the criteria making up the offence of breach of the peace had not been applied at the time the applicants were detained.[262] Complications may arise when the criminal law provision in issue and which is the basis of detention under Article 5(1)(c) has never been applied by the national courts and the constituent elements of the offence are subject to serious difficulties of interpretation. In such circumstances, the Court has regard to the law at the material time and will examine it against the alleged facts held against the applicant in order to determine whether the interpretation of the legal provisions relied on by the domestic authorities was arbitrary or unreasonable, so as to render the detention itself unlawful.[263]

In *KF v Germany*,[264] where domestic law permitted detention of the applicant for a maximum of twelve hours, the Court indicated that it could find as non 'lawful' a detention within that time span but which was unreasonable to the extent that it was not actually justified (for example, the police were no longer pursuing the matter). In principle detention will not be 'lawful' under Article 5(1)(c) when the maximum period laid down by law for detaining the applicant is exceeded, as it was on the facts of the *KF* case. The Court will take a strict approach here when the maximum period is absolute, specifically laid down by law and so known in advance. The authorities would then be under a duty to take all necessary precautions to ensure that the permitted duration was not exceeded and even a short period in excess will violate Article 5.[265] Where the period of detention is not laid down in advance by statute and ends as a result of a court order or the determination of the charge against an accused, in principle Article 5(1)(c) will be violated immediately after the point when a charge is determined.[266] However, the Court has accepted that there may be some limited delay before a detained person is released, when this is a result

[259] See below p 173.
[260] *X v Austria No 10803/84*, 11 EHRR 112 (1989) (Commission decision).
[261] 1998-VII; 29 EHRR 365. See also *RL and M-JD v France* hudoc (2004) (violation of Article 5(1) by four votes to three).
[262] Id, paras 62–4 (the legal question regarding whether there had been a breach of the peace had not been before the domestic court as the prosecution had dropped the charges, whilst no civil claim for false imprisonment against the police was brought).
[263] *Wloch v Poland* 2000-XI; 34 EHRR 229 paras 111–17.   [264] 1997-VII; 26 EHRR 390 para 68.
[265] Id, paras 71–2 (violation of Article 5(1) when individual held forty-five minutes over the twelve-hour maximum). The Commission, 7 votes to 6, considered there had been no violation given the minor delay.
[266] However, Article 5(1)(a) may then apply.

of '[p]ractical considerations relating to the running of the courts and the completion of special formalities'.[267] But the delay must be kept to a minimum.[268]

The 'lawfulness' requirement can provide the basis for controlling the modalities of arrest, such as the need for an arrest warrant. Article 5(1)(c) has not so far been used to regulate the kind of offences for which arrest is permitted or the circumstances in which a private person may be empowered to arrest. It has been accepted, however, that arrest without a warrant is permitted by Article 5 in at least some cases.[269] In the absence of any indication of 'arbitrariness', the fact that one accused is lawfully detained whilst others are not is not by itself contrary to Article 5(1)(c).[270] Nor is the fact that a person is investigated in respect of one offence while detained on reasonable suspicion of another.[271]

The principle of legal certainty, inherent in the concept of 'lawful' detention, is contravened when detention under Article 5(1)(c) is permitted for an unlimited and unpredictable time and without being based on a concrete legal provision or on any judicial decision.[272] Hence, 'detention which extends over a period of several months and which has not been ordered by a court or by a judge or any other person "authorised ... to exercise judicial power" cannot be considered "lawful" in the sense of [Article 5(1)(c)]'.[273] In fact, such a requirement is not explicitly stipulated in Article 5(1), but the Court infers it from Article 5 read as a whole, in particular from Articles 5(1)(c), 5(3), and 5(4).[274]

IV. ARTICLE 5(1)(D): DETENTION OF MINORS

Article 5(1)(d) permits 'the detention of a minor by lawful order for the purpose of educational supervision or his lawful detention for the purpose of bringing him before the competent legal authority'. This creates a specific basis to detain minors, but its existence does not prevent the potential reliance on other Articles 5(1) paragraphs to detain minors.[275]

As with other Article 5(1) terms, 'minor' has an autonomous Convention meaning.[276] In the light of European standards, all persons under eighteen can be taken to be minors.[277] Whether a state with an age of majority higher than eighteen would find that its detention of a person of eighteen years or more was justified under Article 5(1)(d) is unclear. In the case of both grounds for detention allowed by Article 5(1)(d), the detention

---

[267] *KF v Germany* 1997-VII; 26 EHRR 390 para 71. See also *Quinn v France* A 311 (1995); 21 EHRR 529 (Article 5(1)(c) violated when detainee held for eleven hours beyond court order requiring immediate release); *Labita v Italy* 2000-IV; 46 EHRR 1228 GC (violation because twelve-hour delay was due, at least in part, to absence of appropriate member of staff required to complete release formalities); and *Bojinov v France* hudoc (2004) (administrative problems).

[268] *Giulia Manzoni v Italy* 1997-IV; 26 EHRR 691 para 25. See also *Bojinov v Bulgaria* hudoc (2004).

[269] *X v Austria No 7755/77*, 9 DR 210 (1977) and *X v Austria No 9472/81*, 1 Digest Supp 5.1.5.2., p 3 (1982). The fact that the power of arrest concerned did not require a warrant was not commented upon in *Fox, Campbell and Hartley v UK* A 182 (1990); 13 EHRR 157.

[270] *X v Austria No 4622/70*, 40 CD 15 (1972).

[271] *Kamma v Netherlands No 4771/71*, 18 YB 300 (1974) Com Rep; CM Res DH (75) 1.

[272] *Baranowski v Poland* 2000-III para 56. See also *Ječius v Lithuania* 2000-IX; 35 EHRR 400; *Laumont v France* 2001-XI; 36 EHRR 625. See also *Lukanov v Bulgaria* 1997-II; 24 EHRR 121 (former Prime Minister of Bulgaria charged for misappropriation of state funds even though his actions—granting funds in assistance and loans to developing countries—were not criminal under domestic law).

[273] Id, para 57.   [274] Ibid.

[275] *Mubilanzila Mayeka and Kaniki Mitunga v Belgium* hudoc (2006); 46 EHRR 449 para 100.

[276] *X v Switzerland No 8500/79*, 18 DR 238 (1979). Cf, the interpretation of 'vagrant', etc in Article 5(1)(e), p 154, below.

[277] In *X v Switzerland No 8500/79*, 18 DR 238 (1979), it was noted that in no party to the Convention was the age of majority less than eighteen.

must be 'lawful', which, as elsewhere in Article 5(1),[278] requires compliance with municipal law and the Convention and supposes that any deprivation of liberty is 'in keeping with the purpose of Article 5, namely to protect the individual from arbitrariness'.[279]

The first of the two permitted grounds, *viz* detention 'for the purpose of educational supervision', applies when the detention results from a 'lawful order', which may be made by an administrative authority or by a court. This ground for detention would appear to authorize the legal obligation normally found in state law requiring children to attend school.[280] It may be noted, however, that Article 5(1)(d) authorizes the detention of 'minors', not persons of an age that are required to attend school. In other words, where the school leaving age is sixteen, a seventeen-year old may still be detained under Article 5(1)(d).[281]

In *Bouamar v Belgium*[282] it was held that Article 5(1)(d) authorized the detention of a minor in a reformatory 'for the purpose of educational supervision' or in a remand prison as a preliminary to his transfer 'speedily' to such an institution. In that case, the defendant state was held to be in breach of Article 5(1) when the applicant, a seriously disturbed and delinquent sixteen-year-old, was detained by court order in a remand prison, which provided no educational facilities, for periods amounting to 119 days' detention during most of one year. The orders were made under a 1965 Act, the policy of which was that juveniles who committed criminal offences should normally be placed in juvenile reformatories rather than be convicted by a criminal court. The orders for the applicant's detention were made under a provision of the Act that permitted a juvenile's detention in a remand prison for up to fifteen days when it was 'materially impossible' to place him in a reformatory immediately. In the applicant's case, the problem was that the open reformatories that provided the required educational facilities were not willing to take him because of his difficult behaviour and there were no closed reformatories with such facilities in his French-speaking region. The Court accepted that the applicant might be detained temporarily in a remand prison, though this should be 'speedily' followed by detention in an Article 5(1)(d) compatible institution.[283] On the facts, however, the period of prison detention was too long and was not for the permitted purpose as the applicant's detention was an expedient adopted by the authorities in the absence of 'appropriate institutional facilities which met the demands of security and the educational objectives of the 1965 Act'.[284] If, for commendable policy reasons, Belgium had decided not to dispose of seriously disturbed juveniles through the criminal courts (in which case their detention could be justified following conviction under Article 5(1)(a)), it could only detain them consistently with Article 5 in institutions that offered the necessary educational supervision required by Article 5(1)(d). Should this involve the building of appropriate reformatories, the resulting commitment was, the Court made clear,[285] one that Belgium would have to undertake despite the cost involved.

How comprehensive and 'school-like' the regime of 'educational supervision' provided by a reformatory for disturbed juveniles has to be is not entirely clear. In the context of a

---

[278] See above, p 133.   [279] *Bouamar v Belgium* A 129 (1988); 11 EHRR 1 para 47.

[280] As to cases involving parental consent, see *Nielsen v Denmark*, above, p 127.

[281] *DG v Ireland* 2002-III; 35 EHRR 1153 para 76 (according to domestic legalisation a 'minor' was below the age of eighteen).

[282] A 129 (1988); 11 EHRR 1.

[283] Id, para 50. The respondent government failed to satisfy this requirement in *DG v Ireland* 2002-III; 35 EHRR 1153 paras 84–5, where at first no secure education facilities were available and then hastily prepared facilities proved to be inadequate, initially at least, as they did not provide proper, secure, and supervised educational facilities.

[284] Id, para 52.   [285] *Ibid.*

young person in local authority care the Court has accepted that the words do not have to be 'equated rigidly with notions of classroom teaching' and that 'educational supervision must embrace many aspects of the exercise, by the local authority, of parental rights for the benefit and protection of the person concerned'.[286]

The second of the two permitted grounds for the detention of a minor is 'his lawful detention for the purpose of bringing him before the competent legal authority'. The *travaux préparatoires* indicate that this wording was intended to cover the situation where a minor is detained with a view to being brought before a court not on a criminal charge (so that Article 5(1)(c) would apply) but 'to secure his removal from harmful surroundings'.[287] Thus the detention of a minor accused of a crime during the preparation of a psychiatric report necessary to the taking of a decision in his case is permitted,[288] as is detention pending the making of a court order placing a child in care.[289]

V. ARTICLE 5(1)(E): DETENTION OF PERSONS OF UNSOUND MIND, ALCOHOLICS, VAGRANTS, ETC

Article 5(1)(e) permits 'the lawful detention of persons for the prevention of the spreading of infectious diseases, of persons of unsound mind,[290] alcoholics or drug addicts or vagrants'. Each term has an autonomous Convention meaning. The categories of persons covered by this sub-paragraph may all be deprived of liberty 'either in order to be given medical treatment or because of considerations dictated by social policy', or both combined, the 'predominant reason' for allowing detention being that the persons concerned 'are dangerous for public safety but also that their own interests may necessitate their detention'.[291] The Court applies a strict necessity test to detention under this sub-paragraph.[292]

a. Prevention of the spreading of infectious diseases

The Court has held that the criteria for determining the lawfulness of detention under Article 5(1)(e) in relation to 'infectious diseases' is, firstly, 'whether the spreading of the infectious disease is dangerous for public health or safety', and secondly 'whether detention of the person infected is the last resort in order to prevent the spreading of the disease, because less severe measures have been considered and found to be insufficient to safeguard the public interest'.[293] A deprivation of liberty ceases to be lawful when these criteria are no longer fulfilled.

Enhorn v Sweden[294] concerned a person carrying the HIV virus, which the Court accepted satisfied the first test just identified ('dangerous for public health and safety').

---

[286] *DG v Ireland* 2002-III; 35 EHRR 1153 para 80. Cf, *Bouamar v Belgium* A 129 (1988); 11 EHRR 1 para 50. See also *Koniarska v UK No 33670/96* hudoc (2000) DA where the seventeen-year-old applicant was held in a specialist residential facility for seriously disturbed young people. The Court was satisfied that Article 5(1)(d) applied given the multi-disciplinary teaching provided. The fact that the number of classes attended by the applicant became limited because she chose not to go did not affect the underlying position, which was that extensive educational provision was made, and 'the applicant benefited from it to a certain extent'.

[287] 3 TP 724, quoted in Fawcett, p 90.

[288] *X v Switzerland No 8500/79*, 18 DR 238 (1979) (detention for the remarkably long period of eight months for observation justified on this basis).

[289] Cf, *Bouamar v Belgium* A 129 (1988); 11 EHRR 1 para 46.

[290] As to the relationship between Article 5(1)(a) and (e) when a person is detained by a court as mentally disordered following his conviction, see above, p 139.

[291] *Enhorn v Sweden* 2005-I; 41 EHRR 633 para 43. See also *Guzzardi v Italy* A 39 (1980); 3 EHRR 333 para 98 PC and *Witold Litwa v Poland* 2000-III 289; 33 EHRR 1267 para 60.

[292] Cf, comments made above at p 137.   [293] *Enhorn v Sweden* 2005-I; 41 EHRR 633 para 44.

[294] Id, para 45.

The applicant had been placed involuntarily in a hospital for a period totalling approximately one and a half years further to a court order enforcing public health legislation and after the apparent failure of voluntary measures created to protect other members of society, the reason for the detention apparently being to stop the applicant spreading the disease through sexual acts. The European Court accepted that there was a basis for the detention in domestic law in that, firstly, the national courts had considered that the applicant had not voluntarily complied with the measures needed to prevent the virus from spreading; and, secondly, although the relevant medical officer had formulated practical instructions for the applicant to regulate his conduct on release, it was reasonable on the facts to suggest that these would not be complied with, plus that this would entail a risk of the infection spreading.[295] However, Article 5(1)(e) had been violated as the second ('last resort') test identified above was not satisfied. Certain measures that might have reduced the risk posed by the applicant (eg, psychiatric treatment to change the applicant's behaviour and effective treatment to help him control his abuse of alcohol) had not been made a condition of the voluntary regime required of him prior to the order to detain. Moreover, although one sexual partner had been infected prior to the applicant's knowledge that he himself carried the virus, there was no evidence to suggest that the applicant had ever spread HIV intentionally or through gross neglect, including during the period of over five years when the order for detention was in force but when, in fact, he had absconded.[296] More generally the Court considered that the authorities had failed to strike a fair balance between the need to ensure that the HIV virus did not spread and the applicant's right to liberty.[297]

b. 'Vagrants'

The term 'vagrants' was examined in *De Wilde, Ooms and Versyp v Belgium* (the *Vagrancy* cases).[298] The Court noted that in the Belgian Criminal Code 'vagrants' were defined as 'persons who have no fixed abode, no means of subsistence and no regular trade or profession'. It commented that a person who came within this definition was 'in principle' a 'vagrant' for the purposes of Article 5(1)(e). Although the Court did not expressly state that the Convention meaning was co-terminous with that in Belgian law, it is likely that the latter reflects the generally understood meaning of the term. In *Guzzardi v Italy*,[299] the Court rejected a government argument that suspected Mafia members who lacked any identifiable sources of income were vagrants.

c. 'Alcoholics' and 'drug addicts'

In *Witold Litwa v Poland*[300] the Court held that a person does not have to be in a clinical state of 'alcoholism' to be an 'alcoholic' for the purposes of Article 5(1)(e). The term potentially applies to 'persons...whose conduct and behaviour under the influence of alcohol pose a threat to public order or themselves'. Such individuals could 'be taken into custody for the protection of the public or their own interests, such as their health or personal safety'.[301] In this way Article 5(1)(e) can be employed to facilitate the detention of the type

---

[295] Id, paras 37–8.   [296] Id, para 54.

[297] Id, para 55. See also the concurring opinion of Judge Costa warning that systematic confinement of persons capable of spreading infectious diseases would turn them into outcasts and was only acceptable for limited periods ('quarantine'), where the disease is curable.

[298] A 12 (1971); 1 EHRR 373 PC.   [299] A 39 (1980); 3 EHRR 333 PC.

[300] 2000-III; 33 EHRR 1267 paras 57–63. See also *Hilda Hafsteinsdóttir v Iceland* hudoc (2004) and *HD v Poland No 33310/96* hudoc (2001) DA.

[301] Id, para 61. See also para 62. The case suggests that the Court would be prepared to be flexible as regards the requirement of addiction to drugs despite the express wording 'drug *addict*' (Article 5(1)(e)).

of intoxicated individuals just referred to for temporary (sobering up) periods either when the misdemeanour is not actually a criminal offence or, if so, when, for whatever reason, there is no real intention of progressing them through the criminal justice system.[302]

In *Witold Litwa* the Court maintained that its interpretation of 'alcoholics' was in keeping with the original spirit of Article 5;[303] however, Judge Bonnello, the sole dissenter, took strong exception to the interpretation employed which, he insisted, went against the whole thrust of Article 5 jurisprudence and was a 'quantum leap backwards'.[304] Certainly the broad reading of 'alcoholic' places a heavy burden on the controlling requirement that any detention under Article 5(1) must be 'lawful'. The test to be satisfied here is whether the intoxicated person should be detained in order 'to limit the harm caused by alcohol to himself and the public', or even, 'to prevent dangerous behaviour after drinking'.[305] This seems to be worryingly vague, but it is notable that the Court applied the test quite stringently in *Witold Litwa* itself. The applicant was involved in a disagreement at the post office in which the staff claimed he was drunk and abusive. He was almost fifty years old, and practically blind but still taken by the police to Kraków sobering-up centre and detained there for six hours and thirty minutes. The proper legal procedures had been followed, but the 'lawfulness' test was not met as, given apparent elements of arbitrariness in the detention, the Court did not accept that what actually occurred was 'the lawful detention' of an 'alcoholic'. 'Serious doubts' existed as to whether the applicant had indeed behaved, under the influence of alcohol, in such a way that he posed a threat to the public or himself, or that his own health, well-being or personal safety was endangered. As other options had been available to the police, eg simply escorting the applicant off the premises and taking him home, and these seemed to be appropriate on the facts, the applicant's detention had not been 'lawful'. The Court stated that '[t]he detention of an individual is such a serious measure that it is only justified where other, less severe measures have been considered and found to be insufficient to safeguard the individual or public interest which might require that the person concerned be detained. That means that it does not suffice that the deprivation of liberty is executed in conformity with national law but it must also be necessary in the circumstances.'[306]

The test of 'necessity' is therefore a check against the authorities' readiness to detain individuals (perhaps in a pre-emptive way) without proper consideration of the alternatives. It must be hoped that the domestic authorities will interpret this 'necessity' test strictly, placing the onus on the police to explain what alternatives to detention were considered and why they were not appropriate.

Finally, sight should not be lost of the importance of a precise regulatory framework governing detention in this sphere. The 'quality of law' requirements for detention of 'alcoholics' has been stressed in the case law. In *Hilda Hafsteinsdóttir v Iceland*[307] the Court found a violation of Article 5(1) as administrative practice alone governed the scope and the manner of exercise of the police's discretion as regards the duration of detention.

---

[302] Cf, the requirements of Article 5(1)(c).

[303] The majority referred to the preparatory work of the Convention to fortify their understanding, see *Witold Litwa v Poland* 2000-III; 33 EHRR 1267 para 63.

[304] Separate opinion of Judge Bonnello in *Witold Litwa*, arguing that Article 5(1)(e) applied only 'to continuing or habitual states of socially dangerous conditions or attitudes', as opposed 'to one-off, transient manifestations'. The Court had 'for the first time ever, and with a vengeance, departed from a healthy tradition, so far nurtured with religious fervour, of not adding to the list of exceptions which justify deprivations of liberty'.

[305] Id, para 62.   [306] Id, para 78.

[307] Hudoc (2004) paras 51 and 53–6. See, however, the partly dissenting opinion of Judge Garlicki and the dissenting opinion of Judges Casadevall and Maruste.

d. 'Persons of unsound mind'[308]

The meaning of 'persons of unsound mind' was considered in *Winterwerp v Netherlands*.[309] It is not a term that can be given a 'definitive interpretation' because the medical profession's understanding of mental disorder is still developing, but it is evident that a person cannot be detained under Article 5(1)(e) 'simply because his views or behaviour deviate from the norms prevailing in a particular society'.[310] Beyond that, when determining whether a person is of 'unsound mind', it is a matter of referring to the relevant municipal law, which need not define or list the categories of mental disorder to which it extends, and its application in the particular case in the light of current psychiatric knowledge.[311]

The authorities must comply with the procedures set out in domestic law in order for a detention to be lawful. For example, in *Van Der Leer v Netherlands*,[312] the Court held that a person had been detained 'unlawfully' contrary to Article 5(1)(e) when a court had ordered the applicant's detention on the basis of mental illness without hearing her in person, as required by Dutch law. As the Court stated in *Winterwerp v Netherlands*,[313] the detention must be in 'conformity with the purpose of the restrictions permitted by Article 5(1)(e)' and must also be warranted on the facts of the case, otherwise it will be arbitrary. To avoid 'arbitrariness' the case law requires that three minimum conditions have to be satisfied:

(i)   prior to the detention, the detainee must be 'reliably shown' by 'objective medical expertise'[314] to be of 'unsound mind', unless emergency detention is required;[315]

(ii)   the individual's 'mental disorder must be of a kind or degree warranting compulsory confinement', ie the deprivation of liberty must be shown to have been 'necessary in the circumstances';[316] and

(iii)   the disorder, verified by objective medical evidence, must persist throughout the period of detention.

Although the Strasbourg authorities have the final word as to whether the above conditions are met, the defendant state is allowed a certain 'margin of appreciation' when making its own initial assessment of the situation.[317]

As to the second condition noted above, the detention of a mentally disordered person must be in the interest of the safety of the applicant or of others, but medical treatment is not required.[318] It is therefore possible to detain someone suffering from a psychopathic personality disorder that cannot be treated in an appropriate hospital.[319] If so, the detention in a mental hospital is not necessarily contrary to the spirit of Article 5 provided

---

[308] See Bartlett, Lewis, and Thorold, *Mental disability and the European Convention on Human Rights*, 2006.

[309] A 33 (1979); 2 EHRR 387 para 36. On this case, see Muchlinski, 5 HRR 90 (1980). See also *X v UK* A 46 (1981); 4 EHRR 188.

[310] Id, para 37.   [311] Id, para 38.

[312] A 170-A (1990); 12 EHRR 567 para 22. See also *Koendjbiharie v Netherlands* A 185-B (1990); 13 EHRR 820 (failure to renew the applicant's detention order within the legal time limit; breach of Article 5(4) ('speedily'), but Court did not (Judge Bernhardt dissenting) consider the case under Article 5(1)).

[313] A 33 (1979); 2 EHRR 387 para 39.

[314] This will include a personal medical examination, other than in an emergency situation. For elaboration of further standards in this area see *Wassink v Netherlands* (1990) A 185-A paras 33 and 34; *Varbanov v Bulgaria* 2000-X paras 47–4 and *Herz v Germany* hudoc (2003).

[315] See *Varbanov*, id, para 47.   [316] Id, para 46.

[317] *Winterwerp v Netherlands* A 33 (1979); 2 EHRR 387 para 40; *X v UK* A 46 (1981); 4 EHRR 188 para 43; and *Luberti v Italy* A 75 (1984); 6 EHRR 440 para 27.

[318] *Hutchison Reid v UK* 2003 IV; 37 EHRR 211 para 52.   [319] Id, paras 51–2.

there remains 'a sufficient relationship between the grounds of the detention and place and conditions of detention to satisfy Article 5(1)'.[320]

The third condition (validity of continued confinement depends upon the persistence of the disorder) can raise some awkward practical problems given the difficulties that may arise since recovery from mental illness is not an exact science and decisions cannot always be made with absolute certainty. The Court accepts that, on the facts, the wider interest of the community might be balanced against the individual's right to immediate and unconditional release. For example, as regards immediate release, in *Luberti v Italy*[321] even if the medical evidence pointed to his recovery, it was held that a responsible author-ity was entitled to proceed with caution and might need some time to consider whether to terminate an applicant's confinement.

Issues may arise when the applicant's release is subject to certain conditions which are not easily fulfilled. The applicant in *Kolanis v UK*[322] continued to suffer from schizophre-nia and to require treatment (including medication) and medical supervision in order to control her illness. Her condition was such that compulsory confinement was no longer warranted—though only on the basis that she continued to have certain treatment once at liberty. However, appropriate measures for that treatment were not put in place and so the applicant remained detained. There was no violation of Article 5(1), for in the circum-stances her detention was still necessary. The Court stated that there was no absolute obli-gation on the authorities to ensure that the conditions were fulfilled. No comment was made as to the level of obligation, if any, that might arise by way of provision of treatment in the community to ensure the due effectiveness of the decision to release, though the Court expressed reassurance with the existence of legal safeguards entailing that local authorities or doctors could not wilfully or arbitrarily block the discharge of patients into the community without proper grounds or excuse.[323]

The Court accepts that under Article 5(1)(e) a responsible authority, viewing the mat-ter as a whole and wishing to proceed cautiously in good faith, may 'retain some measure of supervision over the progress of the person once he is released into the community and to that end make his discharge subject to conditions'.[324] But Article 5(1)(e) places curbs of the authorities' freedom of action here, it being of 'paramount importance' that firstly, 'appropriate safeguards are in place so as to ensure that any deferral of discharge is consonant with the purpose of Article 5(1) and with the aim of the restriction in sub-paragraph (e)'. Secondly, the discharge must 'not [be] unreasonably delayed'. These points were highly relevant to the applicant in *Johnson v UK*.[325] He had apparently recovered from mental illness and did not require any further medication or treatment. Release was, however, still made subject to conditions for his effective monitoring, it being feared that his mental illness might return. The applicant therefore had to undertake a period of rehabilitation in a hostel. Even after the decision to order conditional discharge had been taken, it had been repeatedly deferred owing to a combination of circumstances, includ-ing lack of available hostel places, but also the applicant's behaviour, which caused some hostels to reject his proposed transfer to them. Meanwhile, as the process dragged on,

---

[320] Id, para 55 (no violation on the facts given the supportive hospital environment and danger that appli-cant's mental health would deteriorate without it).

[321] *Luberti v Italy* A 75 (1984); 6 EHRR 440 para 29. See also *Johnson v UK* 1997 VII; 27 EHRR 196.

[322] Hudoc (2005); 42 EHRR 206.

[323] Id, para 71. She could also rely on Article 5(4) to ensure that any continued detention was consonant with the purpose of Article 5(1).

[324] *Johnson v UK* 1997 VII; 27 EHRR 196 para 63 (phased conditional discharge possible on the facts, para 64).

[325] Id.

the applicant was kept in his original confinement location, a secure psychiatric hospital until, after four years, his unconditional discharge was granted. Whilst the Court indicated that it would be prepared to accept some delay in granting conditional discharge based on practical issues, there had been a breach of Article 5(1) given the unreasonable delay and a lack of safeguards available to the applicant to challenge that delay and his consequential confinement in the secure psychiatric hospital.[326] The Court did not therefore consider whether the proposed requirement that the applicant stay in a hostel was itself a violation of Article 5.[327]

The Court has consistently rejected applicants' arguments that Article 5(1)(e) carries with it an implied 'right to treatment' appropriate to the person's mental state during the period of detention.[328] However, as indicated in *Ashingdane v UK*,[329] there is a general rule that in the case of a 'person of unsound mind', in principle detention must be in a 'hospital, clinic or other appropriate institution authorised for' the detention of such persons.[330] *Aerts v Belgium*[331] indicates that this condition may give rise to a violation of Article 5. As a temporary measure pending placement in the proper institution, the applicant was held in the psychiatric wing of a prison and this proved harmful to him as he did not benefit from a therapeutic environment or receive the treatment required by the condition that had given rise to his detention. The finding of a violation was based on the deficiency in '[t]he proper relationship between the aim of the detention and the conditions in which it took place'.[332] *Morsink v Netherlands*[333] was a similar case. It concerned detention in an ordinary remand centre for fifteen months pending transfer to a custodial clinic (where treatment could be provided), the delay chiefly being due to a structural lack of capacity in custodial clinics. The failure to transfer the applicant to a clinic automatically did not violate Article 5(1)[334] and the Court refused to pursue the 'unrealistic and too rigid' approach of expecting the state to place the detainee immediately after he had been assessed. It accepted that, 'for reasons linked to the efficient management of public funds, a certain friction between available and required capacity in custodial clinics is inevitable and must be regarded as acceptable'.[335] Yet a violation of Article 5(1) was still found given the failure of the authorities to strike a reasonable balance between the competing interests involved, due regard being had to the importance of the applicant's right to liberty. The Court emphasized that, on the facts, a 'significant delay' in admission to a custodial clinic risked prolonging

---

[326] Having made the discharge conditional on finding suitable hostel accommodation there was an onus on the authorities to secure it, but neither the tribunal nor the authorities possessed the necessary powers to ensure that the condition could be implemented within a reasonable time. Furthermore, the applicant had only very limited and very occasional opportunities to seek a review of the terms of his continued detention, and there was no proper regime in existence to monitor independently his plight given the evolving difficulties (there was no possibility to petition the tribunal in between annual reviews or seek judicial review of the terms of conditional discharge order). In practice, the terms of the conditional discharge were tantamount to an indefinite deferral of the release from the psychiatric hospital (for full details, see id, paras 66–7).

[327] Id, para 68.   [328] *Winterwerp v Netherlands* A 33 (1979); 2 EHRR 387 para 51.

[329] A 93 (1985); 7 EHRR 528 para 44. See also *Aerts v Belgium* 1996-V; 29 EHRR 50 para 46 and *Hutchinson Reid v UK* 2003-IV; 37 EHRR 211 paras 48 and 54 ('[g]enerally,... it would be prima facie unacceptable not to detain a mentally ill person in a suitable therapeutic environment').

[330] See the discussion at p 130 above.   [331] 1998-V; 29 EHRR 50.

[332] Id, para 49. Article 5(4) must afford the possibility of reviewing compliance with the conditions to be satisfied if the detention of a person of unsound mind is to be regarded as 'lawful' for the purposes of paragraph 1(e), see *X v UK* A 46 (1981); 4 EHRR 188 para 58.

[333] Hudoc (2004) paras 65–70. See also *Brand v Netherlands* hudoc (2004) and *Mocarska v Poland* hudoc (2007).

[334] See however the strong arguments presented in the concurring opinion of Judge Loucaides.

[335] Id, para 67.

the detention overall since it entailed a delay in treatment and reduced the prospects of its success. Reference was also made to the fact that a structural lack of capacity in custodial clinics had been identified domestically for over a decade such that it could not be said that the authorities were faced with an exceptional and unforeseen situation.[336]

VI. ARTICLE 5(1)(F): DETENTION PENDING DEPORTATION OR EXTRADITION, ETC

Article 5(1)(f) permits 'the lawful arrest or detention of a person to prevent his effecting an unauthorized entry into the country or of a person against whom action is being taken with a view to deportation or extradition'.

Most Strasbourg cases have concerned detention pending deportation or extradition.[337] The first limb of Article 5(1)(f) was nevertheless in issue in *Saadi v UK*.[338] The applicant had sought asylum on his arrival at Heathrow airport. He was granted temporary admission to the UK and three days passed during which he was at liberty. During this period he dutifully returned to the airport each day for the processing of his asylum claim and it was only after the third day that he was detained for seven days in a fast-track centre for the quick processing of his asylum application. By eleven to six the Court held that Saadi's detention did not contravene Article 5(1).

There were two important and contentious aspects to the Court's reasoning. First, temporary admission to enter a country after applying for asylum did not amount to a lawful 'entry' for the purposes of Article 5(1)(f). Leave to stay was required for this. Accordingly asylum-seekers like Saadi *remained* 'unauthorized' entrants and so remained susceptible to being detained under Article 5(1)(f) on the basis that this was preventing an unauthorized entry.[339]

The second aspect of the ruling was related to this. It was the rejection of the principle that detention under the first limb of Article 5(1)(f) had to be necessary in each instance. After all, there was no evidence to suggest that Saadi himself intended to effect an unlawful entry into the UK; indeed the facts indicated that he did not. However, this did not matter because the Court merely required that an individual's detention under Article 5(1)(f) should not be 'arbitrary'.[340] That is, such detention had to be '[i] carried out in good faith; [ii] ... closely connected to the purpose of preventing unauthorised entry of the person to the country; [iii] the place and conditions of detention should be appropriate, bearing in mind that "the measure is applicable not to those who have committed criminal offences but to aliens who, often fearing for their lives, have fled from their own country";[341] and [iv] the length of the detention should not exceed that reasonably required for the purpose pursued'.[342] Applying these tests the majority held that Saadi had not been detained on an arbitrary basis. The good faith test was satisfied as the detention centre in issue had been set up especially for speedy administration of asylum claims

---

[336] The judgment was by five votes to two, Judge Thomassen, joined by Judge Jungwiert, attached a dissenting opinion.

[337] A procedure for the return of deserting military personnel is akin to extradition and within Article 5(1)(f): *C v UK No 10427/83*, 47 DR 85 (1986).

[338] Hudoc (2008) GC (Chamber judgment: hudoc (2006); 44 EHRR1005, no violation of Article 5(1) by four to three). See also *Zamir v UK No 9174/80*, 40 DR 42 (1983); 5 EHRR 242 (1983). In *McVeigh, O'Neill and Evans v UK Nos 8022/77, 8025/77 and 8027/77*, 25 DR 15 (1981); 5 EHRR 71, it was held that the detention of persons at a port of entry for 'further questioning' fell within Article 5(1)(b), not Article 5(1)(f).

[339] Id, para 65 GC.   [340] Id, para 66 GC.

[341] Citing *Amuur v France* 1996-III; 22 EHRR 533 para 43.

[342] *Saadi v UK* hudoc (2008) para 74 GC (numbers added).

and Saadi had been selected to go there as his application seemed ripe for the fast-track process.[343] The second ([ii]) condition noted above was also satisfied, as was the third,[344] whilst seven days detention was reasonable in the circumstances.[345]

In reaching its conclusion the Grand Chamber in *Saadi* specifically referred to 'the difficult administrative problems with which the United Kingdom was confronted during the period in question, with an escalating flow of huge numbers of asylum-seekers'.[346] Evidently it sought to strike a balance between the competing interests of, on the one hand, effective immigration controls and, on the other, meaningful protection of asylum seekers' rights under the Convention.[347] A vociferous minority[348] argued that the Court had given inappropriate weight to the latter. The heart of their argument was that detention under the first limb of Article 5(1)(f) should not be used for the state's administrative convenience. Rather it could only be employed if it was established that the individual concerned was actually seeking to evade immigration controls. This, they insisted, reflected the importance attached to the right to liberty and was in keeping with other international standards. The Court was also criticized for failing to take proper account of the plight of asylum seekers by categorizing them all as ordinary immigrants. Indeed the Court's reading of the first limb of Article 5(1)(f) boldly assumes that all those who have not been fully authorized to stay are seeking illegal entry. In this respect the Court prioritized the States' interest in effective immigration control.[349] However, it circumscribed the alarmingly wide power Article 5(1)(f) gives states to detain by insisting that detention in this context could be rendered arbitrary in certain circumstances, most notably if the period of detention was too long.

Bozano v France[350] concerned the second limb of Article 5(1)(f). A French court refused to order the extradition to Italy of the applicant, an Italian national convicted of murder, because he had been tried *in absentia*. The French government then made a deportation order against him. Despite knowledge of his whereabouts, the order was not served upon the applicant until a month later, when he was arrested suddenly one night. Without being given an opportunity to contact his wife or a lawyer (who might have taken legal steps to challenge the deportation) or to nominate a country of deportation (Spain was by far the nearest), the applicant was forcibly taken the same night by police officers by car across France to the Swiss border, where he was transferred to Swiss police custody. He was later extradited from Switzerland to Italy to serve his life sentence, on the basis of an Italian request for extradition initiated in Switzerland before the applicant's deportation from France. Subsequently, the deportation order against the applicant was declared invalid by a French court as being, *inter alia*, an abuse of power contrary to French law. The French court determined that the circumstances of the deportation demonstrated that the order's purpose had not been to cause the applicant's removal for reasons of a kind associated with deportation but to effect an illegal extradition. In the light of the order's invalidity and of indications that French law might have been infringed when the applicant was

---

[343] Id, paras 76–7.

[344] Id, para 78 (the Court noted the importance of having suitable legal assistance at the centre). See also *Riad and Idiab v Belgium* hudoc (2008) (conditions of detention in airport transit zone).

[345] Id, para 79.   [346] Id, para 80.

[347] Cf, the arguments presented by the third party interveners: UNHCR (paras 54–7) and Liberty, ECRE, and AIRE Centre (jointly at paras 58–60). See also the joint partly dissenting opinion of Judges Rozakis, Tulkens, Kovler, Hajiyev, Speilmann, and Hirvela.

[348] *Ibid.*

[349] See *Saadi v UK* hudoc (2008) para 64 GC. See also para 65 (inappropriate to interpret Article 5(1)(f) as permitting detention only if person shown to be trying to evade entry restrictions) and para 80.

[350] A 111 (1986); 9 EHRR 297. See Cohen-Jonathan, 23 RTDE 255 (1987) and Sudre, 91 RGDIP 533 (1987).

handed over, the European Court expressed the 'gravest doubts whether the contested deprivation of liberty satisfied the legal requirements in the respondent state'.[351] As to the question of 'arbitrariness', the Court 'attached great weight to the circumstances in which the applicant was forcibly conveyed to the Swiss border'.[352] Considering the facts as a whole, relating both to the indications of non-compliance with French law and, particularly, of 'arbitrary' executive action, the Court concluded that the applicant's detention had not been 'lawful' as required by Article 5(1)(f). It was instead an element in a process designed to achieve 'a disguised form of extradition'[353] that could not be justified by that provision.

A question that arose in the *Bozano* case was whether the ruling by the French court that the deportation order was invalid had retroactive effect so as to render the applicant's detention for the purpose of detention contrary to the applicable municipal law and hence unlawful for the purposes of Article 5(1)(f). Since this is a matter of the interpretation and application of municipal law, the question was, in the first place, one for the national authorities.[354] The Court's judgment seems to suppose that, in the absence of any ruling at the national level, the Strasbourg authorities were competent to make their own determination.[355] In this connection, the Court drew a distinction between the situation in which a state's agents, acting in good faith, are later found to have acted illegally and that in which there is evidence of abuse of power *ab initio*, as was true on the facts of the *Bozano* case. The Court seemed to suggest that it would be much more likely that a finding of retroactive effect would be made in national law (and perhaps by the Court) in the latter case than in the former.[356]

The Court regards as irrelevant, for the purposes of Article 5(1)(f), arguments to the effect that, on its facts, the underlying decision to expel the applicant cannot be justified under national or Convention law though, of course, there must be a lawful basis for the detention itself.[357] Detention may be justified by Article 5(1)(f) even though a formal request or an order for extradition has not been issued, provided that enquiries have been made, since the enquiries amount to 'action' being taken in the sense of that provision.[358] Likewise, detention may be within Article 5(1)(f) even though deportation or extradition does not in fact occur.[359] It is not necessary that the detention itself be warranted on its facts in terms of whether it is reasonably considered necessary for example to prevent the applicant fleeing or committing a further offence.[360] However, if there is no actual intention to deport or extradite the individual concerned there will be a violation of Article 5(1), moreover even if such an intention exists there may be a violation if deportation is not possible for legal or other reasons since the provision only permits detention when 'action is being taken with a view to deportation'.[361] Hence continuing

---

[351] Id, para 58.   [352] Id, para 59.   [353] Id, para 60.   [354] See above, pp 133–4.

[355] Although there was no ruling at the national level in the *Bozano* case on the question of the retroactive effect of the order's invalidity, the Court made no finding of its own, preferring to emphasize the 'arbitrary' nature of the detention.

[356] Cf, the restrictive approach adopted by the Commission in *Caprino v UK No 6871/75*, 12 DR 14 at 12 (1978); 4 EHRR 97. Cf, *Krzycki v FRG No 7629/76*, 13 DR 57 (1978), under Article 5(1)(a).

[357] *Chahal v UK* 1996-V; 23 EHRR 413 para 112; *Slivenko v Latvia* 2003-XI; 39 EHRR 490 para 146 GC. See also *Zamir v UK No 9174/80*, 40 DR 42 (1983); 5 EHRR 242 (1983).

[358] *X v Switzerland No 9012/80*, 24 DR 205 (1980). The word 'action' was substituted for 'proceedings' because of the diversity of kinds of extradition and deportation proceedings—executive, judicial—in the drafting states: Fawcett, p 95.

[359] See eg, *X v FRG No 9706/82*, 5 EHRR 512.

[360] *Conka v Belgium* 2002-I; 34 EHRR 1298 para 38.

[361] *Chahal v UK* 1996-V; 23 EHRR 413 para 112 (cf, the British derogation from the Convention submitted on 18 December 2001, see 620 at n 20. Article 5(1)f issues have been raised in the case of *A and Others v UK*, which

loss of liberty under Article 5(1)(f) will only be justified for as long as deportation or extradition proceedings are in progress. Further, such proceedings must be prosecuted with 'due diligence'[362] otherwise the duration of the deportation proceedings will be considered 'excessive'.[363] Accordingly, the Court will examine the record of legal proceedings before the domestic authorities (looking at phases of detention individually but also in combination) in the light of a 'due diligence' test. Here the conduct of the applicant—who might delay proceedings[364]—as well as that of the authorities,[365] is taken into account and there is no absolute limit to the time that proceedings may last. The test is one of diligence appropriate to the circumstances,[366] although for long periods of detention the Court will consider whether there existed sufficient guarantees to safeguard against arbitrary executive decisions to keep an individual in detention.

These points and the weak approach taken by the Court were illustrated in *Chahal v UK*,[367] where the applicant had been detained under Article 5(1)(f) for over three and half years before domestic legal avenues had been exhausted (and he remained in Bedford prison for a further two years while the matter progressed at Strasbourg). The domestic delay was caused by the time it took for his application for judicial review and, above all, resolution of the legal problem of whether it was appropriate to deport him to India given the Article 3 harm he might suffer there. The refusal to release the applicant in the meantime was repeatedly justified by reference to the threat to national security that he was alleged to pose given his purported links to terrorist organizations. The Court expressed its serious concern over the 'extremely long period' of detention,[368] but there was no breach of Article 5(1) on this point. The test of due diligence had not been contravened, it being observed that this was no ordinary deportation matter since it had concerned several complex issues of fact and law, and it was in the applicant's own interest to have them thoroughly examined.[369] However, in view of the 'extremely long period' involved the Court found it 'necessary to consider whether there existed sufficient guarantees against [the] arbitrariness' of the executive's decision to keep the applicant in detention.[370] The

has been heard by the Grand Chamber—judgment is awaited at the time of writing). See also *Ali v Switzerland No 24881/94* 1998-V; 28 EHRR 304, Com Rep (struck off before Court).

[362] *Quinn v France* A 311 (1995); 21 EHRR 529 para 48; *Kolompar v Belgium* A 235-C (1992); 16 EHRR 197 para 36; *Chahal v UK* 1996-V; 23 EHRR 413 para 113.

[363] *Chahal v UK* 1996-V; 23 EHRR 413 para 113. For the purposes of calculating the period of time in issue, time spent in detention by virtue of a conviction (justified under Article 5(1)(a)) will not count, *Raf v Spain* 2000-XI para 64.

[364] See *Kolompar v Belgium* A 235-C (1992); 16 EHRR 197 (no breach of Article 5(1) since applicant had delayed proceedings or impliedly consented to their prolongation for nearly three years) and *S v France No 10965/84*, 56 DR 62 (1988). In *Osman v UK No 15933/89* hudoc (1991) DA, over five years' detention pending extradition was acceptable given the applicant's conduct and determination not to be extradited.

[365] Cf, *Quinn v France* A 311 (1995); 21 EHRR 529 (a period of almost two years disclosed an abuse of the extradition procedure and so violation of Article 5(1)). Cf, *Leaf v Italy No 72794/01* hudoc (2003) DA (nine months' delay was reasonable).

[366] See *X v FRG No 9706/82*, 5 EHRR 512 (1983) (twenty-two months' detention during extradition proceedings justifiable as regular judicial review and delay resulted from attempts by the West German government to obtain Turkish government undertaking not to impose death penalty, also no evidence of dilatoriness by the West German authorities). Cf, *X v UK No 8081/77*, 12 DR 207 (1977) (eleven months' delay attributable to the need to obtain evidence from Pakistan and the applicant's own conduct). For early Commission jurisprudence see *Lynas v Switzerland No 7317/75*, 6 DR 141 (1976); *X v UK No 8081/77*, 12 DR 207 (1977); and *Z v Netherlands No 10400/83*, 38 DR 145 (1984).

[367] 1996-V; 23 EHRR 413 GC.   [368] Id, para 123.

[369] Id, para 117. The Commission had, apparently quite easily, concluded that the proceedings had not been pursued with requisite speed such that the detention ceased to be justified.

[370] Id, para 119.

background here was that the domestic courts were not in a position effectively to control whether the decisions taken by the executive to keep Chahal in detention were justified, because the full material on which these decisions were based was not made available to them. This was because the executive asserted that national security was involved and so full disclosure to the courts did not follow given the sensitivity of certain information. However, a special advisory panel was in place, which included experienced judicial figures, and, even though its report was never disclosed, the Court was satisfied that it had fully reviewed the evidence relating to the national security threat represented by the applicant. The procedure in question 'provided an adequate guarantee that there were at least *prima facie* grounds for believing that if Mr Chahal were at liberty, national security would be put at risk and thus, that the executive had not acted arbitrarily when it ordered him to be kept in detention'.[371] The procedure in question, however, failed to satisfy the requirements of both Article 5(4)[372] and Article 13—an indication of the inferior standard of review required under Article 5(1)(f) itself.

Different factual scenarios occurred in *Amuur v France*[373] and *Conka v Belgium*.[374] The first case was discussed above[375] and was notable for the finding that Article 5 applied, plus certain statements made by the Court regarding the need for national authorities to have due regard to the category of persons national authorities deal with under Article 5(1)(f).[376] In *Conka* the applicants had been part of a group of illegal immigrants who had attended a police station following a deliberately misleading communication to the effect that their presence was required to address aspects of their asylum application. In what was clearly a pre-planned operation they were arrested upon arrival and deported soon after. In its judgment the Court acknowledged that the ruse to get the applicants to the police station would not vitiate the entire arrest procedure, or warrant it being qualified as an abuse of power, but it indicated disapproval and reiterated the point that no loss of liberty can be arbitrary. Thus, although the Court 'by no means exclude[ed] its being legitimate for the police to use stratagems in order, for instance, to counter criminal activities more effectively', it warned that 'acts whereby the authorities seek to gain the trust of asylum seekers with a view to arresting and subsequently deporting them may be found to contravene the general principles stated or implicit in the Convention'.[377] The exceptions to Article 5 had to be interpreted restrictively and that requirement also had to be 'reflected in the reliability of communications such as those sent to the applicants, irrespective of whether the recipients are lawfully present in the country or not'. The Court then added that, 'even as regards overstayers, a conscious decision by the authorities to facilitate or improve the effectiveness of a planned operation for the expulsion of aliens by misleading them about the purpose of a notice so as to make it easier to deprive them of their liberty is not compatible with Article 5'.[378]

---

[371] Id, para 122. The Court's finding under Article 5(1)(f) was by thirteen votes to six; there were some strong dissenting opinions.   [372] See below at p 185.

[373] *Amuur v France* 1996-III; 22 EHRR 533. See also *Gebremedhin v France* hudoc (2007).

[374] *Conka v Belgium* 2002-I; 34 EHRR 1298.   [375] See p 126.

[376] The Court was highly critical of the absence any proper legal regulation of the applicant's detention, *Amuur v France* 1996-III; 22 EHRR 533 para 53 (see also para 50, emphasis on the 'quality of law' requirements of Article 5(1)(f) for asylum seekers at airports). See also *Zamir v UK* No 9174/80, 40 DR 42 (1983); 5 EHRR 242 (1983), when the applicant's claim that he could not reasonably have foreseen the consequences under UK immigration law of failing to reveal on entry into the country the fact that he was married was rejected. Cf, *X v UK No 9403/81*, 28 DR 235 (1982).

[377] *Conka v Belgium* 2002-I; 34 EHRR 1298 para 41.

[378] Id, para 42 (detention was arbitrary; applicants' failure to exhaust domestic remedies was excusable because, in effect, they were ineffective given the timescale and circumstances within which the domestic authorities had acted, and which they had themselves induced, see paras 43–6).

6. ARTICLE 5(2): REASONS FOR ARREST TO BE GIVEN PROMPTLY

I. GENERAL ISSUES

Article 5(2) requires that everyone 'who is arrested shall be informed promptly, in a language which he understands, of the reasons for his arrest and of any charge against him'.[379] This requirement applies to arrest on any ground under Article 5(1) (some of which do not employ the word 'arrest'),[380] and it extends to cases in which a person is recalled after release.[381] It provides 'the elementary safeguard that any person arrested should know why he is deprived of his liberty',[382] enabling him to deny the offence and hence obtain his release without resorting to court proceedings[383] or to make *habeas corpus* proceedings effective. The arrestee must be told 'in simple, non-technical language that he can understand, the essential legal and factual grounds for his arrest, so as to be able, if he sees fit, to apply to a court to challenge its lawfulness in accordance with' (Article 5(4)).[384] 'Lawfulness' means 'lawfulness' under both municipal law and the Convention so that the information required must address the legality of a person's detention in terms of Article 5(1) of the Convention as well as the applicable municipal law.[385]

Article 5(2) does not require that the reasons for an arrest be given in any particular way,[386] eg in the text of any warrant or other document authorizing the arrest[387] or in writing at all.[388] Nor does it guarantee a right of access to a lawyer for an arrested person,[389] though the inability for a detainee to contact a close relative such as a wife may entail a violation of Article 8.[390]

Article 5(2) was breached when a voluntary patient in a mental hospital, who had not received any official communication, learnt only by accident that a court order had been made for her compulsory detention.[391] Where a mentally disordered person cannot understand the information that is given to him, it must be given to a lawyer[392] or other person authorized to act for him. Whether a person who is detained pending deportation or extradition needs to be told the reasons for the proposed action against him as well as the fact that he is detained for such a purpose must depend upon the information that he needs under municipal law to be able to challenge the legality of his detention.[393]

The reasons must be given to the arrested person, or possibly his representative,[394] 'in a language which he understands'. In a case in which the arrest warrant for a

---

[379] Cf, Article 6(3)(a).

[380] *Van der Leer v Netherlands* A 170-A (1990); 12 EHRR 567 para 27 (case concerned a 'person of unsound mind' on its facts, but the reasoning extends to all cases of arrest or detention). The Court rejected an argument to the effect that the wording 'and of any charge' implied that Article 5(2) was limited to Article 5(1)(c) cases.

[381] *X v Belgium No 4741/71*, 43 CD 14 at 19 (1973). Cf, *X v UK* A 46 (1981); 4 EHRR 188 para 66.

[382] *Fox, Campbell and Hartley v UK* A 182 (1990); 13 EHRR 157 para 40.

[383] *X v UK No 8010/77*, 16 DR 101 at 114 (1979).   [384] *Fox*, n 382, para 40.

[385] *McVeigh, O'Neill and Evans v UK Nos 8022/77, 8025/77 and 8027/77*, 25 DR 15 (1981); 5 EHRR 71.

[386] *X v Netherlands No 2621/65*, 9 YB 474 at 480 (1966).   [387] *Ibid.*

[388] *X v Netherlands No 1211/61*, 5 YB 224 at 228 (1962).

[389] *Schiesser v Switzerland* A34 (1979); 2 EHRR 417 at para 36. See also *A v Denmark No 8828/79*, 30 DR 93 at 94 (1982); 5 EHRR CD 278.

[390] *McVeigh, O'Neill and Evans v UK Nos 8022/77, 8025/77 and 8027/77*, 25 DR 15 (1981); 5 EHRR 71. Failure to have access to a lawyer during the intial stage of detention may be relevant for a subsequent Article 6 claim, see above p 313.

[391] *Van der Leer v Netherlands* A 170-A (1990); 12 EHRR 567 para 31.

[392] *X v UK* B 41 (1980) para 111 Com Rep.   [393] See Trechsel, *European System*, p 316.

[394] See *Saadi v UK* hudoc (2008) paras 84–5 GC.

French-speaking person was in Dutch, this requirement was held to be complied with on the basis that the subsequent interrogation, during which the reasons became apparent, was in French.[395]

Finally, the requirement in Article 5(2) overlaps with that in Article 5(4) in that the proceedings provided for by the latter also require that a person be told 'promptly' the reasons for his detention.[396] In criminal cases, Article 5(2) also overlaps to some extent with the obligation in Article 6(3)(a) by which an accused person, whether detained pending trial or not, must be told promptly of the nature and cause of the accusation against him. For obvious reasons the information required by Article 6(3)(a) will be 'more specific and more detailed' than that called for under Article 5(2).[397]

II. THE REQUIREMENT OF PROMPTNESS AND THE LEVEL OF INFORMATION REQUIRED

Two aspects to the application of Article 5(2) have been at the heart of the Court's jurisprudence: firstly, whether the *content* of the information conveyed to a detainee is sufficient and, secondly, the issue of the *promptness* of that information provision. Both are assessed case by case according to the special features of the application before the Court.

As regards the requirement of promptness ('promptly'), this will always apply to the provision of reasons for arrest. Obviously it will only apply to information relating to the charges brought if the decision is made to bring such charges, it being noted that 'facts which raise a suspicion need not be of the same level as those necessary to justify a conviction or even the bringing of a charge'.[398]

As regards the immediate post-arrest period, the Court has indicated that it will usually expect the information to be conveyed to the detainee 'within a few hours of his arrest'[399] and, provided there is no evidence to the contrary, it is apparently prepared to assume that timeframe has been fulfilled when the applicant has been interviewed frequently soon after his arrest.[400] In *Fox, Campbell and Hartley v UK*,[401] the background for which was terrorism in Northern Ireland, intervals of up to seven hours between the arrests and the giving of all of the information required by Article 5(2) were found to meet the requirement of 'promptness'.[402] As the Court noted, the information in question does not have to be given 'in its entirety by the arresting officer at the very moment of the arrest';[403] provided that the arrested person is informed of the required legal and factual grounds for his arrest, whether at one time or in stages, within a sufficient period following the arrest, Article 5(2) is complied with. Whether this has occurred is to be assessed

---

[395] *Delcourt v Belgium No 2689/65*, 10 YB 238 at 270 (1967). As to whether the costs of translation can be charged to the detainee, see Trechsel, *European System*, p 318. In *Conka v Belgium* 2002-I; 34 EHRR 1298 para 52, the provision of a Slovakian-speaking interpreter was viewed as important by the Court.

[396] *X v UK* A 46 (1981); 4 EHRR 188 para 66. In that case, the Court applied Article 5(4) only.

[397] *Nielsen v Denmark No 343/57*, 2 YB 412 at 462 (1959) and *GSM v Austria No 9614/81*, 34 DR 119 (1983).

[398] *Murray v UK* A 300-A (1994); 19 EHRR 193 para 55.

[399] *Kerr v UK No 40451/98* hudoc (1999) DA. Surprisingly, a delay of two days was regarded as acceptable in an earlier Commission case: *Skoogström v Sweden No 8582/79*, 1 Dig Supp para 5.2.2.1 (1981). See also *X v Denmark No 6730/74*, 1 Digest 457 (1975) (twenty-four hours apparently acceptable) and *Delcourt v Belgium No 2689/65*, 10 YB 238 at 252, 272 (1967).

[400] *Ibid* (promptness could 'reasonably be inferred from the intense frequency of the interviews' after arrest).

[401] A 182 (1990); 13 EHRR 157 para 40.

[402] See also *O'Hara v UK* 2001-X; 34 EHRR 812 (notification within six to eight hours of arrest acceptable).

[403] *Fox, Campbell and Hartley v UK* A 182 (1990); 13 EHRR 157 para 40.

by reference to the facts of the particular case.[404] Ten days delay is obviously too long.[405] A delay in informing a person of a court order for his detention is not attributable to a state where the person's whereabouts are not known; it is sufficient that he is informed 'promptly' of the order once he makes contact or, presumably, when his whereabouts otherwise have become known.[406]

In terms of the detail of information to be provided, the case law demonstrates that the Court has again taken a flexible, and somewhat vague approach to the application of Article 5(2) as regards the reasons for initial detention. Arrest on suspicion of committing a crime does not require that information be given in a particular form, nor that it consist of a complete list of charges held against the arrested person.[407] A 'bare indication of the legal basis for an arrest'[408] does not suffice; however, the Court has been satisfied with what it described as a 'fairly precise indication of the suspicions' against the applicant such that he could promptly gain 'some idea of what he was suspected of'.[409] *Fox, Campbell and Hartley v UK*[410] concerned applicants arrested on suspicion of terrorist offences and told that they were being arrested under a named statutory provision. They were later interrogated about specific criminal acts. The Court, disagreeing with the Commission, held that although the information given at the time of arrest was insufficient because it was limited to the legal basis for the arrests, this deficiency was made good[411] by the indications as to the factual basis for the arrests that the applicants could infer from the nature of the questions put to them by the police during the subsequent interrogation. In fact, a person need not be *expressly* 'informed' of the reasons for his arrest insofar as these are apparent from the surrounding circumstances.[412] Indeed, as regards the initial arrest period at least, there may be instances when the applicant is simply assumed to know why he was being detained given the criminal and intentional nature

[404] *Ibid.* Cf, *X v Denmark No 8828/79*, 30 DR 93 (1982). See also *Dikme v Turkey* 2000-VIII para 56 (applicant to some extent contributed to the prolongation of the period in question by concealing his identity) and *HB v Switzerland* hudoc (2001); 37 EHRR 1000 para 49 (Court had in mind that the applicant had specialized knowledge of its financial situation as he was a member of the board and manager of the company he was accused of defrauding).

[405] *Van der Leer v Netherlands* A 170-A (1990); 12 EHRR 567 para 31. See also *Conka v Belgium* 2002-I; 34 EHRR 1298 (Article 5(1)(f) detention: no violation when broad reasons for detention were given upon detention and written reasons supplied two days later); *Saadi v UK* hudoc (2008) paras 84–5 GC (violation given seventy-two-hour delay); and *Shamayev v Georgia and Russia* 2005-III (violation for four-day delay).

[406] *Keus v Netherlands* A 185-C (1990); 13 EHRR 700 para 22 (mentally disordered person absconded; sufficient that he was told when he telephoned the hospital). The Court would appear to have rejected an argument in this case that the applicant's lawyer should have been informed 'promptly' in the interim. Article 5(2) presumably requires that reasonable efforts be made to communicate with a person against whom a detention order is made. Article 5(2) was complied with when a person who was semi-conscious when arrested was told of the reasons for his arrest as soon as he recovered: *X v UK No 7125/75*, 1 Digest 458 (1977).

[407] *X v Germany No 8098/77*, 16 DR 111 (1978). See also *X v UK No 4220/69*, 14 YB 250 at 278 (1971) (told of burglary charge, but not others that were later brought) and *Saadi v UK* hudoc (2006); 44 EHRR 1005 (chamber judgment) para 51 (the information given may be 'even less complete' for detention under Article 5(1)(f)).

[408] *Fox, Campbell and Hartley v UK* A 182 (1990); 13 EHRR 157 para 41. See also *Kerr v UK No 40451/98* hudoc (1999) DA.

[409] *Dikme v Turkey* 2000-VIII para 56 (sufficient on the facts that during questioning interrogator directly accused applicant of belonging to a well-known illegal organization).

[410] A 182 (1990); 13 EHRR 157 para 41. See Finnie, 54 MLR 288 (1991).

[411] Cf, *Murray v UK* A 300-A (1994); 19 EHRR 193 para 77 and *Kerr v UK No 40451/98* hudoc (1999) DA. Contrast *Ireland v UK* A 25 (1978); 2 EHRR 25 para 198 PC in which, contrary to Article 5(2), some arrested persons were told only that they were being arrested under emergency legislation and given no further details.

[412] Cf, *Neumeister v Austria No 1936/63*, 7 YB 224 (1964); *Freda v Italy No 8916/80*, 21 DR 250 (1980); and *B v France No 10179/82*, 52 DR 111 (1987).

of the act which preceded his arrest.[413] In *Öcalan v Turkey*,[414] the facts of which were described above,[415] the applicant was deemed to have been sufficiently informed of the reasons for his arrest by the time he was arrested. He was a notorious figure who had been wanted by the police for a considerable time as the leader of an illegal terrorist organization. Warrants had been issued for his arrest by various prosecuting authorities, a 'red notice' had been issued by Interpol, and details of the charges against him were featured on the extradition request that had been made for him in Italy. He did not deny being aware of this documentation and the Article 5(2) aspect of his application was declared manifestly ill-founded.[416]

The application of Article 5(2) is one that, in the more borderline cases, is prone to cause significant division before the Court.[417] Strong arguments can be made to the effect that the application of that Article in *Fox* and some subsequent case law involves an unacceptable dilution of a basic guarantee.[418] Article 5(2) expressly requires that an arrested person be 'informed' of the reason for his arrest, not that he be able to gather them from the drift of the interrogation, which may involve the putting of various alternative assertions and, possibly, even exaggerated accusations designed to intimidate a detainee. Having made this point it may be added that an assessment of the Court's general approach to Article 5(2) should have in mind the fact that key cases have concerned people suspected of terrorist crimes. This is an area where the Court, for some years now, has emphasized the need to strike a balance between the defence of institutions of democracy in the common interest and the protection of individual rights. On the one hand, one can readily appreciate the need to apply Article 5(2) in a flexible way. This is especially so in the context of genuine suspected terrorism scenarios, when it is clear that an arrest may be warranted even on vague information at first[419] and there would be a danger that an onerous information provision requirement might unduly hamper the authorities in very important and delicate areas of their duties. On the other hand, it will be appreciated that for a society that cherishes the concept of liberty there are also dangers to be guarded against. As noted above, one aim of Article 5(2) is that the applicant quickly knows the essential legal and factual grounds for his arrest as a prerequisite for an effective resort to the safeguard provided by Article 5(4). Once an individual has been released, however, Article 5(4) may not be resorted to. Accordingly, if the information provision requirement of Article 5(2) is too indulgent of the needs of the authorities, the greater is their scope to arrest individuals on general grounds (assuming they are *prima facie* lawful) when the main intention is really to hold the individual for intensive questioning as part of an intelligence-gathering exercise,[420] there being little or no actual intention of bringing them before a court (as required for detention under Article 5(1)(c)).

---

[413] *Dikme v Turkey* 2000-VIII para 54 (arrest as false papers produced during an identity check).

[414] Hudoc (2003); 37 EHRR 238.   [415] See above p 131.

[416] *Öcalan v Turkey No 46221/99* hudoc (2000) DA.

[417] See eg, *Murray v UK* A 300-A (1994); 19 EHRR 191 (no violation of Article 5(2), thirteen votes to five), note the strong dissent of Judge Misfud Bonnici arguing that the decision reduced the meaning of Article 5(2) 'to such a low level that it is doubtful whether in fact it can, if it is adhered to in this form, have any possible concrete application in the future'.

[418] *Ibid.*

[419] Cf, the Court's jurisprudence on the 'reasonable suspicion' requirement for Article 5(1)(c) at p 148 above.

[420] See also *Kerr v UK No 40451/98* hudoc (1999) DA (applicant did not argue that the authorities did not genuinely intend to bring him before a competent judicial authority (Article 5(1)(c)) so Court declined to examine whether the period of detention was deliberately delayed as part of an intelligence-gathering exercise).

7. ARTICLE 5(3): ACCOUNTABILITY DURING PRE-TRIAL DETENTION AND TRIAL WITHIN A REASONABLE TIME

Article 5(3) provides:

> Everyone arrested or detained in accordance with the provisions of paragraph 1(c) of this Article shall be brought promptly before a judge or other officer authorised by law to exercise judicial power and shall be entitled to trial within a reasonable time or to release pending trial. Release may be conditioned by guarantees to appear for trial.

Article 5(3) should be read with Article 5(1)(c), 'which forms a whole with it'.[421] It concerns the criminal process, and is 'intended to minimise the risk of arbitrariness' by providing, in accordance with the concept of the 'rule of law', '[j]udicial control of interferences by the executive with the individual's right to liberty'.[422] Such control concerns two separate phases of detention.[423]

Firstly (see sub-heading I below), there is the judicial control required 'promptly' after the initial arrest: a person arrested in accordance with Article 5(1)(c) on suspicion of having committed an offence must be brought 'promptly' before a judge or similar officer to determine the legality of his arrest.[424] Article 5(3) therefore requires the 'judicial officer' to consider legal criteria relating to the merits of the detention and to order provisional release if it is unreasonable.[425] This is a vital safeguard in a democracy and should be seen alongside the procedural safeguards and positive obligations that the Court has more recently read into Article 5(1)[426] to help provide a custodial regime that promotes the protection of the individual detainee.

Secondly (see sub-heading II below), there is the judicial control required *after* the stage just referred to, that is the period pending eventual trial. Here the Court has again interpreted Article 5(3) creatively so as to imply from it a qualified right to release pending trial, on bail if this is appropriate.

Finally, a third important aspect to Article 5(3) is that it requires that a person detained on remand be tried within a reasonable time (see sub-heading III below).

I. RIGHT TO BE BROUGHT PROMPTLY BEFORE A JUDGE OR 'OTHER OFFICER' AFTER ARREST

a. Brought before a judge or other officer authorized to exercise judicial power

Article 5(3) underlines the sanctity of the right to liberty and the need to provide accountability against abuse of the broad power to detain that Article 5(1)(c) necessarily provides

---

[421] *Ciulla v Italy* A 148 (1989); 13 EHRR 346 para 38 PC; *Smirnova v Russia* 2003-IX; 39 EHRR 450 para 56; and *Aquilina v Malta* 1999-III; 29 EHRR 185 para 47 GC.

[422] *Brogan v UK* A 145-B (1988); 11 EHRR 117 para 58 PC. See also *Aquilina v Malta* 1999-III; 29 EHRR 185 para 47 GC and *Assenov v Bulgaria* 1998-VIII; 28 EHRR 652 para 146.

[423] Cf, *McKay v UK* 2006-X; 44 EHRR 827 para 31 GC. The case provides a recapitulation of the main principles relevant to Article 5(3).

[424] Article 5(3) (particularly its trial within a reasonable time guarantee) does not extend to a person who, although subject to an order for detention on remand, is also serving a prison sentence following conviction for another offence: *X v FRG No 8626/79*, 25 DR 218 (1981).

[425] *Aquilina v Malta* 1999-III; 29 EHRR 185 para 47 GC.   [426] See p 132 above.

to the executive.[427] The detainee 'shall' be brought automatically and 'promptly' before a judge or other comparable officer. He must have the power to release and the 'initial automatic review of arrest and detention' performed must be capable of examining whether the detention falls under Article 5(1)(c), ie it must address 'lawfulness issues and whether or not there is a reasonable suspicion that the arrested person ha[s] committed an offence'.[428] Beyond this *at this initial stage* it is not necessary for there to be an automatic review of the additional and distinct question of whether the applicant should be released on bail pending trial, ie whether continued detention is justified or necessary in the circumstances of the individual case.[429] However, this should follow in due course[430] and the Court has stated that it is 'good practice' and 'highly desirable', albeit not a strict requirement, that the judicial officer who conducts the first initial review also has competence to consider release on bail.[431] Perhaps surprisingly, there is no general rule to the effect that hearings on the lawfulness of detention must usually be held in public.[432]

Judicial control of the detention must be 'automatic'[433] (unlike for Article 5(4)); it is insufficient that Article 5(3) only operates if the detainee makes an application to this effect.[434] This is because vulnerable categories of arrested persons, such as the mentally weak or those who do not speak the local language, may not bring the appropriate application of their own accord.[435] Furthermore, as Trechsel[436] has pointed out, Article 5(3) is a guarantee that is 'particularly important in states in which there exists an actual danger of police brutality or torture', especially since methods of ill-treatment may be used that do not leave long-lasting marks. As the Court stressed in the very first case when it found 'torture' under Article 3, '[j]udicial control of interferences by the executive with the individual's right to liberty is an essential feature of the guarantee embodied in Article 5(3), which is intended to minimise the risk of arbitrariness and to ensure the rule of law ... Furthermore, prompt judicial intervention may lead to the detection and prevention of serious ill-treatment, which ..., is prohibited by the Convention in absolute and non-derogable terms.'[437]

b. Promptly

Article 5(3) requires that an arrested person is brought 'promptly' before a judge or other officer, the 'clock' beginning to tick at the point of arrest.[438] The Strasbourg authorities have not set any upper time limit to the meaning of 'promptly', preferring to decide each

---

[427] *McKay v UK* 2006-X; 44 EHRR 827 para 32 GC.

[428] Id, para 40. Also *Assenov v Bulgaria* 1998-VIII; 28 EHRR 652 para 146.

[429] See *McKay v UK*, above n 427, although Judges Rozakis, Tulkens, Botoucharova, Myjer, and Ziemele disagreed on this point, arguing that the interpretation was contrary to the very purpose of Article 5(3). In their view the majority had placed 'insufficient emphasis on the principle laid down in Article 5(1) read in conjunction with Article 5(1): at the pre-trial stage an arrested person has the right to prompt and full judicial control and the right to be set free immediately unless there are (still) sufficient grounds to keep him in custody'.

[430] See p 173 below.   [431] *McKay v UK* 2006-X; 44 EHRR 827 para 47 GC.

[432] *Lebedev v Russia* hudoc (2007) para 82.

[433] *De Jong, Baljet, and Van Den Brink v Netherlands* A 77 (1984); 8 EHRR 20 para 51 and *Aquilina v Malta* 1999-III; 29 EHRR 185 para 49 GC.

[434] *Aquilina v Malta* 1999-III; 29 EHRR 185 para 49 GC; *McGoff v Sweden No 9017/80*, 31 DR 72 (1982); 6 EHRR CD 101(1984).

[435] *Ibid.*   [436] Trechsel, *European System*, p 333.

[437] *Aksoy v Turkey* 1996-VI; 23 EHRR 553 para 76.

[438] Although see *Ječius v Lithuania* 2000-IX; 35 EHRR 400 paras 85–6 as to the impact that an appropriate reservation to Article 5(3) may have here.

case on its facts.[439] In *Brogan v UK*,[440] the Court held that a delay of four days and six hours in bringing a person before a judge did not comply with Article 5(3). In that case, the four applicants were arrested by the police in Northern Ireland as persons reasonably suspected of involvement in acts of terrorism. After being questioned for periods ranging from four days and six hours to over six days, all four were released without being charged with any offence or being brought before a magistrate. When determining the meaning of 'promptly', the Court stated that the use in the equivalent French text of '*aussitôt*', which literally meant immediately, confirmed that 'the degree of flexibility attaching to the notion of "promptness" is limited'.[441] The Court continued:[442]

> Whereas promptness is to be assessed in each case according to its special features, the significance to be attached to those features can never be taken to the point of impairing the very essence of the right guaranteed by Article 5(3) ...

Applying this approach to the facts of the case, the Court accepted that, 'subject to adequate safeguards, the context of terrorism in Northern Ireland has the effect of prolonging the period during which the authorities may, without violating Article 5(3), keep a person suspected of serious terrorist offences in custody before bringing him before a judge or other judicial officer'.[443] However, even in the light of these 'special features', the Court held, by twelve to seven, that the requirement of 'promptness' could not properly be stretched so as to permit a delay of four days and six hours or more.[444] Implicit in the Court's reasoning is that, beyond a certain time, the remedy for a state faced with an emergency is to make a derogation under Article 15, rather than for Article 5(3) to be interpreted beyond its proper limits. In *Brannigan and McBride v UK*,[445] the defendant state conceded that the detention of IRA suspects under the same power as in the *Brogan* case and for longer periods was contrary to Article 5(3). However, there was no breach of the Convention because the UK had made a valid emergency derogation under Article 15.[446] In another 'special features' context, *viz* that of military criminal law, the Court held that 'even taking into account the demands of military life and justice', a delay of five days was in breach of Article 5(3).[447]

Four days and six hours was found contrary to Article 5(3) in *Brogan v UK*[448] despite the special context of terrorist investigation. So it is arguable that a period of significantly less than this would be suitable for 'ordinary', ie non-terrorist, cases[449] although the Court left

---

[439] *Ireland v UK* A 25 (1978); 2 EHRR 25 para 199 PC.

[440] *Brogan v UK* A 145-B (1988); 11 EHRR 117 PC. See Tanca, 1 EJIL 269 (1990).

[441] Id, para 59. Given that the two language texts were equally authentic, the Court had to interpret them 'in a way that reconciles them as far as possible and is most appropriate in order to realise the aim and achieve the object of the treaty': *ibid*.

[442] *Ibid*. Cf, *Aquilina v Malta* 1999-III; 29 EHRR 185 para 48 GC ('the scope of flexibility in interpreting and applying the notion of promptness is very limited').

[443] Id, para 61.

[444] Whereas the Court found a breach in all four terrorist cases, the Commission found one only in respect of the two applicants detained for over five days.

[445] A 258-B (1993); 17 EHRR 539 PC. See the discussion of this case under Article 15, below, Ch 16.

[446] See below pp 629 and 635.

[447] *Koster v Netherlands* A 221 (1991); 14 EHRR 396 (delay caused by foreseeable military manoeuvres not a good excuse). Cf, *De Jong, Baljet and Van Den Brink v Netherlands* A 77 (1984); 8 EHRR 20 para 53 and *Duinhof and Duijf v Netherlands* A 79 (1984); 13 EHRR 478. See also *Van Der Sluijs, Zuiderveld and Klappe v Netherlands* A 78 (1984); 13 EHRR 461.

[448] A 145-B (1988); 11 EHRR 117 PC.

[449] Of course exceptional circumstances may exist, see eg, two cases concerning detention on the High Seas and consequential delays in bringing before Article 5(3) official on the mainland: *Medvedyev v France* hudoc (2008) (no violation by four votes to three) and *Rigopoulos v Spain* 1999-II (no violation of Article 5(3)). See also

this point open in the *Brogan* case.[450] This would be consistent with the plain meaning of the word 'promptly' and with the purpose of Article 5(3), which, as noted, is to minimize the risk of 'executive arbitrariness'.[451] Trechsel has suggested a test of no 'undue delay' and that the appearance occur, as a general rule, the day after an arrest at the latest.[452] In *McKay v UK*,[453] however, the Grand Chamber proceeded on the understanding that four days was the 'maximum' period of time that could elapse before Article 5(3) review.

c. Characteristics of the judicial officer

The wording 'judge or other judicial officer authorised by law' has the same meaning as 'competent legal authority' in Article 5(1)(c).[454] As in that provision, in English law the requirement is satisfied by bringing an accused before a magistrate. Whereas the meaning of 'judge' has not caused difficulty,[455] the phrase 'other officer authorised by law to exercise judicial power' has given rise to some notable jurisprudence. Two qualities that this 'officer' must have are independence and impartiality.

In *Schiesser v Switzerland*[456] the Court stated that the first characteristic of an Article 5(3) 'officer' is his 'independence of the executive and the parties'. The notion of independence requires that the 'officer' must be able to make a legally binding decision as to detention or release (it is not sufficient that his recommendations are invariably followed).[457] There will be a violation when the prosecutor, or another member of the executive, is able to overturn such decisions.[458] An 'officer' is not considered independent when he is subordinate to authority belonging to the executive.[459] The mere fact that under applicable laws a prosecutor in addition to exercising a prosecutorial role also acted as guardian of the public interest does not give him 'judicial status'.[460] Nor in such circumstances will a violation of Article 5(3) be prevented here because an individual could apply to a judge against the prosecutor's decision to detain (as opposed to such reference being automatic).

The notion of impartiality under Article 5(3) is usually seen in the context of a relationship between the detainee and the 'officer' and has been particularly relevant to cases where the 'officer' also plays a part later on in the prosecution of the case. An officer will not be impartial, as required by Article 5(3), if he is not only competent to decide on the accused's pre-trial detention, but if he is also *'entitled to intervene* in the subsequent criminal proceedings as a representative of the prosecuting authority' (emphasis added).[461] Thus, it is not sufficient that the officer does not in fact intervene at a later stage,

---

X v Belgium No 4960/71, 42 CD 49 at 55 (1972) (delay of nearly five days permissible because applicant had been ill in hospital during this period). Cf, *Öcalan v Turkey* 2005-IV; 41 EHRR 985 GC (Court not convinced that delay of seven days was due to adverse weather conditions: violation).

[450] A 145-B (1988); 11 EHRR 117 para 60 PC.

[451] Id, para 58. A study conducted within the Commission in connection with the *Brogan* case indicated that many parties have a limit of less than four days.

[452] See Trechsel, *Human Rights in Criminal Proceedings*, 2005, p 513.

[453] 2006-X; 44 EHRR 827 para 47 GC.   [454] *Schiesser v Switzerland* A 34 (1979); 2 EHRR 417 para 29.

[455] See the discussion on the meaning of 'court' in Article 5(4), below, pp 189–90.

[456] A 34 (1979); 2 EHRR 417 para 29.

[457] *Ireland v UK* A 25 (1978); 2 EHRR 25 para 199 PC (Advisory Committee on Internment did not qualify). Cf, the military criminal cases of *De Jong, Baljet and Van Den Brink v Netherlands* A 77 (1984); 8 EHRR 20; *Van Der Sluijs, Zuiderveld and Klappe v Netherlands* A 78 (1984); 13 EHRR 461; and *Duinhof and Duijf v Netherlands* A 79 (1984); 13 EHRR 478.

[458] *Assenov v Bulgaria* 1998-VIII; 28 EHRR 652 para 148.

[459] *Niedbala v Poland* hudoc (2000); 33 EHRR 1137 para 52.   [460] Id, para 53.

[461] *Huber v Switzerland* A 188 (1990) para 43 PC. On this point, there has been an evolution in the case law: the early case of *Schiesser* merely required that the 'officer' not take part later in the prosecution case.

as long as it is possible for him to do so: 'impartiality' involves an objective, as well as a subjective, element so that the 'officer's' impartiality must not be open to doubt. Objective appearances *at the time of the decision on detention* are material. This objective element, which brings Article 5(3) into line with the 'impartiality' requirements of Article 6(1),[462] was applied in *Hood v UK*,[463] a case concerning a military police investigation, where Article 5(3) was violated because a commanding officer (or his subordinate) was liable to play a central role in the subsequent prosecution of the case against the accused soldier. The Court also took the view that the commanding officer's concurrent responsibility for discipline and order provided an additional reason for an accused reasonably to doubt that officer's impartiality when deciding on the necessity of the pre-trial detention of an accused in his command.

d. Function of officer and procedure to be followed

The judge or similar officer must 'consider the merits of the detention'.[464] As was first set out in the *Schiesser* case,[465] his role is that of 'reviewing the circumstances militating for and against detention, of deciding, by reference to legal criteria, whether there are reasons to justify detention and of ordering release if there are no such reasons'.[466] The officer is under an 'obligation of himself hearing the individual brought before him',[467] ie there should be an oral hearing. He is not obliged to allow the accused's lawyer to be present at the hearing.[468] A question that remains to be answered is whether, for the purposes of Article 5(3), an officer must have any particular qualifications or training.[469] There are also strong arguments to be made that the detainee should have a right to be assisted by a lawyer at this stage.[470]

It will be appreciated therefore that the procedures envisaged by Article 5(3) are more modest than Article 5(4) (where a procedure of a 'judicial character' must be provided).[471] The safeguards provided by the two Articles are distinct. Article 5(3) review must be automatic and compliance with that provision cannot be ensured by making an Article 5(4) remedy available in the background.

More generally as regards the relationship between Articles 5(3) and 5(4), in many systems of law the body before which the applicant is brought under Article 5(3) may be a court. If so, by virtue of the 'incorporation rule', the requirement of judicial supervision imposed by Article 5(4)[472] will be satisfied at that hearing, but the stricter demands of due process required by that Article, as opposed to Article 5(3)—eg possible attendance of the detainee, equality of arms, and advanced disclosure of documentation if relevant—must also be attendant if it is to count for the purposes of Article 5(4).

Assuming that a person is detained under Article 5(1)(c), during his detention on remand by virtue of Article 5(4) he must be able to take proceedings at reasonable

---

[462] See below p 290.

[463] 1999-I; 29 EHRR 365 GC. See also *Thompson v UK* hudoc (2004); 40 EHRR 245; *Brincat v Italy* A 249-A (1992); 17 EHRR 60. As regards the objective impartiality requirements in military proceedings elsewhere see *De Jong, Baljet and Van Den Brink v Netherlands* A 77 (1984); 8 EHRR 20 and *Pauwels v Belgium* A 135 (1988); 11 EHRR 238 (both violations of Article 5(3)).

[464] *TW v Malta* hudoc (1999); 29 EHRR 185 para 41 GC; *Aquilina v Malta* 1999-III; 29 EHRR 185 para 47 GC.

[465] A 34 (1979); 2 EHRR 417. As to 'legal criteria', see *Skoogström v Sweden* B 68-A (1983) Com Rep.

[466] Id, para 31.   [467] Ibid. Cf, *Skoogström v Sweden* B 68-A (1983) Com Rep.   [468] Id, para 36.

[469] See id, para 31. The Court declined to examine the issue in *Hood v UK* 1999-I; 29 EHRR 365 para 59 GC.

[470] Trechsel, *Human Rights in Criminal Proceedings*, 2005, p 515.

[471] See below, p 189. In *Brannigan and McBride v UK* A 258-B (1993); 17 EHRR 539 para 58 PC the Court stated that a 'procedure that has a judicial character' must be followed (citing the *Schiesser* and *Huber* cases).

[472] See below at p 183.

intervals to challenge the lawfulness of his detention.[473] In view of the assumption under the Convention that such detention is to be of strictly limited duration, 'periodic review at short intervals is called for'.[474]

II. THE RIGHT TO RELEASE PENDING TRIAL IN REASONABLE CIRCUMSTANCES

As noted above, Article 5(3) continues to apply after the detainee's initial appearance before the judge or 'other officer'. During this phase of detention a decision must be taken whether it is appropriate to release the detainee, on conditions if necessary. The decision must be made by an official with the characteristics and functions of the judge or other officer under Article 5(3) as noted above, except, of course, he must have the power to award bail if necessary. The first decision whether to order conditional release must take place with 'due expedition' (if not 'promptly').[475] Further decisions should take place from time to time thereafter, the domestic courts being required to 'review the continued detention of persons pending trial with a view to ensuring release when circumstances no longer justify continued deprivation of liberty'.[476] Those circumstances are discussed below.

The qualified right to release is not easily identified under Article 5(3). This states that an arrested person is 'entitled to trial within a reasonable time or to release pending trial'.[477] On the face of it, this wording obliges a state either to try a detained accused within a reasonable time or, if it does not do so, to release him. Sensibly, in *Wemhoff v FRG*,[478] the Court rejected this reading, which it described as a 'purely grammatical interpretation', on the ground that it would allow a state to avoid trying a person within a reasonable time at the cost of releasing him. This could not have been the intention of the parties and would, moreover, have been 'flatly contradictory' to the guarantee of 'trial within a reasonable time' for all accused persons, whether detained or not, provided by Article 6(1). In the view of the Court, the key to understanding Article 5(3) was to recall that it is part of a guarantee of freedom of the person. Accordingly, 'it is the provisional detention of accused persons'—not the trial—'which must not . . . be prolonged beyond a reasonable time'. Such prolongation occurs, in breach of Article 5(3), when: (i) there is no good reason in the public interest to continue the accused's detention pending trial; or (ii) it is extended in time because the investigation and trial are conducted less expeditiously than might reasonably be expected. As far as the second possibility is concerned, the outcome of the Court's interpretation of Article 5(3) leads to the same result as the 'purely grammatical interpretation' which the Court rejected, in that a person in detention must be tried within a reasonable time. But, by providing a basis for questioning the grounds of detention pending trial, the first possibility goes further by adding a guarantee of a right to bail for persons detained pending trial, without which Article 5 would be seriously deficient.

Before the qualified right to bail is considered in detail, the following points should be noted. First, the different roles of the national courts and the Strasbourg authorities in

---

[473] *Bezicheri v Italy* A 164 (1989); 12 EHRR 210 paras 20–1.

[474] *Ibid.* See also *Assenov v Bulgaria* 1998-VIII; 28 EHRR 652 para 162.

[475] *McKay v UK* 2006-X; 44 EHRR 827 para 46 GC. This leading case implies that the 'bail hearing' does not need to be automatic; it may follow the detainee's application or the judge's order, see para 46.

[476] Id, para 45.

[477] On this part of Article 5(3), see Harris, 44 BYIL 87 (1970) and Wilkinson and Daintith, 18 AJCL 326 (1970).

[478] A 7 (1968); 1 EHRR 55 paras 4–5.

the application of the right to bail in Article 5(3) have been explained by the Court as follows. When the national courts take their decision 'they must examine all the facts arguing for and against the existence of a genuine requirement of public interest justifying, with due regard to the principle of the presumption of innocence, a departure from the rule of respect for individual liberty and set them out in their decisions on the applications for release'.[479] It is then 'essentially on the basis of the reasons given in these decisions [plus, where relevant, appeals] and of the true facts mentioned by the applicant' when pursuing his remedies for release at the national level that the Strasbourg authorities must make their judgment.[480] So the reasons must be those relied upon by the domestic authorities at the time, not new arguments put forward belatedly at Strasbourg.[481] What is striking is that the Court is quite willing to disagree with the national court's assessment of the need for detention on remand; there is little indication that a 'margin of appreciation' doctrine applies in this context.

Secondly, there is the matter of the stages of the criminal process to which Article 5(3) applies. In *Wemhoff v FRG*,[482] it was held that Article 5(3) covers the period from the arrest[483] of the accused on suspicion of having committed a criminal offence[484] to his acquittal or conviction by the trial court.[485] Hence Article 5(3) does not cover detention pending appeal, it is not possible under that provision to challenge the grounds for detaining a convicted person during his appeal or to question the 'diligence' with which appeal proceedings are conducted, which is scarcely consistent with the bias in Article 5 in favour of the 'right to liberty'.[486] However, release pending appeal will not normally be such an important issue as release pending trial. Moreover, the length of the appeal proceedings may be questioned under the 'reasonable time' guarantee in Article 6(1).[487]

Other considerations to be borne in mind when applying Article 5(3) are that if the accused is detained for two or more separate periods pending trial, they are to be cumulated when applying the reasonable time guarantee in Article 5(3).[488] If proceedings are still pending before the national trial court when an application claiming a breach of Article 5(3) is heard at Strasbourg, the period of detention after an Article 34 application is made may be taken into account by the Court.[489] A period of detention that does not count as a part of the period to be taken into account under Article 5(3) (eg because local remedies have not been exhausted or the defendant state was not a Convention party at the time) may nonetheless be relevant as a part of the general context within which the

---

[479] *Letellier v France* A 207 (1991); 14 EHRR 83 para 35. The Court also emphasized that in a case in which the final decision is taken on appeal, the appeal court should state 'clear and specific' reasons for reversing a decision to release by a lower court that is in a better position to assess the facts and the personality of the accused: id, para 52.

[480] *Ibid.* Cf, *Neumeister v Austria* A 8 (1968); 1 EHRR 91 para 5.

[481] *Trzaska v Poland* hudoc (2000) para 66.

[482] A 7 (1968); 1 EHRR 55 paras 6–9. See also *Kalashnikov v Russia* 2002-VI; 36 EHRR 587.

[483] Special considerations apply if the state concerned ratifies the Convention during the period which the applicant subsequently claims violates Article 5(3), see *Jablonski v Poland* hudoc (2000); 36 EHRR 455 para 66.

[484] In *Herczegfalvy v Austria* A 244 (1992); 15 EHRR 437, in which the applicant was already in detention on another basis when the order for his detention on remand was made, it was held by the Commission that Article 5(3) began to run only when the remand order was made. The point was not reconsidered before the Court.

[485] *Wemhoff v FRG* A 7 (1968); 1 EHRR 55 para 9. In *B v Austria* A 175 (1990); 13 EHRR 20 the Court declined to change its position on this point after a minority of the Commission had requested that it re-examine it.

[486] *B v Austria*, id, paras 36–40. For further criticism see Trechsel, *Human Rights in Criminal Proceedings*, 2005, pp 519–21.

[487] See below, p 278.

[488] *Kemmache v France* A 218 (1991); 14 EHRR 520 para 44.   [489] *Ibid.*

reasonableness of the period of detention may be assessed.[490] A period of detention prior to extradition to the defendant state is likewise not subject to control under Article 5(3), although it too is relevant as a part of the general context.[491]

a. More than 'reasonable suspicion' required to sustain prolonged detention

Consistent with the importance of the right to liberty, the whole thrust of Article 5(3) as interpreted by the Court is against any rule that individuals awaiting trial should be held in detention.[492] Rather a detention effected under Article 5(1)(c) during the remand stage must actually be necessary in the individual circumstances of the case and a person must be released pending trial unless the state can show that there are 'relevant and sufficient' reasons to justify his continued detention.[493]

Obviously the persistence of a reasonable suspicion (according to the legal standards required by Article 5(1)(c)) that the person arrested has committed an offence remains a condition of the accused's continued detention under Article 5(1)(c). For 'an initial period' that suspicion alone justifies detention, but the need to justify continues through the remand period and 'there comes a moment when [reasonable suspicion] is no longer enough'.[494] Then Article 5(3) supposes that there also are *other* 'relevant and sufficient' public interest reasons to justify *further* interference with the 'right to liberty' of a person who is presumed to be innocent under Article 6(2).[495] Domestic authorities must be alive to the fact that reasons which may justify detention at the outset may become weaker over time (especially if the subsequent investigation uncovers no new evidence),[496] perhaps leading to a situation where release becomes necessary.

To satisfy Article 5(3) what is required from the domestic authorities are 'specific indications of a genuine requirement of public interest which, notwithstanding the presumption of innocence, outweighs the rule of respect for individual liberty'.[497] It follows that: the actual seriousness of the charge facing the individual cannot be the *sole* basis for denying bail,[498] whilst 'the existence and persistence of serious indications of guilt' do not on their own justify 'long detention',[499] although this is clearly a relevant factor for the assessment of whether detention is justified. Whilst the Court has indicated that a detention based on hearsay evidence or from a single source may *initially* be sufficient for Article 5(1)(c),[500] particularly in the context of the fight against organized crime or terrorism, it also notes that such a potentially unreliable basis for detention presents dangers

---

[490] *Neumeister v Austria* A 8 (1968); 1 EHRR 91 paras 6–7 and *Vallon v Italy* A 95 (1985); 13 EHRR 433 para 49 Com Rep. But see *Stamoulakatos v Greece* A 271 (1993); 17 EHRR 479 para 33 (an Article 6 case).

[491] *X v Italy and FRG No 5078/71*, 46 CD 35 (1972).

[492] Cf the wording of Article 9(3) ICCPR, 'It shall not be the general rule that persons awaiting trial shall be detained in custody...'.

[493] *Wemhoff v FRG* A 7 (1968); 1 EHRR 55 para 12.

[494] *McKay v UK* 2000-X; 44 EHRR 827 para 45 GC (Court declined to detail a particular time-frame). See also *Stögmuller* v Austria A 9 (1969); 1 EHRR 155 para 4 and *Letellier v France* A 207 (1991); 14 EHRR 83 para 35.

[495] *Ibid*, and *Letellier v France* A 207 (1991); 14 EHRR 83 para 35. The Court has left open the question whether the legal basis for continued detention shifts from Article 5(1)(c) to Article 5(3) once the latter applies: *Stögmuller v Austria* A 9 (1969); 1 EHRR 155 para 4 and *De Jong, Baljet and Van Den Brink v Netherlands* A 77 (1984); 8 EHRR 20 para 44. The position would seem to be that it is Article 5(1)(c) as read with Article 5(3).

[496] *Labita v Italy* 2000-IV; 46 EHRR 1228 paras 159 and 163 GC.

[497] *Ilijkov v Bulgaria* hudoc (2001) para 84.

[498] *Morganti v France (No 1)* A 320-C (1995); 21 EHRR 34 para 62, Com Rep.

[499] *Tomasi v France* A-241-A (1992); 15 EHRR 1 para 89.

[500] See *Labita v Italy* 2000-IV; 46 EHRR 1228 para 158 GC (violation of Article 5(3) in a case concerning mafia crime and detention lasting two years and seven months only on the basis of an anonymous informant's evidence). See also *McKay v UK* 2006-X; 44 EHRR 827 para 45 GC.

that need to be guarded against.[501] It therefore requires that, with the passage of time, there will need to be further evidence (eg corroboration of the single source and/or objective evidence backing up the hearsay evidence) during the course of the investigation for 'reasonable suspicion' to be retained. As a general principle the longer a person is held in detention, the greater the level of 'reasonable suspicion' should be. An opportunity for legal challenge lies under Articles 5(3) and 5(4).

Any system of mandatory detention on remand is incompatible with Article 5(3) *per se*.[502] That provision will also be violated when legislation automatically removes the possibility of the judicial control of pre-trial detention in advance, as in *Cabellero v UK*.[503] If the law provides for a presumption in favour of continued detention (eg detention presumed when alleged offence was of a certain category such as murder), the existence of concrete facts outweighing the rule of respect for individual liberty must be convincingly demonstrated before the Court. It is incumbent on the authorities to establish those relevant facts; they may not place a burden of proof on the applicant such that detention will continue unless he can persuade the domestic court otherwise.[504] Similar considerations apply if legislation requires that, given his previous conduct and/or record, the detainee should be granted bail only if 'exceptional circumstances' exist. To the extent that the 'exceptional circumstances' proviso imposes a burden of proof on the applicant, there may be a violation of Article 5(3) as there clearly would be for Article 5(4).[505]

As regards the content of the reasons provided by a domestic court or body for maintaining detention following an Article 5(3) hearing, the Court's approach again emphasizes the need for independent critical assessment by the judge or judicial officer. Although it will not necessarily entail a violation of Article 5(3), the Court has been quick to criticize as inadequate reasoning that does not appear to be tailored to the individual circumstances of a case, on the basis that it is 'abstract',[506] 'stereotyped',[507] or simply too terse and lacking in detail given the length of detention.[508] The Court is not prepared simply to assume that a particular ground has been relied on by the domestic authorities as the basis for detention; it will require it to be expressly stated in the decision of the domestic authorities.[509]

b. Grounds for refusing bail

Five grounds upon which the refusal of bail may be justified have been identified by the Court: the danger of flight, interference with the course of justice, the prevention of crime, the preservation of public order and, exceptionally, the safety of the person under

---

[501] *Labita v Italy* 2000-IV; 46 EHRR 1228 paras 157–9 GC.

[502] *Ilijkov v Bulgaria* hudoc (2001) para 84.

[503] *Cabellero v UK* 2000-II; 30 EHRR 643 GC (applicant's request for bail automatically refused on the basis of domestic law requiring refusal for charges of murder and manslaughter etc when the accused had a prior conviction for such an offence). See also *SBC v UK* hudoc (2001); 34 EHRR 619. For criticism see Trechsel, *Human Rights in Criminal Proceedings*, 2005, p 511.

[504] *Ilijkov v Bulgaria* hudoc (2001) (Article 5(3) violated: authorities relied solely on a statutory presumption based on the gravity of the charges which shifted to the accused the burden of proving that there was not even a hypothetical danger of absconding, re-offending, or collusion, para 87).

[505] See below, p 184. See also *Nikolova v Bulgaria* 1999-II; 31 EHRR 64 para 59 GC and *Ilijkov v Bulgaria* hudoc (2001) para 99 (Article 5(4) violated; Court took into account imposition of a strong burden of proof on applicants held in detention on remand to show that there was no risk of absconding).

[506] *Letellier v France* A 207 (1991); 14 EHRR 83 para 51.

[507] *Yagci and Sargin v Turkey* A 319-A (1995); 20 EHRR 505 para 52.

[508] *Smirnova v Russia* 2003-IX; 39 EHRR 450 para 70.

[509] *Trzaska v Poland* hudoc (2000) para 66.

investigation.[510] These are discussed in turn below, but it should be emphasized that these grounds of detention need to be viewed alongside the fact that bail conditions may be imposed, as well as other 'preventative measures' such as police supervision. Thus, an individual should only be detained if (i) his release would lead to a real risk that harm identified under one of the grounds for detention will occur, *and* (ii), if the imposition of bail conditions or other reasonable preventative measures cannot stop that risk or reduce it to a level which would not justify detention.[511] Bail conditions are also discussed below.[512]

Danger of absconding

Absconding is, of course, a classic reason potentially justifying detention. Most cases of bail denial have concerned this ground and the general test applied is found in the *Stögmuller* case:[513]

> [T]here must be a whole set of circumstances…which give reason to suppose that the consequences and hazards of flight will seem to [the applicant] to be a lesser evil than continued imprisonment.

As to the 'circumstances' that are relevant, insofar as the sentence is imprisonment, its significance is reduced as the length of the period of pre-trial detention increases, if it can be assumed that this period will be treated as a part of the sentence.[514] Clearly the severity of the sentence that the accused may expect if convicted is important, but it neither constitutes a separate ground for refusing bail, nor, after a certain lapse of time, warrants detention on remand on the ground of the danger of the accused absconding.[515]

In the *Neumeister* case,[516] in assessing danger of flight the Court took into account the probable civil liability that would fall upon the accused under Austrian law in respect of the loss of property that would be attributed to him if convicted. Other relevant factors are 'those relating to the character of the person involved, his morals, his home, his occupation, his assets, his family ties and all kinds of links with the country in which he is being prosecuted'.[517] So also are previous abscondings,[518] the 'accused's particular distaste for detention',[519] indications that he has links with another country that will enable him to escape or that he is actually planning to escape,[520] the threat of further proceedings,[521] and the fact that the applicant has significant creditors which he may want to evade.[522] In *Chraidi v Germany*[523] it was acceptable that the national courts had regard to the length

---

[510] Article 5(3) does not require a detainee to be released on account of his state of health (an issue potentially within the scope of Article 3), although ill-health may be relevant to the assessment of 'trial within a reasonable time', *Jablonski v Poland* hudoc (2000); 36 EHRR 455 para 82, where Article 5(3) was violated on the facts (paras 84–5).

[511] See *Jablonski*, id, para 84.   [512] See p 179.

[513] A 9 (1969); 1 EHRR 155 para 15. See also *Smirnova v Russia* 2003-IX; 39 EHRR 450 para 60.

[514] See eg, *Neumeister v Austria* A 8 (1968); 1 EHRR 91 para 10.

[515] *Chraidi v Germany* hudoc (2006); 47 EHRR 47 para 40. Also *Letellier v France* A 207 (1991); 14 EHRR 83 para 43. Nor can bail be refused on any ground on the basis that the accused is anyway likely to be sentenced to imprisonment: id, para 51.

[516] A 8 (1968); 1 EHRR 91 para 10.

[517] *Ibid*, see also *Becciev v Moldova* hudoc (2005) para 58. In *Yagci and Sargin v Turkey* A 319-A (1995); 20 EHRR 505 para 52, when finding a breach of the right to bail the Court took into account that the accused had returned voluntarily to resume residence in Turkey.

[518] *Punzelt v Czech Republic* hudoc (2000); 33 EHRR 1159 para 76.

[519] *Stögmuller v Austria* A 9 (1969); 1 EHRR 155 para 15.

[520] *Matznetter v Austria* A 10 (1969); 1 EHRR 198 para 8. See also *Ceský v Czech Republic* hudoc (2000); 33 EHRR 181 (fear of absconding justified by fact that applicant had entrusted a significant sum of money to an acquaintance, bought a car using another person's identity card, and obtained a false passport, para 79).

[521] *X v Switzerland No 8788/79*, 21 DR 241 (1980).

[522] *Barfuss v Czech Republic* hudoc (2000); 34 EHRR 948 paras 69–70.

[523] Hudoc (2006); 47 EHRR 47 para 40.

of potential sentence together with other relevant factors. These included the fact that he had been extradited to Germany on international terrorism charges and that he 'had neither a fixed dwelling nor social ties in Germany which might have prevented him from absconding if released'.[524] The Court accepted the domestic courts' finding that no other measures to secure his presence would have been appropriate.

Of course, the reasons for continued detention must remain relevant and sufficient. So in *Kudla v Poland*,[525] for example, even if the applicant's failure to provide his address and a medical certificate might have initially justified detention, it did not do so for two years and four months.

In the *Wemhoff* case, the Court held that it followed from the final sentence of Article 5(3) that where the danger of the accused not appearing for trial is the sole justification for detention, 'his release pending trial must be ordered if it is possible to obtain from him guarantees that will ensure such appearance'.[526] In the *Neumeister* case, one of the reasons for finding the defendant state in breach of Article 5(3) was that it had failed to give proper consideration to an offer of financial guarantee by the defendant in return for his release.[527]

Interference with the course of justice
A justifiable fear that the accused will interfere with the course of justice is another permissible ground for detention.[528] This includes destroying documents,[529] warning or collusion with other possible suspects,[530] and bringing pressure to bear upon witnesses.[531] A general statement that the accused will interfere with the course of justice is not sufficient; supporting evidence must be provided.[532] The longer the detention continues and the more the investigation makes progress, the less likely that interference with justice will remain a good reason for detention.[533]

Prevention of crime
In *Matznetter v Austria*,[534] and subsequent case law[535] the Court has held that the detention of the applicant on the basis of the prevention of crime was compatible with Article 5(3). Accordingly, public interest in the prevention of crime may justify detention on remand where there are good reasons to believe[536] that the accused, if released, will commit an offence or offences of the same serious kind with which he is already charged. It is not necessary that there be a reasonable suspicion that any particular, identifiable offence will be committed. Where, however, the ground for believing that an accused charged with murder may commit other offences of violence if released is his mental condition,

---

[524] Though cf, *Sulaoja v Estonia* hudoc (2005); 43 EHRR 722 ('mere absence of a fixed residence does not give rise to a danger of flight', para 62).

[525] 2000-XI; 35 EHRR 198 GC.

[526] *Wemhoff v FRG* A 7 (1968); 1 EHRR 55 para 15. Cf, *Letellier v France* A 207 (1991); 14 EHRR 83 para 46.

[527] *Neumeister v Austria* A 8 (1968); 1 EHRR 91 paras 12–14.

[528] *Wemhoff v FRG* A 7 (1968); 1 EHRR 55 paras 13–14. See also *Contrada v Italy* 1998-V and *IA v France* 1998-VII.

[529] *Ibid.* Cf, *W v Switzerland* A 254-A (1993); 17 EHRR 60.   [530] *Ibid.*

[531] *Letellier v France* A 207 (1991); 14 EHRR 83.

[532] *Clooth v Belgium* A 225 (1991); 14 EHRR 717 para 44. Also *Becciev v Moldova* hudoc (2005) para 59.

[533] Id, para 43 (1991).

[534] A 10 (1969); 1 EHRR 198 para 7 (four votes to three; three dissenting judges expressed concern at permitting the detention of an accused who was presumed to be innocent on the ground, in effect, that he would if released commit other offences).

[535] See *Toth v Austria* A 224 (1991); 14 EHRR 551; *B v Austria* A 175 (1990); 13 EHRR 20; and *Clooth v Belgium* A 225 (1991); 14 EHRR 717.

[536] In *Clooth*, para 40, the Court used a different, possibly less strict, formula, stating that the danger of repetition must be a 'plausible' one.

his detention should not be continued without steps being taken to give the accused the necessary psychiatric care.[537] The fact that the applicant is unemployed and has no family does not mean that he is inclined to commit new offences.[538]

Public order

A further ground for detention recognized by the Court is the preservation of public order. In *Letellier v France*,[539] the Court accepted that, in exceptional circumstances, 'by reason of their particular gravity and public reaction to them, certain offences may give rise to a social disturbance capable of justifying pre-trial detention, at least for a time'; this is so provided that the municipal law concerned recognizes the ground and there is evidence that the accused's release 'will actually disturb public order'. This test is not satisfied where, as in the *Letellier* case, the decision to refuse bail on this ground takes into account only the gravity of the offence in the abstract. In that case, the French courts, whose law recognized that certain offences may lead to a risk of public disorder justifying pre-trial detention, had only taken into account the fact that the offence (accessory to murder) was a very serious one, without considering whether the accused's release would be likely to cause a public disturbance on the facts. Although the threat to public order may justify detention on remand at the outset, it may cease to do so as time passes.[540]

Safety of the person under investigation

As a fifth ground upon which refusal of bail may be justified, the Court accepts that in some cases the safety of a person under investigation may require his continued detention, for a time at least. However, it has stated that 'this can only be so in exceptional circumstances having to do with the nature of the offences concerned, the conditions in which they were committed and the context in which they took place'.[541]

c. Conditions of bail

Article 5(3) states that if an accused is released on bail his release 'may be conditioned by guarantees to appear for trial'. Automatic denial of bail will be a violation of Article 5(3).[542]

In the *Neumeister* case,[543] Austria was held to have violated Article 5(3) partly because the amount of bail set had been calculated 'solely in relation... to the loss imputed to' the applicant. This, the Court held, was contrary to Article 5(3) because the 'guarantee provided by that Article is designed to ensure, not the reparation of loss, but rather the presence of the accused at the hearing'. Using the maxim *unius est exclusio alterius*, which has been employed in the interpretation of treaties,[544] Article 5(3) can be read as meaning that the only conditions that can be attached to release pending trial are those relating to appearance at trial. However, it would be unsatisfactory if Article 5(3) did not allow any considerations other than appearance at trial to be taken into account when allowing bail. Such an approach might work to a person's disadvantage in that it

---

[537] *Ibid.*   [538] *Sulaoja v Estonia* hudoc (2005); 43 EHRR 772 para 64.

[539] A 207 (1991); 14 EHRR 83 para 51. Cf, *Kemmache v France* A 218 (1991); 14 EHRR 520 para 52 and *Tomasi v France* A-241 (1992); 15 EHRR 1.

[540] *Tomasi*, id, para 91.

[541] *IA v France* 1998-VII para 108 (applicant was accused of wife's murder and, the state claimed, would be attacked by wife's relatives; breach of Article 5(3) on the facts as detention continued over five years and likelihood of attack was low).

[542] *Cabellero v UK* 2000-II; 30 EHRR 643 GC. See also *Iwanczuk v Poland* hudoc (2001); 38 EHRR 148 (inappropriate delay in organizing bail when release justified).

[543] *Neumeister v Austria* A 8 (1968); 1 EHRR 91 para 14.

[544] See eg, the *Life Insurance Claims (US v Germany)* 7 UNRIAA 91, 111 (1924).

might prevent his release altogether if, for example, a condition as to the suppression of evidence or the prevention of crime were not permissible.[545] In the *Wemhoff* case,[546] the Court confirmed that financial guarantees to ensure appearance at trial may be set. In the *Stögmuller* case,[547] it implied that the surrender of a passport for the same purpose may also be required. Where the guarantee is a monetary one, the amount set must be assessed 'principally by reference to him [the accused], his assets and his relationship with the persons who are to provide the security', the purpose being to ensure that there is 'a sufficient deterrent to dispel any wish on his part to abscond'.[548] It is probable that the setting of an amount that is more than sufficient to achieve this would be a violation of the right to bail under this provision.[549] The danger of the accused absconding, however, may be such as to make any amount of bail insufficient[550] although the Court has warned that '[a]s the fundamental right to liberty as guaranteed by Article 5 of the Convention is at stake, the authorities must take as much care in fixing appropriate bail as in deciding whether or not the accused's continued detention is indispensable'.[551] The accused must faithfully furnish sufficient information, that can be checked if need be, so as to allow the amount of bail to be fixed.[552]

III. TRIAL WITHIN A REASONABLE TIME[553] (THE NEED FOR 'SPECIAL DILIGENCE IN THE CONDUCT OF THE PROCEEDINGS')

Even if detention is justified under Article 5(3), that provision may still be infringed if the accused's detention is prolonged beyond a 'reasonable time' because the proceedings have not been conducted with the required expedition.[554] The period to be considered here is from the day the accused is taken into custody until the charge is determined.[555]

The guarantee in Article 5(3), which overlaps with that in Article 6(1), requires that in respect of a detained person the authorities show 'special diligence in the conduct of the proceedings',[556] although this should not hinder the efforts of the judicial authorities to

---

[545] Eg, a not uncommon condition set by magistrates in England is that a person accused of assault or a public order offence stay away from a particular person or place.

[546] A 7 (1968); 1 EHRR 55 para 15.

[547] A 9 (1969); 1 EHRR 155 para 15. Cf, *Schmid v Austria No 10670/83*, 44 DR 195 at 196 (1985) (surrender of passport permissible, as were the surrender of a driving licence and a residence requirement).

[548] *Neumeister v Austria* A 8 (1968); 1 EHRR 91 para 14. The accused must make available the information as to his assets needed for a proper assessment of the amount of security that should be set: *Bonnechaux v Switzerland No 8224/78*, 18 DR 100 at 144 (1979) Com Rep; CM Res DH (80) 1; 3 EHRR 259 (1981).

[549] The Commission has stated that the authorities are under a duty to make a careful assessment of the information as to the accused's resources in their possession so as not to set a recognisance at too high a level: *Schertenlieb v Switzerland No 8339/78*, 23 DR 137 at 196 (1980) Com Rep; CM Res DH (81) 9.

[550] *Neumeister v Austria* A 8 (1968); 1 EHRR 91 para 14.

[551] *Iwanczuk v Poland* hudoc (2001); 38 EHRR 148 para 66.   [552] *Ibid.*

[553] For the relevant period to which 'reasonable time' applies, see p 174 above.

[554] In practice, the Court usually only goes on to consider whether the reasonable time guarantee in Article 5(3) has been infringed if it has first found no breach of the right to bail. In *Tomasi v France* A-241 (1992); 15 EHRR 1 the Court went on to consider the reasonable time guarantee in a borderline case on the right to bail.

[555] *Kalashnikov v Russia* 2002-VI; 36 EHRR 587 para 110.

[556] *Herczegfalvy v Austria* A 244 (1992); 15 EHRR 437 para 71. Cf, the earlier formulation in *Wemhoff v FRG* A 7 (1968); 1 EHRR 55 para 17: 'an accused person in detention is entitled to have his case given priority and conducted with particular expedition'. The complexity and special characteristics of the investigation are relevant for the assessment of 'special diligence', *Scott v Spain* 1996-VI; 24 EHRR 391 para 74.

carry out their tasks with proper care.[557] The same, higher standard of diligence would appear to apply under Article 6(1) when the accused is in detention.[558] In practice, 'reasonable time' claims brought by persons remanded in custody that just concern the stages of the proceedings to which Article 5(3) apply, *viz* from arrest to conviction by the trial court,[559] are considered just under that provision, not under Article 6(1).[560] Reasonable time claims that extend in time beyond the accused's conviction to include appeal proceedings are either considered under both Article 5(3) (for the stages to which it applies) and Article 6(1)[561] or just under Article 6(1).[562]

As to the considerations to be taken into account in assessing whether trial within a reasonable time has occurred, the same ones apply for both Articles 5(3) and 6(1). Thus, as with Article 6(1), relevant factors are the complexity of the case, the conduct of the accused, and the efficiency of the national authorities.[563] In one case the Court's conclusion that Article 5(3) was violated was strongly influenced by the fact that the applicant was a minor detained in an adult facility to forty-eight days.[564]

As with Article 6(1), the Court frequently has cause to find violations of Article 5(3) under this particular head for reasons stemming from the disorganization and ineffectiveness of the authorities, for example extended periods of inactivity on the handling of a case prior to trial.[565] For the purposes of Article 5(3) the fact that the context of the criminal proceedings is 'international terrorism' may be of relevance for the Court's determination of reasonableness as it has 'special consideration' of 'the difficulties intrinsic to the investigation of offences committed by criminal associations acting on a global scale'.[566]

As under Article 6(1), the reasonableness of the length of proceedings depends on the facts of the case.[567] A rough survey of recent case law suggests that anything exceeding two years is likely to violate Article 5(3). However, even the shortest period of pre-trial detention will violate this provision if it is not convincingly demonstrated that it is justified, for Article 5(3) cannot authorize pre-trial detention unconditionally provided that it lasts no longer than a certain period.[568] Moreover, very long periods do not *automatically* violate

[557] *Sadegul Ozdemir v Turkey* hudoc (2005) para 44.

[558] *Abdoella v Netherlands* A 248-A (1992); 20 EHRR 585 para 24. This negates earlier statements by the Court that Article 5(3) imposed a stricter 'reasonable time' standard than Article 6 in detention cases: see *Stögmuller v Austria* A 9 (1969); 1 EHRR 155 and *Matznetter v Austria* A 10 (1969); 1 EHRR 198.

[559] See above, p 174.

[560] *Abdoella*, above, n 558, concerned appeal proceedings, to which Article 5(3) does not extend.

[561] *B v Austria* A 175 (1990); 13 EHRR 20 (no breach of Article 5(3), but a breach of Article 6(1) in respect of post-conviction proceedings). See also *Solmaz v Turkey* hudoc (2006).

[562] As just one example from many that could be cited, see *Assenov v Bulgaria* 1998-VIII; 28 EHRR 652 (virtually no activity on the case for approximately a year).

[563] See *Neumeister v Austria* A 8 (1968); 1 EHRR 91 and *Kemmache v France* A 218 (1991); 14 EHRR 520. In both of these cases, the Court had already found a breach of the right to bail in Article 5(3).

[564] *Nart v Turkey* hudoc (2008) para 34.   [565] See below, p 280.

[566] *Chraidi v Germany* hudoc (2006); 47 EHRR 47 para 37 (although see the concurring opinion of Judge Borrego Borrego).

[567] See *Wemhoff v FRG* A 7 (1968); 1 EHRR 55 para 5 and *McKay v UK* 2006-X; 44 EHRR 827 para 45 GC. In *Toth v Austria* A 224 (1991); 14 EHRR 551 (two years and one month's detention on remand), there were periods of inactivity totalling eleven months resulting largely because of a disinclination to photocopy the official file. In *Tomasi v France* A-241 (1992); 15 EHRR 1 (five years and seven months), the public prosecutor admitted to long periods in which no progress was made. See also *Birou v France* A 232-B (1992); 14 EHRR 738 Com Rep (five years' delay unreasonable; F Sett before Court).

[568] *Shishkov v Bulgaria* 2003-I para 66 ('relatively short period in detention' of seven months and three weeks violated Article 5(3)). Article 5(3) can apply to multiple detention periods, if so the Court examines not only the reasonableness of the total time, but also 'whether the repetitiveness of the detention' complies with Article 5(3), *Smirnova v Russia* 2003-IX; 39 EHRR 450 para 67.

Article 5(3). In *W v Switzerland*,[569] the Court held, by five to four, that proceedings resulting in a four-year period of pre-trial detention were not in breach of Article 5(3). In a
strong dissent Judge Pettiti[570] suggested that there should be an absolute limit to the length
of pre-trial detention and that, given European standards and expectations, very strong
evidence indeed was necessary to justify both the refusal of bail and the time taken to
investigate and try a case over a period lasting as long as four years. The finding in *W* was
evidentially controversial, however, in *Chraidi v Germany*[571] the Court unanimously held
that there had been no violation of Article 5(3) when the relevant period was over five
and a half years. It indicated that normally such a period would breach Article 5(3),[572] but
stressed the exceptional circumstances of the case before it, 'a particularly complex investigation and trial concerning serious offences of international terrorism which caused the
death of three victims and serious suffering to more than one hundred'.[573]

8. ARTICLE 5(4): REMEDY TO CHALLENGE THE LEGALITY OF DETENTION

I. THE IMPORTANCE OF ARTICLE 5(4)

Article 5(4) provides:

> Everyone who is deprived of his liberty by arrest or detention shall be entitled to take pro-
> ceedings by which the lawfulness of his detention shall be decided speedily by a court and
> his release ordered if the detention is not lawful.

Article 5(4) is the *habeas corpus* provision of the Convention,[574] providing a 'cornerstone
guarantee'[575] which is in essence a detainee's 'right actively to seek [a prompt] judicial
review of his detention'.[576] The review,[577] which must be obtained 'speedily', is not an
appeal but must examine the procedural and substantive conditions which are essential
for the 'lawfulness', in Convention terms, of the deprivation of liberty.[578] Release must be
ordered if it is concluded that detention is unlawful.

II. WHEN DOES ARTICLE 5(4) APPLY?

There is no need for separate Article 5(4) review if the detention has been made by the
order of a 'court'.[579] This is most clearly the case when a person has been 'convicted by

---

[569] *W v Switzerland* A 254-A (1993); 17 EHRR 60.

[570] See also the joint dissenting opinion of Judges Walsh and Loizou and the dissenting opinion of Judge
De Meyer. The Commission had found a breach of Article 5(3) by nineteen to one, and it had suggested that
Article 5(3) should set a maximum length of pre-trial detention.

[571] Hudoc (2006); 47 EHRR 47.   [572] Id, para 46.

[573] Id, para 47 (cf, the concurring opinion of Judge Borrego Borrego).

[574] Note, however, that in certain circumstances *habeas corpus* under English law has not satisifed Article 5(4),
see below.

[575] *Rakevich v Russia* hudoc (2003) para 43.   [576] *Ibid.*

[577] See the useful recapitulation of principles set out in *Reinprecht v Austria* 2005-XII; 44 EHRR 797 para 31.

[578] Hence Article 5(4) does not 'guarantee a right to judicial review of such breadth as to empower the court,
on all aspects of the case including questions of pure expediency, to substitute its own discretion for that of the
decision-making authority', *Chahal v UK* 1996-V; 23 EHRR 413 para 127.

[579] *De Wilde, Ooms and Versyp v Belgium* A 12 (1971); 1 EHRR 373 para 76 PC. Cf, *Engel v Netherlands*
A 22 (1976); 1 EHRR 706 para 77 PC. The rule has been criticized, see Trechsel, *Human Rights in Criminal
Proceedings*, 2005, pp 469–70.

a competent court' consistently with Article 5(1)(a). It applies equally, however, to other situations where detention is ordered by a 'court',[580] which is given the same meaning for this purpose as it otherwise is under Article 5(4). This 'incorporation rule' reflects the fact that the theory underlying this provision is that a judicial remedy should be available to review the legality of an administrative act of detention, as with, potentially, a decision to continue to detain a mental health detainee or an offender up for parole. Here a full review by a 'court', within the meaning of Article 5(4), will be required. Furthermore, as will be noted below, Article 5(4) may require a review of detention after a certain time and at reasonable intervals thereafter by a 'court', even if the original basis for detention is a court order. Most forms of detention will not require this, but it is required for detainees on remand and when the grounds for detention are susceptible to change over time, as with mental illness or when a detainee is being held during a discretionary phase of his sentence on the basis of his continuing dangerousness.

III. OTHER GENERAL PRINCIPLES

There are a number of core rules that make up the very substance of Article 5(4), however the specific procedural requirements of that Article may vary slightly according to the nature of the detention that is subject to the review. The core rules require that a detainee must be able to seek Article 5(4) review as soon as he is detained and the decision must take place 'speedily' thereafter. Potentially, therefore, Article 5(4), which is a fully independent provision, may come into play before Article 5(3) (which, in any case only applies to detention under Article 5(1)(c)).[581] There is no precondition to the application of Article 5(4) that an applicant 'show that on the facts of his case he stands any particular chance of success in obtaining his release'.[582] The review itself must have a judicial character and provide guarantees appropriate to the kind of deprivation of liberty in question.[583] Although the full range of Article 6 rights is not required, there is a 'close link' between the procedures applying for Article 5(4) and Article 6(1), especially for detention under Article 5(1)(c) (criminal proceedings).[584] The review must be adversarial and always ensure 'equality of arms' between the parties, with a hearing being necessary in certain situations.[585] Even if the state maintains that national security considerations are in issue, in particular legitimate security concerns regarding the hearing of intelligence information in open court,[586] a remedy must exist in some form so as to accord the detainee 'a substantial measure of procedural justice'.[587]

Although Article 5(4) only requires a remedy at one level of jurisdiction, in *Toth v Austria*[588] the Court held that if a party provides a right of appeal against a decision by a first instance 'court' rejecting a claim for release, the appellate body must 'in principle'

---

[580] See *Winterwerp v Netherlands* A 33 (1979); 2 EHRR 387. If in practice the imposition of the length of a sentence of imprisonment is concluded by a member of the executive, the incorporation rule will not have been complied with, see *V v UK* 1999-IX; 30 EHRR 121 para 120 GC.

[581] See Trechsel, *Human Rights in Criminal Proceedings*, 2005, p 466.

[582] *Waite v UK* hudoc (2002); 36 EHRR 1001 para 59.

[583] *Assenov v Bulgaria* 1998-VIII; 28 EHRR 652 para 162.

[584] For further comment see *Reinprecht v Austria* 2005-XII; 44 EHRR 797 paras 36–40. It is clear that review under Article 5(4) does not represent a 'determination' of a 'criminal charge' for the purposes of Article 6(1), para 48. In *Aerts v Belgium* 1996-V; 29 EHRR 50 para 59 the Court stated that 'the right to liberty…is a civil right'. However, as to the more complex question of whether Article 6(1) under its civil head applies to pre-trial detention in the context of criminal proceedings see *Reinprecht*, id, paras 53–4.

[585] *Nikolova v Bulgaria* 1999-II; 31 EHRR 64 para 58 GC.

[586] See text acompanying n 603 below.   [587] *Chahal v UK* 1996-V; 23 EHRR 413 para 131.

[588] A 224 (1991); 14 EHRR 551 para 84. See also *Grauzinis v Lithuania* hudoc (2000); 35 EHRR 144. Cf, *Navarra v France* A 273-B (1993); 17 EHRR 594.

comply with Article 5(4). The position is comparable to that concerning appeal courts in the right to a fair trial guarantee in Article 6(1).[589]

The mere fact that the Court has found no breach of Article 5(1) does not mean that it is excluded from carrying out a review of compliance with Article 5(4).[590] That Article is a *lex specialis* in relation to the 'less strict' general remedy required by Article 13 of the Convention; if the Court finds a breach of Article 5(4), it is unlikely to consider a claim by a detained person under Article 13.[591] However, since the purpose of the remedy required by Article 5(4) is to facilitate a detained person's release, it is no longer required once he is lawfully free.[592] Even if the person is only out on licence, Article 5(4) no longer applies whilst the individual has liberty; instead, Article 13 applies, requiring that a remedy be provided by which the released person may challenge the consistency with the Convention of his earlier detention.[593] Where a person in detention is released 'speedily' while his application for release is pending, the question whether the remedy that he has sought complies with Article 5(4) will not be pursued by the Court on the ground that it serves no purpose. Thus in *Fox, Campbell and Hartley v UK*,[594] two of the applicants sought *habeas corpus* the day after their arrest but were released within the next twenty-four hours, before their application was heard. Given that the applicants had already been released 'speedily', the Court declined to consider whether the *habeas corpus* proceedings would have complied with Article 5(4). As with Article 13, Article 5(4) is of great importance because a municipal law remedy will be of (near) immediate effect and more convenient to obtain than one via Strasbourg for a breach of the international guarantee in Article 5(1).[595]

IV. REVIEW OF THE LAWFULNESS OF THE DETENTION

A remedy in the sense of Article 5(4) is one that permits the detained person to challenge the 'lawfulness' of his detention. The term 'lawful' has the same meaning as it has in Article 5(1), so that the detained person must have the opportunity to question whether his detention is consistent both with the applicable municipal law and the Convention, including its general principles, and is not arbitrary.[596] The onus of proof is on the authorities in this regard; they must prove that an individual satisfies the conditions for compulsory detention, rather than the converse.[597]

Article 5(4) does not impose an obligation on a judge examining an appeal against detention to address every argument contained in the appellant's submissions. However, the judge concerned must have regard to and properly address concrete facts invoked by the detainee and capable of putting in doubt the existence of the conditions essential for

---

[589] See below, p 298.   [590] *Douiyeb v Netherlands* hudoc (1999); 30 EHRR 790 para 57 GC.

[591] *De Jong, Baljet and Van Den Brink v Netherlands* A 77 (1984); 8 EHRR 20 para 60.

[592] *X v Sweden No 10230/82*, 32 DR 303 (1983). A released person may nonetheless challenge under Article 5(4) the 'speediness' of any remedy available to him: *X v UK No 9403/81*, 28 DR 235 (1982). A person who absconds remains entitled to a remedy under Article 5(4) because he is still deprived of his liberty in law: *Van der Leer v Netherlands* A 170-A (1990); 12 EHRR 567.

[593] *L v Sweden No 10801/84*, 61 DR 62 at 73 (1988) Com Rep; CM Res DH (89) 16.

[594] A 182 (1990); 13 EHRR 157.

[595] Cf, Trechsel, *European System*, p 319, who emphasizes the subsidiary character of the remedy under the Convention.

[596] *Van Droogenbroeck v Belgium* A 50 (1982); 4 EHRR 443 para 48 PC. As to 'lawful' under Article 5(1), see above, pp 133–4.

[597] *Hutchison Reid v UK* 2003 IV; 37 EHRR 211 para 71.

the lawfulness, in the sense of the Convention, of the deprivation of liberty.[598] So there will be an obvious violation when, in relation to a detention under Article 5(1)(c), the review body merely verifies the charges against the applicant but does not examine the concrete facts concerning the soundness of the charges against him with a view to ordering release if it could not be said that the test of 'reasonable suspicion' had been met.[599] Again, to the extent that conditions of detention have a bearing on the issue of lawfulness, as in *Aerts v Belgium*,[600] the court should be able to review these too.

With regard to the requirement that the detention not be arbitrary, the nature of the remedy required will vary according to the meaning that this term has in the particular sub-paragraph of Article 5(1) (or part of it) within which the case comes.[601] Consistent with the requirements of Article 5(1)(f) as interpreted by the Court,[602] Article 5(4) does not require that the domestic 'court' have the power to review the merits of the underlying decision to expel. However, there must be a proper review of whether the decision to detain the applicant and to keep him in detention was justified on the grounds given by the state. This was not possible in *Chahal v UK*,[603] since the full material on which the decision to detain was based was not made available to the domestic courts given national security considerations.[604] In that case it was accepted that the use of confidential material may be unavoidable where national security and terrorism is involved, but the Court stated that this did not mean that in such circumstances the national authorities should be 'free from effective control by the domestic courts'.[605] The state had failed to strike a proper balance since, as Canadian experiences illustrated, it was possible to employ techniques which both accommodated legitimate security concerns about the nature and sources of intelligence information and yet accord the individual a substantial measure of procedural justice.[606] In reaction to *Chahal* the British government created the Special Immigration Appeals Tribunal, allowing for proceedings to be held *in camera* with the applicant represented by special security-cleared counsel.

For the detention of a 'person of unsound mind', it must be possible for the 'court' to determine whether the detention is warranted on medical grounds, since compliance with Article 5(1)(e) requires that the person's detention as being of 'unsound mind' is medically justified.[607] It was because no such possibility existed that *habeas corpus* proceedings in English law were held not to provide a sufficient remedy in *X v UK*.[608] *Habeas corpus* did constitute a sufficient Article 5(4) remedy by which to challenge the detention of an accused person within Article 5(1)(c), since it allowed the reasonableness of the grounds for suspicion, as well as the procedural legality of the detention, to be reviewed.[609] However a number of cases brought against the UK have exposed the

---

[598] *Nikolova v Bulgaria* 1999-II; 31 EHRR 64 para 61 GC.

[599] Id. See also *Ječius v Lithuania* 2000-IX; 35 EHRR 400.   [600] See above p 158.

[601] *Bouamar v Belgium* A 129 (1988); 11 EHRR 1 para 60. See also *Zamir v UK No 9174/80*, 40 DR 42 at 58 (1983); 5 EHRR 242 (1983); CM Res DH (85) 3 and *Whitehead v Italy No 13930/88*, 60 DR 272 at 283 (1989) (an Article 5(1)(f) case).

[602] See above p 159.   [603] 1996-V; 23 EHRR 413.

[604] Nor was this deficiency made up for by other potential avenues of address, eg, a Home Office advisory panel on deportation in national security cases, which, owing to its own procedural deficiencies could not be regarded as a 'court' within the meaning of Article 5(4), id, para 130.   [605] Id, para 131.

[606] Id, see paras 131 and 144. See also *Al-Nashif v Bulgaria* hudoc (2002); 36 EHRR 655 paras 94–8.

[607] See the *Winterwerp* case, above, at p 156. The lawfulness requirement will require that the medical report before the court is appropriately up to date, see *Musial v Poland* 1999-II; 31 EHRR 720 para 50 GC (eleven-month-old report).

[608] A 46 (1981); 4 EHRR 188 para 58. *Habeas corpus* would suffice for an emergency admission, para 58.

[609] *Brogan v UK* A 145-B (1988); 11 EHRR 117 para 65 PC. *Habeas corpus* was also held to be a sufficient remedy in an Article 5(1)(f) case since the applicant's claim that the length of the detention was excessive could

failings of judicial review in English administrative law[610] at the time, in that it provided insufficiently close scrutiny of the grounds of detention to satisfy Article 5(4). This case law preceded the entry into force of the Human Rights Act 1998.

V. A CONTINUING REMEDY AT REASONABLE INTERVALS

The fact that the initial decision to detain a person is taken by a 'court' (the 'incorporation rule'), or that an administrative detention is subsequently ratified by such a body will not always suffice for Article 5(4). This is because there may be detention circumstances where 'the very nature of the deprivation of liberty under consideration would appear to require a review of lawfulness at reasonable intervals'.[611] Above all those circumstances are when the basis in law for detention may cease to exist. Two clear examples are a mental health detainee who recovers his health to the point at which it is inappropriate to detain him and life prisoners who have served the relevant tariff but whose continued detention is dependent on elements of dangerousness and risk. Other situations in which a continuing remedy may be required are cases of the preventive detention of recidivists,[612] the detention of minors,[613] and the refusal of bail to an accused person.[614]

The requirement for an Article 5(4) remedy at reasonable intervals was applied in *X v UK*,[615] in which the applicant had been ordered by the trial court following his conviction to be detained at Broadmoor as a restricted offender patient on the statutory grounds that he was mentally disordered and a danger to the public. Although the initial judicial supervision required by Article 5(4) was 'incorporated in the decision' of the trial court, which was clearly a 'court' in the sense of that provision, the possibility that the applicant's mental condition might improve so as no longer to warrant detention meant that Article 5(4) required that he be provided with further possibilities, either by way of 'automatic periodic review of a judicial character' or by the opportunity for him to 'take proceedings at reasonable intervals before a court', to challenge the lawfulness of his continued detention.[616]

have been considered: *X v UK No 9088/80*, 28 DR 160 (1982). But see *Caprino v UK No 6871/75*, 12 DR 14 at 13 (1978); 4 EHRR 97. In *McVeigh, O'Neill and Evans v UK Nos 8022/77, 8025/77 and 8027/77*, 25 DR 15 at 47 (1981); 5 EHRR 71 para 217, *habeas corpus* was a sufficient remedy in an Article 5(1)(b) case.

[610] See eg, *Weeks v UK* A 114 (1987); 13 EHRR 435 PC and *Thynne, Wilson and Gunnell v UK* A190-A (1990); 13 EHRR 666 PC, where Article 5(1)(a) was the basis for detention and *HL v UK* 2004-IX; 40 EHRR 761 paras 136–42 where Article 5(1)(e) was in issue. In *Chahal v UK* 1996-V; 23 EHRR 413 GC, neither judicial review nor *habeas corpus* was an Article 5(4)-compliant basis for challenging a deportation order on the facts.

[611] *Winterwerp v Netherlands* A 33 (1979); 2 EHRR 387 para 55 (1979). In other terms, a continuing remedy is required if 'new issues affecting the lawfulness of the detention might subsequently arise': *X v UK* A 46 (1981); 4 EHRR 188 para 51.

[612] *Van Droogenbroeck v Belgium* A 50 (1982); 4 EHRR 443 PC and *E v Norway* A 181-A (1990); 17 EHRR 30.

[613] *Bouamar v Belgium* A 129 (1988); 11 EHRR 1.

[614] *Bezicheri v Italy* A 164 (1989); 12 EHRR 210. When the lawfulness of the deprivation of liberty depends on the applicant's solvency (as with a sentence and fine with further detention in default of payment of the fine) this is also a factor which can evolve with time, so requiring a continuing remedy, *Soumare v France* 1998-V para 38.

[615] A 46 (1981); 4 EHRR 188.

[616] Id, para 52. For a case of 'automatic periodic review' see *Keus v Netherlands* A 185-C (1990); 13 EHRR 700 para 24. See also *Silva Rocha v Portugal* 1996-V; 32 EHRR 333, involving a homicide committed by a person who could not be held criminally responsible for his actions and who was at the same time dangerous. By six votes to three, the Court held that the incorporation rule applied as regards the three-year minimum imprisonment which was a punishment under domestic law, even though it was accepted that the applicant was not held to be criminally responsible (para 28). Only then was a review at reasonable intervals under Article 5(4) required (though see the dissenting opinion of Judges Pettiti, Russo, and Valticos and the Commission's Report). Hence,

The remedy at reasonable intervals aspect of Article 5(4) has been successfully employed on a case by case basis to challenge the role played by the British Home Secretary in certain parts of the criminal justice system in the UK. Two early cases resulted in the erosion of the Home Secretary's powers in respect of discretionary life sentence prisoners.[617] It was established that an Article 5(4) 'court'—not the Home Secretary—was required to determine periodically the case for release of a discretionary 'lifer' during the discretionary phase of his detention. Likewise the decision to re-detain a 'discretionary lifer' who had been out on licence had to be taken by a 'court' within the meaning of Article 5(4). The same principle was applied to juvenile offenders[618] who, after expiry of the tariff period (the part of the sentence said to reflect the requirements of retribution and deterrence), were also serving indeterminate sentences such as detention 'during Her Majesty's pleasure'. These rulings raised questions regarding the role that a member of the executive (ie the Home Secretary) should play at later stages of detention for mandatory life prisoners. Such prisoners served a determinate sentence which included a tariff period set by the Home Secretary, but when this expired, like the earlier cases the basis for detention appeared in reality to be the nature of the risk the detainee posed to society, ie matters that appeared ripe for consideration by a 'court'. Ultimately in *Stafford v UK*[619] a Grand Chamber of the Court overruled an earlier judgment[620] and relied on developments in domestic law in the UK to hold that the 'review at reasonable intervals' aspect of Article 5(4) applied for mandatory life sentence prisoners too, though only after the expiry of the tariff period, for in reality at that stage the grounds for continued detention were considerations of risk and dangerousness.[621] It followed that the applicant's continued detention after 1997, as decided by the Secretary of State,[622] had not been reviewed by a body that satisfied the requirements Article 5(4). The Court referred to 'the wider recognition of the need to develop and apply, in relation to mandatory life prisoners, judicial procedures reflecting standards of independence, fairness and openness' and recognized that the notion of separation of powers between the executive and the judiciary had 'assumed growing importance in the case-law of the Court'.[623] Although this jurisprudence did not have an impact on the Home Secretary's specific statutory power to fix the tariff for life sentence prisoners, the House of Lords, relying on Strasbourg jurisprudence, has reached the conclusion that that power was incompatible with Article 6(1) of the Convention.[624]

for detention justified under both Articles 5(1)(a) and 5(1)(e), the Article 5(4) 'remedy at reasonable intervals' requirement only applies when the basis for detention shifts to Article 5(1)(e) alone. See also *Morley v UK* No 16084/03 hudoc (2004) DA.

[617] *Weeks v UK* A 114 (1987); 13 EHRR 435 PC and *Thynne, Wilson and Gunnell v UK* A190-A (1990); 13 EHRR 666 PC, see Richardson, 1991 PL 34.

[618] See *Hussain v UK and Singh v UK* 1996-I; 22 EHRR 1 and *V v UK* 1999-IX; 30 EHRR 121 GC.

[619] 2002-IV; 35 EHRR 1121 GC. See Hunt, 22 YEL 483 at 490–3 (2003).

[620] *Wynne v UK* A 294-A; 19 EHRR 333.

[621] It is interesting to note that the Court did not accept arguments to the effect that 'public acceptability of release' could be another basis for continuing detention of mandatory life offenders, para 80.

[622] For the facts of *Stafford* see above at p 141.

[623] *Stafford v UK* 2002-IV; 35 EHRR 1121 para 78 GC. See also *Benjamin and Wilson v UK* hudoc (2002); 36 EHRR 1 (Home Secretary's declared practice of following the recommendations of the Mental Health Review Tribunal was not itself compliant with Article 5(4); although the Tribunal would satisfy Article 5(4) (if its decisions were binding), 'the decision to release would [still] be taken by a member of the executive' and this 'impinge[d] on the fundamental principle of separation of powers and detracts from a necessary guarantee against the possibility of abuse', para 36).

[624] *R (Anderson) v Secretary of State for the Home Department* [2002] UKHL 46. See also *Easterbrook v UK* hudoc (2003); 37 EHRR 812.

Finally, what time periods apply to the notion of 'reasonable intervals'? Although an initial review should be taken 'speedily', the answer to this question depends on the kind of case in issue. A period of one month has been held to be a 'reasonable interval' in the context of detention on remand, the nature of which is such as to call for a remedy at 'short intervals'[625] and given the assumption under the Convention that such detention is to be of strictly limited duration. Although a longer interval may be acceptable in the case of a 'person of unsound mind' a period in excess of one year has been held to be in breach of Article 5(4).[626] Where there is clear evidence of a change in a person's mental condition, a hearing within a shorter period may be required.[627] Arrangements for 'automatic periodic review' must follow the same standards as to frequency[628] and the applicant's conduct may be relevant. As regards discretionary life prisoners in the UK, the Court has stated that it will not attempt to rule as to the maximum period of time between reviews which should automatically apply given the need for flexibility in the system.[629] Generally periods of less than a year between reviews have been acceptable whilst periods of more than one year have breached Article 5(4).[630]

It is perhaps surprising that Article 5(4) does not require the 'court' referred to therein to have the power to set the timing of subsequent reviews of detention.[631]

VI. THE QUALITIES AND PROCEDURES REQUIRED OF AN ARTICLE 5(4) 'COURT'

The detained person must have access to a 'court', but this does not entail that the whole package of Article 6(1) fair trial rights apply for Article 5(4). As the Court has put it:

> [t]he 'court' referred to in this provision does not necessarily have to be a court of law of the classic kind, integrated within the standard judicial machinery of the country. The term denotes 'bodies which exhibit not only common fundamental features, of which the most important is independence of the executive and the parties to the case ..., but also the guarantees'—'appropriate to the kind of deprivation of liberty in question'—'of a judicial procedure', the forms of which may vary but which must include the competence to 'decide' the 'lawfulness' of the detention and to order release if the detention is not lawful.[632]

Article 5(4) may be complied with by the provision of two or more separate remedies that together allow the applicant to test all aspects of the legality of his detention.[633] It is also

---

[625] *Bezicheri v Italy* A 164 (1989); 12 EHRR 210 para 21. See also *X v Netherlands No 11155/85*, 9 EHRR 267 (1985) (review after eleven days satisfactory) and *Assenov v Bulgaria* 1998-VIII; 28 EHRR 652 para 165 (violation as law only allowed for one review of pre-trial detention).

[626] *Herczegfalvy v Austria* A 244 (1992); 15 EHRR 437.

[627] *M v FRG No 10272/83*, 38 DR 104 (1984). See also *Hirst v UK* hudoc (2001) para 44 (twenty-one-month delay between reviews; improvement in mental state of discretionary life prisoner).

[628] See *Keus v Netherlands* A 185-C (1990); 13 EHRR 700 para 24. See also *Oldham v UK* 2000-X; 31 EHRR 813 para 36 (two-year delay between reviews was unreasonable especially as the applicant had addressed areas of concern within eight months).

[629] *Hirst v UK* hudoc (2001) para 38 (twenty-one-month and two-year delays between reviews were not reasonable).

[630] See *Blackstock v UK* hudoc (2005); 42 EHRR 55 para 44.

[631] *Blackstock v UK No 59512/00* hudoc (2004) DA (although the Court stated it would take into account the failure to observe a recommendation from a 'court' as to timing).

[632] *Hutchinson Reid v UK* 2003 IV; 37 EHRR 211 para 64 (with references to *Weeks v UK* A 114 (1987); 13 EHRR 435 para 61 PC).

[633] *Weeks* id, para 69. Cf, *Benjamin and Wilson v UK* hudoc (2002); 36 EHRR 1 para 36, 'Article 5(4) presupposes the existence of a procedure in conformity with its provisions without the necessity to institute separate

sufficient that a remedy exists; it does not matter that the applicant finds it inadvisable to use it in his particular circumstances.[634] However, the principle of accessibility and effectiveness derived from Article 5(4) does require that the existence of the remedy must be sufficiently certain, not only in theory but also in practice.[635] As regards the latter requirement, the onus is on the respondent state to furnish the Court with specific examples of judicial decisions which testify to the existence and effectiveness of the remedy.[636] There is no requirement that remedies that are neither adequate nor effective should be used by the applicant.[637]

The right to apply for a remedy should be exercisable by the detainee on his own initiative; it should not be dependent on the initiative or goodwill of the authorities.[638] Issues may arise given the practical ability of an applicant, in his particular situation, to have effective recourse to an Article 5(4) remedy for it is a principle that circumstances voluntarily created by the authorities must not be such as to deny applicants a realistic possibility of using the remedy. In *RMD v Switzerland*[639] Article 5(4) was violated as the applicant was transferred successively from one canton to another such that, owing to the peculiarities of domestic law and the organization of the national court system, in no single canton was he able to make effective use of the sound Article 5(4) remedies that were available. In *Öcalan v Turkey*[640] the applicant detainee was not legally trained, had no access to a lawyer, and was in effect cut off from the outside world and so it was impossible in practical terms for him to mount an Article 5(4) claim. In *Conka v Belgium*,[641] Article 5(4) was violated as the speed with which the authorities expedited the deportation of the applicants entailed that their lawyer was unable to mount an Article 5(4) challenge before their actual deportation occurred.

a. Judicial character

To be of a 'judicial character', a body must be both impartial[642] and 'independent both of the executive and the parties to the case'.[643] Bodies that have predictably been held not to meet this requirement are a public prosecutor,[644] the medical officer of a 'person of unsound mind',[645] and a government minister.[646] In *Weeks v UK*[647] the English Parole Board was found to have the necessary judicial character; it was 'independent of the executive and impartial in the performance of their duties'.[648] The distinction being drawn was between 'independence' of the executive and 'impartiality' as between the parties.

---

legal proceedings in order to bring it about'. (Court rejected respondent government's argument that fault with domestic remedy could be remedied by subsequent proceedings under the Human Rights Act 1998.)

[634] *Keus v Netherlands* A 185-C (1990); 13 EHRR 700 para 28.

[635] *Van Droogenbroeck v Belgium* A 50 (1982); 4 EHRR 443 para 54 PC; also *Sakık v Turkey* 1997-VII; 26 EHRR 662 para 53.

[636] See eg, *Sakık*, id, para 53 (violation as, despite submissions relating to the effectiveness of the remedy, the Court was provided with no example of a successful application at domestic level). Cf, a less strict approach in early case law: *E v Norway* A 181-A (1990); 17 EHRR 30 para 60.

[637] Id, para 55.   [638] *Rakevich v Russia* hudoc (2003) paras 43–7.

[639] 1997-VI; 28 EHRR 224 para 52.   [640] 2005-IV; 41 EHRR 985 paras 70–2 GC.

[641] 2002-I; 34 EHRR 1298 para 55.

[642] *DN v Switzerland* 2001-III; 37 EHRR 510 para 42 GC (objective and subjective tests are applied, para 44; impartiality is presumed until there is proof to the contrary, para 45).

[643] *De Wilde, Ooms and Versyp v Belgium* A 12 (1971); 1 EHRR 373 para 77 PC. See also the text accompanying n 632 above.

[644] *Winterwerp v Netherlands* A 33 (1979); 2 EHRR 387 para 64.

[645] *X v UK* A 46 (1981); 4 EHRR 188 para 61.

[646] Ibid. Cf, *Keus v Netherlands* A 185-C (1990); 13 EHRR 700 para 28.

[647] A 114 (1987); 13 EHRR 435 para 62 PC.

[648] Cf, the Court's change in approach in respect of the meaning of 'officer' in Article 5(3), above, n 461.

As to impartiality, in *K v Austria*,[649] a court of law did not satisfy Article 5(4) because the judge who ruled on the applicant's detention for failing to pay a fine had earlier imposed the fine.

An investigating judge in a civil law system is a 'court'.[650] This decision has been criticized on the basis that, although 'independent', an investigating judge is not 'impartial' as between the parties since he has a responsibility to bring the investigation successfully to an end and hence has an incentive to detain the accused to avoid him absconding or tampering with evidence.[651] However, the Court has recently confirmed[652] that, other than in special circumstances, the mere fact that a trial judge makes decisions on detention on remand does not in itself taint that figure as being 'impartial' for the purposes of Article 5(4). It takes the view that suspicion and a formal finding of guilt are not to be treated as being the same and that normally questions which the judge has to answer when deciding on detention on remand are not the same as those which are decisive for his final judgment.

A 'court' must have a 'judicial character' in the sense of being competent to take a legally binding decision leading to the person's release. Thus in *X v UK*,[653] a Mental Health Review Tribunal, although independent of the executive and the parties, did not qualify because it could only make advisory recommendations for release to the Home Secretary. In *E v Norway*,[654] the Court was satisfied that whereas the Norwegian courts would normally just declare an administrative decision to be illegal without ordering that any remedial steps be taken, they could go further and order a person's release in a case of illegal detention, as Article 5(4) requires. In *Van Droogenbroeck v Belgium*[655] it was insufficient that a court could convict the responsible government official for illegal detention but could not order the detained person's release.

b. Procedural guarantees

Even if the review is provided by what appears to be a regular court according to domestic law, this does not mean that there will be no violation of Article 5(4), for the procedural guarantees afforded by that court may fall short of that Article's requirements. This was the case in *De Wilde, Ooms and Versyp v Belgium*,[656] where the plenary court held that Article 5(4) obliges a 'court' to provide 'guarantees of judicial procedure', it being later stated that Article 5(4) proceedings 'must have a judicial character and provide guarantees appropriate to the kind of deprivation of liberty in question'.[657]

Article 5(4) allows for some differences of procedure dependent on the 'particular nature of the circumstances in which the proceedings take place',[658] but there should always be 'equality of arms' between the parties concerned.[659] For detention under Article 5(1)(c), Article 5(4) proceedings 'should in principle...meet, to the largest extent possible under the circumstances of an ongoing investigation, the basic requirements of a fair trial'.[660]

---

[649] A 255-B (1993) Com Rep. F Sett before Court.   [650] *Bezicheri v Italy* A 164 (1989); 12 EHRR 210.
[651] Trechsel, *European System*, p 327.
[652] *Ilijkov v Bulgaria* hudoc (2001) para 97 (Bulgarian law at the time entrusted decisions relating to the accused's detention to the same trial judge who subsequently examined the merits of the criminal case).
[653] A 46 (1981); 4 EHRR 188.   [654] *E v Norway* A 181-A (1990); 17 EHRR 30.
[655] A 50 (1982); 4 EHRR 443. Cf, *Benjamin and Wilson v UK* hudoc (2002); 36 EHRR 1 para 36.
[656] A 12 (1971); 1 EHRR 373 para 78 PC.   [657] *Assenov v Bulgaria* 1998-VIII; 28 EHRR 652 para 162.
[658] *De Wilde, Ooms and Versyp v Belgium* A 12 (1971); 1 EHRR 373 para 78 PC.
[659] *Garcia Alva v Germany* hudoc (2001); 37 EHRR 335 para 39.
[660] *Ibid.* See also *Al-Nashif v Bulgaria* hudoc (2002); 36 EHRR 655 para 92 ('person concerned should have access to a court and the opportunity to be heard either in person or through some form of representation') and *Lebedev v Russia* (hudoc) 2007 at paras 70–3 (see also paras 75–9).

The requirements are also stringent when detention depends on an assessment of the detainee's character (ie personality and level of maturity and reliability), mental state, and general dangerousness. Here Article 5(4) 'requires an oral hearing in the context of an adversarial procedure involving legal representation and the possibility of calling and questioning witnesses'.[661] By contrast lower standards are set in extradition proceedings (Article 5(1)(f)).

Adversarial proceedings
Article 5(4) requires an adversarial procedure. The method chosen by the domestic system must ensure 'that the other party will be aware that observations have been filed and will have a real opportunity to comment thereon'.[662]

The relevant cases have mostly concerned 'equality of arms',[663] which is a distinct procedural right that can be subsumed within the general principle of adversarial proceedings. For example, a breach of Article 5(4) was found in *Toth v Austria*[664] because the prosecuting authority was present during the appeal hearing on the question of the applicant's detention when the applicant was not.[665] Equality of arms is clearly not ensured if the applicant's lawyer is denied access to those documents in the investigation file which are essential in order effectively to challenge the lawfulness of his client's detention.[666] One of the contributing factors taken into account by the Court in concluding that Article 5(4) had been breached in *Chahal v UK*[667] (detention under 5(1)(f)) was the fact that the applicant was merely provided with an outline of the grounds for the notice of intention to deport.

With respect to detention under Article 5(1)(c), Article 5(4) proceedings must strike a balance between the rights of defence and the imperatives of investigation. Criminal investigations must be conducted efficiently, so some information collected may in principle be kept secret 'in order to prevent suspects from tampering with evidence and undermining the course of justice'.[668] But 'this legitimate goal cannot be pursued at the expense of substantial restrictions on the rights of the defence'. Accordingly, 'information which is essential for the assessment of the lawfulness of a detention should be made available in an appropriate manner to the suspect's lawyer', and counsel must have access to documents in the investigation file which are 'essential in order effectively to challenge the lawfulness of his client's detention'.[669]

---

[661] *Waite v UK* hudoc (2002); 36 EHRR 1001 para 59. See also *Hussain v UK* 1996-I; 22 EHRR 1 para 60 (convicted juveniles detained 'during her majesty's pleasure').

[662] *Garcia Alva v Germany* hudoc (2001); 37 EHRR 335 para 39.

[663] As to which, see below, p 251. The ruling in the *Neumeister v Austria* A 8 (1968); 1 EHRR 91 that 'equality of arms' was not required can be disregarded.

[664] A 224 (1991); 14 EHRR 551. For recent examples, *Niedbala v Poland* hudoc (2000); 33 EHRR 1137; *Nikolova v Bulgaria* 1999-II; 31 EHRR 64 GC; and *Ilijkov v Bulgaria* hudoc (2001) para 104.

[665] Cf, *Sanchez-Reisse v Switzerland* A 107 (1986); 9 EHRR 71, in which the Court held that the applicant should have been allowed an opportunity to respond to the opinion of the Police Office.

[666] *Garcia Alva v Germany* hudoc (2001); 37 EHRR 335 para 39. See also *Weeks v UK* A 114 (1987); 13 EHRR 435 para 66 PC (violation of Article 5(4) since prisoner seeking release was not entitled to full disclosure of adverse material in the Parole Board's possession). Cf, *Thynne, Wilson, and Gunnell v UK* A190-A (1990); 13 EHRR 666 para 80 PC.

[667] *Chahal v UK* 1996-V; 23 EHRR 413 para 130.

[668] *Garcia Alva v Germany* hudoc (2001); 37 EHRR 335 para 42.

[669] *Garcia Alva v Germany* hudoc (2001); 37 EHRR 335 para 42 (detainee charged with major drug trafficking activities and denied access to investigation files and witness statements containing information upon which the decision to detain was primarily based, given fear that to do so would endanger ongoing investigations). The accused should be given 'a sufficient opportunity to take cognisance of statements and other pieces of evidence underlying them, such as the results of the police and other investigations, irrespective of whether the accused is able to provide any indication as to the relevance for his defence of the pieces of evidence which he seeks to be

Oral hearing

Often, but not always, the circumstances may be such that it is 'essential to the fairness of the proceedings that the applicant be present at an oral hearing'.[670] This would apply to detention falling within the ambit of Article 5(1)(c),[671] Article 5(1)(e),[672] and Article 5(1)(a) as regards the decision to recall a life sentence prisoner out on licence. There was a violation of this provision in *Waite v UK*[673] even though the respondent government argued that the decision reached by the Parole Board would not have been different if there had been an oral hearing.[674] A minor detained under Article 5(1)(d) is also entitled to be heard in person and provided with effective legal assistance.[675] By contrast in *Sanchez-Reisse v Switzerland*,[676] the Court held that written proceedings were sufficient under Article 5(1)(f), at least on the facts before it. In that case, the applicant's request for release was, in accordance with Swiss law, made via the Federal Police Office, which attached its own opinion on the merits of the request. The Federal Court rejected the request on the basis solely of the written documents, without giving the applicant an opportunity to respond to any new points of fact or law raised in the Police Office's opinion. The Court held that an oral hearing was not required since there was 'no reason to believe that the applicant's presence could have convinced the Federal Court that he had to be released'.[677] In *Farmakopoulos v Belgium*,[678] however, the Commission stated in the context of an Article 5(1)(f) case that Article 5(4) generally requires that the detained person or his representative participate in the court proceedings, by which it meant participation in a hearing. Given the origins of Article 5(4) in the writ of *habeas corpus*, the better view is that the 'body' should be produced before the court and the detained person allowed to argue for release in all cases of detention.[679]

Article 5(4) does not 'as a general rule require [the review] hearing to be public' although the Court states it 'would not exclude the possibility that a public hearing may be required in particular circumstances'.[680] Thus no public hearing is needed before a tribunal considering the release of a mental patient[681] and an investigating judge, taking his decision privately in his office, has been held to be a 'court' under Article 5(4).[682] However, there

---

given access to', id para 41. See also *Nikolova v Bulgaria* 1999-II; 31 EHRR 64 para 63 GC and *Migon v Poland* hudoc (2002) para 79.

[670] *Waite v UK* hudoc (2002); 36 EHRR 1001 para 59. See also *Lebedev v Russia* hudoc (2007) para 113.

[671] *Reinprecht v Austria* hudoc (2005); 44 EHRR 797 para 31. See also *Assenov v Bulgaria* 1998-VIII; 28 EHRR 652 paras 162–3.

[672] *Winterwerp v Netherlands* A 33 (1979); 2 EHRR 387 para 60 (person who is detained as being of 'unsound mind' must be allowed 'to be heard either in person or, where necessary, through some form of representation'). As the Court indicated, legal representation will be vital where a 'person of unsound mind' does not understand what is happening. Cf, *Keus v Netherlands* A 185-C (1990); 13 EHRR 700. See also *Merkeir v Belgium No 11200/84*, 57 DR 38 (1988) F Sett.

[673] *Waite v UK* hudoc (2002); 36 EHRR 1001.   [674] Id, para 59.

[675] *Bouamar v Belgium* A 129 (1988); 11 EHRR 1 para 60.

[676] *Sanchez-Reisse v Switzerland* A 107 (1986); 9 EHRR 71 para 51, referring to the *Schiesser* case. See contra, *Neumeister v Austria* A 8 (1968); 1 EHRR 91, which can now be disregarded. In *X v Switzerland No 8485/79*, 22 DR 131 (1981), the Commission had earlier held that written proceedings were sufficient.   [677] Ibid.

[678] *Farmakopoulos v Belgium* A 235-A (1992); 16 EHRR 187 para 46 Com Rep. The Commission relied on the Court judgment in the *Keus* case, which concerned a hearing in a mental patient case.

[679] Cf, the concurring opinions in the *Sanchez-Reisse* case of Judges Ganshof Van Der Meersch and Walsh.

[680] *Reinprecht v Austria* hudoc (2005); 44 EHRR 797 para 41, where no public hearing was required on the facts in an Article 5(1)(c) case.

[681] *Dhoest v Belgium No 10448/83*, 55 DR 5 at 26 (1987), Com Rep; CM Res DH (88); 12 EHRR CD 135. Cf, *X v Belgium No 6859/74*, 3 DR 139 (1975).

[682] *Bezicheri v Italy* A 164 (1989); 12 EHRR 210 para 20. Cf, *Neumeister v Austria* A 8 (1968); 1 EHRR 91.

was a public hearing in the *Vagrancy* cases[683] and it may be that proceedings that are akin to criminal proceedings in the length of deprivation of liberty at risk should be in public, as in criminal cases. This would be consistent with the Court's statement in *Garcia Alva v Germany*[684] as noted above.

Legal assistance

The procedural requirements under Article 5(4) are more flexible than Article 6 yet much more stringent as regards the need for speediness.[685] Hence the Court has stated that, 'as a rule, the [Article 5(4)] judge may decide not to wait until a detainee avails himself of legal assistance, and the authorities are not obliged to provide him with free legal aid in the context of the detention proceedings'.[686] The general rule mentioned in the first part of this sentence may be departed from in certain circumstances.[687] In particular, the Article 5(4) hearing should not be expedited such that an applicant is unable to properly communicate with his lawyer. In short, the state has a duty not to hinder the effectiveness of legal assistance for the applicant.[688] Similarly the principle of the confidentiality of information exchanged between lawyer and client must be protected.[689]

The general position that the authorities are not obliged to provide legal assistance is also subject to qualifications. Guarantees concerning access to a lawyer have been found to be applicable in *habeas corpus* proceedings,[690] legal assistance generally being required if this is necessary for Article 5(4) to be effective given the individual's circumstances.[691] Hence in *Chahal*[692] one of the factors taken into account by the Court in reaching its conclusion that the body reviewing the applicant's detention was not a 'court' within the meaning of Article 5(4), was that the applicant was not entitled to legal representation. Similarly a minor was entitled to 'the effective assistance of his lawyer' at the hearing at which his detention under Article 5(1)(d) was challenged,[693] as was a person detained as being mentally disordered, absent special circumstances.[694] In the latter case it was held that the person concerned should not be required to take the initiative to obtain legal representation, a principle which should apply to minors too. In *Öcalan*[695] the applicant was kept in total isolation with no possibility of consulting a lawyer. He was not legally trained and in the circumstances 'could not reasonably be expected to be able to challenge

---

[683] A 12 (1971); 1 EHRR 373 PC.

[684] Hudoc (2001); 37 EHRR 335 para 39, see text accompanying n 660 above.

[685] See *Lebedev v Russia* hudoc (2007) para 84.   [686] *Ibid.*

[687] Id, paras 85–6 (applicant's lawyers were excluded from hearing by judge). Cf, the partly dissenting opinion of Judges Kovler, Hajiyev, and Jebens.

[688] Id, para 87. See also *Istratii v Moldova* hudoc (2007).

[689] *Castravet v Moldova* hudoc (2007) paras 48–51 (glass partition between lawyer and client was not justified by security considerations and was a real impediment to confidential discussion or to an exchange of documents).

[690] *Winterwerp v Netherlands* A 33 (1979); 2 EHRR 387 para 60.

[691] In this connection see Commission Reports in *Woukam Moudefo v France* A 141-B (1988); 13 EHRR 549 paras 86–91 Com Rep F Sett before Court. Cf, *K v Austria* A 255- B (1993) Com Rep F Sett before Court. See also *S v Switzerland* A 220 (1991); 14 EHRR 670 para 53.

[692] 1996-V; 23 EHRR 413 para 130.   [693] *Bouamar v Belgium* A 129 (1988); 11 EHRR 1 para 60.

[694] *Megyeri v Germany* A 237-A (1992); 15 EHRR 584. See also *Magalhães Pereira v Portugal* hudoc (2002); 36 EHRR 865 paras 56–7 and *Waite v UK* hudoc (2002); 36 EHRR 1001 para 59 (legal representation required 'where characteristics pertaining to the applicant's personality and level of maturity and reliability are of importance in deciding on his dangerousness').

[695] Hudoc (2003); 37 EHRR 238 (Chamber judgment, para 72) comments endorsed by the Grand Chamber (2005-IV; 41 EHRR 985 para 70 GC).

the lawfulness and length of his detention without the assistance of his lawyer'.[696] Finally, in *Zamir v UK*,[697] the Commission accepted that free legal aid was required for an illegal immigrant detained pending deportation in view of the complexity of the proceedings and his limited English.[698]

Time and facilities to prepare an application

A detained person must be allowed the necessary time and facilities to prepare his case.[699] In *Farmakopoulos v Belgium*,[700] the Commission stated that any time limit upon resort to an Article 5(4) remedy 'must not be so short as to restrict the availability and tangibility of the remedy'. In the same case, the Commission indicated that although Article 5(4) does not require that a detained person be informed of the remedy available, the failure to give such information is relevant when assessing the acceptability of any time limit.

As to facilities, the applicant must be told the reasons for his detention because this is information which is essential in order to challenge its legality.[701] Several of the cases considered in the preceding section on the principle of adversarial proceedings could also be regarded as concerning to the right to facilities to prepare one's case.

Decision must be taken 'speedily'

Article 5(4) requires that a decision be taken 'speedily'. For this purpose, time normally begins to run when Article 5(4) proceedings are instituted.[702] The relevant period ends when the final decision as to the detention of the applicant is made; surprisingly, it is not, in the case of a person whose detention is found to be illegal by the national court, the date of his release.[703] Where a state provides the possibility of an appeal, the time taken before the decision on appeal must be taken into account;[704] however, the standard of 'speediness' required for the appeal stage is less stringent.[705] Where a decision is not delivered in public, the period ends when it is communicated to the detained person or his lawyer.[706] If a person has to exhaust an administrative remedy before having recourse to a 'court', the period of time to be considered runs from the time that the administrative authority is seized of the case.[707]

There may be a breach of Article 5(4) where a detained person simply has to wait for a period of time before a remedy is available.[708] Similarly, where a soldier held on a charge

---

[696] As a secondary point, it was also relevant that, owing to practical issues, neither relatives nor lawyer were able to act effectively without contact with the applicant, id, para 73.

[697] No 9174/80, 40 DR 42 (1983); 5 EHRR 242 (1983). The *Megyeri* and *Woukam Moudefo* cases involved officially appointed lawyers paid for by the state.

[698] See also *Duyonov v UK No 36670/97* hudoc (2001) DA (UK did not contest the admissibility of a claim that legal aid was required for Article 5(4) proceedings before the Privy Council; the case was subsequently struck off the Court's list).

[699] *K v Austria* A 255-B (1993) Com Rep F Sett before Court. Cf Article 6(3)(b), below, p 309. See also *Conka v Belgium* 2002-I; 34 EHRR 1298 paras 53–5 (violation as rapid execution of deportation order made meaningful resort to Article 5(4) impossible).

[700] A 235-A (1992); 16 EHRR 187 Com Rep (twenty-four-hour limit too short on the facts). Case withdrawn by applicant before Court.

[701] *X v UK* A 46 (1981); 4 EHRR 188 para 66. This is also required under Article 5(2), with which Article 5(4) overlaps.

[702] *Van der Leer v Netherlands* A 170-A (1990); 12 EHRR 567.

[703] *Luberti v Italy* A 75 (1984); 6 EHRR 440 (eleven days' gap).

[704] Ibid. See also *Letellier v France* A 207 (1991); 14 EHRR 83.

[705] *Lebedev v Russia* hudoc (2007) para 96.

[706] *Koendjbiharie v Netherlands* A 185-B (1990); 13 EHRR 820 para 28.

[707] *Sanchez-Reisse v Switzerland* A 107 (1986); 9 EHRR 71 para 54. There is no right of direct access to a 'court': id, para 45. See also *Ireland v UK* A 25 (1978); 2 EHRR 25 para 200 PC.

[708] *Igdeli v Turkey* hudoc (2002) para 34.

of having committed a military penal offence could only appeal to a military court six days after his detention had begun, there was a breach of Article 5(4), even allowing for the 'exigencies of military life and military justice'.[709] Likewise a remedy available to a mental patient before an English Mental Health Review Tribunal only after he had been recalled for six months was not a 'speedy' remedy.[710] An application for legal aid in connection with Article 5(4) must also be conducted 'speedily'.[711]

When considering whether a decision has been taken 'speedily', the approach to be followed is similar to that when assessing whether the 'trial within a reasonable time' guarantees in Articles 5(3) and 6(1) are satisfied,[712] although Article 5(4) will require 'particular expedition'.[713] There is no absolute limit to the time that a decision may take. The matter is to be determined 'in the light of the circumstances of each case'.[714] Consideration must be given to the diligence of the national authorities and any delays brought about by the conduct of the detained person,[715] as well as any other factors causing delay that cannot engage the state's responsibility. Where the length of time appears *prima facie* 'incompatible with the notion of speediness', it is for the state to explain the reason for any apparent delay.[716]

When determining whether the time taken to decide an application for release infringes Article 5(4), account may be taken of the fact that the detained person was able to make other applications that were disposed of with reasonable expedition.[717] The fact that a decision is about to be reached on the applicant's extradition is not a good reason for postponing a decision on his continued detention.[718] In extradition cases, the same considerations that are relevant to the 'requisite diligence' requirement of Article 5(1)(f)[719] may apply to the 'speedy' remedy requirement of Article 5(4).[720]

In terms of the lengths of time that have been ruled upon in actual cases, a period of five days was permissible in an Article 5(1)(c) case.[721] For this provision in particular the Court has referred to 'a special need for a swift decision determining the lawfulness of detention in cases where a trial is pending', this since the person concerned 'should

---

[709] *De Jong, Baljet, and Van Den Brink v Netherlands* A 77 (1984); 8 EHRR 20 para 58.

[710] *X v UK* B 41 (1980) para 138 Com Rep.

[711] *Zamir v UK* No 9174/80, 40 DR 42 (1983); 5 EHRR 242 (1983) (seven weeks to hear *habeas corpus* application a breach for this reason).

[712] See above, p 180, and below, p 278.   [713] *Hutchison Reid v UK* 2003 IV; 37 EHRR 211 para 59.

[714] *Sanchez-Reisse v Switzerland* A 107 (1986); 9 EHRR 71 para 55.

[715] Eg, a state will not be responsible for any delay resulting from a detained person's disappearance (*Luberti v Italy* A 75 (1984); 6 EHRR 440) or delay in filing an appeal (*Navarra v France* A 273-B (1993); 17 EHRR 594).

[716] *Koendjbiharie v Netherlands* A 185-B (1990); 13 EHRR 820 paras 28–30. The usual principle is that the primary responsibility for delays resulting from the provision of expert opinions rests ultimately with the state, *Musial v Poland* hudoc (2001); 31 EHRR 720 para 46 GC. In certain instances the complexity of medical—or other—issues involved in a determination of whether a person should be detained or released can be a factor which may be taken into account under this aspect of Article 5(4), but it is not a licence to avoid the essential obligation under that provision, see *Ilowiecki v Poland* hudoc (2001); 37 EHRR 546 para 75; *Baranowski v Poland* 2000-III para 72 (an Article 5(1)(c) case)); *Musial v Poland* 1999-II; 31 EHRR 720 para 47 GC. Delay because the responsible judge is on holiday is not a good explanation, see *E v Norway* A 181-A (1990); 17 EHRR 30 para 66 (delay of almost eight weeks unacceptable). Nor is the fact that a judge has an excessive workload, see *Bezicheri v Italy* A 164 (1989); 12 EHRR 210 para 25. Cf, *Sanchez-Reisse v Switzerland* A 107 (1986); 9 EHRR 71 and *Jablonski v Poland* hudoc (2000); 36 EHRR 455 para 90.

[717] *Letellier v France* A 207 (1991); 14 EHRR 83 para 56.

[718] *Sanchez-Reisse v Switzerland* A 107 (1986); 9 EHRR 71.

[719] See above, p 162.   [720] *Kolompar v Belgium* A 235-C (1992); 16 EHRR 197 para 46.

[721] *Egue v France* No 11256/84, 57 DR 47 at 70 (1988). As noted above, six days was too long in the *De Jong, Baljet and Van Den Brink v Netherlands* A 77 (1984); 8 EHRR 20.

benefit fully from the principle of the presumption of innocence'.[722] Periods of up to five months to decide on detention of a minor under Article 5(1)(d) were too long[723] as was a delay of four months in the case of a 'person of unsound mind' under Article 5(1)(e).[724] Periods of thirty-one and forty-six days taken to rule on the release of a person detained pending extradition under Article 5(1)(f) were also in breach of Article 5(4).[725] In contrast, sixteen days to decide on the continued long-term detention of an habitual offender under Article 5(1)(a) was considered 'speedy'.[726]

For persons arrested under Article 5(1)(c) on suspicion of having committed an offence, Article 5(4) applies concurrently with the requirement in Article 5(3) that they be brought 'promptly before a judge or other officer authorised by law to exercise judicial power'.[727] English law is consistent with both requirements in that an accused may challenge his detention by applying for *habeas corpus* in the High Court while in police custody and for bail when he is brought before a magistrate. The two guarantees in Article 5(3) and (4) may be compared in this context as follows. Whereas they may both call for remedies that may lead to the applicant's release (soon after arrest and at regular intervals thereafter),[728] the questions that may arise when considering the 'lawfulness' of the accused's detention under Article 5(4) are 'often of a more complex nature' than those that arise under Article 5(3).[729] Possibly for this reason, the Court has stated that 'the notion of promptly (*aussitôt*)... indicates greater urgency than that of speedily (*à bref délai*)'.[730] An important point of difference is that the procedural guarantees required by Article 5(3) are less rigorous than those in Article 5(4).[731] However, where the procedures in fact followed under Article 5(3) meet the requirements of Article 5(4), the judicial control required by the latter is 'incorporated in' any confirmation of an accused's detention made by a 'judge or other officer' made under the former.[732]

---

[722] *Jablonski v Poland* hudoc (2000); 36 EHRR 455 para 93. Unsurprisingly a delay of five-and-a-half months in an Article 5(1)(c) case was not acceptable in *Bezicheri v Italy* A 164 (1989); 12 EHRR 210 para 24. See, however, *Navarra v France* A 273-B (1993); 17 EHRR 594 (seven months not in breach on the facts: applicant's delay and possibility of other appeals). In a case in which persons detained on suspicion of having committed terrorist offences under Article 5(1)(c) were released forty-four hours before their applications for *habeas corpus* were determined, there was also no breach of the 'speedy' decision requirement, *Fox, Campbell, and Hartley v UK* A 182 (1990); 13 EHRR 157 para 45.

[723] *Bouamar v Belgium* A 129 (1988); 11 EHRR 1 para 63.

[724] *Koendjbiharie v Netherlands* A 185-B (1990); 13 EHRR 820 paras 28–30. See as other examples, *Luberti v Italy* A 75 (1984); 6 EHRR 440 (eighteen months too long) and *Rutten v Netherlands* hudoc (2001) para 51 (violation as first instance court took two months and seventeen days and appellate court took a further three months). In *Boucheras and Groupe Information Asiles v France* No 14438/88, 69 DR 236 (1991), nearly three months was acceptable where the delay resulted partly from the applicant's own conduct.

[725] *Sanchez-Reisse v Switzerland* A 107 (1986); 9 EHRR 71 para 57. Ten days was acceptable in an Article 5(1)(f) case in *A v Sweden* No 11531/85, 53 DR 128 (1987).

[726] *Christinet v Switzerland* No 7648/76, 17 DR 35 (1979).

[727] *De Jong, Baljet and Van Den Brink v Netherlands* A 77 (1984); 8 EHRR 20 para 57.

[728] The obligation under Article 5(3) to consider the grounds for an accused person's continued detention at reasonable intervals follows from the requirement that he be released if there are no longer good reasons to detain him. As to the same requirement in Article 5(4), see *Bezicheri v Italy* A 164 (1989); 12 EHRR 210 (interval of one month acceptable).

[729] *E v Norway* A 181-A (1990); 17 EHRR 30 para 64.

[730] *Ibid.* Note, however, that the times that have been permitted under each provision so far are of the same order, and that the word 'promptly' in Article 5(3) relates only to the time when the detained person must be brought before a judge—it does not allow for the extra time taken making a decision.

[731] See above, pp 169 and 172.

[732] *De Jong, Baljet and Van Den Brink v Netherlands* A 77 (1984); 8 EHRR 20 para 57.

9. ARTICLE 5(5): RIGHT TO COMPENSATION FOR ILLEGAL DETENTION

Article 5(5) provides that everyone 'who has been the victim of arrest or detention in contravention of the provisions of this Article shall be entitled to an enforceable right to compensation'. It is the only provision in the Convention that provides for a right to compensation at the national level for a breach of a particular Convention right.[733] There is, for example, no comparable Convention obligation to provide compensation under national law for torture in breach of Article 3.[734]

Article 5(5) applies when any one or more of paragraphs (1) to (4) has been contravened[735] as determined by either a domestic authority or by the Court.[736] The Article's applicability is not dependent on a domestic finding of unlawfulness or proof that but for the breach the person would have been released.[737] However, consistent with Article 5(5), a state may require proof of damage resulting from the breach of Article 5 before compensation is available. As the Court has stated, 'there can be no question of 'compensation' where there is no pecuniary or non-pecuniary damage to compensate'.[738]

The remedy that Article 5(5) requires is one before a court, leading to a legally binding award of compensation (usually financial).[739] Hence remedies before, for example, an ombudsman or an *ex gratia* payment by the government are insufficient. Although it 'may be broader in scope than mere financial compensation', compensation in the sense of Article 5(5) does not include the detained person's release, since this is provided for by Article 5(4).[740] As to the amount of compensation, it is likely that states are allowed a wide margin of appreciation;[741] however, this is something over which the Court has a power of review. A very low award of compensation might be 'entirely disproportionate to the duration of [an applicant's] detention',[742] entailing a violation of Article 5(5).

A question which arises is *when* a 'contravention' of Article 5 must be established so as to bring Article 5(5) into play. Where an applicant alleges in his application a violation of Article 5(5) at the same time as he claims a breach of some other part of Article 5, the Court will proceed to examine the Article 5(5) claim in the course of considering that application if it finds that another paragraph of Article 5 has been infringed.[743] It will do so without requiring the applicant to go back and exhaust local remedies to see whether he could in fact obtain the compensation that Article 5(5) requires under municipal

---

[733] Article 3 of the Seventh Protocol provides for compensation for miscarriages of justice, which may indirectly involve a breach of the Convention right to fair trial.

[734] However, compensation may be called for under the general right to an effective remedy under Article 13.

[735] See eg, *Wassink v Netherlands* A 185-A (1990).   [736] *NC v Italy* 2002-X para 49 GC.

[737] *Thynne, Wilson and Gunnell v UK* A 190-A (1990); 13 EHRR 666 para 82 PC; also *Blackstock v UK* hudoc (2005); 42 EHRR 55 para 51.

[738] *Wassink v Netherlands* A 185-A (1990) para 38. Non-pecuniary damage includes moral damage (pain, emotional distress, etc).

[739] *Brogan v UK* A 145-B (1988); 11 EHRR 117 para 67 PC and *Fox, Campbell and Hartley v UK* A 182 (1990); 13 EHRR 157 para 46. There is no jurisprudence indicating the meaning of 'court' in this context; for its meaning elsewhere in Article 5, see above, pp 139 and 188.

[740] *Bozano v France No 9990/82*, 39 DR 119 at 144 (1984). The Commission did not give any indication of the other forms of 'compensation' that it had in mind.

[741] See Trechsel, *European System*, p 344.

[742] *Attard v Malta No 46750/99* hudoc (2000) DA (inadmissible). See also *Cumber v UK No 28779/95* hudoc (1996) DA.

[743] *Ciulla v Italy* A 148 (1989); 13 EHRR 346 paras 43–5 PC.

law.[744] Instead, a state will be found to comply with Article 5(5) if it can show 'with a sufficient degree of certainty' that a remedy of the kind required by Article 5(5) is available to the applicant.[745] In this connection, where the Convention has been incorporated into the law of the defendant state and it can be shown with 'sufficient...certainty' that Article 5(5) can be directly relied upon in the national courts as the basis for a claim to compensation, this will suffice.[746] In other cases, the remedy must be shown with sufficient certainty to exist under national law by some other means.[747]

A final question is the relationship between the rights to 'compensation' in Article 5(5) for a breach of Article 5(1)–(4) and to 'just satisfaction' in Article 41 for a breach of the Convention, including any part of Article 5. If compensation for damage is not available nationally in respect of a breach of Article 5(1)–(4), so that Article 5(5) has been infringed, there is the possibility of compensation under Article 41 for that infringement.[748] So far, however, and somewhat ironically, the Court has been very reluctant to find that compensation under Article 41 was appropriate in cases in which it has found a breach of Article 5(5).

10. CONCLUSION

Article 5 remains the subject of a considerable amount of jurisprudence interpreting what can be a confusing text. A large number of judgments today concern basic Articles 5(3) and 5(4) violations. However, novel issues continue to reach the Court as is evidenced, for example, in case law concerning private detention, asylum seekers in transit zones at airports, and detention of 'alcoholics' and HIV sufferers.

Looking back at the jurisprudence as a whole, the understandable wish of some of the drafting states to have express confirmation of all of the circumstances in which they might detain an individual, rather than just a general prohibition of 'arbitrary' detention,[749] has caused predictable problems. Whereas the list in Article 5(1) offers some degree of certainty, its wording does not easily accommodate all of the recognized cases of arrest and is curiously old-fashioned in other respects. However, Article 5(1)(b) has been interpreted in the *McVeigh, O'Neill and Evans* case so as to allow short-term detention for such purposes as stopping and searching on the street that do not fit easily into the text of Article 5(1). The *Winterwerp* case and other cases have introduced some controls as to proportionality that can be applied to the detention of those covered by Article 5(1)(e), including, for example, HIV sufferers. Those controls might go some way to mitigating the broad interpretation of 'alcoholics' in the *Witold Litwa* case.

---

[744] Note, however, Judge Valticos' dissenting opinion in the *Ciulla* case, with whom three other judges agreed, to the effect that an issue can only arise under Article 5(5) after a final Strasbourg determination in an earlier application that a breach of some other part of Article 5 has occurred, following which the applicant has unsuccessfully sought compensation in the national courts.

[745] *Ciulla v Italy* A 148 (1989); 13 EHRR 346 paras 43–5 PC. As to when the remedy should be available, it suffices that the remedy exists 'either before or after the findings by the Court': *Brogan v UK* A 145-B (1988); 11 EHRR 117 para 67 PC. Cf, *Fox, Campbell and Hartley v UK* A 182 (1990); 13 EHRR 157 para 46.

[746] *Ciulla v Italy* A 148 (1989); 13 EHRR 346 paras 43–5 PC. Cf, *Sakık v Turkey* 1997-VII; 26 EHRR 662 paras 58–61 (Court rejecting the respondent government's claim that compensation remedy existed as it was unable to furnish examples of successful employment of the remedy by individuals, whilst domestic law only provided for compensation if this was illegal under domestic law itself).

[747] In *Brogan v UK* A 145-B (1988); 11 EHRR 117 para 67 PC, a pre-Human Rights Act 1998 case, neither false imprisonment nor any other remedy was available because the breach of Article 5(3) involved was not in breach of UK law.

[748] See *Brogan*, id, para 67, where the Court stated that its finding of a breach of Article 5(5) because compensation was not available was 'without prejudice' to its competence under Article 50 (now 41).

[749] Contrast Article 9(1), ICCPR, see n 145 above.

A number of cases concerning Northern Ireland have presented the Strasbourg authorities with difficult questions concerning the application of Article 5 to terrorist situations. It is arguable that the remedy within the Convention system for a state faced with the very real problems posed by a sufficiently serious terrorist threat is to derogate under Article 15 from its Convention obligations, rather than to argue that Article 5 be tempered to meet its needs. However, the Court has been prepared to make some allowance for the Northern Ireland situation in cases that have reached it under Article 5. If such an approach is to be followed, it is better for the rule that emerges to be expressly limited to the terrorist situation,[750] rather than to be stated in unqualified terms that might be applied to non-emergency situations also.[751] Terrorist cases should not be allowed to reduce minimum Convention standards of general application.

One problem has been that Article 5(1)(c) and (3) are imperfectly drafted. In practice, they have been interpreted constructively so that Article 5(1)(c) is understood in a way that properly reflects the criminal process and Article 5(3) incorporates a right to bail. Quite apart from their drafting, these two provisions are also difficult to apply uniformly to the different civil and common law systems represented among the contracting parties. Much of the jurisprudence that has emerged in criminal cases is a response to the particular features of the common law[752] or, more usually, civil law system[753] concerned. If the aim of the Court has properly been to emphasize substance rather than form, the result can sometimes be a rule that does not always apply easily to all kinds of legal system.[754] In the context of criminal justice, the Commission and the Court have also had to consider under Article 5—as under Article 6—the speed with which the authorities should act. The standards that they have applied when determining under Article 5(3) whether an arrested person has been brought 'promptly' before a court[755] or has been tried within a 'reasonable time'[756] are not as strict as they might be.

The requirement in Article 5(1) that detention be 'lawful' has been interpreted in an imaginative way that is in harmony with the reading of similar wording elsewhere in the Convention. In particular, the inclusion of a requirement that detention must not be 'arbitrary' is important. For example, it provided a basis for findings of breaches of Article 5 by reference to the purpose for which an individual was detained in the *Bozano* and *Bouamar* cases concerning the improper use of powers of deportation and short-term detention of juveniles respectively. Article 5(1) has also provided a mechanism for the setting of detailed and rigorous procedural standards concerning the detention of the mentally disordered. Of more general importance has been the interpretation of Article 5(4) in such a way as to impose a demanding obligation upon states to provide a judicial remedy by which an individual may challenge the legality of his detention. One striking result of this has been that United Kingdom procedures concerning the release of mental patients and persons given certain forms of life sentences have been revised following Strasbourg cases so as shift the decision-making power from the Home Secretary to a 'court' in several respects.

---

[750] See *Brogan v UK* A 145-B (1988); 11 EHRR 117 PC, above, p 170. See also the express references to terrorism in connection with the approach taken to Article 5(3) in *Chraidi v Germany* hudoc (2006); 47 EHRR 47 paras 37 and 47.

[751] This was not done in the *Fox, Campbell and Hartley v UK* A 182 (1990); 13 EHRR 157, on the Article 5(2) point.   [752] See *Monnell and Morris v UK* A 115 (1987); 10 EHRR 205.

[753] See eg, the *Schiesser* and *Huber* cases, above, p 171.

[754] See eg, the Court's interpretation of the relationship between Article 5(1)(a) and (3) in the *Wemhoff* case, above, p 173.

[755] See above, p 170.   [756] See *W v Switzerland*, above, p 182.

6

ARTICLE 6: THE RIGHT TO A FAIR TRIAL

Article 6

1. In the determination of his civil rights and obligations or of any criminal charge against him, everyone is entitled to a fair and public hearing within a reasonable time by an independent and impartial tribunal established by law. Judgment shall be pronounced publicly but the press and public may be excluded from all or part of the trial in the interest of morals, public order or national security in a democratic society, where the interests of juveniles or the protection of the private life of the parties so require, or to the extent strictly necessary in the opinion of the court in special circumstances where publicity would prejudice the interests of justice.

2. Everyone charged with a criminal offence shall be presumed innocent until proved guilty according to law.

3. Everyone charged with a criminal offence has the following minimum rights:
   (a) to be informed promptly, in a language which he understands and in detail, of the nature and cause of the accusation against him;
   (b) to have adequate time and facilities for the preparation of his defence;
   (c) to defend himself in person or through legal assistance of his own choosing or, if he has not sufficient means to pay for legal assistance, to be given it free when the interests of justice so require;
   (d) to examine or have examined witnesses against him and to obtain the attendance and examination of witnesses on his behalf under the same conditions as witnesses against him;
   (e) to have the free assistance of an interpreter if he cannot understand or speak the language used in court.

1. ARTICLE 6: GENERALLY[1]

The right to a fair trial has a position of pre-eminence in the Convention, both because of the importance of the right involved and the great volume of applications and jurisprudence that it has attracted. As to the former, the Court has stressed that 'the right to a fair trial holds so prominent a place in a democratic society that there can be no justification for interpreting Article 6(1) of the Convention restrictively'.[2] As to the latter, more

---

[1] On Article 6, see Grotian, *Article 6 of the European Convention on Human Rights: The Right to a Fair Trial*, Council of Europe Human Rights File No 13, 1993. On Article 6 in criminal cases, see Stavros, *The Guarantees for Accused Persons under Article 6 of the European Convention on Human Rights*, 1993 (hereafter Stavros) and Trechsel, *Human Rights in Criminal Proceedings*, 2005.

[2] *Perez v France* 2004-I; 40 EHRR 909 para 64 GC. This can be taken to apply to Article 6 as a whole.

applications to Strasbourg concern Article 6 than any other provision. The cases concern mostly criminal and civil litigation before the ordinary courts, both at the trial court and appellate levels. They also involve, to an extent that could not have been predicted, proceedings before disciplinary and administrative tribunals and administrative decisions determining 'civil rights and obligations'.

The application of Article 6 has presented the Court, and formerly the Commission, with various problems. A delicate question is the closeness with which it should monitor the functioning of national courts. The Court has studiously and properly followed the 'fourth instance' doctrine, according to which, as the Court regularly states, 'it is not its function to deal with errors of fact or law allegedly committed by a national court *unless and in so far as they may have infringed rights and freedoms protected by the Convention*'.[3] The right to a fair hearing, which is one such Convention right, has, as its wording generally suggests, been interpreted as providing only a procedural, not a substantive, guarantee. Accordingly, the Court will intervene in respect to 'errors of fact or law' by a national court only insofar as they bear upon compliance with the procedural guarantees in Article 6: it does not intervene under Article 6 because they affect the 'fairness' of the national court decision on its merits.[4] However, this last statement must be read subject to a limitation that is to be found in some recent Court jurisprudence to the effect that there may be a breach of Article 6 where a national court decision on the merits has been 'arbitrary or manifestly unreasonable'.[5] Thus in *Van Kück v Germany*,[6] the German courts had held that gender reassignment measures did not fall within the notion of 'medical necessity' in German law so as to require the state to pay for them. Finding that in reaching this conclusion the German courts had not followed the Strasbourg Court's approach to the medical and scientific nature of transsexualism in its interpretation of Article 8 of the Convention[7] and had not sought sufficient expert advice on the matter, the Strasbourg Court held that there was a breach of Article 6(1) because the German courts' interpretation of the term 'medical necessity' and evaluation of the evidence were not 'reasonable'.[8] In similar vein, in *Khamidov v Russia*[9] the Court found that a national court had rejected the applicant's claim for compensation for damage to his land by police units on the basis that it was unproven that the units had even entered upon the land when, the Court considered, there was 'abundant evidence' to the contrary. In the Court's view, the 'unreasonableness of this conclusion is so striking and palpable on the face of it', that the national court's decisions were 'grossly arbitrary' In both of these cases, there was an undefined breach of Article 6, presumably of the residual 'fair hearing' guarantee.

The Court also allows states a wide margin of appreciation as to the manner in which national courts operate, for example in the rules of evidence that they use. A consequence of this is that in certain contexts the provisions of Article 6 are as much obligations of result as of conduct, with national courts being allowed to follow whatever particular rules they choose so long as the end result can be seen to be a fair trial.[10]

---

[3] *Garcia Ruiz v Spain* 1999-I; 31 EHRR 589 para 28 GC. Italics added. On the 'fourth instance' doctrine, see above, p 14.

[4] See eg, *Anderson v UK No 44958/98* hudoc (1999) DA.

[5] *Camilleri v Malta No 51760/99* hudoc (2000) DA (no breach on the facts).

[6] 2003-VII; 37 EHRR 973 para 57. Cf, *Storck v Germany* 2005-V; 43 EHRR 96 and *Mikulova v Slovakia* hudoc (2005).

[7] The Court cited the *Christine Goodwin* case, as to which see below, p 385. See also Loucaides, 3 HRLR 27 (2003), arguing for a substantive 'fair' hearing meaning.

[8] Id, para 57. Cf, *Divagsa v Spain No 20631/92* 74 DR 275 (1993). On the right to have one's case properly examined as a distinct element of the 'fair hearing' guarantee: see below, p 267.

[9] 2007-. para 174.   [10] See eg, *Schenk v Switzerland*, below, p 256.

Although Article 6 applies only to a contracting party's own judicial system, it extends beyond that in the sense that a court of a contracting party that is called upon to confirm or execute a judgment of a court of another state that is not a party to the Convention must ensure that the foreign judgment concerned is the result of a fair trial in accordance with Article 6. Thus in *Pellegrini v Italy*,[11] an Italian court made operative in Italy a judgment made by an ecclesiastical court of the Vatican City, which was not a party to the Convention, annulling the applicant's marriage. Although the Italian court checked whether Article 6 had been complied with by the Vatican court, the Strasbourg Court held that there was a violation of it as the principle of 'equality of arms' had been infringed by the Vatican court. Presumably, the requirement to ensure that the Convention is complied with by a foreign court would also apply where it was a court of a state that was a Convention party.

In criminal cases, the interpretation of Article 6 is complicated by the basic differences that exist between common law and civil law systems of criminal justice.[12] The adversarial and inquisitorial systems that these respectively entail, and the dissimilar methods of investigating crime and conducting a trial that they use, necessarily make for difficulties in the interpretation of a text that provides a framework for legal proceedings throughout Europe. It has not proved easy to meet the needs and circumstances of very different legal systems and still set appropriately high standards for a human rights guarantee of a fair trial.

In this connection, it may be helpful by way of introduction to outline very briefly the essential differences between the common and civil law systems for the investigation of crime. In common law jurisdictions, as exemplified by English and Irish law, the investigation of a criminal offence is conducted entirely by the police.[13] In the typical civil law jurisdiction,[14] the case is first investigated by the police, but then, when attention has focused on a particular suspect, it is handed over to an investigating judge, public prosecutor, or other officer who questions the suspect and other witnesses, going over to some extent the ground already covered by the police. The accused person is often detained during this preliminary investigation, which can be a very lengthy process. When it is complete, the investigating judge decides whether a prosecution should be brought.[15] A merit of the civil law approach is that the investigating judge is independent of the police and hence brings a fresh mind to the case. A disadvantage is that the investigation, during which an accused may spend several years in detention, tends to take longer than the investigation just by the police in a common law system.

Another problem has resulted from the application of Article 6 to administrative justice. If the Court, and formerly the Commission, has commendably acted to fill a gap by reading Article 6 as requiring that administrative decisions that determine a person's right, for example, to practise as a doctor or to use his land, are subject to Article 6, they have yet to establish a coherent jurisprudence spelling out the nature of the resulting obligations for states.

---

[11] 2001-VIII; 35 EHRR 44.

[12] On these differences, see Crombag, in de Witte and Forder, eds, *The Common Law of Europe and the Future of Legal Education*, 1992, p 397. For example, there are differences in the rules of evidence, the use of a case file, the permissibility of trials *in absentia* and plea bargaining.

[13] As to the position in Scotland, see Kilbrandon, in Coutts, ed, *The Accused: A Comparative Study*, 1966, Ch 4. Some non-common law jurisdictions adopt the same system: see *Hauschildt v Denmark*, below, p 292.

[14] As to the position in France and Germany, see Vouin and Jescheck, in Coutts, id., Chs 15 and 18. See also Chatel (Belgium), Tsoureli (Greece), and Madlener (Germany) in Andrews, *loc cit* at n 13, above, Chs 8–10. See generally, Van den Wyngaert, ed, *Criminal Procedure Systems in the European Community*, 1993.

[15] In England and Wales, this decision is normally taken by the Crown Prosecution Service (CPS) on the basis of the case prepared by the police; the CPS does not conduct its own investigation.

The above problems have been compounded in civil as well as criminal cases by the need to apply a text that was designed as a template for trial courts of the classical kind to both appellate courts and disciplinary and other special courts, where the same procedural guarantees may not have such full application.[16]

Finally, it is relevant to note that in some contexts a breach of Article 6 will only be found to have occurred upon proof of 'actual prejudice' to the applicant. This is the case in the application of the residual 'fair hearing' guarantee in Article 6(1),[17] and is true of some specific Article 6 guarantees. As to the latter, Stavros[18] states in respect of criminal cases:

> This tendency has manifested itself in the context of Article 6(3)(a), (b) and (d) and sometimes in the context of the right to an impartial tribunal. This is not, however, always the case. The Convention organs appear to regard the presence of actual prejudice inherent in the failure to observe other guarantees,[19] pronouncing automatically the breach of the Convention.

In cases in which 'actual prejudice' is sought, this will be decided on the basis of the hearing 'as a whole', so that a procedural deficiency that is outweighed by other aspects of the hearing[20] or that is rectified on appeal[21] will not involve a breach of Article 6.

2. FIELD OF APPLICATION

I. IN THE DETERMINATION OF A CRIMINAL CHARGE

The rights guaranteed by Article 6 apply, firstly, when a 'criminal charge' is being determined. Article 6 thus only begins to apply when a criminal investigation has reached the point where the applicant has been 'charged' with a criminal offence. It does not extend to ancillary proceedings that are not determinative of a pending 'charge' against the applicant[22], such as proceedings concerning legal aid,[23] pre-trial detention,[24] or committal for trial.[25] Nor does it apply to cases in which a person brings a private prosecution[26] or because the applicant's property is subject to forfeiture by a criminal charge against a third party.[27] It also does not apply to proceedings that may result in the applicant

---

[16] See Stavros, p 328. On the application of Article 6 to juvenile criminal proceedings, see *Nortier v Netherlands* A 267 (1993); 17 EHRR 273 para 38.

[17] See below, p 246. Thus in a 'fair hearing' case, 'where the procedural flaw is not central to the notion of a fair hearing...a violation will be registered if the shortcoming in question caused actual prejudice to the defence': *Harper v UK No 11229/84,* 1986 unreported, quoted in Stavros, p 44.

[18] Stavros, p 44. Footnotes omitted. The same approach applies to civil cases.

[19] Ed. The author refers to the *Artico* and *Luedicke* cases, below, pp 320 and 327, concerning Article 6(3)(c) and (e) respectively. The same must be true of the Article 6(1) guarantee of a public hearing in view of the purpose it serves. The requirement of 'actual prejudice' is most vividly illustrated by the ruling that an accused who is acquitted is no longer a 'victim' and so cannot complain of a breach of Article 6: *Heaney and McGuiness v Ireland* 2000-XII; 33 EHRR 264. For the 'reasonable time' exception to this, see below, p 278, n 721.

[20] See eg, *Stanford v UK* A 282-A (1994).

[21] See eg, *Edwards v UK* A 247-B (1992); 15 EHRR 417.

[22] It does apply to sentencing proceedings, including forfeiture:

[23] *Neumeister v Austria* A 8 (1968); 1 EHRR 91 para 23 and *Gutfreund v France* hudoc 2003-VII; 42 EHRR 1076.   [24] *Van Thuil v Netherlands No 20510/02* hudoc (2004) DA.

[25] *Mosbeux v Belgium No 17083/90,* 71 DR 269 (1990).

[26] *Helmers v Sweden* A 212-A (1991); 15 EHRR 285 PC.

[27] *AGOSI v UK* A 108 (1986); 9 EHRR 1 and *Air Canada v UK* A 316-A (1995); 20 EHRR 150.

being placed under police supervision for the prevention of crime[28] or to the giving by the police of a statutory warning.[29]

Finally, extradition proceedings to face a criminal charge in another state are not 'criminal' in the sense of Article 6.[30] However, in *Soering v UK*,[31] applying its approach to liability under Article 3 in extradition cases, the Court did not exclude the possibility that 'an issue might exceptionally be raised under Article 6 by an extradition decision in circumstances where the fugitive has suffered or risks suffering a flagrant denial of a fair trial in the requesting state'. This approach was applied in *Mamatkulov and Askarov v Turkey*[32] to the extradition of the applicants to face trial in Uzbekistan, but the Grand Chamber held that, although there were reasons to doubt that they would have a fair trial, there was not sufficient evidence to warrant a conclusion, on the basis of the actual or constructive knowledge of the defendant state at the time of extradition, that any irregularities might amount to a 'flagrant denial of justice'.

a. The meaning of 'criminal'

'Criminal' has an autonomous Convention meaning.[33] Otherwise, if the classification of an offence in the law of the contracting parties were regarded as decisive, a state would be free to avoid the Convention obligation to ensure a fair trial (as well as the guarantee against retroactive offences in Article 7) in its discretion. It would also result, in this context, in an unacceptably uneven application of the Convention from one state to another.

In *Engel v Netherlands*[34] it was established that, when deciding whether an offence is criminal in the sense of Article 6, three criteria apply: the classification of the offence in the law of the respondent state; the nature of the offence; and the possible punishment. The first is crucial in that if the applicable national law classifies the offence as criminal, it is automatically such for the purposes of Article 6 too.[35] This is because the legal and social consequences of having a criminal conviction make it imperative that the accused has a fair trial. In cases in which the offence is not classified as criminal in national law, the other two criteria listed above—the nature of the offence and the possible punishment—come into play. These two criteria are 'alternative and not necessarily cumulative'; but a cumulative approach may be adopted where neither criteria by itself is conclusive.[36] In practice, there have been a number of cases of offences characterized as disciplinary or regulatory or that are otherwise analogous to criminal offences without being classified as such in national law in which this 'one-way' autonomous meaning of 'criminal' in Article 6 has been important. Finally, before examining the Court's

[28] *Guzzardi v Italy* A 39 (1980); 3 EHRR 333 para 108 PC and *Raimondo v Italy* A 281-A (1994); 18 EHRR 237. But the preventative confiscation of property may concern 'civil rights and obligations': the *Raimondo* case.

[29] *R v UK No 33506/05* hudoc (2007) DA.

[30] *Mamatkulov and Askarov v Turkey* 2005-I; 41 EHRR 494 GC. Proceedings concerning the entry, stay, and deportation of aliens are not 'criminal': *Maaouia v France* 2000-X; 33 EHRR 1037 GC. A decision to transfer a convicted prisoner abroad is not within Article 6: *Szabo v Sweden No 28578/03* hudoc (2006) DA.

[31] A 161 (1989); 11 EHRR 439 para 113 PC (limited legal aid not a 'flagrant denial').

[32] 2005-I; 41 EHRR 494 GC. See also *Drozd and Janousek v France* A 240 (1992); 14 EHRR 745 and *Eskinazi and Chelouche v Turkey No 14600/05* hudoc (2005) DA.

[33] *Engel v Netherlands* A 22 (1976); 1 EHRR 647 PC.

[34] *Ibid.* See also *Ezeh and Connors v UK* 2003-X; 39 EHRR 1 GC.

[35] See *Funke v France* A 256-A (1993); 16 EHRR 297. A state may make any conduct a criminal offence unless it is conduct protected by a Convention right: *Engel v Netherlands* A 22 (1976); 1 EHRR 647 PC.

[36] *Ezeh and Connors v UK* 2003-X; 39 EHRR 1 para 86 GC. For cases in which one criterion was conclusive, see, eg, *Öztürk v FRG* A 73 (1984); 6 EHRR 409 PC and *Garyfallou AEBE v Greece* 1997-V; 28 EHRR 344.

jurisprudence applying the *Engel* criteria, it may be commented that it is not always easy to rationalize the case law as a whole; the process of applying the second and third criteria to particular offences and sentences in particular legal systems almost inevitably leads in some contexts to decisions based upon the particular facts.

As to the 'nature' of the offence, the purpose of the offence must be deterrent and punitive, not compensatory, these being 'the customary distinguishing feature of a criminal penalty.'[37] The offence should also extend to the population at large,[38] although it may be limited to such general categories of persons as taxpayers and road users.[39] The minor nature of an offence does not detract from its inherently criminal character.[40]

In the context of disciplinary offences, the Court distinguishes between offences focusing on the internal regulation of a group possessing a special status in society, such as the armed forces or prisoners, and offences committed by members of such a group that involve generally anti-social behaviour, with only the latter being subject to Article 6. In this connection, the fact that the conduct proscribed by the disciplinary offence is also a criminal offence under national law (a 'mixed offence')[41] is relevant. Thus in *Ezeh and Connors v UK*[42] the applicants had been found guilty at a governor's hearing of the prison disciplinary offences of using threatening, abusive, or insulting words and of assault, leading to punishments of forty and seven additional days' detention respectively. As to the nature of the offences, while it was a relevant factor that they applied only to prisoners, the proscribed conduct had deterrent and punitive purposes and was also criminal in English law. This, together with what was 'at stake' for the applicants (possible sentences of up to forty-two additional days for each offence), led the Grand Chamber to decide that the offences were 'criminal' for the purposes of Article 6. In this connection, the Court took into account that, although they did not add to the applicants' court sentences, the additional days would lengthen the time that the applicants actually spent in prison before being released on licence.

Some cases have concerned disciplinary or similar offences aimed at protecting proceedings in court or in a national parliament. In *Weber v Switzerland*[43] the applicant was convicted of an offence under the code of criminal procedure by revealing at a press conference confidential information about the judicial investigation into a criminal prosecution by the state of another person which had resulted from the applicant's complaint. Although the offence was not criminal in Swiss law, it was held to be criminal in 'nature' because it applied not just to judges and lawyers—for whom it might be seen as a non-Article 6 disciplinary matter—but to the whole population. In contrast, there was no criminal offence in *Ravnsborg v Sweden*[44] where the applicant was guilty of the offence of disturbing the good order of the court, which was not shown to be criminal under Swedish law, by statements in his written pleadings as a party to civil litigation. The Strasbourg Court distinguished the *Weber* case on the basis that the offence could only

---

[37] *Janosevic v Sweden* 2002-VII; 38 EHRR 473 para 68. And see *Porter v UK No 15814/02* hudoc (2003) DA (local authority surcharge not punitive).

[38] *Lauko v Slovakia* 1998-VI; 33 EHRR 994.

[39] See the *Bendenoun* and *Öztürk* cases, below at nn 59 and 49.

[40] *Ezeh and Connors v UK* 2003-X; 39 EHRR 1 GC and *Lauko v Slovakia* 1998-VI; 33 EHRR 994. A 'breach of the peace' is a criminal offence by its 'nature': *Steel v UK* 1998-VII; 28 EHRR 603.

[41] *Engel v Netherlands* A 22 (1976); 1 EHRR 647 para 80 PC.

[42] 2003-X; 39 EHRR 1 GC. See also *Whitfield v UK*, below, n 842.

[43] A 177 (1990); 12 EHRR 508. See also *Les Travaux du Midi v FRG No 12275/86*, 70 DR 47 (1991).

[44] A 283-B (1994); 18 EHRR 38. See also *Putz v Austria* 1996-I; 32 EHRR 271 and *Schreiber and Boetsch v France No 58751/00* hudoc (2003) DA. In *Kyprianou v Cyprus* 2005-VIII; 44 EHRR 565 GC, a lawyer was convicted of criminal contempt for his conduct in court. Article 6 applied because, unlike *Ravnsborg*, the offence was criminal in national law.

be committed by those, such as the applicant, participating in court proceedings, thus making it an internal court matter. The Court also distinguished *Demicoli v Malta*,[45] in which Article 6 was held to apply when a journalist was convicted by the Maltese House of Representatives of breach of parliamentary privilege for publishing an article ridiculing two members of parliament. Although not a criminal offence under Maltese law, the publication had occurred outside of Parliament and the offence could be committed by the population at large.

Disciplinary offences involving professional misconduct by members of the liberal professions are seen as an internal regulatory matter that does not fall within Article 6, even though a severe punishment—such as a heavy fine, suspension, or striking-off— may be imposed.[46] They may, however, in some cases fall within Article 6 as involving the determination of 'civil rights and obligations'.[47] Disciplinary offences by civil servants and the police are likewise not criminal, even though they may lead to dismissal.[48]

Apart from disciplinary or similar offences, the autonomous concept of a 'criminal' offence in Article 6 has been used to apply its fair trial guarantee to regulatory and certain other offences that, although not classified as criminal in national law, have deterrent and punitive objectives. The leading case on regulatory offences is *Öztürk v FRG*.[49] There the Court held that an offence of careless driving, which was classified under German law as regulatory, not criminal, was none the less 'criminal' for the purpose of Article 6. Despite the decriminalizing steps that had been taken when such road traffic offences ceased to be criminal in West Germany, the offence retained characteristics that were the hallmark of a criminal offence: it was of general application, applying to all road users, and carried with it a sanction of a deterrent and punitive kind. It was also relevant that although some West European states had taken steps to decriminalize road traffic offences (to which the Court was not opposed provided that Article 6 was complied with), the great majority of Convention parties continued to treat minor road traffic offences as criminal.[50] The Court was not concerned by the 'relative lack of seriousness of the penalty at stake' (a modest fine as opposed to imprisonment) because the second element of the *Engel* test was very clearly satisfied.

Other offences that have been regarded as 'criminal' in the sense of Article 6 and that may, more or less convincingly, be placed within the category of regulatory offences are ones governing trade and commerce,[51] hours of work,[52] or public demonstrations[53] and

[45] A 210 (1991); 14 EHRR 47.

[46] *Brown v UK No 38644/97* hudoc (1998) DA (solicitor); and *Wickramsinghe v UK No 31503/96* hudoc (1997) DA (doctor).

[47] *Albert and Le Compte v Belgium* A 58 (1983); 5 EHRR 533 PC. Article 6(1) is understood to include aspects of Article 6(2)(3) in such cases. See further below, p 246.

[48] *X v UK No 8496/79*, 21 DR 168 (1980) (police) and *Kremzow v Austria No 16417/ 90*, 67 DR 307 (1990) (civil servants). Disciplinary offences by the police and some civil servants will also not concern 'civil rights and obligations': see below, p 220. This is an unsatisfactory gap in the Convention 'fair trial' guarantee.

[49] A 73 (1984); 6 EHRR 409 PC. For other road traffic cases, see eg, *Schmautzer v Austria* A 328-A (1995); 21 EHRR 511; *Escoubet v Belgium* 1999-VII; 31 EHRR 1034 GC (temporary withdrawal of driving licence preventive, not criminal); *Blokker v Netherlands No 45282/99* hudoc (2000) DA; and *Siwak v Poland No 51018/99* hudoc (2004) DA.

[50] When deciding on the nature of an offence, the Court regularly takes account of 'common features' of the national law of the contracting parties: see eg, *Ravnsborg v Sweden* A 283-B (1994); 18 EHRR 38.

[51] *Deweer v Belgium* A 35 (1980); 2 EHRR 439; *Société Stenuit v France* A 232-A (1992); 14 EHRR 509 Com Rep; and *Garyfallou AEBE v Greece* 1997-V; 28 EHRR 344. But see *000 Neste St Petersburg et al v Russia No 69042/01* hudoc (2004) DA.

[52] *X v Austria No 8998/80*, 32 DR 150 (1983) (young persons' hours).

[53] *Belilos v Switzerland* A 132 (1988); 10 EHRR 466 PC and *Ziliberberg v Moldova* hudoc (2005).

offences under a customs code.[54] In *Jussila v Finland*,[55] the Court ruled that the imposition of a tax surcharge as a financial penalty for tax evasion involved a 'criminal' charge in the sense of Article 6. In terms of the second *Engel* criterion, it applied to all citizens as taxpayers and was intended to deter and punish, which was sufficient to establish its criminal character; the size of the surcharge was immaterial. Proceedings for committal to prison for non-payment of the UK community charge are also criminal.[56] But an administrative fine for non-compliance with planning laws[57] and a disqualification from being a company director[58] are preventive, not criminal, in character.

As to the third criterion, the Court looks to the nature and severity of the possible, not the actual, punishment.[59] In *Engel v Netherlands*[60] the Court held that a punishment of imprisonment belonged to the criminal sphere unless its 'nature, duration or manner of execution, was not such that its effect could be 'appreciably detrimental'. Applying both the second and third criteria, the Court then found that military disciplinary offences involving the publication of a periodical tending to undermine army discipline and the driving of a jeep irresponsibly that could lead to three or four months' imprisonment were 'criminal', but that offences of being absent without leave that carried possible penalties of just two days' strict arrest were not. A possible punishment of a modest fine that may be converted into imprisonment for more than a minimal period for non-payment may fall within Article 6,[61] as may a substantial fine that cannot be converted into imprisonment.[62] Even an offence that carries a modest fine as the only possible punishment and that will not be entered on the accused's criminal record may fall within Article 6 if it is inherently 'criminal' in its 'nature'.[63] Disqualification from holding public office[64] or the deduction of points that may lead cumulatively to the loss of a driving licence for road traffic offences[65] may be criminal punishments, but the withdrawal of a liquor licence, although severe in its consequences, is not.[66] Nor is a penalty for exceeding election expenses limits of disqualification from standing for election plus an order to repay the excess.[67]

b. The meaning of 'charge'

For Article 6 to apply, a person must be subject to a criminal 'charge'. The point at which this begins to be the case has been developed mostly in connection with the 'trial within a

---

[54] *Salabiaku v France* A 141-A (1988); 13 EHRR 379.

[55] 2006-XX GC; 45 EHRR 39. See also *Bendenoun v France* A 284 (1994); 18 EHRR 54 and *Janosevic v Sweden* 2002-VII; 38 EHRR 473. As to whether decisions on tax matters concern 'civil rights and obligations', see below, p 219.

[56] *Benham v UK* 1996-III; 22 EHRR 293 GC.

[57] *Inocencio v Portugal No 43862/98* hudoc (2001) DA.

[58] *Wilson v UK No 36791/97* hudoc (1998); 26 EHRR CD 195.

[59] *Engel v Netherlands* A 22 (1976); 1 EHRR 647 PC.

[60] *Id*, para 82. See also *Borelli v Switzerland No 17571/90* hudoc (1993) DA and *Brandao Ferreira v Portugal No 41921/98* hudoc (2000) DA (five days' detention for internal army disciplinary offences insufficient).

[61] *Weber v Switzerland* A 177 (1990); 12 EHRR 508 (up to three months' imprisonment).

[62] *Janosevic v Sweden* 2002-VII; 38 EHRR 473. But non-payment of any fine will normally lead to enforcement measures resulting in imprisonment: see *Garyfallou AEBE v Greece* 1997-V; 28 EHRR 344.

[63] *Lauko v Slovakia* 1998-VI; 33 EHRR 994. But a small tax surcharge was not 'criminal': *Morel v France No 54559/00* hudoc (2003) DA.

[64] *Matyjek v Poland No 38184/03* hudoc (2006) DA (lustration proceedings).

[65] *Malige v France* 1998-VII; 28 EHRR 578.

[66] *Tre Traktörer Aktiebolag v Sweden* A 159 (1989); 13 EHRR 309. But it may determine 'civil rights and obligations': *ibid*.

[67] *Pierre-Bloch v France* 1997-VI; 26 EHRR 202. Cf, *Porter v UK No 15814/02* hudoc (2003) DA.

reasonable time' guarantee, for which it will always need to be established.[68] Even so, the precise date on which Article 6 begins to apply to that guarantee will not be crucial if the possible dates that may be chosen involve only a small difference.[69]

Like the word 'criminal', 'charge' has an autonomous Convention meaning.[70] It is 'the official notification given to an individual by the competent authority of an allegation that he has committed a criminal offence' or some other act which carries 'the implication of such an allegation and which likewise substantially affects the situation of the suspect'.[71] As stated in *Deweer v Belgium*,[72] 'charge' is to be given a 'substantive', not a 'formal', meaning, so that it is necessary 'to look behind the appearances and investigate the realities of the procedure in question' to see whether the applicant is 'substantially affected' by the steps taken against him'. In practice, a person has been found to be subject to a 'charge' when arrested for a criminal offence;[73] when notified that he is being charged with an offence;[74] when, in a civil law system, a preliminary investigation has been opened and, although not under arrest, the applicant has 'officially learnt of the investigation or begun to be affected by it';[75] when authorities investigating customs offences require a person to produce evidence and freeze his bank account;[76] or when the applicant's shop has been closed pending the outcome of criminal proceedings.[77] In the case of an MP with parliamentary immunity, the relevant date was that on which the prosecuting authorities requested Parliament to lift the immunity.[78]

Most of the case law on the meaning of 'charge' has concerned civil law systems of criminal justice. With regard to common law jurisdictions, applicants have been held to be subject to a 'charge' when they have been arrested[79] or charged by the police.[80] Presumably, the issuing of a summons would be sufficient. In one case,[81] an applicant already serving a prison sentence for one offence was found to be subject to a 'charge' in respect of a second offence from the time of his first conviction because, from that moment, as the applicant was aware, 'immediate consideration' was being given to the possibility of further charges against him. From that moment onwards the uncertainty and anxiety that the applicant felt about his future and the need for him to prepare his defence meant that he was 'substantially affected'. This raises the question of whether a person who is not under arrest is 'substantially affected' while the police are questioning or otherwise investigating him as a suspect but before he is arrested or charged. An answer in the affirmative would be consistent with the 'substantive', rather than 'formal',

---

[68] It also has relevance for the right of access to a criminal court: see *Deweer v Belgium* A 35 (1980).

[69] See eg, *Zaprianov v Bulgaria* hudoc (2004).   [70] *Deweer v Belgium* A 35 (1980) para 42; 2 EHRR 439.

[71] *Corigliano v Italy* A 57 (1982) para 34; 5 EHRR 334.

[72] A 35 (1980); 2 EHRR 439 paras 44, 46.   [73] *Wemhoff v FRG* A 7 (1968); 1 EHRR 55.

[74] *Pedersen and Baadsgaard v Denmark* 2004-XI; 42 EHRR 486 GC. In *Foti v Italy* A 56 (1982); 5 EHRR 313 the date on which two of the applicants were formally charged was chosen, not that of their arrest two or three days earlier. Yet a person must be 'substantially affected' from the time of his arrest. In *Boddaert v Belgium* A 235-D (1992); 16 EHRR 242 para 10, the date that the arrest warrant was issued was chosen, not the later date when the applicant surrendered to the authorities.

[75] *Eckle v FRG* A 51 (1982); 5 EHRR 1 para 74. In accordance with the 'substantially affected' test, it is the date of notification or of otherwise first being affected by the investigation that is crucial, not the date on which the decision to open the investigation is taken: *Corigliano v Italy* A 57 (1982); 5 EHRR 334 (in that case there was a gap of several months between the two). See also *Angelucci v Italy* A 196-C (1991) para 13 and *P v Austria* No 13017/87, 71 DR 52 (1989) Com Rep; CM Res DH 91 (33).

[76] *Funke v France* A 256-A (1993). See also *TK and SE v Finland* No 38581/97 hudoc (2004) DA (seizure of documents).

[77] *Deweer v Belgium* A 35 (1980).   [78] *Frau v Italy* A 195-E (1991) para 14.

[79] *Heaney and McGuinness v Ireland* 2001-XII; 33 EHRR 264. Cf, *Ewing v UK* No 11224/84, 45 DR 269 (1986); 10 EHRR 141.

[80] *X v Ireland* No 9429/81, 32 DR 225 (1983).   [81] *X v UK* No 6728/74, 14 DR 26 (1978).

meaning of 'charge' that the Court has adopted. It would mean, however, that the point at which Article 6 began to apply in common law systems (as is sometimes already the case in civil law systems) would become a very uncertain one since there would be no formal occurrence that would clearly signify it.

Article 6 continues to apply until the 'charge' against the applicant is finally determined. Any separate sentencing proceedings are included, the 'charge not being determined until the sentence has been fixed'.[82] Although the Convention does not guarantee a right of appeal, Article 6 applies to any appeal proceedings against conviction or sentence that are in fact provided.[83] Constitutional court proceedings involving claims alleging a violation of constitutional rights are included insofar as they are decisive for the outcome of a criminal case.[84]

Article 6 ceases to apply if criminal proceedings are discontinued.[85] Nor does it apply to proceedings that concern a person who is already finally convicted of an offence, and hence is no longer 'charged' with it. Thus Article 6 does not apply to proceedings for the execution of a sentence,[86] for the assessment of costs in criminal cases,[87] or for an application for a re-trial.[88] However, Article 6 does apply to the execution of a judgment that acquits the accused. Thus in *Assanidze v Georgia*,[89] there was a breach of Article 6 when the accused had not been released from detention some three years after his acquittal.

II. IN THE DETERMINATION OF CIVIL RIGHTS AND OBLIGATIONS

Article 6 applies, secondly, when a person's 'civil rights and obligations' are being determined.

a. The meaning of 'civil' rights and obligations[90]

Private law meaning
Some of the more perplexing problems in the interpretation of the Convention concern the application of Article 6(1) to non-criminal cases. According to its text, Article 6(1) applies 'in the determination' of a person's 'civil rights and obligations'. In their early jurisprudence, the Strasbourg authorities established that the phrase 'civil rights and obligations' incorporated, by the use of the word 'civil', the distinction between private

---

[82] *Eckle v FRG* A 51 (1982); 5 EHRR 1 para 77. Tariff fixing (*Easterbrook v UK* hudoc (2003); 37 EHRR 405) and proceeds of crime confiscation (*Phillips v UK* 2001-VII) proceedings are included as a part of sentencing. See also *Callaghan v UK No 14739/89*, 60 DR 296 (1989) (Criminal Cases Review Commission reference).

[83] *Eckle v FRG* A 51 (1982); 5 EHRR 1 para 76. Applications for leave to appeal are included: *Monnell and Morris v UK* A 115 (1987); 10 EHRR 205.

[84] *Gast and Popp v Germany* 2000-II; 33 EHRR 895.

[85] *Eckle v FRG* A 51 (1982) para 78; 5 EHRR 1; *Orchin v UK No 8435/78*, 26 DR 18 (1982); 6 EHRR 391. An appeal against discontinuance is within Article 6: *Zuckerstatter and Reschenhofer v Austria No 76718/01* hudoc (2004) DA.

[86] *Montcornet de Caumont v France No 59290/00*, 2003-VII DA. Cf, *Saccoccia v Austria No 6991/01* hudoc (2007) DA (execution of foreign court sentence).

[87] *X v FRG No 4438/70*, 39 CD 20 (1971).

[88] *Erdemli v Turkey No 33412/03* hudoc (2004) DA. Article 6 does not guarantee a right to a retrial: *Callaghan v UK No 14739/89*, 60 DR 296 (1989).

[89] 2004-II; 39 EHRR 653.

[90] See Bradley, 21 OHLJ 609 (1983); Van Dijk, *Wiarda Mélanges*, p 131; and *European Supervision*, Ch 14. For studies of the early jurisprudence, see Harris, 47 BYIL 157 (1974–5) and Rasenack, 3 HRJ 51 (1970). On the drafting history of 'civil rights and obligations', see Newman, 1967 PL 274 and Velu, 1961 RDIDC 129.

and public law, with 'civil' rights and obligations being rights and obligations in private law.[91] This distinction has long been significant in civil law systems for jurisdictional and other purposes[92] and has more recently become important in UK administrative law.[93] On the basis of it, rights and obligations in the relations of private persons *inter se* clearly fall within Article 6, but some rights and obligations at issue in the relations between the individual and the state (eg the right to nationality and the obligation to pay taxes) do not, the problem in the latter case being to know where to draw the line. Criminal law is in a special position. Decisions taken in the 'determination of... any criminal charge' are included by a separate part of the wording of Article 6(1).[94] Ancillary decisions relating to criminal proceedings are not subject to Article 6 on the criminal side[95] and not otherwise subject to Article 6 as decisions determinative of 'civil rights and obligations'. They are excluded both because of the distinction between private and public law and also, as the Court has preferred to emphasize, because, if certain decisions in criminal proceedings are specifically covered by Article 6(1), others, by inference, are not.[96]

It follows from the above that the Convention does not guarantee a fair trial in the determination of all of the rights and obligations that a person may arguably have in national law. However, as will be seen, the gaps in the coverage of Article 6 have been significantly, if somewhat confusingly, reduced by interpretation. Indeed, whereas the Court occasionally still relies upon the public law/private law divide when excluding rights or obligations as not being 'civil',[97] more recent jurisprudence, by which more and more rights and obligations have been brought within Article 6, is not always easy to explain in terms of any distinction between private and public law that is found in European national law.

Before examining further the Court's, and earlier the Commission's, use of the idea of private law rights and obligations, it should be noted that in two early cases the Court left open the question whether there is an exact equation between 'civil' rights and obligations and rights and obligations in private law. In *König v FRG*[98] and later in *Le Compte v Belgium*,[99] it stated that it did not have to decide 'whether the concept of "civil rights and obligations"... extends beyond those rights which have a private nature'. It is not clear what the Court had in mind by this. One possibility is that human rights protected by the Convention might be 'civil' rights in the sense of Article 6.[100] However, although the Court has not expressly retracted the statements made in the *König* case, it has not repeated them in more recent years.[101]

---

[91] *Ringeisen v Austria* A 13 (1971); 1 EHRR 455 para 94 and *König v FRG* A 27 (1978); 2 EHRR 170 para 95 PC.

[92] See Schlesinger, Baade, Herzog, and Wise, *Comparative Law*, 6th edn, 1998, pp 498ff.

[93] See Wade and Forsyth, *Administrative Law*, 9th edn, 2004, p 649.

[94] A particular factual situation may concern both a criminal charge and civil rights and obligations, although the case will normally be dealt with under one head only: see *Albert and Le Compte v Belgium* A 58 (1983); 5 EHRR 533 para 30 PC. Criminal proceedings may be determinative of 'civil rights' in some jurisdictions in criminal defamation cases or if a victim is joined as a civil party: see below, p 228.

[95] See above, p 204.

[96] *Neumeister v Austria* A 8 (1968); 1 EHRR 91 (right to bail not a 'civil right' for this reason).

[97] See eg, *Ferrazzini v Italy* 2001-VII; 34 EHRR 1068 para 27 GC.

[98] A 27 (1978); 2 EHRR 170 para 95 PC.

[99] *Le Compte, Van Leuven and De Meyere v Belgium* A 43 (1981); 4 EHRR 1 para 48 PC.

[100] See the *Alam and Khan v UK* Nos 2991/66 and 2992/66, 10 YB 478 (1967) line of cases, concerning the right to family life, discussed in Harris, 46 BYIL 157 at 167 (1974–5), in which the Commission seemed for a while to adopt such an approach. This approach concentrates on the rights, as opposed to the obligations, part of civil rights and obligations.

[101] But see below, p 218.

An autonomous Convention meaning

The adoption of a private law meaning of 'civil' rights and obligations raised from the outset the question of the boundary between private and public law for the purposes of Article 6. One approach would have been to have applied a doctrine of *renvoi* by which the Court simply accepted the classification of a particular right or obligation in the respondent state's legal system. This would have led to the application of Article 6 differentially between the contracting parties,[102] given that different states classify borderline cases differently. In fact, the Court has, from the beginning, as with the parallel Article 6 concept of a 'criminal charge', held that 'civil' has an autonomous Convention meaning, so that the defendant state's classification is not decisive.[103] In a particular case, therefore, a right that is regarded as a matter of public law in the legal system of the defendant state may be treated as falling within Article 6[104] and *vice versa*. With the Court applying an autonomous Convention meaning of 'civil' rights and obligations and expanding its scope over time, the position has been reached in which most substantive rights that an individual may arguably claim under national law fall within Article 6 unless they quintessentially concern the exercise of the public power of the state.

Although adopting an autonomous Convention meaning of 'civil' rights and obligations, the Court has refrained from formulating any abstract definition of the term, beyond distinguishing between private and public law.[105] It has instead preferred an inductive approach, ruling on the particular facts, or categories, of cases as they have arisen. Even so, there are certain general guidelines that emerge from the cases. First, 'only the character of the right at issue is relevant'.[106] The 'character of legislation which governs how the matter is to be determined (civil, commercial, administrative law, etc) and that of the authority which is invested with jurisdiction in the matter (ordinary court, administrative body, etc) are therefore of little consequence'.[107] This guideline has minimal significance for cases involving disputes between private persons which will invariably be governed by national private law and usually be within the jurisdiction of the 'ordinary courts'. It is, however, of critical importance in cases that involve the relations between a private person and the state. In national law systems that traditionally have made use of the distinction between private and public law, the classification of such cases generally turns upon whether the state is acting in a sovereign or non-sovereign capacity in its dealings with the private person concerned.[108] For the purpose of Article 6, however, whether the state has 'acted as a private person or in its sovereign capacity is...not conclusive';[109] instead, the focus is entirely upon the 'character of the right'.

---

[102] This does happen in other ways under Article 6: see eg, *James v UK*, below, p 224.

[103] *König v FRG* A 27 (1978); 2 EHRR 170 para 88 PC. In *Porter v UK No 15814/02* hudoc (2003) DA the Court accepted a national court classification for the purposes of argument.

[104] As in the *Feldbrugge* and *Deumeland* cases, below, p 217.

[105] In *Benthem v Netherlands* A 97 (1985); 8 EHRR 1 para 34 PC, the Court declined the Commission's invitation, *id*, para 91 Com Rep, to give guidance on the matter.

[106] *König v FRG* A 27 (1978); 2 EHRR 170 para 90 PC. The wording quoted is phrased only in terms of 'rights', omitting 'obligations'. This tends to happen because most of the cases under Article 6 are brought by claimants, not defendants. For 'obligations' cases, see eg, *Muyldermans v Belgium* A 214-A (1991); 15 EHRR 204 Com Rep (F Sett before Court) and *Schouten and Meldrum v Netherlands* A 304 (1994); 19 EHRR 432.

[107] *Ringeisen v Austria* A 13 (1971); 1 EHRR 455 para 94, quoted in the *König* case A 27 (1978); 2 EHRR 170 para 90 PC.

[108] For example, the state will be acting in a sovereign capacity when it exercises a power of deportation or expropriation. It will be acting in a non-sovereign capacity when it does something that a private person might do, such as buying chairs for an office.

[109] *König v FRG* A 27 (1978); 2 EHRR 170 para 90 PC.

Secondly, when determining the 'character of the right', the existence of any 'uniform European notion' that can be found in the law of the contracting parties is influential. This inference can be drawn from the *Feldbrugge* and *Deumeland* cases.[110] There the Court found that there was no 'uniform European notion' (which by implication would have been followed) as to the private or public law character of the social security rights before it and was forced to make a choice in respect of rights it considered to have a mixed private and public law character.[111]

Thirdly, although the classification of a right or obligation in the law of the respondent state is not decisive, that law is nonetheless relevant in that it necessarily determines the content of the right or obligation to which the Convention concept of 'civil' rights and obligations is applied. For example, in *Konig v FRG*,[112] when deciding whether the right to practise medicine was a matter of private or public law, the Court scrutinized West German law to see whether, in the law of the respondent state in the case, the services offered by the medical profession were a part of a public service or were, although subject to state regulation, essentially a matter of private law contract between doctor and patient. For this reason, despite the autonomous nature of 'civil' rights and obligations, it would be possible for the same right or obligation to be subject to Article 6 as it exists in one legal system but not as it is found in another.

Finally, the Court adopts a restrictive interpretation, in accordance with the object and purpose of the Convention, of the exceptions to the safeguards afforded by Article 6(1). This consideration was relevant in *Vilho Eskelinen v Finland*[113] when the Court ruled that some disputes concerning employment in the public service fall within Article 6.

Rights and obligations in the relations between private persons

Applying its inductive approach, the Court, and earlier the Commission, has developed an extensive jurisprudence classifying rights and obligations as being civil or not for the purposes of Article 6. This jurisprudence is considered in the following pages. The first point to be made is that it is establishes, in accordance with the position uniformly found in European national law, that the rights and obligations of private persons in their relations *inter se* are 'civil' rights and obligations. Thus cases concerning such relations in the law of contract,[114] the law of tort,[115] the law of succession,[116] family law,[117] employment law,[118] commercial law,[119] insurance law,[120] and the law of personal[121] and real[122] property have been regarded as falling within Article 6.

---

[110] *Feldbrugge v Netherlands* A 99 (1986); 8 EHRR 425 para 29 PC and *Deumeland v FRG* A 100 (1986); 8 EHRR 448 para 63 PC. Cf., *König v FRG* A 27 (1978); 2 EHRR 170 para 89 PC.

[111] Cf, *Muyldermans v Belgium* A 214-A (1991); 15 EHRR 204 para 56 Com Rep (F Sett before Court).

[112] A 27 (1978); 2 EHRR 170 para 89 PC. See also *Perez v France* 2004-I; 40 EHRR 909 GC.

[113] 2007-XX GC.

[114] See eg, *Buchholz v FRG*, below, p 283.

[115] See eg, *Golder v UK* A 18 (1975); 1 EHRR 524 PC (defamation).

[116] See eg, *CD v France* hudoc (2003).

[117] See eg, *Airey v Ireland* A 32 (1979); 2 EHRR 305 (separation) and *Mizzi v Malta* hudoc 2006-I; 46 EHRR 529 (paternity).

[118] See eg, *Buchholz v FRG* A 42 (1981); 3 EHRR 597 (unfair dismissal).

[119] See eg, *Barthold v FRG* A 90 (1985); 7 EHRR 383 (unfair competition).

[120] Implied in *Feldbrugge v Netherlands* A 99 (1986); 8 EHRR 425 PC and *Deumeland v FRG* A 100 (1986); 8 EHRR 448 PC.

[121] See eg, *Bramelid and Malmström v Sweden* Nos 8588/79 and 8589/79, 38 DR 18 (1983) (share valuation) Com Rep; CM Res DH (84) 4.

[122] See eg, *Pretto v Italy* A 71 (1983); 6 EHRR 182 PC (sale of land).

State action determining private law rights and obligations
The position is more complicated in cases involving the relations of private persons with the state. In accordance with its approach in the *König* case,[123] in such cases the Court looks solely to the character of the right or obligation that is the subject of the case when deciding whether Article 6 applies. If that right or obligation falls within private law, then any state action that is directly decisive for it[124] must be either taken by a tribunal that complies with Article 6 or, if it is administrative action, challengeable before such a tribunal.[125] What is remarkable, and a tribute to the Court's creativity, is the identity and nature of the rights and obligations of private persons that the Court has recognized as private law rights and obligations in this context. Most significantly, it has recognized certain rights of a very general character, such as rights that have a pecuniary nature or consequences, as being 'civil' rights. When, as is common, state action is determinative of such rights, it is controlled by Article 6.

Pecuniary rights
The key determinant in cases involving state action is often whether the right or obliga-tion in question is pecuniary in nature or, if not, whether the state action that is decisive for the right nonetheless has pecuniary consequences for the applicant.[126] If so, the case will generally fall within Article 6, unless the state is acting within one of the areas that 'still form part of the hard core of public authority prerogatives',[127] such as taxation or the control of aliens. Although the Court commonly states that 'merely showing that a dispute is "pecuniary" in nature is not in itself sufficient to attract the applicability of Article 6',[128] this is mainly intended to allow for the 'public authority prerogative' excep-tion: in cases to which that exception does not extend, Article 6 will generally apply if a pecuniary dimension is present.[129] The following paragraphs concern rights and obliga-tions that are sometimes classified as 'civil' under other headings by the Court but that all have a pecuniary dimension.

The right to property
The right to property is clearly a right with a pecuniary character. As a result, state action that is directly decisive for real or personal property rights is determinative of 'civil' rights and obligations' and hence governed by Article 6. Thus decisions by the state con-cerning the expropriation[130] or the regulation of the use[131] of private land have been held to be subject to the right to a fair hearing. With regard to personal property, decisions by

---

[123] See above at p 212.   [124] As to this requirement, see below, p 226.

[125] As to the requirement that state administrative action be subject to judicial challenge, see below, pp 228ff.

[126] See eg, *Editions Périscope v France* A 234-B (1992); 14 EHRR 597 and *Stran Greek Refineries and Stratis Andreadis v Greece* A 301-B (1994); 19 EHRR 293.

[127] *Ferrazzini v Italy* 2001-VII; 34 EHRR 1068 para 29 GC.   [128] Id, para 25.

[129] Eg, the obligation of a French public accountant to repay public monies lost by his negligence is within Article 6, despite its public law dimensions, because of its pecuniary impact on the accountant: *Martinie v France No 58675/00* hudoc (2004) DA. On surcharges on UK local authority officers, see *Porter v UK No 15814/02* hudoc (2003) DA.

[130] *Sporrong and Lönnroth v Sweden* A 52 (1982); 5 EHRR 35 PC and *Zanatta v France* hudoc (2000). See also *Raimondo v Italy* A 281-A (1994); 18 EHRR 237 para 43 (confiscation) and *Poiss v Austria* A 117 (1987); 10 EHRR 231 (land consolidation).

[131] For planning or building permission cases, see eg, *McGonnell v UK* 2000-II; 30 EHRR 289; *Chapman v UK* 2001-I; 33 EHRR 399 GC; *Haider v Austria No 63413/00* hudoc (2004) DA. See also *Gillow v UK* A 109 (1986); 11 EHRR 335. For other land use cases, see eg, *Zander v Sweden* A 279-B (1993); 18 EHRR 175 (water extraction); *Georgios Papadopoulos v Greece* 2003-VI (mineral exploitation); *Ludescher v Austria* hudoc (2001) (farming); *Posti and Rahko v Finland* hudoc 2002-VII; 37 EHRR 158 (fishing); and *Oerlemans v Netherlands* A 219 (1991); 15 EHRR 561 (nature conservation).

the state as to a person's capacity to administer property,[132] or ones that are otherwise decisive for personal property rights,[133] are controlled by Article 6. Where the state decision concerning real or personal property is taken by an administrative authority (as opposed to a tribunal), there must be the possibility of challenging it before a tribunal that complies with Article 6.[134]

The right to engage in a commercial activity or to practise a profession

The right to engage in a commercial activity, which similarly has a pecuniary character, is also a civil right.[135] Hence state action by way of the withdrawal of a commercial licence or other authorization to engage in a commercial activity is controlled by Article 6.[136] The same is true of the right to practise a liberal profession.[137]

Article 6 applies to the *grant* of a licence or other authorization to undertake a commercial activity or practise a profession as well as a decision to withdraw it. In *König v FRG*,[138] the Court had emphasized that the case was one of the *continued* exercise of a right to operate a medical clinic and to practise medicine, distinguishing between a decision to grant a licence in the first place and the legitimate expectation that a licence holder has in its continuance. In the *Benthem* and later cases,[139] however, Article 6 has been applied to applications for new licences, provided that the grant of the licence is not a discretionary decision by the state.[140]

The right to compensation for illegal state action

The Court's jurisprudence also recognizes as 'civil' the right to compensation from the state for injury resulting from illegal state acts, again on the basis of its pecuniary nature. Thus, in *X v France*,[141] the Court held that a claim for damages in an administrative court for contracting AIDS from a blood transfusion because of government negligence fell within Article 6. Although the case concerned the exercise of a general regulatory

---

[132] *Winterwerp v Netherlands* A 33 (1979); 2 EHRR 387 (mentally disabled person).

[133] *Vasilescu v Romania* 1998-III; 28 EHRR 241 (seizure of property); *Ruiz-Mateos v Spain* A 262 (1993); 16 EHRR 505 PC (restitution); *Tinnelly and McElduff v UK* 1998-IV; 27 EHRR 249 (public contracts); *Pafitis v Greece* 1998-I; 27 EHRR 566 (shareholders' voting rights); *Capital Bank v Bulgaria* 2005-XII (bankruptcy); *Credit and Industrial Bank v Czech Republic* 2003-XI; 39 EHRR 860 (compulsory administration); *British-American Tobacco Co Ltd v Netherlands* A 331 (1995); 21 EHRR 409 (patent applications and rights); *Procola v Luxembourg* A 326 (1995); 22 EHRR 193 (milk levy).

[134] See below, pp 228ff.

[135] There may be an overlap between this right and the right to property; eg, in *Benthem v Netherlands* A 97 (1985); 8 EHRR 1 para 36 PC the Court noted that the licence had a proprietary character (being assignable) and that its grant was 'closely associated with the right to use one's possessions'.

[136] See eg, *Tre Traktörer Aktiebolag v Sweden* A 159 (1989); 13 EHRR 309 (sale of alcohol); *Kingsley v UK* 2002-IV; 35 EHRR 177 GC (gaming); *Pudas v Sweden* A 125-A (1987); 10 EHRR 380 (transport); *König v FRG* A 27 (1978); 2 EHRR 170 PC (medical clinic); *Benthem v Netherlands* A 97 (1985); 8 EHRR 1 PC (liquid petroleum gas); *Hornsby v Greece* 1997-II; 24 EHRR 250 (private school). Where disqualification from a commercial activity results from a criminal conviction, it suffices that Article 6 is complied with in the criminal proceedings: *X v Belgium* No 8901/80, 23 DR 237 (1981).

[137] See eg, *König v FRG* A 27 (1978) 2 EHRR 170 PC (medicine); *GS v Austria* hudoc (1999); 31 EHRR 576 (pharmacy); *H v Belgium* A 127-B (1987); 10 EHRR 339 (law); *Thlimmenos v Greece* 2000-IV; 31 EHRR 411 GC (accountancy); *Guchez v Belgium* No 10027/82, 40 DR 100 (1984) (architecture). And see *Wilson v UK* No 36791/97, 26 EHRR CD 195 (1998) and *X v UK* No 28530/95, 25 EHRR CD 88 (company director).

[138] A 27 (1978); 2 EHRR 170 PC.

[139] *Benthem v Netherlands* A 97 (1985); 8 EHRR 1 PC. Cf, *Allan Jacobsson v Sweden* A 163 (1989); 12 EHRR 56; *Nowicky v Austria* hudoc (2005); *Kraska v Switzerland* A 254-B (1993); 18 EHRR 188; and *De Moor v Belgium* A 292-A (1994); 18 EHRR 372.

[140] Article 6 applies only where a person has an arguable legal right: see below, p 225.

[141] A 234-C (1992); 14 EHRR 483. Cf, *H v France* A 162-A (1989); 12 EHRR 74. See also *Z v UK* 2001-V; 34 EHRR 97 GC.

power by a minister and hence was clearly a matter of public law in France, its outcome was 'decisive for private rights and obligations', namely those concerning pecuniary compensation for physical injury. The same approach was adopted in *Editions Périscope v France*.[142] There the applicant company had ceased trading because of pecuniary losses caused by an illegal decision by a public authority refusing it a tax concession. The Court held that the decision of an administrative court on the applicant's claim for compensation for damage sustained through the fault of the public authority determined the applicant's 'civil' rights. In a brief statement of reasons, the Court noted that 'the subject matter of the applicant's action was "pecuniary" in nature and that the action was founded on an alleged infringement of rights which were likewise pecuniary rights', so that the right in question was a 'civil' one. The Court's approach in these two cases involved finding a pecuniary interest in a very general sense and supposing that such an interest has a private law character.

The *X* and *Editions Périscope* cases have been followed by other cases in which claims for compensation for illegal state acts have been held to be decisive for 'civil' rights. These have concerned claims for compensation for ill-treatment by the police;[143] unlawful detention;[144] unreasonable delay in judicial proceedings;[145] breach of contract;[146] the seizure of property;[147] and a miscellany of other claims.[148]

Statutory rights to compensation against the state for 'wrongful conviction and unjustified detention' in connection with criminal proceedings also fall within Article 6.[149] The cases have involved compensation for detention where the proceedings are discontinued,[150] the accused is acquitted,[151] or the conviction is quashed on appeal.[152] Such cases concern a right to compensation provided by the state under national law where the detention is not necessarily in breach of Article 5 of the Convention, but the detainee is not finally convicted.[153]

Although not involving an illegal act, a claim under a state's criminal injuries compensation scheme may, because of its pecuniary character, fall with within Article 6 if the scheme provides for a legal right to compensation, and not an *ex gratia* payment.[154]

---

[142] A 234-B (1992); 14 EHRR 597 para 40.

[143] *Assenov v Bulgaria* 1998-VIII; 28 EHRR 652 and *Balogh v Hungary* hudoc (2004) (assault); *Baraona v Portugal* A 122 (1987); 13 EHRR 329 (illegal arrest); *Veeber v Estonia* hudoc (2002) (illegal search and seizure); *Ait-Mouhoub v France* 1998-VIII; 30 EHRR 382 (police theft, forgery, etc); *Kaukonen v Finland No 24738/94*, 91-A DR 14 (1997) (malicious prosecution).

[144] *Aerts v Belgium* 1998-V; 29 EHRR 50 and *Göç v Turkey* 2002-V; 35 EHRR 134 GC.

[145] *Pelli v Italy No 19537/02* hudoc (2003) DA ('Pinto law').

[146] *Stran Greek Refineries and Stratis Andreadis v Greece* A 301-B (1994); 19 EHRR 293.

[147] *Air Canada v UK* A 316-A (1995); 20 EHRR 150.

[148] See eg, *Beaumartin v France* A 296-B (1994); 19 EHRR 485 (claim for compensation under a treaty); *Neves e Silva v Portugal* A 153-A (1989); 13 EHRR 535 (official malpractice); and *S A Sotiris and Nicos Koutas Attee v Greece No 39442/98* hudoc (1999) DA (refusal of state subsidy).

[149] *Humen v Poland* hudoc (1999); 31 EHRR 1168 para 57 GC. The payment of compensation must be as of right, not discretionary: *Masson and Van Zon v Netherlands* A 327-A (1995); 22 EHRR 491.

[150] *Goc v Turkey* 2002-V GC and *Werner v Austria* 1997-VII; 26 EHRR 310.

[151] *Lamanna v Austria* hudoc (2001).

[152] *Georgiadis v Greece* hudoc (2000); 33 EHRR 561 and *Humen v Poland* hudoc (1999); 31 EHRR 1168 GC. See also *Halka v Poland* hudoc (2002).

[153] Article 5 provides its own *lex specialis* fair trial guarantees for challenges to the legality of detention (Article 5(3)(4)) or for claims for compensation for detention in breach of Article 5 (Article 5(5)). Article 6 does not apply.

[154] *Gustafson v Sweden* 1997-IV; 25 EHRR 623 (a legal right) and *August v UK No 36505/02* hudoc (2003); 36 EHRR CD 115 (*ex gratia* payment). Article 6 does not apply to discretionary state compensation for a natural disaster: *Nordh v Sweden No 14225/88*, 69 DR 223 (1990).

The right to social security and social assistance
One of the most remarkable developments in the Court's jurisprudence has concerned the classification of rights to social security and social assistance which the Court has held fall within Article 6. Initially, in the companion cases of *Feldbrugge v Netherlands*[155] and *Deumeland v Germany*,[156] the Court adopted a balancing approach, and in both cases found that the private law aspects of the social security rights concerned outweighed their public law aspects, so that Article 6 applied. However, the Court has since gone further and established that 'the development in the law that was initiated by those judgments and the principle of equality of treatment warrant taking the view that today the general rule is that Article 6(1) does apply in the field of social insurance, including even welfare assistance'.[157] In addition, the Court has stressed that such rights are of a pecuniary, or economic, nature.[158] Since the Court adopted this position, disputes concerning social security and social assistance rights have routinely been accepted as falling within Article 6, commonly without argument to the contrary by the respondent state.[159] The right need not be linked to a contract of employment[160] or depend upon contributory payments.[161] There must, however, be entitlement as a matter of legal right for those who qualify: disputes about benefits or assistance given by the state in its discretion are not included.[162] This is not to do with the civil or non-civil character of the benefit or assistance, but because Article 6 extends only to disputes about 'rights'.[163]

Non-pecuniary civil rights and obligations
Although an important touchstone, the pecuniary dimension of a right or obligation is not the only test for a 'civil' right or obligation. Other rights or obligations of private persons may qualify, again by reference to the general perception of them in national law as private law rights or obligations with which the state may not interfere without due process. One right of a non-pecuniary character to which Article 6 applies is the right to respect for family life. Thus state action that is directly decisive for this right, such as decisions placing children in care[164] and restricting the contact of prisoners with their families,[165] have been held to be regulated by Article 6.

---

[155] A 99 (1986); 8 EHRR 425 PC (employment sickness benefit).

[156] A 100 (1986); 8 EHRR 448 PC (industrial injuries benefit).

[157] *Schuler-Zgraggen v Switzerland* A 263 (1993); 16 EHRR 405 para 46 (invalidity pension). See also *McGinley and Egan v UK* 1998-III; 27 EHRR 1 (disability pension); *Pauger v Austria* 1997-III; 25 EHRR 105 (widower's pension); *Grof v Austria No 25046/94*, 25 EHRR CD 39 (1998) (maternity benefit). For a case of welfare assistance, see *Salesi v Italy* A 257-E (1993); 26 EHRR 187 (disability allowance for destitute persons). And see *Wos v Poland No 22860/02* hudoc (2005) DA (forced labour compensation). The distinction between social welfare (or social) assistance and social security is not wholly clear; generally persons receive differing amounts of welfare assistance to cover individual basic needs, rather than the same amount of benefit for all qualifying persons, as in the case with social security.

[158] *Schuler-Zgraggen v Switzerland* A 263 (1993); 16 EHRR 405 para 46 (the applicant 'suffered an interference with her means of subsistence' and was claiming an 'individual economic right').

[159] See eg, *Duclos v France* 1996-VI; 32 EHRR 86. If the issue is raised, the Court typically notes the right's pecuniary nature when finding that it is a 'civil' right: see eg, *Sussmann v Germany* 1996-IV; 25 EHRR 64 para 42.

[160] See eg, *Lombardo v Italy* A 249-B (1992); 21 EHRR 188 (public service pension). The rights in the *Feldbrugge* and *Deumeland* cases were so linked.

[161] *Salesi v Italy* A 257-E (1993); 26 EHRR 187. See also *Stec v UK No 65731/01* hudoc (2005) DA.

[162] *Salesi v Italy, ibid* and *Mennitto v Italy* 2000-X; 34 EHRR 1122 GC. See also *Gaygusuz v Austria* 1996-IV; 23 EHRR 364.

[163] See below, p 223.

[164] *Olsson v Sweden (No 1)* A 130 (1988); 11 EHRR 259 PC. See also *Keegan v Ireland* A 290 (1994); 18 EHRR 342 (adoption) and *Eriksson v Sweden* A 156 (1989); 12 EHRR 183 PC (fostering).

[165] *Ganci v Italy* 2003-XI; 41 EHRR 272.

Other non-pecuniary rights that have been recognized as 'civil rights' are the rights to life,[166] physical integrity,[167] liberty,[168] private life,[169] access to administrative documents,[170] a reputation (and a remedy to protect it),[171] freedom of expression and assembly (unless used for political purposes),[172] and freedom of association.[173] Most of the rights listed in this paragraph are human rights protected by the Convention, although no reference to this link is usually made in Court judgments.[174] Generally, the Court merely states, without giving reasons, that a non-pecuniary right is a 'civil' right, or even just acts on the basis that it is such a right without addressing the matter.[175] At most, the Court usually refers only to the equation between 'civil rights and obligations' and 'private (law) rights and obligations'[176] established in its early jurisprudence. Exceptionally, in *O'Reilly v Ireland*[177] it examined in some detail the public and private law elements of a local authority's statutory duty to repair a road and the applicants' standing as residents on the road to seek an order of *mandamus* to require its repair, finding on balance that the private law elements predominated.

Public law rights and obligations
Following from the private law reading of the word 'civil', claims concerning a number of rights and obligations are not subject to Article 6 because of their public law character. However, their number is limited and in decline. The Court's parsimonious approach to the exclusion of rights and obligations on public law grounds is governed by two general considerations. First, in accordance with the object and purpose of the Convention, a 'restrictive interpretation' must be adopted when deciding whether a right or obligation is excluded from the safeguards of Article 6.[178] Second, the Convention is a living instrument that must be interpreted dynamically.[179] The significance of this second consideration was explained by the Court in *Ferrazzini v Italy*[180] as follows:

> Relations between the individual and the State have clearly developed in many spheres during the 50 years which have elapsed since the Convention was adopted, with State regulation increasingly intervening in private law relations. This has led the Court to find that procedures classified under national law as being part of 'public law' could come within the purview of Article 6 under its 'civil' head if the outcome was decisive for private rights and obligations, in regard to such matters as, to give some examples, the sale

---

[166] *Athanassoglou v Switzerland* 2000-IV; 31 EHRR 372 GC.

[167] *Ibid*; and *Okyay v Turkey* 2005-VII; 43 EHRR 788.

[168] *Laidin v France (No 2)* hudoc (2003). See also *Aerts v Belgium* 1998-V 29 EHRR 50 (a pecuniary rights case: compensation for illegal detention) and *Reinprecht v Austria No 67175/01* hudoc (2004) DA.

[169] *Mustafa v France* hudoc (2003) (choice of surname).   [170] *Loiseau v France* 2003-XII DA.

[171] *Tolstoy Miloslavsky v UK* A 316-B (1995); 20 EHRR 442 and *Werner v Poland* hudoc (2001); 36 EHRR 491.

[172] *Reisz v Germany No 3201/96*, 91-A DR 53 (1997).

[173] *AB Kurt Kellermann v Sweden No 41579/98* hudoc (2003); 37 EHRR CD 161 and *APEH Üldözötteinek Szövetsége and Others v Hungary* 2000-X; 34 EHRR 849.

[174] Such a link was made in the case of the *pecuniary* right to property in Article 1, First Protocol to the Convention in *Procola v Luxembourg* A 326 (1995); 22 EHRR 193. On a possible human rights meaning of 'civil rights', see above, p 211. The Article 13 requirement of an effective remedy suggests that there may well be an 'arguable right' in national law where there is a breach of most Convention rights, but Article 13 does not necessarily require a right enforceable in the courts and some Convention rights (eg, the right to free elections: Article 3, First Protocol) are public law rights.

[175] See eg, the family life cases cited above.

[176] *APEH Üldözötteinek Szövetsége and Others v Hungary* 2000-X; 34 EHRR 849 para 34.

[177] Hudoc (2003) DA.   [178] *Vilho Eskelinen v Flnland* 2007-XX para 49 GC.

[179] *Ferrazzini v Italy* 2001-VII; 34 EHRR 1068 para 26 GC. On dynamic interpretation, see above, p 7.

[180] Id, para 27. Footnotes omitted. But in some contexts the tendency has more recently been for the withdrawal of the state, involving deregulation and privatization.

of land, the running of a private clinic, property interests, the granting of administrative authorisations relating to the conditions of professional practice or of a licence to serve alcoholic beverages. Moreover, the State's increasing intervention in the individual's day-to-day life, in terms of welfare protection for example, has required the Court to evaluate features of public law and private law before concluding that the asserted right could be classified as civil.

However, the Court continued, 'rights and obligations existing for an individual are not necessarily civil in nature'.[181] Giving political rights and obligations, rights in some cases concerning public employment, the expulsion of aliens and the obligation to pay taxes as examples, the Court stated that rights and obligations that relate to matters that 'still form part of the hard core of public authority prerogatives'[182] remain excluded. In the case of such rights or obligations, the fact there may in some cases be a pecuniary dimension to the right or to the consequences of its infringement is outweighed or overridden by its fundamentally public law character.

The obligation to pay tax

On its facts, *Ferrazzini v Italy* concerned the obligation to pay taxes to the state. The Court held that disputes arising out of this obligation are not determinative of a person's 'civil' obligations because of its public law nature. Although the obligation has pecuniary elements, 'the public nature of the relationship between the taxpayer and the tax authority' remains predominant.'[183] In contrast, in *Schouten and Meldrum v Netherlands*[184] it was held that Article 6 does apply to the applicant's obligation to pay social security contributions: following the approach it had used in the *Feldbrugge* case in respect of social security benefits, the Court decided that the private law features of the obligation outweighed its public law features.

Political rights and obligations

As to political rights and obligations, in *Pierre-Bloch v France*[185] it was held that the right to stand for election to a national parliament does not fall within Article 6, because 'such a right is a political and not a "civil" one'. There the applicant, who had been elected to the French National Assembly, was found to have exceeded the election expenses limit and as a penalty was disqualified from standing for election for a year, made to forfeit his seat, and required to pay a sum equal to the expenses excess. Despite the pecuniary consequences of the decision, Article 6 was held not to apply: 'proceedings do not become "civil" merely because they raise an economic issue'.[186] Generally, the right to engage in political activities is not a 'civil' right, so that, for example, disputes concerning the right to vote[187] or the dissolution of a political party[188] also do not fall within Article 6.

---

181 Id, para 28.   182 Id, para 29.

183 *Ferrazzini v Italy* 2001-VII; 34 EHRR 1068 GC. See Lopardi, 26 ELR Human Rights Survey 58 (2001). See also *Emesa Sugar NV v Netherlands* No 62023/00 hudoc (2005) DA (customs duties) and *Smith v UK* No 25373/94 hudoc (1995); 21 EHRR CD 74 (UK poll tax). Surcharges imposed for non-payment of tax may involve a 'criminal charge' within Article 6: see above, p 208.

184 A 304 (1994); 19 EHRR 432. Followed in *Meulendijks v Netherlands* hudoc (2002).

185 1997-VI; 26 EHRR 202. See also *Tapie v France* No 32258/96, 88-A DR 176 (1997); *Asensio Serqueda v Spain* No 23151/94, 77-A DR 122 (1994); and *Guliyev v Azerbaidjan* No 35584/02 hudoc (2004) DA. All kinds of election disputes fall outside Article 6: see eg, *Priorello v Italy* No 11068/84, 43 DR 195 (1985) (challenge to local election).

186 1997-VI; 26 EHRR 202 para 51.

187 *Hirst v UK* No 74025/01 hudoc (2003); 37 EHRR CD 176 DA (prisoner's right to vote).

188 *Yazar, Karataş, Aksoy and the People's Labour Party (HEP) v Turkey* hudoc (2002); 36 EHRR 59. See also *Reisz v Germany* No 32013/96 hudoc (1997) DA and *Papon v France* No 344/04 hudoc (2005) DA.

Disputes concerning the election of an officer of a non-governmental organization[189] or of an employees' council representative[190] are excluded on a similar basis.

Entry, conditions of stay, and removal of aliens

Disputes concerning the entry, conditions of stay, and removal of aliens also fall on the public law side of the line. In *Maaouia v France*,[191] the Court held that proceedings concerning the rescinding of an exclusion order against an alien physically present in France did not concern his 'civil' rights. More generally, the Court stated that 'decisions regarding the entry, stay and deportation of aliens do not concern the determination of an applicant's civil rights or obligations', and that this is so even though, in the case of an exclusion order, the decision 'incidentally' has 'major repercussions on the applicant's private and family life or on his prospects of employment'.[192] The approach in the *Maaouia* case was applied to the extradition of aliens in *Mamatkulov and Askarov v Turkey*.[193]

In the *Maaouia* case, the Court reached its conclusion that Article 6 did not apply to the 'expulsion of aliens' on the basis that the Seventh Protocol to the ECHR[194] provides procedural safeguards for aliens who are to be expelled, which would not have been necessary if the right to a fair hearing in Article 6 already applied. Although the Court did refer to the Commission's jurisprudence to the same effect that was based instead on the public law character of expulsion decisions, the Court relied solely on the Seventh Protocol for its decision.[195] This reasoning cannot apply to the entry or conditions of stay of an alien, to which the Seventh Protocol does not apply. It is likely that the Court would here rely upon the fact that these matters are a 'part of the hard core of public authority prerogatives'.[196]

Employment in the public service

To some extent, rights and obligations arising out of employment in the public service are excluded from Article 6, although the extent of this exception is now more limited than formerly. Before its decision in *Pellegrin v France*,[197] the Court followed an approach by which Article 6(1) did not as a general rule apply to disputes that related to 'the recruitment, careers and termination of service of public servants',[198] unless the claim involved a 'purely' or 'essentially' economic right, such as the payment of the employee's salary.[199] Finding this approach increasingly difficult to apply, the Court replaced it in the *Pellegrin* case by a functional test based upon the nature of the employee's duties and responsibilities: the Court held that Article 6 applied to disputes arising out of public service employment unless that employment involved duties or responsibilities that entailed 'direct or indirect participation in the exercise of powers conferred by public law and duties designed to safeguard the general interests of the state or of other public authorities'.[200]

---

[189] *Fedotov v Russia No 5140/02* hudoc (2005) DA.

[190] *Novotny v Czech Republic No 36542/97* hudoc (1998) DA.   [191] 2000-X; 33 EHRR 1037 GC.

[192] Id, paras 40 and 38. Article 6 does not apply to asylum cases: *P v UK No 13162/87*, 54 DR 211 (1987) and *Taheri Kandomabadi v Netherlands* hudoc (2004) DA. The right to freedom of movement in EU law is a public law right and hence not within Article 6: *Adams and Benn v UK Nos 28979/95 and 30343/96*, 88 DR-A 137 (1997).

[193] 2005-I; 41 EHRR 494 GC. The extradition of nationals is presumably excluded also.

[194] See Article 1, below, p 747.

[195] Concurring, Judge Bratza would have preferred the Court to have followed the Commission's reasoning in exclusion decisions, which was based on the 'substantial discretionary and public order element'.

[196] *Ferrazini v Italy*, above, n 183.   [197] 1999-VIII; 31 EHRR 651 GC.

[198] *Massa v Italy*, A 265-B (1993); 18 EHRR 266 para 26.

[199] See the cases cited in *Pellegrin v France* 1999-VIII; 31 EHRR 651 para 59 GC. The exception also required that the case did not involve the exercise of discretionary power by the state: *ibid*.

[200] Id, para 66. Public service was given an autonomous Convention meaning, so that it was immaterial whether or not the person concerned was classified as a civil servant under national law: id, para 63.

The exclusion from the scope of Article 6 of employment falling on the 'public function' side of the line was justified by the Court on the basis that in such cases the holders of such posts wield 'a portion of the state's sovereign power' and 'the state therefore has a legitimate interest in requiring of these servants a special bond of trust and loyalty'.[201] In the *Pellegrin* case, the Court gave employment in the armed forces and the police as examples of the kinds of public service employment that were accordingly excluded from Article 6(1).[202] Since they concern the post-employment period, disputes about a public service employee's pension always fell, and continue to fall, within Article 6 whether the employment involves the exercise of 'a public function' or not.[203]

Although the *Pellegrin* test did clarify the scope of Article 6 in some respects, it quickly became clear that, as with any functional test, it had its own problems, with a series of borderline cases leading to continued uncertainty and anomalies.[204] To its credit, after less than a decade of applying *Pellegrin,* the Court revised its approach again. In *Vilho Eskelin v Finland,*[205] in place of the *Pellegrin* functional test, the Court introduced a new two part test, with a different emphasis and starting from the presumption that Article 6 does apply. For it not to do so, first, 'the state in its national law must have expressly excluded access to a court for the post or category of staff in question'. Second, where this condition is met, Article 6 nonetheless still applies unless the national law exclusion is justified on 'objective grounds'. These 'grounds' must relate not to the nature of the public servant's employment, as under *Pellegrin*, but the 'subject matter of the dispute' between the public servant and the state, with the latter being required to show that the dispute 'is related to the exercise of state power or that it has called into question the special bond' referred to by the Court in *Pellegrin*. Thus, even though there is no right of access to a court in national law in respect of such disputes, Article 6 will apply—and access to a court compliant with it will be required—to 'ordinary labour disputes, such as those relating to salaries, allowance or similar entitlements',[206] regardless of the nature of the employment or status of the public servant (as diplomat, judge, etc). In the *Vilho Eskilen* case, which concerned a salary dispute between the applicant policemen, who were civil servants, and the state, the government's defence fell at the first hurdle, as the applicants did have a right of access to a court to decide the dispute in national law. Even if this had not been the case, Article 6 would have applied because the dispute was an 'ordinary labour dispute'.

Although the *Vilho Eskelin* case is a welcome step in the right direction, the Court still needs to go further. An approach by which a dispute concerning employment in the public service in which the applicant has an arguable case under national law should be subject to Article 6 without exception. Such an approach is proposed in the joint dissenting opinion of Judges Tulkens, Fischbach, Casadevall, and Thomassen in the *Pellegrin* case, who state that whereas civil servants have traditionally had a special status in the public law of many European states, 'that justification has now largely lost its significance' as 'most member states have "judicialised" civil service disputes, if not entirely then at least in part'.

---

[201] Id, para 65.

[202] Id, para 66. See *Stanczuk v Poland No 45004/98* hudoc (2001) DA (secret police); *Kiratoglu v Turkey No 35829/97* hudoc (2002) DA (armed forces). And see the concurring and dissenting opinions in *Roche v UK* 2005-X; 42 EHRR 599 GC.

[203] *Pellegrin v France* 1999-VIII; 31 EHRR 651 para 67 GC. See eg, *Trickovic v Slovenia* hudoc (2001) (military pension); *Silveri v Italy* hudoc (2000) (police pension); *Vasilopoulou v Greece* hudoc (2002) (judicial pension). But see *R v Belgium* hudoc (2001).

[204] See the examples given in *Vilho Eskelinen v Finland* 2007-XX GC paras 53 and 54.

[205] 2007-XX GC para 62.   [206] *Ibid.*

Other public law rights and obligations
An obligation which is a part of 'normal civic duties in a democratic society' also falls
outside Article 6.[207] Thus an obligation to pay a fine[208] or to give evidence in court proceedings[209] is not a 'civil' obligation to which Article 6 applies. Other kinds of public law
cases that have been regarded as falling outside it include cases concerning the rights to
nationality;[210] liability for military service;[211] certain matters relating to the administration of justice;[212] education;[213] medical treatment;[214]public housing;[215] and the award of
administrative contracts.[216]

Concluding comments
As will be apparent, although the Court has maintained its private law meaning of 'civil'
rights and obligations, its evolving jurisprudence has led to a position in which, in addition to disputes between private persons, Article 6 regulates more kinds of disputes
between the individual and the state than that meaning might suggest. Thus cases concerning the public control of land, the regulation of commercial or professional activities
or practice, compensation claims against the state, social security and welfare assistance
rights, and some cases of public employment now fall within the bounds of the right to a
fair trial. This results partly from the extensive interpretation given by the Court to the
word 'determination'[217] in Article 6(1), but also from the Court's dynamic understanding of what amounts to a private law right or obligation for the purposes of Article 6. The
ingenious use of such all-embracing concepts as the rights to property or to engage in
commercial activities and especially the emphasis upon the pecuniary dimension of a
right or obligation has engineered considerable inroads into the realms of public law and
administrative justice—sometimes to the point where the Court's attempt to explain its
decisions in terms of private and public law as these concepts are understood in national
law appears artificial and unconvincing.

   It is arguable that the Court might do better to reformulate its approach in terms of
an abstract definition of 'civil' rights and obligations that starts from a different premise.
The Court's attempt to rationalize its approach in the *Ferrazzini* case has some merit,
but is not ultimately convincing or of comprehensive application. Given that European
states now commonly provide, or can be expected to provide, judicial remedies in areas
such as taxation, the control of aliens, and electoral matters, the dynamic approach to

---

[207] *Schouten and Meldrum v Netherlands* A 304 (1994); 19 EHRR 432 para 50.   [208] *Ibid.*
[209] *BBC v UK No 25798/94* hudoc (1996) DA. See also *Van Vondel v Netherlands* hudoc (2006) DA and
Burdov v Russia 2002-III; 38 EHRR 639. The failure to execute a judgment debt may be a breach of the right to
property in Article 1, Protocol 1 also: *ibid.*
[210] *S v Switzerland No 13325/87*, 59 DR 257 (1988). See also *Peltonen v Finland No 19583/92*, 80-A DR 38 (1995)
(passport); and *X v UK No 8208/78*, 16 DR 162 (1978) (peerage).
[211] *Nicolussi v Austria No 11734/85*, 52 DR 266 (1987) and *Zelisse v Netherlands No 12915/87*, 61 DR 230
(1989).
[212] *Schreiber and Boetsch v France No 58751/00* hudoc (2003) DA (challenge to a judge); *X v FRG No 3925/69*,
32 CD 56 (1970) (legal aid), but see *Gutfreund v France* 2003-VII; 42 EHRR 1076 paras 39–44; *B v UK No 10615/83*,
38 DR 213 (1984) (lawyers' costs); and *Atkinson, Crook and The Independent v UK No 13366/87*, 67 DR 244 (1990)
and *Loersch et al v Switzerland Nos 23868–9/94*, 80-A DR 162 (1995) (court reporting). On the disciplining of
prisoners (which may involve a 'criminal charge'), see *McFeeley v UK No 8317/78*, 20 DR 44 (1980), now subject
to *Ganci v Italy* 2003-XII; 41 EHRR 272.
[213] *Simpson v UK No 14688/89*, 64 DR 188 (1989) (elementary education) and *X v FRG No 10193/82*; 7 EHRR
141 (1984) (university).
[214] *L v Sweden No 10801/84*, 61 DR 62 (1988) Com Rep para 87; CM Res DH (89) 16.
[215] *Woonbron Volkshuisvestingsgroep v Netherlands No 47122/99* hudoc (2002); 35 EHRR CD 161. And see
X v Sweden No 9260/81, 6 EHRR 323 (1983) (tenants' associations).
[216] *LTC v Malta No 2629/06* hudoc (2007) DA.   [217] See below, p 226.

the interpretation of Article 6 that the Court properly adopts should lead it to a different conclusion from one which still seeks to exclude disputes in the area of 'public authority prerogatives'. Instead, 'civil' rights and obligations might be interpreted as referring to all legal rights and obligations that an individual arguably has under national law, regardless of the area of law concerned and the nature of any involvement by the state.[218] This would be in line both with human rights expectations and evolving national practice in administrative law in European states. The difficulty with such an approach, the Court has stated, is that the principle of dynamic interpretation 'does not give the Court the power to interpret Article 6(1) as though the adjective "civil"... were not present in the text'.[219] However, in view of its juxtaposition with 'criminal' in the wording of Article 6(1), the term 'civil' could—without doing violence to the text—be read as meaning any right or obligation in law that is not a criminal one. Short of that, some extension of the Court's present approach would be to emphasize the pecuniary character of the obligation to pay tax[220] and of some other public law rights and obligations, or of the pecuniary consequences of their breach. A further pragmatic extension of the Court's understanding of the scope of Article 6(1) would be to consider that insofar as states actually have courts or tribunals (including, for example, immigration or tax tribunals) with jurisdiction to determine cases concerning rights and obligations of whatever kind in national law, these should comply with Article 6.[221]

The satisfactory end result of such developments would be that a person would be guaranteed a 'right to a court' in the sense of Article 6 both to assert or question any arguable legal 'right or obligation' that the person has under national law[222] and to challenge by means of judicial review any administrative decision taken by the state that directly affects such rights or obligations. While it may not have been intended when the Convention was drafted that the right to a fair trial in Article 6 should have such a wide application, an extensive reading along these lines would be fully in line with the perception of the right to a fair trial as a human right.

b. The meaning of 'rights and obligations'

By 'rights and obligations' in Article 6 are meant 'rights and obligations' 'which can be said, at least on arguable grounds, to be recognised under domestic law'.[223] The requirement is only that the applicant have a 'tenable' argument, not that he will necessarily win.[224] If the applicant has no arguable right under national law,[225] Article 6 does not apply.[226] The fact that the state has under national law a discretion in responding to an

---

[218] Cf, the dissenting opinion of Judge Loucaides in *Maaouia v France* hudoc (2000); 33 EHRR 1037 GC. For other proposals, see Van Dyk, *Wiarda Mélanges*, p 131 and the dissenting opinion of Messrs Melchior and Frowein in *Benthem v Netherlands* B 80 (1983) para 10 Com Rep.

[219] *Ferrazzini v Italy* 2001-VII; 34 EHRR 1068 para 30 GC.

[220] See the dissenting opinion of Judge Lorenzen, joined by Judges Rozakis, Bonello, Stráznická, Bîrsan, and Fischbach, in the *Ferrazzini* case.

[221] Cf, the approach by which Article 6 applies to whatever appeal courts states have: see below, p 298. And see the dissenting opinion of Mr Alkema in *Maillard v France* 1998-III; 27 EHRR 232.

[222] Any restriction on the access to a court would have to be consistent with the *Ashingdane* case: below, p 239.

[223] *H v Belgium* A 127-B (1987); 10 EHRR 339 para 40 PC.

[224] *Neves e Silva v Portugal* A 153-A (1989); 13 EHRR 535 para 37. The right need only be 'arguable' when proceedings are commenced; changes in the law while they are pending are immaterial: *Reid v UK No 33221/96* hudoc (2001) DA.

[225] National law includes EC law for member states: *Papoulakos v Greece No 24960/94* hudoc (1995) DA.

[226] In *Gutfreund v France* 2003-VII; 42 EHRR 1076 para 39, the Court referred to rights in 'national law *or* the Convention' (italics added), suggesting that Article 6 also applies where a Convention right (in that case the

applicant's claim (eg when granting a licence) will not prevent Article 6 applying if 'it fol-lows from generally recognised legal and administrative principles that the authorities' do 'not have an unfettered discretion' when taking their decision.[227] In such a case, the applicant must be allowed to question whether the state has complied with these prin-ciples before a tribunal that satisfies the requirements of Article 6. Apart from this limita-tion, a discretionary decision is not subject to Article 6.[228]

Thus Article 6 does not control the content of a state's national law; it is only a proce-dural guarantee of a right to a fair hearing in the determination of whatever legal rights and obligations a state chooses to provide in its law. For example, in *James v UK*,[229] the applicants had been deprived of their ownership of certain properties by the exercise by their tenants of a right to acquire the properties that had been given to them by statute. The applicants had no remedy in court by which to challenge the exercise of this right. Although the case concerned their right to property, which was a 'civil' right, Article 6 did not come into play because the applicants had no arguable right under English law that had been infringed.

However, a limit to this approach was set in *Fayed v UK*.[230] There the applicants wanted to bring a claim in defamation arising out of a government inspector's report under the Companies Act 1985 which found that they had been dishonest. Whereas the law of def-amation extended to cover the facts of their claim, it would, as was generally agreed, have been successfully met by a defence of privilege. After referring with approval to its approach in the *James* case, the Court drew a distinction between substantive and pro-cedural limitations:

> Whether a person has an actionable domestic claim may depend not only on the sub-stantive content, properly speaking, of the relevant civil right as defined under national law but also on the existence of procedural bars preventing or limiting the possibilities of bringing potential claims to court. In the latter kind of case Article 6(1) may have a degree of applicability. Certainly the Convention enforcement bodies may not create by way of interpretation of Article 6(1) a substantive civil right which has no legal basis in the state concerned. However, it would not be consistent with the rule of law in a democratic society or with the basic principle underlying Article 6(1)—namely that civil claims must be cap-able of being submitted to a judge for adjudication—if, for example, a state could, without restraint or control by the Convention enforcement bodies, remove from the jurisdiction of the courts a whole range of civil claims or confer immunities from civil liability on large groups or categories of persons...

Thus, in the 'no legal basis' kind of case, the reasoning in the *James* case continues to apply so that, as in that case, if a state's legislation simply deprives a landowner of his right to his property, Article 6 does not apply; there is no legal basis for a claim that such

right to legal aid in criminal cases) is being disputed, whether it is recognized in national law (as the Convention requires) or not. But see *Neves e Silva v Portugal* A 152 (1989); 13 EHRR 535 para 36.

[227] *Pudas v Sweden* A 125-A (1987); 10 EHRR 380 para 34. Cf, *Allan Jacobsson v Sweden (No 1)* A 163 (1989); 12 EHRR 56. And see *Gustafson v Sweden* 1997-VI.

[228] *Masson and Van Zon v Netherlands* A 327-A (1995); 22 EHRR 491; *Anne-Marie Andersson v Sweden* 1997-IV; 25 EHRR 722 para 36; *Le Calvez v France* 1998-V; 32 EHRR 481; *Bozhilov v Bulgaria No 41978/98* hudoc (2001) DA; and *Massa v Italy* A 265-B (1993); 18 EHRR 266. The question whether Article 6 applies where in Italian law a person has 'legitimate interest [*interesse legitimo*]', but not a legal right, was left open in *Mennitto v Italy* 2000-X; 34 EHRR 1122 GC.

[229] A 98 (1986); 8 EHRR 123 para 81 PC. Cf, *Powell and Rayner v UK* A 172 (1990); 12 EHRR 335 (statute excluded liability in tort for aircraft noise). See also *McMichael v UK* A 307-B (1995); 20 EHRR 205.

[230] A 294-B (1994); 18 EHRR 393 para 65.

a right must be restored.[231] But in the *Fayed* 'removal from jurisdiction' or 'immunities' kind of case the rule of law dictates some degree of Convention 'restraint or control'. The vehicle for providing this 'restraint or control' is, the Court indicated in the *Fayed* case, the right of access to a court that Article 6 guarantees. As explained below,[232] in that case the Court, acting on the basis that Article 6 did otherwise apply,[233]concluded that the restriction upon the right of access presented on the facts of that case by the privilege defence to the applicant's' defamation claim could be justified as having a legitimate aim and as being in proportion to its attainment.

c. A 'contestation' or dispute concerning civil rights and obligations

For Article 6 to apply there must be a 'dispute' at the national level, between two private persons or between the applicant and the state, the outcome of which is determinative of the applicant's civil rights and obligations. The need for a 'dispute' follows from the use of the word '*contestation*' in the French text of Article 6. Generally, the Court has interpreted the 'dispute' requirement in such a way that it is not a significant hurdle.[234] It has held that '*contestation*' should not be 'construed too technically' and that it should be given a 'substantive rather than a formal meaning'.[235] This approach is adopted as being in accordance with the spirit of the Convention and because the term '*contestation*' has no counterpart in the English text, a fact that has led to hesitation as to its importance.[236]

A dispute may concern a question of law or of fact.[237] It need not concern the actual existence of a right, but may relate instead to its 'scope...or the manner in which the beneficiary may avail himself of it.'[238] The dispute must be 'genuine and of a serious nature'.[239] This requirement may exclude a case of a hypothetical kind, such as a case raising the question whether proposed legislation would, if enacted, infringe the applicant's rights,[240] or a case in which the applicant does not pursue his claim seriously, eg by not presenting evidence.[241] For the case to be 'genuine and serious', there must also be something 'at stake' for the applicant. In *Kienast v Austria*,[242] the applicant contested the unification of two small plots of land that he owned. It was held that Article 6 did not apply because the unification, which was part of a 'tidying up' exercise by the authorities, did not affect the applicant's ownership or use of his land or, in practice, his freedom to transfer ownership: as a result, his civil rights were not 'at stake'. It is not necessary that damages be claimed for a claim to be 'genuine and serious'; a request for a declaratory judgment is sufficient.[243]

---

[231] The absence of a right in national law may sometimes be an infringement of another Convention guarantee (eg, of the right to property or the right to privacy).

[232] See p 241.   [233] The Court found no need to decide this point.

[234] See *Oerlemans v Netherlands* A 219 (1991); 15 EHRR 561.

[235] *Le Compte, Van Leuven and De Meyere v Belgium* A 43 (1981); 4 EHRR 1 para 45 PC.

[236] In *Moreira de Azevedo v Portugal* A 189 (1990); 13 EHRR 721, the Court cast some doubt upon the very existence of the requirement ('if indeed it does' exist). Cf, the joint dissenting opinion of six judges in *W v UK* A 121 (1987); 10 EHRR 29 PC and the dissenting opinion of Judge de Meyer in *Kraska v Switzerland* A 254-B (1993); 18 EHRR 188.

[237] *Albert and Le Compte v Belgium* A 58 (1983); 5 EHRR 533 PC.

[238] *Le Compte, Van Leuven and De Meyere v Belgium* A 43 (1981); 4 EHRR 1 para 49 PC.

[239] *Benthem v Netherlands* A 97 (1985); 8 EHRR 1 para 32 PC.

[240] But a claim based upon enacted legislation of general application that affects the applicant is subject to Article 6: *Posti and Rahko v Finland* 2002-VII; 37 EHRR 158.

[241] *Kaukonen v Finland No 24738/94*, 91-A DR 14 (1997). See also *Kiryanov v Russia No 42212/02* hudoc (2005) DA.   [242] Hudoc (2003).

[243] *Helmers v Sweden* A 212 (1991); 15 EHRR 285 PC.

A 'dispute' must be justiciable, ie it must be one that inherently lends itself to judicial resolution. This was relevant in *Van Marle v Netherlands*.[244] There the Court held, by eleven to seven, that Article 6 was not applicable to a dispute concerning the applicants' registration as accountants. According to the reasoning in the Court's judgment, this was because the dispute was concerned essentially with the assessment of the applicants' competence as accountants, which was more akin to school or university examining than judging, whereas Article 6 is aimed at regulating only the latter. Curiously, however, this reasoning is only that of a minority of the Court. Three of the eleven judges who voted for the holding that Article 6 did not apply did so, according to their joint concurring opinion, on the basis that there *was* a 'dispute', but that the evaluation of professional competence by a public authority did not concern a civil right.[245] The seven dissenting judges were of the opinion both that there was a 'dispute' and that its outcome was determinative of a civil right, namely the right to exercise a profession. Even so, a requirement of justiciability is a sensible one that is in accordance with European national law.[246]

d. When are civil rights and obligations being determined?

Supposing that a dispute exists, it is still necessary to show that civil rights and obligations are being 'determined' by the decision to which it is sought to apply Article 6(1). This will be the case when the decision it is 'directly decisive' for the civil rights and obligations concerned.[247] This requirement is clearly met where the determination of the applicant's civil rights and obligations is the primary purpose of the decision-making process. Thus Article 6 undoubtedly applies, for instance, to a personal injuries claim in tort between private individuals before the ordinary courts,[248] and to a claim before an administrative court for negligence by a state hospital.[249]

In addition, it was held in *Ringeisen v Austria*[250] that Article 6 extends to proceedings which do not have the determination of 'civil rights and obligations' as their purpose, but which nonetheless are decisive for them. In that case, the applicant had entered into a contract to buy land from third parties. The sale was subject to the approval of an administrative tribunal which refused permission because the land would be used for non-agricultural purposes. The object of the proceedings before the tribunal—the granting of permission by reference to the public interest—clearly pertained to public law. Nonetheless, the Court held that civil rights and obligations were being determined:

> Although it was applying rules of administrative law, the Regional Commission's decision was to be decisive for the relations in civil law (*de caractère civil*) between Ringeisen and the Roth couple.[251]

In *Ringeisen v Austria*, the Court stated only that for Article 6 to apply the proceedings must be 'decisive' for civil rights and obligations. It was in *Le Compte v Belgium*[252] that the Court established that they must be '*directly* decisive' and that a 'tenuous connection or remote consequences do not suffice'. In that case, the applicants were Belgian

---

[244] A 101 (1986); 8 EHRR 483 PC. Cf, *Le Bihan v France No 63054/00* hudoc (2004) DA; *Nowicky v Austria* hudoc (2005); and *Kervoelen v France* hudoc (2001).

[245] This point was left open by the Court.

[246] Eg, in English law the courts will not review the assessment of examinations: *Thorne v University of London* [1966] 2 QB 237.

[247] *Ringeisen v Austria* A 13 (1971); 1 EHRR 455; *Le Compte, Van Leuven and De Meyere v Belgium* A 43 (1981); 4 EHRR 1 PC.

[248] See eg, *Guincho v Portugal* A 81 (1984); 7 EHRR 223.

[249] See eg, *H v France* A 162-A (1992); 12 EHRR 74.   [250] A 13 (1971); 1 EHRR 455.

[251] Id, para 94.   [252] A 43 (1981); 4 EHRR 1, para 47 PC. Italics added.

doctors who had been temporarily suspended from medical practice by the competent disciplinary bodies. The Court accepted that the primary purpose of the disciplinary proceedings was to decide whether breaches of the rules of professional conduct had occurred. Nonetheless, the proceedings were 'directly decisive' for the applicants' private law right to practise medicine because the suspension of the applicants' exercise of that right was a direct consequence of the decision that breaches of the rules had occurred.[253]

In contrast, the applicants 'civil rights' were not 'directly' being determined in *Athanassoglu v Switzerland*.[254] In that case, a decision to renew a licence for a nuclear power station was not subject to Article 6 because, despite the general public interest ramifications, it was not directly decisive for the rights to life, physical integrity, and property of applicants living nearby who were not able to produce evidence showing that the station's operation exposed them to a specific and imminent danger of an infringement of these rights. But civil rights were being determined in proceedings in which an association challenged the building of a dam because of its direct impact on the lifestyle and property of its members as well as on public interest environmental grounds.[255]

Article 6 does not apply where a decision being challenged is important for the applicant economically but does not determine his or her legal rights. Thus an application requesting a court to annul a presidential decree in favour of an airport runway as being unconstitutional did not fall within Article 6. While it was prejudicial to their economic activities relating to adjacent land that they owned, it left their legal rights intact.[256]

Before the *Le Compte* case, it had been possible to imagine that the effect of the *Ringeisen* case was to undermine the Article 6 distinction between private and public law to a very great extent indeed. For example, the decision to deport an alien might be thought to be subject to Article 6 if the alien had private law rights under a contract of employment that could only be performed in the deporting state. The *Le Compte* case makes clear that Article 6 would not apply in such a case; the connection between the public law decision to deport and the applicant's private law contract rights is too tenuous or remote.[257] However, where an applicant had agreed contractual terms to take up a post as a company chief executive but was prevented by law from doing so because a government minister had objected that he was not fit to hold such a post, the objection was directly decisive for the latter's right to take up the post.[258]

Despite the limiting effect of the *Le Compte* case, the impact of the *Ringeisen* case in extending Article 6 to cases in which the 'determination' of civil rights and obligations is a consequence, but not the purpose, of the proceedings has been considerable. In particular, it has provided the basis upon which cases involving decisions by administrative tribunals and, most significantly, by the executive regulating private rights in the public interest are brought within the reach of Article 6.[259]

---

[253] Disciplinary proceedings that result in a lesser penalty than suspension (eg, a fine) fall within Article 6 provided that interference with the exercise of the right (by suspension or termination) is 'at stake': *A v Finland No 44998/98* hudoc (2004); 38 EHRR CD 223 and *WR v Austria* hudoc (1999); 31 EHRR 985.

[254] 2000-IV; 31 EHRR 372 GC, following *Balmer-Schafroth v Switzerland* 1997-IV; 25 EHRR 598 PC. Contrast *Okay v Turkey* 2005-VII; 43 EHRR 788. See also *Martin v Ireland No 8569/79*, 42 DR 23 (1985) (*actio popularis* not within Article 6).

[255] *Gorraiz Lizarraga v Spain* 2004-III.

[256] *SARL de Parc d'activities de Blotzheim v France No 48897/99*, 2003-III DA. Cf, *Krafft and Rougeot v France No 11543/85*, 65 DR 51 (1990).

[257] *Saleem v UK No 38294/97*; hudoc (1998) 25 EHRR CD 193 DA. Cf, *X v UK No 7902/77*, 9 DR 224 (1977). See also *Zelisse v Netherlands No 12915/87*, 61 DR 230 (1989) (call-up for conscription in effect ended employment) and *Maaouia v France* 2000-X; 33 EHRR 1037 para 38 GC.

[258] *X v UK No 28530/95* hudoc (1998) DA.   [259] See below, p 228.

Article 6 does not apply, however, to a report that results from an official investigation making findings of fact that bear upon an individual's 'civil rights and obligations', but that is not determinative of them. This question arose in *Fayed v UK*[260] in which an inspector had been appointed by the government to investigate the affairs of a public company on suspicion of fraud. The inspector's report contained findings that were detrimental to the applicants' right to a reputation, which was a 'civil right' for the purposes of Article 6. Drawing a distinction between investigation and adjudication, the Court held that Article 6 did not apply to the inspector's investigation; although it resulted in a finding that the applicants had been dishonest, this finding was not 'dispositive of anything' in terms of legal rights and duties in the way that a 'determination' in the sense of Article 6 needed to be.

Civil rights and obligations may be determined in criminal proceedings. This is so, for example, where a criminal prosecution is the remedy provided in national law for the enforcement of a civil right, as, for example, in some legal systems in connection with the right to a reputation.[261] Article 6 also applies when a legal system allows the victim of a crime to be joined as a civil party in criminal proceedings against the offender in order to obtain damages or otherwise protect his or her civil rights; however, it does not apply in such cases where the victim's purpose in being joined is to punish the offender or to intervene on an *actio popularis* basis, not to obtain a personal civil remedy.[262]

Finally, proceedings before a constitutional court involve the determination of civil rights and obligations where their outcome is capable of being decisive for those rights.[263]

e. The application of Article 6(1) in the context of administrative decisions[264]

Many decisions that are determinative of a person's civil rights and obligations are taken by the executive or some other body that is not a tribunal in the sense of Article 6. A question which arose following the *Ringeisen* case[265] was whether the Court would say that all such decisions should be transferred to a body that was independent of the executive and otherwise complied with Article 6, or that executive decisions by government departments, local authorities, etc, should all be taken after a hearing conducted by them that complied with Article 6. Either requirement would have been impracticable and quite out of keeping with European traditions. So it is both a relief and sensible that the Court has ruled that neither of these things is called for. Instead, what Article 6 requires is that there must be the possibility of judicial review, or in some cases an appeal on the merits, of administrative decisions that are directly decisive for civil rights and obligations by a body that complies with Article 6.[266] Although this is an approach that conforms to practice generally in most European states, it has presented serious problems for some

---

[260] A 294-B (1994); 18 EHRR 393 para 61. See also *Kervoelen v France* hudoc (2001).

[261] See eg, *Helmers v Sweden* A 212-A (1991); 15 EHRR 285 PC. But Article 6 does not apply if the defamation prosecution is intended to punish: *Rekasi v Hungary* No 315061/96, 87-A DR 164 (1996).

[262] *Perez v France* 2004-I; 40 EHRR 909 GC. See also *Garimpo v Portugal* No 66752/01 hudoc (2004) DA.. The requirements of Article 6 may be satisfied by the criminal court that imposes a conviction that is decisive for a 'civil' right (eg, to practise a profession): *X v Belgium* No 8901/80, 23 DR 237 (1980).

[263] *Sussman v Germany* 1996-IV; 25 EHRR 64; *Gorraiz Lizarraga v Spain* 2004-III; *Voggenreiter v Germany* 2004-I; 42 EHRR 456. For a case in which the constitutional court proceedings were *not* decisive, see *Bakaric v Croatia* No 48077/ 99, 2001-IX.

[264] See Boyle, 1984 PL 89.   [265] See above, p 226.

[266] *Le Compte, Van Leuven and De Meyere v Belgium* A 43 (1981); 4 EHRR 1 para 51 PC.

such states, where the tradition had been of appeal or review that was technically within the executive branch of government, and not of recourse to the courts.[267]

As stated in *Bryan v UK*,[268] what is required by way of recourse to an Article 6 tribunal in this context depends upon the 'subject matter of the decision appealed against, the manner in which that decision was arrived at, and the content of the dispute, including the desired and actual grounds of appeal'. In some cases, depending on the 'subject matter of the decision appealed against', the Court has insisted that there be an appeal on both the facts and the law before a tribunal that complies with Article 6.[269] The first cases in which the Court expressed a clear opinion on the matter concerned decisions by professional disciplinary bodies rather than public bodies. In *Albert and Le Compte v Belgium*,[270] in which the applicant doctors wished to challenge disciplinary decisions against them on their merits, the decisions themselves were taken by a professional association, with a right of appeal to another such body and finally to the Belgian Court of Cassation. The European Court stated that the Convention required either that the associations meet the requirements of Article 6 or 'they do not so comply but are subject to subsequent control by a judicial body that has full jurisdiction and does so provide the guarantees of Article 6(1)'. Article 6(1) was not complied with in the case because the professional associations, which could rule on the facts, did not sit in public and because the Court of Cassation, which met all of the procedural demands of Article 6(1), could only consider points of law.

Then, in *W v UK*,[271] the Court held that the judicial review available in UK administrative law was insufficient in a case in which parents wished to challenge on the merits, or facts, a local authority decision restricting access to a child in care. The Court stated that in 'a case of the present kind', ie one concerning access to children, the Convention required that a tribunal that complied with Article 6 have 'jurisdiction to examine the merits'.[272] As the Court noted, in UK administrative law, 'on an application for judicial review, the courts do not review the merits of the decision but confine themselves to ensuring, in brief, that the authority did not act illegally, unreasonably or unfairly'.[273] A similar decision was taken in an employment context in *Obermeier v Austria*.[274] In that case, there was no appeal to a tribunal on the merits against the decision of a government body to the effect that the applicant's dismissal was lawful as having been 'socially justified'. Although it was possible to appeal to the Austrian Administrative Court on the ground that the government body had exercised its discretion in a manner incompatible with the object and purpose of the law, such 'limited review' did not comply with Article 6(1). In a series of subsequent cases in other contexts, the Court has likewise held

---

[267] See eg, *Benthem v Netherlands* A 97 (1985); 8 EHRR 1 PC and *Ravnsborg v Sweden* A 283-B (1994); 18 EHRR 38. In Soviet style legal systems, recourse was often to the *procuratura*, not the courts: see eg, *Vasilescu v Romania* 1998-III 73; 28 EHRR 241.

[268] A 335-A (1995); 21 EHRR 342 para 45.

[269] In such cases, this is a right of appeal, not of judicial review, in the terminology of UK public law. The Court sometimes uses the term judicial review more generally, to include both appeal and judicial review in the UK law sense.

[270] A 58 (1983); 5 EHRR 533 para 29 PC. Cf, the brief statement in *Le Compte, Van Leuven and De Meyere* case, A 43 (1981); 4 EHRR 1 para 51 PC. On professional disciplinary cases, see *Stefan v UK No 29149/95* hudoc (1997); 25 EHRR CD 130, in which the less strict *Bryan* approach was followed.

[271] A 121 (1987); 10 EHRR 293 PC.   [272] Id, para 82.

[273] *Ibid*. Cf, *Weeks v UK* A 114 (1987); 10 EHRR 293 PC in which judicial review was insufficient for Article 5(4).

[274] A 179 (1990); 13 EHRR 290 para 70. See also *Fischer v Austria* A 312 (1995); 20 EHRR 349 and *Schmautzer v Austria* A 328-A (1995); 21 EHRR 511.

that Article 6 requires that a tribunal that complies with Article 6 must, either when the initial decision is taken or on appeal, have 'jurisdiction to examine all questions of fact and law relevant to the dispute before it'.[275]

The situation is different in cases in which the administrative decision being challenged involves what the Court has called 'the classic exercise of administrative discretion'.[276] In such cases, there may be policy considerations that suggest that the final decision on the merits should rest with the executive, rather than a court, despite the impact upon a person's 'civil rights and obligations' that the decision may have. Decisions concerning the expropriation of land for a road or for public housing are obvious cases in which this can be argued. In such cases, judicial review of the legality of the decision by a tribunal that complies with Article 6 is sufficient: a right of appeal on the merits is not required. This was intimated in *Zumtobel v Austria*,[277] in which the applicant's' right of appeal to the Austrian Administrative Court against an order made by a government office for the expropriation of his land in order to build a road complied with Article 6, even though the Administrative Court's jurisdiction was limited to the question of the lawfulness of the order and did not extend to full jurisdiction on all questions of law and fact. Explaining this decision, the Strasbourg Court stated that regard had to be had to the 'respect which must be accorded to decisions taken by the administrative authorities on grounds of expediency'.

However judicial review of the legality of the decision will only be sufficient in such cases of the 'classic exercise of administrative discretion' if the initial decision on the merits is taken by an administrative body that follows a procedure *that sufficiently complies with Article 6*. It is in this regard that the 'manner in which' the 'decision was arrived at' is important.[278] The key case in this respect is *Bryan v UK*.[279] There the applicant challenged a planning decision against him, involving the 'application of a panoply of policy matters', that had been taken by a planning inspector who, the Court held, did not meet the requirement of objective independence in Article 6. The Strasbourg Court held that the judicial review proceedings which the applicant was able to bring in the English High Court to challenge the decision were sufficient to satisfy Article 6 because, although the High Court could not re-hear the case on the merits,[280] it had jurisdiction to rule on any errors of law, which was all that the applicant wished to argue. What is important about the *Bryan* case for the present purpose is that the Court stated that, supposing the applicant had wanted to question the inspector's findings of fact, there would still have been no breach of Article 6 because the inspector's decision had been taken by 'a quasi-judicial procedure governed by many of the safeguards required by Article 6(1)'.[281] In particular,

---

[275] *Terra Woningen v Netherlands* 1996-VI; 24 EHRR 456 para 53. See also, eg, *Koskinas v Greece* hudoc (2002); *Chevrol v France* 2003-III; *Crisan v Romania* hudoc (2003); *Veeber v Estonia (No 1)* hudoc (2002); *Kilian v Czech Rep* hudoc (2004); *Capital Bank v Bulgaria* 2005-XII; *Linnekogel v Switzerland* hudoc (2005); and *Schmautzer v Austria* A 328-A (1995); 21 EHRR 511 (road traffic offence). See also *Tsfayo v UK* hudoc (2006).

[276] *Kingsley v UK* 2002-IV para 32 GC. A characteristic of such cases is that the decision requires 'professional' (or 'specialist') knowledge or experience and the exercise of administrative discretion pursuant to wider policy aims: *Tsfayo v UK* hudoc (2006) para 46. Decisions involving 'simple questions of fact' must be taken on their merits by a body complying with Article 6: *ibid*.

[277] A 268-A (1993); 17 EHRR 116 para 32. See also *ISKCON v UK No 20490/92*, 76-A DR 90 (1994).

[278] See above at n 268.

[279] A 335-A (1995); 21 EHRR 342 para 47. See also *Chapman v UK* 2001-I; 33 EHRR 399 GC and *Potocka v Poland* 2001-X.

[280] The High Court could, as the Strasbourg Court noted, intervene on the merits if, but only if, the findings of fact were perverse or irrational.

[281] *Id*, para 47. See also *Holding and Barnes v UK* 2002-IV and *APB Ltd et al v UK No 30552/96* hudoc (1998) DA.

the Court held that the procedures followed by the inspector were in accordance with the Article 6(1) residual obligation to ensure a 'fair hearing'; the failure to comply with Article 6(1) was only that the inspector did not meet the requirement of objective independence. The limitation of the power of review in this situation to points of law was, the Court noted, 'frequently a feature in the systems of judicial control of administrative decisions found throughout the Council of Europe member states'.[282]

At the same time, it follows from the Court's judgment in the *Bryan* case that if the initial administrative decision in cases of the 'classic exercise of administrative discretion' does not involve a quasi-judicial procedure that sufficiently complies with Article 6—for example, in an extreme case, if it is taken by an official in his office without any hearing of the applicant—then Article 6 requires an appeal for a final decision on the merits before a tribunal, if and to the extent that it is such an appeal that the applicant wishes to make.[283]

This last comment goes to a separate, important point in the Court's jurisprudence that is confirmed in the *Bryan* case. Article 6 is complied with if the applicant who is challenging an administrative decision has an opportunity to have a ruling by a tribunal that complies with Article 6 on the arguments that he wishes to make.[284] If the applicant has this opportunity, as he had in the *Bryan* case, it does not matter that the tribunal lacks jurisdiction to consider other points of law or fact that some other applicant might wish to raise. It is in this way that, as stated in the *Bryan* case, 'the content of the dispute, including the desired and actual grounds of appeal'[285] is relevant.

In cases of the 'classic exercise of administrative discretion', Article 6 also requires, again under the heading of 'the contents of the dispute', that the reviewing tribunal have competence to act to ensure a remedy is provided for the applicant if successful. This was crucial in *Kingsley v UK*.[286] In that case, the Gaming Board decided, after a hearing before a panel of three of its members, that the applicant was not a 'fit and proper' person to hold a management position in the gaming industry and revoked his certificate to do so. The applicant applied to the High Court for judicial review of the decision, claiming that the panel had not been impartial. Although agreeing that the panel did not meet the requirement of objective impartiality, the High Court found itself unable to quash the Gaming Board's decision on this ground because of the English law 'doctrine of necessity', the Board having been expressly designated by legislation as the body with the authority to decide the matter. The Strasbourg Court held that there was a breach of the right of access in Article 6 because the concept of 'full jurisdiction' articulated in the *Albert and Le Compte* case,[287] above, meant that the reviewing court must not only be able to 'consider the complaint but has the ability to quash the impugned decision and to remit the case for a new decision', in this case by an impartial tribunal.[288]

In terms of the grounds upon which an applicant may wish to seek a judicial review on points of law, a further question that arises is whether the tribunal to which recourse may be had should be competent to rule upon the proportionality of the decision. It has been established by the Court that the effective remedy concerning a violation of Convention rights required by Article 13 of the Convention must be one in which the individual may challenge the proportionality of the decision allegedly amounting to a violation of

---

[282] *Bryan v UK* A 335-A (1995); 21 EHRR 342 para 47.

[283] See eg, *Tsfayo v UK* hudoc (2006) in which there were insufficient procedural safeguards where housing benefit decisions were taken by a board composed of members of the local authority that would pay the benefit.

[284] Cf, *Oerlermans v Netherlands* A 219 (1991); 15 EHRR 561; *Zumtobel v Austria* A 268-A (1993); 17 EHRR 116 and *Ortenberg v Austria* A 295-B (1994); 19 EHRR 524. See also *X v UK No 28530/95* hudoc (1998); 25 EHRR CD 88; *Wickramsinghe v UK No 31503/96* hudoc (1997) DA; and *Crabtree v UK No 32788/96* hudoc (1997) DA.

[285] See above n 268.   [286] 2002-IV GC.   [287] See above, p 229.   [288] Id, para 32.

a Convention right.[289] There has been no case in which this question has been decided under Article 6 in respect of civil rights and obligations.[290] It seems likely and desirable, given the existing and developing position in European national law,[291] and the requirement of proportionality in the jurisprudence of the European Court of Justice,[292] that the Strasbourg Court would require that a person be allowed to raise the question of proportionality in judicial review proceedings before an Article 6 tribunal.

The Court's interpretation of the requirements of Article 6 in the *Bryan* case largely resolves a problem that the Court had created for itself by its early ruling in the *Ringeisen* case, regarding cases of 'the classic exercise of administrative discretion'. At the same time, inventive though it is, it involves a very forced reading of Article 6. The same text of Article 6 now has two different meanings according to the kind of case involved. It applies fully in ordinary private law cases between private individuals and in cases involving state action such as *W v UK* and *Obermeier v Austria*, requiring that the facts and the law be determined finally by a tribunal complying with Article 6. It also applies, but to a lesser extent and in a way for which the text makes no allowance, in public law cases that involve 'the classic exercise of administrative discretion'. This is in line with European national law and the end result is to uphold the rule of law in cases of administrative action. It now remains for the Court to complete the picture by extending further its interpretation of 'civil rights and obligations'[293] for the Convention to provide a full guarantee of administrative justice that is appropriate to the present day.

f. The stages of proceedings covered by Article 6(1)

Article 6 normally begins to apply in cases involving the determination of a person's civil rights and obligations when court proceedings are instituted.[294] But, just as in criminal cases it may apply before the competent court is seized,[295] so too in civil cases Article 6 may begin to run before the writ is issued.[296] This has been held to be so in cases in which the applicant must exhaust a preliminary administrative remedy under national law before having recourse to a court or tribunal[297] or cases in which the applicant objects to a draft plan for land consolidation prior to a tribunal hearing.[298] In the first situation, the Court emphasized that, since the applicant had to exhaust such a remedy, it was only fair to require that this occur expeditiously. In the second situation, the Court's reasoning was that a dispute or '*contestation*' concerning civil rights and obligations arose when the objections to the draft plan were officially lodged, not later when the applicant instituted tribunal proceedings after being served with notice of the decision to take his or her land.

---

[289] *Smith and Grady v UK* 1999-VI; 29 EHRR 493.

[290] The point was raised in argument in *Air Canada v UK* A 316-A (1995); 20 EHRR 150 para 57.

[291] See Schwarze, *European Administrative Law*, 1992, p 680. Proportionality is not yet a ground for judicial review in UK law, but is gradually 'infiltrating British law': Wade and Forsyth, *Administrative Law*, 9th edn 2004, p 366.

[292] See Craig and de Búrca, *EU Law: Text, Cases and Materials*, 4th edn, 2008, pp 544ff.

[293] See above, pp 210 *et seq*.

[294] See eg, *Guincho v Portugal* A 81 (1984); 7 EHRR 223. The point at which Article 6 begins to apply in 'civil rights and obligation' cases is mostly relevant in 'trial within a reasonable time' cases, but it has significance in some other contexts, such as the right of access to a lawyer: see below, p 321.

[295] See above, p 209.   [296] *Golder v UK* A 18 (1975); 1 EHRR 524 PC.

[297] *König v FRG* A 27 (1978); 2 EHRR 170 PC. Cf, *Schouten and Meldrum v Netherlands* A 304 (1994); 19 EHRR 432 para 62.

[298] *Erkner and Hofauer v Austria* A 117 (1987); 9 EHRR 464 para 64. Cf, *Wiesinger v Austria* A 213 (1991); 16 EHRR 258. Article 6 does not apply, however, to private negotiations to solve a dispute before it is referred to arbitration: *Lithgow v UK* A 102 (1986); 8 EHRR 329 para 199 PC.

Article 6 applies not only to the proceedings in which liability is determined but also to any separate court proceedings in which the amount of damages is assessed[299] or costs are allocated[300] since these proceedings are a continuation of the substantive litigation. Article 6 also applies beyond the trial stage to appeal and judicial review proceedings concerning civil rights and obligations.[301] The reasonable time guarantee applies until the time for an appeal or application for judicial review by the parties expires and the judgment becomes final.[302]

Article 6 also applies to the execution of judgments; in particular, the reasonable time guarantee will apply to any delays for which the state is responsible in their execution.[303] This has proved to be an important ruling, with a number of violations being found. The leading case is *Hornsby v Greece*[304] in which the state authorities had for more than five years not taken the measures necessary to comply with a final judgment in the Greek courts entitling the applicants, who were UK nationals, to establish a private English school in Greece. The Court justified its extension of the 'right to a court' to the execution of judgments, which is not expressly mentioned in Article 6, on the basis that the 'right to a court' would be 'illusory' if a final judgment were allowed to remain inoperative to the detriment of one party and that 'to construe Article 6 as being concerned exclusively with access to a court and the conduct of proceedings would be likely to lead to situations incompatible with the principle of the rule of law which the Contracting States undertook to respect when they ratified the Convention'.

The cases have concerned such matters as the execution by the state of judgments requiring its authorities to pay compensation[305] or to provide public housing.[306] In *Okyay v Turkey*,[307] there was a breach of Article 6 where the administrative authorities failed to comply with court orders upheld by the Supreme Administrative Court for the closure of state power plants, which were causing pollution. A Turkish Council of Ministers' decision that the plants should continue to operate despite the court orders was stated by the Strasbourg Court in a strongly worded judgment to be 'obviously unlawful under domestic law', resulting in a situation that 'adversely affects the principle of a law-based state, founded on the rule of law ands the principle of legal certainty'.

The *Hornsby* case also applies to the release from prison of an accused person, in execution of a judgment acquitting him of a criminal offence. Thus in *Assanidze v Georgia*,[308] it was held that the continued detention of the applicant in a remand prison in the Ajarian Autonomous Republic, over which the central government had no control, more than

[299] *Silva Pontes v Portugal* A 286-A (1994); 18 EHRR 156 para 33.

[300] *Robins v UK* 1997-V; 26 EHRR 527 and *Ziegler v Switzerland* hudoc (2002). Proceedings for the award of costs where the applicant had withdrawn her claim were held not to fall within Article 6 in *Alsterlund v Sweden* No 12446/86 56 DR 229 (1988).

[301] *König v FRG* A 27 (1978); 2 EHRR 170 para 98 PC. In *Pretto v Italy* A 71 (1983); 6 EHRR 182 para 30 PC the 'reasonable time' guarantee ran until the Court of Cassation judgment was deposited with the court registry, whereupon it became public.

[302] *Pugliese v Italy (No 2)* A 206-A (1991); para 16. See also *Lorenzi, Bernardini, and Gritti v Italy* A 231-G (1992). In *Pretto v Italy* A 71 (1983); 6 EHRR 182 para 30 PC the 'reasonable time' guarantee ran until the Court of Cassation judgment was deposited with the court registry, whereupon it became public.

[303] *Hornsby v Greece* 1997-II; 24 EHRR 250. The *Hornsby* case only applies to final judgments; any appeal possibilities must be exhausted first: *Ouzounis v Greece* hudoc (2002). Article 6 does not extend to proceedings brought by an applicant who is challenging the enforcement of a judgment, unless, exceptionally, they raise issues going to the merits of the applicant's 'civil obligations': *Hofer v Austria* No 26591/95, 89-A DR 56 (1997) and *Jensen v Denmark* No 14063/88, 68 DR 177 (1991). Arguably, the right to effective access as interpreted in *Hornsby* should extend to such enforcement proceedings also.

[304] Id, para 40.   [305] *Burdov v Russia* 2002-III; 38 EHRR 644.

[306] *Teteriny v Russia* hudoc (2005).   [307] 2005-VII; 43 EHRR 788 para 73.

[308] 2004-II; 39 EHRR 653 GC.

three years after his acquittal on appeal by the Supreme Court of Georgia was a breach of Article 6, under the *Hornsby* principle. The Court found it unnecessary to determine whether the fault lay at the central or regional government level, as the Georgian national government was in any event responsible for all state acts or omissions, including those of the Ajarian Republic.

Under the *Hornsby* case, the state must also ensure the execution of judgments against third parties who are not state actors, so that, for example, the state must take action to ensure that private persons comply with judgments against them for the payment of compensation,[309] the transfer of custody of an adopted child,[310] the eviction of tenants,[311] and the demolition of houses built without planning permission.[312] Police assistance must be provided for court bailiffs where this is needed.[313] In *Turczanik v Poland*,[314] the state was required to ensure that a bar association allocated a barrister to chambers as required by a court judgment. No particular procedure for execution is required; the Court looks only to see that the procedure followed by the state is adequate and effective.[315]

Adopting an appropriately strict approach, the Court has held that lack of available state funds[316] or other resources[317] is not a good reason for the state's failure to execute a judgment against it. But a delay in the execution of a judgment may be justified 'in particular circumstances', provided that the delay does not 'impair the essence of the right protected under Article 6'.[318] The onus is on the state to justify any delay.[319] In *Jasiuniene v Lithuania*[320] the government's obstructive attitude led to the Court to characterize the non-execution as an 'aggravated' breach of Article 6(1).

Whereas Article 6 applies to the execution of final judgments, it does not govern interlocutory court proceedings. These include a challenge to the composition of a court,[321] a request for interim relief,[322] an application for leave to appeal,[323] or an application to re-open a civil case.[324] The question whether the reasonable time guarantee applies to a pre-trial application for legal aid in respect of litigation concerning a 'civil' right or obligation was left open in *H v France*.[325] The Court's generally negative approach in respect of interlocutory proceedings is based upon the view that a person's rights and obligations

---

[309] *Satka v Greece* hudoc (2003); 38 EHRR 579.   [310] *Pini v Romania* 2004-V; 40 EHRR 312.

[311] *Immobiliare Saffi v Italy* 1999-V; 30 EHRR 756 GC and *Kyrtatos v Greece* 2003-IV; 40 EHRR 390. See also *Popov v Moldova* hudoc (2005) (return of house to pre-Soviet owners).

[312] *Antonetto v Italy* hudoc (2000); 36 EHRR 120.

[313] *Immobiliare Saffi v Italy* 1999-V; 30 EHRR 756 GC.

[314] 2005-VI.   [315] *Fociac v Romania* hudoc (2005).

[316] *Burdov v Russia* 2002-III; 38 EHRR 639. The failure to execute a judgment debt may be a breach of the right to property in Article 1, Protocol 1 also: *ibid*. As to a requirement that a litigant pay the cost of enforcement, see *Apostol v Georgia*, below, n 356.

[317] Eg, public housing: *Shpakovskiy v Russia* hudoc (2005) .

[318] *Burdov v Russia* 2002-III; 38 EHRR 639 para 35. The conduct of the parties may excuse some delay: *Jasiuniene v Lithuania* hudoc (2003).

[319] The onus is on the state to justify the delay: *Dubenko v Ukraine* hudoc (2005). The state's obligation to execute a judgment expeditiously increases with the applicant's need: *ibid* (money to avoid bankruptcy) and *Shmalko v Ukraine* hudoc (2004) (payment for medication).

[320] Hudoc (2003) para 30.   [321] *Schreiber and Boetsch v France No 58751/00*, 2003-XII.

[322] *Lamprecht v Austria No 71888/01* hudoc (2004) DA (preservation of evidence) and *Hagman v Finland No 41765/98*, 36 EHRR CD 245 (stay of forced sale). But Article 6 does apply where an interim order for relief effectively determines the merits: *Markass Car Hire v Cyprus No 51591/99* hudoc (2001).

[323] *Porter v UK No 12972/87*, 54 DR 207 (1987) and *Hautakangas v Finland No 61560/00* hudoc (2004) DA.

[324] *Rudan v Croatia No 45943/99* hudoc (2001) DA. But Article 6 may apply to the re-opened proceedings themselves: *Kaisti v Finland No 70313/01* hudoc (2004) DA.

[325] A 162-A (1989); 12 EHRR 74 para 49. See further *Gutfreund v France* 2003-VII; 42 EHRR 1076 paras 38–44.

are only being determined in the sense of Article 6(1) when they are being ruled upon on the merits. While this is a tenable interpretation, it is not a necessary one and does not recognize the importance that decisions taken in interlocutory proceedings may have for the outcome of the case on the merits. An interpretation that included interlocutory proceedings would be more in accordance with a right of effective access to a court and with a purposive, human rights reading of the Convention.

3. ARTICLE 6(1): GUARANTEES IN CRIMINAL AND NON-CRIMINAL CASES

I. THE RIGHT OF ACCESS TO A COURT

a. The *Golder* case

One of the most creative steps taken by the European Court in its interpretation of any article of the Convention has been its ruling in *Golder v UK*[326] that Article 6(1) guarantees the right of access to a court. In that case, a convicted prisoner was refused permission by the Home Secretary to write to a solicitor with a view to instituting civil proceedings in libel against a prison officer. The Court held that the refusal raised an issue under Article 6(1) because that provision concerned not only the conduct of proceedings in court once they had been instituted, but also the right to institute them in the first place. Although there was no express mention of the right of access in Article 6, its protection could be inferred from the text.[327] It was also a key feature of the concept of the 'rule of law', which, as the preamble to the Convention stated, was a part of the 'common heritage' of Council of Europe states. Moreover, any other interpretation would contradict a universally recognized principle of law and would allow a state to close its courts without infringing the Convention. Despite cogent arguments to the contrary by the dissenting judges,[328] the Court's judgment has long been unquestioned and provides a secure foundation for the full guarantee of the 'right to a court'.[329]

The right was established and retains most of its significance in connection with the determination of 'civil rights and obligations'. Cases may concern private litigation, as in the *Golder* case, or claims against the state, including claims arising out of administrative decisions.[330] But it also applies to criminal cases, where it means that the accused is entitled to be tried on the charge against him in a court.[331] The right of access does not

---

[326] A 18 (1975); 1 EHRR 524 PC.

[327] The wording '*à ce que sa cause soit entendue*' in the French text provided the clearest textual indication.

[328] See the separate opinions of Judges Verdross, Fitzmaurice, and Zekia. The last two of these judges noted, *inter alia*, that in at least some other instruments in which it had been intended to include the right of access, a separate provision had been inserted in addition to the equivalent of Article 6. On Judge Fitzmaurice's generally restrictive approach to the interpretation of the Convention, see above, p 6.

[329] By this term is meant the right of access to a court and the guarantees in Article 6 once proceedings are instituted: *Golder v UK* A 18 (1975); 1 EHRR 524 para 36 PC.

[330] See eg, *Sporrong and Lönnroth v Sweden* A 52 (1982); 5 EHRR 35 PC (no appeal to a court against expropriation permit) and *Keegan v Ireland* A 290 (1994); 18 EHRR 342 para 59 (no appeal to a court against an adoption decision). See also *Linnekogel v Switzerland* hudoc (2005). As to the judicial review of administrative decisions required by Article 6, see above, pp 228 *et seq*. A decree that has general application but that is decisive for particular persons' civil rights and obligations must be subject to challenge by them: *Posti and Rahko v Finland* 2002-VII; 37 EHRR 158.

[331] *Deweer v Belgium* A 35 (1980); 2 EHRR 439. The right of access may be complied with in criminal proceedings to which the applicant is joined as a third party: *Anagnostopoulos v Greece* hudoc (2003).

include the right to bring a private criminal prosecution[332] since Article 6 is concerned only with a 'criminal charge' against an accused.[333]

The right of access means access in fact, as well as in law. It was for this reason that there was a breach of Article 6(1) in the *Golder* case.[334] Whereas the applicant was able in law to institute libel proceedings in the High Court, the refusal to let him contact a solicitor impeded his access to the courts in fact. It did not matter that, directly, the applicant's complaint was of an interference with his right of access to a solicitor, not the courts;[335] that he might have made contact with his solicitor other than by correspondence; that after doing so he might never have instituted court proceedings at all; or that the applicant would have been able to have written to his solicitor before his claim became statute-barred after his release from prison. A partial or temporary hindrance may thus be a breach of the right of access to a court.

b. A right of effective access

As the ruling in the *Golder* case also indicates, the right is a right of effective access to the courts. This may entail legal assistance, as was established in *Airey v Ireland*.[336] In that case a wife who was indigent was refused legal aid to bring proceedings in the Irish High Court for an order of judicial separation. Given the particular nature of the proceedings,[337] the Court held that, for the applicant's access to the court to be effective, she required legal representation, which for an indigent person meant free legal representation.[338] The Court rejected the respondent government's argument that the right of access to a court does not impose positive obligations upon states, particularly ones with considerable economic consequences, such as that to provide free legal aid.[339]

The *Airey* case has been applied in a number of cases in which civil legal aid has been claimed as a part of the right of access in Article 6(1).[340] In the *Airey* case, the Court stressed that it was not deciding that the right of access provided a full right to legal aid in civil litigation comparable to that specifically provided by Article 6(3)(c) in criminal cases, which extends to all cases in which 'the interests of justice so require'.[341] Instead, 'Article 6(1) may sometimes compel the state to provide for the assistance of a lawyer when such assistance proves indispensable for an effective access to court'.[342] This will

---

[332] *Rekasi v Hungary No 31506/96*, 87-A DR 164 (1996). Nor is there a right to have criminal proceedings instituted by the state against a third person: *Dubowska and Skup v Poland Nos 33490/95 and 34055/95*, 89-A DR 156 (1997).

[333] See above, p 204.

[334] Similar breaches of the right of access have been found in other UK prisoner cases involving restrictions on contact with solicitors: see eg, *Silver v UK* A 61 (1983); 5 EHRR 347. See also *Grace v UK No 11523/85*, 62 DR 22 (1988); Com Rep; CM Res DH (89) 21. The 'prior ventilation rule', by which prisoners were required to exhaust prison complaints procedures before resorting to the courts, also infringed it: *Campbell and Fell v UK*, A 80 (1984); 7 EHRR 165.

[335] As the Court noted, the applicant could institute court proceedings without recourse to a solicitor.

[336] A 32 (1979); 2 EHRR 305. See Thornberry, 29 ICLQ 250 (1980).

[337] The Court emphasized the complexity of the proceedings, the need to examine expert witnesses, and the emotional involvement of the parties. Cf *P, C and S v UK* 2002-VI (child care and adoption proceedings; legal aid required). Contrast *Webb v UK No 9353/81*, 33 DR 133 (1983).

[338] Ireland had made a reservation concerning criminal legal aid, which is expressly provided for in Article 6(3)(c). It did not anticipate the *Airey* judgment.

[339] But it was recognized in *P, C and S v UK* 2002-VI para 90 that 'limited public funds' may require 'a procedure of selection'.

[340] On the Article 5 *lex specialis* rules on legal aid in detention cases, see above, p 193.

[341] On the meaning of this phrase in Article 6(3)(c), see below, p 318.

[342] *Airey v Ireland* A 32 (1979); 2 EHRR 305 para 26.

be certainly be the case where legal representation is required by national law.[343] In other situations, the need for legal assistance must, as stated in *Steel and Morris v UK*,[344] be determined by reference to the facts of each case and 'will depend *inter alia* upon the importance of what is at stake for the applicant in the proceedings, the complexity of the relevant law and procedure and the applicant's capacity to represent him or herself effectively.' Legal aid will not be required where there is no arguable case on the facts.[345]

The *Steel and Morris* case was one of several British cases in which the Court has considered whether the right of access requires legal aid in defamation claims. In that case, McDonald's, the fast food chain, successfully brought an action for defamation against the two applicants (for criticism of McDonald's on environmental and social grounds, in a leaflet that was part of a London Greenpeace campaign) and was awarded a total of £76,000 damages against them personally. The Court upheld the applicants' claim that the United Kingdom had infringed Article 6(1) by refusing legal aid to the applicants, who were indigent. First, there was a lot 'at stake' financially for the applicants, who were of very modest means, with McDonald's claiming £100,000 damages. Second, the facts and the law in the case were complicated, with voluminous documentation and over 300 days of court hearings, some 100 of which were on legal argument. Third, although the applicants, who represented themselves, were articulate and resourceful and had some *pro bono* help from lawyers, the 'disparity between the respective levels of legal assistance enjoyed by the applicants and Mcdonald's...could not have failed, in this exceptionally demanding case, to have given rise to unfairness'.[346] The *Steel and Morris* case marks a departure from a series of earlier defamation cases, mostly brought by plaintiffs, not defendants, in which the Commission or the Court found that legal aid was not required.[347] Key to the decision in the *Steel and Morris* case were the particularly strong and sympathetic facts.

Whether in defamation or other cases, free legal aid will not be required where the plaintiff's claim has no 'reasonable prospects of success'.[348] Nor does the right of access require the provision of legal aid where the claim by the applicant involves an abuse of the law[349] or of the legal aid system.[350]

Where the right of access does require legal assistance to ensure a fair hearing, Article 6 leaves states 'a free choice of the means' to be used towards this end: 'a legal aid scheme' is only one possibility.[351] Thus an *ex gratia* offer of legal aid in the particular case may be sufficient,[352] or proceedings may be simplified to avoid the need for legal assistance at all.[353] In *A v UK*,[354] the Court held that the availability of two hours' free legal advice under the 'green form' scheme together with the possibility thereafter of engaging a solicitor on a conditional fee basis was sufficient to provide the applicant with effective access to a court in her defamation claim. Where the applicant qualifies for the assistance of a

---

[343] *Ibid.* Cf, *Aerts v Belgium* 1998-V; 29 EHRR 50 and *Staroszczyk v Poland* hudoc (2007).

[344] 2005-II; 41 EHRR 403 para 61. In *Faulkner v UK* hudoc (1999) F Sett before the Court, Guernsey agreed to establish for the first time a civil legal aid system after the applicant was denied legal aid to bring proceedings for false imprisonment, etc.

[345] *Gnahore v France* 2000-IX; 34 EHRR 967.   [346] Id, para 69.

[347] See *McVicar v UK* 2002-III; 35 EHRR 566 (defendant capable of defending himself in defamation case). For earlier Commission rulings rejecting legal aid claims by plaintiffs, see eg, *Munro v UK No 10594/83*, 52 DR 158 (1987) and *Winer v UK No 10871/84*, 48 DR 154 (1986).

[348] *X v UK No 8158/78*, 21 DR 95 at 102 (1980). See also *Del Sol v France* 2002-II; 35 EHRR 1281 and *Stewart-Brady v UK Nos 27436/95 and 28406/95*, 90-A DR 45 (1997).

[349] *W v FRG No 11564/85*, 45 DR 291 (1985).   [350] *Sujeeun v UK No 27788/95* hudoc (1996) DA.

[351] *A v UK* 2002-X; 36 EHRR 917 para 98.

[352] *Andronicou and Constantinou v Cyprus* 1997-VI; 25 EHRR 491.

[353] *Airey v Ireland* A 25 (1978); 2 EHRR 305 para 26.   [354] 2002-X; 36 EHRR 917.

lawyer under the national system, the state has an obligation to appoint a legal aid lawyer who will actually take up the case. Thus in *Bertuzzi v France*,[355] the applicant was denied 'effective access' to a court where a further legal aid lawyer was not appointed after three lawyers had refused to act because of their personal links with the lawyer whom the applicant was suing.

Apart from the position of indigent litigants, the high cost of civil proceedings may be such as to infringe the right to effective access to the courts for litigants paying for their own lawyers and court costs; the amount of any fee must be related to the particular circumstances, including the applicant's ability to pay.[356]

The need for access to the courts to be effective has also been in issue in a variety of contexts other than legal assistance.[357] Thus the right of access is infringed not only when the applicant is not allowed to commence proceedings, but also when proceedings are stayed by the state for an unduly long period of time. In *Kutic v Croatia*[358] a civil claim for damage to property was stayed by statute pending the enactment of legislation governing claims for damage resulting from terrorist acts. It was held that the right of effective access had been infringed because six years had passed without any legislation being enacted. Also, in *Ganci v Italy*[359] there was a breach of this right where a prisoner's complaint against being transferred to a security regime was not adjudicated until after the regime had ceased to apply to him. Finally, there was a breach of the right of access when the Albanian Constitutional Court was unable to reach agreement on a decision on the applicant's appeal, thereby depriving him of a final decision in his case.[360]

The right of effective access also supposes that there is a 'coherent system' governing recourse to the courts that is sufficiently certain in its requirements that litigants have 'a clear, practical and effective opportunity' to go to court.[361] A number of cases in which uncertainty in the law or its application has led litigants to act in a way that has prejudiced their access to a court have been decided in their favour on this basis.[362] In *FE v France*[363] there was a breach of the right of access where an applicant had, without any determination of legal liability, accepted compensation from a state fund for being infected with HIV after a blood transfusion, when he mistakenly believed (because of a lack of clarity in the law) that he was not thereby barred from pursuing a judicial remedy for further compensation. The right of access also requires that the state take reasonable steps to serve documents on the parties to proceedings and to inform them of the dates of hearings, and of decisions.[364]

---

[355] 2003-III para 32. See also *AB v Slovakia* hudoc (2003) and *Renda Martins v Portugal No 50085/99* hudoc (2002) DA (refusal for lack of co-operation permissible).

[356] *Weisman v Roumania* hudoc 2006-VII and *Kreuz v Poland (No 1)* 2001-VI. See also *Apostol v Georgia* hudoc (2006) (obligation to pay judgment enforcement expenses: breach).

[357] On access to information relevant to proceedings, see the right to a 'fair hearing', below, p 254.

[358] 2002-II. Cf, *Multiplex v Croatia* hudoc (2003) and *Aćimović v Croatia* 2003-XI; 39 EHRR 555.

[359] 2003-XII; 41 EHRR 272. See also *Musuceli v Italy* hudoc (2005).

[360] *Marini v Albania* 2007-XX. See also *Dubinskaya v Russia* hudoc (2006) (case 'lost').

[361] *De Geouffre de la Pradelle v France* A 253-B (1992) para 34 (appeal out of time because of uncertainty as to the applicable procedure). See now *Geffre v France No 51307/99* hudoc (2003) DA (procedure reformed).

[362] Some time limit and other cases of procedural uncertainty are decided on a 'disproportionate restriction' basis instead: see below, p 240.

[363] 1998-VIII; 29 EHRR 591 para 40. Cf, *Bellet v France* A 333-B (1995). See also *Beneficio Cappella Paolini v San Marino* 2004-VIII (uncertainty as to competent court); *Levages Prestations Services v France* 1996-V; 24 EHRR 351 (alleged uncertainty as to required documents: no breach); *Serghides and Christoforou v Cyprus* hudoc (2002); 37 EHRR 873 (applicant not told of land expropriation, so could not meet time limit).

[364] See *Bogonos v Russia No 68798/01* hudoc (2004) DA and *Sukhorubchenko v Russia* hudoc (2005). See also *Hennings v Germany*, below, p 418.

c. Restrictions upon the right of access

The right is not an absolute one. Restrictions may be imposed since the right of access 'by its very nature calls for regulation by the state, regulation which may vary in time and place according to the needs and resources of the community and of individuals'.[365] As indicated in *Ashingdane v UK*,[366] in imposing restrictions, the state is allowed a certain 'margin of appreciation' but any restriction must not be such that 'the very essence of the right is impaired'. In addition, a restriction must have a 'legitimate aim' and comply with the principle of proportionality, ie there must be 'a reasonable relationship of proportionality between the means employed and the aim sought to be achieved'.[367] In the *Ashingdane* case, the applicant instituted civil proceedings challenging the Secretary of State's decision under the Mental Health Act 1959, in effect to continue to detain him in a secure mental hospital. However, there was no liability under the Act for acts done under it in the absence of bad faith or reasonable care. Moreover, a claim in respect of such an act could not be brought unless the High Court gave leave, which it could do only if it were satisfied that there were 'substantial grounds' for believing that any of these conditions was were met. The Court held that these limitations on the right of access to a court were not in breach of the right. The limitation of liability under the Act had the 'legitimate aim' of preventing those caring for mental patients from being unfairly harassed by litigation and the availability of a claim only in a case of bad faith or lack of reasonable care both left intact the essence of the right to institute proceedings and was consistent with the principle of proportionality.

In accordance with the *Ashingdane* approach, restrictions upon access to the courts by certain categories of persons have been allowed or countenanced in principle.[368] Conditions attaching to the bringing of claims[369] and restrictions on the level of damages in civil cases are also acceptable if proportionate.[370] Requirements that an appeal be lodged by a lawyer[371] or that a litigant pay security for costs, provided that the amount is not disproportionate,[372] are permissible, as is a fine for an abusive appeal.[373] However, there was a breach of the right of access when the refusal of the applicant's request to have his fixed penalty speeding fine referred to a court was based upon an error of law.[374]

---

[365] *Golder v UK* A 18 (1975); 1 EHRR 524 para 38 PC.

[366] A 93 (1985); 7 EHRR 528 para 57. Cf, *Winterwerp v Netherlands* A 33 (1979); 2 EHRR 387 para 75. The 'very essence' requirement overlaps with the 'effective' right requirement: see *De Geouffre de la Pradelle v France*, at n 361 above, where the Court used both terms.

[367] *Ashingdane v UK* A 93 (1985); 7 EHRR 528 para 57. Cf, *Lithgow v UK* A 102 (1986); 8 EHRR 329 para 194 PC.

[368] See *Golder v UK* A 18 (1975); 1 EHRR 524 (prisoners, minors) PC; *M v UK No 12040/86*, 52 DR 269 (1987) (bankrupts); *H v UK No 11559/85*, 45 DR 281 (1985) (vexatious litigants); *Carnduff v UK No 18905/02* hudoc (2004) DA (police informers). A requirement of legal representation for a mentally disabled person is a permissible restriction: *Stewart-Brady v UK Nos 27436/95 and 28406/95* hudoc (1997); 90-A DR 45.

[369] *Stedman v UK No 29107/95*, 89-A DR 104 (1997); 23 EHRR CD 168 (two years' employment for unfair dismissal claims). See also: *Clunis v UK No 45149/98* hudoc (2001) (*ex turpi causa* limitation).

[370] *Manners v UK No 37650/97* hudoc (1998); 26 EHRR CD 200 (Warsaw Convention limit).

[371] *Gillow v UK* A 109 (1986); 11 EHRR 335.

[372] *Tolstoy Miloslavsky v UK* A 316-B (1995); 20 EHRR 442; *Ait-Mouhoub v France* 1998-VI; 1999 EHRLR 215; and *Grepne v UK No 17070/90*, 66 DR 268 (1990). See also *Podbielski and PPU Polpure v Poland* hudoc (2005) (appeal fee) and *Weissman v Romania* 2006-VII (stamp duty).

[373] *P v France No 10412/83*, 52 DR 128 (1987) and *Les Travaux du Midi v France No 12275/86*, 70 DR 47 (1991).

[374] *Peltier v France* hudoc (2002); 37 EHRR 197. See also *Mortier v France* hudoc (2001); 35 EHRR 163 and *Liakopoulou v Greece* hudoc (2006).

The *Ashingdane* principle was applied in *Khamidov v Russia*[375] to a situation in which the courts in Chechnya were closed for some fifteen months because of military action in the emergency situation in the area. The Court held that the applicant's consequent inability to take legal proceedings to evict the federal police from his land was a breach of the right of access. The courts' closure impaired the 'very essence' of that right and was 'disproportionate': even supposing that the closure was justified in the emergency, steps could have been taken to allow the applicant to have his case heard elsewhere in Russia.

The right of access also requires that procedural requirements governing recourse to the courts that are open to more than one interpretation should not be given a 'particularly strict' interpretation[376] or application,[377] so as to prevent litigants making use of an available remedy. Most cases have concerned time limits for the bringing of first instance or appeal proceedings;[378] others have concerned factual or clerical errors by a litigant.[379] A time limit which the applicant could not reasonably have been expected to meet will be a breach of the right of access,[380] but clear and avoidable errors will not.[381] Time limits in themselves are permissible if they meet the requirement of proportionality, with a margin of appreciation being justified because of the variation in practice in European states. In *Stubbings v UK*,[382] a time limit for civil claims of childhood sexual abuse of six years from attaining the age of eighteen was proportionate.

Various other kinds of restrictions have been considered by the Court. The limitation of the right to bring proceedings to particular interested parties, to the exclusion of others, may be a breach of the right of access. Thus a law that barred certain Greek monasteries from bringing legal proceedings in respect of their property, giving the right to the Greek Church instead, was a breach of the monasteries' right of access, depriving them of the 'very essence' of the right.[383] A fortiori, a judicial decision by which a church was deprived of its legal personality, which prevented it from bringing any civil proceedings, was a breach.[384] However, in a different context, it is permissible to deny a person whose telephone is tapped, in a manner consistent with Article 8 of the Convention, a court remedy to question the legality of the tapping while it continues; such a restriction is justifiable in order to ensure the effectiveness of the system.[385]

Positive state action in the form of legislation with retroactive application that is designed to defeat a litigant's claim in the courts is also in breach of the right of access, unless it can be justified as a proportionate limitation on 'compelling' public interest

---

[375] 2007-XX.   [376] *Beles v Czech Rep* hudoc (2002) para 51.

[377] *Perez de Rada Cavanilles v Spain* 1998-VIII; 29 EHRR 109 para 49. See also *Yagtzilar v Greece* hudoc (2001).

[378] See eg, *Miragall Escolano and Others v Spain* 1998-VIII; 34 EHRR 658; *Tricard v France* hudoc (2001); 37 EHRR 388; *Zemanová v Czech Rep* hudoc (2006); and *Mikulová v Slovakia* hudoc (2005).

[379] See eg, *Kadlec and Others v Czech Rep* hudoc (2004); *Société Anonyme 'Sotiris et Nikos Koutras ATTEE' v Greece* 2000-XII; 36 EHRR 410; and *Saez Maeso v Spain* hudoc (2004). Clerical errors by the state must not disadvantage the applicant: *Platakou v Greece* hudoc (2001).

[380] *Neshev v Bulgaria* hudoc (2004) and *Tsironis v Greece* hudoc (2001); 37 EHRR 183. See also *Cañete de Goñi v Spain* hudoc (2002) and *AEPI SA v Greece* hudoc (2002).

[381] *Edificaciones March Gallego SA v Spain* 1998-I; 33 EHRR 1105.

[382] 1996-IV; 23 EHRR 213. See also *Dobbie v UK No 28477/95* hudoc (1996) DA; and *Mizzi v Malta* 2006-I; 46 EHRR 529.

[383] *Holy Monasteries v Greece* A 301-A (1994); 20 EHRR 1 para 83. See also *Lithgow v UK* A 102 (1986); 8 EHRR 329 PC; *Philis v Greece* A 209 (1991); 13 EHRR 741; and *Związek Nauczycielstwa Polskiego v Poland* 2004-IX; 38 EHRR 122.

[384] *Canea Catholic Church v Greece* 1997-VIII; 27 EHRR 521.

[385] *Klass v FRG* A 28 (1978); 2 EHRR 214 PC

grounds.[386] Most such cases have, however, been treated as involving a breach of the 'principle of the rule of law and the notion of a fair trial enshrined in Article 6',[387] rather than as a breach of the right of access. The overturning of a court judgment that is *res judicata* has sometimes been considered as infringing the right of access,[388] but has generally been regarded as being contrary to the right to a 'fair hearing' instead.[389] In contrast, failure to execute a court judgment is a breach of Article 6 that is unequivocally based on the right of access.[390]

A procedural bar to the successful bringing of a claim that takes the form of an immunity or defence that may be pleaded by the defendant is another kind of restriction upon the right of access to a court—one that has given rise to some important rulings.[391] A distinction is here made by the Strasbourg Court between the situation in which the applicant has no arguable claim under the substantive law of the state concerned, and that in which there is such a claim, but an immunity or defence is raised by the defendant that defeats it. In the former case, the Court has held, the right of access simply does not apply.[392] In the latter case, it does, and the answer to the question whether the immunity or defence is consistent with the right of access turns upon whether it meets the *Ashingdane* requirements indicated above. This approach was first adopted by the Court in *Fayed v UK*.[393] In that case, the Court held that a defence of privilege available in an action for defamation that might be brought by the owners of a company concerning allegations of fraud in a government inspector's report on the company was a permissible restriction on the right of access. It had a legitimate aim (to facilitate the investigation of public companies in the public interest) and, in the light of the respondent state's margin of appreciation, was not disproportionate on the facts.[394]

The same approach has been used to justify parliamentary and state immunity. As to parliamentary immunity, in *A v UK*[395] it was held that absolute immunity for Westminster Members of Parliament from liability in defamation for their statements in proceedings in parliament was not a breach of Article 6. It had the legitimate aims of securing the freedom of speech of MPs on matters of public interest—which is a matter of great importance in a democracy—and of maintaining the separation of powers of the legislature and the judiciary. Although absolute and extending to both civil and criminal proceedings, the immunity did not exceed the margin of appreciation: it could be justified as a proportionate restriction on the right of access to a court in order to achieve these aims, particularly as it extended only to statements *in* Parliament. Also relevant was the fact the immunity was 'consistent with and reflects generally recognised rules within signatory states, the Council of Europe and Members of the European

---

[386] *National and Provincial Building Society et al v UK* 1997-VII; 25 EHRR 127 para 112 (retroactive legislation to fill a tax loophole justified in the public interest). Procedural changes do not infringe the right of access as there is a 'generally recognized principle' that they apply to pending cases: *Brualla Gómez de la Torre v Spain* 1997-VIII; 33 EHRR 1341.

[387] See below, p 267. Sometimes the Court refers to both grounds for its decision: see eg, the *National and Provincial* case, id, para 122.

[388] See eg, *Ryabykh v Russia* 2003-XI; 40 EHRR 615.

[389] See below, p 269.   [390] On the non-execution of judgments, see above, p 233.

[391] See Kloth, ELR Human Rights Survey 33 (2002).   [392] See above, p 224.

[393] A 294-B (1994); 18 EHRR 393. See also *Taylor v UK No 49589/99* hudoc (2003); 38 EHRR CD 25 DA and *Mond v UK No 49606/99* hudoc (2003) DA.

[394] The Court noted, *inter alia*, that businessmen who enter the public sphere lay themselves open to close scrutiny; that the applicants had themselves sought to bring the matters commented upon into the public domain; and that judicial review of the inspector's activities provided some remedy.

[395] 2002-X; 36 EHRR 917. See also *Young v Ireland* hudoc (1996); 84 DR 122 (1996). Cf, *Esposito v Italy* 1997-IV.

Parliament'.[396] An immunity that extends to statements made by parliamentarians *outside* of parliament is given closer scrutiny. In *Cordova v Italy (No 2)*[397] it was held in respect to such statements that the absence of a 'clear connection with a parliamentary activity' required a 'narrow interpretation of the concept of proportionality'. In that case, the absolute parliamentary immunity accorded to a statement made by a senator at an election meeting that was critical of the applicant, a local public prosecutor, and seemed to relate to a private quarrel was held to be disproportionate and so a breach of the applicant's right of access to a court.

As to state immunity, the immunity of states from civil liability in the courts of other states—granted in accordance with international law—has been held to be a proportionate restriction on the right of access to a court, with the legitimate aim of promoting comity and good relations among states. Thus immunity from civil process in national courts in respect of a claim concerning employment in a foreign diplomatic mission,[398] and of a tort claim for personal injury by a foreign soldier,[399] had not exceeded the margin of appreciation and hence were not in breach of the right of access. Immunity from civil proceedings for international organizations, in accordance with international law, may also be permissible.[400]

In the more controversial case of *Al-Adsani v UK*,[401] state immunity from liability in tort for acts amounting to torture was also held to be proportionate. In that case the applicant brought a claim in tort against the government of Kuwait in the English courts in respect of torture allegedly committed in Kuwait by government agents. However, the defendant state successfully pleaded state immunity, this being a shield available to states in English law, as required by long-established customary international law. The European Court, by just nine votes to eight, held that this restriction on the right of access was permissible. It held that a rule of state immunity in national civil proceedings had the legitimate aim of 'complying with international law to promote comity and good relations between states through the respect of another state's sovereignty'.[402] As to proportionality, measures taken by a state to comply with its obligations under the international law of state immunity could not 'in principle' be regarded as disproportionate.[403] As to these obligations, the Court noted that the prohibition of torture in customary international law had become a peremptory norm (*ius cogens*) and that there were judicial precedents suggesting that customary international law had been modified to the point where a claim of state immunity could not bar *criminal* proceedings against an individual for acts of torture. However, the Court could find no evidence of a similar development in the context of *civil* proceedings, so that a state retained its absolute immunity from civil suit in the courts of another state, at least, as on the facts of the case,

---

[396] Id, para. 83. The Court also noted that there was an alternative contempt of parliament remedy, but this was not crucial to its decision: see *Zollmann v UK No 62902/00* hudoc (2003) DA.

[397] Hudoc (2003). See also *Cordova v Italy (No 1), ibid*; and *De Jorio v Italy* hudoc (2004); 40 EHRR 961.

[398] *Fogarty v UK* 2001-XI; 34 EHRR 302 GC.

[399] *McElhinney v Ireland* 2001-XI; 34 EHRR 322 GC. Judges Rozakis, Caflisch, Cabral Barreto, Vajic, and Loucaides dissented on the ground that international law no longer imposed a duty on states to grant immunity in tort cases. See also *Kalogeropoulou and Others v Greece and Germany* 2002-X DA. State immunity—again based on international law—extends to the *execution* of judgments against state property: *Manoilescu and Dobrescu v Romania and Russia* 2005-VI DA.

[400] *Waite and Kennedy v Germany* 1999-I; 30 EHRR 261 GC; and *Beer and Regan v Germany* hudoc (1999); 33 EHRR 54 GC. In these cases the existence of an alternative European Space Agency remedy was important.

[401] 2001-XI; 34 EHRR 273 GC. See Bates, 3 HRLR (2003) and Voyakis, 52 ICLQ 279 (2003).

[402] Id, para 54.   [403] *Ibid.*

for acts of torture committed outside of the forum state.[404] The dissenting judges mostly rejected the majority's distinction between criminal and civil proceedings, arguing that the consequences of the prohibition of torture as *ius cogens* was that it was hierarchically superior in customary international law to the law of state immunity and should prevail over the latter generally, so as to remove all of its legal effects, whether in civil or criminal cases.[405] The argument of the dissenting judges is persuasive. As suggested by Judge Ferraro Bravo, the Court 'had a golden opportunity to issue a clear and forceful condemnation of all acts of torture'.[406]

A different kind of immunity, in the form of an executive certificate that was conclusive of an issue before the courts, was the subject of *Tinnelly and McElduff v UK*.[407] In that case, a right of action for damages for discrimination in Northern Ireland did not extend to acts done to protect national security. Whereas this by itself did not present a problem, the Court held that the rule by which an executive certificate to the effect that the act was done for that purpose was conclusive was a disproportionate limitation upon the right of access; it would have been possible, as the UK had done in other contexts, to have made special arrangements to allow an independent judicial, rather than an executive, determination of the facts.

The distinction between the situation where there is no arguable substantive claim under national law and that where there is a procedural limitation by way of an immunity or defence that may be invoked is sometimes difficult to draw.[408] In *Z v UK*,[409] the applicant children, who brought a civil claim for damages against a local authority for failing to prevent their being abused by their parents, were denied the chance to plead their case on the merits when their claim was struck out by the courts. This followed proceedings in which it was held, deciding a new point of law, that the local authority owed no duty of care in negligence and had no liability for breach of statutory duty in respect of their statutory child care duties. The Court held that the inability to sue the local authority was not an immunity under the applicable law, in which case questions of a legitimate aim and proportionality would have been relevant, but a case of the absence of a right within the bounds of the substantive law, so that Article 6 did not apply at all. In its judgment in the *Z* case, the Court took the opportunity to signal a reversal of its reasoning in its judgment in *Osman v UK*.[410] Whereas in *Osman* the Court had ruled that the absolute immunity in English law of police officers from civil liability in negligence in the course of their conduct in the investigation and prevention of crime was held to be a disproportionate limitation upon the right of access to a court, in *Z v UK*, the Court

---

[404] In line with the relaxation of the law of state immunity in the European Convention on State Immunity 1972, the UK State Immunity Act 1978, s 5(a), does allow a civil claim against a state in the UK courts in respect of personal injuries caused *within* the UK.

[405] See the dissenting opinion of Judges Rozakis and Caflisch, joined by Judges Wildhaber, Costa, Cabral Barreto, and Vajic. For further arguments, see the dissenting opinions of Judges Ferraro Bravo and Loucaides.

[406] But for a well-argued presentation of the problems, eg, of execution of judgments, that would have arisen were the dissenting judges to have prevailed, see the dissenting opinion of Judge Pellonpää, joined by Judge Bratza.

[407] 1998-IV; 27 EHRR 249. Cf, *Devlin v UK* hudoc (2001); 34 EHRR 1029 and *Devenney v UK* hudoc (2002); 35 EHRR 643.

[408] See eg, *Markovic v Italy* 2006-XX GC ('act of government' doctrine). The Court has sometimes declined to make it in cases in which the restriction is disproportionate, so that the outcome does not depend upon it. See eg, the *Ashingdane* and *Fayed* cases, above.

[409] 2001-V; 34 EHRR 97 GC. Cf, *TP and KM v UK* 2001-V; 34 EHRR 42 GC and *DP and JC v UK* hudoc (2002) 36 EHRR 183.

[410] 1998-VIII; 29 EHRR 245 GC.

stated that, in the light of clarifications made by the English judiciary in later cases,[411] it now understood this exclusion as deriving from the extent of the duty of care in the substantive law of negligence, not as going to an immunity. As a result, it can be taken that the Court's ruling in *Osman* that the police immunity from liability was in breach of the right of access as being disproportionate because of its absolute nature is no longer good law; instead Article 6 simply did not apply.

A similarly difficult issue arose in *Roche v UK*[412] in which the question was whether the exclusion under s 10, Crown Proceedings Act 1947 of Crown liability in tort in some cases of personal injuries suffered by members of the armed forces was held to be a breach of the right of access to a court. In that case, a soldier brought a claim in tort for physical injuries allegedly caused by chemical weapons tests to which he had been subjected while in service. His claim failed when the Secretary of State certified that the case fell within s 10. The Strasbourg Court held, by just nine votes to eight, that s 10 contained a substantive rather than a procedural limitation, so that Article 6 did not apply. In doing so, it was strongly influenced by the unanimous ruling of the House of Lords in a comparable armed forces case,[413] in which the House had interpreted s 10 in the light of Article 6 of the Convention, finding no breach of the right of access. In that case, the House had noted that prior to the Crown Proceedings Act the Crown had not been liable in tort at all. Reversing this position, the Act had established a general substantive right to sue the Crown but left the position (of no substantive right) unchanged in cases covered by s 10. In following the House of Lords' interpretation, the Strasbourg Court noted that, in deciding whether there was a civil 'right' for the purposes of Article 6, 'the starting point must be the provisions of the relevant domestic law and their interpretation by the domestic courts' and that where 'the superior national courts have analysed in a comprehensive and convincing manner the precise nature of the impugned restriction, on the basis of the relevant Convention case law and principles drawn therefrom, this court would need strong reasons to differ from the conclusion reached by those courts by substituting its own views for those of the national courts on a question of interpretation of national law'.

As well as in immunity and defence cases, the Court has applied the *Ashingdane* approach where the national courts' jurisdiction has been ousted by treaty. In *Prince Hans Adam II of Liechtenstein v Germany*,[414] the applicant brought a claim in Germany concerning the expropriation by the Czechoslovak authorities of a painting to which he claimed title that was kept in Czechoslovakia, but which was temporarily in Germany for exhibition. The German courts held that, under the Settlement Convention, which was binding upon Germany and the Western Allies, they had no jurisdiction to hear a claim concerning 'German external assets'. Applying *Ashingdane*, the European Court, unanimously, found against the applicant on the basis that the restriction on the German courts' jurisdiction had a legitimate aim—the realization of German sovereignty and unity—and was not disproportionate to that end, given that the natural and most likely forum for such a claim was where the painting was kept, and that a claim had earlier been brought unsuccessfully in the Czechoslovak courts.

In his separate opinion in the *Prince Hans Adam II* case, Judge Costa questioned the Court's application of the *Ashingdane* approach in the case.[415] For an applicant who is prevented from bringing his claim because of a lack of court jurisdiction—and, he

---

[411] See *Barrett v Enfield LBC* [1999] 3 WLR 79 in which members of the House of Lords expressed their surprise at the *Osman* judgment.

[412] 2005-X; 42 EHRR 599 para 120 GC. See also *Dyer v UK No 10475/83*, 39 DR 246 (1984).

[413] *Matthews v Ministry of Defence* [2002] EWCA Civ 773.   [414] 2001-VIII GC.

[415] Cf, the concurring opinion of Judge Ress, joined by Judge Zupančič.

suggested, in immunity or defence cases—the situation was not one of a restriction upon the right of access to a court, but of the 'very essence' of that right being impaired. However, the Court's approach in immunity and defence cases may be defended on the basis that the applicant's substantive right—to sue in defamation, assault, etc—exists generally, or in essence: it is unavailable only against defendants who claim an immunity or defence. As to the jurisdiction issue in the *Prince Hans Adam II* case, as the Court's judgment indicates, the 'essence' of the right of access was not impaired, as the natural and most likely forum for a claim was in the Czechoslovak courts.

The right of access may be restricted in criminal, as well as non-criminal cases. Thus a decision may be taken not to prosecute, or proceedings may be discontinued without infringing Article 6.[416] A practice whereby there is no hearing as to guilt or innocence (only as to the sentence) if an accused pleads guilty at the beginning of his trial is consistent with Article 6(1) provided that adequate safeguards exist to prevent abuse.[417] It is also permissible to issue a penal order by which a person is convicted and sentenced in respect of a minor criminal offence without any court hearing, provided that the person has sufficient opportunity to request a hearing.[418] However, a requirement that a convicted person who appeals on a point of law must surrender to custody pending a decision on the appeal is a disproportionate restriction that takes away the very essence of the right of access to a court on appeal.[419] Finally, the immunity of an investigating judge from criminal prosecution has been held to be justified.[420]

d. Waiver of the right of access

A person may waive his right of access in civil and criminal cases.[421] In *Deweer v Belgium*,[422] the Court stated that a claim of waiver should be subjected to 'particularly careful review'. In that case, a butcher chose to pay an out of court fine for an 'over-pricing' offence rather than wait for trial. A waiver was found not to have occurred because his decision to waive his right to a trial was subject to constraint. In particular, the accused was faced with the provisional closure of his shop pending prosecution, with consequential economic loss, if he elected to go for trial.

e. Relationship with Article 13

Finally, the right of access to a court overlaps with the right to an effective national remedy in respect of a breach of a Convention right that is guaranteed by Article 13.[423] The overlap exists insofar as the Convention right is also a 'civil right' in the sense of

---

[416] *Deweer v Belgium* A 35 (1980); 2 EHRR 439 para 49. See also *X v UK No 8233/78*, 3 EHRR 271 (1979). Where the discontinuance of proceedings may imply guilt, there may be a breach of Article 6(2): see below, p 303.

[417] *X v UK No 5076/71*, 40 CD 64 at 67 (1972). The adequate safeguards in that case were that 'the judge is satisfied that the accused understands the effect of his plea and the accused's confession is recorded'.

[418] *Hennings v Germany* A 251-A (1992); 16 EHRR 83. Cf, *X v FRG No 4260/69*, 35 CD 155 (1970).

[419] *Omar v France* 1998-V; 29 EHRR 210 GC and *Papon v France* 2002-VII; 39 EHRR 217. See also *Eliazer v Netherlands* 2001-X (no breach).

[420] *Ernst v Belgium* hudoc (2003); 39 EHRR 724.

[421] *Deweer v Belgium* A 36 (1980); 2 EHRR 439 para 49; and *Nordström-Janzon and Nordström-Lehtinen v Netherlands No 28101/95*, 87-A DR 112 (1996) (arbitration agreed, not court hearing).

[422] A 35 (1980); 2 EHRR 439 para 49. See also *Marpa Zeeland v Netherlands* 2004-X; 40 EHRR 817 (denial of effective access by persuasion not to appeal against conviction).

[423] On the inter-relationship between the two guarantees, see *Golder v UK* A 18 (1975); 1 EHRR 524 para 33 PC and *Kudla v Poland* 2000-XI; 35 EHRR 198. See also *Powell and Rayner v UK* A 172 (1990); 12 EHRR 355 and the joint separate opinion of Judges Pinheiro Farinha and De Meyer in *W v UK* A 121 (1987); 10 EHRR 29. As to Article 13, see below, Ch 14.

Article 6(1). The right of access provides a stricter guarantee than Article 13 in that it requires a remedy before a court.[424]

II. THE RIGHT TO A FAIR HEARING

In contrast with the other guarantees in Article 6(1), the right to a 'fair hearing' has an open-ended, residual quality. It provides an opportunity for adding other particular rights not listed in Article 6 that are considered essential to a 'fair hearing', and for deciding whether a 'fair hearing' has occurred when the proceedings in a particular case are looked at as a whole, even though no particular right has been infringed.

In criminal cases, the 'fair hearing' guarantee has to be read together with the specific guarantees in Article 6(2) and (3). Whereas the latter are subsumed within the former, the general guarantee of a 'fair hearing' in Article 6(1) has elements that supplement those specified in Article 6(2) and (3).[425] Where a case falls within one (or more) of the specific guarantees in Article 6(2) or (3), it may be considered by the Court under that guarantee alone,[426] or in conjunction with Article 6(1),[427] or just under Article 6(1). When the last of these options is chosen, it is on the basis that the complaint is essentially that the proceedings in their entirety, including any appeal proceedings, were unfair.[428]

Whereas the right to a 'fair hearing' applies to civil as well as criminal proceedings, 'the contracting states have a greater latitude when dealing with civil cases concerning civil rights and obligations than they have when dealing with criminal cases'.[429] Thus although certain of the guarantees listed in Article 6(3) (eg, the right to legal aid or to cross-examine witnesses) are inherent in a 'fair hearing' in civil as well as criminal cases, they may not apply with the same rigour or in precisely the same way under Article 6(1) in civil proceedings as they do in criminal ones.[430] The same is true of rights that flow exclusively from Article 6(1), such as the right to be present at the hearing.[431]

A number of specific rights have in fact been added to Article 6(1) through the medium of its 'fair hearing' guarantee. The first of these to be established were 'equality of arms' and the right to a hearing in one's presence. Others have been added since, such as the right to freedom from self-incrimination, or are in the process of crystallization, such as the right to a hearing free from pre-trial publicity. A breach of such a specific right may itself amount to a breach of the right to a 'fair hearing' without any need to consider other aspects of the proceedings.

In cases not involving a breach of a specific right, the Court may nonetheless find a breach of the right to a 'fair hearing' on a 'hearing as a whole' basis. Thus in *Barberà, Messegué and Jabardo v Spain*,[432] involving the prosecution of alleged members of a Catalan organization for terrorist offences, the Court identified a number of features of the hearing that cumulatively led it to conclude that there had not been a 'fair hearing'. The Court referred to the fact that the accused had been driven over 300 miles to the court the night before the trial, the unexpected changes in the court's membership, the brevity of the trial, and above all the failure to adduce and discuss important evidence orally in

---

[424] See *De Geouffre de la Pradelle v France* A 253-B (1992) para 37.

[425] *Artico v Italy* A 37 (1980); 3 EHRR 1 para 32. Article 6(3) guarantees 'minimum' rights.

[426] See eg, *Luedicke v FRG* A 29 (1978); 2 EHRR 149.

[427] See eg, *Benham v UK* 1996-III; 22 EHRR 293 GC.

[428] *Edwards v UK* A 247-B (1992); 15 EHRR 417 paras 33–4.

[429] *Dombo Beheer v Netherlands* A 274 (1993); 18 EHRR 213 para 32.   [430] *Ibid.*

[431] See below, p 247. In some cases, there are no such differences: see *Niderost-Huber v Switzerland* 1997-I; 25 EHRR 709 para 28 (right to an adversarial trial).

[432] A 146 (1988); 11 EHRR 360 para 89 PC.

the accused's presence as considerations that, 'taken as a whole', rendered the proceedings unfair contrary to Article 6(1).

a. A hearing in one's presence

Although not expressly provided for in Article 6, the right to a hearing in one's presence is a part of the right to a 'fair hearing' in Article 6 (1).[433] Clearly a litigant has an interest in witnessing and monitoring proceedings that are of great importance to him. The right of a litigant to be present at the hearing is also implicit in his right to 'participate effectively' in the hearing,[434] the right to an adversarial trial,[435] and, in criminal cases, his rights in Article 6(3)(c), (d), and (e).[436] Where, exceptionally, Article 6 does not require an oral hearing,[437] there is by definition no right to be present.

Whereas there is a general right of the accused in a criminal case to attend the hearing,[438] the right of a litigant to be present has been held to extend to only certain kinds of non-criminal cases. These include cases where the 'personal character and manner of life' of the party concerned is directly relevant to the decision[439] or where the case involves an assessment of the applicant's 'conduct'.[440] In other cases it will be sufficient that there is a hearing at which the party is represented by a lawyer.[441] However, the recognition of the right to an adversarial trial[442] suggests that the right of a party to civil proceedings to be present should be more generally recognized.[443]

A party to a criminal or non-criminal case may waive his right to be present at the hearing, provided that the waiver is made 'of his own free will, either expressly or tacitly', is 'established in an unequivocal manner', is 'attended by minimum safeguards commensurate to its importance', and does 'not run counter to any important public interest.'[444] Waiver will depend upon the applicant having knowledge of the hearing. In *T v Italy*,[445] a chamber of the Court held that 'indirect' knowledge was not sufficient. Instead notice must be given officially 'in accordance with procedural and substantive requirements capable of guaranteeing the effective exercise of the accused's rights': 'vague and informal knowledge' did not suffice. But in *Sejdovic v Italy*[446] a Grand Chamber revised this formula, indicating that, while appropriate official notice is normally required, it 'could not rule out the possibility that certain established facts might sufficiently provide an unequivocal indication that the accused is aware' of the criminal proceedings

---

[433] *Colozza v Italy* A 89 (1985); 7 EHRR 516.

[434] On the right to participate effectively, see below, p 250.   [435] *Ziliberberg v Moldova* hudoc (2005).

[436] *Sejdovic v Italy* 2006-II para 81 GC. There is also a public interest in an accused attending so that his evidence can be checked in person against that of others: id, para 92. For this reason, the legislature may discourage 'unjustified absences': *ibid*.

[437] On the right to an oral hearing, see below, p 274.

[438] See *Hermi v Italy* 2006-XII; 46 EHRR 1115 GC. Prison authorities must ensure that an accused attends a hearing of which it has knowledge: see *Goddi v Italy* A 76 (1984); 6 EHRR 457.

[439] *X v Sweden* No 434/58, 2 YB 354 at 370 (1959). Child access cases fall within the above category (*ibid*), but see *X v Austria* No 8893/80, 31 DR 66 (1983). So may some commercial cases (*X v FRG* No 1169/61, 6 YB 520 at 572 (1963)). But see *No 10754/84*, 2 Digest Supp 6.1.1.4.4.1 (1984).

[440] *Muyldermans v Belgium* A 214-A (1991); 15 EHRR 204 para 64 Com Rep.

[441] It is for the applicant to show that his presence is necessary: *X v Switzerland* No 7370/76, 9 DR 95 (1977).

[442] See below, p 254.

[443] Cf, *Feldbrugge v Netherlands* A 99 (1986); 8 EHRR 425 PC.

[444] *Sejdovic v Italy* 2006-II para 86 GC. This was a criminal case, but these statements must apply also to non-criminal litigation. The required 'procedural guarantees' will include representation by a lawyer: id, para 91. See also *Poitrimol v France*, A 277–A (1993); 18 EHRR 130.

[445] A 245-C (1992) para 28. See also *FCB v Italy* A 208-B (1991); 14 EHRR 909. On notification to the mentally disabled, see *Vaudelle v France* 2001-I; 37 EHRR 397.

[446] 2006-II para 99 GC.

against him and does not intend to appear at them. It gave as one example, relevant to waiver, the situation where the accused states publicly or in writing that he does not intend to respond to summonses which he has become aware of other than through official sources. However, the mere fact that, as in the *Sejdovic* case, the accused has left his place of residence and is untraceable is not sufficient to show that he knows of the hearing.

Waiver need not be expressly indicated. It may be inferred from conduct, for example by a litigant not attending the hearing, having the required knowledge of it; non-attendance by itself is not a waiver.[447] However, notice must be given in good time to allow the applicant to attend,[448] and in a language that the accused understands,[449] before waiver may be inferred. 'Particular diligence' is required where notice of the hearing is given via the applicant's lawyer.[450] Refusal to participate in a hearing other than in the accused's own language is not a waiver.[451] A waiver is also not 'unequivocally' established where an accused could not reasonably have foreseen the consequences of his failure to attend. Thus there was no waiver in *Jones v UK*[452] when the applicant's trial commenced in his absence when the applicant, having been given bail, did not surrender on the date set for the trial. There was held to be no waiver because at the time it was not clear in English law that a trial could proceed to a conclusion in the accused's absence and without his being legally represented, and the seemingly invariable practice was to adjourn the proceedings until the accused could be brought to court.

As well as in cases of waiver, trial *in absentia* is permitted without infringing Article 6 in two other situations, The first is where the state has acted diligently, but unsuccessfully, to give an accused notice of the hearing. In *Colozza v Italy*,[453] the Court stated that this is because the 'impossibility of holding a trial by default may paralyze the conduct of criminal proceedings, in that it may lead, for example, to the dispersal of evidence, expiry of the time-limit for prosecution or a miscarriage of justice'. On the facts of the *Colozza* case, the Court found a breach of Article 6(1) because the authorities had sought to serve documents upon the applicant at his previous address, even though the police and the public prosecutor knew of his current address. The Court found that the authorities had not been diligent in the steps they had taken to locate the applicant's new address and that trial *in absentia* was a disproportionate penalty for failure to report a change of address. The onus was upon the state to show diligence, not upon the accused to show that he was 'not seeking to evade justice or that his absence was due to *force majeure*'.[454]

The second situation is where the accused, having knowledge of the trial, intentionally absents himself from it with a view to escaping trial.[455] Such cases differ from waiver in that there is no express or implied acceptance that the trial may proceed in the accused's absence. As with waiver, knowledge of the trial normally means official knowledge, except that it may be inferred from conduct, such as evading an attempted arrest.[456] This may be

---

[447] *Godlevskiy v Russia No 14888/03* hudoc (2004) DA and *Hermi v Italy* 2006-XII GC.

[448] See *Yakovlev v Russia* hudoc (2005). See also *Ziliberberg v Moldova* hudoc (2005).

[449] *Brozicek v Italy* A 167 (1989); 12 EHRR 371 PC.   [450] *Yavuz v Austria* hudoc (2004).

[451] *Zana v Turkey* 1997-VII; 27 EHRR 667.

[452] *No 30900/02* hudoc (2003) DA. In *R v Jones* [2002] UKHL 5, it was later held that an accused could be tried *in absentia* where there was an 'unequivocal' waiver. Cf, *Kremzow v Austria* A 268-B (1993); 17 EHRR 322 (failure to apply to attend not a waiver when the state was under an obligation to ensure attendance).

[453] A 89 (1985); 7 EHRR 517 para 29. Cf, *FCB v Italy* A 208-B (1991); 14 EHRR 909 and *T v Italy* A 245-C (1992).

[454] Id, para 30.   [455] *Sejdovic v Italy* 2006-II para 82 GC.

[456] Id, para 99.

so in ordinary cases of an accused absconding from justice, as well as in less obvious cases such as *Medenica v Switzerland*, below.

In a case in which a trial is permitted *in absentia* under the rule in the *Colozza* case, the accused must be able to obtain 'a fresh determination of the merits of the charge, in respect of both law and fact',[457] should he later learn of the proceedings. A re-hearing adequately overcomes the 'fair' trial problems that may result from the accused's absence at the original trial and failure to provide one would be a denial of justice.[458] The requirement of a re-hearing may be satisfied by a trial court hearing, or by an appeal that provides for a sufficient consideration of the merits of the case.[459]

There is, however, no right to a re-trial in a case when under the Convention a trial is permitted *in absentia*, where it is established that the right to be present at the trial was waived or in which the applicant intended to escape justice, by absconding or otherwise.[460] The latter situation existed in *Medenica v Switzerland*.[461] In that case, while released on bail on charges of fraud, the applicant doctor had moved to the US and continued his practice as a cancer specialist there. While his Swiss trial was pending, one of his American patients obtained a US court order that the applicant should not leave the US because this would endanger the patient's life. The applicant then did not attend his trial when officially summoned and he was tried and convicted *in absentia*, with two lawyers defending him. Later, the Swiss courts rejected the applicant's claim for a re-trial on the ground that he did not have 'good cause' for absenting himself: the applicant could have arranged for other doctors to treat his patients, making the court order unnecessary. Allowing a 'margin of appreciation', the Strasbourg Court held that the applicant's conviction *in absentia* and the refusal to grant him a re-trial at which he would be present did not amount to a disproportionate penalty. The Court noted the Swiss Federal Court's opinion that the applicant had misled the American court into making a decision that prevented him attending his trial.

In addition to the above cases in which a trial may commence and be fully conducted in the absence of the accused, a trial that has already commenced may continue in the absence of the accused in the interests of the administration of justice in some cases of illness or obstructive behaviour. As to the former, in *Ensslin, Baader and Raspe v FRG*,[462] the accused had, by going on hunger strike, reduced themselves to the point where they were medically unfit to attend the hearing for more than a limited number of hours each day. The decision to continue the trial during their absence was held by the Commission not to be a breach of the right to a hearing in person, taking into account the need for the proceedings not to grind to a halt, the presence of the applicants' lawyers at the hearing, and their unrestricted opportunities to consult with their clients. Obviously also, an accused who seeks to delay proceedings by claiming unsubstantiated illness may be tried

---

[457] Id, para 82.

[458] Ibid. The destruction of the case file is not a good reason for not having a re-hearing: *Stoichkov v Bulgaria* hudoc (2005).

[459] The possibility of introducing fresh evidence before the English Court of Appeal meets this requirement: *Jones v UK No 30900/02* hudoc (2003) DA. A reasonable period of time to appeal is required: *Sejdovic v Italy* 2006-II GC.

[460] *Sejdovic v Italy* 2006-II para 82 GC; *Einhorn v France No 71555/01* 2001-XI; and *Demebukov v Bulgaria*. Cf, the European standard suggested in the Council of Europe Criteria Governing Proceedings held in the Absence of the Accused, CM Res (75) 11. It is for the state to have effective procedures in place to establish a waiver or an intention not to appear. Thus there was a breach of Article 6 where the procedure for considering the applicant's claim that his signature acknowledging receipt of the hearing notice had been forged was inadequate: *Somogyi v Italy* 2004-IV.

[461] 2001-VI para 59.

[462] *Nos 7572/76, 7586/76 and 7587/76*, 14 DR 64 (1978). See also *Ninn-Hansen v Denmark No 28972/95* hudoc (1999) DA.

in his absence.[463] Similarly, an accused or other litigant who behaves in the courtroom in such as way as to seriously obstruct proceedings may be excluded from the court, at least temporarily.[464]

Although Article 6 applies to such appeal proceedings as a state chooses to provide,[465] there are limits to the right of the accused to be present at an oral hearing on appeal. In some cases written proceedings will suffice, so that the question of the right to be present does not arise. The cases in which an oral hearing has been required by the Court have been ones in which the justification for the hearing has been the need for the appellate court to hear the appellant as a witness, in which situations his right to be present is implied. These cases are considered in the section on the right to an oral hearing.[466]

b. The right to participate effectively at the hearing

In *Stanford v UK*,[467] the Court held that Article 6 guarantees not only the right of an accused to be present at the hearing, but also the right to hear and follow the proceedings and generally to participate effectively in them. This followed from 'the very notion of an adversarial procedure' and the specific guarantees in Article 6(3)(c), (d), and (e). The right must also apply to civil cases. In the *Stanford* case, the applicant claimed that he was unable to hear the proceedings because of a combination of his hearing difficulties and the acoustics in the courtroom. While the right to participate effectively meant, *inter alia*, that the state must provide a courtroom in which the accused is able to hear and follow the proceedings, the Court found no breach of Article 6 on the facts of the case as a whole. While it was accepted that the accused had indeed not been able to hear all of the evidence, the trial court had not been informed of this and the complaint about the acoustics was unjustified. In addition, the accused had experienced lawyers with him with whom he had been able to communicate and who had clearly defended him well. Similarly, in *Pullicino v Malta*,[468] the confiscation of the accused's notes during the trial hearing raised an issue of effective participation, but did not amount to a breach on the facts.

The right to participate effectively was infringed in *V v UK*.[469] In that case, the applicant was one of two boys tried at the age of eleven years[470] for the murder of a two-year-old boy in a case that had attracted huge publicity in the national media. The trial took place in public over three weeks in a packed Crown Court. Although some special measures were taken in view of the accused's young age,[471] nevertheless 'the formality and ritual of the Crown Court must at times have seemed incomprehensible and intimidating for a child of 11'; and there was evidence that the raising of the dock in which the accused was placed, in order for him to see the proceedings, increased his discomfort by exposing him to the press and the public. There was also psychiatric evidence to suggest that the accused had been terrified and unable to pay attention to the proceedings. The Court held that in these circumstances, the applicant's right to participate effectively in the hearing had not been respected; although his lawyers sat close by him, he would have been in no state to consult with them or generally to follow what was going on.[472]

---

[463] *X v UK No 4798/71*, 40 CD 31 (1972).

[464] See *Colozza v Italy*, Report of the Commission, para 117 (1983).   [465] See below, p 298.

[466] Below, p 274.   [467] A 282-A (1994) para 26.   [468] *No 45441/99* hudoc (2000) DA.

[469] 1999-IX; 30 EHRR 121 GC. Cf, *SC v UK* 2004-IV; 40 EHRR 226.

[470] For the case of the other accused, see *T v UK* hudoc (1999) GC.

[471] The trial procedure was explained to him, he was shown the courtroom before the trial, and the hearings were shortened.

[472] A Practice Direction on the trial of children and young persons was issued in 2000 to take account on the *T* and *V* cases: see [2000] 2 All ER 205.

It is not a breach of Article 6 for an accused to be placed in a glass cage for security reasons provided that he is able to communicate freely and confidentially with his lawyer and with the court.[473]

c. Equality of arms

The right to a fair hearing supposes compliance with the principle of equality of arms.[474] This principle, which applies to civil as well as criminal proceedings,[475] 'requires each party to be given a reasonable opportunity to present his case under conditions that do not place him at a substantial disadvantage vis-à-vis his opponent'.[476] In general terms, the principle incorporates the idea of a 'fair balance' between the parties.[477] When deciding whether it has been complied with, 'appearances' are relevant, as is the seriousness of what is at stake for the applicant.[478] In criminal cases, the principle of equality of arms in Article 6(1) overlaps with the specific guarantees in Article 6(3).[479] It has, however, a wider scope than these guarantees, applying to all aspects of the proceedings.[480] Non-compliance with the principle does not depend upon proof of unfairness on the facts: the procedural deficiency in itself is a breach of the right to a fair trial.[481]

The principle has been applied most strikingly in cases from civil law jurisdictions in which the role of the *avocat général* or similar officer in final appellate court proceedings has been called in question. The key case was *Borgers v Belgium*.[482] There the Court held that the lack of equal standing in criminal proceedings before the Court of Cassation between the *avocat général* within the Belgian *procureur général's* department and the appellant was in breach of equality of arms. In particular, the *avocat général* was entitled to state his opinion at the hearing as to whether the appellant's appeal should be allowed and then retire with the Court and take part (without a vote) in its discussion of the appeal. The appellant did not have prior notice of the *avocat général's* opinion and could neither reply to it nor retire with the judges. The decision reversed the European Court's earlier ruling to the contrary in the much-criticized case of *Delcourt v Belgium*[483] and invalidated a century-old Belgian practice. In its reasoning, the Court accepted that the *avocat général* was not a part of the prosecution and that his function was to give independent and impartial advice to the Court of Cassation on the legal issues raised in the case and on the consistency of its case law. However, once he had expressed an opinion on the merits of the appeal and where this opinion favoured its dismissal, the *avocat général* became the applicant's 'opponent', to whose arguments the applicant should have been able to respond. Similarly, and 'above all', the *avocat général's* participation in the Court's private deliberations 'could reasonably be thought' to have afforded him an opportunity to reinforce his view that the appeal should be dismissed. In reaching its conclusion, the

---

[473] *Auguste v France No 11837/85*, 69 DR 104 (1990) Com Rep; CM Res DH (91) 3. See also *Campbell v UK No 12323/86*, 57 DR 148 (1988) (handcuffing). On cages and handcuffing under Article 3, see above, p 101.

[474] *Neumeister v Austria* A 8 (1968); 1 EHRR 91.

[475] *Dombo Beheer v Netherlands* A 274 (1993); 18 EHRR 213 para 33.

[476] *Kress v France* 2001-VI para 72 GC. Total equality between the parties is not required so that publicly funded legal aid does not have to match that provided privately by the other party: *Steel and Morris v UK* 2005-II; 41 EHRR 403 GC. The principle extends to ancillary proceedings, eg, for costs: *Beer v Austria* hudoc (2001).

[477] *Dombo Beheer v Netherlands* A 274 (1993); 18 EHRR 213 para 33.

[478] *AB v Slovakia* hudoc (2003).   [479] See below, pp 306ff.

[480] *Ofner and Hopfinger v Austria* 6 YB 676 (1962) Com Rep para 46; CM Res DH (63) 1.

[481] *Bulut v Austria* 1996-II; 24 EHRR 84.

[482] A 214-B (1991); 15 EHRR 92 PC. See Wauters, 69 RDIDC 125 (1992).

[483] A 11 (1970); 1 EHRR 355. For criticisms, see Cappelletti and Jolowicz, *Public Interest Parties and the Active Role of the Judge in Civil Litigation*, 1975, p 31; Nadelmann 66 AJIL 509 (1972); and Velu, *L'Affaire Delcourt*, 1972.

European Court emphasized the importance of 'appearances' and 'the increased sensitivity of the public to the fair administration of justice'.[484] The emphasis upon 'appearances',
which echoes the English law doctrine that 'justice must be seen to be done', follows the
use of the same idea in the Court's jurisprudence on the requirement of an 'independent
and impartial' tribunal.[485]

In a number of similar cases since *Borgers*, concerning both Belgium and other civil
law jurisdictions and in both civil and criminal cases, the Strasbourg Court has continued to find breaches of Article 6(1), but has modified its reasoning. In particular, it has
treated cases of the lack of prior disclosure of the opinion of an *avocat général* or similar
officer, and of an opportunity to comment on it, as a breach not of equality of arms, but of
the right to an adversarial trial.[486] This is appropriate in that such officers are not parties
to the proceedings and the lack of prior disclosure, etc, affects the preparation of their
case equally by all parties.[487] In cases in which the *avocat général* has also retired with
the court, the Strasbourg Court has regarded the breach of the right to an adversarial
trial as 'aggravated' by this second feature of the proceedings, and not identified it as a
separate breach of equality of arms.[488] In *Kress v France*,[489] the fact that the *commissaire
du gouvernement*[490] retired with the Conseil d'Etat, having made submissions adverse to
a litigant's case, was held by the Grand Chamber, by ten votes to seven, to be a breach of
Article 6(1) generally, not of equality of arms, although the Court did refer to a legitimate
'feeling of inequality' that the litigant might have.

In cases in which the officer does retire with the court, as in both *Borgers* and *Kress*,
the application of an equality of arms approach, based upon a 'legitimate doubt', would
appear justified. However, it has been suggested that this reliance upon 'appearances' has
been taken too far, arguably leading the Court to require states to change long-established
practices by valued institutions that are recognized without question as independent of
government and objective in their approach, and that play an important role in ensuring
the proper administration of justice.[491] The Court's response to such criticism in *Kress*
was that:[492]

> the mere fact that the administrative courts, and the Government Commissioner in par-
> ticular, have existed for more than a century and, according to the Government, function
> to every one's satisfaction cannot justify a failure to comply with the present requirements
> of European law…the Convention is a living instrument to be interpreted in the light of
> current conditions and the ideas prevailing in democratic States today.

In criminal cases, apart from the obvious requirement established in the *Borgers* line of
cases that the defence is entitled to a right of audience substantially equal to that of the

---

[484] *Borgers v Belgium* A 214-B (1991); 15 EHRR 92 para 24 PC. Cf, the reasoning in *Brandstetter v Austria* A
211 (1991); 15 EHRR 378.
[485] See below, p 290.   [486] See below, p 254.
[487] Cf, *Kress v France* 2001-VI para 73 GC. *Martinie v France* 2006-VI GC was decided on a 'fair hearing'
rather than an adversarial trial or other basis.
[488] *Vermeulen v Belgium* 1996-I; 32 EHRR 313. Cf, *Lobo Machado v Portugal* 1996-I; 23 EHRR 79. Both are
civil cases.
[489] 2001-VI paras 81–2 GC. See also *Fretté v France* 2002-I; 38 EHRR 438.
[490] The *commissaire du gouvernement*'s function in the French *Conseil d'État* differs from that of an *avocat
général* in that it is solely to make submissions on cases and not also to ensure consistency of jurisprudence.
[491] See the dissenting opinion of Judge Martens in *Borgers* and joint partly dissenting opinion of Judges
Wildhaber, Costa, Pastor Ridruejo, Kuris, Birsan, Botoucharova, and Ugrekhelidze in *Kress*. The Court has held
that *avocats généraux* and *commissaires du gouvernement* are independent and impartial under Article 6(1): see
Borgers, para 24 and *Kress*, para 82.
[492] 2001-VI para 70 GC.

prosecution, a number of other particular rulings have been made. Thus the failure to lay down rules of criminal procedure by legislation may be a breach of equality of arms, since their purpose is 'to protect the defendant against any abuse of authority and it is therefore the defence which is the most likely to suffer from omissions and lack of clarity in such rules'.[493] In addition, an expert witness appointed by the accused must be accorded equal treatment with one appointed by the trial court who has links with the prosecution.[494] Requiring the lawyer for the accused, but not the prosecution, to wait many hours before being heard by the court may also be a breach of equality of arms.[495] The failure by the prosecution to disclose all 'material evidence' to the defence may be a breach of equality of arms (as well as of the right to an adversarial trial),[496] as may limitations upon an accused's access to his case file or other documents on public interest grounds.[497]

With regard to 'civil rights and obligations' cases, there is a breach of equality of arms if one party may attend the hearing when the other may not.[498] In *Dombo Beheer v Netherlands*,[499] in which it had to be proved that an oral agreement had been made by X and Y at a meeting which only they attended, there was a breach of the principle because the applicant was not allowed to call X to give evidence when the other party was allowed to call Y. The principle was also infringed in *Ruiz-Mateos v Spain*[500] when the applicants were not allowed to reply to written submissions to the Constitutional Court made by the Counsel for the State, their opponent in a civil case, on the constitutionality of a relevant law. In other cases, the Court has indicated that equality of arms requires that a party to civil proceedings be permitted to call witnesses,[501] and to cross-examine witnesses against him;[502] to have material evidence in support of his case admitted in court;[503] and to be informed of, and hence be able to challenge, the reasons for an administrative decision.[504] A court appointed expert must be neutral,[505] and litigants must also be allowed access to facilities on equal terms.[506] Unequal time limits for the bringing of proceedings may also be a breach of equality of arms,[507] as may rules as to costs that unduly favour the state or other party.[508]

Finally, the Court has relied upon the principle of equality of arms in some cases in which a state has enacted legislation with retroactive effect that is intended to influence

[493] *Coëme v Belgium* 2000-VII para 102.

[494] *Bönisch v Austria* A 92 (1985); 9 EHRR 191. A court appointed expert must be neutral: *Brandstetter v Austria* A 211 (1991); 15 EHRR 378.

[495] *Makhfi v France* hudoc (2004). For other criminal cases on 'equality of arms' see *Blastland v UK* No 12045/86, 52 DR 273 (1987); *U v Luxembourg* No 10140/82, 42 DR 86 (1985); *Kremzow v Austria* A 268-B (1993); 17 EHRR 322; and *Monnell and Morris v UK* A 115 (1987); 10 EHRR 205.

[496] Non-disclosure is considered under the right to an adversarial trial, below, p 254. See also *Bendenoun v France* A 284 (1994); 18 EHRR 54; and *Kuopila v Finland* hudoc (2000); 33 EHRR 615. On the handing over of evidence for scientific testing, see *Korellis v Cyprus* hudoc (2003).

[497] *Matyjek v Poland* 2007-XX (lustration proceedings).

[498] *Komanický v Slovakia* hudoc (2002).

[499] A 274 (1993); 18 EHRR 213. See also *Ankerl v Switzerland* 1996-V; 32 EHRR 1.

[500] A 262 (1993); 16 EHRR 505 PC.

[501] *Wierzbicki v Poland* hudoc (2002); 38 EHRR 805. But the Court will respect a national court's refusal to hear a witness, unless it is 'tainted by arbitrariness': id, para 45. Cf, Article 6(3)(d), below, p 326.

[502] *X v Austria* No 5362/72, 42 CD 145 (1972).

[503] *De Haes and Gijsels v Belgium* 1997-I; 25 EHRR 1.

[504] *Hentrich v France* A 296-A (1994); 18 EHRR 440 para 56.

[505] *Sara Lind Eggertsdottir v Iceland* 2007-XX.

[506] See *Schuler-Zgraggen v Switzerland* A 263 (1993); 16 EHRR 405. For other civil cases, see *H v France* A 162-A (1989); 12 EHRR 74; *Van de Hurk v Netherlands* A 288 (1994); 18 EHRR 481; *Yvon v France* 2003-V; 40 EHRR 938.

[507] *Platakou v Greece* 2001-I and *Dacia SRL v Moldova* hudoc (2008).

[508] *Stankiewicz v Poland* 2006-VI.

the outcome of pending civil litigation against the state.[509] In other such cases, the Court has treated the legislation as falling foul of a separate Article 6(1) 'fair hearing' requirement, distinct from equality of arms.[510]

d. The right to an adversarial trial

The right to an adversarial trial 'means in principle the opportunity for the parties to a civil or criminal trial to have knowledge of and comment on all evidence adduced or observations filed with a view to influencing the Court's decision'.[511] It is for the court to take the initiative to inform an accused or a party to civil proceedings of the existence of such evidence or observations; it is not sufficient that the material is on file at the court for the party to consult.[512] In criminal cases, the right also requires that the 'prosecution authorities should disclose to the defence all material evidence in their possession for or against the accused',[513] whether or not they use it in the proceedings. In criminal cases, the right to an adversarial trial overlaps with the specific guarantees in Article 6(3), particularly those in Article 6(3)(b) and (d) to adequate facilities and to call and cross-examine witnesses respectively.[514] Generally, the approach of the Court is to decide the case under Article 6(1), after considering whether the trial as a whole has been 'fair'. It is not necessary to show actual prejudice: the essence of the right is that the parties should be in a position to decide whether they wish to respond to the material.[515]

While the facts of a case may give rise to issues under both the right to an adversarial trial and the right to equality of arms, the two rights differ in that whereas the latter is satisfied if the parties are treated equally, the former requires access to all relevant material, whether the other party has access to it or not.[516] The Court applied both the rights to an adversarial trial and to equality of arms in a group of UK criminal cases[517] in which material in the possession of the prosecution was not made available to the defence on public interest immunity grounds. In these cases, the Court established that whereas, as indicated above, the prosecution must disclose 'all material evidence' to the defence, this is not an absolute requirement. It is permissible to withhold evidence if

---

[509] See *Stran Greek Refineries v Greece* A 301-B (1994); 19 EHRR 293; and *OGIS-Institut Stanislas et al v France* hudoc (2004).

[510] See below, p 266.

[511] *Vermeulen v Belgium* 1996-I; 32 EHRR 313 para 33 GC. Cf, *Barberà, Messegué and Jabardo v Spain* A 146 (1988); 11 EHRR 360 para 78 PC: 'all evidence must in principle be produced in the presence of the accused...with a view to adversarial argument'. In the *Barberà* case, the Court found a breach of the fair hearing guarantee partly because various witness statements and documents on the investigation file were simply read into the record. See also *Feldbrugge v Netherlands* A 99 (1986); 8 EHRR 425 PC (access to case file); *Georgios Papageogiou v Greece* 2003-VI (forged cheques not adduced); and *Sofri v Italy* No 37235/97 2003 DA (evidence destroyed).

[512] *Göç v Turkey* 2002-V; 35 EHRR 134 GC. See also *HAL v Finland* hudoc (2004). However, a party must use all available procedures for obtaining disclosure: *McGinley and Egan v UK* 1998-III; 27 EHRR 1.

[513] *Edwards and Lewis v UK* 2004-X; 40 EHRR 593 para 46 GC. Although this is sometimes formulated as a separate fair hearing requirement from the right to an adversarial trial, it is treated here as a part of the latter.

[514] See below, pp 309 and 322. These guarantees apply to civil proceedings under the rights to an adversarial trial and equality of arms: see *Wierzbicki v Poland* hudoc (2002); 38 EHRR 805.

[515] *Walston (No 1) v Norway* hudoc (2003) para 58.

[516] See *Niederöst-Huber v Switzerland* 1997-I; 25 EHRR 709.

[517] *Rowe and Davis v UK* 2000-II; 30 EHRR 1 GC; *Jasper v UK* hudoc (2000); 30 EHRR 441 GC; *Fitt v UK* 2000-II; 30 EHRR 480 GC; *Dowsett v UK* 2003-VII; 38 EHRR 845; *Edwards and Lewis v UK* 2004-X; 40 EHRR 593 GC; and *Mansell v UK* No 60590/00 hudoc (2003) DA. See also *Edwards v UK* A 247-B (1992); 15 EHRR 417 in which the police failed to inform the defence of material evidence (fingerprints, failure to identify the accused) where there was no public interest immunity claim: no breach as any possible unfairness was rectified on appeal. Cf, *Botmeh and Alami v UK* hudoc (2007).

this is 'strictly necessary' 'to preserve the fundamental rights of another individual or to safeguard an important public interest': for example, non-disclosure might be justified to protect informers, police undercover activities, or national security.[518] Where public interest immunity is claimed, the Strasbourg Court's role is not to assess the necessity for withholding the evidence, which is the function of the national courts, but to ensure that the procedure followed when the non-disclosure decision is taken incorporates adequate safeguards to protect the interests of the accused. In *Jasper v UK*,[519] the Grand Chamber held that the public interest immunity procedure in English law complied with Article 6(1) as it applied on the facts of the case. Under that procedure, the decision on non-disclosure on public interest immunity grounds was taken by the trial judge after examining the non-disclosed evidence. The defence was not shown the evidence or even told of the kind of evidence it was, but was permitted to outline its case to the judge, who was competent to order disclosure of evidence relevant to it. In ruling, by a bare majority of nine to eight, that the judge's decision authorizing non-disclosure was not a breach of the rights to an adversarial trial or equality of arms, the Court was strongly influenced by the fact that the non-disclosed evidence formed no part of the prosecution case and was not put to the jury. In contrast, in *Edwards and Lewis v UK*,[520] the Grand Chamber unanimously held that the same English law procedure did not comply with the same rights on the facts of that case. In particular, the facts differed from those in *Jasper* in that the non-disclosed material in *Edwards and Lewis* was directly relevant to the trial, for the reason that it related to the applicants' possible entrapment by the police into committing the alleged offence which, if established, would have led to the discontinuance of the prosecution. In these circumstances, a procedure that did not permit the defence to have access to the material, and an opportunity then to argue its case for entrapment with full information, was a breach of Article 6(1).[521]

A breach of the right to an adversarial trial was also found in a series of cases from civil law jurisdictions in which an *avocat général* or similar officer[522] presented an opinion in final appellate court proceedings to which the parties had not had prior access or upon which they had not been able to comment.[523]

A breach of the right to an adversarial trial has been found in various other contexts. For example, in *Kamasinski v Austria*,[524] there was a breach of Article 6(1) when the Supreme Court obtained, and relied upon, information obtained over the telephone from the presiding judge at the trial; this was without the accused being informed or having

---

[518] *Edwards and Lewis v UK* 2004-X; 40 EHRR 593 para 46 GC.

[519] Hudoc (2000); 30 EHRR 441 GC. Cf, *Fitt v UK*, above. The procedure was introduced after a breach of Article 6 was found in *Rowe and Davis*, above, in which the prosecution withheld evidence that a key witness was a paid informer without informing the trial judge. In contrast with *Edwards*, above, n 517, the unfairness in *Rowe and Davis* could not be rectified on appeal.

[520] 2004-X; 40 EHRR 593 GC.

[521] On the possible use of special counsel to represent the interests of the accused in the light of *Edwards and Lewis*, see *R v H and C* [2004] 2 WLR 335; [2004] UKHL 3.

[522] On the independent role of such officers, who are not parties to the case, see above, p 251.

[523] See *Vermeulen v Belgium* 1996-I; 32 EHRR 313 GC; *Lobo Machado v Portugal* (civil case) 1996-I; 23 EHRR 79 GC; *JJ v Netherlands* 1998-II; 28 EHRR 168; *KDB v Netherlands* 1998-II; *Van Orshoven v Belgium* 1997-III; 26 EHRR 55. See also *Reinhardt and Slimane-Kaïd v France* 1998-II; 28 EHRR 59 GC and *Kress v France* 2001-VI GC. On the inter-relationship with 'equality of arms' in these cases, see above, p 252.

[524] A 168 (1989); 13 EHRR 36. The Court expressed itself in terms of a breach of the 'principle that contending parties should be heard (*le principe du contradictoire*)', para 102. Cf, *Brandstetter v Austria* A 211 (1991); 15 EHRR 398 in which the principle was prominent in finding a breach of Article 6(1) when an accused was not given notice of submissions by the Senior Public Prosecutor that were relied on by the appeal court.

an opportunity to comment on the judge's response.[525] In *McMichael v UK*,[526] there was a breach where social reports on children in care, relevant to a dispute between their parents and the local authority, were not revealed to the parents. In *Mantovanelli v France*,[527] there was a breach when the applicants were not permitted to participate in the procedure for obtaining a medical expert's report.

e. Rules of evidence

The right to a fair hearing in Article 6(1) does not require that any particular rules of evidence are followed in national courts in either criminal or non-criminal cases; it is in principle for each state to lay down its own rules.[528] Such an approach is inevitable, given the wide variations in the rules of evidence in different European legal systems, with, for example, common law systems controlling the admissibility of evidence very tightly and civil law systems setting very few restrictions.[529] However, the Strasbourg Court has set certain parameters within which a state must operate.

Admissibility of evidence

In *Schenk v Switzerland*[530] the Court stated that Article 6 'does not lay down any rules on the admissibility of evidence as such, which is therefore primarily a matter for regulation under national law'. Accordingly, it 'is not the role of the Court to determine, as a matter of principle, whether particular types of evidence…may be admissible…The question for the Court instead is whether the proceedings as a whole, including the way in which the evidence was obtained, were fair.'[531]

As to the admissibility of *illegally obtained* evidence, in *Chalkley v UK*,[532] the Court summarized the position as being that 'the use at trial of material obtained without a proper legal basis or through unlawful means will not generally offend the standard of fairness imposed by Article 6(1) where proper procedural safeguards are in place and the nature and source of the material is not tainted, for example, by any oppression, coercion or entrapment which would render reliance on it unfair'; instead the lack of a legal basis raises an issue generally to be addressed under Article 8 (the right to privacy). Article 6 comes into play only if the use of evidence illegally obtained renders the trial unfair.

This summary by the Court was based upon the *Schenck* and *Khan* cases. In the *Schenk* case, there was no breach of Article 6(1) when a tape recording of a conversation between the applicant and another person, P, that was obtained in breach of Swiss criminal and other law, and that incriminated the applicant, was admitted in evidence. This was because the proceedings as a whole were not unfair, for the following reasons. First, the rights of the defence had not been disregarded. In particular, the defence had the opportunity to challenge both the authenticity of the recording and its admission as evidence

---

[525] Cf, the facts of *J v Switzerland No 13467/87* hudoc (1989) DA (F Sett) in which a conviction was based on reports obtained after the hearing unknown to the accused.

[526] A 307-B (1995); 20 EHRR 205. Cf, *Feldbrugge v Netherlands* A 99 (1986); 8 EHRR 425 PC.

[527] 1997-II; 24 EHRR 370. Cf, *Cottin v Belgium* hudoc (2005). And see *Augusto v France* 2007-XX (non-communication of expert's report).

[528] Eg, the burden of proof in civil proceedings is in principle a matter for national courts: *Hämäläinen v Finland No 351/02* hudoc (2004) DA. See also *X v Belgium No 8876/80*, 20 DR 233 (1980).

[529] See Schlesinger, Baade, Herzog, and Wise, *Comparative Law*, 6th edn, 1998, p 425.

[530] A 140 (1988); 13 EHRR 242 para 46 PC.

[531] 2000-V; 31 EHRR 1016 para 34. Cf, *Jalloh v Germany* 2006-IX;44 EHRR 667 para 94 GC. A relevant consideration as to fairness is whether the accused objected to the evidence being admitted: *X v Belgium No 8876/80*, 23 DR 233 (1980).

[532] *No 63831/00* hudoc (2002) DA. Entrapment may be a breach of Article 6(1): see below, p 264.

and to examine both P and the police officer who had instigated the recording. Secondly, the recording was not the only evidence on which the conviction was based.

The *Schenk* case was applied in *Khan v UK*,[533] in which again no breach of Article 6 was found. There a conversation between the applicant and X on the latter's premises had been recorded by an electronic listening device secretly installed on the premises by the police. The recording was admitted in evidence at the applicant's trial for a drug trafficking offence. In contrast to the *Schenk* case, the installation and use of the device were not contrary to national criminal law,[534] and the recording was the only evidence on which the applicant's conviction was based. However, this last consideration was discounted by the Court on the basis that the recording was both 'very strong evidence' and undoubtedly reliable and that in *Schenk* the recording had in fact been important, possibly decisive evidence. Moreover, the applicant had, as in the *Schenk* case, been able to challenge the authenticity and admissibility of the recording and the national courts at three levels of jurisdiction had rejected claims that it should be excluded as rendering the proceedings unfair.

The position is different for the admissibility of evidence obtained by 'torture or inhuman or degrading treatment or punishment' in breach of Article 3 of the Convention. In *Jalloh v Germany*[535] the accused was convicted of drug-trafficking and given a six months' suspended prison sentence. The decisive evidence against him were drugs that he had swallowed that he had been made to regurgitate by the use of an emetic, the forcible administration of which, whilst not in breach of German law, was held by the Strasbourg Court to have been 'inhuman and degrading treatment' contrary to Article 3, but not torture. Had the administration of the emetic amounted to torture, its admission as evidence would without question have been a breach of Article 6. The Court stated that 'incriminating evidence—whether in the form of a confession or real evidence—obtained as a result of acts of violence or brutality or other forms of treatment which can be characterized as torture—should never be relied on as proof of the victim's guilt, irrespective of its probative value.'[536] On the facts of the case, the Court held the applicant's trial had been rendered unfair in breach of Article 6 by the use of evidence obtained by 'inhuman and degrading treatment'. This was because the regurgitated drugs were the decisive evidence that secured the conviction and the public interest in a conviction was limited, given that the applicant was a small-time street dealer given only a light sentence. The Court discounted the fact that the infliction of pain and suffering may not have been intended and that the applicant had been able to challenge the use of the evidence. The decision was particular to its facts. The Court left open the general question whether the use of evidence obtained by 'inhuman or degrading treatment' in breach of Article 3 in all cases 'automatically renders a trial unfair'.[537] In later cases, citing *Jalloh*, the Court has found a breach of Article 6 where a statement has been admitted in court which, although not decisive, has been obtained by inhuman treatment in breach of Article 3; an important factor in these cases was that the accused had not had access to a lawyer in custody.[538]

---

[533] Id, para 37. Cf, *PG and JH v UK* 2001-IX. See also *Parris v Cyprus No 56354/00* hudoc (2002) DA (illegal post-mortem: no breach).

[534] They were in breach of Article 8 ECHR, as not being 'in accordance with the law', having no express legal basis: see below, p 400.

[535] 2006-IX 44 EHRR 667 GC. On the Article 3 ruling, see above, p 100.

[536] Id, para 105. The Court cited Article 15, UN Torture Convention, to this effect. The use of evidence obtained by torture rendered the trial unfair in *Harutyunyan v Armenia* hudoc (2007).

[537] Id, para 107.

[538] *Haci Ozen v Turkey* hudoc (2007); *Gocmen v Turkey* hudoc (2006); and *Soylemez v Turkey* hudoc (2006).

In other cases in which there has been an allegation that evidence has been obtained by coercion or oppression in which there has been no finding of a breach of Article 3, the Strasbourg Court has made it clear that it will not intervene where appropriate safeguards are in place. These include the presence of the accused's lawyer during police questioning or, in the absence of this, satisfactory procedures followed by the court that ensure that the statement has been freely made.[539] The Court's reluctance to find that there has been coercion or oppression was apparent in *Ferrantelli and Santangelo v Italy*.[540] Noting that a national court had investigated and found unproven claims of ill-treatment by the police and recalling that the admissibility of evidence was 'primarily a matter for regulation by national law', the Court held that there was no breach of Article 6: although 'doubts may subsist as to the conduct of the *carabinieri*...the evidence adduced does not provide a sufficient basis for the Court to depart from the findings' of the national judge.

Certain other national rules as to admissibility of evidence have been found to be acceptable. The admission of evidence by an accomplice or other accused who has been promised immunity is not in itself contrary to Article 6.[541] Consistently with the practice in a number of European criminal justice systems, it has also been held that it is not in breach of Article 6 for the court to be informed of the accused's criminal record during the trial[542] or for a conviction to be founded solely on circumstantial evidence.[543] In *Blastland v UK*,[544] it was stated that the common law hearsay rule, by which statements made by persons who do not give evidence in court are, with certain exceptions, not admissible in court, is not, 'in principle', contrary to Article 6. This was because its purpose is 'partly to ensure that the best evidence is before the jury, which can evaluate the credibility and demeanour of the witness, and partly to avoid undue credibility being given to evidence which cannot be tested by cross-examination'. In the *Blastland* case, the exclusion of exculpatory statements that had been made to the police and others by a third party who was not called as a witness and that the defence wished to introduce as evidence was not a breach of equality of arms Article 6(1).[545]

Assessment of evidence

Just as the Strasbourg Court regards the rules as to the admissibility of evidence as primarily a matter for national decision, so it will not generally review the assessment of evidence by a national court.[546] It will only do so where the national court has drawn 'arbitrary or grossly unfair conclusions from the facts submitted to it'.[547] The same general 'hands off' approach extends to 'the means to ascertain the relevant facts' in that the Strasbourg Court will not generally question a national court decision as to the calling of an expert report or witness.[548]

---

[539] See *Latimer v UK No 12141/04* hudoc (2005) and *G v UK No 9370/81*, 35 DR 75 (1983).

[540] 1996-III; 23 EHRR 288 paras 48, 50. There was no allegation of a breach of Article 3. See also *Allan v UK*, below, p 263 (confession to a police informer was self-incrimination).

[541] *Cornelis v Netherlands No 994/03*, 2004-V.   [542] *X v Austria No 2676/65*, 23 CD 31 (1967).

[543] *Alberti v Italy No 12013/86*, 59 DR 100 (1989). But the admission of photocopied evidence must be subjected to strict scrutiny: *Buzescu v Romania* hudoc (2005).

[544] *No 12045/86*, 52 DR 273 at 274. As to the application of the rule and the exceptions to in respect of *prosecution* evidence, see Article 6(3)(d), below, p 323. The hearsay rule was abolished in English *criminal* proceedings by the Criminal Justice Act 2003.

[545] The Commission took into account that the applicant failed to call the third party as a witness and to challenge the hearsay ruling. See Loucaides, 3 HRLR 27 at 34, who argues against the hearsay rule.

[546] *Barberà, Messegué and Jabardo v Spain* A 146 (1988); 11 EHRR 360 para 68 PC. Cf, *Wierzbicki v Poland* hudoc (2002); 38 EHRR 805.

[547] *Waldberg v Turkey No 22909/93* hudoc (1995) DA. Cf, *Camilleri v Malta No 51760/99* hudoc (2000) DA.

[548] See *Sommerfeld v Germany* 2003-VIII; 36 EHRR 565 GC (Article 8 case). Cf, *Accardi v Italy No 30598/02* 2005-II. For an exception, see *Elsholz v Germany* 2000-VIII; 34 EHRR 1412.

Disclosure of evidence
The obligation to disclose all material evidence to the other party has been considered above under the right to an adversarial trial.[549]

f. Presumption of innocence in criminal cases

The presumption of innocence in criminal cases is guaranteed by Article 6(2) and is considered under that provision.[550] However, the presumption of innocence is also a part of the 'general notion of a fair hearing' in Article 6(1). This is crucial where the applicant is subject to a criminal 'charge' but where Article 6(2) does not apply. This was the case in *Phillips v UK*,[551] in which the applicant had been convicted of a drug trafficking offence and sentenced to nine years' imprisonment. In separate proceedings, the Crown Court later made an order confiscating property believed to have been gained from drug trafficking. In those proceedings the court applied a rebuttable statutory assumption that property held by the applicant following his conviction or during a six-year period before it was obtained by drug trafficking. In response to the applicant's claim that the assumption infringed the presumption of innocence, the Strasbourg Court held that Article 6(2) did not govern the confiscation proceedings as it ceased to apply after conviction, but that the presumption of innocence in Article 6(1) did apply as Article 6(1) generally 'applies throughout the entirety of proceedings'. However, no breach of the presumption of innocence was found, as the application of the statutory assumption on the facts of the case was 'reasonable.'

g. The principle of immediacy

It is 'an important element of fair criminal proceedings' that the accused should be able to confront a witness in the presence of the judge who finally decides the case.[552] Thus 'normally' a change in the composition of the trial court after the hearing of an important witness should lead to lead to the re-hearing of that witness, although exceptions may be allowed where the facts as a whole suggest that the outcome of the case has not been affected.[553] This principle of immediacy applies also to civil proceedings, although less strictly.[554]

h. Freedom from self-incrimination

The right to a fair hearing includes freedom from self-incrimination in criminal cases. In one sense, this is an unexpected reading of Article 6(1), in that when Council of Europe member states added to the rights of the accused in the Seventh Protocol to the Convention, they considered including freedom from self-incrimination but decided not to do so. Nonetheless, the Court's subsequent jurisprudence under Article 6 fills an obvious and unfortunate gap. As the Court stated in *Saunders v UK*,[555] 'the right to silence and the right not to incriminate oneself are generally recognized international standards which lie at the heart of the notion of a fair procedure under Article 6'.

Freedom from self-incrimination follows from the autonomy of the individual, the need to avoid miscarriages of justice, and the principle that the prosecution should prove its case without the assistance of the accused.[556] In Article 6 it is 'primarily concerned

---

[549] See above, p 254.   [550] See below, p 299.   [551] 2001-VII para 39.
[552] *PK v Finland No 37442/97* hudoc (2002) DA. The principle overlaps with the right to contront witnesses, below, p 323.
[553] *Ibid.*   [554] *Pitkänen v Finland* hudoc (2004).
[555] 1996-VI; 23 EHRR 313 para 68 GC. Freedom from self-incrimination is expressly guaranteed in Article 14(3)(e) of the International Covenant on Civil and Political Rights.
[556] *Ibid.* It is also closely linked to the presumption of innocence: *ibid.*

with respecting the will of an accused to remain silent'.[557] Accordingly, it excludes the obtaining of tangible evidence by the state's use of compulsory powers. As the Court stated in *Saunders*:[558]

> As commonly understood in the legal systems of the Contracting Parties to the Convention and elsewhere, it does not extend to the use in criminal proceedings of material which may be obtained from the accused through the use of compulsory powers but which has an existence independent of the will of the suspect such as, *inter alia*, documents acquired pursuant to a warrant, breath, blood and urine samples and bodily tissue for the purpose of DNA testing.

However, Article 6 is not limited totally to the refusal to answer questions or make a statement. It also applies to situations in which there is 'coercion to hand over real evidence to the authorities'.[559] Thus in *Funke v France*,[560] in which the applicant was required himself to produce documents, as opposed to being subjected to the execution by others of a search warrant for them, the evidence was not obtained independently of his will, so that his right to freedom from self-incrimination was in issue. In *Jalloh v Germany*,[561] the *Funke* case was extended to cover a situation in which the applicant was subjected to the forced administration of an emetic causing him to regurgitate 'real evidence' (drugs) from his body. In this case the Grand Chamber distinguished the examples of material given in *Saunders* that fall outside the guarantee of freedom from self-incrimination on the following grounds. It noted that the material obtained in *Jalloh* was 'real evidence', as opposed to material that was wanted for forensic examination; that the degree of force used to obtain it was much greater than that used in the conduct of blood tests, etc; and that the procedure used to recover the drugs involved a breach of Article 3.

Freedom from self-incrimination is not absolute; what is prohibited is 'improper compulsion'.[562] 'Compulsion' may take various forms. Clearly, the use of physical force against a person aimed at obtaining a confession or other evidence from him is compulsion,[563] as is requiring an accused to give evidence at his trial by law.[564] The threat[565] or imposition[566] of a criminal sanction for failure to provide information is compulsion and may be a breach of freedom from self-incrimination whether or not the person concerned is later prosecuted for,[567] or convicted of,[568] an offence. A rule permitting the drawing of adverse inferences from the exercise of the right to silence is also a form of compulsion, by bringing pressure to bear to answer questions.[569] Similarly, the use of an undercover agent to solicit information may involve compulsion. This was the case in *Allan v UK*,[570] where the applicant confessed to a murder to an undercover

---

[557] Id, para 69. The right to silence is a part of the larger concept of freedom from self-incrimination, which includes incrimination by eg, a breath test or a search (matters within Article 8 of the Convention). Although Article 6 is mostly only about the right to silence, the general term is used in this chapter.

[558] *Ibid.*   [559] *Jalloh v Germany* 2006-IX; 44 EHRR 667 para 111 GC.

[560] A 256-A (1993); 16 EHRR 297. See also *JB v Switzerland* 2001-III, in which freedom from self-incrimination was infringed where the applicant was fined for failing to produce business documents relevant to a pending tax evasion charge.

[561] 2006-IX GC.   [562] *Murray (John) v UK* 1996-I; 22 EHRR 29 para 46 GC.

[563] See *Jalloh v Germany* 2006-IX; 44 EHRR 667 GC. See also *Austria v Italy* 6 YB 740 at 784 (1963) Com Rep; CM Res DH (63) 3.

[564] See *Murray (John) v UK* 1996-I; 22 EHRR 29 para 47 GC. See also *Serves v France* 1997-VI; 28 EHRR 265 (applicant obliged to give evidence in the preliminary investigation of a fellow suspect for the same murder).

[565] *Saunders v UK* 1996-VI; 23 EHRR 313 GC.   [566] *Funke v France* A 256-A (1993); 16 EHRR 297.

[567] *Ibid.*   [568] *Heaney and McGuiness v Ireland* 2000-XII; 33 EHRR 264.

[569] *Condron v UK* 2000-V; 31 EHRR 1.

[570] 2002-IX. The Court stressed that the informer could be seen as a state agent whose questioning was the equivalent of interrogation. Contrast *A v FRG No 12127/86* hudoc (1986) DA.

police informer who was placed in his remand cell for the purpose of eliciting information from him. Having resisted police questioning, the psychological pressures upon the applicant, who was induced to confess by persistent questioning by someone with whom he shared his cell, meant that the confession was obtained 'in defiance of the will' of the applicant.

Compulsion is 'improper' if the 'very essence of the right' not to incriminate oneself is destroyed. This test was articulated in *Murray (John) v UK*.[571] There the Court held that the possibility of drawing of adverse inferences from the failure of a suspect or an accused to answer questions, either before or at his or her trial for a criminal offence, does not amount to 'improper compulsion', destroying the 'very essence of the right', provided that proper safeguards are in place. In that case, the applicant was arrested in a house in which a police informer was being questioned by the IRA. He was convicted of aiding and abetting false imprisonment. Under the legislation applicable to terrorist offences in Northern Ireland, the applicant was tried by an experienced judge without a jury who drew 'strong inferences' from the applicant's failure, exercising his right to silence, to explain his presence in the house when he was arrested and interrogated by the police and from his refusal to give evidence at his trial. The Court held, by fourteen votes to five, that there was no 'improper compulsion' upon the applicant to break his silence, because of the safeguards that applied. These were that adverse inferences could only be drawn (i) if the accused had been cautioned that this could follow from his exercise of the right to silence and (ii) there was a *prima facie* case against the accused that could lead to a conviction if unanswered, and that the judge both had a discretion as to whether it was appropriate to draw inferences from silence and had to give reasons should he do so. Given these safeguards and the 'formidable' case against the applicant, the Court concluded that the drawing of adverse inferences on the facts was 'a matter of common sense' and could not be regarded as 'unfair or unreasonable'; whereas it was contrary to the right to freedom of self-incrimination to base a conviction 'solely or mainly' on the accused's silence, this should not prevent that silence being taken into account in situations 'which clearly call for an explanation' provided that satisfactory safeguards apply. As the Court noted, the UK legislation providing for the drawing of inferences simply placed upon a 'formalized' basis the practice of criminal courts in 'a considerable number of countries' in Europe.

In the *Murray (John)* case, the Court distinguished *Funke v France*.[572] In *Funke*, the applicant was convicted and fined for an offence of refusing to produce bank statements, which it was believed existed, at the request of the customs authorities who suspected him of having committed offences concerning financial dealings abroad.[573] The 'degree of compulsion' to which the applicant was subjected in *Funke* destroyed the 'very essence' of his freedom from self-incrimination.[574]

Adverse inferences were also at issue in *Condron v UK*.[575] There it was held that where adverse inferences may be drawn not by a judge, as happened in the *Murray* case, but by

---

[571] 1996-I; 22 EHRR 29 PC.   [572] A 256-A (1993); 16 EHRR 297.

[573] Although not arrested, the applicant in *Funke* was considered to be 'charged' as being 'substantially affected' by the allegation made against him: see *Weh v Austria* hudoc (2004); 40 EHRR 890 para 52. The applicant's death forestalled his prosecution for the substantive offence. For criticism of the *Funke* case, see Naismith, 3 EHRLR 229 (1997) and Stressens, ELR Human Rights Survey 45 (1996).

[574] *Murray (John) v UK* 1996-I; 22 EHRR 29 para 49. The Court had not used 'very essence' language in *Funke*. The severity of the sanction is a relevant factor in deciding whether the 'very essence' of the right is destroyed: *Allen v UK No 76574/01* hudoc (2002) DA (a small fine: no breach). In *Heaney and McGuiness v Ireland* 2000-XII; 33 EHRR 264 no distinction was drawn between accumulated fines (*Funke*) and a six-month prison sentence (*Heaney and McGuiness*).

[575] 2000-V; 31 EHRR 1 para 61. *Condron* has been applied in eg, *Beckles v UK* hudoc (2002); 36 EHRR 162; *Smith v UK No 64714/01* hudoc (2002) DA; and *Wood v UK* hudoc (2004) DA.

a jury, a necessary additional safeguard that is required to prevent an infringement of the right to freedom from self-incrimination is that the jury is directed that 'if it was satisfied that the applicants' silence at the police interview could not sensibly be attributed to their having no answer or none that would stand up to cross-examination it should not draw an adverse inference'. In the *Condron* case, the applicants, who were heroin addicts, were suspected of drug dealing. They exercised their right to silence during police questioning on the advice of their solicitor, who was present during the interview and was concerned that they would not be able to follow the questions because of the influence of drugs. In contrast with the *Murray* case, they did give evidence later at the trial. Applying legislation that contained the safeguards present in the *Murray* case, the judge directed the jury that they might draw adverse inferences from the accused's silence, but did not draw their attention to the possibility that there might have been a good reason for their remaining silent (on their solicitor's advice) other than that they had no satisfactory answers to give.

The 'very essence' of the right was also destroyed in *Heaney and McGuiness v Ireland*.[576] In that case, the applicants were arrested in a house on suspicion of membership of the IRA, and of involvement in a suspected terrorist bombing that had occurred nearby hours earlier. When they refused to answer questions about the bombing or their presence in the house, the applicants were requested to provide an account of their movements during the relevant period under a statute that made failure to give such an account a criminal offence, but they refused to do so. They were later acquitted of an offence involving membership of the IRA, but convicted of the offence of failing to provide the requested account of their movements. The latter convictions, resulting in sentences of six months' imprisonment, were held to be a violation of freedom from self-incrimination. Article 6 applied, as the applicants were 'substantially affected', by being arrested on the basis of their suspected criminal activities, and there was, as in the *Funke* case, 'improper compulsion' in breach of that Article, because the 'degree of compulsion' applied through the imposition of a criminal sanction for failure to supply the requested information destroyed the 'very essence' of the right to freedom from self-incrimination.

In the *Murray (John)* and *Heaney and McGuiness* cases, the Court adopted a 'degree of compulsion' criterion to be applied when deciding whether the compulsion was 'improper' so that the 'very essence' of the right to freedom from self-incrimination had been destroyed. In *Jalloh v Germany*,[577] the Court revised and added to this criterion. The Court stated that it would have regard to the following three criteria: 'the nature and degree of the compulsion, the existence of any relevant procedural safeguards,[578] and the use to which any material so obtained is put'.[579] Applying these three criteria to the facts, the Court noted that the 'nature and degree' of the compulsion had interfered with the applicant's physical and mental integrity to the point where it was 'inhuman and degrading treatment'; that while there were generally sufficient procedures to prevent the arbitrary or improper use of compulsion, the applicant's ability to withstand the force used had not been fully established because of his poor German; and that the evidence obtained was the decisive evidence in the case. The Court also introduced later in its judgment in the *Jalloh* case a fourth criterion, namely the weight of public interest in the investigation, but concluded that this could not on the facts justify such a grave interference with the

---

[576] 2000-XII; 33 EHRR 264 para 48. See Ashworth, [2001] Crim LR 482. See also *Shannon v UK* hudoc (2005); 42 EHRR 660.
[577] 2006-IX para 101 GC. For the facts, see above, p 257.
[578] Cf, the reference to procedural safeguards in *Murray (John)* and *Heaney and McGuiness*.
[579] Cf, the reference to the weight of evidence in *Murray (John)*.

applicant's physical and mental integrity. The use of this fourth criterion was not apparent in the earlier case of *Heaney and McGuiness v Ireland*.[580] There the Court rejected the defendant government's argument that it could require the applicants to give an account of their movements or face a criminal sanction of up to six months' imprisonment as a 'proportionate response' to a terrorist and security threat: such public interest considerations could not justify the imposition of a criminal sanction for remaining silent that destroyed the 'very essence' of the right.

In *O'Halloran and Francis v UK*,[581] the Grand Chamber confirmed and applied the criteria formulated in the *Jalloh* case. In that case, each of the two applicants had been required, on pain of criminal sanction, to identify to the police the driver of his car in connection with a speeding offence. The first applicant revealed that he was the driver and was convicted the speeding offence. The second did not reveal who the driver was, and was convicted of a different criminal offence of failing to identify the driver and fined for not doing so. The Grand Chamber held, by fifteen votes to two, that neither the threat nor the imposition of the criminal sanction for not identifying the driver destroyed the 'essence' of the right to freedom from self-incrimination.[582] It did so on the basis of the 'special nature of the regulatory regime at issue and the limited nature of the information sought', both of which considerations the Court addressed under the first of the *Jalloh* criteria. As to the former, the Court stressed that the regulatory regime for motor vehicles was motivated by their 'potential for grave injury'.[583] As to the latter, the Court noted that only the name of the driver was required,[584] which in itself was not incriminating. The Court also noted, in terms of the third *Jalloh* criterion, that many other elements beyond the identification of the driver were needed to prove guilt.[585] Although the Court did not expressly refer to the fourth, public interest *Jalloh* criterion, it can be seen to underlie the Court's reference to the motivation for the regulatory regime, as can its comment that 'those who choose to keep and drive motor cars can be taken to have accepted certain responsibilities and obligations'[586] including informing the authorities of the drivers of their vehicles.

Public interest considerations were also relevant in *Allen v UK*.[587] In that case, after being pressured, the applicant eventually made the required declaration of his assets for tax purposes, but was convicted of making false statements in it. This was held not to be a breach of freedom from self-incrimination because the applicant did not allege that he was being forced to reveal prior acts or omissions that might contribute to his conviction for some other offence:[588] instead the offence of which he was convicted was committed only in the false statements in his declaration. In any event, as the Court stated, an obligation to declare income and capital for the assessment of tax is 'a common feature of the taxation systems of contracting states and it would be difficult to envisage them functioning effectively without it'.[589] Hence, it would seem that even an accurate return of income

---

[580] 2000-XII; 33 EHRR 264 paras 55–8.   [581] 2007-GC para 62.

[582] In recent cases, the Court has referred to the 'essence', not the 'very essence', of the right.

[583] Id, para 57.

[584] In other cases, the applicants had been requested to provide documents or information about their movements within very broad categories.

[585] As to the second criterion, there were sufficient procedural safeguards.   [586] *Ibid.*

[587] No 76574/01 hudoc DA. Contrast *JB v Switzerland*, above, n 560.

[588] Contrast the *Saunders* case, below.

[589] For other possible examples see *Vasileva v Denmark* hudoc (2003) (giving one's name in some circumstances) and *Shannon v Ireland* hudoc (2005) para 38 (requirement to account for one's movements where no suspicion). See also *R v Hertfordshire CC, ex p Green Environmental Industries Ltd* [2000] AC 326, HL (obligation to answer public health inquiry not in breach of freedom from self-incrimination).

or capital that is (required for tax purposes on pain of criminal sanction) that reveals prior tax evasion would not be a breach of freedom from self-incrimination.

On its facts, the *O'Hallaran and Francis* case concerned two different kinds of cases in which breaches of the right to freedom of self-incrimination have been found. As pointed out by the Court in *Weh v Austria*,[590] first, there are cases in which compulsion is used 'for the purpose of obtaining information which might incriminate the person concerned in pending or anticipated criminal proceedings against him, or—in other words—in respect of an offence with which that person has been "charged" within the autonomous meaning of Article 6(1)'.[591] Second, there are cases of 'incriminating information compulsorily obtained outside of the context of criminal proceedings' that is later used in criminal proceedings against the person concerned.[592] Most cases that raise freedom from self-incrimination issues are of the first kind. Cases of the second kind include cases such as *Saunders v UK*.[593] In that case, the applicant, on pain of criminal sanction (a fine or two years' maximum imprisonment), was required by law to answer (and did answer) questions put to him by Department of Trade and Industry inspectors in the course of their administrative investigation under company law into the conduct of a company takeover. Although this requirement did not *per se* raise an issue of freedom of self-incrimination, the use to which the information was put might do. In the *Saunders* case, the answers that the applicant gave, although not directly self-incriminating, were introduced by the prosecution to great effect in the later successful prosecution of the applicant for offences involving fraud. This was held to be 'improper compulsion' in violation of Article 6.

i. Entrapment

By entrapment is meant conduct instigating the commission of a criminal offence by a person who would otherwise not have committed it. The use in a criminal trial of evidence obtained by such conduct, which is that of an *agent provocateur*, may render the trial unfair in breach of Article 6. In *Teixeira de Castro v Portugal*,[594] the applicant was requested by undercover police officers to supply heroin. The trial leading to his conviction was held by the Strasbourg Court to have been unfair because the officers had not investigated the applicant's possible criminal activity in an 'essentially passive manner, but exercised an influence such as to incite the commission of the offence'. In reaching this conclusion the Court noted that the police action was not judicially authorized[595] and that there were no indications that the applicant was predisposed to commit drug dealing offences:[596] he had no criminal record and all the evidence suggested that he was essentially a drug user who was prepared to help others in need, rather than a person minded and equipped to deal in drugs. In addition, the evidence of the police officers had been the main evidence against him.

The approach taken in the *Teixeira de Castro* case was adopted by the Grand Chamber in *Ramanauskas v Lithuania*,[597] which is now the leading authority on entrapment. In

---

[590] Hudoc (2004); 40 EHRR 890.

[591] Id, para 42. A person is 'charged' where he is under arrest or otherwise 'substantially affected' by an allegation against him: see above, p 209.

[592] Id, para 43.   [593] 1996-IV; 23 EHRR 313 GC.   [594] 1998-IV; 28 EHRR 101 para 38.

[595] See also *Khudobin v Russia* 2006-XX para 135, on the need for 'clear and foreseeable' procedures authorizing undercover investigations and at least judicial review thereof and *Rajcoomar v UK No 59457/00* hudoc (2004) DA (Court satisfied with national court finding that the accused had not been pressured to offend).

[596] Cf, *Vanyan v Russia* hudoc (2005) and *Eurafinacom v France No 58753/00*, 2004-VII DA.

[597] 2008-XX GC. See also *Calabro v Italy and Germany No 59895/00* hudoc (2002) DA and *Sequeira v Portugal No 73557/01* hudoc (2003) DA. In *Khudobin v Russia* 2007-XX the applicant's conviction was not 'fair' when the

that case, the applicant was a prosecutor who, after repeated requests from members of the police anti-corruption unit, eventually accepted a bribe to secure the acquittal of a third person. The Grand Chamber held the applicant's subsequent conviction for a corruption offence, in which the key evidence was his taking of the bribe, was unfair. In reaching this decision, the Grand Chamber noted that there was no evidence that the applicant had committed any corruption or other offences beforehand and that all meetings between the police and the applicant had been initiated by the police. The police conduct went beyond the 'mere passive investigation of existing criminal activity' and incited the applicant to commit an offence which there was no objective indication (only rumours) that he would have committed without their intervention.

In *Shannon v UK*,[598] the question arose whether the use of entrapment evidence obtained not by state agents, but by private persons, might give rise to unfairness in breach of Article 6. In that case, the applicant, a well known TV actor, agreed to provide a *News of the World* journalist, disguised as a sheikh, with cocaine. The journalist revealed this in his newspaper story and handed over his audio and visual recordings to the police. The applicant was convicted of supplying drugs illegally, the recordings being a key part of the evidence. While noting that the *Teixeira de Castro* case was different in that it involved a direct 'misuse of state power', the Court nonetheless stated that the use by the prosecution as evidence in court of information handed over to the state by a third party may 'in certain circumstances' render the proceedings unfair. However, on the facts of the case the Court found no breach of Article 6, essentially because the applicant was, in contrast with the applicant of the *Teixeira de Castro* case, predisposed to supply drugs, responding readily in the manner of an experienced supplier. The Court also noted that the applicant had had the benefit of a five-day adversarial hearing by the trial judge who ruled that the admission of the evidence provided by the journalist would not have an adverse effect on the fairness of the trial.

For the purposes of Article 6, *agents provocateurs* are to be distinguished from undercover police who monitor or participate in, but do not instigate, an offence. Whereas the use of evidence obtained by the former may, in accordance with the above cases, render the trial unfair, the use in court of the evidence of the latter may in some cases be permitted, even though they are excused from appearing in person as witnesses at the trial, subject to necessary safeguards to protect the rights of the defence.[599]

j. Prejudicial media publicity

In *Craxi v Italy*[600] the Court stated that 'in certain cases a virulent press campaign can adversely affect the fairness of a trial by influencing public opinion and consequently the jurors called upon to decide the guilt of an accused'. Whereas Commission decisions to the same effect were expressed in terms of the residual 'fair hearing' guarantee, in the *Craxi* and some other cases the Court has considered this matter under the specific guarantees of an 'impartial tribunal' and the 'presumption of innocence' in Articles 6(1) and 6(2).[601] For convenience the matter is dealt with here as a separate issue under the 'fair hearing' heading. Although some of the Strasbourg jurisprudence might be read as suggesting

trial court failed to give proper conderation to an arguable claim of entrapment. And see *Edwards and Lewis v UK* 2004-X; 40 EHRR 593 GC.

[598] *No 67537/01* hudoc (2004) DA.

[599] *Ludi v Switzerland* A 238 (1992); 15 EHRR 173. See Article 6(3)(d), below, p 323.

[600] Hudoc (2002) para 98. Translation. The ruling applies to the media generally: see eg, *Ninn-Hansen v Denmark No 28972/95,* 1999-V (television).

[601] The *Craxi* case was decided under the presumption of innocence. See also eg, *Claes v Belgium* hudoc (2005) and *Anguelov v Bulgaria No 45963/99* hudoc (2004) DA.

that prejudicial media publicity may be a breach of Article 6 even in trials before judges alone,[602] this is obviously less likely to be so than in cases in which juries (or lay assessors) are involved.[603] This is confirmed by the *Craxi* case in which the Court, when finding that the trial of a former First Minister, which attracted a great deal of media coverage, was not a breach of the presumption of innocence, emphasized that the case was decided entirely by professional judges.

Several limits to possible breaches of Article 6 on a 'virulent campaign' basis have been set, which together help to explain why, despite the great publicity that sometimes attends trials, no case of a violation of Article 6 has yet been found on this ground. Thus the Court has stressed that, in accordance with freedom of expression, some press comment on a trial involving a matter of public interest must be expected.[604] Moreover, in a jury case the effect of prejudicial comment may be countered by the judge's direction to the jury to discount it.[605] Also, the test has sometimes been expressed as a subjective one, requiring proof of prejudicial effect in fact, not just a legitimate doubt.[606] However, in *Wloch v Poland*,[607] the Court would appear to have countenanced an objective as well as a subjective test of liability, which would be consistent with its approach elsewhere.[608] There are also statements suggesting that state involvement in the generation of the publicity is necessary for the state to be responsible for any resulting prejudice,[609] although in the theory of the Convention the simple failure of the court, a state organ, to counter the possible prejudicial effect should be sufficient to engage responsibility under the Convention. Finally, it should be noted that where a national appeal court does not consider that the trial has been unfair on this ground, it is unlikely that a breach will be found at Strasbourg.[610]

k. Legal representation

Whereas Article 6(3)(c) provides a specific guarantee of the right to be legally represented and to be granted legal aid where appropriate in criminal cases, there is no such guarantee in non-criminal cases. However, it has been established that Article 6(1) provides a guarantee, although a less extensive one, in the latter kind of case. This has been achieved by means of the right of access to a court, rather than the right to a fair hearing.[611]

l. Retroactive legislation designed to defeat a litigant's claim

Retroactive legislation that is designed to defeat a litigant's claim against the state in the courts in pending proceedings is in breach of the 'principle of the rule of law and the

---

[602] See *Anguelov v Bulgaria, ibid.*   [603] See eg, *Priebke v Italy No 48799/99* hudoc (2001) DA.

[604] See eg, *Papon v France (No 2) No 54210/00* hudoc (2001) DA. See also the *Sunday Times case*, below, p 472, in which a contempt of court decision in respect of comment on pending civil litigation was contrary to the guarantee of freedom of speech in Article 10. But conviction for criminal contempt for publishing jury deliberations was not a breach of Article 10: *Associated Newspapers Ltd v UK No 24770/94* hudoc (1994).

[605] *Noye v UK No 4491/02* hudoc (2003); 36 EHRR CD 231 DA.

[606] See eg, *X v Norway No 3444/67*, 13 YB 302 (1970).

[607] *No 27785/95* hudoc (2000) DA. But see *Anguelov v Bulgaria No 45963/99* hudoc (2004) DA.

[608] See below, p 284.

[609] See *Ensslin, Baader and Raspe v FRG Nos 7572/76, 7586/76 and 7587/76*, 14 DR 64 at 112 (1978). Cf, *Hauschildt v Denmark No 10486/83*, 49 DR 86 (1986).

[610] See eg, *X v UK No 3860/68*, 30 CD 70 (1969).

[611] See above, p 236. In some cases, the Commission has referred to the 'fair hearing' requirement as well as the right of access: see eg, *Webb v UK No 9353/81*, 33 DR 133 (1983). It has then considered whether there has been a 'fair hearing' in the circumstances of the case as a whole.

notion of a right to a fair trial enshrined in Article 6'.[612] Thus in *Stran Greek Refineries and Stratis Andreadis v Greece*[613] the state challenged in the courts an arbitration award against it arising out of a contract with the applicants. While the state's appeal to the Court of Cassation against lower court judgments was pending, the Greek Parliament, in breach of Article 6, enacted legislation that made it 'inevitable' that the arbitration award in the applicants' case was judicially declared void. While the *Stran* and other cases have been ones in which the state has been a party to the proceedings, there seems to be no reason why the rule concerning retroactive legislation should not extend to cases in which this is not so, but in which legislative interference equally prevents a 'fair trial' between the parties. Exceptionally, retroactive legislation that interferes with the administration of justice in pending cases is not in breach of Article 6 if it can be justified on 'compelling' public interest grounds.[614]

m. The right to have one's case properly examined

Given that Convention rights must be guaranteed 'effectively', Article 6 implies that the national court hearing a case has 'a duty effectively to examine the grounds, arguments and evidence adduced by the parties'.[615] *Kraska v Switzerland*[616] was the first case in which this aspect of the right to a fair hearing was articulated by the Court. There an appeal court judge had, as he remarked, not had time to read all of the appellant's memorial before the hearing. However, although the judge's remark was 'open to criticism', when the proceedings were considered as a whole it was held that it was not established that there had been an unfair hearing. In contrast, there was a breach of Article 6(1) on this basis in *Dulaurans v France*.[617] There the Court of Cassation's sole reason for refusing an application to quash a lower court civil judgment was that it was based upon an argument that was new. The Strasbourg Court held that this was 'a clear error' on the part of the Court of Cassation. The records showed that the applicant had earlier raised the argument before both lower courts, so that the Court of Cassation had not properly examined the applicant's arguments, thereby denying her a fair hearing. In *Kuznetsov v Russia*,[618] there was a breach of Article 6 on a 'proper-examination' basis where their approach to the facts of the case 'permitted the domestic courts to avoid addressing the applicants' main complaint'. In *Pronina v Ukraine*,[619] the failure of a civil court to address an important argument by the applicant was also a breach of Article 6, although the Court relied upon the obligation to give reasons for a decision[620] more than the right to have one's arguments examined.

---

[612] *Zielinski and Pradal & Gonzalez and Others v France* 1999-VII; 31 EHRR 532 para 57 GC. Although the Court refers to a fair 'trial' the rule may be considered under the residual fair 'hearing' heading.

[613] A 301-B (1994); 19 EHRR 293 paras 46, 49. The Court also relied upon 'equality of arms'. See also, eg *Scordino v Italy (No 1)* 2006-V GC. Some cases of interference have been decided on a right of access basis: see above, p 238.

[614] *Forrer-Niedenthal v Germany* hudoc (2003) (furthering German reunification); *Gorraiz Lizarraga and Others v Spain* 2004-III (need for regional planning). See also *National and Provincial Building Society et al v UK* (public interest in clarifying tax law and securing tax payments) above, p 241, n 386 and *OGIS-Institut Stanislas et al v France* hudoc (2004).

[615] *Dulaurans v France* hudoc (2000); 33 EHRR 1093 para 33. Cf, *Van de Hurk v Netherlands* A 238 (1994); 18 EHRR 481. See also the *Van Kück* and *Khamidov* cases, above, p 202.

[616] A 254-B (1993); 18 EHRR 188 para 30.

[617] *Ibid.* Cf, *Fouquet v France* 1996-I; 22 EHRR 279 F Sett before the Court. See also *De Moor v Belgium* A 292-A (1994); 18 EHRR 372; *Quadrelli v Italy* hudoc (2000); 34 EHRR 215; and *Jokela v Finland* 2002-IV; 37 EHRR 581.

[618] 2007-XX para 84.   [619] Hudoc (2006).

[620] On the obligation to give reasons, see below, p 268.

n. A reasoned judgment

The requirement of a 'fair' hearing also supposes that a court will give reasons for its judgment, in both criminal and non-criminal cases. Whereas national courts are allowed considerable discretion as to the structure and content of their judgments, they must 'indicate with sufficient clarity the grounds on which they base their decision' so as to allow a litigant usefully to exercise any available right of appeal.[621] Further justifications for the need for a reasoned judgment are the interest of a litigant in knowing that his or her arguments have been properly examined, and the interest of the public in a democratic society in knowing the reasons for judicial decisions given in its name.[622]

Precisely what is required will depend upon the nature and circumstances of each case.[623] It is not necessary for the court to deal with every point raised in argument.[624] If, however, a submission would, if accepted, be decisive for the outcome of the case, it may require a 'specific and express reply' by the court in its judgment, although an 'implied rejection' may be sufficient if clear.[625] Merely stating that a party has been grossly negligent where such negligence is crucial to the decision without explaining why this is so on the facts is unlikely to comply with Article 6.[626] Likewise, giving a reason for a decision that is not a good reason in law will not do so.[627]

The Court has yet to rule whether an unreasoned decision by a jury will in all cases comply with Article 6. In the few cases in which the issue has arisen, no breach of Article 6 has been found because the jury has been asked particular questions by the court, assisted by counsel, which have guided the jury's verdict.[628] Whether a system in which no such questions are put, but the judge in his 'summing up' assists the jury in reaching an unreasoned verdict, complies with Article 6 has also yet to be decided by the Court.[629]

The right to a reasoned judgment applies to appellate, as well as lower court, decisions, although an appellate judgment may not have to be so fully reasoned. It may be sufficient for an appeal court that agrees with the reasoning of the trial or lower appeal court simply to incorporate that reasoning by reference or otherwise indicate its agreement with it.[630] The essential requirement in such cases is that, in one way or another, the appeal court shows that it 'did in fact address the essential issues' in the appeal, and did not endorse without evaluation the decision of the lower court[631] or allow an appeal without addressing them.[632] In other cases, decisions by appeal courts rejecting appeals in very summary terms where there is clearly no merit in the appeal have been found not to be in breach of

---

[621] *Hadjianastassiou v Greece* A 252 (1992); 16 EHRR 219. See also *Karakasis v Greece* hudoc (2000); 36 EHRR 507 and *Hirvisaari v Finland* hudoc (2001); 38 EHRR 139. In criminal cases, the Article 6(1) guarantee of a reasoned judgment overlaps with the Article 6(3)(b) 'facilities' guarantee in respect of appeals.

[622] *Tatishvili v Russia* hudoc (2007).   [623] *Garcia Ruiz v Spain* GC 1999-I; 31 EHRR 589.

[624] *Van de Hurk v Netherlands* A 288 (1994); 18 EHRR 481 para 61. But the applicant's 'main arguments' must be addressed: *Buzescu v Romania* hudoc (2005) and the *Pronina* case, above, p 267.

[625] *Ruiz Torija v Spain* A 303-A (1994); 19 EHRR 553 para 30. Cf, *Hiro Balani v Spain* A 303-B (1994); 19 EHRR 566 para 28; *Elo v Finland No 30742/02* hudoc (2004) DA; and *Kusnetsov v Russia* 2007-XX.

[626] *Georgiadis v Greece* 1997-III; 24 EHRR 606.

[627] *De Moor v Belgium* A 292-A (1994); 18 EHRR 372.

[628] See *Papon v France (No 2) No 54210/00* hudoc (2001) DA; and *Saric v Denmark* hudoc (1999) DA. See also *Planka v Austria No 25852/94* hudoc (1996) DA.

[629] As to whether English jury practice complies, see Blom-Cooper, 2001 EHRLR 1.

[630] *Garcia Ruiz v Spain* 1999-I; 31 EHRR 589 GC.

[631] *Helle v Finland* 1997-VIII; 26 EHRR 159. Not shown in *Sakkapoulos v Greece* hudoc (2004).

[632] *Lindner and Hammermayer v Romania* hudoc (2002).

Article 6.[633] When refusing leave to appeal, there is no obligation to give detailed reasons or, in some cases, to give reasons at all.[634]

o. *Res judicata*: the finality of judgments

The right to a fair hearing also requires that, in accordance with the principle of *res judicata*, the judgment by the final court that decides a case should be irreversible, in accordance with the principle of legal certainty. In the leading case of *Brumarescu v Romania*,[635] a Court of First Instance held that the nationalization of the applicant's parents' house was invalid. In the absence of any appeal to a higher court, the decision became *res judicata* and the house was returned to the applicant. Later, the Procurator-General of Romania, who was not a party to the case, successfully applied to the Supreme Court of Justice for the decision to be quashed on the ground that the trial court had exceeded its jurisdiction. At Strasbourg, a Grand Chamber ruled in favour of the applicant on the following basis:

> The right to a fair hearing before a tribunal...must be interpreted in the light of the Preamble...which declares...the rule of law to be a part of the common heritage of the Contracting States. One of the fundamental aspects of the rule of law is the principle of legal certainty, which requires *inter alia* that where the courts have finally determined an issue, their ruling should not be called into question...In the present case the Court notes that...the exercise of that power by the Procurator-General was not subject to any time limit, so that judgments were liable to challenge indefinitely...The Court observes that, by allowing the application lodged under that power, the Supreme Court of Justice set at naught an entire judicial process which had ended in a judicial decision that was...'irreversible' and thus *res judicata*—and which moreover had been executed.

The power of the Prosecutor-General in issue in the *Brumarescu* case to initiate 'supervisory review' proceedings was a common feature in former Soviet-style legal systems, and was exercisable by a 'range of persons', including judges who were 'chairmen of the courts and their deputies'.[636] The *Brumarescu* ruling applies to its exercise by judges as well as members of the executive, as the issue is one of legal certainty and not just of an interference by the executive.[637] A procedure for quashing a final judgment may, however, be consistent with the principle of legal certainty where it is 'made necessary by circumstances of a substantial and compelling character', which would include the need to correct a miscarriage of justice.[638]

Although the *Brumarescu* case was decided by the Grand Chamber on the basis of the residual right to a 'fair hearing' in Article 6(1), in their concurring opinions Judges Rozakis, Bratza, and Zupančič took the view, which has a lot to recommend it, that the situation is best considered as concerning the 'right of access to a court'.[639] In their judgments in later

---

[633] See *X v FRG No 8769/79*, 25 DR 240 (1981). Fines for a vexatious appeal may not require detailed justification: *Les Travaux du Midi v France No 12275/86*, 70 DR 47 (1991) and *GL v Italy No 15384/89*, 77-A DR 5 (1994).

[634] *Sawoniuk v UK* 2001-VI and *Webb v UK* (1997); 24 EHRR CD 73.

[635] 1999-VII; 33 EHRR 862 para 61.

[636] *Tregubenko v Ukraine* hudoc (2005); 43 EHRR 608 para 36 (deputy chairman, Supreme Court). See also *Ryabykh v Russia* 2003-IX; 40 EHRR 615 (regional court president) and *Rosca v Moldova* hudoc (2005) (public prosecutor).

[637] *Tregubenko v Ukraine*, ibid. Cf, *Sovtransavto Holding v Ukraine* 2002-VII; 38 EHRR 911 and *Driza v Albania* hudoc (2007).

[638] *Pravednaya v Russia* hudoc (2005) para 25. See also *Nikitin v Russia* hudoc (2004) and *Bratyakin v Russia* hudoc (2006) DA. Miscarriage of justice procedures exist in European legal systems generally.

[639] Cf, the classification of the non-execution of judgments as concerning the right of access: see above, p 233. Judges Bratza and Zupančič could see an 'equality of arms' argument for a 'fair hearing' basis for the ruling.

cases, Chambers of the Court vary in their reasoning, referring to a 'fair hearing';[640] a 'fair hearing' and a 'right of access';[641] or generally to a 'right to a court'.[642]

p. Other fair hearing issues

A number of other particular 'fair hearing' issues have been resolved or raised in the jurisprudence of the Court, and formerly of the Commission. One point that is clear is that a jury trial in criminal cases is not an element of the right to a 'fair hearing'.[643] Despite being highly prized in common law jurisdictions, the jury's lack of general use in European legal systems made this inevitable in view of the consensus approach to the interpretation of the Convention.[644] However, where juries are used they must comply with the requirements of Article 6. This is particularly true of the requirement that a tribunal be 'impartial'.[645]

There is jurisprudence to suggest that the failure by a court to respect an undertaking or indication that it gives to a litigant, and that prejudices the presentation of his case, may render the hearing unfair, although there must be good evidence to show that the undertaking or indication was given. Thus in *Pardo v France*,[646] the applicant's lawyers had not presented oral argument on the merits at a hearing because, the applicant claimed, the President of the Court of Appeal had indicated that there would be a later hearing at which this could be done, but no such hearing occurred. The Court held against the applicant on the basis that he did not 'provide sufficient prima facie evidence of the accuracy of his version of events', but appeared to act on the basis that the hearing might have been unfair if such evidence had been produced.

Similarly, in *CG v UK*,[647] it was implied that interventions or other conduct by the judge during the hearing that interferes with a litigant's freedom to plead his case may render the hearing unfair. In that case, the trial judge's interruptions during the defence's questioning of witnesses was 'excessive and undesirable' but was not, when the hearing was viewed as a whole, such as to render it unfair in breach of Article 6(1). In particular, although the interruptions were disconcerting, defence counsel was not prevented from maintaining his line of defence and was allowed to address the jury in his final speech almost without interruption.

Certain other issues have been left open. In several cases, the Commission left open the possibility that the right to a fair hearing requires that a person not be tried twice for the same offence.[648] The fact that freedom from double jeopardy (*ne bis in idem, autrefois acquit*) is guaranteed by the Seventh Protocol to the Convention for the parties thereto may, however, prevent the Court taking a double jeopardy point under Article 6 against a state that has not ratified the Protocol.[649] Likewise, it is not established whether the trial

---

[640] *Rosca v Moldova*, above.   [641] *Ryabykh v Russia* and *Pravednaya v Russia*, above.

[642] *Tregubenko v Ukraine* above. cf *Poltorachenko v Ukraine*, hudoc (2005).

[643] *X and Y v Ireland No 8299/78*, 22 DR 51 (1980) and *Callaghan v UK No 14739/89*, 60 DR 296 (1989). The same must be true in civil cases.

[644] As to this approach, see above, p 8.

[645] See below, p 295. Where a jury trial occurs, the judge's summing up must be 'fair': *X v UK No 5574/72*, 3 DR 10 (1975). As to the need to give reasons, see above, p 268. As to jury vetting and Article 6, see Gallivan and Warbrick, 5 HRR 176 (1980).

[646] A 261-B (1993); 17 EHRR 383 para 28. See also *Colak v FRG* A 147 (1988); 11 EHRR 513 (alleged informal assurance that an accused would not be convicted of murder).

[647] Hudoc (2001); 34 EHRR 789.

[648] See eg, *X v Netherlands No 9433/8*, 27 DR 233 (1981). Article 6 does not prevent a prosecution in two states successively: *S v FRG No 8945/80*, 39 DR 43 (1983).

[649] But see the approach to appellate courts in the *Ekbatani* case: see below, p 275.

of an accused who has been brought within the defendant state's territory, following an abduction for which it is responsible, infringes his right to a fair hearing.[650]

III. THE RIGHT TO A PUBLIC HEARING AND THE PUBLIC PRONOUNCEMENT OF JUDGMENT[651]

a. The right to a public hearing

Article 6(1) provides that 'everyone is entitled to a...public hearing'. This guarantee has two elements: it requires both that a hearing take place in public and by implication that there is in the first place an oral hearing, not just written proceedings. Focusing mainly on the first of these elements, the Court has explained the purpose of the guarantee as being to 'protect litigants against the administration of justice in secret with no public scrutiny', thereby contributing, through the resulting transparency, to a fair hearing and to the maintenance of confidence in the courts.[652] The presence of the press, which includes reporters for the electronic media, is particularly important.[653] The guarantee applies in criminal and non-criminal cases.[654]

The right to a public hearing has been a particular problem for administrative or disciplinary tribunals or other bodies that are not 'classic' courts within the ordinary court system but that are competent to adjudicate upon either disciplinary or regulatory offences that qualify as 'criminal' for the purposes of Article 6 or a person's 'civil rights and obligations,' for example the right to practise a profession. In the case of such a tribunal, its failure to provide a public hearing may be remedied from the standpoint of Article 6 if its decision is 'subject to review by a judicial body that has full jurisdiction', on the law and the facts, and that does provide a public hearing.[655] In the case of a court 'of the classic kind' this will not be sufficient: 'Given the possible detrimental effects that the lack of a public hearing before the trial court could have on the fairness of the proceedings, the absence of publicity could not in any event be remedied by anything other than a complete re-hearing before the appellate court'.[656]

Whereas court hearings must generally be in public, the public may be excluded from an oral hearing on one or more of the grounds listed in Article 6(1), which reads:

> Judgment shall be pronounced publicly but the press and public may be excluded from all or part of the trial in the interests of morals, public order or national security in a democratic society, where the interests of juveniles or the private life of the parties so require, or

---

[650] See *Stocké v FRG* A 199 (1991); 13 EHRR 839 in which the Court was not satisfied, on the facts, that there had been state involvement.

[651] See Cremona, *Wiarda Mélanges*, p 107.

[652] *Malhous v Czech Rep* 2001-XII para 55 GC. Cf, *Barberà, Messegué and Jabardo v Spain* A 146 (1988); 11 EHRR 360 para 89 PC, in which the right to a public hearing was breached because much of the evidence against the accused was made a part of the record without being adduced or read in court, and hence not subjected to 'the watchful eye of the public'.

[653] *Axen v FRG*, B 57 (1981) para 77 Com Rep. References to the 'public' in this section include the press.

[654] It includes compulsory arbitration proceedings: *Bramelid and Malmström v Sweden* Nos 8588/79 and 8589/79, 38 DR 18 (1983) Com Rep; CM Res DH (84) 4. Cf, *Scarth v UK* hudoc (1999). In the case of voluntary arbitration, whereby the parties themselves choose to go outside the courts, Article 6 does not apply: *ibid*.

[655] *Riepan v Austria* 2000-XII para 39. Cf, *Le Compte, Van Leuven and De Meyere v Belgium* A 43 (1981); 4 EHRR 1 PC and *Albert and Le Compte v Belgium* A 58 (1983); 5 EHRR 533 PC. In *Stallinger and Kuso v Austria* 1997-II para 51 the Court left open the possibility of 'exceptional circumstances'.

[656] *Riepan v Austria*, 2000-XII para 40. By a 'complete re-hearing' is meant one in which the court with the power of review hears the witnesses, etc, as if it were the trial court: *Göç v Turkey* 2002-V GC. For the reasons for the distinction between special and classic courts, see below, p 298.

to the extent strictly necessary in the opinion of the court in special circumstances where publicity would prejudice the interests of justice.

The list is an exhaustive one: a private hearing will be in breach of Article 6 if it is not justified on one or more of the above grounds.[657]

In the interpretation of similar lists of restrictions to the rights guaranteed in Articles 8–11 of the Convention, the Court, and formerly the Commission, has required the restriction to be a proportionate response on the facts to a pressing social need.[658] This interpretation is based upon the wording 'necessary in a democratic society' in those Articles. Although the text of Article 6(1) does not contain this precise formula,[659] such a balancing approach seems generally appropriate. A proportionality test was used in *Campbell and Fell v UK*.[660] In that case, it was held that prison disciplinary proceedings could be conducted in camera on prison premises for 'reasons of public order and security'. The Court had in mind the problems of security that would result for the state in admitting the public to the prison or in transporting convicted prisoners to court. Because of these considerations, the Court held that a requirement that disciplinary proceedings be in public would 'impose a disproportionate burden on the authorities of the state'.[661]

In the interpretation of Articles 8–11 of the Convention, the Court has also applied a margin of appreciation doctrine, by which the state is allowed a certain discretion in its assessment of the need for a restriction in a particular factual situation.[662] However, there has been no case in which margin of appreciation language has been used in a Court judgment concerning restrictions on a public hearing:[663] instead the Court, and formerly the Commission, has made its own assessment of the need for a restriction without indicating that any discretion is left to the defendant state. The wording of the 'interests of justice' restriction ('in the opinion of the court') most clearly invites a margin of appreciation approach.[664]

As to the particular grounds on which a hearing in camera is permissible, in *B and P v UK*[665] it was stated that proceedings in cases concerning the residence of children following the divorce or separation of the parents are 'prime examples' where private court hearings may be justified, in order to 'protect the privacy of the child and parties' and to 'avoid prejudicing the interests of justice'. In such cases, 'it is essential that the parents and other witnesses feel able to express themselves candidly on highly personal issues without fear of public curiosity or comment'. The exclusion of the public from divorce proceedings[666] and from medical disciplinary proceedings[667] is also permissible as being for the 'protection of the private life of the parties'. The 'interests of justice' may, even in

---

[657] For a case not falling within the listed exceptions, see *Osinger v Austria* hudoc (2005) (succession to property).

[658] See below, Ch 8.

[659] As to the wording 'strictly necessary' in Article 6(1), see the standard set for 'absolutely necessary' in Article 2: above, p 61.

[660] A 80 (1984); 7 EHRR 165.

[661] Id, para 87.

[662] See below, Ch 8.

[663] But see the separate opinions of Judge Morenilla in *Nortier v Netherlands* A 267 (1993); 17 EHRR 273 and Lord Reed in *V v UK*, above, in the context of juvenile cases.

[664] But the wording '*strictly* necessary' suggests a limited margin: see above, p 11.

[665] 2001-III; 34 EHRR 529 para 38. Cf, *Moser v Austria* hudoc (2006) (child transfer to public care; public hearing required).

[666] *X v UK No 7366/76*, 2 Digest 452 (1977).

[667] *Guenoun v France No 13562/88*, 66 DR 181 (1990). See also *Imberechts v Belgium No 15561/89*, 69 DR 312 (1991) (private lives of patients).

criminal cases, justify the giving of evidence in camera 'to protect the safety or privacy of witnesses or to promote the free exchange of information and opinion in the pursuit of justice'.[668] The exclusion of the public from the trial of an accused for sexual offences against children was justified under Article 6(1) without specifying which particular ground of restriction was being applied.[669] As to the other grounds for private hearings permitted by Article 6(1), in *Campbell and Fell v UK*,[670] the Court relied upon the 'public order' restriction in Article 6(1), interpreting the term as having a wide public interest meaning, thereby including prison security, rather than one limited to public disorder.[671] A trial in camera may be justified on grounds of 'national security' in a prosecution for passing state secrets.[672]

More generally, the Court has accepted that it is permissible to exclude a whole class of cases from a public hearing by reference to one or more of the grounds listed in Article 6(1), subject to the Court deciding that the general exclusion of cases within the class falls within one of the grounds listed in Article 6(1). Thus in *B and P v UK*,[673] the Court found it acceptable that there was a rebuttable presumption in favour of a private hearing in all proceedings under the Children Act 1989.

Article 6(1) provides an entitlement to a 'public' hearing as an individual right which may be restricted on the initiative of the state on a permitted ground. However, there may be cases in which an accused or other litigant would prefer a private hearing. In such a case, the question will be whether a public hearing would be a violation of the right to a 'fair' hearing in Article 6(1), or of the right to privacy in Article 8, rather than the guarantee of a 'public' hearing. Thus in *V v UK*,[674] involving the trial of two young boys accused in a murder case that attracted great press attention, the issue was not whether the state *could* exclude the press and the public under Article 6(1), but what adaptations to the normal court procedures, including the public nature of the hearings, it was *obliged* to make in order to ensure that the accused had a 'fair' hearing in the sense of Article 6(1), free from the glare of publicity. In other cases in which an accused or private litigant has been refused a private hearing by a national court, a right to privacy claim under Article 8 may or may not be outweighed by a public interest justification allowed by Article 8(2).[675] Obviously, there is also an interest on the part of the public in knowing what is happening in the courts generally.

Court hearings must be open to the public in fact as well as in law. Accordingly, in *Riepan v Austria*,[676] the Court stated that Article 6 will only be complied with if the public is 'able to obtain information about its date and place and if this place is easily accessible to the public'. The latter requirement will normally be met by holding the hearing in a 'regular courtroom large enough to accommodate spectators'.[677] In the *Riepan* case, there was not a 'public' hearing when, because of the risk of the applicant escaping, the hearing leading to the applicant's conviction for an ordinary criminal offence, for threatening

---

[668] *B and P v UK* 2001-III; 34 EHRR 529 para 37. The private nature of pre-trial investigations is permissible in the interests of the privacy of those questioned and of justice: *Ernst v Belgium* hudoc (2003); 37 EHRR 724.

[669] *X v Austria No 1913/63*, 2 Digest 438 (1965). Several grounds, including the 'interests of juveniles', could have applied. See also *V v UK*, below at n 674.

[670] See above, p 272. See also *Riepan v Austria* 2000-XII.

[671] Cf, *Le Compte, Van Leuven and De Meyere v Belgium* A 43 (1981); 4 EHRR 1 para 59 PC. This public interest meaning is consistent with the French text of Article 6(1) which uses the term '*ordre public*'. Public disorder in the courtroom might be brought within the 'interests of justice' restriction.

[672] *Moiseyev v Russia No 62936/00* hudoc (2004) DA.   [673] 2001-III; 34 EHRR 529.

[674] 1999-IX; 30 EHRR 121 GC.

[675] In *B and P v UK*, above, the wife had no need to bring an Article 8 claim, the court having rejected the applicant husband's claim to a public hearing.

[676] 2000-XII para 29. Cf, *Hummatov v Azerbaijan* hudoc (2007).   [677] *Ibid.*

prison officers, was held not in the criminal court building but in the prison where he was serving a sentence for murder. The hearing was open to the public and its prison location was on the weekly court list sent to the media and available to the public at the court's registry. But no particular measures were taken, such as directions to the prison, to facilitate attendance and the hearing was held in a small room early in the morning. In these circumstances, not enough had been done to counterbalance the detrimental effect for the public of holding the hearing in prison.[678]

An oral hearing

Although not expressly mentioned in the text of Article 6, an oral hearing 'constitutes a fundamental principle enshrined in Article 6(1)'.[679] This follows in criminal cases from the nature of the guarantees in Article 6(3)(c), (d), and (e) and has been held to be the case in non-criminal cases also.[680] The right to an oral hearing has a general scope, applying both when a court sits in public and to hearings *in camera* in circumstances allowed by Article 6(1).[681]

The obligation to hold an oral hearing is not absolute. In *Jussila v Finland*,[682] the Grand Chamber characterized the position as follows. It stated that, whereas in earlier cases the Court had expressed the limitation in terms of the right to an oral hearing not applying in 'exceptional circumstances', a more accurate formulation was that 'the character of the circumstances that may justify dispensing with an oral hearing essentially comes down to the nature of the issues to be decided', not their 'frequency', and that Article 6(1) did not 'mean that refusing to hold an oral hearing may be justified only in rare cases'. Prior to the *Jussila* case, the kinds of cases in which it had been established that the absence of an oral hearing is permissible had all been non-criminal cases. In these, the issues involved are 'highly technical'[683] or concern exclusively questions of law of 'no particular complexity'.[684] In these circumstances, in which the case could perfectly adequately be decided on the basis of written documents, the Court has recognized that 'it is understandable that the national authorities should have regard to the demands of efficiency and economy'.[685] However, in such cases the applicant should have the opportunity to request an oral hearing, either at first instance or, if applicable, on appeal, on the ground that the case presents special features, although the request may be rejected following proper consideration of it.[686]

---

[678] The Court distinguished the *Campbell and Fell* case, above, p 272, because the latter concerned prison disciplinary offences. However, the *Campbell and Fell* offences were 'criminal' for the purposes of Article 6 and the conduct concerned would now be dealt with under English law as criminal offences in the ordinary courts.

[679] *Jussila v Finland* 2006-XX GC para 40. Cf, *Göç v Turkey* 2002-V GC.

[680] *Demebulov v Bulgaria* hudoc (2008).

[681] The Court's jurisprudence has not always clearly distinguished between the requirements of a public hearing and an oral hearing: see eg, *Ekbatani v Sweden* A 134 (1988); 13 EHRR 504 PC.

[682] *Jussila v Finland* 2008-XX GC para 42. Cf, *Miller v Sweden* 2005-XX. Arguing for allowing non-oral hearings more flexibly and generally, see the dissenting opinions of Judge Wildhaber and others in *Göç v Turkey* 2002-V GC.

[683] *Schuler-Zgraggen v Switzerland* A 263 (1993); 16 EHRR 405 para 58. The Court also stressed that there was no issue of 'public importance' involved: *ibid*. As in *Schuler-Zgraggen* most cases have concerned social security benefit claims turning upon medical evidence: see eg, *Miller v Sweden* 2005-XX. See also *Martinie v France* 2006-VI GC (judicial audit of accounts) and *Hofbauer v Austria No 68087/01* hudoc (2004) (whether door was fire-resistant).

[684] *Valová, Slezák and Slezák v Slovakia* hudoc (2004). See also *Allan Jacobson v Sweden (No 2)* 1998-I; 32 EHRR 463.

[685] *Schuler-Zgraggen v Switzerland* A 263 (1993); 16 EHRR 405 para 58.

[686] *Martinie v France* 2006-VI GC.

In the *Jussila* case,[687] the Grand Chamber accepted that, although the right to an oral hearing 'is particularly important in the criminal context', it may also be dispensed with in some criminal cases. Generally, it distinguished between criminal cases that do not carry 'any significant degree of stigma', and others that form a part of the 'hard core of criminal law'. On the facts, the Grand Chamber held that an oral hearing was not required in a case involving the imposition of a tax surcharge. It also referred to cases involving administrative (eg under road traffic law), customs, competition, and other financial offences that fell within Article 6 under the *Engel* case[688] but that do not strictly belong to the 'traditional categories of the criminal law' as being cases in which an oral hearing might not be required.

Clearly, a court of first instance must provide the required oral hearing where there is no right of appeal.[689] In cases in which there has been an oral hearing at first instance, or in which one has been waived at that level,[690] there is no absolute right to an oral hearing in any appeal proceedings that are provided. Instead, whether this is required 'depends on the special features of the proceedings involved; account must be taken of the entirety of the proceedings in the domestic legal order and of the role of the appellate court therein'.[691] Where the proceedings involve an appeal only on points of law, an oral hearing is generally not required.[692] If an appeal court is called upon to decide questions of fact, an oral hearing may or may not be required, depending whether one is necessary to ensure a fair trial.[693] In practice, the cases have mostly concerned an oral hearing at which the applicant, as opposed to his lawyer, wished to be present in person to give evidence or otherwise assist the court.[694] In *Ekbatani v Sweden*[695] an oral hearing was required where there was a dispute as to the facts in a criminal case that involved the accused's credibility: the accused's guilt or innocence 'could not, as a matter of a fair trial, have been properly determined without a direct assessment of the evidence given in person by the applicant'. In contrast, in *Jan-Ake Andersson v Sweden*[696] an oral hearing was not required in the case of a minor road traffic offence in which the appeal did not raise 'any questions of fact or law which could not adequately be resolved on the basis of the case file'. What is at stake for the applicant is also relevant. Thus in *Helmers v Sweden*,[697] in a private criminal prosecution for defamation, it was relevant that the applicant's professional reputation and career were at stake.

Waiver of a public hearing
A person may waive his right to a public hearing, so long as the waiver is done of his own free will 'in an unequivocal manner' and there is no 'important public interest'

---

[687] *Jussila v Finland* 2006-XX GC paras 40, 43.

[688] See above, p 205.   [689] *Göç v Turkey* 2002-V GC.   [690] *Dory v Sweden* hudoc (2002).

[691] *Ekbatani v Sweden* A 134 (1988); 13 EHRR 504 para 27 PC. See also *Hermi v Italy* 2006-XII; 46 EHRR 1115 GC.

[692] *Axen v FRG* A 72 (1983); 6 EHRR 195. An oral hearing is not required for leave to appeal proceedings: *Monnell and Morris v UK* A 115 (1987); 10 EHRR 205.

[693] *Ekbatani v Sweden* A 134 (1988); 13 EHRR 504 PC. See also *Elsholz v Germany* 2000-VIII; 34 EHRR 1412 GC and *Belziuk v Poland* 1998-II.

[694] There is in such cases an overlap with the rights to be present at a hearing, above, p 247, and to participate effectively therein, above, p 250. On oral hearings at which the applicant must be represented by a lawyer, see below, p 315. A video-link may be suifficient on security grounds: see *Marcello Viola v Italy* hudoc (2006).

[695] *Ekbatani v Sweden* A 134 (1988); 13 EHRR 504 para 32 PC. See also *Kamasinski v Austria* A 168 (1989); 13 EHRR 36; *Botten v Norway* 1996-I; 32 EHRR 37; and *Belziuk v Poland* 1998-II; 30 EHRR 614.

[696] A 212-B (1991); 15 EHRR 218 para 29.

[697] A 212-A (1991); 15 EHRR 285. See also *Kremzow v Austria* A 268-B (1993); 17 EHRR 322; *Constantinescu v Romania* hudoc (2000); and *Arnarsson v Iceland* hudoc (2003); 39 EHRR 426.

consideration that requires a public hearing.[698] This possibility of waiver applies to the right to a public hearing both in the sense of a right to an oral hearing, and to access of the public thereto.[699] A waiver may be tacit, provided that it is clear from the facts that one is being made.[700] An 'unequivocal' waiver was found to have been made in *Håkansson and Sturesson v Sweden*[701] when the applicant failed to ask for a public hearing before a court, which by law conducted its proceedings in private unless a public hearing was considered by it to be 'necessary'. The judgment can be criticized as requiring the applicant to take the initiative to request the application of an exception to a general rule, when the general rule should itself, consistently with Article 6(1), provide for a public hearing.[702] The case may be distinguished from *H v Belgium*[703] where an applicant barrister was held not to have waived his right to a public hearing in disciplinary proceedings when he failed to request a public hearing where the practice was to hold such proceedings in private and there was 'little prospect' of a request for a public hearing succeeding. The cases in which a waiver has been established have concerned professional disciplinary proceedings or civil litigation; it is arguable that a stricter test should apply to criminal cases.

b. The right to the public pronouncement of judgment

In contrast with the right to a public hearing, the right to have judgment 'pronounced publicly' is not subject to any exceptions in the text of Article 6(1). However, the Court has applied the wording 'pronounced publicly' 'with some degree of flexibility'.[704] Whereas this wording appears to require that judgment be delivered orally in full in open court,[705] the Strasbourg Court has not taken this view. Instead it has established a number of limitations or exceptions.

First, it may be sufficient that delivery in court is not of the full text of the judgments at all levels of the proceedings. In *Lamanna v Austria*,[706] there was no breach of Article 6(1) when the Court of Appeal's judgment on a claim for compensation for detention was delivered by it in open court, but only contained a summary of the trial court's otherwise unpublished judgment. Further, it was not delivered until six years after its adoption, on the order of the Supreme Court after an application had been declared admissible at Strasbourg. In contrast, in *Ryakib Biryukov v Russia*[707] it was held not sufficient just to read out the operative part of judgment in a civil case, without giving any reasons for the decision. Secondly, an exception may be allowed for reasons of security. In *Campbell and Fell v UK*,[708] in the special context of Boards of Visitors in the former English system of prison disciplinary proceedings, the Court accepted that a Board of Visitors award need not be delivered in the presence of 'press and public' in view of the problem of prison security, but found a breach of the 'pronounced publicly' requirement since no alternative arrangements had been made to publish the text of the award subsequently.[709]

---

[698] *Håkansson and Sturesson v Sweden* A 171-A (1990); 13 EHRR 1 para 66. See also *Schuler-Zgraggen v Switzerland* A 263 (1993); 16 EHRR 405 para 58 and *Pauger v Austria* 1997-III; 25 EHRR 105 para 58.

[699] See the *Håkansson and Sturesson* and *Pauger* cases *ibid*.

[700] See *Hermi v Italy* hudoc (2006); 46 EHRR 1115 GC.

[701] *Ibid.* See also the *Schuler-Zgraggen* and *Zumtobel* cases, above, n 683. Failure to ask for a hearing by a court that lacks full jurisdiction in the case is not a waiver: *Göç v Turkey* 2002-V GC.

[702] Cf, Judge Walsh's dissenting opinion.   [703] A 127-B (1987); 10 EHRR 339 PC.

[704] *Lamanna v Austria* hudoc (2001) para 31.

[705] The French text—'*rendu publiquement*'—suggests the same: *Pretto v Italy* A 71 (1983); 6 EHRR 182 PC.

[706] Hudoc (2001). See also *Crociani v Italy* No 8603/79, 22 DR 147 (1980).   [707] 2008-XX.

[708] A 80 (1984); 7 EHRR 165. The disciplinary function of Boards of Visitors has since been abolished.

[709] Following the judgment, arrangements were made for the publication of Boards of Visitors awards in the local press.

Thirdly, noting that the publication of some kinds of judgments by making them available to the public in the court registry is a longstanding tradition in many Council of Europe member states, in *Pretto v Italy*[710] the Strasbourg Court ruled that 'the form of publicity to be given to the "judgment"…must be assessed in the light of the special features of the proceedings in question and by reference to the object and purpose of Article 6(1)', with account being taken of the 'entirety of the proceedings', including the function of the court concerned and whether judgments have been pronounced in open court at any level in the case. Thus in the *Pretto* case, the Court held that Article 6(1) was complied with even though the judgment of the Italian Court of Cassation rejecting the applicant's appeal in a civil claim was only made available to the public in the court registry without having been delivered orally in open court. The Strasbourg Court noted that the Court of Cassation had jurisdiction to consider only points of law and to reject an appeal or quash a judgment and that it had given its judgment after a public hearing. Bearing in mind the purpose of the 'pronounced publicly' requirement, which is to contribute to a fair trial through public scrutiny,[711] publication via the registry was consistent with Article 6(1) on these facts. In *Axen v FRG*,[712] the Court reached the same conclusion in a criminal case in respect of a similar practice of the German Federal Court of Justice, which again heard appeals on points of law only.[713]

Both the *Pretto* and *Axen* judgments concerned a state's highest court. The Court has applied the same dispensation to the publication of lower court judgments. In *Werner v Austria*,[714] the judgments of the trial court and the first court of appeal on the applicant's claim for compensation for detention after criminal proceedings against him had been discontinued were not delivered in court. They were served on the applicant but were otherwise only available from the registry to third parties who, in the court's opinion, could show a legitimate interest. Since it might be of importance to the person concerned that the public should know that any suspicion against him has been dispelled, the Strasbourg Court held that there was a breach of Article 6(1) because 'no judicial decision was pronounced publicly and…publicity was not sufficiently ensured by other appropriate means'. The second alternative allowed by the Court would seem to suggest that it is sufficient for judgments of lower courts to be made available to the public generally from the court registry. Involving the same deviation from the literal wording of Article 6(1), the Court's approach here again accords with the practice in a number of European legal systems.

Fourthly, the Court has accepted that the publication of orders or judgments concerning children's and parental rights may be restricted to interested persons, ie not made available to the public at large. Thus in *B and P v UK*,[715] it was sufficient that any one who could establish an interest could consult or obtain a copy of the full text of the orders or judgments made by the court of first instance in child residence cases. Further, the publication of first instance and appeal court judgments in law reports in such cases sufficiently allowed the general public to study the approach taken by the courts. Interestingly, in the *B and P* case, the Court drew upon the 'interests of juveniles' and the 'administration of

---

[710] Id, paras 26–7. See the separate opinions of Judges Van Der Meersch and Pinheiro Farinho.

[711] See *Werner v Austria* 1996-VII; 26 EHRR 310.   [712] A 72 (1983); 6 EHRR 195 para 31 PC.

[713] In contrast with the Italian Court of Cassation in the *Pretto* case, the Federal Court of Justice in the *Axen* case did not hold a public hearing, dismissing the appeal as without merit and thereby confirming the Court of Appeal judgment, which had been delivered in public.

[714] 1997-VII; 26 EHRR 310 para 60. Cf, *Sutter v Switzerland* A 74 (1984); 6 EHRR 272 PC.

[715] 2001-III; 34 EHRR 529. The Court cited *Sutter v Switzerland* A 74 (1984); 6 EHRR 272 PC in which there was no breach in military disciplinary proceedings when only a person who could establish an interest could consult or obtain a copy of a judgment from the court registry.

justice' exceptions to the requirement of a public hearing in the text of Article 6(1) when reaching this decision on the public pronouncement of judgment. It is likely that the Court would adopt the same approach in cases falling within other such public hearing exceptions in Article 6(1) (eg national security), thereby eroding further, but for good reason, the significance in the difference in the formulation of the rights to a public hearing and the public pronouncement in the text of Article 6(1). Clearly, the publication of the judgment may undermine the legitimate purpose of holding a hearing *in camera*.

Whereas it is well established that the right to a public hearing may be waived, the Court, and formerly the Commission, has not ruled on the question whether this is the case with the right to public pronouncement of a judgment. There appears to be no good reason to distinguish between the two rights in this regard.

IV. THE RIGHT TO TRIAL WITHIN A REASONABLE TIME

The purpose of the 'reasonable time' guarantee, which applies to both criminal and non-criminal cases, is to protect 'all parties to court proceedings…against excessive procedural delays'[716] and 'underlines the importance of rendering justice without delays which might jeopardize its effectiveness and credibility'.[717] In criminal cases, it is also 'designed to avoid that a person charged should remain too long in a state of uncertainty about his fate'.[718] In such cases, the effect that being an accused has upon a person's reputation is relevant too.

In criminal cases, the reasonable time guarantee runs from the moment that an accused is subject to a 'charge', that is 'substantially affected'.[719] In non-criminal cases, it normally begins to apply from the initiation of court proceedings, but sometimes earlier.[720] In both kinds of case, the guarantee continues to apply until the case is finally determined.[721] If proceedings are still pending in the national courts when an application is under consideration at Strasbourg, the period covered by the reasonable time guarantee runs until the judgment is given in the case by the Court.[722] If the respondent state becomes a party to the Convention after Article 6 has begun to apply to a particular case, the guarantee will only begin to run as of the date of ratification.[723] Nonetheless, in assessing the reasonableness of the time that is taken to determine a case after that date, 'account must be taken of the then state of proceedings'.[724] Thus a decision as to whether a case has been treated with the necessary expedition after that date will be influenced by the fact that the case has already been pending for a long time.[725]

The obligation to decide cases within a reasonable time extends to constitutional courts, subject to the need to take account of their special role as guardian of the constitution.[726] In particular, they may delay consideration of a case to ensure that sufficient time is taken to rule on a matter of constitutional importance, possibly in combination with other similar cases.

---

[716] *Stögmüller v Austria* A 9 (1969) p 40; 1 EHRR 155, 191.
[717] *H v France* A 162-A (1989); 12 EHRR 74 para 58.
[718] *Stogmuller v Austria* A 9 (1969) p 40; 1 EHRR 155, 191. *Cf, Wemhoff v FRG* A 7 (1968); 1 EHRR 55.
[719] See above, p 209.
[720] See above, p 232.
[721] See above, p 233. A reasonable time claim subsists despite acquittal: *Lehtinen v Finland* hudoc (2006).
[722] *Neumeister v Austria* A 8 (1968); 1 EHRR 91 and *Nibbio v Italy* A 228-A (1992).
[723] *Foti and others v Italy* A 56 (1982); 5 EHRR 313. As to appeal proceedings, see the *Stamoulakatos* case, below, p 802.
[724] *Foti and others v Italy* A 56 (1982); 5 EHRR 313 para 53.   [725] *Brigandi v Italy* A 194-B (1991).
[726] *Sussmann v Germany* 1996-IV; 25 EHRR 64 GC. But see *Wimmer v Germany* hudoc (2005).

The reasonableness of the length of proceedings in both criminal and non-criminal cases depends on the particular circumstances of the case.[727] There is no absolute time limit. Factors that are always considered are the complexity of the case, the conduct of the applicant, and the conduct of the competent administrative and judicial authorities.[728] The Court also takes into account what is 'at stake' for the applicant when applying the last of these criteria.[729] No margin of appreciation doctrine is applied, at least expressly, when determining the reasonableness of the time taken; the European Court simply makes its own assessment.[730] When it does so, it must bear in mind that Article 6 can only require such expedition as is consistent with the proper administration of justice.[731]

As to the first of the three factors listed above, a case may be complicated for many reasons, such as the volume of evidence,[732] the number of defendants or charges,[733] the need to obtain expert evidence[734] or evidence from abroad,[735] or the complexity of the legal issues involved.[736]

With regard to the second factor, the state is not responsible for delay that is attributable to the conduct of the applicant. While an applicant is entitled to make use of his procedural rights, any consequential lengthening of proceedings cannot be held against the state.[737] In a criminal case, although an accused is not required 'actively to co-operate with the judicial authorities',[738] if delay results, for example, from his refusal to appoint a defence lawyer, this is not the responsibility of the state.[739] But a state is responsible for its negligent delay in discontinuing proceedings against an accused: it cannot claim that the accused should have taken the initiative to remind it.[740] Where an accused flees from the jurisdiction or disappears while subject to a 'charge', the time during which he has absented himself from the proceedings is not to be taken into account in determining the length of proceedings,[741] unless there is a 'sufficient reason' for the flight.[742]

In civil litigation, some municipal legal systems apply the principle that the parties are responsible for the progress of proceedings.[743] This does not, however, 'absolve the courts from ensuring compliance with the requirements of Article 6 concerning reasonable time'; the state must itself take appropriate steps to ensure that proceedings progress

---

[727] *König v FRG* A 27 (1978); 2 EHRR 170 PC and *Pedersen and Baadsgaard v Denmark* 2004-XI; 42 EHRR 486 GC.

[728] *Ibid.*

[729] *Frydlender v France* 2000-VII; 31 EHRR 1152 GC. What is 'at stake' is sometimes treated as a separate fourth factor: see eg, *Sürmeli v Germany* 2006-VII GC.

[730] See eg, *Casciaroli v Italy* A 229-C (1992), in which the Court disagreed with the defendant state's assessment of the complexity of the case.

[731] *Boddaert v Belgium* A 235-D (1992); 16 EHRR 242. The accused is entitled to reasonable time to prepare his defence: see Article 6(3)(b), below, p 309.

[732] *Eckle v FRG* A 51 (1982); 5 EHRR 1.   [733] *Neumeister v Austria* A 8 (1968); 1 EHRR 91.

[734] *Wemhoff v FRG* A 7 (1968); 1 EHRR 55.

[735] *Neumeister v Austria* A 8 (1968); 1 EHRR 91. The defendant state will not be responsible for another state's delays in supplying evidence: *ibid.* A claim may be brought against that state under Article 6 if it is a Convention party: *X v FRG* No 9604/81, 5 EHRR 587 (1983).

[736] *Neumeister v Austria, ibid.*

[737] See eg, *König v FRG* A 27 (1978); 2 EHRR 170 PC (changing lawyers, making appeals, calling new evidence).

[738] *Eckle v FRG* A 51 (1982); 5 EHRR 1 para 82.   [739] *Corigliano v Italy* A 57 (1982); 5 EHRR 334.

[740] *Orchin v UK* No 8435/78, 34 DR 5 (1982) Com Rep; CM Res DH (83) 14.

[741] *Girolami v Italy* A 196-E (1991). The Commission suggested a possible exception, where the accused flees for a 'sufficient reason'.

[742] *Vayic v Turkey* hudoc (2007), citing *Ventura v Italy* No 7438/76, 23 DR 5 at 91 (1980).

[743] See *Buchholz v FRG* A 42 (1981); 3 EHRR 597 para 50 and *Foley v UK* hudoc (2002).

speedily.[744] Whether such a principle applies or not, the responsibilities of the applicant in civil cases are only to 'show diligence in carrying out the procedural steps relevant to him, to refrain from using delaying tactics, and to avail himself of the scope afforded by domestic law for shortening proceedings'.[745] Delay caused by the conduct of the applicant's legal aid lawyer in civil proceedings is not attributable to the state: although he is publicly appointed, such a lawyer acts for his client, not the state.[746] Nor is a state responsible for delay that results from the conduct of the defendant against whom the applicant brings a civil claim.[747]

As to the third factor, the state is responsible for delays that are attributable to its administrative or judicial authorities.[748] In criminal cases, breaches of Article 6(1) have been found because of unjustified delays in the conduct of the preliminary investigation in a civil law system,[749] entering a *nolle prosequi*,[750] appointing judges,[751] controlling expert witnesses,[752] communicating the judgment to the applicant,[753] and the commencement of appeals.[754] Whereas it may be sensible to hear cases against two or more accused persons together, this cannot 'justify substantial delay' in the bringing of a case against any one of them.[755] In appropriate circumstances, a court may be justified in permitting a delay in order to allow political or other passions to cool.[756]

Where applicable, the same considerations apply in non-criminal cases also. In such cases, states have been held responsible for delays in civil and administrative courts in performing routine registry tasks,[757] in the conduct of the hearing by the court,[758] in the presentation of evidence by the state,[759] for the adjournment of proceedings pending the outcome of another case,[760] and for delays caused by lack of co-ordination between administrative authorities.[761] As in criminal cases, the period of time to be considered continues until the judgment becomes final.[762]

As indicated, when assessing the reasonableness of the length of proceedings, the Court also takes into account what is 'at stake' for the applicant.[763] The Court has identified a large number of kinds of case in which particular expedition is required on this

---

[744] *Unión Alimentaria Sanders SA v Spain* A 157 (1989); 12 EHRR 24 para 35. Cf, *Sürmeli v Germany* 2006-VII GC.

[745] *Unión Alimentaria* case *ibid*. Cf, *Deumeland v FRG* A 100 (1986); 8 EHRR 448 para 80 PC. For cases of litigant delay for which the state was not responsible, see *Monnet v France* A 273-A (1993); 18 EHRR 27 and *Patrianakos v Greece* hudoc (2004).

[746] *H v France* A 162-A (1989); 12 EHRR 74. But in a criminal case there is a duty to provide effective legal aid under Article 6(3)(c): see below, p 319. The state is not responsible for delays caused by a lawyers' strike: *Giannangeli v Italy* hudoc (2001).

[747] *Bock v FRG* A 150 (1989); 12 EHRR 247 para 41.

[748] A private law reporter's delay is not attributable to the state: *Foley v UK* hudoc (2002). *Quaere* whether the UK is responsible for delays by its health authorities: see *Somjee v UK* hudoc (2002).

[749] *Eckle v FRG* A 51 (1982); 5 EHRR 1.

[750] *Orchin v UK No 8435/78*, 34 DR 5 (1982) Com Rep; CM Res DH (83) 14.

[751] *Georgiadis v Cyprus* hudoc (2002). See also *Foti and others v Italy* A 56 (1982); 5 EHRR 313 (transferring cases between courts).

[752] *Rawa v Poland* hudoc (2003).   [753] *Eckle v FRG* A 51 (1982); 5 EHRR 1.

[754] *Ibid*. The reasonable time guarantee continues to apply until the time limit for an appeal is exhausted: *Ferraro v Italy* A 197-A (1991).

[755] *Hentrich v France* A 296-A (1994); 18 EHRR 440. See also *Rezette v Luxembourg* hudoc (2004).

[756] *Foti and others v Italy* A 51 (1982); 5 EHRR 313.   [757] *Guincho v Portugal* A 81 (1984); 7 EHRR 23.

[758] *König v FRG* A 27 (1978); 2 EHRR 170 PC.   [759] *H v UK* A 120 (1987); 10 EHRR 95 PC.

[760] *König v FRG* A 27 (1978); 2 EHRR 170 PC.

[761] *Wiesinger v Austria* A 213 (1991); 16 EHRR 258.   [762] *Maciariello v Italy* A 230-A (1992).

[763] *Frydlender v France* hudoc (2000); 31 EHRR 1152.

basis. These include cases concerning the applicant's employment,[764] civil status,[765] child custody,[766] health,[767] reputation,[768] title to land,[769] and compensation for road accidents.[770] It may be relevant that the applicant has been charged interest on the sum in dispute while the case is pending.[771] In criminal cases, the likelihood of a life sentence or other heavy sentence is relevant.[772]

Criminal cases generally require more urgency than non-criminal ones[773] and a more rigorous standard applies where an accused is in detention.[774] In the latter case, the reasonable time guarantee in Article 6(1) overlaps with that in Article 5(3), under which 'special diligence' in the time taken in cases where the accused is in detention is also required.[775] However, since Article 5(3) ceases to apply once an accused is convicted, the reasonable time guarantee in Article 6(1) is the only one that protects a convicted person detained during subsequent appeal or other proceedings. Thus in *B v Austria*,[776] a breach of Article 6(1) was found when it took two years and nine months for an appeal court judge to draw up the court's judgment after the hearing of an appeal by a convicted person in detention. Another factor concerns the practice in criminal justice systems by which the time spent awaiting trial is taken into account when deciding upon the sentence in a criminal case. Any reduction in sentence, or other favourable outcome, may mean that the applicant is not a 'victim' who is competent to bring an application alleging a breach of the 'reasonable time' guarantee.[777]

When applying the above factors, the Court has been prepared to tolerate some proven, but small, instances of delay as not involving a breach provided the overall length of the proceedings is not excessive given the number of stages of proceedings in the case. Thus in *Pretto v Italy*,[778] there were delays of several months in civil proceedings before an appeal was heard and before a judgment was filed with the court registry, but, 'although these delays could probably have been avoided, they are not sufficiently serious to warrant the conclusion that the total duration of the proceedings (of three years six months) was excessive'. But the Court has found breaches on the basis of a single instance of unexplained delay of sufficient duration regardless of the overall length of the proceedings. Thus in *Bunate Bunkate v Netherlands*,[779] there was a breach of the guarantee in a criminal case, lasting two years and ten months over three levels of proceedings, on the basis that there had been an unexplained delay of fifteen months in transferring the appeal from one appeal court to another.

In cases in which the overall length of time in criminal or non-criminal cases is on its face unreasonable for the kind of proceedings and the number of court levels, the Court

---

[764] *Buchholz v FRG* A 42 (1981); 3 EHRR 597. Cf, *Eastaway v UK* hudoc (2004) (company director).

[765] *Sylvester v Austria No 2* hudoc (2005). See also *Berlin v Luxembourg* hudoc (2003) (family life).

[766] *Hokkanen v Finland* A 299-A (1994); 19 EHRR 139. Cf, *H v UK* A 120 (1987); 10 EHRR 95 PC (parental access).

[767] *Bock v FRG* A 150 (1989); 12 EHRR 247; *RPD v Poland* hudoc (2004); and *Gheorghe v Romania* 2007-XX. 'Exceptional diligence' is required in claims of compensation for AIDS: *X v France* A 234-C (1992); 14 EHRR 483.

[768] *Pieniążek v Poland* hudoc (2004).

[769] *Poiss v Austria* A 117 (1987); 10 EHRR 231 and *Hentrich v France* A 296-A (1994); 18 EHRR 440.

[770] *Silva Pontes v Portugal* A 286-A (1994); 18 EHRR 156. But see *Sürmeli v Germany* 2006-VII GC.

[771] *Schouten and Meldrum v Netherlands* A 304 (1994); 19 EHRR 432.

[772] *Henworth v UK* hudoc (2004); 40 EHRR 810 and *Portington v Greece* 1998-VI.

[773] *Baggetta v Italy* A 119 (1987); 10 EHRR 325. Special diligence is required in a re-trial: *Henworth v UK* hudoc (2004); 40 EHRR 810.

[774] *Abdoella v Netherlands* A 248-A (1992); 20 EHRR 585 and *Kalashnikov v Russia* 2002-VI; 36 EHRR 587.

[775] See above, p 180.   [776] A 175 (1990); 13 EHRR 87.   [777] *Eckle v FRG* A 51 (1982); 5 EHRR 1.

[778] A 71 (1983); 6 EHRR 182 para 37 PC. Cf, *Biryukov v Russia No 63972/00* hudoc (2004) DA.

[779] A 248-B (1993); 19 EHRR 477. Cf, *Kudla v Poland* 2000-XI; 25 EHRR 198 GC.

will look at the explanation for any delays particularly closely.[780] Although the length of particular stages of proceedings may not seem unreasonable, the overall length of time taken to decide the case may be such that some action should have been taken to expedite proceedings.[781] For example, in *Obasa v UK*,[782] a claim of racial discrimination in employment took over seven years, during which time there were three appeal stages of one year or more each. While it was generally not unreasonable for an appeal stage to take a year, given the length of the proceedings as a whole the time taken for these appeals was unreasonable, in breach of Article 6(1). In some extreme cases, the Court would appear to decide the case essentially on the basis of the excessive total length, quite separately from particular instances of unjustified delay (even though these may exist) on the basis that no proceedings that took so long could have been conducted diligently.[783]

The discussion so far has supposed that the Court is considering whether the proceedings on the facts of a particular case have been conducted with sufficient expedition. There is, however, another dimension to the 'reasonable time' guarantee. The Convention places a duty on the contracting parties, which applies regardless of cost,[784] 'to organise their judicial systems in such a way that their courts can meet each of its requirements, including the obligation to hear cases within a reasonable time'.[785] It follows that a state may be held liable not only for any delay in the handling of a particular case in the operation of a generally expeditious system for the administration of justice, but also for a failure to increase resources in response to a backlog of cases and for structural deficiencies in its system of justice that cause delays.

As to a backlog of cases, the Court has drawn a distinction between a situation of 'chronic overload', involving an ongoing problem, for which the state may be liable, and a sudden or 'temporary backlog', for which it will not be liable if it takes 'appropriate remedial action with the requisite promptness'.[786] In *Zimmermann and Steiner v Switzerland*,[787] the defendant state was held liable when administrative appeal proceedings of a straightforward kind, before the Swiss Federal Court, had taken nearly three and a half years, during most of which time the applicants' case had remained stationary. The agreed reason for the delay was that the Court was overworked and had for that reason given priority to urgent or important cases,[788] within neither of which categories the applicants' case fell. The Court's case-load had built up over several years, and adequate steps to increase the number of judges and administrative staff or otherwise reorganize the court system to cope with what had become a permanent problem had not been taken to remedy the situation by the time that the applicants' appeal was heard. Similarly, a backlog defence was rejected in *Guincho v Portugal*[789] in which delays in the civil courts were attributed to the increase in litigation that resulted from the return to democracy, the increase in

---

[780] See eg, *Guincho v Portugal* A 81 (1984); 7 EHRR 223 para 30; *Deumeland v FRG* A 100 (1986); 8 EHRR 448 para 90 PC; and *Lechner and Hess v Austria* A 118 (1987); 9 EHRR 490 para 39.

[781] *Uhl v Germany* hudoc (2005).

[782] Hudoc (2003). See also *Jordan v UK (No 2)* hudoc (2002) and *Ruotolo v Italy* A 230-D (1992).

[783] See eg, *Comingersoll SA v Portugal* 2000-IV; 31 EHRR 772 GC and *Gümüşten v Turkey* hudoc (2004). See also *Uoti v Finland* No 20388/92 hudoc (2004) para 2 DA.

[784] *Airey v Ireland* A 32 (1979); 2 EHRR 305.

[785] *Sussmann v Germany* 1996-IV; 25 EHRR 64 para 55.

[786] *Klein v Germany* hudoc (2000); 34 EHRR 415 para 43.

[787] A 66 (1983); 6 EHRR 17. See also *Ziacik v Slovakia* hudoc (2003).

[788] A system of priorities may be permissible as a short-term measure: *Sussmann v Germany* 1996-IV; 25 EHRR 64 para 60 GC (priority for German reunification cases permissible).

[789] A 81 (1984); 7 EHRR 223. Backlog arguments were also rejected in *B v Austria* A 175 (1990); 13 EHRR 87; *Ruiz-Mateos v Spain* A 262 (1993); 16 EHRR 505; and *Hentrich v France* A 296-A (1994); 18 EHRR 440 para 61.

litigation resulting from the impact of the new constitution, the repatriation of nationals from Portuguese colonies, and the 1970s economic recession. Portugal was found to be in breach of Article 6(1) because the resulting overloading had become a permanent problem by the time that the applicant's claim was brought and because it could, in some respects, have been foreseen. A situation of 'chronic overload' under which the German Constitutional Court had 'laboured since the end of the 1970s' was also a factor in finding a breach of the reasonable time guarantee in *Pammel v Germany.*[790]

However, in *Buchholz v FRG*,[791] the state was not liable for a delay that resulted from a backlog of cases that was not reasonably foreseeable where it had taken reasonably prompt remedial action. In that case, the delay in the consideration of the applicant's claim for unfair dismissal was attributable to a backlog of cases that had developed suddenly with the economic recession of the mid-1970s and because prompt steps had been taken to increase the number of judges when the problem became apparent. Although these steps did not benefit the applicant, they were all that could reasonably be expected of the defendant state in the circumstances. Similarly, no special measures were required to tackle a clearly temporary backlog in *Foti and Others v Italy.*[792] There delays were caused when the competent regional courts were flooded by several hundred prosecutions as a result of large-scale public disorder. It was held that delays in certain of the cases concerned were acceptable simply by reference to the temporary overloading of the courts that had occurred.

More delicate than the problem of delays resulting from a backlog of cases is the question of whether a state can be required to restructure its administration of justice system to eliminate delays that are inherent in it. This question arose in *Neumeister v Austria*[793] in which much of the delay had occurred at the preliminary investigation stage. Under some civil law systems of criminal justice, including that in Austria, a person may spend a considerable length of time waiting for a 'charge' against him in the sense of Article 6 to be fully examined by an investigating judge when much of that examination is a repetition of work already done by the police in its investigation. If such a system, which has advantages in other respects, were altered to eliminate this overlap of time, the period during which an accused had a charge hanging over him would generally be reduced. In the *Neumeister* case, the Court confirmed that preliminary investigation systems of the kind described are not in themselves contrary to Article 6; the requirement is only that they be administered efficiently. It could not have been the intention of the drafting states that such a fundamental change in the legal systems of many of their number would be required.

The same question arose again in *König v FRG*[794] in the different context of the elaborate system of administrative courts in West Germany. Faced with one set of proceedings that had lasted nearly eleven years and were still pending, the Court first noted that it was not its function to comment on the structure of the courts concerned which, it conceded, was aimed at providing a full set of remedies for the individual's grievances. It added, however, that if efforts to this end 'resulted in a procedural maze, it is for the state alone to draw the conclusions and, if need be, to simplify the system with a view to complying with Article 6(1) of the Convention'. The implication is that if a case takes what is on the face of it an unreasonably long time, a state will not escape liability by providing that it has been dealt with efficiently within the limits of an unduly elaborate court structure.

---

[790] 1997-IV; 26 EHRR 100 para 69. Cf, *Klein v Germany* hudoc (2000); 34 EHRR 415.
[791] A 42 (1981); 3 EHRR 597.   [792] A 56 (1982); 5 EHRR 313.   [793] A 8 (1968); 1 EHRR 91.
[794] A 27 (1978); 2 EHRR 170 para 100 PC.

What emerges generally from the case law of the Court on the reasonable time guarantee is the length of time that both criminal[795] and civil[796] proceedings may take in European jurisdictions and the large number of cases in which the Court has found breaches of Article 6. Either the Court is being too rigorous in its expectations, or—as is the more convincing alternative in the light of the facts of the Strasbourg cases—the 'law's delay' is a serious and pervasive problem in the legal systems of European states generally.[797]

Finally, in an important development by the Court in tackling its own case-load, it should be noted that in *Bottazzi v Italy*,[798] in response to the violations of the 'reasonable time' guarantee found at Strasbourg in many hundreds of cases coming from Italy, the Strasbourg Court noted that the 'frequency with which violations are found shows that there is an accumulation of identical breaches which are sufficiently numerous to amount not merely to isolated incidents'. This accumulation, the Court stated, 'accordingly constitutes a practice that is incompatible with the Convention'. The consequence of this ruling has been that later 'reasonable time' cases from Italy have commonly been disposed in groups and after less detailed examination of the facts than would otherwise be the case.[799]

V. THE RIGHT TO AN INDEPENDENT AND IMPARTIAL TRIBUNAL ESTABLISHED BY LAW

The right to a fair trial in Article 6(1) requires that cases be heard by an 'independent and impartial tribunal established by law'. The right applies equally to criminal cases and cases concerning 'civil rights and obligations'. There is a close inter-relation between the guarantees of an 'independent' and an 'impartial' tribunal. A tribunal that is not independent of the executive is likely to be in breach of the requirement of impartiality also in cases to which the executive is a party. Likewise, a tribunal member who has links with a private party to the case is likely to be in breach of both requirements. For this reason, the European Court commonly considers the two requirements together, using the same reasoning to decide whether the tribunal is 'independent and impartial'.[800] In respect of both requirements, there is a breach not only where there is proof of actual dependence or bias (subjective test), but also where the facts raise a 'legitimate doubt' that the requirement has been met (objective test).

---

[795] See eg, *Gümüşten v Turkey* hudoc (2004) (seventeen years) and *Hannak v Austria* hudoc (2004) (fifteen years). Both cases involved appeals.

[796] See eg, *Mazzotti v Italy* hudoc (2000) (twenty-four years, for one level of proceedings); *Szarapo v Poland* hudoc (2002) (nineteen years, with appeals); and *Surmeli v Germany* 2006-VIII GC (sixteen years, with appeals and still pending).

[797] Whereas breaches of the 'reasonable time' guarantee were for a long time a problem mainly in cases coming from civil law jurisdictions, there has been a growing number of such breaches from common law jurisdictions: for UK cases, see eg, civil cases: *Darnell v UK* A 272 (1993); 18 EHRR 205 (eight years) and *Foley v UK* hudoc (2003) (fourteen years); and criminal cases: *Massey v UK* hudoc (2004) (four years) and *Crowther v UK* hudoc (2005) (eight years), all more than one level.

[798] 1999-V para 22 GC.

[799] For criticism of this consequence, see Judge Ferrari Bravo's dissenting opinion in *Angelo Giuseppe Guerrera v Italy* hudoc (2002), pointing out that 133 Italian 'reasonable time' cases had been decided on this basis on one day. In *Scordino v Italy (No 1)* 2006-V GC, it was held that while the Italian 'Pinto law', by which a person may claim compensation in an Italian court for breaches of the Article 6 reasonable time guarantee, may constitute a domestic remedy for such a breach, it did not mean that a person who had suffered in that way could not bring a Strasbourg claim as a 'victim' of the breach: Italy still needed to reform its judicial system to prevent such violations.

[800] See eg, *Cooper v UK* 2003-XII; 39 EHRR 171 GC.

An important question is whether the right to an independent and impartial tribunal may be waived. Although it is tempting to accept that an applicant should not be allowed at Strasbourg to claim against a state a right which he has earlier unequivocally, and without pressure, waived at the national level, it is arguable that the requirement that a case always be decided by an independent and impartial tribunal is crucial to the operation of the rule of law, and that an Article 6 application should always be available to maintain this value. However, such indications as have been given by the Court—and they are not clear, unequivocal pronouncements of such a right—appear to accept that waiver is permitted. The following cases, in none of which was a waiver established on the facts, point this way and indicate the conditions that must be satisfied to establish that the applicant has waived his right. In *Pfeifer and Plankl v Austria*,[801] the Court noted generally that 'the waiver of a right guaranteed by the Convention—*in so far as it is permissible*—must be established in an unequivocal manner' and must be accompanied by 'minimum guarantees commensurate to its importance', such as the services of a lawyer. These conditions were not satisfied in the *Pfeifer* case: a waiver by the applicant in the absence of his lawyer of his right to challenge two trial judges who had acted as investigating judges in his case (and hence were disqualified by law) was held to be invalid.[802] In *McGonnell v UK*,[803] referring to its jurisprudence on the waiver of the right to a public hearing, the Court stated that the waiver of a Convention right must also 'not run counter to any important public interest', and that it may be made expressly or tacitly. As to whether a tacit waiver may be inferred from the failure to raise the issue in the national proceedings, the Court stated that it depends upon what is 'reasonable in the circumstances of the case'.[804] Thus, in the *McGonnell* case, where a national court had already ruled authoritatively that an executive role exercised by a judge did not affect his independence, it was not unreasonable for the applicant not to raise the matter in his case at the national level. Finally, in *Bulut v Austria*[805] the Court first ruled that a trial court judge's participation in the questioning of witnesses at the pre-trial stage did not amount to a breach of the right to an impartial tribunal. It then added that, in any event, the applicant could not complain of the court's partiality when he 'had the right to challenge its composition, but had refrained from doing so'.[806]

a. A tribunal

A 'tribunal' was defined in *Belilos v Switzerland*[807] as follows:

> ...a 'tribunal' is characterized in the substantive sense of the term by its judicial function, that is to say determining matters within its competence on the basis of rules of law[808] and after proceedings conducted in a prescribed manner. It must also satisfy a series of further requirements—independence, in particular of the executive; impartiality; duration of its members' terms of office; guarantees afforded by its procedure—several of which appear in the text of Article 6(1) itself.

---

[801] A 227 (1992); 14 EHRR 692 para 37. Italics added. See also *Oberschlick v Austria* A 204 (1991); 19 EHRR 389.

[802] Cf, *Öcalan v Turkey* hudoc (2003); 37 EHRR 238 (waiver not unequivocal).

[803] 2000-II; 30 EHRR 289 para 44. On waiver of a public hearing: see above, p 275.   [804] *Ibid.*

[805] 1996-II; 24 EHRR 84 para 34. The Commission had found that the right could be, and was, waived.

[806] The applicant's lawyer had been invited to object, but failed to do so.

[807] A 132 (1988); 10 EHRR 466 para 64. See also *Cyprus v Turkey* 2001-IV; 35 EHRR 731 para 233 GC and *Mihailov v Bulgaria* hudoc (2005).

[808] Ed. A 'tribunal' requires a set of rules of procedure by which it operates: *H v Belgium* A 127-B (1987); 10 EHRR 339.

This definition is overly comprehensive insofar as it contains organizational and procedural elements that, as the Court notes, are included or may be subsumed under other
guarantees in Article 6(1). As to the functional element, an important feature of a tribunal is that it must be competent to take legally binding decisions: the capacity to make
recommendations or give advice (even if normally followed) is not enough.[809] A tribunal's decisions must also not be subject to being set aside by a non-judicial body;[810] and
the government must not be empowered by law not to implement them, even though
the power is never exercised.[811] The fact that a body has other functions (administrative,
legislative, etc) does not in itself prevent it being a tribunal when exercising its judicial
function.[812]

    As to membership, although a tribunal will normally be composed of professional
judges, this is not an absolute requirement. Lay assessors are a common feature of ordinary courts in European legal systems,[813] and a bench composed of lay magistrates,
advised by a legally trained clerk (as in the English legal system), would appear to comply
with Article 6. As to administrative and disciplinary tribunals, these may include persons who are not professional judges or qualified lawyers. Civil servants may be members
of administrative tribunals[814] and members of the armed forces may serve on military
tribunals that try members of the armed forces for disciplinary[815] or criminal offences.[816]
However, the participation of such members may raise issues on the facts of the case
under the objective test.[817]

b. An independent tribunal

Many of the decided cases on the meaning of an 'independent' tribunal concern administrative or disciplinary tribunals, in which context the Strasbourg authorities have not
imposed standards as high as might be applied to the ordinary, 'classic' courts of law. This
is particularly true of such matters as the duration of office of tribunal members and their
protection from outside pressures.

    By 'independent' is meant 'independent of the executive and also of the parties'.[818]
Clearly a government minister is not 'independent' of the executive, so that a decision
taken by him does not comply with Article 6(1).[819] A tribunal that is otherwise separate
from the executive is not 'independent' where it seeks and accepts as binding Foreign
Office advice on the meaning of a treaty that it has to apply; in such a case it has surrendered its judicial function to the executive.[820] With regard to other bodies, in *Campbell*

---

[809] *Benthem v Netherlands* A 97 (1985); 8 EHRR 1 PC.
[810] *Cooper v UK* 2003-XII; 39 EHRR 171 GC. The power of the 'reviewing authority' to review a UK court-
martial's verdict under the Army Act 1996 reforms is not a problem, because the final decision lies with the
Courts-Martial Appeal Court: *ibid*. See also *British-American Tobacco v Netherlands* A 331-A (1995); 21 EHRR
409; *Beaumartin v France*, below, p 820; and the *Sovtransavto Holding* case, below, p 291. As to the related
Article 6 requirement of the finality of court judgments, see the *Brumarescu* case, above, p 269.
[811] *Van de Hurk v Netherlands* A 288 (1994); 18 EHRR 481 para 45.
[812] *Campbell and Fell v UK* A 80 (1984); 7 EHRR 165; *H v Belgium* A 127-B (1987); 10 EHRR 339; and *Demicoli v
Malta* A 210 (1991); 14 EHRR 47. However, it may raise issues of objective independence and impartiality on the
facts.
[813] See eg, *Langborder v Sweden*, A 155 (1983); 12 EHRR 416 PC.
[814] *Ettl and Others v Austria* A 117 (1987); 10 EHRR 225 and *Stojakovic v Austria* hudoc (2006).
[815] *Engel v Netherlands No 1* A 22 (1976); 1 EHRR 647 PC. Cf, *Le Compte v Belgium* A 43 (1981); 4 EHRR 1 PC
(medical disciplinary body).   [816] *Cooper v UK* 2003-XII; 39 EHRR 171 GC.
[817] See eg, *Sramek v Austria* A 84 (1984); 7 EHRR 351.
[818] *Ringeisen v Austria* A 13 (1971) para 95. It also means independence of Parliament: *Crociani v Italy*
No 8603/79, 22 DR 147 at 221 (1980).
[819] *Benthem v Netherlands* A 97 (1985); 8 EHRR 1 PC.
[820] *Beaumartin v France* A 296-B (1994); 19 EHRR 485. Cf, *Chevrol v France* hudoc (2003).

and Fell v UK,[821] the Court indicated the considerations it takes into account when assessing independence:

> In determining whether a body can be considered to be 'independent'—notably of the executive and of the parties to the case—the Court has had regard to the manner of appointment of its members and the duration of their term of office, the existence of guarantees against outside pressures and the question whether the body presents an appearance of independence.

As far as 'manner of appointment' is concerned, appointment by the executive is permissible, indeed normal.[822] The arrangements for the selection or substitution of judges for a particular case from amongst the judiciary as a whole can give rise to questions of independence.[823] For a judge's independence to be challenged successfully by reference to his 'manner of appointment' it would have to be shown that the practice of appointment 'as a whole is unsatisfactory' or that 'at least the establishment of the particular court deciding a case was influenced by improper motives',[824] ie motives suggesting an attempt at influencing the outcome of the case.

With regard to the 'duration of their term of office', a short term of office has been accepted as permissible as far as members of administrative or disciplinary tribunals are concerned. In *Campbell and Fell v UK*,[825] appointment for a term of three years as a member of a prison Board of Visitors acting as a disciplinary tribunal was sufficient, the Court being influenced by the fact that members were unpaid and that it might be hard to find candidates for any longer period. With regard to ordinary courts, appointment of judges may be for life or a fixed term,[826] but a renewable four-year term has been questioned.[827]

As to 'guarantees against outside pressures', tribunal members must be protected from removal during their term of office, either by law or in practice.[828] The appointment of a judge for a fixed term, so as to prevent dismissal at will, is a relevant factor,[829] although apparently not in itself required. In *Engel v Netherlands*[830] the military members of the Netherlands Supreme Military Court were removable by Ministers at will. The Court would appear to have considered, without discussion, that their independence was not an issue in fact. In the *Campbell and Fell* case, the Court did not require any 'formal recognition' in law of the irremovability of a prison Board of Visitors member during his term of office; it was sufficient that this was 'recognised in fact and that the other necessary

---

[821] A 80 (1984); 7 EHRR 165 para 78. Footnotes omitted. Cf, *Langborger v Sweden* A 155 (1989); 12 EHRR 416 PC.

[822] *Campbell and Fell v UK* A 80 (1984); 7 EHRR 165; *Belilos v Switzerland* A 132 (1988); 10 EHRR 466; and *Asadov v Azerbaijan No 138/03* hudoc (2002). Appointment by Parliament is also permissible: *Filippini v San Marino No 10526/02* hudoc (2003) DA and *Ninn-Hansen v Denmark No 28972/95* hudoc (1999).

[823] See *Barberà, Messegué, and Jabardo v Spain* A 146 (1988); 11 EHRR 360 paras 53–9 (1988) (an impartiality case).

[824] *Zand v Austria No 7360/76*, 15 DR 70 at 81 (1978) Com Rep; CM Res DH (79) 6 (no breach). As to the appointment of judges for their political views, see *Crociani v Italy No 8603/79*, 22 DR 147 at 222 (1980) (question seen in terms of impartiality).

[825] A 80 (1984); 7 EHRR 165. Cf, *Sramek v Austria* A 84 (1984); 7 EHRR 351. *Ad hoc* appointment of a military officer as a court-martial member for just one case was sufficient: *Cooper v UK* 2003-XII; 39 EHRR 171 GC. Cf, *Dupuis v Belgium No 12717/87*, 57 DR 196 (1988). See also *Mihailov v Bulgaria* hudoc (2005) (no tenure).

[826] *Zand v Austria No 7360/76*, 15 DR 70 (1978) Com Rep; CM Res DH (79) 6.

[827] *Incal v Turkey* 1998-IV; 29 EHRR 449. But see *Yavuz v Turkey No 29870/96* hudoc (2000) DA.

[828] *Engel v Netherlands* A 22 (1976); 1 EHRR 647 PC. See also *Zand v Austria No 7360/76*, 15 DR 70 at 82 (1978); *Sramek v Austria* A 84 (1984); 7 EHRR 351 para 38; and *Brudnicka v Poland* 2005-II.

[829] See *Crociani v Italy No 8603/79*, 22 DR 147 at 221 (1980).

[830] A 22 (1976); 1 EHRR 647 PC.

guarantees are present'.[831] In both of the above cases, the possibility of removal by the executive without procedures for judicial review was not questioned. The availability of judicial review was at issue in *Eccles, McPhillips and McShane v Ireland*,[832] which dealt with terrorist offences tried by the Irish Special Criminal Court. The independence of its judges was questioned because they could be dismissed at will and have their salaries reduced. Emphasizing the need to look at the 'realities of the situation', the Commission found no evidence of any attempt by the executive to interfere with the Court's functioning on either basis and noted that the ordinary courts had powers to review the Court's independence. In other cases, the possibility of transferring tribunal members to other duties has also not been considered to present a problem.[833]

As far as other 'guarantees against outside pressure' are concerned, the Court requires that tribunal members are not subject to instructions from the executive, although here too it may be sufficient that this is the case in practice.[834] In the *Greek* case[835] the extraordinary courts-martial during the regime of the Colonels were found not to be independent partly because their jurisdiction was to be exercised 'in accordance with decisions of the Minister of National Defence'. The secrecy of a tribunal's deliberations also affords protection against outside pressures.[836] Any authority given to the executive to grant an amnesty or a pardon must not be used so as to undermine the judicial function.[837]

Finally, the 'appearance of independence' requirement listed by the Court in the *Campbell and Fell* case relates to the objective test that has been developed by the Court in respect to the requirements of both independence and impartiality.[838] In *Campbell and Fell*, a Prison Board of Visitors served a dual role as a disciplinary tribunal and as a body independent of the government whose function was to monitor the administration of the prison in the interest of both prisoners and the public. It was argued that prisoners regarded the Board of Visitors as being too closely connected with the prison administration to be independent when exercising their role as a disciplinary tribunal. The Court held that this impression was not a reasonable one: the Board was objectively independent.[839]

However, a breach of the 'appearance of independence' requirement was found in *Findlay v UK*.[840] There it was held that there were 'fundamental flaws' in the UK court-martial system because of the role of the convening military officer. This officer decided which charges should be brought and was otherwise closely linked with the prosecuting authorities. He also appointed the court-martial members, who were below him in rank and in some cases under his command, and he could dissolve the court-martial. Finally, the convening officer had to confirm the court-martial decision for it

---

[831] A 80 (1984) 7 EHRR 165 para 80. In practice, the Home Secretary would require the removal of a member 'only in the most exceptional circumstances': *ibid*. See also *Clarke v UK No 23695/02* 2005-X DA (circuit judges).

[832] *No 12839/87*, 59 DR 212 (1988). See also *Cooper v UK* 2003-XII; 39 EHRR 171 GC (sufficient safeguards against outside pressure on military officer court-martial members).

[833] See *Sutter v Switzerland No 8209/78*, 16 DR 166 (1979). See also *Clarke v UK No 23695/02* hudoc (2005) DA. And see *Beaumartin v France*, above, n 820.

[834] See *Sramek v Austria* A 84 (1984); 7 EHRR 351 (law) and *Campbell and Fell v UK* A 80 (1984); 7 EHRR 165 (practice). Cf, *Schiesser v Switzerland* A 34 (1979); 2 EHRR 417 (an Article 5(3) case).

[835] 12 YB (the *Greek* case) at 148 (1969); Com Rep CM Res DH (70) 1.

[836] *Sutter v Switzerland No 8209/78*, 16 DR 166 (1979).

[837] 12 YB (the *Greek* case) at 148 (1969) Com Rep; CM Res (70) 1.

[838] On the objective test, which requires only a 'legitimate doubt' of bias, etc, see below, p 290.

[839] The disciplinary role of Boards of Visitors (now Independent Monitoring Boards) has since been abolished. On the current disciplinary procedures, see Livingstone, Owen, and MacDonald, *Prison Law*, 4th edn, 2008, pp 384ff.

[840] 1997-I; 24 EHRR 221 para 78.

to be valid and could vary the sentence. In these circumstances, an outside observer could legitimately doubt the court-martial's structural independence of the executive and its impartiality.[841] In *Whitfield v UK*,[842] a similar lack of 'structural independence', giving rise to a legitimate doubt in breach of Article 6, was found to exists in UK prison governor's disciplinary proceedings. This followed from the fact that governors, prison officers and, in the case of private prisons, controllers who were answerable to the Home Secretary were responsible for laying, investigating, prosecuting, and ruling upon the charges against a prisoner.

The membership of military judges in ordinary criminal courts has been an issue in some Turkish cases. In *Incal v Turkey*,[843] the applicant was convicted of a criminal offence of inciting racial hatred, by distributing the leaflets of a Kurdish political party, by a National Security Court composed of two civilian judges and a military judge. The Strasbourg Court held the participation of the military judge in a civil (ie non-military) court was in breach of the requirements of independence and impartiality, since the civilian applicant 'could legitimately fear that because one of the judges of the Izmir National Security Court was a military judge it might allow itself to be unduly influenced by considerations which had nothing to do with the nature of the case'.[844] In *Öcalan v Turkey*[845] it was held that the objective requirement had not been satisfied even though, following the *Incal* case, the military member of a State Security Court (a civil court) that tried the applicant had been replaced by a third civilian judge before judgment was given In a persuasive joint dissenting opinion, President Wildhaber and five other judges took the view that the fact that the verdict and sentence were decided upon by a wholly civilian court was sufficient: to go further was 'to take the 'theory' of appearances very far' and was neither 'realistic' nor 'fair'.[846]

The *Incal* and *Öcalan* cases involved the trial of civilians for criminal offences by civil courts that had a military judge as a member. In *Martin v UK*[847] the Court held that the prosecution of civilians for criminal offences before *military* courts is a matter of even greater concern under Article 6. Although their jurisdiction over civilians was not 'absolutely' excluded by the Convention, it would be consistent with Article 6 'only in very exceptional circumstances'. In particular, it should not extend to civilians unless there was a 'clear and forseeable legal basis' and there were 'compelling reasons'. Moreover, the existence of such reasons 'must be substantiated in each specific case'; it was 'not sufficient for the law to allocate certain offences to military courts *in abstracto*'. In the *Martin* case, the applicant was a seventeen-year-old living with his family on a British military base in Germany, where his father was an army corporal. He was convicted in Germany by a British court-martial board—Germany having waived jurisdiction under the NATO Status of Forces Agreement 1951—of murder there. The Strasbourg Court found a breach of Article 6 on the basis that the court-martial board was not an independent and

---

[841] As revised by the Armed Forces Act 1996 the UK court-martial system for the army and the RAF complies with Article 6 for the army and the RAF: *Cooper v UK* 2003-XII; 39 EHRR 171 GC. The naval system was amended by the Army Act 2006 to comply with *Grieves v UK* 2003-XII; 39 EHRR 51 GC.

[842] Hudoc (2005); 41 EHRR 967. See also *Mihailov v Bulgaria* hudoc (2005).

[843] 1998-IV; 29 EHRR 449 GC.

[844] Id, para 68. The Court took into account that the judge was subject to military discipline and appointed only for four years, and that the army took orders from the executive—considerations that outweighed certain guarantees of his independence and impartiality.

[845] 2005-IV; 41 EHRR 985 GC. But see *Ceylan v Turkey No 68953/01* hudoc (2005) in which a military judge's participation in interlocutory proceedings before his replacement by a civilian judge on the merits was not a breach.

[846] The fact that it was a death penalty case may have influenced the Court majority.

[847] Hudoc (2006) paras 44–5.

impartial tribunal. While it did not find it necessary to decide whether there was also a breach of Article 6 because the applicant had been tried by a military court, it expressed 'considerable doubts' as to whether there were 'compelling reasons' for him to be so tried. Justifying its concern at the military trial of civilians, in *Ergin v Turkey (No 6)*,[848] the Court stated that to allow civilians to be tried by military courts other than in exceptional cases would 'seriously undermine the confidence that courts ought to inspire in a democratic society' and be inconsistent with the limited national security function of the armed forces; military courts should only try military personnel. It added that although 'military courts may comply with Convention standards to the same extent as ordinary courts, differences in treatment linked to their different nature and reasons for existence may give rise to a problem of equality before the courts, which should be avoided as far as possible, particularly in criminal cases'. This last statement suggests a possible breach of the residual 'fair hearing' requirement in Article 6(1).

c. An impartial tribunal

'Impartiality' means lack of prejudice or bias. To satisfy the requirement, the tribunal must comply with both a subjective and an objective test:[849]

> The existence of impartiality for the purpose of Article 6(1) must be determined according to a subjective test, that is on the basis of the personal conviction of a particular judge in a given case, and also according to an objective test, that is ascertaining whether the judge offered guarantees sufficient to exclude any legitimate doubt in this respect.

In *Kyprianou v Cyprus*,[850] the Court distinguished between two situations in which there might be a breach of the impartiality requirement, namely situations involving either 'functional or personal' partiality. In the case of the former, the issue was whether 'the exercise of different functions within the judicial process by the same person or hierarchical or other links with another actor in the proceedings' raised a legitimate doubt as to the court's objective impartiality. In the case of the latter, it was whether a judge's personal conduct raised such a doubt or indicated actual bias, thus going to both objective and subjective impartiality.

As to the *subjective* test, the question is whether it can be shown on the facts that a member of the court 'acted with personal bias' against the applicant.[851] In this connection, there is a presumption that a judge is impartial, 'until there is proof to the contrary'.[852] Given this presumption and the need to prove actual bias, it is not surprising that a breach of the subjective test is difficult to establish.[853] One case in which a breach was found was *Werner v Poland*.[854] There an insolvency judge who requested that the applicant be removed from his post as a judicial liquidator later sat as a member of the court that heard

---

[848] 2006-VI. There a newspaper editor was convicted of a criminal (non-military) offence involving propaganda against military service by a military court composed entirely of military officers. As in *Martin*, an Article 6 breach was found for lack of independence and impartiality.

[849] *Hauschildt v Denmark* A 154 (1989); 12 EHRR 266 para 46. The test was first formulated in *Piersack v Belgium* A 53 (1982); 5 EHRR 169.

[850] 2005-XIII; 44 EHRR 565 para 122 GC.   [851] *Hauschildt v Denmark*, id, para 47.

[852] *Kyprianou v Cyprus* 2005-XIII; 44 EHRR 565 GC. The presumption applies to jury members: *Sander v UK* 2000-V; 31 EHRR 1003.

[853] Cf, *Kyprianou v Cyprus* 2005-XIII; 44 EHRR 565 para 119 GC.

[854] Hudoc (2001); 36 EHRR 491. See also *Boeckmans v Belgium No 1727/62*, 8 YB 410 (1965) F Sett; *Kyprianou v Cyprus* hudoc (2004); *Driza v Albania* 2007-XX; and *Svetlana Naumenko v Ukraine* hudoc (2004). In *Barberà, Messegué and Jabardo v Spain* A 146 (1988), 11 EHRR 360 the applicants' doubts concerning a judge's political connections (he wore a Francoist tie and cufflinks) were not substantiated. On the political sympathies of judges and their impartiality, see *Crociani, Palmiotti, Tanassi, Lefebvre, D'Ovidio v Italy No 8603/79*, 22 DR 147 at 222 (1980).

her request. The European Court held that it was 'only reasonable' to conclude that the insolvency judge held a personal conviction that her request was well founded and should be granted.

The *objective* test is comparable to the English law doctrine that 'justice must not only be done: it must also be seen to be done'. In this context, the Court emphasizes the importance of 'appearances'.[855] As the Court has stated, '[w]hat is at stake is the confidence which the courts in a democratic society must inspire in the public and, above all, as far as criminal proceedings are concerned, in the accused'.[856] In applying the objective test, the opinion of the party to the case who is alleging partiality is 'important but not decisive'; what is crucial is whether the doubt as to impartiality can be 'objectively justified'.[857] If there is a 'legitimate doubt' as to a judge's impartiality, he must withdraw from the case.[858]

There was such a 'doubt' in *McGonnell v UK*,[859] where the Guernsey Royal Court rejected the applicant's appeal against the refusal of his planning application by a development committee. The presiding judge in the applicant's appeal was the Bailiff of Guernsey, who, as Deputy Bailiff, had earlier presided over the Guernsey legislature (the States of Deliberation) when it adopted the development plan under which the applicant's planning application had been refused and which the Royal Court had to apply. As well as chairing the States of Deliberation, the Deputy Bailiff also had a casting vote in the event of a tie, although he was not called upon to exercise it in this case. The European Court held that the 'mere fact' that the Deputy Bailiff presided over the legislature when the plan was adopted was sufficient to raise a 'legitimate doubt' as to his impartiality when he later served as the sole judge on the law when the applicant's planning appeal was rejected. More generally, the Court stated that 'any direct involvement in the passage of legislation, or of executive rules, is likely to be sufficient to cast doubt upon the judicial impartiality of a person subsequently called on to determine a dispute' concerning its or their application. In considering such cases, the Court has stated that the Convention does not suppose that contracting parties follow any particular constitutional theory concerning the separation of powers: the question is always whether there is a 'legitimate doubt' about impartiality (or independence) on the facts.[860]

Again in terms of the separation of powers, the objective test will be infringed where the executive intervenes in a case in the courts with a view to influencing the outcome. In *Sovtransavto Holding v Ukraine*,[861] while civil proceedings brought by the applicant Russian company in Ukraine were pending, the President of Ukraine drew the attention of the Supreme Arbitration Tribunal to the need to protect state interests. The Strasbourg Court held that, irrespective of whether it had influenced the outcome of the case, the President's intervention gave rise to a 'legitimate doubt' as to the Tribunal's independence and impartiality. In contrast, public remarks in another case by the Romanian President to the effect that judgments by the Romanian courts in decided cases for the restitution of

---

[855] *Sramek v Austria* A 84 (1984) para 42; 7 EHRR 351.

[856] *Fey v Austria* A 255-A (1993); 6 EHRR 387 para 30.

[857] *Hauschildt v Denmark* A 154 (1989); 12 EHRR 266 para 48.   [858] *Ibid.*

[859] 2000-II; 30 EHRR 289 para 55. Cf, *Procola v Luxembourg* A 326 (1995); 22 EHRR 193 (*Conseil d'Etat* members who had advised on legislation later applied it as judges: not impartial), distinguished in *Kleyn v Netherlands* 2003-VI; 38 EHRR 239 GC. See also *Sacilor-Lormines v France* 2006-XIII. A member of parliament is not *per se* disqualified from being a judge: *Pabla Ky v Finland* 2004-V; 42 EHRR 688.

[860] *Kleyn v Netherlands* 2003-VI; 38 EHRR 239 GC.

[861] 2002-VII; 38 EHRR 911. There was also a breach the principle of legal certainty because all judicial decisions in the case were later quashed by the Supreme Administrative Tribunal following an objection by its President.

property should not be implemented, which, it was claimed, might influence the courts, were not in breach of the objective test.[862]

The Court has applied the objective test in many cases in which the trial judge in a criminal court has previously taken part in the proceedings at the pre-trial stage in a variety of different capacities.[863] The Court has stated that 'the mere fact that a judge has also made pre-trial decisions in the case cannot be taken as in itself justifying fears as to his impartiality... What matters is the extent and nature of those decisions.'[864] In practice, the Court has found a 'legitimate doubt' in a number of cases, including some involving long-established national practices. In *Piersack v Belgium*,[865] the presiding trial court judge had earlier been the head of the section of the public prosecutor's department that had investigated the applicant's case and instituted proceedings against him. Although there was no evidence that the judge had actual knowledge of the investigation, the Court held there had been a breach of the objective test:

> [I]f an individual, after holding in the public prosecutor's department an office whose nature is such that he may have to deal with a given matter in the course of his duties, subsequently sits in the same case as a judge, the public are entitled to fear that he does not offer sufficient guarantees of impartiality.

In *De Cubber v Belgium*,[866] the *Piersack* case was extended to the situation where a judge had earlier acted as an investigating judge. Although the investigating judge was, unlike a member of the public prosecutor's department, independent of the prosecution, he had links with that department and it could reasonably be supposed that he had already formed a view as to the accused's guilt before the trial, thereby giving rise to a 'legitimate doubt' as to his impartiality.

The position is normally different where pre-trial decisions are taken by a judge who is not linked to the investigation or prosecution of the case. In *Sainte-Marie v France*,[867] two members of an appeal court that sentenced the accused following his conviction on charges of possession of arms had earlier been members of a court that had refused his application for bail in criminal damage proceedings arising out of the same facts. Noting that the judges had played no part in the preparation of the case for trial, the Court stated that in such circumstances the 'mere fact that such a judge has already taken pre-trial decisions in the case, including decisions relating to detention on remand, cannot in itself justify fears as to his impartiality'. The Court distinguished *Hauschildt v Denmark*.[868] There a judge who had taken numerous pre-trial decisions as to detention on remand,

---

[862] *Mosteanu and others v Romania* hudoc (2002).

[863] For similar civil cases, see *Nordborg v Sweden No 13635/88*, 65 DR 232 (1990); *Jensen v Denmark No 14063/88*, 68 DR 177 (1991); and *S v Switzerland No 17722/91*, 69 DR 345 (1991).

[864] *Fey v Austria* A 255-A (1993); 6 EHRR 387 para 30.

[865] A 53 (1982); 5 EHRR 169 para 30. A 'legitimate doubt' may also exist where the judge takes over the role of the prosecution during the trial: see *Thorgeir Thorgeirson v Iceland* A 239 (1992); 14 EHRR 843. See also *Kristinsson v Iceland* A 171-B (1990) Com Rep (F Sett before Court), in which the chief of police was also a criminal court judge. The Commission found a breach, the limited number of qualified persons in a small population being no excuse. See also *D'Haese, Le Compte, Van Leuven and De Meyere v Belgium No 8930/80*, 6 EHRR 114 (1983) and *Mellors v UK No 57836/00* hudoc (2003) DA.

[866] A 86 (1984); 7 EHRR 236. Cf, *Pfeifer and Plankl v Austria* A 227 (1992); 14 EHRR 692 (breach of Article 6(1)—and national law—for an investigating judge to be the trial judge) and *Ben Yaacoub v Belgium* A 127-A (1987) Com Rep; F Sett before Court. Contrast *Fey v Austria* A 255-A (1993); 6 EHRR 387 in which the trial judge had played a marginal interrogating role at the pre-trial stage (no breach).

[867] A 253-A (1992); 16 EHRR 116 para 32. Cf, *Padovani v Italy* A 257-B (1993); *Nortier v Netherlands* A 267 (1993); 17 EHRR 273; *Castillo Algar v Spain* 1998-VIII; 30 EHRR 27; and *Jasinski v Poland* hudoc (2005).

[868] A 154 (1989); 12 EHRR 266 para 50 PC. See also *Cianetti v Italy* hudoc (2004) (breach).

solitary confinement, and other ancillary matters, later served as the presiding judge at the accused's trial. Under the Danish system, the judge had taken no part in the preparation of the case for trial or the decision to prosecute. Instead, his role had been to act as an independent judge, taking decisions as to bail, etc, in open court on the application of the police, and after hearing the defence. The Court stated although a trial court judge who has earlier taken pre-trial decisions in such a system does not normally give rise to a 'legitimate doubt', there were 'special circumstances' on the facts. These were that the judge's decisions to remand the accused in detention had been on a statutory ground that required him to be convinced that there was a 'particularly confirmed suspicion of guilt'. This, it might well be supposed, involved him in formulating a considered opinion on the applicant's guilt and contrasted with the normal situation in Danish law, which had not have raised a 'legitimate doubt' as to impartiality, in which the judge would be looking only for *prima facie* grounds for the police's suspicion, and which would not have raised a 'legitimate doubt' as to impartiality.

Another question is whether a judge can sit at more than one stage in the hearing of the merits of a case, or in both of two related cases. As to the former situation, in *Ringeisen v Austria*,[869] the Court indicated that 'it cannot be stated as a general rule resulting from the obligation to be impartial' that a case must be re-heard, having been referred back by an appellate court, by a tribunal with a totally different membership from that of the first hearing. In contrast, it has been held that a judge should not take part in two different appellate stages of the same case.[870] Clearly, there is also a breach of the requirement of objective impartiality where a judge is the presiding judge of an appeals tribunal that hears an appeal from his own decision.[871] As to a judge sitting in two related cases, a judge may participate in related civil and/or criminal cases concerning the applicant without this in itself raising a legitimate doubt as to his impartiality.[872] However, the judge's statements in the earlier proceedings may do so on the facts. Thus, in *Ferrantelli and Santangelo v Italy*[873] there was a 'legitimate doubt' where the President of the Court of Appeal that heard the applicants' appeal from their conviction for murder had earlier been the President of the Court of Appeal following the conviction of others for the same murder, when the Court of Appeal judgment in the earlier case contained passages referring to the applicants' involvement in the murder and the Court of Appeal's judgment in the applicants' case had cited these passages.

The procedures applicable in common law jurisdictions in cases of criminal contempt in the face of the court were in issue in *Kyprianou v Cyprus*.[874] There the applicant was a lawyer who had been convicted of criminal contempt in the face of the court for his offensive personal remarks and other behaviour during an exchange with the judges in a criminal case. After a short break in the proceedings, the same judges convicted him of contempt and sentenced him to five days' imprisonment. Finding a breach of the impartiality requirement, the Strasbourg Court held that the 'the confusion of roles between complainant, witness, prosecutor and judge could self-evidently prompt objectively justified

[869] A 13 (1971); 1 EHRR 455 para 97. See also *Thomann v Switzerland* 1996-III; 24 EHRR 553.

[870] *Oberschlick v Austria* A 204 (1991); 19 EHRR 389. See also *Indra v Slovakia* hudoc (2005); 43 EHRR 388.

[871] *De Haan v Netherlands* 1997-IV; 26 EHRR 417. See also *San Leonard Band Club v Malta* 2004-IX; 42 EHRR 473. And see *Kingsley v UK* 2002-IV; 35 EHRR 177 GC.

[872] *Gillow v UK* A 109 (1986); 11 EHRR 335 and *Kalogeropoulou and Others v Greece and Germany* No 59021/00 hudoc (2002) DA. See also *Lindon et al v France* 2007-XX GC.

[873] 1996-III; 23 EHRR 288. See also *Indra v Slovakia* hudoc (2005); 43 EHRR 388 and *Warsicka v Poland* hudoc (2007). There may also be a breach where a judge has been an opposing party to the applicant in an earlier case: *Chmelíř v Czech Republic* 2005-IV.

[874] 2005-XIII; 44 EHRR 565 paras 127, 130 GC.

fears as to the conformity of the proceedings with the time-honoured principle that no one should be a judge in his or her own cause and, consequently, as to the impartiality of the bench'. The correct course would have been for the court to have referred the matter to the prosecuting authorities with a view to trial before a differently composed court. The Court went on to find a breach of the subjective impartiality test also, on the basis of the statement made by the judges in their decision that they were 'deeply insulted', their generally 'emphatic language', the severe penalty imposed, and their statements in the exchanges with the applicant that he was guilty.

In view of the robust remarks sometimes made by English judges in court about defendants in criminal cases, it is noticeable that no English case of this kind has been admitted on the merits. In one such case,[875] in which the judge had indicated very clearly that the accused was guilty and expressed his concern at the cost of the case for the legal aid fund, the application was declared inadmissible, the Commission emphasizing that the trial had to be considered as a whole. In a civil case,[876] in which a judge was alleged by the applicant to have formed a prejudice against him in proceedings concerning his rights to his children, the Court found that although the judge had undoubtedly taken a strongly negative view of the applicant's character, this did not in itself indicate bias and that, in any event, any such defect had been rectified on appeal by the Court of Appeal.

There may also be a breach of the impartiality requirement where a judge makes extra-judicial pronouncements in the press or elsewhere that may raise a legitimate doubt about his impartiality in a case before him. In *Buscemi v Italy*,[877] the applicant had published a letter in the press complaining about the placing of his daughter in a children's home by court order. The President of the court in pending child custody proceedings concerning the child responded with a letter in the press in terms that, in the Strasbourg Court's view, 'implied that he had already formed an unfavourable view of the applicant's case' before deciding it, thereby raising a legitimate doubt as to his impartiality. In the Court's words, 'all judicial authorities are required to exercise maximum discretion with regard to the cases with which they deal in order to preserve their image as impartial judges', which requirement should 'dissuade them from making use of the press, even when provoked'.

Breaches of the objective impartiality test may also arise where the judge has acted as a lawyer for the applicant's opponent in other proceedings. In *Wettstein v Switzerland*,[878] there was a breach of the objective test when the part-time judge in the applicant's civil case was at the same time acting as a lawyer for the applicant's opponent in that case, in other pending civil litigation. Although the two cases were unrelated on their facts, the applicant had a 'legitimate fear' that the judge might 'continue to see in him the opposing side'. In contrast, in *Walston v Norway*[879] there was no such breach where the judge had acted as the lawyer for the applicant's opponent in another case some five years earlier.

The objective test may also be infringed where the judge has a personal interest in the case. A financial interest will disqualify a judge as not being impartial,[880] although there will be no breach of Article 6(1) if the interest is disclosed and the applicant is given

---

[875] *X v UK No 4991/71*, 45 CD 1 (1973). Cf, *X v UK No 5574/72*, 3 DR 10 (1975) (accused had 'not a ghost of a chance'). See also *Grant v UK No 12002/86*, 55 DR 218 (1988).

[876] *Ranson v UK No 14180/03* hudoc (2003) DA.

[877] 1999-VI paras 67–8. See also *Lavents v Latvia* hudoc (2002), below, p 304.

[878] 2000-XII para 47. See also *Puolitaival and Pirttiaho v Finland* hudoc (2004); 43 EHRR 153; *Chmelíř v Czech Rep* hudoc (2005); and *Svarc and Kavnik v Slovenia* hudoc (2007).

[879] *No 37272/97* hudoc (2001) DA.   [880] *Sigurdsson v Iceland* 2003-IV.

an opportunity to object.[881] Non-financial interests are also relevant. Thus in *Demicoli v Malta*,[882] the Maltese House of Representatives that tried the applicant for breach of parliamentary privilege was not impartial because two of its members who participated in the proceedings were the Members of Parliament who were criticized in the article that was the subject of the alleged offence.

The objective test was also not satisfied in *Langborger v Sweden*,[883] which concerned lay assessors who were members of a Housing and Tenancy Court, whose function was to adjudicate upon the continuation of a clause in a tenancy agreement; they were nominated by, and had close links with, organizations that had an interest in the removal of the clause. It did not matter that the tribunal was composed of two judges as well as the two lay assessors, with the presiding judge having the casting vote. The *Langborger* case may be contrasted with the earlier case of *Le Compte, Van Leuven, and De Meyere v Belgium*,[884] in which the medical members of a professional tribunal had 'interests very close to' those of one of the doctors being disciplined.[885] This fact was counterbalanced by the presence of an equal number of judges, one of which had the casting vote, so that there was no breach of Article 6(1). In *Gautrin v France*,[886] however, there was a breach of the requirement of objective impartiality when the medical disciplinary bodies who determined the applicants' cases had doctors linked to rival professional organizations among their members.

Personal links between a judge and a party to the case have been an issue in a variety of other particular contexts. The fact that a judge is a freemason does not *per se* raise doubts as to his impartiality in a case in which a party to the case or a witness is also a freemason; the position may be different if the judge has personal knowledge of the freemason or his lodge.[887] In contrast, there was a 'legitimate doubt' where the judge was also a professor employed by the University that was the other party to the case[888] and where a judge had threatened a reprisal after his son had been expelled from the school.[889] The fact that a judge in a divorce case had a conversation with the applicant's wife immediately after the hearing did not by itself raise a 'legitimate doubt'.[890] In *Belukha v Ukraine*,[891] there was a lack of impartiality when the employer against whom the applicant was claiming supplied the trial court with goods and services.

The requirement of impartiality applies to juries.[892] Whether a jury member's personal link with a party to the case or to a witness raises a 'legitimate doubt' depends in each case on 'whether the familiarity in question is of such a nature and degree as to indicate

---

[881] *D v Ireland No 11489/85*, 51 DR 117 (1986) (judge owned shares in defendant company). On waiver of the right to an impartial court, see further, above, p 285.

[882] A 210 (1991); 14 EHRR 47.

[883] A 155 (1989); 12 EHRR 416 PC. Cf, *Thaler v Austria* hudoc (2005); 41 EHRR 727. Contrast *AB Kurt Kellermann v Sweden* hudoc (2004) and *Timperi v Finland No 60963/00* hudoc (2004) DA (no breaches).

[884] A 43 (1981); 4 EHRR 1 para 58 PC.

[885] Report of the Commission in the *Le Compte* case, para 78.

[886] 1998-III; 28 EHRR 196. See also *Thaler v Austria* hudoc (2005); 41 EHRR 727.

[887] *Salaman v UK No 43505/98* hudoc (2000) DA. For other cases in which personal links were not a breach, see *Steiner v Austria No 16445/90* hudoc (1993) DA; *Academy Trading Ltd and Others v Greece* hudoc (2000); 33 EHRR 1081; and *Lawrence v UK No 74660/01* hudoc (2002) DA.

[888] *Pescador Valero v Spain* hudoc (2003). See also *Timperi v Finland No 60963/00* hudoc (2004) DA (no breach).

[889] *Tocono et al v Moldova* hudoc (2007). See also *Podoreski v Croatia* hudoc (2007) (F Sett) (judge close relative of plaintiffs).

[890] *X v Austria No 556/59*, 4 CD 1 (1960).   [891] Hudoc (2006).

[892] So does the independence requirement, but impartiality will usually be most relevant: see *Pullar v UK* 1996-III; 22 EHRR 391.

a lack of impartiality'.[893] There was no 'legitimate doubt' in *Simsek v UK*.[894] There a jury member was the sister-in-law of a prison officer, who worked on the house block of 180 prisoners in which the applicant had been detained on remand; but who had not escorted or worked with him. In contrast, in *Holm v Sweden*[895] a breach of Article 6(1) was found because of the links between members of a jury and the defendants in an unsuccessful private prosecution brought by the applicant for libel in a book commenting on right wing political parties. A majority of the jury were active members of a political party that owned the first defendant (the publisher) and that had been advised by the second defendant (the author), thereby giving rise to a 'legitimate doubt' as to the jury members' members independence and impartiality.

The question of impartiality has also arisen in cases alleging racial discrimination within juries. In *Remli v France*,[896] a certified statement by a third party was presented by the defence to a criminal court that was trying the applicant and another accused, who were both of North African origin. The statement indicated that the author had over-heard one of the jurors saying on entering the courtroom before the trial, 'What's more, I'm a racist.' Without considering its merits, the court refused a defence application that it should take formal note of the statement because it had no jurisdiction to take note of events occurring out of its presence. The trial proceeded and the applicant and his co-defendant were convicted of homicide. The Strasbourg Court held, by five votes to four, that the decision of the court to refuse the application without considering its substance raised a 'legitimate doubt' as to the court's impartiality.

In contrast, no breach was found in *Gregory v UK*[897] in which the applicant, who was black, was convicted of robbery by a jury, by ten votes to two, and sentenced to six years' imprisonment. While the jury was deliberating, a note was passed by the jury to the judge stating: 'Jury showing racial overtones. One member to be excused.' After consulting with both counsel, the judge gave a 'firmly worded' and 'forceful' redirection to the jury instructing them to put out of their minds 'any thoughts of prejudice of one form or another'. The Strasbourg Court held, by eight votes to one, that, in doing so, the judge had taken sufficient steps to 'dispel any objectively held fears or misgivings about the impartiality of the jury'.

The *Gregory* case was distinguished in *Sander v UK*,[898] in which the applicant, who was Asian, was convicted by a jury of conspiracy to defraud and sentenced to five years' imprisonment. During the hearing, a jury member passed a note to an usher stating that at least two jury members had been making 'openly racist remarks and jokes' and that he feared that they were going to convict the applicant because he was Asian. Rejecting defence counsel's application to dismiss the jury on grounds of bias, the judge told the jury of the note, reminded them of their oath, and asked them to consider overnight whether they could decide the case without prejudice. The following morning the judge was given

---

[893] Id, para 83.

[894] *No 43471/98* hudoc (2002) DA. See also *Pullar v UK* 1996-III; 22 EHRR 39, in which a juror was employed by a key prosecution witness's firm, but had no personal connection with the case: no 'legitimate doubt', taking into account, *inter alia*, that the juror was only one of fifteen selected at random and that the jurors swore an oath—reinforced by the judge's directions—requiring impartiality. These considerations were not relied upon in *Simsek*.

[895] A 279-A (1993); 18 EHRR 79. See also *Fahri v France* 2007-XX (*ministere public* private talk with jury: breach).

[896] 1996-II; 22 EHRR 253.

[897] 1997-I; 25 EHRR 577 paras 47–8. See also *Elias v UK No 48905/99* hudoc (2001) DA (racial comment by counsel).

[898] 2000-V; 31 EHRR 1003.

a note signed by all of the jurors refuting the allegation and stating that they would reach a verdict according to the evidence and without prejudice. A second letter from a juror stated that although he might have made racist jokes, he apologized for any offence and was not racially biased. The Strasbourg Court held, by four votes to three, that there had been a breach of the requirement of objective impartiality.[899] The majority distinguished the *Gregory* case on the basis that in that case there had been no admission by a juror of racist comments; the complaint was vague and imprecise and its author unknown; and defence counsel had insisted throughout that the jury should be dismissed.[900] On the facts in *Sander*, the judge should, in the majority's view, have reacted in a 'more robust manner than merely seeking vague assurances', probably by dismissing the jury. Judge Bratza, in a dissenting opinion joined by Judges Costa and Fuhrmann, questioned the weight of the points of distinction between *Gregory* and *Sander* on their facts and considered that the judgment of an experienced judge as to what was necessary to dispel the perceived doubts as to racial bias should have been respected.

d. A tribunal established by law

Article 6(1) requires that the tribunal is 'established by law'. The intention is that, with a view to ensuring its independence, 'the judicial organisation in a democratic society must not depend on the discretion of the Executive, but that it should be regulated by law emanating from Parliament'.[901] This does not mean that every detail of the court system must be spelt out in legislation: provided that the basic rules concerning its organization and jurisdiction are set out by legislation, particular matters may be left to the executive acting by way of delegated legislation and subject to judicial review to prevent illegal or arbitrary action.[902] Article 6(1) does not prohibit the establishment of special courts if they have a basis in legislation.[903]

But it is for the constitution and the legislature, not the judiciary, to provide for the organization of the judicial system and the jurisdiction of the courts. In *Coëme and Others v Belgium*,[904] the constitution gave the Court of Cassation, not the ordinary criminal courts, jurisdiction to try government ministers for certain criminal offences. When prosecutions were brought against both ministers and non-ministers for offences of fraud, the Court of Cassation decided to try all of the accused together because of the connection between the offences, even though it had no legislative authority to try the non-ministers. The Strasbourg Court held that because the 'connection rule' that the Court of Cassation applied to join the cases was its own rule, not one provided by legislation, the Court of Cassation was not 'established by law' vis-à-vis the applicant non-ministers.

'Established by law' also means 'established in accordance with law', so that the requirement is infringed if a tribunal does not function in accordance with the particular rules

---

[899] There was no breach of the subjective impartiality requirement, the judge not being in a position to inquire into the precise nature and context of the comments made in the jury room.

[900] There was some uncertainty in *Gregory* whether defence counsel had called for the jury to be dismissed.

[901] *Zand v Austria No 7360/76*, 15 DR 70 at 80 (1978) Com Rep; CM Res DH (79) 6.

[902] *Ibid.* Cf, *Crociani v Italy No 8603/79*, 22 DR 147 at 219 (1980). In *Campbell and Fell v UK* A 80 (1984); 7 EHRR 165, no question was raised about the rules, which were mostly in delegated legislation, concerning prison Boards of Visitors.

[903] See *X and Y v Ireland No 8299/78*, 22 DR 51 (1980) (special criminal court to deal with terrorist offences). As to the extraordinary courts-martial in the *Greek* case, see above, p 288.

[904] 2000-VII. The Strasbourg Court will not question the national courts interpretation of national law on these matters in the absence of a 'flagrant violation': *Jorgic v Germany* 2007-XX.

that govern it.[905] Thus there was a violation of the requirement when the internal rules for the appointment of judges were not complied with.[906]

The courts in the Turkish Republic of Northern Cyprus were 'established by law' even though the laws which provided for them were not those of an internationally recognized state.[907]

VI. THE APPLICATION OF ARTICLE 6(1) TO APPEAL PROCEEDINGS

Article 6(1) does not guarantee a right of appeal from a decision by a court complying with Article 6 in either criminal or non-criminal cases.[908] If, however, a state in its discretion provides a right of appeal, proceedings before the appellate court are governed by Article 6(1).[909] The extent to which Article 6(1) applies to appeal proceedings, however, depends upon the nature of the particular proceedings, including the function of the appeal court and the relationship of proceedings before it with those earlier in the case. For example, the requirement of a public hearing may not apply fully where the court hears an appeal on points of law only and where a public hearing has taken place on the merits in the trial court.[910] The exercise of a right of appeal may be subjected to reasonable time limits.[911]

Where the initial determination of 'civil rights' within the meaning of Article 6 is made by an administrative or disciplinary tribunal or other body which does not comply with it, Article 6 is satisfied 'so long as its proceedings 'are subject to review by a judicial body that has full jurisdiction', on the law and the facts, that does comply with it.[912] This dispensation 'is a proper recognition of the 'demands of flexibility and efficiency'[913] that permit the use of such bodies.

As the Court established in *De Cubber v Belgium*,[914] the same is not true in respect of 'courts of the classic kind', ie courts that are 'integrated within the standard judicial machinery of the country'. In the case of such courts, Article 6 must be fully complied with both at the trial court stage and on any appeal. The fact that allowance may be made for special professional or disciplinary bodies 'cannot justify reducing the requirements of Article 6(1) in its traditional and natural sphere of application'. There is, however, a limit to this properly stringent rule. In a case in which the breach of Article 6 concerns the conduct of a first instance court, it may be that the appeal court can 'make reparation'

---

[905] *Zand v Austria No 7360/76*, 15 DR 70 at 80 (1978) Com Rep; CM Res DH (79) 6 and *Buscarini and Others v San Marino No 31657/96* hudoc (2000) DA.

[906] *Posokhov v Russia* 2003-V; 39 EHRR 441 and *Fedotova v Russia* hudoc (2006). See also *Lavents v Latvia* hudoc (2002) (Supreme Court direction as to membership of re-hearing court not followed). But waiver is permitted: *Bulut v Austria* 1996-II; 24 EHRR 84.

[907] *Cyprus v Turkey* 2001-IV; 35 EHRR 731 GC. For criticism, see Loucaides, 15 LJIL 225 at 235 (2002).

[908] A right of appeal in criminal cases is provided by Article 2, Seventh Protocol: see below, p 748. The interpretation of the Article 6 guarantee concerning appeal courts is not to be influenced by the content (particularly the limitations) of the guarantee in the Seventh Protocol: *Ekbatani v Sweden* A 134 (1988); 13 EHRR 504 PC.

[909] *Delcourt v Belgium* A 11 (1970); 1 EHRR 355. This includes leave to appeal proceedings in a criminal case: *Monnell and Morris v UK* A 115 (1987); 10 EHRR 205. But *semble* not in a civil case: *Porter v UK No 12972/87*, 54 DR 207 (1987).

[910] See the cases discussed above, p 275.   [911] *Bricmont v Belgium No 10857/84*, 48 DR 106 (1986).

[912] *Riepan v Austria* 2000-XII para 39. Cf, the *Le Compte* and *Albert and Le Compte* cases, above, p 229. As to the need for judicial review of administrative decisions, see the *Bryan* case, above, p 230.

[913] *Albert and Le Compte* case, above, p 229.

[914] A 86 (1984) para 32; 7 EHRR 236. Cf *Riepan v Austria*, above, p 271.

for the breach, in which case Article 6 will be complied with. For example, in *Adolf v FRG*,[915] there was no breach of Article 6 when the appeal court corrected the impression given by the trial court that the accused was considered by it to be guilty, in breach of the presumption of innocence. Likewise, in *Edwards v UK*,[916] there was no breach of Article 6 when the implications of the police's failure to disclose relevant information to the defence at the trial were examined by the Court of Appeal, which was competent to overturn the conviction on the basis of the evidence of non-disclosure. However, where the earlier defect is or cannot be remedied on appeal, the position is different. This is particularly likely to be true where the defect concerns the organisation of the trial court, rather than its conduct of the trial. Thus in *Findlay v UK*,[917] the role of the convening officer in military court-martial proceedings meant that the proceedings were neither independent nor impartial, which was a defect that could not be corrected by later review proceedings: as the Court stated, the applicant was entitled 'to a first instance tribunal which fully met the requirements of Article 6(1)'. Similarly, in *Riepan v Austria*,[918] the absence of a public hearing could not be rectified at a later stage: as with 'independence and impartiality', the requirement of a public hearing was a 'fundamental guarantee' upon which the applicant could insist at the trial stage, thus requiring a 'full re-hearing', with, for example, the hearing of witnesses.

4. ARTICLE 6(2): THE RIGHT TO BE PRESUMED INNOCENT IN CRIMINAL CASES

Article 6(2) provides that a person 'charged with a criminal offence shall be presumed innocent until proved guilty according to law'. It guarantees a right that is fundamental to both common law and, despite legend in the United Kingdom to the contrary,[919] civil law systems of criminal justice. The obligation in Article 6(2) is independent of those in other Article 6 guarantees, so that there may be a breach of it even though the rest of Article 6 is respected.[920]

Article 6(2) extends only to persons who are subject to a 'criminal charge'.[921] Hence it does not apply to a person detained for a purpose (eg deportation or extradition) other than prosecution for a criminal offence.[922] Nor does Article 6(2) benefit a person who is under suspicion of having committed an offence, but is not yet subject to a 'criminal charge'.[923] However, prejudicial statements at the pre-trial stage about an accused who is subject to a criminal charge are controlled by Article 6(2).[924]

---

[915] A 49 (1982); 4 EHRR 313.

[916] A 247-B (1992); 15 EHRR 417. Cf, *Schuler-Zgraggen v Switzerland* A 263 (1993); 16 EHRR 405.

[917] 1997-I; 24 EHRR 221 para 79. Cf, the *De Cubber* case, in which the trial court was not impartial because the judge had taken part in an earlier stage of the case. And see *Holm v Sweden* A 279-A (1993); 15 EHRR 79 para 33 (defect stemming from jury system could not be cured by appeal court because it was bound by the jury's verdict).

[918] See above, p 273.   [919] See Allen, *Legal Duties*, 1931, p 253.

[920] *I and C v Switzerland No 10107/82*, 48 DR 35 (1985) Com Rep; CM Res DH (86) 11.

[921] 'Criminal charge' has the same autonomous meaning as elsewhere in Article 6, as to which see above, pp 204 *et seq*.

[922] *X v Austria No 1918/63*, 6 YB 484 (1963) (extradition); *X v Netherlands No 1983/63*, 8 YB 228 (1965) (deportation).

[923] *Adolf v Austria* A 49 (1982); 4 EHRR 313 para 30.

[924] *Krause v Switzerland No 7986/77*, 13 DR 73 (1978). In *X v Austria No 9077/80*, 26 DR 211 (1981) the question whether prejudicial statements by public officials might apply before a person is subject to a charge was left unanswered.

In accordance with the general approach in the legal systems of contracting parties, Article 6 has been held not to apply to practices in the course of a criminal investigation such as the conduct of breath, blood, or urine tests,[925] or medical examinations,[926] or an order to produce documents.[927] By analogy, Article 6(2) also does not apply to finger-printing, searches of the person and of property,[928] and identity parades.[929] A conviction for an offence of failing to provide information is in some contexts considered to be in breach of the presumption of innocence, as well as freedom from self-incrimination.[930] Restrictions on pre-trial detention (eg as to clothing and correspondence[931] or cell conditions[932]) do not raise an issue under Article 6(2). Nor does it extend to the closure of a shop as a provisional measure or the offer of an 'out of court' fine.[933]

Article 6(2) continues to apply to the end of any appeal proceedings against conviction.[934] It does not apply to proceedings for the sentencing of a convicted person, because that person is then no longer subject to a 'criminal charge'.[935] However, Article 6(2) does apply to accusations about a convicted person that are made during sentencing proceedings if they are of such a nature and degree as to amount to the bringing of a new 'criminal charge'.[936] Article 6(2) was held to apply on this basis and to have been infringed when a court revoked the suspension of the applicant's sentence for an earlier offence, because of the court's 'certainty' that the applicant was guilty of another offence for which he had not been tried.[937] Article 6(2) also applies to proceedings concerning the discontinuance of a case against an accused[938] or the award of costs or compensation following discontinuance[939] or acquittal.[940] Such proceedings are a part of the determination of the criminal charge. However, Article 6(2) does not apply to an application by a convicted person for a re-trial.[941]

The meaning of Article 6(2) is explained in *Barberà, Messegué and Jabardo v Spain* as follows:[942]

> Paragraph 2 embodies the principle of the presumption of innocence. It requires, *inter alia*, that when carrying out their duties, the members of a court should not start with

---

[925] *Tirado Ortiz and Lozano Martin v Spain* No 43486/98 hudoc (1999) DA.

[926] *X v FRG* No 986/61, 5 YB 192 (1962).

[927] *Funke v France* A 256-A (1993); 16 EHRR 297 para 69 Com Rep.

[928] The seizure of the property of an arrested person as security for costs is not a breach of Article 6(2): *X v Austria* No 4338/69, 36 CD 79 (1970).

[929] Articles 8(2), 10(2), 11(2) Convention support this view. For criticism of this limited application of Article 6(2), see Stavros, p 50.

[930] See *Heaney and McGuiness v Ireland* 2000-XII; 33 EHRR 264.

[931] *Skoogström v Sweden* No 8582/72, 5 EHRR 278 (1982). Cf, *Englert v FRG* A 123 (1987); 13 EHRR 392 para 47 Com Rep.

[932] *Peers v Greece* 2001-III; 33 EHRR 1192. Articles 5(1)(c) and 5(3) apply instead.

[933] *Deweer v Belgium* B 33 (1980) para 64 Com Rep.

[934] *Nölkenbockhoff v FRG* A 123 (1987); 10 EHRR 163 PC.

[935] *Engel v Netherlands* A 22 (1976); 1 EHRR 647 PC. However, the presumption of innocence is also a part of the general fair hearing requirement in Article 6(1), which does extend to the sentencing stage: *Phillips v UK* 2002-II. See further above, p 259.

[936] *Engel v Netherlands*, ibid. Cf, *Geerings v Netherlands* 2007-XX.

[937] *Böhmer v Germany* hudoc (2002); 38 EHRR 410.

[938] *Adolf v Austria* A 49 (1982); 4 EHRR 313.   [939] *Minelli v Switzerland* A 62 (1983); 5 EHRR 554.

[940] *Sekanina v Austria* A 266-A (1993); 17 EHRR 221; *Lamanna v Austria* hudoc (2001); *Hammern v Norway* hudoc (2003). Article 6(2) does not apply to miscarriage of justice cases referred for judicial review: *Callaghan v UK* No 14739/89, 60 DR 296 (1989).

[941] *X v FRG* No 914/60, 4 YB 372 (1961).

[942] A 146 (1989); 11 EHRR 360 para 77 PC. See also *Austria v Italy* 6 YB 740 at 782–84 (1963) Com Rep; CM Res DH (63) 3.

the preconceived idea that the accused has committed the offence charged; the burden of proof is on the prosecution, and any doubt should benefit the accused. It also follows that it is for the prosecution to inform the accused of the case that will be made against him, so that he may prepare and present his defence accordingly, and to adduce evidence sufficient to convict him.

This confirms, in common law terms, that the presumption of innocence under Article 6(2) means that the general burden of proof must lie with the prosecution, or, in terms more appropriate for civil law systems, that the court, in its inquiry into the facts, must find for the accused in a case of doubt.[943]

The close link between the presumption of innocence and freedom from self-incrimination has been demonstrated in several cases. In *Murray (John) v UK*,[944] the accused's right to remain silent was limited to the extent that inferences could be (and were) drawn by the trial court from the accused's failure to explain his presence at the scene of the crime and to give evidence in court. The Strasbourg Court held that, having regard to the considerable weight of other evidence against the accused, the drawing of inferences from his failure to explain his presence was a matter of 'common sense and cannot be regarded as unfair or unreasonable in the circumstances'. Nor did it have 'the effect of shifting the burden of proof from the prosecution to the defence so as to infringe the principle of the presumption of innocence'. In contrast, there was such a shifting of the burden of proof in breach of Article 6(2) in *Telfner v Austria*[945] when the accused, who refused to give evidence to the police or at the trial, was convicted of a road traffic accident offence on the basis that he was the driver of the car involved, when there was no direct evidence to show that he was. The conviction was based on the facts that, although registered in his mother's name, the accused was the main user of the car and that he had not been home that night, which facts required him, the national court determined, to show that he was not the driver. The Strasbourg Court distinguished the *Murray* case on Article 6(2) because in the *Telfner* case there was no *prima facie* case against the accused that justified the drawing of 'common sense' inferences in the absence of an explanation by the accused. There was also a breach of the presumption of innocence, as well as the freedom from self-incrimination in Article 6(1), in *Heaney and McGuiness v Ireland*[946] because of certain legal consequences for the applicants of maintaining their right to silence.

Although the burden of proof must generally fall upon the prosecution, it may be transferred to the accused when he is seeking to establish a defence.[947] Similarly, Article 6(2) does not prohibit presumptions of fact or of law that may operate against the accused. However, it does require that states confine such presumptions 'within reasonable limits which take into account the importance of what is at stake and maintain the rights of the defence'. This was stated in the leading case of *Salabiaku v France*,[948] in which the applicant had been convicted of the strict liability customs offence of smuggling prohibited goods.

---

[943] As to whether Article 6(2) incorporates the civil law principle *in dubio pro reo*, see *Lingens and Leitgeb v Austria No 8803/79*, 26 DR 171 (1981).

[944] A 300-A (1994); 22 EHRR 29 para 54 GC. See further, above p 261.

[945] Hudoc (2001); 34 EHRR 207. But see now the approach to road traffic offences in *O'Hallaran and Francis v UK*, above, p 263.

[946] 2000-XII; 33 EHRR 264. For the facts, see above, p 262.

[947] *Lingens and Leitgens v Austria No 8803/79*, 26 DR 171 (1983) (burden of proof on defence in criminal defamation proceedings to show that statement is true; no breach of Article 6(2)).

[948] A 141-A (1988); 13 EHRR 379 para 28. Cf, *Pham Hoang v France* A 243 (1992) and *Janosevic v Sweden* 2002-VII; 38 EHRR 473. See also *Duhs v Sweden No 12995/87*, 67 DR 204 (1990); *AP, MP and TP v Switzerland* 1997-V; 26 EHRR 541; *Falk v Netherlands No 66273/01* hudoc (2004) DA; and *Phillips v UK* 2001-VII (Article 6(1) case).

The applicant had collected and taken through the 'green' customs exit at Paris airport a trunk that contained prohibited drugs, of which he claimed to have no knowledge. Under French law, a person who was in possession of prohibited goods in these circumstances was presumed to be guilty of smuggling them. Thus the case was not a straightforward one of strict liability for an act that the prosecution had proved that the accused had committed. Instead it was one in which the *actus reus* of smuggling had been presumed from the proven fact of possession. The Court found that, as applied to the applicant's case, this presumption of fact was not contrary to Article 6(2). Under French law, the applicant had a defence of *force majeure*, by which it was open to him to prove that it was impossible for him to have known of the contents of the trunk. This he failed to prove to the satisfaction of the trial court. The Court held that, having regard to the possibility of the *force majeure* defence, the Customs Code was not applied by the courts in a manner which conflicted with Article 6(2), despite what was 'at stake' (imprisonment and a substantial fine) for the applicant. In other cases it has been held that rebuttable presumptions, including that an accused was living knowingly off the earnings of a prostitute who was proved to be living with him or under his control;[949] that a company director was guilty of an offence committed by the company;[950] and that a dog was of a dangerous breed[951] were not inconsistent with Article 6(2).

As the *Salabiaku* case also decided, Article 6(2) does not prohibit offences of strict liability, which are a common feature of the criminal law of the Convention parties. An offence may thus be committed, consistently with Article 6(2), on the basis that a certain act has been committed, without it being necessary to prove *mens rea*. Provided a state respects the rights protected by the Convention, it is free to punish any kind of activity as criminal and to establish the elements of the offence in its discretion, including any requirement of *mens rea*.

Although mainly concerned with the burden of proof, Article 6(2) extends to certain other evidential matters. As to the standard of proof, there is no clear statement that there is a requirement of proof of guilt beyond reasonable doubt; in *Austria v Italy*[952] the Commission stated that Article 6(2) requires that a court find the accused guilty only on the basis of evidence 'sufficiently strong in the eyes of the law to establish his guilt'. As to the kind of evidence that may be relied upon, this may be 'direct or indirect'.[953] A confession obtained by torture and, at least in some cases, inhuman or degrading treatment must not be admitted in evidence.[954] However, it is not contrary to Article 6(2) to reveal the accused's past criminal record to the court before his conviction.[955] What is clear is that, in accordance with their general policy of not acting as a 'fourth instance',[956] the Strasbourg authorities do not regard themselves as competent to question findings of fact by the trial court that appear to be based upon probative evidence.[957] The accused must be allowed an opportunity to rebut the evidence presented against him.[958]

---

[949] *X v UK No 5124/71*, 42 CD 135 (1972).

[950] *G v Malta No 16641/90* hudoc (1991) DA. Cf, *Radio France v France* 2004-II.

[951] *Bullock v UK No 29102/95* hudoc (1996); 21 EHRR CD 85.

[952] 6 YB 740 at 784 (1963) Com Rep; CM Res DH (63) 3.   [953] *Ibid.*

[954] *Jalloh v Germany*, above, p 257. See also *Austria v Italy, ibid.* Cf, *X v UK No 5076/71*, 40 CD 64 (pressure to plead guilty may be contrary to Article 6(2)). There is an overlap here with the general 'fair hearing' requirement in Article 6(1).

[955] *X v Austria No 2742/66*, 9 YB 550 (1966).   [956] See above, p 14.

[957] See *Albert and Le Compte v Belgium* A 58 (1983); 5 EHRR 533 PC. See also the discussion of the rules of evidence requirements under Article 6(1), above, p 256.

[958] *Austria v Italy* 6 YB 116 at 784 (1963) Com Rep; CM Res DH (63) 3. The Commission emphasized the words 'according to law' in Article 6(2). See also *Albert and Le Compte v Belgium, ibid*, and *Schenk v Switzerland* A 140 (1988); 13 EHRR 242 PC. Article 6(2) overlaps with Article 6(3)(d) in this respect.

Various claims that the presumption of innocence has been infringed in the conduct of the trial other than in respect of the operation of the rules of evidence have been rejected. The handcuffing of the accused in front of the jury was consistent with Article 6(2) as a necessary security measure.[959] The arrest of a witness in the courtroom for perjury immediately after giving evidence for the accused was also permissible,[960] as were the re-trial of the accused before a court that had earlier considered his application for bail[961] and the detention of a convicted person pending his appeal.[962] A procedure by which a person may plead guilty to an offence, with the proceedings being limited to sentencing, is not in breach of Article 6(2), provided that pressure has not been brought improperly to bear upon the accused to obtain the guilty plea.[963] A requirement that a tax surcharge be paid pending an appeal against its imposition may be in breach of Article 6(2) if it is not kept 'within reasonable limits that strike a fair balance between the interests involved', which include the financial consequences for the taxpayer and any effect upon the rights of the defence.[964]

Article 6(2) may be infringed in a decision in which a court expresses the view that the applicant is guilty of an offence, when he has not been tried and found guilty of it. The general rule was formulated in *Minelli v Switzerland*[965] as follows:

> ...the presumption of innocence will be violated if, without the accused's having previously been proved guilty according to law and, notably, without his having had the opportunity of exercising his rights of defence, a judicial decision concerning him reflects an opinion that he is guilty. This may be so even in the absence of any formal finding; it suffices that there is some reasoning suggesting that the court regards the accused as guilty.

In that case, a private prosecution against the applicant was discontinued because it had become statute-barred. A Swiss court thereupon ordered the applicant to pay part of the private prosecutor's and court costs on the basis that the applicant would 'very probably' have been convicted had the case gone to trial. The European Court held that Article 6(2) had been infringed. Although there was no formal decision as to guilt, the court's judgment as to costs 'showed that it was satisfied' of the accused's guilt, and this was sufficient. Prior to the *Minelli* case, the Court had adopted the same approach in *Adolf v Austria*,[966] in which, in the judgment discontinuing proceedings against the accused for a petty assault, there was a passage that was 'well capable of being understood as meaning' that the accused had committed the offence. However, the Court found no breach of Article 6(2) because the passage had been corrected on appeal.

The Court has drawn a distinction between statements by courts indicating guilt and statements by them that merely voice suspicion. The latter are permissible where no final decision in the accused's trial has been taken. Thus the voicing just of suspicion by a court when ruling on claims for compensation for detention on remand and/or costs in cases in which the prosecution has been discontinued,[967] or when ruling on claims for provisional measures[968] is not a breach of Article 6(2). In contrast, statements indicating

---

[959] *X v Austria No 2291/64*, 24 CD 20 (1967). On handcuffing as 'degrading treatment', see above, p 100.

[960] *X v FRG No 8744/79*, 5 EHRR 499 (1983).   [961] *X v FRG No 2646/65*, 9 YB 484 (1966).

[962] *Cuvillers and Da Luz v France No 55052/00* hudoc (2003) DA.

[963] *X v UK No 5076/71*, 40 CD 69 (1972). See also *Duhs v Sweden No 12995/87*, 67 DR 204 (out of court car-parking fines). And see *Panarisi v Italy*, below, n 1176.

[964] *Janosevic v Sweden* 2002-VII; 38 EHRR 473 para 106.

[965] A 62 (1983); 5 EHRR 554 para 38.   [966] A 49 (1982); 4 EHRR 313 para 39.

[967] *Lutz v FRG* A 123 (1987); 10 EHRR 182 PC and *Leutscher v Netherlands* 1996-II; 24 EHRR 181. But see *Capeau v Belgium* 2005-I.

[968] *Gökçeli v Turkey* hudoc (2003).

guilt in such situations are a breach.[969] The position is different following acquittal. Court statements voicing continuing suspicion (and *a fortiori* guilt)[970] after the accused has been finally acquitted are in breach of Article 6(2).[971] But statements by a court following acquittal in proceedings for compensation for lawful detention on remand that there was reasonable suspicion at the time of the arrest are not a breach of Article 6(2).[972]

The above cases concern statements made in judicial decisions in criminal proceedings that directly concern the applicant. Article 6(2) is not infringed when a court refers in its judgment in criminal proceedings against another person to the involvement of the applicant, who has yet to be tried, for the same offence where this is relevant in establishing the other person's guilt.[973] Although civil proceedings are not directly subject to it,[974] Article 6(2) requires that a civil court act in accordance with an acquittal of an accused who is later party to proceeding before it arising out of the same facts.[975] But the mere suspension of civil proceedings pending the outcome of a criminal case is not a breach.[976]

The *Minelli* case concerned statements made in judicial decisions. Article 6(2) has been also applied to statements made by judges while a case is pending, whether in or outside of court proceedings. Thus in *Kyprianou v Cyprus*,[977] the trial court stated in the course of exchanges with defence counsel during a court hearing, that his conduct in court amounted to criminal contempt. After a short adjournment, the court sentenced counsel to five days' imprisonment without giving him an opportunity to defend himself on the charge of contempt. The Strasbourg Court held that the statements indicating contempt were a breach both of the requirement that an accused be tried by an impartial tribunal in Article 6(1)[978] and of the presumption of innocence in Article 6(2). As to statements made outside of court proceedings, in *Lavents v Latvia*[979] there was a breach of both Article 6(1) (partial tribunal) and Article 6(2) when the trial judge stated in press interviews which she gave during the trial, that she was not sure whether to convict the accused on all or only some counts, and expressed her astonishment that he totally denied his guilt. As well as statements by judges, prejudicial comment by counsel or witnesses may raise a question under Article 6(2) if the court's failure to control it shows judicial bias.[980] With regard to these cases although it is possible to see a presumption of innocence element in them, it might be simpler and more natural to treat them just under the 'impartial tribunal' requirement in Article 6(1).[981]

---

[969] *Baars v Netherlands* hudoc (2003); 39 EHRR 538 and *Panteleyenko v Ukraine* hudoc (2006). But the particular circumstances may indicate otherwise: *AL v Germany* hudoc (2005); 42 EHRR 186.

[970] *Del Latte v Netherlands* hudoc (2004); 41 EHRR 176 and *Geerings v Netherlands* hudoc (2007).

[971] *Sekanina v Austria* A 266-A (1993); 17 EHRR 221; *Rushiti v Austria* hudoc (2000); 33 EHRR 1331. See also *Moody v UK; Lochrie v UK*, Commission reps 16 and 18 January 1996, see Reid, *op cit* at p 1, n 1, above, p 157 (judge's comments when disallowing applicants' costs breach of Article 6(2)). Adverse comments short of suspicion are not a breach: *Fashanu v UK No 38440/97* hudoc (1998); 26 EHRR CD 217 DA.

[972] *Hibbert v Netherlands No 38087/97* hudoc (1999) DA.

[973] *Gjerde v Norway No 18672/91* hudoc (1993) DA.

[974] *X v FRG No 6062/73*, 2 DR 54 (1974).

[975] *X v Austria No 9295/81*, 30 DR 227 (1982) and *Diamantides v Greece (No 2)* hudoc (2005). But civil liability may be found on the same facts using a lower standard of proof, provided that the civil court does not question the acquittal in so doing: see *Ringvold v Norway* 2003-II and *Y v Norway* 2003-II; 41 EHRR 87.

[976] *Farragut v France No 10103/82*, 39 DR 186 (1984).

[977] Hudoc (2004).   [978] See above, p 293.   [979] Hudoc (2002).

[980] See *Austria v Italy* 6 YB 740 Com Rep; CM Res DH (63) 3; *Nielsen v Denmark No 343/57*, 2 YB 412; *X, Y, Z v Austria No 7950/77*, 4 EHRR 270 at 274 (1980). In determining whether proceedings have been allowed to get out of hand to the prejudice of the accused, allowance may be made for different national temperaments and legal traditions: *Austria v Italy, ibid.*

[981] As in *Buscemi v Italy* 1999-VI, above, p 294.

The approach in the *Minelli* case applies not only to judicial statements, but also to statements by other public officials.[982] In *Krause v Switzerland*,[983] the Commission stated:

> Article 6, paragraph 2 ... may be violated by public officials if they declare that somebody is responsible for criminal acts without a court having found so. This does not mean, of course, that the authorities may not inform the public about criminal investigations. They do not violate Article 6, paragraph 2, if they state that a suspicion exists, that people have been arrested, that they have confessed, etc. What is excluded, however, is a formal declaration that somebody is guilty.

In that case, the applicant was detained on remand pending trial for terrorist offences. When aircraft hijackers demanded her release, the Swiss Federal Minister of Justice stated on television that the applicant had 'committed common law offences' for which she must accept responsibility, although tempering this remark in a later television statement by the comment that he did not know whether she would be convicted. However, the Commission found that Article 6(2) had not been infringed on the facts because the minister's remarks were an assertion of suspicion, not of guilt.[984] The same approach has since been adopted by the Court. In *Allenet de Ribemont v France*[985] a senior police officer, flanked by other officials who made supporting remarks, stated at a press conference that the applicant was one of the 'instigators' of a murder. The Court held that Article 6(2) applied and had been infringed. Although not yet charged under French law, the applicant had been arrested and hence was 'charged' in the sense of Article 6(2).[986] As to the infringement:

> The Court notes that ... some of the highest ranking officers in the French police referred to Mr Allenet de Ribemont, without qualification or reservation, as one of the instigators of a murder and thus an accomplice in that murder ... This was clearly a declaration of the applicant's guilt which, firstly, encouraged the public to believe him guilty and, secondly, prejudged the assessment of the facts by the competent judicial authority.[987]

A breach of Article 6(2) was also found in *Butkevicius v Lithuania*[988] when statements by the Chairman of the Lithuanian Parliament were made to the press shortly after the applicant, who was the Lithuanian Minister of Defence, had been apprehended in a hotel lobby accepting an envelope full of US dollars. The Chairman said that he 'had no doubt' that the applicant, who was later convicted of attempting to obtain property by deception, had accepted a bribe and that he was a 'bribe-taker.' In the Court's view, these remarks amounted to declarations by a public official of the applicant's guilt, in breach

---

[982] As to a state's obligation to control (and not to promote) assertions of guilt in the private press, see *Wloch v Poland No 27785/95* hudoc (2000). See also *Ensslin, Baader and Raspe v FRG* 14 DR 64 at 113 (1978); *X v UK No 3860/68*, 30 CD 70 (1969); *Crociani v Italy No 8603/79*, 22 DR 147 at 227 (1980).

[983] *No 7986/77*, 13 DR 73 (1978). The word 'formal' is best understood in the sense of 'official' in the light of the *Minelli* case.

[984] Cf, *X v Austria No 9077/80*, 26 DR 211 (1981). And see *Berns and Ewert v Luxembourg No 132351/87*, 68 DR 137 (1991); *Hayward v Sweden No 14106/88* hudoc (1991) DA; *Howden v UK No 20755/92* hudoc (1994) DA; and *Murati v Switzerland No 37285/97* hudoc (1998) DA; *Montera v Italy No 64713/01* hudoc (2002) DA. As to whether Article 6(2) extends to statements by public officials that may prejudice a prosecution in another state, see *C v UK No 10427/83*, 47 DR 85 (1986) and *Zollmann v UK No 62902/00* hudoc (2003) DA.

[985] A 308 (1995); 20 EHRR 557 paras 37, 41. Cf, *YB v Turkey* hudoc (2004).

[986] See above, p 209.

[987] The Court noted that Article 6(2) entails a limit upon freedom of speech in this regard: id, para 38.

[988] 2002-II. The case has to be distinguished from the *Krause* case on the basis that the Court found that there was a 'formal declaration of guilt'.

of Article 6(2). In contrast, in *Daktaras v Lithuania*,[989] the Court found no breach of Article 6(2) when a prosecutor indicated the applicant's guilt in his decision refusing an application for discontinuance of the prosecution. The Strasbourg Court drew a distinction between public statements made in a context, such as a press conference, that was separate from the court proceedings concerning the applicant and statements that were a part of those proceedings. It is probable that the Court might have reached a different conclusion had the statement been made not by the prosecutor but by the judge in the case, as in the *Lavents* case.[990]

A violation of the presumption of innocence by a lower court may be made good by a higher court on appeal.[991] It may be, however, that 'the failure of the lower court to observe the principle of presumption of innocence has so distorted the general course of proceedings' that this is not possible.[992]

5. ARTICLE 6(3): FURTHER GUARANTEES IN CRIMINAL CASES

I. ARTICLE 6(3): GENERALLY

Article 6(3) guarantees certain rights that are necessary to the preparation and conduct of the defence and to ensure that the accused is able to defend himself on equal terms with the prosecution. The rights listed are 'minimum rights'. They are elements of the wider concept of the right to a fair trial in Article 6(1).[993] Because of this the Court commonly decides cases on the basis of Article 6(1) *and* the relevant specific right in Article 6(3) or even on the basis of Article 6 as a whole.[994]

The rights in Article 6(3) are guaranteed only to persons 'charged with a criminal offence'. This wording is identical to that in Article 6(2) and has the same autonomous Convention meaning as it has in that paragraph and in the equivalent wording in Article 6(1).[995] Accordingly, a person is charged with a criminal offence for the purposes of Article 6(3) from the moment that he is 'substantially affected' by the steps taken against him as a suspect.[996] Article 6(3) does not protect a person who is suspected of a criminal offence but not yet charged with it in this sense. Nor does it benefit a person who is being extradited for prosecution in another jurisdiction.[997]

However, the fact that a person is 'charged with a criminal offence' does not mean that each of the rights in Article 6(3) extends to him from the very moment of his being so charged.[998] Whether Article 6(3) applies at all to the pre-trial stage of criminal proceedings was formerly a matter of dispute, with a number of civil law contracting parties questioning whether it did. This argument was expressly rejected by the Court in *Imbrioscia v Switzerland*.[999] Noting that the reasonable time guarantee in Article 6(1) applied at the

---

[989] 2000-X; 34 EHRR 1466. See also *Hentrich v France* A 296-A (1994); 18 EHRR 440.
[990] Above at p 304.
[991] *Adolf v Austria* A 49 (1982); 4 EHRR 313 and *Arrigo and Vella v Malta* hudoc (2005) DA.
[992] *Austria v Italy* 6 YB 740 at 784 (1966) Com Rep; CM Res DH (63) 3.
[993] On the relationship between Article 6(1) and 6(3), see above p 246.
[994] For an 'Article 6 as a whole' case, see *Vidal v Belgium* A 235-B (1992).
[995] See *Adolf v Austria* A 49 (1982); 4 EHRR 313.   [996] See above, p 209.
[997] But see the *Soering* exception, above, p 80.
[998] Thus Article 6(3)(d) does not generally apply at the pre-trial stage: see below, p 322.
[999] A 275 para 36 (1993); 17 EHRR 441. Cf, *Öcalan v Turkey* hudoc 2005-VI para 131 GC.

pre-trial stage, the Court stated:

> Other requirements of Article 6—especially of paragraph 3—may also be relevant before
> a case is sent for trial if and insofar as the fairness of the trial is likely to be seriously preju-
> diced by the initial failure to comply with them.

Article 6(3) applies to appeal proceedings, although its requirements at this stage are
shaped by the function of the appellate court concerned and its place in the proceedings
as a whole.[1000]

II. ARTICLE 6(3)(A): THE RIGHT TO BE INFORMED OF THE ACCUSATION

Article 6(3)(a) requires that a person charged with a criminal offence 'be informed
promptly, in a language which he understands and in detail, of the nature and cause of the
accusation against him'. It overlaps with Article 5(2), which provides a similarly worded
guarantee for persons detained pending trial.[1001] Although both provisions respond to
the legitimate claim of an individual to know why the state has acted against him, the
purpose of the two guarantees is essentially different. Whereas Article 5(2) seeks to assist
the arrested person in challenging his detention, Article 6(3)(a) is intended to give the
accused person the information he needs to answer the accusation against him. For this
reason, the information required by Article 6(3)(a) is to be understood in the light of the
accused's right to prepare his defence that is guaranteed in Article 6(3)(b).[1002]

The requirement in Article 6(3)(a) that persons 'charged with a criminal offence' be
given the necessary information 'promptly' has not been the subject of much interpretation. In *Kaminski v Austria*,[1003] it was considered to have been met when the information,
in the civil law system concerned, was given at the time of the indictment hearing, some
eleven days after the accused's arrest. 'Promptly' has been interpreted more strictly than
this in Article 5(2).[1004]

The accused must be informed of the 'nature and cause of the accusation against him'.
The 'nature' of the accusation is the offence with which the accused is charged. This may
be altered as the case proceeds provided that the accused is given the opportunity to prepare his defence to the new charge in 'a practical and effective manner and, in particular,
in good time'.[1005] Article 6(3)(a) was infringed when the applicant was only informed of
the new charge on the final day of the trial[1006] and where a court of appeal convicted the
applicants of a new offence of which they only learnt when that court's judgment was
delivered.[1007] There was no breach, however, where the accused could reasonably have

---

[1000] See eg, *Artico v Italy* A 37 (1980); 7 EHRR 528 and *Kremzow v Austria* A 268-B (1993); 17 EHRR 322 para 58. On the application of Article 6 to appeal proceedings generally, see above, p 298.

[1001] But, unlike Article 5(2), Article 6(3)(a) may apply to unarrested persons concerning whom a pre-liminary investigation has commenced, provided they are 'substantially affected': see *Brozicek v Italy* A 167 (1989); 12 EHRR 371 PC. For cases in which Article 6(3)(a) claims did not meet this requirement, see *C v Italy* No 10889/84, 56 DR 40 (1988) and *Padin Gestoso v Spain* No 39519/98 1999-II DA.

[1002] *Péllisier and Sassi v France* 1999-II; 30 EHRR 715 para 54 GC. Compliance with Article 6(3)(a) is a condi-tion of compliance with Article 6(3)(b): *Ofner v Austria* No 524/59, 3 YB 322 at 344 (1960).

[1003] A 168 (1989); 13 EHRR 36.   [1004] See above, p 165.

[1005] *Péllisier and Sassi v France* 1999-II; 30 EHRR 715 para 62 GC. See also *Mattoccia v Italy* 2000-IX; 36 EHRR 825.

[1006] *Sadak v Turkey (No 1)* 2001-VIII; 36 EHRR 431. Cf, *Chichlian and Ekindjian v France* A 162-B (1989); 13 EHRR 553 Com Rep (F Sett before Court).

[1007] *Péllisier and Sassi v France* 1999-II; 30 EHRR 715 GC. See also *Mattoccia v Italy* 2000-IX 89; 36 EHRR 825 and *Sipavicius v Lithuania* hudoc (2002).

anticipated that an aggravating factor which was present on the facts, but not argued, would be taken into account in sentencing.[1008] Nor was there a breach where the accused had sufficient opportunity to respond at the appeal stage to a reformulated charge on the basis of which he had been convicted at first instance.[1009]

The 'cause' of an accusation consists of the 'acts he is alleged to have committed and on which the accusation is based'.[1010] What needs to be communicated to the accused will depend upon what he can be taken to know from the questioning he has undergone and from the other circumstances of the case.[1011] Similarly, the accused must take advantage of what opportunities exist to learn of the accusation against him; if a prisoner fails to attend a hearing at which he could have obtained further information, this will count against his claim of a breach of Article 6(3)(a).[1012]

The words 'in detail' clearly suggest that the information to which a person is entitled under Article 6(3)(a) is 'more specific and more detailed' than that which he must receive under Article 5(2).[1013] In *Mattoccia v Italy*,[1014] the Court stated that the accused must be told of the 'material facts' that form the basis of the accusation against him: the level of detail may vary with the circumstances, but the accused 'must at any rate be provided with sufficient information as is necessary to understand fully the extent of the charges against him with a view to preparing an adequate defence'. There was clearly a breach of Article 6(3)(a) in *Kyprianou v Cyprus*[1015] where a lawyer was held guilty of contempt in the face of the court following a ten minutes recess after an outburst by him in court. The transcript of the proceedings indicated that the court had already decided on his guilt before informing the accused of the nature and cause of the accusation against him and the lawyer only learnt of the 'material facts' on which the charge was based when a sentence of five days' imprisonment was imposed following his conviction.

Article 6(3)(a) does not impose any special formal requirement as to the manner in which the information is to be given. Although the importance of the required information is such that it should normally be given in writing, this is not essential in all cases: depending on the facts, the accused may be given the information orally or he may have waived his right to a written communication. In *Kamasinski v Austria*,[1016] sufficient information was given orally to the applicant during the questioning sessions following his arrest. Where the information is sent in writing by post, proof of delivery is generally required.[1017] Where a person has mental difficulties, appropriate action must be taken to make sure that he is aware of the nature and cause of the accusation against him.[1018]

The information must be given to the accused in a 'language which he understands'. Unless the authorities can prove or have reasonable grounds to believe that the accused has a sufficient command of the language in which the information is given to him, they

---

[1008] *Gea Catalan v Spain* A 309 (1995); 20 EHRR 266 and *De Salvador Torres v Spain* 1996-V; 23 EHRR 601.
[1009] *Dallos v Hungary* 2001-II; 37 EHRR 524.
[1010] *Péllisier and Sassi v France* 1999-II; 30 EHRR 715 para 51 GC.
[1011] *Kamasinski v Austria* A 168(1989); 13 EHRR 36.
[1012] *Campbell and Fell v UK* A 80 (1984); 7 EHRR 165.
[1013] *Neilsen v Denmark* No 343/57, 2 YB 412 at 462 (1959).
[1014] 2000-IX; 36 EHRR 825 paras 59–60. See also the earlier case of *Brozicek v Italy* A 167 (1989); 12 EHRR 371.
[1015] Hudoc (2004). Chamber decision. The Grand Chamber did not consider Article 6(3)(a).
[1016] A 168 (1989); 13 EHRR 36.
[1017] *C v Italy* No 10889/84, 56 DR 40 (1988). But the accused may be shown to have avoided delivery of a warrant with the required information: *Erdogan v Turkey* No 14723/89, 73 DR 81.
[1018] *Vaudelle v France* 2001-I; 37 EHRR 397.

must provide him with an appropriate translation if he requests it.[1019] Since the right is that of the defence as a whole, Article 6(3)(a) is complied with if the required information is given in a language that the accused *or* his lawyer understands.[1020] The cost of any translation must be met by the state under Article 6(3)(e).[1021]

III. ARTICLE 6(3)(B): THE RIGHT TO ADEQUATE TIME AND FACILITIES

Article 6(3)(b) guarantees a person charged with a criminal offence 'adequate time and facilities for the preparation of his defence'. This right was explained by the Commission in *Can v Austria*[1022] as requiring that the accused has 'the opportunity to organise his defence in an appropriate way and without restriction as to the possibility to put all relevant defence arguments before the trial court, and thus to influence the proceedings'.

a. Adequate time

The guarantee in Article 6(3)(b) of 'adequate time' to prepare a defence, which protects the accused against a 'hasty trial',[1023] is the counterpoise to that in Article 6(1) by which an accused must be tried within a reasonable time.[1024] The guarantee begins to run from the moment that a person is subject to a criminal charge, ie from the moment that he is arrested or otherwise 'substantially affected.'[1025] Generally, the adequacy of the time allowed will depend upon the particular facts of the case.[1026] Relevant considerations are the complexity of the case,[1027] the stage of proceedings,[1028] the fact that the accused is defending himself in person,[1029] and the accused's lawyer's workload.[1030] A legal aid lawyer must be appointed,[1031] or the accused allowed to appoint his own lawyer,[1032] in good time before the hearing.[1033] If a lawyer is replaced for good reason, additional time must be allowed for the new lawyer to prepare the case.[1034] Any breach of Article 6(3)(b) that results from the brevity of the time allowed for a lawyer to prepare a case may be rectified in appeal proceedings.[1035]

[1019] *Brozicek v Italy* A 167 (1989); 12 EHRR 371 PC. The case for a written translation of a key document such as an indictment is particularly strong: *Kamasinski v Austria* A 168 (1989); 13 EHRR 36. And see *Hermi v Italy* 2006-XII; 46 EHRR 1115 GC.

[1020] *X v Austria No 6185/73*, 2 DR 68 (1975). The question was not ruled on in *Kamasinski v Austria* A 168 (1989); 13 EHRR 36, the applicant having requested that the indictment be sent to his lawyer. For the view that the information should be given in a language that the accused understands so that he can control his defence, see Stavros, p 174.

[1021] See below, p 327.

[1022] A 96 (1985); 8 EHRR 14 Com Rep para 53 (F Sett before Court). Cf, *Galstyan v Armenia* hudoc (2007).

[1023] *Kröcher and Müller v Switzerland No 8463/78*, 26 DR 24 at 53 (1981).   [1024] See above, p 278.

[1025] See above, p 209. And see *X and Y v Austria No 7909/77*, 15 DR 160 (1978).

[1026] *Mattick v Germany No 62116/00* hudoc (2005) DA.

[1027] *Albert and Le Compte v Belgium* A 58 (1983) PC.

[1028] *Huber v Austria No 5523/72*, 17 YB 314 (1974); 46 CD 99 (1974).

[1029] *X v Austria No 2370/64*, 22 CD 96 (1967).

[1030] *X and Y v Austria No 7909/77*, 15 DR 160 (1978) and *Berlinski v Poland* hudoc (2002).

[1031] *X and Y v Austria ibid* and *Galstyan v Armenia* hudoc (2007).

[1032] *Perez Mahia v Spain No 11022/84*, 9 EHRR 145 (1985).

[1033] An accused cannot complain if he or she is responsible for the delay: *X v Austria No 8251/78*, 17 DR 166 (1979).

[1034] See *Goddi v Italy* A 76 (1984) (Article 6(3)(c) decision) and *Samer v FRG No 4319/69*, 14 YB 322 (1971).

[1035] *Twalib v Greece* 1998-IV; 33 EHRR 584.

As to what is 'adequate time', in cases at the trial stage two weeks for the accused's lawyers to examine a case file of 17,000 pages was insufficient,[1036] as were, in a different kind of case, just a few hours for an accused who was defending himself in person in a minor public order case 'to enable him to familiarise himself properly with and to assess adequately the charge and evidence against him, and to develop a viable legal strategy for his defence'.[1037] In contrast, a period of seventeen days' notice of the hearing before a criminal court in a 'fairly complicated' case of misappropriation was 'adequate',[1038] as was five days' notice of a prison disciplinary hearing.[1039] Generally, less time will be needed to prepare for an appeal than for a trial.[1040] Where an accused considers that the time allowed is inadequate, he should, as a matter of local remedies, seek an adjournment or postponement of the hearing,[1041] but there may be exceptional circumstances which make this unnecessary.[1042] The reclassification on the final day of a trial of the offence with which the accused was charged gave him inadequate time to consult with his lawyer to prepare his defence and was a breach of both Article 6(3)(a) and (b).[1043]

In an early decision, the Commission held that, in the absence of actual prejudice, there was no breach of Article 6(3)(b) when the applicant had met and instructed his legal aid barrister only ten minutes before a trial that led to a sentence of seven years' imprisonment[1044] However, in *Artico v Italy*,[1045] the Court recognized that proof of actual prejudice caused by the absence of a lawyer—which might be 'impossible' to show—was not required to establish a breach of Article 6(3(c), and this, it is submitted, should apply also to the failure to appoint a lawyer in sufficient time in breach of Article 6(3)(b).[1046]

b. Adequate facilities

Adequate facilities include the accused's right of access to a lawyer at the pre-trial stage and later to the extent necessary to prepare his or her defence.[1047] There is an overlap here between Article 6(3)(b) and the right to legal assistance in Article 6(3)(c).[1048] The following paragraphs are based on the jurisprudence of the Court and the Commission under Article 6(3)(b).[1049]

The right of access to a lawyer has particular significance for persons in detention on remand pending the hearing. A prisoner must be allowed to receive a visit from his lawyer out of the hearing of prison officers or other officials in order to convey instructions or

---

[1036] *Öcalan v Turkey* 2005IV; 41 EHRR 985 GC. Cf, *Kremzow v Austria* A 268-B; 17 EHRR 322 (21 days to examine forty-nine-page document sufficient). See also *GB v France* 2001-X.

[1037] *Galstryan v Armenia* hudoc (2007) para 87. Fast track procedures are permissible if the defence is not prejudiced: *ibid*. Cf, *Borisova v Bulgaria* hudoc (2006).

[1038] *X and Y v Austria No 7909/77*, 15 DR 160 (1978).

[1039] *Campbell and Fell v UK* A 80 (1984); 7 EHRR 165. Cf, *Albert and Le Compte v Belgium* A 58 (1983); 5 EHRR 533 PC.

[1040] *Huber v Austria No 5523/72*, 17 YB 314 (1974); 46 CD 99 (1974).

[1041] *Campbell and Fell v UK* A 80 (1984) 7 EHRR 165. In *Murphy v UK No 4681/70*, 43 CD 1 (1972), in which a legal aid barrister was allocated to the accused just minutes before a hearing, the application was refused because an adjournment would have been granted if requested. See also *Craxi v Italy* hudoc (2002) and *Backstrom and Andersson v Sweden No 67830/01* hudoc (2006) DA.

[1042] *Goddi v Italy* A 76 (1984). Cf, *Mattei v France* hudoc (2006).

[1043] *Sadak v Turkey (No 1)* 2001-VIII; 36 EHRR 431.

[1044] *X v UK No 4042/69*, 13 YB 690 (1970). Cf, the *Murphy* case, above, n 1041.

[1045] See below, p 320. But see *Twalib v Greece* 1998-IV; 33 EHRR 584 para 40.

[1046] Cf, *Korellis v Cyprus*, below, p 312 (facilities).

[1047] *Campbell and Fell v UK* A 80 (1984) 7 EHRR 165 and *Goddi v Italy* A 76 (1984).

[1048] See *Goddi v Italy* A 76 (1984) para 31.

[1049] The right of access to a lawyer is now usually dealt with by the Court under Article 6(3)(c), not under Article 6(3)(b): see eg, *Öcalan v Turkey* 2005-IV; 41 EHRR 985 GC. On Article 6(3)(c), see below, p 321.

to pass or receive confidential information relating to the preparation of his defence.[1050] Restrictions upon visits by lawyers may be imposed if they can be justified in the public interest (eg to prevent escape or the obstruction of justice).[1051]

A restriction by which a lawyer may not discuss certain evidence with his client may be permissible to protect the identity of an informer.[1052] In early decisions, the Commission held that a refusal to allow a prisoner to take his notes and annotated documents to an interview with his lawyer[1053] and that an accused's lack of opportunity to discuss his appeal with his legal aid lawyer in person because the lawyer lived too far away[1054] were not a breach of the Convention. It is for the accused who appoints his own lawyer to ensure that the lawyer speaks a language that the accused understands or to arrange for an interpreter; the state is under no obligation to provide an interpreter in such circumstances.[1055] The right to communicate with one's lawyer extends to written as well as oral communication. In practice, questions concerning prison correspondence, in respect of which most problems of correspondence between accused persons and their lawyers concerning criminal proceedings[1056] are likely to arise, have generally been considered under Article 8 (the right to respect for correspondence).[1057]

Apart from access to a lawyer, Article 6(3)(b) 'recognises the right of the accused to have at his disposal, for the purpose of exonerating himself or of obtaining a reduction in his sentence, all relevant elements that have been or could be collected by the authorities', including any document that 'concerns acts of which the defendant is accused, the credibility of testimony, etc'.[1058] In any criminal case, the prosecution will have at its disposal the results of the police investigation or, in a civil law system, the case file prepared during the preliminary investigation.[1059] This will include both documents and other evidence obtained by questioning or searches backed by the power of the state or by the use of forensic resources which the defence may well lack.[1060] In this context, the primary purpose of Article 6(3)(b) is to achieve 'equality of arms' between the prosecution and the defence by requiring that the accused be allowed 'the opportunity to acquaint himself, for the purposes of preparing his defence, with the results of investigations carried out throughout the proceedings'.[1061] Article 6(1) requires that the prosecution disclose to the

---

[1050] *Can v Austria* A 96 (1985); 8 EHRR 14 paras 51–2 Com Rep (F Sett before Court); *Campbell and Fell v UK* A 80 (1984); 7 EHRR 165 para 113; and *Öcalan v Turkey* 2005-IV; 41 EHRR 985 GC. The restrictions permitted in the pre-*Can* case of *Krocher and Moller v Switzerland*, above, p 96, n 252 would not now be accepted, even in a terrorist context.

[1051] See the *Can* and *Campbell and Fell* cases, above, n 1050.

[1052] *Kurup v Denmark No 11219/84*, 42 DR 287 (1985).

[1053] *Koplinger v Austria No 1850/63*, 12 YB 438 (1968).

[1054] *X v Austria No 1135/61*, 6 YB 194 (1963) (correspondence was possible).

[1055] *X v Austria No 6185/73*, 2 DR 68 (1975).

[1056] As to prisoners' correspondence in civil proceedings and the right of access to a court, see above, p 236.

[1057] See eg, *Schönenberger and Durmaz v Switzerland* A 137 (1988). See also *McComb v UK No 10621/83*, 50 DR 81 (1986) (Article 6(3)(c)). Article 6(3)(c) may be infringed by delays caused by monitoring correspondence with a lawyer: *Domenchini v Italy* 1996-V; 32 EHRR 68.

[1058] *Jespers v Belgium No 8403/78*, 27 DR 61 at 88 (1981) Com Rep; CM Res DH (82) 3. Cf, *CGP v Netherlands No 29835/96* hudoc (1997) DA.

[1059] As to access in a civil law system to the complete case-file, see Stavros, pp 181–3. See also *Foucher v France* 1997-II; 25 EHRR 234. Article 6(3)(b) requires that the accused by given sufficient personal access to the documents in the case file to allow his defence to be prepared properly: *Öcalan n v Turkey* 2005-IV; 41 EHRR 985 GC. See also *Kremzow v Austria* A 268-B (1993); 17 EHRR 322. In some circumstances it may be sufficient that the accused's lawyer has access: *Kamasinksi v Austria* A 168 (1989); 13 EHRR 36 para 88.

[1060] As to the 'equality of arms' requirement that the defence have access to relevant evidence to conduct a forensic examination, see above, p 251.

[1061] *Jespers v Belgium No 8403/78*, 27 DR 61 at 87 (1981) Com Rep; CM Res DH (82) 3. See also *Öcalan v Turkey* 2005-IV; 41 EHRR 985 para 140 GC.

defence all material evidence in its possession for or against the accused, and this obligation must apply also under Article 6(3)(b).[1062]

Article 6(3)(b) also extends to 'facilities' that the defence requires at the trial in order
to plead its case so that, for example, defence counsel must be allowed sufficient time to
present the defence[1063] and to call expert witnesses,[1064] or be allowed an adjournment.[1065]
But Article 6(3)(b) does not imply a right to attend a pre-trial hearing by an investigating
judge of witnesses abroad who may give evidence later at the trial.[1066]

If there is a right of appeal against the trial court decision, Article 6(3)(b) requires that
the applicant be allowed sufficient facilities to prepare his appeal. Thus the applicant must
be informed of the reasons for the decision against him or her[1067] and given a copy of the
pleadings[1068] in good time.[1069] If the applicant is detained, the prison authorities must
take reasonable steps to supply him or her with the legal and other materials needed to
prepare an appeal.[1070]

It would appear from *Korellis v Cyprus*[1071] that the accused does not have to show 'actual
prejudice' to the defence resulting from the state's failure to allow access to documents or
other 'facilities': the test instead is one of 'relevance' to the preparation of the defence.

IV.   ARTICLE 6(3)(C): THE RIGHT TO DEFEND ONESELF
IN PERSON OR THROUGH LEGAL ASSISTANCE

Article 6(3)(c) guarantees the right of a person charged with a criminal offence to:

> defend himself in person or through legal assistance of his own choosing or, if he has not
> sufficient means to pay for legal assistance, to be given it free when the interests of justice
> so require.

The purpose of this guarantee is to ensure that proceedings against an accused 'will not
take place without an adequate representation of the case for the defence'.[1072] In terms of
equality of arms, it is 'primarily to place the accused in a position to put his case in such
a way that he is not at a disadvantage vis-à-vis the prosecution'.[1073] The accused's lawyer
may also serve as the 'watchdog of procedural regularity'[1074] both in the public interest
and for his client.

[1062] *Edwards v UK* A 247-B (1992); 15 EHRR 417. Claims of non-disclosure of evidence to the defence are now
generally dealt with not under Article 6(3), but the 'fair hearing' guarantee in Article 6(1), see above, p 254. On
the late introduction of prosecution witnesses, see *X v UK No 5327/71*, 43 CD 85 (1972).

[1063] *X v FRG No 7085/75*, 2 Digest 809 (1976) (no breach).

[1064] *GB v France* 2001-X.   [1065] *X v UK No 6404/73*, 2 Digest 895 (1975) (no breach).

[1066] *X v FRG No 6566/74*, 1 DR 84 (1974). See also *Crociani v Italy No 8603/79*, 22 DR 147 (1980).

[1067] *Hadjianastassiou v Greece* A 252 (1992). An abridged (not a full) copy of the trial court judgment
will be sufficient if the applicant's defence rights are not 'unduly affected': *Zoon v Netherlands* 2000-XII; 36
EHRR 380.

[1068] *Kremzow v Austria* A 268-B (1993).

[1069] As to the need to give notice of the date of the hearing, see *Goddi v Italy*, A 76 (1984) and *Vacher v France*
1996-V; 24 EHRR 482.

[1070] *Ross v UK No 11396/85*, 50 DR 179 (1986).

[1071] Hudoc (2003) (access to evidence for forensic examination; decided under Article 6(1), but relevant to
Article 6(3)(b)). But see the earlier Commission cases of *Koplinger v Austria No 1850/63*, 12 YB 438 (1968);
X v FRG No 8770/79, 2 Digest 405 (1981); and *F v UK No 11058/84*, 47 DR 230 (1986).

[1072] *Pakelli v FRG* A 64 (1983); 6 EHRR 1 para 84 Com Rep.

[1073] *X v FRG No 10098/82*, 8 EHRR 225 (1984).

[1074] *Ensslin, Baader and Raspe v FRG Nos 7572/76, 7586/76 and 7587/76*, 14 DR 64 at 114 (1978).

Article 6(3)(c) protects any person subject to a criminal charge.[1075] It applies to all stages of the criminal process. At the pre-trial stage, Article 6(3)(c) will be infringed 'if and insofar as the fairness of the trial is likely to be seriously prejudiced' by a failure to comply with it then.[1076] It was on this basis that in *Quaranta v Switzerland*[1077] Article 6(3)(c) was held to require that the accused have the assistance of a legal aid lawyer in connection with his appearances before an investigating judge in the civil law system concerned as well as later at the trial.

Applying the same criterion, in most cases the accused will also be entitled to access to a lawyer at the pre-trial stage. In *Ócalan v Turkey*[1078] the applicant was interrogated by the security forces, a public prosecutor and a judge over a period of almost seven days after his forced return to Turkey, during which time his lawyer was refused permission to visit him. Under interrogation, the applicant made incriminating statements that proved to be a 'major contributing factor in his conviction'. The Court held that 'to deny access to a lawyer over such a long period and in a situation in which the rights of the defence might well be irretrievably prejudiced' was a breach of Article 6(3)(c).

In *Murray (John) v UK*,[1079] the Court stated that access to a lawyer at the pre-trial stage 'may be subject to restrictions for good cause. The question, in each case, is whether the restriction, in the light of the entirety of the proceedings, has deprived the accused of a fair hearing'. In that case, the applicant terrorist suspect was denied access to his lawyer during the first forty-eight hours following his arrest under emergency legislation. During this time he was questioned by the police, but refused to answer any questions. The Court held that the forty-eight hours' restriction was a breach of Article 6(3)(c). Crucial to this decision was the fact that under the legislation an adverse inference could be drawn by the trial court if the accused exercised his right to silence during police questioning. Whereas the government justified the denial of access on the ground that it would prejudice the gathering of information about acts of terrorism, the Court held that the concept of 'fairness' in Article 6 meant that to 'deny access to a lawyer for the first 48 hours of police questioning, in a situation where the rights of the defence may well be irretrievably prejudiced, is—whatever the justification for such denial—incompatible with the rights of the accused under Article 6'.[1080] A delay of over a year in appointing a lawyer for remand prisoners, during which period they were questioned by the prosecutor and medically examined, was also a breach of Article 6(3)(c).[1081] But there was no breach where the applicant was not allowed access to a lawyer during detention on

---

[1075] As to the meaning of this term, see above, p 209. Article 6(3)(c) does not apply to proceedings challenging detention on remand; these come within Article 5(4), not Article 6: *Woukam Moufedo v France No 10868/84*, 51 DR 62 (1987).

[1076] *Imbrioscia v Switzerland* A 275 (1993); 17 EHRR 441 para 36.

[1077] A 205 (1991).   [1078] 2005-IV; 41 EHRR 985 para 131 GC.

[1079] 1996-I; 22 EHRR 29 para 63 GC. See also *Magee v UK* 2000-VI; 31 EHRR 822, where the accused confessed during forty-eight hours' denial of access (breach). Denial of access for twenty-four hours under the same emergency legislation where—in contrast with *Murray*—no adverse inference was drawn at the trial was not a breach of Article 6(3)(c): *Brennan v UK* 2001-X; 34 EHRR 507. Cf, *Averill v UK* 2000-VI; 31 EHRR 839. The Youth, Justice and Criminal Evidence Act 1999, s 58 now provides that inferences may not be drawn from silence if the accused has been denied access to legal advice. See also *Berlinski v Poland* hudoc (2002) (breach) and *Salduz v Turkey* hudoc (2008) GC (breach; accused's age relevant).

[1080] Id, para 66. The Court found a breach of Articles 6(1) and 6(3)(c) by a majority of twelve to seven. The minority dissented on the basis that the Court should have decided the case not the *possibility* of 'irretrievable prejudice', but on its facts and the applicant had failed to show that the drawing of an adverse inference at his trial had rendered it unfair as a whole.

[1081] *Berlinski v Poland* hudoc (2002).

remand, but no statements he made to the investigating judge or *procureur* during that period were relied on in court.[1082] The absence of a lawyer has also been a factor in cases in which evidence obtained by treatment in breach of Article3 has been admitted in evidence (in breach of Article 6).[1083]

The rights of private access to a lawyer and to sufficient visits by a lawyer, which are treated by the Court as aspects of the right to effective legal assistance in Article 6(3)(c),[1084] also apply at the pre-trial stage.

The question whether an accused's lawyer is entitled to be present during pre-trial questioning was raised in *Imbrioscia v Switzerland*.[1085] There the applicant was questioned by the police and later the district prosecutor in the absence of his lawyer. The lawyer had neither been invited to attend the initial interrogation sessions nor asked to attend. When the lawyer later complained that he had not been given notice of the sessions, he was invited to attend the remaining one. The Court held that Articles 6(1) and 6(3)(c) had not been infringed. What emerges from the case is that Article 6(3)(c) does not require a state to take the initiative to invite an accused's lawyer to be present during questioning in the course of the investigation. However, although the Court does not say this in so many words, it would appear from the tenor of its judgment that if the accused or his lawyer requests the latter's attendance, this must be allowed if, as is likely, there is a risk the information obtained will prejudice the accused person's defence. The question whether the accused must be asked if he wishes to have his lawyer present during questioning was not considered in the Court's judgment. Referring to *Miranda v Arizona*,[1086] Judge De Meyer, dissenting, suggested that he should. The *Imbrioscia* case concerned a civil law system. The Court's approach can be taken to apply to police questioning in a common law system also.[1087] In *Brennan v UK*,[1088] a Court Chamber agreed that both the attendance of the suspect's lawyer and video or taped recordings of police interviews were safeguards against police misconduct, but was 'not persuaded that these were an indispensable precondition of fairness': the facts of each case had to be considered as a whole.

As far as other stages of proceedings are concerned, Article 6(3)(c) applies to the trial and to any appeal proceedings following the accused's conviction, although when assessing its requirements at the appellate level regard must be had to the special features of the appeal proceedings concerned and the part they play in the case as a whole.[1089] Thus the appointment of a legal aid lawyer for the hearing of an appeal will not remedy the absence of a lawyer at the trial stage where the appeal court lacks jurisdiction to consider the case again fully on the law and the facts.[1090] With regard to leave to appeal applications, in *Monnell and Morris v UK*,[1091] a hearing of the applicants in person was not required; it was sufficient that they could present written submissions to the Court of Appeal.

[1082] *Yurttas v Turkey* hudoc (2004).

[1083] See the cases cited above, n 538.   [1084] See below, p 321.   [1085] A 275 (1993); 17 EHRR 441.

[1086] 384 US 436 (1966). *Miranda* also requires that an arrested person be informed of his rights.

[1087] In English law, an arrested person is entitled to have his lawyer present during police questioning and must be so informed: Code C, para 6.8, issued under s 67, PACE 1984.

[1088] 2001-X; 34 EHRR 507 para 53. The question whether an accused's lawyer is entitled to be present during questioning was left unanwered in the *Murray (John)* case.

[1089] *Meftah and Others v France* 2002-VII para 41 GC. See also *Granger v UK* A 174 (1990); 12 EHRR 469.

[1090] *Quaranta v Switzerland* A 205 (1991).

[1091] A 115 (1987); 10 EHRR 205. On the right to an oral hearing in person in criminal appeal proceedings, see above, p 275.

a. Defence in person

Article 6(3)(c) guarantees the right of the accused to defend himself in person.[1092] However, this is not an absolute right. The law of a number of Convention parties provides that in certain kinds of cases the accused must be represented by a lawyer at the trial stage[1093] or on appeal[1094] in the interests of justice. In *Correia de Matos v Portugal*[1095] the Court confirmed that this approach was consistent with Article 6(3)(c), the interests of justice being a 'relevant and sufficient' reason for insisting upon legal representation. A 'margin of appreciation' applies, as the contracting states are 'better placed than the [Strasbourg] Court' to decide whether the interests of justice require that the defence be conducted by a legal representative, rather than the accused, in a particular case or kind of case.[1096]

Where the accused does defend himself, his manner of conducting his defence may bear upon a state's liability under Article 6(3)(c). In *Melin v France*,[1097] the Court held that an accused who elects to defend himself in person, having 'thus deliberately waived his right to be assisted by a lawyer', is 'under a duty to show diligence'. Accordingly, there will be no breach of Article 6 by the state because of a deficiency in the proceedings that results from a lack of diligence that may reasonably be expected of the accused, given his capabilities and knowledge.[1098]

In contrast, a state may be in breach of Article 6(3)(c) if it impedes the exercise of the accused's legal right to defend himself. In *Brandstetter v Austria*,[1099] the accused had been convicted of defamation on the basis of allegedly false statements made by him when defending himself at an earlier trial for another offence. While finding no breach of Article 6(3)(c) on the facts, the Court accepted that 'the position might be different if it were established that, as a consequence of national law or practice in this respect being unduly severe, the risk of subsequent prosecution is such that the defendant is genuinely inhibited from freely exercising' his rights of defence, including defending himself in person.

b. Legal assistance

Article 6(3)(c) provides that an accused who does not defend himself in person is entitled to have legal assistance through his own lawyer or, subject to certain conditions, by means of free legal assistance provided by the state.[1100] The state thus cannot require an accused to defend himself in person.[1101] 'Although not absolute, the right of everyone charged with a criminal offence to be effectively defended by a lawyer, assigned officially if need be, is one of the fundamental features of a fair trial'.[1102]

Where an accused is represented by a lawyer, Article 6(3)(c) guarantees the accused's right to be present at the trial as well.[1103] However, the right to legal representation is

[1092] *Foucher v France* 1997-II; 25 EHRR 234.
[1093] See *Croissant v Germany* A 237-B (1992); 16 EHRR 135.
[1094] See *Philis v Greece No 16598/90*, 66 DR 260 (1990) and *Meftah v France* 2002-VII GC.
[1095] *No 48188/99* hudoc (2001) DA (lawyer denied the right to defend himself on a charge of insulting the court: no breach). Contrast the contrary ruling by the UN Human Rights Committee in *Correia de Matos v Portugal (1123/02)*, 13 IHRR 38 (2006). See also Treschel, p 263.
[1096] *Ibid.*   [1097] A 261-A (1993); 17 EHRR 1 para 25.
[1098] On the duty to intervene where the accused's lawyer is not diligent, see below, p 320.
[1099] A 211 (1991); 15 EHRR 378 paras 51, 53.
[1100] Legal assistance refers to advice and representation, both in and out of court.
[1101] *Pakelli v FRG* A 64 (1983); 6 EHRR 1.
[1102] *Poitrimol v France* A 277-A (1993); 18 EHRR 130 para 34.
[1103] *FCB v Italy* A 208-B (1991); 14 EHRR 909 and *Ezeh and Connors v UK* 2003-X; 39 EHRR 1 GC.

not dependent upon the accused's presence.[1104] Thus in *Campbell and Fell v UK*,[1105] the Court held that Article 6(3)(c) had been infringed by the United Kingdom because a prisoner, who had refused to attend in person, was denied legal representation at a Board of Visitors hearing of a disciplinary charge against him. The refusal of legal representation in *Campbell and Fell* resulted from the application of a rule by which representation was not permitted at Board of Visitors hearings generally; it was not a penalty aimed at encouraging attendance or punishing non-attendance. Other cases in which the Court has also found a breach have concerned an accused who absconds, in which context the refusal of legal representation is to deter or punish.[1106] Such a penalty is in breach of Article 6(3)(c); although a state must be able to impose sanctions to discourage the unjustified absence of an accused from appearing in court, it is 'disproportionate' to deny the accused legal representation needed for his or her defence.

Article 6(3)(c) guarantees an accused the right to legal assistance 'of his own choosing', ie assistance by a lawyer whom the accused appoints and pays for. As a general rule, the accused's choice of lawyer should be respected.[1107] However, the state may refuse to recognize it for 'relevant and sufficient' reasons.[1108] Rules limiting the accused's choice of lawyer to members of a specialist bar when appealing to a Court of Cassation or other appeal court are permissible.[1109] Regulations governing the qualifications and conduct of lawyers authorized to practise law in a state's legal system are obviously permissible, as are regulations concerning the practice in its courts of lawyers qualified in another legal system. A lawyer may be excluded for failure to comply with professional ethics,[1110] for refusal to wear robes,[1111] for showing disrespect to the court,[1112] or because he or she is appearing as a witness for the defence[1113] or has a personal interest in the case.[1114] A restriction upon the number of lawyers appointed by the accused is permissible, so long as the defence is able to present its case on an equal footing with the prosecution.[1115] Nor is a state liable if an accused is unable to find a lawyer who will act for him, provided that this failure is not the result of 'pressure or manoeuvres' by the state.[1116] Although the state thus has a general regulatory power, the Strasbourg Court retains the capacity to intervene if it is used improperly, eg by excluding a lawyer simply because of his willingness to represent an 'unpopular accused' or his opposition to the government.

Article 6(3)(c) refers to 'legal' assistance. This can be taken to allow assistance by a person chosen by the accused who is not a qualified lawyer[1117] although the state must have

---

[1104] *Poitrimol v France* A 277-A (1993); 18 EHRR 130.

[1105] A 80 (1984); 7 EHRR 165. See further *Ezeh and Connors v UK* 2003-X; 39 EHRR 1 GC. For the current legal representation problems at disciplinary hearings, see Livingstone *et al, op cit*, at n 839, p 400.

[1106] *Van Geyseghem v Belgium* 1999-I; 32 EHRR 554. This so though even though the accused violates a legal obligation by not attending (*Poitrimol v France* A 277-A (1993); 18 EHRR 130) and a conviction *in absentia* may be set aside in later proceedings (*Van Geyseghem* case). See also *Lala v Netherlands* A 297-A (1994); 18 EHRR 586 and *Karatas and Sari v France* hudoc (2002); 35 EHRR 1253.

[1107] *Goddi v Italy* B 61 (1982) p 5.

[1108] See *Croissant v Germany* A 237-B (1992); 16 EHRR 135 para 30.

[1109] *Meftah and Others v France* 2002-VII GC.

[1110] *Ensslin, Baader and Raspe v FRG Nos 7572/76, 7586/76 and 7587/76*, 14 DR 64 (1978).

[1111] *X and Y v FRG Nos 5217/71 and 5367/72*, 42 CD 139 (1972).

[1112] *X v UK No 6298/73*, 2 Digest 831 (1975).   [1113] *K v Denmark No 19524/92* (1993) unreported.

[1114] *X v UK No 8295/78*, 15 DR 242 (1978) (prosecution of barrister's father).

[1115] *Ensslin, Baader and Raspe v FRG Nos 7572/76, 7586/76 and 7587/76*, 14 DR 64 (1978).

[1116] *X and Y v Belgium No 1420/62 et al*, 6 YB 590 at 628 (1963).

[1117] See *Engel v Netherlands* A 22 (1976); I EHRR 647 PC and *Morris v UK* 2002-I; 34 EHRR 1253 (representation by non-lawyers in army disciplinary proceedings).

a regulatory power to control representation by such persons too. The drafting history[1118] and the object and purpose of Article 6(3)(c) suggest that professional qualifications are not necessary so long as the legal assistance provided is 'effective' in fact.[1119]

c. Legal aid

In practice, most accused persons are indigent so that the guarantee of legal aid in Article 6(3)(c) is of particular importance. Although an assessment of whether legal aid is required is in the first instance for the national authorities to make and a 'margin of appreciation' may apply,[1120] the Strasbourg Court is competent to review and disagree with their assessment, applying the terms of Article 6(3)(c).[1121]

The right to legal aid in Article 6(3)(c) is subject to two conditions. First, the accused must lack 'sufficient means' to pay for legal assistance. The Convention contains no definition of 'sufficient means' and there is no case law indicating the level or kind of private means that may be taken into account when deciding whether to award legal aid.[1122] When seeking to establish a breach of Article 6(3)(c), the onus is on the accused to show that he lacks 'sufficient means'. The accused need not, however, do so 'beyond all doubt'; it is sufficient that there are 'some indications' that this is so. This test was formulated and satisfied on the facts in *Pakelli v FRG*[1123] on the basis that the applicant had spent two years in custody shortly before the case, had presented a statement of means to the Commission that led it to award him legal aid in bringing his Strasbourg application, and had offered to prove lack of means to the West German Federal Court.

The Commission took the view that Article 6(3)(c) does not prohibit a contracting party from requiring an accused upon conviction to pay the costs of any free legal assistance that he has been allowed if he then has the necessary means to do so.[1124] The point was left open by the Court in *Luedicke, Belkacem and Koç v FRG*[1125] in which it held that there was such a prohibition under Article 6(3)(e) with regard to the costs of an interpreter. The text of Article 6 supports the Commission's interpretation in that, in contrast with the right in Article 6(3)(e), the right to legal aid in Article 6(3)(c) is made conditional upon the accused's means. Nonetheless, the possibility that an accused might have to repay the cost of legal aid could, as was recognized in the *Luedicke* case, cause him to defend himself in person rather than apply for legal aid in a case in which legal representation would be in the interests of a fair trial and hence of the object and purpose of the Convention. Moreover, the word 'given' in the English text can be read as meaning an irrevocable grant of free legal aid where the accused is without means at the time that the grant is made.

[1118] In the drafting of Article 14, ICCPR, upon which Article 6 is based, the words 'qualified representative' were replaced by 'legal assistance' so that they 'did not necessarily mean a lawyer, but merely assistance in the legal conduct of a case': UN Doc E/CN.4/SR 107, p 6.

[1119] See *X v FRG No 509/59*, 3 YB 174 (1960) (probationary lawyer).

[1120] Cf, *Correia de Matos* case, above, at p 315.

[1121] The question whether the right to legal aid is a 'civil right' so that it should be determined by a tribunal complying with Article 6 was raised but not decided in *Gutfreund v France* hudoc 2003-VII; 42 EHRR 1076: see further, above, p 222.

[1122] On the rules applicable to the grant of legal aid to applicants in order to allow them to bring a case to Strasbourg, see below, p 841.

[1123] A 64 (1983); 6 EHRR 1 para 34. The fact that the accused has been granted legal aid at another stage in the national proceedings is relevant: *Twalib v Greece* 1998-IV; 33 EHRR 584 and *RD v Poland* hudoc (2001); 39 EHRR 240. See also *Morris v UK* 2002-I; 34 EHRR 1253.

[1124] *Croissant v Germany* A 237-B (1992) Com Rep.

[1125] See below, p 327. Also left open by the Court in *Croissant*, above.

Second, legal aid need only be provided 'where the interests of justice so require'. This is to be judged by reference to the facts of the case as a whole, including those that may materialize after the competent national authority has taken its decision. Thus in *Granger v UK*[1126] the refusal of legal aid should have been reviewed when it proved during the appeal proceedings that the case was more complicated than appeared earlier.

A number of criteria have been identified by the Court as being relevant when determining whether the 'interests of justice' call for legal assistance. First, what is 'at stake' for the applicant in terms of the seriousness of the offence and hence the possible sentence that could result is of great importance.[1127] In *Benham v UK*,[1128] it was stated that where any 'deprivation of liberty is at stake, the interests of justice in principle call for legal representation'. In *Quaranta v Switzerland*,[1129] the 'mere fact' that the possible sentence that could be imposed upon the accused for drugs offences was three years' imprisonment meant that legal aid should have been provided.[1130] In contrast, in *Gutfreund v France*[1131] the 'interests of justice' did not require legal aid where the maximum possible sentence on a minor assault charge was not imprisonment but a modest fine (5,000FF) and where the procedure was 'simple'. Secondly, as the *Gutfreund* case suggests, the more complicated the case on the law or the facts, the more likely that legal assistance is required.[1132] Third, regard must be had to the contribution that the accused would be able to make if he defended himself; in this connection, the test is the capacity of the particular accused to present his case.[1133] Finally, Fawcett[1134] has argued that 'the interests of justice' might also require legal assistance for the accused where an issue of public importance is involved irrespective of whether a lawyer could assist the defence.

In appeal cases, it does not matter that the accused's chances of success are negligible.[1135] To the extent that the accused is granted a right of appeal by national law, he must be provided with legal aid if this is required for him to exercise it effectively. Thus in *Boner v UK*,[1136] the applicant was refused legal aid on the statutory ground that he did not have 'substantial grounds for making the appeal'.[1137] In holding that there had been a breach of Article 6(3)(c), the European Court focused on the fact that the accused would need the services of a lawyer in order to argue the point he wished to raise, as well as the importance of what was at stake for him (an eight-year sentence).

When applying the 'interests of justice' requirement, the test is not whether the absence of legal aid has caused 'actual prejudice' to the presentation of the defence. In *Artico*

[1126] A 174 (1990); 12 EHRR 469.   [1127] See eg, *Twalib v Greece* 1998-IV; 33 EHRR 584.

[1128] 1996-III; 22 EHRR 293 para 61 GC (possible three months' imprisonment for non-payment of community charge).   [1129] A 205 para 33 (1991).

[1130] The Court emphasized the possible, rather than the likely, penalty. Cf, *Pham Hoang v France* A 243 (1992). In appeal proceedings the actual sentence imposed takes over: see eg, *Boner v UK* A 300-B para 41 and *Maxwell v UK* A 300-C para 38 (1994), although any possibility of the sentence being increased must be relevant.

[1131] 2003-VII; 42 EHRR 1076 para 39. In contrast, a heavy fine without imprisonment is a relevant factor: *Pham Hoang v France* A 243 (1992).

[1132] See also *Granger v UK* A 174 (1990); 12 EHRR 469; *Quaranta v Switzerland* A 205 (1991); and *Pham Hoang v France* A 243 (1992).

[1133] See the *Granger* and *Quaranta* cases above; *Twalib v Greece* 1998-IV; 33 EHRR 584 (foreigner with no knowledge of the language or legal system); and *Vaudelle v France* 2001-I; 37 EHRR 397 (mental state).

[1134] Fawcett, p 170. There may have been an element of this approach in the account taken in the *Pakelli* case of the fact that the case might have some value in the development of case law.

[1135] The same must apply to the chances of acquittal at the trial stage.

[1136] A 300-B (1994); 19 EHRR 246 paras 41–4. Cf, *Maxwell v UK* A 300-C (1994); 19 EHRR 97 paras 38–41.

[1137] Section 25(2), Legal Aid (Scotland) Act 1986. The applicant's solicitors refused to support his application for legal aid and counsel was not prepared to represent him because of a professional rule applicable to appeals which are considered to have no merit.

v Italy,[1138] the Court stated that the test is a less stringent one, *viz* whether 'it appears plausible in the particular circumstances' that the lawyer would be of assistance, as was true on the facts of that case. There the Court noted that a lawyer would have been more likely than the applicant to have emphasized a statute of limitations argument in the applicant's favour before the Court of Cassation and that only a lawyer was competent to request a hearing at which the defence could have replied to the Public Prosecutor's arguments against the appeal. On this basis, legal aid comes close to being generally required because a lawyer will nearly always, by virtue of his professional expertise, be able to add to the accused's defence.[1139]

Although the choice of a legal aid lawyer is ultimately for the state, the wishes of the accused must be taken into account. In *Lagerblom v Sweden*,[1140] the Strasbourg Court stated that when providing legal assistance in the name of the state 'the [national] courts must certainly have regard to the accused's wishes, but these can be overridden when there are relevant and sufficient reasons for holding that this is necessary in the interests of justice'. In that case, the accused, whose mother tongue was Finnish and who was required by Swedish law to be legally represented in connection with assault and road traffic offences, wanted the lawyer chosen for him by the court to be replaced by a Finnish speaking lawyer. The Strasbourg Court held that there had been no breach of Article 6(3)(c) because the appointed lawyer had already done a lot of work on the case and the accused had both sufficient knowledge of Swedish and an interpreter.

The funding of legal aid is an expensive item for states. In the context of legal aid in civil proceedings, it has been held that it must be provided in accordance with Article 6(1) irrespective of the economic cost.[1141] The same approach must apply to criminal cases under Article 6(3)(c), so that budgetary considerations should not prevent effective legal assistance for accused persons who otherwise qualify under Article 6(3)(c).[1142]

d. Practical and effective legal assistance

The right in Article 6(3)(c) is to 'practical and effective' legal assistance.[1143] But a state cannot be held responsible for every shortcoming of a lawyer acting for the defence. As stated in *Kamasinski v Austria*,[1144] it 'follows from the independence of the legal profession of the state that the conduct of the defence is essentially a matter between the defendant and his counsel, whether counsel be appointed under a legal aid scheme or be privately financed'. Because of the state's lack of power to supervise or control his or her conduct, a lawyer, even though appointed by the state, is not an 'organ' of the state who can engage its direct responsibility under the Convention by his or her acts, in the way, for example, that a policeman or soldier may.[1145] Instead, the 'competent national

---

[1138] A 37 (1980); 3 EHRR 1 para 35. Cf, *Alimena v Italy* A 195-D (1991) and *Biondo v Italy No 8821/79*, 64 DR 5 (1983) Com Rep; CM Res DH (89) 30.

[1139] But for a case in which the 'interests of justice' did not require legal aid in respect of written appeal proceedings, see *X v FRG No 599/59*, 8 CD 12 (1961). See also *M v UK No 9728/82* 36 DR 155 (1983).

[1140] Hudoc (2003) para 54. See also *Croissant v Germany* A 237-B (1993); 16 EHRR 135. The state has a 'margin of appreciation' when deciding what the 'interests of justice' require: see *Correia de Matos v Portugal*, above, p 315.

[1141] See the *Airey* case, discussed above, p 236.

[1142] But see *M v UK No 9728/82*, 36 DR 155 at 158 (1983) (number of consultations may be limited for reasons of cost).

[1143] *Artico v Italy* A 37 (1980); 3 EHRR 1 para 33.

[1144] A 168 (1989); 13 EHRR 36 para 65. Cf, *Daud v Portugal* 1998-II; 30 EHRR 400 para 38.

[1145] *Alvarez Sanchez v Spain No 50720/99* hudoc (2001) DA. Cf. *Rudkowski v Poland No 45995/99* hudoc (2000) DA. The state may have a positive obligation to ensure, in the last resort, that the legal profession properly regulates itself. It might also be directly responsible if the lawyer were a 'public defender' in the employ of the state.

authorities', who may be the courts or other state actors, 'are required by Article 6(3)(c) to intervene only if a failure by legal aid counsel to provide effective representation is manifest or sufficiently brought to their attention'.[1146] The same must apply to privately appointed lawyers.[1147]

There may be liability on this *Kamasinski* basis where a lawyer simply fails to act for the accused. Thus in the leading case of *Artico v Italy*,[1148] the applicant was granted free legal aid under Italian law for his appeal to the Italian Court of Cassation. Unfortunately, the appointed lawyer never acted for the applicant, claiming other legal commitments and ill-health. Despite constant requests by the applicant, the Court of Cassation refused to appoint another lawyer to replace him. As a result, the applicant was forced to plead the case himself in circumstances in which legal assistance would have been likely to have been of value. Noting that the right in Article 6(3)(c) was to 'assistance', not 'nomination', the European Court rejected an Italian argument that by appointing a lawyer for the accused the Court of Cassation had done sufficient to comply with Article 6(3)(c).[1149]

There may also be liability on the *Kamasinski* basis where the lawyer fails to comply with a 'formal' but crucial procedural requirement. Thus in *Czekalla v Portugal*[1150] the accused's appeal to the Supreme Court had been dismissed because his legal aid lawyer had failed to include submissions in her pleadings. This failure to comply with a 'simple and purely formal rule' was a 'manifest failure' which 'called for positive measures on the part of the relevant authorities'. As to possible measures, the Strasbourg Court suggested that the Supreme Court could, in order to meet the requirements of Article 6(3)(c), have invited the lawyer to make submissions out of time, instead of declaring the appeal inadmissible. Whether the state has a positive obligation to act in such cases will depend upon the facts. In the *Czekalla* case, the Court noted that the accused faced a lengthy prison sentence and—as a foreigner who did not know the language used in court—was utterly dependent on his lawyer. In contrast, in *Alvarez Sanchez v Spain*,[1151] in which the time limit for appealing to the Constitutional Court had not been met because of an omission by the accused's officially appointed legal representative, the Strasbourg Court did not suggest that appropriate positive action, such as waiving the time limit, should have been taken. Despite the fact that the accused in this case also faced a lengthy prison sentence, his appeal to the Constitutional Court only concerned his right to a fair trial: he had had his sentence reduced by the Court of Appeal, and he could bring a civil claim for negligence against the lawyer.

To be distinguished from a 'formal' or procedural error such as those in the *Czekalla* and *Alvarez Sanchez* cases, is 'an injudicious line of defence or a mere defect in argumentation'[1152] or any other professional error [1153] in presenting the accused's defence.

[1146] *Kamasinski v Austria* A 168 (1980); 13 EHRR 36 para 65. The obligation to intervene arises where the lawyer's failure has rendered the defence ineffective, 'taking the proceedings as a whole': *Rutkowski v Poland* No 44995/99 hudoc (2000) para 3 DA. Cf, *Sannino v Italy* hudoc (2007).

[1147] But see *Tripodi v Italy* A 281-B (1994); 18 EHRR 295.   [1148] A 37 (1980); 3 EHRR 1.

[1149] Cf, *Daud v Portugal* 1998-II; 30 EHRR 400, in which the court was put on notice by the applicant of the failure of his legal aid lawyer to act. Although a substitute lawyer was appointed, the proceedings were not postponed to allow his replacement sufficient time to prepare the case.

[1150] 2002-VIII para 68.   [1151] No 50720/99 hudoc (2001) DA.

[1152] *Czekalla v Portugal* 2002-VIII para 60.

[1153] See *Tripodi v Italy* A 281-B (1994); 18 EHRR 295 (failure to ask for adjournment) and *Stanford v UK* A 282-A (1994) (failure to raise accused's hearing problem).

In such cases, the state is unlikely to be liable for the lawyer's conduct of the case, whatever is 'at stake' for the accused and even though the lawyer is state appointed.[1154]

The right to effective legal assistance in Article 6(3)(c) includes a right of private access to a lawyer, both at the pre-trial stage and later. In *S v Switzerland*,[1155] Article 6(3)(c) was infringed when the accused, who was in detention on remand, was not allowed to consult with his lawyer out of the hearing of a prison officer. As the Court stated, 'if a lawyer were unable to confer with his client and receive confidential instructions from him without such surveillance, his assistance would lose much of its usefulness, whereas the Convention is intended to guarantee rights that are practical and effective'.[1156] It may also be a breach of Article 6(3)(c) to tap the telephone conversations between an accused and his lawyer.[1157] The Article 6(3)(c) guarantee of access to a lawyer may be subject to restrictions in the public interest, but surveillance of 'the contacts of a detainee with his defence counsel is a serious interference with an accused's defence rights' so that 'very weighty reasons should be given for its justification'.[1158] The fear of collusion between the accused and the lawyer, resulting in the influencing of witnesses or the removal of documents, was insufficient to justify an investigating judge's order authorising such surveillance in *Lanz v Austria*.[1159] In contrast, the need for confidentiality to catch other members of the accused's criminal gang was enough to justify surveillance in *Kempers v Austria*.[1160] A glass screen preventing common access to documents may infringe Article 6(3).[1161]

For access to be effective, the number and length of lawyers' visits to the accused must be sufficient. Thus in *Öcalan v Turkey*,[1162] after the first two visits, the accused was allowed only two one-hour visits a week from his lawyers. This was insufficient given the highly complex charges against the accused and the voluminous case-file that they had generated. Insofar as the frequency of visits was dictated by the times of ferries to the island on which the accused was detained, it was necessary for the state to provide other more adequate means of transport.

In guaranteeing a right of access to a lawyer, Article 6(3)(c) overlaps with Article 6(3)(b) which guarantees the accused 'adequate facilities' to prepare his defence, a phrase that has been interpreted to include the right of access.[1163] But Article 6(3)(c) is wider than Article 6(3)(b) since it 'is not especially tied to considerations relating to the preparation of the trial but gives the accused a more general right to assistance and support by a lawyer throughout the whole proceedings'.[1164]

[1154] But see *Rutkowski v Poland No 45995/99* hudoc (2000) para 2 DA in which the Court checked whether a legal aid lawyer was 'negligent or superficial' in deciding whether there were grounds for appeal.

[1155] A 220 (1991); 14 EHRR 670 para 48. See also *Brennan v UK* 2001-X; 34 EHRR 507 and *Öcalan v Turkey* 2005-IV; 41 EHRR 985 GC.

[1156] In support of this statement, the Court cited the Council of Europe Standard Minimum Rules for the Treatment of Prisoners, Rule 93, CM Res (73)5 and Article 3(2), European Agreement Relating to Persons Participating in Proceedings of the European Commission and Court of Human Rights 1969.

[1157] *Zagaria v Italy* hudoc (2007) (breach). Cf, *D v Austria No 16410/90* (1990) unreported. The right of access also includes access by correspondence, although such cases are most commonly dealt with under Article 8: see eg, *Campbell v UK* A 233 (1992); 15 EHRR 137. For an Article 6 case on correspondence with a lawyer in criminal proceedings, see *McComb v UK No 10621/83*, 50 DR 81 (1986) F Sett.

[1158] *Lanz v Austria* hudoc (2002) para 52. See also *Can v Austria* A 96 (1985); 8 EHRR 14 para 52 Com Rep (F Sett before Court); *Egue v France No 11256/84*, 57 DR 47 (1988); and *Castravet v Moldova* hudoc (2007).

[1159] *Ibid.*   [1160] *No 21842/93* hudoc (1997) DA. The limited period of surveillance was relevant.

[1161] *Castravet v Moldova* hudoc (2007) (Article 5(4) case).

[1162] 2005-IV; 41 EHRR 985 para 135 GC.   [1163] See above, p 310.

[1164] *Can v Austria* A 96 (1985); 8 EHRR 14 para 54 Com Rep (F Sett before Court). In *S v Switzerland* the Court focused on paragraph (c), not (b), seemingly because the restrictions on the applicant's communications

The requirement that assistance be 'effective' has been considered in a variety of other contexts. A state will be in breach of it if it negligently fails to notify the accused's lawyer of the hearing with the result that the accused is not represented at it.[1165] To be 'effective' a lawyer appointed to defend an accused must be qualified to appear at the particular stage of proceedings for which his assistance is sought.[1166] Frequent changes of lawyers appointed for the defence may raise a problem of effectiveness,[1167] as may the allowance of inadequate time for a defendant's lawyer, whether a legal aid lawyer or not, to prepare his case.[1168] However, it is permissible to limit the role of the accused's lawyer, at least in army disciplinary proceedings, to the legal, as opposed to the factual, issues in the case where the facts are simple.[1169]

V. ARTICLE 6(3)(D): THE RIGHT TO CALL AND CROSS-EXAMINE WITNESSES

Article 6(3)(d) guarantees a person charged with a criminal offence the right:

> to examine or have examined witnesses against him and to obtain the attendance and examination of witnesses on his behalf under the same conditions as witnesses against him.

The right applies to the trial and any appeal proceedings. It does not generally apply at the pre-trial stage.[1170] Thus Article 6(3)(d) does not require that the accused be allowed to question a witness being interrogated by the police[1171] or by an investigating judge,[1172] provided that he may be cross-examined at the trial.[1173] The refusal by an investigating judge to hear a defence witness is likewise not a breach of Article 6(3)(d) if the witness may be called at the trial.[1174]

Neither the accused's right to cross-examine witnesses against him nor his right to call defence witnesses is absolute. However, any limitations must be consistent with the principle of 'equality of arms', the full realization of which is the 'essential aim' of Article 6(3)(d).[1175] There was a breach of Article 6(3)(d) where the accused was not allowed an opportunity to examine or cross-examine any witnesses, either at the trial or on appeal.[1176] The right supposes that the examination of witnesses occurs before the judges who decide the case, so that if a judge is replaced after a witness has been heard, generally the witness must be recalled.[1177]

---

with his lawyer were later lifted for a long enough period prior to the trial to permit the proper preparation of his defence, so that the facilities were 'adequate'.

[1165] *Goddi v Italy* A 76 (1984).

[1166] See *Biondo v Italy* No 8821/79, 64 DR 5 (1983) Com Rep; CM Res DH (89) 30. See also *Frexias v Spain* No 53590/99 2000-X (labour, not criminal, lawyer appointed; no breach on the facts).

[1167] See *Koplinger v Austria* No 1850/63, 9 YB 240 (1966).

[1168] Such cases have been considered under both Articles 6(3)(b) and 6(3)(c): see eg, *X v UK* No 4042/69, 32 CD 76 (1970): *Murphy v UK* No 4681/70, 43 CD 1 (1972).

[1169] *Engel v Netherlands* A 22 (1976); 1 EHRR 647 PC.

[1170] See *Can v Austria* A 96 (1985) para 47 Com Rep (F Sett before Court) and *Adolf v Austria* B 43 (1980) para 64 Com Rep.

[1171] *X v FRG* No 8414/78, 17 DR 231 (1979).   [1172] *Ferraro-Bravo v Italy* No 9627/81, 37 DR 15 (1984).

[1173] See further below, pp 324 *et seq.*   [1174] *Schertenlieb v Switzerland* No 8339/78, 17 DR 180 (1979).

[1175] *Engel v Netherlands* A 22 (1976); 1 EHRR 647 para 91 PC and *Bonisch v Austria* A 92 (1985); 9 EHRR 191 para 32. And see *Oyston v UK* No 42011/98 hudoc (2002) DA (restrictions on questions to rape victim; no breach). But Article 6(3)(d) is not limited to 'equality of arms': *Vidal v Belgium* A 235-B (1992) para 33.

[1176] *Vaturi v France* hudoc (2007). On the forfeiture of the right to examine witnesses by opting for an accelerated procedure with a reduce sentence, see *Panarisi v Italy* hudoc (2007).

[1177] *Graviano v Italy* hudoc (2005) (no breach on the facts). See also the principle of immediacy, above, p 259.

The term 'witness' in Article 6(3)(d) has an autonomous Convention meaning. It is not limited to persons who give evidence at the trial; a person whose statements are introduced as evidence but who does not give oral evidence is also a 'witness' for the purposes of Article 6(3)(d).[1178] The term also includes expert witnesses called by the prosecution or the defence. An expert appointed by the court may be a 'witness against' the accused for the purposes of Article 6(3)(d) depending upon his evidence.[1179] A co-accused is a witness, so that depositions made by him during the investigation stage[1180] and statements made at his own separate trial[1181] that are introduced as evidence at the accused's trial are subject to Article 6(3)(d).

The right to call or cross-examine witnesses may be waived, but waiver must be established in an unequivocal manner and not run counter to any important public interest.[1182] There was no waiver of the right when the defence failed to challenge the admission of written statements by witnesses whom it had not been able to cross-examine when such a challenge was unlikely to succeed.[1183]

The *right of the accused to cross-examine 'witnesses against him'* is a key element of Article 6(3)(d)[1184] and is in principle infringed where evidence is introduced at the trial by the prosecution without the witness whose direct evidence it is being called as a witness at the trial.[1185] However, Article 6(3)(d) has been interpreted, in the light of European national practice, as allowing the introduction of such evidence in certain exceptional cases.[1186] Thus the Court has recognized that it may be introduced in order to prevent reprisals against witnesses or their families;[1187] to safeguard police operational methods;[1188] to excuse victims of sexual offences from having to confront the offender;[1189] to excuse a witness from giving evidence against a family member;[1190] and where a witness is ill[1191] or has disappeared[1192] or died.[1193] Some of these exceptions can be seen safeguarding the witness's Convention

---

[1178] *Kostovski v Netherlands* A 166 (1989); 12 EHRR 434 PC. Such statements have included statements to the police and depositions.

[1179] *Bonisch v Austria* A 92 (1985); 9 EHRR 191 and *Brandstetter v Austria* A 211 (1991); 15 EHRR 378.

[1180] *Luca v Italy* 2001-II; 36 EHRR 807.

[1181] *Cardot v France* A 200 (1991); 13 EHRR 853 para 51 Com Rep. See also *X v UK No 10083/82*, 6 EHRR 142 (1983).

[1182] *Craxi v Italy* hudoc (2002); 38 EHRR 995.   [1183] *Ibid.*

[1184] And of the right to an adversarial trial in Article 6(1): see above, p 254. See Holdgaard, 71 Nord JIL 83 (2002).

[1185] A variant is where the witness gives evidence subject to protective safeguards: see *SN v Sweden*, below, p 1211 and *R v Davis*, below, p 326.

[1186] Dispensation may be allowed in cases of ordinary crime (*Windisch v Austria* A 186 (1990); 13 EHRR 281), as well as of organized crime (*Kostovski v Netherlands* A 166 (1989); 12 EHRR 434 PC); drug trafficking (*Saidi v France* A 261-C (1993); 17 EHRR 251; and terrorism (*Hulki Gunes v Turkey* hudoc 2003-VII; 43 EHRR 263), which are recognized as presenting special problems.

[1187] *Van Mechelen v Netherlands* 1997-III; 25 EHRR 647. There must be good evidence that the fear is justified: *Visser v Netherlands* hudoc (2002).

[1188] Eg, *Van Mechelen v Netherlands, ibid,* and *Ludi v Switzerland, ibid* (undercover police).

[1189] *SN v Sweden* hudoc 2002-V; 39 EHRR 304.

[1190] *Unterpertinger v Austria* A 110 (1986); 13 EHRR 175 and *Asch v Austria* A 203 (1991); 15 EHRR 597 (unmarried partner).

[1191] *Bricmont v Belgium* A 158 (1989); (1990) 12 EHRR 217; *Wester v Sweden No 31076/96* hudoc (1998) DA; *Kennedy v UK No 36428/97* hudoc (1998); 27 EHRR CD 266.

[1192] *Isgro v Italy* A 194 (1991) and *Verdam v Netherlands No 35253/97* hudoc (1999); 28 EHRR CD 161. The state must make sufficient efforts to find or bring to court a missing witness: *Calabro v Italy and Germany No 59895/00* hudoc (2002) DA. The absence of a power in law to summon a witness whose whereabouts are known is not an excuse: *Mild and Virtanen v Finland* hudoc (2005). See also *Haas v Germany No 73047/01* hudoc (2005) DA. On statements by witnesses abroad, see *X v FRG No 11853/85*, 53 DR 182 (1987);10 EHRR 521. On evidence from foreign court proceedings, see *S v FRG No 8945/80*, 39 DR 43 (1983).

[1193] *Ferrantelli and Santangelo v Italy* 1996-III; 23 EHRR 288.

rights to 'life, liberty or security' (Articles 2 and 5) or to respect for private or family life (Article 8).[1194] The rules governing these exceptions vary, with, for example, the use of the evidence of a witness who has died[1195] raising different issues from the use of the evidence of anonymous witnesses who are available to appear at the trial but have good reason not to do so.[1196] Most of the Court's jurisprudence has concerned problems that have arisen in cases of the latter kind,[1197] which are largely the focus of the following paragraphs.

In *Kostovski v Netherlands*[1198] the Plenary Court held that the inability of the defence to cross-examine a non-appearing witness against the accused at the trial is not in itself a breach of Article 6(3)(d) in these exceptional cases if 'the rights of the defence have been respected'. By this, the Court meant that the accused has been given 'an adequate and proper opportunity to challenge and question a witness against him, either at the time the witness was making his statement or at some later stage of the proceedings'.[1199] In the *Kostovski* case,[1200] there was a breach of Article 6(3)(d) where the 'decisive evidence' against the accused consisted of statements made to the police and to an examining magistrate by private anonymous witnesses whom the defence was not allowed to confront at the pre-trial stage and who did not give evidence at the trial for fear of reprisals by organized crime. Whereas the Plenary Court judgment in the *Kostovski* case is to be read as meaning that the evidence of anonymous, as well as identifiable, non-appearing witnesses may be relied on in court even though it is 'the decisive evidence'[1201] against the accused provided that the rights of the defence are respected, in the *Doorson*[1202] and some later cases[1203] Court Chambers would appear to have gone further in stating that 'a conviction should not either solely or to a decisive extent upon anonymous statements' regardless of the steps taken to secure the rights of the defence. The better interpretation of the Strasbourg jurisprudence as a whole is that a balancing approach applies in all cases, but that in 'decisive evidence' cases, the burden of proving that the rights of the defence have been sufficiently safeguarded is very high, particularly in the case of anonymous witnesses. The Court has been particularly concerned about reliance upon the evidence of anonymous witnesses who are police officers. In *Van Mechelen v Netherlands*,[1204] it stated that their position was different from that of a 'disinterested witness or a victim' who wished to remain anonymous for fear of reprisals.[1205] This was because of the links between the police and the state and the prosecution of offenders. With this in mind, the Court held that, although very elaborate, the special arrangements for the anonymous questioning by the investigating

---

[1194] *Doorson v Netherlands* 1996-II; 22 EHRR 330.

[1195] See the requirements in the *Ferrantelli v Santangelo* case, above, n 1193.

[1196] As to whether the exceptions under the English common law 'hearsay' rule complied with Article 6(3)(d), see the Law Commission for England and Wales, Report No 245 (1997), pp 56 ff. The 'illness' exception was held not in breach of Article 6(3)(d) in *Trivedi v UK No 31700/96* hudoc (1997) DA. For the current exceptions, see s 114, Criminal Justice Act 2003.

[1197] The cases mostly concern civil law criminal justice systems, involving pre-trial hearings by investigations judges etc.

[1198] A 166 (1989); 12 EHRR 434 para 41 PC.   [1199] Id, para 44.

[1200] *Ibid.*

[1201] In some cases, Court chambers have applied a 'sole' or 'only' evidence test: see eg, *Asch v Austria* A 203-A (1991); 15 EHRR 597 para 30. The less demanding (for applicants) *Kostovski* 'decisive extent' test is now generally applied: see eg, *Van Mechelen v Netherlands* 1997-III; 25 EHRR 647 para 63.

[1202] *Doorson v Netherlands* 1996-II; 22 EHRR 330 para 76.

[1203] See eg, *Visser v Netherlands* hudoc (2002) and *Krasniki v Czech Rep* hudoc (2006).

[1204] 1997-III; 25 EHRR 647 paras 56, 63.

[1205] See eg, *Windisch v Austria* A 186 (1990); 13 EHRR 281 and *Asch v Austria* A 203 (1991); 15 EHRR 597.

judge of police officers who then did not give evidence at the trial in the applicants' case did not sufficiently guarantee the rights of the defence to comply with Article 6(3)(d), given that the convictions of the applicants for attempted murder and robbery were 'to a decisive extent' based on the police evidence. In that case, the police officers were questioned in a separate room by the investigating judge, with the accused and their lawyers hearing the questions and answers by a sound link. The Court was concerned that in this situation the defence was unaware of the demeanour of the witnesses under questioning, as well as their identity. The Court was also not satisfied that a real threat of reprisals had been shown on the facts or that there were not less extreme measures that could have been used.[1206]

Where the accused's conviction is not based to a 'decisive extent' upon the evidence of the non-appearing witness, a balancing test clearly applies, with the question being whether 'the rights of the defence have been respected'. As stated in *Doorson v Netherlands*,[1207] the test is whether 'the handicaps under which the defence labours' are 'sufficiently counterbalanced by the procedures followed by the judicial authorities'. Thus in *Kok v Netherlands*,[1208] where the evidence of an anonymous witness was relevant but not 'decisive', so that the rights of the defence were therefore 'handicapped to a much lesser extent', the Court reviewed the procedures that were followed at the pre-trial stage and concluded that they had been sufficient to comply with Article 6(3)(d). Relevant factors when applying a balancing test include whether an investigating judge knows the identity of an anonymous witness[1209] and whether the defence has taken advantage of opportunities of confrontation at the pre-trial stage or of other opportunities to counterbalance the lack of the ability to cross-examine the witness at the trial.[1210]

The Court has accepted that special arrangements for confrontation of a witness at the trial that would not normally comply with Article 6(3)(d) may suffice in cases involving sexual offences. In *SN v Sweden*[1211] the Court held that Article 6(3)(d) had to be interpreted as making some allowance for the 'special features' of criminal proceedings concerning such offences, because giving oral evidence at the trial in open court in such cases, particularly in cases involving children, may be an ordeal for the victim and may raise issues of respect for private life. In the *SN* case, the evidence of a ten-year-old child who had been sexually abused by his school teacher was 'virtually the sole evidence' on the basis of which the teacher was convicted. The child did not give evidence as a witness at the trial, but the videotape of his first police interview was shown during both the trial and appeal hearings and the record of the second interview was read out at the trial and the audiotape played back at the appeal hearing. What was crucial for the Court was that the applicant's lawyer had been present during the police hearing (by a specially trained

---

[1206] The Court suggested that it might have been sufficient just to disguise the police witnesses during the investigating judge questioning. Cf, *Ludi v Switzerland* A 238 (1992); 15 EHRR 173.

[1207] 1996-II; 22 EHRR 330 para 76.

[1208] No 43149/98 hudoc (2000) DA. Cf, *Birutis v Lithuania* hudoc (2002) and *Sapunarescu v Germany* No 22007/03 hudoc (2006) DA.

[1209] *Isgro v Italy* (1991) A 194 and *Doorson v Netherlands* 1996-II; 22 EHRR 330.

[1210] *SN v Sweden* 2002-V; 39 EHRR 304; *Asch v Austria* A 203 (1991); 15 EHRR 597; *Baegen v Netherlands* A 327-B (1995) Com Rep; *PS v Germany* hudoc (2001); 36 EHRR 1139; *Solakov v FYROM* hudoc 2001-X. See also *Pullar v UK* 1996-III; 22 EHRR 391.

[1211] 2002-V; 39 EHRR 304 para 46. For other sex offences cases, see *Baegen v Netherlands* A 327-B (1995) Com Rep (defence failure to use alternative options; no breach); *MK v Austria* No 28867/95 hudoc (1997); 24 EHRR CD 59 (expert report sufficient; no breach); *PS v Germany* hudoc (2001) 36 EHRR 1139 (no special arrangements; breach). And see *Mayali v France* hudoc (2005) and *Bocos-Cuesta v Netherlands* hudoc (2005) (breaches).

unit) and had been able to suggest lines of questioning. The Court considered that this was sufficient to enable the applicant to challenge the child's statements and his credibility. The Court also took into account that the 'necessary care' was taken by the national court in its evaluation of the child's statements.[1212]

In the British national case of *R v Davis*,[1213] the House of Lords held that special arrangements[1214] for the protection of witnesses who feared reprisals to preserve their anonymity as a condition of their giving evidence in court was contrary to the long established right to confront one's accusers in English common law. The House of Lords understood its ruling to be required by the *Kostovski* case in a case where, as in the *Davis* case, the evidence is to a 'decisive extent' the basis for the accused's conviction. However, arrangements of the *Davis* case kind for witnesses who give evidence at the trial have not been reviewed by the European Court;[1215] the closest parallel is the *SN* case, concerning the special arrangements for child victims.

As to the calling of *witnesses for the defence*, it is for the national courts, 'as a general rule, to assess whether it is appropriate to call witnesses'.[1216] Although the national court's decision is subject to review under Article 6(3)(d), it will only be in exceptional circumstances that the Strasbourg Court will question a national court's exercise of its discretion in the assessment of the relevance of the proposed evidence.[1217] This 'hands off' approach may be justified on the ground that the text of Article 6(3)(d) refers to the calling of witnesses by the accused 'on his behalf' and not 'at his request'. It is also in accord with the 'fourth instance' doctrine[1218] which the Strasbourg authorities generally apply when reviewing the decision of national courts. An exceptional case in which the Court did intervene was *Vidal v Belgium*.[1219] There the Court found a breach of Article 6 as a whole when the national court to which the accused's case had been remitted refused—without giving reasons—to hear the four witnesses requested by the accused and replaced a three-year suspended sentence by a four-year sentence that was not suspended, without any new evidence.

A state is not liable under Article 6(3)(d) for the failure of defence counsel to call a particular witness,[1220] but where witnesses are properly called by the defence, a court is under a positive obligation to take appropriate steps to ensure their appearance.[1221] There is no breach of Article 6(3)(d), however, if a defence witness fails to appear for reasons beyond

---

[1212] Cf, *Doorson v Netherlands* 1996-II; 22 EHRR 330 para 76.   [1213] [2008] UKHL 36.

[1214] These were that the witnesses gave evidence under a pseudonym; any personal details that would identify them were kept from the defence; no questions were allowed that would identify them; the witnesses gave evidence behind a screen so that they could only be seen by the judge and jury; and their natural voices were distorted. The witnesses were the only eye witnesses identifying the accused as the killer.

[1215] For a terrorist screening case, see *Murphy v UK No 2066657/92*, 15 EHRR CD 113 (1992) DA.

[1216] *Vidal v Belgium* A 235-B (1992) para 33. Cf, *Engel v Netherlands* A 22 (1976); 1 EHRR 647 PC; *Doorson v Netherlands* 1996-II; 22 EHRR 330; and *Perna v Italy* 2003-V; 39 EHRR 563 GC. On expert witnesses, see above, p 323.

[1217] See *L v Switzerland No 12609/86*, 68 DR 108 (1991) F Sett and *Wiechart v FRG* 7 YB 104 (1964). National courts are also permitted considerable discretion in controlling the accused's questioning of such defence witnesses as are called: see eg, *Kok v Netherlands No 43149/98* hudoc (2000); 30 EHRR CD 273.

[1218] See above, p 14. The Commission has also referred to the 'margin of appreciation' doctrine: see eg, *Payot and Petit v Switzerland No 16596/90* hudoc (1991) DA.

[1219] A 235-B (1992). Cf, *Popov v Russia* hduoc (2007). The refusal to order a psychological report requested by the applicant in a case of parental access to a child contributed to a breach of Article 6(1) in *Elsholz v Germany* 2000-VIII; 34 EHRR 1412 GC. Contrast *Sommerfeld v Germany* 2003-VIII; 38 EHRR 756 GC (decided under Article 8; no breach on the facts).

[1220] *F v UK No 18123/91* hudoc (1992) 15 EHRR CD 32. As to Article 6(3)(c), see above, p 320.

[1221] *Sadak and Others v Turkey* 2001-VIII; 36 EHRR 431.

the court's control[1222] or just because the witness is called by the court at a time other than that requested by the accused, unless this affects the presentation of the defence.[1223]

Article 6(3)(d) recognizes that at the trial court hearing it is 'in principle' essential that an accused is allowed to be present when witnesses are being heard in a case against him.[1224] Exceptionally, however, the interests of justice may permit the exclusion of the accused consistently with Article 6(3)(d) to ensure that a witness gives an unreserved statement provided that the accused's lawyer is allowed to remain and conduct any cross-examination.[1225]

In *Luedicke, Belkacem and Koç v FRG*,[1226] the Court left open the question whether it would be a breach of Article 6(3)(d) for a state to require an accused to pay the costs associated with compliance with Article 6(3)(d) (eg interpreters' costs in questioning witnesses) if convicted.

VI. ARTICLE 6(3)(E): THE RIGHT TO AN INTERPRETER

Article 6(3)(e) guarantees the right of a person charged with a criminal offence 'to have the free assistance of an interpreter if he cannot understand or speak the language used in court'. As in the case of other Article 6(3) rights, the guarantee protects persons once they are 'charged with a criminal offence'.[1227] It does not benefit suspects being questioned by the police prior to their being 'charged' in the sense of Article 6(1); it does apply to the pre-trial stage of proceedings thereafter. Thus in *Kamasinski v Austria*,[1228] an interpreter was required during police questioning following the accused's arrest and in the course of the civil law preliminary investigation in the case. As with Article 6 rights generally,[1229] Article 6(3)(e) applies during any appeal proceedings. The right to an interpreter may be waived,[1230] but it must be a decision of the accused, not his lawyer.[1231]

The obligation to provide 'free' assistance is unqualified. It does not depend upon the accused's means; the services of an interpreter for the accused are instead a part of the facilities required of a state in organizing its system of criminal justice.[1232] Nor can an accused be ordered to pay for the costs of interpretation if he is convicted, as was required by West German law in *Luedicke, Belkacem and Koç v FRG*.[1233] The language of Article 6(3)(e) indicates 'neither a conditional remission, nor a temporary exemption, nor a suspension, but a once and for all exemption or exoneration'. Any contrary interpretation would also be inconsistent with the object and purpose of Article 6, which is to ensure a fair trial for all accused persons, whether subsequently convicted or not, since an accused might forgo his right to an interpreter for fear of the financial consequences.[1234]

The 'assistance' required by Article 6(3)(e) applies to the translation of documents as well as the interpretation of oral statements; in both respects the obligation is to provide

[1222] *Ubach Mortes v Andorra No 46253/99*, 2000-V DA (ill-health).
[1223] *X v UK No 5506/72*, 45 CD 59 (1973).
[1224] *Kurup v Denmark No 11219/84*, 42 DR 287 (1985). Cf, *X v Denmark No 8395/78*, 27 DR 50 (1981).
[1225] *Kurup v Denmark* ibid. Cf, *X v UK No 20657/92* hudoc (1992); 15 EHRR CD 113 (screening of witness from accused, but not his lawyer, permissible).
[1226] See below.   [1227] As to the meaning of this phrase, see above, p 209.
[1228] A 168 (1989); 13 EHRR 36. Article 6(3)(e) extends to pre-trial appearances before a judge, remand hearings, and the translation of the indictment: *Luedicke, Belkacem and Koc v FRG* A 29 (1978); 2 EHRR 149.
[1229] See above, p 298.   [1230] See *Kamasinski v Austria* A 168 (1989); 13 EHRR 36 para 80.
[1231] *Cuscani v UK* hudoc (2002); 36 EHRR 11 and *Sardinas Alba v Italy No 56271/00* hudoc (2004) DA.
[1232] But an accused may be charged for an interpreter provided for him at a hearing that he fails to attend: *Fedele v Germany No 11311/84* hudoc (1987) DA.
[1233] A 29 (1978); 2 EHRR 149 para 40.   [1234] Id, para 42.

such assistance as is necessary to ensure a fair trial.[1235] Article 6(3)(e) does not require that every word of the oral proceedings is interpreted or that all documents are translated; the test is whether enough is done to allow the accused fully to understand and answer the case against him.[1236] Thus a written translation of the indictment may be unnecessary if sufficient oral information as to its contents is given to the accused, and it may be enough for an interpreter to summarize parts of the oral proceedings.[1237]

It is arguable that the state's obligation should extend to informing an accused who appears in need of assistance to his right to an interpreter.[1238] As to whether there is such a need, in *Cuscani v UK*[1239] the Court stated that the onus was on the judge to reassure himself, following consultation with the applicant, that the latter was not prejudiced by the absence of an interpreter. In that case, the Court held that Article 6(3)(e) had been infringed when, although aware of the applicant's difficulty in following the proceedings and that his legal aid barrister had had problems in communicating with the applicant, the judge was persuaded by the barrister, without consulting the applicant, that it would be possible to 'make do and mend' with the assistance of the 'untested language skills' of the applicant's brother in a sentencing hearing that led to a four-year prison sentence and ten-year disqualification as a company director.

Article 6(3)(e) only extends to the language used in court: an accused who understands that language cannot insist upon the services of an interpreter to allow him to conduct his defence in another language, including a language of an ethnic minority of which he is a member.[1240]

Where, as is usually the case, the accused does not defend himself in person but is represented by a lawyer, it will generally not be sufficient that the accused's lawyer (but not the accused) knows the language used in court. Interpretation of the proceedings is required as the right to a fair trial, which includes the right to participate in the hearing,[1241] requires that the accused be able to understand the proceedings and to inform his lawyer of any point that should be made in his defence.[1242] A related question is whether the accused must be provided with an interpreter, where necessary, in order to communicate with his lawyer. In a legal aid case, the responsibility should lie with the state under Article 6(3)(c) to appoint a lawyer who can communicate with his client or to provide an interpreter.[1243] Where the accused appoints his own lawyer, it must be for him to appoint a lawyer who can communicate with him, if one is available.[1244]

Clearly, the interpreter who is provided must be competent. In this connection, the Court has stated that in order for the right guaranteed by Article 6(3)(e) to be 'practical and effective', the 'obligation of the competent authorities is not limited to the appointment

---

[1235] *Kamsinski v Austria* A 168 (1989); 13 EHRR 36 para 74. As to whether written translation is required, see *Hermi v Italy* 2006-XII; 46 EHRR 1115 GC.

[1236] Id paras 74, 83.

[1237] Id. paras 81, 83. An oral summary of the judgment may suffice to permit an appeal: *ibid*. See also *Hayward v Sweden No 14106/88* hudoc (1991) DA.

[1238] Cf, Stavros, p 257.

[1239] Hudoc (2002); 36 EHRR 11 para 38. In *X v Austria No 6185/73*, 2 DR 68 (1975), the Commission ruled that Article 6(3)e ('language in court') does not extend to communications between the accused and his lawyer.

[1240] *K v France No 10210/82*, 35 DR 203 (1983) and *Bideault v France No 11261/84*, 48 DR 232 (1986). See also *Lagerblom v Sweden* hudoc (2003).

[1241] See above, p 250.

[1242] *Kamasinski v Austria* A 168 (1991); 13 EHRR 36 para 74 and *Cuscani v UK* hudoc (2002); 36 EHRR 11 para 38.

[1243] In *Lagerblom v Sweden* hudoc (2003), see above, p 319, the accused sought to have his Swedish-speaking legal aid lawyer replaced by a Finnish speaking lawyer so that he could talk directly with him. The claim was rejected on the basis that an interpreter was provided and anyway the accused had sufficient Swedish.

[1244] *X v FRG No 1022/82*, 6 EHRR 353 (1983).

of an interpreter but, if they are put on notice in the particular circumstances, may also extend to a degree of subsequent control over the adequacy of the interpretation provided'.[1245] Although there is no formal requirement that an interpreter be impartial or independent of the police or other authorities, the assistance provided must be 'effective' and 'not of such a nature as to impinge on the fairness of the proceedings'.[1246]

6. CONCLUSION

Although Article 6 cases do not generally catch the headlines as much as cases under some other articles of the Convention, such as Article 3 or 10, they are the staple diet of the Convention system. As noted, the majority of cases decided at Strasbourg raise issues under Article 6. One reason for this is that it is in the administration of justice that the state is most likely to take decisions affecting individuals in the areas of conduct covered by the Convention.

Article 6 has been given an unexpectedly but commendably wide field of application. Although it does not yet extend to every situation in which an individual would benefit from a 'right to a court', Article 6 nonetheless has acquired an extensive reach. It controls appellate as well as trial and some pre-trial proceedings. And it applies to certain disciplinary and other proceedings before special tribunals. While this is good for the individual, it presents problems for the uniform interpretation of a text that was devised with the classical court of law in mind. Article 6 also requires states to provide a right of appeal from, or judicial review of, administrative decisions that are directly decisive for an individual's 'civil rights and obligations'. Should the Court's jurisprudence in this last regard appear confusing and in need of a coherent statement of principle, the result is still an extension of the rule of law into areas of administrative justice where it was sometimes lacking.

As to the meaning of a 'fair trial', Article 6 has been imaginatively interpreted. A right of access to a court has been read into the text. The emphasis upon 'objective justice' has given more bite to the guarantees of an 'independent and impartial tribunal' and 'equality of arms', leading in some cases to changes in longstanding national practices.[1247] The residual right to a 'fair hearing' has proved fertile ground for the addition of further nominate rights[1248] and has served as a means of dealing with cases on a flexible 'facts as a whole' basis.[1249] But the most striking feature of Article 6 cases has been the long line of decisions involving violations of the right to trial 'within a reasonable time'. If one feature of the administration of justice in European states has been highlighted by the working of the Convention, it is the delay that sometimes occurs before justice is delivered.[1250] Proceedings in some cases have lasted an astonishing number of years.

As to the mechanics of the trial process, the Court has been far less intrusive. Given the great diversity of practice in European criminal justice systems concerning, for example, the rules of evidence, the Court has allowed considerable discretion as to means, requiring only that the outcome of the procedure followed is a fair trial. One issue in respect of which it has taken a stand concerns the admissibility of the prosecution hear-

---

[1245] *Kamasinski v Austria* A 168 (1989) 13 EHRR 36 para 74. See also *Ucak v UK No 44234/98* hudoc (2002) DA.

[1246] *Ucak v UK No 44234/98* hudoc (2002) DA.   [1247] See *Piersack v Belgium*, above, p 292.

[1248] See above, pp 246 ff.   [1249] See *Kraska v Switzerland*, A 254 (1983); 18 EHRR 188.

[1250] See above, p 284.

say evidence of anonymous witnesses.[1251] This example demonstrates clearly the choice that the Court has between leading and following national practice in the administration of justice. Whereas Article 6, like the US Constitution, should not be seen as a 'uniform code of criminal procedure federally imposed',[1252] there are areas in which corrective action may properly be taken in respect of trial proceedings in the interests of human rights.

[1251] See above, p 324.
[1252] Frankfurter, *Law and Politics*, 1939, pp 192–3.

7

ARTICLE 7: FREEDOM FROM RETROACTIVE CRIMINAL OFFENCES AND PUNISHMENT

Article 7

1. No one shall be held guilty of any criminal offence on account of any act or omission which did not constitute a criminal offence under national or international law at the time when it was committed. Nor shall a heavier penalty be imposed than the one that was applicable at the time the criminal offence was committed.

2. This article shall not prejudice the trial and punishment of any person for any act or omission which, at the time when it was committed, was criminal according to the general principles of law recognised by civilised nations.

Article 7 incorporates the principle of legality, by which, in the context of criminal law, a person should only be convicted and punished on a basis of law: *nullem crimen, nulla poena sine lege*.[1] The object and purpose of the guarantee in Article 7, 'which is an essential element of the rule of law', is 'to provide effective safeguards against arbitrary prosecution, conviction and punishment'.[2] The importance of the guarantee in Article 7(1) is recognized by the fact that it cannot be derogated from in time of war or public emergency.[3]

Given that Article 7 requires that national courts act on the basis of their national law and that they interpret and apply that law in accordance with Article 7, the Strasbourg Court may find itself reviewing the interpretation and application of national law by national courts. In accordance with the Court's general approach whereby it does not question the interpretation and application of national law by national courts,[4] this supervisory function is undertaken with caution,[5] with the Court only exceptionally finding the interpretation and application of national law by the national courts to be in breach of Article 7.[6]

---

[1] *Kafkaris v Cyprus* 2008-XX GC. On the principle of legality, see Hall, *General Principles of Criminal Law*, 2nd edn, 1960, pp 225 *et seq*. The principle is implicit in the 'rule of law' mentioned in the Convention preamble. On the principle as interpreted in Article 7, see Cremona, *Pallieri Studies*, Vol 2, 1978, p 194.

[2] *Streletz, Kessler and Krenz v Germany* 2001-II; 33 EHRR 751 para 50 GC.

[3] See Article 15(2), Convention.

[4] As to the *'quatrième instance'* doctrine, see above, p 14. For another context in which the Strasbourg authorities must also consider whether national law has been complied with, see Article 5: see above, p 121.

[5] *Streletz, Kessler and Krenz v Germany* 2001-II; 33 EHRR 751 GC.

[6] See eg, *Baskaya and Okcuoglu v Turkey* 1999-IV; 31 EHRR 292 GC and *Gabarri Moreno v Spain* hudoc (2003); 39 EHRR 885.

1. *EX POST FACTO* CRIMINAL OFFENCES

The wording of Article 7(1) is limited to cases in which a person is ultimately 'held guilty' of a criminal offence.[7] A prosecution that does not lead to a conviction, or has not yet done so, cannot raise an issue under Article 7—at least not by means of an individual application.[8] A state application under Article 33 may question the compatibility with Article 7 of a law *in abstracto*, so that even a prosecution is not required. Thus in *Ireland v UK*,[9] Ireland challenged the consistency of the Northern Ireland Act 1972 with Article 7, insofar as it could be read as making it an offence retroactively to fail to comply with an order issued by the security forces. The application was withdrawn when the UK Attorney-General gave an undertaking that the Act would not be applied retroactively.

Article 7 does not prevent the retroactive application of laws in respect of such ancillary matters concerning criminal proceedings as detention on remand, the refusal of legal aid or of leave to appeal, or the entry of a conviction on a person's record since they do not concern the characterization of the applicant's act or omission as an offence.[10] Similarly, a change in a statute of limitations rule to the detriment of an accused in pending proceedings is not a breach of Article 7, both for the above reason and because changes in procedural rules generally have immediate application in national law.[11] Likewise, an amendment to the rules of evidence to the detriment of the accused is not within Article 7.[12] Article 7, that is, applies only where a change in the substantive law has retroactive effect to the detriment of the accused.[13] What it does not do is guarantee that an accused has the benefit of any alteration to that law to his advantage.[14] Nor does Article 7 incorporate the principle *non bis in idem* (a person should not be tried twice for the same offence).[15] Since Article 7 applies only within the criminal justice system, decisions to deport or to extradite a person to another jurisdiction,[16] to order the preventive detention of a suspected terrorist,[17] or to detain a person as a vagrant[18] are also not controlled by it.[19] Similarly, Article 7(1) does not apply to the imposition of a regime of civilian service upon a conscientious objector to military service[20] or to judicial decisions in civil, ie non-criminal, law.[21]

---

[7] 'Guilty' has an autonomous Convention meaning: *X v Netherlands No 7512/76*, 6 DR 184 (1976).

[8] *X v UK No 6056/73*, 3 Digest 21 (1973) and *Lukanov v Bulgaria No 21915/93*, 80-A DR 108 (1995).

[9] *No 5310/71*, 15 YB 76 (1972).

[10] See eg, *X v FRG No 448/59*, 3 YB 254 (1960). Cf, Fawcett, p 202.

[11] *Coëme v Belgium* 2000-VII. The question whether a new prosecution following the removal of an immunity from prosecution could lead to an infringement of Article 7 was left open. See also *Walczak v Poland No 77395/01* hudoc (2002) DA (appeal hearing abolished).

[12] See *X v UK No 6683/74*, 3 DR 95 (1975).   [13] See *G v France* A 325-B (1995); 21 EHRR 288.

[14] *Le Petit v UK No 35574/97* hudoc (2000) DA. Cf *X v FRG No 7900/77*, 13 DR 70 (1978).

[15] *X v Austria No 7720/76*, 3 Digest 32 (1978).

[16] *Moustaquim v Belgium* A 193 (1991); 13 EHRR 802 and *X v Netherlands No 7512/76*, 6 DR 184 (1976). *Quaere*, however, whether extradition to face a real risk of conviction contrary to Article 7 might be a breach of that Article: see the *Soering* case, above, p 10.

[17] *Lawless v Ireland* (Merits) A 3 (1961); 1 EHRR 15.

[18] *De Wilde, Ooms and Versyp v Belgium* A 12 (1971); 1 EHRR 373 PC.

[19] In terms of Article 7(1), there is neither a conviction for a criminal offence nor a resulting 'penalty'.

[20] *Johansen v Norway No 10600/83*, 44 DR 155 (1985).

[21] *X v Belgium No 8988/80*, 24 DR 198 (1981). *Quaere* whether Article 7 might control a non-criminal court ruling (eg as to the presence of negligence) based upon an *ex post facto* law that would later be binding upon a criminal court when determining guilt.

Following *Engel v Netherlands*,[22] 'criminal' in Article 7(1) has an autonomous Convention meaning.[23] Hence a disciplinary offence that meets the requirements of the *Engel* case is a 'criminal' offence for the purposes of Article 7.[24] Likewise, offences that are classified as regulatory offences or are otherwise non-criminal offences in national law but are 'criminal' offences for the purposes of Article 6[25] may be regarded as 'criminal' for the purposes of Article 7 too.[26] As under Article 6, it is likely that an offence that is classified as a 'criminal' offence under the law of the state in which the person is found guilty is always to be regarded as such for the purposes of Article 7.

Article 7(1) refers to criminal offences that have a basis in 'law'. The term 'law' has the same autonomous meaning as it has elsewhere in the Convention, so that it includes, in terms of sources of law, judge-made law as well as legislation, whether primary or delegated.[27] It does not include 'state practice' that is inconsistent with a state's written or judge-made law and its international human rights obligations. This was ruled in *Streletz, Kessler and Krenz v Germany*.[28] There the three applicants had been convicted by a German court of offences of incitement to commit intentional homicide and sentenced to five to seven years' imprisonment under the criminal law of the German Democratic Republic (GDR), or East Germany, that applied in the GDR when they committed their offences (and which the courts of the new Germany continued to apply). The cases concerned the deaths of a large number of individuals who had been killed by GDR border guards by shooting or by mines as they tried to cross the border to West Germany at the time of the Berlin Wall. The applicants occupied senior positions in the GDR government and party apparatus that was responsible for orders to border guards to arrest or, if necessary, 'annihilate' border violators and to protect the border 'at all costs'. Whereas the applicants were tried under the GDR criminal law that existed when the deaths occurred, they argued that GDR 'state practice'—by way of the orders to border guards referred to above for which they shared responsibility—had superseded that law and justified their acts. The Court held that this 'state practice' was not 'law' for the purposes of Article 7 as it was contrary to both the fundamental right provisions of the GDR constitution and other GDR laws and the GDR's international human rights obligations. Accordingly, it did not replace the GDR criminal law existing at the time, which met the requirements of Article 7(1). The Court's judgment confirms that delegated legislation or administrative acts that are *ultra vires* in national law do not count as 'law' for the purposes of Article 7, whether to take away an otherwise valid legal basis for prosecution or to provide a basis for prosecution that otherwise does not exist. The case may also provide a basis for ruling that Article 7 is not complied with on the ground that a national 'law' which is valid within the national legal system is nonetheless contrary to the international human rights obligations of the state. In the companion case of *K-HW v Germany*,[29] no breach of Article 7 was also found where a young GDR border guard who shot and killed a border violator was convicted by a German court of intentional homicide. In this case, while acknowledging the great difficulties the border guard would have faced if he had

---

[22] A 22 (1976); 1 EHRR 647 PC. See above, pp 125–6.

[23] *Brown v UK No 38644/97* hudoc (1998) DA. The drafting history of 'criminal' in Article 7 supports a wide reading: see Fawcett, pp 200–1.

[24] Army disciplinary offences did not do so in *Celikates v Turkey No 45824/99* hudoc (2000) DA.

[25] See above, p 201.

[26] See *Harman v UK No 10038/82*, 38 DR 53 (1984); F Sett 46 DR 57 (1986) (whether civil contempt in English law 'criminal' under Article 7 left open).

[27] *Kafkaris v Greece* 2008 GC.

[28] 2001-II; 33 EHRR 751 GC. See also *Glässner v Germany No 46362/99* 2001-VII.

[29] 2001-II; 36 EHRR 1081GC paras 75–6.

not followed orders, the Court stated that the GDR constitution and criminal law under which he was later prosecuted were accessible to him and that 'even a private soldier could not show total, blind obedience to orders which flagrantly infringed not only the GDR's own legal principles but also internationally recognised human rights, in particular the right to life, which is the supreme value in the hierarchy of human rights'. In support of this approach, it may be argued that the soldier's difficulties should be taken into account in sentencing rather than in determining guilt.[30]

The law under which a person is convicted must derive its authority from the state's lawful constitution. This can be problematic where an offence is committed in the course of a struggle for power as a new state emerges from its predecessor. In *Kuolelis, Bartosevicius and Burokevicius v Lithuania*,[31] the democratically elected government of the re-established state of Lithuania had in March 1990 declared its independence from the USSR and enacted new constitutional legislation. After strong opposition from the USSR, during which the course of which it invaded Lithuania in January 1991, by September 1991 the new government achieved international recognition by other states, including the USSR. The applicants were leading member of the Communist Party of Lithuania opposed to independence who were convicted of criminal offences in connection with an attempted coup against the new government in January 1991. The offences were committed under laws enacted by the new government in November 1990 that applied prospectively to the applicant's conduct; the only question was whether they had legal force in Lithuania at the time. The Court held that by November 1990 the 'political will of the new Lithuanian Government was clearly established', that the applicants were convicted for offences under its laws that were 'sufficiently clear and foreseeable' and that the consequences of non-compliance were 'adequately predictable', both with legal advice and 'as a matter of common sense'.

As elsewhere in the Convention, the term 'law' also implies 'qualitative requirements, including those of accessibility and forseeability'.[32] As to forseeability, an individual must be able to know from the wording of the relevant provision and, if need be, with the courts' interpretation of it, what acts and omissions will make him criminally liable and what penalty will be imposed.[33]

As indicated, for Article 7(1) to be infringed, the act or omission on the basis of which a person is convicted must not constitute a criminal offence 'at the time when it is committed'. This covers the position in which the offence of which the accused is convicted is introduced with retroactive effect by legislation or by the courts, after the accused's act or omission. In the case of a continuing offence, where the accused's conduct that is now an offence occurred both before and after it became an offence, there will be a breach of Article 7 unless it is shown that the conviction (and penalty) is based solely upon the

---

[30] Cf, Article 8, Charter of the Nuremberg International Military Tribunal, 39 AJIL Supp 257 (1945). In the *K-HW* case, the sentence was one year ten months' imprisonment, suspended on probation.

[31] 2008 para 120.

[32] *Kakkaris v Cyprus* 2008-XX para 140 and *Korbely v Hungary* hudoc (2008) GC. This applies to offences and penalties: *ibid*. See also *Custers, Devaux and Turk v Denmark* 2007-XX. The requirements of accessibility and foreseeability overlap, with the former, which supposes, *inter alia*, that the 'law' is publicly available, see *G v France* A 325-B (1995); 21 EHRR 288, contributing to the latter.

[33] *Kafkaris v Cyprus, ibid.* As to the application of these qualitative requirements to case law, see the *CR* case, below. The applicant's technical knowledge and background is relevant to foreseeability: *X v Austria No 8141/78*, 16 DR 141 (1978) and *Chauvy v France No 64915/01* hudoc (2003) DA. The applicant may be expected to have recourse to a lawyer, as far as is reasoanable in the circumstances, to understand the law: *Cantoni v France* 1996-V GC and *Jorgic v Germany* hudoc (2007).

accused's later conduct.[34] Article 7 also applies to the situation where a criminal offence has been abrogated or has ceased to apply by reason of desuetude.[35] In both cases, a person is convicted of an offence that does not exist at the time that his act or omission occurs.

Article 7 also extends to the situation in which the scope of existing law is extended to acts or omissions that were previously not criminal, and lays down the principle that the 'criminal law must not be extensively construed to the accused's detriment'.[36] The application of the existing law may be extended to new conduct by the courts by way of interpretation where its meaning has previously been unclear or is given a changed meaning by the courts in the applicant's case. It will only be in exceptional cases that the Strasbourg Court will find a violation on either of these bases. As stated by the Court in *CR v UK*,[37] 'there will always be a need for elucidation of doubtful points and for adaptation to changed circumstances. Indeed...progressive development of the criminal law through judicial-lawmaking is a well entrenched and necessary part of legal tradition' in Convention states, so that Article 7 'cannot be read as outlawing the gradual clarification of the rules of criminal liability through judicial interpretation from case to case, provided that the resultant development is consistent with the essence of the offence and could reasonably be foreseen'. As to clarity of meaning, the Court has in several cases not found a breach of Article 7 despite some very generally worded or obscurely drafted laws. This has been either because the national courts have already given it more precise meaning in their case law,[38] or because they have given it a meaning when the point is ruled upon for the first time in the applicant's case that is both foreseeable and consistent with the essence of the offence.[39]

As to a changed interpretation of the law, in the *CR* case[40] the applicant was found guilty of attempting to rape his wife when he attempted to have sexual intercourse with her without her consent after she had left the matrimonial home. The applicant relied during his trial on the long established common law exception to rape whereby a husband could not be found guilty of raping his wife. The House of Lords held that this exception no longer applied, as it was inconsistent with the status of men and women in modern times and English law had been moving in the direction of its abolition. Applying its foreseeability/essence of the offence approach, the Strasbourg Court held unanimously that Article 7(1) had not been infringed. However, the Court's decision is open to criticism in respect of foreseeability. While the Court's argument that the exception was at variance with a 'civilised concept of marriage' and the 'fundamental objectives of the Convention', which concern 'human dignity and freedom',[41] was a very strong one, opportunities to change the law by legislation had not been taken by the time the applicant's offence was committed and, while some judicial erosion of the exception had been effected, the House of Lords decision can most easily be viewed as a direct reversal of the law that was not

---

[34] *Ecer and Zeyrek v Turkey* 2001-II; 35 EHRR 672; *Veeber (No 2) v Estonia* 2003-I; 39 EHRR 125; and *Puhk v Estonia* 2004-XX. A substituted conviction for another pre-existing offence is not a breach of Article 7: *Garner v UK No 38330/97* hudoc (1999) DA.

[35] *X v FRG No 1169/61*, 6 YB 520 at 588 (1963). Cf *X v Netherlands No 7721/76*, 11 DR 209 at 211 (1977).

[36] *Kafkaris v Cyprus* 2008 GC para 138 (a penalty case).

[37] A 335-C (1995); 21 EHRR 363 para 34.

[38] *Kokkinakis v Greece* A 260-A (1993); 17 EHRR 397; *Larissis v Greece* 1998-XX ; 27 EHRR 329 (198); *Baskaya and Okcuoglu v Turkey* 1999-IV; 31 EHRR 292 GC; *Schimanek v Austria No 32307/96* hudoc (2000) DA. See also *Handyside v UK No 5493/72*, 17 YB 228 at 290 (1974) and *Prasser v Austria No 10498/83*, 46 DR 81 (1986).

[39] *Jorgic v Germany* hudoc (2007) (interpretation of 'genocide' one of two predictable interpretations). See also *Custers, Devaux and Turk v Denmark* 2007-XX.

[40] See also the companion case *SW v UK* A 335-B (1995) (rape by a husband). See also *Kingston v UK No 27837/95* hudoc (1997) DA and *Laskey, Jaggard and Brown v UK No 21627/93* hudoc (1995) DA.

[41] *CR v UK* A335-C; (1995) 21 EHRR 363 para 42.

a foreseeable outcome of a process of gradual judicial development. Insofar as national courts develop their national law so as to present possible problems under Article 7, a simple remedy would be for any judicial alteration to the criminal law to the detriment of an accused to apply prospectively only.[42]

A conviction that has no basis in national law, or results from its retroactive application, will not be in breach of Article 7 if the conduct upon which the conviction is based is a crime under 'international law' at the time of its commission. This is particularly significant for a state if, and to the extent that, international law is not a part of its national law. The question then arises as to the meaning of crimes under 'international law'. In *Streletz, Kessler and Krenz v Germany*,[43] the Court held that it may include 'offences' under the international law of human rights. In that case, the guarantees of the right to life and freedom of movement in the International Covenant on Civil and Political Rights and the European Convention on Human Rights were infringed. Although these guarantees did not give rise to criminal responsibility on the part of individuals in international law, the GDR Criminal Code provided for individual criminal responsibility for those who violated the GDR's international obligations, so that, the Court considered, the applicant's acts constituted offences under the international law of human rights. Having reached this conclusion, the Court found it unnecessary to consider whether the applicants had committed crimes under international humanitarian law, notably crimes against humanity. The Court's ruling concerning violations of international human rights law is limited to the special case under the GDR constitution, and is not wholly convincing. As the Court acknowledged, international human rights law does not give rise to individual criminal responsibility. Such responsibility does exist under international humanitarian law—extending to genocide, war crimes, crimes against humanity, and aggression—and these have since been held to be crimes under international law for the purposes of Article 7.[44] As well as such crimes, it is likely that Article 7 refers to crimes in respect of which international law permits individuals to be prosecuted by states under their national criminal law on the basis solely of their custody of the alleged offender. Such offences include piracy in customary international law and, for the states parties to the relevant treaties, torture, enforced disappearance, drug trafficking, hijacking, the sabotage of aircraft, apartheid, attacks upon diplomats, and the taking of hostages.[45]

2. *EX POST FACTO* CRIMINAL PENALTIES

Article 7(1) also provides that there shall not be imposed a 'heavier penalty...than the one that was applicable at the time the criminal offence was committed'. Article 7(1) applies to any 'penalty', or sentence. The meaning of 'penalty' was examined in *Welch v UK*.[46] The Court indicated that it had an autonomous Convention meaning. The measure in question must be one that is imposed following conviction for a criminal offence. Other factors that may be taken into account are 'the nature and purpose of the measure in question; its characterisation under national law; the procedures involved in the making and implementation of the measure; and its severity'. In the *Welch* case, the applicant

---

[42] Cf, the prospective overruling doctrine of the US Supreme Court: see, eg, *Linkletter v Walker* 381 US 618 (1965).
[43] 2001-II; 33 EHRR 751 GC.
[44] See *Korbely v Hungary* and *Kononov v Latvia*, below.
[45] See Brownlie, *Principles of Public International Law*, 6th edn, 2003, p 303.
[46] A 307-A paras 27–35 (1995); 20 EHRR 247. Cf, *Jamil v France* A 317-B (1995); 21 EHRR 65.

was convicted of criminal offences involving drug trafficking. He was given a twenty-two-year prison sentence and a confiscation order was made under the Drug Trafficking Offences Act 1986. The order was for the payment of £59,000, in default of which he would receive a further two-year prison sentence. There was no doubt that the Act had been applied retroactively to an offence committed prior to it; the only question was whether the order made under it was a 'penalty' so that Article 7 applied. In deciding that it was, and that Article 7 had been infringed as a result, the Court noted that the order had been imposed following a conviction; that the measure had punitive as well as preventative and reparative aims;[47] and that there were indications of a regime of punishment in the fact that the amount of the order was related to the proceeds of drug dealing, not just the actual profits, and could be related to culpability; and that imprisonment might result in default of payment.

In contrast, a statutory requirement that a convicted sex offender register with the police is not a penalty.[48] This is because the purpose is not to punish but to reduce the level of re-offending, the requirement does not result from a judicial process, and the obligation to register is not severe. The removal from the jurisdiction of an illegal immigrant as an administrative measure is also not a 'penalty' in the sense of Article 7.[49] In another case, the Commission left open the question whether Article 7 applies where a convicted person is sent to a mental institution as mentally disordered.[50] It would seem that it should not apply, since the purpose of committing a person to a mental institution is not to punish. The Commission also left open the question whether the award of costs in criminal cases is a 'penalty'.[51]

Article 7 applies only to the 'penalty' imposed, not to the manner of its execution. Hence it does not prevent any retroactive alteration in the law or practice concerning the parole or conditional release of a prisoner to his or her detriment.[52] It may, however, apply to a retroactive change in the conditions of detention where the new conditions are 'essentially different' from those that would have applied previously.[53] The distinction between a penalty and the manner of its execution was was issue in *Kafkaris v Cyprus*.[54] In that case, the applicant was sentenced in 1989 to 'life imprisonment' for murder. At the time he committed the offence in 1987, under the prison regulations life imprisonment meant twenty years' imprisonment, with the possibility of remission earlier. However, his trial court, following another judicial decision in 1988, stated that life imprisonment meant imprisonment for the whole of an individual's life. Confusingly, upon entering prison the applicant was advised of a release date based upon the twenty years rule. The prison regulations were later judicially declared unconstitutional and repealed, and the applicant's life sentence became a sentence for his biological life, with no possibility of remission. The Strasbourg Court held that the change in the rule by which the applicant had lost the possibility of remission was not subject to Article 7, as it concerned the execution of a penalty, not the penalty itself, which remained life imprisonment. Nonetheless, the Court did find a breach of Article 7 for lack of forseeability. At the time of the commission of the offence,

---

[47] Contrast *M v Italy No 12386/86*, 70 DR 59 (1991) in which the confiscation of Mafia-owned property was preventive, punitive, and did not follow a conviction.

[48] *Adamson v UK No 42293/98* hudoc (1999) DA. Cf, *X v Austria No 9167/80*, 26 DR 248 (1981) (detention of recidivists to prevent crime, not punish, not a penalty).

[49] *Moustaquim v Belgium* A 193 (1991); 13 EHRR 802.

[50] *Dhoest v Belgium No 10448/83*, 55 DR 5 (1987).

[51] *X and Y v Austria Nos 5424/72 and 5425/72*, 43 CD 159 (1973).

[52] *Kafkaris v Greece* 2008-XX GC. See also *Hogben v UK No 11653/85*, 46 DR 231 (1986); *Grava v Italy* hudoc (2003); and *Saccoccia v Austria No 69917/01* hudoc (2007) DA.

[53] *X v Austria No 7720/76*, 3 Digest 32 (1978).   [54] *Kafkaris v Cyprus* 2008-XX GC para 150.

the relevant Cypriot law 'as a whole' was not formulated with 'sufficient precision as to enable the applicant to discern, even with appropriate advice, the scope of the penalty of life imprisonment'.

Much of what has been said earlier concerning *ex post facto* criminal offences applies to penalties also. As with such offences, an *ex post facto* 'penalty' is in breach of Article 7 where, as in the *Welch* case, a new penalty is applied to an offence committed before the penalty came into operation,[55] or where there is no legal basis for the penalty imposed,[56] or where an existing penalty is applied to the detriment of the convicted person in a way that is not reasonably foreseeable. Foreseeability was in issue in *Achour v France*.[57] In that case, the French law for the punishment of recidivists was amended so as to double in some cases the sentence that would otherwise be given to persons convicted for a second time of a serious offence. The applicant complained of a breach of Article 7 when the amended law was applied to his detriment to increase his sentence to twelve years' imprisonment for a second drugs offence committed after the amended law came into force, when his first offence had been committed before it had done so. The Court ruled that there was no breach of Article 7; the doubling of his sentence was foreseeable because he knew of, or could have discovered, before he committed the second offence, the consequences of doing so and the long established French judicial practice by which new laws on recidivism were applied with immediate effect.

The Court confirmed in the *Achour* case that a state is free to increase the penalties for an offence prospectively, without any issue arising under Article 7. Similarly the existence or harsh application of a tariff of possible penalties is not controlled by Article 7, unless it is applied retroactively.[58] Nor does Article 7 prevent a court from choosing to convict a person of an offence carrying a higher penalty instead of one carrying a lower one.[59] Generally, the nature and severity of a 'penalty' is a matter within a state's discretion; considerations of proportionality arise under Articles 2 and 3, not Article 7.

3. GENERAL PRINCIPLES OF LAW EXCEPTION

Article 7(2) provides that Article 7 'shall not prejudice the trial and punishment of any person for any act or omission which, at the time when it was committed, was criminal according to the general principles of law recognised by civilised nations'. The phrase 'general principles of law recognised by civilised nations' is taken word for word from Article 38, Statute of the International Court of Justice, in which it identifies a third formal source of public international law. The purpose of Article 38 is to provide that if there is no treaty binding upon the parties to a dispute and if no rule of customary international law based upon state practice applies, recourse may be had to 'general principles of law recognised by civilised nations', ie by the states members of the international community, to fill the gap in international law rules. In the context of the Statute of the International Court and, presumably, of Article 7 of the Convention, these are 'general principles of law' to be found in municipal legal systems. Interestingly, the text of Article 7 refers to 'nations' generally; it is not limited to the legal systems of the contracting parties to the

---

[55] *Ecer and Zeyrek v Turkey* 2001-III; 35 EHRR 672.

[56] See *Gabarri Moreno v Spain* hudoc (2003); 39 EHRR 885 (court applied the wrong sentencing rules, to the detriment of the accused: hence no legal basis for the sentence imposed).

[57] 2006-IV; 41 EHRR 751 GC.

[58] See the facts of *Grant v UK No 12002/86*, 55 DR 218 (1988) (lawful increase in sentence on appeal).

[59] *X v UK No 6679/74*, 3 Digest 31 (1975). Cf, *Gillies v UK No 14099/88* hudoc (1989).

Convention, to which the Strasbourg authorities primarily refer when looking for standards in the context of other articles which make no reference to national law.[60]

The *travaux préparatoires* indicate that Article 7(2) is intended 'to make it clear that Article 7 does not affect laws which, under the very exceptional circumstances at the end of the Second World War, were passed to punish war crimes, treason and collaboration with the enemy,[61] and has been held to apply to laws punishing crimes against humanity committed then also.[62] In *Kolk and Kislyiy v Estonia*,[63] Article 7(2) was extended to immediate post-war crimes that had a Second World War connection. The case was curious in that the Court held both that a crime against humanity contrary to international law had been committed (the 1949 deportation of civilians to the USSR), so that Article 7(1) applied, and that crimes against humanity fell within Article 7(2). Whereas it had been the Strasbourg practice to dispose of Second World War-related cases solely under Article 7(2), later in *Kononov v Latvia*,[64] the Court just applied Article 7(1). There the applicant was the commander of a Soviet 'Red Partisan' group that, as a reprisal, in 1944 killed Latvian villagers suspected of giving information to the German army, leading to the killing by the latter of the members of another such group. The applicant was convicted under a 1993 Latvian law for a war crime. The Court held that the conviction was not justified by the 'international law' limb of Article 7(1). It rejected the Latvian court's ruling that a war crime had been committed, as, in view of their conduct, the villagers were not 'civilians'. The Court ruled that it was not necessary to consider the case under Article 7(2), as Article 7(1) applied.[65]

In the most recent case under Article 7, in *Korbely v Hungary*[66] the applicant had been convicted of a crime against humanity by the Hungarian courts, for killing a 'non-combatant' during the 1956 uprising. Disagreeing with the national court's assessment of the facts—which turned upon what the victim intended when he drew a gun—the Grand Chamber held the conviction could not be justified under Article 7(1) as the victim was not a 'non-combatant', as required by international law. The Court did not apply Article 7(2), demonstrating its application to Second World War-related cases only. The case confirmed the Court's willingness to take issue with national courts. Whereas the Court may be at least as well qualified as a national court to interpret international (as opposed to national) law, the fourth instance doctrine may suggest a more cautious approach when it comes to findings of fact. *Korbely* and other recent cases also show the Court moving beyond human rights law into the field of international humanitarian law.

[60] See above, p 8.

[61] *X v Belgium No 268/57*, 1 YB 239 at 241 (1957). Translation in 3 Digest 34. Germany has made a reservation to Article 7(2) (text in 1 YB 40 (1955–58)) that in effect excludes the exception that Article 7(2) provides: see *X v FRG No 1063/61*, 3 Digest 36 (1962).

[62] *Touvier v France No 2940/95*, 88 DR-A 148 (1997) and *Papon v France (No 2) No 54210/00*, 2001-XII DA.

[63] *No 23052/4* hudoc (2004). See also *Penart v Estonia No 14685/04* hudoc (2004).

[64] Hudoc (2008). Unlike an ordinary criminal law prosecution, eg for murder, a prosecution under international humanitarian law is not statute barred.udoc (2008). nlike an ordinary criminal lawprosecution, eg for murder, a prosecution under international humanitarian law is not statute barreH

[65] But the Court did state that in any event the applicant's conduct was not covered by Article 7(2).

[66] Hudoc (2008) GC. It was also 'open to question', para 85, whether there was a crime against humanity, as the national courts had not considered whether the killing was more than an isolated incident.

8

ARTICLES 8–11: GENERAL CONSIDERATIONS

1. INTRODUCTION

There are common features to and connections between Articles 8–11 which justify considering them together.[1] Some of these are formal: Articles 8–11 are constructed in identical form, the first paragraph defining the protected rights, the second laying down the conditions upon which a state might legitimately interfere with the enjoyment of those rights. Others are substantive: Articles 9–11 protect 'freedoms', essentially liberties, against interference by the state with activities which an individual may or may not choose to engage in. However, the Articles are expressed in terms of 'rights' to the various freedoms, language which has enabled the Strasbourg authorities to interpret the protected rights beyond a mere guarantee of non-interference by the government. States have routinely, but unsuccessfully, argued that these are freedoms in the Hohfeldian sense of liberty, requiring only that the state not interfere with the exercise of the freedom by an individual.[2] Article 8 is unique in using the language 'right to respect' for various interests. It has sometimes been suggested that this formulation imposes a less onerous burden on the state but, again, the Strasbourg authorities have taken the opportunity to expand the obligations which flow from these words.[3] The substantive rights protected are both multiple and complex. Four rights are set out in Article 8, three in Article 9, two in Article 11. Certain of the rights are said to 'include' particular rights. For instance, the right to freedom of association in Article 11 includes the right to form and join trade unions. As the subsequent chapters show, it would not be misleading to say that, in general, the Court has extended the content of the protected rights in Articles 8–11, such as including an element of activity in public spaces in 'private life' and providing environmental protection as an aspect of the right to 'home'. This generous approach has, perhaps, been acceptable to states because of their powers to intervene with the enjoyment of human rights in the second paragraphs of these Articles, albeit powers subject to the supervision of the Court.

Further, as with other rights in the Convention, some of the rights in Articles 8–11 must be read in conjunction with those in other provisions. For instance, the right to respect for family life has, in some of its aspects, close relations with Article 12, on the right to marry and found a family, and with Article 5, Seventh Protocol, which protects the equality of spouses in private law. It may also overlap with the prohibition or inhuman of degrading treatment in Article 3. Finally, some of the language of Articles 8–11 is found elsewhere in

---

[1] For an account of how the Court approaches Article 8 questions, see Warbrick (1998) EHRLR 32. The analysis made there applies, *mutatis mutandis*, to the Court's approach to matters under each of the other Articles.

[2] See eg, government arguments in *Lingens v Austria* A 103 (1986); 8 EHRR 407 para 37 PC and *Plattform 'Arzte für das Leben' v Austria*, oral argument, 21 March 1988, Corr/Misc (88) 71, pp 15–17.

[3] See below, pp 381–96.

the Convention—notions of 'law' in Article 7 or 'lawfulness' in Article 5, the understanding of proportionality in Article 14, for instance—and approaches to interpretation are pervasive through the Convention provisions. There are, therefore, in some of what follows references to the Court's jurisprudence touching other articles of the Convention.

2. NEGATIVE AND POSITIVE OBLIGATIONS[4]

The classical conception of the fundamental right is that it imposes a duty on the state not to interfere with the enjoyment of the right. So the state must not torture anyone or, in the context of Articles 8–11, interfere, say, with a person's exercise of his freedom of expression by preventing the publication of his writing. Important though it is, this wholly negative view of a state's responsibility towards the enjoyment of civil liberties is inadequate to secure the effective exercise of the individual's freedoms. Thus freedom of expression, if it be restricted to requiring the state to tolerate the enunciation of certain opinions by an individual, will be of little practical consequence if the state is under no obligation to protect a speaker against a hostile group which wishes to prevent the dissemination of the message. The principle that the Convention protects the effective rather than the theoretical enjoyment of rights set out in *Golder v UK*[5] and *Airey v Ireland*[6] is of great importance here.

The Court has not determined any general theory of positive obligations and, accordingly, it will be necessary to consider the question in relation to each particular right.[7] However, it is worth noticing here what levels of obligation may be contained in each of the rights in Articles 8–11. In addition to the wholly negative obligation of non-interference already referred to, three other, inter-related, possibilities arise:

(i)   the obligation of the authorities to take steps to make sure that the enjoyment of the right is effective;[8]

(ii)   the obligation of the authorities to take steps to make sure that the enjoyment of the right is not interfered with by other private persons;[9] and

(iii) the obligation of the authorities to take steps to make sure that private persons take steps to ensure the effective enjoyment by other individuals of the right.

It should be borne in mind that Article 13 will apply to positive obligations, so that the enjoyment of any right will be protected by minimum procedural guarantees, although in some cases, more will be required of a state (eg where the positive obligation touches a 'civil right' in the Article 6(1) sense), in some cases less, where the state successfully

---

[4] On negative and positive obligations generally, see above, pp 18–21 and Mowbray, *The Development of Positive Obligations under the European Convention on Human Rights by the European Court of Human Rights*, 2004.

[5] A 18 para 28 (1975); 1 EHRR 524 PC.   [6] A 32 (1979); 2 EHRR 305 para 24.

[7] Eg, *VgT Verein gegen Tierfabriken v Switzerland* 2001-VI; 34 EHRR 159. In general, see Clapham, *Human Rights and Non-State Actors*, 2006, pp 357–8 and 387–418.

[8] See the *Golder* and *Airey* cases, *loc cit* at nn 4 and 5 above. This general obligation includes the obligation to have in place laws that grant individuals the legal status, rights, and privileges required to ensure, for example, that their family and private life is properly respected. See eg, the family law regime for children born out of wedlock required by the *Marckx* case, below, pp 392–3. The obligations in (ii) and (iii) above can also be subsumed within the general obligation in (i), but are usually and helpfully separated out.

[9] *X and Y v Netherlands* A 91 (1985); 8 EHRR 235 para 32 and *Von Hannover v Germany* 2004-VI; 43 EHRR 2. See Clapham, above, n 7.

shows that its powers of interference would be prejudiced by a strict procedural duty.[10] It is a characteristic of positive obligations that the duties they impose are seldom absolute. What is required of the state will vary according to the importance of the right and the resources required to be disbursed to meet any positive obligation. States have a 'margin of appreciation'[11] with respect to the identification of rights and many of the same factors and techniques are relevant here, just as they are to determining the compatibility of acts of interference with established rights.[12] It should be noted, though, that at this stage, the state and the individual stand in positions of equality—the process is to determine whether or not there is a right under the Convention. When it comes to interferences, the individual's right is already established and it for the state to show a 'pressing social need' to impose limitations on its enjoyment. While the Strasbourg authorities have interpreted some positive obligations strictly, notably some of the state's obligations under Article 6,[13] more generally, they have considered only whether the state has taken reasonable measures to safeguard the individual's enjoyment of his right.[14] Nor is the state's obligation uniform with respect to the three categories of positive obligation listed above which may arise in connection with a single right. Thus the Commission was cool towards suggestions that the rights to enjoy the various freedoms in Articles 9–11 involve much by way of positive obligations to supply the means for the exercise of those freedoms.[15] It is more likely that the state will be required to act to protect the exercise of the freedom against interference by other private groups.[16] In contrast, and hardly surprisingly, the obligation on the state to require one private person to provide facilities for another to exercise his right (see (iii) above) is little more than a suggestion in the practice of the Strasbourg authorities.[17]

The European Court deals with individual cases and the facts of each application loom large in the application of the law. In deciding whether or not an individual has the right he claims or whether state interference has justifiably interfered with an acknowledged right, both national decision-makers and the Court have some flexibility to pursue the just solution. Nonetheless, 'bright-line' determinations are sometimes necessary and, at the margins, it may be impossible to avoid hardship in any particular instance.[18] This is especially so where the Court detects a clash of human rights and its solution must prefer one claim to the other.[19]

---

[10] Eg, *Leander v Sweden* A 116 (1987); 9 EHRR 433 para 84.

[11] See below, pp 349–59.

[12] Eg, *Odièvre v France* 2003-III; 38 EHRR 871 paras 40–9 GC. Here, the Court looked at the 'European consensus', see below, pp 352–4, but 'although most of the Contracting States do not have legislation comparable to that of France' (para 47), concluded that France had not exceeded the margin of appreciation in denying an adopted child access to full information about its natural mother. Also *L and V v Austria* 2003-I paras 51–3, the Court held that the state had not 'offered convincing and weighty reasons' why the applicants did not have the right to the enjoyment of an Article 8 right (to sexual relations) without discrimination on the basis of sexual orientation.

[13] See eg, *Zimmermann and Steiner v Switzerland* A 66 (1983); 6 EHRR 17 para 29.

[14] See eg, *Plattform 'Ärzte für das Leben' v Austria* No 10126/82, 44 DR 65 (1985) and *Rees v UK* A 106 (1986); 9 EHRR 56 paras 38–45 PC.

[15] *X and Association Z v UK No 4515/70*, 38 CD 86 at 88–9 (1971).

[16] Eg, *Young, James and Webster v UK* A 44 (1981); 4 EHRR 38 paras 55–6 PC; and *Gustafsson v Sweden* 1996-II; 22 EHRR 409 GC.

[17] *X v UK No 4515/70*, 38 CD 86 at 88 (1971).

[18] Eg, *Pretty v UK* 2002-III; 35 EHRR 1 para 76 (blanket prohibition of assisted suicide not disproportionate interference with right to respect for private life).

[19] See especially *Evans v UK* hudoc (2007); 46 EHRR 728 GC.

3. LIMITATIONS

The conditions upon which a state may interfere with the enjoyment of a protected right are set out in elaborate terms in the second paragraphs of Articles 8–11. These paragraphs have a common structure but differ in detail.[20] Limitations are allowed if they are 'in accordance with the law' or 'prescribed by law' and are 'necessary in a democratic society' for the protection of one of the objectives set out in the second paragraph.[21] The Court's usual practice is to consider those elements separately and in the order 'law', 'objective', and 'necessity'.

I. 'IN ACCORDANCE WITH THE LAW'/'PRESCRIBED BY LAW'

On the face of it, there is a significant difference between the formulation in Article 8(2), 'in accordance with the law' and the words used in Articles 9(2)–11(2), 'prescribed by law'. The first could carry the meaning 'not unlawful' whereas the second could imply that some specific authorization is required. The difference might have been of importance for the United Kingdom with its tradition of recognizing the lawfulness of action (including action by the state) where such action is not specifically prohibited. However, the argument that there was a difference in meaning was abandoned by the British government in *Malone v UK*[22] and it was established by the Court in that case that both formulations are to be read in the same way.[23] They mean that, as a minimum, the defendant state must point to some specific legal rule or regime which authorizes the interfering act it seeks to justify.[24] The rule need not be a rule of domestic law but may be a rule of international law or Community law so long as it purports to authorize the interference.[25] It may consist of a whole legal regime regulating the area of activity, including rules made by a delegated rule-making authority[26] and rules from more than one legal order.[27] If a state does indicate the legal basis for its action, the Court is reluctant in the extreme to accede to arguments that the national law has not been properly interpreted or applied by the national courts.[28] [29]

Domestic legality is a necessary condition but it is not sufficient. The Court has said that the notion of 'law' is autonomous.[30] The Court has taken a wide view of what delegated

---

[20] Eg, Article 8(2) alone permits restrictions for 'economic well-being'.

[21] There are further special powers of limitation in the final sentences of Articles 10(1) and 11(2): see below pp 467–70 and 546–7.

[22] B 67 (1983–5) Com Rep paras 118–19; cf, oral argument, id, pp 201–3.

[23] A 82 (1984); 7 EHRR 14 para 66 PC. The French text of each is identical, '*prévues par la loi*'.

[24] *Silver v UK* A 61 (1983); 5 EHRR 347 para 86.

[25] *Groppera Radio AG v Switzerland* A 173 (1990); 12 EHRR 321 para 68 PC; Com Rep para 153. Note Judge Bernhardt dissenting on the importance of establishing that the legal effect of the international rule in the appropriate domestic legal order is to authorize the interference against the applicant.

[26] *Barthold v FRG* A 90 (1985); 7 EHRR 383 paras 45–6 (1985).

[27] *Groppera Radio AG v Switzerland* A 173 (1990); 12 EHRR 321 paras 65–8 PC.

[28] In *Malone v UK* A 82 (1984); 7 EHRR 14 para 69 PC, the Court preferred the judgment of the English High Court in *Malone v Commissioner of Police* [1979] 2 All ER 620 Ch D, to the government's account of the position in national law.

[29] *Bosphorus Airways v Ireland* 2005-VI; 42 EHRR 1 para 143 GC. But see *MM v Netherlands* hudoc (2003) para 45, where the domestic court was held to have misinterpreted 'interference by a public authority', so making a telephone-tap outside the authority of national law and *Foxley v UK* hudoc (2000); 31 EHRR 637 para 35, where the Court held that a national official had acted beyond her powers under domestic law and so an interference with the applicant's Article 8 right was 'not in accordance with the law'.

[30] *Sunday Times v UK* A 30 (1979); 2 EHRR 245 para 49 PC.

powers are capable of generating 'law'[31] in a Convention sense and has recognized that unwritten law, most importantly judge-made law, will satisfy its understanding of 'law'.[32] Reliance on the law of European Community[33] or international law[34] will be adequate, always assuming the rule in question otherwise satisfies the Convention notion of 'law'. The fact is that delegated rule-making finds its authority in actual endorsement by a legislative superior and some legal challenge on grounds of *ultra vires* is often available as a check on unlawful rule-making. The democratic basis of the modern common law is problematic.[35] Extracting the 'right' amount of legislative input into a rule is probably an unnecessary complication.

It is conceivable that the notion of 'law' here could include the element of propriety or absence of arbitrariness in terms of purpose which the Court has ascribed to it in other contexts,[36] but this is unlikely to be of consequence for it is hard to see how a manifestly arbitrary law could ever be 'necessary in a democratic society'. However, the Court has introduced the notion of arbitrariness in a different sense into its idea of 'law'. In *Sunday Times v UK*[37] the Court added two further criteria for a rule to be a 'law':

> Firstly, the law must be adequately accessible: the citizen must be able to have an indication that is adequate in the circumstances of the legal rules applicable to a given case. Secondly, a norm cannot be regarded as a 'law' unless it is formulated with sufficient precision to enable the citizen to regulate his conduct.

These are further guarantees against substantively arbitrary rules. Accessibility of course requires that the texts be available to an applicant[38] but it is accepted that understanding of the texts may require access to appropriate advice.[39] If texts or rules are relied on to establish the foreseeability of the law, for instance, to supplement the wide language of the primary, published rule, then they also must be available to the applicant. In *Silver v UK*,[40] the government conceded that some restrictions on prisoners' correspondence imposed on the basis of unpublished prison orders and instructions that supplemented the relevant delegated legislation could not be used to establish that interferences had been 'in accordance with law'. In *Autronic v Switzerland*,[41] the Court allowed that the horrendously complicated regime which regulated international broadcasting was sufficiently accessible to those whose activities as broadcasters were regulated by it, with

---

[31] *Barthold v FRG* A 90 (1985); 7 EHRR 383 para 46. A professional association's rules were 'law', being traditionally regarded as made by 'parliamentary delegation' and monitored by the state.

[32] *Sunday Times v UK* A 30 (1979); 2 EHRR 245 para 47 PC.

[33] *Bosphorus Airways*, above n 29, paras 143–8 (a case under Protocol 1, Article 1). The international law obligations of states may be relevant to the elaboration of states' duties under the Convention, eg, *Ignaccolo-Zenide v Romania* 2000-I; 31 EHRR 212 paras 95, 101–13 and *Iglesias Gil and AUI v Spain* 2003-V; 40 EHRR 55 paras 47–61, especially para 51, or the assessment of the legality of an interference with an individual's rights, eg, *Bianchi v Switzerland* hudoc (2006) (all referring to the Hague Convention on Civil Aspects of International Child Abduction).

[34] Eg, *Slivenko v Latvia* 2003-XI; 39 EHRR 490 paras 104–9 GC.

[35] See Simpson, in Simpson, ed, *Oxford Essays in Jurisprudence* (Second Series), 1973, pp 77–99.

[36] As to Article 5, see above, pp 121. See also *Council of Civil Service Unions v UK No 11603/85*, 50 DR 228 at 240–2 ('lawful' in Article 11(2)).

[37] A 30 (1979); 2 EHRR 245 para 49 PC. See also *Rekvenyi v Hungary* 1999-III paras 34–8 GC, indicating that imprecision in constitutional rules may be compensated for by more detailed regulation at the level of ordinary law.

[38] *Silver v UK* A 61 (1983); 5 EHRR 347 paras 87–8.

[39] *Sunday Times v UK* A 30 (1979); 2 EHRR 245 PC and *Markt intern Verlag v FRG* A 165 (1989); 12 EHRR 161 para 30 PC ('commercial operators and their advisers').

[40] A 61 (1983); 5 EHRR 347 paras 87–8 and 91.   [41] A 178 (1990); 12 EHRR 485 paras 55 and 59 PC.

proper advice. The same is true about the common law, the true purport of which is available only through the medium of legal advice.[42]

The meaning of 'sufficient precision' is more difficult to ascertain. Wholly general, unfettered discretion will not satisfy the Convention, no matter what the formal validity of the delegating rule, the more particularly if the exercise of the delegated powers may be secret. Good examples of this are the judgments of the Court in *Kruslin v France*[43] and *Huvig v France*.[44] The Court accepted that there was in French law a legal basis for secret telephone-tapping by the police to be found in Articles 81, 151, and 152 of the Code of Criminal Procedure and the case law interpreting them.[45] However, the Court was not satisfied with the 'quality' of the French law. In the *Kruslin* case,[46] the Court said:

> Tapping and other forms of interception of telephone conversations represent a serious interference with private life and must accordingly be based on a 'law' that is particularly precise. It is essential to have clear, detailed rules on the subject, especially as the technology available for use is continually becoming more sophisticated.

The government argued that subsequent case law and reasonable 'extrapolation' from the interpretation by the French courts of other, analogous provisions provided sufficient assurance against oppressive use of the interception powers, even in the absence of specific language in the Code of Criminal Procedure. The Court was not satisfied with this. Amongst other deficiencies, the law neither identified the persons whose telephones might be tapped nor imposed any limits of time during which the process could be carried out. Because the French law lacked the quality of 'law' in the Convention sense, the interference with the applicants' rights had not been in accordance with Article 8(2).[47] The test, the Court had said in *Silver v UK*,[48] was that where a law conferred a discretion, it must also indicate with sufficient clarity the limits of that discretion. In *NF v Italy*, the Court held that a national rule which provided for disciplinary measures against any judge 'who failed to fulfil his duties' did not make it foreseeable that membership of the freemasons was incompatible with the proper discharge of the judicial function and, accordingly, since action had been taken against the judge, there had been a breach of Article 11.[49]

Other factors may serve to relax the degree of precision which is required of a national law. In *Müller v Switzerland*,[50] the Court acknowledged that obscenity laws could not be framed with 'absolute precision', not least because of the need to keep the law in accord with the prevailing views of society. It has taken a similar position about laws protecting against restraint of trade.[51] Since the exercise of the state's 'margin of appreciation' will often involve the promulgation of various kinds of legal rules, the Court takes a generous view about what regulations a state may rely on. In *Leyla Sahin v Turkey*, the Court accepted that the phrase 'according to the law' could embrace both the constitution and the regulations of individual universities, as well as ordinary legislation—the

---

[42] The Court accepts that there may be a wide division of opinion about what the common law is without that resulting in inaccessibility of the law but that wholly new developments in the common law may not satisfy the test, see below p 347. Cf, also the similar problem under Article 7, above, p 335.

[43] A 176-A (1990); 12 EHRR 547.   [44] A 176-B (1990); 12 EHRR 528.

[45] *Kruslin* case, *loc cit* n 43, above, paras 15–22.   [46] Id, para 33.   [47] Id, para 36.

[48] A 61 (1983); 5 EHRR 347 para 80. See also *Leander v Sweden* A 116 (1987); 9 EHRR 433 paras 50–7 (1987).

[49] *NF v Italy* 2001-IX; 35 EHRR 106 para 31.

[50] A 133 (1988) para 29; 13 EHRR 212. Even here there must be some indication of what is comprehended by the law: it would not do to replicate Justice Stewart's famous dictum that, while he could not define obscenity, he knew it when he saw it!: *Jacobellis v Ohio* 378 US 184 (1964).

[51] *Barthold v FRG* A 90 (1985); 7 EHRR 383 para 47. See also *Markt intern Verlag v FRG* A 165; 12 EHRR 161 para 30 PC.

case concerned dress codes as a condition for admission.[52] The meaning of widely drawn legal texts and rules of common law may be worked out and developed by courts without affecting their quality as 'law'. Nonetheless, there is a limit to this process. In *Sunday Times v UK*,[53] the applicants argued that the House of Lords had introduced a novel principle into the English common law of contempt, which they could not have anticipated and, accordingly, could not have based their conduct upon. The Court rejected this claim and held:

> ...the applicants were able to foresee, to a degree that was reasonable in the circumstances, a risk that publication of the draft article might fall foul of the principle.

The line between the reasonably foreseeable and the wholly novel is not an easy one to draw. The difficulties of the foreseeability test can be illustrated by reference to *Open Door and Dublin Well Women Centre v Ireland*. Injunctions against the applicants had been issued by the national court forbidding them from circulating in Ireland information about the possibility of abortion outside Ireland. The injunctions had been issued to enforce a constitutional amendment which provided:

> The State acknowledges the right to life of the unborn and, with due regard to the equal right to life of the mother, guarantees in its laws to respect, and, as far as practicable, by its laws to defend and vindicate that right.

The applicants argued that the language of the amendment did not clearly reach their activities and that it was in any case unforeseeable that the courts would issue injunctions to prevent the commission of constitutional torts. A majority of the Commission took the view that the 'prescribed by law' requirement had been infringed because a lawyer could reasonably have concluded that no illegal act was being committed, particularly because there had been no previous attempts to take enforcement action since the passing of the amendment. It said that 'in such a vital area' the law requires 'particular precision'.[54] Although the Court conceded that these arguments were not without their cogency, it took the view that in the light of the very high threshold of protection given to the unborn in Irish law, it was foreseeable that the courts would use their powers against the applicants, a conclusion reinforced by legal advice given to one of the applicants to that effect.[55] An example of a national rule which was held to lack the substantive precision required by the Court for it to be 'law' was the power of an English magistrate to bind-over a defendant to be of good behaviour. The Court said law the vagueness of what was required of the applicants during the period for which they were bound over did not satisfy the requirement of providing foreseeability about what was expected of them.[56] Furthermore, the Court will not allow the nature of the objective to which the interference is directed to justify unfettered executive discretion under the guise of a widely framed law. In *Al-Nashif*, a case involving deportation on national security grounds, the Court said:

> It would be contrary to the rule of law for the legal discretion granted to the executive in areas affecting fundamental human rights to be expressed in terms of an unfettered

---

[52] 2005-XI; 44 EHRR 99 para 88 GC.

[53] A 30 (1979); 2 EHRR 245 para 52. See also *Observer and Guardian v UK* A 216 (1991); 14 EHRR 153 para 53 PC. Cf, *Kruslin v France*, at n 43, above.

[54] *Open Door and Dublin Well Woman Centre v Ireland* A 246 (1992); 15 EHRR 44 para 52 Com Rep.

[55] Id, Ct Jmt para 60.

[56] *Hashman and Harrup v UK* 1999-VIII; 30 EHRR 241 paras 36–42 GC. Cf, *Steel et al v UK* 1998-VII; 28 EHRR 603.

power. Consequently, the law must indicate the scope of any such discretion conferred on the competent authorities and the manner of its exercise with sufficient clarity, having regard to the legitimate aim of the measure in question, to give the individual adequate protection against arbitrary interference…Even where national security is at stake, the concept of lawfulness and the rule of law in a democratic society require that measures affecting fundamental human rights must be subject to some form of adversarial proceedings before an independent body competent to review the reasons for the decision and the relevant evidence, if need be with appropriate procedural limitations on the use of classified information…[57]

The Court has reaffirmed this case law in some detail in *Gorzelik et al v Poland*.[58] The principles apply outside security cases. A discretionary power, unconfined in its terms, even if formally subject to judicial scrutiny, will not pass the foreseeability test.[59]

II. LEGITIMATE AIMS

A defendant state must identify the objective(s) of its interference with an individual's protected right. It often identifies more than one. Applicants have frequently challenged the aims asserted by the state as being no more than rationalizations of limitations imposed for quite different and impermissible purposes.[60] However, the breadth of most of the grounds for interference is so wide—for example, 'the protection of public order', 'the interests of national security', 'the prevention of disorder or crime'[61]—that the state can usually make a plausible case that it did have a good reason for interfering with the right. The applicant's claim is thus essentially that the reason given is not the 'real' reason, an allegation tantamount to bad faith on the part of the government. Not surprisingly, the Strasbourg authorities have not been willing to accept such a claim easily but there have been cases where it has succeeded.[62] Identification of the aim will be of importance, because an interference which might be appropriate to one aim will not necessarily be appropriate to another. There have been cases where the Court has not pursued this matter as vigorously as it might.[63] States sometimes cite more than one aim as the purpose for which they limit the enjoyment of a right. If the Court is satisfied that the measures are necessary for the protection of one of these aims, it has no need to go on and consider the others pleaded by the state, the absence of a violation having already been established. But if the Court is not convinced that the restriction is justified for one of the claimed purposes, it should go on and see if it may be justified for another. In the *Open Door* case,[64] the

---

[57] *Al-Nashif v Bulgaria* hudoc (2002); 36 EHRR 655 paras 119–23; and see the detailed treatment, both in principle and on the particular facts in *Association for European Integration and Human Rights and Ekimdzhiev v Bulgaria* hudoc (2007) paras 74–94.

[58] 2004-I; 40 EHRR 76 paras 64–71 GC.   [59] *Ostrovar v Moldova* hudoc (2005) paras 94 and 105–8.

[60] Eg, *Campbell v UK* A 233 (1992); 15 EHRR 137 paras 39–41, where the applicant prisoner alleged that the real reason for opening letters to him from his lawyer was to discover their contents. The Court accepted the government's claim that the interference was 'for the prevention of disorder or crime'. In *Vereinigung Bilender Kunstler v Austria* hudoc (2007) para 31, the Court refused to accept the government's claim that an interference with the applicant's Article 10 right was for 'the protection of morals', rather than a politician's rights or interests.

[61] In *Groppera Radio AG v Switzerland* A 173 (1990); 12 EHRR 321 para 70 PC and *Autronic v Switzerland* A 178 (1990); 12 EHRR 485 para 59 PC, the Court accepted that prevention of disorder in the telecommunications regime was a legitimate aim within Article 10(2).

[62] *Moscow Branch of the Salvation Army v Russia* 2006-XI; 44 EHRR 912 para 97.

[63] *Barfod v Denmark* A 149 (1989); 13 EHRR 493 paras 30–6 and *Observer and Guardian v UK* A 216 (1991); 14 EHRR 153 paras 55–6, 69 PC.

[64] A 246 (1992); 15 EHRR 44 para 67 PC.

Court collapsed the alternative aims cited by the state—the protection of morals and the protection of the rights of others—into one enquiry: were the restrictions on the giving of advice about abortion necessary for the protection of morals? Although it found that the restrictions could properly be seen on the facts of the case as being for the protection of morals, it found a breach of Article 10 because they were disproportionate and hence not 'necessary'. Although this approach enabled the Court to avoid a difficult issue—was the unborn an 'other' whose rights the state could protect?—it may be doubted whether the Court did full justice to the government's arguments.

III. 'NECESSARY IN A DEMOCRATIC SOCIETY': THE MARGIN OF APPRECIATION[65]

It is not enough that a state has *some* reason for interfering with an individual's right under Articles 8(2)–11(2) for one of the appropriate aims. It must show that the interference is 'necessary in a democratic society', a phrase heavy with uncertainty. In *Handyside v UK*,[66] the Court explained the meaning of 'necessary' as follows:

> The Court notes...that, while the adjective 'necessary'...is not synonymous with 'indispensable', neither has it the flexibility of such expressions as 'admissible', 'ordinary', 'useful', 'reasonable' or 'desirable'.

Having thus excluded excessively strict or generous interpretations of the term 'necessary', the Court has since settled upon a requirement of proportionality. In *Olsson v Sweden*,[67] it stated:

> According to the Court's established case-law, the notion of necessity implies that an interference corresponds to a pressing social need and, in particular, that it is proportionate to the legitimate aim pursued.

In assessing whether an interference is 'proportionate to the legitimate aim' to which the government claims that it responds, the Court and Commission have relied on the principle of the 'margin of appreciation', which they concede to states when their institutions make the initial assessment of whether the interference is justified. In *Handyside v UK*[68] the Court stated:

> By reason of their direct and continuous contact with the vital forces of their countries, state authorities are in principle in a better position than the international judge to give an opinion on the...'necessity' of a 'restriction' or 'penalty'...it is for the national authorities to make the initial assessment of the reality of the pressing social need implied by the notion of 'necessity' in this context.
>
> Consequently, Article 10(2) leaves to the contracting states a margin of appreciation. This margin is given both to the domestic legislator ('prescribed by law') and to the bodies, judicial amongst others, that are called upon to interpret and apply the laws in force.
>
> Nevertheless, Article 10(2) does not give the contracting states an unlimited power of appreciation. The Court, which, with the Commission, is responsible for ensuring

---

[65] On the margin of appreciation doctrine, see Arai-Takahashi, *The Margin of Appreciation Doctrine and the Principle of Proportionality in the Jurisprudence of the ECHR*, 2002 (a thorough review of the case law, Article by Article). For a more critical evaluation, see Greer, *The European Convention on Human Rights: Achievements, Problems, Prospects*, 2006, Ch 5.

[66] A 24 (1976); 1 EHRR 737 para 48 PC.   [67] A 130 (1988); 11 EHRR 259 para 67 PC.

[68] A 24 (1976); 1 EHRR 737 paras 48–9 PC. Cf, *Sunday Times v UK* A 30 (1979); 2 EHRR 245 para 59 PC. Both of these are Article 10 cases; the Court's pronouncements apply to Articles 8–11 generally.

the observance of those states' engagements, is empowered to give the final ruling on whether a 'restriction' or 'penalty' is reconcilable with freedom of expression. The domestic margin of appreciation thus goes hand in hand with a European supervision. Such supervision concerns both the aim of the measure challenged and its 'necessity'; it covers not only the basic legislation but also the decision applying it, even one given by an independent court.

It is worth emphasizing that the 'margin of appreciation' is a power conceded to the state. It envisages that that power will be exercised in the first instance by organs of the states properly addressing the various elements of the Convention relevant to determining the content of a particular right and assessing the justification given for interfering with it. The function of the European Court is to see that the state has not exceeded its power of appreciation.[69] In principle, the doctrine of a 'margin of appreciation', which applies in other areas of the Convention too,[70] is not a doctrine of judicial deference to the national decision, for the Convention authorities may carry out their own fact-finding and do apply the Convention law for themselves. Yet they have declined the role of a fully-fledged appeal mechanism from the national decision. Instead, the Court has said that the role of the Convention in protecting human rights is 'subsidiary' to the roles of the national legal systems.[71] This allows for a diversity of systems for the protection of human rights and even for different conceptions of the rights themselves and acknowledges the superiority of the organs of a state in fact-finding and in the assessment of what the local circumstances demand by way of limitation of rights.[72] However, the danger that excessive respect for national decision-making will result in the swamping of the individual right by national determinations of the public interest is apparent.[73]

The question then is how the Convention organs are to preserve the quality of rights as worthy of special protection. As noted, the answer that the Court has given is that the idea of necessity implies that a state should demonstrate a 'pressing social need' that the right should be interfered with in the particular public interest identified by the state. In *Handyside v UK*,[74] the Court indicated that while the initial assessment was for the national authorities, it was its duty to review the national decision:

> in the light of the case as a whole [including the facts] and the arguments and evidence adduced by the applicant in the domestic legal system and then at the international level. The Court must decide, on the basis of the different data available to it, whether the reasons given by the national authorities to justify the actual measures of 'interference' they take are relevant and sufficient...

---

[69] See *Hirst v UK (No 2)* 2005-IX; 42 EHRR 849 GC (a case under Protocol 1, Article 3), where the Court noted that neither the UK Parliament (para 79) nor the UK courts (para 80) had carried out any balancing exercise between the prisoners' right to vote and the protection of any public interest. *Hirst (No 2)* was followed in *Dickson v UK* hudoc (2007); 46 EHRR 927 para 84 GC, finding a violation where the formulation of an executive policy (about access to artificial insemination for a prisoner and his wife) had not involved any serious balancing of the rights and competing interests, nor allowed for individuated decision-making where that could be done on a case-by-case basis.

[70] See above, pp 11–14.   [71] *Handyside v UK* A 24 (1976); 1 EHRR 737 para 48 PC.

[72] *Müller v Switzerland* A 133 (1988); 13 EHRR 212 para 35. There is a strong functional justification for the margin of appreciation as well. The Court could not, as a practical matter, take on the intensive review of all cases which might reach it—the margin of appreciation puts much of the fact-finding and the assessment of the factors within Articles 8(2)–11(2) in the hands of national decision-makers. For the argument that a distinction should be drawn between the substantive (identifying the protected rights) and the structural (determining the character of the judicial review to be exercised by the Court) uses of 'margin of appreciation', see Lestas, *A Theory of Interpretation of the European Convention on Human Rights*, 2007, pp 80–98.

[73] Mahoney, 19 HRLJ 1 (1998).   [74] A 24 (1976); 1 EHRR 737 para 50 PC.

This was in answer to the government's claim that the review function of the Court was restricted to examining whether the authorities had acted in good faith in assessing what the Convention allowed. Good faith, even the good faith of an independent decision-maker like a court, will not be sufficient of itself.[75]

Putting the burden on the government to demonstrate a pressing social need for the interference preserves the superior character of the protected rights. On the other hand, it introduces a new dilemma for the Court: how is it to make its decisions in a principled manner so that its judgments do not appear to the states as the substitute of one discretion for another? The language of the Convention is so broad that the text alone will seldom dictate solutions, though it should be noticed that there are minor differences in the way Articles 8(2)–10(2) are drafted which allows differences of approach to particular questions.[76] The Court has adopted a variety of principles to give some structure to its judgments in which it considers the exercise of the margin of appreciation by states. While they supplement the general language of the Convention, it is important not to ascribe to them too great a weight: they are not rules and must be applied as a whole to each case with which the Court is faced.[77]

a. The importance of the protected right

When a state claims to be interfering with a right 'to protect the rights of others', those rights may be other human rights under the ECHR. The Court has identified some human rights or some aspects of some human rights as being of more importance than others. For instance, in *Dudgeon v UK*,[78] which concerned the criminality of private, consensual, adult homosexual activity, the Court said:

> The present case concerns a most intimate aspect of private life. Accordingly, there must exist particularly serious reasons before interferences on the part of public authorities can be legitimate for the purposes of [Article 8(2)].

In *Lingens v Austria*,[79] the Court stressed the freedom of the press as a particularly significant aspect of the 'right to receive and impart information and ideas...'. In *Campbell v UK*,[80] the Court confirmed a line of authorities which determined that a prisoner's correspondence with his legal advisor was of such importance as to entitle it to greater protection against interference than his correspondence in general. Where a strong right is invoked by the applicant, there will be a demanding burden on the state to demonstrate the pressing social need for limiting his enjoyment of it. The Court has emphasized the importance of the right to respect for private life, including its social dimension, in the

---

[75] *Sunday Times v UK* A 30 (1979); 2 EHRR 245 para 59 PC.

[76] The language of Article 10(2) is more open-ended in ascribing powers to the state to interference with the protected right than the other provisions—Article 8(2) 'There shall be no interference...*except such as is*...', Article 9(2) 'Freedom to manifest one's religion...shall be subject *only* to such limitations...', Article 11(2) 'No restrictions shall be placed on the exercise of these rights *other than*...' (emphasis added).

[77] See Delmas-Marty, in Delmas-Marty, ed, *The European Convention for the Protection of Human Rights: International Protection Versus National Restrictions*, 1992, p 319. Macdonald, *European System*, Ch 6 at pp 123–4, states that 'the justification of the margin of appreciation is usually a pragmatic one', but argues that the maturing of the Convention system requires the Court to articulate 'the underlying reasons why a particular amount of deference is considered proper'.

[78] A 45 (1981); 4 EHRR 149 para 52 PC.

[79] A 103 (1986); 8 EHRR 407 para 42 PC and *Ekinci and Akalin v Turkey* hudoc (2007) ('terrorist' prisoners' correspondence with lawyers).

[80] A 233 (1992); 15 EHRR 137 paras 46–7.

light of developments of technologies which allow for the collection and storage of information about individuals.[81]

b. The character of 'democratic society'[82]

While an interference with a protected right must be 'necessary in a democratic society', the nature of democratic society may be a constraint on the justification of some forms of interference. Again in *Dudgeon v UK*,[83] the Court spoke of 'tolerance and broad-mindedness' as two of the 'hallmarks' of democratic society, characteristics which inclined against the justifiability of interferences to protect the intolerance and narrow-mindedness of others, however widely and strongly felt. The importance of political expression derives from its role in a properly functioning democracy.[84] In *Klass v FRG*,[85] the Court referred to the dangers of destroying democracy under the guise of trying to preserve it, so requiring the strictest supervision of the justification for interferences with rights which removed the normal protections of the law against abuses of power by the authorities. Freedom of association, particularly for trade unions and professional bodies, was likewise important to democratic societies to protect plural centres of power and influence,[86] though it has to be said that the Court has not given strong protection to the claims by trade unions to enjoy particular rights. These foundational features of the Court's conception of democratic society reinforce the special weight to be given to individual rights when assessing the legitimacy of an interference with a particular right. The Court has recently emphasized the significance of secularism as a condition for the tolerance which characterizes democratic societies[87] (though, at the same time its treatment of Article 9 rights to religious freedom within democratic societies has been quite favourable to those claiming such rights.)[88]

c. The European consensus

There might be little objection to the features isolated by the Court as characteristic of democratic society. However, that is in part because of their generality. If more precise guidance is to be obtained as to what is or is not necessary in a democratic society to interfere with protected rights, then the Court needs to look elsewhere for evidence one way or the other if it is not to be accused of simply substituting its judgment for the judgment of the state. One of the devices to which it has had recourse is to search for a 'European standard' among the national laws of the parties to the Convention.[89] It is an approach which requires some caution. Unless the case is particularly stark, the comparative investigation is likely to be complicated and will often be inconclusive.[90] Nonetheless, a European-wide standard of toleration may sometimes be established[91] and the burden

---

[81] *Von Hannover v Germany*, above n 9, para 70.

[82] See Jacot-Guillarmod, in *Democracy and Human Rights*, Thessaloniki Colloquy Proc, 1990, pp 43–66, especially pp 57–63.

[83] A 45 (1981); 4 EHRR 149 para 53 PC.   [84] *Barthold v FRG* A 90 (1985); 7 EHRR 383 para 58.

[85] A 28 (1978); 2 EHRR 214 para 42 PC.

[86] *Le Compte, Van Leuven, De Meyere v Belgium* A 43 (1981); 4 EHRR 1 para 65 PC.

[87] *Refah Partisi (The Welfare Party) v Turkey* 2003-II; 37 EHRR 1 GC and *Leyla Sahin v Turkey* 2005-XI; 44 EHRR 99 GC.

[88] See Ch 10.   [89] See Macdonald, *European System*, Ch 6 at p 103.

[90] Cf, the search for a European standard against the criminalization of adult homosexuality in *Dudgeon v UK* A 45 (1981); 4 EHRR 149 para 60 PC, and that for the age of consent to homosexual activities, *Zukrigl v Austria No 17279/90* hudoc (1992) DA.

[91] The finding in the *Dudgeon* case, *ibid*, was confirmed in *Norris v Ireland* A 142 (1988); 13 EHRR 186 para 46 PC.

on the state to justify its exceptional interference contrary to the consensus is increased.[92] This may be particularly useful where a developing consensus indicates a clear trend to isolate the state maintaining an interference, the unacceptability of which has gradually become recognized elsewhere. An example of this is *Marckx v Belgium*[93] where the Court found that the great majority of the Council of Europe states acknowledged the impermissibility of discrimination between the legitimate child and the illegitimate child in the law of affiliation. In the cases dealing with the criminalization of male homosexuality, the Court has reinforced its findings that such an interference with an individual's right to respect for his private life may not be justified by noting 'the marked changes' in the laws of national states.[94] In *Modinos v Cyprus*,[95] the government sought to justify its law which criminalized homosexual behaviour in proceedings before the Commission, which found against it on the basis of an established European consensus. The government did not argue justification before the Court.

The establishment of the existence of a European consensus is not an arithmetical exercise of simply adding up the number of states participating in the practice, a certain number being sufficient to establish the threshold. The Strasbourg authorities have been criticized for not developing a more scientific concept of what the consensus consists.[96] Sometimes, the Court is presented with evidence of a consensus but finds no need to rely on it. In *Lingens v Austria*,[97] the Court relied on the disproportionality of an interference rather than on the extensive comparative evidence of its incompatibility with a consensus, presented by an intervenor.[98] Demonstrating a consensus may not be sufficient to establish the unjustifiability of the interference. In *Handyside v UK*,[99] the applicant argued that the book which had been condemned in England had circulated freely in the majority of member states of the Council of Europe. So, he said, it could not be necessary in a democratic society to ban it. The conclusion of the Court that, nonetheless, banning it in part of England was not a breach of Article 10 is not explicated. Judge Mosler dissented on this point, indicating that since it had not been found necessary to prohibit the circulation throughout the whole of the UK, it could hardly be necessary to forbid it in only a part of England—at least not without much stronger justification than was provided.[100] It is, therefore, open to a state to argue that, notwithstanding an established European consensus against the interference, there are reasons particular to its democratic society which are sufficiently strong to justify limiting an individual's rights there.

Being able to rely on a consensus among the laws of the European states is especially valuable to the Court if it is confronted with a fundamental moral issue where a solution favouring one outcome over another will appear to the disappointed side to depend entirely on the premise from which the argument starts—abortion, euthanasia, recreational use of drugs, and homosexuality are among the questions of this kind. The Strasbourg authorities have shown themselves adept at avoiding taking them head-on. However, they cannot always be side-stepped. *Marckx v Belgium*, dealing with illegitimacy, and the

---

[92] In the *Norris* case, *ibid*, the Court said: 'Yet the government have adduced no evidence which would point to the existence of factors justifying the retention of impinged laws which are *additional to or are of greater weight* than those present in the aforementioned *Dudgeon* case'. (Emphasis added.)

[93] A 31 (1979); 2 EHRR 330 para 41 PC.   [94] See the *Dudgeon* and *Norris* cases, above n 91.

[95] A 259 (1993); 16 EHRR 485 para 45 Com Rep.

[96] See Helfer, 26 Corn ILJ 133 at 138–40 (1993). See also pp 8–10, above.

[97] A 103 (1986); 4 EHRR 149 paras 43–7 PC.

[98] Written comments submitted by INTERIGHTS on behalf of the International Press Institute, Corr (85) 114.

[99] A 24 (1976); 1 EHRR 737 paras 54–7 PC; also *Hirst (No 2)*, above, n 69, para 81.

[100] In *Dudgeon v UK* A 45 (1981); 4 EHRR 149 paras 56–61 PC, the majority of the Court did not accept the government's argument that different standards on so important an issue as the criminalization of homosexual activity might apply in Northern Ireland and England and Wales.

Dudgeon-Norris cases, concerning adult homosexual relations, are examples where the Court has been able to rely on the consensus. To the contrary, where there is no consensus, the Court is the more likely to defer to the choice made by the state, unless there is a textual basis on which the Court may rely. It rejected an application of a woman that the national requirement of consent of both partners for the use of frozen gametes in IVF be dispensed with when the woman became unable to have natural children because of medical treatment some time after the partners had separated. One reason for this, despite the strong interest of the woman in being able to proceed without the man's consent, was the absence of a 'uniform European approach'.[101] On the other hand, the Court relied on a textual basis to find for the compatibility of Ireland's law excluding divorce, even in the face of a European standard to the contrary.[102] For some time, the Court had refused to interfere with the UK's position that it was under no obligation to issue a revised, post-operative birth certificate to a transsexual in his/her new gender, finding that there was no European consensus in the various applicants' favour. It abandoned this stance in *Goodwin (Christine) v K*, in language suggesting that the 'consensus' which would be determinative could be sought on a wider basis than that which might (or might not) be found in Europe. It said:

> [It] attaches less importance to the lack of evidence of a common European approach to the resolution of the legal and practical problems posed, than to the clear and uncontested evidence of a continuing international trend in favour not only of increased social acceptance of transsexuals but of legal recognition of the new sexual identity of post-operative transsexuals.[103]

This conclusion is not without its difficulties. It is hard to see how a 'clear and uncontested' international trend would not have a European component to it and, in every case, the inquiry required of applicants and states will be a demanding one, especially on applicants seeking to establish the international standard. Even establishing a European consensus is a formidable proposition in a Convention system of now nearly fifty states, the traditions of which are more diverse than they were when the Court first seized on the idea of a European standard as an element in the interpretation of the Convention. It has been suggested that the Court is less sympathetic to interferences based on what it perceives to be laws and practices influenced by the communist pasts of states admitted since 1989.[104] It may be, then, that it is easier to disregard certain deviations from the European consensus on the same grounds.

d. The interest to be protected by the interference

The weight of the interest to be protected
The reason for some interferences with rights is to protect the enjoyment of other rights protected by the Convention. This is a possibility which occurs with increased frequency as the Court's understanding of the content of rights expands. Freedom of expression may be limited in favour of the right to a fair trial[105] or to take into account the right of others to exercise their freedom of religion.[106] In these cases, the interest which is sought to be protected is a strong one and usually an accommodation must be reached between

[101] *Evans v UK* hudoc (2007); 46 EHRR 728 paras 79, 90 GC.
[102] *Johnston v Ireland* A 112 (1986); 9 EHRR 203 paras 51–4 PC.
[103] *Goodwin (Christine) v UK* 2002-VI; 35 EHRR 447 para 75 GC.
[104] Sweeney, 21 Conn JIL 1 (2005).
[105] *Observer and Guardian Newspapers v UK* A 216 (1991); 14 EHRR 153 PC.
[106] *Otto-Preminger-Institut v Austria* A 295-A (1994); 19 EHRR 34 para 47.

the two competing human rights, when the initial assessment by the state of how that accommodation should be made will carry great weight. The problem is not a new one. It is a feature of disputes about rights to respect for family life, especially the resolution of conflicting claims between parents and children or between each parent about their children.[107] The judgment in *Von Hannover v Germany* may indicate a significant change of direction by the Court in cases involving conflicts of human rights (which, in one form or another, will always raise questions about the positive obligations of the state to at least one party).[108] The applicant claimed that her right to respect for private life had been violated because she had inadequate remedies against intrusive press photography when she was in public places, where the publishers of the photographs claimed to be acting in their right of freedom of expression. German law and the German courts had addressed the conflict between the two human rights, seeking an appropriate balance between them, which, on the facts of the applicant's complaint, denied her any protection.[109] The fact that the protection of a countervailing right is the object of the state's interference is relevant to the application of the general principle that limitation powers should be construed narrowly, but the state must take care not to give one of the rights total priority over the other.[110] Only if one of the rights is 'absolute' will it take complete priority over another right, subject to limitations, expressly or impliedly in the text.[111]

If even some interferences in the interest of protecting fundamental rights may not always be within the margin of appreciation, then it would follow that no other of the interests set out in the second paragraphs of Articles 8–11 are of overwhelming weight, for, if that were the case, the rights protected by the Convention would lose their fundamental status. Finally, it should be noted that it is not so much the denominated interest but the actual situation in which it is invoked which is important[112]—action for the prevention of crime may be directed against homicide or parking offences: the weight of each compared with the right sought to be limited is not the same.

The objectivity of the interest

In *Sunday Times v UK*,[113] the Court suggested that the greater the prospect of obtaining an objective understanding of the content of the interest sought to be protected, the narrower the state's margin to determine what interferences are necessary to protect it. The Court drew a contrast between the relative objectivity of 'maintaining the authority and impartiality of the judiciary' and the 'protection of morals'. The former, objectively ascertainable, left a narrower margin to the state than the latter which was subject to a wide notion of what 'morals' were and, therefore, what was necessary to protect them.

---

[107] Choudry and Fenwick, 25 OJLS 453 (2005).

[108] The case was not sent to the Grand Chamber by Germany, so it remains a matter of speculation whether the Grand Chamber would have endorsed this substantial revision of the way clashes of human rights should be resolved, given the consideration of this very question by the German Constitutional Court.

[109] *Von Hannover v Germany* 2004-VI; 43 EHRR 1 paras 40–1, 72.

[110] One of the weaknesses of the government's case in *Sunday Times v UK* A 30 (1979); 2 EHRR 245 para 65 PC, was that the House of Lords' judgment gave practically no weight to the applicants' right to freedom of expression against the interest sought to be protected, the administration of justice. Ironically, the only reference the European Court made to Article 6 was to narrow the margin of appreciation of the state: see para 59. See *Bowman v UK* 1998-I (state privileging right to fair elections to the practical exclusion of the exercise of certain forms of expression—violation).

[111] Eg, a state would have a duty, let alone a right, to interfere with a religious practice which constituted inhuman or degrading treatment.

[112] *Handyside v UK* A 24 (1976); 1 EHRR 737 para 50 PC.

[113] A 30 (1979); 2 EHRR 245 para 59 PC: 'The domestic law and practice of the contracting states reveal a fairly substantial measure of common ground in this area.'

The actual example chosen by the Court has been challenged[114] but the principle seems well established. It has been made to carry considerable weight in upholding limitations of individual rights. *Müller v Switzerland*[115] is an example. The Court held that the idea of 'morals' might be determined by the opinions within even a narrow locality, let alone from state to state. However, it has not gone so far as accepting states' claims that questions of morals are so subjective that the Court should simply defer to their conclusions. The Court's jurisprudence on the standard of objectivity is weak. It has easily found ways of avoiding its consequences if it deems it desirable to do so.[116] The Court shows no inclination to abandon reliance on the objectivity standard as an indication of the reach of the margin of appreciation with respect to different aims of interferences.[117] There are doubts though whether it adds anything to the calculations to be made about the necessity of interferences with protected rights.

The justiciability of the interest

In the *Greek* case,[118] the Commission rejected the argument that the assessment of the existence of an emergency within the terms of Article 15 was beyond its competence on grounds of non-justiciability. Given the difficulty and the sensitivity of the issue with which the Commission was faced, it is hard to see why, in principle, the assessment of whether there is evidence that any of the interests listed in Articles 8(2)–11(2) is in jeopardy is also not appropriate for the Strasbourg authorities. Even when action is taken 'in the interests of national security', they may insist that the state produce some evidence that there is a national security interest to be protected by the interference.[119] The mere assertion of a national security interest is not sufficient.[120]

There are, however, two kinds of fact-finding and assessment involved. The first relates to the facts of the particular case, for example, what was the content of a proscribed publication and could access to it plausibly threaten moral standards?[121] The second is what is sometimes called 'constitutional fact-finding', ie establishing the factual accuracy of general claims about the protected interest, for example, that the perpetual or long-term confidentiality of security information as a whole is necessary to protect the integrity of the security services and the efficacy of its operations.[122] The Court took a view favourable to the government on the question of evidence about the economic effects of limiting night flights to Heathrow in *Hatton*. It said that 'it was reasonable to assume' that flights through Heathrow made some contribution to the general economy, so that complaints

---

[114] *Weber v Switzerland* A 177 (1990), Swiss government, verbatim record, 23 January 1990, p 35.

[115] A 133 (1988); 13 EHRR 212 paras 35–6.

[116] In the homosexuality cases, above the Court struck down serious interferences with rights which it regarded as of high importance even though the states claimed to be acting to protect morals and brought evidence that the relevant prevailing moral climate was opposed to the toleration of private homosexual activity.

[117] *Otto-Preminger-Institut v Austria* A 295-A (1994); 19 EHRR 34 para 50.

[118] 12 YB (the *Greek* case) 1 at 72 (1969); CM Res DH (70) 1. See below pp 626–7.

[119] *Observer and Guardian v UK* A 216 (1991); 14 EHRR 153 para 69. In general, see Cameron, *National Security and the European Convention on Human Rights*, 2000.

[120] In *Observer and Guardian*, Judge Walsh, dissenting, para 4, suggested that the threat to national security was 'simply… an expression of opinion' and, therefore, inadequate to allow the state to rely on Article 10(2). See *Al-Nashif v Bulgaria* hudoc (2002); 36 EHRR 655, for rejection of the claim that matters of national security are wholly non-justiciable.

[121] See eg, *Müller v Switzerland* A 133 (1988); 13 EHRR 212 para 36, where the inclusion of a description of the painting in the judgment, para 16, was insisted upon by the government and the Court sustained the state's assessment of the need to punish the artist for the protection of morals for exhibiting the painting.

[122] *Observer and Guardian v UK* A 216 (1991); 14 EHRR 153 paras 66–70 PC. In *Lustig-Prean et al v UK* hudoc (1999); 29 EHRR 548, the Court dismissed scarcely evidenced claims by the UK that the recruitment of homosexuals into the armed services would adversely affect military efficiency.

that the restrictions on night flights had not gone far enough to satisfy the right to respect for private life of residents in the Heathrow neighbourhood could be justified as being for the protection of the economy.[123] *Hatton* has been strongly criticized as lacking a coherent allocation of the burdens of proof between applicants and government[124] but the Court put considerable weight on the procedures adopted by the UK to evaluate the competing rights and interests, which given their length and complexity, were probably enough to persuade the Court that it could not repeat the exercise at the international level. Some of the questions which arise in the context of constitutional fact-finding are more intractable than others. They are questions which may arise about *any* protected interest, for example, whether the circulation of sexually explicit material has an impact on conduct, such that restrictions may be placed upon it to prevent crime or protect others, or whether immigration of aliens permitted in the exercise of the right to respect for family life may be limited because of the impact of such immigrants on the labour market and, hence, in the 'interests of…the economic well-being of the country'. The Court has used the existence of a European consensus as evidence that a factual claim made by a state is unfounded. In *Unal Tekeli v Turkey*, the Court used the widely established practice in the party states of allowing women to retain their maiden names after marriage to rebut the state's claim that such a possibility threatened family stability.[125] In controversial matters, the Commission, especially, was willing to accept the claims of defendant governments based on only scant evidence and did not engage in extensive constitutional fact-finding of its own.[126] The margin of appreciation here operated substantially in favour of the state. The Commission departed from its original position in *Sutherland v UK*[127] and the Court has reaffirmed that legislation which differentiates against homosexuals on the basis of their asserted predatory characteristics lacks a factual foundation, striking a better balance between the applicant and the state.[128] The ascertainment of historical truth is a subset of constitutional fact. It has been an important element in cases involving 'Holocaust denial'[129] where the Court usually says that it will abstain 'from matters of purely historical fact'. However, its incidence is not restricted to this issue. Most recently, in *Zdanoka v Latvia*, the Court has said that such fact-finding is primarily for the national authorities. Its role is to 'satisfy itself that the national authorities based their decisions on an acceptable assessment of the relevant facts and did not reach arbitrary conclusions'.[130] Here, there does seem a wide margin of appreciation to the state.

The significance of the interference

While some interferences are of themselves more significant than others—a term of imprisonment rather than a fine, prior censorship rather than post-publication punishment—in other cases, the significance of the interference may be closely related to the particular facts. The forfeiture orders of the *Little Red School Book* in *Handyside v UK*[131] were of less significance to a publisher who could reproduce the publication elsewhere and modify it for publication in England than the forfeiture order of his paintings against the artist in

---

[123] 2003-VIII; 37 EHRR 611 para 132 GC.   [124] Greer, above n 65, pp 259–65.

[125] 2004-X; 42 EHRR 1185 paras 665–7.

[126] Eg, homosexual age of consent cases based on assertions of predatory promiscuity: *X v FRG No 5935/72*, 3 DR 46 at 55–6 (1975). In *X v UK No 7215/75*, 19 DR 66 at 75–8 (1978) CM Res DH (79) 5, the Commission considered the matter on the merits but deferred to the government's fact-finding.

[127] *No 25186/94* hudoc (1996) paras 59–60 DA.

[128] *L and V v Austria*, above n 12, paras 52–5.

[129] For instance, *Lehideux and Isorni v France* 1998-VIII; 30 EHRR 665 GC; and *Garaudy v France No 65831/01* hudoc (2003) DA.

[130] 2006-IV; 45 EHRR 478 para 96 GC.   [131] A 24 (1976); 1 EHRR 737 paras 19 and 22–3.

Müller v Switzerland.[132] The weight of the interference, then, must be assessed by considering its effects in the circumstances of the particular application, conceding though that some interferences will have a great impact, whatever the situation. In *Dudgeon v UK*[133] and the other homosexuality cases, the Court put some weight on the criminalization of the applicants' private activities as an indication of the excessiveness of the interference. In *Observer and Guardian v UK*,[134] while rejecting the argument that Article 10 implied a complete proscription against prior censorship, the Court acknowledged that such an interference with freedom of expression called for 'the most careful scrutiny', especially for news media 'for news is a perishable commodity'. In finding a violation of Article 10 with respect to the freedom of expression of a politician in Turkey, in *Incal* the Court took into account what it called the 'radical' nature of the consequences for the applicant— criminal punishments, including imprisonment, exclusion from the civil service and from participation in political and trade union activities.[135] In *Connors*, the Court pointed to the seriousness of the consequences of the exercise of a summary power of eviction against gypsies who had lived on a site for fourteen years, in the absence of suitable alternative locations to which they could move. It held that there was a violation of Article 8.[136]

e. The resolution of the conflict between the different factors

The general approach
It will be appreciated now that the inquiry into the exercise of a state's margin of appreciation may be complex, involving a variety of factors, not merely a simple balance between the rights of the individual and the interests of the state, however convenient it might be to express it in these terms. The explanation of how the Court resolves the various forces is complicated by a difference between its rhetoric and practice in some judgments. The basic principle remains that explicated in the *Handyside* case,[137] that the word 'necessary' means neither 'indispensable' at the strict end nor 'reasonable' at the lenient end, so far as the state is concerned. What is 'necessary' in a particular case will fall along a spectrum between those two extremes and it is better to understand the Court's approach as being a multifaceted one, rather than try to demarcate its decisions into groups of 'strict scrutiny'/'rational basis' or other categories, on the American constitutional model.[138] If, after treating all the appropriate factors considered already, the Court finds that the interference might conceivably have been 'necessary in a democratic society', it reaches the final resolution of forces by asking whether the restriction of the applicant's rights was 'proportionate' to the interest sought to be protected.[139]

Assessing proportionality[140]
Proportionality, it should be underlined, is the final factor the Strasbourg authorities take into account in determining whether an interference with a right is necessary. The practice of the Court has isolated various factors which are to be taken into account in determining the proportionality issue.

---

[132] A 133 (1988); 13 EHRR 212 para 17; see also *Vereinigung BildenderKünstler v Austria* hudoc (2007) para 37, holding that an injunction against the exhibition of a controversial illustration which was 'unlimited in time and space' was an element in holding the interference disproportionate.

[133] A 45 (1981); 4 EHRR 149 paras 49 and 60 PC.   [134] A 216 (1991); 14 EHRR 153 para 60 PC.

[135] *Incal v Turkey* 1998-IV; 29 EHRR 449 paras 30–1 GC.

[136] *Connors v UK* hudoc (2004); 40 EHRR 189 paras 85–95.

[137] A 24 (1976); 1 EHRR 737 para 48 PC.   [138] See Gunter, 86 Harv LR 1 (1972).

[139] *Sunday Times v UK* A 30 (1979); 2 EHRR 245 para 67 PC.

[140] On the principle of proportionality, see Eissen, *European System*, Ch 7. See also pp 10–11, above.

While the balance of factors in a close case may be difficult and, therefore, incline the Court to accept the balance struck by the state, manifest disproportionality will result in the Court finding that the measure of limitation is not necessary. An example of this may be seen in *Campbell v UK*[141] where the government claimed the right to open and inspect incoming mail to prisoners from the European Commission to guard against the possibility that the Commission's envelopes might have been forged. The Court took the view that the eventuality was far-fetched and held the interference with the prisoner's right of correspondence unnecessary. Another way in which a lack of proportionality may be demonstrated is where there is an alternative, less intrusive way of protecting the public interest. The *Campbell* case also provides an example of this. The Court rejected a blanket right of the authorities to open and read a prisoner's letters to his legal advisors where they suspected that the letters contained illicit enclosures. The Court conceded only that a narrower rule, allowing inspection only on reasonable suspicion, with guarantees to the prisoner against abuse, such as opening letters in his presence, would satisfy the test of necessity.[142] In *Marckx v Belgium*,[143] though in a slightly different context, the Court pointed out that where there were alternative ways in which social policies might be pursued, the state was not entitled to choose a way which violated an individual's rights.

Interference with an individual's rights is disproportionate where it is purposeless, that is, where the object cannot be achieved by the interference. It is not necessary to interfere with freedom of expression on grounds of protecting confidential information where the confidence has been lost because of its publication elsewhere.[144] The proportionality requirement is not satisfied where the government does not provide evidence to show that the claim of necessity was made out. In *Kokkinakis v Greece*,[145] the government claimed the right to interfere with the applicant's right to religion because he had been attempting to convert others by 'improper means'. The Court held that because no evidence was presented to show that what he had done fell within 'improper means', the interference was not necessary.

Questions of proportionality involve some element of balancing one factor against another but it is not a scientific process, despite the metaphor. The language is pervasive: the Court speaks of the 'fair balance' between the enjoyment of rights and the protection of other interests which runs through the Convention.[146] A state will be in a stronger position if the domestic institutions have themselves addressed the issue of proportionality of the interference with the applicant's right but, because of its ultimate responsibility, the Court will review, and may differ from, the results of even the most careful domestic scrutiny.[147]

4. CONCLUSION

Cases alleging violations of Articles 8–11 will raise a variety of questions to be disposed of for their determination. In general, the Court has adopted the practice of taking each

---

[141] A 233 (1992); 15 EHRR 137 para 62.   [142] Id, para 48.
[143] A 31 (1979); 2 EHRR 330 para 40 PC.
[144] *Weber v Switzerland* A 177 (1990); 12 EHRR 508 para 51 and *Observer and Guardian v UK* A 216 (1991); 14 EHRR 153 para 68 PC.
[145] A 260-A (1993); 17 EHRR 397 para 49.
[146] Eg, *Hatton v UK* 2003-VIII; 37 EHRR 611 para 122 GC.
[147] See eg, *Beldjoudi v France* A 234-A (1992); 14 EHRR 801.

item in an application successively, no matter how simple some of them may be. The stages are:

(i)   the identification of the right, including positive aspects of the right;

(ii)   the identification of the interference;

(iii) consideration of whether the interference is prescribed by law, including both the internal and external (Convention) understanding of 'law';

(iv) determining what objectives are sought to be protected by the interference; and

(v)   deciding whether the interference is 'necessary in a democratic society', ie whether the state gives, and gives evidence for, relevant and sufficient reasons for the interference and those reasons are proportionate to the limitation of the applicant's enjoyment of his right, in which connection the margin of appreciation is most important.

While the Court has often used the same language in its judgments to explain what each of these various stages involves, the precedential value of previous judgments must be assessed against the changing social, technical, and economic conditions as reflected in national laws and decisions. In carrying on its task, the Court is conscious of its 'subsidiary' role, recognizing the quasi-federal nature of the Convention regime. The states may adopt a variety of solutions to similar problems and all or several of them may be compatible with the Convention.[148] However hard the Court tries to establish clear rules of easy applicability, the reality is that it can often do no more than indicate the factors a decision-maker should take into account without being able to provide much guidance on the relative weight of each of them.[149] The result is that the processes of arguing and deciding cases brought under these articles is seldom simple and the outcome is difficult to anticipate.[150]

---

[148] Eg, *Buckley v UK* 1996-IV; 23 EHRR 101 para 75—'It is not for the Court to substitute its own view of what would be the best policy in the planning sphere or the most appropriate individual measure in planning cases.'

[149] Eg, *Üner v Netherlands* 2006-XII; 45 EHRR 421 paras 57–9 GC.

[150] Macdonald, *European System*, Ch 6 at pp 160–1.

9

ARTICLE 8: THE RIGHT TO RESPECT FOR PRIVATE AND FAMILY LIFE, HOME, AND CORRESPONDENCE

Article 8

1. Everyone has the right to respect for his private and family life, his home and his correspondence.

2. There shall be no interference by a public authority with the exercise of this right except such as in accordance with the law and is necessary in a democratic society in the interests of national security, public safety or the economic well-being of the country, for the prevention of disorder or crime, for the protection of health or morals, or for the protection of the rights and freedoms of others.

1. INTRODUCTION

Article 8 places on states the obligation to respect a wide range of personal interests. Those interests—'private and family life, home and correspondence'—embrace a variety of matters, some of which are connected with one another and some overlap. In its application of Article 8, the Court has taken a flexible approach to the definition of the individual interests protected, with the result that the provision continues to broaden in scope. Issues falling within the scope of Article 8 now include search and seizure, secret surveillance, immigration law, paternity and identity rights, child and family law, assisted reproduction, suicide, prisoners' rights, inheritance, tenants' rights, and environmental protection.

None of the four interests referred to in Article 8(1) is entirely self-explanatory in meaning. Each of them is 'autonomous', so the Court is not constrained by any national interpretation of them. Typically, the Court applies Article 8(1) to the individual facts of each case and has avoided laying down general understandings of what each item covers. In some cases, the Court has utilized the co-terminancy of them to avoid spelling out precisely which individual interest is at stake.[1] Nonetheless, a survey of the case law shows a generous approach to the definition of the personal interests protected, and the lack of precision in Article 8(1) has allowed the case law to develop in line with social and technical

---

[1] Eg, *Klass v FRG* A 28 (1978); 2 EHRR 214 para 41 PC and *Kopp v Switzerland* 1998-II; 27 EHRR 91 (telephone conversations a part of 'private life,' 'family life', and 'correspondence').

developments.[2] The disadvantage may be the absence of a theoretical conspectus, which makes an account of the jurisprudence inevitably descriptive and prediction about its likely progress hazardous. Because so many separate issues may be involved in a single application and the margin of appreciation intrudes into the determination of some of them, the outcome of any particular case may not tell us much beyond its own facts. Such generalizations as are advanced in what follows are made cautiously.

The terms of Article 8(2) make it clear that the state must refrain from arbitrary interference with everyone's private and family life, home, and correspondence. This obligation not to engage in 'arbitrary action' is an obligation of the classic negative kind, described by the Court as 'the essential object' of Article 8.[3] The Court has made it clear that there may 'in addition be positive obligations inherent in "effective" respect for family life [and the other Article 8(1) values].' The 'positive obligations inherent' in Article 8(1) include both those requiring the state to take steps to provide rights or privileges for individuals and those which require it to protect persons against the activities of other private individuals which prevent the effective enjoyment of their rights.[4] The source of these positive obligations is found in the language of Article 8(1). It protects the right 'to respect for' each of the interests, not the right to private life, etc. If the intention in choosing this formulation, reinforced by the reference in Article 8(2) to 'interferences by a public authority', was to suggest a rather narrow duty not to interfere with the rights in Article 8,[5] the Strasbourg authorities have taken a different view, using the wording 'respect for' as a basis for expanding the duties in Article 8(1).[6] The Court has not perceived the rights in Article 8(1) in wholly negative terms—the right 'to be left alone'. Instead it has acknowledged the part they play in the confident exercise of liberty and, what is more, has found that the states must ensure the effective enjoyment of liberty so understood. The private sphere embracing the interests recognized in Article 8(1) is better understood as the personal rather than the secret.[7] Accordingly, if it is to respect private life (*not* privacy with its rather narrower connotations of the secrecy of information or seclusion), the state must not merely desist from the revelation or surveillance of activities that the individual would rather keep from public view. It must also allow and even facilitate the establishment of open relationships between individuals which make liberty worth having.[8]

As well as overlaps between the interests protected by Article 8(1), the case law also highlights the connections between Article 8 and other articles of the Convention. Many Article 8 rights are 'civil rights' in the sense of Article 6 and decisions concerning them must be taken by a procedure which satisfies that Article.[9] Also, the effect of Article 8 may be to impose a duty on the state to take measures involving the limitation of another Convention right in order to secure the enjoyment of an Article 8 right. For example, measures necessary to protect a person's private life under Article 8 may involve placing

[2] See eg, *Rees v UK* A 106 (1986); 9 EHRR 56 para 47 PC and *Marckx v Belgium* A 31 (1979); 2 EHRR 330 para 40 PC.

[3] *Kroon v Netherlands* A 297-C (1994); 19 EHRR 263 para 31.   [4] See above, pp 18–21.

[5] For discussion of the preparatory work, see Velu, in Robertson, ed, *Privacy and Human Rights*, 1973, pp 12, 14–18.

[6] See Connelly, 35 ICLQ 567 at 570–5 (1986) and Cohen-Jonathan, *European System*, Ch 14 at pp 409–15.

[7] Louciades, 62 BYIL 176 (1991), especially pp 192–6.

[8] On the legal concept of privacy, see Fenwick, *Civil Liberties and Human Rights*, 4th edn, 2007, Part 3, which includes treatment of the Convention.

[9] Eg, *Golder v UK* A 18 (1975); 1 EHRR 524 PC (prisoner's correspondence with lawyer); *Airey v Ireland* A 32 (1979); 2 EHRR 305 (access to legal procedure for terminating obligations part of a family life); and *Olsson v Sweden (No 1)* A 130 (1988); 11 EHRR 259 PC (conditions of foster-care of children taken from natural parents).

limitations on the freedom of the press under Article 10.[10] The state could provide some remedy without exceeding its powers under Article 10(2), although a law of defamation too respectful of individual reputations at the expense of freedom of expression will involve a breach of Article 10.[11] Conversely, the state may be obliged under Article 8 to protect an individual's reputation where statements going beyond the limits of what is considered acceptable criticism under Article 10 are published.[12] In other cases, the Court has had to choose whether to examine a complaint about physical integrity under Article 3 (freedom from torture, inhuman and degrading treatment or punishment) or as part of 'private life' under Article 8, when both provisions are applicable.[13]

The doctrine of the margin of appreciation plays an important role in the development of Article 8 case law giving states a degree of discretion in sensitive areas where the Court is reluctant to interfere with decisions made by those who have direct contact with the parties involved, or where a different approach is justified by local conditions. While its willingness to keep the extent of the margin of appreciation enjoyed by states under review is apparent,[14] so too is its commitment to the development of procedural safeguards, which now forms a significant part of the Court's jurisprudence in areas like child protection.[15]

In most cases, the application of Article 8 requires a two-stage test. Stage one involves consideration of whether the complaint falls within the scope of Article 8(1) and stage two concerns an examination of whether the interference is consistent with the requirements of Article 8(2). With this in mind, the following issues may arise within the course of a single application under Article 8:

(i) Does the complaint fall within the scope of one of the protected interests (eg 'private life')?

(ii) Is there a positive obligation to 'respect' that interest?

Under Article 8(2):

(iii) Has there been an interference with the Article 8 right?

(iv) If so,
    (a) is it 'in accordance with the law',
    (b) does it pursue a legitimate aim, and
    (c) is it 'necessary in a democratic society'?

2. THE FOUR INTERESTS PROTECTED BY ARTICLE 8(1)

Because Article 8(1) protects four precise interests, it is necessary to determine first what is the content of each of these interests. It is up to the applicant to characterize the interest which he seeks to protect or advance in the terms of the Court's understanding of Article 8(1). A good example of this is *Gaskin v UK*,[16] where the applicant convinced the Court that his interest in obtaining access to information in the hands of a local authority about

---

[10] *Von Hannover v Germany* 2004-VI; 43 EHRR 1.　　[11] See above, pp 349–50.

[12] *Pfeifer v Austria* hudoc (2007) para 44.

[13] Eg, *LCB v UK* 1998-III; 27 EHRR 212 and *Z v UK* 2001-V; 34 EHRR 97 GC.

[14] *Goodwin (Christine) v UK* 2002-VI; 35 EHRR 447 GC.

[15] *W v UK* A 121 (1987); 10 EHRR 29 PC; *McMichael v UK* A 307-B (1995); 20 EHRR 205; *TP and KM v UK* 2001-V; 34 EHRR 42 GC.

[16] A 160 (1989); 12 EHRR 36 paras 36–7 PC.

his upbringing in public foster-care concerned his private and family life, and not some general interest in access to information, which would not be protected by Article 8.

I. PRIVATE LIFE

The case law concerning the meaning of private life has been distinguished neither by its clarity nor its discipline. There is no single formula to apply in determining whether the private life interest is invoked, other than to take each case on its individual merits. The Court, and formerly the Commission, has not always been careful to distinguish the ambit of private life from the content of the state's obligation to respect private life.[17] Nor have the questions whether a state has failed to respect private life in breach of Article 8(1) and whether an interference with a right is justified under Article 8(2) always been kept separate.[18]

Although the Court has established that private life is a broad concept, incapable of exhaustive definition,[19] it has, through its case law, provided some guidance as to the meaning and scope of private life for the purposes of Article 8. In *Niemietz v Germany*, the Court said:

> ...it would be too restrictive to limit the notion [of private life] to an 'inner circle' in which the individual may live his own personal life as he chooses and to exclude therefrom entirely the outside world not encompassed within that circle. Respect for private life must also comprise to a certain degree the right to establish and develop relationships with other human beings.[20]

Private life thus extends beyond the narrower confines of the Anglo-American idea of privacy, with its emphasis on the secrecy of personal information and seclusion.[21] Indeed, the Court has recognized that the guarantee afforded by Article 8 is primarily intended to ensure 'the development, without outside interference, of the personality of each individual in his relations with other human beings'.[22] In *McFeeley v UK*,[23] the Commission underlined the importance of relationships with others, concluding that private life applied to prisoners and required a degree of association for persons imprisoned. Freedom to associate with others is thus a further, social feature of private life and more recently the Court has referred to a 'zone of interaction of a person with others, even in a public context, which may fall within the scope of "private life"'.[24] In *Niemietz v Germany*,[25] the Court considered that some personal relations in business contexts might fall within 'private life', and this was confirmed in *Halford v UK*[26] where the Court considered that

---

[17] See the different approaches by the Commission and the Court in *Botta v Italy* 1998-I; 26 EHRR 241.

[18] For a particularly glaring example see *Bruggemann and Scheuten v FRG* No 6959/75, 10 DR 100 (1977) Com Rep; CM Res DH (78) 1. See Connelly, 35 ICLQ 567 at 586–8 (1986).

[19] *Costello-Roberts v UK* A 247-C (1993); 19 EHRR 112 para 6; *Peck v UK* 2003-I; 36 EHRR 719 para 57.

[20] A 251-B (1992); 16 EHRR 97 para 29. Cf, D'Oswald-Beck, 4 HRLJ 283 at 183–7 (1983) on earlier practice.

[21] *X v Iceland* No 6825/74, 5 DR 86 (1976).

[22] *Niemietz v Germany* A251-B (1992); 16 EHRR 97 para 29; *Botta v Italy*, 1998-I; 26 EHRR 241 para 32; and *Van Hannover v Germany* 2004-VI; 43 EHRR 1 para 50.

[23] No 8317/78, 20 DR 44 at 91 (1980). See also *Botta v Italy*, id, para 28 where the Commission rejected that the applicant's complaint regarding access to a public beach fell within the remit of private life. The Court disagreed.

[24] *PG and JH v UK* 2001-IX para 56; *Peck v UK* 2003-I; 36 EHRR 719 para 57.

[25] A 251-B (1992); 16 EHRR 97 para 29.

[26] 1997-III; 24 EHRR 523 paras 44–6. They also constituted 'correspondence'. See also *PG and JH v UK* 2001-IX para 57 (recording the applicants' voices when being charged by police and in their police cell). Here, the Court recognized the importance of the applicant's reasonable expectations of privacy as a 'significant although not necessarily conclusive, factor'.

measures to intercept the applicant's office phone calls concerned respect for her private life given the guarantees of privacy she had received. Although the Court has held that the monitoring of the actions of an individual in a public place by the use of photographic equipment does not, as such, give rise to an interference with the individual's private life, the recording, storage, or use of that data may do so.[27] In *Sidabras and Džiautas v Lithuania*[28] the Court held that a far-reaching ban on taking up private sector employment affects 'private life', and a series of cases against Italy found that the automatic entry of the applicant's name onto a bankruptcy register raised an issue of private life.[29]

In *X and Y v Netherlands*,[30] the Court established that 'private life' also covered 'the physical and moral integrity of the person', including, in that case, 'his or her sexual life'. This statement was relied on by the Commission in *Costello-Roberts v UK*[31] when assessing corporal punishment inflicted on a pupil at a private school by a master. The Court conceded that there might be circumstances where Article 8 provided protection in relation to school discipline but, accepting also the government's view that not every measure which adversely affected an individual's physical or moral integrity necessarily involved an interference with his right to respect for his private life, decided that the punishment complained of here 'did not entail adverse effects for his physical or moral integrity sufficient to bring it within the scope of the prohibition contained in Article 8'.[32]

While on occasion the Court has preferred to examine such cases under Article 3 of the Convention,[33] interference with physical integrity as part of the concept of private life is now well established in the case law.[34] The Court has also held that it is without doubt that 'sexual orientation and activity concern an intimate aspect of private life', although it has left open the question of whether all such activities fall within the scope of the provision.[35]

These widening categories of 'private life', combined with a lack of rigour in classifying cases in practice, make an account of 'private life' difficult. The best that can be done is to identify the categories of interests and activities that the Court has held to be within the ambit of 'private life'. These categories are not closed[36] and, doubtless, the cases could equally profitably be arranged under different heads.[37]

It must be said also that the Court's expansive approach to the scope of private life holds out a promise of protection of individual interests which ultimately is rarely conceded by the Strasbourg authorities. The margin of appreciation allowed to states to determine what is required by 'respect' and what interferences are 'necessary in a democratic society' means that there are substantial burdens for an individual in making out his case

---

[27] See *Herbecq and the Association 'Ligue des droits de l'homme' v Belgium* Nos 32200/96 and 32201/96, 92-B DR 92 (1988); *Rotaru v Romania*, 2000-V paras 43–4 GC; *Amann v Switzerland* 2000-II; 30 EHRR 843 paras 65–7 GC; and *Peck v UK* 2003-I; 36 EHRR 719.

[28] 2004-VIII; 42 EHRR 104 para 47.

[29] Eg, *Luordo v Italy* 2003-IX; 41 EHRR 547 and *Vitiello v Italy* hudoc (2006).

[30] A 91 (1985); 8 EHRR 235 para 22.   [31] A 247-C (1993); 19 EHRR 112 para 49 Com Rep.

[32] The Court considered the matter principally under Article 3. See also *X v Belgium* No 8707/79, 18 DR 255 (1979) (regulation in interests of public safety not generally affecting private life (seat-belts)).

[33] Eg, *LCB v UK* 1998-III; 27 EHRR 212; *Z v UK* 2001-V; 34 EHRR 97 GC.

[34] Eg, *Matter v Slovakia* hudoc (1999); 31 EHRR 783; *Glass v UK* 2004-II; 39 EHRR 341; *Storck v Germany* 2005-V; 43 EHRR 96; *Worwa v Poland* 2003-XI; 43 EHRR 758 (regarding forcible medical treatment).

[35] *Dudgeon v UK* A 45 (1981); 4 EHRR 149 para 52 PC (sexual orientation); *Laskey, Jaggard and Brown v UK* 1997-I; 24 EHRR 39 para 36 (sado-masochism).

[36] See Louciades, 62 BYIL 176 at 192 (1991) on the need to keep 'private life' in tune with moral and social developments.

[37] For general surveys, see Duffy, 3 YEL 191 (1983); D'Oswald-Beck, 4 HRLJ 283 (1983); Connelly, 35 ICLQ 567 (1986); Louciades, 62 BYIL 176 (1991); Cohen-Jonathan, *European System*, Ch 16; Ovey and White, 2006, Ch 11.

successfully in Strasbourg even if he is able to identify his interest as falling within 'private life'. In fact, it would appear that establishing the relevance of a private life interest under Article 8(1) is relatively straightforward, the greater challenge is proving that there has been a disproportionate interference with that interest.

a. Personal identity

The fundamental interest within the sphere of private life is the capacity of the individual to determine his identity. While some matters, like his mode of dress,[38] are left within the individual's power, others, like an individual's choice of name, are often regulated.[39] At stake here is not merely privacy with regard to one's identity, therefore, but an interest in having one's identity given official recognition. For example, in the many transsexual cases to come before the Strasbourg authorities it has been accepted that giving legal recognition to the transsexual's acquired gender raises a matter of private life which goes beyond the 'inner circle'.[40] Accordingly, private life embraces aspects of one's physical and social identity.[41]

An example of a case concerning 'private life' in the sense of personal identity from within the 'inner circle' is *Gaskin v UK*.[42] There the majority of the Court acknowledged the applicant's claim that the records of his upbringing in public foster-care were significant to him as part of what he was, as a substitute for the parental memory of children brought up within their own family. Defining the relationship between parent and child is also a matter of private life[43] and the Court has recognized that persons seeking to establish the identity of their ascendants have a vital interest, protected by the Convention, in receiving the information necessary to uncover the truth about an important aspect of their personal identity.[44] It is this connection between information regarding a person's identity and the formal development of one's personality that reinforces this issue as one of private life.[45]

b. Moral or physical integrity

While the Court initially showed some reluctance to consider interferences with the moral or physical integrity of an individual as an interference with his private life,[46] a body of case law has recognized the importance of physical and psychological integrity as part of 'private life'. These cases confirm that the imposition of medical treatment without consent, including unwanted medication and psychiatric evaluation, raises serious issues with the scope of private life, however slight the intervention.[47] *X and*

---

[38] On prison dress, see *McFeeley v UK No 8317/78*, 20 DR 44 at 91 (1980) and *Sutter v Switzerland No 8209/78*, 16 DR 166 (1979) (haircut).

[39] On first names, see *Burghartz v Switzerland* A 280-B (1994); 18 EHRR 101; *Stjerna v Finland* A 299-B (1994); 24 EHRR 195; *Guillot v France* 1996-V; and *Johannson v Finland* hudoc (2007) and on maiden names see *Ünal Tekeli v Turkey* 2004-X; 42 EHRR 1185. Note also *Konstandinis v Stadt Altensteigstandsamt* C-168/91, ECtJ [1993] 3 CMLR 401.

[40] *B v France* A 232-C (1992); 16 EHRR 1 para 62 PC. See also *Rees v UK* A 106 (1986); 9 EHRR 56 para 37 PC; *Sheffield and Horsham v UK* 1998-V; 27 EHRR 163 GC; *Goodwin (Christine) v UK* 2002-VI; 35 EHRR 447 GC.

[41] *Pretty v UK* 2002-III; 35 EHRR 1 para 61.   [42] A 160 (1989); 12 EHRR 36 paras 36–7 PC.

[43] Eg, *Rasmussen v Denmark* A 87 (1984); 7 EHRR 371 para 33; *Mikulic v Croatia* 2002-I; *Shofman v Russia* hudoc (2005); *Jaggi v Switzerland* 2006-X.

[44] Eg, *Jaggi v Switzerland* 2006-X para 38.   [45] *Mikulic v Croatia* 2002-I para 54.

[46] Eg, *Costello-Roberts v UK* A 247-C (1993); 19 EHRR 112 para 36. As noted above, it has frequently considered such complaints within the scope of Article 3, eg, *Jalloh v Germany* 2006-IX; 44 EHRR 667 GC.

[47] *X v Austria No 8278/78*, 18 DR 154 at 156 (1979) (blood test); *Peters v Netherlands No 21132/93*, 77-A DR 75 (1994) (urine test). More recently, see *Pretty v UK* 2002-III; 35 EHRR 1 (2002) concerning assisted suicide; *Glass*

Y v Netherlands,[48] which concerned the sexual assault upon a mentally handicapped young woman by a man, shows that an unwelcome physical attack by one individual is capable of infringing the private life of another. Private life thus encapsulates a sense of physical and psychological autonomy, breach of which may raise an issue of private life. In *Pretty v UK*,[49] concerning assisted suicide, the Court noted that, although case law has not established the right to self-determination as part of Article 8, the notion of personal autonomy is an important principle underlying the interpretation of its guarantees. The Court held that applicant's complaint that the law prevented her from exercising her choice to avoid what she considered would be an undignified and distressing end to her life raised an issue of private life.[50] The applicant claimed that the refusal of the DPP to give an undertaking in advance of the applicant's suicide that her husband would not be prosecuted for assisting her death was a blanket and disproportionate interference with respect for her private life, especially given her state as a competent adult who has made a fully informed and voluntary decision. The Court disagreed noting that the seriousness of the act for which immunity was claimed was such that the decision of the DPP to refuse the undertaking sought could not be said to be arbitrary or unreasonable.

In *Tysiac v Poland*,[51] the Court agreed that the applicant's complaint that abortion law excluded her from terminating her pregnancy despite the risk it posed to her health touched on her private life. Moreover in *Evans v UK*,[52] the Grand Chamber held that decisions whether or not to have children fell within the scope of private life. The Court has also established that an application for adoption falls within the ambit of private life notwithstanding that the right to adopt is not implicit in either private or family life elements of Article 8(1).[53] As a further dimension of physical integrity, the Court has found that environmental hazards such as noise, smells, and pollution raise *inter alia* issues of private life under Article 8(1).[54] The finding that severe environmental pollution can affect the physical well-being of a person and thus interfere with his private life has led to a clear widening in the scope of Article 8 to cover environmental human rights.

c. Private space

At the heart of the concept of private life is the notion of a private space into which no-one is entitled to enter. The environmental cases may be viewed from this perspective too insofar as the noise and smells generated by nearby factories, nightclubs, or airports not only involve physical harm but may also raise an aspect of the right to be left alone, to enjoy one's private space free from unwelcome interferences. Strasbourg case law on telephone-tapping has also proceeded on the assumption that secret surveillance infringes upon the private life of an individual although usually other aspects of Article 8(1) will

---

v UK 2004-II; 39 EHRR 341 concerning medical intervention in the face of parental opposition; and *Storck v Germany* 2005-V; 43 EHRR 96; concerning treatment in a psychiatric institution.

[48] A 91 (1985); 8 EHRR 235.   [49] 2002-III; 35 EHRR 1 paras 73–8.

[50] The Court went on to find no violation of Article 8.

[51] Hudoc (2007); 45 EHRR 947 para 106. Cf, *D v Ireland No 26499/02* hudoc (2006) DA, where the Court found that absence of abortion services did not constitute a violation of Article 8.

[52] *Evans v UK* hudoc (2007); 46 EHRR 728 para 71 GC.

[53] *Fretté v France* 2002-I; 38 EHRR 438 para 32 and *EB v France* hudoc (2008) para 41 GC. In *EB*, the Court found that the decision of the domestic authority refusing the single gay applicant eligibility to adopt constituted discrimination on the grounds of sexual orientation reading Article 8 together with Article 14. On Article 14 see further pp 577–615.

[54] Eg, *Lopez Ostra v Spain* A 303-C (1994); 20 EHRR 277; *Guerra v Italy* 1998-I; 26 EHRR 357; *Hatton v UK* 2003-VIII; 37 EHRR 611 GC.

be involved as well, such as 'home' or 'correspondence'.[55] At the same time, private space includes places such as hotel rooms or prison cells which are not 'home', and spying on the activities of an individual which could not be brought within the notion of 'correspondence' may interfere with a person's private life. The reason for this is that it is not enough just for the individual to be himself: he must be able to a substantial degree to keep to himself what he is and what he does, if he wishes to do so.[56]

The Court continues to define the extent to which Article 8 protects the individual's private space and it has established the concept of a zone of privacy to which everyone— even those who live their lives in the public eye—is entitled. The absence of a remedy in relation to the publication of information relating to private affairs may thus constitute a lack of respect for private life.[57] With respect to the publication of photographs, the Court has held that even a leading politician may be protected against the publication of his picture where it constitutes an intrusion upon his privacy, where his picture is distorted, or where it is accompanied by disparaging statements.[58] In *Von Hannover v Germany*[59] the Court acknowledged that, despite being very well known, there was no doubt that the publication by various magazines of photographs of the applicant in her daily life fell within the scope of her private life. For private persons, this zone of privacy also exists notwithstanding allegations of criminal wrongdoing or other notoriety.[60]

It is increasingly apparent that this zone of privacy relates to the person whose private life is at issue, and not the place where the interference occurs. In this regard, it may be justified to use the evidence acquired through telephone-tapping, or confidential medical records in legal proceedings but any publication or use of such data beyond this purpose will raise a clear issue of interference with private life.[61]

d. Collection and use of information

The collection of information by officials of the state about an individual without his consent will interfere with his right to respect for his private life. This is the case with an official census[62] and with fingerprinting and photography by the police.[63] The collection of medical data and the maintenance of medical records also fall within the sphere of private life.[64] In *Hilton v UK*,[65] the Commission said that a security check *per se* did not interfere with respect for private life, but that it might do so if it involved the collection of information about a person's private affairs.[66] It is more obviously so where

---

[55] *Klass v Germany* A 28 (1978); 2 EHRR 214 PC; *Malone v UK* A 82 (1984); 7 EHRR 14 PC; *Khan v UK* 2000-V; 31 EHRR 1016.

[56] This is the essence of the 'Anglo-Saxon' idea of privacy to which the Commission referred in *X v Iceland* No 6825/74, 5 DR 86 (1976).

[57] *Earl and Countess Spencer v UK* Nos 28851/95 and 28852/95, 92 DR 56 (1998).

[58] *Schussel v Austria* No 42409/98 hudoc (2002) DA.   [59] 2004-VI; 43 EHRR 1 para 53.

[60] See *Sciacca v Italy* 2005-I; 43 EHRR 400 (release of the applicant's photograph to the media by the police) and *Peck v UK* 2003-I; 36 EHRR 719 (closed circuit television footage of the applicant broadcast on television without his consent). Cf, *Friedl v Austria* A 305-B (1995) paras 48 and 51 Com Rep (F Sett).

[61] See *Z v Finland* 1997-I; 25 EHRR 371 (witness' HIV status disclosed during trial); *Craxi (No 2) v Italy* hudoc (2003); 38 EHRR 995 (the content of taped telephone conversations released into the public domain) and *Panteleyenko v Ukraine* hudoc (2006) (the applicant's psychiatric records read out at trial).

[62] *X v UK* No 9702/82, 30 DR 239 (1982).

[63] *Murray v UK* A 300-A (1994); 19 EHRR 191 paras 84, 85 GC and *McVeigh v UK* No 8022/77, 25 DR 15 at 49 (1981); CM Res DH (82) 1.

[64] *Chare née Jullien v France* No 14461/88, 71 DR 141 at 155 (1991).

[65] No 12015/86, 57 DR 108 at 117 (1988).   [66] See *Segerstedt-Wiberg v Sweden* 2006-VII; 44 EHRR 14.

the information is gained surreptitiously by telephone-tapping, reading a person's post or intercepting email.[67]

The obligation of the state to respect private life by safeguarding against the intrusive activities of its agents and officials extends also to similar operations by private persons, such as private detectives or newspaper reporters.[68] The precise content of the positive obligation involved here is subject to a wide margin of appreciation on the part of the state and, for the press at least, may involve consideration of other Convention rights, particularly freedom of expression. For example, in *White v Sweden*,[69] the Court found that the publication by the media of allegations of the applicant's criminal activities, even though he had not been convicted of a criminal offence, concerned his private life. However, it found that the domestic courts had struck a fair balance between the public interest in the information being published and the applicant's private life.

Collection and storage of personal information[70] raises an issue of private life under Article 8(1), which will need to be justified under Article 8(2). In *Rotaru v Romania* the Court established that 'both the storing by a public authority of information relating to an individual's private life and the use of it and the refusal to allow an opportunity for it to be refuted amount to interference with the right to respect for private life'.[71]

Even though the collection of information might be justified, this does not inevitably mean that its retention or use will be equally defensible. Thus, according to the Commission, fingerprints taken in the course of investigating crime should be destroyed when there are no longer suspicions about the defendant.[72] However, more recent developments, including the establishment of DNA databases, pose new challenges here. In *S and Marper v UK*, the applicants were charged with offences and had DNA samples collected as part of the police investigation. Their requests for these samples to be destroyed following the acquittal/dropping of their charges was refused and their appeals were rejected, *inter alia*, by the House of Lords. In December 2008, the Grand Chamber of the European Court of Human Rights upheld the applicants' claims that the retention of cellular samples, DNA profiles and fingerprints constituted an interference with their right to respect for their private lives.[73] The Court went on to conclude that the blanket and indiscriminate nature of the power to retain such samples in respect of those suspected but not convicted of an offence, as applied in the case of the present applicants, failed to strike a fair balance between the private life interests and the legitimate aim of the prevention of crime. According to the Court, the respondent state had overstepped any acceptable margin of appreciation in this regard and the retention at issue thus constituted a

---

[67] Eg, *PG and JH v UK* 2001-IX; *Doerga v Netherlands* hudoc (2004); 41 EHRR 45; *Keegan v UK* 2006-X; 44 EHRR 716.

[68] In *A v France* A 277-B (1993); 17 EHRR 462, the government argued there was no interference because there was no state involvement (but the Court found that the state was implicated). In *Winer v UK No 10871/84*, 48 DR 154 at 170 (1986), the Commission found that the absence of a right of privacy in English law did not show a failure to respect the applicant's right to private life insofar as it left him without a remedy against the publication of information he would rather have had kept secret in view of other remedies that existed: *quaere* whether the same would apply to the manner in which information was obtained, if that involved intrusion into the applicant's home. See further below p 376.

[69] Hudoc (2006); 46 EHRR 23.

[70] The complexity of data protection issues requires regulation of a more sophisticated kind than can be derived from the simple standards of the Convention. Other Council of Europe treaties include the Convention for the Protection of Individuals with regard to Automatic Processing of Personal Data, CETS No 108, and its Additional Protocol regarding Supervisory Authorities and Transborder Data Flows, CETS 181.

[71] 2000-V para 46 GC. See also *Kopp v Switzerland* 1998-II; 27 EHRR 91 para 53.

[72] *Friedl v Austria* A 305-B (1995); 21 EHRR 83 para 66 Com Rep, F Sett; *McVeigh O'Neill and Evans v UK No 8022/77*, 25 DR 15 at 49 (1980); *Williams v UK No 19404/92* hudoc (1992) DA (DNA samples).

[73] *S and Marper v UK* hudoc (2008) GC.

disproportionate interference with the applicants' right to respect for private life which could not be regarded as necessary in a democratic society.

Although certain information may properly be retained it does not necessarily follow that an individual will have an automatic right of access to it. The applicant in *Gaskin v UK*[74] was able to demonstrate that the specific importance of information to him created a positive obligation on the state to allow him to see it. However, the significance of the information to the individual is only a factor to be taken into consideration: establishing this is a necessary but not a sufficient condition of access. In *Leander v Sweden*,[75] the Court confirmed that the retention and use of information about an individual in connection with employment in national security sensitive jobs (which in the applicant's case resulted in his being denied employment) did not carry with it a positive obligation to allow the applicant to know the content of the files so that he might have the opportunity of refuting data that was damaging to him. So, an individual has no automatic right of access to information held about him although the refusal to advise him about the full extent of the information kept will raise an issue of private life.[76] In this regard, the Court has recognized the excessive burden this puts on the applicant who is set at a disadvantage in seeking to vindicate his right to respect for his private life.[77]

e. Sexual activities

Private life embraces not only individual, personal choices but choices about relationships with others. It is beyond doubt that sexual relations fall within the sphere of private life. In *Dudgeon v UK*,[78] concerning consensual homosexual relations between adult men in private, the Court described sexual life as being 'a most intimate aspect' of private life. The Commission in *Bruggeman and Scheuten v Germany*[79] had earlier acknowledged the importance of untroubled sexual relations as a part of private life. There, it was the right of a woman to an abortion in the event of an unwanted conception.[80] As will be seen, the Court has contributed to a process which has seen the toleration of private, adult, consensual, homosexual relationships become practically universal in the Convention states.[81] More recent challenges in this area have concerned discharge from the defence forces on the grounds of sexual orientation, which complaint raised clear issues of private life notwithstanding the employment context.[82]

Consideration of the reach of private life is by no means concluded. The same matter already raised under 'private space' above arises here also—does the reach of private life include the manifestation of sexual relationships in public places and can the state forbid the performance of acts of sexual intercourse, whether homosexual or heterosexual, in a public place? As to sexual activity in private places, in *Laskey, Jaggard and Brown v UK*,[83] which concerned the prosecution of three men for assault and wounding as a result of sado-masochistic sexual activity in private, the Court noted that not all sexual activity which takes place in private is consistent with Article 8. The Court appeared to be open to

[74] A 160 (1989); 12 EHRR 36 PC. See also *MG v UK* hudoc (2002).

[75] A 116 (1987); 9 EHRR 433. See also *N v UK No 12327/86*, 58 DR 85 (1980).

[76] See *Segerstedt-Wiberg v Sweden* 2006-VII; 44 EHRR 14 para 99.

[77] *Turek v Slovakia* 2006-II paras 116–17. This resulted in a violation in this case.

[78] A 45 (1981); 4 EHRR 149 para 52 PC.   [79] 5 DR 103 (1981); 3 EHRR 244.

[80] See also *Tysiac v Poland* hudoc (2007); 45 EHRR 942 and *D v Ireland No 26499/02* hudoc (2006) DA.

[81] In addition to the *Dudgeon* case, see *Norris v Ireland* A 142 (1988); 13 EHRR 186 PC; *Modinos v Cyprus* A 259 (1993); 16 EHRR 485; and *L and V v Austria* 2003-I. See generally, Van Dijk, in Waaldijk and Clapham, eds, *Homosexuality: a European Community Issue*, 1993, p 184 at pp 185–93 and Helfer, 32 VJIL 157 (1991).

[82] *Smith and Grady v UK* 1999-VI; 29 EHRR 493; *Perkins and R v UK* hudoc (2002); and *Beck, Copp and Bazeley v UK* hudoc (2002).

[83] 1997-I; 24 EHRR 39 para 36.

the possibility that respect for private life was not engaged given the nature of the activity involved, which included the filming and circulation of videotapes of the group's sexual activities. However, this issue was not considered because there was no dispute between the parties on this issue. This issue was raised by the government in *ADT v UK*,[84] where it argued that the prosecution of the applicant for gross indecency did not constitute an interference with his private life given the number of people involved in the sexual activities and the fact that they were recorded on video tape. Although the Court did not rule out that in some circumstances sexual activities in private may justify state interference, it found no evidence that this was the case here.[85]

It could be said that the limit of Article 8's protection with respect to sexual activity, homosexual and heterosexual, has yet to be really tested although the fact that violations resulted in both of the above cases suggests a narrowing of the margin of appreciation in this area. The equality dimension is also open as a basis for further challenge, including discrimination in the ages of consent for heterosexual and homosexual activity and between genders.

f. Social life; the enjoyment of personal relationships

While sexual activities may be the central element in the notion of personal relationships as part of private life, they do not exhaust it. The Court, and formerly the Commission, has accepted a view of private life which encompasses the possibility of the effective enjoyment of a social life being an aspect of 'private life'. In many of the cases involving the deportation or exclusion from a Convention state of those who have lived there for long periods of time, the strength of their ties in and with that country is a factor taken into account.[86] In *Slivenko et al v Latvia*, the Grand Chamber recognized these ties as an intrinsic part of private life. In finding that the removal of the applicants constituted an interference with Article 8, the Court noted that the family had been removed from the country where 'they had developed . . . the network of personal, social and economic relations that make up the private life of every human being'.[87] In light of the Court's approach to 'family life' in immigration cases, which limits protection to an inner circle or the 'core family' the importance of interpreting 'private life' to include links with community and society in general is clear.[88] Notwithstanding that this indicates a different approach as between immigration and non-immigration cases, it is important that 'private life' may usefully cover those relationships which are not proximate enough to fall within the scope of 'family life' and that the concept encapsulates a sphere of social activity important to the person separate from family life.

II. FAMILY LIFE

The elaboration of the idea of 'family life' is one of the best examples of the way the Commission and Court have interpreted the Convention to take account of social changes.[89] Family life is now understood as extending beyond formal relationships and

---

[84] 2000-IX; 31 EHRR 803 para 21.   [85] Id, para 37.

[86] Eg, *Boughanemi v France* 1996-II; 22 EHRR 228 (no violation); *El Boujaidi v France* 1997-VI; 30 EHRR 223 (no violation); *Baghli v France* 1999-VIII; 33 EHRR 799 (no violation); and *Boultif v Switzerland* 2001-IX; 33 EHRR 1179 (violation). See also *Üner v Netherlands* 2006-XII; 45 EHRR 421 GC (no violation).

[87] 2003-XI; 39 EHRR 490 para 96 GC.   [88] See Thym, 57 ICLQ 87 (2008) at p 91.

[89] In contrast with the Court's jurisprudence, the *travaux* reveal an emphasis on the *father's* right to family life: see Opsahl, in Robertson, ed, *Privacy and Human Rights*, 1973, p 182 at 183–8. See now Seventh Protocol, Article 5, below, p 754. See also Stalford (2002) IJLP&F 410. For the right to marry, see Article 12, below, pp 549–56.

the family based on marriage[90] and in some circumstances it can include potential or planned relationships[91] as well as those whose ties are more social than biological in nature.[92] The Court has taken into account increasingly the substance and reality of relationships, acknowledging developments in social practices and the law in European states. Scientific progress in assisted human reproduction has meant that the Court, and formerly the Commission, has been confronted with new challenges.[93] Although some of the problems thrown up by the possibilities of technology will be less tractable than those faced already, it is likely that the same general approach will be followed, ie the existence of family life will be determined on the facts of each case, looking at the substance of the relationship and the reality for the parties involved.

It should be noticed at the outset that the obligation on the state is to respect family life: it does not allow persons to claim a right to establish family life, eg by marrying or having the opportunity to have children by whatever means,[94] nor a general right to establish or enjoy family life in a particular jurisdiction.[95] That is not to say that issues concerning procreation, such as the availability of artificial insemination, fall outside the scope of private and family life.[96] Moreover, the right to respect for one's family life may involve the recognition by the state of the reality of family life already established. There is no right to formal termination of family life, in particular no right to divorce,[97] though the effective enjoyment of family life may require that the state establish procedures which may result in the termination of some obligations of family life in certain circumstances.[98]

While the Convention understanding of family life is not restricted to formal relationships, such arrangements represent the typical situation which will fall within Article 8. Despite the rise in *de facto* unions and the growth in the number of children born outside marriage, most marriages are celebrated according to the formalities of the law and most children are born into such arrangements. It is usually the case that formal marriages are accompanied by enough of substance for them to be regarded as constituting family life but a marriage subsisting in form only, for example, a sham marriage entered into for the purposes only of avoiding immigration controls or obtaining nationality, might fall outside Article 8 altogether.[99] Children born to married parents are also *ipso jure* part of that relationship and 'hence, from the moment of the child's birth and by the very fact of it, there exists between him and his parents a bond amounting to "family life"'.[100] Where

[90] *Johnston v Ireland* A 112 (1986); 9 EHRR 203 PC and *Marckx v Belgium* A 31 (1979); 2 EHRR 330 PC.

[91] *Keegan v Ireland* A 290 (1994); 18 EHRR 342 and *Kearns v France* hudoc (2008).

[92] *X, Y and Z v UK* 1997-II; 24 EHRR 143 GC.

[93] *G v Netherlands No 16944/90*, 16 EHRR CD 38 (1993) (refusal of access rights to biological father of child born by artificial insemination) (inadmissible). *X, Y and Z v UK, ibid* (failure to register the transsexual parent as the father of a child born by artificial insemination by donor).

[94] See Article 12. The Court has confirmed that Article 8 does not involve a right to adopt a child. *Fretté v France* 2002-I; 38 EHRR 438 para 29; *Pini v Romania* 2004-V; 40 EHRR 312 para 140.

[95] See below, pp 392–6 and Fourth Protocol, Article 3(2).

[96] See *Evans v UK* hudoc (2007); 46 EHRR 728 GC and *Dickson v UK* hudoc (2007); 46 EHRR 927 GC.

[97] *Johnston v Ireland* A 112 (1986); 9 EHRR 203 paras 51–8 PC, where, unusually in the interpretation of Article 8, the Court set little store by social developments.

[98] *Airey v Ireland* A 32 (1979); 2 EHRR 305 para 33. The remedy here was judicial separation to relieve the wife of her duty to cohabit with an abusive husband.

[99] In *Moustaquim v Belgium* A 193 (1991); 13 EHRR 802 para 51 Com Rep, the government initially questioned whether there was a real family life between parents and an adolescent child: the link had been asserted purely for the purpose of relying on the Convention. See also *Benes v Austria No 18643/91*, 72 DR 271 (1992) (annulment of marriage entered into for the sole purpose of obtaining spouse's nationality interference with right to respect for family life but justified under Article 8(2)).

[100] *Berrehab v Netherlands* A 138 (1988); 11 EHRR 322 para 21.

the parents cohabit but are unmarried, it will usually be the case that they enjoy family life together and with their children.[101] If a relationship established in accordance with the forms recognized by the national law ought ordinarily to fall within Article 8(1), then so ought marriages celebrated abroad but recognized by the national law, a matter of particular importance for polygamous unions.[102] Prospective relationships as husband and wife, that is to say, those between present fiancé and fiancée, may be regarded as family life if they are sufficiently established.[103] Where the union between partners is informal, it will depend on all the facts whether it constitutes family life. Stability of the relationship over a period and the intention of the parties are significant factors. It is not always essential that the man and woman live together.[104]

The Court established from an early stage that the relationship between an unmarried mother and her child constituted family life.[105] It has not given similar automatic recognition to the relationship between a child and his father, and has instead enquired in each case about the quality of that relationship, illustrated by arrangements regarding contact and maintenance and formal recognition of paternity.[106] Nevertheless, the Court's approach has been to find family life to exist between father and child unless there are exceptional circumstances to conclude that the bond has been broken.[107] The Court's requirement of 'close personal ties' would appear to be satisfied in all but the most extreme cases, envisaged as one where, perhaps, the parent has been violent towards the child. Even then, it is likely that the merits of the claim being made under Article 8—to contact, to rights of residence, etc—will be determined within the framework of Article 8(2) rather than by denying family life to exist under Article 8(1).

Modern family arrangements have presented issues as to whether family life exists between those who enjoy solely a biological or genetic link or those born using donor gametes who have no biological link with their social parents. In *X, Y and Z v UK*[108] the Court confirmed that the reality of family arrangements between a transsexual male and the child born to his wife by artificial insemination by donor meant that their relationship constituted family life for the purposes of Article 8. Thus, it appears, the absence of a genetic link may not in itself preclude the existence of family life. But, if the common genetic material is the only connection between parent and child, will this be sufficient to attract the protection of Article 8? This matter has not yet been considered by the Court. In the earlier case of *G v Netherlands*[109] the Commission rejected that a biological link was sufficient, notwithstanding the applicant's clear attachment and commitment to the child concerned. The Court took a different approach in *Keegan v Ireland*[110] where the child was born as a result of a conscious decision taken by the applicant and his girlfriend who were then in a loving relationship. Notwithstanding that their relationship had broken down by the time the child was born, and the father had met his child on

---

[101] *Johnston v Ireland* A 112 (1986); 9 EHRR 203 para 75 PC.

[102] See *Alam and Khan v UK* No 2991/66, 10 YB 478 (1967). There does not appear to be an obligation to recognize polygamous unions as formal marriages, although a family relationship between parties to such a union may be established as existing in substance: see *A and A v Netherlands* No 14501/89, 72 DR 118 at 121–3 (1992).

[103] *Wakefield v UK* No 15817/89, 66 DR 251 at 255 (1990).

[104] *Berrehab v Netherlands* A 138 (1988); 11 EHRR 322 para 21; *Kroon v Netherlands* A 297-C (1994); 19 EHRR 263 para 30.

[105] *Marckx v Belgium* A 31 (1979); 2 EHRR 330 para 31 PC.

[106] Eg, *Boughanemi v France* 1996-II; 22 EHRR 228 para 35; *Ciliz v Netherlands* 2000-VIII para 60. Family life was found to exist in both cases despite the applicants' varying levels of commitment towards their children.

[107] *Ahmut v Netherlands* 1996-VI; 24 EHRR 62 para 60.

[108] 1997-II, 24 EHRR 143 para 37 GC.   [109] *G v Netherlands* No 16944/90, 16 EHRR CD 38 (1993).

[110] A 290 (1994); 18 EHRR 342 para 45.

only one occasion, the Court held family life to exist because at the material time their relationship had all the hallmarks of family life.

Surprisingly few challenges have been brought under Article 8 by same sex couples with or without children, meaning that the question of what protection Article 8 offers such relationships is uncertain. The Court has yet to determine whether same-sex relationships constitute family life although the Commission found that that a stable relationship between two women and the child born to one of them by donor insemination amounted to private rather than family life.[111] Increasing consensus on the rights of those in same-sex partnerships to have their relationships, including with any children of the family, legally recognized is likely to be an important factor when this issue comes before the Court and no doubt this will reduce the margin of appreciation allowed to a state seeking to deny this protection. A factor of further influence may be the precedent set by the Court in the case of X, Y and Z v UK where the Court formally recognized the existence of family life without a blood tie for the first time.[112] The Court may thus rely on this approach to bring same-sex couples and their children within the scope of family life; in doing so it would reflect an interpretation of Article 8 which is in line with modern social and legal conditions in many Council of Europe states.[113]

The central relationships of family life are those of husband and wife and parent and child. The Convention does not stop there: relationships between siblings,[114] between uncle and nephew,[115] and between grandparents and grandchildren[116] are covered by it. The more remote the relationship, the less might be demanded of a state to respect it or the more easily a state might justify interfering with it,[117] but generalizations restricted to the formal closeness of the relationship are unhelpful. In each case, attention will have to be paid to the actual circumstances of the relationship as well.[118]

Family life may be terminated, say by divorce between husband and wife,[119] or by adoption between natural parent and child, just as it is, by the same process, established between adoptive parent and child. However because a single family life might involve a number of relationships, the severance of one of them does not necessarily mean the end of all of them. In Berrehab v Netherlands,[120] the Court accepted that family life between a father and daughter had survived the divorce between the father and the mother. Although the latter had custody, the father maintained a genuine relationship with his daughter, which the state was obliged to respect. Similarly, although the adoption of a child may sever the bond of family life (although the Court is much more likely

---

[111] S v UK No 11716/85, 47 DR 274 (1986); B v UK No 16106/90, 64 DR 278 (1990); and Kerkhoven, Hinke and Hinke v Netherlands No 15666/89 hudoc (1992) DA.

[112] 1997-II, 24 EHRR 143 GC. However, the Court went on to find that Article 8 did not require the applicant's name to be entered onto the child's birth certificate as her father.

[113] As the attitude to homosexual unions changes in European national law, this matter may be reconsidered or, alternatively, raised under Article 14: see Van Dijk, loc cit at p 370, n 81, above.

[114] Moustaquim v Belgium A 193 (1993); 13 EHRR 802 para 56; Olsson v Sweden A 130 (1988); 11 EHRR 259 para 81 PC.

[115] Boyle v UK A 282-B (1994); 19 EHRR 179 Com Rep.

[116] Marckx v Belgium A 31 (1979); 2 EHRR 330 para 45 PC and Price v UK No 12402/86, 55 DR 224 at 237 (1988).

[117] Boyle v UK, ibid (uncle-nephew), where the Commission divided by fourteen to four on what was required to respect the interests in the custody of a child in this relationship compared to parents and child. A friendly settlement was reached which acknowledged the uncle's interest.

[118] Duffy, 3 YEL 191 (1983), suggests that the content of family life might depend on the context in which it is being considered, drawing a contrast between domestic and immigration cases.

[119] Berrehab v Netherlands A 138 (1988); 11 EHRR 322 para 21.

[120] Id, para 59. See also Hendriks v Netherlands No 8427/78, 29 DR 5 (1982).

to consider the issue under Article 8(2)),[121] the placement of a child in care does not.[122] The law may allow the creation of formal relationships other than by marriage. Adoption creates family life between the adoptive parents and the adopted child[123] and the same may be true of a relationship between foster-parent and foster-child although the content of family life will depend on the terms of the fostering arrangement.[124]

One aspect of the proof of a relationship raises special problems. It is the matter of paternity. A presumption of paternity of the husband to a formal marriage whose wife has a child does not, of itself, contravene the Convention. However, the Court established in *Kroon v Netherlands*[125] that biological and social reality should prevail over legal presumptions and the quest for legal certainty of relations, so that any presumption of paternity must be effectively capable of being rebutted and not amount to a *de facto* rule. While the application of time limits for challenging such presumptions is justifiable under Article 8(2) *inter alia* in the public interest, an inflexible system will be difficult to defend given the importance of the private life interest at stake.[126] This is particularly so where the time limit continues to apply notwithstanding that relevant circumstances may have become known only after its expiry.[127] Despite the clear implications for family life in these cases, most of which are brought either by children seeking details of their true identity,[128] or parents seeking to assert or rebut a presumption of paternity,[129] the Court has clearly categorized them as private life issues for reasons explained above. Similarly, matters such as the identification of children given for adoption by natural mothers and the tracing of their natural parents by adopted children also appear to be questions of private life rather than family life.[130]

The Commission rejected the claim that the right to respect for family life includes the father's right to be consulted as to whether the mother should have an abortion.[131] This may largely exhaust the content of family life for the father in such a case but it is possible that other matters, such as succession, could arise which would require reconsideration of the existence of family life between a father and a foetus. Moreover, a father could conceivably have a private life interest in a decision to have or not to have children, as in *Evans v UK* where the Grand Chamber was required effectively to weigh up the interests of the applicant, who wished to have the frozen embryo transferred to her womb, with that of her husband who did not.[132]

The essential ingredient of family life is the right to live together so that family relationships may 'develop normally'[133] and that members of the family may 'enjoy each

---

[121] See eg, *Kearns v France* hudoc (2008).

[122] *W v UK* A 121 (1987); 10 EHRR 29 para 59 PC; *Olsson v Sweden (No 1)* A 130 (1988); 11 EHRR 259 para 59 PC.

[123] *X v France* No 9993/82, 31 DR 241 (1982). This is the case even where the children have not been placed in the custody of their adoptive parents provided they have formally been adopted. See *Pini v Romania* 2004-V; 40 EHRR 312 para 143.

[124] *Gaskin v UK* A 160 (1989); 12 EHRR 36 para 49 PC.

[125] A 297-C (1994); 19 EHRR 263 para 40. See also *Tavli v Turkey* hudoc (2006) and *Mizzi v Malta* 2006-I; 46 EHRR 529 where the applicant's inability to contest paternity violated Article 8.

[126] *Shofman v Russia* hudoc (2005) para 43 where no exceptions to the time limit were permitted.

[127] *Phinikaridou v Cyprus* hudoc (2007) paras 47–67.

[128] Eg, *Mikulic v Croatia* 2002-I; *Jaggi v Switzerland* 2006-X.

[129] *Rasmussen v Denmark* A 87 (1984); 7 EHRR 371 para 33; *Paulik v Slovakia* hudoc (2006) (applicant sought to contest paternity); *Rozanski v Poland* hudoc (2006) (father unable to establish paternity).

[130] *Odièvre v France* 2003-III; 38 EHRR 871 paras 40–4.

[131] *X v UK* No 8416/78, 19 DR 244 at 253–4 (1980).

[132] *Evans v UK* hudoc (2007); 46 EHRR 728 para 90 GC. See Morris, 70(6) MLR 992 (2007).

[133] *Marckx v Belgium* A 31 (1979); 2 EHRR 330 para 31 PC.

other's company'[134] but the reach of this right cannot be considered separately from the specific duty on a state under Article 8, ie its duty to respect family life. This is considered further below.[135]

III. HOME

In general, 'home', which is an autonomous concept within the meaning of Article 8(1), is where one lives on a settled basis—the French text uses the word '*domicile*'—and, according to the Court, 'will usually be the place, the physically defined area, where private and family life develops'.[136] Whether or not a particular habitation constitutes a 'home' which attracts the protection of Article 8(1) will depend on the factual circumstances, namely, the existence of sufficient and continuous links with a specific place.[137] It may be the case that not all living places are 'home', for example, 'holiday homes'[138] and work hostels might be exceptions, although the Court has found that the hotel room used by a homeless person and paid for by the local authority constituted his 'home' within the meaning of Article 8.[139] In *Prokopovich v Russia*[140] the Court held that the flat in question was the applicant's home within the meaning of Article 8 given that she shared the maintenance costs with her partner, received post at that address, and was, according to witnesses, regularly seen about the place.

In *Gillow v UK*,[141] the Commission decided that 'home' could include a place where one intended to live, not confining 'home' to where one actually was living particularly where there is intention to use the residence in question as one's home.[142] Although in this case the applicant's home had initially been established legally, this does not appear to be a requirement for the establishment of a 'home' interest under Article 8(1). *Buckley v UK*[143] concerned the complaint of a gypsy who moved her caravan onto her land but was then denied planning permission to use the caravan as her residence on that property. Because she had purchased the land to establish her residence there, had lived there almost continuously for a number of years, and it had not been suggested that she had established, or intended to establish another residence elsewhere, the Court found that the case concerned her right to respect for her 'home' under Article 8(1).

The Court has also extended the notion of 'home' to cover business premises. In *Niemietz v Germany*,[144] the Court, relying on the French text of Article 8 and on German law, decided that 'home' may extend, for example, to a professional person's office. This, the Court said, was consonant with the object of Article 8 to protect against arbitrary interference by the authorities. Because 'activities which are related to a profession or

[134] *Olsson v Sweden* A 130 (1988); 11 EHRR 259 para 59 PC.   [135] See pp 392–6.
[136] Eg, *Giacomelli v Italy* 2006-XII; 45 EHRR 871 para 76.
[137] Eg, *Gillow v UK* A 109 (1986); 11 EHRR 335 para 46 and *Buckley v UK* 1996-IV; 23 EHRR 101 paras 52–4.
[138] In *Kanthak v FRG No 12474/86*, 58 DR 94 (1988), the question whether a camping van could be a 'home' was raised, but not answered.
[139] *O'Rourke v UK No 39022/97* hudoc (2001) DA.   [140] 2004-XI; 43 EHRR 167 para 37.
[141] A 109 (1986); 11 EHRR 335 paras 109–19 Com Rep.
[142] The government had argued that the applicants had been absent from their house for so long that it was no longer their 'home' within the meaning of Article 8(1) This was rejected by the Commission (and not contested before the Court) on the grounds that the applicants had always intended to return to the house in question. *Gillow*, id, paras 44, 46.
[143] 1996-IV; 23 EHRR 101 para 54. See also *Connors v UK* hudoc (2004); 40 EHRR 189 para 58 where a case with similar facts was found to raise issues of 'private life', 'family life', and 'home'.
[144] A 251-B (1992); 16 EHRR 97 para 30. See also *Chappell v UK* A 152-A (1989); 12 EHRR 1 para 96 Com Rep ('home' where part of premises used as residence and part for business purposes). See also *Buck v Germany* 2005-IV; 42 EHRR 440.

business may well be conducted from a person's private residence and activities which are not so related may well be carried on in an office or commercial premises', it 'may not always be possible to draw precise distinctions'. The *Niemietz* case[145] was one where the professional's activities (he was a lawyer) could be carried on as easily at home as at his office. The Court has subsequently held that 'home' is to be construed as including also the registered office of a company run by a private individual, as well as a juristic person's registered office, branches, and other business premises.[146] Article 8 thus covers the circumstances where business is conducted from home, and this is important in ensuring that the terms of the provision keep pace with modern work practices and lifestyle where the lines can often be blurred between 'home' and 'office'. In *Halford v UK*,[147] which concerned the tapping of the home and work telephones of the applicant who was an Assistant Chief Constable, it was significant that she had been assured of the privacy of her conversations giving her a legitimate expectation of confidentiality. The Court reached a similar conclusion in *Copland v UK*[148] where the applicant had not been warned that her email correspondence would be liable to monitoring. Where these factors do not exist, the relevance of the 'home' interest might be more open to question. Regardless, the Court's definition of the concept of 'home' would appear to exclude wholly work premises.

Where it is established that premises are 'home', then the first protection is of a right of access and occupation,[149] and a right not to be expelled or evicted from them.[150] The property right in houses is protected, if at all, by Article 1 of the First Protocol,[151] although the line is sometimes hard to draw. In *Howard v UK*,[152] the Commission decided that a compulsory purchase order for the house where the applicants lived interfered potentially with their rights under Article 8 as well as Article 1 of the First Protocol.

The interests protected by 'home' include the peaceful enjoyment of residence there. In addition, the Court has established that[153] breaches of the right to respect for the home are not confined to concrete or physical breaches, such as unauthorized entry into a person's home, but also include those that are not concrete or physical, such as noise, emissions, smells, or other forms of interference. A serious interference may result in the breach of a person's right to respect for his home if it prevents him from enjoying the amenities of his home.

The various environmental cases have made this clear, establishing also the procedural requirement that the decision-making around the planning process must ensure adequate respect for the individual's right to respect for their home under Article 8.[154] In the cases of *Taskin v Turkey* and *Ockan v Turkey*, the Court held that the decision-making process which led to the granting of a mining license in each case was flawed with the effect that the applicants' rights to respect for their home had been violated.[155] Other cases concerning the pollution created by nearby factories were similarly found to raise

---

[145] Id, paras 29–30.   [146] *Sallinen v Finland* hudoc (2005) para 70.

[147] 1997-III; 24 EHRR 523 para 44. See also *Amann v Switzerland* 2000-II; 30 EHRR 843 para 43 GC.

[148] Hudoc (2007) para 42.   [149] *Wiggins v UK* No 7456/76, 13 DR 40 (1978).

[150] *Cyprus v Turkey Nos 6780/74 and 6950/75 (First and Second Applications)*, 4 EHRR 482 at 519–20 (1976); *Cyprus v Turkey No 8007/77*, 72 DR 5 at 41–3 (1983); CM Res DH (92) 12.

[151] *James v UK* A 98 (1986); 8 EHRR 123 PC.

[152] *No 10825/84*, 52 DR 198 (1985). See also *X v UK No 9261/81*, 28 DR 177 (1982).

[153] *Hatton v UK* 2003-VIII; 37 EHRR 611 para 96 GC and *Giacomelli v Italy* 2006-XII; 45 EHRR 871 para 76.

[154] Eg, *Arrondelle v UK No 7889/77*, 26 DR 5 (1982) F Sett. See also *Lopes Ostra v Spain* A 303-C (1994); 20 EHRR 277; *Guerra v Italy* 1998-I; 26 EHRR 357; *Hatton v UK* (2003); 37 EHRR 611 GC; *Moreno Gomez v Spain* 2004-X; 41 EHRR 899; and *Giacomelli v Italy* 2006-XII; 45 EHRR 871.

[155] *Taskin v Turkey* 2004-X; 42 EHRR 250 para 125 and *Ockan v Turkey* hudoc (2006).

serious issues regarding the applicants' peaceful enjoyment of their home and private and family life, which were inadequately protected.[156]

The interference with respect for one's home may come in the first instance from private parties, but the state's responsibility will be engaged if it fails to address a continuing interference. Thus in *Surugiu v Romania*,[157] the interference with the applicant's home was caused by repeated acts of trespass and harassment by people in a land dispute with the applicant, while in *Moreno Gomez v Spain*[158] noise from nearby bars and nightclubs prevented the applicant from enjoying his home. Article 8 was engaged in each case. There are limits to the scope of protection offered by Article 8, however. In *Kyrtatos v Greece*[159] the applicants complained that urban development around their property on the Greek island of Tynos damaged the area's natural beauty and as a result interfered with their enjoyment of their home contrary to Article 8. The Court noted that:

> the crucial element which must be present in determining whether, in the circumstances of a case, environmental pollution has adversely affected one of the rights safeguarded by paragraph 1 of Article 8 is the existence of a harmful effect on a person's private or family sphere and not simply the general deterioration of the environment.

As no such evidence was presented to the Court, no interference with the applicant's home had been established in this respect.

Many aspects of home life will overlap with private life; the right to live one's life as one wishes, to adopt a particular lifestyle, may have implications for the kind of home one wants[160] and the level of protection to which one's 'home' is entitled. This was raised as an issue in *Chapman v UK*,[161] one of several gypsy cases concerning the interference with the applicant's Article 8 interests caused by the failure to grant her planning permission to live in a caravan on her land. With regard to the margin of appreciation to which the domestic authorities are entitled in taking decisions about planning matters, the Grand Chamber noted that there was an emerging consensus in Council of Europe states 'recognising the special needs of minorities and an obligation to protect their security, identity and lifestyle'.[162] However, it did not consider this to be sufficiently concrete to offer any guidance to states as to the standards to be applied in cases of this kind and, accordingly, it concluded that its role was to ensure that such decisions were based on reasons that were relevant and sufficient. The majority found that they were in this case although seven judges dissented to highlight the vulnerability of the applicants as a minority group with a particular lifestyle directly related to their traditions and identity. In the opinion of the minority, the seriousness of what was at stake for the applicant was readily apparent and thus the failure to provide adequate alternative accommodation to her family who had been evicted forcibly from her own land meant that her treatment was not consistent with Article 8.[163] Thus, while there had been slight indications in the Commission's practice that the right to live in a mobile home might fall within Article 8, as an aspect of

---

[156] *Lopez Ostra v Spain* A 303-C (1994); 20 EHRR 277 (concerning a waste treatment plant operating illegally); *Guerra v Italy* 1998-I; 26 EHRR 357 (concerning a chemical factory established without adequate information being provided to the applicants); and *Giacomelli v Italy* 2006-XII; 45 EHRR 871 (concerning a toxic waste plant).

[157] Hudoc (2004).   [158] 2004-X; 41 EHRR 899.   [159] 2003-VI; 40 EHRR 390 para 52.

[160] *G and E v Norway* Nos 9278/81 and 9415/81, 35 DR 30 (1983) (the applicants were members of a minority).

[161] 2001-I; 33 EHRR 399 GC. See also *Beard v UK* hudoc (2001); 33 EHRR 442 GC.   [162] Id, para 93.

[163] Joint dissenting opinion of Judges Pastor Ridruejo, Bonello, Tulkens, Strážnická, Lorenzen, Fischbach, and Casadevall.

one's lifestyle,[164] these cases make clear that this right will not always be easily vindicated for this group.

The Court has established that there is no right to be provided with a home and that such a claim falls outside the scope of Article 8.[165] According to the Court, while it is:

> 'clearly desirable that every human being have a place where he or she can live in dignity and which he or she can call home, there are unfortunately in the Contracting States many persons who have no home. Whether the State provides funds to enable everyone to have a home is a matter for political not judicial decision.'[166]

The latter statement appears to exclude issues of homelessness from the scope of Article 8 insofar as matters of socio-economic rights go beyond the Court's jurisdiction. While it is not without merit—it is undeniable that there is no right to a home under the Convention—it would appear to misrepresent the Convention's position in this area. In other cases, admitted under Article 1 of the First Protocol, the Court has stated that 'in spheres such as housing, which play a central role in the welfare and economic policies of modern societies, it will respect the legislature's judgment as to what is in the general interest unless that judgment is manifestly without reasonable foundation'.[167]

Moreover, in *Connors v UK*,[168] the applicant complained that his family's eviction due to alleged anti-social behaviour from the caravan site where he lawfully resided interfered with his 'private life', 'family life', and 'home'. The Court distinguished *Chapman* (where the applicants had lived in their caravan without the necessary permission) and went on to find that the weighty reasons of public interest required to justify the very severe interference with the applicant's rights—he was effectively evicted and rendered homeless with a detrimental impact on his and his family's health and education—did not exist in this case.

There is no right to enjoy a home of a particular standard. But in *Marzari v Italy*[169] the applicant who had a severe disability complained that the apartment he was allocated was inadequate for his needs and undertook various protest measures designed to compel the authorities to undertake the necessary adjustments to the property. He complained that his treatment violated his right to respect for his home. According to the Court:

> although Article 8 does not guarantee the right to have one's housing problem solved by the authorities, a refusal of the authorities to provide assistance in this respect to an individual suffering from a severe disease might in certain circumstances raise an issue under Article 8 of the Convention because of the impact of such refusal on the private life of the individual.

On the facts, the authorities were found to have taken reasonable measures to address the shortcomings of the applicant's accommodation and no violation of Article 8 was found.

The notion of 'home' is not seen entirely as the protection of a particular category of established property right. It includes a family home but it is not restricted to it. While its core idea is one of sanctuary against intrusion by public authorities, there are further

---

[164] Cases involving the right of gypsies to live in caravans against the UK have gone in different directions at the admissibility stage: see *Smith v UK No 18401/91*, 18 EHRR CD 65 (1993) (inadmissible) and *Buckley v UK No 20348/92*, 18 EHRR CD 123 (1994) (admissible); *Smith (Carol and Steven) v UK No 22902/93* hudoc (1994) (admissible); *Smith (Carol and Walter) v UK No 23442/94* hudoc (1994) (admissible).

[165] *Chapman v UK* 2001-I; 33 EHRR 399 para 99 GC.

[166] *Ibid*. See also *X v FRG No 159/56*, 1 YB 202 (1956) (no right to a decent ('*convenable*') home).

[167] *Mellacher v Austria* A 169 (1989); 12 EHRR 391 para 45 PC and *Immobiliare Saffi v Italy* 1999-V; 30 EHRR 756 para 49 GC.

[168] Hudoc (2004); 40 EHRR 189.   [169] *No 36448/97*, 28 EHRR CD 175 (1999).

connotations to the idea of 'home', in particular that the state will facilitate the right to live in one's home, rather than merely protect it as a possession or property right.[170] Numerous cases against Turkey have established state responsibility for the destruction of the applicants' homes and, finding that this was without any justification, the Court concluded that Article 8 had been violated.[171] The Court has also considered the impact on the applicants' right to respect for their home of having their homes destroyed. In *Moldovan and Others (No 2) v Romania*,[172] the Court held that apart from the responsibility of the state for the destruction of the applicants' homes (this had happened before Romania ratified the ECHR),[173] the failure to address the appalling conditions in which they were forced to live since that time constituted a failure to put a stop to the continuing breaches of their right to respect for their home. Similarly, in *Akdivar v Turkey*,[174] the Court noted that the response of the authorities—the prosecutors, courts, and local authorities—perpetuated the applicants' feelings of insecurity after the attack on their home and constituted in itself a hindrance of their rights to respect for their private and family life and their home.[175]

Ownership is not necessary to establish a 'home' interest under Article 8(1). The Court has considered several cases concerning the rights of tenants to enjoy their home that make this clear. In *Prokopovich v Russia*[176] the Court held that the flat rented by the applicant's partner constituted her 'home' and in *Pibernik v Croatia*[177] it was uncontested that the applicant's flat which was owned by the Ministry for Defence was her 'home' within the meaning of Article 8. The nature of the tenancy, whether public or private in nature, is equally unimportant and it may be difficult for the state to justify treating its tenants differently from those in private arrangements. In *Larkos v Cyprus*,[178] the applicant successfully contested that as a tenant of the state he was treated differently from a private tenant in that his tenancy entitled him to less protection. The Court found that there was no reasonable and objective justification for not extending full protection to state tenants and his treatment was found to be contrary to Article 14 taken together with Article 8.

Beyond the right to occupy one's home, the central protection afforded by the right to respect for one's home is against intrusion by the authorities of the state to arrest, search, seize, or inspect. The weight attached to the strong interest a person has in the sanctuary of his home puts the burden on the state to justify such interventions for good public purposes. Such cases frequently involve issues of search and seizure and secret surveillance and are considered below.

IV. CORRESPONDENCE

The right to respect for one's correspondence is a right to uninterrupted and uncensored communications with others. A letter writer retains no right to respect for his

---

[170] *Howard v UK No 10825/84*, 52 DR 198 (1987). The Commission dealt with the denial of access to their homes in the north of Cyprus to Greek Cypriots under Article 8 and under Article 1, First Protocol: *Cyprus v Turkey Nos 6780/74 and 6950/75*, paras 208, 486 Com Rep; and id, *No 8007/77*, 72 DR 5 at 42, 46–7; *Loizidou v Turkey No 15318/89*, paras 86–101 Com Rep.

[171] Eg, *Akdivar v Turkey* 1996-IV; 23 EHRR 143; *Dulas v Turkey* hudoc (2001) and *Altun v Turkey* hudoc (2004). In several other cases the Court found the applicants' allegations regarding the state authorities' destruction of their homes to be unsubstantiated, eg *Gundem v Turkey* 1998-III; 32 EHRR 350 and *Cacan v Turkey* hudoc (2004).

[172] (2007) 44 EHRR 16 paras 102–9.

[173] *Moldovan and Rostas v Romania Nos 41138/98 and 64320/01* hudoc (2001) DA.

[174] 1996-IV para 88 and *Moldovan and Others (No 2) v Romania* hudoc (2005); 44 EHRR 16 para 108.

[175] See further Kenna, 2 EHRLR 193–208 (2008).   [176] 2004-XI; 43 EHRR 167 para 37.

[177] Hudoc (2004); 40 EHRR 698 para 62. See also *Cvijetic v Croatia* hudoc (2004).

[178] 1999-I; 30 EHRR 597.

correspondence once the letter is in the hands of the addressee[179] nor, it would seem to follow, would the right be violated if the contents of one's telephone conversations were revealed by the other party to them. That there may be expectations of confidentiality about the contents of a letter or telephone conversation, as, for instance, between lawyer and client or doctor and patient, suggests that the conclusion is not unqualified, though the protection of the individual's right to confidence is as likely to be a matter of respect for his private life as for his right to correspondence. Interferences caused by secret surveillance are often considered in relation to both private life and correspondence under Article 8(1) given that the interception of email, post, or telephone communication will often involve a potential breach of both interests. In much of the case law, therefore, these issues are considered together. In telephone-tapping cases, the literal meaning of 'correspondence' has been expanded to include telephone communications.[180] The concept has been interpreted to keep pace with developments in technology. In *Copland v UK*,[181] the applicant's email and internet usage were subjected to monitoring raising issues of the right to respect for her correspondence. This logical expansion of the concept may bring other methods of communication within Article 8, although the appropriate level of protection required by 'respect' will have to take into account the techniques involved.[182] The protection is about the means of communication rather than its content (which will ordinarily fall to be considered under Article 10).[183] However, the content of a communication may be relevant to determining the limits of the right of the state to interfere with a letter or telephone call, particularly where legally privileged correspondence is involved. Equally, the identity of the sender or consignee of correspondence will play a part in determining what is required by Article 8. It is to persons in detention that the right of correspondence is of the greatest importance because for such people it is, visits apart, the only method of communication with others beyond the closed institution. In this regard, the Court has been solicitous in protecting letters between detained persons and their lawyers, and even more so with respect to prisoners' correspondence with the European Court of Human Rights.[184]

3. 'RESPECT'

Article 8(1) protects the right to *respect* for the various interests it lists. This makes it clear that not every act of a public authority which has an impact on the exercise of the interest will constitute an interference with the Article 8(1) right. So wide is the content of the interests that much state activity will have an incidental impact upon them. The criminal law on assault will, if it applies, have an impact on the exercise of parental discipline and hence on family life.[185] Road safety legislation requiring the wearing of seat-belts

---

[179] *AD v Netherlands No 21962/93*, 76A DR 157 (1994).

[180] Eg, *Klass v FRG* A 28 (1978); 2 EHRR 214 para 41 PC—telephone-tapping constitutes an interference with 'the applicant's right to respect for private life and family life and correspondence'.

[181] Hudoc (2007) para 41.

[182] There are not the same expectations of confidentiality for radio telephone conversations or open fax communications as there are for ordinary telephone calls because of the greater susceptibility of the former to interception.

[183] *A v France* A 277-B (1993); 17 EHRR 462 paras 34–7, rejecting government's claim that telephone conversations about criminal activities fell outside Article 8(1).

[184] There is now extensive jurisprudence in this area, eg *Campbell v UK* A 233 (1992); 15 EHRR 137 para 47; *Herczegfalvy v Austria* A 244 (1992); 15 EHRR 457 para 91; *Jankauskas v Lithuania* hudoc (2005); and *Michta v Poland* hudoc (2006). See further below pp 404–6.

[185] *Seven Individuals v Sweden No 8811/79*, 29 DR 104 at 114 (1982).

touches on private life (the 'right' to take risks as an element of one's personality).[186] In some instances, this kind of incidental consequence may be regarded as not constituting a failure to respect an Article 8(1) interest and, therefore, not requiring justification under Article 8(2).[187]

The obligation on states is to 'respect' the interests set out in Article 8(1). States have argued that this is purely a negative obligation not to interfere arbitrarily with those rights.[188] This limited conception of the obligation would condemn only interferences by the state with the protected interest, a conclusion buttressed by the language of Article 8(2) which says, 'There shall be no interference by a public authority with the exercise of this right...'. Thus a state would have a duty, for example, to desist from criminalizing private sexual relations or from authorising arbitrary powers for social workers to separate members of a family or for policemen to enter private houses. However, it would not be responsible where, for example, the interference with private life was by a newspaper reporter or the disruption of family life was caused by another member of the family or the entry into a person's home was by a private detective. Such a narrow reading has not been acceptable to the Court. Accordingly, it set out the principle of positive obligations in *X and Y v Netherlands*[189] when it said:

> [Article 8] does not merely compel the state to abstain from...interference: in addition to this primarily negative undertaking, there may be positive obligations inherent in an effective respect for private and family life...These obligations may involve the adoption of measures designed to secure respect for private life even in the sphere of the relations of individuals between themselves.

The identification of the circumstances in which the duty to respect an individual's interest involves positive action is not without its difficulties. In *Abdulaziz, Cabales and Balkandali v UK*,[190] the applicants argued that the state had a positive obligation to admit their alien husbands to join them when these men had no independent right to be admitted under immigration law. The Court said:

> ...especially as far as those positive obligations are concerned, the notion of 'respect' is not clear-cut: having regard to the diversity of practices followed and the situations obtaining in the Contracting states, the notion's requirements will vary considerably from case to case.

The boundaries between the state's positive and negative obligations under Article 8 'do not lend themselves to precise definition' although, as the Court has held on many occasions, 'the applicable principles are similar'. In both contexts, the Court has established that 'regard must be had to the fair balance that has to be struck between the competing interests of the individual and the community as a whole, and in both contexts the state is recognised as enjoying a certain margin of appreciation'.[191]

These generalizations do not take us very far, particularly since they concern the establishment of the primary obligations under Article 8(1) and not the justifications for derogating from them under Article 8(2). The legitimate aims of justifiable interferences in Article 8(2) have a 'certain relevance' for the inquiry under Article 8(1)[192] but they do

---

[186] *X v Belgium No 8707/79*, 18 DR 255 (1979).
[187] For other examples, see Louciades, 62 BYIL 176 at 193–4 (1991).
[188] See eg, *Lingens v Austria* A 103 (1986); 8 EHRR 407 PC.
[189] A 91 (1985); 8 EHRR 235 para 23, as to which, see below, p 384. See also eg, *Johnston v Ireland* A 112 (1986); 9 EHRR 203 para 55 PC.   [190] A 94 (1985); 7 EHRR 471 para 67 PC.
[191] *Hokkanen v Finland* A 299-A (1994); 19 EHRR 139 para 55.
[192] *Rees v UK* A 106 (1986); 9 EHRR 56 para 37 PC.

not exhaust the matters of public interest which may have a bearing on the existence of a positive obligation. Although the Court has used the language of 'margin of appreciation', the inquiry is not identical to the one to be made in deciding whether an interference with a protected right 'is in accordance with law and is necessary in a democratic society' within Article 8(2). Under Article 8(2), the balance is struck between a right already established, which, formally at least, carries a special weight, and the countervailing interests which the state is seeking to protect. In reaching the balance in Article 8(1), the Court is determining the content of the protected right. It is thus incumbent on an applicant to establish the distinctive importance of the interest to him as it can be easy for the Court to underestimate this and there is no formal weight to attach to his claim as there would be if his interest were already acknowledged as a right.[193] The applicant in *Stjerna v Finland*[194] was not able to establish that the state had failed to respect his private life when it refused to allow him to register a change of surname in the official records; nor was this refusal an 'interference' with his right as, the Court surmised, an order to him to change his surname might have been.[195] Similarly, in *Guillot v France*,[196] the Court concluded that the prejudice caused by the refusal to allow the applicants to register their daughter's name as 'Fleur de Marie' did not interfere with their private and family life as the alternative name 'Fleur-Marie' was allowed. The fact that the Court stopped short of finding an interference in both of these cases meant that it did not have to consider whether the measure was justified under Article 8(2). That is not to say that justification could not have been found. In *Guillot*, for example, the prevailing view of the domestic authorities was that the proposed name was eccentric and excessively whimsical. It might thus easily have been found to be compatible with Article 8 as a measure proportionate to the aim of protecting the interests of the child and of society. So the outcome might have been the same, even with a different approach.[197] As the Court stated in *Johansson v Finland*,[198] which also involved the compatibility with Article 8 of refusing to register parents' choice of name for their child, whatever approach is taken 'the applicable principles are nonetheless similar', ie the weighing up of competing interests in light of the margin of appreciation. What was likely to have persuaded the Court to take the negative obligations approach in *Johansson*, and to find the interference to be disproportionate with the aim sought to be achieved, was not the severity of the interference with the applicants' interests but the indefensible nature of the state's position. Thus, the applicants' choice of name, 'Axl', was not whimsical like 'Fleur de Marie' (in *Guillot*), or likely to harm the child like 'Ainut Vain Marjaana' ('The One and Only Marjaana') in *Salonen v Finland*, but rather was a name already accepted by the authorities in other cases and one which was not too different from other Finnish names, which the policy was designed to preserve.

It is also possible for there to be an interference with the enjoyment of one individual's rights by the activities of another individual.[199] Although states have argued that conduct of this kind cannot implicate the state—Article 8(2) talks only of 'interference by a public authority'—the Court has rejected this contention. The matter of what kinds of interferences with Article 8(1) rights might be justified under Article 8(2) is independent

---

[193] See the transsexual cases and *Gaskin*, below, p 386.

[194] A 299-B (1994); 24 EHRR 195 para 38.

[195] See also the more recent case of *Bulgakov v Ukraine* hudoc (2007) concerning the translation of the applicant's surname for passport purposes.

[196] 1996-V para 27.

[197] See also *Salonen v Finland No 27868/95* hudoc (1997) DA.   [198] Hudoc (2007) para 29.

[199] In *Lopes Ostra v Spain* A 303-C (1994); 20 EHRR 277 paras 52, 55–6, the Court seemed to discern elements of both kinds of positive duty to protect the applicant from environmental damage from a private plant built on public land.

of the question of what rights are protected by Article 8(1). In *Airey v Ireland*,[200] the Court said that 'there may be positive obligations inherent in an effective respect for private or family life...'. Here, the obligation to respect family life included relieving partners to a marriage of their duty to live together in some circumstances. Ireland had failed to make its procedures for doing this effectively accessible to the applicant and had violated its positive obligation to respect her right to family life. Similarly, in numerous family law cases to come before the Court, it has been argued successfully by applicants that respect for family life imposes a positive duty on state authorities to reunite parents and their children even where it is another parent, rather than the state, that has caused their separation. Here, the Court has referred to the positive obligation to adopt measures:

> designed to secure respect for family life even in the sphere of relations between individuals, including both the provision of a regulatory framework of adjudicatory and enforcement machinery protecting individuals' rights and the implementation, where appropriate, of specific steps.[201]

In *X and Y v Netherlands*,[202] the Court held that the positive obligation on the state extended to the circumstances of private activities. Here, there had been a sexual assault on a sixteen-year-old, mentally handicapped girl by an adult male. It had not been possible to bring a criminal charge against the man because of a procedural gap in Dutch law. The Court conceded that there was a wide margin of appreciation for a state to determine what steps it should take to intervene between individuals. The government's position was that there were civil remedies available to the girl and so she was not bereft of protection. However, affirming the *Airey* case, the Court found that the civil remedies were not without their practical drawbacks and that the absence of an effective criminal remedy in these circumstances constituted a failure by the Dutch authorities to respect Y's right to private life. In the *X and Y* case, 'fundamental values and essential aspects of private life are at stake. Effective deterrence is indispensable in this area and it can be achieved only by criminal law provisions'.

This is a strong statement of what the positive obligation entails. It is unusual, of course, for the Court to be so specific about the content of a state's obligation (and the state, even here, retains the discretion about the precise form of the criminal sanction to be provided). The very particular circumstances of this case, ie that there was an admitted gap in the law and the gap was procedural rather than substantive, might militate against too wide an obligation being imposed upon states to criminalize private activities. However, it is clear that violent offences against children fall into the category of those cases where the effective application of the criminal law is required to ensure adequate protection from breaches of their physical integrity although it may be more appropriate to consider this issue under Article 3.[203] Beyond such clear-cut areas, it is difficult to envisage the wider potential of this approach and to predict, for example, whether the Court would find positive obligations to criminalize private surveillance or data collection which

---

[200] A 32 (1979); 2 EHRR 305 para 32.

[201] *Hokkanen v Finland* A 299-A (1994); 19 EHRR 139 para 58; *Glaser v UK* hudoc (2000); 33 EHRR 1 para 63; *Bajrami v Albania* 2006-XIV para 52.

[202] A 91 (1985); 8 EHRR 235 para 27.

[203] See *A v UK* 1998-VI; 27 EHRR 611 para 24. Here the Court found that the application of the common law defence of moderate and reasonable chastisement against a criminal charge of assault failed to effectively protect the child from treatment contrary to Article 3. A similar argument was made under Article 8 but it was not found that no separate issue arose under that provision. See also *Z v UK* 2001-V; 34 EHRR 97 paras 76–7 GC, although the argument here was that social services rather than the criminal law failed to protect the children from abuse.

impinged upon an individual's rights to private life or correspondence, where civil remedies already exist.[204] One factor which is likely to be of some influence in favour of an applicant making this argument is the existence of a widely adopted common position among the Convention states.

Nonetheless, Article 8 may impose positive obligations on a state with respect to private conduct and this may even extend to requiring positive action from private persons. In effect, the case law in these areas, such as that concerning the duty on a parent to allow the other parent to have contact with their child, presents the duty as one on the state to ensure individuals' compliance with the law.[205]

I. PRIVATE LIFE

The transsexual cases are good illustrations of the positive obligations which arise from the right to respect for one's private life and the balance to be drawn in this area. In none of the cases before the Court had the state forbidden the treatment which brought about the applicant's gender reassignment. Indeed, in the UK cases, the treatment was provided by the public health service.[206] The governments, then, did not interfere with the applicants' rights. Rather, the applicants argued, the state had failed to respect their rights to private life by refusing to amend their birth certificates after they had undergone the surgery. In *Van Oosterwijck v Belgium*,[207] the Commission found that there was a violation because the state 'had refused to recognise an essential element of his personality' and the effect of its refusal to concede his request for rectification was to 'restrict the applicant to a sex which can scarcely be considered his own'. When a similar question arose in two cases against the United Kingdom—*Rees* in 1986 and *Cossey* in 1990—the Court weighed the interest of the applicants in having the altered birth-certificate against the burden on the state substantially to reassess the system for registering births.[208] It found the balance to be in favour of the state and held, therefore, that in light of the margin of appreciation enjoyed by the state in this area, it had not failed to respect the applicant's private life. The Court reached the same conclusion in 1998 in *Sheffield and Horsham v UK*[209] noting that the detriment suffered by the applicants through being obliged to disclose pre-operative gender in certain contexts was not of sufficient seriousness to override the state's margin of appreciation. The balance tipped the other way in *B v France*[210] in 1992 where the majority held that, compared with practice in the UK, the disadvantages resulting from the non-recognition for certain purposes of the applicant's new gender were greater in French law and practice while the consequences for the state in changing the system were less.

The Court had not reached its conclusions unanimously in the above cases, with *Sheffield and Horsham* finely balanced at eleven votes to nine.[211] Perhaps, not surprisingly then, the Court broke new ground in the *Goodwin (Christine)* and *I* decisions in

---

[204] See Clapham, *Human Rights in the Private Sphere*, 1993, pp 211–22.

[205] Eg, *Hokkanen v Finland* A 299-A (1994); 17 EHRR 293 and *Karadzic v Croatia* hudoc (2005).

[206] In *Van Kuck v Germany* 2003-VII; 37 EHRR 973 paras 78–81 the Court held that the refusal of the domestic courts to order the reimbursement of medical expenses for gender reassignment (and the impact of that refusal) because of doubt as to its necessity violated the right to respect for private life under Article 8.

[207] B 36 (1979) para 52 Com Rep. The case was rejected by the Court for non-exhaustion of domestic remedies, A 40 (1980); 3 EHRR 557 PC.

[208] *Rees v UK* A 106 (1986); 9 EHRR 56 paras 42–6 PC and *Cossey v UK* A 184 (1990); 13 EHRR 622 para 39 PC.

[209] 1998-V; 27 EHRR 163 paras 51–61 GC.   [210] A 232-C (1992); 16 EHRR 1 paras 49–62 PC.

[211] There were four separate dissenting opinions.

2003[212] when it concluded that due to continually emerging European and international consensus around the legal recognition of transsexuals' acquired gender, the margin of appreciation had narrowed, meaning that states had less discretion to adopt their own approach. The Court also considered that the balance to be struck between the individual's right to respect for her private life and the public interest had shifted in the applicant's favour. While the interference with her private life remained serious, what was material was that 'the unsatisfactory situation in which post-operative transsexuals live in an intermediate zone as not quite one gender or the other (was) no longer sustainable'.[213] The Court also noted the absence of evidence that changing the UK system for birth registration to accommodate the rights of transsexuals would have a detrimental impact on the public interest and noted that, while not to be underestimated, such change could not be considered to be insurmountable. So the sands had shifted on both sides, resulting in a unanimous decision that Article 8 had been violated.[214]

The characterization of the interest of an applicant as of central importance to his private life also determined the outcome in *Gaskin v UK*.[215] The applicant had been in public foster-care as a child. The local authority had maintained records about his care, some of it given on express or implied understandings of confidentiality. As an adult, Gaskin sought access to the files held about him but the authority would reveal only that for which it had obtained a release from its obligation of confidentiality from the person who had been the source of the information. The government emphasized the importance of confidential record-keeping for an effective system of public child care and argued that, if any positive obligation existed with respect to the applicant, it had been discharged by the measures the local authority had taken to obtain waivers of confidentiality. However, the majority of the Court shared the Commission's perception that this kind of information was of especial importance to the applicant. It stated 'persons in the position of the applicant have a vital interest, protected by the Convention, in receiving the information necessary to know and understand their childhood and early development'. The Court concluded that the positive obligation on the state demanded independent adjudication to decide whether the continued confidentiality of information was really necessary where the contributor refused to waive confidentiality or could not be traced.[216]

In *Mikulic v Croatia*,[217] a more recent decision of equal importance, the Court also found that the positive obligation on the state to respect the young applicant's private life with respect to the establishment of her identity had not been fulfilled. Under Croatian law, the only avenue available to the applicant, who sought to establish details of her paternity, was to take a civil action against the putative father, JH. However, as nothing compelled him to undergo DNA testing he refused to attend over a period of three and a half years, after which time the first instance court relied on his non-attendance and the evidence of the child's mother to conclude that he was her father. The appellate court found this evidence inconclusive. The European Court acknowledged the importance to the applicant of obtaining accurate information about her identity, and also accepted that

---

[212] *Goodwin (Christine) v UK* 2002-VI; 35 EHRR 447 paras 89–93 GC and *I v UK* hudoc (2002); 36 EHRR 967 paras 69–73 GC.

[213] *Goodwin*, id, para 90.

[214] See also *Grant v UK* 2006-VII paras 40–4 and *L v Lithuania* hudoc (2007) paras 57–60 concerning a gap in the law regulating gender reassignment surgery.

[215] A 160 (1989); 12 EHRR 36 para 48 PC.

[216] Judges Ryssdal, Cremona, Gölcüklü, Matscher, and Evans dissenting on the basis of their concern about the consequences for the child-care system of the possible revelation of information given in confidence. Judge Walsh thought Article 8 did not apply at all and instead found Article 10 relevant.

[217] 2002-I para 65.

states approach such situations in different ways. Nonetheless, the fact that there were no effective means of compelling JH to comply with the court order to undergo DNA testing, together with the absence of alternative means available to the applicant to establish her identity, resulted in a violation of Article 8. In conclusion, it noted that:

> in determining an application to have paternity established, the courts are required to have regard to the basic principle of the child's interests. The Court finds that the procedure available does not strike a fair balance between the right of the applicant to have her uncertainty as to her personal identity eliminated without unnecessary delay and that of her supposed father not to undergo DNA tests, and considers that the protection of the interests involved is not proportionate.

In *Odièvre v France*,[218] the Court reached a different conclusion applying the same basic test. The applicant in this case was an adult whose mother had placed her for adoption anonymously. She claimed that France had failed to respect her private life because its legal system both precluded an action to establish maternity being brought if the natural mother had requested confidentiality and prohibited others from providing her with identifying information. The Court noted that the case showed a direct clash between the interests of the mother, who clearly wished to remain anonymous, and the applicant, who had a strong desire to know her true identity, which were not easily reconciled. It distinguished *Mikulic* noting that the applicants in this case were both adults 'each endowed with their own free will' and also gave some consideration to the impact that disclosure might have on the applicant's adoptive family and her mother's family. Granting France a wide margin of appreciation owing to the variety of ways in which states deal with child abandonment (although few states have similar legislation to France), and taking into account both that the applicant had been given access to non-identifying information about her mother and would have access to a new procedure designed to facilitate individuals' access to information about their origins, the Court concluded that a fair balance had been struck in the circumstances.

The case of *Evans v UK* was not dissimilar to these in that it concerned at one level a private dispute where the irreconcilable rights of two individuals were at stake, although with a significant public interest dimension. Here, the applicant sought to use frozen embryos created with her husband during an IVF procedure, despite his refusal to consent. She claimed that the law that permitted her husband to withdraw his consent after the fertilization of her eggs with his sperm, to which he obviously consented, violated her rights to respect for private and family life. According to the Court, the question was whether the law in question struck a fair balance between the competing public (legal certainty, the importance of consent) and private (Article 8 rights of both parents) interests involved. The Court noted the complexity and difficult nature of the issue involved, the detailed consideration it had been given in Parliament and in the courts to date, and the fact that at the time of the procedure the rules were clear and had been made clear to the applicant. On this basis, the Court rejected that the applicant's right to respect for the decision to become a parent in the genetic sense should be accorded greater weight than her husband's right to respect for his decision not to have a genetically related child with her. Although detailed and well reasoned, the judgment of the Grand Chamber was not unanimous, and it is inevitable that similar challenges to private life interests will continue to emerge in this area, especially given the continuous advances in reproductive and related medicine.[219]

---

[218] 2003-III; 38 EHRR 871 paras 40–9 GC.   [219] Id, paras 83–92.

These cases show that it is not enough to establish that the interest the applicant seeks to protect falls within private life, because 'respect' does not require the state to take positive measures in every case in which these are sought by the applicant. Thus in *Winer v UK*,[220] the Commission found that the limited range of legal remedies available in English law to protect the applicant's reputation from both true and false statements about his and his wife's sexual relations that had been published in a book did not amount to a failure to respect his private life. There was a remedy in defamation in respect of the untrue statements, which he had indeed used and which had led to a settlement. The defamation remedy did not, however, extend to the statements that were true, the publication of which he claimed was an invasion of privacy. The Commission rather easily found that there was no positive obligation to provide additional remedies, in particular a remedy directly for invasion of privacy in the case of true statements. Explaining its cautious approach, the Commission noted that a positive obligation of the kind sought by the applicant would involve a limitation upon another Convention right, *viz* freedom of expression. Bearing this in mind and considering that on the facts 'the applicant's right to privacy was not wholly unprotected, as shown by his defamation action and settlement', the Commission found no breach of Article 8. What the *Winer* case does not decide is that there is no positive obligation to protect against invasions of privacy by the press or other private persons by the revelation of private information in a case in which there is no remedy at all on the facts. Nor does it address the situation where the interference with privacy takes the form of an intrusion (eg by electronic eavesdropping or long-lens photography) in search of information, in which case a limitation on freedom of expression or any other Convention right would not be directly involved.[221] These issues were the focus of the Court's attention in *Von Hannover v Germany*,[222] concerning the lack of a remedy to prevent the paparazzi from invading the applicant's private life, *inter alia*, by publishing extensive photographs of her in the popular press. At issue was the extent of positive obligations on the state to take measures designed to respect the applicant's private life in light of the opposing interest of the freedom of expression protected by Article 10. The Court noted that publication of photographs of the applicant was not a matter of pressing social concern or of public importance, and was unrelated to the role of the press as watchdog or a reporter of facts.[223] Rather, its sole purpose was to satisfy the curiosity of particular readers and, accordingly, it held that freedom of expression should be narrowly construed in this context. In addition, the Court noted that many of the photographs at issue had been taken from some distance and clearly without the applicant's consent or knowledge and in this context considered that 'anyone, even if they are known to the general public, must be able to enjoy a "legitimate expectation" of protection of and respect for their private life'. Because the German courts had interpreted domestic law only to offer her protection of her privacy when in a 'secluded place', the Court considered this to be insufficient to satisfy the positive obligations to respect her private life under Article 8.

---

[220] *No 10871/84*, 48 DR 154 at 170–1 (1986).

[221] See *Earl Spencer and Countess Spencer v UK Nos 28851/5 and 28852/95* hudoc (1998) DA concerning the failure to prohibit the publication of information relating to the applicants' private affairs and to provide a legal remedy to prevent such action or claim damages for loss caused. The Commission declared the case inadmissible for failing to exhaust domestic remedies, finding that the applicants could have pursued the remedy of breach of confidence.

[222] 2004-VI; 43 EHRR 1 paras 61–81.

[223] Cf, *White v Sweden* hudoc (2006); 46 EHRR 23, where details of the applicant's alleged criminal activities published in the media did not amount to a failure to respect his private life as there had been an appropriate balance reached between the interests of the applicant and the public interest in the information published.

The task of the Strasbourg authorities is not made any easier because, with regard to any particular interest, the facts of the case may have a determinative role in deciding the content of the positive obligation, as the contrast between the earlier United Kingdom and French cases involving transsexuals demonstrates. It might be better, where this is a feasible course, if the existence of the positive obligation were established in relatively general terms and the facts of the application were taken into account to determine whether the state had justifiably interfered with the enjoyment of the positive right under Article 8(2).[224] The practice of the Court is far from consistent. In *Kroon v Netherlands*,[225] the Court considered the case under Article 8(1) and found no need to take the matter further once it had found a violation of Article 8(1). In *Beldjoudi v France*[226] and *Keegan v Ireland*,[227] the Court did not expressly decide the Article 8(1) claim but went on to decide if the interference were justified under Article 8(2)—in each case, it decided that it was not. The cases on the 'name' aspect of private life show similar inconsistencies.[228] To some extent, the approach the Court takes will be determined by the pleadings of the government. If its argument is that there is no duty under Article 8(1), the government may offer no justification under Article 8(2) and so be without ground to stand on if the Court finds against it on its principal argument.

It has been indicated already that a state's duty to respect private life may require it to take positive action to intervene in the relations between individuals.[229] In the *X and Y* case, the Dutch government argued that an obligation to criminalize private action would drive the legal regime from protection to paternalism. While the facts of that case made the contention somewhat unworthy, the claim in general is not without its merits. There is an obvious tension between those 'fundamental values and essential interests' of private life which require that the state desist from interference with a person's activities (for instance, the obligation not to criminalize adult, consensual homosexual activities in private)[230] and others, such as those that were present in *X and Y*, where the positive obligation demands that the state does interfere to the point of criminalizing private action. Where the activities are wholly consensual between adults, it might be expected that a state would be slow to intervene. However, where there are elements of duress or exploitation, owing to youth or some other vulnerability, then the state can be expected to take action. The primary responsibility for identifying which situations are which lies with the state but, as *X and Y* itself shows, the final assessment is for the Court. This is clear from *Storck v Germany*[231] where the Court held that where remedies for breach of physical integrity (in this case the applicant's detention and treatment against her will in a psychiatric institution) either in the form of criminal sanctions or damages apply only after the event, they are inadequate to fulfil the state's positive obligations under Article 8(1). Rather, the positive obligation to protect the applicant's physical integrity places the state

---

[224] To the same end, see Judge Wildhaber, concurring, in *Stjerna v Finland* A 299-B (1994); 24 EHRR 195, arguing that, whether negative or positive obligations are involved, the Court should consider whether there has been an interference with an Article 8(1) right and, if there has, whether it may be justified under Article 8(2). Cf, *B v UK No 16106/90*, 64 DR 278 (1990) (deportation of partner in homosexual union; claim considered under Article 8(1) and (2); inadmissible on both counts). See also cases on family life, below, pp 392–9.

[225] A 297-C (1994); 19 EHRR 263 para 40. See also *Marckx v Belgium* A 31 (1979) paras 36–7; 2 EHRR 330 PC and *Johnston v Ireland* A 112 (1986); 9 EHRR 203 para 75 PC.

[226] A 234-A (1992); 14 EHRR 801 para 79.   [227] A 290 (1994); 18 EHRR 342 para 55.

[228] See further above, p 383.   [229] See above, p 384.

[230] Eg, *Dudgeon v UK*, A 45 (1981); 4 EHRR 149 para 52 PC; *Laskey, Jaggard, and Brown v UK* 1997-I; 24 EHRR 39 para 36 and *ADT v UK* 2000-IX; 31 EHRR 803 para 21.

[231] 2005-V; 43 EHRR 96 para 149.

under a more extensive duty to 'exercise supervision and control over private psychiatric institutions'.[232]

Cases involving environmental damage and noise pollution have also involved the state's positive obligations under Article 8 with varying approaches to the issues raised. The Commission utilized the notion of positive obligations in *Powell and Rayner v UK*[233] in the context of deciding whether the applicants had an arguable claim for the purposes of Article 13. Earlier cases involving aircraft noise had implicated the state directly as the operator of national airports but, by the time these applications came to be determined, the British Airports Authority had been privatized. It was therefore necessary to determine whether Article 8(1) imposed on the government an obligation to protect the applicants' enjoyment of their rights to private life and home against excessive noise from aircraft using the now privately owned airport. If there were such an obligation and that obligation had not been complied with, then it would have been open to the government to justify its interference under Article 8(2). The Court said that the 'applicable principles' were 'broadly similar' in each inquiry and it held that there was no violation of the Convention however the claim was framed.[234] In *Lopez Ostra v Spain*,[235] the Court balanced the 'town's economic well-being' against the applicant's interests in home and private and family life to decide whether there had been a breach of Article 8(1) (which it determined that there had). The investigation, as the Court acknowledged, was not dissimilar to the one it would have made under Article 8(2) to see if an interference with an Article 8(1) right was necessary for the protection of the 'economic interests of the country' under Article 8(2). In *Guerra v Italy*,[236] which also concerned environmental pollution, the key question for the Court, once it had decided that the toxic emissions had a direct effect on the applicants' right to respect for their private and family life, was to consider whether the national authorities took the necessary steps to ensure effective protection of those rights. It decided on the facts that they had not on the basis that the applicants had:

> waited, right up until the production of fertilisers ceased in 1994, for essential information that would have enabled them to assess the risks they and their families might run if they continued to live at Manfredonia, a town particularly exposed to danger in the event of an accident at the factory.[237]

In both *Lopez Ostra* and *Guerra* the finding of a violation of Article 8 had been predicated on a failure by the national authorities to comply with some aspects of the domestic regime. In *Lopez Ostra*, the waste-treatment plant at issue was illegal in that it operated without the necessary licence, and was eventually closed down whereas in *Guerra* the violation was based on the fact that the applicants had been unable to obtain information that the state was under a statutory obligation to provide. A similar conclusion was

---

[232] See also *Worwa v Poland* 2003-XI; 43 EHRR 758 paras 80–4 where involuntary medical treatment constituted an interference that was unjustified under Article 8(2). See further below.

[233] See *Rayner v UK No 9310/81*, 47 DR 5 (1986).

[234] *Powell and Rayner v UK* A 172 (1990); 12 EHRR 335 paras 37–46. See also the Commission's approach at paras 58–9 Com Rep.

[235] A 303-C (1994); 20 EHRR 277 para 58.   [236] 1998-I; 26 EHRR 357 para 57.

[237] Id, para 60. Cf, *McGinley and Egan v UK* 1998-III; 27 EHRR 1 paras 98–104, which concerned the non-disclosure of the applicants' military records and details of the radiation levels on Christmas Island where they had been stationed during nuclear testing. The existence of a procedure allowing the applicants to request this information was found to satisfy the state's positive obligation under Article 8.

drawn in *Moreno Gomez v Spain*[238] where the Court found that the authorities' tolerance of widespread flouting of laws regulating noise levels by licensed premises operating in a residential area meant that there had been a failure to respect the applicants' private and family life.

Hatton v UK also concerned the issue of state responsibility for the pollution generated by private industry. Here the applicants complained that the government's policy on night flights at Heathrow airport in London violated their rights under Article 8. Whereas the Court Chamber found a breach of Article 8, when the Grand Chamber considered the case in 2003[239] it explained that in cases involving state decisions that affect environmental issues there are two aspects to the Court's inquiry: the first is to assess the substantive merits of the government's decision to ensure that it is compatible with Article 8 and the second is to scrutinize the decision-making process to ensure that due weight has been accorded to the interests of the individual. Significantly, with respect to the former, the Grand Chamber avoided identifying which approach to the application of Article 8 was applicable in this case viewing the central issue of simply whether the appropriate balance had been struck between the relevant interests. In this regard, it remarked that economic interests were specifically enumerated as a legitimate aim under Article 8(2) and that accordingly it was appropriate for the state to take them into account in policy-making. With respect to reviewing the balance to be struck between the relevant interests, however, the Grand Chamber held that:

> Environmental protection should be taken into consideration by states in acting within their margin of appreciation and by the Court in its review of that margin, but it would not be appropriate for the Court to adopt a special approach in this respect by reference to a special status of environmental human rights.[240]

While the Court acknowledged that the evidence and data regarding the noise generated by night flights, its impact on the applicants' rights, and the economic benefits of night flights at Heathrow were not conclusive, nonetheless the authorities had not overstepped the margin of appreciation by failing to strike a fair balance between these interests here. With respect to the procedural aspect of the case, the Court noted the importance in this context of assessing the type of policy or decision involved and the extent to which the views of individuals were taken into account throughout the decision-making procedure and the procedural safeguards available.[241] In this regard, it did not find that there were fundamental flaws in the preparation of the government's policy in the area and concluded by twelve votes to five that there had been no violation of Article 8.[242]

While it may not have influenced the decisions in all of the above cases, it does seem to be important generally that the two tests under Articles 8(1) and 8(2) are not collapsed into a single one. For the government, the matter is simple: it ought not to be made to justify that which is not in breach of a duty anyway. For an applicant, the establishment of the positive duty will be of significance in his dealings with the government in a range of circumstances. While the basic test as to the proportionate balancing of interests appears the same, the margin of appreciation is clearly wider in the context of positive obligations

---

[238] 2004-X; 41 EHRR 899 paras 57–63. Cf, *Kyrtatos v Greece* 2003-VI; 40 EHRR 390 para 54, where the Court found that the noise complained of was not serious enough to amount to an interference with the applicants' rights under Article 8.

[239] 2003-VIII; 37 EHRR 611 para 119 GC.   [240] Id, para 122.   [241] Id, paras 99 and 128.

[242] The joint dissenting opinion of Judges Costa, Ress, Turmen, Zupančič, and Steiner essentially weighted the interest differently giving greater weight to the gravity of the interference complained of and to the environmental objectives generally, and less to economic interests.

than with respect to the state's duty not to intervene under Article 8(2).[243] In this regard, the development of a procedural aspect to the positive obligation test is welcome and allows the Convention to add a valuable safeguard to the process in a variety of areas, notably in the environmental cases.

II. FAMILY LIFE

Extensive claims have been made about the reach of the state's duty to respect family life on the basis of the observation of the Court in *Marckx v Belgium*[244] that Article 8(1):

> does not merely compel the state to abstain from...interference: in addition to this pri-marily negative undertaking, there may be positive obligations inherent in an effective 'respect' for family life.

The Commission interpreted this very widely where, in one case, it said:

> In shaping the domestic law, the state must act in a manner calculated to allow those concerned to lead a normal family life...The Commission is of the opinion that this con-sideration applied not only to legislation regulating family relationships, but also to legis-lation regulating the use of property insofar as it interferes with the possibility to use this property for family purposes.[245]

In the *Marckx* case[246] itself, the Court held that the state had a positive obligation to provide a system of domestic law which safeguarded the integration into its family of the child born outside marriage. By requiring further steps beyond mere registration at birth to establish maternal affiliation, Belgium had failed to respect the family life of the child and the mother. In the *Airey* case,[247] the state's failure consisted of the absence of an effective and accessible remedy for protection of one family member from the threats of violence of another. In *Hokkanen v Finland*,[248] the Court held that the non-enforcement of a father's right of access to his daughter against other persons (the maternal grandpar-ents) who refused to comply with court orders did not respect his family life. Similarly, there have been an increasing number of cases where the state's failure to facilitate the reunion of a parent with a child, especially following the child's unlawful removal by the other parent. *Ignaccollo-Zenide v Romania*[249] concerned the abduction of the applicant's two daughters by their father, and she complained that the authorities had not taken suf-ficient steps to ensure rapid execution of the court decisions granting her custody and facilitate the return of her daughters, contrary to her right to respect for her family life. According to the Court, the national authorities had a duty to facilitate reunion of the family in this context but this was not absolute since 'the reunion of a parent with chil-dren who have lived for some time with the other parent may not be able to take place immediately and may require preparatory measures to be taken'. It noted that 'the nature and extent of such preparation will depend on the circumstances of each case, but the

---

[243] Clapham, *Human Rights in the Private Sphere*, 1993, pp 211–22, especially p 216.

[244] A 31 (1979); 2 EHRR 330 para 31 PC. See also *Airey v Ireland* A 32 (1979); 2 EHRR 305 para 32.

[245] *Z and E v Austria* No 10513/83, 49 DR 67 (1986).

[246] A 31 (1979); 2 EHRR 330 para 36 PC. See also *Johnston v Ireland* A 112 (1986); 9 EHRR 203 paras 73–6 PC.

[247] A 32 (1979); 2 EHRR 305 para 32.

[248] A 299-A (1994) paras 58–62. More recently, see *Volesky v Czech Republic* hudoc (2000); *Sophia Hansen v Turkey* hudoc (2003); and *Mihailova v Bulgaria* hudoc (2006).

[249] 2001-I; 31 EHRR 212 para 94.

understanding and cooperation of all concerned are always an important ingredient'. Accordingly:

> whilst national authorities must do their utmost to facilitate such cooperation, any obliga-
> tion to apply coercion in this area must be limited since the interests as well as the rights
> and freedoms of all concerned must be taken into account, and more particularly the
> best interests of the child and his or her rights under Article 8 of the Convention. Where
> contacts with the parent might appear to threaten those interests or interfere with those
> rights, it is for the national authorities to strike a fair balance between them.

The Court has also held that in cases of this kind 'the adequacy of a measure is to be judged by the swiftness of its implementation' in light of the fact that the passage of time can have irremediable consequences for relations between the child and the parent who does not live with him.[250] The essence of such an application is thus to protect the individual against any damage that may result merely from the lapse of time and here the Court referred to the requirement of expedition set out explicitly in Article 11 of the Hague Convention on Child Abduction.[251] In such cases, the Court has held not only that the authorities had failed to take all the measures that could reasonably be expected to reunite parent and child, but that it did not do so 'without delay'.[252] One of the interesting aspects of the case law in this area is the inter-play between the duty on the state under Article 8 as outlined above, and the Hague Convention on Child Abduction. Because the domestic decisions in the area of child abduction normally take place within the framework of the Hague Convention, at least among states that have ratified it, the Court has sometimes been drawn into assessing whether states are complying with their Hague obligations.[253] For instance, in *Ignaccolo-Zenide*, the Court made reference to Article 7 of the Hague Convention (which sets out the duties on Convention states with respect to securing the prompt return of an abducted child) in the context of assessing compliance with Article 8 of the Convention.[254] Indeed, in *Bajrami v Albania* the effect of its judgment was to find a violation of Article 8 on the basis of the failure to ratify the Hague Convention.[255] In particular, the Court held that non-ratification of the Convention meant that Albania lacked the legal framework to ensure the practical and effective protection of the applicants' family life that is required by the state's positive obligation enshrined in Article 8 of the European Convention.

The absence of a legal framework such as that in the Hague Convention for resolving cases within states where contact rights were frustrated by one parent's disappearance with the children has also been a feature of Strasbourg case law. *Glaser v UK*[256] concerned a father whose children had been removed by their mother from England to Scotland. The Court accepted that the applicant faced significant difficulties in enforcing his rights to contact, which involved courts in two jurisdictions within the United Kingdom (Scotland and England), but noted that these flowed inevitably from the unilateral actions of the mother, and her determination to avoid complying with the court

---

[250] Id, para 102. See also *Sylvester v Austria* hudoc (2003); 37 EHRR 417 para 60.

[251] Convention of 25 October 1980 on the Civil Aspects of International Child Abduction.

[252] Eg, *Sylvester v Austria* id, para 72. See also *Maire v Portugal* 2003-VII; 43 EHRR 23 where the Court emphasized the four-year delay returning the child who was particularly young at the time.

[253] The Court has also noted that the ECHR must be interpreted in light of other international obligations. See *HN v Poland* hudoc (2005) para 75.

[254] Para 113. See also *Iosub Caras v Romania* hudoc (2006) para 38; *Karadzic v Croatia* hudoc (2005) para 54; and *Monory v Hungary and Romania* hudoc (2005); 41 EHRR 771 paras 69–85.

[255] 2006-XIV paras 66–8.

[256] Hudoc (2000); 33 EHRR 1 para 86. See also *Siemianowski v Poland* hudoc (2005) paras 97–109.

order. It went on to note that once a certain amount of time had elapsed, it was unlikely that the original contact order could be enforced. Accordingly, the Court did not find that the authorities had failed to take the reasonable steps available to them in either locating the family or dealing with the applicant's requests for enforcement, or that there was any lack of expedition on their part which prevented the applicant's claims being properly considered on their merits.

In *Keegan v Ireland*,[257] the Court concluded that the failure to consult a natural father (who had been party to a relationship within 'family life' with the mother) before placing his child for adoption did not respect his family life. The Court did not decide whether natural fathers had 'an automatic but defeasible right to guardianship' where the mother was not able or willing to keep the child.[258] However, the Commission found that the natural father has no right to joint custody as against the mother.[259] Moreover, if the purpose of the child's adoption is to enable the child to be integrated into the mother's second family—by being adopted by her new husband—the state will enjoy a particularly wide margin of appreciation in overruling the objection of the child's natural father.[260] Moreover, in the 2008 judgment of *Kearns v France*[261] the Court held as compatible with Article 8 that a woman who had placed her child for adoption could not revoke her consent after the expiry of a two-month time period.

Where decisions are to be made about interfering with family relationships, such as placing children for adoption or taking children into care, the obligation to respect family life imposes procedural obligations on the state. In *W v UK*,[262] the Court said that Article 8(1) requires that the procedure be sufficient to protect the interests of the family members; accordingly, parents should be actively involved in proceedings about their children. In *McMichael v UK*,[263] the Commission held that there was a right of access for parents to reports about their children in proceedings which potentially could lead to the children being freed for adoption. Nor should parents be responsible for obtaining the evidence on which a decision to remove their child is based. In *TP and KM v UK*,[264] where the applicant's child was placed in care on grounds that turned out to be erroneous, the Court held that the positive obligation on the state to respect family life requires that material on which such decisions are based should be made available to the parent concerned, even in the absence of any request by the parent. If there are doubts as to whether this poses a risk to the welfare of the child, the domestic authorities should submit the matter to the court at the earliest stage in the proceedings possible for it to resolve the issues involved.

The existence or non-existence of family life between two people may be of great importance, since the conclusion will carry benefits and burdens for them. In *Marckx v Belgium*,[265] the Court held that the situation in Belgian law which faced an unmarried mother with the choice of either 'recognizing' her child with certain disadvantages in the succession of property between mother and child, or avoiding these drawbacks at the expense of establishing a formal family tie between them was not consonant with

---

257 A 290 (1994); 18 EHRR 342 paras 49–51.

258 Id, para 52. For a comparative study of the father's position, see Forder, 7 IJL Fam 40 at 73–7 (1993).

259 *N v Denmark No 13557/88*, 63 DR 167 at 170 (1989).

260 See *Soderback v Sweden* 1998-VII; 29 EHRR 95 and *Eski v Austria* hudoc (2007) paras 36–8.

261 Hudoc (2008).   262 A 121 (1987); 10 EHRR 29 paras 64, 77–9 PC.

263 A 307-B (1995); 20 EHRR 205 paras 101–5 Com Rep, confirmed by Court, para 92.

264 2001-V; 34 EHRR 42 para 82 GC. See also *Venema v Netherlands* [2003] 1 FLR 552.

265 A 31 (1979); 2 EHRR 330 para 36 PC. See also *Johnston v Ireland* A 112 (1986); 9 EHRR 203 para 75 PC.

Belgium's duty to respect mother and child's right to family life.[266] Where paternity is contested, there is an obligation to provide a procedure whereby the issue may be resolved. In *Rasmussen v Denmark*,[267] the Court suggested that this was an aspect of private life, acceding to the government's claim that the right to respect for family life could not require a process to establish that there was no family life by reason of natural relationship. If the implication is that where the object of the process is to establish or confirm the natural relationship, then family life is necessarily involved, the point might be reconsidered. For a father or a child, the ultimate reason to know the reality of the relationship is at least as likely to be an issue of private life, of personality, which has no necessary connection with matters of family relations.[268]

The state's positive obligation stops short of support for the substance of family life. The Commission rejected an application demanding financial support from the state so that one parent could stay at home to look after the children rather than the daycare offered so that both parents could work.[269] An application based on Article 8 read together with Article 14 complaining about the lack of paid parental leave for fathers (when it was paid to mothers) was also rejected as falling within the state's margin of appreciation.[270] However, the Court found that the payment of child benefit is one way of showing respect for family life and as such it falls within the scope of Article 8, requiring any denial of benefit to be justified under Article 14.[271] The state does have an obligation to assist serving prisoners to maintain contact with their families,[272] although only in exceptional circumstances will that duty extend to transferring a prisoner from one jail to another.[273] The duty may be more extensive between prisoners and their children than between prisoners and their spouses, who can ordinarily be expected to travel more easily to visit a prison.[274]

One aspect of the positive obligation of a state to respect family life concerns the position of family members who do not have an independent right to enter or to stay in a Convention state where other family members have a right to reside. The essence of family life is the right to live together, although the Convention does not protect the right to live in a contracting state. Imposing the obligation on a state to admit a person to its territory or to allow him to stay when he has no right of residence there is a sensitive matter. The Court acknowledged this in *Abdulaziz, Cabalas and Balkandali v UK*[275] when it stated:

> The duty imposed by Article 8 cannot be considered as extending to a general obligation on the part of a contracting state to respect the choice by married couples of the country of their matrimonial residence and to accept the non-national spouses for settlement in that country.

---

[266] On matters of inheritance concerning Article 8 taken together with Article 14 see *Camp and Bourimi v Netherlands* 2000-X; 34 EHRR 1446; *Haas v Netherlands* 2004-I; 39 EHRR 897; and *Merger and Cross v France* hudoc (2004).

[267] A 87 (1984); 7 EHRR 371 para 33. The case was decided under Article 14, see below, p 579.

[268] See Fortin, 57 MLR 296 (1994). Forder, *loc cit* at n 258, above, relies on the Gaskin case to establish the right of the child to know the identity of his father. See also Besson, 21 IJLP&F 137 (2007).

[269] *Andersson and Kullman v Sweden No 11776/85*, 46 DR 251 (1986). See Duffy, 3 YEL 191 at 199 (1983).

[270] *Petrovic v Austria* 1998-II; 33 EHRR 307.

[271] *Niedzwiecki v Germany* hudoc (2005); 42 EHRR 679 para 33 where the Court held the denial of the payment to aliens without a residence permit had no reasonable or objective justification.

[272] *X v UK No 9054/80*, 30 DR 113 (1982) and *McCotter v UK No 18632/91*, 15 EHRR CD 98 (1993).

[273] *Campbell v UK No 7819/77*, 14 DR 186 (1978) paras 30–2.

[274] *Ouinas v France No 13756/88*, 65 DR 265 at 277 (1990). See also *Wakefield v UK No 15817/89*, 66 DR 251 (1990) (fiancé imprisoned, private life rather than family life).

[275] A 94 (1985); 7 EHRR 471 para 68 PC.

In the *Abdulaziz* case, the applicants had not shown that there were obstacles to establishing family life in their own (the applicants were non-UK national women with rights of residence there) or their husbands' (their husbands were non-UK nationals with no right of residence there) home countries.[276] The strongest cases appear to be where members of the family in the Convention state have no right in the law of the alien member state to join him there. Equally, where the alien is not able to return to his own state because he is a refugee, there is good reason why Article 8(1) should be interpreted to require the Convention state to allow him to join the other members of his family, whether it is formally bound to do so under refugee law or not.[277] Otherwise, the obstacles to the family members joining the other outside the Convention state will have to be substantial— economic or cultural disadvantage will generally be insufficient.[278] That Convention rights would not be enjoyed there ought to be a more compelling reason; benefits withdrawn or advantages not available, such as imperative medical treatment, might constitute an obstacle to establishing effective family life abroad[279] although such issues are more likely to be considered under Article 3 given that what is at stake is the likely treatment of one individual rather than the family relationship.[280] Although there is a distinction to be drawn between a decision refusing admission to a Convention state to a family member for reunification purposes and one ordering deportation of an individual already resident in a Convention state, the net effect in the application of immigration rules is the same in that it denies the individual the right to live in the state in question. While it is certainly arguable (and indeed more logical) that the former type of case, if not the latter, involves the existence and scope of a positive obligation under Article 8(1), they are commonly considered as a matter of an interference which falls to be justified under Article 8(2).

III. HOME

Although the idea of 'home' has been interpreted broadly, there has to date been limited case law defining the positive obligations to respect one's 'home'. The aircraft noise cases indicate that positive obligations to protect the quiet enjoyment of one's own home are to be found in Article 8(1).[281] Analogous interventions, say, harassment by private gangs or intrusions by journalists, are also capable of raising the same issue.[282]

IV. CORRESPONDENCE

The right to respect for one's correspondence is largely a right not to have one's communications interfered with. The Commission rejected the claim that there is a positive obligation on the authorities to guarantee the perfect functioning of the postal service.[283]

---

[276] The Court found that there was a violation of Article 14 because men in the same position would have been entitled to have their wives join them.

[277] Cohen-Jonathan, *European System*, Ch 14 at pp 436–7.   [278] See further below, p 418–21.

[279] Note the friendly settlement in *Fadele v UK No 13078/87*, 70 DR 159 (1991) where an alien father was granted leave to return to the UK to join his children, who had rights of residence, after they had followed him to Nigeria and suffered hardship, including problems about medical treatment. More recently see *Bensaid v UK* 2001-I; 33 EHRR 205 paras 47–8 (mental health) and *Gul v Switzerland* 1996-I; 22 EHRR 93 paras 40–3 (health of mother). Both applications were unsuccessful when considered under Article 8(2). See further below.

[280] See *Slivenko v Latvia* 2003-X; 39 EHRR 490 para 97 GC, where the Court found that the deportation of an entire family raised issues of private life rather than family life given that family life had not been disrupted.

[281] Eg, *Arrondelle v UK No 7889/77*, 26 DR 5 (1982) F Sett.

[282] On private harassment, see *Whiteside v UK No 20357/92*, 76A DR 80 (1994).

[283] *X v FRG No 8383/78*, 17 DR 227 (1979).

However, for people in detention, the possibility of corresponding with others will often depend on the provision of facilities by the authorities. In *Boyle v UK*,[284] the Commission said that while the general principle was that the state did not have to pay for a prisoner's letters, an obligation might arise where the prisoner's inability to pay severely limited or denied him the possibility of correspondence altogether. Here, the applicant's circumstances did not bring him within the exception. At the same time, the Court has confirmed that prisoners have no absolute right to make telephone calls in particular where the facilities for contact by way of correspondence are available and adequate.[285] In *Grace v UK*,[286] the Commission said that there were positive obligations on the prison authorities where correspondence was routed through the prison administration to make sure that letters were posted and delivered and that where there were difficulties with the postal service, for instance the return of an inadequately addressed letter, the prisoner had a right to be informed. There is a fine line between interference with the letters of a person in detention by a positive act of censorship, which will require justification under Article 8(2), and the effective organization of the transmission of letters which are allowed by the authorities to be sent out. The vast majority of prisoner's correspondence applications are dealt with under the legality requirement of Article 8(2).

4. ARTICLE 8(2): JUSTIFICATION FOR INTERFERENCE WITH ARTICLE 8(1) RIGHTS

I. INTERFERENCE

Article 8(1) establishes some wide categories of interest which an individual has a right to have respected although the state has the power to 'interfere' with Article 8(1) rights in accordance with the conditions in Article 8(2). That measures taken by it are an interference with a protected interest is often not disputed by the state: the question is instead whether they may be justified under Article 8(2). Examples are the storing and release of information on a secret police file,[287] the removal into public care of children from their parents,[288] stopping prisoners' correspondence,[289] and searches of a person's home.[290]

It is for the applicant to establish the fact of interference. In *Campbell v UK*,[291] the government maintained that the applicant prisoner had not substantiated his claim that his right to respect for his correspondence had been interfered with because he could not show that any particular letter had been opened. The Court was satisfied that there had been an interference for the purpose of the Convention because the prevailing prison regime allowed for letters to be opened and read, a condition which had been specifically brought to the applicant's and his legal advisor's attention. The Court stated that in these

---

[284] *No 9659/82*, 41 DR 90 at 94 (1985).

[285] *AB v Netherlands* hudoc (2002); 37 EHRR 928 para 92.

[286] *No 11523/85*, 62 DR 22 at 41 (1987) Com Rep; CM Res DH (89) 21.

[287] *Leander v Sweden* A 116 (1987); 9 EHRR 433 para 48.

[288] *Olsson v Sweden* A 130 (1988); 11 EHRR 259 para 59 PC.

[289] *Campbell and Fell v UK* A 80 (1984); 7 EHRR 165 para 109.

[290] *Chappell v UK* A 152-A (1989); 12 EHRR 1 para 51. The Court sometimes considers whether an Article 8(1) right is involved at all when looking at whether there is an interference, eg *Niemietz v Germany* A 251-B (1992); 16 EHRR 97 paras 27–33, but the two questions are distinct.

[291] A 233 (1992); 15 EHRR 137 para 32.

circumstances, the applicant can claim to be a victim of an interference with his right to respect for his correspondence under Article 8.[292]

Tying together the questions of the status of 'victim' and the existence of an interference, however theoretically unsound,[293] does give an applicant assistance in some circumstances in establishing that his rights have been interfered with. There are two separate situations. The first is where the applicant cannot establish the certainty of the material damage which would constitute the interference. As the *Campbell* case shows, if he can demonstrate that there is a sufficient degree of likelihood that the interference has occurred, that will be enough. However, evidential burdens, while different, can be difficult to surmount in some cases and, in a number of applications brought against Turkey concerning the destruction of the applicants' homes, the Court found the allegations unproven and the applications were unsuccessful on that basis.[294] The second situation is where the damage claimed by the applicant which amounts to the interference is not an actual, material effect upon him, such as a conviction, but psychological damage attributable to the threat or risk that material interference will occur, such as the threat of prosecution. The two cases are distinct but they share the element of threat or risk of interference against which protection is required if an individual is to take effective advantage of his rights.

In *Dudgeon v UK*,[295] the government did not contest that the applicant, who was an adult, male homosexual, was a 'victim' for the purposes of Article 25, even though he had not been prosecuted or convicted of an offence but it did argue that on the facts there had been no interference with his right under Article 8(1). Although the Commission accepted that the prosecution of consenting adult males had not occurred for some time, nonetheless the threat was not, 'illusory or theoretical or [had] no real or practical effect. It still has concrete effects on the private life of male homosexuals including the present applicant, even if the risk that it will be enforced in criminal proceedings is not great'.[296] Accordingly, there was an interference with Dudgeon's right. This approach was endorsed by the Court: 'In the personal circumstances of the applicant, the very existence of this legislation continuously and directly affects his private life'.[297] The Court was sustained in this view because there had been a criminal investigation into Dudgeon's activities. This was not the case in *Norris v Ireland*,[298] but the Court nonetheless reached the same conclusion there.[299]

There were analogous difficulties for the applicants in *Klass v FRG*.[300] They complained about surreptitious state activity—wire-tapping—which in the nature of things they could not prove.[301] What the applicants could do, according to the Court in the *Klass* case, was 'claim to be a victim'.[302] Once this was established, the interference which they claimed was not dependent upon the actual interception of their calls (the government said that there had not been any): 'In the mere existence of the legislation itself there is involved, for all those to whom the legislation could be applied, a menace of surveillance...'.[303]

[292] Id, para 33.   [293] Duffy, 3 YEL 191 at 201 (1983).
[294] Eg, *Nuri Kurt v Turkey* hudoc (2005); *Cacan v Turkey* hudoc (2004); and *Gundem v Turkey* 1998-III; 32 EHRR 350.
[295] A 45 (1981); 4 EHRR 149 para 40 PC.   [296] B 40 (1980) para 95 Com Rep.
[297] A 45 (1981); 4 EHRR 149 para 41 PC.   [298] A 142 (1988); 13 EHRR 186 para 37 PC.
[299] See also *Modinos v Cyprus* A 259 (1993); 16 EHRR 485 paras 17–24 and Judge Pikis, dissenting. Cf, *Seven Individuals v Sweden* No 8811/79, 29 DR 104 at 113 (1982).
[300] A 28 (1978); 2 EHRR 214 PC. See also *Kruslin v France* A 176-A (1990); 12 EHRR 547 para 31; *Weber Saravia v Germany* No 54934/00 2006-XI paras 78–9 DA; and *Association for European Integration and Human Rights and Ekimdzhiev v Bulgaria* hudoc (2007) para 58.
[301] Cf *Leander v Sweden* A 116 (1987); 9 EHRR 433.   [302] A 28 (1978); 2 EHRR 214 para 38 PC.
[303] Id, para 41.

Thus, while the individual will have to establish some reason for explaining why the legal regime *might* be applied to him, once he has done that, there has been an interference with his rights because of the threat to the effective enjoyment of them.

A different if more rare problem arises where the state maintains that the individual is directly responsible for the conditions about which he complains. In *McFeeley v UK*,[304] the Commission was faced with a wide variety of allegations of violations of the Convention during a protest in prison in Northern Ireland by prisoners claiming political status and certain privileges which would flow from that. Parts of the protest took the form of refusing to wear prison clothes or use lavatories and the applicants argued that the resulting conditions interfered with their right to respect for their private life. Since they resulted directly from the prisoners' own decisions, the Commission found that there were no interferences with their rights for which the state was responsible.[305]

Where consent is normally required, as in the case of medical treatment, action without consent will not be an interference if the state can show that the individual was not in a position to give informed consent. In *Herczegfalvy v Austria*,[306] the Court said it gave:

> decisive weight here to the lack of specific information capable of disproving the government's opinion that the hospital authorities were entitled to regard the applicant's psychiatric illness as rendering him entirely incapable of taking decisions for himself.

It should not be without importance that the Court had earlier noted that the treatment of the applicant was in accord with 'psychiatric principles generally accepted at the time'.[307] The danger is that any 'irrational' unwillingness to consent will be classed as a failure to consent at all, thus undermining the individual's right to exercise his rights as he sees fit. Since *Herczegfalvy*, the Court has changed its position, adopting instead the more preferable approach of considering the matter under Article 8(2). In *Matter v Slovakia*,[308] the Court considered that the forcible treatment of the applicant without his consent did constitute an interference with his private life. However, it found the interference proportionate given that the purpose of the medial examination was to determine whether the applicant's legal capacity should be restored and in light of his continued refusal to consent to the assessment.[309] Moreover, in *Glass v UK*[310] the Court found that the administration of treatment to the applicant in the face of his mother and legal guardian's opposition constituted an interference with his private life which required justification under Article 8(2). A more recent case, communicated to Slovakia, has raised the question of a woman's capacity to consent during labour, as well as questions about the role played by a Roma woman's ethnic origin in the medical decision to sterilize her following the birth of her child.[311] This case is likely to throw up important issues about the role of ethnic origin in the practice of medicine while it may also add significantly to the case law on the issue of consent.

II. IN ACCORDANCE WITH THE LAW

In order to be compatible with Article 8, the interference complained of must be 'in accordance with the law' under Article 8(2). If it is not, then there will be a violation of Article 8 and there is no need to examine the application further. In order to be 'in

---

[304] *No 8317/78*, 20 DR 44 (1980).

[305] Id, pp 90–1. Cf, *Robert Napier v The Scottish Ministers* [2001] ScotCS 162.

[306] A 244 (1992); 15 EHRR 457 para 86.   [307] Id, para 83.

[308] Hudoc (1999); 31 EHRR 783 paras 62–72.   [309] Cf, *Storck v Germany* 2005-V; 43 EHRR 96.

[310] Hudoc (2004); 39 EHRR 341 paras 70–2.

[311] *VC v Slovakia*, reported in the Information Note of the Court's Case-Law, April 2008.

accordance with the law' the interference complained of must have a legal basis, the law in question must be sufficiently clear and precise, and it must contain a measure of protection against arbitrariness by public authorities. While this analysis is undertaken in every case concerning an interference with an Article 8 right, it has been a particularly prominent issue in four kinds of cases: secret surveillance, especially telephone-tapping; taking children into public care; interfering with detained persons' correspondence; and recently, immigration cases.

a. Secret surveillance

In *Malone v UK*,[312] the government failed to convince the Court that its power to intercept telephone conversations had a legal basis. At the relevant time, telephone-tapping was regulated by administrative practice, the details of which were not published. There was no specific statutory authorization. As a national court held, telephone-tapping was lawful because it was not prohibited by law. The Court did not reject out of hand the government's arguments that there was a basis to be found in an amalgam of statutory provisions and actual practice, although if the Court had relied solely on the domestic judgment in the case[313] it might have done. It is clear that an administrative practice, however well adhered to, does not provide the guarantee required by 'law'. The Court said that there was insufficient clarity about the scope or the manner in which the discretion of the authorities to listen secretly to telephone conversations was exercised; because it was an administrative practice, it could be changed at any time. About the practice of 'metering', that is supplying details of numbers called and their time and duration, the Court was more forthright. It stated that 'apart from the simple absence of prohibition, there would appear to be no legal rules concerning the scope and manner of the exercise of the discretion enjoyed by public authorities'.[314]

The Interception of Communications Act 1985 came into force in response to the *Malone* judgment and its objective was to provide a statutory framework within which the interception of communications on public systems would be authorized and controlled. Although the Commission had declared inadmissible an application seeking to challenge the compatibility of the legislation with the requirements of Article 8(2),[315] the Court had to consider the application of the legislation to communications outside the public telephone system in *Halford v UK*.[316] Here, the applicant was Assistant Chief Constable of the Merseyside Police and she complained that telephone calls from her office (and her home) had been intercepted. Before the Court, the government accepted that the 1985 Act did not apply to internal communications systems operated by public authorities, such as that at Merseyside police headquarters, and given that there was no other provision in domestic law to regulate interceptions of telephone calls made on such systems the interference was found not to be 'in accordance with the law'.

The Court has also considered the compatibility with the 'law' requirement in Article 8(2) of the use of covert listening devices. *Khan v UK*[317] concerned an applicant

---

[312] A 82 (1984); 7 EHRR 14 para 79 PC. See also *Hewitt and Harman v UK No 12175/86*, 67 DR 88 at 99–101 (1989) Com Rep; CM Res DH (90) 36 and *N v UK No 12327/86*, 67 DR 123 at 132–3 (1989) Com Rep; CM Res DH (90) 36.

[313] *Malone v MPC* [1979] 2 All ER 620 at 635–8, 647–9.

[314] A 82 (1984); 7 EHRR 14 para 87 PC. See the related decisions of, *Esbester v UK No 18601/91*, 18 EHRR CD 72 (1993) and *Hewitt and Harman v UK No 20317/92* hudoc (1993) DA.

[315] *Christie v UK No 21482/93*, 78-A DR 119, 133–135 (1994).   [316] 1997-III; 24 EHRR 523 paras 49–51.

[317] 2000-V; 31 EHRR 1016 paras 26–8. See also *Allan v UK* 2002-VIII paras 35–6 on the use of such devices in prison and *Perry v UK* 2003-IX; 39 EHRR 76 concerning the use of CCTV footage for identification and prosecution purposes.

who was placed under surveillance on suspicion of being involved in the importation of heroin and who sought to challenge the legal basis for the placement of a listening device in the home of an acquaintance, suspected of similar offences. It was not envisaged or expected that the applicant would visit the premises, but he did and was caught on tape admitting to drugs offences. He lost the appeal against his conviction (on the basis of the admissibility of the contested evidence) before the House of Lords and then complained to the Court that the interference with his private life was contrary to Article 8. The Court accepted that the measure constituted an interference with his rights and, considering its legality within the meaning of Article 8(2), highlighted the need for domestic law to provide adequate protection from arbitrary interferences with an individual's rights. It noted that the law must be sufficiently clear in its terms to give individuals an adequate indication as to the circumstances in which and the conditions on which public authorities are entitled to resort to such covert measures. At the relevant time there was no statutory system to regulate the use of covert listening devices (although it had since been introduced in the form of the Police Act 1997) and Home Office Guidelines were neither legally binding nor directly publicly accessible. Accordingly, the interference lacked a basis in domestic law in violation of Article 8.

An identical conclusion was reached in a series of related cases, one of which was *PG and JH v UK*.[318] The applicants here also complained that the telephone metering of the telephone in the flat of their acquaintance, B, was not carried out under law that had the necessary safeguards to protect their Article 8 rights. The Court first made a crucial distinction between metering, which can be undertaken legitimately, for example for billing purposes, and the interception of telephone communications, which will always require justification. The Court noted that to be compatible with the legality requirement of Article 8(2), an interference must both have a basis in domestic law and, referring to the quality of the law in question, be accessible to the person concerned, who must be able to foresee its consequences for him. According to the Court, the safeguards necessary to protect the applicants' rights will depend, to some extent at least, on the nature and extent of the interference in question. Here, the information obtained concerned solely the telephone numbers called from one telephone between two specific dates; no information was recorded about the contents of those calls or who made or received them and, as a result, both the data and its use was strictly limited. The Court went on to find that while the storage and destruction of this information was not governed by any specific statutory provisions (other than guidelines), this did not raise any risk of arbitrariness or misuse. Nor was there any lack of foreseeability; disclosure to the police was permitted under the relevant statutory framework where necessary for the purposes of the detection and prevention of crime, and the material was used at the applicants' trial only to corroborate other evidence relevant to the timing of telephone calls. It was not apparent to the Court that the applicants did not have an adequate indication as to when and how the public authorities were empowered to resort to such a measure.

Kruslin v France[319] considered the compatibility with Article 8 of French law on telephone-tapping. There the French government relied on Article 81 of the Code of Criminal Procedure which provided: 'The investigation judge shall, in accordance with the law, take all investigative measures which he deems useful for establishing the truth'. Its generality

---

[318] 2001-IX paras 37–8. See also *Armstrong v UK* hudoc (2002) paras 19–20; *Chalkley v UK* hudoc (2003); 37 EHRR 680 paras 24–5; *Hewitson v UK* hudoc (2003); 37 EHRR 687 paras 20–1; and *Lewis v UK* (2003); 39 EHRR 213 paras 18–19 on the use of covert listening devices prior to the introduction of statutory regulation. These claims were conceded by the government before the Court.

[319] A 176-A (1990); 12 EHRR 547 para 17.

was supplemented by extensive case law which showed that the French courts accepted that powers conferred by this provision included the power to order telephone-tapping. However, this formal legality was not sufficient to avoid the Court holding that the French law was defective as Convention 'law' because it did not provide guarantees against arbitrary use of the power it conferred. The need for protection here was strong because a particularly serious intrusion into private life and correspondence was involved. Adequate safeguards against abuse were required. Whose telephones might be tapped? For what offences? For how long? How were results to be used? What were the rights of the defence of access to them? What happened to tapes and records at the end of the proceedings?[320]

Similarly, in *PG and JH v UK*, the government had sought to rely on the general powers of the police to store and gather evidence as the legal basis for recording the applicants' voices when being charged by the police and in their police cells. The Court found no material difference between the interception of telephone calls on public and private telephone systems and the use of covert surveillance devices on private premises, and their use without the knowledge or consent of the individual on police premises. It held that the 'underlying principle that domestic law should provide protection against arbitrariness and abuse in the use of covert surveillance techniques applies equally in that situation.'[321] Although laws had been enacted since the events in question—the Regulation of Investigatory Powers Act 2000—they were not in place at the material time, giving rise to a violation of Article 8. The absence of applicable regulations specifying with precision the circumstances in which correspondence will be redirected or opened or the categories of correspondence concerned meant that the minimum degree of protection required was absent.[322]

While many cases have involved the complete absence of domestic law regulating secret surveillance, others have concerned the quality of the law in place.[323] The terms of Article 8(2) require that the law be sufficiently clear in its terms to give citizens an adequate indication of the conditions and circumstances in which the authorities are empowered to resort to secret and potentially dangerous interference with the right to respect for private life and correspondence.[324] Moreover, the Court noted in *Kopp v Switzerland*,[325] that it is 'essential to have clear, detailed rules on the subject, especially as the technology available for use is continually becoming more sophisticated'.[326] While the Swiss regime had safeguards built into the law at various stages, including the involvement of an independent judge, it did not clearly state how, under what conditions, and by whom the distinction was to be drawn between matters specifically connected with a lawyer's work under instructions from a party to proceedings, and those relating to activity other than that of counsel.[327] In this regard, the Court has developed minimum safeguards that should be set out in statute law to avoid abuses: the nature of the offences which may give rise to an interception order; a definition of the categories of people liable to have their

[320] Id, para 34.   [321] *PG and JH v UK* 2001-IX para 62.
[322] Cf, *Copland v UK* hudoc (2007); 45 EHRR 37 paras 45–8 where the Court rejected the government's argument that the monitoring of the applicant's email correspondence by her employer, a third level educational institution, could be derived from the college's power to take all necessary and expedient measures to carry out its statutory functions to provide higher and further education. A similar argument failed in *Narinen v Finland* hudoc (2004) paras 35–6, where the government tried to argue that the power to intercept the applicant's correspondence was based on established practice applying to the administration of bankruptcy estates.
[323] See *Vetter v France* hudoc (2005) (no statutory basis for interception) and *Sciacca v Italy* 2005-I; 43 EHRR 400 (no provision in law for the release of the applicant's photograph to the media).
[324] *Malone v UK* A 82 (1984); 7 EHRR 14 para 67 PC; *Valenzuela Contreras v Spain* 1998-V; 28 EHRR 483 para 46; and *Khan v UK* 2000-V; 31 EHRR 1016 para 26.
[325] 1998-II; 27 EHRR 91 paras 56–75.   [326] Id, para 72.
[327] On search and seizure of lawyer's privileged documents see *Sallinen v Finland* hudoc (2005).

communications monitored; a limit on the duration of such monitoring; the procedure to be followed for examining, using, and storing the data obtained; the precautions to be taken when communicating the data to other parties; and the circumstances in which data obtained may or must be erased or the records destroyed.[328] In addition, it has made it clear that independent judicial oversight must be integrated into the framework to provide the necessary protection for the applicant's interests. Returning to *Kopp*, while the Swiss legal system contained various safeguards including judicial oversight at specific stages, the failure to provide judicial supervision at a key stage, ie in relation to the scope of the telephone monitoring of the applicant lawyer's professional activities, meant that the law was inadequate for the purposes of Article 8(2).[329] In *Kruslin v France*,[330] the Court explained that the issue was about whether in line with the requirements of Article 8(2), a state provided 'the minimum degree of protection to which citizens are entitled under the rule of law in a democratic society'. In *Mersch v Luxembourg*,[331] the Commission noted that while the law had to be expressed with such a degree of particularity that the circumstances in which it would be applied were generally foreseeable, that obligation did not extend to providing advance warning to a person whose telephone might be tapped where that would threaten the object of the interception (and the interception was otherwise compatible with the Convention). The precision in the law required here was only that which allowed a person to know in general when, say, the security forces might intercept telephone calls, not whether they were about to intercept his calls.[332]

The quality of the law regulating interferences with private life has also been a feature of cases involving the storage and use of private information. In *Rotaru v Romania*[333] the applicant complained that the Romanian Intelligence Service (RIS) held and used a file containing personal information on him, some of which he claimed was false and defamatory. The core issue was whether the law which permitted this interference was accessible to the applicant and foreseeable as to its results. Noting that the risks of arbitrariness are particularly great where a power of the executive is exercised in secret, the Court noted that 'since the implementation in practice of measures of secret surveillance of communications is not open to scrutiny by the individuals concerned or the public at large, it would be contrary to the rule of law for the legal discretion granted to the executive to be expressed in terms of an unfettered power. Consequently, the law must indicate the scope of any such discretion conferred on the competent authorities and the manner of its exercise with sufficient clarity, having regard to the legitimate aim of the measure in question, to give the individual adequate protection against arbitrary interference.'[334]

The question was, therefore, whether domestic law laid down with sufficient precision the circumstances in which the RIS could store and make use of information relating to the applicant's private life. Noting that the relevant law provided that information affecting national security may be gathered, recorded, and archived in secret files, the Court observed that no provision of domestic law lays down any limits on the exercise of those powers. For instance, it observed that the relevant domestic law did not set out any of the following: the kind of information that may be recorded; the categories of people against

---

[328] *Weber and Saravia v Germany No 54934/00* hudoc (2006) para 95 DA; *Association for European Integration and Human Rights and Ekimdzhiev v Bulgaria* hudoc (2007) para 76. See also *Prado Bugallo v Spain* hudoc (2003); *Lavents v Latvia* hudoc (2002); and *Niedbala v Poland* hudoc (2000); 33 EHRR 1137.

[329] *Kopp*, id, para 73. See also *Association for European Integration and Human Rights and Ekimdzhiev v Bulgaria* hudoc (2007) and *Dumitru Popescu v Romania (No 2)* hudoc (2007) (lack of independent oversight).

[330] A 176 (1990); 12 EHRR 547 para 36.   [331] *No 10439/83*, 43 DR 34 (1985).

[332] *Leander v Sweden* A 116 (1987); 9 EHRR 433 para 51.   [333] 2000-V paras 52–63 GC.

[334] Id, para 55 citing *Malone v UK* A 82 (1984); 7 EHRR 14 para 67. See also *Amann v Switzerland* 2000-II; 30 EHRR 843 para 56 GC.

whom surveillance measures such as gathering and keeping information may be taken; the circumstances in which such measures may be taken, or the procedure to be followed. Nor did it place any limits on the age of information held or the length of time for which it may be kept. In relation to the safeguards which were necessary to protect against arbitrary use of the power to gather and archive information, the Court noted that Romanian law did not provide any supervision procedure, either while the measure ordered was in force or afterwards. Overall, then, it was found not to indicate with reasonable clarity the scope and manner of exercise of the relevant discretion conferred on the public authorities and the holding and use by the RIS of information on the applicant's private life was thus not 'in accordance with the law', in violation of Article 8.

b. Children: public care

The second area in which the compatibility of an interference with an Article 8 interest has raised the issue of 'legality' is in relation to taking children into public care. In *Eriksson v Sweden*[335] and *Olsson v Sweden (No 2)*,[336] the Swedish courts had found that there was a lacuna in the national child-care law because there was no legal basis for the conditions imposed by social workers restricting the access of parents to their children who were in public care. Swedish law was amended in 1990 but the European Court necessarily found that restrictions imposed before that date were not 'in accordance with the law'. But the usual complaint of applicants in cases like this is not that there is no national law but that the national law is too general in the scope of the powers that it confers on social workers to remove children from their parents or to take other decisions about children in public care. A further issue in such cases is that the test as to the risk of harm to the child that needs to be established before intervention takes place is too low. For example, Swedish law at issue in *Olsson v Sweden (No 1)*[337] authorized the taking of children into care on various grounds including 'lack of care for him' or 'any other condition in the home'. While acknowledging its 'rather general' terms, the Court accepted that the provisions satisfied the notion of 'law' in Article 8. The circumstances in which social workers needed to be able to act were so various that a general power, including a pre-emptive authority, was necessary; it would scarcely be possible to formulate a law to cover every eventuality. Accordingly, to confine the authorities' entitlement to act to cases where actual harm to the child has already occurred might well unduly reduce the effectiveness of the protection which the child requires.[338]

Protection against arbitrariness is to be found in the procedural protection which accompanies the general power, including judicial supervision.[339] The principle that the wider the power, the greater the procedural protection required is welcome but, as is sometimes the case when the Court looks at national remedies, the actual degree of supervision of the exercise of administrative power is less than the form of the law might suggest.[340]

c. Prisoners' correspondence

Prisoners have frequently alleged that the monitoring, interception, and censoring of their correspondence was not 'in accordance with the law'. The same basic principles apply here as with the cases on secret surveillance—the law must be both sufficiently clear

---

[335] A 156 (1989); 12 EHRR 183 para 67 PC.   [336] A 250 (1992); 17 EHRR 134 para 76.

[337] A 130 (1988); 11 EHRR 259 PC. See also *Andersson (M and R) v Sweden* A 226-A (1992); 14 EHRR 615.

[338] See also *TP and KM v UK* 2001-V; 34 EHRR 42 para 67 GC, where the Court rejected the claim of the applicant that the removal of her child into care was not in accordance with law because it was based on an erroneous assessment of the risk of harm to the child.

[339] *Olsson v Sweden (No 1)* A 130 (1988); 11 EHRR 259 para 62 PC.   [340] See below, p 503.

and precise and accessible so as to allow the foreseeability of potential interference with Article 8 interests; it must also incorporate sufficient safeguards to prevent the arbitrary exercise of any discretion that the law conveys. In addition, the Court is mindful of the particular importance of correspondence to prisoners, who are otherwise cut off from the outside world and from their families. In general, prisoners' cases have focused on the 'legality' requirement of Article 8(2) either due to the vagueness of the law or its inaccessibility to prisoners. In the first such case, *Silver v UK*,[341] one of the applicant prisoners maintained that some of his letters had been stopped in accordance with Standing Orders and Circular Instructions, which were directions to governors not having the force of law. The Court accepted that these instruments, which filled in some details of the necessarily wide legal authority to intercept prisoners' mail, could be taken into account to determine whether the legal regime satisfied the Convention standard of foreseeability. However, this was acceptable only to the extent that the Orders and Instructions were accessible to a prisoner, which in general they were not. The result was that the stopping of several of Silver's letters had not been in accordance with the law.[342] Where the authorities relied primarily on the Prison Rules as the basis for stopping the letters, the Court held that these were sufficiently available to prisoners through 'cell cards' and that the guidance they gave was adequate for the prisoner to be able to foresee how the Rules would be applied to his correspondence.

In *Campbell v UK*,[343] the Court rejected a claim that stopping the applicant's letters was without legal foundation altogether in the national law because the claim was based on an interpretation of national law which had been rejected by the Scottish courts and which the European Court was not prepared to re-examine. In contrast, in *Herczegfalvy v Austria*[344] the requirement of foreseeability was held not to be satisfied by decisions under an Austrian law which allowed a mental patient's curator to decide whether his correspondence should be sent on. A curator's powers were set out in the most general terms and, the Court stated, 'in the absence of any detail at all as to the kind of restrictions permitted or their purpose, duration and extent or arrangements for their review, [these] provisions do not offer the minimum degree of protection against arbitrariness required by the rule of law in a democratic society'.

In *Niedbala v Poland*[345] the Court found a violation of Article 8 in the case of a prisoner whose letters complaining about his ill-treatment were intercepted and delayed between leaving him and arriving at the office of the Ombudsman. According to the Court, the fact that Polish law permitted automatic censorship of all prison correspondence and did not set out any guidance on how this wide discretion should be exercised brought it in conflict with the legality requirement of Article 8(2). The Court applied this reasoning in *Salapa v Poland*[346] where it examined *ex officio* a complaint about control of a prisoner's correspondence with the former European Commission of Human Rights. It highlighted

---

[341] A 61 (1983); 5 EHRR 347 paras 91, 93–5.

[342] See also *McCallum v UK* A 183 (1990); 13 EHRR 597 para 31 where 'management guidelines' were insufficient to supplement the generalities of the law.

[343] A 233 (1992); 15 EHRR 137 para 37. See further, Cram, 13 Legal Studies 356 (1993). Note also *Boyle and Rice v UK* A 131 (1988); 10 EHRR 425 para 50 PC and *William Faulkner v UK* hudoc (2002) para 12 (breach because letter stopped when Rules not applied correctly).

[344] A 244 (1992); 15 EHRR 457 para 91. Section 51(1) of the Austrian Hospitals Law simply said: 'Patients who are compulsorily detained...may be subjected to restrictions with respect to freedom of movement or contact with the outside world', id, para 51.

[345] Hudoc (2000) para 81; 33 EHRR 1137.

[346] Hudoc (2002) para 97. See also *Matwiejczuk v Poland* hudoc (2003) para 102 and *Mianowski v Poland* hudoc (2003) para 66 where the required procedure of opening the prisoner's correspondence in his presence was not adhered to in either case. A similar conclusion was reached with respect to correspondence monitored

first that it is of 'prime importance for the effective exercise of the right of individual petition under the Convention that the correspondence of prisoners with the Court not be subject to any form of control, which might hinder them in bringing their cases to the Court'. However, because Polish law did not draw any distinction between the different categories of persons with whom the prisoners could correspond and the authorities were not obliged to give 'a reasoned decision specifying grounds on which the letter could be intercepted, opened and read' this meant that correspondence with the Convention organs could be opened and read. Other flaws, including that the prisoner was not entitled to be told about any alterations to the outgoing correspondence and that there was no remedy whereby the prisoner could challenge the scope and nature of the screening used, meant that the law did not satisfy the requirements of Article 8(2).

Similarly, in a series of cases against Italy, Italian law has also been found be inadequate to satisfy the requirements of Article 8(2).[347] In particular, what brought it outside Article 8 was that it contained no rules as to the length of time for which prisoners' correspondence could be censored or the grounds on which an order for censorship could be made, and it did not indicate with sufficient clarity the extent of the relevant authorities' discretion in that sphere or provide guidance on how it was to be exercised.

d. Immigration law

Although the compatibility of immigration decisions with Article 8 has been tested many times, the legality and procedural propriety of such measures has only recently been the focus of the Court's attention. In *Liu and Liu v Russia*,[348] for example, the Court held that domestic law, which permits the executive to choose between two different procedures for the deportation of a foreign national, one of which involves procedural safeguards and the other which does not, does not meet the required standard to be 'in accordance with the law' under Article 8(2). In *CG v Bulgaria*,[349] the decision to expel the applicant made no mention of the factual grounds on which it was based but merely stated that he presented 'a serious threat to national security'. Thus, although the applicant was entitled to seek judicial review of the decision to deport him, the domestic courts' failure to undertake a meaningful review of the executive's assertion that he presented a national security risk meant that the decision was not in accordance with law as required by Article 8. Strict attention to the requirements of legality under Article 8(2) is vital to underpin the compatibility with the Convention of decisions to deport or refuse admission into a Convention state. Ensuring that decisions by the executive are checked through the process of meaningful judicial review, which *inter alia* tests the veracity of the grounds on which the measures is based, is key here.

e. Summary

Although the formal tests for 'law' are well established, their application does present some difficulties. The question cannot be resolved in the abstract but must take into account the nature of the applicant's right and the precise reasons for which the state seeks to interfere with it. The principal cause for uncertainty is the requirement that the national law protect against arbitrary exercise of any discretion that it confers. An

---

outside the terms of a court order in the context of banktruptcy proceedings in *Foxley v UK* hudoc (2000); 31 EHRR 637 para 35.

[347] Eg, *Domenichini v Italy* 1996-V; 32 EHRR 68 paras 32–3. See also *Ospina Vargas v Italy* hudoc (2004) and *Salvatore (Manuele) v Italy* hudoc (2005). In these cases, the Court also held that although the new legal provisions adopted in 2004 were Article 8 compliant, they did not remedy earlier violations.

[348] Hudoc (2007).   [349] Hudoc (2008).

applicant's complaint is likely to be that a wide and uncontrolled power *might* be used in an unacceptable way, ie contrary to the Convention. Inevitably this shades into consideration of whether an interference is necessary in a democratic society, though it is the risk rather than the actuality of incompatibility with the Convention which is at stake. That risk can be reduced by the provision of adequate safeguards of a procedural kind attached to the exercise of the power. For example, in some cases, like *Leander v Sweden*[350] and *Erdem v Germany*,[351] the available safeguards have been considered under the 'in accordance with the law' and the 'necessary in a democratic society' inquiries.

III. THE AIM OF THE INTERFERENCE

Once an interference has been found to be 'in accordance with the law' under Article 8(2), the Court moves on to examine whether the interference has a legitimate aim. It is for the state to identify the objective for which it is interfering with an applicant's Article 8(1) right. The list of legitimate aims in Article 8(2) is broadly similar to those in Articles 9(2)–11(2), except that Article 8(2) permits interference 'in the interests...of the economic well-being of country'. States have nearly always been able to convince the Court that they were acting for a proper purpose, even where this has been disputed by the applicant.[352] Examples include the secret collection of information about an individual in the interests of national security,[353] the separation of children from their parents in the interests of the rights of others (*viz* of the children, when the parents are the applicants)[354] or the protection of health or morals (*viz* of the children, when the children themselves are the applicants),[355] stopping prisoners' letters for the prevention of disorder (within the prison) or the prevention of crime,[356] and the deportation of aliens convicted of crimes for the prevention of crime.[357] Of particular note here are the cases involving children where the Court appears to have adopted the language of 'the best interests of the child' to describe the legitimate aim pursued by an interference with parents' family life notwithstanding that these terms do not appear in the Convention itself.[358]

IV. NECESSARY IN A DEMOCRATIC SOCIETY

In the preceding chapter, the complexity of the criteria to be taken into account in deciding whether an interference was necessary in a democratic society was underlined.[359] It is for the state to indicate the objective of its interference and to demonstrate the 'pressing social need' for limiting the enjoyment of the applicant's right. The Court recognizes that some aspects of the various rights protected by Article 8 are more important than others. In *Dudgeon v UK*,[360] the Court identified the right to private enjoyment of sexual relations

---

[350] A 116 (1987); 9 EHRR 433 paras 50–7, 61–7.   [351] 2001-VII; 35 EHRR 383 paras 56–9, 61–9.

[352] Eg, *Andersson (Margareta and Roger) v Sweden* A 226-A (1992); 14 EHRR 615. For a rare exception see *Nowicka v Poland* hudoc (2002) para 75 where the Court found that restricting the applicant's family to visiting her once a month in detention did not pursue any legitimate aim.

[353] *Leander v Sweden* A 116 (1987); 9 EHRR 433.

[354] *Olsson v Sweden (No 1)* A 130 (1988); 11 EHRR 259 PC.

[355] *Andersson (M and R) v Sweden* A 226-A (1992); 14 EHRR 615.

[356] *Campbell and Fell v UK* A 80; 7 EHRR 165 (1984).

[357] *Moustaquim v Belgium* A 193 (1993); 13 EHRR 802.

[358] Reference is made to the 'interests of children' in Article 5 of Protocol 7: see below, p 754. Also of significance is the weight to be attached to 'the best interests of the child'. See eg, Choudry and Fenwick, 25 Legal Studies 453 (2005).

[359] See above pp 349–59.

[360] A 45 (1981); 4 EHRR 149 para 52 PC.

as requiring 'particularly serious reasons' to justify an interference with it. In deciding that the criminalization of adult, private, consensual male homosexual relations was not necessary, the Court was not deterred by the good faith of the United Kingdom's assessment to the contrary, nor by the claim that the existing position enjoyed wide support in Northern Ireland.[361] Instead, it relied on the developing European consensus towards removing criminal sanctions and the absence of any evidence that the practice of the Northern Ireland authorities in refraining from the implementation of the law had led to damage to moral standards in the province. These considerations led it to conclude that the legislation was not necessary in a democratic society.[362]

It is clear from the case law that the importance of the exercise of an Article 8 right will be weighted more heavily in some cases than others. The Court has acknowledged that detention, by its nature, entails an interference with one's private and family life and that some measure of control over prisoners' contacts with the outside world is called for and is not in itself incompatible with the Convention.[363] At the same time, the Court has held that there is 'no question that a prisoner forfeits his Convention rights merely because of his status as a person detained following conviction'.[364] Moreover, a policy that interferes with prisoners' private and family life interests must give sufficient weight to the competing interests at stake: in *Dickson v UK*,[365] the policy on access to assisted reproduction services, which was reserved to exceptional cases only, breached Article 8 as it had failed to strike a fair balance between the prisoner applicant's interest in having children and the public interest *inter alia* in ensuring confidence in the prison system.

It is an essential part of a prisoner's right to respect for family life that the prison authorities assist him in establishing and maintaining contact with his family in detention.[366] Subjecting prisoners' correspondence to censorship and restricting visits with family must be based on reasons that are relevant and sufficient, and be proportionate with the aim such measures are designed to achieve.[367] Relevant factors may include the type of offence with which the applicant has been charged,[368] the seriousness of what is at stake for the prisoner concerned,[369] and the breadth of the interference caused.[370] Invasive searches of those seeking to visit prisoners must also satisfy the

[361] Id, paras 57–9.
[362] Id, paras 60–1. The European consensus was also important in *Norris v Ireland* A 142 (1988); 13 EHRR 186 paras 43–6 PC. See also *Modinos v Cyprus* A 259 (1993); 16 EHRR 485 and note the development of the jurisprudence from earlier Commission decisions such as *X v FRG No 5935/72*, 3 DR 46 (1975) and *B v UK No 9237/81*, 34 DR 68 (1983).
[363] *Silver v UK* A 61 (1978); 5 EHRR 347 para 98; *Kalashnikov v Russia No 47095/99*, 2001-XI DA; and *DG v Ireland* 2002-III para 105. See also *Puzinas (No 2) v Lithuania* hudoc (2007) paras 33–4, where disciplinary measures taken against the applicant for failing to send his correspondence through official channels (sending it instead with a prisoner being released) was a proportionate interference with his Article 8 rights in the circumstances.
[364] *Hirst v UK (No 2)* 2005-IX; 42 EHRR 849 GC.
[365] *Dickson v UK* hudoc (2007); 46 EHRR 927 GC. See also Codd [2006] EHRLR 1.
[366] *Messina (No 2) v Italy* 2000-X para 61. See *Ucar v Turkey* hudoc (2006) paras 133–41 where the applicant's son's detention *in communicado* gave rise to a violation of Article 8. In *Sari and Colak v Turkey* 2006-V para 36, the absence of a legal framework to facilitate prompt contact after arrest led to the violation of Article 8.
[367] See *Van der Ven v Netherlands* 2003-II; 38 EHRR 967 paras 69–72 (prevention of escape) and *Messina (No 2) v Italy* hudoc (2000) paras 72–4 (preventing use of Mafia contacts in prison).
[368] Cf, *Messina (No 2) v Italy* 2000 hudoc (2000) paras 72–4 (Mafia crime) with *Ploski v Poland* hudoc (2002) (non-violent offences) paras 36–9.
[369] *Ploski v Poland* hudoc (2002) paras 36–9 where the Court found that the refusal to grant him temporary release to go to the funerals of his parents violated Article 8. See also *Marincola and Sestito v Italy No 42662/98* hudoc (1999) DA and *Georgiou v Greece No 45138/98* hudoc (2000) DA.
[370] *Jankauskas v Lithunia* hudoc (2005) paras 20–2 where widespread censorship of the applicant's correspondence took place.

requirements of Article 8 with reference to justifying the interference with the visitor's rights rather than, by extension, those of the prisoner. In this regard, the Court has held that 'where procedures are laid down for the proper conduct of searches on outsiders to the prison … it behoves the prison authorities to comply strictly with those safeguards and by rigorous precautions protect the dignity of those being searched from being assailed any further than is necessary'.[371]

The Court has accorded a particularly high priority to the protection of a prisoner's right to communicate with his legal advisors. In *Golder v UK*,[372] the Court rejected the government's claim that it was necessary to refuse to transmit a letter from a prisoner to his solicitor about the possibility of bringing a civil action against a prison officer 'for the prevention of disorder'. Subsequent reform of the law in the UK sought to distinguish between correspondence with legal advisors about legal proceedings already instituted (which was privileged) and other correspondence, including that about prospective legal proceedings (which could be opened and read). This was also found to infringe Article 8 in *Campbell v UK*[373] where the Court held that the 'general interest' required that consultations with lawyers should be in conditions 'which favour full and uninhibited discussion'. Moreover, *all* letters to and from legal counsel were privileged which meant that 'reasonable cause' must be shown by the state for suspecting that a particular letter contained illicit material before it could be opened. There must be guarantees to the prisoner that this limited power to intercept and read his correspondence was not being abused, for instance, by opening any letters in his presence. In *Erdem v Germany*,[374] the Court was faced with a question of how to strike a proportionate balance between the prisoner's right to respect for his correspondence with his lawyer and the state's legitimate aim of 'protecting national security' and 'preventing crime and disorder' in the context of a prisoner suspected of terrorist offences.[375] The applicable law was aimed at preventing those suspected of terrorist offences from continuing to work for the terrorist organization to which it was alleged they belonged while in detention. The Court noted that the relationship between the accused's privileged correspondence with his lawyer and his right to prepare his defence meant that such correspondence could only be interfered with in exceptional circumstances. Given the precise wording of the law in question, and the safeguards involved in its application, an appropriate balance had been struck in this case. Although it was not explicit what the exceptional circumstances were in this case, the Court's reference to 'the threat posed by terrorism in all its forms' would suggest that, in this case at least, the terrorism context provided the state with the margin of appreciation underlying the exception, if not the exception itself.

In contrast, the Court has staunchly defended the individual's right to communicate with itself, and formerly the Commission, demonstrating something akin to a zero-tolerance approach to interference with and screening of its correspondence with those in detention, regardless of the offences with which they have been charged.[376]

The lawyer-client privilege is also regarded by the Court as of high importance outside the context of prison. In *Niemietz v Germany* the Court held that, in the circum-

---

[371] *Wainwright v UK* hudoc (2006); 44 EHRR 809 para 48.   [372] A 18 (1975); 1 EHRR 524 para 45 PC.

[373] A 233 (1992); 15 EHRR 137 paras 46–8. On communication between a prisoner and the European Commission of Human Rights, see paras 61–4.

[374] 2001-VII; 35 EHRR 383 paras 61–70.

[375] Cf, earlier, *Klass v FRG* A 28 (1978); 2 EHRR 214 PC. See also *Messina (No 2) v Italy* hudoc (2000) concerning restrictions on the applicant's (an alleged Mafia member) contacts with his family and censorship of his correspondence.

[376] *Rehbock v Slovenia* 2000-XII para 99; *Peers v Greece* 2001-III; 33 EHRR 1192 para 83; *AB v Netherlands* hudoc (2002); 37 EHRR 928 para 83; and *Karalevičius v Lithuania* hudoc (2005) para 60.

stances in which it had taken place, the search of a lawyer's office was not justified under Article 8(2), even though it was for the prevention of crime and the protection of the rights of others. The Court noted that where 'a lawyer is involved, an encroachment on professional secrecy may have repercussions on the proper administration of justice and hence on the rights guaranteed by Article 6 of the Convention'.[377]

While the same degree of solicitude for the confidentiality of correspondence is not required for prisoners' letters in general, the powers to intercept, scrutinize, and prohibit correspondence must be related to some specific objection and not be couched in general terms which would unnecessarily catch letters of an unobjectionable kind. If some interests of individuals are given higher priority than others, the same is true about the interests the state seeks to protect by interfering with rights under Article 8. In *Klass v FRG*,[378] the Court accepted the government's claim that secret surveillance of telephone calls was undertaken in the interests of 'national security' and 'public safety'. The threats to these interests came from increasingly sophisticated foreign espionage and serious, internal terrorist activities. These were 'exceptional conditions' which could justify exceptional measures of secret surveillance. Similarly, in *Leander v Sweden*,[379] the Court accepted the need of the state to collect information and maintain secret dossiers on candidates for employment in sensitive jobs, where there might be threats to national security. However, the Court insists on the provision of measures to protect against abuse of the powers asserted by the state. But in each of these cases, the applicant could not demand protective powers of such scope as to undermine the purpose of the interference—there could be no right to prior notification that one's telephone was to be tapped, for instance. In the *Klass* case, the Court accepted that parliamentary supervision and an independent board under the chairmanship of a person qualified to hold judicial office to review the exercise of the surveillance powers was an adequate protection against abuse. In the *Leander* case,[380] the Court accepted that the provision of several measures of control by bodies independent of the government were sufficient guard against abuse. In neither case did the Court require in all circumstances even *ex post facto* notification to an individual of the fact that his telephone had been tapped or that information continued to be held about him by the authorities.[381] This was confirmed more recently in *Segerstedt-Wiberg v Sweden*[382] where the applicants sought to challenge the storage of a range of information on them drawn from public and media sources as a disproportionate interference with their Article 8 rights. The Court held that the respondent state, having regard to the wide margin of appreciation available to it, was entitled to consider that the interests of

---

[377] A 251-B (1992); 16 EHRR 97 para 37. See also *Schonenberger and Durmaz v Switzerland* A 137 (1988); 11 EHRR 202 para 28 (not necessary to stop a letter from lawyer to remand prisoner advising prisoner to exercise his lawful right to remain silent).

[378] A 28 (1978); 2 EHRR 214 para 48 PC.

[379] A 116 (1987); 9 EHRR 433 para 60. These considerations are closely similar to those which arise in deciding whether the national law is 'law' in the Convention sense. For a series of cases where the Court chose to deal with the absence of procedural protection as demonstrating a lack of proportionality rather than a failure of 'law', see *Funke, Crémieux, Miailhe v France* A 256-A, B, C (1993), below p 411.

[380] Id, para 65.

[381] For cases where the Commission held the procedural safeguards adequate and interferences in accordance with them 'necessary in a democratic society', see *Mersch v Luxembourg No 10439/83*, 43 DR 34 (1985); *MS and PS v Switzerland No 10628/83*, 44 DR 175 (1985); *Spillmann v Switzerland No 11811/85*, 55 DR 182 (1988); *L v Norway No 13564/88*, 65 DR 210 (1990); for retention, *Hewitt and Harman*, see above, p 400, n 314.

[382] 2006-VII; 44 EHRR 14 paras 87–92 (regarding the storage of information) and paras 99–104 (regarding the refusal to advise on the extent of information held). Cf, *Turek v Slovakia* 2006-II paras 110–17 (concerning negative security clearance issued in respect of the applicant) and *Sidabras and Džiautas v Lithuania* 2004-VIII; 42 EHRR 104 paras 51–62 (concerning a law banning the applicants, former members of the KGB, from employment in the private sector in violation of Articles 8 and 14).

national security and the fight against terrorism prevailed over the interests of the applicants in being advised of the full extent to which information was kept about them on the security police register.

More typically, interferences with private life or a person's home or correspondence will occur in the course of the enforcement of the ordinary criminal law. In this context, search warrants will generally require prior judicial authorization if they are to be regarded as proportionate to their purpose by the Strasbourg authorities. In *Funke v France*, the Court said about the very wide powers given to the customs authorities to institute searches of property: 'Above all, in the absence of any requirement of a judicial warrant the restrictions and conditions provided for in law...appear to be too lax and full of loopholes for the interferences with the applicant's rights to have been strictly proportionate to the legitimate aim pursued'.[383] The customs authorities had searched the applicant's house in order to obtain information of his assets abroad and seized documents concerning foreign bank accounts in connection with customs offences which, under French law, were criminal offences. Under the law that applied at the time, the customs authorities had, as the Court noted with concern, 'exclusive competence to assess the expediency, number, length and scale of inspections'.[384] The customs officers were required by law to be accompanied during their search by a local municipal officer or, as on the facts, by a senior police officer. The Court held that the search and seizure was not justified under Article 8(2), emphasizing particularly the absence of prior judicial authorization. While judicial authorization may ordinarily be required if search and seizure measures are to be justified under Article 8(2), the fact that a judicial warrant has been obtained will not always be sufficient. In *Niemietz v Germany*,[385] the Court found that a search of the premises of a lawyer in quest of documents to be used in criminal proceedings was disproportionate to its purposes of preventing crime and protecting the rights of others,[386] even though it took place under the authority of a warrant. The warrant was drawn in terms that were too broad and the search impinged on the professional secrecy of some of the materials which had been inspected. There were, in German law, no special procedural safeguards attending the exercise of search powers on the premises of lawyers.

In other circumstances, the manner in which the warrant is implemented can raise questions about its compatibility with Article 8. In *Smirnov v Russia*[387] the applicant, a lawyer, complained about the search of his private residence which was part of the ongoing criminal investigation into his client's alleged criminal activity. While the Court accepted the legitimacy of using powers of search and seizure in the investigation of criminal activity, it recalled that such activities must be underlined by reasons that are relevant and sufficient, and proportionate in the circumstances of the case. The Court has taken the following criteria, among others, into consideration in determining this latter issue, 'the circumstances in which the search order had been issued, in particular further evidence available at that time, the content and scope of the warrant, the manner in which the search was carried out, including the presence of independent observers

---

[383] A 256-A (1993); 16 EHRR 297 para 57. To the same effect, *Crémieux v France* A 256-B (1993); 16 EHRR 357 para 40; *Miailhe v France* A 256-C (1993); 16 EHRR 332 para 38.

[384] A 256-A (1993); 16 EHRR 297 para 57.   [385] A 251-B (1992); 16 EHRR 97 para 37.

[386] The warrant extended to 'documents' that might reveal the identity of a third party to be prosecuted for the criminal offence of writing an insulting letter to a judge. The reason for searching the applicant's office was that it had been used as a post box for the political party for which the letter had been written. The police examined the contents of four filing cabinets.

[387] Hudoc (2007) paras 41–9.

during the search, and the extent of possible repercussions on the work and reputation of the person affected by the search'.[388]

In *Smirnov*, the principal concern of the Court was that while the search of the applicant's premises was being undertaken no provision was made for safeguarding the privileged materials. The terms of the search warrant were found to be very broad and open-ended, and its implementation was similarly extensive. Having regard to the materials that were inspected and seized, and the absence of safeguards to protect professional privilege, the Court found that the search impinged on professional secrecy to an extent that was disproportionate to whatever legitimate aim was pursed.

In *Chappell v UK*,[389] the Court accepted that in civil proceedings the execution of an Anton Piller order (an order made *ex parte* authorizing the plaintiff in civil proceedings to enter the defendant's premises to seize property that is the subject of the proceedings *inter alia* to prevent its disappearance) was compatible with Article 8. The applicant was a video tape dealer who was being sued in breach of copyright by the plaintiffs who obtained an order to search for pirate videos. The order was executed in premises that served as his offices and, upstairs, his home. It was executed by five persons, including his solicitor, while at the same time, as prearranged, eleven policemen executed a separate criminal search warrant for obscene videos. The Court held that the resulting interference with the applicant's privacy and his home could be justified under Article 8(2) as being to protect the plaintiff's copyright. While the manner of execution was, as the English Court of Appeal had said, 'disturbing' and 'unfortunate and regrettable', with a large number of persons invading the applicant's privacy, the issue and execution of the order was not disproportionate to that end. The Court reached the opposite conclusion in *McLeod v UK*.[390] Here the applicant's ex-husband entered her home in order to collect property that the court had ordered her to hand over to him. He was accompanied by the police fearing a breach of the peace. On arrival, however, the applicant was not at home; the police officers entered anyway and the property was removed. According to the Court, the police did not take steps to verify whether the applicant's ex-husband was entitled to enter her home to remove property (in fact he had no such right) and moreover, they should not have entered the house upon being informed that the applicant was not present since there was little risk of crime or disorder occurring (the reason for which the warrant was granted). Accordingly, the interference was found to be disproportionate to the aim sought to be achieved.

Electronic and scientific advances have facilitated the collection, storage, and dissemination of data meaning that there are now more ways for the state to interfere with individual's private lives. The consequence has been a greater number of challenges to such state activities, including the storage and use of data by the police in the investigation of crime, files maintained by national security agencies and medical data made public during litigation. The protection of personal data is of fundamental importance to a person's enjoyment of his private and family life and its disclosure to the public or third parties will constitute an interference with private life that is less difficult to justify than its mere storage.[391] The Court has held that the public interest in disclosure must outweigh the individual's right to privacy, having regard to the aim pursued and the safeguards surrounding its use. Disclosure of personal information about an individual

---

[388] *Chappell v UK* A 152-A (1989); 12 EHRR 1 para 60; *Camenzind v Switzerland* 1997-VIII; 28 EHRR 458 para 46. Moreover, in *Buck v Germany* 2005-IV; 42 EHRR 440 para 45 the Court expressed concern about the minor nature of the offence being investigated in finding that the interference with the applicant's private life was not proportionate.

[389] A 152-A (1989); 12 EHRR 1.   [390] 1998-VII; 27 EHRR 493 paras 49–58.

[391] The 'legality' requirement has also presented difficulties in this context. See *Leander v Sweden* A 116 (1987); 9 EHRR 433 para 48 and *Rotaru v Romania* 2000-V GC. See above p 403.

other than for the direct purpose for which it was legitimately collected may constitute an interference with the right to respect for private life and accordingly require justification under Article 8(2).

Whether the taking of photographs by the police amounts to an intrusion into an individual's private life will depend on whether it related to private matters or public incidents, and whether the material obtained was envisaged for a limited use or was likely to be made available to the general public. In *Friedl v Austria*[392] these factors were all relevant in the Commission's conclusion that there was no violation of Article 8 in respect of photographs taken of the applicant by the police at a public demonstration. The Commission gave weight to the fact that the government had given assurances that the individual persons on the photographs taken remained anonymous in that no names were noted down, the personal data recorded and photographs taken were not entered into a data processing system, and no action was taken to identify the persons photographed on that occasion by means of data processing.

A number of cases have concerned the disclosure of matter pertaining to an individual's private life to the media or the public. For example, in *Craxi (No 2) v Italy*,[393] the Court found a violation of Article 8 with respect to the divulging to the media of the content of telephone conversations intercepted by the police. This was based both on the failure to put in place effective safeguards to prevent such disclosure and the failure, following such disclosure, to take measures to investigate how it happened with a view to preventing reoccurrence. In *Doorson v Netherlands*,[394] the police's decision to show the applicant's photograph to third parties as a means of addressing drug-related crime in Amsterdam was not in violation of Article 8 because the photograph had been used solely for investigation purposes, it was not disclosed to the public generally, and it had been taken lawfully by the police during an earlier arrest.

A common feature of life in many countries is the use of closed circuit television (CCTV) cameras to monitor public places. The Court has accepted that CCTV plays an important role in detection and prevention of crime and that the monitoring of the actions of an individual in a public place by the use of photographic equipment does not, as such, give rise to an interference with the individual's private life. However, recording of the data and the systematic or permanent nature of the record may give rise to such considerations.[395] In *Peck v UK*,[396] CCTV footage of the applicant involved in a suicide attempt was used in a television broadcast about crime prevention without first obtaining his consent or masking his identity. The applicant had not been charged with, much less convicted of an offence and this meant that broadcasting the footage constituted a serious breach of his private life involving local and national media coverage. The release of the CCTV coverage to the public was not accompanied by effective safeguards necessary to prevent disclosure that was inconsistent with respect for his private life.

The Court established in *Leander v Sweden*[397] that the retention and use of information about an individual in connection with employment in national security-sensitive jobs (which in the applicant's case resulted in his being denied employment) did not carry with it a positive obligation to allow the applicant to know the content of the files so that he might have the opportunity of refuting data that was damaging to him. Nonetheless, in *Turek v Slovakia*,[398] the Court clearly recognized the excessive burden this situation

---

[392] (1994) p 20 Com Rep.   [393] Hudoc (2003); 38 EHRR 995 paras 60–76.
[394] 1996-II; 22 EHRR 330. Application inadmissible on this point.
[395] *Rotaru v Romania* 2000-V paras 43–4 GC; *Amann v Switzerland* 2000-II; 30 EHRR 843 paras 65–7 GC.
[396] 2003-I; 36 EHRR 719 paras 76–87. See also *Perry v UK* 2003-IX; 39 EHRR 76 above.
[397] A 116 (1987); 9 EHRR 433. See also *N v UK No 12327/86*, 58 DR 85 (1980).
[398] 2006-II paras 116–17.

placed on the applicant who was set at a disadvantage in seeking to vindicate his right to respect for his private life, finding it in violation of Article 8.

The disclosure of an individual's medical information can also cause difficulties in the context of Article 8. In *TV v Finland*,[399] the Commission held that the disclosure that a prisoner was HIV-positive to prison staff directly involved in his custody and who were themselves subject to obligations of confidentiality was justified as being necessary for the protection of the rights of others. The Court took a much stronger line in *Z v Finland*[400] and placed particular emphasis on the confidentiality of health data, its relationship with the individual's right to privacy, and overall confidence in both the medical profession and health services generally. The applicant complained that her medical data, including details of her HIV status, had been disclosed during the course of a criminal trial in breach of her Article 8 rights. According to the Court, '[i]n view of the highly intimate and sensitive nature of information concerning a person's HIV status, any state measures compelling communication or disclosure of such information without the consent of the patient call for the most careful scrutiny on the part of the Court, as do the safeguards designed to secure an effective protection'.[401]

The Court accepted that the interests of a patient and the community as a whole in protecting the confidentiality of medical data may be outweighed by the interest in investigation and prosecution of crime and in the publicity of court proceedings. Each case must thus be taken on its merits and must take into account the margin of appreciation that the state enjoys in such an area. On the facts of *Z*, the Court held that the disclosure of the witness's medical records was 'necessary' within the meaning of Article 8(2) for the purposes of a trial. However, the publication of her name and HIV status in the appeal court judgment was not justified as necessary for any legitimate aim.

Sensitive and confidential information is often used in family law proceedings but that does not mean it will always be justified. In *LL v France*[402] the applicant complained that the admissibility and use by the judge in divorce proceedings of a document relating to his alcoholism, which he alleged his wife had obtained by fraudulent means, violated his right to respect for his private life. The document had been relied on by the court in granting the divorce on the grounds of his fault alone. While the Court acknowledged that, although it is not unusual that confidential information will be disclosed during divorce proceedings, it is nonetheless vital that any unavoidable interference be limited as far as possible to that which is rendered strictly necessary by the specific features of the proceedings and by the facts of the case. Given that the document was relied upon as only a secondary and alternative basis for the conclusion reached in granting the divorce, its admissibility in the proceedings was found to be in breach of Article 8(2).

It is well established that removing children from the care of their parents to place them in the care of the state will constitute an interference with respect for family life that requires justification under Article 8(2).[403] According to the Court, it must be established that the decision to remove the child was supported by relevant and sufficient reasons pertaining to the welfare of the child.[404] This requires that a careful assessment of the impact of the proposed care measure on the parents and the child be carried out prior to

---

[399] *No 21780/93*, 76A DR 140 at 150–1 (1994).
[400] 1997-I; 25 EHRR 371 paras 94–114. See also *MS v Sweden* 1997-IV; 28 EHRR 313 *and Panteleyenko v Ukraine* hudoc (2006) (concerning the use of psychiatric information).
[401] Id, para 96.   [402] Hudoc (2006) paras 41–8.
[403] See further Kilkelly, *The Child and the ECHR*, 1999, pp 263–94.
[404] *Olsson v Sweden (No 1)* A 130 (1988); 11 EHRR 259 paras 74, 77 PC.

the implementation of a care measure.[405] The Court has established that a very wide margin of appreciation applies to states in the area of child protection.[406] This is derived from the hugely complex and sensitive nature of these cases and the Court's acceptance that domestic authorities are in principle better placed to make such decisions, not least given their direct contact with the parties involved at the very stage when care measures are being envisaged or immediately after their implementation.[407] It follows that the Court's task is not to substitute itself for the domestic authorities here, but rather to review under the Convention the decisions that those authorities have taken in the exercise of their power of appreciation. Accordingly, the Court has found a violation of Article 8 on this issue only in extreme cases, such as where the child has been removed from his mother at birth.[408] What is key in this context is the extent to which alternatives to such draconian measures were considered.[409]

The Court has instead focused its scrutiny on two related areas: the implementation of the care order, including rights of access and reunification of children with their parents, and the development of strong jurisprudence on procedural rights. In relation to the former, the Court has established that 'taking a child into care should normally be regarded as a temporary measure to be discontinued as soon as circumstances permit and that any measures of implementation of temporary care should be consistent with the ultimate aim of reuniting the natural parent and the child'.[410]

In *Olsson (No 1)*, the Court found that although there were good and adequate explanations for the decision of the authorities placing the children in foster care, the manner in which that was undertaken, ie placing two of the children in care a great distance away from their parents and their brother, was not justified and was in fact inimical to the aim of reuniting the family.[411] The same dispute came back to the Court more than four years later by which time the reunification of the family had still not been achieved. The Court said that, in cases like this, there was a positive, but not an absolute, duty on the state to take steps to bring about the reuniting of parent and child. What that duty involved in a particular case, which was subject to a margin of appreciation, was 'whether the national authorities have made such efforts to arrange the necessary preparations for reunion as can reasonably be demanded under the special circumstances of each case'.[412]

In the context of reuniting parents with their children, Article 8 incorporates an obligation to undertake regular reviews to consider whether the conditions for

---

[405] *Venema v Netherlands* [2003] 1 FLR 552 para 93. See also *Couillard Maugery v France* hudoc (2004) where it was clear that the authorities had undertaken a careful and thorough examination of the case before reaching its decision, and *Schaal v Luxembourg* 2003-XI; 40 EHRR 569 and *Nuutinen v Finland* 2000-VIII; 34 EHRR 358 both concerning access between fathers accused or convicted of violent offences and their children, where the regular reviews of their situation meant that there was no violation of their Article 8 rights.

[406] Eg, *Scozzari and Giunta v Italy* 2000-VIII; 35 EHRR 243 paras 148–51 GC; *Johansen v Norway* 1996-III; 23 EHRR 33 paras 62–4.

[407] Eg, *Johansen v Norway* id, para 74.

[408] *K and T v Finland* 2001-VII; 36 EHRR 255 paras 164–70 GC; *P, C and S v UK* 2002-VI; 35 EHRR 1075 paras 123–33 and *Haase v Germany* 2004-I; 39 EHRR 897 paras 88–105.

[409] See also *Wallova and Walla v Czech Republic* hudoc (2006) where the Court found that because the underlying reason for the children being taken into care was the housing difficulties faced by their parents this decision was not proportionate.

[410] *Olsson v Sweden (No 1)* A 130 (1988); 11 EHRR 259 para 81 PC and *Johansen v Norway* 1996-III; 23 EHRR 33 para 78.

[411] Id, para 82. See also *Kutzner v Germany* 2002-I; 35 EHRR 653 paras 65–82.

[412] *Olsson v Sweden (No 2)* A 250 (1992); 17 EHRR 134 para 90. This line of case law has also been developed and applied in private family law cases concerning child abduction and the enforcement of contact. See above, p 404.

maintaining the child in public care continue to be met.[413] The minimum to be expected of the authorities is to examine the situation anew from time to time to see whether there has been any improvement in the family's situation.

The importance of maintaining regular and meaningful contact between parents and their children in care, and bringing the care order successfully to an end is made throughout the case law. For example, in *Andersson (M and R) v Sweden*,[414] the Court found a violation of Article 8 on the basis that the government had not shown that the conditions restricting access and communication between the parent and child while the child was in care were necessary. They 'had to be supported by strong reasons'.[415] Subsequent case law has established clearly that in light of the margin of appreciation that gives domestic authorities considerable latitude with respect to decisions to take children into care, the decision to restrict or prohibit contact must be susceptible to an even greater level of scrutiny.[416] The fact that the possibility of reunification will be diminished progressively if sufficient contact is not permitted means that such interferences with family life are particularly difficult to justify. Harsh restrictions on contact will be justified only where they are motivated by an overriding requirement pertaining to the best interests of the child.[417] The more severe the interference with family life, the greater the justification required to ensure its compatibility with Article 8.

The second area where the Court has developed case law is in respect of procedural obligations, either as a positive duty to respect family life or by providing safeguards against arbitrary treatment as a condition of justifying interference with Article 8 rights. In *W v UK*, the decision to place children into foster-care was one which might lead to the severing of links between parents and children and as such was 'a domain in which there is an even greater call than usual for protection against arbitrary interferences'.[418] Here, what is required is a process which, taken as a whole, involves the parents to a degree sufficient to provide protection of their interests. In *W*, the parents had not been informed of a decision which arranged the legal basis of the foster-care seriously to the parents' disadvantage; they were not kept informed about the development of the long-term foster-care of their children and the possibility that it might lead to adoption, and they were not consulted about the decision to deny them access to the children. There were significant delays in legal proceedings, in part attributable to the authorities, all of which ultimately led to the High Court's conclusion that it was in the best interests of the child that the parents' consent to his adoption be dispensed with. Even allowing for the margin of appreciation in the state about how such cases were managed, this catalogue of exclusion and delay was not necessary for the protection of the rights of the child and there was a violation of Article 8.[419]

---

[413] Eg, *KA v Finland* hudoc (2003) para 139 and *K and T v Finland* 2001-VII; 36 EHRR 255 para 170.

[414] A 226-A (1992); 14 EHRR 615 para 95.

[415] See also *Kutzner v Germany* 2002-I; 35 EHRR 653 para 79 where the young age of the child was a significant factor in the Court's conclusion that the restrictive contact with their parents violated Article 8.

[416] Eg, *L v Finland* hudoc (2000) para 118; 31 EHRR 737.

[417] *Johansen v Norway* 1996-III; 23 EHRR 33 para 78 and *Kutzner v Germany* 2002-I; 35 EHRR 653 para 77. The Court has acknowledged that the child's interests require that he be protected but also that he maintain contacts with his family. See *Gnahoré v France* 2000-IX para 59.

[418] A 121 (1987); 10 EHRR 29 para 62 PC. See also *H v UK*, *O v UK* A 120 (1987); 10 EHRR 95, 82 PC and *B v UK*, *R v UK* A 121 (1987); 10 EHRR 87, 74 PC.

[419] *W v UK*, id, paras 62–5. Note the even more precise requirements of the separate opinion of Judges Pinheiro Farinha, Pettiti, De Meyer, and Valticos. Cf, also *McMichael v UK* A 307-B (1995); 20 EHRR 205 para 105 Com Rep, where the Commission considered the procedural requirements of child-care decisions under Article 8(1); cf, the Court's judgment, paras 89–93.

As to the level and type of involvement required to satisfy Article 8, the Court has recognized that regular contact between social workers and parents is both an appropriate channel for the communication of the parents' views and essential, given that decisions as to the child's welfare may evolve from a continuous process of monitoring on the part of the domestic authority. However, the requirement is not absolute and authorities are entitled to a degree of discretion as to whether the participation of parents in the decision-making process, or a particular stage of it, is meaningful or possible.[420] According to the Court, it is essential that a parent be placed in a position where he may obtain access to information which is relied on by the authorities in taking decisions relevant to the care and custody of a child. Otherwise, the parent will be unable to participate effectively in the decision-making process or put forward in a fair or adequate manner those matters militating in favour of his ability to provide the child with proper care and protection. For example, in *McMichael v UK*,[421] the Court recognized the importance of ensuring access by parents to relevant documentation as a precondition to their effective participation in decisions concerning their children. However, involving parents in the decision-making process may be problematic where urgent intervention in the family is required to protect a child from harm and in such cases consultation may be neither possible nor advisable.[422] Full and open consultation may also be difficult where the child's parent or carer is alleged to be the child's abuser.[423] The Court has acknowledged the parent's interest in being informed of the nature and extent of the allegations of abuse made against them and noted that this is relevant not only to the parent's ability to put forward those matters militating in favour of his capability in providing the child with proper care and protection but also to enable the parent to understand and come to terms with traumatic events affecting the family as a whole.[424] While situations may arise where a parent can claim no absolute right to obtain disclosure of evidence, such as that of a child where this would place the child at risk, in general, the positive obligation to protect the interests of the family requires that all case material be made available to the parents concerned, even in the absence of any request by them.

Procedural rights have also played a significant role in case law concerning contact and custody disputes where they have perhaps prevented the Court from second-guessing cases on their merits. The Court has considered the extent to which the process giving rise to the decision denying custody or contact rights complies with Article 8(2). In *Sahin v Germany*, in a dispute about an unmarried father's right to contact with his child, the national court's failure to hear the child directly meant that he was not sufficiently involved to protect his interests under Article 8.[425] However, the Grand Chamber disagreed noting that the applicant had enjoyed access to all relevant information relied on by the courts and had been able to put arguments forward in favour of obtaining access.

---

[420] *W v UK* A 121 (1987); 10 EHRR 29 paras 105–11 Com Rep. Decisions to exclude parents from decision-making will nonetheless require justification under Article 8(2).

[421] A 307-B (1995); 20 EHRR 205 para 92. Significantly, the father in this case was an unmarried man who had recognized paternity of his children and lived together with them. It is clear, therefore, that once family life is found to exist, Article 8 will require the parties' effective involvement in the decision-making process including access to all relevant documentation. The right to disclosure of relevant documentation is also required under Article 6 and indeed the Court found a violation of this provision in the *McMichael* case also.

[422] Eg, *K and T v Finland* 2001-VII; 31 EHRR 484 para 168. Cf, *HK v Finland* hudoc (2006) paras 119–20 concerning an emergency measure where the applicant *was* involved.

[423] Eg, *TP & KM v UK* 2001-V; 34 EHRR 42 GC.

[424] Id, paras 78–83 and *KA v Finland* hudoc (2003) para 105. See also *Buchberger v Austria* hudoc (2001); 37 EHRR 356 paras 38–45.

[425] *Sahin v Germany* hudoc (2001); 36 EHRR 765 paras 45–8 and *Hoffmann v Germany* hudoc (2001); 36 EHRR 565.

As regards the issue of hearing the child in court, the Court noted that, while it would be going too far to say that domestic courts are always required to hear a child on the issue of access, the issue depends on the specific circumstances of each case, having due regard to the age and maturity of the child concerned.[426]

Sommerfeld v Germany[427] concerned the slightly different complaint that the authorities should not have relied on the child's wishes in the absence of supporting psychiatric evidence in deciding against awarding contact with his child. The view of the Chamber was that such expert testimony was important because 'correct and complete information on the child's relationship with the applicant as the parent seeking access to the child is an indispensable prerequisite for establishing a child's true wishes and thereby striking a fair balance between the interests at stake'. According to the Grand Chamber, however, it is for the national courts to assess the evidence before them and again, it would be going too far to say that domestic courts are always required to involve a psychological expert on the issue of access to a parent not having custody.[428] On the facts of the case, the District Court had the benefit of direct contact with the girl and was thus well placed to evaluate her statements and to establish whether or not she was able to make up her own mind.

In *Hokkanen v Finland*,[429] the Court held that the transfer of custody rights from the father to the maternal grandparents was justifiable under Article 8(2), taking into account the girl's wishes and the length of time she had been in the *de facto* custody of her grandparents. This was so even though the authorities had failed to enforce court orders allowing the father custody and access against the recalcitrant grandparents. The interests of the child were elevated over those of the father and the Court emphasized the better position of national courts to assess the evidence upon which such decisions would be based. Given the emphasis placed by the family law of many states and in international human rights treaties[430] on the 'best interests of the child' in reaching decisions about him, it was to be anticipated that action justified by the state on this ground (as being necessary 'for the protection of the rights of others') would weigh particularly heavily in favour of the legitimacy of an act of interference with an Article 8(1) right. However, the Strasbourg institutions have been criticized for deferring too readily to the state's determination of what these best interests are in a particular case, to the detriment of the child's right to family life.[431]

Article 8 has been invoked in many cases in support of an individual's right to remain in a Convention state. The established position is that the right to respect for family life does not in general involve a positive obligation to allow the family to establish itself in a particular country, and the state is entitled to remove an alien for a good reason under Article 8(2), usually for the protection of public order or the prevention of crime, even where it might be difficult for him thereafter to enjoy his family life. In such cases, the issue is whether a fair balance has been struck between the applicant's family or private

---

[426] 2003-VII para 73 GC. On the wishes of the child see also *C v Finland* hudoc (2006) paras 57–8.

[427] *Sommerfeld v Germany* hudoc (2001); 36 EHRR 565 para 43. See also *Elsholz v Germany* 2000-VIII; 34 EHRR 1412 GC.

[428] 2003-VIII; 38 EHRR 756 para 72 GC.

[429] A 299-A (1994); 19 EHRR 139 paras 63–5. See also *Hendriks v Netherlands No 8427/78*, 29 DR 5 (1982) Com Rep; CM Res DH (82) 4. For criticism of the Commission majority in this case, see Gomien, 7 Neth QHR 435 at pp 440–3 (1989). These criticisms would apply also to the *Hokkanen* case.

[430] See the Convention on the Rights of the Child (CRC), Article 3(1). On the interplay between the CRC and the ECHR see Kilkelly, 23(2) HRQ (2001) 308.

[431] Gomien, above n 429, pp 449–50. Some lack of clarity also surrounds the use by the Court of the best interests principle and its weight in justifying interferences with family life.

life interest, and that of the state in preventing disorder or crime, or protecting the economic well-being of the country (although the latter is rarely invoked).

Berrehab v Netherlands[432] concerned a previously married alien who had lost his right to stay in the Netherlands after his divorce from his Dutch wife. Despite his continued close links with his daughter, the authorities proposed to deport him. What counted with the Court was the strength of Berrehab's ties with his daughter, even after the divorce, and the importance to her of maintaining contact with him. Because refusal to grant him a residence permit seriously threatened those ties, the state had failed to strike a proper balance between their interests and those of the state.[433] If this case is relatively uncontroversial (not least because the applicant was not involved in criminal activity), the extension of the principle which it established to cases involving second generation immigrants has been less easily accepted. In *Moustaquim v Belgium*,[434] the Court found that Belgium would interfere with the applicant's right to respect for his family life if it deported him to Morocco, his country of nationality. He had been brought to Belgium by his parents as a young child with the rest of his family and, as an adolescent, he had engaged in an intensive life of crime, much of it petty but some of it serious. Weighing up these considerations, the Court was persuaded by the strength of his ties with his family and decided that his deportation would interfere with his family life in an unjustifiable manner. Perhaps even more remarkably, the Court took the same position in *Beldjoudi v France*.[435] Here the applicant had been brought from Algeria to France as an infant although he retained his Algerian nationality. He was educated in France, his close relatives lived there, and he had been married to a Frenchwoman for twenty years. He was a professional criminal who had spent about half of his adult life in prison. There would have been severe practical and even legal obstacles to Mr Beldjoudi's wife, also an applicant, accompanying him to Algeria. The Court found that it would be disproportionate to the aims of preventing crime or preserving public order if he were deported for that 'might imperil the unity or even the existence of the marriage'.

Since these early cases, the Court has considered numerous applications, many of them against Belgium, the Netherlands, and France, regarding the compatibility with second generation immigrants' right to respect for their private and family life of the decision to deport them. In most cases, the applicant has been involved to some degree in criminal activity and this has prompted the authorities to authorize his deportation. While each case is different, what emerges from the case law is a clear balancing exercise of the classic kind between what is at stake for the applicant under Article 8(1) and the importance of the state's objectives under Article 8(2). Nevertheless, the outcome of individual cases has been difficult to predict and the Court brought some much needed clarity to the area in 2001 when it established the '*Boultif* criteria' as the factors to be taken into account in such cases. These include:

> ...the nature and seriousness of the offence committed by the applicant; the duration of the applicant's stay in the country from which he is going to be expelled; the time which has elapsed since the commission of the offence and the applicant's conduct during that period; the nationalities of the various persons concerned; the applicant's family situation, such as the length of the marriage; other factors revealing whether the couple lead a real and genuine family life; whether the spouse knew about the offence at the time when he or she entered into a family relationship; and whether there are children in the marriage and, if so, their age. Not least, the Court will also consider the seriousness of the

---

[432] A 138 (1988); 11 EHRR 322 para 29.
[433] See more recently *Rodrigues da Silva and Hoogkamer v Netherlands* 2006-I.
[434] A 193 (1991); 13 EHRR 802.   [435] A 234-A (1992); 14 EHRR 801 para 78.

difficulties which the spouse would be likely to encounter in the applicant's country of origin, although the mere fact that a person might face certain difficulties in accompanying her or his spouse cannot in itself preclude expulsion.[436]

Although the Court has not indicated what weight is to be given to each factor, in *Üner v Netherlands* in 2006, the Grand Chamber appeared to favour the state's interest over the applicant's in both expelling and excluding him from its territory. In particular, it was unconvinced by the fact that the applicant had lived in the Netherlands since the age of twelve, had a well-established family life predating his offending, and had both a Dutch wife and two children aged six years and one and a half years at the time of the exclusion, who he would not be able to visit in the event that they did not follow him to Turkey. The Court was persuaded, instead, by the seriousness of his offences (including manslaughter and assault) even though he had been granted early release from prison and had been deported five years after the offences occurred.

Although *Üner* suggests a harshness in approach, each case is nonetheless to be decided on its merits in line with the *Boultif* criteria. At the same time, the case law indicates that the most likely chance of success for applicants arises in cases where they have established long-term relationships or marriage with children in the Convention state[437] and/or have committed only minor offences.[438] The Court has been less sympathetic to applicants who do not have strong ties with or in the respondent state (although the Court has sometimes been difficult to persuade on this issue),[439] who have been less than honest with immigration officials,[440] and where the offences committed were serious, especially involving drugs.[441] Other notable factors include where the applicant committed the offences triggering the deportation proceedings as a juvenile and in such cases, the Court appears to demand a more generous approach from states.[442] The deportation of children also requires special measures designed to protect their family life from interference.[443] In this respect, the Grand Chamber questioned in *Üner v Netherlands*[444] whether the *Boultif* criteria were sufficiently comprehensive to 'render them suitable for application in all cases concerning the expulsion and/or exclusion of settled migrants following a

---

[436] *Boultif v Switzerland* 2001-IX ; 33 EHRR 1179 para 48.

[437] Eg, *Mehemi v France* 1997-VI; 30 EHRR 739 paras 36–7 (applicant was father of three French children) and *Ciliz v Netherlands* 2000-VIII paras 66–72 (where applicant's deportation prejudged proceedings for access to his children).

[438] Eg, *Mokrani v France* hudoc (2004); 40 EHRR 123; *Sezen v Netherlands* hudoc (2006); 43 EHRR 621 paras 40–50; and *Keles v Germany* hudoc (2005) paras 53–66.

[439] Eg, *Baghli v France* 1999-VIII; 33 EHRR 799 paras 41–9 (applicant's links with France found to be tenuous even though his entire family lived there). See the dissenting judgment of Judges Costa and Tulkens.

[440] *Nsona v Netherlands* 1996V; 32 EHRR 170 para 113.

[441] Eg, *C v Belgium* 1996-III; 32 EHRR 19 paras 31–6 (applicant committed drugs offences and had some links with Morocco); *El Boujaidi v France* 1997-VI; 30 EHRR 223 paras 37–41 (applicant had not lost all links with Algeria and had committed armed robbery and drugs offences); *Boujlifa v France* 1997-VI; 30 EHRR 419 paras 40–5 (applicant lived in France since age five but was convicted of serious offences in France). See also *Boughanemi v France* 1996-II; 22 EHRR 228 paras 41–4, where the Court acknowledged the strength of the applicant's family life with his daughter but nonetheless found the seriousness of the crime committed relevant and sufficient justification for the interference, and *Konstatinov v Netherlands* hudoc (2007) paras 49–53 where the combination of circumstances made the applicant's status in the Netherlands precarious.

[442] *Yildiz v Austria* hudoc (2002) paras 41–5; *Radovanovic v Austria* hudoc (2004); 41 EHRR 79 paras 29–37. See also *Jakupovic v Austria* hudoc (2003) paras 26–32 where the Court held that the deportation of the sixteen-year-old applicant to Serbia where he knew no one was unjustifiably harsh.

[443] See *Mubilanzila Mayeka and Kaniki Mitunga v Belgium* hudoc (2006) paras 75–86 where the Court found a violation of Article 8 in respect of the applicant child's detention separated from her mother prior to deportation.

[444] *Üner v Netherlands* 2006-XII ; 45 EHRR 421 paras 55–9 GC.

criminal conviction'. In particular, it made explicit reference to two criteria, namely, the best interests and well-being of the children, in particular the seriousness of the difficulties which any children of the applicant are likely to encounter in the country to which the applicant is to be expelled; and the solidity of social, cultural, and family ties with the host country and with the country of destination. In the latter respect, the Court held that the test must include reference to both family life, but also private life in the form of 'the totality of social ties between settled migrants and the community in which they are living'. Consequently, it noted that in the application of these criteria, the Court will have regard to the special situation of aliens who have spent most, if not all, of their childhood in the host country, were brought up there, and received their education there.

In *Maslov v Austria*, a 2008 Grand Chamber decision, the Court applied these principles to the case of the applicant, deported to Bulgaria as an eighteen-year-old in light of the fact that he continued to live with his parents and thus had not yet started a family of his own. In this regard, the Court held the relevant criteria to be the nature and seriousness of the offence committed, the length of the applicant's stay in the country from which he is to be expelled, the time elapsed since the offence was committed, and the applicant's conduct during that period and the solidity of social, cultural, and family ties with the host country and with the country of destination.[445] According to the Court, the applicant's age is a relevant factor in this context both with respect to the age at which he arrived in the Convention state and the age at which the relevant offences were committed. Taken together, in the case of a settled migrant who has lawfully spent all or the major part of his childhood and youth in the host country, very serious reasons are required to justify expulsion notwithstanding that Article 8 offers no guarantee against deportation. The decisive feature of the *Maslov* case, which distinguished it from *Üner* and *Boultif*, was the Court's assessment of the applicant's criminal activities as 'acts of juvenile delinquency'. Where offences committed by a minor underlie an exclusion order, regard must be had to the best interests of the child (under Article 8 ECHR and under Article 3 of the Convention on the Rights of the Child) as well as the duty under Article 40 of the latter Convention which makes reintegration an aim to be pursued by the juvenile justice system. Together with the length of the applicant's stay in Austria and the strength of his family life ties there, the Court concluded his expulsion violated his rights under Article 8.[446]

There has been a longstanding debate throughout the immigration case law on the appropriateness of the Court's approach, especially to cases involving the deportation of second generation immigrants following a criminal conviction. Strong dissenting judgments have been written about the need for equal treatment of nationals and non-nationals, criticizing the use of deportation as an additional penalty on the latter group, and the need to give relevant weight to the impact of deportation on the applicant who has spent a substantial period in the country from which he is being deported.[447]

Perhaps with an awareness of the harshness of its approach, the Court has begun to comment on the nature of the applicant's exclusion from the respondent state. In *Radovanovic v Austria*[448] it suggested that a limited exclusion from Austria, rather than the unlimited one imposed, would have sufficed in the circumstances, although elsewhere it has made it clear that questions of substantive immigration law and the form of legal status granted

---

[445] *Maslov v Austria* hudoc (2008) GC.   [446] Id, paras 77–100.

[447] Eg, *Boughanemi v France* 1996-II; 22 EHRR 228, dissenting opinion of Judge Martens; *El Boujaïdi v France* 1997-VI; 30 EHRR 223, dissenting opinion of Judge Foighel; *Bouchelkia v France* hudoc (1996), dissenting opinion of Judge Palm; and *Boujlifa v France* 1997-VI; 30 EHRR 419, joint dissenting opinion of Judges Baka and Van Dijk.

[448] *Radovanovic v Austria* hudoc (2004) para 37. See also *Keles v Germany* hudoc (2005) para 66.

to immigrants do not fall within its remit.[449] It has also, on occasion, gone beyond the simple question of whether the refusal to grant a residence permit infringes the right to respect for private and family life and expressed sympathy for those who suffer the impact on their private and family life of a precarious and uncertain immigration situation while they await resolution of their status.[450] More generally, the Court has, as the above case law shows, been slowly refining its approach in these cases.

Overall, recent developments in Strasbourg law highlight that the relationship between Article 8 and national immigration law is a continuously evolving one. While cases involving second generation immigrants will undoubtedly continue to cause controversy, other pertinent issues like the sanctioning of illegal entry and stay, the legal conditions of leave to remain, and the practical effects of immigration decision-making demonstrate a renewed activism by the Court in this area.[451] Nonetheless, it is perhaps surprising that, with few exceptions, the majority of the case law in this area concerns immigration rather than asylum or refugee decisions. Notwithstanding that the latter may raise issues more relevant to Article 3, there is clearly greater potential, for example, for challenging the deportation of children and parents who have spent long periods in the respondent state having asylum applications processed. The Court's reference in *Maslov* to the requirement to take into account the best interests of the child in deportation cases is both a welcome and an interesting development from a children's rights perspective.

5. CONCLUSION

The complexity of Article 8(1) is twofold: the interests which it protects are wide and there is much scope for interpretation by the Strasbourg authorities, although the way in which these interests are protected—'the right to respect' for them rather than 'the right' to them—allows some leeway to the states in determining what 'respect' requires. There is a dual focus on the state with regard to many aspects of Article 8(1). On the one hand, there is the concern to control the state's capacity to interfere in central matters of interpersonal relationships: consensual sexual activities, parent and child relations, conversation, and correspondence, where the principal concern of the right-holder is keeping the state out. On the other hand, the state's assistance is called for to protect persons from harm inflicted by others: exploitative sexual conduct, children harmed or neglected by parents, communications which harass the recipient. The practice shows how hard the various balances are to strike but, even once struck, the Court is faced with the more familiar problem under Articles 8–11 of supervising the power of the states to limit the exercise of the rights established under Article 8(1).

The Court is notoriously unwilling to elaborate general statements of rights. In relation to Article 8, this has had an advantage as well as the usual drawback of making it difficult for an account of the case law to rise above the single instances before the Court. The advantage is that the Court has been able to develop the interests protected to take into account changing circumstances and understandings without being confined by an established theoretical framework. The expansion of the right to respect for private life to include personal relationships of a non-secret kind and to provide for an element of protection against environmental damage are examples of this. It is also evident that the Court is being asked to determine issues that are at the forefront of technology—such as human assisted reproduction—while bearing in mind that they are also the centre of

---

[449] See *Sisojeva v Latvia* hudoc (2007); 45 EHRR 753 para 91 GC.
[450] See *Ariztimuno Mendizabal v France* hudoc (2006).   [451] See Thym, 57 ICLQ 87 (2008).

the human experience. In this regard, Article 8 has passed the test as to its continuing relevance and application to modern legal dilemmas and human rights challenges with flying colours. This is apparent too in the fact that the extended notion of family life has enabled the Court to provide protection for the substance rather than the form of relationships in accordance with the developing practice and expectations of people. It is one thing to get states to comply with obligations which affect only a few people and which are on the periphery of political concerns: it is much more of a test to secure the co-operation of the authorities on matters of such central and prominent interest. Yet it is against such threats to human rights that the Convention was originally designed.

The Strasbourg authorities have made use of the term 'respect' in Article 8(1) to enhance rather than reduce the reach of states' obligations. Imposing positive obligations on states, whether to take action to enhance the enjoyment of a right or to take action to prevent interference with a right by non-state actors, presents further difficulties in giving an account of the law. Positive obligations are hardly ever absolute and the reach of obligations to stand between private actors remains relatively unexplicated by the Court. Once again, recourse is made to the 'balance' metaphor but the problem is not so much in weighing the individual interest against the public interest as in deciding just what weight to attach to the individual interest. The Court's evolving views on the private life interests of transsexuals demonstrates this; the Court is deciding here the rights that are protected by the Convention, rather than balancing an established right against the public interest as it does under Article 8(2). This approach is also relevant to those cases before the Court which are inherently private in nature, albeit with a strong public interest in how it is resolved. Cases at either end of the life scale—abortion and assisted reproduction, sterilization, and assisted suicide—are particularly challenging here. Given what is at stake for the individuals involved in these cases, the 'margin of appreciation' doctrine, developed in the context of negative obligations, ought not to be relied on in the same way to determine what is necessary to 'respect' an individual's interest. Instead, the Court should welcome more argument on the real nature of the individual's interest before embarking on its balancing exercise against the countervailing demands of the public interest.

One thing which distinguishes the deportation cases is the willingness of the Court to review substantive decisions of national authorities, even though taken in accordance with national laws, laws furthermore which satisfy the Convention understanding of 'law'. Recent developments in the Grand Chamber judgments in *Üner* and *Maslov* show a deepening of the Court's understanding of what is at stake for individuals in these cases and a move away from the *à la carte* approach whereby each case was determined largely in isolation and on its merits. Elsewhere, the Strasbourg authorities have been very reluctant to challenge substantive decisions, as in the child-care cases, or practically unwilling to do so, as in the wire-tapping cases. Great emphasis is put on formal legality and procedural guarantees and the Court has been able to establish a flexible due-process standard to accommodate the variety of cases which fall within Article 8. First, there are very specific requirements for particular rights, such as the independent review required in *Gaskin* (there, under Article 8(1)). Then, there is the obligation to satisfy Article 13. What has been influential is the *Klass* case, which decided that the remedy required had to be tailored to the legitimacy of the state's power to interfere with the right rather than the right of the individual. If wire-tapping was, in some conditions, permissible, those conditions did not include a remedial system which undermined the effectiveness of a particular wire-tap. Where the authorities have been able to point to a lawful basis for wire-tapping and procedural protections which satisfy the *Klass* interpretation of Article 13, the institutions have never disputed that the interception was 'necessary in a democratic society'.

Finally, if the right protected by Article 8(1) is a 'civil right' within the terms of Article 6(1) and if the act of interference by the state has 'determined' the applicant's civil right, then the procedural protection which he is due is that established by Article 6(1), a fairly rigid standard, not as amenable as Article 13 to flexible interpretation. However, some aspects of Article 6 may be interpreted in ways related to the Article 8 character of the right, for instance, the need for special expedition in children's cases. The procedural failure under Article 6(1) may also be a substantive failure under Article 8. If it seems a cautious conclusion that procedure will often prevail over substance, it is a reflection of the subsidiary role of the Convention in protecting rights. It is only in the exceptional case that the Court will reject a conclusion of state authorities which have addressed themselves, in substance at least, to the very question that comes before the Court.

10

ARTICLE 9: FREEDOM OF RELIGION

Article 9

1. Everyone has the right to freedom of thought, conscience and religion; this right includes freedom to change his religion or belief and freedom, either alone or in community with others and in public or private, to manifest his religion or belief, in worship, teaching, practice and observance.

2. Freedom to manifest one's religion or beliefs shall be subject only to such limitations as are prescribed by law and are necessary in a democratic society in the interests of public safety, for the protection of public order, health or morals, or for the protection of the rights and freedoms of others.

In spite of the clear breadth of interests protected by Article 9, this provision was not examined in detail by the European Court until 1993.[1] Whilst this may have been a reflection of the fact that freedom of religion and belief is accorded much greater protection in Europe than in many other parts of the world, it was also, at least in part, almost certainly due to the Commission's tendency to interpret Article 9 narrowly.[2] The Commission may have now been replaced by the single full time Court, but its earlier decisions have undoubtedly influenced the jurisprudence of the Strasbourg judges when deliberating on matters of thought, conscience, and religion. That said, in recent years the Court has gone some way towards developing its own guidelines in this area, largely as a result of having received an unprecedented number of complaints under Article 9. This increase in applications is seemingly attributable to factors such as the expansion of the Council of Europe eastwards, the contemporary importance of religion on the global political arena, and the changing religious demography of Europe. Thus, from being an area where there was a paucity of literature and limited Convention jurisprudence, there is now a developing case law and a wide range of published material on Article 9.[3]

---

[1] See *Kokkinakis v Greece* A 260-A (1993); 17 EHRR 397, described by Judge Pettiti (p 425) in his partly concurring judgment as 'the first real proceedings brought before the European Court since its creation which concerns freedom of religion'.

[2] Eg, see *Arrowsmith v UK No 7050/75*, 19 DR 5 (1978) Com Rep; CM Res DH (79) 4.

[3] See Uitz, *Europeans and their Rights—Freedom of Religion*, 2007; Taylor, *Freedom of Religion: UN and European Human Rights Law and Practice*, 2005; Renucci, *Article 9 of the European Convention on Human Rights: Freedom of Thought, Conscience and Religion*, 2005; C Evans, *Freedom of Religion under the European Convention on Human Rights*, 2001; M Evans, *Religious Liberty and International Law in Europe*, 1997.

1. THE SCOPE OF ARTICLE 9

Although the *travaux préparatoires* make it clear that those responsible for drafting the ECHR viewed freedom of religion as a fundamental right which demanded inclusion,[4] and some of the Convention's drafters acknowledged the influence of their own religious convictions in this regard,[5] it is indisputable that Article 9 protects both religious *and* non-religious beliefs. For example, in *Kokkinakis v Greece*,[6] the Court said that the values of Article 9 were at the foundation of a democratic society:

> It is, in its religious dimension, one of the most vital elements that go to make up the identity of believers and their conception of life, but it is also a precious asset for atheists, agnostics, sceptics and the unconcerned.

As a consequence, Article 9 of the ECHR is confined not merely to long established religions (eg, Buddhism,[7] Christianity,[8] Hinduism,[9] Islam,[10] Judaism,[11] Sikhism[12]), but it has also afforded protection to relatively new religious organizations (eg, the Jehovah's Witnesses,[13] the Church of Scientology[14]), as well as covering a wide range of philosophical beliefs (eg, pacifism,[15] veganism,[16] and opposition to abortion[17]). Indeed, some previous rulings of the Commission appear to suggest that controversial political philosophies such as fascism,[18] communism,[19] and neo-Nazi principles[20] may even constitute beliefs for the purposes of Article 9.

By giving such a broad interpretation to Article 9,[21] the Convention organs have conspicuously avoided any determination of what is meant by the term 'religion'.[22] This approach is understandable, because any definition of 'religion' would need to be flexible enough to satisfy a broad cross-section of world faiths, as well as sufficiently precise for practical application in specific cases. Such a balance would be practically impossible to strike and echoes the approach of the Human Rights Committee, which has also refrained from seeking to define 'religion' under the International Covenant on Civil and Political Rights (1966).[23] Thus, the inclusion of the term 'belief' in Article 9(1) enables the Court to avoid having to grapple with the formidable problems associated with defining the

---

[4] See C Evans, n 3 above, p 39.   [5] Id, pp 39, 40.   [6] A 260-A (1993); 17 EHRR 397 para 31.

[7] *X v UK No 5442/72*, 1 DR 41 (1975).   [8] *Stedman v UK No 29107/95* hudoc (1997); 23 EHRR CD 168.

[9] *ISKCON v UK No 20490/92* hudoc (1994); 18 EHRR CD 133.

[10] *X v UK No 8160/78*, 22 DR 27 (1981).   [11] *D v France No 10180/82*, 35 DR 1993 (1983).

[12] *X v UK No 8231/78*, 28 DR 5 (1982).   [13] *Manoussakis v Greece* 1996-IV; 23 EHRR 387.

[14] *Church of Scientology Moscow v Russia* hudoc (2007); 46 EHRR 304 para 64, where Article 11 was read in the light of Article 9.

[15] *Arrowsmith v UK No 7050/75*, 19 DR 5 (1978) Com Rep; CM Res DH (79) 4.

[16] *H v UK No 18187/91* hudoc (1993); 16 EHRR CD 44.

[17] *Knudsen v Norway No 11045/84*, 42 DR 247 (1985).   [18] *X v Italy No 6741/74*, 5 DR 83 (1976).

[19] *Hazar and Açik v Turkey Nos 16311/90, 16312/90 and 16311/93*, 72 DR 200 (1991).

[20] *X v Austria No 1747/62*, 13 CD 42 (1963).

[21] In *Chassagnou v France* 1999-III; 29 EHRR 615 GC, Judge Fischbach (p 72, in a separate opinion) even suggested 'that "environmentalist" or "ecological" beliefs come within the scope of Article 9 insofar as they are informed by what is a truly societal stance'.

[22] See *X and Church of Scientology v Sweden No 7805/77*, 16 DR 68 at 72 (1979); *X v UK No 7291/75*, 11 DR 55 (1977); *Omkarananda and the Divine Light Zentrum v Switzerland No 8118/77*, 25 DR 105 (1981); and *Chappell v UK No 12587/86*, 53 DR 241 (1987).

[23] Human Rights Committee, General Comment 22, Article 18 (Forty-Eighth session, 1993) paras 1, 2.

word 'religion'.[24] But this can also sometimes lead to uncertainty, especially in relation to whether certain controversial new religious movements are (or should be) protected by Article 9.[25]

Even though 'belief' has been interpreted widely under Article 9, the meaning accorded to this term is not exhaustive. For example, the Commission rejected an application from a man who wished to have his cremated ashes scattered over his land on the basis that his motivation—a desire not to be buried in a cemetery with Christian symbols—was insufficiently 'coherent'.[26] Similarly, the 'idealistic' aims of an organization offering free legal advice to prisoners could not bring it within the scope of Article 9.[27] More recently, the Court rejected the submission that Article 9 encompassed the notion of assisted suicide, on the basis that 'not all opinions or convictions constitute beliefs in the sense protected by Article 9(1) of the Convention'.[28] Thus, it is generally recognized that in order to be afforded protection under the Convention, a belief must 'attain a certain level of cogency, seriousness, cohesion and importance',[29] and that once this threshold has been met the state may not 'determine whether religious beliefs ... are legitimate'.[30]

It is also important to bear in mind the structure of Article 9. The first part of Article 9(1) guarantees 'the right to freedom of thought, conscience and religion,' whereas 'belief' is only mentioned in the next clause, which stipulates that 'this right includes freedom to change [one's] religion or belief'. The issue as to whether there is a significant difference between 'thought and conscience' on the one hand, and 'religion or belief' on the other, has led to the claim that such distinctions are 'improbable' and unimportant.[31] However, a more widely held view is that 'religion or belief' should be distinguished from 'thought and conscience' on the basis that Article 9 protects the manifestation of 'religion or belief', whereas expressions of one's 'thought and conscience' are protected by (and confined to) Article 10 of the Convention.[32] In this context Evans suggests that 'it is best to reserve the term "manifestation" to describe a particular form of expression which is only relevant to religion or belief [and that] there can be no question of manifesting or "actualizing" thought or conscience under Article 9'.[33]

---

[24] On this generally see Gunn, 16 Harv HRJ 189–215 (2003).

[25] Eg, in *Church of Scientology Moscow v Russia* hudoc (2007); 46 EHRR 304, the Court held that there had been a violation of Article 11, read in the light of Article 9, following the failure of the Church of Scientology to be re-registered as a religious association under a new Russian law. However, the Court avoided commenting on the 'religious' nature of this organization, other than noting that Article 9 was of relevance because 'the religious nature of the applicant was not disputed at the national level and it had been officially recognized as a religious organization since 1994': id, para 64.

[26] *X v Federal Republic of Germany No 8741/79*, 24 DR 137 (1978).

[27] *Vereniging Rechtswinkels Utrecht v Netherlands*, 46 DR 200 (1986).

[28] See *Pretty v UK* 2002-III; 35 EHRR 1 para 82, where the claim that assisted suicide constituted a belief for the purposes of Article 9(1) was rejected.

[29] *Campbell and Cosans v UK* A 48 (1982); 4 EHRR 293 para 36. In this case the Court was considering 'belief' in the context of Article 2 of Protocol 1, and not under Article 9.

[30] *Hasan and Chaush v Bulgaria* 2000-XI; 34 EHRR 1339 para 78 GC; *Manoussakis v Greece* 1996-IV; 23 EHRR 387 para 47.

[31] See Edge, 1996 Juridical Review 42 at 43.

[32] See M Evans, n 3 above, pp 284–6 and C Evans, n 3 above, pp 52, 53. On Article 10 see pp 443–515.

[33] M Evans, n 3 above, p 285. See also *Ivanova v Bulgaria No 52435/99* hudoc (2007) para 79, where the Court observed that 'Unlike the second paragraphs of Articles 8, 10 and 11 of the Convention, which cover all the rights mentioned in the first paragraphs of those Articles, that of Article 9 of the Convention refers only to "freedom to manifest one's religion or belief".

2. FREEDOM OF THOUGHT, CONSCIENCE, AND RELIGION: THE RIGHT TO BELIEVE

I. ARTICLE 9: INTERNAL AND EXTERNAL DIMENSIONS

There are two elements to Article 9(1). First, it has an 'internal' dimension (*forum internum*), in that it guarantees 'freedom of thought, conscience and religion'.[34] This right, which is 'largely exercised inside an individual's heart and mind',[35] falls beyond the jurisdiction of the state and must not be restricted.[36] Secondly, Article 9(1) has an 'external' element (*forum externum*) since it recognizes that everyone has the right to manifest a 'religion or belief' in 'worship, teaching, practice and observance'. Accordingly, subject to the 'prescribed by law' and 'necessary in a democratic society' criteria, the state may impose restrictions on the *manifestation* of religion or belief on the grounds of public safety, public order, health, or morals and 'for the protection of the rights and freedoms of others'.[37]

The distinction between this 'internal' and 'external' dimension is not clearly defined. For some the scope of the *forum internum* is relatively narrow and that as long as 'individuals are able to continue in their beliefs',[38] Article 9(1) will not be violated. In contrast, others take a broader view, insisting that there are more subtle ways in which the state may interfere with one's *forum internum*.[39] The jurisprudence of the Court tends to reflect the former rather than the latter approach.[40] For example, in *Buscarini and others v San Marino*[41]—where the applicants were required to swear an oath on the Christian Gospels in order to take their seats in the San Marino Parliament—the Court held that this legal obligation 'did indeed constitute a limitation within the meaning of the second paragraph of Article 9, since it required them to swear allegiance to a particular religion'.[42] Although some argue that on the facts of this case there was an interference with the *forum internum*[43]—which would have then precluded the imposition of restrictions on the applicants' rights—the Court refrained from considering such matters, and held instead that Article 9 had been violated because the obligation to swear an oath was not 'necessary in a democratic society' under Article 9(2).[44]

Whilst there is uncertainty at the margins, certain conduct is undoubtedly contrary to the *forum internum*. For example, the use of physical threats or sanctions that force people to deny or adhere to a particular religion or belief is forbidden.[45] Even though

---

[34] See Article 9(1) of the ECHR. Article 18 of the UN Declaration on Human Rights (1948) and Article 18(1) and (3) of the International Covenant on Civil and Political Rights 1966 (ICCPR) are also drafted according to this model.

[35] Gomien, *Short Guide to the European Convention on Human Rights*, 1991, p 69.

[36] *Darby v Sweden* A 187 (1990); 13 EHRR 774 para 44 Com Rep.

[37] Article 9(2). Under Article 15 of the ECHR a state may also derogate from its Article 9 obligations '[i]n time of war or other public emergency threatening the life of the nation'. This is in contrast to the ICCPR, whereby Article 4(2) precludes derogation from the principle of thought, conscience, and religion (Article 18) in such circumstances.

[38] See M Evans, n 3 above, p 295.   [39] See C Evans, n 3 above, pp 72–81.

[40] Indeed Carolyn Evans suggests that 'States have to act very repressively before the Court...will hold that they have interfered with the *forum internum*'. Id, p 78.

[41] 1999-I; 30 EHRR 208 GC.   [42] Id, para 34.

[43] C Evans, n 3 above, p 73, Taylor, n 3 above, p 130.

[44] In *Buscarini and others v San Marino* 1999-I; 30 EHRR 208 para 39 GC.

[45] See Tahzib, *Freedom of Religion or Belief: Ensuring Effective International Protection*, 1996, p 26.

Article 9 does not outlaw 'coercion' in express terms,[46] the right to change one's religion or belief is, in effect, a bulwark against 'indoctrination of religion by the state'.[47] The benchmark for 'indoctrination' would appear to have been set narrowly,[48] but in this context as long as an individual is free to hold his own beliefs, the terms of Article 9(1) are unlikely to be violated.[49]

Less draconian (albeit equally pervasive) state actions can also fall foul of Article 9. The state may, for example, neither dictate nor demand to know what an individual believes.[50] Although a legal obligation to complete a census form interferes with one's right to respect for a private life (Article 8(1)), and can be justified as being necessary for the economic well-being of the country under Article 8(2),[51] no such principle applies to Article 9. In contrast, however, because such a measure is seemingly incompatible with the *forum internum* under Article 9(1), a state's actions in seeking to compel an individual to reveal their beliefs cannot be justified under Article 9(2).[52] Perhaps the explanation for this positive affirmation of freedom of thought, conscience, and religion is that there are unlikely to be good reasons why the state should need such information, but there are undoubtedly many bad ones, especially when one bears in mind the Inquisition and the coercive investigations of modern totalitarian regimes.

Finally, the question of whether Article 9 prevents states from expelling non-nationals to countries where they may face religious persecution has been considered by the Court. In *Z and T v UK*,[53] the Court held that Article 9 offers 'very limited assistance' where an applicant claims that they will be 'impeded [in their] religious worship', if returned to their country of origin.[54] The Court's justification for this approach is that to have decided otherwise would have meant 'imposing an obligation on Contracting States effectively to act as indirect guarantors of freedom of worship for the rest of the world'.[55] As has often been the case in relation to such politically sensitive matters,[56] the demands of realpolitik perhaps lie at the heart of the Court's ruling that Article 9 will only be engaged in 'exceptional circumstances' in regard to expulsion and claims of persecution on the grounds of religion or belief.[57]

[46] This is in contrast to Article 18(2) of the ICCPR 1966 which provides that, 'No one shall be subject to coercion which would impair his freedom to have or to adopt a religion or belief of his choice'.

[47] *Angelini v Sweden No 10491/83*, 51 DR 41 at 48 (1986).

[48] Eg, in *CJ, JJ and EJ v Poland No 23380/94*, 84A DR 46 (1996), the Commission held that the attendance of a twelve-year-old girl in religious instruction lessons was 'voluntary', even though she had been under pressure from the school to do so, and had previously been forced to wait in the corridor during such classes.

[49] Forms of 'indoctrination' may also raise issues under Article 3. See Judge Martens in *Kokkinakis v Greece* A 260-A (1993); 17 EHRR 397 para 18.

[50] Eg, in *Folgerø v Norway* hudoc (2007); 46 EHRR 1147 para 98 GC, the European Court held that 'imposing an obligation on parents to disclose detailed information to the school authorities about their religious and philosophical convictions may constitute a violation of Art.8 of the Convention and, possibly also, of Art.9'.

[51] *X v UK No 8160/78*, 22 DR 27 at 36 (1981).

[52] See *Alexandridis v Greece* hudoc (2008), where a requirement on the applicant to disclose that he was not a member of the Orthodox Church, in taking an oath to practise as a lawyer, violated Article 9.

[53] *No 27034/05* hudoc (2006) DA.

[54] In *Z and T v UK, ibid*, the Court recognized that, aside from Article 9, expulsion may lead to claims of torture, inhuman or degrading treatment, or punishment under Article 3. On Article 3 see pp 69–112.

[55] *Ibid*.

[56] Eg, in *El Majjaoui and Stichting Touba Moskee v Netherlands* hudoc (2007) para 32 GC, the Court held that Article 9 did not guarantee the employees of religious organizations a right to have residence permits in other contracting states.

[57] *Z and T v UK No 27034/05* hudoc (2006) DA.

a. Church/state relations

A church or association with religious and philosophical objects is capable of exercising rights under Article 9.[58] Its interests, as well as those of its members, may be protected under the Convention,[59] a seeming legacy of the fact that Article 9(1) offers rights to '[e]veryone'. The Convention also appears to afford protection to freedom *of* and freedom *from* a particular religion or belief. This proposition derives from the Court's assertion that Article 9 guarantees 'freedom to hold or not to hold religious beliefs and practice or not to practice a religion'.[60]

Neutrality is evidently the watchword for the state's relationship with faith communities and individuals.[61] The Court has, for example, held that 'the believer's right to freedom of religion encompasses the expectation that the community will be allowed to function peacefully free from arbitrary State intervention'.[62] Moreover, it has emphasized that:

> the autonomous existence of religious communities is indispensable for pluralism in a democratic society and is thus an issue at the very heart of the protection which Article 9 affords.[63]

With this in mind there are at least five areas where those in government must tread warily.

First, the state must ensure that religious organizations retain autonomy in relation to the selection of their own leaders.[64] For example, in *Hasan and Chaush v Bulgaria*,[65] following a dispute within the Bulgarian Muslim community as to who should be its national leader (Chief Mufti), the government effectively replaced the applicant who had been elected to this office (Hasan) with another candidate who had previously held the post. The Court held that, as a result of this decision, it had been shown to 'favour one faction of the Muslim community...to the complete exclusion of the hitherto recognized leadership', and that Article 9 had been violated because of 'an interference with the internal organization of the Muslim community'.[66] Thus, even if a government contends that it has appointed the leader of a particular religious group with the (ostensibly) legitimate aim of avoiding intra faith strife, such a claim will almost certainly fail. In acknowledging that community relations may be threatened by divisions between religious groups, the Court has nonetheless affirmed that the 'role of the authorities in such circumstances is not to remove the cause of tension by eliminating pluralism, but to ensure that the competing groups tolerate each other'.[67]

Secondly, when a state accords official recognition to certain faiths under national law, it must ensure that due regard is paid to the Convention. For example, in *Metropolitan Church of Bessarabia v Moldova*,[68] the applicant (Orthodox Christian) Church argued, successfully, that the government's refusal to recognize it as a registered church violated Article 9. The ruling is significant, not just as a reiteration of the need for the state 'to remain neutral and impartial' in such matters,[69] but also because the Court rejected the government's submission that its refusal to recognize the Metropolitan Church was necessary in order to protect national security and Moldovan territorial integrity. In response to the government's contention that the applicant church posed a threat to

---

[58] *X and the Church of Scientology v Sweden No 7805/77*, 16 DR 68 (1979).

[59] *Cha'are Shalom Ve Tsedek v France*, 2000-VII para 72 GC; *Chappell v UK No 12587/86*, 53 DR 241 (1987).

[60] *Buscarini v San Marino* 1999-I; 30 EHRR 208 para 34 GC.

[61] *Hasan and Chaush v Bulgaria* 2000-XI; 34 EHRR 1339 para 78 GC.   [62] Id, para 62.

[63] Ibid.   [64] *Metropolitan Church of Bessarabia v Moldova* 2001-XII; 35 EHRR 306 para 117.

[65] 2000-XI; 34 EHRR 1339 GC.   [66] Id, para 82.

[67] *Serif v Greece* 1999-IX; 31 EHRR 561 para 53.   [68] 2001-XII; 35 EHRR 306.

[69] Id, para 116.

the state because it was (allegedly) working towards the reunification of Moldova with Romania, the Court accepted that a religious organization's 'programme might conceal objectives and intentions different from the ones its proclaims', but held that, on these particular facts, there was no evidence to support such a claim.[70] Thus, as a result of its progressive interpretation of Article 9 in this and other similar cases,[71] the Court has sent a powerful signal to the (still relatively new) democracies in Eastern Europe, in regard to the need to take proper account of the Convention, when granting formal legal recognition to churches and other religious organizations.

Thirdly, the state must make sure that it complies with Article 9 in relation to the regulation of places of worship. Of course, the need to protect the public interest by upholding planning provisions in respect of religious buildings or related public spaces may override the right to manifest one's religion or belief.[72] Yet such powers should not be exercised arbitrarily, or used against minority groups. As a consequence, in *Manoussakis v Greece*,[73] a requirement that the applicants (a group of Jehovah's Witnesses) obtain prior authorization to use premises as a place of worship was held to contravene Article 9 because they had been waiting over a decade for such permission to be granted, and the law had been used to curb the activities of non-Orthodox faiths such as the Jehovah's Witnesses.

Fourthly, in the provision of education to children and young people, the state is under a duty to ensure 'that information or knowledge included in the curriculum is conveyed in an objective, critical and pluralistic manner'[74]—and is forbidden from pursuing 'an aim of indoctrination that might be considered as not respecting parents' religious and philosophical convictions'.[75] The Court has usually considered these matters under Article 2 of Protocol 1,[76] rather than Article 9,[77] although there is some degree of overlap between these two provisions. Thus, for example, in *Hasan and Eylem Zengin v Turkey*,[78] when the Court held that compulsory lessons in religious culture violated Article 2, Protocol 1, it added that a rule which required some parents (ie, those of the Christian and Jewish religion) to reveal their faith in order to exempt their children from such classes, 'may also raise a problem under Art.9'.[79]

Finally, it is incumbent on the state not to ignore the communal nature of Article 9.[80] The Court has recognized 'that religious communities traditionally and universally exist in the form of organised structures',[81] and in *Cyprus v Turkey*[82] it held that Article 9 had been violated because Greek Cypriots living in Northern Cyprus did not have free access

---

[70] Id, para 125.

[71] Eg, see *Moscow Branch of the Salvation Army v Russia* 2006-XI; 44 EHRR 912; *Svyato-Mykhaylivska Parafiya v Ukraine* hudoc (2007); and *Biserica Adevărat Ortodoxă din Moldova v Moldova* hudoc (2007).

[72] See *Vergos v Greece* hudoc (2004); 41 EHRR 913 (planning permission rejected for a house of prayer) and *Johannische Kirche and Peters v Germany* 2001-VIII (planning permission rejected for a new cemetery).

[73] 1996-IV; 23 EHRR 387. See also *Pentidis v Greece*, 1997-III; 23 EHRR CD 37.

[74] *Folgerø v Norway* hudoc (2007); 46 EHRR 1147 para 84 GC.   [75] *Ibid*.

[76] Article 2 of Protocol 1 guarantees that 'No person shall be denied the right to education' and provides that 'the State shall respect the right of parents to ensure such education and teaching in conformity with their own religions and philosophical convictions.' See also pp 697–709.

[77] In *Folgerø v Norway* hudoc (2007); 46 EHRR 1147 paras 78, 79 GC, the Court held there had been a violation of Article 2, Protocol 1 (rather than Article 9), following a complaint from humanist parents that they could only exempt their children from certain parts of a religion and philosophy course in a primary school. See also *Konrad v Germany No 35504/03* hudoc (2006) DA, where the Court focused on Article 2, Protocol 1 rather than Article 9, in refusing an application from Christian parents who wanted to educate their children at home.

[78] Hudoc (2007); 46 EHRR 1060.   [79] Id, para 73.

[80] The Court first recognized the collective dimension of manifestation in *Kokkinakis v Greece* A 260-A (1993); 17 EHRR 397 para 31, as did the Commission before that (*X v UK No 8160/78*, 22 DR 27 (1981)).

[81] *Hasan and Chaush v Bulgaria* 2000-XI; 34 EHRR 1339 para 62 GC.

[82] 2001-IV; 35 EHRR 731 para 245 GC.

to places of worship outside their villages. With states under a positive obligation to protect faith groups from harassment or physical attack,[83] and the Court having acknowledged the important role that religious organizations play in the democratic process,[84]
Article 9 clearly has both an individual and a collective dimension.

b. Conscientious objection

An issue which frequently generates conflict between the individual and the state is that
of conscientious objection. Even though a refusal to serve in the armed forces may constitute a manifestation of one's religion or belief, there is no right of conscientious objection
to military service within the Convention generally[85] or under Article 9 in particular.[86]
Moreover, the application of a general law to anyone who objects to it on grounds of conscience will not violate Article 9(1).[87] Thus, in *C v UK*,[88] where a Quaker objected to a
proportion of his taxes being used for military expenditure and wished instead for those
funds to be redirected towards peaceful purposes, the Commission held that the general
obligation to pay taxes raised no specific issue of conscience, since the distribution of tax
revenue was a political matter which fell beyond the realm of any individual.[89]

It has long been held that a state *may*—but need not—recognize conscientious
objection,[90] and only if it does so should it provide some kind of substitute non-military
service, as an alternative to conscription.[91] If a state adopts this approach, it is permitted
to take measures to enforce the civilian service without breaching Article 9.[92] What is
more, where the state makes provision for substitute service, this will not violate Article 9,
alone or in conjunction with Article 14, even if it insists on maintaining a longer period of
civilian service than for military conscription.[93]

There has, of late, been an apparent willingness to tackle the issue of conscientious objection more vigorously, albeit by looking beyond Article 9. For example, in
Thlimmenos v Greece,[94] the applicant's previous conviction for refusing to wear a military
uniform could not justify his exclusion from the chartered accountants' profession, and
it was held that the state's failure to distinguish his case from that of more serious criminal offences—to which it was 'significantly different'[95]—meant that Article 14 (which
prohibits discrimination) taken with Article 9 had been violated. Furthermore, in offering redress to applicants who have refused to perform military service, the Court has
based its reasoning on Article 3 (the prohibition of degrading treatment)[96] and Article 5
(unlawful detention),[97] with the result that its jurisprudence in this area has remained
fairly undeveloped under Article 9. This is regrettable, and it has been suggested that

---

[83] See *97 Members of the Gldani Congregation of Jehovah's Witnesses and 4 Others v Georgia* hudoc (2007);
46 EHRR 613.

[84] *Moscow Branch of the Salvation Army v Russia* 2006-XI; 44 EHRR 912 para 61.

[85] Eg, Article 4(3)(b) provides that 'any service of a military character or, in the case of conscientious objectors
in countries where they are recognised, service extracted instead of compulsory military service', is excluded
from the Convention's prohibition of 'forced or compulsory labour'. On Article 4 see pp 113–19.

[86] *Conscientious Objectors v Denmark* No 7565/76, 9 DR 117 at 118 (1978).

[87] *Seven Individuals v Sweden* No 8811/79, 29 DR 104 (1982).   [88] *No 10358/83*, 37 DR 142 (1983).

[89] Id, at 147.   [90] See Article 4(3)(b), n 85 above.

[91] *Grandrath v FRG* No 2299/64, 10 YB 626 at 674 (1966) Com Rep; CM Res (67) DH 1.

[92] *Johansen v Norway* No 10600/83, 44 DR 155 (1985). See also *Thlimmenos v Greece* 2000-IV; 31 EHRR 411
para 43 GC.

[93] See *Autio v Finland* No 17086/90, 72 DR 245 (1991), where there was no violation of the Convention
even though the length of the substitute service was twice that of the military service. See also *N v Sweden*
No 10410/83, 40 DR 203 (1984).

[94] 2000-IV; 31 EHRR 411 GC.   [95] Id, para 44.

[96] *Ülke v Turkey* hudoc (2006).   [97] *Tsirlis and Kouloumpas v Greece* 1997-III; 25 EHRR 198.

one reason for the 'slow development of the right to conscientious objection' has been the restrictive way in which the Court has approached the manifestation of belief under Article 9.[98]

3. MANIFESTING RELIGION OR BELIEF IN WORSHIP, TEACHING, PRACTICE, AND OBSERVANCE

I. THE NATURE OF MANIFESTATION

The second part of Article 9(1) protects the right to the freedom 'to manifest' one's religion or belief, in public or in private, alone or with others. The manifestations to which Article 9(1) refers are 'worship, teaching, practice and observance', a catalogue of not wholly distinct activities.[99] In *Arrowsmith v UK*,[100] the Commission indicated that the term 'practice' in this list 'does not cover each act which is motivated or influenced by a religion or belief'.[101] As a consequence it held that the distribution of leaflets to soldiers advising them to go absent or to refuse to serve in Northern Ireland was held not to be the 'practice' of pacifist belief, whereas 'public declarations proclaiming generally the idea of pacifism and urging the acceptance of a commitment to non-violence...' would fall within Article 9(1).[102]

Whilst this approach, which focuses on the nature of the *manifestation* of a religion or belief rather than its *motivation*, may have the advantage of excluding bogus or trivial beliefs from Article 9(1), it can also bring the Court dangerously close to adjudicating on whether a particular practice is formally required by a religion—a task which its judges, given the relevant theological issues, appear ill-equipped to handle. For example, when a Jehovah's Witness child refused to attend a parade in her school commemorating an earlier war, the Court held that it was unable to discern anything 'either in the purpose of the parade or in the arrangements for it, which could offend the applicant's pacifist convictions'.[103] Critics of this ruling (and another identical case)[104] argue that the Court made a 'dangerous mistake' because it 'in effect substituted its judgment for the conscience of the persons involved, defining what was "reasonable" for them to believe'.[105]

The Strasbourg organs in the past often questioned the 'necessity' of certain religious practices,[106] but there has, in recent years, been a move away from this approach.[107] Thus,

[98] See Gilbert, 5 EHRLR 554–67 (2001).

[99] The obligation under this part of Article 9(1) includes desisting from interference with acts of worship and from rites associated with worship. See *Chappell v UK No 12587/86*, 53 DR 241 (1987).

[100] *No 7050/75*, 19 DR 5 at 19 (1978) Com Rep; CM Res DH (79) 4.

[101] The Court has also endorsed this formula. See *Metropolitan Church of Bessarabia v Moldova* 2000-XI; 35 EHRR 306 para 117; and *Hasan and Chaush v Bulgaria* 2000-XI; 34 EHRR 1339 para 78 GC.

[102] *Arrowsmith v UK No 7050/75*, 19 DR 5 at 19 (1978) Com Rep; CM Res DH (79) 4. See also *X and Church of Scientology v Sweden No 7805/77*, 16 DR 68 at 72 (1979), where a line was drawn between religious and commercial advertisements.

[103] *Valsamis v Greece* 1996-VI; 24 EHRR 294 para 32. It is perhaps worth noting that this case was decided by the pre-Protocol 11 Court.

[104] *Efstratiou v Greece* 1996-VI; 24 EHRR 298.

[105] Martínez-Torrón and Navarro-Valls, 'Protection of Religious Freedom in the System of the Council of Europe', in Lindholm, Durham, and Tahzib-Lie, eds, *Facilitating Freedom of Religion or Belief: A Deskbook*, 2004, p 234.

[106] Eg, in *X v Austria No 1753/63*, 8 YB ECHR 174 (1965), the Commission denied a prisoner access to a prayer chain on the ground that it was not 'an indispensable element in the proper exercise of the Buddhist religion'.

[107] See *Metropolitan Church of Bessarabia v Moldova* 2001-XII; 35 EHRR 306 paras 96–8.

in *Leyla Şahin v Turkey*,[108] the Court accepted the applicant's contention that in wearing an Islamic headscarf she was manifesting her faith. That said, although the Court in *Şahin* indicated that it was willing to proceed 'on the assumption that the regulations in issue...constituted an interference with the applicant's right to manifest her religion', it also added that it was proceeding on this basis 'without deciding whether such decisions are in every case taken to fulfill a religious duty'.[109] It is to be hoped that in this regard the Court will avoid reverting to the Commission's rigid 'necessity' approach, and that there will instead be a presumption that bona fide manifestations of 'worship, teaching, practice and observance' fall within Article 9(1).

II. THE PUBLIC MANIFESTATION OF RELIGION OR BELIEF

In contemporary Europe people often wish to exercise, share, or display their faith at the workplace, so it is perhaps unsurprising that this is an area where the manifestation of religion or belief frequently generates controversy. The Strasbourg organs have traditionally taken the view that there is no interference with the manifestation of religion or belief when a person voluntarily accepts a position whereby curbs are placed on the free exercise of their religious beliefs. For example, a minister of religion has no claim against his religious organization under Article 9(1) in a dispute over doctrine, because in such circumstances he remains free to resign and leave the church.[110] Similar principles apply in relation to employment in the armed forces. Thus in *Kalaç v Turkey*,[111] where a senior airforce officer had been dismissed on account of his close ties with a controversial Muslim group, the Court held that Article 9(1) had not been breached on the basis of the contractual nature of his employment and his free choice to forgo certain rights by embarking on a career in the armed services.[112]

This 'free to leave' test has not however been confined to religious vocation or service life. For example, in *Stedman v UK*,[113] where a Christian working in a travel agency refused to work on Sundays, the Commission justified its rejection of her complaint on the basis that she 'was free to resign and did in effect resign from her employment'. Similarly, when a Muslim teacher sought an extended Friday lunch break so that he could attend the nearest Mosque for prayers, it was held that Article 9(1) had not been violated because the applicant 'remained free to resign if and when he found that his teaching obligations conflicted with his religious duties'.[114] The Commission previously called this approach, 'the ultimate guarantee of ...freedom of religion',[115] but it rests on the questionable assumption that everyone seeking to manifest their religion or belief will, in a competitive labour market, have a 'real' choice.[116] Indeed, given that most employers fix their working week around the Christian calendar, the Christian employee who ultimately 'chooses' to seek alternative employment is likely to find a convivial working environment more easily than someone from outside this tradition.[117]

The Court has said that it is not for the state to determine how one manifests their religion or belief,[118] and in recent years there have been some indications of a fresh

---

[108] 2005-XI; 44 EHRR 99 para 78 GC.   [109] *Ibid*.

[110] *Knudsen v Norway No 11045/84*, 42 DR 247 (1985).   [111] 1997-IV; 27 EHRR 552.

[112] Id, para 28. See also *Başpinar v Turkey No 45631/99* hudoc (2002); 36 EHRR CD 1.

[113] *No 29107/95* hudoc (1997); 23 EHRR CD 168 at 169.

[114] *Ahmad v UK No 8160/78*, 22 DR 27 (1981); 4 EHRR 126 at 135.

[115] *Konttinen v Finland No 24949/94* (1996) 87A DR 68 at 75.   [116] See Leader, 70 MLR 713–30 (2007).

[117] On claims that the European Court often displays bias against non-mainstream religions see Gunn, in Van der Vyver and Witte, eds, *Religious Human Rights in Global Perspective: Legal Perspectives*, 1996, p 329.

[118] See *Metropolitan Church of Bessarabia v Moldova* 2001-XII; 35 EHRR 306 paras 97–8.

willingness to interpret Article 9 more imaginatively in this area. For example, in *Ivanova v Bulgaria*,[119] where the applicant lost her job at a school due to her membership of an evangelical Christian group, Article 9 was violated and, unlike in *Stedman,* the option of her moving to a less hostile working environment was not considered. A more positive approach was also evident in *Thlimmenos v Greece*,[120] when the Court held that a ban on a Jehovah's Witness working as a chartered accountant, because of an earlier criminal conviction for refusing to wear a military uniform, breached Article 14 (non-discrimination) taken in conjunction with Article 9.

However, such cases aside, the Court remains generally cautious in its determinations of whether a purported manifestation of religion or belief falls within Article 9(1). Accordingly, in *Kosteski v Former Yugoslav Republic of Macedonia*[121]—where the applicant sought to invoke Article 9 because he had been fined by his employer for being absent from work on a Muslim holiday—the Court rejected the applicant's submissions that his actions constituted a manifestation of his religious beliefs, because he had 'not substantiated the genuineness of his claim to be a Muslim'.[122] Similarly, in *Pichon and Sajous v France*,[123] the conviction of pharmacists for refusing to supply contraceptives lawfully prescribed by doctors was held not to violate Article 9(1), thereby obviating the Court of the need to consider related matters such as 'health' and the 'rights and freedoms of others' under Article 9(2). Furthermore, in *Cha'are Shalom Ve Tsedek v France*,[124] the Court held that a decision to refuse an Orthodox Jewish association a licence to carry out its form of ritual slaughter was not in breach of Article 9(1), because its members could obtain specially certified ('glatt') meat from other sources. Thus, by interpreting Article 9(1) narrowly in cases such as these, it is perhaps not surprising that the Strasbourg judges have been criticized for being 'slow in giving acknowledgement to the complete range of manifestations of religion or belief'.[125]

4. JUSTIFIABLE INTERFERENCES

It is worth reiterating, as noted above, that the *forum internum* is inviolable, although the state can nonetheless interfere under Article 9(2) with the exercise of an Article 9(1) freedom. Under Article 9(2) a restriction on the manifestation of one's religion or belief may thus be justified if is 'prescribed by law', has a legitimate aim, and is 'necessary in a democratic society'. These criteria, which resemble those in the second paragraphs of Articles 8, 10, and 11, will now be considered in more detail.

I. PRESCRIBED BY LAW

Under Article 9(2), a legitimate interference must be 'prescribed by law'. This has been taken to mean that such a law must be 'adequately accessible' and 'formulated with sufficient precision to enable the citizen to regulate his conduct'.[126] In the past the Court tended to avoid any serious discussion of this issue in the context of Article 9. As a consequence, in both *Kokkinakis*[127] and *Larissis*,[128] the Court failed to examine critically the compatibility of a national law outlawing proselytism with the Convention. However, in *Hasan and Chaush v Bulgaria*,[129] the Court held for the first time that the 'prescribed by

---

[119] Hudoc (2007).   [120] 2000-IV; 31 EHRR 411 GC.   [121] Hudoc (2006); 45 EHRR 712.
[122] Id, para 39.   [123] *No 49853/99*, 2001-X DA.   [124] 2000-VII para 81 GC.
[125] Taylor, n 3 above, p 234.
[126] *Sunday Times v UK* A 30 (1979); 2 EHRR 245 para 49 PC.   [127] Paras 40, 41.   [128] Para 42.
[129] 2000-XI; 34 EHRR 1339 GC.

law' requirement in Article 9(2) had not been satisfied, following the decision of a government agency to replace the Chief Mufti and other senior Muslim clerics with the state's own preferred religious leaders. The Court reasoned that:

> the interference with the internal organisation of the Muslim community and the applicants' freedom of religion was not 'prescribed by law' in that it was arbitrary and was based on legal provisions which allowed an unfettered discretion to the executive and did not meet the required standards of clarity and foreseeability.[130]

This decision has paved the way for a number of decisions in recent years where the failure of states to comply with the 'prescribed by law' criterion has led to violations of Article 9. These include: a government's refusal to obey a court order and register a church as an official religious denomination;[131] the lack of any legal basis for refusing a prisoner awaiting execution access to a priest;[132] the actions of state officials in breaking up a meeting of Jehovah's Witnesses on premises that had been lawfully rented;[133] and the use of a residence permit to prevent a non-national preacher from performing his religious activities.[134] As these cases indicate, the Court is increasingly willing to scrutinize the actions of state parties, so as to ensure that restrictions on the manifestation of religion or belief are 'prescribed by law'.[135]

II. LEGITIMATE AIM

Under Article 9(2), the state may interfere with the manifestation of religion or belief in 'the interests of public safety, for the protection of public order, health or morals, or for the protection of the rights and freedoms of others'. The need to maintain public order has been held to justify restrictions on access to a Druid summer solstice festival at Stonehenge,[136] a public protest against alcohol and pornography,[137] and the removal from a prisoner of a religious book which contained a chapter on martial arts.[138] In addition, curbs may be imposed on the manifestation of religion or belief in order to protect public health.[139] Thus, a high caste Sikh prisoner was required to clean the floor of his prison cell,[140] while a law requiring all motorcyclists to wear crash-helmets was held to be necessary for the protection of public safety and could be applied to Sikhs even though, by the time of the Commission's ruling, national legislation had granted Sikh motorcyclists the right to wear turbans rather than helmets.[141] Furthermore, the most nebulous of the Article 9(2) criteria are those whereby limits may be imposed on the manifestation of religion or belief for 'the protection of the rights and freedoms of others'. As a consequence, controls on planning,[142] curbs on religious dress,[143] and compulsory motor insurance[144] have all been regarded as being necessary to protect the rights and freedoms of other parties.

---

[130] Id, para. 86.
[131] *Biserica Adevărat Ortodoxă din Moldova v Moldova* hudoc (2007) para 36.
[132] *Poltoratskiy v Ukraine* 2003-V; 39 EHRR 916 para 170.   [133] *Kuznetsov v Russia* hudoc (2007).
[134] *Perry v Latvia* hudoc (2007) para 62.
[135] See eg, *Svyato-Mykhaylivska Parafiya v Ukraine* hudoc (2007) para 139.
[136] *Chappell v UK No 12587/86*, 53 DR 241 (1987).
[137] *Håkansson v Sweden No 9820/82*, 5 EHRR 297 (1983).   [138] *X v UK No 6886/75*, 5 DR 100 (1976).
[139] See *Cha'are Shalom Ve Tsedek v France*, 2000-VII para 84 GC.
[140] *X v UK No 8231/78*, 28 DR 5 at 38 (1982).   [141] *X v UK No 7992/77*, 14 DR 234 (1978).
[142] See n 72 above; See also *ISKON v UK No 20490/92*, 90 DR 90 (1994).
[143] *Dahlab v Switzerland No 42393/98*, 2001-V DA.
[144] *X v Netherlands No 2988/66*, 10 YB 472 (1967).

III. NECESSARY IN A DEMOCRATIC SOCIETY

The proportionality of a restriction on religion or belief and the extent to which it is 'necessary in a democratic society' is an issue that has often provoked controversy. Curbs on the manifestation of religion or belief must clearly be proportionate to their intended aim,[145] but states continue to enjoy a wide margin of appreciation in a number of areas.[146] Two of these will now be considered in more detail: the regulation of religious dress and the right to proselytize.

a. Religious dress

States have long been afforded considerable discretion in the often controversial area of religious dress.[147] For example, in *Dahlab v Switzerland*,[148] the Court rejected a complaint from a female teacher in Switzerland who failed to overturn a ban on wearing the Islamic veil in a primary school, when it held that the state's actions were justified (under Article 9(2)) because they sought to guarantee religious neutrality in the classroom of a multi-faith society.

More recently the issue of religious dress has been examined by the Court in the context of state sanctioned curbs on Islamic headscarves in Turkey. In *Leyla Şahin v Turkey*,[149] the applicant (Sahin), who considered it her religious duty to wear the Islamic headscarf, complained that a rule prohibiting students at Istanbul University from wearing such headscarves in class or during exams was contrary to Article 9. Sahin argued on the basis of her right as an adult to dress as she wished,[150] and insisted that the headscarf was compatible with the principle of secularism as guaranteed by the Turkish constitution.[151] However, the Turkish government strongly contested Sahin's claims. It maintained that secularism was a key element in Turkey remaining a liberal democracy, and that because the Islamic headscarf was associated with extreme 'religious fundamentalist movements', its display posed a threat to Turkish secular values.[152]

Both the Grand Chamber[153] and the Chamber[154] of the Court accepted the Turkish government's arguments. The Grand Chamber held (by sixteen votes to one) that the headscarf ban could be justified under Article 9(2). In attaching considerable significance to the impact that the headscarf might have on those choosing not to wear it, the Court ruled that the relevant dress restrictions were proportionate to the legitimate aim of upholding public order and of protecting the 'rights and freedoms of others'.[155] Furthermore, in reaching the conclusion that the curbs on the headscarf were 'necessary in a democratic society', the Court accorded the state a wide margin of appreciation,[156] and focused on the need to protect two important principles: secularism and equality.

With regard to secularism, the Court noted that this principle was not merely 'consistent with the values underpinning the Convention',[157] but was also 'the paramount consideration' for the headscarf ban.[158] Moreover, given the presence of 'extremist political movements' that wished to impose their values on Turkish society,[159] the Court found it

---

[145] *Manoussakis v Greece* 1996-IV; 23 EHRR 387 para 44.
[146] See *Cha'are Shalom Ve Tsedek v France*, 2000-VII para 84 GC.
[147] See *Karaduman v Turkey* No 16278/90 and *Bulut v Turkey* No 18783/91, 74 DR 93 (1993).
[148] *No 42393/98, 2001-V DA.*   [149] 2005-XI; 44 EHRR 99 GC.   [150] Id, para 101.
[151] Hudoc (2004); 41 EHRR 108 para 85.   [152] Id, paras 90–3.   [153] 2005-XI; 44 EHRR 99 GC.
[154] Hudoc (2004); 41 EHRR 108.   [155] 2005-XI; 44 EHRR 99 para 115 GC.
[156] This was because of the 'diversity of approaches' in Europe on the issue of religious dress. Id, para 109.
[157] Id, para 114.   [158] Id, para 116.   [159] Id, para 115.

'understandable' that the state should 'wish to preserve the secular nature' of the university and thereby impose restrictions on the Islamic headscarf.[160]

In respect of equality, the Court was concerned about a link between the Islamic headscarf and women's rights. It cited (with apparent approval) a passage in *Dahlab*, which
referred to the Islamic headscarf as a 'powerful external symbol', that 'appeared to be
imposed on women by a religious precept that was hard to reconcile with the principle of
gender equality' and which 'could not easily be reconciled with the message of tolerance,
respect for others and, above all, equality and non-discrimination'.[161] The Court's choice
of words in this context was harshly criticized by the sole dissenting judge, Judge Tulkens,
who suggested that it was 'not the Court's role to make an appraisal of this kind'.[162] What
is more, in questioning the approach of the majority on the issue of gender equality and
curbs on the Islamic headscarf, she accused her fellow judges of '[p]aternalism'.[163]

Many of Judge Tulkens's criticisms of Şahin have been echoed by academics,[164] and the
Court's (majority) decision has been attacked on a number of grounds, which include:

> Inadequate application of the margin of appreciation doctrine; narrow interpretation of
> the freedom of religion; imposition of 'fundamental secularism'; adverse implications of
> Muslim women's right to education; and promotion of the image of Islam as a threat to
> democracy.[165]

Indeed, given the level of criticism, it is hard to think of an area, in recent years, where
the Court's jurisprudence has provoked as much unfavourable comment as that of
religious dress.[166]

b. Proselytism

Another area synonymous with controversy, which raises issues under Article 9(2), is that
of proselytism. In *Kokkinakis v Greece*[167] the Court held that the application of a Greek
law criminalising the proselytizing activities of a Jehovah's Witness was not proportionate to the aim of protecting the rights of others. Even though the Greek anti-proselytism
law was regarded as pursuing a legitimate aim ('the protection of the rights and freedoms
of others'), it was held not to be 'necessary in a democratic society'. With this in mind,
the Court contrasted 'true evangelism' and 'improper proselytism'.[168] Whilst the former
was 'an essential mission and the responsibility of every Christian and every Church',
'improper proselytism' was 'a corruption or deformation of it', and could 'take the form
of activities offering material or social advantage with a view to gaining new members
for a Church or exerting improper pressure on people in distress or in need', possibly
also entailing 'the use of violence or brainwashing'.[169] On the facts the Court held that
although the applicant had been persistent, he had done no more than try to persuade
another person of the virtues of his faith and thus his criminal conviction could not be
justified by a 'pressing social need'.

The *Kokkinakis* case has also attracted much criticism,[170] but the Court relied on
it a short time later in *Larissis v Greece*.[171] In *Larissis* the issue was whether measures
taken against three Pentecostal air force officers for seeking to win converts to their
faith had been disproportionate. The Court distinguished between their attempts to
proselytize other service personnel and those that related to civilians. With regard to

---

[160] Id, para 116.
[161] Id, para 111.   [162] Id, dissenting opinion of Judge Tulkens, para 12.   [163] *Ibid.*
[164] See eg, Lewis, 56 ICLQ 395–414 (2007).   [165] Vakulenko, 16(2) Social and Legal Studies 190 (2007).
[166] For a criticism of *Dahlab* and *Sahin* see C Evans, 7 MJIL 52–73 (2006).
[167] A 260-A (1993); 17 EHRR 397.   [168] Id, para 48.   [169] *Ibid.*
[170] See Gunn, n 117 above.   [171] 1998-I; 27 EHRR 329.

service personnel there was no violation of Article 9 because, in view of the 'particular characteristics of military life', it was necessary for the state to protect junior airmen from being put under 'improper pressure' by the more senior applicants.[172] However, in respect of the curbs on proselytizing civilians, Article 9(2) had been contravened because the civilians whom the applicants wished to convert 'were not subject to pressures and constraints of the same kind as the airmen'.[173]

It is significant that in *Larissis,* as in *Kokkinakis,* the Court's focus was narrow, in that it limited its analysis primarily to the facts of these two cases. A regrettable consequence of this approach is that the Court has, to date, refrained from offering detailed guidance on the limits of acceptable proselytism.[174]

5. ARTICLE 9: CONFLICTS AND OVERLAPS

I. CONFLICTS OF RIGHTS

On occasion there are conflicts between Article 9 and other rights protected by the Convention. This issue was addressed by the Court in *Otto-Preminger-Institut v Austria,*[175] when it suggested that strong regard should be had for religious beliefs (and thus Article 9) in relation to competing Convention provisions. In *Otto-Preminger* the state had interfered with the applicant's right to freedom of expression (Article 10) by seizing and ordering forfeiture of a film found likely to offend the religious feelings of the local (predominantly Catholic) population in the region where the film was to be shown. The Court held that the imposition of curbs on the film were necessary for the protection of 'the [religious] rights and freedoms of others',[176] and that '…in the context of religious opinions and beliefs—[there] may legitimately be included an obligation [on individuals] to avoid as far as possible expressions which are gratuitously offensive to others…'.[177]

Any suggestion that free expression is subordinate to the freedom of majority religious beliefs has however been questioned by a former member of the Court who (writing extra-judicially) pointed out that such a view would be 'at odds with the emphasis that the Court has placed on the pluralism in a democratic society of religious belief encompassing scepticism and agnosticism'.[178] Moreover, not merely has the Court's ruling in *Otto-Preminger* been attacked for 'introducing the concept of 'peaceful enjoyment of freedom of religion'…against offensive or 'immoral' criticism',[179] but 'for failing to distinguish issues under Article 9 from those under Article 10'.[180] Thus, it has been argued that '*Otto-Preminger* should perhaps be seen in the light of its particular facts and the wide margin of appreciation accorded in consequence of those facts'.[181]

In spite of the criticism levelled at *Otto-Preminger,* the European Court followed this decision in *Wingrove v UK,*[182] where it was held that the UK's refusal to award a certificate permitting the distribution of a film about a nun's erotic visions of Christ on the cross was justified by the need to protect the sensibilities of Christians. In seeking to balance

---

[172] Id, para 54.   [173] Id, para 59.

[174] On this generally see Stahnke, 1999 Brigham Young ULR 251–350.

[175] A 295-A (1994); 19 EHRR 34.   [176] Id, para 46.   [177] Id, para 49.

[178] Fuhrmann, 2000 Brigham Young ULR 829 at 837.

[179] Nowak and Vospernik, in Lindholm, Durham, and Tahzib-Lie, eds, *Facilitating Freedom of Religion or Belief: A Deskbook,* 2004, p 162.

[180] See Taylor, n 3 above, p 87.

[181] See Fuhrmann, n 178 above, at 837. See also Palmer, 56 CLJ 469–71 (1997).

[182] 1996-V; 24 EHRR 1. For criticism of *Wingrove* see Kearns, 5 EHRLR 512–21 (1997).

a range of diverse and apparently conflicting interests, the Strasbourg organs have, on the one hand, established that 'members of a religious majority or a minority, cannot reasonably expect to be exempt from all criticism'[183] whilst, on the other, recognized that Article 9 imposes a duty on states to 'avoid as far as possible an expression that is, in regard to objects of veneration, gratuitously offensive to others and profanatory'.[184] Attacks on religious beliefs tend to be particularly emotive,[185] and in a continent that is home to a wide range of religions and equivalent forms of belief, the Court's willingness to grant states a wide margin of appreciation is perhaps understandable.[186] That said, it also creates uncertainty, and adds weight to Evans' claim that 'the Strasbourg organs have themselves blurred the freedom of religion into a general mélange of mutual respect not only between religions but between the freedom of religion and other human rights'.[187]

II. OVERLAPS OF RIGHTS

Article 9 may also overlap with other rights guaranteed under the Convention, such as Article 11 (freedom of assembly and association) and Article 6 (fair hearing). For example, in *Metropolitan Church of Bessarabia v Moldova*,[188] where the non-registration of the applicant Church was held to be contrary to Article 9, the Court indicated that:

> ...since religious communities traditionally exist in the form of organised structures, Article 9 must be interpreted in the light of Article 11 of the Convention... [and that] one of the means of exercising the right to manifest one's religion, especially for a religious community, in its collective dimension, is the possibility of ensuring judicial protection of the community, its members and its assets, so that Article 9 must be seen not only in the light of Article 11, but also in the light of Article 6.[189]

The Court has had several opportunities to consider the relationship between Articles 9 and 11, but in contrast to *Metropolitan Church of Bessarabia v Moldova*—where the Court held that because there had been violations of Article 9 it was unnecessary to determine whether there had been a violation of Article 11[190]—it has tended to focus on Article 11 in such cases at the expense of Article 9.[191] Indeed, a more general characteristic of Convention case law has been the number of occasions where the Court has resisted applicants' attempts to raise issues under Article 9, by instead dealing with them under other provisions.[192] For example, in *Hoffmann v Austria*,[193] the Court regarded the dispute over the custody of children of two parents—one of whom was a Jehovah's Witness—as falling within Article 8 (right to respect for family life) rather than Article 9.[194] Similarly,

---

[183] *Otto-Preminger-Institut v Austria* A 295-A (1994); 19 EHRR 34 para 47.

[184] See *Wingrove v UK*, 1996-V; 24 EHRR 1 para 52.

[185] Eg, in 2006, Muslims were outraged by the publication of Danish cartoons satirising the prophet Mohammad and the Pope's use of a quotation on holy war from a fourteenth-century Byzantine Emperor.

[186] See *İA v Turkey* 2005-VIII; 45 EHRR 703, where the Court rejected the applicant's claim that Article 10 had been violated by his prosecution for blasphemy against Islam.

[187] M Evans, see above, n 3, p 365.   [188] 2001-XII; 35 EHRR 306.

[189] Id, para 118. See also *Moscow Branch of the Salvation Army v Russia* 2006-XI; 44 EHRR 912.

[190] See id, para 142.

[191] Eg, see *United Communist Party of Turkey v Turkey* 1998-I; 26 EHRR 121 para 62; *Refah Partisi v Turkey* 2003-II; 37 EHRR 1 para 137 GC; *Chassagnou v France* 1999-III; 29 EHRR 615 para 125 GC; and *Öllinger v Austria* No 76900/01, 2006-IX para 53.

[192] See Renucci, n 3 above, pp 36–41.   [193] A 255-C (1993); 17 EHRR 293.

[194] See also *Palau-Martinez v France* 2003-XII; 41 EHRR 136, where, in a custody battle between a Jehovah's Witness mother and her ex-husband who did not share her religious convictions, the Court held that because there had been a violation of Article 8 (right to respect for family life) taken together with Article 14 (prohibition of discrimination), it was not necessary to examine the applicant's claims under Article 9.

in *Murphy v Ireland*,[195] in ruling that a ban on religious adverts on the radio was compatible with Article 10, the Court failed to consider the significance of the applicant's claims under Article 9.[196] Likewise, in *Riera Blume v Spain*,[197] the applicants' claims that the 'deprogramming' measures employed by an organization 'formed to fight against sects' were not considered under Article 9, because the Court found that there had been an unlawful deprivation of liberty and thereby a violation of Article 5(1) of the Convention. What is more, in several other areas—ranging from trade union membership,[198] to the dissolution of political parties[199] and the legal personality of churches[200]—the Convention organs have avoided utilizing Article 9. This tendency of the Court (and Commission) to decide cases by making detailed reference to Convention provisions other than Article 9, though perhaps understandable, is also regrettable. Indeed, by adopting such an approach, the Court lays itself open to the long standing charge that it has interpreted Article 9 too restrictively.[201]

6. CONCLUSION

Despite some progressive rulings in recent years, it is questionable whether the European Court has, to date, interpreted Article 9 in such a way as to realize its full potential. Of course, any criticism of the Court should be tempered by the fact that it continues to face a number of taxing challenges in relation to Article 9. After all, it has the invidious task of ensuring that the Convention affords proper respect to a variety of faiths and beliefs in a religiously diverse continent. There are also the challenges presented by the accommodation of religious practices which, until recent decades, were largely alien to Europe. And finally, there is the perennial problem of ensuring that the Convention sets appropriate standards for states that grant privileges to one particular church (eg, the UK), as well as others which accord constitutional protection to secularism (eg, France and Turkey).[202] Yet, such considerations aside, the Court has, in the main, tended to interpret Article 9 conservatively. With religion and belief playing an increasingly significant role on the European political agenda, fresh imagination and boldness may thus be required in Strasbourg when tackling the (seemingly inevitable) challenges that lie ahead in respect of Article 9.

[195] 2003-XI; 38 EHRR 212. For a criticism of *Murphy* see Geddis, 2 EHRLR 181–92 (2004).
[196] See also *Glas Nadezhda Eood and Elenkov v Bulgaria* hudoc (2007) para 59, where the state's refusal to issue a broadcasting licence to a Christian group was considered (and rejected) under Article 10, rather than Article 9.
[197] 1999-VII; 30 EHRR 632.
[198] In *Young, James and Webster v UK* A 44 (1981); 4 EHRR 38 para 66, the Court held that because a national law making trade union membership compulsory contravened Article 11, it was not necessary to consider the applicants' claim that their rights under Article 9 were prejudiced, even though their objections to union membership had been partly based on personal convictions.
[199] See *Sadak v Turkey No 2*, 2002-IV para 47, where the Court, in holding that there had been a violation of Article 3 to Protocol 1 (right to free elections), ruled that it was not necessary to examine whether there had been a violation of Article 9.
[200] See *Canea Catholic Church v Greece* 1997-VIII; 27 EHRR 521, where the Court refrained from examining Article 9 on account of the fact that Article 6 had been violated.
[201] See Richardson, 18 UQLJ 195 (1995).
[202] On these challenges more generally see Loenen and Goldschmidt, *Religious Pluralism and Human Rights in Europe: Where to Draw the Line?*, 2007.

11

ARTICLE 10: FREEDOM OF EXPRESSION

Freedom of Expression

(1) Everyone has the right to freedom of expression. This right shall include freedom to hold opinions and to receive and impart information and ideas without interference by public authority and regardless of frontiers. This Article shall not prevent States from requiring the licensing of broadcasting, television or cinema enterprises.

(2) The exercise of these freedoms, since it carries with it duties and responsibilities, may be subject to such formalities, conditions, restrictions or penalties as are prescribed by law and are necessary in a democratic society, in the interests of national security, territorial integrity or public safety, for the prevention of disorder or crime, for the protection of health or morals, for the protection of the reputation or rights of others, for preventing the disclosure of information received in confidence, or for maintaining the authority and impartiality of the judiciary.

1. INTRODUCTION

Article 10 guarantees freedom of expression,[1] one of the cardinal rights guaranteed under the Convention. The historical significance of this right is self-evident, as it has been dearly won after centuries of struggles. After the devastating turmoil of the two World Wars and the Holocaust, the drafters of the Convention reaffirmed it as one of the foundational values of the Council of Europe. The marked importance attached to this right and the demand for its special protection are readily explicable by its close linkage to democracy's political process and its role as an indispensable vehicle for minorities, political opponents, and civil society to nurture and foster public debates. Such a constitutional underpinning of freedom of expression lends succour to the consistent assertion of the Strasbourg organs (the Court and the erstwhile Commission) that interference with this right can be justified only by 'imperative necessities', and that exceptions to this right must be interpreted narrowly.[2] The 'constitutional' importance of freedom of expression is elaborated in a steady stream of cases. The Court has explained its approach to the interpretation of Article 10 as follows:

> The Court's supervisory functions oblige it to pay the utmost attention to the principles characterising a 'democratic society'. Freedom of expression constitutes one of the essential foundations of such a society, one of the basic conditions for its progress and for the

---

[1] For analysis, see Macovei, *Freedom of Expression—A guide to the implementation of Article 10 of the European Convention on HumanIghts, Human Rights Handbook* No 2, 2nd edn, 2004.

[2] *Vereinigung Demokratischer Soldaten Österreichs and Gubi v Austria* A 302 (1994); 20 EHRR 56 para 37. See also *Informationsverein Lentia v Austria* A 276 (1993); 17 EHRR 93 para 35.

development of every man. Subject to paragraph 2 of Article 10, it is applicable not only to information or ideas that are favourably received or regarded as inoffensive or as a matter of indifference, but also to those that offend, shock or disturb the State or any sector of the population. Such are the demands of that pluralism, tolerance and broadmindedness without which there is no 'democratic society'. This means, amongst other things, that every 'formality', 'condition', 'restriction' or 'penalty' imposed in this sphere must be proportionate to the legitimate aim pursued.[3]

This approach has led to the development of a host of interpretive devices in the case law. As in the jurisprudence of Articles 8, 9, and 11, the Court initially examines whether there is an interference with freedom of expression under the first paragraph of Article 10, and, if so, whether such an interference can be justified under the second paragraph on the basis of the following three standards: (i) whether an impugned measure is 'prescribed by law'; (ii) whether it pursues a legitimate aim(s); and (iii) whether it is 'necessary in a democratic society'.

The first standard, 'prescribed by law', is essentially the legal basis test, requiring the state authorities to identify the national law that provides the basis for restricting a person's right under Article 10. The second requirement, of legitimate aim, has rarely generated substantive discussion in the case law. The Court's analysis generally focuses instead on the third standard, which constitutes the most demanding litmus test for the Court and litigants alike. The Court has taken the phrase 'necessary in a democratic society' as supposing a 'pressing social need', which can be met by a restriction that strikes a fair or proportionate balance between the means chosen to satisfy it and the individual's freedom of expression. The national authorities are given a margin of appreciation in assessing the existence of such a social need and choosing the measures to be taken to deal with it. The state nonetheless does not have an unlimited power of appreciation; instead the Court retains the competence to decide whether the national authorities have adduced both 'relevant and sufficient reasons' to justify its measures of interference. While the sub-test of relevance, which requires a measure to be suitable for attaining a legitimate goal, has rarely caused serious obstacles to respondent states,[4] the sub-test of sufficiency has attracted the Court's more rigorous assessment, with the excessive nature of the interference casting doubt on the reason for it or its proportionality.[5]

The inquiries in this chapter start with delineating the boundaries of protection of Article 10. The focus will then turn to different categories of expression, specific issues relating to the press and media licensing, the standard 'prescribed by law', legitimate aims, the notion of 'duties and responsibilities' of the bearers of expression rights, and some distinct methodologies advanced by the Court to deal with defamation cases.

2. THE SCOPE OF PROTECTION

I. GENERAL OVERVIEW

The scope of protection under Article 10 is to be broadly interpreted so as to encompass not only the substance of information and ideas, but also a diverse variety of forms and

---

[3] *Handyside v UK* A 24 (1976); 1 EHRR 737 para 49 PC.

[4] See eg, *Roemen and Schmit v Luxembourg* 2003-IV para 59; *Ernst v Belgium* hudoc (2003); 37 EHRR 724 para 104. See also *Salov v Ukraine* hudoc (2005) para 116; and *Dammann v Switzerland* hudoc (2006).

[5] See further on these standards, Ch 8 above.

means in which they are manifested, transmitted, and received.[6] Because of the demands of pluralism, tolerance, and broadmindedness, the scope of protection under Article 10 is broadened to cover information or ideas that are unpalatable to the state, or offending or shocking to some people.[7] Article 10 as such does not forbid discussion or dissemination of information that is suspected of being false.[8] Further, Article 10 guarantees the negative aspect of freedom of expression encompassed by the right to remain silent. There is growing recognition of this implicit right in the practice of the Convention,[9] as this right is of special importance to freedom from self-incrimination and the right to be presumed innocent.[10]

Whether a measure complained of constitutes interference within the meaning of Article 10(2) cannot be answered without determining the parameters of protection under Article 10(1). Although Article 10 is, as indicated, generally given a broad scope, the Court has held that it is not enough for an application to fall within it that a person's expression is in some way affected by a decision of the state. Where the impact on expression is consequential upon or collateral to the exercise by the state of its authority for other purposes, the Court has been reluctant to consider the matter as falling within Article 10. This has been an issue in respect of the duty of loyalty required of German civil servants, which can present problems for persons with certain political views. In the two German cases, *Glasenapp* and *Kosiek*,[11] the Court found that a refusal to grant the applicants access to the civil service, which turned upon this requirement, was based essentially on the fact that the applicants did not possess one of the necessary qualifications for access, not on their political views, so that the complaints fell outside the scope of protection of Article 10. As will be discussed below, in the subsequent *Vogt v Germany*[12] case, the Court distinguished it from these two earlier cases on the basis that it concerned the dismissal of a permanent civil servant, who was already employed, by virtue of her association with the German Communist Party: it was therefore centrally about an 'interference' with her freedom of expression, not the right of access to employment. Similarly, in *Otto v Germany*,[13] where a police officer complained of the refusal to promote him to the position of chief inspector on account of his membership of an extreme right-wing party, the Court found that the main issue was not recruitment to the civil service, so that the refusal of promotion fell within the material scope of Article 10. In contrast, in *Harabin v Slovakia*,[14] the Court found that terminating the appointment of the President of the Supreme Court was concerned essentially with the right to hold a public post relating to the administration of justice, a right not secured in the Convention. It was ruled that the removal of the judge was based largely on the appraisal of his professional qualifications and personal qualities. Even though the minister's report, which prompted the removal, referred to the applicant's views on a constitutional amendment, it was not

---

6 *Nilsen and Johnsen v Norway* 1999-VIII; 30 EHRR 878 para 43 GC; and *Sokolowski v Poland* hudoc (2005) para 44. See also *Janowski v Poland* 1999-I; 29 EHRR 705 para 45 Com Rep.

7 See eg, *Handyside v UK* A 24 (1976); 1 EHRR 737 para 49 PC; *Müller and Others v Switzerland* A 133 (1988); 13 EHRR 212 para 33; *Jersild v Denmark* A 298 (1994); 19 EHRR 1 para 37; *Sokolowski v Poland* hudoc (2005) para 41; and *Klein v Slovakia* hudoc (2006) para 47.

8 *Salov v Ukraine* hudoc (2005) para 113.

9 *Funke v France* A 256-A (1993); 16 EHRR 297 para 44. See also *K v Austria* A 255-B (1993) para 46 Com Rep.

10 See Article 6 above, p 201.

11 *Glasenapp v FRG* A 104 (1986); 9 EHRR 25 para 50 PC; and *Kosiek v FRG* A 105 (1986); 9 EHRR 328 para 36 PC.

12 A 323 (1995); 21 EHRR 205 para 44 GC. See below, p 725.

13 *No 27574/02* hudoc (2005) DA.   14 *No 62584/00* hudoc (2004) DA.

demonstrated that such views 'exclusively or preponderantly' served as the relevant factor to bring Article 10 into play.[15]

II. POSITIVE OBLIGATIONS

The positive obligation to protect freedom of expression and to prevent encroachments on its guarantee requires the horizontal application (*Drittwirkung*) of Article 10 in the relations of private persons. While refraining from formulating a general theory on positive obligations and the extent to which the Convention can be applied to relations between private persons,[16] the Court has consistently recognized that states must ensure that private individuals can effectively exercise their right of communication among themselves.[17] The notion of positive obligations is of special importance to issues of access to information, which will be examined separately.

In determining whether a positive obligation to act exists in a particular situation, 'regard must be had to the fair balance that has to be struck between the general interest of the community and the interests of the individual'.[18] The ambit of the state's positive obligation varies, depending on considerations of distributive justice and the equitable allocation of resources required for different administrative tasks.[19] Relevant factors are: the kind of the expression rights at stake; their public interest nature; their capacity to contribute to public debates; the nature and scope of restrictions on expression rights; the availability of alternative venues for expression; and the weight of countervailing rights of others or the public.[20]

A state's positive obligation has been held to apply in a variety of contexts. The requirement that private employees refrain from making statements or divulging information may be stipulated in an employment contract. A breach of such a duty of loyalty may result in suspension or dismissal. According to the Commission, the enforcement of such legal consequences with the assistance of the competent national authorities does not amount to an 'interference by public authority' within the meaning of Article 10(1). In *Rommelfanger v FRG*,[21] a physician employed by a Catholic hospital was dismissed because of his views about abortion. The Commission considered that the requirement to refrain from making statements on abortion in conflict with the church's opinion was not unreasonable, as the issue of abortion was of crucial importance to the church. It found no interference within the meaning of Article 10(1) on the ground that the positive obligation imposed on the state did not go beyond the requirement of protecting employees from any unreasonable compulsion impairing the very essence of their freedom of expression.

The case of *Rommelfanger* can be compared with the later case of *Fuentes Bobo v Spain*.[22] There, the applicant was laid off by the Spanish television company (TVE) because of his criticism of its management, which was made during a radio programme. In response to a government argument that TVE was a private legal person, the Court found that by virtue of its positive obligation, it was incumbent on the Spanish government to safeguard

---

[15] *Ibid.* See also *Pitkevich v Russia No 47936/99* hudoc (2001) DA (dismissal of a judge because of her activities irreconcilable with the judicial post, rather than of her expression of religious views).

[16] *VGT Verein gegen Tierfabriken v Switzerland* 2001-VI; 34 EHRR 159 para 46.

[17] See Clapham, *Human Rights in the Private Sphere*, 1993, p 231. On positive obligations under the Convention, see above, p 18.

[18] *Ozgur Gundem v Turkey* 2000-III; 31 EHRR 1082 para 43.

[19] *Appleby v UK* 2003-VI; 37 EHRR 783 para 40.   [20] Id, paras 42–3, and 47–9.

[21] *No 12242/86* hudoc (1989) DA. See also *Carrillo and Burgoa v Spain No 11142/84*, (1986) unreported.

[22] Hudoc (2000).

freedom of expression from threats stemming from private persons, so that the applicant's lawful dismissal constituted an interference with his freedom of expression.

Clearly, the concept of positive obligations under Article 10 assumes great importance in relation to any violence or threats of violence directed by private persons against other private persons, such as the press, exercising free speech. In *Özgür Gündem v Turkey,*[23] the Court held that Turkey was under a positive obligation to take investigative and protective measures where a pro-PKK newspaper, and its journalists and staff, were exposed to a campaign of violence and intimidation by private individuals, including killings, assaults, and arson attacks. Despite the numerous requests for protection by the newspaper applicant, the Turkish government failed to take adequate or effective steps. Such an omission was considered to warrant the fear that the concerted campaign of violence was tolerated, if not approved, by state officials.[24] In the *Özgür Gündem* case, Turkey submitted that the applicant and its staff supported the PKK and acted as its propaganda tool. The Court held that even if this was proven to be true, this did not justify the omission of positive steps to undertake effective investigations and protection.

In *Appleby v UK,*[25] the Court rejected a claim that Article 10 imposed a positive obligation to secure a 'freedom of forum' for the exercise of freedom of expression. The applicants, who were campaigners opposed to an application for planning permission, set up stands at the entrance of a privately owned shopping mall, which was originally built by a public corporation. They displayed posters, warning the public of the likely loss of an open space, and sought signatures to present to the council. They were prevented by security guards from collecting signatures. The applicants contended that the disputed shopping centre functioned as a town centre, providing venues for public services and facilities. They argued that in some states of the United States the authorities must ensure individual persons access to privately owned shopping centres to enable them to exercise free speech rights. The Court did not endorse this line of reasoning. In its view, Article 10 does not bestow any freedom of forum. Still, the Court did not foreclose the possibility that a positive obligation may arise for a state to regulate property rights where the bar on access to property prevents any effective exercise of freedom of expression, or stultifies the essence of this freedom, as in the case of a corporate town. The Court's reasoning was swayed by the limited nature of the restrictions and the availability of alternative means, such as obtaining individual permission for a stand, distributing leaflets on public access paths, or door-to-door calling.

III. ACCESS TO INFORMATION

Unlike its counterparts in the International Covenant on Civil and Political Rights (ICCPR)[26] and EU law,[27] Article 10 has yet to be recognized by the Court as providing a basis for the right of access to information. It has consistently rejected the view that Article 10(1), which includes the phrase 'freedom...to receive...information', can be read to guarantee a *general* right of access to information.[28] Instead, its approach has been to deal with complaints of denial of access to information under Article 8.[29] In

---

[23] 2000-III; 31 EHRR 1082 paras 42–6. See also *Fuentes Bobo v Spain*, id, para 38.

[24] *Özgür Gündem v Turkey* 2000-III; 31 EHRR 1082 para 41.   [25] 2003-VI; 37 EHRR 783.

[26] Article 19 of the ICCPR clearly recognizes the right of the citizens to seek information.

[27] The right of access to documents has been established as a fundamental right: Case C-58/94, *Netherlands v Council* [1996] ECR I-2169, paras 34–7; Case T-105/95, *WWF UK v Commission* [1997] ECR II-313 para 55. See Peers, 21 YEL 385 (2002); and Arai-Takahashi, 24 YEL 27 at 53–69 (2005).

[28] See eg, *Leander v Sweden* A 116 (1987); 9 EHRR 433 and *Gaskin v UK* A 160 (1989); 12 EHRR 36 PC.

[29] See eg, *Gaskin v UK, ibid*, and *McGinley and Egan v UK* 1998-III; 27 EHRR 1 Com Rep.

Leander v Sweden,[30] the applicant applied for a temporary post of museum technician at the Naval Museum, which was adjacent to a naval base designated as a restricted military security zone, but he was informed that he was denied the post for security reasons. He challenged the security procedure that was followed and sought to obtain reasons for the decision against him under, *inter alia*, Article 10. The Court held that 'Article 10 does not, *in circumstances such as those of the present case,* confer on the individual a right of access to a register containing information on his personal position, nor does it embody an obligation on the Government to impart such information to the individual'. This reasoning was followed in *Gaskin v UK*,[31] which concerned the refusal to grant an applicant access to his child-care records.

In *Guerra v Italy*,[32] the erstwhile Commission did endorse the right of access to information under Article 10, relying on teleological interpretation. There, the local authorities failed to provide residents with sufficient information on a potential health hazard arising from a chemical factory. The Commission stressed the interdependent nature of the protection of the environment, public health, and the well-being of individuals. The right to information under Article 10 was considered vital for preventing potential violations of the Convention in the event of serious environmental pollution. Further, the scope of positive obligations under Article 10 was interpreted as going beyond the general duty to make environmental information accessible to the public. It was considered broad enough to cover more *specific* duties, such as the duties 'to collect, process and disseminate information which...is not directly accessible and which cannot be known to the public unless the public authorities act accordingly'.[33] The Commission averred that the 'right of effective access' to the relevant information on environmental and health hazards must be accorded unless there is an overriding public interest in maintaining confidentiality of the information.[34] The Commission's dynamic approach was corroborated by the Parliamentary Assembly of the Council of Europe, which adopted a resolution expressly recognizing 'public access to clear and full information' as a 'basic human right'.[35] While not expressly spelling it out, the Commission suggested that the general rule ought to be open access to information, with the onus on a government to establish the necessity of confidentiality. The Commission's reasoning could be deployed to justify claims for access to information affecting national security, and information held by medical and welfare authorities.

However, the prospect of such dynamic interpretation was dampened by the Court in the *Guerra* case when it confined the freedom to receive information under Article 10(2) to the negative duty on the government not to interfere with communication of information among individuals *inter se*.[36] In the subsequent case of *Sîrbu v Moldova*,[37] the Court followed the same reasoning. It held that the freedom to receive information under Article 10(1) '*basically* prohibits a government from restricting a person from receiving information that others wish or may be willing to impart to him', and that this freedom 'cannot be construed as imposing on a State, *in circumstances such as those of the present case,* positive obligations to disclose to the public any secret documents or information concerning its military, intelligence service or police'. It remains to be seen whether this dictum might suggest the possibility, albeit slim, of inferring the right of access to

[30] A 116 (1987); 9 EHRR 433 para 74, emphasis added. See also paras 81 and 85 Com Rep.

[31] A 160 (1989); 12 EHRR 36 para 52 (finding of a violation of Article 8).

[32] 1998-I; 26 EHRR 357 para 43 Com Rep.   [33] Id, para 49.   [34] Id, para 51.

[35] Resolution 1087 (1996) of the Parliamentary Assembly of the Council of Europe, para 4; *Guerra v Italy* 1998-I; 26 EHRR 357 Com Rep para 44.

[36] *Guerra v Italy,* id, para 53.   [37] Hudoc (2004) para 18, emphasis added.

information and the corresponding positive duty of states to impart information *in other circumstances.*[38]

IV. ODIOUS EXPRESSION AND THE RELATIONSHIP BETWEEN ARTICLES 10 AND 17

The drafters of the Convention intended to provide an institutional framework based on liberal democratic values to overcome the extremism of Nazism and fascism and to set a counterbalance against a looming threat of Stalinist communism. In view of these considerations, it is understandable that some European states are wary and sceptical of the ability of democracy to resist the risk of racist propaganda and manifestations leading to totalitarian dictatorship and massive human rights abuses.[39] The case law reveals a variety of values which have been considered egregiously offensive and contrary to the 'constitutional paradigm' of the Convention. Apart from typical examples of (neo-)Nazism,[40] fascism, racism, anti-Semitism, and communism, the recent cases address Islamic fundamentalism[41] and Kurdish nationalism involving discussions of hatred and an incitement to violence.[42]

In a very early case dealing with the dissolution of the German communist party, the Commission argued that the examinations of complaints under Article 17[43] would dispense with the need to analyze a case under Article 10(2).[44] This approach suggests that issues of restrictions on free speech could be subsumed under Article 17. As a corollary of this, the exercise of free speech by certain individuals would fall outside the scope of protection of Article 10 on the mere basis of their membership to a group espousing anti-Convention values. Such an implication would be squarely at variance with the 'constitutionally' entrenched status of free speech in the Convention's order. It would also suggest inherent limitations, which must be rejected under Article 10.

Another feature emerging from the earlier case law of the Commission was that if national authorities justified the contested measures by reference to the need to address issues of racial discrimination or to suppress other anti-Convention values, there was a presumption in favour of their decisions.[45] In a Belgian case which involved a criminal conviction of an applicant who participated in the publication of a work justifying the Nazi atrocities against the Jewish population, the Commission was satisfied that the criminal conviction was proportionate to its legitimate purpose.[46]

However, the development of the case law demonstrates a more finely-tuned approach based on a closer appraisal of the proportionality of specific measures, which has the effect of bolstering press freedom. The Court has held that racist remarks must be examined

[38] See Van Dijk and Van Hoof p 787.

[39] Lester, in Macdonald, Matscher, and Petzold, eds, *The European System for the Protection of Human Rights*, 1993, Ch 18, p 474.

[40] See, eg, *KPD v FRG No 250/57*, 1 YB 222 at 224 (1957); and *H, W, P and K v Austria No 12774/87*, 62 DR 216 at 220–1 (1989).

[41] See eg, *Kalaç v Turkey* 1997-IV; 26 EHRR 552 para 28; *Refah Partisi (The Welfare Party) v Turkey* 2003-II paras 94 and 123 GC (incompatibility of sharia with democracy); *Yanasik v Turkey No 14524/89*, 74 DR 14 (1993).

[42] See eg, *Sürek v Turkey (No 1)* 1999-IV paras 61–5 GC; *Gündüz v Turkey No 59745/00* hudoc (2003) DA; and *Medya FM Reha Radyo ve İletişim Hizmetleri AŞ v Turkey No 32842/02* hudoc (2006) DA.

[43] See below, p 648.   [44] See *KPD v FRG No 250/57*, 1 YB 222 at 224 (1957).

[45] See, in particular, *H, W, P and K v Austria No 12774/87*, 62 DR 216 (1989) (neo-Nazi activities); and *Purcell v Ireland No 15404/89*, 70 DR 262 (1991) (the ban on live interviews with spokespersons of a terrorist organization). See also the argument submitted by Denmark in *Jersild v Denmark* A 298 (1994); 19 EHRR 1 para 29.

[46] *T v Belgium No 9777/82*, 34 DR 158 at 170–1 (1983).

to decide if they are presented in an objective manner as part of news reporting and analysis—which supports a finding that there has not been a breach—or in a tendentious manner abetting the incitement of racial hatred.[47]

It is submitted that a sounder approach would be that all forms and types of free speech, however hideous and appalling, are embraced within the scope of protection under Article 10(1), but that limitations on them may be justified under Article 10(2). This methodology prevents states from having abusive recourse to Article 17 or to implied limitations. Any restrictions must be subordinated to the Court's scrutiny on the basis of the standards developed under Article 10(2). Indeed, the case law suggests that, faced with a political agenda imbued with anti-democratic ideology, both the Commission and the Court have followed this methodology, whilst making reference just in passing to both Article 17 and the notion of 'duties and responsibilities' of bearers of expression rights under Article 10(2).

V. 'REVISIONIST' SPEECH

A vexed question is what coherent rationale can be found for balancing the acceptability of statements that cast revisionist light on accepted historical *interpretations or understandings* (rather than facts) on the one hand, and the paramount importance in safeguarding the rights and honour of victims of past atrocities on the other. *Lehideux and Isorni v France*[48] concerned a political advertisement in *Le Monde* designed to rehabilitate Marshal Pétain. The French courts convicted the applicants of the offence of the public defence of crimes of collaboration with the enemy during the Second World War, inferring the *mens rea* of the offence from the authors' failure to criticize Petain's authorization of the internment of Jewish people to be sent to extermination camps. While 'this page of history was very painful for France' and it was 'morally reprehensible' of the applicants not to mention Petain's involvement in the implementation of these policies, the Court noted that the applicants had referred in their advertisement to 'Nazi atrocities and persecutions', supporting the view that they were defending the man, not the policies; that the events were now more than forty years old, so that the advertisement might, despite the pain that the events still caused, be seen as a part of the process of a country coming to terms with its history. For these reasons, even allowing for the respondent state's margin of appreciation, the Court held that the imposition of criminal sanctions was disproportionate, given that other lesser remedies, particularly civil remedies, were available. But, as Judges Foighel, Loizou, and Freeland noted in their dissent,[49] the majority's decision may be seen as insensitive to the groups of victims affected and not taking proper account of the fact that the conviction could, in the context of the massive collaboration in France with the Holocaust, have the purpose of demonstrating that anti-Semitism is not to be condoned. In these regards, this case aptly fits one of the residual rationales for the application of the margin of appreciation doctrine. The assessment of sensitive historical subjects of a particular society could not be 'objectively defined' on a European scale. Furthermore, as the dissenting judges noted, the penalty was limited to a symbolic payment of one franc to the civil parties and the ordering of publication of excerpts from the national judgment in *Le Monde*.[50]

---

[47] *Jersild*, id, para 37.   [48] 1998-VII; 30 EHRR 665 paras 53–5 GC.

[49] Id, joint dissenting opinion of Judges Foighel, Loizou, and Sir John Freeland. See also the dissenting opinion of Mrs S Trechsel joined by Mr C Bîrsan in the Commission's Report of 8 April 1997.

[50] *Ibid.*

Notwithstanding the conclusion reached in *Lehideux and Isorni*, what the Court at least agreed on is that in the light of Article 17 and the phrase 'duties and responsibilities' in Article 10(2), the rejection or revision of 'clearly established historical facts—such as the Holocaust'—falls outside the scope of protection of Article 10.[51] This dictum has been confirmed in the subsequent case law. In *Garaudy v France*,[52] the applicant was a renowned academic and a former politician in France, who published a controversial book that not only criticized policies of the state of Israel but even denied the Nazi's attempt at exterminating the Jewish population. Relying partly on the Commission's case law,[53] France argued that the application should be declared inadmissible under Article 17. The Court examined two related issues separately: (i) the conviction of the applicant for denying the crimes against humanity committed against the Jewish population; and (ii) his conviction for publishing racially defamatory statements and incitement to racial hatred by virtue of his criticism levelled at the actions of Israel and of the Jewish community. With regard to the first issue, the Court found that in view of Article 17, the complaint was incompatible *ratione materiae*. The book cast doubt on the existence, extent, and seriousness of the Holocaust, which 'are not the subject of debate between historians, but—on the contrary—are clearly established'.[54] In the Court's view, far from providing political or ideological criticisms of Zionism and an 'objective' study of the revisionist theories to raise public and academic debate, the applicant was a subscriber to such revisionist theorists that 'systematically' denied that crimes against humanity had been committed. The Court found that the purpose of the book was to rehabilitate the Nazi regime and to accuse the victims of falsifying history, stressing that:

> Denying crimes against humanity constitutes one of the most serious forms of racial defamation of Jews and of incitement to hatred of them. The denial or rewriting of this type of historical fact undermines the values on which the fight against racism and anti-Semitism are based and constitutes a serious threat to public order. Such acts are incompatible with democracy and human rights because they infringe the rights of others. Its proponents indisputably have designs that fall into the category of aims prohibited by Article 17 of the Convention.[55]

As regards the second issue, the Court, while expressing 'serious doubt' over whether such opinions could fall under the scope of protection of Article 10, recognized that the conviction of the applicant was an interference to be appraised under Article 10(2). When assessing justificatory grounds for the interference, the Court suggested that the generally revisionist tenor of the book, buttressed by 'a proven racist aim', impaired the merits in the academic and political criticism of Zionism, thereby rendering the conviction permissible under Article 10(2).

What emerges from the case law is that not only denying the existence of the specific atrocities that form part of 'clearly established historical facts', but also minimizing their degree and seriousness, fall outside the protection of Article 10.[56] This implication may raise two concerns. First, aside from the Holocaust, to what extent will the Court expand the list of the 'clearly established historical facts', the negation or downplaying of which can be excluded from the ambit of protection under Article 10? Second, even if

---

[51] Id, para 51.

[52] No 65831/01, 2003-IX DA. And see *Chauvy v France* 2004-VI; 41 EHRR 610 para 69.

[53] See eg, *Glimmerveen and Hagenbeek v Netherlands* Nos 8345/78, 8406/79, 18 DR 187 (1979); *Pierre Marais v France* No 31159/96, 85 DR 184 (1996).

[54] *Garaudy v France* No 65831/01, 2003-IX DA.   [55] *Ibid.*

[56] This is the approach followed by the Court in the *Garaudy* case in relation to the denial of the crimes against humanity.

the existence of a certain atrocity is well established in its historical context, its death toll and legal characterization (for instance, the denomination of crimes against humanity or genocide) may be in dispute. It must be examined to what extent this principle can be applied by analogy to certain revisionist comments that purport to shed a different light on the magnitude and causes of such an atrocity.[57] The Court has shrewdly abstained from dwelling on polemics over historical facts, stating that:

> it is an integral part of freedom of expression to seek historical truth and it is not the Court's role to arbitrate the underlying historical issues, which are part of a continuing debate between historians that shapes opinion as to the events which took place and their interpretation.[58]

Given the paramount importance of free speech, it may be preferable to carry out a specific contextual analysis, assessing the impact of the impugned speech on surviving victims of atrocities and their families in each case, rather than to take an 'across-the-board' approach of banning the speech as such.

Second, national authorities allegedly acting to protect the 'objective' character of historical accounts may be suspected of verging on arbitrariness in favour of the 'official version'. *Monnat v Switzerland*[59] related to the broadcasting of a television programme, which shed critical light on the role of Switzerland during the Second World War, revealing details of collaboration by the Swiss government, banks, and insurance companies with Nazi Germany. Following public outcry, complaints of this reportage were lodged before the Swiss media complaint authority. A journalist responsible for the programme claimed an infringement of his freedom of expression because of both the surveillance envisaged by the Swiss legislature, and the authority's decision to recognize the complaints on the ground that the programme at issue did not deal with 'an incontestable truth' but with an issue susceptible of different interpretations. The Court noted that determining the role of Switzerland during the Second World War was not its responsibility but a matter to be left to historians. Instead, the Court's inquiry astutely concentrated on the question whether a proportionate balance was struck between the rights of audiences to receive objective information and freedom of expression.[60] It was held to be unreasonable to require the applicant to clarify that the reportage concerned 'subjective' points of view and not 'unique historical truth'.[61]

VI. INCITEMENT TO VIOLENCE

In a series of cases against Turkey, the Grand Chamber was confronted with the question whether or not it was objectionable under Article 10 to impose criminal sanctions on applicants of Kurdish origin in view of their virulent criticisms of the Turkish government. These cases demonstrate that, when confronted with remarks liable to incite to violence against an individual, a public official, or a sector of the population, the Court's methodology is not to argue that the incitement falls outside the scope of protection under Article 10. Instead, its approach is to recognize the broad pale of protection of the expression rights under the first paragraph and to analyze the restricting measures under

---

[57] See eg, the debates on the legal characterization (genocide or not) of the massacres and deportation of Armenians at the hand of the Ottoman Empire during the First World War.

[58] *Chauvy v France* 2004-VI; 41 EHRR 610 para 69. See also *Monnat v Switzerland* hudoc (2006) para 57.

[59] Hudoc (2006) para 57.   [60] *Ibid.*

[61] Id, paras 68–9. The Court suggested its scepticism of a 'unique historical truth' at the level of historical discussions: *ibid.*

the second paragraph. However, the Court has repeatedly stated that 'where...remarks constitute an incitement to violence against an individual or a public official or a sector of the population, the State authorities enjoy a wider margin of appreciation when examining the need for an interference with freedom of expression'.[62]

In *Sürek v Turkey (No 1)*,[63] the applicant was the owner of a weekly review that published two letters submitted by readers. The letters vehemently accused the Turkish military of brutally suppressing the Kurds. Distinguishing the present case from the other Turkish cases, the majority of the Grand Chamber found that the criminal sanction imposed on the applicant for the publication of the letters, a relatively modest fine, did not upset the proportionate balance. What the majority considered serious was the accusation made by the letter that the Turkish army massacred the Kurds, and that the government connived in brutalities against the dissidents. The majority found that the use of labels such as 'the fascist Turkish army' and the references to 'massacres' and 'brutalities' signalled 'a clear intention to stigmatise the other side to the conflict'. In their view, this amounted to 'an appeal to bloody revenge by stirring up base emotions and hardening already embedded prejudices which have manifested themselves in deadly violence'. Special importance was attached to the background of the security situations. Since 1985, serious disturbances and fighting had raged between the security forces and the PKK, resulting in heavy loss of lives and the establishment of an emergency rule in much of the south-east region. Against such a violent background, the content of the letters was perceived capable of inciting to violence by instilling 'a deep-seated and irrational hatred' against perpetrators of the alleged atrocities, and to funnel a message to the reader that recourse to violence was justified as a self-defence measure.[64] Further, what was deemed an aggravating factor was that the letters specifically identified persons by name, stirred up hatred, and exposed them to possible risk of physical violence. The majority concluded that the protection of the territorial integrity against separatist propaganda constituted a both relevant and sufficient ground for the penal sanction.[65]

In *Sürek (No 1)*, virulent and stigmatizing words employed in the publication can be understood as reflecting the partisan nature of the conflict. Admittedly, the penalty was relatively mild. However, the applicant was not the author of the letters. Nor was he the editor of the review responsible for selecting the materials.[66] Further, he was not a prominent figure in Turkey, who could, as in *Zana v Turkey*,[67] exert an influence on the public.[68] The potentially disturbing fallout of *Sürek (No 1)* is to allow the scope of vicarious responsibility to be broadened on the basis of the 'duties and responsibilities' of editorial and journalist staff to such an extent as seriously to inhibit press freedom. This fear is all the stronger because, in this case, as noted by the Court, the applicant did not personally associate himself with the contested views published in the review. Judge Bonello emphatically stated in his dissenting opinion that whether words encouraging violence deserved criminal sanction should be assessed on the basis of the US doctrine of 'a clear and present danger'; he suggested that where the invitation to violence remains in the abstract and removed in time and space from actual or impending scene, the paramount interest of free speech should prevail.

In the parallel case of *Sürek and Özdemir v Turkey*,[69] the Grand Chamber, however, departed from *Sürek (No 1)* and accorded primacy to freedom of expression. The same

---

[62] *Surek v Turkey (No 1)* 1999-IV GC para 61.   [63] Id, paras 60 and 62 GC.   [64] Id, para 62.

[65] By eleven votes to six, the Grand Chamber concluded that there was no violation of Article 10. The Commission also found no violation of Article 10 (by nineteen votes to thirteen).

[66] See the partly dissenting opinion of Judge Palm.   [67] 1997-VII; 27 EHRR 667 GC.

[68] 1999-IV GC, partly dissenting opinion of Judge Palm.   [69] Hudoc (1999) para 61 GC.

applicant and the editor of the weekly complained that criminal sanctions were imposed on them because they published interviews with a leading member of the PKK, an illegal organization, and a joint statement issued on behalf of four other proscribed organizations committed to the Kurdish cause. One of the contested expressions included a message that '[t]he war will go on until there is only one single individual left on our side'. The majority confirmed that the fact that the contested interviews were given by a leading figure of the banned organization could not in itself justify interference with freedom of expression. What may be depicted as hard-hitting criticism or as a one-sided view did not constitute a sufficient ground to negate the guarantee under Article 10. The majority took an overall approach, downplaying the virulent nature of some contested passages as an implacable resolve of the opposite side. The contents were not regarded as tantamount to an incitement to violence, or liable to such an incitement.[70] Further, special importance was accorded to the right of the public to be informed of a different, albeit unpalatable, perspective on disturbances in the 'Kurdish region'.[71] In a stark contrast to the reasoning in the *Zana* case, the fact that the interviewed person was the key figure of the PKK was considered to enhance the newsworthiness of the information through which the public could gain an insight into the psychology of the political opponents. The majority concluded that the reason for the criminal sanction was not sufficient.[72]

In some of the Turkish cases, the Court did not find that the contested statements encouraged, or even called for, the use of violence, armed resistance, or insurrection, despite their virulent and acerbic tenor.[73] In others, contested words that were written in highly critical or derogatory terms were not deemed to be an incitement to violence,[74] or even *liable* to incite to violence in the light of their content, tone and context.[75]

It is submitted that even if the contested words fail to reach the threshold of incitement to violence, they may be curtailed to prevent the exacerbation of serious public disturbance and inter-ethnic hatred in a volatile region.[76] However, interferences with free speech that are justified on this basis should be subject to the Court's rigorous approach. Some notable features of the Court's methodology can be highlighted. First, the Court has ascertained specific elements such as the position of the applicant, and the tone, form, and addresses of the contested statement.[77] These elements help appraise the impact of the impugned statements or publications on the public.[78] Even so, with respect to the publication or broadcasting of an interview with representatives of organizations that resort to violence, regard may be had to the 'duties and responsibilities' of media professionals not to provide an outlet for disseminating hate speech or glorifying violence.[79] Second, when scrutinizing the proportionality of both the nature and severity of criminal sanctions

---

[70] See also *Özgür Gündem v Turkey* 2000-III; 31 EHRR 1082 para 63.

[71] Hudoc (1999) para 61 GC.

[72] Further, the severity and nature of the penalties were considered particularly serious: id, para 62.

[73] *Ceylan v Turkey* 1999-IV; 30 EHRR 73 para 36 GC; *Polat v Turkey* hudoc (1999) para 47 GC. Cf, *Karataş v Turkey* 1999-IV para 52 GC.

[74] *Gerger v Turkey* hudoc (1999) para 50 GC; *Özgür Gündem v Turkey* 2000-III; 31 EHRR 1082 para 70.

[75] See eg, *Erdoğdu and İnce v Turkey* 1999-IV para 52 GC; *Başkaya and Okçuoğlu v Turkey* 1999-IV; 31 EHRR 292 para 64 GC; *Özgür Gündem v Turkey* 2000-III; 31 EHRR 1082 paras 60, 64. In *Özgür Gündem v Turkey*, however, the Court found that some passages of the impugned articles constituted the encouragement of the use of violence, and that the criminal measures were justified under Article 10(2): id, para 65.

[76] See eg, *Incal v Turkey* 1998-IV; 49 EHRR 449 paras 54 and 58 GC; *Karataş v Turkey* 1999-IV para 51 GC.

[77] See eg, *Ceylan v Turkey* 1999-IV; 30 EHRR 73 GC (an article in the weekly newspaper); *Karataş v Turkey* 1999-IV GC (poetry); *Başkaya and Okçuoğlu v Turkey* 1999-IV; 31 EHRR 292 para 64 GC (an academic book).

[78] See *Gerger v Turkey* hudoc (1999) para 50 GC.

[79] *Erdoğdu and İnce v Turkey* 1999-IV para 54 GC; and *Sürek v Turkey (No 1)* 1999-IV para 62 GC.

imposed on bearers of free speech rights,[80] the Court does not jib at requiring that the means be the least injurious for free speech rights and not entail a chilling effect.[81] Even when a criminal sentence is deferred or suspended, its mere threat may be sufficient to upset the fair balance.[82] Third, in relation to fiction, poetry, etc, which contain aggressive tones and *actually call for the use of violence,* primacy may still be given to their artistic nature. In *Karataş v Turkey,*[83] the contested poems included aggressive tones and the glorification of armed rebellions and martyrdom. Yet, given that their adverse impact on the public was limited, freedom of artistic expression held sway.

Needless to say, freedom of academic expression occupies a privileged status in the case law, even when the tenor of the expression is unpalatable to the government or the public. In *Başkaya and Okçuoğlu v Turkey,*[84] a scholarly book referred to a 'racist policy of denial' vis-à-vis the Kurds and the annexation of 'Kurdistan' by Turkey as its 'colony', which could be viewed as supporting separatism against Turkey's territorial integrity. Nevertheless, the Court underscored that the incriminated book, far from being liable to incite to violence, was a serious academic work of an analytical nature.

3. DIFFERENT CATEGORIES OF EXPRESSION

I. POLITICAL EXPRESSION

a. Overview

Freedom of political debate and free elections form 'the bedrock of any democratic system'.[85] Healthy democracy requires a government to be exposed to close scrutiny not only by the legislative and judicial authorities, but also by the general public and mass media.[86] By virtue of its dominant power, government, both national and local,[87] must tolerate the greatest extent of criticisms against it. It must also be vigilant to avoid any chilling effect that any restrictive measures it adopts may have upon political expression.[88]

The nature of speech is crucial for assessing the Court's standard of review. It is firmly established that restrictions on political discussions call for stringent review.[89] Political expression exercised by elected representatives or journalists has been given a 'privileged' status because of its contribution to public debates on matters of general interest.[90] The Court has fleshed out an array of interpretative tools, including the doctrines of 'chilling effect' and the 'less restrictive alternative' to enhance effectiveness in guaranteeing

---

[80] See eg, *Ceylan v Turkey* 1999-IV; 30 EHRR 73 para 37 GC; *Karataş v Turkey* 1999-IV para 53 GC; *Polat v Turkey* hudoc (1999) para 48 GC; *Gerger v Turkey* hudoc (1999) para 51 GC.

[81] See, *inter alia, Ceylan v Turkey,* id, para 34; *Karataş v Turkey,* id, para 50; *Polat v Turkey,* id, para 45; *Erdoğdu and İnce v Turkey* 1999-IV para 50 GC; *Başkaya and Okçuoğlu v Turkey* 1999-IV; 31 EHRR 292 para 62 GC; *Sürek and Özdemir v Turkey* hudoc (1999) para 60 GC; *Özgür Gündem v Turkey* 2000-III; 31 EHRR 1082 para 60.

[82] *Erdoğdu and İnce v Turkey* 1999-IV para 53 GC.   [83] 1999-IV para 52 GC.

[84] 1999-IV; 31 EHRR 292 paras 64–5 GC.

[85] *Mathieu-Mohin and Clerfayt v Belgium* A 113 (1987); 10 EHRR 1 para 47 PC; *Lingens v Austria* A 103 (1986); 8 EHRR 407 paras 41–2 PC; and *Bowman v UK* 1998-I para 42 GC.

[86] See eg, *Şener v Turkey* hudoc (2000) para 40; *Lombardo v Malta* hudoc (2007) para 54; and *Vides Aizsardzības Klubs v Lithuania* hudoc (2004) para 46.

[87] *Lombardo,* id, para 54.   [88] *Castells v Spain* A 236 (1992); 14 EHRR 445 para 46.

[89] *Id,* para 42; *Piermont v France* A 314 (1995); 20 EHRR 301 para 76; *Ceylan v Turkey* 1999-IV; 30 EHRR 73 para 34 GC.

[90] *Lombardo,* id, para 53.

freedom of political expression. In *Ahmet Sadik v Greece*,[91] a Greek parliamentarian, who circulated communiqués referring to Muslim minorities in Western Thrace as 'Turkish', was convicted of a criminal offence of deceiving an elector. The Commission considered such a measure clearly excessive because there was no indication of incitement to violence. Even a low amount of damages imposed on local councillors for libel and defamation in comments critical of a public authority may suffice to entail an unacceptable chilling effect on a councillor's political expression.[92] The onus may be imposed on a government to prove the overriding weight of countervailing social ends. Even statements which are considered to pose a threat to national security and public order, or to the territorial integrity of member states, may cause the Court to consider whether the contested measure is the least injurious,[93] and generally to scrutinize it closely.[94]

Immunity is often conferred upon parliamentarians to prevent their free speech being compromised by 'partisan complaints'.[95] Similarly, the national authorities are entitled to give immunity to statements made in parliamentary debates in the legislative chambers to safeguard the interests of Parliament as a whole.[96] In contrast, with respect to senior politicians, it would be excessive to accord them total immunity from accountability for their defamatory or insulting remarks against a prosecutor, as this constitutes a breach of Article 6(1).[97] In *Karhuvaara and Iltalehti v Finland*,[98] it was held to be disproportionate, in breach of Article 10, that by law an aggravating factor in the applicants' conviction for offence of invasion of privacy was that the offending newspaper articles concerned a member of parliament. The articles focused on the ill-conduct of her husband, just mentioning that he was married to a member of parliament.

Obviously, free elections and the freedom of political debate, albeit closely intertwined with each other, may come into collision, warranting restrictions on the latter freedom to secure equal opportunity for candidates in an election. In *Bowman v UK*,[99] an anti-abortion campaigner provided a leaflet showing candidates' voting records and attitudes on abortion before parliamentary elections in the UK. She was charged with a statutory offence that forbad an unauthorized person expending more than five pounds during the period before an election when conveying information to electors to promote the election of a candidate. The restriction on expenditure was applicable only for a limited duration prior to the general election, and the applicant could have campaigned freely at any other time. However, the Grand Chamber noted that the distribution at other times would not have served the objective of informing the electorate at the time when the choice of representatives was made. Similarly, it rejected the effectiveness of alternative methods. It was not demonstrated that she could publish the material contained in the leaflets in a newspaper or broadcast it on radio or television. Nor could the option of her standing for election have been realistic, as this would have required her to pay a deposit that was likely to be forfeited. Further, contrast was made with the absence of restrictions upon the freedom of the press to support or oppose any candidate, or upon political parties to advertise. In view of these facts, the Court found a violation of Article 10, ruling that the applicant was debarred from publishing information vital to political debates. Judge

---

[91] 1996-V; 24 EHRR 323 Com Rep (non-exhaustion of the domestic remedies before the Court).

[92] *Lombardo v Malta* hudoc (2007) para 61.   [93] *Incal v Turkey* 1998-IV; 49 EHRR 449 GC.

[94] See eg, *Piermont v France* A 314 (1995); 20 EHRR 301.

[95] *Cordova v Italy (No 1)* 2003-I; 40 EHRR 974 para 55; and *Karhuvaara and Iltalehti v Finland* 2004-X; 41 EHRR 1154 para 50.

[96] *Karhuvaara*, id, para 50.

[97] *Cordova v Italy (No 1)* 2003-I; 40 EHRR 974; and *Cordova v Italy (No 2)* 2003-I.

[98] *Karhuvaara and Iltalehti v Finland* 2004-X; 41 EHRR 1154 para 52.

[99] 1998-I; 19 EHRR 179 para 45 GC.

Freeland opined in his dissent that the Court was left a delicate task of examining the extent to which the funding of single-issue pressure groups at elections may be controlled to counter 'the risk of excessive diversion of the main electoral debates'.[100]

b. Political parties and the freedom of expression

The vital importance of the rights guaranteed under Article 10 can be most keenly felt by political parties. The Court has recognized their crucial role in promoting pluralism[101] and ensuring the healthy function of democracy.[102] To the extent that their activities are considered a collective exercise of freedom of expression, political parties are fully entitled to the protection of the rights under Article 10.[103] In *United Communist Party of Turkey v Turkey*,[104] the Court held that:

> one of the principal characteristics of democracy [is] the possibility it offers of resolving a country's problems through dialogue, without recourse to violence, even when they are irksome. Democracy thrives on freedom of expression. From that point of view, there can be no justification for hindering a political group solely because it seeks to debate in public the situation of part of the State's population and to take part in the nation's political life in order to find, according to democratic rules, solutions capable of satisfying everyone concerned.

Yet, a vexed question relates to political parties whose leaders incite to violence, or craft policies which flout democratic principles, or which aim at destroying democratic systems and infringing rights safeguarded in the democracy. In the Court's view, such political parties 'cannot lay claims to the Convention's protection against penalties imposed on those grounds'.[105] Nevertheless, it ought to be recalled that these parties may not inherently be divested of Article 10's free speech rights. In *Stankov and the United Macedonian Organization Ilinden v Bulgaria*,[106] the Court held:

> The essence of democracy is its capacity to resolve problems through open debate. Sweeping measures of a preventive nature to suppress freedom of assembly and expression other than in cases of incitement to violence or rejection of democratic principles—however shocking and unacceptable certain views or words used may appear to the authorities, and however illegitimate the demands made may be—do a disservice to democracy and often even endanger it.

The preventive intervention associated with the concept of 'militant democracy'[107] must not end up in dismantling the edifice of democracy through its corrosive impact.[108]

II. CIVIL EXPRESSION

The notion of public interest has an autonomous and broad meaning in the Convention. It has been liberally construed in the case law to encompass social, economic, cultural, or

---

[100] Id, para 13.

[101] The Court has stressed that there can be no democracy without the principle of pluralism: *Refah Partisi (The Welfare Party) v Turkey* 2003-II para 89 GC.

[102] *United Communist Party of Turkey v Turkey* 1998-I paras 42–3 GC; and *Refah Partisi (The Welfare Party) v Turkey* 2003-II para 88 GC.

[103] *Refah Partisi (The Welfare Party) v Turkey* 2003-II paras 43 and 89 GC. [104] 1998-I para 57 GC.

[105] See, *inter alia, Socialist Party v Turkey* 1998-III paras 46–7 GC; *Yazar v Turkey* 2002-II para 49; and *Refar Partisi (The Welfare Party) v Turkey* 2003-II paras 98 and 110 GC. [106] 2001-IX para 97.

[107] The term 'militant democracy' was coined by Karl Loewenstein, in 31 AmPol Sci Rev 417 (1937).

[108] Macklem, 4 Int'l J Const. L 488, at 514 (2006).

even commercial and religious aspects. Expression that claims to be in the public interest can be aptly described as civil expression.[109] Broadcasting a programme that critically examined the Swiss collaboration with Nazi Germany during the Second World War was clearly of public interest.[110] The broader meaning of civil expression can be illustrated in *Steel and Morris v UK*.[111] There, the Court contemplated the allegation that McDonald's was responsible, *inter alia,* for abusive farming, deforestation, cancer, and exploitation of children to be of public concern and worthy of a higher degree of protection. More controversial is the decision in *Paturel v France*.[112] A member of the Jehovah's Witnesses, who in his book compared the methods of deprogramming by an association aiding victims of religious sects to the methods used in Soviet internment camps, was found to have acted in the public interest in shedding light on methods of fight against sects.

III. ARTISTIC EXPRESSION

Needless to say, artistic freedom is vital to the enrichment of humanity and diversity of civilizations. The Court's dictum that the protection of Article 10 extends to expressions which 'offend, shock or disturb the state or any sector of the population'[113] is of special importance to artistic work. The fact that artistic expression is triggered by commercial incentives or designed for profit-making purposes ought not to lessen its protection under Article 10. The liberal democratic values underpinning the Convention system means that artists should be encouraged freely to manifest their artistic conviction to challenge the orthodoxy as avant-gardes, and to create new and critical thinking. The mission of the artists to defy the establishment by radical work should be encouraged as essential contributions to the plural cultural values in democracies.[114] The upshot of the constitutional significance of artistic expression has been stated by the Court as follows:

> ...Article 10 includes freedom of artistic expression—notably within freedom to receive and impart information and ideas—which affords the opportunity to take part in the public exchange of cultural, political and social information and ideas of all kinds...Those who create, perform, distribute or exhibit works of art contribute to the exchange of ideas and opinions which is essential for a democratic society. Hence there is an obligation on the State not to encroach unduly on the author's freedom of expression....[115]

Nevertheless, as compared with political expression, the decision-making policy of the Court is to accord a less privileged position to artistic expression. Nonetheless, what ought to be avoided is deployment of the notion 'duties and responsibilities' to mask oppressive measures, whose deterrent impact may stifle artistic imagination and creativity.

Some artistic work may be perceived as exceptionally offensive to the religious or moral convictions of members of a particular religious faith. Similarly, it may be considered defamatory or insulting to specific persons identifiable in the work. In such circumstances, the legitimate aims of protecting public morals or the rights of others can be invoked to justify appropriate measures against artistic expression. In case the reputation or the honour of persons is at stake, special regard must be had to the nature of the

---

[109] See Jacq and Teitgen, in Delmas-Marty, ed, *The European Convention for the Protection of Human Rights—International Protection versus National Restrictions,* 1992, p 64.

[110] *Monnat v Switzerland* hudoc (2006) para 58. [111] 2005-II; 41 EHRR 403 para 88.

[112] Hudoc (2005) paras 41–2. [113] *Handyside v UK* A 24 (1976); 1 EHRR 737 para 49 PC.

[114] Lester refers to 'the inherently subversive nature of the artistic impulse': Lester, above n 39, at p 471, f 35.

[115] *Alinak v Turkey* hudoc (2005) para 42.

offending elements (including the tone of accusation), the public status or otherwise of the persons recognizable in the artistic work and its harmful impact.

Much more controversial would be circumstances in which a hindrance to artistic activities is defended by the public interest in preventing crimes or disorder, or protecting national security. Arguably, novels and paintings can serve as a medium for conveying certain political messages considered an incitement to hatred, revolt, or even the use of violence. Nevertheless, in liberal democracies, it seems unsustainable that artistic expression can be restricted on the basis that it is of such a nature as to ignite the nationalistic or fundamentalist fervour of a minority and to incite to hatred and violence among rivalling religious or ethnic groups, as was argued by the respondent government in *Alinak v Turkey*.[116] In that case, the applicant, though formerly a member of parliament, was a private person when writing a novel which, although a work of fiction, recounted a real event, a massacre committed by Turkish Security forces. National courts ordered the seizure of his book, ruling that its content incited to hatred and hostility by distinguishing Turkish citizens along ethnic or religious lines. The Court recognized that graphic details of fictional atrocities 'might be construed as inciting readers to hatred, revolt and the use of violence'.[117] Nevertheless, it quickly added that the novel was destined for a relatively small public, and the applicant was a private citizen at the material time. Further, an official involved in the massacre was not identified. The Court found that the seizure of the novel went too far. It is submitted that even if the book had been addressed to a large readership *and* if the applicant had been a public figure, such factors *alone* should not justify inherently harsh measures such as the seizure of a novel. The Court should give presumptive privileged status to artistic expression and scrupulously examine specific factors such as the contents, nature, medium, and the impact of a contested artistic expression. In the subsequent *Lindon, Otchakovsky-Laurens and July v France*[118] case, which also concerned a novel based on real events, the Court distinguished that case from *Alinak*. As will be examined in the context of defamation, in the former case the Court highlighted the more serious nature of accusations (complicity in racially motivated murder, etc) and the identification of the person by name.

Reflecting cultural relativism, the boundaries between obscenity and art are often hard to draw, varying from one society to another. The case of *Müller and Others v Switzerland*[119] related to the criminal conviction of an artist for publicly displaying pictures depicting sodomy and bestiality in crude forms, and to the confiscation of his paintings. There was no public warning about the content of the exhibition, and entry was free of charge. The Commission's rigorous appraisal was commensurate with the approach followed in the assessment of political expression. It found that the order to confiscate his paintings violated Article 10, stressing the need to choose less onerous alternatives.[120] In contrast, the Court recognized the measures as necessary to protect morals. To justify this decision, the Court made a hasty resort to the margin of appreciation and to the 'duty and responsibilities' of artists in selecting the means of expression.[121] Judge Spielmann, in his dissenting opinion, took issue with the lax approach followed by the majority, adverting to the historical struggle to obtain artistic freedom in liberal democracies.[122] In the subsequent case of *Otto-Preminger-Institut v Austria*,[123] the Commission's robust review favouring artistic expression was once again reversed by the Court.[124] The case concerned

---

[116] *Ibid.*   [117] Id, para 41.   [118] Hudoc (2007) GC.
[119] A 133 (1988); 13 EHRR 212 para 16.
[120] Id, para 70 Com Rep. See also *X Ltd and Y v UK No 8710/79*, 28 DR 77 (1982).   [121] Id, para 34.
[122] Id, dissenting opinion of Judge Spielmann, para 10.
[123] A 295-A (1994); 19 EHRR 34 paras 72, 77 Com Rep.   [124] Id, paras 56–7.

the seizure and forfeiture of a film which provocatively portrayed God the Father, the Virgin Mary, and Jesus Christ. The Austrian courts considered it blasphemous for the predominantly Catholic population in the Tyrol. The Court stressed the national margin of appreciation in ensuring that religious beliefs of pious population would not be offensively attacked.[125]

The inconsistency of the Court's approach becomes apparent when *Otto-Preminger-Institut* is compared with *Müller*. Whereas in *Müller* the applicants failed to warn the public of the content of the exhibition, which was free and open to the public, the *Otto-Preminger Institut* informed the public of the content of the film and imposed an age limit for the admission. This point was emphasized by the minority in *Otto-Preminger Institut*, who held that the applicant association took steps to ensure that no one would be faced with the film unwittingly.[126] They held that the contested action constituted prior restraint, disproportionate to the purpose of protecting religious sensitivities and detrimental to the principle of tolerance underpinning pluralist democracy.[127] It seems unreasonable that the (anticipatory) outrage of the people in a local region, however genuine, which was based only on the knowledge of the content of the film, was considered to outweigh artistic expression and to justify even prior restraint. The Court was aware that after the seizure of the film, the play on which the film was based was shown even in Innsbruck (the capital of the Tyrolean *Land*) without meeting criminal prosecution.[128] The Court's approach in *Müller* and *Otto-Preminger-Institut* must be criticized for lacking in rigour and being oblivious of the rationale underpinnings of artistic expression in a pluralistic democracy.

In a stark contrast to these judgments, the case law since then has clearly marked a turn-around that bolsters artistic expression.[129] In *Vereinigung Bildender Künstler v Austria*,[130] an association of artists directed a famous gallery of contemporary arts. An exhibition organized by it included a collage of a group of public figures in sexual positions. Among the figures was the former general secretary of the Austrian Freedom Party (FPÖ), Mr Meischberger, who was shown naked, gripping the ejaculating penis of the former head of the FPÖ, Mr Haider, and ejaculating on Mother Teresa. Mr Meischberger was granted an injunction preventing the further exhibition of the painting on the ground that it was a debasement of his public standing. The Court found the depiction of Mr Meischberger 'somewhat outrageous' and accepted that the injunction had the legitimate aim of protecting the rights of others. But it held, by a very narrow majority of four to three, that the injunction was a disproportionate response in breach of Article 10. The Court stressed the 'satirical' nature of the painting, noting that members of the FPÖ had criticized the painter's work, adding that 'satire is a form of artistic expression and social commentary and, by its inherent features of exaggeration and distortion of reality, naturally aims to provoke and agitate'.[131] The Court also took into account the fact that Mr Meischberger was only one of over thirty public figures in the collage, thus diminishing the attention drawn to him; that the offensive painting of his body was completely covered by red paint, the result of damage caused by an exhibition visitor, so that it was uncertain that Mr Meischberger was still recognizable; and that the injunction was unduly

---

125 Id, para 56.
126 Id, joint dissenting opinion of Judges Palm, Pekkanen, and Makarczyk, paras 8–9.
127 Id, para 4.   128 Id, para 19.
129 Apart from *Vereinigung Bildender Künstler* hudoc (2007), see eg, *Karataş v Turkey* 1999-IV para 49 GC (poems); *Alinak v Turkey* hudoc (2005) para 41 (novel); *Dağtekin v Turkey* hudoc (2005) para 26 (novel); *Yalçın Küçük v Turkey* hudoc (2002) (an interviewed book written in a literary and metaphorical style).
130 Hudoc (2007) para 31.   131 Id, para 33.

broad, extending to all future exhibitions anywhere. In contrast, Judge Loucaides, in his dissent, placed special weight on the protection of the reputation of others, noting that:

> In the same way that we exclude insults from freedom of speech, so we must exclude from the legitimate expression of artists insulting pictures that undermine the reputation or dignity of others, especially if they are devoid of any meaningful message and contain nothing more than senseless, repugnant and disgusting images, as in the present case.[132]

Judge Loucaides also noted that the gallery was accessible even to the children. This could have offered a more potent argument if the aim of the injunction had been to protect public morals.

IV. COMMERCIAL EXPRESSION

a. Overview

The identification of what constitutes commercial speech is not free from difficulty. In the EU law context, commercial expression is aptly defined as 'the dissemination of information, the expression of ideas or the dissemination of images in the course of the promotion of an economic activity and the corresponding right to receive such information'.[133] The principal aim of commercial expression is to enhance the economic interests of individuals and enterprises. Commercial advertising as a means of imparting information on characteristics of services and goods to consumers[134] is clearly the most salient form. Article 2(f) of the European Convention on Transfrontier Television 1989[135] defines advertisement as 'any public announcement in return for payment or similar consideration or for self-promotional purposes, which is intended to promote the sale, purchase or rental of a product or service, to advance a cause or idea, or to bring about some other effect desired by the advertiser or the broadcaster itself'.

A survey of the case law suggests that commercial expression remains relatively less safeguarded than political or artistic expression. As discussed below, the lax review that is afforded to limitations upon it, based on a margin of appreciation,[136] is marked by the absence of the distinct interpretative principles widely used in cases involving political expression. Nevertheless, the fact that communicators pursue a purely economic motive should not deprive them of the protection afforded under Article 10. Regard should be had to the interest of consumers in the free flow of commercial information.[137]

b. Restrictions on commercial expression

Limitations on commercial advertising may be justified for the purpose of preventing unfair competition, and untruthful or misleading advertising. Such purposes can fall within the phrase 'the protection of the reputation or rights of others'. The word 'others' can refer to both competitors in the same market and consumers in general. The Court has recognized that even the publication of objective and truthful advertisement may be restricted to ensure respect for the rights of others, or because of the special circumstances of specific business activities and professions.[138]

---

132 Id, dissenting opinion of Judge Loucaides.
133 Case C-71/02, *Herbert Karner Industrie-Auktionen GmbH v Troostwijk GesmbH*, para 75, *per* Albert AG.
134 *Krone Verlag GmbH & Co. KG v Austria (No 3)* 2003-XII; 42 EHRR 578 para 31.
135 ETS 132. In force 1993. thirty-two parties.
136 See eg, *Church of Scientology v Sweden No 7805/77*, 16 DR 68 at 73 (1979).
137 See Lester, above n 39, at p 480.
138 *Krone Verlag GmbH & Co KG v Austria (No 3)* 2003-XII; 42 EHRR 578 para 31.

In *Markt Intern Verlag GmbH v Germany*,[139] the Court upheld an injunction against a trade magazine, which was precluded from publishing information about a mail-order firm dealing with chemist and beauty products. The article in the magazine described one retailer complaining about the products and service of this mail-order firm, soliciting information of similar experiences of dissatisfaction with this firm. The German courts considered such statements to run counter to honest practices of competition. They held that the contested article cast doubt on the reliability of the mail-order firm in question when the latter promised to carry out an investigation of the reported case. The Court was equally divided (seven votes to seven), with the casting vote of the President tipping the balance in favour of the government. As an explanation for its curt examination of the merits of the case and the application of a margin of appreciation, the Court referred to the 'complex and fluctuating' nature of the issues involved.[140] It is doubtful whether the applicants (a small publishing firm and its editor-in-chief) acted in a dishonest manner. Indeed, the majority of the Court conceded that there lacked a competitive relationship between *Markt intern* and the mail-order firm, and that the applicant company intended 'legitimately' to safeguard the interests of chemists and beauty product retailers.[141] Nevertheless, they were receptive to the domestic courts' formalistic argument that even in the absence of such a competitive relationship, the contested statements could, albeit *en passant*, provide objective advantage to the specialized retail trade to the detriment of the mail-order firm which was described as a competitor. They did so, even though the impact of the article reporting one incident and soliciting similar incidents was limited. Another striking element is that while recognizing the truth contained in the impugned statements, the majority did not consider it sufficiently material. Overall, the commercial nature of the statements was preponderant for the Court's standard of review. The Court held that:

> even the publication of items which are true and describe real events may under certain circumstances be prohibited: the obligation to respect privacy of others [and] the duty to respect the confidentiality of certain commercial information are examples. In addition, a correct statement can be and often is qualified by additional remarks, by value judgments, by suppositions or even insinuations.[142]

Oddly, none of these elements cited by the Court in this passage was relevant to the essence of the contested information, namely, the information on individual retailers' dissatisfaction with the product and the reimbursement of the mail-order firm. Without adducing any substantive justifications, the Court relied on the non-substitution principle, according to which it 'should not substitute its own evaluation for that of the national courts...where those courts, on reasonable grounds, had considered the restrictions to be necessary'.[143]

The restrained approach followed in *Markt Intern* may be criticized for lowering the standard of proportionality to the most lax level. It suggests that the Court would be required only to verify whether the contracting party exercised its discretion 'reasonably, carefully and in good faith'.[144] This reticent policy was boosted in *Jacubowski*,[145] which concerned the dismissal of an editor of a news agency. His employer issued a press release questioning his professional competence. In order to safeguard his reputation and prospect of obtaining a job in the same sector, the applicant distributed a circular letter among news agency professionals, which criticized the competence and management

---

[139] A 164 (1989); 12 EHRR 161 PC.   [140] Id, para 33.   [141] Id, para 36.   [142] Id, para 35.

[143] Id, para 47. See also Eissen, in Macdonald *et al*, eds, above n 39, Ch 7, at pp 145–6.

[144] See, however, the bolder approach of the Commission in *Markt Intern Verlag GmbH and Klaus Beermann v German* and in *Jacubowski v Germany*.   [145] *Jacubowski v Germany* A 291-A (1994); 19 EHRR 64.

of the employer. Mainly because the circular contained his intention to set up a news agency, national courts found that its distribution amounted to an act of unfair competition against the interests of the employer, who would become his possible competitor. An injunction was granted, impeding the applicant from distributing the circular. The Commission's unanimous finding that Article 10 was breached was overturned by the Court.[146] The rationale adduced by the Court was essentially the same as seen in *Markt Intern*. The standard of review was confined only to the question 'whether the measures taken at national level are justifiable in principle and proportionate'.[147] As the minority judges pointed out, this judgment must be criticized for overlooking the applicant's main intention, which was to reply to the harsh criticism made by his employer in a press release and to secure his reputation. Further, the newspaper articles supporting his view were already circulated in the public domain.[148] On a closer scrutiny, it is hard to read into the document an essentially competitive purpose and intention. The dissenting judges cogently argued that to 'accept in this case a preponderance of the competitive element amounts to reducing the principle of freedom of expression to the level of an exception and to elevating the [German] Unfair Competition Act to the status of a rule'.[149]

Many countries still forbid comparative advertising or price comparison under their unfair competition laws. Even where such practice is recognized, rigorous requirements may effectively result in its denial. In *Krone Verlag GmbH & Co KG v Austria (No 3)*,[150] a court injunction prohibited the comparison of the sales prices of two regional newspapers without indicating the differences in their reporting styles on coverage of different issues. The Court found such a stringent requirement to impair the very essence of price comparison. The impact of the injunction was all the more excessive in view of a risk of fines for non-compliance with it.

Professional advertising and publicity has been treated as a genre of commercial expression in the case law. Confronted with a regulatory power of professional organizations, the Court and Commission have often shied away from robust review.[151] In *Casado Coca v Spain*,[152] a lawyer was subject to disciplinary proceedings after distributing advertisements. The Commission found a violation of Article 10, on the casting vote of the President. In contrast, the Court endorsed the measure, emphasizing a margin of appreciation owing to the absence of European consensus on professional advertising. It held that '[b]ecause of their direct, continuous contact with their members, the Bar authorities and the country's courts are in a better position than an international court to determine how, at a given time, the right balance can be struck between the various interests involved, namely the requirements of the proper administration of justice, the dignity of the profession, the right of everyone to receive information about legal assistance and affording members of the Bar the possibility of advertising their practices'.[153]

In *Colman v UK*,[154] the British General Medical Council's guidance designed to protect patients from misleading or manipulative advertising prevented a doctor's advertisement

---

[146] Id, para 28.

[147] Id, para 26. Clapham endorsed this approach based on non-substitution principle: Clapham, above n 19, at p 224.

[148] Id, dissenting opinion of Judges Walsh, MacDonald, and Wildhaber.   [149] Id, *in fine*.

[150] 2003-XII; 42 EHRR 578 paras 32–4.

[151] As well as the *Casado Coca* case examined here, see also *Hempfing v Germany No 14622/89*, 69 DR 272 (1991).

[152] A 285-A (1994); 18 EHRR 1 para 66 Com Rep.

[153] Id, para 55. See also *Colman v UK* A 258-D (1993); 18 EHRR 119 para 39 Com Rep.

[154] *Colman v UK* A 258-D (1993); 18 EHRR 119 para 39 Com Rep. In that case, the dissenting Commissioners questioned how a publicity containing only the name, qualifications, address, and telephone number of the

in a press. This was considered compatible with Article 10(2), as the applicant's concern was purely commercial. In contrast, in *Stambuk v Germany*,[155] disciplinary punishment meted out to an ophthalmologist by a national medical court for disregarding the ban on advertising was found excessive. The publicity was considered a possible side effect of giving an interview on his laser operation technique, which was published in a local press with his photograph. The strict interpretation of the ban on advertising of a liberal profession was all the more apparent, as the photograph was so closely connected to the contents of the article that it could not be reduced to mere advertisement.[156]

The Court's general approach to limitations on commercial expression can be summarized here. As a consequence of lax review, its assessment of proportionality may not be attended by elaborate reasoning.[157] *Prima facie*, the *Conventionnalité* of contested measures is presumed, so that the Court's review may be confined only to the question whether the measures are 'justifiable *in principle* and proportionate'.[158] As a justification for such a restrained stance, it has invoked its limited knowledge and expertise in assessing complex details of commercial and competition regulations.[159] Yet, the cogency of this argument is increasingly challenged by the Court's better acquaintance with national practice and the harmonization of European competition laws. Further, advertisement can be hybrid, being comprised of both commercial and non-commercial (and public interest) elements.[160] As will be analyzed below with respect to such category crossover, it may be argued that a more subtle calibration is required to assess what weight can be ascribed to non-commercial elements.[161]

c. Commercial expression and public interest

In contrast to the general tendency described above, once commercial expression is considered to relate to matters of public interest as understood broadly, the standard of review may revert to a heightened level. In *Barthold v FRG*,[162] a local paper carried an opinion by a veterinary surgeon, who criticized the absence of veterinary service at night. He was interviewed by a local journalist who wrote about this problem, with his name and photograph. Barthold's fellow veterinarians filed an action against him under unfair competition law. This was endorsed by the national court that presumed his intention was to act for commercial competition, unless this was entirely overridden by other motives. The injunction was ordered, withholding the applicant from repeating his criticisms. The Court rejected the claim that this case was about commercial advertising susceptible to greater restrictions. Instead, it considered that the statements contributed to public discussions of a matter of general interest and described the publicity effect as merely secondary. The German courts' presumption as to intention was considered to be too rigorous a yardstick, which was disproportionate.

The fine-tuned appraisal of proportionality in *Barthold* is followed in the subsequent case law. Thus in *Hertel v Switzerland*,[163] the applicant was prevented from publishing views about allegedly hazardous effects of microwave ovens in a health journal. Again, the

---

applicant could pose a danger to public health: the dissenting opinion of Mr. Martinez, joined by Messrs Nørgaard, Busuttil, Weitzel, Rozakis, and Loucaides. The case was settled before the Court.

[155] Hudoc (2002); 37 EHRR 845 para 50.   [156] Id, para 48.   [157] Lester, above n 39 at 478–80.

[158] *Markt Intern Verlag GmbH and Klaus Beermann v FRG* A 164 (1989); 12 EHRR 161 para 33 (emphasis added). See also *Jacubowski v Germany* A 291-A (1994); 19 EHRR 64 para 26.

[159] *Ibid.*

[160] See eg, *Barthold v FRG* A 90 (1985); 7 EHRR 383 paras 54 and 58; and *Stambuk v Germany* hudoc (2002); 37 EHRR 845 para 42.

[161] Randall, 6 HRLR 53 at 65 (2006). See also Munro, 62 CLJ 134 at 149–50 (2003).

[162] A 90 (1985) 7 EHRR 383 para 58.   [163] 1998-VI; 28 EHRR 534 paras 47ff.

ground for interference was that his views would constitute an act of unfair competition and prejudice the interests of the manufacturers and suppliers. The Court deemed the ban out of proportion, as it amounted to censorship of the applicant's work and removed his opportunity to disseminate ideas of public concern. Such a disproportionate effect was aggravated by the risk of his imprisonment.[164]

In contrast, where contested publications do not contain any contribution to public debate, the discretionary power exercised by a professional body may be upheld. In *Hempfing v Germany*,[165] a reprimand was issued by a local bar association against a lawyer who sent circulars to collection agencies. The interference was found proportionate, because these were purely motivated by the intention of advertising.

4. DIFFERENT MEANS OF EXPRESSION

I. THE PRESS AND JOURNALISTIC FREEDOM

a. Overview

The Court has repeatedly emphasized that Article 10 safeguards not only the substance and contents of information and ideas, but also the means of transmitting it. The press has been accorded the broadest scope of protection in the case law, which encompasses preparatory acts for publication, such as activities of research and inquiries carried out by journalists,[166] as well as the confidentiality of journalistic source as discussed below. Prior restraints on the press are not in themselves incompatible with Article 10,[167] but must not provide a subterfuge for repressive measures against anti-governmental media. Indeed, prior restraints are the most serious threat to the free flow of information and to meaningful debate among the public. Accordingly, this is the area where not only the proportionality test,[168] but even the two standards 'prescribed by law'[169] and 'legitimate aims', may be stringently applied.

Needless to say, the role of the press as a 'public watchdog' is vital to democracy's political process.[170] The press and investigative journalism guarantee the healthy operation of democracy, exposing policy decisions and actions or omissions of government to close scrutiny of the public opinion,[171] and facilitating the citizens' participation in the decision-making process. Such a democracy-fostering function of the press assumes special importance when it operates in conjunction with the right of the public to receive information and ideas of public concern,[172] including those on divisive political issues.[173]

---

[164] Id, para 50.   [165] *No 14622/89*, 69 DR 272 (1991).

[166] *Sunday Times v UK (No 2)* A 217 (1991); 14 EHRR 229 para 51 PC and *Dammann v Switzerland* hudoc (2006) para 52.

[167] See eg, *Krone Verlag GmbH & CoKG and MEDIAPRINT Zeitungs- und Zeitschriftenverlag GmbH & Co KG v Austria No 42429/98* hudoc (2003) DA.

[168] See eg, *Observer and Guardian v UK* A 216 (1991); 14 EHRR 153 para 60 PC; *Gaweda v Poland* 2002-II; 39 EHRR 90 para 35.   [169] See eg, *Gawęda v Poland*, id, para 40.

[170] See, *inter alia*, *Sunday Times v UK (No 1)* A 30 (1979); 2 EHRR 245 para 65 PC; *Sunday Times v UK (No 2)* A 217 (1991); 14 EHRR 229 para 50 PC; *Jersild v Denmark* A 298; 19 EHRR 1 para 35; *Goodwin v UK* 1996-II; 22 EHRR 123 para 39 GC. See also *Vides Aizsardzības Klubs v Lithuania*, Judgment of 27 May 2004, para 42 (recognition of a similar 'public watchdog' function of NGOs).

[171] *Özgür Radyo-Ses Radyo Televizyon Yapim Ve Tanitim AŞ v Turkey* hudoc (2006) para 78.

[172] *News Verlags GmbH & Co KG v Austria* 2000-I; 31 EHRR 246 para 56.

[173] See, *inter alia*, *Lingens v Austria* A 103 (1986); 8 EHRR 407 paras 41–2 PC; *Erdoğdu and İnce v Turkey* 1999-IV para 48 GC; *Özgür Gündem v Turkey* 2000-III; 31 EHRR 1082 para 58.

The press provides the public 'the best means of discovering and forming an opinion of the ideas and attitudes of political leaders'.[174] Even outside the political process, the press helps shape an informed public opinion, and nurtures and stimulates critical public debate on issues of general public interest.[175] Further, news items are a 'perishable commodity'. To avoid news items becoming stale, a *continued* injunction against the press must be subordinated to a stringent review as to the existence of 'compelling', countervailing interests.[176] As a corollary of its close linkage to democracy, the scope of press freedom must be construed in a broad manner to permit of a degree of exaggeration or even provocation.[177] Correspondingly, the most rigorous scrutiny is required to evaluate restrictions on press freedom.[178]

The 'imposition of a prison sentence for a press offence will be compatible with journalists' freedom of expression . . . only in exceptional circumstances, notably where other fundamental rights have been seriously impaired, as in the case of hate speech or incitement to violence'.[179] Indeed, the Court has stressed that the infliction of any criminal sanction, albeit minor in nature, may entail an unacceptable chilling effect; what matters most is not the gravity of the penalty inflicted on journalists but the very fact that they are convicted.[180]

b. The protection of the confidentiality of journalistic sources

The confidentiality of journalistic sources is crucial for press freedom.[181] Without such protection, the role of the press as a public watchdog in providing accurate and reliable information to the public[182] and shaping a well-informed public may be jeopardized. It is readily understandable that any encroachments on the confidentiality of journalistic sources require 'the most careful scrutiny'[183] and will not comply with Article 10 'unless it is justified by an overriding requirement in the public interest'.[184] In the *Goodwin* case,[185] an order for discovery served on a journalist to divulge the identity of his informant was considered excessive.[186] In contrast, to require journalists to supply some factual basis substantiating their allegedly defamatory statements, which were described as value-judgments, was not considered incompatible with Article 10, insofar as such a duty did not go so far as to require the disclosure of the identity of sources.[187]

A court order to disclose a journalist's research materials may be warranted for the purpose of preventing disorder or crimes. In *Nordisk Film & TV A/S v Denmark*,[188] a journalist went undercover and became involved in a paedophile association to produce a documentary on paedophilia in Denmark. A court order was issued, compelling the applicant company to hand over the unedited footage and the notes written by the undercover journalist to produce evidence of a serious child abuse case. Since the majority of the programme's participants neither knowingly assisted the press nor gave consent to being filmed or recorded, they were not considered sources of journalistic information

---

[174] See eg, *Lingens v Austria* A 103 (1986); 8 EHRR 407 paras 41–2 PC; *and Özgür Gündem v Turkey* 2000-III; 31 EHRR 1082 para 58.

[175] *Cumpănă and Mazăre v Romania* 2004-XI; 41 EHRR 400 para 96.

[176] See eg, *Editions Plon v France* 2004-IV; 42 EHRR 705 para 53 and *Stoll v Switzerland* hudoc (2007) para 131 GC.

[177] *Radio France v France* 2004-II; 40 EHRR 706 para 37.

[178] *Observer and Guardian v UK* A 216 (1991); 14 EHRR 153 para 60 PC.

[179] *Cumpănă and Mazăre v Romania* 2004-XI; 41 EHRR 400 para 115 GC.

[180] *Dammann v Switzerland* hudoc (2006) para 57.   [181] *Goodwin v UK* 1996-II; 22 EHRR 123 GC.

[182] *Ibid.*   [183] Id, para 40.

[184] *Nordisk Film & TV A/S v Denmark* No 40485/02 hudoc (2005) DA.   [185] *Ibid.*   [186] *Ibid.*

[187] *Katamadze v Georgia* No 69857/01 hudoc (2006) DA.   [188] No 40485/02 hudoc (2005) DA.

in the traditional sense. According to the Court's reasoning, the applicant company was ordered not to divulge its journalistic source of information, but rather to hand over part of its own research material. The two situations differed in that the former involved the freedom of expression of both the journalist and the participants, whereas the latter concerned only the freedom of expression of the journalist. In the latter situation, where the persons filmed or recorded were unaware that this was happening, the chilling effect doctrine did not apply, making it more likely that an order for disclosure—as opposed to something more intrusive such as a search—would be a proportionate interference with freedom of expression that was justifiable for the prevention of crime, particularly where the crime involved a breach of a Convention right, such as Article 3, as in the child abuse case concerned. On the facts, the Court was satisfied with the proportionality of the court order.

When confronted with more drastic measures aimed at identifying an individual than a court order for disclosure, such as searches of the home or workplace of journalists and even the seizure of materials, not surprisingly the Court's probing may start with the presumption that the required reasonable balance has been upset. In *Roemen and Schmit v Luxembourg*,[189] following the publication of a newspaper article concerning tax fraud by a government minister, a journalist's home and workplace were searched by the police. The searches were carried out not to seek evidence of any offence that the journalist had committed, but to identify the name of officials who allegedly had breached professional confidence. Further, the applicant's home and workplace was raided unannounced and by investigators armed with search warrants authorizing extensive investigations. This added up to an undue interference not corroborated by sufficient reasons, in breach of Article 10. The same exacting review was applied in *Ernst v Belgium*.[190] The lesson that can be learnt from these cases is that where the information published by the journalist relates to matters of serious public concern, an onerous burden may be imposed on the national authorities to demonstrate the overriding nature of the countervailing public interest. It becomes also clear that the less restrictive doctrine can sit well with such an exacting review. The national authorities must establish that the measures other than searches of journalists' home and workplace, and seizure of materials, such as the interrogation of appropriate officials, would not have been effective in preventing disorder or crime.[191]

II. LICENSING FOR BROADCASTING

a. Overview

The free speech rights of mass media are fully covered by the first paragraph of Article 10.[192] There is specific recognition of the right of individual persons and the public at large to receive 'information and ideas...regardless of frontiers'. But the third sentence of Article 10(1) states that this provision does 'not prevent States from requiring the licensing of broadcasting, television or cinema enterprises'. Even though the third sentence refers to 'broadcasting', rather than to the reception or retransmission of broadcasts, this sentence has been interpreted as giving the state the general licensing power to regulate broadcasting and cinematographic activities within their territories, including the grant or refusal of a licence.[193] States have a variety of reasons why they wish to use

---

[189] 2003-IV paras 57 and 59. There was also a breach of Article 8.   [190] Hudoc (2003); 37 EHRR 724.
[191] *Roemen and Schmit v Luxembourg*, id, para 56; and *Ernst v Belgium* id, para 102.
[192] See eg, *Murphy v Ireland* 2003-IX; 38 EHRR 212 para 61.
[193] See eg, *Hins and Hugenholtz v Netherlands No 25987/94* hudoc (1996) DA.

their licensing power to impose content-based conditions on operators, such as the need to protect the press or the protection of national culture. At a time of globalization, there is a keenly felt need to ensure that, irrespective of the principle of market forces, the programme content is not only balanced but also diverse to promote cultural or linguistic pluralism in national societies.[194]

A question arises as to the inter-relationship between the third sentence of Article 10(1), which is exclusive to broadcasting, and Article 10(2). The Court has recognized that there are distinct legitimate aims applicable to the licensing of broadcasting under the third sentence of Article 10(1). This suggests that interferences can be legitimated under that sentence, even if they do not accord with any of the aims that are exhaustively stipulated in Article 10(2).[195] In its earlier case law, the Commission considered a broad range of restrictions imposed in the exercise of the licensing and regulatory powers of states under the third sentence of Article 10(1) without subordinating them to examinations under Article 10(2).[196] However, such methodology, which would imply the doctrine of inherent limitations, was not consistent.[197] At any event, this methodology has been abandoned in the subsequent case law. It is now settled that measures based on the third sentence of the first paragraph, including measures to deal with unlicensed operators, must be examined on the basis of the standards developed under Article 10(2).[198]

With respect to public monopolies of broadcasting which the national authorities considered necessary to ensure the impartiality and objectivity of reporting and diversity of opinions, the Commission in its early decisions recognized the maintenance of such monopolies as compatible with the Convention.[199] The Court found that the Austrian Broadcasting Corporation's monopoly in broadcasting through its supervisory powers over the media contributed to the quality and balance of programmes, and that this was compatible with the third sentence of Article 10(1).[200] Nevertheless, it found that as a result of technological progress, the public monopoly that prevented the establishment of a radio and television station was inconsistent with Article 10(2).[201] Reserving terrestrial television broadcasting to a state monopoly, while giving private broadcasters access only to cable broadcasting, was considered harmonious with the requirements of Article 10(2), on the ground that a high percentage of households could use cable television broadcasting as a viable alternative.[202] The fact that there were scarce frequencies available for terrestrial television broadcasting because of an alpine topography warranted the decision of the Austrian legislator to assign most to a state monopoly while granting private broadcasters access only to cable and satellite broadcasting. Such a decision, taken at the time of a rapid technological change from analogue to digital transmission, was considered to

---

[194] See eg, *X SA v Netherlands* No 21472/93, 76-A DR 129 (1994).

[195] *Informationsverein Lentia v Austria* A 276 (1993); 17 EHRR 93 para 32; and *Tele 1 Privatfernsehgesellschaft mbH v Austria* hudoc (2000); 34 EHRR 181 para 25.

[196] See, in this regard, *X and Association Z v UK* No 4515/70 38 CD 86 (1971); and *Radio X, S, W and A v Switzerland* No 10799/84, 37 DR 236 (1984).

[197] See eg, *X v UK* No 8266/78, 16 DR 190 (1978); *X and Y v Belgium* No 8962/80, 28 DR 120 (1982).

[198] *Groppera Radio AG v Switzerland* A 173 (1990); 12 EHRR 321 para 61 PC. See also *Autronic AG v Switzerland* A 178 (1990); 12 EHRR 485 paras 53 and 60–1 PC; *Informationsverein Lentia v Austria* A 276 (1993); 17 EHRR 93 paras 32, 39, and 43; and *Radio ABC v Austria* 1997-VI; 25 EHRR 185 para 28.

[199] *X v Sweden* No 3071/67 26 CD 71 (1968); and *Sacchi v Italy* No 6452/74 5 DR 43 at 50 (1976) (failure to exhaust domestic remedies).

[200] *Informationsverein Lentia v Austria* A 276 (1993); 17 EHRR 93 para 33 and *Radio ABC v Austria* 1997-VI; 25 EHRR 185 para 28.

[201] Id, para 39.

[202] *Tele 1 Privatfernsehgesellschaft mbH v Austria* hudoc (2000); 34 EHRR 181 paras 36–41.

fall within a margin of appreciation.[203] Further, when deciding the allocation of a given frequency, the primacy given to regional public broadcasting organizations over private organizations acting for commercial purposes may be justified under Article 10(2). Such a policy can be justified in the light of the legitimate aim (efficient use of airwaves to safeguard pluralism in the media etc), and of the conditions under which it is implemented (the limited duration of such a priority right accorded to a local public broadcasting organization, etc).[204]

Apart from technical aspects, the factors that need to be taken into account for assessing national decisions on the grant or refusal of a broadcasting licence include: (i) the nature and objectives of a proposed station; (ii) its potential audience, examined nationally, regionally, or locally; and (ii) the needs of a specific audience.[205] States may argue that the outer limits of their margin in ascertaining commercial broadcasting should be broader. To justify such wide discretionary powers, they have referred to such grounds as: (i) the technically complex and fluctuating nature of issues;[206] (ii) the need for equitable allocation of limited range of transmitting spectrum;[207] and (iii) a policy-oriented concern to preserve diverse national media, a theme closely intertwined with cultural diversity and distinguished national identities. In *United Christian Broadcasters Ltd v UK*,[208] because of a statutory ban on the award of a *national* radio licence to a body whose objects were wholly or mainly of a religious nature, a charitable company was pre-empted from applying for a digital multiplex radio licence. The Court found the ban harmonious with Article 10(2), as it was based on the legitimate concern to forestall different religious groups from monopolizing limited national broadcasting resources with discriminatory results. The applicant company was also free to apply for licences for *local* radio broadcasting.

Patently, in case a broadcasting programme contains words of hatred or even incitement to violence and uprising, the national media supervisory body may employ necessary measures to stave off disorder or crime. In such a scenario, even a severe measure, such as the suspension of authorization of broadcasting for a year, may be justified to prevent the abuse of freedom of expression to thwart the Convention's foundational principle of democratic pluralism.[209]

Despite the relatively generous latitudes of national discretion over policy choices that have been allowed, the development of the case law suggests that the Court has gradually intensified the standard of reviewing the content of proposed broadcasting.[210] The Court's decision-making policy is no doubt prompted by the role of the media in shaping the informed and critical public through the 'free flow of information' and contributing to 'open and free debate' in democracy.[211] As an indication of such trend, the Council of Europe adopted the European Convention on Transfrontier Television.[212]

When exercising licensing and regulatory powers under the third sentence of Article 10(1), the national authorities may take into account factors other than technical

[203] *Id*, paras 33–4.   [204] *Hins and Hugenholtz v Netherlands No 25987/94* hudoc (1996) DA.
[205] *Informationsverein Lentia v Austria* A 276 (1993); 17 EHRR 93 para 32.
[206] See eg, *Demuth v Switzerland* 2002-IX; 38 EHRR 423 para 42.
[207] The rationale based on finite resources in broadcasting has, however, been increasingly challenged by the availability of technological advancements in satellite and cable: Lester, above n 39, at pp 483–4, f 77.
[208] *No 44802/98* hudoc (2000) DA.
[209] *Medya FM Reha Radyo ve İletişim Hizmetleri AŞ. v Turkey No 32842/02* hudoc (2006) DA.
[210] See eg, *Demuth v Switzerland* 2002-IX; 38 EHRR 423 para 48.   [211] *Id*, para 40.
[212] See above, at p 461. See also the EU's Council Directive 89/552 concerning transfrontier television broadcasting: Council Directive 89/552 on the co-ordination of certain provisions laid down by law, regulation or administrative action in Member States concerning the pursuit of television broadcasting activities, [1989] OJ L298/23, as amended by Directive 97/36 of the European Parliament and of the Council, [1997] OJ L202/60.

or financial considerations, such as the nature and objectives of a proposed station, its potential audience at national, regional, or local level, the rights and needs of a specific audience, and the obligations derived from international legal instruments.[213] The imposition of content-based conditions and regulations is hard to reconcile with the entrenched safeguard afforded to freedom of expression by Article 10. With respect to such content-based regulations, the analysis of the case law suggests a clear policy shift from the reluctance in the earlier case law to challenge national decisions on licensing[214] to an increasing willingness to appraise at length the exercise of regulatory powers in specific circumstances under Article 10(2). Because of the particularly grave nature of content-based interference, special need for rigorous review is recognized. In *Özgür Radyo-Ses Radyo Televizyon Yayin Yapim Ve Tanitim AŞ v Turkey*,[215] the applicant company had its operation suspended after broadcasting programmes criticizing capitalism, and the assassination and forced disappearance of the Kurds. The suspension was ordered on the ground that, under Turkish law, the media were not allowed to diffuse programmes which the authority considered to incite people to resort to violence, terrorism, or ethnic discrimination, or to provoke sentiments of hatred. After close examinations of the contents of the programmes, the Court concluded that none of the grounds cited by Turkey were well-founded.

b. Broadcasting of religious and political advertisement

In contrast to commercial or professional advertising primarily designed for financial gain and promotion purposes, many countries have prohibited the broadcasting of religious or political advertisement[216] which is essentially of non-profit-making nature. This is mainly on the ground of guaranteeing neutrality and fairness to all religious and political groups, irrespective of their financial resources. Yet this poses a serious question, and even a moral dilemma.[217] To what extent can a state's regulatory power meddle with religious and political advertising through a mechanism of content-based filtering without risking arbitrariness?

Useful comparison can be made between *VgT Verein gegen Tierfabriken v Switzerland* and *Murphy v Ireland*. The former concerned the refusal of political advertisement in television while the latter involved the ban on religious advertisement in radio. In *VgT Verein gegen Tierfabriken*,[218] the applicant was an association for the protection of animals, which requested the broadcasting of an advertisement shedding critical light on the ways in which pigs were reared in commercial industries. The applicant's request was rejected on the basis of its political character, which was prohibited in the Swiss Federal Radio and Television Act. The Court was not receptive to the argument that because of its immediate impact, advertising in audio-visual media had to be neutral and free from any political character. It held that the ban on political advertising in audio-visual media but not in other media such as the press was discriminatory and not supported by both relevant and sufficient reasons. Moreover, the political nature of the advertisement dealing with a matter of public interest was such as to require that there be stringent scrutiny.[219]

---

[213] *Demuth v Switzerland* 2002-IX; 38 EHRR 423 para 33.

[214] *X and Association Z v UK No 4515/70*, 38 CD 86 (1971).   [215] Hudoc (2006) paras 81–5.

[216] For the earlier case law, see eg, *X and Association Z v UK No 4515/70*, 38 CD 86 (1971).

[217] Eg, advertising for raising public awareness of gross human rights violations may be prohibited on political grounds, whilst the aggressive promotion of commercial projects are not. See eg, *R v Radio Authority, ex p Bull* [1998] QB 294 (recognizing the ban on broadcasting a radio advertisement concerning genocide in Rwanda by Amnesty International). See Lewis (2005) EHRLR 290, at 290–1.

[218] 2001-VI; 34 EHRR 159 paras 70, 74–5 (unanimous finding of a violation of Article 10).

[219] Id, para 70.

The scrupulous appraisal undertaken in *VgT Verein gegen Tierfabriken* marks a contrast to the case of *Murphy v Ireland*[220] which addressed the issue of religious advertising. There, a pastor requested an independent, local, and commercial radio station to transmit an advertisement concerning a video-showing during the Easter week, which was purported to provide evidence of the resurrection of Christ. The Independent Radio and Television Commission stopped the broadcasting of the advertisement in accordance with the law banning the broadcasting of religious and political advertising. The Court found no violation of Article 10. The rationale adduced by the Court for recoiling from a bold and critical assessment of the national decision involved was the absence of European consensus on regulating the broadcasting of religious advertisements. On an empirical level, it is not clear, however, whether common European standards on religious advertising were unverifiable.

The Court in *Murphy* was at pains to distinguish that case from *VgT Verein gegen Tierfabriken*. It argued that while the former involved religious expression[221] and an open-ended notion of respect for religious beliefs of others, the latter related to political expression and to a matter of public interest.[222] There is persuasive force in the argument that content-based restrictions through a mechanism of filtering excessive religious advertising on a case-by-case basis could entail risk of arbitrariness.[223] Nevertheless, in the specific circumstances of *Murphy*, the content of the advertisement in question was essentially an announcement of a video-showing, which was innocuous and inoffensive. In that light, the Court's approach seems too categorical. In contrast, *VgT Verein gegen Tierfabriken* reveals its more fine-tuned approach. The Court carefully ascertained whether each of the legitimate objectives that would generally justify the ban on political advertisement was defensible in the *specific* circumstances of the case. The national authorities were required to adduce specific justifications for prohibiting political advertising. Merely invoking general and mundane grounds relating to the need for neutrality and independence of the media was insufficient.[224] In *Murphy*, the Court recognized the wariness of the respondent state as to the potential impact of the contested religious advertisement, stressing that audio-visual media could have more immediate and pervasive impacts on passive recipients.[225] However, in *VgT Verein gegen Tierfabriken*, such a special impact of audio-visual media, though pleaded by Switzerland, was rejected by the Court. Further, in *Murphy*, the Court took the view that even a limited freedom to advertise would benefit a dominant religion more than smaller religions, breaching the principles of neutrality and equal participation of all religions.[226] If the Court's approach in *Murphy* is to be upheld, one may wonder whether the similar reasoning of equal opportunity could have been applied to political advertising examined in *VgT Verein gegen Tierfabriken*.

5. PRESCRIBED BY LAW

With respect to the legal basis test, or the standard 'prescribed by law', the word 'law' has been extensively construed so as to include not only statutory laws but also unwritten laws to accommodate the legal cultures of common law countries.[227] It also encompasses the rules enacted by different administrative or professional bodies, to which the

---

[220] 2003-IX; 38 EHRR 212 paras 67 and 81.   [221] Id, paras 71 and 73.   [222] Id, para 68.
[223] Id, paras 76–7.   [224] *VgT Verein gegen Tierfabriken v Switzerland* 2001-VI; 34 EHRR 159 para 75.
[225] *Murphy v Ireland* 2003-IX; 38 EHRR 212 para 74.   [226] Id, para 78.
[227] *Sunday Times v UK (No 1)* A 30 (1979); 2 EHRR 245 para 47 PC.

law-making and disciplinary authorities are delegated.[228] In some circumstances, rules of international law furnish a sufficient legal basis.[229]

The Court has identified two sub-tests that must be satisfied for a norm to be a 'law': those of accessibility and of foreseeability (or clarity).[230] The sub-test of accessibility can be fulfilled if the citizen is 'able to have an indication that is adequate in the circumstances of the legal rules applicable to a given case'.[231] A more rigorous assessment is required for the sub-test of foreseeability. The Court has elaborated the meaning of this sub-test as follows:

> 'foreseeability' is one of the requirements inherent in the phrase 'prescribed by law' in Article 10§2...of the Convention. A norm cannot be regarded as a 'law' unless it is formulated with sufficient precision to enable the citizen—if need be, with appropriate advice—to foresee, to a degree that is reasonable in the circumstances, the consequences which a given action may entail....[232]

The case law has provided some guidelines for determining the foreseeability subtest, which is held to depend, in particular, on three specific factors: (i) the content of the contested statement; (ii) the field it is purported to cover; and (iii) the number and status of its addressees.[233] The sub-test of foreseeability does not require the impossible task of obtaining absolute precision in the framing of laws, especially in areas in which regulations change to reflect evolving perceptions in the society. Such ambiguity may even be a deliberate policy choice of the legislature, precisely for the purpose of proffering flexibility in the future decision-making policy of both the administrative and judicial organs.[234] The Court has recognized that many laws are inevitably couched in flexible or even vague terms to avoid excessive rigidity and to keep pace with changing circumstances.[235] However, in case a failure to comply with a formal procedure for exercising a certain form of expression brings about a criminal offence, Article 10, in tandem with Article 7, requires that the relevant law must clearly define the circumstances in which it is applied, and that the scope of restrictions must not be broadened at an accused person's expense, for instance by analogy.[236]

In *Sunday Times v UK (No 1)*,[237] the Court had to examine whether the common law concept of contempt of court was compatible with the forseeability sub-test. The applicants submitted that the 'prejudgment principle' which required the domestic courts to ascertain whether a proscribed article was liable to cause public prejudgment of an issue in pending litigation, and hence contempt of court, was novel and inadequately indicated. The Court expressed 'certain doubts' about the precision with which this principle was formulated. Nevertheless, it quickly added that a risk that the publication of the draft

---

[228] Delegating rule-making powers to professional bodies by the general law does not prevent their rules being 'law' for the purposes of Article 10(2): *Barthold v FRG* A 90 (1985); 7 EHRR 383 para 46; and *Casado Coca v Spain* A 285-A (1994); 18 EHRR 1 paras 42–3.

[229] See *Groppera Radio AG v Switzerland* A 173 (1990); 12 EHRR 321 para 68 PC and *Autronic v Switzerland* A 178 (1990); 12 EHRR 485 para 57.

[230] See, *inter alia, Sunday Times v UK (No 1)* A 30 (1979); 2 EHRR 245 para 49 PC; *Gawęda v Poland* 2002-II; 39 EHRR 90 para 39. See further above, Ch 8.

[231] *Sunday Times v UK (No 1)* A 30 (1979); 2 EHRR 245 para 49 PC.

[232] *Müller and Others v Switzerland* A 133 (1988); 13 EHRR 212 para 29 and *Perrin v UK No 5446/03* hudoc (2005).

[233] See eg, *Piroğlu and Karakaya v Turkey* hudoc (2008) para 51.

[234] See Shany, 16 EJIL 907 at 916 (2005).

[235] *Müller and Others v Switzerland]* A 133 (1988); 13 EHRR 212 para 29.

[236] See eg, *Karademirci v Turkey* 2005-I para 40.   [237] A 30 (1979); 2 EHRR 245 para 49 PC.

article could be incompatible with the prejudgment principle was foreseeable 'to a degree that was reasonable in the circumstances'.[238]

In the *Markt Intern* and *Barthold* cases,[239] the Court was satisfied that the German law on Unfair Competition Law 1909, Section 1, which required 'honest practices', met the forseeability sub-test, despite a broad discretion given to the national courts in assessing this imprecise wording. The impossibility of framing laws in absolutely precise terms was considered all the more relevant, as competition law governs 'a subject where the relevant factors are in constant evolution in line with developments in the market and in means of communication'. The availability of both 'clear and abundant' case law and 'extensive' academic commentaries was considered sufficient to assist individuals to obtain clarity over indefinite legal terms.[240] Similarly, in *Müller v Switzerland*,[241] the Court found that the word 'obscene' under the Swiss Criminal Code satisfied the predictability sub-test, as it was felt necessary to skirt excessive rigidity in legal terms to accommodate changing circumstances concerning obscenity laws.

The sub-test of foreseeability must be applied in the light of the advice available to the applicant. In *Open Door and Dublin Well Woman v Ireland*,[242] the Commission accepted that the Irish law was insufficiently precise to allow the corporate applicants reasonably to predict that their non-directive counselling service on abortion would be unlawful and tantamount to an actionable, constitutional tort. But this argument was rejected by the Court, which in essence turned to two rationales: first, unlike the statutory laws, the case law clarified the actionable nature of constitutional rights that were infringed even by private individuals; and second, one of the applicants was actually given legal advice as to a possible injunction against its counselling.[243]

In *Karademirci v Turkey*,[244] a group of individuals were convicted and sentenced under the Associations Act after making a statement to the press. According to the first sentence of section 44(1) of the Turkish Associations Act, associations were prohibited from publishing or distributing leaflets, written statements, or 'similar publications' without a prior resolution by their executive board. The failure to comply with this requirement was a criminal offence. The main question was whether a statement to the press could be categorized as a 'leaflet', 'written statement', or 'similar publication' so as to meet the foreseeability sub-test. The Court answered in the negative. The fact that the applicants were sentenced to three months' imprisonment, albeit commuted to a suspended fine, was held to constitute an unacceptable extension of criminal sanction by analogy, which ran afoul of the foreseability requirement.[245] In *Piroğlu and Karakaya v Turkey*,[246] the 'prescribed by law' standard came to the fore in relation to the conviction of executive members of a human rights association who took part in a movement and participated in a collective press declaration. Under the Turkish Associations Act, associations could not form a legal entity other than federations and confederations. The Court found that that wording was insufficiently clear to allow the members of the applicants' association to foresee that rallying to a movement would expose them to criminal sanctions. Indeed, to equate

---

[238] Id, para 52. See also *Harman v UK No 10038/82,* 38 DR 53 (1984): *ibid,* 46 DR 57 (1986) F Sett. In the *Goodwin case,* the Commission expressed 'some doubt' on the sufficient precision with which s 10 of the Contempt of Court Act 1981 was implemented, but considered it unnecessary to deal with this issue: *Goodwin v UK* 1996-II; 22 EHRR 123 paras 56–7 Com Rep.

[239] *Barthold v FRG* A 90 (1985); 7 EHRR 383 para 47 and *Markt Intern Verlag v FRG* A 165 (1989); 12 EHRR 161 para 30 PC.

[240] *Markt Intern Verlag,* id, para 30.   [241] A 133 (1988); 13 EHRR 212 para 29.

[242] A 246-A (1992); 15 EHRR 244 paras 45–52 Com Rep.   [243] Id, paras 59–60 PC.

[244] 2005-I para 42.   [245] *Ibid.*   [246] Hudoc (2008) para 54.

the mere supporting of such a movement to the formation of an organization was totally irreconcilable with the subtest of foreseeability.

Once an impugned measure is found to breach the legal basis test, the examination should terminate. Yet, in case the question relating to the sub-test of foreseeability remains inconclusive, the Court may focus on examining the compatibility with the standard 'necessary in a democratic society'.[247]

6. LEGITIMATE AIMS

I. OVERVIEW

The second paragraph of Article 10 lists nine legitimate purposes for which restrictions on the freedom of expression can be justified. These are: (i) the protection of national security; (ii) the protection of territorial integrity; (iii) the protection of public safety; (iv) the prevention of disorder or crime; (v) the protection of health;[248] (vi) the protection of morals; (vii) the protection of the reputation or rights of others; (viii) the prevention of the disclosure of information received in confidence; and (ix) the maintenance of the authority and impartiality of the judiciary. Among them, the following objectives are worthy of closer analysis: the protection of national security; the protection of morals; the protection of the reputation or rights of others; and the maintenance of the authority and impartiality of the judiciary. As discussed above, with respect to licensing for broadcasting, the Court has acknowledged the possibility of other distinct legitimate aims in relation to the third sentence of the first paragraph.[249]

II. PROTECTION OF NATIONAL SECURITY

Clearly 'the interests of national security' under Article 10(2) constitutes one of the most solid grounds that state authorities can adduce as a counterweight to freedom of expression. An expulsion order that prevented the leader of Sinn Fein from entering Great Britain to attend a political meeting was justified in view of a sensitive peace process in Northern Ireland, and of the real and continuous threat of renewed violence. Given that the expulsion order was lifted subsequent to the IRA's announcement of a ceasefire, the measure was found within the bounds of proportionality.[250] In contrast, in Çetin v Turkey,[251] the ban imposed by a governor on distributing a daily newspaper in an emergency region was considered to have gone too far, even seen against the fierce background of terrorism. The absence of sufficient safeguards against abuse, such as judicial review of administrative bans, was a key to the finding that a fair balance was upset.

It must be carefully analyzed to what extent and in what ways a generally potent legitimate ground such as the protection of national security has served to justify encroachments on free speech. When assessing constraints on the free expression of public officials dealing with delicate information on national security, the Court has invoked the

---

[247] See eg, Dammann v Switzerland hudoc (2006) para 35.

[248] Stambuk v Germany hudoc (2002); 37 EHRR 845 para 30; Verités Santé Pratique Sarl v France No 74766/01 hudoc (2005) DA. See also Colman v UK A 258-D (1993); 18 EHRR 119 Com Rep and J v Germany No 21554/93 hudoc (1994) Com Rep.

[249] Informationsverein Lentia v Austria A 276 (1993); 17 EHRR 93 para 32.

[250] Adams and Benn v UK Nos 28979/95 and 30343/96 hudoc (1997) DA. See also eg, Medya FM Reha Radyo ve İletişim Hizmetleri AŞ v Turkey No 32842/02 hudoc (2006) DA.

[251] 2003-III paras 59–62 and 66.

qualifying words 'duties and responsibilities' of such officials in sync with Article 10(2).[252] Considerations of national security may be reinforced by particular historical experience. In many former communist countries, civil servants' political expression and activities are constrained to safeguard national security and to prevent public disorder. It is against the background of peaceful transition to plural democracies that the Court found pressing social needs for such restrictions in fledgling democracies.[253]

Nevertheless, when complaints relate to political or civil expression, it is of paramount importance for the Court to scrutinize specific factual circumstances. Viewed in that way, the approach followed by the former Commission may be criticized for the brevity of its appraisal in many cases. The Commission upheld the conviction of a 'convinced pacifist' for distributing to troops leaflets dissuading service in Northern Ireland[254] and the ban on a civil servant revealing information on the establishment of atomic weapons.[255] In *Hadjianastassiou v Greece*,[256] the Court endorsed the conviction of an officer for disclosing secret military information of minor importance to a private company. In *Zana v Turkey*,[257] a former mayor of a city in south-eastern Turkey was imprisoned on the ground of his statements supporting the PKK. In an interview with a nationwide newspaper, he described the PKK as a 'national liberation movement', stating that PKK would only kill women and children 'by mistake'. Yet he denounced the massacres. The assessment focused in particular on the question whether the tone of his criticism of terrorist acts could be considered to reflect his genuine intention rather than to serve as a political gesture to avoid censure. The Court found no violation of Article 10, referring to the applicant's contradictory attitudes toward the terrorist organization and his influential political position. But as Judge Van Dijk stressed in his dissenting opinion, the Court failed to take into account the content of his controversial statements and personal background against which the statements had to be interpreted. In examining impacts of the contested statements on the 'explosive situation' in the region, the Court should have noted that when the interview took place, the applicant was in prison. Further, Judge Van Dijk criticized Turkey for failing to choose a less harsh measure than two-month imprisonment.

In contrast, when confronted with a sweeping form of interference on national security grounds, the Court is prepared to apply a robust review,[258] requiring the national authorities to satisfy an onerous standard of establishing the necessity of interference.[259] There has been recognition that even where national security is at stake, the entrenched nature of political speech should be given primacy. In *Piermont v France*,[260] the Court endorsed the free speech interests of a member of European Parliament who made public statements that supported independence for Tahiti and New Caledonia and criticized France's nuclear experiments. She was considered the beneficiary of a high standard of protection, given that her speech contributed to a democratic debate. Likewise, even against pleas of

---

[252] *Hadjianastassiou v Greece* A 252 (1992); 16 EHRR 219; *Rekvényi v Hungary* 1999-III para 43; and *B v UK No 10293/83*, 45 DR 41 (1985).

[253] *Rekvényi v Hungary* 1999-III paras 42–3 and 46–8. For analysis of the implications of cultural relativism linked to the former communist countries, see Sweeney, 54 ICLQ 459 (2005).

[254] *Arrowsmith v UK No 705075*, 19 DR 5 at 25 para 99 (1978). See also *X v UK No 6084/73*, 3 DR 62 (1975).

[255] *B v UK No 10293/83*, 45 DR 41 at 54 (1985). See also *Z v Switzerland No 10343/83*, 35 DR 224 (1983) and *Brind v UK No 18714/91*, 77-A DR 42 (1994).

[256] A 252 (1992); 16 EHRR 219 para 47. See also *Steel v UK* 1998-VII; 28 EHRR 603 paras 101 and 105 ff.

[257] 1997-VII; 27 EHRR 667 GC.

[258] See *Arslan v Turkey* hudoc (1999); 31 EHRR 264 paras 46–50 GC; and *Baskaya and Okçuoglu v Turkey* 1999-IV; 31 EHRR 292 paras 62–7 GC.

[259] *Vereinigung Demokratischer Soldaten Österreichs and Gubi v Austria* A 302 (1994); 20 EHRR 56 para 37.

[260] A 314 (1995); 20 EHRR 301 paras 77 and 85.

national security, the Court favoured an enhanced protection of civil expression raising 'matters of public interest', as in the case of a speech made by leading members of trade unions.[261]

Once the confidentiality of security information is lost, the question whether the information should continue to be withheld simply becomes moot. In a case concerning contempt of court in the United Kingdom, the publication of a memoir of a former agent outside of the United Kingdom destroyed the confidentiality of intelligence service information, negating the sufficiency of the ground for the UK courts imposing an injunction on the newspaper applicants.[262] The cogency of this rationale cannot be diminished even if security information has been revealed by illegal means. In the *Bluf!* case, despite the illegality of the applicants' disclosure of security information, withdrawing their periodicals from circulation was regarded as out of proportion.[263]

III. THE PREVENTION OF DISORDER OR CRIMES

Akin to the ground of national security, the objective of preventing disorder or crimes has been invoked by the national authorities in their fight against terrorism and other crimes. Again, this objective, set against a real threat of terrorism or insurrections, is closely linked to the rationale underpinning of Article 17. For all the pivotal nature of such an objective, it can be susceptible to risk of abuse. In view of this, the Court has stressed the importance of sufficient procedural safeguards against abuse. In *Association Ekin v France*,[264] the Court partially endorsed the French argument that the ban on the circulation of a book concerning the Basque culture pursued the legitimate aim of preventing disorder, even though on a closer look it did not find anything in the content suggesting incitement to violence or to separatism. However, the Court decided the case on the basis of the third standard, finding a violation of Article 10 on the basis that the interference was not 'necessary in a democratic society'. The content of the book was considered innocuous. The French Ministry was given wide discretionary power in proscribing publications classified as 'foreign origin'. Yet, there were insufficient safeguards against such discretionary power. Further, judicial review procedures were limited and ineffective.

Certainly, when confronted with real or potential danger of terrorism, contracting parties are, without invoking far-reaching measures authorized under Articles 15 and 17, fully entitled to take appropriate measures under Article 10(2), including a ban on broadcasting images or voices of proscribed organizations. Such measures are necessary to deny terrorist or other prohibited organizations unimpeded access to the broadcasting media, and to prevent them encouraging or inciting to violence, or giving an impression of legitimacy through the powerful audio-visual means. In *Purcell v Ireland*,[265] a ministerial order prevented journalists from broadcasting an interview, or a report of an interview, with spokespersons of the terrorist organizations such as the IRA and a political party such as Sinn Fein which, albeit not declared unlawful in Ireland, was part of such a terrorist organization. The ministerial order imposed a blanket ban on covering press conferences live, and even on reading out press statements afterwards. It was designed to prevent terrorist organizations or their associates from promoting or inciting crimes.

[261] *Ceylan v Turkey* 1999-IV; 30 EHRR 73 para 34 GC.
[262] *Observer and Guardian v UK* A 216 (1991); 14 EHRR 153 paras 66–70 PC and *Sunday Times v UK (No 2)* A 217 (1991); 14 EHRR 229 paras 52–6 PC.
[263] *Vereiniging Weekblad Bluf! v Netherlands* A 306-A (1995); 20 EHRR 189 para 44.
[264] 2001-VIII; 35 EHRR 1207 para 48.   [265] *15404/89*, 70 DR 262 (1991).

The applicants claimed that, as a result, they were barred from providing a programme concerning political candidates' campaign manifesto or objectives. In view of the considerable and immediate impact of audio-visual media on the public, and of the need to prevent the conveyance of coded messages, the Commission found the order consistent with the objectives of protecting national security, and preventing disorder and crime. In the subsequent case of *Brind v UK*,[266] the Commission was similarly sympathetic to notices restraining the broadcasting of any words spoken by a person representing or supporting the proscribed terrorist organizations such as the IRA. The applicants complained that an interview with Gerry Adams, President of Sinn Fein, could no longer be retransmitted, and that the notices, backed by the sanction, would generate a chilling effect, forcing broadcasters to err on the safe side. When finding no violation of Article 10, the Commission considered that the requirement that an actor's voice be used to broadcast interviews was interference of limited scope.

In *Purcell* and *Brind*, an impression cannot be effaced that the pivotal role of the media in informing the public of extreme political movements and their leaders was underrated. Behind the semblance of the cogent rationales for shielding the edifice of democracy from terrorist violence, these decisions were marred by the failure finely to calibrate the scope of national discretion in favour of a more robust review.

IV. THE PROTECTION OF MORALS

Among the legitimate aims enlisted under Article 10(2), it is the protection of morals which is arguably the most controversial. This is the area where the nebulous notion of margin of appreciation has enjoyed extensive application to justify judicial self-restraint under Article 10. There is no European consensus on the requirements of morals, whose variable nature can be seen even within a country.[267] The Court has also noted that national authorities, which have direct contact with national societies, are better suited than international judges to assess the requirements of local morals. The Court's position is aptly summarized in *Handyside v UK*,[268] where the Court held that:

> it is not possible to find in the domestic law of the various Contracting States a uniform European conception of morals. The view taken by their respective laws of the requirements of morals varies from time to time and from place to place, especially in our era which is characterized by a rapid and far-reaching evolution of opinions on the subject. By reason of their direct and continuous contact with the vital forces of their countries, State authorities are in principle in a better position than the international judge to give an opinion on the exact content of these requirements as well as on the 'necessity' of a 'restriction' or 'penalty' intended to meet them.

In the area of freedom of expression, the Strasbourg organs have been confronted with diverse moral values encompassing sexual propriety, obscenity, abortion, and the significance of religion.[269] In the *Handyside* case, the Court recognized the seizure, forfeiture, and subsequent destruction of an allegedly obscene book (*Little Red Schoolbook*) as pursuant to the protection of morals. Further, reliance was made on the protection of

---

[266] *No 18714/91*, 77-A DR 42 (1994).

[267] See *Müller and Others v Switzerland* A 133 (1988); 13 EHRR 212 para 36; *Otto-Preminger-Institut v Austria* A 295-A (1994); 19 EHRR 34 para 56.

[268] A 24 (1976); 1 EHRR 737 para 48 PC. See also *X Company v UK No 9615/81*, 32 DR 231 at 234 (1983).

[269] As welll as the cases cited here, see *X Company v UK No 9615/81*, 32 DR 231 at 234 (1983) and *X, Y and Z v Belgium Nos 6782–84/74*, 9 DR 13 at 20 (1977).

the rights of adolescent children, to which the book was addressed. The Court noted as follows:

> despite the variety and the constant evolution in the United Kingdom of views on ethics and education, the competent English judges were entitled, in the exercise of their discretion, to think at the relevant time that the Schoolbook would have pernicious effects on the morals of many of the children and adolescents who would read it.[270]

The Court's approach in *Handyside* raises a serious doubt over whether the proportionality assessment was duly carried out. This concern was warranted in several ensuing cases.[271] In *Müller*, as examined above, the Court found no violation of Article 10 with respect to the confiscation of paintings. The audience was not warned of the content of the exhibition, and the paintings depicting homosexuality and bestiality in crude forms were 'spontaneous'. The exhibition was free of charge, and without any age limit, and hence accessible even to small children.[272] Nevertheless, it is doubtful whether such a sweeping measure as the confiscation of the paintings met the test of proportionality, even in relation to the protection of morals.

In *Scherer v Switzerland*,[273] the Commission averred that the conviction of the proprietor of a sex shop for showing explicit videos for homosexuals violated Article 10. Its reasoning was that no one was likely to be confronted with them against their will, and that only a limited number of consenting adults who paid the entrance fees would be admitted. This reasoning was consonant with *Müller*. Nonetheless, as will be examined below, this reasoning was shunned in *Otto-Preminger-Institut* relating to the conflict between the freedom of expression and the religious freedom. Turning back to the *Scherer* case, another notable factor was that the obscene videos were not visible from the street. *Scherer* was the missed opportunity to reset the Court's standard of review because, following the death of the applicant, the case was struck out of the list.[274] In *Wingrove v UK*,[275] the Court, however, confirmed its restrained stance in *Handyside*. The case arose from a short experimental video entitled 'Visions of Ecstasy', which depicted the mingling of religious ecstasy and sexual passion of St Teresa of Avila. The British Board of Film Classification rejected the application for a classification certificate lodged by a film director. The Commission submitted an argument similar to that advanced in *Scherer*, according to which the risk that any Christian would unwittingly view the contested video could have been averted if its distribution was limited to licensed sex shops. Because video boxes included a description of its content, only consenting adults would have been faced with those contents. However, the Court rejected this argument. It provided rather specious reasoning to the effect that, by their nature, videos, once available on the market, would easily escape the control of the authorities and be transmitted among audiences through copying, renting, etc.[276]

---

[270] *Handyside*, id, para 52.

[271] See also *X Company v UK No 9615/81*, 32 DR 231 at 234 (1983), where the Commission endorsed the seizure and forfeiture of 'hard pornographic' magazines destined for export, partly on the ground of a legitimate concern to prevent the country from becoming a source of export trade of obscene materials.

[272] A 133 (1988); 13 EHRR 212 para 36.

[273] A 287 (1994); 18 EHRR 276 para 61 Com Rep. This was decisive for this case to be distinguished from the precedent in *W and K v Switzerland No 16564/90* hudoc (1991) DA.

[274] Compare *Scherer* with *Hoare v UK No 31211/96* hudoc (1997) DA, where the Commission noted that despite the applicant's efforts to prevent the contested, pornographic video cassettes from accidentally falling into the hands of persons other than the purchasers, the cassettes, once distributed, could easily escape control.

[275] 1996-V; 24 EHRR 1 para 62. Contrast this with the Commission's Report of 10 January 1995, paras 65–9, where the Commission argued that any blasphemous effect of the video would be limited because it was a short experimental film destined for a smaller audience.   [276] Id, para 63.

The tenacity with which the margin of appreciation continues to be recognized in assessing the notion of obscenity is corroborated by *Perrin v UK*.[277] There, the applicant was convicted under the Obscene Publications Act for publishing web pages full of extremely obscene photographs. The Court recognized the national state's broad margin of appreciation in deciding on the measure appropriate to deal with issues of obscenity. The fact that the contested internet site was published and operated by a company based in the United States, and that the dissemination of the images was legal in other states, was found immaterial to the legitimacy of the British decision. The onus was shifted to the applicant to prove that an alternative less injurious to his freedom of expression was '*more* effective'.[278] The burden imposed on the applicant was arguably greater than in *Handyside* and *Müller*. Nevertheless, apart from the extremely obscene nature of the website, what was critical in the *Perrin* case was that, unlike the applicants in *Wingrove* (and in the *Otto-Preminger-Institut*, as will be examined below), the applicant failed to impose an age limit and to block the impugned photographs on the free preview page.

V. PROTECTION OF REPUTATION AND HONOUR OF PRIVATE INDIVIDUALS

In a modern age of information, characterized by the paparazzi feeding the curiosity of the public about the private lives of public figures, any sanction imposed on journalists for intruding into privacy or divulging personal information highlights an inevitable tension between the interest of journalists in imparting information to the public under Article 10 and the right of privacy under Article 8.[279]

Clearly, as compared with public figures, the permissible bounds of criticism of private persons are much narrower. Journalists must strictly adhere to their 'duties and responsibilities' and to professional ethics so as not to make disobliging references to the private life of individual persons.[280] Publishing photographs and images containing intimate private aspects of individuals or their family is a serious affront to their right to good reputation, honour,[281] and privacy.[282]

On the other hand, journalists themselves are equivalent of public figures. Yet, in case a journalist has become the target of allegedly defamatory statements made by another journalist, the latter must establish that the impugned article is not a gratuitous personal attack, and that its contents contribute to matters of public interest.[283]

Ample references have been made to the absence of a European consensus on appropriate responses to libellous opinions or other unacceptable expression directed against private individuals.[284] Nevertheless, this does not handicap the rigorous review and 'autonomous' decision-making policy of the Strasbourg Court where free speech rights of journalists and the press are at stake.[285] Its proportionality appraisal has focused on the amount of compensation or damages for libel or defamation, and on the availability

---

[277] *No 5446/03* hudoc (2005) DA.   [278] *Ibid*, emphasis added.

[279] *Shabanov and Tren v Russia* hudoc (2006) para 46 and *Hachette Filipacchi Associés v France* hudoc (2007) para 43.

[280] *Katamadze v Georgia No 69857/01* hudoc (2006) DA.

[281] Note that Article 17 of the ICCPR specifically recognizes the right to good reputation and honour.

[282] *Von Hannover v Germany* 2004-VI; 43 EHRR 1 para 59 and *Hachette Filipacchi Associés v France* hudoc (2007) para 42.

[283] *Katamadze v Georgia No 69857/01* hudoc (2006) DA.

[284] *Tolstoy Miloslavsky v UK* A 316-B (1995); 2 EHRR 442 para 48.

[285] *Bergens Tidende v Norway* 2000-IV; 31 EHRR 430 para 52 and *Marônek v Slovakia* 2001-III paras 56–60.

or otherwise of 'adequate and effective safeguards' against an exorbitant award.[286] Nevertheless, if a contested newspaper article does not relate to any matter of legitimate public interest, journalists have to establish that such information is not, by virtue of its nature and purpose, liable to constitute gratuitous personal attacks.

VI. PROTECTION OF THE PRIVACY, REPUTATION, AND HONOUR OF PUBLIC FIGURES

The phrase 'the protection of... rights of others' under Article 10(2) has been frequently invoked to ascertain the extent to which the privacy or reputation and honour of public figures can be guaranteed. With respect to privacy, the Court has stressed that the public has the right to be informed even of aspects of private lives of public figures.[287] Yet the conditions under which private aspects of public figures can be considered sufficiently related to their public function to justify their disclosure is debatable.[288] Nevertheless, the Court has moved a step closer to establishing an autonomous and harmonized yardstick on this matter. In assessing whether national authorities have struck a fair balance in constraining the circulation of information or photographs bearing on the privacy of public figures, it is essential to examine several factors, including: (i) the impact of their publication; (ii) public knowledge of the information or photographs, in case this has already been uncovered by other means;[289] and (iii) the degree of injuries to the personal feelings of (families of) individuals concerned.

According to the Court, 'the protection of the reputation... of others' within the meaning of Article 10(2) extends even to politicians who are *not* acting in their private capacity,[290] and that such protection remains even where a politician is criticized by another one in the 'privileged arena of Parliament'.[291] A politician who has levelled a defamatory or insulting criticism against a political opponent in a parliamentary debate is not exempted from proving the factual basis for the criticism, especially if this is classified as an allegation of fact of a serious nature. In *Keller v Hungary*,[292] a member of a parliament suggested at a parliamentary session that a cabinet minister had failed to investigate the practices of extreme right-wing groups because the latter's father participated in the pro-Nazi *Hungarista* movement. The domestic courts ordered him to arrange a rectification in the press and pay damages for the infringement of the personality of the minister in question. According to the Court, the accusation that the cabinet minister deliberately neglected his ministerial duty for personal reasons was a serious allegation of fact, which remained unproven. The fact that the applicant's statement during the parliamentary session was 'elusive', and that the identity of his target only became clear in his subsequent televized interview, was considered to detract from the otherwise entrenched value of political expression.

In contrast, the Court did not baulk at challenging the national courts' finding that the recorded telephone conversations between high ranking governmental officials were private in nature,[293] closely examining the context and content of the conversations. The

---

[286] *Tolstoy Miloslavsky v UK*, id, para 50.

[287] *Karhuvaara and Iltalehti v Finland* 2004-X; 41 EHRR 1154 para 45.

[288] *Von Hannover v Germany* 2004-VI; 43 EHRR 1; and *Hachette Filipacchi Associés v France* hudoc (2007). See also *Schüssel v Austria* No 42409/98 hudoc (2002) DA.

[289] See eg, *Karhuvaara and Iltalehti v Finland* 2004-X; 41 EHRR 1154 para 47; and *Édition Plon v France* 2004-IV; 42 EHRR 705 para 53.

[290] *Lingens v Austria* A 103 (1986); 8 EHRR 407 para 42 PC; and *Keller v Hungary* No 33352/02 hudoc (2006) DA.

[291] *Ibid.*   [292] *Ibid.*   [293] *RADIO TWIST AS v Slovakia* hudoc (2006) para 58.

fact that the contested information has been obtained illegally by a third person does
not in itself detract from the importance of the media in transmitting such information.
Journalists or the media can reinforce their free speech claims, arguing that they are not
responsible for the illegal procurement of the information, that no untrue or distorted
information has been broadcast or published, or that they are not acting in bad faith for
any extraneous purpose.[294]

Once civil servants have resigned their post, they must clearly be protected from the
intrusive media coverage of their private life. In *Tammer v Estonia*,[295] a journalist made
insulting remarks about the wife of a senior politician in a newspaper interview, referring
to her role in destroying an earlier marriage of that politician and her act of deserting her
child. By the time of the publication of the interview, the woman in question had resigned
from her post as a government official. Despite the fact that she was a public figure until
only six months before, and that she intended to publish her memoirs, the Court found
that, at the material time, she was a private person whose rights under Article 8 had to be
specially protected, and that the use of offensive terms was not warranted by any public
interest.

Two French cases deserve special analysis in highlighting the difficulty in pinpointing
the juncture at which the delicate balance between the free speech rights and the privacy
rights of public figures should be struck. In *Hachette Filipacchi Associés v France*,[296] *Paris-
Match*, a popular magazine, published a photograph of the blood-covered and mutilated
body of a prefect of Corsica. National courts ordered the publication of a notice acknowledging that the photograph was published without the consent of the prefect's bereaved
family. The photograph had appeared only ten days after the funeral of the prefect, and
the family of the victim was expressly opposed to its publication. The publication of the
photograph was considered to aggravate the trauma suffered by the family, and a majority of the Court found no violation of Article 10.[297] Judge Loucaides,[298] in his dissenting
opinion, stressed that in view of the special importance of press freedom, an 'objective'
appraisal had to be given to the *specific* circumstances of the case, rather than following a
general approach favouring privacy rights. In Judge Loucaides's opinion, the photograph
was not presented in an undignified manner. The public at large was invited to show a
sense of horror of the crime, and the sentiment of sympathy for the family. Further, the
image of the assassinated body had already been broadcast on a television channel.

In *Éditions Plon v France*,[299] the applicant company published a book entitled *Le
Grand Secret*, which described the secret medical history of the former French President
Mitterrand. The book was written in order to protect his reputation by the physician of
the late President who was diagnosed with cancer soon after his election in 1981. Upon
Mitterrand's family's complaining of a breach of medical confidentiality, damage to the
late President's privacy, and injury to his family's feelings, an injunction was issued. This
prevented the distribution of *Le Grand Secret* and ordered the applicant company to pay
damages. The Court distinguished the interim injunction banning the distribution of
the contested book, and the subsequent decision to maintain the ban on distributing
the book. The interim injunction was upheld because of the timing of the publication
and of the temporary nature of the injunction. The book was published barely ten days
after Mitterand's death, and this was considered to intensify the grief of his heirs while

[294] Id, paras 60–3.   [295] 2001-I; 37 EHRR 857 paras 66–8.   [296] Hudoc (2007) paras 46–9.
[297] Id, para 62.   [298] Id, dissenting opinion of Judge Loucaides.
[299] 2004-IV; 42 EHRR 705 para 47. See also *Gubler v France* hudoc (2006) (no violation of Article 6(1) in
response to the complaint, raised by the physician at issue, that the conseil national de l'Ordre des médecins
lacked independence and impartiality).

inflicting serious damage on his reputation. In contrast, no pressing social need was found for the continued ban on distribution. Unlike the interim measure issued only a day after the book's publication, the decision to maintain the injunction was made more than nine months afterwards. With the President's death becoming more distant in time, the need to safeguard the interests of the deceased's family was considered of less consequence in contrast to the growing public interest in the history of the President. The judgment also confirmed another established principle, according to which once confidentiality is breached, the need for maintaining a general and absolute ban becomes moot.

VII. PROTECTION OF THE FREEDOM OF RELIGION OF OTHERS

Another area where the phrase 'the protection of... rights of others' has become the subject of disputes concerns the clash between free speech rights and the freedom of religion under Article 9. Intimate religious beliefs and convictions of persons, which are specially guaranteed under Article 9, may be offended by a blasphemous expression in regard to objects of veneration. The 'duties and responsibilities' of those who exercise freedom of expression, as set forth in Article 10(2), encompass 'a duty to avoid expressions that are gratuitously offensive to others and profane',[300] and 'which therefore do not contribute to any form of public debate capable of furthering progress in human affairs'.[301] As a corollary, the state authorities are allowed to take measures to punish improper attacks on objectives of religious veneration,[302] or to repress some form of expression, such as the imparting of information and ideas, which are incompatible with the rights guaranteed under Article 9.[303] The fact that there is no European consensus on what is required for the protection of religious convictions and beliefs may justify a broad margin of appreciation.[304] Yet it must always be remembered that it is for the Strasbourg Court to take the final decision.[305]

A survey of the case law reveals a clear evolution from the past jurisprudence, which was characterized by the timid and overcautious stance,[306] to a more robust review. The Court is displaying a readiness scrupulously to analyze the allegedly offensive nature of the contested statements in the light of more 'objective' public sentiments, rather than the subjective feelings of specific individuals.

In *Otto-Preminger-Institut*,[307] the majority of the Court followed the reasoning in *Müller*, discussed above. It recognized the Austrian decisions to seize and then to order the forfeiture of a film as necessary for the protection of rights of others, especially adherents of Catholicism. The Court went so far as to state that the need to give due consideration to religious sensitivities constitutes a more potent ground than the protection of public morals. In *Wingrove v UK*,[308] it is to be recalled, the absence of European consensus

---

[300] *Otto-Preminger-Institut v Austria* A 295-A (1994); 19 EHRR 34 para 49; *İA v Turkey* 2005-VIII; 45 EHRR 703 para 24.

[301] See eg, *Gündüz v Turkey* 2003-XI; 41 EHRR 59 para 37; *Giniewski v France* 2006-I; 45 EHRR 589 para 43.

[302] Id.　　　[303] *Otto-Preminger-Institut v Austria* A 295-A (1994); 19 EHRR 34 para 47.

[304] Id, para 50; *İA v Turkey* 2005-VIII; 45 EHRR 703 para 25.

[305] *Giniewski v France* 2006-I; 45 EHRR 589 para 44.

[306] See, *inter alia*, *Otto-Preminger-Institut v Austria* A 295-A (1994); 19 EHRR 34; *Wingrove v UK* 1996-V; 24 EHRR 1; *Geerk v Switzerland* No 7640/76, 12 DR 103 (1978) (and 16 DR 56 (1979) F Sett); and *Gay News Ltd and Lemon v UK* No 8710/79, 28 DR 77 (1982); 5 EHRR 123 para 12. See, however, the Commission's finding of a violation of Article 10: *Otto-Preminger-Institute v Austria*, id, paras 75–8 Com Rep (nine votes to five as to the seizure of the film and thirteen votes to one with respect to the forfeiture of the film) and *Wingrove v UK*, id, paras 65–9 Com Rep (fourteen votes to two).

[307] *Loc cit* above at n 306, paras 56–7.　　　　[308] *Loc cit* at n 306 above, para 58.

on appropriate measures to balance the freedom of expression and the rights of third persons to religious faith was decisive for widening the ambit of margin of appreciation:

> as in the field of morals, and perhaps to an even greater degree, there is no uniform European conception of the requirements of 'the protection of the rights of others' in relation to attacks on their religious convictions. What is likely to cause substantial offence to persons of a particular religious persuasion will vary significantly from time to time and from place to place, especially in an era characterised by an ever growing array of faiths and denominations. By reason of their direct and continuous contact with the vital forces of their countries, State authorities are in principle in a better position than the international judge to give an opinion on the exact content of these requirements with regard to the rights of others as well as on the 'necessity' of a 'restriction' intended to protect from such material those whose deepest feelings and convictions would be seriously offended.[309]

In contrast, the Court's preparedness to undertake an exacting appraisal of national decisions can be seen by its effective reliance on the principle of pluralism, tolerance, and open-mindedness. It has required persons exercising the right to manifest religion to tolerate and accept not only the rejection of their religious faith by others but even the propagation of doctrines hostile to their own.[310] It is salutary that for fear of downgrading the standard of protection of free speech, the emphasis has now shifted from subjective feelings of pious followers of specific religious faith to a more 'objective' evaluation of the public sentiments.[311] A contrast should be made between *İA v Turkey*,[312] on the one hand, and *Giniewski v France* and *Klein v Slovakia* on the other. In *İA* a proprietor and a managing director of a publishing house published a novel expounding the author's views on philosophical and theological issues. The novel contained the following passage: 'God's messenger broke his fast through sexual intercourse, after dinner and before prayer. Muhammad did not forbid sexual intercourse with a dead person or a live animal'. The Istanbul public prosecutor lodged criminal proceedings against the applicant *proprio motu* on the basis of blasphemy against 'God, the Religion, the Prophet and the Holy Book' under the Turkish Criminal Code. The Court recognized that the above passage constituted an abusive attack on the Prophet of Islam, and that this was so even in a secular society like Turkey where there is 'a certain tolerance of criticism' of religious doctrine. The majority, by a close vote, found that the conviction of the applicant was buttressed by both relevant and sufficient reasons and hence not in breach of Article 10. The three dissenting judges, however, forcefully defended what they regarded as 'anti-conformist' perspectives. They considered that the book revealed the author's scepticism of any religious beliefs or atheism. They observed that Turkey is 'a highly religious society' with 'relatively few' atheists, and that materialist or atheist views were liable to shock the religious faith of the majority of the population. Even so, according to them, this did not provide 'sufficient' reasons for the criminal sanction.[313] The minority judges also stressed the very limited publicity impact, given that the book was never reprinted. Further, they considered it grave that the prosecuting authorities took their initiative to institute proceedings against the applicant.[314] The penalty was

---

[309] Id, para 58. See also *Murphy v Ireland* 2003-IX; 38 EHRR 212 para 67.

[310] *İA v Turkey* 2005-VIII; 45 EHRR 703 para 28; *Aydin Tatlav v Turkey* hudoc (2006) para 27. See also *Otto-Preminger-Institute v Austria* A 295-A (1994); 19 EHRR 34 para 47.

[311] *Aydin Tatlav v Turkey* hudoc (2006) para 28 and *Klein v Slovakia* hudoc (2006) paras 51–2.

[312] 2005-VIII; 45 EHRR 703 paras 29–30.

[313] Id, joint dissenting opinion of Judges Costa, Cabral Barreto, and Jungwiert, para 3.

[314] They stressed that 'a democratic society is not a theocratic society': id, para 5.

acknowledged by them to be relatively light, because the two-year prison sentence was commuted to a modest fine. Yet the dissenting judges underscored that any criminal sanction entailed 'a chilling effect', and that 'a risk of self-censorship' is highly perilous for the free speech in democracy.[315] It is noteworthy that they specifically pleaded the need to depart from what they saw as a 'conformist' rationale behind the Court's application of the margin of appreciation.[316]

In contrast, in *Giniewski*,[317] a journalist published an article in a Parisian newspaper, accusing the papal encyclical 'The splendour of truth' ('Veritatis Splendor') of enshrining a theological doctrine of the 'fulfilment' of the Old Covenant in the New, which in his view led to anti-Semitism and ushered the way for Auschwitz. Following proceedings launched by the General Alliance against Racism and for Respect for the French and Christian Identity, he was convicted of defamation. The article was considered by the Court to contribute to a wide-ranging debate as to the causes of the Holocaust, and, in the light of the tenor and tone of the article, 'without sparking off any controversy that was gratuitous or detached from the reality of contemporary thought'.[318] The article was not considered to incite to disrespect or hatred, or to 'cast doubt in any way on clearly established historical facts'.[319] In view of this, the Court unanimously found that the reasons for convicting the journalist of public defamation were insufficient.[320]

In *Klein v Slovakia*,[321] the Court took another step to strengthen the standard of free speech when this right is juxtaposed against freedom of religion. The case concerned posters placed in Bratislava for the promotion of a film *The People vs. Larry Flynt*. The posters showed the main character crucified on a woman's pubic area dressed in a bikini. The Archbishop of the Catholic Church in Slovakia considered the posters defamatory of the symbol of Christianity and called for the withdrawal of the posters and the film. The applicant was a journalist who published an article in an intellectual weekly, which sharply criticized the moral integrity of the Archbishop, using slang and innuendo with oblique vulgar and sexual connotations. He expressed his wonder as to why decent Catholics did not leave the Catholic Church, which was headed by an 'ogre'. At the request of two religious associations, the applicant was convicted of defaming another person's belief. With regard to the contents of the controversial article, the Court did not consider that the applicant disparaged Catholics, referring to the more objective test of assessing the allegedly offensive nature of expression:

> The fact that some members of the Catholic Church could have been offended by the applicant's criticism of the Archbishop and by his statement... cannot affect the position. The Court accepts the applicant's argument that the article neither unduly interfered with the right of believers to express and exercise their religion, nor did it denigrate the content of their religious faith.

In this case, the Court held that imposing the criminal offence of defaming another person's belief was misplaced, as the applicant's criticism was levelled exclusively at the person of the Archbishop.

---

[315] Id, para 6.   [316] Id, para 8.   [317] 2006-I; 45 EHRR 589 para 51.

[318] Id, paras 50. On matters of historical controversy, it added that it is not supposed to 'arbitrate' the underlying historical issues: id, para 51. Cf, *Chauvy v France* 2004-VI; 41 EHRR 610 para 69.

[319] *Loc cit*, above n 317, para 52. See, *a contrario*, *Garaudy v France* No 65831/01, 2003-IX DA.

[320] The penalty imposed on the journalist at issue was very limited. Yet, accent was placed on the fact that the notice mentioned the criminal offence of defamation, which was found to have a chilling effect: id, para 55.

[321] Hudoc (2006) paras 51–2.

VIII. PREVENTION OF DISCLOSURE OF CONFIDENTIAL INFORMATION

The phrase 'the disclosure of information received in confidence' in Article 10(2) has been interpreted as encompassing the disclosure of confidential information by a person who has received the information subject to a duty of confidence, or by a third party, including a journalist, who has received it subject to no such duty.[322] The right of journalists to engage in the free flow of information may be at odds with the legitimate aims of preventing the divulgence of confidential information. As discussed above, the fact that information has been obtained illegally by a third person, such as a journalist, does not divest that person of the protection of Article 10.[323] But ordering a journalist, or the press, to account for the profits and costs accruing from the publication of confidential material has been considered proportionate in view of the relatively minor nature of the interference and of the need to sanction the breach of confidence.[324] Similarly, recovering from a former government secret service agent the profits from publishing a material in a book in breach of his undertaking to the government not to disclose information obtained in his employment was justified. Even though the subject matter had ceased to be confidential, special note was taken of the fact that those profits derived from the notoriety and gravity of the applicant's criminal past.[325] It ought to be mentioned that, as confirmed in the cases of *Sunday Times (Spycatcher)* (the disclosure of national intelligence) and *Fressoz and Roire*[326] (use of confidential tax documents), once the contents of the confidential information have come to the public knowledge, the legitimacy of sanctions against a journalist who has breached professional confidence becomes questionable.

Despite the critical importance of political expression, the Commission endorsed the criminal conviction of an accredited parliamentary journalist who, while being aware of its confidential nature, published a confidential parliamentary document.[327] Similarly, applying criminal sanction against a journalist who has breached the confidentiality of diplomatic correspondence may be warranted in view of the paramount national interest. In *Stoll v Switzerland*,[328] the Grand Chamber upheld the conviction of a journalist for publishing a confidential report written by the Swiss ambassador to the US in preparation for the negotiations between Jewish organizations and Swiss banks concerning the unclaimed assets of the Holocaust victims deposited in Swiss banks. The journalist obtained a copy of the report from an unidentified person in breach of professional confidence. He published some of its extracts in a weekly newspaper, reporting that the ambassador insulted the Jewish representatives by calling them 'our adversaries ... not to be trusted'. The Swiss courts found him culpable of making public 'secret official deliberations' within the meaning of the Swiss Criminal Code. Until the contested article appeared, the public had not been privy at all to the content of the diplomatic report in question. The senior official position held by the author of the document was not considered to diminish the confidential nature of the diplomatic dossier.[329] Nor was the government's failure to establish that the applicant's articles prevented the Swiss government

---

[322] *Stoll v Switzerland* hudoc (2007) para 61 GC. Faced with inconsistent English and French authentic texts, the Grand Chamber relied on Article 33(4), Vienna Convention on the Law of Treaties to interpret Article 10(2) as including third parties.

[323] *RADIO TWIST AS v Slovakia* hudoc (2006) para 62. See further above, n 293.

[324] *Times Newspapers Ltd and Neil v UK No 14644/89*, 73 DR 41 (1991).

[325] *Blake v UK No 68890/01* hudoc (2005) para 158 DA. Cf, *Blake v UK* hudoc (2006) (finding of a violation of Article 6(1)).

[326] 1999-I; 31 EHRR 28 para 53 GC.   [327] *Z v Switzerland No 10343/83*, 35 DR 224 (1983).

[328] Hudoc (2007) para 16 GC.   [329] Id, para 114.

and Swiss banks from resolving issues of unclaimed assets deemed material. According to the Grand Chamber, what mattered was the *potentiality* that the revelation of the report and the publication of the articles might cause 'considerable damage' to Swiss national interests.[330] In the light of the presentation of the ambassador's remarks in the applicant's articles, the Grand Chamber took the view that the disclosure of the extracts of the report at a delicate juncture could cause 'considerable damage' to those interests.[331] The applicant did not act unlawfully to obtain the document, and the Swiss authorities could have opened an investigation to prosecute a staff member responsible for the leak of the document. Even so, according to the Grand Chamber, the duties and responsibilities of the applicant as a journalist held sway, countering the claim that he was unaware of the risk of criminal prosecution.

The Grand Chamber found that the articles isolated extracts from the impugned report, taken out of context. Given that one of the articles was placed on the front page, the applicant's intention was considered to make the ambassador's report 'the subject of needless scandal'.[332] When finding no violation of Article 10, the Grand Chamber ruled that the reductive form of the articles was liable to mislead the reader concerning the ambassador's personality and abilities, and to lessen the worthiness of their contribution to the public debate. This was a curious line of reasoning. No action was taken to prosecute other journalists and the newspapers that published the contested document virtually *in full* the day after the applicant's articles appeared. As Judge Zagrebelsky noted in his dissent,[333] publishing only a few extracts from the document, albeit relating specifically to the manner in which the ambassador expressed himself, 'paradoxically' served to diminish the value of the press freedom, and the majority suggested that the applicant should have published the document in full.

Where divulging confidential information clashes with the right to privacy of a judge, it is crucial to examine the extent to which it can contribute to general public debate. In *Leempoel & SA ED Ciné Revuev Belgium*,[334] the Court found it reasonable to order the withdrawal of the sales of a magazine that published the confidential documents of a judge who was under parliamentary inquiry. An article in the magazine included a copy of the judge's private correspondence. The parliamentary inquiry was no doubt of great public interest, as it related to the judge's controversial handling of the case of kidnapped girls. The case turned on whether there was any reason to justify the publication of purely private material. The Court found that the applicants had failed to demonstrate both the overriding public interest in publishing the contested information, when to do so was harmful not only to the reputation and privacy of the judge under the inquiry but also to his fair trial rights.[335]

A trend emerging from the principle of transparency in modern Europe is that publication is the rule and prohibition of publication the exception.[336] It is becoming increasingly difficult to maintain the legitimacy of 'preventing the disclosure of information received in confidence', save in highly exceptional circumstances such as pending criminal investigations and a very sensitive diplomatic document. As stressed earlier,[337] there would

---

[330] Id, para 130.   [331] Id, paras 132–6.   [332] Id, para 151.

[333] Id, dissenting opinion of Judge Zagrebelsky joined by Judges Lorenzen, Fura-Sandström, Jaeger, and Popović.

[334] Hudoc (2006) para 79.   [335] Id, paras 74–80.

[336] See eg, Committee of Ministers Resolution Res (2001) 6 of 12 June 2001 on access to Council of Europe documents; and Resolution 1551 (2007) of the Parliamentary Assembly of the Council of Europe on fair trial issues in criminal cases concerning espionage or divulging state secrets. See also I-A Ct HRts, *Claude Reyes and Others v Chile*, Judgment of 19 September 2006, Series C No 151, para 58.

[337] Above, p 476.

be no need to keep the confidentiality of the information held by a public prosecutor, once the information enters the public domain by different channels.[338] In *Dammann v Switzerland*,[339] a journalist was convicted of having instigated the violation of confidentiality of information after he obtained from the public prosecutor's office the information concerning the criminal records of persons suspected of drug dealing. Given that the information could have been obtained by consulting reports of the judgments and the archives of newspapers, both the relevance and the sufficiency of the interference were deemed dubious. The information was considered to raise a matter of public interest, as it related to a burglary of a post office in Zurich. The applicant did not resort to a ruse, menace, or any other illegal means. Further, any alleged injury to the rights of persons, if at all, was held to have dissipated once the applicant himself decided not to publish the data in question. In these circumstances, the imposition of the criminal sanction, albeit minor in nature, was found so disproportionate as to deter unjustifiably the journalist from undertaking research to support his article.

IX. MAINTENANCE OF THE AUTHORITY AND IMPARTIALITY OF THE JUDICIARY

a. Overview

Under Article 6(1), the Convention explicitly allows courts to hold criminal proceedings in camera, excluding journalists or the public in general. Such exclusion is aimed at protecting the privacy rights of juvenile offenders, preventing disorder or crime, maintaining the authority and impartiality of the judiciary, or protecting the rights of others.[340] The interest of the media in reporting criminal proceedings may be outweighed by the combination of these public purposes, which can be subsumed into the legitimate aim of 'maintaining the authority and impartiality of the judiciary in Article 10 terms'. A court may order the exclusion of the public from the pending criminal proceedings involving highly sensitive matters, which if disclosed to the public, may jeopardize the safety of third parties, including family members of those involved in organized crimes. The failure by a court, which ordered the exclusion of the public from the pending criminal proceedings, to make public the reasons for such an exclusion was deemed compatible with Article 10, it being noted that the senior judge of that court had offered to give the reasons in confidence to the chairperson of the association of journalists.[341]

A witness summons issued to a journalist or a media company to provide evidence in criminal proceedings belongs to a normal civil duty in democracy, and this can be defended as being to 'maintain the authority and impartiality of the judiciary'. In *BBC v UK*,[342] the witness summons required the BBC to divulge recordings of riots for the purpose of a criminal proceeding. In contrast to the *Goodwin* case, where the disclosure order concerned information received on a confidential basis, this case related to information on events which took place in public, so that no duty of confidentially arose. The BBC challenged a disclosure obligation without being informed of the issues in the criminal trial. This argument was rejected by the Commission, which opined that witnesses often gave evidence without appreciating the impact of their evidence, and that its impact was the matter to be decided by a national court.

---

[338] See, *inter alia*, *Fressoz v Roire v France* 1999-I; 31 EHRR 28 para 53; *Observer and Guardian v UK* A 216 (1991); 14 EHRR 153 para 69 PC; and *Dammann v Switzerland* hudoc (2006) para 53.

[339] *Ibid.*   [340] See above, p 235.

[341] *Atkinson, Crook and The Independent v UK* No13366/87, 67 DR 244 1990.

[342] *No 25798/94* hudoc (1996) DA.

With respect to the live transmission of court proceedings by the media, there is a risk that journalists' subjectivity in filtering and editing may compromise the fair administration of justice. In *P4 Radio Helge Norge ASA v Norway*,[343] the Court recognized that a legal presumption against the live transmission of court hearings by radio was consistent with Article 10. Indeed, 'no common ground' was held to exist in European national legal systems to support the argument that live transmission by audio-visual means was vital for imparting information on criminal proceedings. Account was also taken of the fact that the national authorities allowed the proceedings to be held in an open court, and even made arrangements for live transmission of 'picture and sound' to a press hall nearby to cater for the considerable media interest in a case that had attracted great public interest.

b. Criticisms of the judiciary

According to the case law, among all public officials, judges enjoy the highest protection of their authority, and the limit of acceptable criticism of them is the narrowest. This can be explained by their special role as guarantors of justice that must inspire confidence both in the accused in criminal proceedings and in the public at large.[344] Further, special regard must be had to their inability to reply to criticism.[345] Indeed, the Court has stressed the need to distinguish between criticism and insult. If the sole intention of any form of expression is to insult a court, or members of the court, an appropriate punishment can be justified under Article 10(2).[346] The authority of the judiciary needs to be safeguarded from any abusive or insulting language by the defence even in heated circumstances. In *Saday v Turkey*,[347] the defendant used acerbic and virulent words, such as 'the State wish that we should be killed by the executioners wearing robes' and 'The fascist dictator... now wants to judge me before a security court of the State'. The Court accepted that such words could undermine the judicial authority and the dignity of the judges by creating an atmosphere of insecurity to the detriment of the good administration of justice.

Clearly, for the purpose of safeguarding the authority of the judiciary and the dignity of the legal profession, many countries allow the legal professional bodies to take disciplinary measures. In *Schöpfer v Switzerland*,[348] a lawyer was subjected to disciplinary penalty for having criticized the administration of justice in pending proceedings at a press conference. He deliberately chose such a public venue before having resort to a legal remedy of appeal. The Court suggested that the applicant was under a special duty, as a member of the Bar, to contribute to the proper administration of justice and to maintain public confidence in it. In view of the tone of the accusation and of the modest amount of the fine, the Court concluded that a proper balance had been struck.

With respect to virulent criticisms or disparaging comments directed at judges, the approach taken by the Court in its early case law may be criticized for lacking in both depth and rigour in its analysis.[349] In *Barfod v Denmark*,[350] a Danish citizen in Greenland criticized a judgment in a taxation case rendered by the High Court, which found in

---

[343] No 76682/01 hudoc (2003) DA.

[344] See, *inter alia*, *Fey v Austria* A 255-A (1993); 6 EHRR 387 para 40 and *Skałka v Poland* hudoc (2003); 38 EHRR 1 para 40.

[345] *Prager and Oberschlick v Austria* A 313 (1995); 21 EHRR 1 para 34.

[346] *Skałka v Poland, loc cit*, above n 344, para 34.

[347] Hudoc (2006) paras 35–6. Nevertheless, the severity of the criminal sanction was found disproportionate: id, para 36.   [348] 1998-III; 33 EHRR 845 paras 29 and 33.

[349] See eg, *Hodgson, Woolf Productions Ltd, National Union of Journalists and Channel Four Television Co Ltd v UK Nos 11553/85 and 11658/85 (joined)*, 51 DR 136 (1987); and *C Ltd v UK No 14132/88*, 61 DR 285 (1989).

[350] A 149 (1989); 13 EHRR 493 para 71 Com Rep, emphasis added.

favour of the local government. The sitting judges of the High Court included two lay judges employed by the local government, namely the defendant of the case. The applicant wrote an article in a magazine, stating that these lay judges 'did their duty', implying that they cast vote as employees of the local government rather than as independent and impartial judges. He was convicted on the ground that his remarks were defamatory of the character of the judges. The Commission, by fourteen votes to one, found a violation of Article 10, recognizing that the contested remarks raised matters of public interest relating to the functioning of the public administration. This reasoning was upheld 'even if the article in question could be interpreted as an attack on the integrity or reputation of the two lay judges'. In contrast, the Court overturned the Commission's opinion by six votes to one, holding that the contested remarks did not entail any contribution to public debates. It did not find that his criminal conviction could entail any deterrent impact on his freedom of expression, referring to the possibility of criticizing the composition of the High Court without attacking the lay judges personally. It also rejected the argument that the applicant's critical remarks were made in political context concerning a disputed tax levied in Greenland. According to the Court, the impugned remarks consisted of two elements: a criticism of the composition of the High Court in the tax case in question; and the statement that the two lay judges 'did their duty'.[351] The Court held that it was not demonstrated that these 'two elements of criticism... were so closely connected as to make the statement relating to the two lay judges legitimate'.[352] On closer scrutiny, this argument seems rather artificial. Indeed, the two elements concerned were inseparably intertwined. Further, even if these elements could have been disjoined, with the second element considered a personal attack, it would still be difficult to deem the tenor of the wording sufficiently offensive to amount to defamation.

This lax approach was followed in *Prager and Obserschlick v Austria*.[353] There, a journalist and a publisher were convicted of defamation after the former wrote an article in a magazine, criticizing the judges of the Vienna Regional Criminal Court in virulent and disparaging words. The article stated that the judges 'treat each accused at the outset as if he had already been convicted', and described Judge J as 'arrogant' and 'bullying'. Both the Commission[354] and the Court[355] found no violation of Article 10 by close votes. The Court recognized that these words were 'unnecessarily prejudicial' and defamatory, noting that this was true 'even in the absence of a sufficient factual basis'.[356] No doubt the Court's deference to the national authorities' classification of the contested passages in the article as value-judgments or allegations of fact was important to this decision.[357] In his dissenting opinion, Judge Martens carefully examined the context in which the contested article was written. He noted that after months of research the journalist considered that it was the personalities of judges at the Vienna Regional Criminal Court that explained why criminal justice in Vienna was more unduly harsh than elsewhere in Austria.[358] According to Judge Martens, the article raised matters of crucial public interest, requiring special protection. Further, he cogently pointed out that while scathing criticism directed against Judge J was defamatory, other judges rebuked no less severely in the article did not institute defamation proceedings.

The Court's decision-making policy has, however, shifted to an approach that now gives more lengthy thought to the specific circumstances of the case, in tune with other

---

[351] Id, para 30. [352] *Ibid*. [353] A 313 (1995); 21 EHRR 1.
[354] Id, Com Rep (fifteen votes to twelve). [355] Id (five votes to four). [356] Id, para 37.
[357] Id, para 36.
[358] Id, dissenting opinion of Judge Martens, joined by Judges Pekkanen and Makarczyk.

defamation cases. In *De Haes and Gijsels v Belgium*,[359] journalists were found by the national courts to have defamed the judges in divorce proceedings, when criticizing them for bias and lack of independence in awarding child custody to a father accused of abuse and incest. The impugned statements were considered of special public interest because of the serious allegations concerning both the fate of young children and the role of the local judiciary. The Court carefully dissected different elements of the statements to ascertain whether they constituted facts or opinions. Some of the applicants' allegations, including the allusion to an extreme right-wing ideology espoused by a father of one judge as evidence of his political bias, were clearly irrelevant and deemed deserving of penalty. Nevertheless, the Court was quick to stress that such were only part of the statements, and that it was essential not to overlook their *overall* tenor. In view of the special weight given to the role of the journalists in informing the public of a controversial decision in a child custody case, even an aggressive tone levelled at judges was found reasonable.

The Court's scrutiny of the reaction of judges to abusive comments may extend to the nature and severity of a criminal sanction imposed, irrespective of whether the words used against judges were clearly offensive. In *Skałka v Poland*,[360] a prisoner wrote a letter to the President of the Katowice Regional Court, describing an unidentified judge, with whom he had made initial communication, as a 'small-time cretin' and 'some fool'. The Court found that such wording was clearly derogatory. Yet, this could not warrant a prison sentence of eight months, which was considered to upset the equilibrium.

c. Prevention of improper influence on trials

The legitimate aim of maintaining the authority and impartiality of the judiciary is of special relevance to the doctrine of contempt of court in common law, according to which an injunction can be ordered to prevent the release and circulation of information on a pending trial to avoid any prejudgment or public pressure on the parties to the trial. In criminal proceedings, due account must be taken of the defendant's right to a fair trial and an impartial tribunal under Article 6 to hinder any deleterious impact arising from the publicity.

In *Sunday Times (No 1) v UK*,[361] the minority of the Commission and the government described the contempt of court doctrine as 'peculiar' to common-law countries. The same argument was taken up by the dissenting judges, who held that 'the notion of the authority of the judiciary was by no means divorced from national circumstances and could not be determined in a uniform way'.[362] This 'peculiar nature' of the doctrine was relied upon by the dissenting judges to support the application of a wide margin of appreciation. However, the majority of the Court did not follow this argument, stressing that the objective nature of the doctrine of contempt of court required stringent scrutiny. It held that, in contrast to 'public morals', which were susceptible to diverse interpretation and standards, the notion of judicial authority was 'by far more objective' and capable of stringent review. Further, the fact that the case concerned restrictions on the press, one of the privileged means of expression, was pivotal. The contested newspaper articles related to the criticism of the pending settlement of the thalidomide tragedy, which was judged by the Court to be of 'undisputed public concern'.[363] The *Sunday Times (No 1)* case suggests that the Court's analysis of the clash between the free speech and the doctrine of

---

[359] 1997-I; 25 EHRR 1 para 45.   [360] Hudoc (2003) 38 EHRR 1.
[361] A 30 (1979); 2 EHRR 245 para 60 PC.
[362] Id, joint dissenting opinion of Judges Wiarda, Cremona, Thor Vilhjalmsson, Ryssdal, Ganshof van der Meersch, Fitzmaurice, Bindschedler-Robert, Liesch, and Matscher, para 9.
[363] Id, para 67.

contempt of court may demonstrate a fine-tuning and relatively bold approach where the information concerns matters of considerable public interest.

Notwithstanding the seminal implication of *Sunday Times (No 1)*, the Commission found to be justifiable a series of judicial measures, based on the contempt of court doctrine, which clashed with the rights of the media in reporting pending proceedings. In *C Ltd v UK*,[364] it endorsed the order of the Court of Appeal banning the TV broadcasting of a scheduled programme, which was essentially a dramatic reconstruction of criminal proceedings based exclusively on the official shorthand transcripts. The dramatized re-enactment of criminal proceedings was distinguished from the reporting of such proceedings in the press, because it was considered to entail the risk of subtly inviting the viewers to be placed in 'conditioned' settings. Similarly, in the *Hodgson Channel Four Television Co Ltd* cases,[365] a court order required the postponement of a programme 'Court Report', which was a rehearsal of a criminal trial concerning official secrets and highlighting the most dramatic parts of a hearing. The programme would consist of studio readings from a transcript of the proceedings, which were checked for accuracy and fairness. Actors were instructed to avoid any dramatic re-enactment of the proceedings. The Commission endorsed the court order on the grounds that this was purported to avoid 'a *real* risk of prejudice' to the jury, and that imparting the same information could be effectuated in a revised programme. The Commission's deferential stance can be borne out by the rejection of the argument that, short of prior restraint, there were other less injurious courses open to the trial judge, such as the instruction given to the jury not to watch the programme. Further, in *Associated Newspapers Limited, Steven and Wolman v UK*,[366] the unauthorized disclosure of juries' deliberations for the purpose of research was found objectionable in jeopardizing the jury trial, which was based on the confidentiality of their deliberations.

On the basis of the doctrine of contempt of court, the Commission also upheld the conviction of journalists to safeguard the fair trial rights of the accused and the right to privacy of victims or of witnesses. In *Crook and National Union of Journalists v UK*,[367] a court order withheld the publication of the name of a witness who was abducted for rape. Rather contradictorily, the order nonetheless allowed her name to be freely used in a public hearing so as not to prejudice the defence of the defendants. A request from journalists to reconsider the order was nevertheless rejected. The case was settled before the admissibility decision, following the UK government's proposal to amend the Criminal Justice Bill to allow an appeal to the Court of Appeal against orders of the kind raised in this case.

In *Kyprianou v Cyprus*,[368] the Court, in contrast to the Commission's earlier decisions, exhibited a readiness to engage in scrupulous review of contempt rulings. In that case, a lawyer defending a person accused of murder made a mildly intemperate attack on judges. During heated debates, he used the Greek word which could mean both a love letter and a note, referring to a note exchanged between judges. Because of his remarks and conduct, he was convicted for contempt of court, and sentenced to five-day imprisonment in summary proceedings conducted by the same judges against whom his remarks were directed. The Grand Chamber appraised the impact of his sentence upon the applicant's free speech. It found that the imposition of a custodial sentence must have a chilling

364 *No 14132/88*, 61 DR 285 (1989).

365 *Hodgson, Woolf Productions Ltd and National Union of Journalists v UK and Channel Four Television Co Ltd v UK Nos 1553/85 and 11658/85*, 51 DR 136 (1987), emphasis added. See also Commission's Report of 15 July 1988 (F Sett as to an alleged violation of Article 13).

366 *No 24770/94* hudoc (1994) DA.   367 *No 11552/85* hudoc (1988) DA.

368 2005-VIII para 150.

effect on the conduct of the applicant and lawyers generally in criminal proceedings. The penal sanction (five days' imprisonment) was perceived as excessive in response to his discourteous remarks and conduct. Moreover, the applicant's status as a respected lawyer and the availability of less onerous alternatives[369] aggravated the disproportionate nature of the interference.

Clearly, civil law countries are also well-equipped to deal with an affront to the authority and impartiality of the judiciary. A number of cases have arisen in relation to the improper influence exercised by the mass media on criminal trials. The case of *Worm v Austria*,[370] suggests that even the ample protection afforded to journalists' expression rights may have to be circumscribed to safeguard fair trial guarantees of defendants. A journalist wrote an article commenting on pending criminal proceedings for tax evasion against a former Vice-Chancellor and Minister of Finance. He was convicted for having exercised prohibited influence on the criminal proceeding. The Commission considered that the incriminated article had only raised a mere suspicion of the guilt of the defendant, and found the proportionality test to be breached. In contrast, the Court held that the article provided a clear opinion likely to affect the minds of the lay judges, contrary to the defendant's right to an impartial tribunal, so that there was no violation of Article 10. The balance between press freedom and the right to a fair trial was tipped in favour of the latter. The Court considered that national judiciaries were given discretion in evaluating the likelihood that the lay judges might read the article in question, resulting in possible prejudgment. The majority clearly departed from its approach in *Sunday Times (No 1)*. Special weight was given to the margin of appreciation, despite the emerging European consensus on the notion of the 'authority and impartiality of the judiciary'. The Court furnished the following explanations:

> With respect to the notion of the 'authority and impartiality of the judiciary', the Court has already noted its objective character and the fact that, in this area, the domestic law and practice of the Member States of the Council of Europe reveal a fairly substantial measure of common ground...This does not mean that absolute uniformity is required and, indeed, since the Contracting States remain free to choose the measures which they consider appropriate, the Court cannot be oblivious of the substantive or procedural features of their respective domestic laws...It cannot thus hold that the applicant's conviction was contrary to Article 10 of the Convention simply because it might not have been obtained under a different legal system.[371]

It was not deemed decisive that this case concerned a highly influential politician, and that the bounds of acceptable criticism of such a public figure should be set wider. Further, the Court glossed over the argument raised by the applicant that the gist of the article was essentially a quotation of a statement made by the public prosecutor at the trial.

In the subsequent case of *News Verlags GmbH & Co KG v Austria*,[372] the Court reasserted the primacy of press freedom and the right of the public to receive information. The case concerned injunctions prohibiting a magazine from printing photographs of a person suspected of sending of letter bombs. The Court found that the injunctions pursued two legitimate aims: (i) the protection of the reputation or rights of the suspect in question; and (ii) the maintenance of the authority and impartiality of the judiciary. Nevertheless, it unanimously condemned the injunctions as being disproportionate. The fact that the photographed person was a well-known right-wing extremist, whose views challenged the Convention's values, corroborated the argument that the suspect

---

[369] The applicant referred to the possibility of an overnight adjournment of the trial: id, para 79.
[370] 1997-V; 25 EHRR 454 para 50.   [371] *Ibid.*   [372] 2000-I; 31 EHRR 246 paras 54–8.

was a public figure, and the photographs were of special public interest in a case that had attracted great public attention.

In *Tourancheau and July v France*,[373] a journalist was convicted for publishing an article dealing with the investigation of a murder case. The article reproduced extracts from a declaration made by a girl who was under investigation and the words of her fiancé. A photograph of the latter was published with a caption stating that he had been liberated while his fiancée stayed in prison. When convicting the journalist, national courts held that the tenor of the article supported the story of one accused to the detriment of the other. They noted that this would adversely affect the decisions of non-professional judges in pending criminal proceedings, undermining public confidence in the administration of criminal justice and the fair trial rights of the accused. The Court held that the ban on publication was minimal, and that the applicant was otherwise free to comment on the investigation. The article was not deemed to raise general interest to the public. Further, according to the Court, it was up to the national courts to examine the probability of non-professional judges drawing adverse inferences. Primacy was given to the presumption of innocence and to the interest in maintaining the authority and impartiality of the judiciary. The nature and severity of the penalty were not considered so excessive as to have a chilling effect. By a close vote of four to three, the Court concluded that Article 10 was not breached. The dissenting judges' opinions gave greater weight to the right of the public to receive information on pending trials. They considered that the present case departed from the more finely-tuned approach in *Worm*.[374] In their view, the article in question did not flout the presumption of innocence of the accused.[375] As they noted, given the lapse of almost twenty months between the publication of the article and the date of the hearing, it was difficult to detect any seriously adverse impact flowing from the publication of the article.

7. DUTIES AND RESPONSIBILITIES UNDER ARTICLE 10(2)

I. OVERVIEW

Article 10(2) refers to the 'duties and responsibilities' of persons exercising their freedom of expression. The inclusion of such duties and responsibilities is unusual for the Convention rights. However, to argue that the inclusion of such wording suggests an inherently greater limitation envisaged in the freedom of expression is untenable. Indeed, there is no room for implied limitations in Article 10. Even so, the Court has shrewdly parried the question whether individual persons are able to waive their right to freedom of expression,[376] confining itself to holding that a waiver of a right guaranteed under the Convention, if permissible, must satisfy three requirements: (i) this must not be incompatible with any significant public interest; (ii) it must be established in an unequivocal manner; and (iii) there must be minimum guarantees commensurate to the waiver's importance.[377]

---

[373] Hudoc (2005) para 66.   [374] Above, p 492.

[375] Joint dissenting opinion of Judges Costa, Tulkens, and Lorenzen, paras 2 and 6.

[376] See eg, *Blake v UK No 68890/01* hudoc (2005) para 128 DA.

[377] *Håkansson and Sturesson v Sweden* A 171-A (1990); 13 EHRR 1 para 66; *Pfeifer and Plankl v Austria* A 227 (1992); 14 EHRR 692 para 37.

The notion of 'duties and responsibilities' has been invoked in relation to different bearers of expression rights, including politicians, civil servants, lawyers,[378] the press, journalists, editors,[379] authors and publishers (vicariously),[380] and even artists such as novelists.[381] This notion assumes marked importance with respect to special categories of civil servants, such as diplomats, judges, intelligence agents, and police officers.[382] With respect to journalists, the Court has repeatedly highlighted that they are to act in good faith to provide accurate and reliable information in accordance with the ethics of journalism.[383] In view of the vast quantities of information and of the diverse means of information developed in a modern age, monitoring compliance with journalistic ethics has become of greater significance.[384] The issue of duties and responsibilities of journalists will be more closely examined in a separate section below. In relation to the free speech of judges, it is considered reasonable to expect them to display a certain degree of discretion and even self-restraint so as not to undermine the authority and impartiality of the judiciary. Even so, as demonstrated in *Wille v Liechtenstein*,[385] whether their statements have overstepped the acceptable bounds of freedom and flouted their professional ethics or adversely affected their performance is a question that must not escape rigorous assessment.

Representatives of professional bodies[386] and members of civil society such as non-governmental organizations (NGOs) have also been regarded as subject to the similar duties and responsibilities. In *Steel and Morris v UK*,[387] the Court held that duties and responsibilities of journalists to act in good faith to provide accurate and reliable information in accordance with the ethics of journalism could apply by analogy to those that engage in public debate, such as campaigners of a small NGO, who distributed leaflets.

II. DUTIES AND RESPONSIBILITIES OF CIVIL SERVANTS

The notion of 'duties and responsibilities' under Article 10(2) has been invoked to justify encroachments on civil servants' political speech and activities to ensure their neutrality and impartiality. The Court has found that the obligations imposed on special categories of public officials, including police officers, to refrain from political activities to ensure that their 'balanced' or 'political neutral' views were compatible with the 'duties and responsibilities' under Article 10(2).[388]

Ahmed v UK[389] concerned the prohibition of municipal authorities' employees from participating in political activities. In ruling against the applicant, the Court recognized that there limitations may be imposed on the free speech of public servants by widely interpreting the term 'duties and responsibilities' in Article 10(2). It held that this term 'assume[s] a special significance, which justifies leaving to the authorities of the respondent State a certain margin of appreciation in determining whether the impugned interference

---

[378] *Steur v Netherlands* 2003-XI; 39 EHRR 706 paras 37–8.
[379] *Sürek v Turkey (No 1)* 1999-IV para 63 GC; and *Leempoel v SA ED Ciné Revue v Belgium* hudoc (2006) para 66.
[380] *Édition Plon v France* 2004-IV; 42 EHRR 705 para 50.
[381] *Lindon, Otchakovsky-Laurens and July v France,* hudoc (2007) para 51.
[382] With respect to secret agents, see eg, *Blake v UK No 68890/01* hudoc (2005) paras 126 and 159.
[383] For this principle, see eg, *Bladet Tromsø and Stensaas v Norway* 1999-III; 29 EHRR 125 para 65.
[384] *Stoll v Switzerland* hudoc (2007) para 104 GC.   [385] 1999-VII; 30 EHRR 558 GC.
[386] See eg, *Nilsen and Johnsen v Norway* 1999-VIII; 30 EHRR 878 para 47 GC.
[387] 2005-II; 41 EHRR 403 para 90.
[388] *Rekvényi v Hungary* 1999-III para 46 GC; and *Otto v Germany No 27574/02* hudoc (2005) DA.
[389] 1998-VI para 61. Another decisive factor was that among the member states there existed diverse approaches to the regulations of local authorities: id, para 62.

is proportionate to the aim as stated'. In contrast, in the same case, the Commission had not extensively interpreted the words 'duties and responsibilities'. It rejected any room for inherently wide restrictions on the rights of a public servant[390] and stressed the foundational nature of free speech in a democracy. It called on the government to establish a less restrictive form of limitation, which was in essence prior restraint.[391] The Commission's finding that the proportionality test was not met was based on its examination of the contested law in the light of its scope of application, impact, and possibility of exemption.[392] The Commission's approach was more consonant with other cases revealing rigorous standard of review.

It must be examined whether and, if so, in what ways, the notion 'duties and responsibilities' under Article 10(2) has become of special relevance to the assessment of anti-Convention values espoused by civil servants.[393] Several complaints have arisen in connection with the German loyalty test for civil servants, which is premised on the constitutional safeguard called the *wehrhafte Demokratie* ('democracy capable of defending itself'[394] or 'military democracy'). In view of the Nazi experience, all civil servants, irrespective of their job and rank, must swear to abide by the values incorporated in the Basic Law. Any involvement in, or connection to, an organization whose aim is held unconstitutional may lead to 'wilful deceit' of this loyalty requirement. In the two German cases of *Glasenapp* and *Kosiek*, which concerned the dismissal of civil servants on probation, the Court evaded the question of conflict between the freedom of expression and the loyalty test. The Court's approach in the *Glasenapp* case,[395] concerning a school teacher associated with a proscribed communist party, may be aptly described as 'a puzzling *non sequitur*'.[396] The Court considered that the essence of the complaint was the right of access to the civil service, a right not guaranteed under the Convention. In its view, the national authorities took account of the applicant's opinions only for the purpose of verifying her qualifications for the post. The Court took the same approach in *Kosiek v FRG*,[397] which concerned the dismissal of a probationary lecturer belonging to an extreme right-wing party. The potential repercussion of the non-application of Article 10 in respect of civil servants is disturbing.[398] By contrast, in both cases, the Commission considered that the freedom of expression was at issue. In *Glasenapp*, the Commission favoured freedom of expression,[399] concluding that the categorical application of loyalty test, which took no account of the rank, position, or nature of civil service, was excessive.[400] By contrast, in, the *Kosiek* case, the Commission endorsed the national decision. The difference in the Commission's approach can be explained by the degree of the applicant's involvement in each extreme political group.

A distinction needs to be drawn between laying off civil servants who have a permanent contract, and dismissing those on probation. In *Vogt v Germany*,[401] this distinction was clearly decisive. There, the Court found that it went too far to dismiss a secondary-school teacher on the ground of her political affiliation to a German communist party (DPK). Her discharge would make it almost impossible for her to find a teaching post, depriving her of her livelihood. Another crucial element was that she was a teacher of

---

[390] Id, para 76 Com Rep.   [391] *Ibid.*   [392] Id, paras 77 and 86.

[393] See eg, *Vogt v Germany* A 323 (1995) 21 EHRR 205 para 53 GC.

[394] Id, para 51; and *Otto v Germany* No 27574/02 hudoc (2005) DA.

[395] *Glasenapp v FRG* A 104 (1986); 9 EHRR 25 para 53 PC.   [396] Lester, above n 39 at p 475.

[397] A 105 (1986); 9 EHRR 328 para 115 Com Rep.

[398] See dissenting opinion of Judge Spielmann in the *Glassenapp* case, paras 24 and 39, who stressed a more meticulous appraisal of such factors as the nature of the post held by the applicant, her behaviour, the circumstances in which the disputed opinion was made, and the nature of the opinion.

[399] Id, para 111.   [400] Id, para 128.   [401] A 323 (1995); 21 EHRR 205 para 61 GC.

languages, a post which did not intrinsically pose any security threat. Further, the DPK was not prohibited by the Federal Constitutional Court. The German system of control was perceived as too categorical in applying to all civil servants irrespective of their function and rank, and disallowing separation between service and private life. Further, such a stringent duty of loyalty was not imposed in any other member states of the Council of Europe. Nevertheless, the German system of loyalty control as such has yet to be called into question. In the subsequent case of *Otto v Germany*,[402] where a police officer complained of the non-promotion to a senior position due to his active involvement in an extreme right-wing party, the emphasis was placed again on the 'duties and responsibilities' of a civil servant. Clearly, the severity of the measure imposed on civil servants is crucial in these cases.[403] As compared with the more serious impact on the applicant in the *Vogt* case (the loss of livelihood), in the *Otto* case, the Court found the contested measure of non-promotion to be proportionate.[404]

III. DUTIES AND RESPONSIBILITIES OF JOURNALISTS

With respect to journalists, the Court has consistently stressed their 'duties and responsibilities' to act in good faith to provide accurate and reliable information in accordance with ethics of journalism.[405] The concept 'duties and responsibilities' of journalists is closely linked to the requirement that 'they are acting in good faith to provide accurate and reliable information in accordance with the ethics of journalism'.[406] Aside from the question of accuracy, which is more empirically ascertainable in case of quotation or citation from an original source, perhaps a more intriguing question would be the extent to which the press can reasonably regard its sources as reliable.[407] There inevitably remain questions as to the extent of precision or trustworthiness that is expected of journalists quoting or citing information from another source. As will be seen shortly in the analysis of the *Bladet Tromsø and Stensaas* case, the Court's preferred course is to adopt its own autonomous and general guidelines on this matter, rather than leaving it to national judicial discretion. The notion of the 'duties and responsibilities' of the press has been frequently invoked to reinforce the claim that measures encroaching on press freedom are necessary for protecting the honour and reputation of individual persons, or their right to private and family life.[408] As will be analyzed in the context of defamation, with regard to an affront to honour and reputation of individuals caused by allegedly defamatory statements, the Court has scrupulously appraised the nature, degree, and effect of such statements.

The Court has stressed that journalists' speech should not be subordinated to the requirement that they must systematically and formally distance themselves from the content of a quotation that might insult, provoke others, or damage their reputation. Such a rigorous requirement would clearly be at odds with the principle that the widest possible scope of protection must be accorded to the press and journalistic expression.[409]

---

[402] *No 27574/02* hudoc (2005) DA.

[403] Apart from the cases of *Vogt* and *Otto*, see also *Wille v Liechtenstein* 1999-VII (refusal by the Prince to re-appoint the President of the Administrative Court because of his statement on a constitutional controversy).

[404] The Court noted that the applicant was promoted several times, and that the contested refusal of his non-promotion occurred at a very advanced stage of his career: *Otto v Germany No 27574/02* hudoc (2005).

[405] See eg, *Bladet Tromsø and Stensaas v Norway* 1999-III; 29 EHRR 125 para 65.

[406] See *Goodwin v UK* 1996-II; 22 EHRR 123 para 39 GC and *Fressoz and Roire* 1999-I; 31 EHRR 28 para 54.

[407] *McVicar v UK* 2002-III; 35 EHRR 566 para 84.

[408] See *Von Hannover v Germany* 2004-VI; 43 EHRR 1 para 63.

[409] *Thoma v Luxembourg* 2001-III; 36 EHRR 359 paras 58–63.

The *Verlagsgruppe News GmbH v Austria*[410] case arose from the forfeiture of a magazine. In his open letter, an artist criticized the politicians of the Austrian Freedom Party (FPÖ), describing them as 'dastardly'. The applicant news company quoted this letter when reporting the FPÖ's defamation proceedings against the artist. The Court held that the mere reproduction of the controversial wording, coupled with sharp critical comments, did not provide sufficient basis for forfeiting the magazine; the requirement applied by the Austrian courts that journalists had systematically and formally to distance themselves from the content of a quoted passage, which might be insulting, was considered too formalistic to be seen proportionate.

A vexed question in this context is to what extent the press is required, according to journalistic ethics and diligence, to carry out independent research to verify the accuracy or truthfulness of the information that it prints. It is of special import in this connection to juxtapose the cases of *Bladet Tromsø and Stensaas v Norway*[411] and *Standard Verlagsgesellschaft mbH v Austria (No 2)*.[412] In the former case, the issue arose from the publication of a minister-appointed inspector's report concerning seal-hunting in local newspaper articles, which highlighted acts of cruelty to seals committed by seal-hunters (including allegations of the flaying of seals alive and the unlawful killing of female harp seals) and an alleged assault on the inspector by the crew. The inspector's report accused the crew members of the seal-hunting vessel, without identifying the names of those allegedly implicated in the acts of cruelty. The Ministry of Fisheries issued an order, temporarily exempting the report from public disclosure to give the accused seal-hunters an opportunity to reply to the accusations. The independent Commission of Inquiries, set up to investigate the issue, found that the three serious accusations described above were not proven. It also turned out that some crew members were not on board. The Norwegian courts held that the reproduction of the expert's report was damaging to the reputation and honour of the crew members of the vessel and convicted the newspaper company and its editor of defamation. The question was whether the newspaper was required to undertake an independent research to establish factual basis for the allegations made in the inspector's report, or whether there were any special grounds that would exempt it from verifying factual statements that were defamatory of private individuals. The Norwegian courts found that by failing to establish the truth of the allegations, the applicants did not comply with the ethics of journalism.

The Grand Chamber considered that the allegations concerning the seals being flayed alive and hunters' assault on the inspector were serious. Nevertheless, it moderated their libellous effect, noting that they could be comprehended by readers as an exaggerated presentation. In the majority's view, the applicants' decision not to publicize the names of those accused of having committed the cruelty detracted from the defamatory impact. Paradoxically, some crew members of the vessel, who were not on board at the material time, argued that their reputation was infringed, because the articles mentioned the name of the vessel, so that the blame was laid on the entire crew members. In relation to the reliability of the impugned report, the Grand Chamber considered that the report was an official one, with the expert appointed as an inspector by the Ministry of Fisheries. It held that, in the light of its public watchdog role, the press was normally entitled to rely on the contents of official reports without need to engage in independent research.

Three dissenting judges[413] pointed out that the majority of the Grand Chamber gave scant regard to the reputation of the private individuals. Given the paramount interest of press freedom in a democracy, it was essential, *as a general principle*, that the press should

---

[410] Hudoc (2006) para 33.   [411] 1999-III; 29 EHRR 125 para 68.   [412] Hudoc (2007).
[413] Joint dissenting opinion of Judges Palm, Fuhrmann, and Baka.

be exonerated from undertaking inquiries into the details of an official source. However, it is questionable whether this general principle can be applied to *all* situations in which the reputation of private persons is at stake and where, as in this case, a newspaper has reproduced the contents of publicly inaccessible reports in disregard of a ministerial order explicitly banning such disclosure. The Grand Chamber held that the applicants were exempted from verifying the accuracy or precision of the reported facts, finding no sufficient ground to justify the interference. In contrast, the three dissenting judges took the view that the majority minimized the fact that after the ministerial order of non-disclosure, the newspaper consciously took the risk of publishing the articles without checking the veracity of the contested claims.

In *Standard Verlagsgesellschaft mbH (No 2)*,[414] the applicant company, which was the owner of the daily newspaper *Der Standard*, published an article attributing administrative misconduct to Jörg Haider, who was serving in a regional government. The Austrian courts found the contested statements to be incorrect factual statements and defamatory. They found that the applicant company had used an expert opinion in a one-sided manner. The article cited the expert opinion as reporting that Mr Haider deliberately deceived the regional government even though that expert opinion did not contain such allegations. The applicant company argued that it relied on a press release of the Socialist Party, which summarized the expert opinion incorrectly. The Austrian courts ordered the forfeiture of the relevant issues of *Der Standard*, the publication of the judgment and the revocation of the untrue statements.

In its judgment in the case, with respect to the 'duties and responsibilities' of journalists, the Strasbourg Court held that:

> special grounds are required before the media can be dispensed from their ordinary obligation to verify factual statements that are defamatory of private individuals. Whether such grounds exist depends in particular on the nature and degree of defamation in question and the extent to which the media can reasonably regard their sources as reliable with respect to the allegations....[415]

On the facts of the case, the Court held that the allegations in the article were false statements of fact and serious accusations of a defamatory nature, going beyond exaggerations or provocations. The Court distinguished the case from *Bladet Tromsø and Stensaas v Norway*. Statements by political opponents of Mr Haider were not considered comparable to the reports prepared by a government-appointed expert in the latter case. The lack of journalistic diligence was compounded by the failure to identify the press release as the source of citation and to verify the veracity of the information in the expert opinion even though this was available. By a close vote of four to three, the Court found no violation of Article 10. The three dissenting judges stressed journalists' entitlement to rely on press releases as a vital source of information for the media.[416] The applicant's misunderstanding of the expert opinion could have been corrected by the publication of a counter-statement, requested by Mr Haider. Because of the vital nature of journalistic freedom, it was crucial that such a less burdensome alternative should have been sought before immediate recourse to civil proceedings against the journalists.

In *Radio France v France*,[417] the duties of journalists to provide 'accurate and reliable information' were further clarified. Again, the main question was whether the bounds of

---

[414] Hudoc (2007).
[415] Id, para 38. See also *Pedersen and Baadgaard v Denmark* 2004-XI; 42 EHRR 486 para 78.
[416] Joint dissenting opinion of Judges Rozakis, Vajić, and Spielmann, para 6.
[417] 2004-II; 40 EHRR 706 para 37.

exaggeration or provocation were overstepped in reporting information originating from another source. The weekly magazine *Le Point* published an article stating that Michel Junot, a former deputy mayor of the Paris City Council, had supervised the maintenance of order during the Second World War in a town where a thousand Jewish people were interned before their deportation to Auschwitz. A journalist with France Info, a radio station of Radio France, reported that, according to *Le Point,* Mr Junot supervised the deportation of a thousand Jewish people in 1942. The French courts convicted the publishing director of France Info and a journalist for defaming Mr Junot. While *Le Point* mentioned the transport of Jews 'under Junot's responsibility', France Info went further in broadcasting that Mr Junot 'admits that he organised the departure of a transport of deportees to Drancy'.[418] The Court found that such a change in wording and connotations could not be justified on the basis of a 'degree of exaggeration' or 'provocation' because this constituted a dissemination of false information. When unanimously finding no violation of Article 10, the Court held that in view of the extremely grave allegations, the repeated form in which the information was broadcast and the immediate and powerful impact of audio-visuals, the journalists were required to act with utmost care and special moderation.

8. DISTINCT METHODOLOGIES AND PRINCIPLES DEVELOPED TO EXAMINE ISSUES OF DEFAMATION

I. OVERVIEW

Clearly a contracting party may interfere with freedom of expression under Article 10(2) to sanction defamatory statements in their civil or even criminal law in order to protect 'the rights of others.' The limits to such interference have been spelt out by the Court in an abundance of cases in which statements have been held to be defamatory by national courts, especially ones instituted against journalists and the press. These provide a number of methodologies and doctrines that are worthy of separate examination. The first step of the Court is to examine whether the defamatory statement relates to an issue of general public interest, in which case curtailment of it must be stringently assessed. In this connection, the notion of public interest has been broadly construed. It is also well established in the case law that rulings that statements are defamatory of politicians invite a particularly stringent review. No European minimum threshold below which it would be unjustifiable under Article 10 to impose a criminal sanction for defamatory expression has been established by the Court.[419]

In assessing the proportionate nature of a national measure adopted in response to an defamatory or insulting statement, the Court will examine: (i) the nature of the interference; (ii) the position of the applicant, and the status of the victim of defamation or insult; (iii) the subject matter of the contested statements; and (iv) the reasons for the interference, provided by the national authorities.[420] There are numerous other factors, including the medium or form of communications and the background against which the

---

[418] Id, para 38.

[419] Macdonald, in Matscher and Petzold, eds, *Protecting Human Rights: The European Dimension—Studies in Honour of Gérard J Wiarda,* 1988, p 361 at 368.

[420] *Scharsach and News Verlagsgesellschaft GmbH v Austria* 2003-XI; 40 EHRR 569 para 31.

contested statement is made. With respect to the medium or form of expression, audio-visual communications are considered to entail more immediate and direct impact on the audience. At the same time, statements which could be described as offensive if expressed in a written form,[421] may not overstep the boundaries of acceptable criticism if they are made orally, particularly when they are a spontaneous reaction in the course of heated debates.[422] Clearly, there is little scope for reformulating or retracting oral words before publication.[423] As regards the background, or context, within which the contested words need to be assessed, as affirmed in *Nilsen and Johnsen*,[424] special regard must be had to the question whether the allegedly defamatory statements have been made as a result of, or in response to, previous acerbic criticism, so as to counter what may be perceived as unfounded accusations.

The nature and extent of the publicity attached to the defamatory or insulting statement is a key to assessing the permissible reaction by the state.[425] In *Lindon, Otchakovsky-Laurens and July v France*,[426] it was not deemed objectionable that even the mere act of reproducing a defamatory statement could yield criminal liability. One of the rationales for this was that the medium used was a national newspaper with broad public appeal. In *Yankov v Bulgaria*,[427] it was disproportionate to impose a disciplinary punishment on a detainee who used insulting words to describe the personnel of the penitentiary and judiciary system in his private manuscript, which was far from being ready for publication. In *Grigoriades v Greece*,[428] an army officer was convicted of insulting the army, after writing a letter to his commanding officer, which contained some unpalatable passages, including the description of the army as 'a criminal and terrorist apparatus'. Despite the harsh tone of his accusations, the Grand Chamber held in his favour, giving special weight to the fact that the impugned letter was neither published nor disseminated to a wider audience.

Confronted with the conflict between press freedom and the honour of public figures, the Court generally accords the press a privileged status. It is an established principle in the case law that journalists' freedom of expression under Article 10 can encompass a degree of exaggeration, or even provocation, on their part.[429] This principle has been applied by analogy to members of civil society, such as NGO campaigners, who are also entitled to 'a certain degree of hyperbole and exaggeration'.[430] However, as already noted,[431] the Court has frequently made reference to the duties and responsibilities of the press to act 'in good faith and on an accurate factual basis', and to provide 'reliable and precise' (or 'accurate and reliable') information in accordance with the ethics of journalism.[432] The press must not abuse its freedom of expression in order to make gratuitous personal attacks. Nevertheless, journalistic expression made in good faith does not forfeit its privileged status unless there is no element of truth underlying the words considered

---

[421] *De Diego Nafria v Spain* hudoc (2002) para 41. See also *Katamadze v Georgia No 69857/01* hudoc (2006) DA.

[422] *Fuentes Bobo v Spain* hudoc (2000) para 48.

[423] *Nilsen and Johnsen v Norway* 1999-VIII; 30 EHRR 878 para 48 GC.   [424] Id, para 52.

[425] *Yankov v Bulgaria* 2003-XII; 40 EHRR 854. See also eg, *Nikula v Finland* 2002-II; 38 EHRR 944 para 52.

[426] Hudoc (2007) para 66 GC. See further below, pp 506–7.

[427] 2003-XII; 40 EHRR 854 paras 135–41.

[428] 1997-VII; 27 EHRR 464 para 47. Cf, the dissenting opinion of Judge Sir John Freeland, joined by Judges Russo, Valticos, Loizou, and Morenilla, para 7.

[429] See eg, *Prager and Oberschlick v Austria* A 313 (1995); 21 EHRR 1 para 38; *Perna v Italy* 2003-V; 39 EHRR 563 para 39 GC; and *Lindon, Otchakovsky-Laurens and July v France* hudoc (2007) para 62 GC.

[430] *Steel and Morris v UK* 2005-II; 41 EHRR 403 para 90.   [431] See above, p 496.

[432] *Bladet Tromsø and Stensaas v Norway* 1999-III; 29 EHRR 125 para 62; *Colombani v France* 2002-V, para 65; *McVicar v UK* 2002-III; 35 EHRR 566 para 73; *Hachette Filipacchi Associés v France* hudoc (2007). See also *Shabanov and Tren v Russia* hudoc (2006) para 40.

offensive and insulting.[433] With respect to the duty to act on an 'accurate factual basis', the extent to which journalists are expected to prove the veracity of information that they disclose has been analyzed above in relation to their duties and responsibilities.[434]

A crucial question is whether on the facts of a particular case the contested statements remain within the ambit of acceptable criticism on matters of public concern, or instead constitute abusive attacks on the personality of individuals. In some cases, the nature, content, tone, and context of the contested statements are clearly not such as to cause them to be deemed insulting or defamatory. For instance, a lawyer's critical comment that the decision of the Moldovan Constitutional Court would cause 'total anarchy in the legal profession' in encroaching on the independence of legal profession was hardly insulting enough to overstep the limits of acceptable criticisms.[435] When assessing the boundary between acceptable criticism and gratuitous attacks, the Court distinguishes between factual elements and value-laden elements, the crucial question that will be examined below.

II. PUBLIC PERSONS AND BROADER BOUNDS OF ACCEPTABLE CRITICISM

a. Political figures and the public status doctrine

The Court has not fully adopted the US 'public figures' doctrine, according to which a successful claim for defamation by public officials will only be consistent with freedom of expression where malice is demonstrated.[436] Nevertheless, the essence of this doctrine has been implicitly introduced in the case law and developed into a distinct form, which can be aptly baptized as a 'public status doctrine' in the Convention context. However, it is clear that once politicians or civil servants withdraw from their political or civic life, they regain the status of private persons entitled to a broader scope of privacy rights.[437]

It is well established that the permissible pale of criticism of politicians is broader than it is for private individuals.[438] The rationale is that, unlike private persons, politicians knowingly choose to become public figures exposed to close scrutiny by journalists and the general public.[439] Politicians must accordingly display greater tolerance of criticisms made by the press and the public.[440] If the contested expression is described as political or civil in nature or based on press freedom, robust review may intervene,[441] with the Court displaying greater vigilance in discovering any chilling effect of an interfering measure.[442] This is especially true when journalists or the press are accused of defamation of politicians.[443] Even the conditional discontinuation of criminal proceedings against a journalist may be considered to constitute a form of censorship that may deter press

---

[433] *Feldek v Slovakia* 2001-VIII paras 81 and 84.   [434] See above, pp 496–7.

[435] *Amihalachioaie v Moldova* 2004-III; 40 EHRR 833 para 36.

[436] See *New York Times v Sullivan* 376 US 254 (1964). See also Macdonald, above n 419.

[437] *Tammer v Estonia* 2001-I; 37 EHRR 857 para 68.   [438] *Brasilier v France* hudoc (2006) para 41.

[439] *Lingens v Austria* A 103 (1986); 8 EHRR 407 para 42 PC; *Oberschlick v Austria (No 1)* A 204 (1991); 19 EHRR 389 paras 57–9 PC; *Vereinigung Demokratischer Soldaten Österreichts and Gubi v Austria* A 302 (1994); 20 EHRR 56 para 37; *Oberschlick v Austria (No 2)* 1997-IV; 25 EHRR 357 para 29; *Incal v Turkey* 1998-IV; 49 EHRR 449 para 54 GC; *Hrico v Slovakia* hudoc (2004); 41 EHRR 300 para 40; *Turhan v Turkey* hudoc (2005) para 25; and *Brasilier v France* hudoc (2006) para 41.

[440] See, *inter alia, Dąbrowski v Poland* hudoc (2006) para 35.

[441] See, *inter alia, Turham v Turkey* hudoc (2005) para 25.

[442] See eg, *Lingens v Austria* A 103 (1986); 8 EHRR 407 para 44 PC; *Brasilier v France* hudoc (2006) para 43.

[443] See eg, *Lingens v Austria*, id, para 44.

freedom, if a criminal record remains.[444] In *Dąbrowski v Poland*,[445] a journalist was convicted of defamation after publishing newspaper articles reporting criminal proceedings against a local politician. He described the allegedly defamed mayor as 'mayor burglar', but only after the trial court had found the mayor guilty of burglary. In finding a breach of Article 10, the Court gave special weight to the journalist's entitlement to a certain degree of exaggeration, and to the expectation that the mayor, as a public figure, should have displayed a greater degree of tolerance to criticism, some of which were classified as value-judgments not devoid of factual basis.

The first *cause célèbre* in the field of defamation of politicians was the case of *Lingens v Austria*.[446] In this case, the Austrian Chancellor (ie Prime Minister) had described the Jewish Documentation Centre as a 'political mafia' when its President, Simon Wiesenthal, had reproached the President of the Austrian Liberal Party, with whom the Chancellor was seeking to arrange a post-election coalition, for having served in the SS during the Second World War. The applicant was convicted of criminal defamation when he accused the Chancellor of 'the basest opportunism' and of acting in an 'immoral' and 'undignified' manner. The Plenary Court held unanimously that the conviction was a disproportionate restriction upon freedom of expression, relying on the principle that political figures must tolerate a greater extent of criticism than private individuals. Against the background of heated political debates, the applicant's expressions, though offensive, were not deemed defamatory. The criminal sanction was all the more disproportionate because the applicant was required to prove the truth of his value-judgments relating to matters of political concern.

Similarly, in other cases involving defamation of politicians, the Court has boldly undertaken an independent and critical examination of national decisions.[447] In the second *Oberschlick* case,[448] a journalist was convicted of defaming the then leader of the Austrian Freedom Party, Jörg Haider, for describing him as an 'idiot'. Once again, the Commission and Court stressed the broad bounds of acceptable criticism of a politician.[449] The decisive factor was that the contested word was not classified as a 'gratuitous personal attack' in a polemical tone, but as an 'opinion' (hence value-judgment) worthy of protection under Article 10.[450] The emphasis was shifted to the *overall* context in which the expression was used.

As explained below, when participating in public debates, private persons must also tolerate greater extent of criticisms. In *Österreichischer Rundfunk v Austria*,[451] the applicant was a public law foundation which broadcast information on the release on parole of the head of a neo-Nazi organization in Austria. The news item also mentioned his deputy, S, who had been convicted and sentenced to a lengthy term of imprisonment for being a leading member of a neo-Nazi organization, but had been released on parole earlier. The broadcast showed S's picture for a couple of seconds, together with information about his conviction. At S's request, the national courts ordered the applicant to refrain from publishing S's picture without his consent following his release on parole. Holding that the injunction was a breach of Article 10, the Court stated that even though S was a private individual, the fact that he was a well-known neo-Nazi activist warranted the application of the public status doctrine.

---

[444] *Dąbrowski v Poland* hudoc (2006) paras 3.   [445] Id, paras 33–5.

[446] A 103 (1986); 8 EHRR 407 paras 42–3 PC, and also paras 74, 81–4 Com Rep.

[447] Apart from the second *Oberschlick* case discussed in the text, see eg, *Turham v Turkey* hudoc (2005) paras 24–30.

[448] 1997-IV; 25 EHRR 357.   [449] Id, para 29. See also *Turham v Turkey* hudoc (2005) paras 25–7.

[450] *Oberschlick v Austria (No 2)* 1997-IV; 25 EHRR 357 para 33.   [451] Hudoc (2006) para 65.

b. Civil servants and the public status doctrine

Civil servants must be shielded from any abusive and defamatory attacks that are intended to impinge on their performance of duties and to damage public confidence in them.[452] The Court has suggested that the bounds of permissible criticism of civil servants under Article 10 depend on the scope and nature of the public authorities concerned and the powers entrusted to them.[453] Unlike politicians, civil servants do not lay themselves open to public scrutiny. They also require public confidence in performing their duties.[454]

Nevertheless, the Court has held that it is reasonable to assume that the public status doctrine can be applied by analogy to civil servants entrusted with certain administrative powers. Civil servants who exercise certain powers must tolerate greater criticism directed against their words and deeds.[455] When confronted with defamation proceedings filed by civil servants, the Court must closely ascertain whether there exists a real risk that an impugned remark may perturb public confidence in their performance. A case in which the parallel with politicians was held not to apply was *Janowski v Poland*.[456] In that case, a journalist was convicted for orally insulting 'municipal guards', who were civil servants, during a heated exchange in a public place about the exercise by the guards of their law enforcement powers to move street traders on. The Court accepted that civil servants may need protection from offensive and abusive verbal attacks if they are successfully to perform their tasks and, on the facts of the case, the requirements of such protection did 'not have to be weighed in relation to the interests of the freedom of the press or of open discussion of matters of public concern since the applicants' remarks were not uttered in such a context'.[457] Judge Bratza, in his dissenting opinion, persuasively argued that the applicant used virulent words as a spontaneous reaction in a heated exchange, rather than as a 'deliberate and gratuitous personal attack' on the guards.[458] In contrast, once civil servants or judges run for election, they are clearly to be considered as having entered the 'political arena' so that they must endure greater bounds of public criticism.[459]

It is also essential that the accountability of government-appointed experts, albeit non-elected, should be subject to constant scrutiny. Yet, the proposal that the public status doctrine ought to be applied on the basis of their function *as such* was not taken up by the Court in *Nilsen and Johnsen v Norway*.[460] In that case, the Court held that it was not the activity of the government-designated expert in question that could justify treating him as akin to a politician who had to tolerate close scrutiny. What was decisive for broadening the bounds of acceptable criticism of his work was his participation in public debates, which went beyond the remits of his duty as an appointed expert. As the expert in question himself contributed to a heated public discussion, he had to tolerate a greater degree of exaggeration.

III. DISTINCTION BETWEEN STATEMENTS OF FACT AND VALUE-JUDGMENTS

When confronted with statements that national courts have found defamatory, libellous, or insulting, the Court firstly examines whether such statements are to be categorized as

---

[452] *Busuioc v Moldova* hudoc (2004); 42 EHRR 252 para 64.   [453] Id, paras 64–5.

[454] *Raichinov v Bulgaria* hudoc (2006) para 48.

[455] *Steur v Netherlands* 2003-XI; 39 EHRR 706 para 39.   [456] 1999-I; 29 EHRR 705.

[457] Id, para 33.

[458] Dissenting opinion of Judge Sir Nicolas Bratza joined by Judge Rozakis. Cf, the approach of the Commission, which stressed that the amount of the fine was excessive: id Com Rep para 46.

[459] *Hrico v Slovakia* hudoc (2004); 41 EHRR 300 para 46; and *Kwiecień v Poland* hudoc (2007) paras 52 and 54.

[460] This was the reasoning adopted by the Commission: 1999-VIII; 30 EHRR 878 Com Rep.

factual assertions or value-judgments. Factual statements require proof of their truth, raising the questions of the burden of proof and of the evidentiary standard for applicants. On the other hand, value-judgments such as opinions and comments are regarded as not susceptible of proof.[461] In *Krone Verlag*,[462] the Court acknowledged that the distinction between value-judgments and factual statements was blurred and intractable in many cases, and that the issue needed to be resolved by examining the degree of factual proof. After all, such difficulty is inevitable, as 'rights are mediators between the domain of pure value judgements and the domain of factual judgements'.[463]

When classifying certain statements as value-judgments or as allegations of fact, the Court has desisted from succumbing to the margin of appreciation doctrine.[464] The recent case law suggests the Court's preparedness to undertake a scrupulous examination of the contested statements to identify elements that can be described as value-judgments. This can often take the form of disaggregating the contested statement into different elements and appraising whether each of its components can amount to a value-judgment.[465] If such an approach had been applied to *Tolstoy Miloslavsky v UK*,[466] the applicant, who was a historian, could have successfully challenged the injunction preventing him from disseminating his research outputs, including the allegation of a war crime committed in the aftermath of the Second World War by a warden of a prestigious English school. In that case, when finding the balance to be upset, the Court focused instead on the absence of 'adequate and effective safeguards' against the award of an exorbitant sum for libel.

Generally, the Court has applied a liberal construction, favouring freedom of expression, by recognizing a broad meaning of the notion of value-judgment, especially where the expression rights of a journalist or a politician are in issue. In *Jerusalem*,[467] where a local politician remarked that sects shared totalitarian character and fascist tendencies, Austrian courts found her remark to be a statement of fact which was not proven true, and so amounted to defamation. In contrast, the Court described it as a value-judgment and a fair comment on matters of general public interest, not requiring proof of its truth. In *Hrico v Slovakia*,[468] a journalist published articles in a weekly periodical, criticizing a decision of the Slovakian Supreme Court which found that a poet defamed a government minister when accusing the latter of having a fascist past. He described this decision as 'a legal farce', noting that it was explicable partly by the presiding judge's political candidacy for the Christian-Social Union party, which failed to condemn Slovakia's fascism during the Second World War. This led to legal proceedings against him, and he was ordered to make public apology and to pay compensation. The Court classified the contested statement as an opinion, even if overblown, hence a value-judgment whose truth could not be proven. Even with respect to private persons, the Court's readiness to recognize elements of value-judgments can be seen. As discussed above, in *Paturel*,[469] a member of the Jehovah's Witnesses compared the method of 'deprogramming' proposed by an association aiding victims of religious sects to the Soviet method of psychological

---

[461] See, *inter alia, De Haes and Gijsels v Belgium* 1997-I; 25 EHRR 1 para 47; *Nilsen and Johnsen v Norway* 1999-VIII; 30 EHRR 878 paras 49–50 GC; and *Hrico v Slovakia* hudoc (2004); 41 EHRR 300 para 40.

[462] *Krone Verlag GmbH & Co KG and MEDIAPRINT Zeitungs- und Zeitschriftenverlag GmbH & Co KG v Austria No 42429/98* hudoc (2003) DA. See also *Katamadze v Georgia No 69857/01* hudoc (2006) DA.

[463] Kennedy, *A Critique of Adjudication—fin de siècle*, 1997, p 305.

[464] *Amihalachioaie v Moldova* 2004-III; 40 EHRR 833 para 36.

[465] See eg, *Busuioc v Moldova* hudoc (2004,); 42 EHRR 252 paras 70–1, 74–5, 78–9, 81–5, 90–3.

[466] A 316-B (1995); 2 EHRR 442. The Court upheld the injunction: id, paras 49–50 and 54.

[467] *Jerusalem v Austria* 2001-II; 37 EHRR 567 para 44. The Court also found a sufficient factual basis for this: id, para 45. See also *Sokolowski v Poland* hudoc (2005) para 47.

[468] Hudoc (2004); 41 EHRR 300 paras 40 and 45–6.

[469] *Paturel v France* hudoc (2005) para 37. See above, p 458.

internment of dissidents. Such a description may be staggering, yet the Court favoured the free speech rights by classifying it as a value-judgment rather than as a statement of fact.

The broad interpretation of the notion of value-judgments to favour the press and journalistic expression can be reinforced by the public interest nature of the impugned article *taken as a whole*. In *Scharsach and News Verlagsgesellschaft GmbH v Austria*,[470] a magazine article described those persons who had an ambiguous relation to National Socialist ideas as 'closet Nazi', referring, among others, to Mrs Rosenkranz, an Austrian Freedom Party (FPÖ) politician. The Austrian courts considered the term 'closet Nazi' a statement of fact. They took a highly formalistic and narrow interpretation of this term, holding that it called for clandestine Nazi activities. They ruled that, in the absence of any proof of such activities by Mrs Rosenkranz, the use of this term went beyond the acceptable bounds of journalistic criticism. In contrast, the Court considered the contested term a value-judgment, which was supported by sufficient facts. In particular, Mrs Rosenkranz was an extreme right-wing politician, who publicly criticized the National Socialism Prohibition Act. The Court found that the degree of precision that the Austrian courts required for establishing the well-founded nature of a criminal charge was incompatible with the journalistic expression dealing with a matter of public interest.

In contrast, where the disparaging statements of fact voiced in a newspaper article are motivated by a competitive intention, this may weaken the claim that they are value-judgments. In *Krone Verlag GmbH & Co KG and MEDIAPRINT Zeitungs- und Zeitschriftenverlag GmbH & Co KG v Austria*,[471] the applicant newspaper company published an article virulently criticizing an article of another newspaper which, written by a history professor, defended an exhibition concerning the crimes committed by the Wehrmacht during the Second World War. The applicant company's impugned article contained such statements as 'A Salzburg professor...—a Waldheim persecutor—praises this exhibition.... anyone who ... has been guilty of such criminal falsification ... deserves our utter contempt.' The Austrian courts found the article not only to contain untrue and disparaging statements of fact but also to be written with a competitive aim. The contents of the article, which related to the exhibition that caused public uproar in Salzburg, were surely of public interest. Yet, the Court, endorsing the national courts' decision, found that the public interest of the article was outweighed by the defamatory statements aggravated by a competitive aim.

IV. 'SUFFICIENT FACTUAL BASIS'

Once the contested statements are found to include value-judgments, the next task of the Court is to ascertain whether there is a 'sufficient factual basis' to support them.[472] Even value-judgments require at least some factual grounds.[473] When an applicant has made a *prima facie* case for some factual basis, the onus is shifted to the government to refute such a basis. Once the facts have come to the public knowledge, the requirement to adduce the facts on which a value-judgment is premised becomes of less importance.[474] The necessity of linkage between a value-judgment and its supporting facts may

---

[470] 2003-XI; 40 EHRR 569 paras 39–43.   [471] Hudoc (2003) DA.

[472] See eg, *Jerusalem v Austria* 2001-II; 37 EHRR 567 para 43; *Sokolowski v Poland* hudoc (2005) para 48; and *Lindon, Otchakovsky-Laurens and July v France* hudoc (2007) para 55.

[473] See eg, *Turhan v Turkey* hudoc (2005) para 24; *Shabanov and Tren v Russia* hudoc (2006) para 41.

[474] *Feldek v Slovakia* 2001-VIII para 86.

vary, depending on the specific circumstances of the case.[475] For instance, the fact that a mayor was examined by a national tribunal for fraudulent manoeuvres concerning a ballot was regarded as sufficient for the allegation that he stole the election.[476] Similarly, the revelations of false accusations of police brutalities, which cast doubt on the research methodology of a government-appointed expert, were held to constitute sufficient factual ground for harsh criticisms made by the representatives of police organizations against that expert to defend their reputation and honour.[477]

The rigour with which the sub-test of sufficient factual basis is applied may vary, according to the close connection between the contested remarks and matters of public interest.[478] Special note must be taken of another sign of maturing methodology. The case law suggests that the evaluation of the public interest nature of the contested statements can be integrated into the process of examining the two stages (the distinction between factual allegations and value-judgments; and the sufficient factual basis for value-judgments).[479] In relation to markedly privileged expression such as political expression, and journalistic or press freedom,[480] the Court has not recoiled from: (i) broadening the notion of public interest; and (ii) undertaking a detailed analysis of controversial statements to identify both value-judgments and some (even limited) factual basis for supporting them. With respect to the expression rights of journalists, describing a local politician as 'burglar mayor' in newspaper articles was not considered devoid of any factual basis, if there was a finding by a trial court that he was guilty of burglary. In such cases, special regard must be had to the question whether the statements disclose any elements of gratuitous personal attacks or any intention to offend or humiliate the criticized politician.

The assessment of the defamatory nature or otherwise of a reality novel, which, while using fictional characters, is based on real events, poses delicate questions as to the pertinence of the disjunction between value-judgments and facts, and the extent to which the factual basis needs to be established. The case of *Lindon, Otchakovsky-Laurens and July v France*[481] concerned a novel entitled 'Jean-Marie Le Pen on Trial', in which the ex-chairperson of the far-right political party was likened to the 'chief of a gang of killers' and portrayed as a 'vampire'. The book noted that he 'advocated' the murder of an immigrant, which was committed by a fictional character. The author of the book and the chairperson of the board of directors of the publishing company were convicted of defamation and complicity in defamation respectively. The French courts dismissed the defence of good faith because of the failure of the first two applicants to carry out sufficient investigations into the allegations of fact and to use dispassionate language. The Grand Chamber took the view that the contested words revealed not only value-judgments but also allegations of fact, requiring investigations into the sufficient basis of the allegations. Special weight was placed on the virulent nature of the contested words, which were considered such as to indicate the intention of stigmatization and liable to stir up violence and hatred. These words were held to exceed the tolerable limit of political debate. According to the Grand Chamber, even against the background of fierce political struggles, it was legitimate for the French courts to try to ensure a minimum degree of moderation and propriety, 'especially as the reputation of a politician, even a controversial

---

[475] *Wirtschafts-Trend Zeitschriften-Verlags GmbH v Austria (No 3)* hudoc (2005) para 35.
[476] *Brasilier v France* hudoc (2006) paras 38 and 41.
[477] *Nilsen and Johnsen v Norway* 1999-VIII; 30 EHRR 878 paras 50–1 GC.
[478] *Amihalachioaie v Moldova* 2004-III; 40 EHRR 833 para 35.
[479] For such an overall and synthesized approach, see *Kobenter and Standard Verlags GmbH v Austria* hudoc (2006) para 30.
[480] See eg, *Dąbrowski v Poland* hudoc (2006) paras 33–5.   [481] Hudoc (2007) para 55.

one, must benefit from the protection afforded by the Convention'.[482] The majority of the Grand Chamber concluded that the penalty imposed on the applicants was relevant and sufficient so as not to disclose a violation of Article 10.[483] The medium of the impugned expression was a fiction, rather than a news report. As the four dissenting judges noted,[484] serious doubt remains as to whether the majority duly took account of this, so as not to stifle the role of artistic creation in political debates. The dissenting judges pointed out that the distinction between fact and value-judgment 'becomes *partly* pertinent when the novel and the reality coincide'.[485]

In the *Lindon* case, the publishing director of *Libération* (the third applicant) was convicted of defamation as well. The Grand Chamber accepted that his conviction was justified on the ground that *Libération* published a petition that reproduced extracts from the novel, which the domestic court found defamatory. Whether or not the bounds of acceptable 'provocation' had been transgressed was examined on the basis not only of the nature and the content of the impugned passages. Account was taken of other factors such as the potential impact of reproducing the defamatory passages in a widely circulated newspaper. The Grand Chamber noted that the 'duties and responsibilities' of the journalists to provide 'reliable and precise' information in accordance with the ethics of journalism became pivotal when assessing attacks of the reputation of a specific individual. The majority endorsed the national courts' finding, noting that:

> special grounds are required before the media can be dispensed from their ordinary obligation to verify factual statements that are defamatory of private individuals. Whether such grounds exist depends in particular on the nature and degree of the defamation in question and the extent to which the media can reasonably regard their sources as reliable with respect to the allegations.[486]

The implication of the majority's conclusion is to detract from the established principle that public figures, even though entitled to the protection of their reputation under Article 8, must endure greater extent of criticisms. As compared with the first two applicants, the blameworthiness imputable to the third applicant lay merely in publishing the extracts of the passages that the domestic courts found defamatory. He was not the author of the petition. As noted in dissent, there is a serious risk that imposing criminal sanctions, albeit moderate in nature, in itself, yields chilling effects on journalists whose vigilance of the politicians is essential for healthy democracy.[487]

V. PROOF OF THE TRUTH OF CONTESTED STATEMENT

Journalists accused of defamation are required to provide *prima facie* reliable evidence for supporting their claim, failing which the Court may demand the proof of the veracity of allegations.[488] As stated in *Steel and Morris v UK*,[489] it is 'not in principle incompatible with Article 10 to place on a defendant in libel proceedings the onus of proving to the civil standard the truth of defamatory statements', namely that the statement is 'substantially

---

[482] Id, para 57.

[483] Id, paras 58 and 60 (thirteen votes to four). The Court also found the amount of the fine to be moderate: id, para 59.

[484] Partly dissenting opinion of Judges Rozakis, Bratza, Tulkens, and Šikuta. They referred to *Vereinigung Bildender Kunstler v Austria* hudoc (2007) para 33.

[485] Id, para 5, emphasis added.   [486] *Loc cit*, above n 481 para 67.

[487] Id, partly dissenting opinion of Judges Rozakis, Bratza, Tulkens, and Šikuta, paras 4 and 7.

[488] *McVicar v UK* 2002-III; 35 EHRR 566 para 86.   [489] 2005-II; 41 EHRR 403.

true on the balance of probabilities'.[490] Nevertheless, as examined in the context of 'duties and responsibilities', they are not required to establish the truth of *all* aspects of information they report in the press. In *Thorgeir Thorgeirson v Iceland*,[491] the applicant was convicted of defaming the police by publishing articles stating that the Reykjavik police force was involved in serious assaults and other criminal offences. His conviction was based on his failure to establish the truth of allegations concerning police brutalities. The Court exempted him from establishing the accuracy of some allegations made in strong language, adducing several rationales. The applicant was reporting what was being said by others. He was not deemed responsible for the content of the allegations. Nor was it established that the allegations were entirely false. The nature of the information disseminated in the press was considered of serious public concern. Further, the purpose of the applicant was not held to damage the reputation of the police but essentially to urge the Minister of Justice to initiate an inquiry into alleged police brutalities.

Clearly, the onus and the standard of proof imposed on journalists and the press to establish the veracity of contested statements are keys to a proportionality appraisal. This can be demonstrated by *Dichand v Austria*.[492] In a newspaper article, the applicants criticized a lawyer and the secretary-general of the Austrian People's Party, stating that he violated 'moral concepts' in democracies by refusing to give up his job at a law firm when becoming a member of the government, and that he was involved in amending the law giving advantage to his clients. National courts found these statements to be an insult, granting an injunction that obliged the applicants to retract certain statements and not to repeat them. The Court found that the contested statements were value-judgments related to public interest. It ruled that the criticisms, although harsh, nonetheless remained within the bounds of acceptable criticism under Article 10. The applicants were required under Austrian law to establish that the amendment to the law in question *exclusively* served the interests of his clients. Such an onerous burden of proof was decisive for the Court to find a violation of Article 10.[493]

In relation to statements considered false assertions of facts, the Court may take into account whether the applicants were responsible for the production or publication of such statements, and whether they intended to deceive other persons through such information. In *Salov v Ukraine*,[494] the applicant, one of the presidential candidates for Ukraine, was convicted and sentenced on account of having imparted false information. In an article disseminated in a copy of a 'forged newspaper', he noted that the incumbent president had died of an alcohol-related disease, and that a *coup d'état* by his 'criminal entourage' ensued. The Court recognized that the impugned article contained false factual statements. Nonetheless, special weight was given to the fact that the contested information was not produced by the applicant, and that domestic courts failed to establish that he intended to deceive voters during the 1999 presidential elections. The impact of the information was also minor, as he possessed only limited copies of the newspaper, which were addressed to a very small number of persons. The Court emphasized that Article 10 safeguards even the information received, which may be strongly suspected of being untrue. Further, the nature and severity of the penalty were found to be very grave. In the light of these facts, the reason for the interference was deemed not only insufficient but also irrelevant.

It should be noted, however, that where contested statements are manifestly insulting or defamatory of specially protected persons, such as judges or prosecutors, the Court's

---

[490] *McVicar v UK*, id, para 87.   [491] A 239 (1992); 14 EHRR 843 para 65.
[492] Hudoc (2002) para 52.   [493] Id, para 50.   [494] Hudoc (2005) para 113.

appraisal can be fixed on the question whether defendants have proved the veracity of their statements. In *Perna v Italy*,[495] the Grand Chamber was confronted with the conviction of a journalist for having defamed a public prosecutor, Mr Caselli. The latter brought proceedings against a well-known politician Mr Andreotti, who was accused of aiding and abetting the Mafia. In a newspaper article, the applicant suggested that Mr Caselli knowingly committed an abuse of authority in indicting Mr Andreotti, pursuant to the Italian Communist Party's partisan strategy, referring to Mr Casselli's 'ideological blinkers'. The applicant never established that the conduct that he attributed to Mr Caselli actually took place. The contested statements as a whole were considered factual assertions, and the whole text clearly besmirched Mr Caselli's honour and reputation. It may be argued that the disparaging tone and nature of the contested article was so manifest as to dispense with both the analysis of the contested article and the laborious task of teasing out elements that were value-judgments as opposed to factual statements.

VI. SOME SALIENT APPROACHES DEVELOPED TO ESTABLISH THE VERACITY OF CONTESTED STATEMENTS

When ascertaining the truth of statements that national authorities have found defamatory, the Court may apply either of the following methodologies to retain the elevated standard of protection given to the freedom of expression: (i) the broad and liberal interpretation of the notion of value-judgments; (ii) the overall evaluation of the contested statements; (iii) de-emphasizing the distinction between factual statements and value-judgments in relation to political expression; and (iv) side-stepping the question whether or not (part of) the impugned statement is defamatory and focusing instead on a disproportionate element of the measures taken to sanction it.

The first such methodology was demonstrated in *Unabhängige Initiative Informationsvielfalt v Austria*.[496] There, the applicant association published a periodical, which included a leaflet calling on readers to send the FPÖ politicians 'small gifts in response to their racist agitation'. The Austrian courts granted an injunction preventing the applicant from repeating the remark in question, describing the words 'racist agitation' as an insult to the reputation and honour of Mr Haider. They characterized the words as statements of fact, demanding that their veracity had to be established in a manner akin to the proof of a criminal offence of incitement to hatred. In contrast, the Court classified the contested words not as a gratuitous personal attack, but as a value-judgment made in reaction to a political discussion on immigration controls. It held that the degree of precision required for establishing the well-founded nature of a criminal charge should not have been applied to the duty of journalists to verify the sufficient basis of their opinions on a matter of public interest. No sufficient ground was found to justify the injunction.

The second methodology, based on an overall appraisal, is propitious in circumstances where disparaging words appear isolated in the contested statements.[497] Focusing on the overall context in which such words are expressed enables the Court to treat the statements as a whole as value-judgments immune from the requirement of establishing their truth. In *Schwabe v Austria*,[498] a member of the Austrian People's Party was convicted of

[495] 2003-V; 36 EHRR 563 paras 13 and 47.   [496] 2002-I; 37 EHRR 710 paras 9 and 41.
[497] *Nikula v Finland* 2002-II; 38 EHRR 944 para 44; *Skałka v Poland* hudoc (2003); 38 EHRR 1 para 35.
[498] A 242-B (1992) paras 14 and 34.

defamation. In a press release, he argued that a member of the Austrian Socialist Party had remained in public office even after committing a serious traffic accident whilst under the influence of alcohol. He added that this should have disentitled the Socialist's critical remarks against the applicant's colleague who remained in office despite his conviction for a similar offence. The Austrian courts held that the words 'while under the influence of alcohol' suggested the conviction of drunken driving after consuming more than the limit of alcohol, and that the applicant failed to prove the veracity of his statements along this casuistic line of interpretation. The Court, based on an overall evaluation, conflated facts and elements of value-judgments in Schwabe's statements and classified all of them as 'a value-judgment for which no proof of truth is possible'.[499] While no doubt salutary, this conclusion leaves the question in what circumstances such an overall approach can be applied to expand the parameters of value-judgments. This question is of special merit because, unlike the First Amendment to the US Constitution, the Court has so far refrained from providing absolute protection to value-judgments.[500]

The third methodology is to consider the distinction between factual statements and value-judgments of little import in assessing political debates. This salient methodology was advanced in *Lombardo v Malta*,[501] which involved the conviction of elected members of a local council for defamation and libel against a mayor. The thrust of the Court's reasoning was that 'the distinction between statements of fact and value judgments is of less significance ... where the impugned statements are made in the course of a lively political debate at local level and where elected officials and journalists should enjoy a wide freedom to criticise the actions of a local authority, *even where the statements made may lack a clear basis in fact*'. It remains to be seen whether this suggests a *general* approach, so that the requirement of establishing the accuracy of statements of fact can be dispensed with, every time the contested statements are judged to form part of political debates on matters of public interests.

According to the fourth methodology, even in the absence of proof of the veracity of serious allegations classified as statements of fact, the Court may focus on the nature and severity of sanction which may not strike the right balance, making the interference disproportionate. In *Steel and Morris v UK*,[502] two campaigners of London Greenpeace, who distributed leaflets containing serious allegations against McDonald's, ended up in defending themselves against the mighty multinational in defamation proceedings. The absence of legal aid for defamation resulted in a gross inequality of arms, disabling them from carrying out an effective defence of their case. This, together with the possible chilling effect that the substantial sum of damages awarded against them would have on their right freely to circulate information of public interest, led the Court to find a violation of Article 10. It is not, however, clear whether, if given sufficient legal aid, the applicants could have successfully established the veracity of their allegations that the Court classified as factual statements, such as their contention that McDonald's was accountable for health, environment, and labour problems. Nevertheless, such a question was immaterial for the Court's examination that spotlighted the disproportionate impact of the unfair proceedings on the applicants' free speech. This fourth methodology thus ingeniously bypasses difficult questions for the Court (and the applicant) concerning the establishment of the truth of allegations.

---

[499] Id, para 34. Cf, para 55 Com Rep.   [500] Macdonald, above n 419, at 367–8.
[501] Hudoc (2007) para 60, emphasis added.
[502] 2005-II; 41 EHRR 403 paras 95–8. See further above, p 458.

VII. DENIAL OF THE OPPORTUNITY TO PROVE
THE TRUTH OF ALLEGATIONS

Where a penal sanction is imposed on the basis that the factual statements are false, denying the defendants the opportunity to prove the truth of the allegations contravenes Article 10. In *Castells v Spain*,[503] the applicant was a senator and a member of a Basque nationalist party supporting the independence of the Basque country. In newspaper articles, he contended that the police were responsible for the murder of Basque activists, and that the right-wing government in Madrid was behind the impunity of perpetrators. He was convicted of criminal offences involving serious insults to the government and public servants. He complained that he was denied the opportunity to establish the truth of his criticism. The Court also held that because of 'the dominant position' held by the government, there was a special need to restrain recourse to criminal sanctions against a politician and to apply less burdensome measures in response to unjustified attacks or criticisms.[504] On close scrutiny of the judgment, it did not matter whether the allegations were true or false. It was the denial of the opportunity to try to establish the truth of his allegations, combined with the chilling effect on political expression and press freedom, which was crucial.[505]

In *Colombani v France*,[506] the French daily newspaper *Le Monde* published an article that summarized a report commissioned by the European Commission. The article cited a report to assert that the Moroccan royal family assumed 'direct responsibility' for the lucrative business of drug trafficking. Upon the request of the King of Morocco, the public prosecutor took action against the editor-in-chief of *Le Monde* and the author of the article, and they were found guilty of the offence of publicly insulting a foreign head of state. The applicants' main contention was that under the French law, unlike the position in the ordinary law of defamation, there was no defence of justification—that is to say proving the truth of the allegation—where the charge was insulting a foreign head of state. The Court found that the absence of such a defence upset the proportionality balance.

9. CONCLUSION

The foregoing survey suggests that an array of dynamic and refined methodologies and interpretive techniques have been devised by the Court to give enhanced effectiveness to the protection of freedom of expression. The nature and the form of expression, together with the position of persons exercising their right to free speech, will continue to be the lynchpin for assessing the standard of review and the choice of methodologies. Yet, these considerations are far from conclusive. Indeed, the interplay of numerous factors involved in free speech cases adds great complexity to an area in which the Court has already been experimenting with reasoning particular to Article 10 and with innovative interpretive devices. These make it difficult to draw general inferences from the case law and to present a coherent theoretical framework. Furthermore, the Court cannot be impervious to such exogenous factors as changing social attitudes, technological developments, and the emergence of common European regulatory frameworks.

---

[503] A 236 (1992); 14 EHRR 445 paras 12, 47–8.   [504] Id, para 46.

[505] Id, paras 48–50. Cf, the concurring opinion of Judge Pekkanen, paras 3 and 4; and concurring opinion of Judge de Meyer, paras 3 and 4 (emphasis on the conviction of the applicant for having disseminated his political opinion).

[506] 2002-V para 66.

Despite the robust decision-making policy that has unfolded since the late 1990s, the Court's case law leaves some questions unanswered. A general right of access to information held by public bodies has yet to be recognized under Article 10. How much European consensus will the Court require before it is persuaded to depart from its negative case law on this point? Or does the Court feel unable to recognize such a right at all, considering that it is beyond the bounds of teleological interpretation to recognize such a right? Issues concerning the defamation of public figures and the disclosure of their privacy by the press[507] will continue to shape the body of case law that pits free speech rights against privacy rights. A question which the Court may be called upon to address is whether or to what extent the scope of application of the public status doctrine can be expanded to cover artists, celebrities in show business and sports, and popular newsreaders on television. One may attribute different weight to the privacy rights of those persons who possess certain public profiles and who are situated in the intermediate range between politicians and ordinary private individuals.[508] Further, there is a lack of European consensus on what weight can be ascribed to the free speech rights of the entertainment press or tabloids, which are primarily interested in increasing commercial gains by satisfying their readers' voyeuristic tendencies. This poses a delicate question whether it is necessary or legitimate for the international judicial organ in Strasbourg to categorize and protect different types of national or local press on the basis of the newsworthiness of contents and their readership without being charged with arbitrariness and elitism.

Other questions concern the concept of 'public interest', which is crucial to the application of Article 10. For example, in the case of 'category crossover', such as hybrid expression that is essentially commercial in nature but can be seen as having a 'public interest' dimension also, the identification of a 'public interest' dimension will strengthen the standard of review that would otherwise be applied by the Court in a case of purely commercial expression.[509] Yet the Court has so far appeared content intuitively to invoke the notion of 'public interest' without formulating reasoned argument for determining what exactly amounts to such interest.[510] This approach entails a haze of vagueness. To what extent the notion of 'public interest' is autonomous under the Convention and broad enough to embrace diverse social needs cannot be uniformly diagnosed. Arguably, such amorphous nature has proven to be a practical advantage in enabling the Court to invoke this notion as a vehicle for providing semblance of explanation for the enhanced protection accorded to free speech in convoluted cases.

Finally, in an overstated 'paradigm' of a post-September 11 world, an increasing securitization of societies faced with a perceived or real threat of terrorism has seen many European nations hastily rush to enact anti-terrorism laws with sweeping powers of stop, search, arrest, and detention. There is a legitimate fear that this may yield a corrosive effect on the Court's critical stance when assessing interferences with freedom of expression, as with other Convention rights. Rather than causing a stasis in the creativity of interpretational doctrines, a newly instituted form of 'militant democracy' within states may lead to a veiled attempt on their part to roll back the *acquis* of freedom of expression. Macklem cautions against the propensity of the militant democracy readily to resort to preventive intervention in an across-the-board fashion, which presents itself as an *ad hoc* exercise of interest balancing. He suggests that even confronted with terrorists or other subversive associations, their political agendas should be appraised not *ex ante* and in

[507] *Von Hannover v Germany* 2004-VI; 43 EHRR 1.
[508] See eg, Sanderson, 6 EHRLR 631 at 636–7 (2004).   [509] See above, pp 464–5.
[510] Sanderson, *loc cit*, above n 508, at 638.

an abstract manner, but as close to the threshold between concrete proposal and policy as possible, so that a close regard is had to disaggregated components such as timing, context,[511] and the probability of harmful impact of their activities.

Another related element of controversy relates to hate speech or incitement to violence in the dimension of a secular Europe, at a time when its multicultural premise is being increasingly challenged. At what juncture can an applicant exercising free speech be said to fall short of, or run counter to, the requirement of tolerance and pluralism? As the repercussions of the Danish cartoon case vividly illustrate, the risk of auto-censorship of the press faced with perceived threats of inter-religious or inter-ethnic violence cannot be brushed aside.

[511] Macklem, *above* n 108, at 513–14.

12

ARTICLE 11: FREEDOM OF ASSEMBLY AND ASSOCIATION

Article 11

1. Everyone has the right to freedom of peaceful assembly and to freedom of association with others, including the right to form and to join trade unions for the protection of his interests.

2. No restrictions shall be placed on the exercise of these rights other than such as are prescribed by law and are necessary in a democratic society in the interests of national security or public safety, for the prevention of disorder or crime, for the protection of health or morals or for the protection of the rights and freedoms of others. This article shall not prevent the imposition of lawful restrictions on the exercise of these rights by members of the armed forces, of the police or of the administration of the state.

1. INTRODUCTION

Article 11 protects the two distinct, if sometimes connected, freedoms of peaceful assembly and association.[1] They are sufficiently different to be treated separately but they share the objective of allowing individuals to come together for the expression and protection of their common interests. Where those interests are political in the widest sense, the function of the Article 11 freedoms is central to the effective working of the democratic system. In particular, it provides for the creation and operation of political parties, interest groups, and trade unions which serve as diverse centres of power, and for the propagation of ideas and programmes, from among which others may choose and by which influence may be exerted on the holders of public power for the time being. Equally, Article 11 protects the right of individuals to assemble and to associate for the furtherance of their personal interests, be they economic, social, or cultural. The same ends are sought: the effective enjoyment of a diversity of interests. Article 11 makes specific reference to trade unions, the roles of which overlap considerably between the political and the economic interests of their members. The Court and Commission regard the rights of trade unions as being embraced within the general freedom of association but, since certain matters particular to trade unions have arisen in the case law, they will be treated separately.

---

[1] See Tomuschat, *European System*, Ch 19, pp 493–513 and Lewis-Anthony, in *Freedom of Association*, Rekjavik Seminar Proceedings, reprinted in 33A YB 27 (1994).

2. FREEDOM OF PEACEFUL ASSEMBLY

Article 11 protects the right to freedom of peaceful assembly as a 'fundamental right',[2] whether it is exercised for political,[3] religious or spiritual,[4] cultural,[5] social,[6] or other purposes. It covers private and public meetings,[7] including marches,[8] demonstrations,[9] and sit-ins.[10] The holding of public meetings and the mounting of demonstrations through marches, picketing, and processions has played a significant part in the political history of European states. Events in Central and Eastern Europe in recent decades show the continued potency of these activities. It is true that much orthodox politics has moved to the private meeting and the orchestrated occasion, the impact of which depends upon transmission through the news media. However, public meetings and demonstrations are a tool for those outside the established parties, whose direct access to the media is limited but who may be able to gain attention by staging '*événements*' which capture the television and newspaper headlines,[11] while ritual and commemorative events continue to play a part in the expression of minority consciousness[12] and the manifestation of religious beliefs.[13]

The content of any message which the organizers wish to project is not, of itself, a reason for regarding the occasion as being outside the scope of Article 11. The Court has said that the freedom of assembly guaranteed under Article 11 must be considered in the light of Article 10, the protection of opinions and the freedom to express them being one of the objectives of freedom of assembly. Thus freedom of assembly under Article 11 protects an assembly that 'may annoy or give offence to persons opposed to the ideas or claims that it is seeking to promote'.[14] Nor is the form of the assembly of importance.[15] The only limitation is that the assembly must be 'peaceful'. Occupation of a building that in itself is peaceful even though it is clearly in breach of domestic law may be regarded as a 'peaceful' assembly.[16] Even disruption incidental to the holding of the assembly will not render it 'unpeaceful', whereas a meeting planned with the object of causing disturbances

---

[2] *Rassemblement Jurassien Unité Jurassienne v Switzerland No 8191/78*, 17 DR 93 at 119 (1979) and *Djavit An v Turkey* 2003-III; 40 EHRR 1002 para 56.

[3] Eg, *Cissé v France* 2002-III.

[4] Eg, *Barankevich v Russia* hudoc (2007); 47 EHRR 266 and *Pendragon v UK No 31416/96* hudoc (1998); 27 EHRR CD 179.

[5] Eg, *Gypsy Council v UK No 66336/01* hudoc (2002); 35 EHRR CD 96.   [6] *Ibid.*

[7] *Rassemblement Jurassien Unité Jurassienne v Switzerland No 8191/78*, 17 DR 93 at 119 (1979) and *Djavit An v Turkey* 2003-III; 40 EHRR 1002.

[8] *Christians against Racism and Fascism v UK No 8440/78*, 21 DR 138 at 148 (1980).

[9] *Oya Ataman v* Turkey 2006-XIV.

[10] *G v FRG No 13079/87*, 60 DR 256 (1989). See also *Cissé v France* 2002-III (lengthy occupation of premises).

[11] See eg, *Cissé v France* 2002-III.

[12] See eg, *Stankov and The United Macedonian Organization Ilinden v Bulgaria* 2001-X; *United Macedonian Organization Ilinden and Ivanov v Bulgaria* hudoc (2005); 43 EHRR 119; and *Ivanov and Others v Bulgaria* hudoc (2005).

[13] *Barankevich v Russia* hudoc (2007); 47 EHRR 266.

[14] See *Plattform 'Ärzte für das Leben' v Austria* 44 DR 65 (1985); 13 EHRR 204 para 32 and *Stankov and The United Macedonian Organization Ilinden v Bulgaria* 2001-X paras 85–6.

[15] *Djavit An v Turkey* 2003-III; 40 EHRR 1002 para 60 (exhibitions, concerts, fairs, seminars, and receptions organized other than by the participants were assemblies, not mere gatherings for entertainment or occasions to enjoy the company of others, as they had a common aim: to bring Turkish and Greek Cypriots together with a view to resolving the conflict in Cyprus. Nor was the capacity in which the applicant attended the gatherings relevant to the question of whether there was an 'assembly' for the purposes of Article 11).

[16] *Cissé v France* 2002-III.

will not be protected by Article 11.[17] The line between the two may not be clear. The Commission held that a non-violent sit-in, blocking the entrance to American barracks in Germany, did count as 'peaceful assembly', so interference with it required justification under Article 11(2).[18]

For the authorities, freedom of assembly raises a number of problems, especially where public meetings and marches are involved. These pose threats to public order through the disruption of communications and activities, the prospect of confrontation with the police, and the danger of violence with rivals, they claiming, of course, their own freedom to demonstrate. It is this last situation which raises particular difficulties under Article 11(1).

I. POSITIVE OBLIGATIONS

There is a positive duty on a state to protect those exercising their right of freedom of peaceful assembly from violent disturbance by counter-demonstrators.[19] This duty is imposed to ensure the right to freedom of assembly provided under Article 11 is effective.[20] Because both sides may claim to be exercising Article 11 rights, initially this may be a duty to hold the ring between rival meetings or processions, but if one of them is aimed at disruption of the activities of the other, the obligation of the authorities is to protect those exercising their right of peaceful assembly. *United Macedonian Organization Ilinden and Ivanov v Bulgaria*[21] indicates what may be required to discharge the duty. In this case individual participants in a commemoration ceremony were physically attacked and their property damaged by counter-demonstrators. The police had formed a cordon to keep the two groups apart but failed to prevent the incidents. In the Court's view 'the authorities appeared somewhat reluctant' to protect the participants in the ceremony from the counter-demonstrators. In these circumstances the Court unanimously held that Article 11 had been violated because the authorities had failed to discharge their positive obligations to take 'reasonable and appropriate measures to enable lawful demonstrations to proceed peacefully'.[22] Presumably other measures the police could take in such a situation are to give warnings to those causing trouble and/or proceed to arrest the perpetrators of the violence. The threat of disorder from opponents does not of itself justify interference with the demonstration.[23] Indeed the failure to take preventative measures to neutralize the threat may weigh heavily against the necessity of a prohibition on the demonstration.[24] Nevertheless, the requirements of this positive duty leave a good deal to the discretion of the authorities. The Court has said that the reasons given by them for imposing an unconditional ban on a counter-demonstration instead of

---

[17] *Christians against Racism and Fascism v UK No 8440/78*, 21 DR 138 at 150 (1980) and *Stankov and The United Macedonian Organization Ilinden v Bulgaria* 2001-X para 77.

[18] *G v FRG No 13079/87*, 60 DR 256 at 263 (1989). See also *Osmani v FYRM* 2001-X, where a public meeting was considered a 'peaceful assembly' although it played a 'substantial part' in the occurrence of the violent events that followed. The issue in *Osmani* was whether the prosecution and conviction of the applicant following riots occurring over one month after the meeting was justified under Article 11(2): for the facts, see below, p 525.

[19] *Plattform 'Ärzte für das Leben' v Austria No 10126/82*, 44 DR 65 at 72 (1985); 13 EHRR 204 para 32; *G v FRG No 13079/87*, A 139 (1988); *United Macedonian Organisatiozn Ilinden and Ivanov v Bulgaria* hudoc (2005); 43 EHRR 1119 para 115; and *Barankevich v Russia* hudoc (2007); 47 EHRR 266 paras 32 and 33.

[20] *United Macedonian Organization Ilinden and Ivanov* id, para 115 and *Barankevich*, id, para 32. See generally Mowbray, 1999 PL 703–25.

[21] hudoc (2005); 43 EHRR 1119.   [22] Id, para 115.

[23] *Christians against Racism and Fascism v UK No 8840/78*, 21 DR 138 at 148 (1980).

[24] *Barankevich v Russia* hudoc (2007); 47 EHRR 266 para 33. See also *Öllinger v Austria* 2006-IX; 46 EHRR 849 para 48.

taking preventative measures will be subject to intense scrutiny,[25] otherwise the fact that action may have to be taken in anticipation of possible disturbances or, in other cases, that policing measures must be taken at short notice leaves a wide margin of appreciation to the state to decide what Article 11(1) requires in a particular case.[26]

One issue is whether there is a positive obligation on a state to require private individuals to allow the exercise of peaceful assembly by others on their property. As a freedom, in principle peaceful assembly confers no obligations on, say, owners of private halls, to make them available (on hire or not) to political groups for meetings. In *Anderson v UK*[27] a commercial company, which leased a shopping centre from the local council, obtained an injunction forbidding the applicants, a group of young men, from entering the centre for an indefinite period on the grounds of their misconduct and disorderly behaviour at the centre. In finding that the exclusion of the applicants had not interfered with their rights under Article 11, the Commission said there was no support for the argument that freedom of assembly is 'intended to guarantee a right to pass or re-pass in public places, or to assemble for purely social purposes *anywhere* one wishes'. Further, the Commission took into account the fact that the applicants had 'no history of using the Centre for any form of organised assembly or association'.[28] The decision in *Anderson* undoubtedly had a harsh impact on the applicants as the town was their place of residence and the centre occupied approximately two thirds of the town's centre and contained not only shops, but also basic facilities used by the applicants, such as banking and electricity services. In the later case of *Appleby v UK*[29] it was precisely for the purposes of 'organized assembly', rather than for 'purely social purposes', that the applicants sought access to a shopping mall owned by a private company. The applicants contended that their rights to freedom of expression and assembly had been violated when the corporation refused them permission to distribute leaflets and collect signatures at the shopping mall in order to protest against the development of local playing fields. In particular, they argued that the state had indirect responsibility for the interference with their rights as it was a public company that had transferred, with ministerial approval, the mall to the corporation. The issue before the Court was, therefore, whether the state had failed in any positive obligation to protect the exercise of those rights from interference by the owner of the property. The determination of this question, the Court reasoned, required a balance to be struck between the applicants' Convention rights and the property rights of the owner of the shopping centre under Article 1 of the First Protocol. It held that Article 10 rights, and by implication Article 11 rights, do not confer 'any freedom of forum' for the exercise of the right, nor do changing modes of social interaction require 'the automatic creation of rights of entry to private property'.[30] However, while exclusion from quasi-public places is not itself a violation of Convention rights, the Court said a positive obligation to regulate property rights might arise in exceptional situations where a restriction on access to private property 'has the effect of preventing any effective exercise' of the right or when 'it

[25] *Öllinger*, id, paras 44 and 48, where the Court said the requirement for 'particular justification' was at its most pressing since the organizer of the meeting was a member of parliament expressing an opinion on an issue of public interest.

[26] *Plattform 'Ärzte für das Leben' v Austria No 10126/82*, 44 DR 65 at 74 (1985); 13 EHRR 204. The Court in this case held that there was not even an 'arguable' claim that the authorities had failed in their positive duty sufficient to raise an issue under Article 13: A 139 (1988) paras 34–9.

[27] *No 33689/96* hudoc (1997); 25 EHRR CD 172. Declaring the complaint under Article 11 inadmissible, the Commission indicated that freedom of movement under Article 2 of Protocol 4 might be more relevant.

[28] Id, para 1 (emphasis added).

[29] 2003-VI; 37 EHRR 38, in which the Court examined the case under Article 10, but said that 'largely identical considerations' arose under Article 11.

[30] Id, para 47.

can be said that the essence of the right has been destroyed'.[31] The Court cited 'a corporate town where the entire municipality is controlled by a private body' as an example of when the positive obligation could arise.[32] Only Judge Maruste in dissent said that the state had a responsibility to limit private property rights that have been created by it, subject only to the 'reasonable' exercise of Convention rights and freedoms. The decision in *Appleby* indicates that the Court will require proof of the complete negation of an applicant's Convention rights before it will limit the owner's proprietorial right to exclude others. The circumstances in *Appleby* did not qualify, as there were alternative places for collecting signatures and alternative means of campaigning; the applicants could not claim that they were 'effectively prevented from communicating their views' to others. The cases of *Anderson* and *Appleby* indicate that when the right of freedom of assembly and the right to protection of property are to be balanced against one another the exercise of the right of assembly may be circumscribed in deference to the full exercise of the property right.

II. RIGHTS OF THIRD PARTIES

An interesting issue arises where the exercise of the right of freedom of peaceful assembly impacts upon other Convention rights of third parties. In *Öllinger v Austria*[33] the domestic authorities imposed a total ban on a small meeting organized by a member of parliament and planned for All Saint's Day at a Salzburg cemetery so as to coincide with a ceremony held by Comradeship IV to commemorate SS soldiers who were killed in the Second World War. The purpose of the applicant's meeting was to remember the crimes committed by the SS and to commemorate the Jews killed by SS members. The meeting was to be 'silent', conducted only by the use of messages attached to the garments of those assembled and without chants or banners. Previous similar meetings at Comradeship IV ceremonies had resulted in heated discussions between the groups. It was undisputed that there was no justification for banning the meeting to protect the rights of Comradeship IV; rather the issue was characterized as one of balancing the interests of counter-demonstrators under Article 11 against the rights of others visiting the cemetery to manifest their religion under Article 9. The Austrian Constitutional Court had held that the unconditional prohibition of the meeting was justified in order to protect members of the public who would be visiting the graves of their relatives in the exercise of their religion. Although the Constitutional Court had recognized proportionality as the principle for resolving the issue, the European Court considered too much weight had been given by it to previous incidents between Comradeship IV and counter-demonstrators and to the solemn nature of All Saint's Day for the general population. In particular, the Court thought it important that the Constitutional Court had failed to accord any weight to the far-reaching nature of the unconditional prohibition on the meeting when assessing the reasons for its imposition, particularly given its impact upon the expression of an opinion on a matter of public interest by a member of parliament. Further, the majority considered the subdued manner in which the counter-demonstration was to be conducted, the absence of the threat of violence, and the intended target of the counter-demonstration also to be relevant factors in determining the proportionality of the interference. The availability of policing measures to prevent disruption was a further reason for deciding that the prohibition failed to strike a fair balance between the interests notwithstanding the state's wide margin of appreciation in this area. Thus, the extent of the interference, the nature of the assembly, and the availability of ways to

[31] Id, para 47.   [32] *Ibid.*
[33] 2006-IX; 46 EHRR 849 paras 46–8, by six votes to one. See generally Mead, 2 EHRLR 133–45 (2007).

monitor the assembly's impact on the rights of cemetery-goers favoured the freedom of assembly. However, in his dissenting opinion Judge Loucaides' questioned whether the majority conclusion left anything to the state's margin of appreciation. The inappropriateness of holding a political demonstration in a sacred place, the real danger of disturbance to the cemetery, and the availability of other avenues for challenging Comradeship IV assemblies, as well as his disagreement with the majority's assessment of the facts and its treatment of the domestic court's reasoning, were all factors that he considered weighed against a finding of a violation of Article 11. Certainly, in *Öllinger* the Court appears to have striven for a compromise between the two rights rather than have one right prevailing over the other, which is what a ban would have achieved.

III. INTERFERENCES WITH PEACEFUL ASSEMBLY

Because the threats to public order from the exercise of the freedom of peaceful assembly are real, the authorities may demand a variety of powers to meet or to mitigate them. These may range from requirements of prior authorization and authorization subject to conditions to complete bans.[34] Criminal penalties may be imposed for participation in assemblies held in defiance of such regulation[35] or for offences committed in the exercise of the right[36] but must satisfy the requirements of Article 11(2). The Court has rejected the contention that post-demonstration penalties do not amount to an interference with freedom of assembly.[37] Bans, because of the seriousness of the interference, will also require justification under Article 11(2).

Requirements of notification or authorization will not normally be regarded as interferences.[38] However, a refusal to authorize an assembly may be an interference with the freedom of assembly. In *Bączkowski v Poland*[39] a march and six stationary assemblies, organized to raise public awareness of discrimination against minorities, women, and disabled persons, were held on the days planned despite the mayor issuing refusals to give authorization eight and two days, respectively, before they were due to take place and the appeals against the refusals not yet being decided. Although the assemblies went ahead the Court considered that there had been an interference with the applicants' freedom of assembly. It stated that a 'presumption of legality' of an assembly constitutes 'a vital aspect of effective and unhindered exercise of the freedom of assembly and freedom of expression'.[40] Holding an assembly with an official ban in force held its risks and, in particular, there was no guarantee of official protection. The potential for the refusals to give authorization to have a 'chilling effect' on the participants in the assemblies was clear.

---

[34] Unconditional bans will require 'particular justification': *Öllinger v Austria* 2006-IX; 46 EHRR 849 para 44.

[35] *Ziliberberg v Moldova No 61821/00* hudoc (2004) DA (fine at lower end of scale for penalties not disproportionate despite harsh financial impact on applicant). Cf, *Çetinkaya v Turkey* hudoc (2006) (applicant fined for being present at a press conference which was later labelled an unlawful assembly by the authorities).

[36] *Osmani v FYRM No 50841/99*, 2001-X DA.

[37] *Ezelin v France* A 202 (1991); 14 EHRR 362 para 39 and *Osmani v FYRM No 50841/01*, 2001-X DA.

[38] *Rassemblement Jurassien Unité Jurassienne v Switzerland No 8191/78*, 17 DR 93 at 119 (1979); *Ziliberberg v Moldova No 61821/00* hudoc (2004) DA; *Oya Ataman v Turkey* 2006-XIV para 37; and *Bukta v Hungary* hudoc (2007) para 35. The Court has said that formal requirements attached to the notification procedure 'should not represent a hidden obstacle to the freedom of peaceful assembly' under Article 11: *Oya Ataman v Turkey* 2006-XIV para 38 and *Balçik v Turkey* hudoc (2007) para 49. A decision to disband a demonstration because of a lack of prior notification required by law will constitute an unjustified interference if the demonstrators do not otherwise engage in illegal conduct: *Bukta v Hungary* hudoc (2007) para 36; *Oya Ataman v* Turkey 2006-XIV paras 39, 41, and 42; and *Balçik*, id, para 52. See below, p 523.

[39] Hudoc (2007).   [40] Id, para 67.

Moreover, if a legal remedy is to ameliorate the negative effect of a ban it must take effect before the date on which the assembly is planned to be held.[41] In *Bączkowski* the legal remedy was not effective as the decision to quash the refusals for being unlawful was not made until after the date on which the assemblies were held.

IV. LIMITATIONS ON INTERFERENCES

The interference must be 'prescribed by law'.[42] In most cases this condition has been met. However, a violation of Article 11 was found in *Djavit An v Turkey*[43] because the government could not refer to any law or policy that applied to the refusals to issue permits to the applicant to allow him to cross the 'green line' into southern Cyprus to attend bi-communal meetings. Even when the interference is made with reference to law, the decisions or provisions must be shown to be lawful under domestic law otherwise the interference will offend the legality requirement.[44] In addition to the interference having a basis in domestic law, lawfulness requires that the law should be accessible and formulated with sufficient precision to enable those to whom it applies to foresee to a reasonable degree the consequences of their actions.[45] Laws conferring a discretion may be compatible with the foreseeability requirement provided the scope of the discretion and the manner of its exercise are indicated with sufficient clarity to give the individual protection against arbitrary interference.[46] The applicant in *Mkrtchyan v Armenia*[47] could not foresee his conviction and fine for holding a procession because there was no domestic legal provision or practice clearly stating whether the rules contained in the former laws of the Soviet Union, under which he was convicted, remained in force in Armenia. A finding of unlawfulness is sufficient to establish a violation of Article 11 so the Court will not proceed to examine the legitimacy of its aim or its necessity.[48]

The aims of government interferences permitted by Article 11(2) are 'the interests of national security or public safety', 'the prevention of disorder or crime', 'the protection of health or morals', and 'the protection of the rights and freedoms of others'. They have given rise to no serious difficulties for the state.[49]

The Strasbourg authorities have spoken inconsistently about the fundamental quality of the Article 11 rights and, hence, the need to interpret them widely, while conceding a 'fairly broad' margin of appreciation to states to assess the necessity of any limitation of peaceful assembly. The Court has allowed states the widest latitude in their assessment of the necessity of restrictions where the assembly intentionally causes disruption to activities.[50]

---

[41] Id, para 68. The Court also unanimously found that the failure of domestic law to ensure the applicants could obtain a ruling on the refusals before the date of the planned assemblies violated Article 13 in conjunction with Article 11.   [42] See generally above, Ch 8.

[43] 2003-III; 40 EHRR 1002. See also *Adali v Turkey* hudoc (2005) para 274.

[44] *Bączkowski v Poland* hudoc (2007) paras 70–1.

[45] *Galstyan v Armenia* hudoc (2007) paras 106–7 (public order offences sufficiently precise).

[46] *Rai, Allmond and 'Negotiate Now' v UK No 25522/99* hudoc (1995); 19 EHRR CD 93 (scope of broad statutory power conferred to regulate the use of a public place for assemblies, and subject to a policy of restricting demonstrations relating to Northern Ireland, indicated with sufficient precision).

[47] Hudoc (2007) para 43.   [48] See further, eg, *Bączkowski v Poland* hudoc (2007) para 72.

[49] Except in the *Greek* case, 12 YB (the *Greek* case) 1 at 171 (1969); CM Res DH (70)1. In *Ezelin v France* A 202 (1991); 14 EHRR 362 para 47, the applicant claimed that proceedings had been taken against him because of his opinions and trade union affiliation but the Court was satisfied that the action was for 'the prevention of disorder'. See generally above pp 348–9.

[50] Eg, *Drieman v Norway No 33678/96* hudoc (2000) DA (fine and confiscation of property for obstruction of commercial whaling amounting 'to a form of coercion' declared inadmissible) and *Nicol and Selvanayagam v*

522   ARTICLE 11: FREEDOM OF ASSEMBLY AND ASSOCIATION

If a peaceful assembly concerns the expression of opinions on a question of public interest the necessity for the restriction has been more closely examined in recent cases.[51] In both the early cases of *Rassemblement Jurassien* and *Christians against Racism and Fascism v UK*,[52] the Commission had found that total bans on marches were justified under Article 11(2). In the first case, it pointed to the relatively narrow area and short time for which the ban had been imposed, against the evidence of tension in the area and the government's expectation of trouble. In the second case, a general ban on processions in London was directed principally at marches by the National Front, a racist group whose demonstrations had frequently been attended by violence. The applicants, against whom no aspersions were made, were simply caught in a wide ban imposed on the whole of London for two months which was framed in such terms to prevent its circumvention by the National Front. For the Commission, that was sufficient justification for the interference. Further, it said, the applicants were not precluded from holding meetings to press their point during the period of the ban on marches.

In the later case of *Stankov and United Macedonian Organization Ilinden v Bulgaria*[53] the authorities placed total bans and then conditions, including prohibitions on speeches and the use of banners, on meetings organized by the applicants to commemorate events of historical importance to the Macedonian minority in Bulgaria. Unlike *Rassemblement Jurassien* and *Christians against Racism and Fascism*, the time and place of the assemblies were crucial for the participants. However, the government sought to justify the interferences by relying on those cases when characterizing the meetings as threats to the preservation of public order owing to their potential to generate public tension between the minority and majority of the population. For the Court the fact that a ban was, at least in part, in reaction to views held or statements made by the participants, or members of the applicant association, engaged the principles for the protection of freedom of expression under Article 10 in the light of which Article 11 must be considered. The Court accepted that there might be some tension caused by the meetings but rejected as a rule that 'every probability of tension and heated exchange between opposing groups' during an assembly called for a 'wider margin of appreciation'.[54] This was so even where sensitivities involving national symbols and identity were heightened. Moreover, states had an obligation to 'display particular vigilance to ensure that national public opinion is not protected at the expense of the assertion of minority views, no matter how unpopular they may be'.[55] Nor was the reasonable prospect of separatist declarations or any expression of political ideas challenging the existing order sufficient justification for an automatic ban on assemblies. The Court said:

> In a democratic society based on the rule of law, political ideas which challenge the existing order and whose realisation is advocated by peaceful means must be afforded a proper opportunity of expression through the exercise of assembly as well as by other lawful means.[56]

UK No 32213/96 hudoc (2001) DA (two days' detention and twenty-one days' imprisonment for obstruction of leisure fishing declared inadmissible).

[51] There is little scope for restrictions on political speech: see *Stankov and The United Macedonian Organization Ilinden v Bulgaria* 2001-X para 88, especially for the elected representative: see *Osmani v FYRM No 50841/99*, 2001-X DA.

[52] No 8440/78, 21 DR 138 at 150–1 (1980). See also *Rai, Allmond and 'Negotiate Now' v UK No 25522/94* hudoc (1995); 19 EHRR CD 93 (general ban on marches relating to Northern Ireland at high profile location in London not disproportionate as alternative venues available).

[53] 2001-X.   [54] Id, para 107.   [55] Ibid.

[56] Id, para 97. See also *United Macedonian Organization Ilinden and Ivanov v Bulgaria* hudoc (2005); 44 EHRR 75 para 115 and *Ivanov and Others v Bulgaria* hudoc (2005) para 64.

The Court found no evidence that the applicant association's meetings were likely to become a platform for violence. Those statements that could be interpreted as calling for violence were considered isolated and more appropriately dealt with by prosecuting those responsible. The Court roundly rejected the government's argument that the significance of the prohibition was tempered by its flexibility in allowing the banned meetings to take place on condition there were no speeches or banners. Further, the Court was not persuaded that there was no possibility of holding official celebrations and the applicants' celebrations at the same time, timing and place being important to both groups. In circumstances where there was 'no real foreseeable risk of violent action or of incitement to violence or any other form of rejection of democratic principles' the bans on the meetings were not justified under Article 11(2); the authorities had overstepped their margin of appreciation.[57] The rationale for the Court's approach is to be found in the possibility democracy offers of 'resolving a country's problems through dialogue, without recourse to violence, even when those problems are irksome'.[58] To do otherwise would be to 'do a disservice to democracy and often even endanger it'.[59]

The idea of tolerance towards the peaceful and collective public expression of political opinions is also evident in *Oya Ataman v Turkey*[60] and *Bukta v Hungary*.[61] In *Oya Ataman* a group of fifty demonstrators held a march in a park during rush hour without giving seventy-two hours' prior notification as required by law. The demonstrators were arrested when they proceeded after being informed by police a number of times that their march was unlawful and would disrupt public order at a busy time of day.[62] The *Bukta* case involved a spontaneous demonstration in front of a hotel where the Prime Minister was attending a reception. The government contended that the demonstration was dispersed not because of the failure to give notice, as required by law, but because of a 'minor detonation' posing the possibility of a security risk. In both cases the Court found no evidence of a danger to public order beyond the level of minor disturbance to be expected at an assembly in a public place. In concluding that the dispersal of the demonstrators was not necessary in a democratic society, the Court said:

> [W]here demonstrators do not engage in acts of violence, it is important for the public authorities to show a certain degree of tolerance towards peaceful gatherings if the freedom of assembly is not to be deprived of all its substance.[63]

The Court has adopted a similar approach to restrictions placed on religious assemblies as it has to assemblies involving the dissemination of political views. In *Barankevich v Russia*[64] the Court looked at the effect of restrictions on freedom of assembly when rejecting the government's argument that it was 'necessary in a democratic society' to deny authorization for a religious service of an evangelical Christian church to be held in a town park to avoid causing discontent amongst the population as the majority practised a different religion. The Court observed that it 'would be incompatible with the underlying values of the Convention if the exercise of Convention rights by a minority group were made conditional on its being accepted by the majority'.[65] It considered that the role of the authorities in a democratic society where several religions co-exist was to be informed by 'pluralism, tolerance and broadmindedness'. These qualities required that the authorities act in a 'neutral and impartial' manner in order to ensure the competing

---

[57] Id, paras 111 and 112. See also *United Macedonian Organization Ilinden and Ivanov v Bulgaria* hudoc (2005); 44 EHRR 75 para 133.

[58] Id, para 88.   [59] Id, para 97.   [60] 2006-XIV.   [61] Hudoc (2007).

[62] On the significance of non-compliance with a formal notification requirement, see above, p 520.

[63] *Oya Ataman*, id, para 42 and *Bukta*, id, para 37.   [64] Hudoc (2007); 47 EHRR 266.

[65] Id, para 31.

groups tolerate each other; rather than removing the cause of tension by eliminating pluralism altogether.[66] Consistent with the judgment in *Stankov,* the Court found that the ban was not justified under Article 11(2) in the light of Article 9 in the absence of evidence of incitement or resort to violence by those assembled or of the use of unlawful means of conversion of others.

The limits to tolerance required by Article 11(2) were reached in *Cissé v France*[67] where 200 illegal immigrants occupied a church for nearly two months. By occupying the church, with the consent of the church authorities and without disruption to religious services, the applicants had sought to draw attention to their plight under French immigration rules.[68] In the Court's view the state had acted within its 'wide margin of appreciation' when it forcibly evacuated the immigrants from the Church because health conditions in the Church had deteriorated.[69] Furthermore, the 'symbolic and testimonial value of the applicant's and other immigrants' presence had been tolerated sufficiently long enough'.[70] While the heavy-handed method of evacuation used by the police 'went beyond what was reasonable' to curtail the assembly, the interference was nevertheless proportionate.[71]

In *Ezelin v France*[72] it was established that the imposition of penalties for participation in lawful assemblies may violate Article 11. The applicant had taken part in a demonstration in Basse-Terre (Guadeloupe) directed against the courts and individual judges. Prior notice of the march had been given and the march was not prohibited. Ezelin attended in his capacity as lawyer and trade union official, carrying an inoffensive placard. The march disintegrated into violence. Ezelin did not leave the demonstration when this happened and he refused to answer police questions in an inquiry into the events. He was reprimanded by the Court of Appeal exercising its disciplinary function over lawyers for 'breach of discretion' in not disassociating himself from the march and for not co-operating with the police. No allegations of unlawful conduct during the march were made against Ezelin. The European Court held by six votes to three that there had been a lack of proportionality between the imposition of the sanction and the need to act in the interests of the prevention of disorder. A 'just balance' must not discourage persons from making their beliefs peacefully known. The judgment is a strong one in favour of freedom of assembly, given the relatively insignificant punishment imposed on the applicant.

However, if demonstrators resort to conduct which is independently criminal, like the sit-in in *G v FRG,*[73] even if it is done with the purpose of drawing attention to the cause,

[66] *Ibid.*   [67] 2002-III.

[68] The Court rejected the argument that the illegal immigrant status of the applicant *per se* justified the interference with her right to freedom of assembly, id, para 50. See also *Oya Ataman v Turkey* 2006-XIV para 39.

[69] Id, para 51.

[70] *Ibid.* See also *Friedl v Austria* A 305-B (1995); 21 EHRR 83 (sit-in located in a busy square continued day and night for one week, where there was evidence of disruption of the progress of passers-by, was inadmissible); and *Çiloğlu v Turkey* hudoc (2007) (forceful dispersal of unlawful sit-in held every Saturday for over three years causing disruption to traffic and a breach of peace was within the state's margin of appreciation).

[71] *Ibid.*

[72] A 202 (1991); 14 EHRR 362 paras 52–3. See also *Galstyan v Armenia* hudoc (2007) paras 116–17 (three days' imprisonment for being 'present and proactive' at a lawful demonstration a violation of Article 11) and *İzmir Savaş Karşitlari Derneği v Turkey* hudoc (2006) (three months' imprisonment for failing to obtain permission to leave the country in order to attend meetings a violation of freedom of assembly and association).

[73] No 13079/87, 60 DR 256 at 263 (1989). For the facts, see above, p 517. See also, eg, *Lucas v UK No 39013/02* hudoc (2003); 37 EHRR CD 86 (minor fine for breach of peace for sitting in a public road); *Nicol and Selvanayagam v UK No 32213/96* hudoc (2001) DA (two days' detention and twenty-one days' imprisonment for breach of peace for obstructing fishing); *Drieman v UK No 33678/96* hudoc (2000) DA (fine and confiscation of boat for obstructing lawful whaling); and *McBride v UK No 27786/95* hudoc (2001) DA (arrest and detention for one and a half hours for entering upon military land during a demonstration).

Article 11(2) is unlikely to protect them against prosecutions and conviction. A dramatic illustration of where Article 11 will afford no protection from sanctions following an assembly is to be found in *Osmani v FYRM*,[74] where the Court declared inadmissible the applicant's complaint that his prosecution and conviction some months after his involvement in a public meeting had violated his right to freedom of assembly under Article 11. The applicant had organized a public meeting entitled 'defending the official use of the national flag' and addressed it in his capacity as elected mayor of Gostivar. This occurred soon after the Constitutional Court had suspended the decision of the Gostivar local council to place the Albanian and Turkish flags alongside the Macedonian flag in front of the Town Hall. In the following weeks the applicant failed to execute the Constitutional Court's order, as his duty as mayor required, and in his personal capacity became actively involved in planning and setting up crises headquarters and armed shifts for the protection of the Albanian flag. After a public riot in which there was loss of life, injury, and damage to property, the applicant was charged and convicted with the offence of 'stirring up, as a public official, national, racial and religious hatred, disagreement and intolerance'. The European Court held that the prosecution and conviction served a 'pressing social need' and that sufficient reasons were given by the authorities to justify the conviction of the applicant. In particular, the applicant's speech at the public meeting and his other actions played a 'substantial part in the subsequent violence'. Further, the Court considered that the applicant's imprisonment for one year and three months was not disproportionate in the light of the violent nature of the consequent events and the facts upon which his conviction was based, including the local council's decision to act in breach of the Constitution by displaying the flags.

3. FREEDOM OF ASSOCIATION

The right of freedom of association embraces a complex of ideas, not all of which are fully worked out in the practice under the Convention. It involves the freedom of individuals to come together for the protection of their interests by forming a collective entity which represents them. The existence of associations in which citizens can pursue common objectives collectively in the democratic process has been recognized by the Court as an important component of a healthy civil society.[75] Such an 'association' will have fundamental rights which must be respected and protected by the state[76] and will generally have rights against and owe duties to its members. An individual has no right to become a member of a particular association so that an association has no obligation to admit or continue the membership of an individual.[77] Equally, an individual cannot be compelled

---

[74] *No 50841/99*, 2001-X DA.

[75] *Sidiropoulos v Greece* 1998-IV; 27 EHRR 633 para 44 and *Gorzelik v Poland* hudoc (2004); 40 EHRR 76 para 93 GC.

[76] *Plattform 'Arzte für das Leben' v Austria No 10126/82*, 44 DR 65 at 72 (1985); 13 EHRR 204. Eg, İzmir Savaş Karşitlari Derneği v Turkey hudoc (2006) (members of association imprisoned for failing to obtain permission to leave the country to attend meetings a violation); *Grande Oriente D'Italia Di Palazzo Guistiniani v Italy* 2001-VIII; 34 EHRR 629 (law barring freemasons from applying for public office that had a minimal impact on the association a violation); and *Grande Oriente D'Italia Di Palazzo Guistiniani v Italy (No 2)* hudoc (2007) (freemasons and members of secret associations required to declare their membership when applying for public office a breach of Article 14 in conjunction with Article 11); cf, *Siveri and Chiellini v Italy No 13148/04* hudoc (2008) DA (freemasons dismissed from public office for concealing membership in breach of rules requiring a declaration of membership inadmissible).

[77] *Cheall v UK No 10550/83*, 42 DR 178 at 185 (1985); 8 EHRR 74.

to become a member of an association nor disadvantaged if he chooses not to do so.[78] This last arrangement, the so-called 'negative' freedom of association, is not specifically spelled out in Article 11(1), as it is in Article 20(2) of the Universal Declaration of Human Rights. Nonetheless, it is settled that this is the proper interpretation of Article 11(1).[79]

I. MEANING OF ASSOCIATION

The notion of 'association' has an autonomous Convention meaning. As a result, the fact that a substantive co-ordination of activities of individuals is not recognized in the national law as an 'association' will not necessarily mean that freedom of association is not at stake under Article 11. Whereas association in the sense of the right to 'share the company' of others does not qualify as 'association' for the purposes of Article 11,[80] informal, if also stable and purposive, groupings will fall within its scope.[81] However, the mere existence of separate legal status for an institution beyond that of its individual members will not necessarily implicate Article 11(1). On several occasions, the Strasbourg authorities have decided that professional associations, established by law and requiring membership of all practising professionals, are not 'associations' within the meaning of Article 11(1).[82] Amongst other things, this means that the issue of compulsory membership in such associations does not present a difficulty under the Convention. The autonomous meaning of 'association' is vital here too, because the question whether an institution is an association will not finally be decided by its classification in the national law.[83] Thus, the mere fact of incorporation under a general law mainly directed at facilitating economic enterprises is not enough to make the resulting corporate body an association; the use of the corporate structure by associations whose principal purposes are the furtherance of the non-economic interests of their members will not take them outside Article 11.[84]

II. LIMITATIONS UPON ASSOCIATIONS

As with freedom of assembly, interferences will be justified if they meet the conditions set out in Article 11(2), ie are 'prescribed by law', are for the protection of one of the objectives specified in the second paragraph, and are 'necessary in a democratic society'. These requirements will be examined in the following discussion on limitations on particular types of associations. Limitations on trade unions are considered separately under heading 4 below.

---

[78] *Young, James and Webster v UK* A 44 (1981); 4 EHRR 38 para 55 PC and *Chassagnou v France* 1999-III; 29 EHRR 615 para 117 GC.

[79] See below, p 540.

[80] *McFeeley v UK* No 8317/78, 20 DR 44 at 98 (1980); 3 EHRR 161 (concerning contact between prisoners).

[81] See, however, Tomuschat, *European System*, Ch 19, p 494, requiring 'an organizational structure'.

[82] Eg *Le Compte, Van Leuven and De Meyere v Belgium* A 43 (1981); 4 EHRR 1 paras 64–5 PC and *A v Spain* No 13750/88, 66 DR 188 (1990).

[83] *Sigurjonsson v Iceland* A 264 (1993); 16 EHRR 462 paras 30–1. See also *Chassagnou v France* 1999-III; 29 EHRR 615 para 101 GC (hunters' associations established by law and requiring the membership of private landowners fell within Article 11(1)). For a discussion of whether the distinction between public and private associations can be sustained in the way that the professional association cases have suggested, see Alkema, *Freedom of Association*, *loc cit* p 515, n 1, above, pp 55–86 at 72–82.

[84] Cohen-Jonathan, *La Convention européenne des droits de l'homme*, 1989, p 515, would restrict 'association' to non-profit-making bodies. Tomuschat, *European System*, Ch 19, p 495, instead distinguishes between noneconomic (protected) and economic (not protected) activities of institutions.

a. Political parties

It is settled law that Article 11 on freedom of association applies to political parties.[85] The Court's conclusion on the applicability of Article 11 to political parties is based in part on the wording of Article 11(1), but is more compelled by the importance it attributes to the role of political parties in a 'democratic society', democracy itself being regarded as a fundamental feature of the Convention system and pluralism a precondition of that democracy.[86] The Court has said that freedom of expression of opinion in the choice of legislature:

> is inconceivable without the participation of a plurality of political parties representing different shades of opinion to be found in a country's population. By relaying this range of opinion … political parties make an irreplaceable contribution to political debate, which is at the very core of the concept of a democratic society.[87]

The Court's conception of the relationship between political parties and the core democratic rights of freedom of expression, guaranteed in Article 10, and of free elections, guaranteed in Article 3 of the First Protocol, has also been reason for construing the exceptions in Article 11(2) 'strictly' so that 'only convincing and compelling reasons' serve to justify restrictions on their freedom of association.[88] This narrow approach towards the exceptions to the rule of freedom of association is mitigated only by the state's power under Article 11(2) and its positive obligation under Article 1 of the Convention to impose restraint on an association's activities or intentions in order to secure the rights and freedoms of others.[89] As a 'power' granted to the state the Court has said must be used 'sparingly'.[90] The narrow ambit of the permitted limitations on the right to freedom of association for political parties was first articulated in *United Communist Party of Turkey v Turkey*.[91] In this case the Turkish Constitutional Court dissolved the newly formed party and, by operation of law, a ban was placed on its founders and managers from holding similar office in any new political party because of the threat to the unity of the nation and the territorial integrity of Turkey that was allegedly created by, *inter alia*, the express recognition in the party's programme of a 'Kurdish nation' in Turkey and of a right to self-determination for the Kurdish people. The Grand Chamber emphasized at the outset:

> The only type of necessity capable of justifying an interference with any of those [Article 8, 9, 10, and 11] rights is … one which may claim to spring from 'democratic society'.[92]

This conclusion allows the state 'only a limited margin of appreciation' when determining whether the interference with the political party is 'necessary in a democratic society'.[93]

---

[85] *KPD v FRG* No 250/57, 1 YB 222 (1957) (*German Communist Party*); *United Communist Party of Turkey v Turkey* 1998-I; 26 EHRR 121 para 33 GC; and *Refah Partisi (The Welfare Party) v Turkey* 2003-II; 37 EHRR 1 GC.

[86] *United Communist Party of Turkey v Turkey* 1998-I; 26 EHRR 121 paras 25 and 45 GC and *Refah Partisi,* id, para 89. On the Court's conception of democracy, see generally Marks, 1995 BYBIL 209 and Mowbray, 1999 PL 703.

[87] *United Communist Party of Turkey v Turkey* 1998-I; 26 EHRR 121 para 44 GC.   [88] Id, para 46.

[89] *Refah Partisi (The Welfare Party) v Turkey* 2003-II; 37 EHRR 1 para 103 GC and *Gorzelik v Poland* hudoc (2004); 40 EHRR 76 para 94 GC.

[90] *Gorzelik,* id, para 95. With the recognition of the positive obligation in the context of political party programmes, the Court has no longer found it necessary to examine complaints under Article 17; cf, *WP v Poland* No 42264/98 hudoc (2004) DA (prohibition on the formation of an association).

[91] 1998-I; 26 EHRR 121 GC.   [92] Id, para 45.

[93] Id, para 46; *Socialist Party v Turkey* 1998-III; 27 EHRR 51 para 50 GC and *Christian Democratic People's Party v Moldova* 2006-II; 45 EHRR 392 para 68.

Applied to the *United Communist Party* case,[94] the Grand Chamber reasoned that there could be no justification for restrictions on a political party 'solely because it seeks to debate in public the situation of part of the State's population … in order to find, according to democratic rules, solutions capable of satisfying everyone concerned'. Observing that the programme expressly strived for peaceful and democratic solutions, the Grand Chamber unanimously held that, despite the state's argument that what was at stake was the essential conditions for the state's existence, the penalties were disproportionate to the aim pursued and, therefore, constituted a violation of Article 11.[95] The same penalties were in issue in *Socialist Party v Turkey*, this time in response to statements made in party publications and by the party's chairman during an election campaign in which the establishment of a federal system of government as a solution to the 'Kurdish problem' in Turkey was advocated. The Grand Chamber accepted the government's argument that the statements were directed at the Kurdish population but found no evidence of incitement to violence or otherwise of an infringement of the rules of democracy.[96] It also rejected the government's contention that a political programme that is incompatible with the current principles and structures of the state must be incompatible with the rules of democracy. The Grand Chamber reasoned:

> It is of the essence of democracy to allow diverse political programmes to be proposed and debated, even those that call into question the way a state is currently organised, provided that they do not harm democracy itself.[97]

In this context, the Grand Chamber said that the 'necessity' referred to in the phrase 'necessary in a democratic society' requires that the interference satisfy a 'pressing social need' and is proportionate to the legitimate aim it seeks to achieve.[98] It found that the dissolution of the party was unnecessary in a democratic society for failing to meet the proportionality requirement. The *Socialist Party* case illustrates that, where the Court is satisfied that an association does not question the need for compliance with democratic principles, vigorous demands by it for the fundamental re-organization of the structure of the state will not *per se* provide convincing and compelling reasons to justify restrictions of the right to freedom of association under Article 11(2).

Such reasons were found to exist by the majority of the Grand Chamber in *Refah Partisi (The Welfare Party) v Turkey*.[99] Consolidating upon statements of principle articulated in the earlier cases, the Grand Chamber formulated two criteria to be satisfied in order to

[94] 1998-I; 26 EHRR 121 para 57 GC. See also *Socialist Party v Turkey* 1998-III; 27 EHRR 51 para 45 GC and *Dicle on behalf of the DEP (Democratic Party) of Turkey v Turkey* hudoc (2002).

[95] An examination of the stated objectives of the programme sufficed as the party's limited period of existence meant that the Court could not, as a practical matter, look to the party's activities to discern the party's true intentions and responsibility for the terrorism situation in Turkey: id, paras 58–9.

[96] *Socialist Party v Turkey* 1998-III; 27 EHRR 51 para 47 GC, although the Court suggests that had the statements encouraged secession from Turkey then its conclusion may have differed. On the Court's conception of democracy advanced in the *United Communist Party* and the *Socialist Party* cases, see Mowbray, 1999 PL 703 at 703–6.

[97] *Socialist Party v Turkey* 1998-III; 27 EHRR 51 para 47 GC. See also, *Freedom and Democracy Party (ÖZDEP) v Turkey* 1999-III; 31 EHRR 674 para 41 GC (the Party's programme for government assumed there was a Kurdish people in Turkey with a separate language and culture and advocated the abolition of the Department of Religious Affairs) and *Democracy and Change Party v Turkey* hudoc (2005). In the context of non-governmental associations, see *United Macedonian Organization Ilinden and Others v Bulgaria* hudoc (2006) para 76 (demanding autonomy or secession not sufficient ground to refuse association's registration).

[98] Id, para 49. See also *Freedom and Democracy Party (ÖZDEP)*, id, para 43 (no pressing social need); *Refah Partisi (The Welfare Party) v Turkey* hudoc (2001); 37 EHRR 1 para 104 GC (pressing social need); and *Democracy and Change Party v Turkey* hudoc (2005) (no pressing social need).

[99] Hudoc (2001); 37 EHRR 1 GC.

invoke the protection of Article 11 where a political party has promoted a change in the law or the legal and constitutional structures of the state:

> [F]irstly, the means used to that end must be legal and democratic; secondly, the change proposed must itself be compatible with fundamental democratic principles. It necessarily follows that a political party whose leaders incite violence or put forward a policy which fails to respect democracy or which is aimed at the destruction of democracy and the flouting of rights and freedoms recognised in a democracy cannot lay claim to the Convention's protection against penalties imposed on those grounds.[100]

Unlike the *United Communist Party* and *Socialist Party* cases, which raised concerns about separatism, *Refah* involved the principle of secularism. The earlier cases further differed from *Refah* in that they concerned the dissolution of fledgling political parties. In *Refah's* case the Turkish Constitutional Court dissolved the largest political party in Turkey, which had held office in a coalition government for thirteen months (before it resigned under pressure from the military) and had been in existence for over fourteen years. Its assets were transferred to the state treasury and a five-year ban on participation in political activities was imposed on a number of its members, one of whom was the party's chairman (who had been Prime Minister during the time of the coalition government). The Constitutional Court did so on the ground that acts[101] and statements[102] imputable to the party disclosed that it had become a 'centre of activities contrary to the principle of secularism' guaranteed in the Turkish Constitution insofar as: (i) the party intended to set up a plurality of legal systems in the state; (ii) the party intended to apply Islamic principles and law (sharia) to the internal and external relations of the Muslim community within that framework; and (iii) statements had referred to the possible use of force as a political method. Relying on the same evidence as the Constitutional Court, the Grand Chamber emphasized the importance of the principle of secularism for the democratic system in Turkey.[103] It was satisfied that the penalties served the legitimate aims of protecting national security and public safety, prevention of disorder or crime, and protection of the rights and freedoms of others, and were prescribed by law. The issue was, therefore, whether the penalties were 'necessary in a democratic society'. The Grand Chamber identified three questions to be answered in order to determine whether the interference with the party's freedom of association met a 'pressing social need' as follows:

(i)   whether there was plausible evidence that the risk to democracy, supposing it had been proved to exist, was sufficiently imminent;

(ii) whether the acts and speeches of the leaders and members of the political party concerned were imputable to the party as a whole; and

---

[100] Id, para 98. See also *Partidul Comunistilor (Nepeceristi) and Ungureanu v Romania* 2005-I; 44 EHRR 340 para 46 (refusing communists registration as a political party was a violation) and *United Macedonian Organization Ilinden-PIRIN v Bulgaria* hudoc (2005) (political party dissolved on grounds of national security because individual members held separatist views and sought autonomy of region a violation). In the context of political associations, see *Zhechev v Bulgaria* hudoc (2007) para 47 (non-governmental organization aiming for restoration of monarchy requiring amendment to Bulgarian constitution).

[101] Including the following conduct by the Prime Minister and Minister of Justice while in government: encouraging the wearing of Islamic headscarves in public and educational establishments; altering public service working hours to accommodate Ramadan fasting; visiting a Party member in prison awaiting trial for incitement to religious hatred; and hosting a reception for Islamic leaders at the Prime Minister's residence.

[102] The statements were made by some Refah members over a period of years prior to Refah holding government office.

[103] Id, para 67.

(iii) whether the acts and speeches imputable to the political party formed a whole which gave a clear picture of a model of society conceived and advocated by the party which was incompatible with the concept of a 'democratic society'.[104]

First, the Grand Chamber considered that at the time of its dissolution Refah's standing in election polls indicated that it had the 'real potential to seize political power without being restricted by the compromises inherent in a coalition' and 'the real chances that Refah would implement its programme after gaining power' made the danger to Convention rights and freedoms posed by the party's proposed programme 'more tangible and more immediate'.[105] Secondly, the Grand Chamber found that the acts and statements of Refah's members were imputable to the whole party as it had not taken 'prompt practical steps', including disciplinary proceedings, to distance itself from those members.[106] Regarding the grounds for dissolving the party, the Grand Chamber held, agreeing with the majority of the Chamber,[107] that a plurality of legal systems one of which would be religion based is a societal system that is incompatible with the Convention because it removes the state's role as the impartial guarantor of human rights and neutral arbiter of beliefs, and infringes the principle of non-discrimination.[108] Furthermore, the Grand Chamber held that sharia is incompatible with the fundamental principles of democracy as contained in the Convention owing to its 'stable and invariable' nature and the divergence of its doctrines from Convention values in a number of respects including the principle of pluralism.[109] The finding that sharia is incompatible with democracy was reinforced in *Refah* by the fact that Turkey had opted for secularism, confining religion to the private sphere, when the republican state was founded. The Court said that a state might oppose political movements based on 'religious fundamentalism' in the light of its own historical experience.[110] It also rejected the applicants' argument that prohibiting a plurality of private-law systems in the name of secularism constituted discrimination against Muslims. The Court observed that the right to freedom of religion as enshrined in the Convention is a matter of individual conscience that is separate from the field of private law, which is concerned with the organization of society as a whole. With regard to the possible use of force, it found that speeches made by several party members referred to the possible use of force as a political method to be used by Refah to gain and retain

---

[104] Id, para 104. Later applied in *Partidul Comunistilor (Nepeceristi) and Ungureanu v Romania* hudoc (2005); 44 EHRR 340 para 48 (refusal to register a new political party a violation).

[105] Id, paras 108–10. Cf, *United Macedonian Organization Ilinden-PIRIN v Bulgaria* hudoc (2005) (no 'pressing social need' for party's dissolution where, *inter alia*, its public influence was negligible).

[106] Id, paras 113–15 and 131. This was so despite Refah's constitution and programme making no reference to a plurality of legal systems, to sharia or Islam, or the use of force as a political method: see paras 73, 117, and 131. The Court has said that when determining a party's intentions and motives the Court may go beyond the party's constitution and programme to consider the acts and stances of the party's leaders: id, para 101. Nor had Refah sought during its period in office to introduce sharia.

[107] The Chamber held there was no violation of Article 11 by a slim majority of four votes to three.

[108] In his concurring opinion, Judge Kovler regretted the Chamber's failure to examine more closely the concept of plurality of legal systems.

[109] Id, para 123; cf, the concurring opinion of Judge Kovler. For a discussion of this finding, see Evans, in Ghanea, ed, *The Challenge of Religious Discrimination at the Dawn of the New Millennium*, 2004, pp 153–4. Although the Court observed, at para 100, that 'a political party animated by the moral values imposed by a religion cannot be regarded as intrinsically inimical to the fundamental principles of democracy, as set forth in the Convention'.

[110] *Refah Partisi (The Welfare Party) v Turkey* 2003-II; 37 EHRR 1 para 124 GC. The Court noted that 'the Convention institutions have expressed the view that the principle of secularism is certainly one of the fundamental principles of the state which are in harmony with the rule of law and respect for human rights and democracy': id, para 93.

power.[111] It noted that the party did not exclude the use of force.[112] The Grand Chamber unanimously concluded that, despite the limited margin of appreciation, the penalties met a 'pressing social need' and could not be regarded as disproportionate. Refah had failed to meet the two conditions by which a political party may promote a change in the law and invoke the protection of Article 11. Accordingly, the penalties were 'necessary in a democratic society' and no violation of Article 11 had occurred.

The decision in *Refah* is controversial. It raises important questions about the relationships between secularism, religion, human rights, and democracy and their connection within the framework of the Convention.[113] The joint dissenting opinion of Judges Fuhrmann, Loucaides, and Bratza in the Chamber provides a different approach towards the analysis of the issues posed in the *Refah* case. The minority found it unnecessary to examine the nature or effect of a plural legal system or to embark upon an assessment of sharia; rather their focus was on the standard of proof required to justify dissolution where a policy, not contained in the party's constitution or programme, is imputed. Indeed, the minority noted that Refah's constitution and programme for government expressly endorsed the principle of secularism contained in the Turkish constitution. In a case in which statements or acts of individual leaders or members are relied on to take the drastic measure of dissolving an entire party, the minority said that 'particularly convincing and compelling reasons' must be shown to justify the penalty, especially in *Refah*'s case where the representations were isolated events occurring in very different contexts over a period of six years, long before the party came to power. In the absence of reasons of that quality, a proportionate penalty would be the prosecution of the members responsible.

b. Other associations

Political objectives may be pursued by associations other than those registered as political parties.[114] The Court has recognized that associations formed for other objectives, including protecting cultural or spiritual heritage, pursuing various socio-economic aims, proclaiming or teaching religion, seeking an ethnic identity, or asserting a minority consciousness, which may or may not have political objectives, also fall within Article 11, as they too are important for the 'proper functioning of democracy'.[115] Whatever the objective of the association, when determining whether an interference with the freedom of association is justified under Article 11(2) the stricter standard of review adopted in the political party cases, and transposed from Article 10, applies. The Court has reasoned:

> [G]iven that the implementation of the principle of pluralism is impossible without an association being able to express freely its ideas and opinions, the Court has also recognised that the protection of opinions and the freedom of expression within the meaning of Article 10 of the Convention is one of the objectives of freedom of association.[116]

Applied to associations asserting a minority consciousness, in *Sidiropoulos Greece*[117] the Court found there had been a violation of Article 11 when the Greek authorities refused to register an association purporting in its memorandum of association to preserve and develop the traditions and culture of the Macedonian minority of the region. The

[111] Id, para 130.   [112] Id, para 132.
[113] See Boyle, 1 EHRR 1 (2004) and McGoldrick, 5 HRLR 27 (2005) 52–3.
[114] *Zhechev v Bulgaria* hudoc (2007).
[115] *Gorzelik v Poland* hudoc (2004); 40 EHRR 76 para 92 GC. See also, eg, *Grande Oriente D'Italia Di Palazzo Guistiniani v Italy* 2001-VIII; 34 EHRR 629 (masonic association) and *Koretskyy v Ukraine* hudoc (2008) (protection of the natural environment).
[116] Id, para 91.   [117] 1998-IV; 27 EHRR 633.

authorities considered that the true intent of the association was to undermine Greece's territorial integrity by disputing the Greek identity of the region. However, the Court was not persuaded that 'convincing and compelling reasons' for the refusal existed given the absence of a national system for review of associations prior to registration and the weak evidence relied on by the national courts that gave rise to no more than a 'mere suspicion' about the association's intention.[118] The Court observed that 'the inhabitants of a region in a country are entitled to form associations in order to promote the region's special characteristics, for historical as well as economic reasons'.[119] The Court also held the refusal was disproportionate because a national law conferred power on the courts to dissolve an association once registered if it subsequently pursued aims contrary to those contained in its memorandum or the law.[120]

By contrast with the *Sidiropoulos* case, in *Gorzelik v Poland*[121] the Court upheld the state's decision to refused to register an association. In this case an association described itself in its memorandum of association as an 'organisation of the Silesian national minority'. The Polish court had found that the Silesian people did not constitute a 'national minority' under Polish law, a designation that would have given the association an entitlement to special privileges under electoral laws, including an exemption from the threshold of votes required to obtain seats in Parliament. Moreover, it was held that the registration itself set in motion a further train of events leading to the acquisition of privileges under electoral laws. Before the Court, the government sought to justify the interference by contending that the purpose of refusing the association's application for registration was to prevent it from acquiring those electoral benefits available to national minorities; while the association denied that it was interested in running for elections and argued the restriction was premature. When considering whether the refusal to register the association was justified the Grand Chamber found that the interference sought to protect the existing democratic institutions and procedures in Poland by preventing an abuse of electoral law by the association itself, or other associations in similar situations. It accepted that once the association was registered there was no national law capable of preventing the mischief the authorities perceived would occur. In other words, there was no way for the authorities to ensure the rights of others participating in parliamentary elections would not be infringed. In this circumstance, it held, the authorities had not overstepped their margin of appreciation in considering that there was a 'pressing social need' at the moment of registration to regulate the 'free choice of associations to call themselves an "organisation of a national minority"'.[122] Furthermore, the refusal to register the ethnic minority association owing to the threat of abuse of electoral laws was not disproportionate to the aim of protecting existing democratic institutions in Poland as the refusal was not directed at the objectives of the association but rather the label it would use at law.[123] *Gorzelik* is a case where the Court clearly considered that the state had justifiably exercised the power, recognized in *Refah*, to restrain the freedom of association to protect its institutions.

---

[118] See also *Bozgan v Romania* hudoc (2007) (refusal to register association on basis of 'mere suspicion' that it intended to set up parallel structures to monitor the authorities a violation).

[119] Id, para 44.

[120] Id, paras 45–6. See also *United Macedonian Organization Ilinden and Others v Bulgaria* hudoc (2006) (alternative powers taken into account in finding no 'sufficient' ground for refusal to register association); *Bekir-Ousta v Greece* hudoc (2007) (refusal to register an association of a Muslim minority a violation); and *Bozgan v Romania* hudoc (2007) (refusal to register an association aiming at protecting citizens against organized crime a violation).

[121] Hudoc (2004); 40 EHRR 76 GC. See also *Artyomov v Russia No 17582/05* hudoc (2006) DA.

[122] Id, para 103.   [123] Id, para 105.

Tomuschat[124] raises the difficult question whether minorities may claim to be 'associations'. If an association through which a minority acts were to do so in other than a representational capacity, this would assume the existence of collective minority rights, a matter which has proved controversial under the International Covenant on Civil and Political Rights, which has a specific minority provision.[125] The Court is unlikely to introduce the idea of collective minority rights under the cover of Article 11. The protection of national minorities is dealt with by the Framework Convention for the Protection of National Minorities and, while collective minority rights are not envisaged, the rights and freedoms guaranteed under the Framework Convention may be exercised individually or in community.[126]

The right to freedom of association of religious groups must be read in the light of Article 9 of the Convention. In *The Moscow Branch of the Salvation Army v Russia* the Court said:

> [T]he right of believers to freedom of religion, which includes the right to manifest one's religion in community with others, encompasses the expectation that believers will be able to associate freely, without state intervention.[127]

The Court found that the refusal by the authorities to re-register the applicant religious association after changes in the law on religious associations was not 'prescribed by law' and lacked 'relevant and sufficient reasons'.[128] Moreover, the Court considered that where a religious community had operated as an independent and law abiding religious community for more than seven years, the reasons for refusing re-registration should be 'particularly weighty and compelling'.[129] Not only had there been a violation of Article 11 read in the light of Article 9, but the Russian authorities had neglected their duty of neutrality and impartiality towards the religious community.[130]

The regulation of associations by law may raise an issue as to the 'quality of law'. The case of *Koretskyy v Ukraine*[131] illustrates how the question can arise as an aspect of the requirements contained in Article 11(2), ie the interference must be lawful, as embodied in the expression 'prescribed by law',[132] and 'necessary in a democratic society'. In this case the authorities refused to register an environmental non-governmental organization on the basis that its articles of association did not comply with the law. The relevant law provided that an application for registration of an association may be refused if its articles of association 'contravene the legislation of Ukraine'. Relying on this provision the authorities required, as a condition of the association's registration, *inter alia*, the exclusion of numerous activities from the applicant's articles of association including distributing propaganda, lobbying authorities, involving volunteers in its work, publishing and engaging its managing body in the everyday financial activities of the association, as well as a limitation restricting the association to acting within the region in respect of which it was registered. With respect to whether the lawfulness requirement was met,

---

[124] *European System*, Ch 19, p 496.

[125] Article 27, which is expressed in terms of the rights of individual members of a minority. For a summary of the practice of the Human Rights Committee on Article 27, see Joseph, *The International Covenant on Civil and Political Rights: Cases, Materials and* Commentary, 2nd edn, 2004, Ch 24.

[126] ETS No 157. On 1 February 1998 the Convention entered into force and has thirty-nine parties.

[127] Hudoc (2006); 44 EHRR 912 para 58. See also *Church of Scientology Moscow v Russia* hudoc (2007); 46 EHRR 304 para 72.

[128] Id, paras 86, 95, and 97.   [129] Id, para 96.

[130] Id, para 97. See also *Church of Scientology Moscow*, id, para 97.   [131] Hudoc (2008).

[132] See also *NF v Italy* hudoc (2001); 35 EHRR 106 and *Maestri v Italy* hudoc (2004) GC (prohibition on membership of masonic association not foreseeable).

the Court said that the provision 'allowed a particularly broad interpretation'. In practice this would prohibit any departure from domestic legislation dealing with the activities of associations. In this circumstance the Court found that the provision was 'too vague to be sufficiently "foreseeable"' for the persons concerned.[133] Nor could judicial review of a decision to refuse registration prevent arbitrary decision-making given the excessively wide discretion granted to the authorities by the provision. The Court's examination was not, however, limited to the lawfulness of the provision. Regarding the question of whether the restrictions met a 'pressing social need' and, if so, whether they were proportionate, the Court held that the state had advanced no 'relevant and sufficient reasons' for the restrictions on the association's activities, and none could be found. Instead an examination of the evidence satisfied the Court that the association intended to pursue peaceful and purely democratic aims and tasks. Thus, the refusal to register the association did not meet the requirement of lawfulness and was not necessary in a democratic society, constituting a violation of Article 11.

c. Interferences with freedom of association: the requirement of proportionality

The extent of the interference with an association's capacity to function can be decisive in determining the necessity of the interference with the right to freedom of association.[134] The refusal to register an association is a 'radical measure' preventing as it does, the association from commencing any activity.[135] Likewise, the immediate and permanent dissolution of a political party is a 'drastic' measure and will be justified only in the most exceptional circumstances. The choice of name of a political party does not in principle justify the dissolution of a political party.[136] Nor will a single speech made overseas in a foreign language by a former leader of a political party to an audience not directly concerned with the situation justify 'so general a penalty' as the dissolution of an entire party despite the message of the speech amounting to a call to the use of force as a political tool.[137] In these circumstances the impact of the speech on 'national security', public 'order', or 'territorial integrity' would be very limited.[138] Similarly, a temporary ban on a political party's activities will be justified only by very serious breaches such as 'those which endanger political pluralism or fundamental democratic principles'.[139] In Refah's case the Court considered the dissolution of the party and the temporary bar on its leaders from similar political activity to be a proportionate measure because the party's objectives and the means chosen to achieve them were found to be a threat to democratic principles.

In *Parti Nationaliste Basque—Organisation Régionale D'Iparralde v France*[140] the Court held that the prohibition on the funding of political parties by foreign political parties may have a significant impact on an association's financial resources and hence

---

[133] Id, para 48.

[134] *Parti Nationaliste Basque—Organisation Régionale D'Iparralde v France* No 71251/01 hudoc (2007) para 49. See also *Refah Partisi (The Welfare Party) v Turkey* 2003-II; 37 EHRR 1 para 100 GC.

[135] *Gorzelik v Poland* hudoc (2004); 40 EHRR 76 para 105 GC and *United Macedonian Organization Ilinden and Others v Bulgaria* hudoc (2006).

[136] *United Communist Party of Turkey v Turkey* 1998-I; 26 EHRR 121 para 54 GC.

[137] *Dicle on behalf of the DEP (Democratic Party) of Turkey v Turkey* hudoc (2002) (criminal proceedings had been taken against the maker of the speech).

[138] *Ibid.*

[139] See *Christian Democratic People's Party v Moldova* 2006-II; 45 EHRR 392 para 76 (one month ban on the party's activities as a result of holding unauthorized but peaceful meetings outside Parliament buildings was a violation).

[140] Hudoc (2007).

its ability to engage fully in its political activities. Moreover, the Court was not fully persuaded that funding of political parties by foreign political parties would undermine state sovereignty. However, the lack of consensus in member state practice and Article 7 of the Recommendation Rec(2003)4 of 8 April 2003 of the Committee of Ministers of the Council of Europe supporting the prohibition on funding of political parties from foreign sources were grounds for finding that the prohibition was not in itself incompatible with Article 11. Further, the interference was proportionate to the aim of the 'prevention of disorder' because the adverse impact on finances of the relevant political party placed it in a position that was no different from that of any small political party faced with a shortage of funds.

d. Legal recognition of associations

The first duty of a state is to interfere neither with individuals who seek to exercise their freedom of association nor with the essential activities of any established association. However, although it is conceivable that informal associations will satisfy the aspirations of individuals, the effective exercise of their freedom will be enhanced by the provision of a legal basis for the formation and recognition of associations, both so that individuals may be certain of what is required of them to set up an association and also so that the resulting body has legal personality and is able to act in an independent way to further the interests of its members.[141] While an absolute, positive obligation on a state to institute a legal framework for every form of association that might be envisaged by groups of individuals goes beyond what Article 11 demands,[142] the Convention states invariably do provide some options for association which lead to legal personality. Individuals have the right to avail themselves of the power to form associations and to have these actions recognized by the state.[143] In *The Moscow Branch of the Salvation Army v Russia*[144] the Court found there had been an interference with a religious organization's freedom of association when it lost legal-entity status after the authorities refused to register it under new laws requiring the re-registration of all religious associations. As a consequence, the association was liable to be dissolved by the courts and its functioning and religious activities were adversely affected as, for example, lack of legal-entity status had been the ground relied upon by the authorities for refusing to register amendments to a religious association's charter and for staying the registration of a religious newspaper. In *Ramazanova v Azerbaijan*[145] the Court held that there was a *de facto* refusal to register an association that triggered Article 11 when the authorities had delayed the registration process for almost four years. An association should not, however, be forced by the state to take on a legal shape it does not seek as insurmountable requirements may be placed in its way and, thus, effectively obstruct freedom of association.[146]

---

[141] *United Macedonian Organization Ilinden and others v Bulgaria* hudoc (2006).

[142] Eg, it is not conceivable that the Convention protects the right to associate with limited liability or charitable status: *Association X v Sweden No 6094/73*, 9 DR 5 (1977).

[143] See *The Moscow Branch of the Salvation Army v Russia* hudoc (2006); 44 EHRR 912 para 59. See also *Church of Scientology Moscow v Russia* hudoc (2007); 46 EHRR 304. In *Le Compte, Van Leuven and De Meyere v Belgium* A 43 (1981); 4 EHRR 1 para 65 PC, the Court emphasized that while medical practitioners were obliged to be members of the *public* association, they were quite free to establish private associations for the protection of their interests, so no violation of Article 11 had been demonstrated.

[144] Hudoc (2007) 44 EHRR 912; para 74. See also *Church of Scientology Moscow v Russia* hudoc (2007); 46 EHRR 304. See also *United Macedonian Organization Ilinden and Others v Bulgaria* hudoc (2006) (non-governmental organization representing ethnic minority refused registration).

[145] Hudoc (2007); 47 EHRR 407.

[146] *Zhechev v Bulgaria* hudoc (2007) para 56 (requiring an association with political aims to register as political party a violation).

III. POSITIVE OBLIGATIONS

Once the association is set up, the essential relationships are between itself and its members and non-members. There are indications from the trade union cases that members have a limited right to remain as members but, in general, neither they nor non-members may claim a right to membership over the objection of the association.[147] Because we are here dealing with the relationships between individuals or between individuals and the association, another aspect of the positive obligation of states intrudes: what is a state's duty to regulate these private relationships in the interest of the effective enjoyment of Article 11 rights? This is perhaps the most pressing context in which the question whether a state has a positive obligation under the Convention to control private action that infringes other individuals' rights arises.[148] Since the important practice concerns trade unions, it will be dealt with separately below. The association will have rights of its own, for which the right to operate effectively provides a general rubric. Again, the trade union cases to one side, there is a duty on states to provide associations with suitable measures of protection against immediate threats of violence from acts of private individuals. In *Ouranio Toxo v Greece*[149] the Court held that where the authorities could reasonably foresee the danger of violence to members of an association and clear violations of freedom of association they should take appropriate measures to prevent, or at least contain, the violence. A related positive obligation is the duty to undertake an effective investigation into complaints of interference with freedom of association by acts of private individuals.[150]

4. FREEDOM TO FORM AND JOIN
TRADE UNIONS[151]

The right to freedom to form and to join trade unions is a sub-division of freedom of association, not a special and independent right.[152] Accordingly, the elements of freedom of association discussed above apply to trade unions as well as to other associations, so far as they are relevant.[153] There is no definition of a trade union in the Convention, beyond the indication in the text of Article 11(1) that they are organizations in the field of employment that have as their purpose the protection of their members' interests.[154]

Individuals must be free to form or join trade unions of their choice.[155] The state is not permitted to establish or to favour a single trade union in which membership of the appropriate individuals concerned is compulsory. In the professional association cases, the Court has made it clear that the right to set up these public law bodies must not be at the expense of the private right to establish other associations for the promotion of the interests of those professionals who elect to join and which can provide a different perspective to the government-required body.[156]

[147] See the *ASLEF* case, below, p 537.
[148] See Clapham, *Human Rights in the Private Sphere*, 1993, pp 232–40.
[149] Hudoc (2006) para 43.   [150] *Ibid.*
[151] See Forde, 31 AJCL 301 (1983); Hepple, in *Freedom of Association, loc cit* at p 515, n 1, above, p 162; and Morris, in Ewing *et al*, eds, *Human Rights and Labour Law: Essays for Paul O'Higgins*, 1994, pp 28–55.
[152] *National Union of Belgian Police* case A 19 (1975); 1 EHRR 578 PC.
[153] Eg, those concerning registration of associations, above, p 531.
[154] A works council is not an 'association' within Article 11: *Karakurt v Austria No 32441/96* hudoc (1999) DA.
[155] This includes holding a union office: *X v Ireland No 4125/69*, 14 YB 198; 37 CD 42 (shop steward).
[156] *Le Compte, Van Leuven and De Meyere v Belgium* A 43 (1981); 4 EHRR 1 PC. See above, p 526. See also *Young, James and Webster v UK* B 39 (1979) para 160 Com Rep—'a trade union monopoly is excluded'.

The right to freedom to form and join trade unions in Article 11 is complemented by similar guarantees in relevant International Labour Organization Conventions[157] and the European Social Charter.[158] The Court takes into account the guarantees in those instruments as interpreted by the relevant enforcement bodies, and normally interprets the Convention consistently with them.

Article 11 imposes both negative and positive obligations upon the state. The negative obligation of states not to interfere with individual and trade union freedom of association within Article 11(1) is qualified by Article 11(2), which permits interferences on specified public interest grounds, such as the 'protection of the rights of others'. Although the 'essential object' of Article 11 is to 'protect the individual against arbitrary interference by public authorities with the exercise of the rights protected, there may in addition be positive obligations to secure the effective enjoyment of the rights protected'.[159] In the trade union context, there are positive obligations to secure the rights of individuals and trade unions against employers[160] and to protect the individual against abuse of power by a trade union.[161] The positive obligation to act to ensure that trade unions may protect their members' interests, or to protect individuals against trade union abuse, derives from Article 11(1). As with other similarly structured Convention articles, notably Articles 8–10, the Court has taken the view that in respect of both kinds of obligation, 'the criteria to be applied do not differ in substance': in both contexts, whether Article 11(1) or (2) is being applied, 'regard must be had to the fair balance to be struck between the competing interests of the individual and of the community as a whole'.[162] When deciding whether this 'fair balance' has been struck, the Court generally applies 'a wide margin of appreciation' in trade union cases; there is a more limited margin in closed shop cases.[163]

In the area of industrial relations, the state may appear in the guise of employer—of civil servants and others—rather than in a public capacity. The Court has rejected government arguments that Article 11 only applies to the state in its latter capacity.[164] Given that ruling, subjecting the 'state as employer' to Article 11, it would scarcely be consistent to regard the activities of private employers, who, vis-à-vis the individual worker, are hardly in a different case from the government, as not being subject to it. It is here that the state's positive obligations, referred to above, to ensure that private persons do not infringe the rights under Article 11 of other private persons becomes crucial.

I. THE TRADE UNION RIGHT TO REGULATE ITS INTERNAL AFFAIRS

In *Associated Society of Locomotive Engineers and Firemen (ASLEF) v UK*[165] the Court stated that the right to form a trade union includes 'the right of trade unions to draw up their own rules and to administer their own affairs'. This right is subject, however, to the state's power to impose restrictions in the public interest permitted by Article 11(2),

---

[157] Freedom of Association Convention 1948 (ILO 87), 68 UNTS 17 and Right to Organize and Collective Bargaining Convention 1949 (ILO 98), 96 UNTS 257.

[158] Article 5. On the Charter, see above, p 3.

[159] *Wilson, National Union of Journalists and Others v UK* 2002-IV; 35 EHRR 523 para 41.

[160] *Ibid.*   [161] See eg, *Cheall v UK*, below, p 538.

[162] *Sorensen and Rasmussen v Denmark* 2006-I; 46 EHRR 572 para 58 GC.

[163] *Ibid.* See further below, p 542. See also the *Tum Haber Sen* case, below, p 546.

[164] *Swedish Engine Drivers' Union* case A 20 (1976); 1 EHRR 617 para 37. In view of this approach, in *Young, James and Webster v UK* A 44 (1981); 4 EHRR 38 PC the Court stated that it did not have to decide whether the employer, British Rail, a nationalized industry, was a part of the state, in which case its acts would implicate the state directly.

[165] Hudoc (2007); 45 EHRR 793 para 38.

coupled with its positive obligation under Article 11(1) 'to protect an individual against any abuse of a dominant position by trade unions'.[166] This is an area in which there may be difficult questions, given the tension between the individual and collective aspects of Article 11, when trade unions mobilize or discipline their members. In the *ASLEF* case, the Court stated that, as part of their right to regulate their internal affairs, '[p]rima facie trade unions enjoy the freedom to set up their own rules concerning conditions of membership, including administrative formalities and payment of fees, as well as more substantive criteria, such as the profession or trade exercised by the would-be member'.[167]

Whereas the state may interfere with a trade union's administration of its internal affairs to prevent abuse of a dominant position, there was no such abuse justifying or requiring interference in the *ASLEF* and *Cheall* cases respectively In the *ASLEF* case, the applicant union had under its rules expelled a member because he was a member of the British National Party, a far right but lawful political party whose policies were diametrically opposed to the objects of the union. The expulsion was held to be illegal by the UK courts as being contrary to legislation which prohibited the expulsion of a union member because he was a 'member of a political party'. The Strasbourg Court upheld the applicant union's claim that the state's intervention limiting the union's freedom to expel a member for the reason given was an unjustified interference with its right to freedom of association. The Court ruled that the 'crucial question is whether the state has struck the right balance between Mr Lee's rights and those of the applicant trade union'.[168] Applying this text, the Court noted that the expulsion did not limit the former member's freedom of expression or lawful political activities and did not affect his employment or entitlement to benefits of union collective bargaining. At the same time, the Court noted that associations within Article 11 generally have the right to choose their members, and that where 'associations are formed by people, who, espousing particular values or ideals, intend to pursue common goals, it would run counter to the very effectiveness of the freedom at stake if they had no control over their membership'.[169] This, the Court stated, certainly was the case with trade unions, which 'are not bodies solely devoted to politically-neutral aspects of the well-being of their members, but are often ideological, with strongly-held views on social and political issues'.[170] Given that the expelled member's political values and ideals clashed fundamentally with those of the union and that there was nothing to suggest that the union had undertaken any responsibility to admit members to fulfil any wider role than the achievement of its own objectives, the state's intervention had failed to strike the 'right balance'.

Cheall v UK [171] involved an inter-union membership dispute in which the applicant had been expelled by his current union in response to a request from his previous union in implementation of a membership-protection agreement to which both unions were parties. The Commission said that, while matters of admission to membership and expulsion were generally a matter for the union and that there was no general right of an individual to be admitted nor not to be expelled, '[n]onetheless for the right to join a union to be effective the state must protect the individual against any abuse of a dominant position by trade unions...such abuse might occur, for example, where exclusion or expulsion was not in accordance with union rules or where the results were wholly arbitrary or where the consequences of exclusion or expulsion resulted in exceptional hardship such as job loss because of a closed shop'. On the facts of the case, however, the Commission found nothing arbitrary about the decision, which was lawful under national law.

---

[166] Id, para 43.   [167] *Ibid.*   [168] Id, para 49.   [169] Id, para 39.
[170] Id, para 50.   [171] *No 10550/83*, 42 DR 178 at 186 (1985).

The question of alleged abuse by a trade union was also in issue in *Sibson v UK*.[172] The applicant argued that the decision of his employer to transfer him to another depot (in accordance with the terms of his contract and with the same pay) was arbitrary in the sense referred to by the Commission in the *Cheall* case because it had been motivated by a desire to appease a trade union from which the applicant had resigned after a dispute arising out of his conduct as its branch secretary. The employer's decision had been taken as a result of pressure by the trade union after the applicant had joined another trade union (as he was entitled to do under his contract). The members of his former union had refused to work with the applicant and voted for a closed shop in the union's favour, which was the reason for the offer of work at the other depot. The applicant argued that the government's failure to provide him with a remedy against the employer's decision was a violation of Article 11. The Court held against the applicant because he had not left his former union for reasons of personal conviction (and would have re-joined if given an apology) and, above all, was not threatened with the loss of his job: '[he] was not subjected to a form of treatment striking at the very substance of the freedom of association guaranteed by Article 11'.[173]

II. TRADE UNION ACTION AGAINST THIRD PARTIES

Trade union action in their members' interests may affect third parties adversely, sometime in breach of the third parties' freedom of association. This was the claim in *Gustafsson v Sweden*[174] in which a trade union sought to have the applicant restaurant owner apply to his employees, some of whom were its members, a collective agreement that the union had negotiated with the relevant employers' associations. This could be achieved by the applicant becoming a member of one of the employers' associations concerned or negotiating a separate agreement with the union. The applicant declined to do either as he was opposed in principle to participation in collective bargaining and argued that the resulting (lawful) union boycott of his restaurant, which eventually forced him to sell it, put pressure upon him to join an employers' association in breach of his negative right not to join an association.[175] The Grand Chamber rejected his claim, by twelve votes to seven. It did so because the applicant was not legally compelled to join an association: he could have chosen to make a separate agreement. Moreover, the union pressure upon him did not raise an issue under the Convention, since Article 11 does not guarantee a right not to enter into a collective agreement. In this situation, the trade union pressure and the forced sale of the restaurant did not strike at the 'very substance' of the applicant's rights under Article 11. In reaching this decision, the Court stressed that a wide margin of appreciation applied, given the important role of collective agreements in labour relations in Sweden; the different approaches to their use across Europe; and the sensitive social and political issues involved in restricting trade union action.

In the related case of *Englund v Sweden*,[176] the Commission held inadmissible an application by employees of the restaurant owner who was the applicant in the *Gustafsson* case

---

[172] A 258-A (1993); 17 EHRR 193. Cf, *Roepstorff v Denmark No 32955/96* hudoc (2000) DA (dispute between union and member; no abuse) and *X v Ireland No 4125/69*, 14 YB 108; 37 CD 42 (1971) (pressure not to be shop steward may be abuse); *Johansson v Sweden No 13537/88*, 65 DR 202 at 205 (1990) (compulsory insurance, no abuse).

[173] Id, para 29. Cf, *Kajanen and Tuomaala v Finland No 36401/97* hudoc (2000) DA; *Thorkelsson v Iceland No 35771/97* hudoc (2001) DA; *Evaldsson v Sweden No 75252/01* hudoc (2006) DA.

[174] 1996-II; 22 EHRR 409 GC. Cf, *Ab Kurt Kellermann v Sweden No 41579/98* hudoc (2003) DA.

[175] Although it is not clear if the Court regarded the employers' association as a trade union or an association otherwise within Article 11, the case is included in this section for convenience.

[176] *No 15533/89*, 77-A DR 10 at 18–19 (1994).

who were not members of the trade union taking action against him and who had not authorized the union to act on their behalf. They claimed that the union action interfered with their right to conclude employment contracts on terms agreed between them with their employer, and that, if the restaurant owner had acceded to the union's demand, there would have been an interference with their negative freedom of association because they would have been bound to accept the terms of the collective agreement. The Commission did not decide the government's main point that Article 11 did not apply at all but, assuming that it did, said that it had not been violated because the employer's refusal to give in to the unions meant that the applicants did not have to join a union and the conditions of their employment were not affected. This last point may have seemed somewhat academic to the applicants because, as noted, the restaurant had been sold owing to the effectiveness of the industrial action and they had lost their jobs.

III. THE RIGHT NOT TO JOIN A TRADE UNION

The Court has recognized that Article 11 protects the negative right not join a union, as well as the positive right to do so. The negative right has been most significant in the context of 'closed shop' situations, in which an employer and a trade union or trade unions have agreed that employment is dependent upon trade union membership. This negative right applies both to the situation where an individual is refused employment or is 'continuously and directly running a risk of being prevented from obtaining a job' because of an existing closed shop agreement (pre-entry closed shop)[177] and to the situation where an individual is dismissed because of a closed shop agreement made after employment has commenced (post-entry closed shop). It is in these closed shop situations that the potential clash under Article 11 between the individual and collective aspects of the right to freedom of association is most noticeable.

The closed shop situation was first considered in *Young, James and Webster v UK*,[178] which concerned a post-entry closed shop. The Court rejected the government's arguments that the *travaux* showed that the drafting states did not intend to protect the negative freedom of association at all and, in particular, did not intend to inhibit a state's right to impose or permit closed shops. The Court carefully avoided generalities. It was not prepared to endorse the position that compulsion to join a union was always prohibited by Article 11. The test was whether the compulsion 'strikes at the very substance of the freedom guaranteed by Article 11' on the facts of each case.[179] In *Young, James and Webster*, the Court said that it did so because the closed shop was addressed to workers already in employment who had strong objections in principle to union membership (which touched interests under Articles 9 and 10) and the consequence of holding to their position was the very serious one of dismissal. Furthermore, in practice there was no choice open to the applicants as to which union to join and they were not in a position to form their own union.[180]

In *Young, James and Webster*, the government was not prepared to seek to justify the arrangements under Article 11(2)[181] but, as the case of *Sigurjonsson v Iceland*[182] shows, such justification will be difficult. In that case, the Court found that a requirement in law

---

[177] See *Hoffman Karlskov v Denmark No 62560/00* hudoc (2003) DA.

[178] A 44 (1981); 4 EHRR 38 para 52 PC.   [179] Id, para 55.   [180] Id, para 56.

[181] There had been a change of government during the progress of the application and the new Conservative government was not prepared to rely on Article 11(2). See Forde, 11 ILJ 1 (1982).

[182] A 264 (1993); 16 EHRR 462 paras 36, 37, 41.

that a taxi licence holder be a member of an association of taxi drivers[183] was in violation of Article 11. The Court found that international legal developments were increasingly favouring the individual against closed shop arrangements and referred to a finding under the European Social Charter that Iceland's practice was not in accordance with the Charter. Again, what appeared to weigh most with the Court was that the consequences for the applicant were so severe, going to the very substance of the negative right: if he was not a member of the association, he could not earn his living as a taxi driver. Furthermore, the applicant had at all times objected to becoming a member of the association; had been allowed a licence before membership was required;[184] and had objections that were based on strongly held beliefs. When the Court turned to the government's case under Article 11(2), it found the reasons advanced, mainly that the arrangement facilitated the administration of the taxi service in the public interest, to be 'relevant but not sufficient'. The objective could have been achieved at not significantly greater cost whether membership was compulsory or not; the government could demonstrate expediency but not a pressing social need. In the Court's view, 'notwithstanding Iceland's margin of appreciation, the measures complained of were disproportionate to the legitimate aim pursued'.

In *Sorensen and Rasmussen v Denmark*,[185] the Grand Chamber had to consider a pre-entry closed shop. In that case the two applicants accepted employment in the knowledge that membership of the SID trade union, to which they were opposed because of the union's political views, was required by their different employers who had lawful closed shop agreements with the union under which membership was a condition of employment. The first applicant was dismissed when he indicated that he did not wish to pay the union's membership dues; the second applicant joined the union to gain employment but challenged the compulsion to do so as infringing Article 11. The Court first confirmed its earlier ruling that although the right not to join a trade union was not an absolute one, compulsion to join a union that 'strikes at the very substance' of the right is an interference with the guarantee of freedom of association in Article 11(1). Second, the Court declined to rule in the abstract on the question, which it had left open in earlier trade union cases, whether the positive and negative rights to join or not to join a trade union in Article 11 should be given the same level of protection, ie with equal weight being given to the individual and collective interests involved. Instead it ruled that this was a matter to be determined on the facts, weighing what was at stake for the individual and the union in the particular case. Third, the Court ruled that the negative right applied equally to both pre- and post-entry closed shops. The distinction between the two was only relevant when assessing the facts of each case: the 'very substance' of the right might be interfered with in pre-entry closed shop cases as well as post-entry cases, as was the case on the facts of the *Sorensen and Rasmussen* case. Although the applicants in that case knowingly took employment on the condition that they accepted SID membership, in the Court's view this did not 'significantly alter the element of compulsion inherent in having to join a trade union against their will'.[186] Moreover, the existence of the condition struck at the 'very substance' of the applicants' negative right not to join a trade union in that the first applicant was dismissed without notice when he indicated that he would not pay membership dues and the second applicant would have been dismissed, and probably have found it hard to gain employment elsewhere, if he resigned his union membership. The

---

[183] The Court said that it did not need to decide whether the association was a trade union.

[184] The Commission more explicitly makes the point that this was a post-entry closed shop case: id, para 57 Com Rep.

[185] 2006-I; 46 EHRR 572 GC.   [186] Id, para 59.

Court then examined whether on the facts a 'fair balance' had been struck between the applicants' interests and those of the union in being able to protect its members' interests. Whereas under Article 11 the Court normally applies a 'wide margin of appreciation' in trade union cases, it held in this case that the 'margin of appreciation' was narrower in the case of closed shop agreements. This was because the dominant approach in Convention states parties was now not to regard closed shop agreements as an essential means for securing the interests of trade unions and their members: very few parties permitted such agreements in their law and Denmark itself had abandoned them in the public and much of the private sectors.[187] Weighing these considerations against the impact upon the applicants of non-compliance with their right not to join a trade union,[188] the Court, by twelve votes to five and by fifteen votes to two, found a violation of Article 11.[189]

IV. THE RIGHT TO PROTECT MEMBERS' INTERESTS

Article 11 imposes a positive obligation upon states to ensure that trade unions may function effectively. Focusing on the words 'for the protection of his interests' in Article 11(1), in the *National Union of Belgian Police* case[190] the Court stated:

> These words, clearly denoting purpose, show that the Convention safeguards freedom to protect the occupational interests of trade union members by trade union action, the conduct and development of which the state must both permit and make possible...What the Convention requires is that under national law trade unions should be enabled, in conditions not at variance with Article 11, to strive for the protection of their members' interests.

Despite this language, trade unions have, until recently, enjoyed little success in claims that they or their members have brought under Article 11 seeking to enforce this positive obligation. In a group of seminal cases in the 1970s, the Court simply did not support claims brought by unions[191] or union members alleging that state restrictions upon trade union activities had infringed Article 11. In these cases, the Court noted that Article 11 is phrased in very general terms and 'does not secure any particular treatment of trade unions or their members'.[192] Apart from the specified rights to form and to join trade unions, Article 11 demanded of states only that they protect rights 'that [are] indispensable for the effective enjoyment of trade union freedom'.[193] In the 1970 cases, the Court took a very narrow view of what rights were indispensable.

In the *National Union of Belgian Police* case,[194] the Court conceded that they included the right of a trade union to be heard by the employer on behalf of its members in order to function effectively. This did not, however, suppose a right to be consulted, which the

---

[187] The Court also referred to the European Social Charter and EU human rights standards to the same effect.

[188] It was relevant that the applicants' objected to SID membership for reasons of principle; had they, as in *Sibson*, above, p 539, just been in dispute with the union, their claim would have been weaker. Confirming its approach in *Young, James and Webster*, the Court stressed, id, para 54, that 'the protection of personal opinions guaranteed by Articles 9 and 10 is one of the purposes of Article 11, and that such protection can only be effectively secured' by both a positive and negative Article 11 right.

[189] The five dissents concerned the first applicant, who was a student in temporary summer employment who could more easily have found other non-union work.

[190] A 19 (1975); 1 EHRR 578 para 39 PC.

[191] Trade unions, as well as individuals, may claim to be victims of a breach of their rights under Article 11: *National Union of Belgian Police* case, id, 39.

[192] This wording is found, eg, *Swedish Engine Drivers' Union* case A 20 (1976); 1 EHRR 617 para 39.

[193] *Ibid.*   [194] A 19 (1975); 1 EHRR 578 para 39 PC.

applicants claimed and which in Belgium was allowed only to certain large trade unions. Similarly, in the *Swedish Engine Drivers' Union* case[195] the Court held that the right to be heard, which remains the only indispensable right so far recognized, did not entail that the applicant trade union be allowed to have a right to collective bargaining or to enter into a collective agreement with an employer. In the Swedish system of industrial relations the terms and conditions of work of state employees, including railway engine drivers, were governed by a collective agreement entered into with four large federations of trade unions to which the applicant union was not affiliated, the resulting agreement then being applied to its members. Although these arrangements limited the power of the applicant union to protect its members' interests, there was no breach of Article 11. In both of the above cases, the Court stated that Article 11(1) allowed the state 'a free choice of means' as to how it ensured the right to be heard, and that these means might involve the right to bring claims or make representations rather than the specific right that was claimed.[196] Neither of the claimed rights were 'indispensable' or to be found generally in the 'national law and practice' of the states parties to the Convention.[197]

Finally, in *Schmidt and Dahlstrom v Sweden*,[198] the Court held that it was not a breach of Article 11 for the applicant non-striking members of a striking trade union to be denied by the state as employer the retroactive benefit of the eventual collective agreement, when the agreement was applied retroactively to the benefit of members of non-striking unions. Referring both to the obligation of states to facilitate trade union action[199] and to the 'free choice of means' that states are allowed when complying with it, the Court commented on the right to strike as follows:

> The grant of a right to strike represents without any doubt one of the most important of these means, but there are others. Such a right, which is not expressly enshrined in Article 11, may subject under national law to regulation of a kind that limits its exercise in certain instances. The Social Charter of 18 October 1961 only guarantees the right to strike subject to such regulation, as well as to 'further restrictions' compatible with its Article 31.

The facts of the *Schmidt and Dahlstrom* case were considered by the Court to involve a permissible 'regulation' of the applicants' right to strike. This was also the ruling in *Federation of Offshore Workers' Trade Unions v Norway*,[200] where there was no breach of Article 11 when the applicant federation and individual oil workers were banned from striking and their claim for a wage rise was referred to compulsory arbitration. However, applying its *Belgian Union of National Police* approach, the Court noted that, in accordance with Norwegian law, the ban was implemented only when the trade union members concerned had already been allowed to exercise their right to strike for thirty-six hours

---

[195] A 20 (1976); 1 EHRR 617. See also *Gustafsson v Sweden* 1996-II;-22 EHRR 409 GC.

[196] A 19 (1975); 1 EHRR 578 para 39 PC and A 20 (1976); 1 EHRR 617 para 40. In the *Swedish Engine Drivers' Union* case, the Court also noted that, although not able to conclude an agreement, the applicant union was permitted to negotiate. Cf, *Haalebos v Netherlands* No 21741/93 hudoc (1995) DA; *Schettini v Italy* No 29529/95 hudoc (2000) DA; and *Swedish Transport Workers' Union v Sweden* No 53507/99 hudoc (2004) DA.

[197] A 19 (1975); 1 EHRR 578 para 38 PC and A 20 (1976); 1 EHRR 617 para 39.

[198] A 21 (1976) para 36; 1 EHRR 632.

[199] The Court cited its statement of principle in the *National Union of Belgian Police* case quoted above.

[200] No 38190/97 hudoc (2002) DA. See also *National Association of Teachers in Further and Higher Education v UK* No 28910/95 hudoc (1998) DA (requirement that a union provide an employer with a list of members to be balloted on industrial action not a breach); *S v FRG* No 10365/83, 39 DR 237 (1984) (ban on German civil servants striking not a breach); and *UNISON v UK* No 53574/99 hudoc (2002) DA.

and the strike had been preceded by collective bargaining and compulsory mediation without success.

Despite having had opportunities in several later cases,[201] the Court has yet to be recognize that the right to strike in its essentials is an 'indispensable' right that a state is required to secure under Article 11. Whereas the tone of the judgment in the *Schmidt and Dahlstrom* case and subsequent cases is not sympathetic to the right to strike, given that it is generally recognized in the law of European states, that it has been given strong protection under the European Social Charter,[202] and that the freedom to withdraw one's labour is crucial to the proper balance of power in industrial relations in a democratic society, it can be strongly argued that the right to strike should be protected under Article 11 as 'indispensable'.[203]

A rationale for the Court's very cautious approach to the collective trade union right to protect members' interests that originated in its 1970s cases was recently articulated by the Grand Chamber in *Sorensen and Rasmussen v Denmark*,[204] in which it recognized that a 'wide margin of appreciation' applied:

> In the area of trade union freedom and in view of the sensitive character of the social and political issues involved in achieving a proper balance between the respective interests of labour and management, and given the wide divergence between the domestic systems in this field, the contracting states enjoy a wide margin of appreciation as to how the freedom of trade unions to protect the occupational interests of their members may be secured.

However, two more recent cases offer some encouragement to trade unions in this context. The first is *Wilson, National Union of Journalists and Others v UK*.[205] There the applicants' employers decided not to renew their collective bargaining agreement with the applicant trade union. Withdrawing recognition from that (and any other) union, they adopted a policy of determining employees' salaries unilaterally. This was lawful under UK law, as both collective bargaining and the recognition of trade unions by employers were voluntary. The Strasbourg Court confirmed that there was no breach of Article 11 on these facts, as the positive obligation on states to ensure that trade unions could 'strive for the protection of their members interests' did not include as 'indispensable' any right to collective bargaining[206] or to union recognition.[207] However, there was another dimension to the case. As allowed by UK law, in order to avoid possible union action aimed at preventing the employers' new policy being successfully implemented,

---

[201] See eg, *Wilson v UK* 2002-IV; 35 EHRR 523 para 45, which repeats the *Schmidt and Dahstrom* formula.

[202] The Court's reading of the right to strike in the European Social Charter in the *Schmidt and Dahlstrom* case gives the wrong impression. Article 6(4) expressly guarantees the right to strike and various restrictions upon the right to strike have been found to be contrary to it: see Harris, *op cit*, p 3, n 22 above, pp 104ff.

[203] The second sentence of Article 11(2) would provide a basis for allowing exceptions for members of the armed forces, the police, and at least some civil servants. This sentence was not relied on by the Court in the *Schmidt and Dahlstrom* case, in which one of the applicants was in the armed forces (the other was a state-employed university lecturer).

[204] 2006-I; 46 EHRR 572 para 58 GC.

[205] 2002-IV; 35 EHRR 523 paras 47, 48. See Ewing, 32 ILJ 1 (2003). See also *Danilenkov v Russia No 67336/01* hudoc (2004) DA (discrimination against workers for striking; pending on the merits) and *Sanchez Navajas v Spain No 57442/00* hudoc (2001) DA (employee trade union representatives should 'enjoy appropriate facilities to enable them to perform their trade union functions rapidly and effectively', including an appropriate amount of paid leave during their hours of work; inadmissible on the facts).

[206] Cf, *Swedish Engine Drivers' Union* case, above, p 543.

[207] The Court took into account that in UK law, although collective bargaining and union recognition were not compulsory, there were other important means by which unions could protect their members, including the right to strike.

the applicants' employers had offered their employees substantial pay rises if they signed personal contracts effectively renouncing their trade union rights. This was held by the Court to result in a breach of Article 11. The financial incentives were 'a disincentive or restraint on the use by employees of union membership to protect their interests' and, 'by permitting employers to use financial incentives to induce employees to surrender important trade union rights, the respondent state has failed in its positive obligation to secure the enjoyment of the rights under Article 11'.

The second case is *Demir and Baykara v Turkey*,[208] in which a Chamber of the Court cut back on the apparently unqualified ruling in the *Swedish Engine Drivers' Union* case that Article 11 does not guarantee a right to enter into collective agreements, by holding that where on the facts the right to enter into a collective agreement represents for a union the 'principal, if not the only, means of promoting and safeguarding the interests of its members', an interference with that right may by itself be a breach of Article 11 unless it can be justified under Article 11(2). In that case, the applicant trade union[209] had entered into a collective agreement with a municipal council that for two years had governed all employer-employee relations within the municipality, but which was then annulled retrospectively as a result of a judicial decision ruling that the union was not competent to make collective agreements. The Chamber held that on the facts of the case the collective agreement was for the union the 'principal, if not the only, means' of protecting its members' interests—no other possibility or possibilities of action available to the union under Turkish law would have been sufficient. The Court then held that the failure to provide the union with legal capacity to enter into collective agreements, which was required by ILO Convention 98 that the respondent state had ratified but not implemented, was not justified under Article 11. This ruling was confirmed by the Grand Chamber which held that Article 11 did guarantee a right to bargain collectively and to enter into collective agreements, overruling, in the light of developments in international and national law, the Court's contrary rulings in the *Swedish Engine Drivers' Union* case.

Although, with the exception of the recent *Wilson* and *Demir and Baykara* cases, the Court's jurisprudence creates the appearance that Article 11(1) guarantees only the barest minimum of protection for trade unions in the protection of their members' interests, it should be noted that in the cases in which the matter has been raised unsuccessfully the trade union or its members have had extensive rights in the national legal system concerned which could be seen cumulatively as allowing for the effective exercise of the right to organize. What the applicants were complaining about in those cases was the absence of a specific right or a specific restriction. A state which conceded only the bare minimum of rights to organized labour should not be confident that it is complying with Article 11, although the opaque language of the Court in its judgments may make it difficult for an applicant to demonstrate that the state is in dereliction. Hopefully, the *Wilson* and *Demir and Baykara* cases (the latter is pending before the Grand Chamber) signify a new departure offering at least some necessary protection for the legitimate work of trade unions. Otherwise, if Article 11 is ultimately interpreted as offering little or nothing by way of a guarantee of the collective right to organize, the only remedies available at the international level will be the less effective rights of petition under the European Social Charter and within the procedures of the ILO.[210]

---

[208] Hudoc (2006) para 40; Grand Chamber judgment hudoc (2008).

[209] This was the civil servant trade union in the *Tum Haber Sen* case, below.

[210] Neither the Charter nor the ILO system of petitions lead to legally binding decisions, which is one reason why the ILO adverse ruling in the *GCHQ* case, below, was simply ignored. The Charter collective complaints system cannot be invoked by individuals and has only been accepted by twelve Convention parties. The guarantees of freedom of association in the two UN Covenants (see Article 22 of the International Covenant on Civil and Political Rights and Article 8 of the International Covenant on Economic, Social and Cultural Rights) have yet to bear fruit.

5. RESTRICTIONS ON PUBLIC SERVICE EMPLOYEES

The second sentence of Article 11(2) reads:

> This article shall not prevent the imposition of lawful restrictions on the exercise of these rights by members of the armed forces, of the police or of the administration of the state.

This provision was considered by the Commission in *Council of Civil Service Unions v UK* (the *GCHQ* case).[211] The British government had decreed that civil servants working at its national centre for electronic eavesdropping should cease to have the right to belong to a trade union, which they had had formerly. Instead, they were allowed membership only of an approved staff association. The Commission decided that the staff fell within the second sentence of Article 11(2) as 'members of the administration of the state'. It also read 'restrictions' as permitting a complete ban on union membership.[212] It then held that the term 'lawful' in the second sentence meant, firstly, that the restrictions must be imposed in accordance with national law and, secondly, that they should not be arbitrary. Both of these requirements were met on the facts. As to the second, the Commission concluded that the decision to impose such a ban, though 'drastic', was not 'arbitrary', given the fact that earlier industrial action at GCHQ had revealed the threat to national security that would be posed if GCHQ telecommunications monitoring were interrupted. The decision of the Commission reflected the general attitude of deference at Strasbourg to the choices made by the states in the field of trade union rights and freedoms, a position doubtless enhanced in this case because of the general reluctance to review determinations of the states made in the interests of national security. Nonetheless, it is a matter of regret that an application affecting the rights of 8,000 workers, raising novel questions under Article 11, did not reach the Court. The only other form of protection available against too ready resort to this exception lies in the determination of who are 'members of the administration of the state'.[213]

A judgment that is more supportive of the right of 'members of the administration of the state' to form a trade union was given in the admittedly clear-cut case of *Tum Haber Sen and Cinar v Turkey*.[214] In that case, a trade union whose members were civil servants working in the communications field for the post office and the (non-national security) telecommunication service was dissolved by the state solely on the ground that

---

[211] *No 11603/85*, 50 DR 228 (1987). See Burrows, in Jaspers and Betten, eds, *25 Years European Social Charter*, 1988, pp 38–44; and Morris, *loc cit* at p 536, n 151, above, pp 45–9. The claim was also unsuccessful under the European Social Charter, but an ILO claim succeeded under a differently worded text: see Harris, *op cit* at p 3, n 22 above, p 89.

[212] The Commission noted that 'restrictions' in Article 11(2), first sentence, has been so interpreted in the context of freedom of assembly. For criticism of this interpretation, see Hepple, *loc cit* at p 536, n 151, above, p 173.

[213] See *Vogt v Germany* A 323 (1995); 21 EHRR 205 para 88 Com Rep (although a civil servant, a secondary school teacher was not 'member of the administration of the state', as her work did not involve the exercise of state authority; question not decided by the Court) and *Grande Oriente D'Italia Di Palazzo Giustiniani v Italy No 35972/97* hudoc (2001) (law barring masonic association members from holding office in regional organizations and standing for nomination and regional Council appointments not part of the 'administration on the state'). For the view that Article 11(2) should be amended so as to exclude 'members of the administration of the state', see Zanghi, in *Freedom of Association loc cit* at p 515, n 1, above, p 149.

[214] 2006-II; 46 EHRR 374 para 35. Cf, *Demir and Baykara v Turkey*, above, p 545. And see *Metin Turan v Turkey No 14111/06* (transfer owing to membership of trade union a violation of Article 11 right to freedom of association).

civil servants were not allowed to form or join a trade union under Turkish law. When assessing the 'restriction', which, despite being a complete ban, it did not rule was in itself impermissible (cf, the *GCHQ* case), the Court applied the 'prescribed by law'/'necessary in a democratic society' formula found in the first sentence of Article 11(2), taking the view that this formula governed restrictions justified by the second sentence also. As to the 'necessity' of the restriction, the Court held that 'the exceptions in Article 11 are to be construed strictly', requiring 'convincing and compelling reasons' to 'justify restrictions on such parties'[215] freedom of association' and that 'only a limited margin of appreciation' applies. In the absence of any 'concrete evidence' to suggest that the union represented a threat to Turkish society or the Turkish state or of any other credible public interest argument by the respondent state, the Court found that the absolute ban on the trade union was a breach of Article 11. If, as can be assumed, the Court continues to apply the 'necessity' test to the second sentence of Article 11(2), as in *Tum Haber Sen*, it is unlikely that the reasoning in the *GCHQ* case would be replicated in any future cases.

6. CONCLUSION

The last decade has seen an abundance of cases on freedom of assembly and association with a high proportion of violations. Most of these cases have originated from the 'new democracies' of Central and Eastern Europe. The themes are tolerance of peaceful dissent, pluralism in opinion, with some allowance for disturbance to others, and the lawfulness of government interference. Of general significance in the jurisprudence is the incorporation of the strict protection of the freedom to express opinions found in Article 10 into the freedoms of assembly and association in Article 11. Notable also is the development of positive obligations on the state to take preventative measures to protect assemblies and associations and an obligation to conduct effective investigations into interferences by private individuals with freedom of association. These are essential democratic standards that support the activities of civil society. Beyond these standards the freedom of assembly cases concede a fairly broad margin of appreciation to states when deciding the necessity for an interference on the facts of a particular case. The limit to the ambit of the freedom is revealed in the direct action cases and in *Cissé v France*.[216] A further challenge to freedom of assembly is the increasing privatization of the public spaces available for its exercise.

Interferences with freedom of association have primarily involved the dissolution of political parties and the refusal to register associations. The limitations on freedom of association under Article 11(2) are strictly construed, following the approach taken to freedom of expression of political opinions in Article 10. The Court has allowed the curtailment of freedom of association where it is considered to be incompatible with Convention values, specifically political and religious pluralism and the prohibition on the use of violence.[217] However, as the *Refah* case[218] demonstrates, the circumstances in which the maintenance of democratic institutions and the rights of others demand limitation upon the right to freedom of association is debatable and the issue raises fundamental questions about the organization of European political democracy.

---

[215] Id, presumably those in the second sentence of Article 11(2).   [216] 2002-III.
[217] See *Refah Partisi (The Welfare Party) v Turkey* 2003-II; 37 EHRR 1 GC and *Gorzelik v Poland* hudoc (2004); 40 EHRR 76.
[218] *Ibid*.

The unwillingness of the Court, and formerly the Commission, to find greater protection for trade unions in the protection of their members' interests within Article 11 has been criticized.[219] However, the Court may be in the process of demanding more of states, more closely in line with international labour law standards. The *Wilson* and *Demir and Baykara* cases expand the positive obligation of states in this regard and may signal a more general move away from the Court's unwillingness to use Article 11 as a vehicle for protecting trade union rights that was manifest in its 1970s judgments in the *National Union of Belgian Police* and other cases. But any such development will not affect the Court's clear stance in favour of the negative right not to join a trade union in the *Young, James and Webster* and later cases, in which the individual, as opposed to the collective, dimension of freedom of association has prevailed in the context of labour relations. In this respect the Court has not responded to arguments that it should take a more active role in protecting the collective interest and that there is a danger that too great a concentration on the position of the dissenting individual will weaken the fundamental right of association of others and the effective capacity of the association to protect their interests.[220]

The references to standards of 'unreasonableness' and 'arbitrariness'[221] as those that are applicable when deciding whether the state's positive obligation to protect private persons from interferences with their Article 11 rights by others do not indicate a willingness by the Court, and formerly the Commission, to subject national laws and decisions to intensive scrutiny.[222] For some labour lawyers, this is an acceptable outcome.[223] Many of the conflicts are essentially between trade unions and members or non-members or between trade unions and employers. In the field of industrial relations, not only do the states adopt a variety of ways of managing these matters but they frequently acknowledge that considerable degrees of economic and social pressure are legitimate instruments in industrial conflict.[224] The Court has recognized this too. In a sense, this is a realistic attitude. The European Court cannot write a comprehensive trade union law on the narrow basis of Article 11. At the same time, there must be more that Article 11 can offer in the context of the protection by organized labour in the protection of members' interests than is to be found in the Court's early judgments, and, as suggested, the Court's recent judgments may indicate a new willingness to recognize this.

---

[219] Leader, 20 ILJ 39 at 57 (1991).

[220] *Ibid.* See also the dissenting opinion of Judge Soerensen, joined by Judges Thór Vilhjálmsson and Lagergren in *Young, James and Webster v UK.*

[221] See *Cheall v UK,* above at p 538.

[222] But see Mr Busuttil, dissenting in *Sibson v UK* A 258-A (1993); 17 EHRR 193 Com Rep, who was effectively reviewing the judgment of the Court of Appeal.

[223] See Forde, *loc cit* at p 536, n 151, above, pp 330–2.

[224] See Baglioni and Crouch, eds, *European Industrial Relations,* 1990, particularly Ch 1 by Baglioni.

13

ARTICLE 12: THE RIGHT
TO MARRY AND TO
FOUND A FAMILY

Article 12

Men and women of marriageable age have the right to marry and to found a family, according to the national laws governing the exercise of this right.

1. INTRODUCTION

The text of Article 12 asserts a relatively narrow right (or possibly rights) to marry and to found a family, subject to a wide power on the part of states to regulate the exercise of the right. The interpretation of Article 12 by the Strasbourg authorities has not greatly expanded its scope. Although closely connected with the notions of 'family life' and 'private life' in Article 8, which has been interpreted imaginatively, the Court, and formerly the Commission, has not been so receptive to developing the content of Article 12.[1] This has had a particularly inhibiting effect on the right to found a family. The original understanding of Article 12 appears to have been, as its text suggests ('the right'), that it set out a single right of men and women to marry and found a family. Accordingly, although the right to marry has been held to be protected in circumstances where there is no intention or no possibility of procreation,[2] the Court has not been willing to admit that the right to found a family can arise under Article 12 in the absence of a marriage.[3]

If an unmarried couple do have a family, their various rights will be protected under Article 8, not under Article 12 and any differentiation that national law makes between married and unmarried couples in this respect will fall to be considered under Articles 8 and 14, not Articles 12 and 14.[4] In contrast, discrimination in national laws on marriage and the founding of a family within marriage do fall within Articles 12 and 14, for example in cases of discrimination between men and women.[5]

With regard to the relationship between Articles 12 and 8 in other respects, Article 12 does not apply to family life beyond the point of marriage, other than in respect of the founding of a family. For example, the taking of children into care is entirely a matter for

---

[1] See eg, *Marckx v Belgium* A 31 (1979); 2 EHRR 330 para 67 PC and *BR and J v FRG No 9639/82*, 36 DR 130 at 140 (1984).

[2] See *Hamer v UK No 7114/75*, 24 DR 5 at 16 (1979) Com Rep; CM Res DH (81) 5.

[3] See *Rees v UK* A 106 (1986); 9 EHRR 56 para 49 and *Christine Goodwin v UK* 2002-VI; 35 EHRR 447 para 98 GC.

[4] See *KM v UK No 30309/96* hudoc (1997) DA and *McMichael v UK* A 308 (1995); 20 EHRR 205.

[5] *KM v UK No 30309/96* hudoc (1997) DA.

Article 8.[6] Insofar as there is a potential overlap between the two Articles in respect of the founding of a family, the Court may deal with the case just under Article 8, as in its treatment of artificial insemination.[7]

Article 12 guarantees the right to marry and to found a family 'according to the national laws governing the exercise of this right'. This qualificatory wording is of a quite different kind from that in Articles 8–11. While it does provide a wider margin of appreciation to states, the words are not to be read literally for that would deprive Article 12 of all meaning at the international level. National 'laws' must satisfy a European standard as to the meaning of a 'law' and 'must not restrict or reduce the right in such a way or to such an extent that the very essence of the right is impaired'.[8] This interpretation is bolstered by the words 'governing the *exercise* of this right' which indicate that the national laws may regulate but not prohibit or exclude the right altogether.[9]

2. THE RIGHT TO MARRY

I. GENERALLY

It is for the national law to regulate such matters as form and capacity to marry, but any procedural or substantive limitations that are adopted must not remove the very essence of the right.[10] As to procedural limitations, the state may require compliance with formal registration requirements.[11] As to substance, it may impose limitations on such matters as marriageable age,[12] consanguinity, and the number of spouses.[13] It is for the state to decide on the content of its conflict rules and whether to apply them.[14] The question of the recognition of foreign marriages, whether of a different kind to national ones[15] or not, will generally arise under Article 8 rather than Article 12.

Certain limitations have been found to be in breach of Article 12. In *F v Switzerland*,[16] a Swiss court ruled that the applicant could not marry again for three years after a divorce in which the court found him solely responsible for the breakdown of the marriage. After the divorce, the applicant was a single man and wanted to remarry. He was, the majority in the European Court stated, entitled to re-marry 'without unreasonable restrictions'. The condition imposed by the Swiss court was unreasonable because the reasons the government gave for it were inappropriate (to protect the future spouse) or its effects on others were disproportionate (the chance that children would be born out of wedlock). The judgment was by the narrowest majority, nine to eight. The dissenting judges thought that this restriction fell within the wide power of the state to legislate for the exercise of the right to marry: it did not affect the essence of the right. The majority judgment

---

[6] *P, C and S v UK* 2002-VI; 35 EHRR 1075.

[7] See *Dickson v UK* hudoc (2007); 46 EHRR 927. An interference with family life that is justified under Article 8(2) cannot be a breach of Article 12: *Boso v Italy* 2002-VII.

[8] *Rees v UK* A 106 (1986); 9 EHRR 56 para 50 PC.   [9] *Hamer v UK*, n 2 above.

[10] *F v Switzerland* A 128 (1987); 10 EHRR 411 para 32 PC.

[11] *X v FRG No 6167/73*, 1 DR 64 (1974) (religious marriage ceremony by itself insufficient).

[12] See *Khan v UK No 11579/85*, 48 DR 252 (1986). Marriageable age varies within Europe.

[13] *X v UK No 3898/68*, 35 CD 102 (1970); 13 YBECHR 674 (1970) (bigamy prohibition not a breach). And see *Johnston v Ireland* A 112 (1986); 9 EHRR 203 para 52 PC. See also *Zu Leiningen v Germany* 2005-VIII F Sett (need for family approval of spouse).

[14] *X v Switzerland No 9057/80*, 26 DR 207 (1981).

[15] Eg, a state may recognize polygamous marriages celebrated lawfully abroad while not allowing them under its own law.

[16] A 128 (1987); 10 EHRR 411 paras 30–40 PC. See *also KM v UK No 30309/96* hudoc (1997) DA.

confirms that the imposition of delay in the exercise of the right to marry between two people who are ready to do so will be regarded as a serious infringement of their interests and a breach of Article 12.[17]

Another substantive limitation was found to be in breach of Article 12 in *B and L v UK*.[18] This case concerned a statutory limitation prohibiting the marriage of a man and the former wife of his son until after the death of both his son and the son's mother. The ban was aimed at protecting the integrity of the family (preventing sexual rivalry between parents and children) and preventing harm to any children of the son's family. The Court noted that such a limitation, with the same 'legitimate aims', was present in the law of a 'large number of contracting states' (twenty-one). Nonetheless, the Court held unanimously that there was a breach of Article 12 'in the circumstances of the case'. First, the ban did not criminalize extra-marital relationships —indeed in this case the father and the daughter-in-law were cohabiting, with the child of the latter's marriage living in their home. Second, the ban was not an absolute one: an exception could be made in a particular case pursuant to a personal Act of Parliament, the procedure for which was 'expensive and cumbersome' and did not involve any examination of the particular circumstances.

Marriage is a consensual union between the parties and ordinarily the state will have no positive obligations to facilitate it. However, where there are collateral circumstances which prevent willing parties from entering into what otherwise would be a lawful marriage, the state may have a duty to mitigate or eliminate these obstacles. The Commission considered this in two cases involving prisoners in the United Kingdom. There was no specific rule of English law preventing prisoners from marrying but the Marriage Act 1949 required that marriages be celebrated only at certain places outside prisons and the prison authorities would not allow the applicants temporary release to be married outside the prison. In *Hamer v UK*,[19] the prisoner's opportunity to be married would have been delayed for a period until he obtained parole. In *Draper v UK*,[20] the prisoner was serving a life sentence and had no foreseeable date when he would be released on licence and be able to marry. The Commission decided that there was a violation in each case, an assessment confirmed by the Committee of Ministers. Considerations of security did not preclude the state from making some arrangement which would have allowed the prisoners to marry. The effect of the law and the decision of the authorities was to cause such delay in the prisoners' opportunity to be married as to infringe the substance of their right to marry. As a result of these cases, the government introduced legislation to allow prisoners to be married in prison.[21]

As noted, the right to marry is protected even though there is no intention or possibility of procreation. One of the government's arguments in the *Draper* and *Hamer* cases was that there was no opportunity for cohabitation and consummation of the marriage. To that, the Commission said: 'The essence of the right to marry...is the formation of a legally binding association between a man and a woman. It is for them to decide whether or not they wish to enter an association in circumstances where they cannot cohabit.'[22]

[17] Cf, the *Draper* and *Hamer* cases, below.

[18] Hudoc (2005) paras 36, 37, 41. For other questionable restrictions, see *Selim v Cyprus* 2002-VI F Sett (civil marriage by Muslim Turkish Cypriots prohibited) and *Staiku v Greece No 35426/97* hudoc (1997) DA (woman dismissed from army for marrying within five years). A marriage of convenience restriction is permissible: *Klip and Kruger v Netherlands No 33257/96* hudoc (1997) DA.

[19] No 7114/75, 24 DR 5 at 16 (1979) Com Rep; CM Res DH (81) 5.

[20] No 8186/78, 24 DR 72 at 81 (1980) Com Rep; CM Res DH (81) 4. See also *Mazak v Poland* 2007 F Sett.

[21] Marriage Act 1983, s 1, which also allows marriages for some mental patients in places of detention and for house-bound persons at home.

[22] *Hamer v UK, loc cit* at n 19, above, p 16. Cf, *Draper, loc cit* at n 20, above, p 81. On conjugal visits for prisoners, see below, p 555.

There is no positive duty on a state to provide the material conditions to make the right to marry effective. Thus a state may foster marriage by granting benefits to married couples which it denies to single cohabitees but it is not obliged to do so.[23] Indeed, it is not under a duty to guarantee that married couples are no worse off than cohabitees in a similar position to them.[24]

The right to marry does not 'in principle include the right to choose the geographic location of the marriage'.[25] Accordingly, a state is not obliged to admit an alien fiancé to its territory, or to allow him or her to remain in it so that a marriage may be celebrated there, at least where the couple are able to marry elsewhere.[26] By implication, there may be an exception where one of intended spouses is a national of the state concerned and the marriage may not be contracted elsewhere. Similarly, Article 12 does not require a state to admit an alien married to one of its nationals to enter or remain on its territory to establish or live in the marital home and found a family there;[27] any such case would arise under Article 8 rather than Article 12.[28]

II. TRANSSEXUALS

The question whether marriage is limited to unions between a man and woman has arisen in two situations: unions between a transsexual and another; and unions between homosexuals.

For the transsexual, the complaint is that a state which denies the transsexual the right to marry a person of the *now* opposite sex is inconsistent with his or her new status and the transsexual's possibilities for marriage. In its early jurisprudence, the Court rejected this complaint, but has since changed its mind. In *Rees v UK*[29] the Court unanimously ruled against the applicant transsexual. It stated that 'the right to marry guaranteed by Article 12 refers to the traditional marriage between persons of opposite biological sex. This appears also from the wording of the Article which makes it clear that Article 12 is mainly concerned to protect marriage as the basis of the family'. In *Cossey v UK*,[30] the Court, by fourteen votes to four, confirmed its ruling in *Rees*. Although there were some states in which a marriage between a transsexual and another person of the now opposite sex was permitted, there was no 'general abandonment' of the traditional notion of marriage propounded in *Rees*.

But in *Christine Goodwin v UK*,[31] the Court reversed *Rees*. It did so on the basis that the right to marry in Article 12 was distinct from the right to found a family in the same Article and that it could no longer be assumed that the wording 'men and women' in Article 12 referred to a 'determination of gender by purely biological criteria'. There had been 'major social changes in the institution of marriage since the adoption of the Convention', with now 'widespread acceptance of the marriage of transsexuals' to members of their new opposite sex in Council of Europe states. In addition, 'dramatic changes'

---

[23] *Marckx v Belgium* A 31 (1979); 2 EHRR 330 PC.

[24] *Kleine Staarman v Netherlands* No 10503/83, 42 DR 162 (1985) (loss of benefit on marriage) and *Lindsay and Lindsay v UK* No 11089/84, 49 DR 181 at 193 (1986) (married couple taxed more heavily than cohabitees).

[25] *Savoia and Bounegru v Italy* No 8407/05 hudoc (2006) DA.

[26] *Ibid*. Cf, *X v FRG* No 7175/75 6 DR 138 (1976).

[27] *Abdulaziz, Cabales and Balkandali v UK* A 94 (1985); 7 EHRR 471 PC, which concerned the right of persons settled in the UK to have their alien spouses join them, was not argued under Article 12 and, in any event, turned on the discrimination point: see below, p 592.

[28] *Mahfaz v UK* No 20598/92 hudoc (1993) DA and *Schober v Austria* No 34891/97 hudoc (1999) DA.

[29] A 106 (1986); 9 EHRR 561 para 49 PC.   [30] A 184 (1990); 13 EHRR 622 para 46 PC.

[31] 2002-VI; 35 EHRR 447 paras 100–3.

had been brought about by developments in medicine and science in the field of trans-sexuality. While not so many states allowed in their law post-operative transsexuals to marry members of their new opposite sex as gave full legal recognition to gender reassignment in other respects,[32] this did not support an argument for leaving the matter entirely within the contracting parties' margin of appreciation. While some discretion could be left to them on matters such as 'the conditions under which a person claiming legal recognition as a transsexual establishes that gender reassignment has been properly effected or under which past marriages cease to be valid and the formalities applicable to future marriages', not to allow a post-operative transsexual who was living as a member of his or her new sex the possibility in any circumstances of marrying a member of the new opposite sex was to deny him or her the very essence of the Article 12 right to marry. As to the validity of past marriages, in *Parry v UK*[33] it was held that it was within the margin of appreciation for a state to make the legal recognition of a transsexual's acquired gender contingent upon the dissolution of a marriage contracted with a person who was now of the same gender as the post-operation transsexual.

III. HOMOSEXUALS

The Court's ruling in the *Christine Goodwin* case that the right to marry is not limited to persons who are biologically of the opposite sex opens up the possibility that Article 12 might be extended beyond the facts of that case to homosexual marriages or civil partnerships. However, this would be a step beyond allowing transsexuals the right to marry under Article 12: whereas transsexual unions may be regarded as associations between a man and a woman, in the case of homosexuals, it would be the substance of the proposed union rather than the character of the participants in it that would be in issue. Given the increasing number of contracting parties to the Convention that allow homosexual marriages or (especially) civil partnerships in their law,[34] the time may come when the Court, if called upon, would rule that Article 12 extended to them.[35]

IV. DIVORCE

There is no reference to the dissolution of marriage in Article 12. After a review of the *travaux préparatoires*, in *Johnston v Ireland*[36] the Court decided that the omission was deliberate: the drafting states did not intend the Convention to grant a right to divorce. The Court held that the prohibition on divorce in the Irish Constitution did not infringe the Convention and that a different conclusion would not be reached by taking into account developments in other European states which had established a very wide right to divorce, because 'the Court cannot, by means of an evolutive interpretation, derive from [the Convention and the Protocols] a right which was not included therein at the outset.

---

[32] The Court had evidence from *Liberty*, para 57, that twenty Convention parties allowed such marriages; Ireland and the UK did not and four had no legislation. The position in other parties was unclear. Where gender reassignment was publicly funded, only Ireland and the UK did not give full legal recognition to the new gender identity. See also *L v Lithuania* 2007-XX.

[33] No 42971/05 hudoc (2006) DA. Cf, *R and F v UK* No 35748/05 hudoc (2006) DA.

[34] Tbree states recognize gay marriages; another sixteen recognize civil partnerships.

[35] In his dissent in *W v UK* No 11095/84, 63 DR 34 (1989) Com Rep; CM Res DH (89) 27, Mr Schermers argued that Article 12 should extend to homosexual marriages. They do not give rise to 'family life' under Article 8: *S v UK* No 11716/85, 47 DR 274 (1986). See also *Fretté v France* 2002 and *EB v France* 2008 (Article 8 adoption by homosexuals cases).

[36] A 112 (1986); 9 EHRR 203 PC.

This is particularly so here, where the omission was deliberate.'[37] The Court found that Article 5 of the Seventh Protocol also had been drafted in such a way as to avoid the implication that a right to divorce was contained in the Convention.[38] The consequences of the judgment are less serious because of the requirement of a protective remedy between husband and wife under Article 8[39] and the steps the Court has taken to ameliorate the position of illegitimate children under the same Article,[40] but it does not sit happily with the importance the Court attached to the right to remarry to avoid children being born out of wedlock in its judgment in *F v Switzerland*.[41] If a state, in the exercise of its discretion, permits divorce, a divorce must be obtainable with reasonable expedition in order to allow re-marriage.[42]

3. THE RIGHT TO FOUND A FAMILY

The right to found a family exists only within marriage.[43] It does not apply to the many couples who now live together in European society without marrying. It also does not extend to having grandchildren, so that potential grandparents have no claim under Article 12 if their children take a vow of celibacy in holy orders.[44]

The Commission described the right to found a family as an 'absolute right' in the sense that Article 12 gives no grounds for the state to interfere with it.[45] The most obvious interferences with the right to found a family are programmes of compulsory sterilization or abortion.[46] Voluntary sterilization or abortion by one partner to a marriage clearly has an impact on the interests of the other partner but, however serious this may be, it is hard to see that the Court would find a positive obligation on a state under Article 12 to regulate a private decision of the above kind except in circumstances where some other right under the Convention was more directly implicated, such as that in Article 2 or Article 8. In *Boso v Italy*,[47] an application by a husband who claimed that his wife's decision to have an abortion deprived him of his opportunity to have a family was declared inadmissible on the ground that the abortion was to protect the wife's health, as allowed by national law and Article 2.

While states have the power to encourage the legitimate family, they have no positive obligation to do so. Article 12 cannot be made the vehicle for requiring positive social programmes from the state in support of the family.[48] We have already seen that couples have the right to marry even in the absence of a prospect of cohabitation. In these circumstances, the state has no duty to facilitate opportunities for the couple to found a family by allowing for consummation of the marriage.[49] Where couples are separated as the result

---

[37] Id, para 53. Ireland legalized divorce in 1996. Malta is now the only Convention party that prohibits divorce.

[38] See below p 754. Article 5 refers to equality of spouses 'during marriage and in the event of its dissolution' (emphasis added).

[39] *Airey v Ireland* A 32 (1979); 3 EHRR 592.

[40] See *Marckx v Belgium* A 31 (1979); 2 EHRR 330 PC.

[41] A 128 (1987); 10 EHRR 411 para 36 PC.   [42] *Charalambous v Cyprus* hudoc (2007).

[43] *Christine Goodwin v UK* 2002-VI; 35 EHRR 447 para 98 GC.

[44] *Sijakova v FYRM No 67914/01* hudoc (2003) DA.

[45] *X v UK No 6564/74*, 2 DR 105 at 106 (1975).

[46] A claim of infertility resulting from nuclear tests was inadmissible *ratione temporis* in *McGinley and Egan v UK Nos 21825/93 and 23414/95* hudoc (1995) DA.

[47] 2002-VII DA. See further above, p 54.

[48] *Andersson and Kullmann v Sweden No 11776/85*, 46 DR 251 (1986).

[49] *X v UK No 6564/74*, 2 DR 105 (1975) and *X and Y v Switzerland No 8166/78*, 13 DR 241 (1978).

of a deportation or an immigration order which prevents a party to a marriage or proposed marriage from entering a state, any Convention remedy will arise under Article 8, not Article 12.[50] It is unlikely that a right of a partner to a marriage or a proposed marriage to stay in or to be admitted to a state in order to found a family can be found in Article 12 if it cannot be found in Article 8.

A further interference with the right to found a family exists for persons detained by the state. This can be remedied by conjugal visits, but as yet, while noting that prisoners are allowed conjugal visits by their wives in more than half of the Convention parties,[51] the Court has held that such visits are not required by Article 12 or Article 8.[52]

While Article 12 protects married couples from interference by the state with their right to found a family, for some couples the chance will be an empty one because of their incapacity to procreate. Neither Article 12 nor any other Article of the Convention guarantees a right to adopt or otherwise integrate into a family a child which is not the natural child of the married couple concerned.[53] However, states do commonly provide for adoption and the adoption system that they have is subject to scrutiny by the Court, although a breach of Article 12 is likely to be found where adoption is refused only in an extreme case of substantive or procedural unfairness[54] or where discrimination brings Article 14 into play.[55]

More recently, attention has switched to artificial reproduction. The state may be implicated at two levels. It has to decide whether and what techniques of artificial reproduction may legally be used and to whom, if any, they should be made available by the state. Both questions were in issue, directly or indirectly, in *SH v Austria*.[56] That case concerned an Austrian law which permitted artificial insemination in some cases, but prohibited the use of the sperm of a third party male donor for the purpose of *in vitro* fertilization (but not for its introduction into the woman's reproductive organs) and prohibited ovum donation by another woman entirely. The Court rejected the claims by the applicants, who were married,[57] that these limitations were a breach of Article 12 on the basis that Article 12 does not guarantee a right to procreation. Article 12, that is, is limited to the prohibition of interferences by the state with the having of children within marriage by natural means: there is no positive obligation to facilitate it by legislation to permit artificial insemination or, *a fortiori*, by providing for it through state funded medical institutions. The decision is a disappointing one. Although there may be no right of procreation under Article 12, it is arguable that the right to found a family implies that where a couple can procreate by whatever means the state should not impose unreasonable restrictions on their possibility of doing so.

---

[50] See eg, *Beldjoudi v France* A 234A (1992); 14 EHRR 801.

[51] *Dickson v UK* hudoc (2007) GC.

[52] *Ibid* and *Aliev v Ukraine* hudoc (2003). See also *ELH and PBH v UK* Nos 32094/96 and 32568/96 hudoc (1997) DA. On access to artificial insemination for a prisoner and spouse, see *Dickson v UK*, below, p 408 (breach of Article 8).

[53] *Di Lazzaro v Italy* No 31924/96 hudoc (1997) DA; *Akin v Netherlands* No 34986/97 hudoc (1998) DA; *Fretté v France* 2002-I; 38 EHRR 438; and *EB v France* 2008-XX. A state is not obliged to recognize a foreign adoption: *X and Y v UK* No 7229/75, 12 DR 32 (1997).

[54] *X and Y v UK* No 7229/75, 12 DR 32 at 34 (1977) and *X v Netherlands* No 8896/80, 24 DR 176 at 177–8 (1981).

[55] See *Singh v UK* No 60148/00 hudoc (2002) F Sett. See also *EB v France* 2008-XX GC (Article 8 case). Testamentary discrimination against adopted children falls within Article 8: *Pla and Puncernau v Andorra* hudoc (2004).

[56] No 57813/00 hudoc (2007) DA. The claim was admitted and is pending under Article 8.

[57] Artificial insemination claims by single women would fail under both Articles 12 and 14 on the Court's limited reading of the Article 12 right to found a family to the married state.

4. NON-MARRIED PERSONS

In *Marckx v Belgium*,[58] the mother of an illegitimate child claimed a right 'not to marry', that is to say, that her right to found a family should not be inhibited by disadvantages which she and her child would suffer by reason only of the fact that the mother had chosen not to marry the father of the child. The Court held that there was no legal obstacle confronting the mother 'in the exercise of the freedom to marry or to remain single' and that the disadvantages to which she referred did not constitute an interference with that legal opportunity such as to violate Article 12, although issues might arise under Article 8. In *B, R and J v FRG*,[59] the Commission confirmed that a state could treat the legitimate family more favourably than the illegitimate one, provided that its treatment of the latter did not violate Article 8. The 'full protection' of German family law extended only to the legitimate family. Here, an unmarried father and mother were living in a stable relationship with their child. A parental link was recognized by German law between the father and his child but the law would not allow him to obtain custody of the child. Just as he could not rely on Article 8, the Commission said that he could not find the right to custody in Article 12, so long as the couple remained unmarried. This limited approach to the position of unmarried persons will only be broadened, as social changes in Europe suggest it should, through an alteration in the understanding of who can marry (homosexuals), and the ambit beyond marriage of the right to found a family, or by reliance upon of Article 8.

5. CONCLUSION

Article 12 has generated only a small number of Court judgments. One reason for this has been the limited textual scope of Article 12, which to its credit the Court has largely made good by its broad and dynamic interpretation of the rights to respect for private and family life in Article 8. Thus matters arguably pertinent to Article 12 such as having a family (outside the traditional marriage), child care, family support, and sustaining family life have been dealt with under Article 8. A second reason has until recently been the Court's restriction in Article 12 of the right to marry to individuals of the biological opposite sex and of the right to found a family to married couples. The *Christine Goodwin* case concerning transsexuals marks an important departure in this regard and may presage other decisions that similarly reflect changing social values in personal relations in European states. What was particularly striking in the *Goodwin* case was the Grand Chamber's willingness to act on the basis of legal change in less than the 'great majority' of contracting parties. Other beneficial developments based on a similarly more dynamic approach to Article 12 would be the recognition of homosexual marriages and civil partnerships and adoption by same sex couples; the extension of the right to found a family beyond marriage; and a wider guarantee of artificial insemination for childless couples. The recognition of conjugal visits for prisoners would also be in line with practice in many contracting parties, although the *Dickson* case may suggest a different (artificial insemination) approach to their right to found a family. Another approach to some of these matters would be their further development under Article 8, in some cases together with Article 14.

---

[58] A 31 (1979); 2 EHRR 330 para 67 PC.
[59] *No 9639/82*, 36 DR 130 (1984). See also *X v Belgium and Netherlands No 6482/14*, 7 DR 75 (1975).

14

ARTICLE 13: THE RIGHT TO AN EFFECTIVE NATIONAL REMEDY

Article 13

Everyone whose rights and freedoms as set forth in this Convention are violated shall have an effective remedy before a national authority notwithstanding that the violation has been committed by persons acting in an official capacity.

1. INTRODUCTION[1]

Article 13 requires the provision of effective national remedies for the breach of a Convention right. So, with Article 35 (addressing, *inter alia*, exhaustion of domestic remedies), this Article is central to the co-operative relationship between the Convention and national legal systems. If national remedies were more comprehensive there would be less need for applications to be made to the Court; consequently there would be less pressure of cases on that institution, which would be better able to deal with the cases reaching it; its case law could be more considered and so in turn it would be clearer to the national authorities what is required of them. Accordingly, via Article 13 the primary responsibility of the states to secure the enjoyment of human rights may be realized and the effective discharge of the subsidiary role of the institutions may be facilitated.[2]

Despite its importance, the language and precise objective of Article 13 are far from clear: two judges have called it the 'most obscure' provision of the Convention.[3] Some complex questions occur regarding its place within the scheme of the Strasbourg system of human rights control (see heading 2 below). In the past, the approaches to the interpretation of Article 13 by the Strasbourg authorities have oscillated, sometimes demanding more of the state,[4] sometimes less,[5] as they have sought an understanding of it which fits into the whole structure of the Convention. Over the last decade, the general trend of the jurisprudence has been to ask significantly more of the state in relation to Articles 2, 3, 5, and 6(1) (as regards trial within a reasonable time) of the Convention in particular. Given

---

[1] On Article 13, see Frowein in *Ryssdal Essays* and Mowbray, *The Development of Positive Obligations*, Ch 8.

[2] See Recommendation Rec(2004)6 of the Committee of Ministers to Member States on the Improvement of Domestic Remedies. This 'encourages member states to examine their respective legal systems in the light of the case-law of the Court and to take, if need be, the necessary and appropriate measures to ensure, through legislation or case-law, effective remedies as secured by Article 13' (Appendix para 4).

[3] Judges Matscher and Pinheiro Farinha, partly dissenting in *Malone v UK* A 82 (1984); 7 EHRR 14 PC.

[4] Eg, *Plattform 'Ärzte für das Leben' v Austria* A 139 (1988); 13 EHRR 204.

[5] Eg, *Leander v Sweden* A 116 (1987); 9 EHRR 433.

the workload pressures facing the Court, often in respect of so-called 'repetitive cases', this trend is a welcome development.

2. ARTICLE 13 WITHIN THE GENERAL SCHEME OF THE CONVENTION

I. ARTICLE 13, INCORPORATION OF THE CONVENTION AND DISCRETION AVAILABLE TO THE STATE IN PROVIDING REMEDIES

The text of Article 13 ('violation...committed by persons acting in an official capacity') indicates that it is primarily directed toward executive action, but the Court has not viewed it in this limited way. The Article gives 'direct expression to the states' obligation to protect human rights first and foremost within their own legal system'.[6] It backs that up at the international level by 'establish[ing] an additional guarantee for an individual in order to ensure that he or she effectively enjoys those rights'. So the Article exists 'to provide a means whereby individuals can obtain relief at national level for violations of their Convention rights before having to set in motion the international machinery of complaint before the Court'.[7]

Article 13 cases will therefore involve the Court examining the domestic legal regime relevant to the applicant's Convention claim to see if it was possible for him or her to obtain relief at the national level. Generally speaking, the Court will be examining whether domestic law provided an 'effective remedy' in the sense that, if resorted to, it could have prevented the alleged violation occurring or continuing, or for any violation that had already occurred the applicant could have achieved appropriate redress.[8]

The best way for a state to help to insulate itself from violating Article 13 in a Strasbourg case is, therefore, to effectively incorporate the Convention into domestic law.[9] All states parties have incorporated the Convention in one form or another,[10] but this has not been through any legal obligation derived from Article 13 or the Convention generally. Indeed, Article 13 does not require incorporation of the Convention.[11] It is not even necessarily the case that it requires that the state be required to provide one single remedy, provided an aggregate of remedies suffices on the facts.[12] Nor does Article 13 guarantee a remedy to challenge domestic (primary) legislation[13] before a national

---

[6] *Kudla v Poland* 2000-XI; 35 EHRR 198 para 152 GC.   [7] *Ibid.*

[8] Cf, *Ramirez Sanchez v France* hudoc (2006); 45 EHRR 1099 para 160 GC.

[9] Even when incorporated the exact place of the Convention in the domestic hierarchy of laws, matters of standing and justiciability may serve to deny an effective remedy in a particular case, see Polaciewicz and Jacob-Foltzer, 12 HRLJ 65, 125 (1991). Further, the remedy must be available in practice as well as in law.

[10] See Blackburn, ed, *Fundamental Rights in Europe: The ECHR and its Member States: 1950–2000*, 2001, Ch 3 (by Polakiewicz).

[11] See *Ireland v UK* A 25 (1978); 2 EHRR 25 para 239 PC; *James v UK* A 98 (1986); 8 EHRR 123 para 85 PC (Article 13 does not 'guarantee a remedy allowing a contracting state's laws to be challenged before a national authority on the ground of being contrary to the Convention'); *Leander v Sweden* A 116 (1987); 9 EHRR 433 para 77 and *Young, James and Webster v UK* A 44 (1981) para 177 Com Rep, cf, Messrs Opsahl and Trechsel, dissenting. Cf, *Peck v UK* 2003-I; 36 EHRR 719 para 101; *Goodwin (Christine) v UK* 2002-VI; 35 EHRR 447 para 113 and *PM v UK* hudoc (2005); 42 EHRR 1015 paras 32–4.

[12] See below, p 566.

[13] See *James v UK* A 98 (1986); 8 EHRR 123 para 85 PC and *A v UK* 2002-X; 36 EHRR 917 para 112.

authority on the basis of the Convention (secondary legislation is a different matter).[14] This position may be hard to reconcile with the effective protection of human rights, but it is must be recalled that most states parties to the Convention do not allow even their Supreme Courts to strike down legislation.[15] Similarly the unwillingness of a constitutional tribunal to exercise a discretion to undertake a review of the Convention question will not involve a violation of Article 13.[16]

Consistent with the fact that there is no requirement to incorporate the Convention, the exact way in which the states provide for Article 13 'relief at national level' is up to them; they are 'afforded a margin of appreciation in conforming with their obligations'.[17] It is not a requirement that the Convention be capable of being directly relied upon in the domestic courts; nonetheless, Article 13 requires that the legal remedies an applicant makes use of provide for the same remedy *in substance*. As the Grand Chamber put it in *Rotaru v Romania*:[18]

> Article 13 guarantees the availability at national level of a remedy to enforce the substance of the Convention rights and freedoms in whatever form they might happen to be secured in the domestic legal order. This Article therefore requires the provision of a domestic remedy allowing the 'competent national authority' both to deal with the substance of the relevant Convention complaint and to grant appropriate relief, although Contracting states are afforded some discretion as to the manner in which they conform to their obligation under this provision. The remedy must be 'effective' in practice as well as in law ...

Although the requirement is that the applicant be able to put the substance of his Convention claim to the national decision-maker, there does not need to be a guarantee that that decision-maker will reach the right result on the Convention question in issue.[19]

The effectiveness of the remedy required by Article 13 may be conditioned by the character of the Convention right to which it is sought to attach it. More important rights require more stringent remedies,[20] but the effectiveness of any remedy that Article 13 requires may be limited by virtue of the nature of the state power—for example those related to national security considerations—the exercise of which is being questioned.[21]

---

[14] In *Abdulaziz, Cabales and Balkandali v UK* A 94 (1985); 7 EHRR 163 paras 92–3 PC the Court refused to accept the British government's argument that the Immigration Rules were a form of legislation and so should be subject to the principle of immunity of legislation. Considering the amount of administrative law covered by secondary legislation any other finding would have had a devastating effect on the role Article 13 could play.

[15] See the concurring opinion of Judges Bindschedler-Robert, Gölcüklü, Matscher, and Spielmann in *James v UK* A 98 (1986); 8 EHRR 123 PC, noting that, 'when the Convention was ratified, only a few Contracting states made legislative provision for private individuals to test the constitutionality of a statute (or its compatibility with the Convention), and this is still the position'. The opinion concluded, 'we are not at all convinced by the argument that it would be inconsistent with the sovereignty of [the UK] Parliament if its Acts were subject to review by another national authority, since, on the one hand, as a matter of international law, there is no longer any doubt as to the state's responsibility even for Acts passed by its legislature, and, on the other hand, the legislation of a number of states provides for judicial control of Acts of Parliament by a constitutional court'. See also the concurring opinion of Judge Pinheiro Farinha and that of Judges Pettiti and Russo.

[16] *VDSO and Gubi v Austria* A 302 (1994); 20 EHRR 56 paras 54–5.

[17] *Smith and Grady v UK* 1999-VI; 29 EHRR 493 para 135. See also *Kudla v Poland* 2000-XI; 35 EHRR 198 para 154 ('Contracting states...afforded some discretion as to the manner in which they provide the relief required by Article 13 and conform to their Convention obligation under that provision').

[18] 2000-V para 67 GC. See also *Soering v UK* A 161 (1989); 11 EHRR 439 para 122 PC and *Vilvarajah v UK* A 215 (1991); 14 EHRR 248 paras 117–27. Cf, Judges Walsh and Russo, dissenting in the *Vilvarajah* case. See also *Council of Civil Service Unions v UK* No 11603/85, 50 DR 228 at 242–3 (1987); 10 EHRR CD 269 at 279.

[19] *Silver v UK* A 61 (1983); 13 EHRR 582 para 113.

[20] *Klass v FRG* A 28 (1979); 2 EHRR 214 para 55 PC.

[21] Id, para 72 and *Leander v Sweden* A 116 (1987); 9 EHRR 433 para 84. In these cases the Court accepted that remedies against secret surveillance for national security reasons would inevitably be restricted.

So the protection afforded by Article 13 'is not absolute'. The Court accepts that, '[t]he context in which an alleged violation—or category of violations—occurs may entail inherent limitations on the conceivable remedy'.[22] If so, Article 13 'is not treated as being inapplicable but its requirement of an "effective remedy" is to be read as meaning "a remedy" that is as effective as can be, having regard to the restricted scope for recourse inherent in [the particular context]'.[23]

II. A PRE-EMPTIVE REMEDY FOR 'ARGUABLE' CLAIMS ONLY

A literal reading of Article 13—'Everyone whose rights and freedoms ... *are violated* shall have an effective remedy' (emphasis added)—might imply that it merely imposes an obligation to establish a means of redress open to the individual in the domestic legal system to obtain the enforcement of a judgment he has *already* won at Strasbourg. This narrow view has been rejected,[24] the Court in *Klass v FRG* stating:[25]

> ... Article 13 requires that where an individual considers himself to have been prejudiced by a measure allegedly in breach of the Convention, he should have a remedy before a national authority in order both to have his claim decided and, if appropriate, to obtain redress. Thus, Article 13 must be interpreted as guaranteeing an 'effective remedy before a national authority' to everyone who *claims* that his rights and freedoms under the Convention have been violated. (Emphasis added.)

The Court sensibly qualified this statement ('everyone who claims' a violation) in *Silver v UK*[26] such that the Article applies only to those with 'an arguable claim' that he or she is a victim of a violation of the Convention. Of course, there will be no violation of Article 13 if, for example, an applicant alleges a denial of his right to health care or to a passport, no matter how well-founded his claim on the facts, because no Convention right is implicated by the claim. But it is important to appreciate that a violation of Article 13 is not dependent on there actually being a violation of *another* Convention right. In *Leander v Sweden*,[27] the Court accepted that the applicant had had an arguable claim even though it was eventually persuaded that no violation of another article had been made out. In *Bubbins v UK*,[28] the Court found no violation of Article 2 on the facts, but it acknowledged that the applicant's complaint under that Article had been 'arguable'. The case concerned a fatal police shooting and was brought by the deceased's sister. Examining the case under Article 13, the Court accepted that there had been an effective remedy as regards the procedural aspect of the Article 2 claim. However, it found a violation of Article 13 as the domestic legal regime was inadequate owing to lacunas in the compensatory regime. There had been no judicial determination as to the potential liability in damages of the police following their role and conduct in the death of the deceased.

---

[22] *Kudla v Poland* 2000-XI; 35 EHRR 198 para 151 GC (citing *Klass v FRG*, id, para 69).

[23] Ibid.

[24] Although it was originally accepted by the Commission in the 1960s, see Frowein in *Ryssdal Essays* 545 at 546.

[25] A 28 (1979); 2 EHRR 214 para 64 PC. The Court's decision was facilitated by the use of the word '*recours*' for 'remedy' in the French text: Raymond, 5 HRR 161 at 165–7 (1980).

[26] A 61 (1983); 13 EHRR 582 para 113. See also *Verein Alternatives Lokalradio, Bern v Switzerland No 10746/84*, 49 DR 126 at 143 (1986).

[27] A 116 (1987); 9 EHRR 433 para 79.

[28] 2005-II; 41 EHRR 458 para 170. *Hatton v UK* 2003-VIII; 37 EHRR 611 GC is another example of a case where there was a violation of Article 13, though not of another substantive Article. See also *Nuri Kurt v Turkey* hudoc (2005) for the significance of this case law in the context of claims of property destruction in south-east Turkey.

Furthermore, the applicant could not obtain compensation for non-pecuniary damage suffered as she was not a dependent of the deceased.[29]

No abstract definition of the notion of arguability has been provided. The Court insists that, arguability 'must be determined, in the light of the particular facts and the nature of the legal issue or issues raised, whether each individual claim of violation forming the basis of a complaint under Article 13 was arguable and, if so, whether the requirements of Article 13 were met in relation thereto'.[30]

III. AN AUXILIARY REMEDY, AND RELATIONSHIP WITH ARTICLE 35

In some instances the Convention text itself fixes on states a more stringent procedural obligation to provide a remedy in particular contexts than that required by Article 13: see Articles 5(4), 5(5), and 6. In such cases, and with the exception of Article 6(1) 'reasonable time' cases,[31] the 'context-specific' remedy required by the Article concerned is what the Convention requires, not the less rigorous Article 13 remedy. For example, any claim to an Article 13 remedy is absorbed by the claim that a detained person has the *habeas corpus* remedy required by Article 5(4).[32] The Court has also regarded Article 13 obligations as auxiliary in the sense that the Court has narrowed the obligation to provide a remedy to claims of a violation which pass a threshold of 'arguability' (see above), a notion which is determined by Convention procedural standards and not by any independent substantive character of Article 13.[33]

Complex questions arise as to the inter-relationship between Article 13 and the rule in Article 35 that an applicant must exhaust local remedies before bringing an Article 34 application. As the Court has noted, there is a 'close affinity'[34] between these two Articles. The Court is obliged by Article 35 to determine whether an application is 'manifestly ill-founded', which can involve taking a position on the legal and/or factual merits of a claim.[35] In *Boyle and Rice v UK*,[36] the Court said that 'it is difficult to conceive how a claim that is "manifestly ill-founded" can nevertheless be "arguable", and *vice versa*'. Subsequently, in *Powell and Rayner v UK*,[37] it elaborated as follows:

> Article 13 and [Article 35(3)] are concerned within their respective spheres with the availability of remedies for the enforcement of the same Convention rights and freedoms. The coherence of this dual system of enforcement is at risk of being undermined if Article 13 is interpreted as requiring a national law to make available an 'effective remedy' for a grievance classified under [Article 35(3)] as being so weak as not to warrant examination on its merits at the international level.

Evidently a complaint that has been declared 'manifestly ill-founded' will not satisfy the threshold test for reliance on Article 13 and there will be no violation of that provision.[38]

---

[29] Id, para 172. Judge Zagrebelsky dissented on this point asking how there could be an arguable claim for compensation if there was no violation in the first place.

[30] *Boyle and Rice v UK* A 131 (1988); 10 EHRR 425 para 55 PC.

[31] See text accompanying n 108 below.

[32] Eg, *Campbell and Fell v UK* A 80 (1984); 7 EHRR 165 para 123 (Article 6(1)) and *De Jong et al v Netherlands* A 77 (1984); 8 EHRR 20 para 60 (Article 5(4)).

[33] *Powell and Rayner v UK* A 172 (1990); 12 EHRR 355 para 33.

[34] *Kudla v Poland* 2000-XI; 35 EHRR 198 para 152 GC.   [35] See below, pp 757 and 785.

[36] A 131 (1988); 10 EHRR 425 para 54 PC.

[37] A 172 (1990); 12 EHRR 355 para 33. See Hampson, 39 ICLQ 891 (1990).

[38] See *Conka v Belgium* 2002-I; 34 EHRR 1298 para 76.

If there is a remedy that satisfies Article 13 then, of course, an individual will need to go on to Strasbourg only where the process has failed to reach a result satisfactory to him. If there is no remedy that complies with Article 13, then there can be no obligation to have recourse to it[39] for the purposes of Article 35 (although an individual may be advised to test whether a particular process satisfies Article 13, even if he has doubts whether it does).

3. ARTICLE 13: GENERAL PRINCIPLES/REQUIREMENTS OF AN 'EFFECTIVE REMEDY'

The general principles which Article 13 embodies are set out in the paragraphs that follow. Their application to the facts of an individual case is not always easy; in particular, the development of remedies in a national legal system over time may mean that previous Court judgments or decisions of the Commission finding them to be inadequate must be revised. This point is well illustrated by various Strasbourg cases which highlighted the inadequacies of UK law on judicial review but concerned facts occurring prior to the entry into force of the Human Rights Act 1998 in 2000.[40] It should also be noted that the Court's approach can be very context dependent, as is illustrated by the deferential standards set in some cases concerning national security and Article 13.[41] As the Court has noted, 'the scope of the obligation under Article 13 varies depending on the nature of the Convention right relied on'.[42]

I. SUBSTANTIVE REQUIREMENTS OF AN EFFECTIVE REMEDY

As noted, Article 13 requires the possibility of canvassing the substance of the Convention argument before a national authority and, if accepted, this should give rise to an *effective* remedy. The remedy must be effective 'in practice as well as in law',[43] effectiveness encompassing a remedy that can prevent the alleged violation or its continuation, or one which can provide 'adequate redress for any violation that has already occurred'.[44]

As is noted below, arguable claims of violations of Articles 2 and 3 by the direct actions of the state are treated as such an important issue that not only must compensation be paid to relatives, where appropriate,[45] but there must also be an effective investigation

---

[39] *Warwick v UK No 9471/81*, 60 DR 5 at 19 (1989) (no remedy to test parent's claim that lawful school beating of daughter violated Article 2, First Protocol).

[40] Eg, *Vilvarajah v UK* A 215 (1991); 14 EHRR 248; *Smith and Grady v UK* 1999-VI; 29 EHRR 493; and *Hatton v UK* 2003-VIII; 37 EHRR 611 GC.

[41] See below, p 568.

[42] *Hasan and Chaush v Bulgaria* 2000-XI; 34 EHRR 1339 para 98. This case concerned state interference in religious affairs, in particular the state's refusal to recognize a rival leadership to a religious group. The Court accepted that Article 13 was satisfied if representatives of the aggrieved religious community had access to a remedy, ie it was not necessary that every single member of the group should have such access, see paras 98-9.

[43] *Kudla v Poland* 2000-XI; 35 EHRR 198 para 157 GC. Obviously, in practical terms the exercise of the effective remedy 'must not be unjustifiably hindered by the acts or omissions of the authorities of the respondent state', *Aksoy v Turkey* 1996-VI; 23 EHRR 553 para 95.

[44] Id, paras 157-8 GC.

[45] For Article 2, compensation for pecuniary and non-pecuniary damage should in principle be possible as part of the range of redress available, see for example *Edwards (Paul and Audrey) v UK* 2002-II; 35 EHRR 487 para 97.

meeting certain standards elaborated by the Court.[46] In other cases, pecuniary compensation alone might suffice for the purposes of Article 13, though the Court has hinted that a compensatory award may be so derisory that it raises an issue as to the effectiveness of the redress.[47] Of course, if improper legal obstacles exist to the realization of such compensatory awards then there may be a violation of Article 13.[48] The same applies if an individual has access to a commission, for example a press or media complaints commission, which does not have legal power to award damages to the person concerned.[49] Again the timely payment of a compensation award is an essential element of a remedy under Article 13.[50]

The prospect of a wholly discretionary response to the national authority's decision may raise issues under Article 13.[51] A remedy by dint of the exercise of political discretion will not suffice, so a petition to the Home Secretary by prisoners contesting the compatibility of Prison Rules with the Convention, rules made by him and amendable by him but only in the discharge of his political function, was not an effective remedy.[52] Nor will bodies whose powers are limited to advising the ultimate decision-maker of a remedially effective remedy for the purposes of Article 13:[53] some element of enforceability is generally required.[54]

Of course, a judicial discretion will not undermine the effectiveness of proceedings before a court. However, no effective remedy will exist if the scope of review conducted by a domestic court or other authority is so weak that it is unable to properly address the key elements of whether there has been a violation of the Convention. On this basis the Court found violations of Article 13 with Article 8 of the Convention in *Smith and Grady v UK*[55] and *Hatton v UK*[56] given the weak powers of judicial review exercised by the domestic

---

[46] For full details see below, p 572.

[47] See *Wainwright v UK* 2006-X; 44 EHRR 809 para 55. See also *Keenan v UK* 2001-III; 33 EHRR 913 para 129.

[48] See eg, *Edwards (Paul and Audrey) v UK* 2002-II; 35 EHRR 487 (parents' inability to obtain compensation for death of son in prison); *Keenan v UK* 2001-III; 33 EHRR 913 (parents' inability to obtain compensation for ill-treatment of son in prison); and *Z v UK* 2001-V; 34 EHRR 97 GC (children's inability to sue local authority for its failure to prevent child abuse by parents).

[49] *Peck v UK* 2003-I; 36 EHRR 719 para 109.

[50] *Öneryıldız v Turkey* 2004-XII; 41 EHRR 325 para 152 GC (five-year delay in a case concerning loss of a close relative).

[51] Eg, an English prisoner's right of complaint to the Parliamentary Commissioner was not remedially effective because a finding in the prisoner's favour was merely reported to an individual MP or, exceptionally, to Parliament as a whole: *Silver v UK* A 61 (1983); 13 EHRR 582 paras 54 and 115 and *Campbell and Fell v UK* A 80 (1984); 7 EHRR 165 paras 51 and 126.

[52] *Silver v UK*, id, para 116. See also *Malone v UK* A 82 (1984) para 156 Com Rep, where the Commission was not satisfied that the power of a judge to act on his own initiative and to report to the Prime Minister about possible misuse of powers to intercept telephone calls was, by reason of the judge's status, remedially effective.

[53] Eg, the Unit Review Board and the Standing Committee on Difficult Prisoners: *McCallum v UK* A 183 (1990) para 80 Com Rep.

[54] In *Leander v Sweden* A 116 (1987); 9 EHRR 433 para 82 the Court conceded that the 'main weakness' of the Ombudsman/the Chancellor of Justice was that neither could make a binding decision. This remedy was not effective on its own even though their opinions 'command[ed] by tradition great respect in Swedish society and in practice are usually followed' (see also *Segerstedt-Wiberg v Sweden* 2006-VII; 44 EHRR 14 para 118).

Although in ordinary circumstances a judicial remedy will satisfy the Convention in the exceptional conditions of the *Greek case* (12 YB (the *Greek case*) 1 at 174 (1969); CM Res DH (70) 1) the Commission conceded the applicants' claims that the courts in post-coup Greece were not independent and impartial and for that reason failed to comply with Article 13.

[55] 1999-VI; 29 EHRR 493 (threshold of 'irrationality' set so high that there was no proper consideration by domestic courts of Article 8 issues).

[56] 2003-VIII; 37 EHRR 611 GC.

courts in those pre-Human Rights Act 1998 cases. In *Murray v UK*,[57] the Court said that the 'feeble prospects of success' on the facts of a particular case did not detract from the effectiveness of a remedy for Article 13 purposes if it could, on stronger facts, have afforded the applicant relief.

It may be necessary for a respondent government which maintains that a particular remedy satisfies Article 13 to provide examples of the remedy's application so as to establish its effectiveness.[58] In this respect the Court will not regard an absence of judicial practice as decisive in relation to a law that has recently entered into force,[59] but it does require a remedy that has acquired a 'sufficient level of certainty'.[60]

In expulsion cases the effects of the violation of the Convention may be irreversible. In this context Article 13 requires 'independent and rigorous scrutiny of a claim that there exist substantial grounds for fearing a real risk of treatment contrary to Article 3 and the possibility of suspending the implementation of the measure impugned'.[61] There must be a remedy which may prevent the execution of the offending measures, and the Article 13 national authority must examine the Convention compatibility of the expulsion order prior to its implementation.[62] Article 13 will be violated if there is not a clear legal practice whereby the application before the national authority is always heard and completed prior to the expulsion order being implemented, ie in effect the expulsion order is suspended in practice,[63] or if that order is not automatically suspended pending the application for a stay of execution.[64]

In *Andersson (Margareta and Roger) v Sweden*[65] the applicants were mother and son who claimed that the removal of the child to public care and the conditions of the care violated Article 8. Although there were remedies available in Swedish law to challenge the decisions, the child could take advantage of them only through his guardian, his mother. It was argued that the conditions of the separation of mother from child made it impossible for her to take effective action to protect the child's rights. By a narrow majority (five to four), the Court found that the claim was not made out on the facts. However, the principle is an important one for vulnerable or isolated individuals, such as prisoners and mental patients.

The Court's emphasis on a remedy needing to be practical and effective for the purposes of Article 13 is also illustrated by a recent case concerning public protest. Effective enjoyment of the right to freedom of assembly, the Court held, potentially entails that a demonstration be permitted to take place on or around a certain date relevant to the issue concerned, for outside that date the impact of the protest may be seriously diminished.[66]

---

[57] A 300-A (1994); 19 EHRR 193 para 100.

[58] See *Kudla v Poland* 2000-XI; 35 EHRR 198 para 159 GC and *Segerstedt-Wiberg v Sweden* 2006-VII; 44 EHRR 14 para 120.

[59] *Krasuski v Poland* hudoc (2005); 44 EHRR 223 para 70.

[60] Id, para 72. See also *Conka v Belgium* 2002-I; 34 EHRR 1298 para 83.

[61] *Jabari v Turkey* 2000-VIII para 39.

[62] *Conka v Belgium* 2002-I; 34 EHRR 1298 para 79 (this case concerned Article 4 of the Fourth Protocol (collective expulsion of aliens), though most will concern Article 3). See also *Gebremedhin v France* hudoc (2007). Cf, *Mamatkulov and Askarov v Turkey* 2005-I; 41 EHRR 494 para 124 GC, where the Court cited *Conka* as partial justification for the conclusion that its own interim measures are mandatory.

[63] See *Soering v UK* A 161 (1989); 11 EHRR 439 para 123. See also *Vilvarajah v UK* A 215 (1991); 14 EHRR 248 para 153.

[64] See *Conka v Belgium* 2002-I; 34 EHRR 1298 para 83 where the implementation of the remedy was regarded by a large majority of the Court as 'too uncertain to enable the requirements of Article 13 to be satisfied'. See, however, the partly dissenting opinion of *ad hoc* Judge Velaers and the partly dissenting opinion of Judge Jungwiert joined by Judge Kuris.

[65] A 226-A (1992); 14 EHRR 615 paras 98–103.

[66] *Bączkowski and Others v Poland* (hudoc) 2007 paras 81–3.

Hence an effective, Article 13 remedy here must include a legal framework providing for reasonable time limits within which the authorities should act when taking decisions or giving permission for demonstrations.[67] *Post-hoc* decisions (ie made after the key date for the demonstration) cannot provide adequate redress in respect of alleged violations of Article 11.[68]

II. INSTITUTIONAL REQUIREMENTS OF AN EFFECTIVE REMEDY

In *Leander*[69] the Court stated that it was a general principle that, 'the authority referred to in Article 13 need not be a judicial authority but, if it is not, the powers and the guarantees which it affords are relevant in determining whether the remedy before it is effective'. While the Court is prepared to be flexible in special cases, for instance *Klass* and *Leander*,[70] it is influenced by the judicial model in determining the question of the effectiveness of the remedy. In *Z v UK*,[71] although the Court did not address the applicants' suggestion that only court proceedings could have furnished effective redress on the facts of that case, it did acknowledge that 'judicial remedies indeed furnish strong guarantees of independence, access for the victim and family, and enforceability of awards in compliance with the requirements of Article 13'. In a recent case involving accountability for the prolonged detention of an applicant held in solitary confinement, the Grand Chamber had regard to the seriousness of the issues at stake before concluding that, on the facts, it was 'essential' that the Article 13 remedy be 'before a judicial body'.[72]

If the national remedy need not always be judicial, still less need it satisfy all the criteria of Article 6(1).[73] In the past a variety of non-judicial authorities have been accepted as satisfying Article 13, including parliamentary and executive bodies.[74] As has been noted above, the authority concerned must be able to produce a binding decision, so an ombudsman lacking this power will not usually suffice.

Institutional effectiveness requires that the decision-maker be 'sufficiently independent'[75] of the authority alleged to be responsible for the violation of the Convention.[76] In *Silver v UK*,[77] the Court accepted that a right of petition to the Home Secretary against a decision by the prison authorities applying his directives on the censorship of prisoners' correspondence could be an effective remedy. More recently in *Khan v UK*[78] the Court concluded that the avenues of complaints against the Police available to the applicant did not 'meet the requisite standards of independence needed to constitute sufficient

---

[67] Id, para 83.   [68] *Ibid*.

[69] A 116 (1987); 9 EHRR 433 para 77. See also *Chahal v UK* 1996-V; 23 EHRR 413 para 152.

[70] See eg, *Leander*, id, para 81 ('The Chancellor of Justice...may likewise be regarded as being, *at least in practice*, independent of the government ...' (emphasis added)).

[71] 2001-V; 34 EHRR 97 para 110 GC (citing *Klass v FRG* A 28 (1979); 2 EHRR 214 para 67 PC). See also *Soering v UK* A 161 (1989); 11 EHRR 439 PC and *Andersson (M and R) v Sweden* A 226-A (1992); 14 EHRR 615.

[72] *Ramirez Sanchez v France* hudoc (2006); 45 EHRR 1099 para 165 GC.

[73] Such a conclusion would absorb Article 13 within Article 6(1) and would have the effect of making all Convention rights 'civil rights' within its terms, an interpretation rejected by the Court in *Golder v UK* A 18 (1975); 1 EHRR 524 para 33 PC.

[74] See eg, *Klass v FRG* A 28 (1979); 2 EHRR 214 para 21 PC ('G10 Commission' (parliamentary)) and *Silver v UK* A 61 (1983); 13 EHRR 582 para 53 (Home Secretary (executive)).

[75] *Silver v UK* A 61 (1983); 13 EHRR 582 para 116.

[76] *Leander v Sweden* A 116 (1987); 9 EHRR 433 para 81.

[77] A 61 (1983); 13 EHRR 582. If the appeal involved a challenge to the legality of his directions, the Home Secretary would not be sufficiently independent since he would in effect be a judge in his own cause: *ibid*. A body which is independent for the purposes of Article 6(1), like Prison Boards of Visitors (*Campbell and Fell v UK* A 80 (1984); 7 EHRR 165 para 81) would be independent for the purposes of Article 13 also.

[78] 2000-V; 31 EHRR 1016 para 47. See also *PG and JH v UK* 2001-IX.

protection against the abuse of authority'. Of relevance here was that on the facts the local Chief Constable had a discretion to refer matters to the Police Complaints Authority, failing which the standard procedure was to appoint a member of his own force to carry out the investigation. Further, as regards the Police Complaints Authority itself the Secretary of State had an important role in appointing, remunerating and, in certain circumstances, dismissing its members, plus he had an influence on the withdrawal or referring of disciplinary charges and criminal proceedings.

In *Chahal v UK*,[79] which concerned the deportation of an alleged terrorist on national security grounds, the Court was critical of the fact that the advisory panel which reviewed the applicant's deportation order reached decisions which were not binding, plus it also suffered from a lack of 'sufficient procedural safeguards'. Amongst other things, the applicant had no right of legal representation and was only given an outline of the grounds for the notice of intention to deport. Furthermore, the details of the panel's decision were never disclosed.[80]

III. CUMULATION OF PROCEDURES MAY SUFFICE

A cumulation of possible channels of redress in the national legal system must be taken into account when deciding whether an applicant has an effective remedy for the purposes of Article 13, rather than examining any or each procedure in isolation. In *Leander*[81] the Court stated that it was a general principle of Article 13 that, 'although no single remedy may itself entirely satisfy the requirements of Article 13, the aggregate of remedies provided for under domestic law may do so'. It falls to the respondent state to raise and substantiate a case here, otherwise the Court will not address it and will assume a violation of Article 13.[82]

So, where an appeal lies to a sufficiently independent body from the decisions of one which is not independent, then the applicant must use this opportunity, which will satisfy Article 13.[83] Additionally, where an applicant makes different kinds of complaint, the national remedies must be effective with respect to each kind. In *Silver v UK*,[84] the Court distinguished between complaints about the application of the Prison Rules (was it within the Rules to stop this letter?), for which the possibility of a petition to the Home Secretary was an effective remedy, and complaints about the Rules themselves (was a Rule which authorizes the stopping of letters to a legal advisor about litigation compatible with the Convention?), in which case a petition to the minister was not effective because he was not sufficiently detached to review his own rule-making.

The dangers of the Court's approach were made apparent in *Leander v Sweden*.[85] Four remedies in the national legal system were indicated by the Swedish government: appeal to the government from refusal to appoint to the post; request to the National Police Board for access to its secret register, with appeal to the courts in the event of

[79] 1996-V; 23 EHRR 413 para 154 GC.

[80] See also the discussion of Article 13 in the context of national security at p 568 below.

[81] A 116 (1987); 9 EHRR 433 para 77. See *Silver v UK* A 61 (1983); 13 EHRR 582 para 118.

[82] *Sürmeli v Germany* 2006-VII; 44 EHRR 438 para 115 GC.

[83] Eg, the possibility referred to in *Klass v FRG* A 28 (1979); 2 EHRR 214 para 70 PC of raising some questions before the Constitutional Court.

[84] A 61 (1983); 13 EHRR 582 para 118. See also *Lithgow v UK* A 102 (1986); 8 EHRR 329 paras 206–7 PC, where the Court talks about 'aggregate' remedies, when what was involved was different remedies for different claims.

[85] A 116 (1987); 9 EHRR 433 paras 80–2. See also the criticism of *Silver v UK* A 61 (1983); 13 EHRR 582 in the first edition of this volume at p 457.

refusal; complaint to the Chancellor of Justice; and complaint to the Ombudsman. The majority inclined to the view that the last two might have been effective remedies, even though neither the Chancellor nor the Ombudsman could give a binding decision, but held that, in any event, appeal to the government was capable of providing a remedy. The Court said:

> Even if, taken on its own, the complaint to the government was not considered sufficient to ensure compliance with Article 13, the Court finds that the aggregate of the remedies…satisfies the conditions of Article 13 in the particular circumstances of the instant case…[86]

It is not made clear how each of the remedies reinforces any other. If any of them individually was adequate to satisfy Article 13, then no reference need be made to the others. On the other hand, if none of them individually were sufficient, as the dissenting judges thought, and none were appeals from another, then aggregating the series of inadequate measures would not be satisfactory to an applicant in the absence of an explanation of how the deficiencies of one were made up by the advantages of another, which the Court did not give.[87] Until the Court is able to demonstrate the effective operation of the aggregation approach in an actual case, a degree of caution is appropriate in assessing a government's claim that this is the case.

The approach based on 'aggregate of remedies' may have been more defensible for sensitive cases such as *Leander* in the earlier years of the Court's 'life', when not all states had incorporated the Convention. But it is harder to justify it today and it is submitted the Court should be reluctant to employ it. In *Edwards (Paul and Audrey) v UK*,[88] the Court was not persuaded that the aggregate of remedies suggested to it by the respondent government was sufficient for the purposes of Article 13. An Article 2 violation had been found on the basis of the government's failure to protect the life of the applicants' son who was murdered by another inmate in prison. In *Sürmeli v Germany*,[89] a case concerning the effectiveness of remedies for excessive length of proceedings under Article 6(1), the Court individually rejected the four different remedies put to it by the respondent government. It stated that it was unnecessary to rule of the question of whether the aggregate of remedies sufficed for Article 13, since that point had neither been alleged by the respondent government to satisfy Article 13 nor shown to do so.

IV.   'NOTWITHSTANDING THAT THE VIOLATION HAS BEEN COMMITTED BY PERSONS ACTING IN AN OFFICIAL CAPACITY'

Article 13 imposes an obligation to provide a remedy 'notwithstanding that the violation has been committed by persons acting in an official capacity'. The words may be read as denying effect to national laws which provide immunity to public officials or the state for some wrongful acts.[90] It has been argued that this wording acknowledges that there may be violations of Convention rights by individuals, with respect to which the state has an obligation under Article 13 to provide an effective national remedy.[91]

[86] Id, para 84.   [87] For further comment, see Drzemczewski and Warbrick, 7 YEL 364 (1987).
[88] 2002-II; 35 EHRR 487 paras 97–102.   [89] 2006-VII; 44 EHRR 438 para 115 GC.
[90] See, *loc cit*, n 25, above, pp 168–70.
[91] See Clapham, *Human Rights in the Private Sphere*, 1993, pp 240–4.

4. ARTICLE 13: GENERAL PRINCIPLES/ REQUIREMENTS IN SPECIFIC CONTEXTS

I. ARTICLE 13 AND THE NATIONAL SECURITY CONTEXT

Some of the most interesting Article 13 judgments have concerned cases in which the domestic legal position has been that there can be only very limited review of executive action because of national security considerations. In this context the Court has been prepared to accept significant limitations on the type of Article 13 remedy available with respect to Articles 8 and 10 in areas such as secret surveillance and secret checks on individuals for screening job candidates for sensitive posts. However, it has also demonstrated that it is not sufficient for a state simply to invoke the claim of 'national security' for the purposes of rebutting an Article 13 claim.

In *Klass v FRG*,[92] the Court held as compatible with Article 8 a German law allowing secret surveillance of individuals by the state, naturally without prior notification to the target but sometimes even without *ex post facto* notification. The applicants maintained that unless persons were told that their telephone calls had been intercepted, then they had no opportunity to challenge the surveillance as being contrary to their Convention rights and, accordingly, that there had been a breach of Article 13. Since there could be *no* remedy, *a fortiori* there could not be an effective one. If this argument had prevailed, there would have been an incompatibility with the Court's decision under Article 8 (which it determined had not been violated). The Court avoided this by saying:

> an effective remedy under Article 13 must mean a remedy that is as effective as can be having regard to the restricted scope for recourse inherent in any system of secret surveillance.[93]

It held on the facts that Article 13 was satisfied. In cases where there was later notification, the individual could go to the courts in the ordinary way. Where there was no notification, the process was supervised by an independent committee, which was, in the circumstances, the best that could be done. As the Court has since noted (citing *Klass*), 'where secret surveillance is concerned, objective supervisory machinery may be sufficient as long as the measures remain secret. It is only once the measures have been divulged that legal remedies must become available to the individual.'[94]

The Court found for the defendant state (by four votes to three) in much the same terms in *Leander v Sweden*,[95] where the applicant was unable to gain access to secret information contained on a national register which he might have wished to challenge in the context of an unsuccessful job application to a security-sensitive post. Again, in circumstances involving the protection of national security, the Court held that Article 13 could not guarantee a right to a remedy which undermined a state's rights to take action established elsewhere under the Convention.[96] Echoing *Klass*, the Court determined that, '[on the facts of *Leander*], an "effective remedy" under Article 13 must mean a remedy that is as effective as can be having regard to the restricted scope for recourse inherent in any system of secret checks on candidates for employment in posts of importance from

---

[92] A 28 (1979); 2 EHRR 214 para 58 PC.   [93] Id, para 69.
[94] *Rotaru v Romania* 2000-V para 69 GC.
[95] A 116 (1987); 9 EHRR 433 para 59. See also the subsequent case of *Segerstedt-Wiberg v Sweden* 2006-VII; 44 EHRR 14 (storage of information on file and refusal to give advice as to its full extent).
[96] Id, paras 80–4.

a national security point of view'.[97] It may be pointed out that in both *Klass* and *Leander* there were still elements of procedural guarantees and independent review, albeit they were limited. The impact of the approach used in those two cases is limited because there is only a narrow range of situations where there will be a need to rely on wholly secret processes, nonetheless, given the seriousness of what is at stake, the Court's conclusions are strong confirmations of the subsidiary character of the Article 13 obligation.[98]

The impression should not be gained, however, that the Court greatly dilutes Article 13 simply because the state claims that national security interests are involved. In *Smith and Grady v UK*[99] the respondent government claimed that the ban on homosexuals serving in the armed forces, which entailed a violation of Article 8 on the facts, was justified by national security considerations. The Court nevertheless found a violation of Article 13 as the standard of judicial review operated by the domestic courts at the time (a modified irrationality test) had been too weak. It set such a high threshold that the domestic courts were 'effectively excluded' from addressing the key Article 8 aspects of the applicants' case.

Article 3 'deportation' cases have also highlighted the tension between the right to an effective remedy and 'national security' considerations. Here, however, the Court's stance is that national security considerations are immaterial so there is no place for the 'as effective as can be' in the circumstances doctrine as regards the remedies instituted to address the Article 3 claim.[100] In *Chahal v UK* the claim was that neither judicial review under English law, nor a special advisory panel instituted to assess the applicant's claim regarding Article 3 constituted an effective remedy. The national security context entailed that the scope of judicial review operated by the domestic courts was too limited for an effective judicial evaluation of the Article 3 claim, whilst the aforementioned panel suffered from a number of procedural flaws. The Court highlighted the importance of Article 3 and made reference to 'the irreversible nature of the harm that might occur if the risk of ill-treatment materialised'.[101] This dictated that Article 13 requires 'independent scrutiny of the claim that there exist substantial grounds for fearing a real risk of treatment contrary to Article 3',[102] and that the scrutinizing body has sole regard to the issue of risk and not be influenced by national security assessments.

Al-Nashif v Bulgaria[103] also concerned expulsion on grounds of national security, though the Article 13 claim related to the lack of an effective remedy for the interference with the applicant's right to respect to family life that would result from his deportation. In essence, all the domestic proceedings brought by the applicant to challenge his deportation were rejected automatically as the government stated that the ground for expulsion was national security. There was, therefore, no effective possibility of challenging the deportation order in terms of 'having the relevant issues examined with sufficient procedural safeguards and thoroughness by an appropriate domestic forum offering

---

[97] Id, para 78.

[98] See also *Amann v Switzerland* 2000-II; 30 EHRR 843 GC, which concerned telephone-tapping and storing of personal data in security card index. There was no violation of Article 13: the applicant had access to the card and could appeal to a court as regards its creation, legality, and the phone-tapping. *Rotaru v Romania* 2000-V GC concerned the intelligence services' storage of secret information, some of which was false, dating back decades. There was a violation of Article 13 as the applicant was unable to challenge the information holding, refute it, or get it destroyed. *Segerstedt-Wiberg v Sweden* 2006-VII; 44 EHRR 14 paras 120–1 highlights the Article 13 requirement that a legal remedy include procedures to secure the destruction of a secret file or its rectification in appropriate circumstances.

[99] *Smith and Grady v UK* 1999-VI; 29 EHRR 493 paras 137–9.

[100] See *Chahal v UK* 1996-V; 23 EHRR 413 para 150.   [101] Id, para 151.   [102] *Ibid.*

[103] Hudoc (2002); 36 EHRR 655. See also *CG v Bulgaria* hudoc (2008).

adequate guarantees of independence and impartiality'.[104] The Court pointed out that, compared to *Klass* and *Leander,* it was easier to reconcile the interest of preserving sensitive information with the individual's right to an effective remedy since in those two cases 'the system of secret surveillance or secret checks could only function if the individual remained unaware of the measures affecting him'.[105] It was accepted that in the deportation/national security context the sensitivity of the material could justify 'procedural restrictions' on the presentation of evidence before the independent authority purportedly providing the Article 13 remedy, which for its part 'may need to afford a wide margin of appreciation to the executive in matters of national security'.[106] However, there was no justification for 'doing away with remedies altogether'. As a minimum there had to be a 'competent independent appeals authority' hearing the reasons grounding the deportation decision (even if these were not made public), able to 'reject the executive's assertion that there is a threat to national security where it finds it arbitrary or unreasonable', and before which there has to be 'some form of adversarial proceedings, if need be through a special representative after a security clearance'. Additionally, the body in question should examine whether the deportation infringed the applicant's Article 8 rights.

II. ARTICLE 6(1) 'TRIAL WITHIN A REASONABLE TIME' AND ARTICLE 13

Over its history the Court has found more violations of the right to a trial within a reasonable time, as protected by Article 6(1), than any other provision of the Convention. In recent years 60 per cent of Strasbourg judgments on the merits have concerned unreasonable length of judicial proceedings. The problem seems to be endemic in a number of Convention states.

It is against this background that the Grand Chamber judgment in *Kudla v Poland*[107] marked a significant development in the Court's jurisprudence on Article 13. Before this ruling the Court's general position was that Article 6(1) was deemed to constitute a *lex specialis* in relation to Article 13, so the latter Article was not considered even when Article 6(1) was found to be violated. This was logical in most Article 6(1) cases as the standards set by that provision, encompassing as it did a range of due process safeguards, were more stringent that that required by Article 13. However, as the Court acknowledged in *Kudla,* for unreasonable length of judicial proceedings in particular, the Article 13 claim is not absorbed into that under Article 6(1) since:

> [t]he question of whether the applicant in a given case did benefit from trial within a reasonable time in the determination of civil rights and obligations or a criminal charge is a separate legal issue from that of whether there was available to the applicant under domestic law an effective remedy to ventilate a complaint on that ground.[108]

Indeed, in *Kudla* the applicant's complaint was that the determination of fraud charges against him remained unresolved after nearly a decade, but it was only at Strasbourg that he was able to pursue a claim regarding the excessive length of proceedings. The Court in *Kudla* addressed the applicant's claim of excessive length not only under Article 6(1), but also under Article 13, finding a violation of both provisions. It rejected the Polish government's argument that requiring a remedy of unreasonable length of judicial proceedings would mean that domestic proceedings would be even more cumbersome and insisted

---

104 Id, para 133.   105 Id, para 137.   106 *Ibid.*   107 2000-XI; 35 EHRR 198 GC.
108 Id, para 147.

that the new reading of Article 13 reinforced the requirements of Article 6(1).[109] It also proceeded to justify its stance by reference to the principle of subsidiarity, pointing out that if Articles 13 and 6(1) were not read in the way it suggested:

> individuals will systematically be forced to refer to the Court in Strasbourg complaints that would otherwise, and in the Court's opinion more appropriately, have to be addressed in the first place within the national legal system. In the long term the effective functioning, on both the national and international level, of the scheme of human rights protection set up by the Convention is liable to be weakened.[110]

For unreasonable length of judicial proceedings under Article 6(1), Article 13 requires a domestic remedy which would prevent the alleged violation or its continuation (ie expedite the determination of the applicant's legal proceedings), or provide 'adequate redress for any violation that had already occurred'.[111] Damages alone would suffice, but, without being prescriptive, the Court has also indicated its strong preference for a 'preventative'[112] remedy since this addresses the root cause of the problem and avoids 'a finding of successive violations in respect of the same set of proceedings and does not merely repair the breach *a posteriori*, as does a compensatory remedy'.[113]

Following *Kudla* in Poland a new statutory remedy was created which apparently provided applicants alleging a violation of the right to a hearing within a reasonable time in judicial proceedings with an action for damages. This new law was subsequently in issue in *Krasuski v Poland*[114] where the Court held that since its entry into force an effective remedy existed in Polish law for the purpose of Article 6(1) protracted legal proceedings. However, it also indicated that it might review this conclusion if it transpired that the functioning of a newly created statutory remedy proved not to be effective, sufficient, and accessible.[115] Here it specifically referred to the adequacy of the level of compensation awarded and the Polish civil courts' ability to handle actions arising under the new legislation with 'special diligence and attention, especially in terms of the length of time taken for their determination'.[116]

Kudla may be seen as an attempt to use Article 13 of the Convention to repatriate the problem of Article 6(1) unreasonable length of judicial proceedings to the member states.[117] Those states that did not already have a right to an effective remedy in respect of a complaint about the undue length of court proceedings will need to reform domestic law or risk a double finding of a violation at Strasbourg. As and when appropriate

---

[109] Id, para 152.

[110] Id, para 155. See, however, the partly dissenting opinion of Judge Casadevall who argued passionately that the Court's new reading of Article 6(1) 'smack[ed] ... more of expediency than of law' and would not necessarily benefit applicants at all.

[111] Id, para 158.   [112] *Sürmeli v Germany* 2006-VII; 44 EHRR 438 para 100 GC.

[113] *Ibid* (the Grand Chamber continued, '[s]ome states have understood the situation perfectly by choosing to combine two types of remedy, one designed to expedite the proceedings and the other to afford compensation' (citing *Scordino v Italy (No 1)* 2006-V; 45 EHRR 207 paras 183 and 186 GC). See also the comments at paras 138–9 made in connection with Article 46(1).

[114] 2005-V; 44 EHRR 223.

[115] *Ibid*. See also *Sürmeli v Germany* 2006-VII; 44 EHRR 438 para 101 GC.

[116] *Ibid*. See also eg, the Court's consideration of the Italian 'Pinto' legislation in *Scordino v Italy (No 1)* 2006-V; 45 EHRR 207 GC, including the important comments made in relation to obligations arising under Article 46 of the Convention, at paras 229–40.

[117] For further analysis of the many complex issues raised by *Kudla* and equivalent case law arising from other states see Directorate General of Human Rights and Legal Affairs, *The improvement of domestic remedies with particular emphasis on cases of unreasonable length of proceedings* (Council of Europe, 2006) and European Commission for Democracy through Law (Venice Commission), *Study on The Effectiveness of National Remedies in Respect of Excessive Length of Proceedings*, CDL-AD(2006)036.

applications are made to it, the Court will also have to start to assess whether news laws put in place in reaction to *Kudla* satisfy Article 13.

III. EFFECTIVE INVESTIGATIONS UNDER ARTICLE 13 FOR SERIOUS VIOLATION OF FUNDAMENTAL RIGHTS

In the context of cases concerning deaths or ill-treatment allegedly occurring under the responsibility of state agents, the Court has developed a number of 'effective investigation' principles for the application of Articles 2, 3, and 5.[118] Not only does this case law reinforce the subsidiary nature of the Convention, but there are clear practical reasons for this approach. In the case of *Aksoy v Turkey*,[119] where the Court found that the applicant had been tortured, in the context of its examination of Article 13 the Court stated, 'allegations of torture in police custody are extremely difficult for the victim to substantiate if he has been isolated from the outside world, without access to doctors, lawyers, family or friends who could provide support and assemble the necessary evidence. Furthermore, having been ill-treated in this way, an individual will often have had his capacity or will to pursue a complaint impaired'.[120] The Court emphasized that the nature of the right safeguarded under Article 3 had implications: both 'the fundamental importance of the prohibition of torture... and the especially vulnerable position of torture victims, [necessitated that] Article 13 imposes, without prejudice to any other remedy available under the domestic system, an obligation on states to carry out a thorough and effective investigation of incidents of torture'. The Court therefore ruled that where an individual has an arguable claim that he has been tortured by state agents—or in fact suffered any ill-treatment contrary to Article 3[121]—then Article 13 entails, 'in addition to the payment of compensation where appropriate, a thorough and effective investigation capable of leading to the identification and punishment of those responsible and including effective access for the complainant to the investigatory procedure'.[122] The Court saw this requirement as being implicit in Article 13.

In *Aksoy* itself the Court found that there had been a violation of Article 13 owing to the intransigence of the local prosecutor, who failed to investigate credible allegations of very serious of ill-treatment brought to him, despite a legal obligation to do so under domestic law. As the Court put it, 'such an attitude from a state official under a duty to investigate criminal offences was tantamount to undermining the effectiveness of any other remedies that may have existed'.[123] Hence, even if an Article 13 remedy may exist, if its exercise is unjustifiably hindered via the acts or omissions of the authorities of the respondent state, or if the investigation is otherwise generally incompetent and error-prone, then this will entail a violation of Article 13.[124]

---

[118] See Chs 2, 3, and 5 above.   [119] 1996-VI; 23 EHRR 553 para 97.

[120] For a similar point made in relation to Article 2, see eg, *Makaratzis v Greece* 2004-XI; 41 EHRR 1092 para 73 GC.

[121] See *Assenov v Bulgaria* 1998-VIII; 28 EHRR 652 para 117.

[122] *Aksoy v Turkey* 1996-VI; 23 EHRR 553 para 98. Although the Court has also noted that Article 13 does not guarantee an applicant 'a right to secure the prosecution and conviction of a third party', see *Öneryıldız v Turkey* 2004-XII; 41 EHRR 325 para 147 GC.

[123] *Aksoy v Turkey* 1996-VI; 23 EHRR 553 para 99. See also *Hüseyin Esen v Turkey* hudoc (2006) (violation of Article 13 with Article 3 as police officers' conviction for torture so drawn out that it became discontinued under a statute of limitations).

[124] See also eg, *Aydin v Turkey* 1997-V; 25 EHRR 251 para 107 (allegations of Article 3 ill-treatment by way of the victim's rape did not include the proper independent professional medical examination required by Article 13) and *Ilhan v Turkey* 2000-VII; 34 EHRR 869 para 103 (the domestic investigation into Article 3

The approach to Articles 13 and 3 in *Aksoy* as regards a 'thorough investigation' etc has been extended to Article 2[125] and Article 5[126] with respect to deaths and 'disappearances' occurring at the hands of or with the connivance of the members of the security forces, plus also violations of Article 8 of the Convention occurring by virtue of the destruction of the applicant's home and possessions.[127]

The Court has stated that its willingness to find a violation of Article 13 in cases such as those concerning Article 2 was founded generally on the 'close procedural and practical relationship between the criminal investigation and the remedies available to those applicants in the legal system as a whole'.[128] A deficient investigation into a death or ill-treatment may have a negative 'knock-on' effect on the individual's access to any other available remedies relevant to Article 13, such as claims for compensation. It may be that without a criminal investigation by the authorities to establish liability for death an applicant simply has no prospect of obtaining an effective remedy, but this will be dependent on the facts of each case.[129]

When examining an allegation under Article 13 the Court has on a number of occasions stated that 'the requirements' of that Article are 'broader' than the effective investigation duties respectively arising under Articles 2, 3, and 5. It has never really explained exactly why this is so, it not being clear in practical terms why an Article 13 remedy is more extensive that the procedural obligations which the Court has read in to Articles 2, 3, and 5, other than the possibility afforded by Article 13 of obtaining compensation.[130] In fact, the Court's general approach seems to be that it will not examine Article 13 separately once it has examined the procedural aspects of Articles 2 and/or 3.[131] The Court is prepared to make exceptions, however, as in cases raising very serious violations of Articles 2 and 3 emanating from the Chechnya region of Russia. The policy is that the

---

ill-treatment was flawed on several grounds, eg inconsistencies in the gendarmes' reports and prosecutor's failure to interview important witnesses, so there was a violation of Article 13).

[125] Eg, *Kaya v Turkey* 1998-I; 28 EHRR 1 para 107.

[126] Eg, *Kurt v Turkey* 1998-III; 27 EHRR 373 para 140.

[127] Eg, *Menteş v Turkey* 1997-VIII; 26 EHRR 595 para 89.

[128] See *Öneryıldız v Turkey* 2004-XII; 41 EHRR 325 para 148 GC. The case concerned the responsibility of the state for the deaths and destruction of property occurring after an accidental explosion at a rubbish tip close to a shanty town. The Court stated, 'it does not inevitably follow...that Article 13 will be violated if the criminal investigation or resultant trial in a particular case do not satisfy the State's procedural obligation under [the Court's] Article 2 [case law]...What is important is the impact the State's failure to comply with its procedural obligation under Article 2 had on the deceased's family's access to other available and effective remedies for establishing liability on the part of State officials or bodies for acts or omissions entailing the breach of their rights under Article 2 and, as appropriate, obtaining compensation' (para 148).

[129] See *Kaya v Turkey* 1998-I; 28 EHRR 1 para 108. In *Cobzaru v Romania* hudoc (2007) para 83 the Court found a violation of Article 13 after the authorities had failed in their obligation to carry out an effective investigation into allegations of ill-treatment by police officers. The Court pointed out that the absence of a criminal investigation entailed that 'any other remedy available to the applicant, including a claim for damages, had limited chances of success and could be considered as theoretical and illusory, and not capable of affording redress to the applicant'. The Court acknowledged that the civil courts could independently assess the facts, but domestic case law evidenced that 'in practice the weight attached to a preceding criminal inquiry is so important that even the most convincing evidence to the contrary furnished by a plaintiff would often be discarded and such a remedy would prove to be only theoretical and illusory'. By contrast see *Öneryıldız v Turkey, ibid,* para 151 where the effectiveness of the administrative law remedy available to the applicants did not depend on the outcome of the pending criminal proceedings (although there was still a violation of Article 13 given the delay in payment of compensation).

[130] See Mowbray above n 1 pp 212–13 and the partly dissenting opinion of Judge Zagrebelsky in *Khashiyev and Akayeva v Russia* hudoc (2005); 42 EHRR 397.

[131] See *Ramsahai v Netherlands* hudoc (2007); 43 EHRR 39 para 363 GC and *Makaratzis v Greece* 2004-XI; 41 EHRR 1092 para 86 GC.

Article 13 claim will be addressed when 'the criminal investigation into the deaths [for Article 2 claims] was ineffective and the effectiveness of any other remedy that may have existed, including... civil remedies... [are] consequently undermined'.[132]

The value of the additional protection afforded by Article 13 is also apparent in the context of claims under Article 8 and Article 1 of the First Protocol emanating from the troubled region of south-east Turkey and where applicants to Strasbourg have alleged that they have been forcibly evicted from their homes, or that there has been deliberate destruction of their homes and property by the security forces. In accordance with its standard approach to assessing facts, the Court will only find a violation of Article 8 and Article 1 of the First Protocol here if it is satisfied beyond reasonable doubt that the events have occurred, ie the security forces are responsible. Sometimes the Court has found violations of one or both of these Articles; but sometimes doubts remain, it being simply unclear how the applicants' property was damaged, so no violation of the aforementioned Articles is found. However, Article 13 applies to 'arguable' claims. So, providing the claim as regards property destruction has been declared admissible and the Court accepts that the allegations 'could not be discarded as being *prima facie* untenable',[133] it is prepared to find a violation of Article 13 based on the ineffectiveness of the domestic enquiry into the allegations of property destruction.[134]

IV. ARTICLE 2 AND 3 VIOLATIONS IN THE CONTEXT OF THE DUTY TO PROTECT FROM HARM

It is clear that Article 13 can have some applicability in cases involving the indirect responsibility of the state arising out of its positive duties to take action to prevent violations by individuals of the human rights of others.[135] This is most relevant to the state's duty, in certain circumstances, to protect the individual from the harmful acts of others. In such circumstances, and where violations of Articles 2 and 3 have been found, 'Article 13 may not always require that the authorities undertake the responsibility for investigating the allegations'.[136] So it would seem that as regards the duties of investigation in this context the requirements of Article 13 are not necessarily as stringent as they are in cases where the violation of Article 2 or 3 occurred as a consequence of the direct action of state officials. Nonetheless Article 13 still requires a domestic mechanism that is effectively accessible to an applicant and by which it may be established where responsibility for the harm to his or her relative lay.[137] Where Articles 2 and 3 are concerned then 'compensation for the non-pecuniary damage flowing from the breach should in principle be part of the range of available remedies'.[138] The administrative law remedies available to the applicant here should be effective in practice as well as in law.[139]

---

[132] See eg, *Musayev v Russia* hudoc (2007) para 175.   [133] *Nuri Kurt v Turkey* hudoc (2005) para 117.

[134] Id, paras 119–21. Cf, *Soylu v Turkey* hudoc (2007) para 53 where the Court found no violation of Article 13 as the applicant was unable to lay the 'basis of a *prima facie* case of misconduct on the part of the security forces'.

[135] See Clapham, *The Human Rights Obligations of Non-State Actors*, 2006, pp 358 and 420.

[136] *Z v UK* 2001-V; 34 EHRR 97 para 109 GC. See also *Edwards (Paul and Audrey) v UK* 2002-II; 35 EHRR 487 para 97.

[137] *Ibid.* See also *Keenan v UK* 2001-III; 33 EHRR 913 para 132, where the Court recognized that the inquest into the death of the applicant's child in prison was useful for establishing the facts surrounding the death, but did not properly go to the potential liability of the authorities for the same, and lacked compensatory powers.

[138] *Ibid.* A violation of Article 13 was found in *Keenan v UK*, ibid, paras 129–33 as the Court argued, *inter alia*, the civil claim for negligence that the applicants might have made would not have led to an award of 'adequate damages' (para 129) and legal aid was not available to pursue such a claim.

[139] See *Öneryıldız v Turkey* 2004-XII; 41 EHRR 325 paras 152–5 GC (ineffectiveness of the compensation proceedings and failure in practice to pay damages was a violation of Article 13).

5. CONCLUSION

Article 13 is of autonomous but subsidiary character. While a breach of Article 13 does not depend on establishing a breach of another Article, what the obligations of a state are under Article 13 can be established only by taking the exact nature of each Convention claim into consideration. Nonetheless, this does not reduce the importance of Article 13 in securing co-operation between national legal systems and the Convention regime. The more effective and embracing the scheme of national remedies, particularly if the national authorities are sensitive to the developments in the Convention case law, the more likely it is that Convention cases may be decided without recourse to the Strasbourg authorities. This is, after all, one of the primary goals of the Convention system and it is, therefore, surprising that, outside some of the specific contexts noted above (Articles 2, 3, 6(1) (reasonable time), etc) the Court has not been more consistent in interpreting Article 13 in a way which enhances the effectiveness of national remedies.

15

ARTICLE 14 (FREEDOM FROM DISCRIMINATION IN RESPECT OF PROTECTED CONVENTION RIGHTS) AND PROTOCOL TWELVE (NON-DISCRIMINATION IN RESPECT OF 'ANY RIGHT SET FORTH BY LAW')

Article 14

The enjoyment of the rights and freedoms set forth in this Convention shall be secured without discrimination on any ground such as sex, race, colour, language, religion, political or other opinion, national or social origin, association with a national minority, property, birth or other status.

1. INTRODUCTION

Non-discrimination does not have the same, specific, foundational designation in the Statute of the Council of Europe or Preamble to the Convention as it does in the UN Charter.[1] Nor is there an equivalent in the main Convention text to Article 26 of the International Covenant on Civil and Political Rights, which provides comprehensive protection against discrimination in all those activities which the state chooses to regulate by law. Protocol Twelve[2] to the Convention, which entered into force in April 2005, has to some degree plugged this gap, but it has not been widely ratified to date.

It follows that for the majority of states the key provision addressing discrimination within the Convention is Article 14,[3] which, as we shall see in this chapter, has a number

---

[1] However, non-discrimination is central to the work of the Council of Europe, eg on equality between men and women see <http://www.coe.int/t/e/Human_Rights/Equality> and on combating racial discrimination see <http://www.coe.int/T/E/human_rights/Ecri/>. One should also note the important role of the European Union in the field of discrimination law as regards nationality, gender, and race equality in particular, but also religion or belief, sexual orientation, age, and disability, see <http://europa.eu/pol/rights/index_en.htm> and Chapter III of *The Charter of Fundamental Rights of the European Union*. See Bell, *Anti-Discrimination Law and the European Union*, 2002, and Ellis, *EU Anti-Discrimination Law*, 2005.

[2] See below, p 611.

[3] On Article 14 generally, see Partsch, *European Supervision*, Ch 23; Livingstone, 1 EHRLR 25 (1997) and Council of Europe, *Non-Discrimination: a Human Right*, Strasbourg, October 2005. Note that Article 16 (see

of significant limitations. Above all, it is a 'parasitic' provision, ie it only applies to 'rights and freedoms set forth' in the Convention and its Protocols;[4] it 'only complements'[5] those other substantive provisions.

The main principles for the application of Article 14 were set out in one of the Court's first judgments, the so-called *Belgian Linguistic* case[6] of 1968, when it recognized that there could be a breach of Article 14 even if there is no breach of another Article. The Court soon established, however, that it would not always consider the Article 14 claim in such cases. As the Court has since put it, '[w]here a substantive Article of the Convention has been invoked, both on its own and together with Article 14, and a separate breach has been found of the substantive Article, it is not generally necessary...to consider the case under Article 14 also, though the position is otherwise if a clear inequality of treatment in the enjoyment of the right in question is a fundamental aspect of the case'.[7] Viewed over-all the jurisprudence indicates that the Court has been disinclined to address Article 14 where another violation has been established (or even to consider whether the other vio-lation precludes the Article 14 question).[8] Several examples of cases may be cited where one would have thought that the issue of discrimination was a 'fundamental aspect' of the case for the applicant, but where the Court did not address Article 14 in view of the fact that it had already found a breach of another Article. In *Dudgeon v UK*,[9] for example, the Court decided that its ruling that the criminalization of adult, private homosexual acts was a breach of Article 8 absolved it from the need to adjudicate on the applicant's Article 14 allegations. It said that these concerned 'the same complaint, albeit seen from a different angle', as that underlying the Article 8 claim and that there was 'no useful legal purpose in deciding them'.[10] *Chassagnou v France*[11] and *Aziz v Cyprus*[12] are relatively rare recent examples of the Court proceeding to address Article 14 even after finding a breach of other Articles (in fact, Article 11 and Article 1, First Protocol).[13]

The importance of Article 14 has nevertheless been brought out in a number of signifi-cant cases over the last decade including, for example, important judgments and deci-sions concerning discrimination based on sexual orientation. The relevance of Article 14 has been developed in a series of key cases concerning allegations of racial discrimina-tion against members of the Roma[14] community from countries in Central and Eastern Europe, for example in the context of police violence and in the field of education provi-sion. The Court has also recently developed its position on the notion of 'indirect dis-crimination' and the relevance of statistical evidence to claims of discrimination.

Ch 17 below) and, by implication, Article 17 (Ch 17 below) allow discrimination. Also some provisions of the Convention have 'equality' obligations built into them, eg Article 5, Seventh Protocol.

[4] Cf, Protocol 12 discussed at p 611 below.   [5] *EB v France* hudoc (2008) para 47 GC.

[6] A 6 (1968); 1 EHRR 252 PC.

[7] *Aziz v Cyrpus* 2004-V; 41 EHRR 164 para 35. See also *Airey v Ireland* A 32 (1980); 2 EHRR 305 para 30. Cf, *Dudgeon v UK* A 45 (1981); 4 EHRR 149 para 67 PC and *Chassagnou v France* 1999-III; 29 EHRR 615 para 89. In *Pla and Puncernau v Andorra* 2004-VIII; 42 EHRR 522 the Court examined the Article 14 (with another right) claim without addressing the main substantive right first or at all. The Court stated that the 'alleged discrimina-tory treatment of the...applicant is at the heart of [his] complaint'.

[8] See *Airey v Ireland* A 32 (1980); 2 EHRR 305 at paras 29–30.

[9] A 45 (1981); 5 EHRR 573. See also *Goodwin (Christine) v UK* 2002-VI; 35 EHRR 447 para 108 GC; *Smith and Grady v UK* 1999-VI; 29 EHRR 493 para 115 and *X, Y and Z v UK* 1997-II; 24 EHRR 143.

[10] Id, para 69. However, note the dissent of Judge Matscher.

[11] 1999-III; 29 EHRR 615 GC.   [12] 2004-V; 41 EHRR 164 para 35.

[13] For an earlier example see *Marckx v Belgium* A31 (1979); 2 EHRR 330 PC (illegitimacy).

[14] On Article 14 in this context more generally, see Sandland, 8 HRLR 4 (2008).

2. OVERVIEW OF THE APPLICATION
OF ARTICLE 14

It is axiomatic that not every difference in treatment amounts to discrimination, but establishing clear principles for the application of Article 14 is not easy. The case in which the Court set out most clearly its approach to Article 14 is *Rasmussen v Denmark*.[15] A husband invoked Article 14 in combination with Articles 6 and 8 in relation to his complaint that he was subject to time limits to contest the paternity of a child born during the marriage, whereas his wife could institute paternity proceedings at any time. The Court decided that:

(i) the allegations of a violation of Article 14 fell *'within the ambit'* of Articles 6 and 8 (see heading 3 below);

(ii) there was *a difference of treatment* between a husband and a wife (and, since the list of categories of discrimination in Article 14 was not exhaustive, it was not necessary to determine the basis for this different treatment) (see heading 4.I below);

(iii) it was not necessary in this case to decide whether the husband and the wife were in *'analogous situations'*, though the Court proceeded on the assumption that they were (see heading 4.II below); and

(iv) there was *an 'objective and reasonable' justification for the difference in treatment* of individuals in analogous positions, relying on the Danish state's margin of appreciation: in particular, the discrimination was proportionate to the legislator's aims of ensuring legal certainty and protecting the interests of the child, a conclusion reinforced by the absence of 'common [European] ground' as to how paternity proceedings should be regulated (on this fourth element to the Court's approach to Article 14, see heading 5 below).

As a result, the Court decided in the *Rasmussen* case that there was no violation of Article 14 of the Convention taken with another right.

The step-by-step approach set out in *Rasmussen* can be rather technical in practice and is not always rigorously applied by the Court. Steps (i) and (ii) establish whether Article 14 generally applies in the first place, but the issue of what falls 'within the ambit' of a Convention right can be controversial. The last two steps have also been the source of some confusion. In some cases the Court has demonstrated the importance of step (iii) since it has concluded that an applicant has failed to satisfy the conditions set down by that step and so hold that there has been no violation of Article 14. But, as commentators have observed, the Court has frequently glossed over step (iii) by collapsing the 'analogous situation' test into the general issue of whether there can be a justification for the differentiation (step (iv)).[16]

In more recent case law the Court has simply stated that discrimination means 'treating differently, without an objective and reasonable justification, persons in relevantly similar situations'.[17] As the jurisprudence evidences, however, the relevance of Article 14 is not confined to discrimination on the state's part; the state also has a positive obligation to protect against private discrimination.[18] As regards indirect discrimination, the Court

---

[15] A 87 (1984); 7 EHRR 371.

[16] For the UK courts' approach to the Article 14 tests and criticism thereof, see Baker, 2006 PL 476.

[17] *Zarb Adami v Malta* hudoc (2006); 44 EHRR 49 para 71 (citing *Willis v UK* 2002-IV; 35 EHRR 547 para 48).

[18] See p 610.

has accepted that 'a general policy or measure that has disproportionately prejudicial effects on a particular group may be considered discriminatory notwithstanding that it is not specifically aimed at that group...and that discrimination potentially contrary to the Convention may result from a *de facto* situation'.[19] Furthermore, as regards affirmative action, the Court has also pointed out, 'Article 14 does not prohibit a member state from treating groups differently in order to correct "factual inequalities" between them; indeed in certain circumstances a failure to attempt to correct inequality through different treatment may in itself give rise to a breach of the Article'.[20]

3. PROTECTION FOR GUARANTEED RIGHTS ONLY AND THE AMBIT TEST

The 'reach' of Article 14 is restricted to discrimination *only with respect to the rights and freedoms set out elsewhere in the Convention*.[21] So, as a 'parasitic' provision Article 14 is not a general proscription against every kind of discrimination.[22] Where a right falls outside the Convention, such as the right of access to civil service employment,[23] a state has no obligation to avoid discrimination. In practice, this is a significant restriction because a great deal of discrimination law is concerned with the enjoyment of economic and social rights, such as rights to employment or to pay and working conditions or to housing, none of which are the direct concerns of the Convention.[24]

Subject to this limitation, the Court has generally approached the application and interpretation of Article 14 in an effective way. In particular, an applicant may establish a violation of Article 14, even though he cannot show or does not even claim a violation of another Article,[25] provided that the claim falls 'within the ambit' of a Convention right. This is possible as the Court has held that 'the notion of discrimination includes in general cases where a person or group is treated, without proper justification, less favourably than another, even though the more favourable treatment is not called for by the Convention'.[26] Put another way:

> [t]he prohibition of discrimination enshrined in Article 14...extends beyond the enjoyment of the rights and freedoms which the Convention and the Protocols thereto require

[19] *DH v Czech Republic* hudoc (2007) para 175 GC (citing, *inter alia, Hugh Jordan v UK* 2001-III; 37 EHRR 52 para 154 and *Zarb Adami v Malta* hudoc (2006); 44 EHRR 49 para 76).

[20] Id (citing *Belgian Linguistic* case A 6 (1968); 1 EHRR 252 para 10 PC; *Thlimmenos v Greece* 2000-IV; 31 EHRR 411 para 44; and *Stec v UK* hudoc (2006); 43 EHRR 1017 para 51 GC).

[21] Those Protocols to the Convention which contain new substantive rights all provide that they shall be regarded as additional rights to the Convention itself and, accordingly, persons are protected by Article 14 in the enjoyment of them: see Article 5, First Protocol; Article 6(1), Fourth Protocol; Article 6, Sixth Protocol; Article 7(1), Seventh Protocol; Article 5, Thirteenth Protocol.

[22] Cf, Protocol Twelve considered below at p 611.

[23] *Glasenapp v FRG* A 104 (1986); 9 EHRR 25 para 53 PC and *Kosiek v FRG* A 105 (1986); 9 EHRR 328 para 39 PC.

[24] Such rights are protected by the European Social Charter 1961, which has a non-discrimination provision in its Preamble. See also Additional Protocol to the European Social Charter 1988, Article 1 (Right to equal opportunities and equal treatment in matters of employment and occupation without discrimination on the grounds of sex). Article 8 of the Convention has some application to housing. On the Convention and economic, social, and cultural rights see Warbrick, in *Economic Social and Cultural Rights in Action*, 2007, Ch 10.

[25] See *Belgian Linguistic* case B 3 (1965) para 400 Com Rep. cf, the Court judgment: A 6 (1968); 1 EHRR 252 PC.

[26] *Zarb Adami v Malta* hudoc (2006); 44 EHRR 49 para 73 (citing *Abdulaziz, Cabales and Balkandali v UK* A 94 (1985); 7 EHRR 163 para 82 PC). See also *Delcourt v Belgium* A 11 (1970); 1 EHRR 355.

each State to guarantee. It applies also to those additional rights, falling within the general scope of any Convention Article, for which the State has voluntarily decided to provide.[27]

Hence in the *Belgian Linguistic* case,[28] where one of the complaints was about the right of access to language-based state education, it was accepted that the Convention does not require a state to provide *any* system of education but that, if it did, it may not restrict access to it on a discriminatory basis.[29] The principle then is that a state which goes beyond its obligations under a Convention right should do so in a non-discriminatory way. Thus, whilst the right to adopt is not covered by Article 8 taken alone,[30] French law permits adoption by single persons, so in *EB v France*[31] and *Fretté v France*[32] the Court considered the ambit test satisfied, and went on to examine the claim of discrimination based on sexual orientation.[33] A last example of this is *Inze v Austria*.[34] The applicant in this case did not allege that his rights under Article 1 of the First Protocol had been infringed by an Austrian law affecting succession to 'hereditary' farms, which was designed to preserve farms as economically viable units. He did argue that the Austrian law which gave priority to legitimate over illegitimate heirs as to who should succeed to an entire farm was a violation of Article 14 in combination with Article 1 of the First Protocol. The test, the Court said, was not whether Article 1 of the First Protocol had been violated but whether the applicant's claim fell within its 'ambit'.[35]

The practical significance of the Court's 'ambit test' approach is illustrated by case law on welfare benefits. The Convention places no restrictions on the contracting states' freedom to decide whether or not to have in place any form of social security scheme, or to choose the type or amount of benefits to provide under any such scheme. However a state which creates a benefits scheme engages Article 1 of the First Protocol insofar as an individual has an enforceable right under domestic law to the benefit. In these circumstances the state must act in a manner which is compatible with Article 14,[36] there being potential Convention issues if, for example, an individual has been denied all or part of a particular benefit on a discriminatory ground covered by Article 14.

4. DIFFERENTIAL TREATMENT ON A PROHIBITED GROUND

Assuming that the alleged ill-treatment falls within the ambit of a Convention right, the next issue to be considered is whether there has been a difference of treatment in fact and whether this has been on a ground prohibited by Article 14 of the Convention.

---

[27] *EB v France* hudoc (2008) para 48 GC.　　[28] A 6 (1968); 1 EHRR 252 para 9 PC.

[29] *Ibid.* Cf, *Skender v FYROM No 62059/00* hudoc (2001) DA.

[30] *EB v France* hudoc (2008) paras 41–6 GC, see, however, the dissenting opinion of Judge Mularoni.

[31] Id.　　[32] See also *Fretté v France* 2002-I; 38 EHRR 438.

[33] See below, p 597. In *EB v France* the Grand Chamber held that the applicant's case 'undoubtedly' (id, para 49) fell within the ambit of Article 8 for the purposes of the Article 14 claim. The Court was clear that it was not called upon to decide whether the right to adopt fell 'within the ambit of Article 8...taken alone' (para 46; cf, Judge Mularoni's dissenting opinion in *EB*). See, by comparison, the earlier case of *Fretté v France* 2002-I; 38 EHRR 438 (especially the separate opinion of Sir Nicholas Bratza and Judges Fuhrman and Tulkens, and the partly concurring opinion of Judge Costa (joined by Judges Jungwiert and Traja).

[34] *Inze v Austria* A 126 (1987); 10 EHRR 394. As another example see *Petrovic v Austria* 1998-II; 33 EHRR 307, discussed below at p 593.

[35] Id, para 36. See also *Van der Mussele v Belgium* A 70 (1983); 6 EHRR 163 para 43 PC.

[36] *Stec v UK Nos 65731/01* and *65900/01* hudoc (2005); 41 EHRR SE 295 paras 54–5 GC.

I. IDENTIFYING DIFFERENTIAL TREATMENT

In the typical discrimination case, the applicant will claim that he has been treated differently from others who, though in a similar position to him, are treated better.[37] Often the applicant will argue that the basis for the different treatment is that he is a member of one group, while the better treated are members of another group, whereas in reality the members of both groups are in the same position. Normally the applicant will have no difficulty identifying *how* he has been treated less favourably than others. Interference with the enjoyment of possessions, criminalization of sexual activities, and obligations to provide free services are instances where the complaint relates to positive action by the state to the disadvantage of the applicant. In other cases, the complaint is about the denial of opportunities afforded to others, for example the right to bring civil actions or to be tried by an ordinary criminal court or to exercise the same freedom of expression. However if, ordinarily, this question is not troublesome, there are circumstances where the applicant and the state dispute what is different treatment. In *Schmidt v Germany*,[38] for example, the applicant was a man who had had to pay a levy as an alternative obligation to serving in his local fire brigade. All men were potential firemen but women were not. Accordingly, women never had an obligation to pay the levy. Schmidt's complaint was that he was a victim of different treatment on the basis of his sex. But what was the different treatment? A majority of the Court, taking into account the fact that no man was ever obliged to serve in a fire brigade because the fire service was never short of volunteers, considered that the different treatment was the payment of the levy. There was no justification for taxing men and women differently by reason of their sex alone.[39] That being the case, it is somewhat surprising that these judges thought that Schmidt had been discriminated against with respect to Article 4(3)(d), work or service which forms part of normal civic obligations, rather than with respect to Article 1 of the First Protocol, which protects the right to property.[40] Two of the dissenting judges[41] said that the different treatment was with respect to the obligation to serve in the fire service. The distinction the state made was not primarily between men and women but between those who were fit to serve and those who were not.

The 'badge' of differentiation relied on in the legislation or decision by the state may be challenged by the applicant as not being the 'real' reason for distinguishing him from others. In *Hoffmann v Austria*,[42] the applicant was a Jehovah's Witness. She alleged that the decision of the Austrian courts to award custody of her child to her husband was taken largely on the basis of her religious beliefs. The government argued that the decision had been made in the interests of the child. The European Court examined the national judgments and decided that the final judgment had been taken on grounds of religion. In *Abdulaziz, Cabales, and Balkandali v UK*[43] the applicants claimed that the explanations

---

[37] *Van der Mussele v Belgium* A 70 (1983); 6 EHRR 163 para 46 PC.

[38] A 291-B (1994); 1 EHRR 632 (cf, the comments made about this case in the separate opinions annexed to *Zarb Adami v Malta* hudoc (2006); 44 EHRR 49). As another example see *Dahlab v Switzerland* No 42393/98, 2001-V (inadmissible). The applicant was a Muslim teacher banned from wearing a headscarf while teaching and claimed discrimination based on sex as Muslim men could teach at a state school without similar restraints. The Court considered that the headscarf ban for teaching was not directed at her as a member of the female sex but pursued the legitimate aim of ensuring the neutrality of the state primary-education system. The measure could also be applied to a man who wore clothing identifying him as a member of a different faith. Cf, *Kara v UK* No 36528/97 hudoc (1998) DA (concerning alleged discrimination regarding different dress codes for men and women at work imposed by a council—inadmissible).

[39] Id, para 28.   [40] *Ibid.*   [41] Judges Spielmann and Gotchev, dissenting.

[42] A 255-C (1993); 14 EHRR 437 paras 33 and 36.   [43] A 94 (1985); 7 EHRR 163 para 84 PC.

given by the British government for subjecting them as women to a different regime from that for men in the matter of the immigration rights of their partners—for the protection of the labour market and the protection of public order—disguised the racial motivation behind the Rules. The Court gave this claim short shrift.[44]

II. NO DISCRIMINATION IF SITUATIONS ARE NOT ANALOGOUS

The state only has to justify preferential treatment if situations are analogous, that is for 'persons in relevantly similar situations'.[45] So an applicant will need to avoid the Court being able to conclude that his or her position (and the position of people like him or her) cannot be said to be similar to, that is 'analogous' to, the situation of people in the group he or she has identified as enjoying more favourable treatment. This was so in *Burden v UK*,[46] where two elderly (unmarried) sisters who had co-habited all their life and in the family home for the last thirty-one years claimed discrimination with respect to Article 1 of Protocol 1. Upon the death of one sister the survivor would have to pay inheritance tax on their home, unlike married or Civil Partnership Act couples who benefited from exemptions. As the comparators were not analogous[47] the Grand Chamber did not go on to assess whether the difference of treatment could be justified.[48]

The importance of this requirement is evident from case law illustrating that, for the purpose of Article 14 generally, unmarried partners are not in an analogous position to spouses.[49] However, generally speaking this is another area of Article 14 that is difficult to apply[50] and which has given rise to conflicting views which determine the decision in the case.[51] Further, it has been noted that the Court regularly glosses over the analogous situation test and even collapses it into the issue of whether there can be a *justification* for the differentiation.[52] An example was *Holy Monasteries v Greece*,[53] a case which concerned large-scale land expropriation from the Greek Church alone as opposed to other monasteries. In finding no violation of Article 14 the Court simply held that the close links between the monasteries and the Greek Church justified treating them differently from those subject to other authority.

It may be hard to separate the questions of whether situations are analogous and whether there is different treatment in fact. An applicant may simply contend that by being treated differently from the way other members of his group have been treated he has been discriminated against. In *Pine Valley Developments Ltd v Ireland*[54] two of the applicant property developers argued successfully that their rights under Article 1 of the First Protocol had been breached in connection with Article 14. Their claim was that remedial legislation, introduced to correct a misapplication of the planning law, had been drafted in such a way as to exclude them but not other holders of permissions in the same categories as theirs from the benefit of the law.[55]

---

[44] Id, paras 85–6.   [45] *Zarb Adami v Malta* hudoc (2006); 44 EHRR 49 para 71.

[46] Hudoc (2008) GC.

[47] See, however, the strong dissenting opinions of Judges Zupancic and Borrego Borrego.

[48] Cf, the Chamber judgment which skipped over the analogous situation test yet found the difference of treatment justified, *Burden and Burden v UK* hudoc (2006); 44 EHRR1023.

[49] See below p 600.   [50] See Baker, 2006 PL 476.

[51] See eg, the different approaches taken by the Commission and Court in *Stubbings v UK* 1996-IV; 23 EHRR 213 para 73.

[52] Van Dijk and Van Hoof at p 1041.   [53] *Holy Monasteries v Greece* A 301-A (1994); 20 EHRR 1.

[54] A 222 (1991); 14 EHRR 319.

[55] Id, paras 14–17 and 61. Similarly see *Fredin v Sweden* A 192 (1991); 13 EHRR 784.

III. OBLIGATION TO TREAT DIFFERENTLY PERSONS WHOSE SITUATIONS ARE SIGNIFICANTLY DIFFERENT

In *Thlimmenos v Greece*,[56] the Grand Chamber stressed that '[t]he right not to be discriminated against in the enjoyment of the rights guaranteed under the Convention is also violated when states without an objective and reasonable justification fail to treat differently persons whose situations are significantly different'.[57] The Greek Institute of Chartered Accountants had refused to appoint the applicant, a Jehovah's Witness, on account of his prior conviction for insubordination (failing to wear military uniform). It was the applicant's case that the Institute should have distinguished his conviction from other convictions because it had stemmed from the exercise of his religious belief. The Court accepted this argument and concluded that the failure to treat the applicant differently was disproportionate and did not pursue a legitimate aim (leading to a violation of Article 9 in conjunction with Article 14).

IV. PROHIBITED GROUNDS (OR 'BADGES') OF DISCRIMINATION

Article 14 contains a long, and apparently non-exhaustive,[58] list of characteristics which might render differential treatment discriminatory, so identifying the 'badge' on the basis of which the differential treatment is made is not usually a problem. Furthermore these identified 'badges' are supplemented by an open-ended 'other status' category, which has been held to include sexual orientation, marital status, illegitimacy, status as a trade union, military status, conscientious objection, professional status, and imprisonment. Financial status is a characteristic that has not been rejected peremptorily by the Court but it did show some reluctance to address the claim in *Airey v Ireland*[59] that the applicant had been discriminated against by reason of her poverty. Article 14 forbids discrimination on the ground of 'property'. This is the most problematic of categories[60] and one would anticipate that the institutions would be reluctant to admit a separate violation of Article 14 on this ground alone[61] but that they would rather consider, as the Court did in the *Airey* case, whether there had been a violation of a substantive provision. In *Johnston v Ireland*,[62] the Court found that a lack of financial resources was not in fact the basis on which the applicants had been treated differently from others.

---

[56] 2000-IV; 31 EHRR 411 GC; see also *Chapman v UK* 2001-I; 33 EHRR 399 para 129 GC.

[57] Id, para 44. No indirect discrimination was found in *Chapman v UK, ibid* (applicants argued that domestic law failed to accommodate gypsies' traditional way of life as they were treated in the same way as the majority population) or *Pretty v UK* 2002-III; 35 EHRR 1 (applicant claimed blanket ban on assisted suicide was discriminatory on the facts given her particular disabilities; the application was refused on this point on other grounds).

[58] The text reads 'any ground such as'. Article 14 may be compared to Article 21(1) of the Charter of Fundamental Rights of the European Union, which states 'Any discrimination based on any ground such as sex, race, colour, *ethnic* or social origin, *genetic features*, language, religion *or belief*, political or any other opinion, membership of a national minority, property, birth, *disability, age or sexual orientation* shall be prohibited' (emphasis added to indicate additions).

[59] A 32 (1980); 2 EHRR 305 paras 29–30.

[60] See Thornberry, 29 ICLQ 250 (1980) (on the *Airey* case). More generally, see Michelman, 83 Harv LR 7 (1969).

[61] Cf, the rather different case of *Chassagnou v France* 1999-III; 29 EHRR 615, where the Court found discrimination on 'the ground of property', para 95. Small landowners were required to join an inter-municipality hunting association whereas large landowners were not. The latter could demonstrate their anti-hunting stance while the former could not—a difference in treatment regarding the use of land in accordance with conscience. The Court found a breach of Article 1, First Protocol with Article 14, as well as of Article 11 with Article 14.

[62] A 112 (1986); 27 EHRR 296 paras 59–61 PC.

The Court has reiterated that Article 14 'is not concerned with all differences of treatment but only with differences having as their basis or reason a personal characteristic by which persons or group of persons are distinguishable from each other'.[63] So it may be argued that the term 'other status' should restrict the application of Article 14 as the specific grounds listed all relate to some sort of 'personal characteristic' of a potential victim.[64] In *Magee v UK*[65] the applicant claimed a violation of Article 6(1) in conjunction with Article 14 regarding access to a lawyer. His point was that the different criminal regime operating in Northern Ireland entailed that there he obtained access to his solicitor at a later stage than would have been the case on the UK mainland. The Court rejected the claim that there had been a violation of Article 14 read with Article 6 as the difference of treatment was 'not to be explained in terms of personal characteristics, such as national origin or association with a national minority, but on the geographical location where the individual is arrested and detained'.[66] The relevant legislation, the Court stated, took into account 'regional differences and characteristics of an objective and reasonable nature'.

However, deciphering the limits to 'personal characteristic[s]' is not an easy exercise. In one recent case the Court implicitly accepted that the applicants' status as fisherman with rights to fish waters that became subject to fishing controls sufficed as a 'personal characteristic'.[67] In *Sidabras and Dziautas v Lithuania*,[68] the applicants' status as two former KGB agents seemed to suffice as they complained that they had suffered discrimination (Article 8 with Article 14) since the law excluded them from certain private sector jobs. The Court accepted that they had been treated differently from other persons in Lithuania who had not worked for the KGB and, by five votes to two, proceeded to find a violation of Article 14 read with Article 8. In partial dissent Judge Thomassen argued that the 'principle of non-discrimination, as it is recognised in European Constitutions and in international Treaties, refers above all to a denial of opportunities on grounds of personal choices insofar as these choices should be respected as elements of someone's personality, such as religion, political opinion, sexual orientation and gender identity, or, on the contrary, on grounds of personal features in respect of which no choice at all can be made, such as sex, race, disability and age'.[69]

As is noted below, certain personal characteristics, such as race, sex, or birth status, ie those specifically mentioned in Article 14, will be treated more seriously than others ('other status') in the broader assessment of whether there has been discrimination in fact.

5. DIFFERENTIAL TREATMENT MAY BE JUSTIFIED ON OBJECTIVE AND REASONABLE GROUNDS

If there is differential treatment within the ambit of a protected right on a prohibited ground for the purposes of Article 14, the central issue becomes whether it can be justified or whether it should be stigmatized as discrimination. As the Court has put it recently,

---

[63] *Halis v Turkey* No 30007/96 hudoc (2002) DA and *Jones v UK* No 42639/04 hudoc (2005) DA (both citing *Kjeldsen, Busk Madsen and Pedersen v Denmark* A 23 (1976); 1 EHRR 711 para 56). For discussion of the matter of 'personal characteristic' before the UK courts see *R v Secretary of State for Work and Pensions, ex p Carson* [2005] UKHL 37.

[64] *Dudgeon v UK* A 45 (1981); 4 EHRR 149 PC, see the separate opinion of Judge Matscher.

[65] 2000-VI; 31 EHRR 822.   [66] Id, para 50.   [67] *Alatulkkila and Others v Finland* hudoc (2005).

[68] 2004-VIII; 42 EHRR 104; see also *Rainys and Gasparavičius v Lithuania* hudoc (2005).

[69] See also the partial dissent of Judge Loucaides.

'Article 14 does not prohibit distinctions in treatment which are founded on an objective assessment of essentially different factual circumstances and which, being based on the public interest, strike a fair balance between the protection of the interests of the community and respect for the rights and freedoms safeguarded by the Convention.'[70]

I. THE TESTS SET IN THE *BELGIAN LINGUISTIC* CASE

The tests to be applied by the Court were set out in one of its earliest judgments: the *Belgian Linguistic* case.[71] First, the Court easily rejected the argument made on the basis of the French text that every difference of treatment in the exercise of Convention rights is excluded. It recognized the existence of a wide variety of national legislative and administrative regimes based on differential treatment which could well be seen to be for a good reason. As a result, a test had to be formulated to allow the distinction to be drawn between permissible differentiation and unlawful discrimination. The Court said:

> It is important...to look for the criteria which enable a determination to be made as to whether or not a given difference in treatment, concerning of course the exercise of one of the rights and freedoms set forth, contravenes Article 14. On this question the Court, following the principles which may be extracted from the legal practice of a large number of democratic states, holds that the principle of equality of treatment is violated if the distinction has no reasonable and objective justification. The existence of such a justification must be assessed in relation to the aim and effects of the measure under consideration, regard being had to the principles which normally prevail in democratic societies. A difference of treatment in the exercise of a right laid down in the Convention must not only pursue a legitimate aim: Article 14 is likewise violated when it is clearly established that there is no reasonable relationship of proportionality between the means employed and the aim sought to be realised.[72]

This test embraces two elements: the identification of a legitimate aim for the different treatment, which is the obligation of the state, and an assessment of whether there is a 'reasonable relationship of proportionality' between the different treatment and the aim pursued, where it is for the applicant to 'clearly establish' the lack of proportionality.[73] In the *Belgian Linguistic* case, the Court also noted[74] that its role was not to put itself in the place of the national law-maker but to exercise its subsidiary role of ensuring that national determinations were not incompatible with the Convention. Accordingly, it conceded to states a 'margin of appreciation' in making their assessments of what different treatment was proportionate to the legitimate objective they had chosen.

II. 'DIFFERENCE OF TREATMENT IN THE EXERCISE OF A RIGHT LAID DOWN IN THE CONVENTION MUST...PURSUE A LEGITIMATE AIM'

When the Court scrutinizes the differential treatment before it, if the government does not plead any justification for alleged discrimination then, other than exceptional circumstances, the applicant's claim of a violation will be made out.[75] If the government

---

[70] *Zarb Adami v Malta* hudoc (2006); 44 EHRR 49 para 73.
[71] A 6 (1968); 1 EHRR 252 PC. See Verhoeven, 23 RBDI 353 (1990).   [72] Id, para 10.
[73] See Eissen, *European Supervision*, Ch 7, p 141.   [74] A 6 (1968); 1 EHRR 252 para 10 PC.
[75] *Darby v Sweden* is an example, A 187 (1990); 13 EHRR 774 para 33. The explanation for treating resident and non-resident non-nationals differently for the purposes of religious tax was administrative convenience,

suggests an explanation, the justification which it gives must have a rational basis and an evidential foundation.

Legitimate aims have included: in the *Belgian Linguistic* case, to achieve the effective implementation of the policy of developing linguistic unity of the two large language regions;[76] in the *Marckx* case, to support and encourage the traditional family;[77] and in the *Abdulaziz* case, to protect the labour market and the protection of public order.[78] In *Karner v Austria*,[79] which concerned differential treatment for homosexuals regarding succession to tenancies, again there were detailed submissions from both sides, but the Court accepted that protection of the family in the traditional sense is, in principle, a weighty and legitimate reason which might justify a difference in treatment. In *Sidabras and Dziautas v Lithuania*[80] the Court accepted that a law restricting employment prospects for former KGB agents pursued the legitimate aims of the protection of national security, public safety, the economic well-being of the country, and the rights and freedoms of others.

Often the Court is relatively easily satisfied by the legitimate aim put forward by the state. However, it may be necessary for the state to demonstrate the proper link between the legitimate aim pursued and the differential treatment being challenged by the applicant.[81] Furthermore, the applicant may contest the authenticity of the government's explanation, so requiring the Court to adjudicate upon the argument.[82] In the *Abdulaziz* case, the applicants were able to show that the supposed reason for distinguishing between men and women, that they had a different effect on the labour market, was without factual basis.[83] In some cases, however, the 'evidence' on which the state's allegedly discriminatory treatment is based and justified may be inconclusive either way. Here the Court asserts that 'Contracting states enjoy a margin of appreciation in assessing whether and to what extent difference in otherwise similar situations justify a difference in treatment'.[84] However, as is noted below, the Court has identified certain types of differences of treatment, for example discrimination based exclusively on sex, that it will find justified only if 'very weighty reasons' have been put forward.

III. PROPORTIONALITY

As the Court stated in the *Belgian Linguistic* case,[85] after finding a legitimate aim what is essentially required is that the differences in treatment between the members of the groups 'strike a fair balance between the protection of the interests of the community

---

which the state declined to put by way of excuse to the Court. See also *Zarb Adami v Malta* hudoc (2006); 44 EHRR 49 para 82. By contrast see *Petrovic v Austria* 1998-II; 33 EHRR 307, where the Court conveniently avoided the legitimate aim test, proceeding to conclude that there was no Article 14 discrimination based on the proportionality test.

[76] A 6 (1968); 1 EHRR 252 para 7 PC.   [77] A 31 (1979); 2 EHRR 330 para 40 PC.

[78] A 94 (1985); 7 EHRR 163 paras 78 and 81 PC.

[79] 2003-IX; 38 EHRR 24 para 528 (there was a violation on the facts, see below).

[80] 2004-VIII; 42 EHRR 104 para 55.   [81] *Larkos v Cyprus* 1999-I; 30 EHRR 597.

[82] In *Abdulaziz, Cabales and Balkandali v UK* A 94 (1985); 7 EHRR 163 PC.

[83] Id, paras 74–80. But the Court rejected the applicant's argument that the Immigration Rules were racially motivated, id, paras 85–6. See also the criticism made in the first edition of this volume, at p 479, regarding early Commission jurisprudence addressing differential treatment of homosexuals.

[84] See, as recent examples, *L and V v Austria* 2003-I; 36 EHRR1022 para 44; *Chassagnou v France* 1999-III; 29 EHRR 615 para 91 and *Stec v UK* (hudoc) 2006; 43 EHRR 1017 para 51 GC.

[85] A 6 (1968); 1 EHRR 252 para 7 PC. See also *G v Netherlands No 11850/85*, 51 DR 180 (1987), upholding a longer period of compulsory service for conscientious objectors than the period of military service for conscripts, to avoid too much opting out.

and respect for the rights and freedoms safeguarded by the Convention'. The test here is whether it is established that there is in fact no reasonable relationship of proportionality between the means employed by the state and the legitimate aim that it is attempting to realize. In other words, this is an area where the Court will condemn arbitrary distinctions, but in their absence the public interest can justify some forms of differential treatment. Moreover, in assessing the issue of public interest the Court is prone to recognize the subsidiary nature of the Convention system of protection paying due deference to the task of the domestic authorities: it 'cannot disregard those legal and factual features which characterise the life of the society in the state which, as a Contracting Party, has to answer for the measure in dispute'.[86]

This is therefore another area where the Court has frequently asserted that 'the Contracting states enjoy a certain margin of appreciation in assessing whether and to what extent differences in otherwise similar situations justify a different treatment in law'.[87] The effect of this was seen in the rejection of the application in *Murdock v UK*[88] where the applicant was a life prisoner in Northern Ireland following conviction for a non-terrorist-related crime and complained of discrimination in breach of Article 14 compared to those who obtained accelerated release in connection with the evolving Northern Ireland peace process. Although it was not the only ground relied upon, the Court referred to 'the sensitive nature of the ongoing peace process and the complexity of the security situation which it [sought] to resolve... [such that] a wide margin of appreciation in the measures perceived as necessary in the pursuit of that process' was afforded to the respondent state. As regards the margin of appreciation in the context of Article 14 the Court has stated that its 'scope... will vary according to the circumstances, the subject matter and its background; in this respect, one of the relevant factors may be the existence or non-existence of common ground between the laws of the Contracting states'.[89]

In many cases the Court easily concludes that there has been no breach of Article 14 on grounds of proportionality. When 'general measures of economic or social strategy'[90] are in issue the Court will grant a wide margin of appreciation. This has been so in some notable cases which have related to national taxation policy, where the Court has indicated that 'it is primarily for the state to decide how best to strike the balance between raising revenue and pursuing social objectives'.[91]

As a general rule the less evidence there is that the state's differential treatment departs from a common standard in the Convention states, the less likely the Court is to condemn it. For example, in *Rasmussen v Denmark*,[92] there was evidence that a Danish law distinguishing between husbands and wives in the matter of time limits applicable to paternity proceedings was not different to that in some other European states. Accordingly, the Court found that making the distinction did fall within the state's margin of appreciation.[93]

[86] Id, para 10.   [87] *Petrovic v Austria* 1998-II; 33 EHRR 307 para 38.
[88] No 44934/98 hudoc (2000) DA.   [89] *Petrovic*, above n 87.
[90] *Burden v UK* hudoc (2008) para 60 GC (unmarried cohabiting family members' claimed discrimination (Article 1, First Protocol with Article 14) as they were liable to pay inheritance tax unlike survivors of a marriage or a civil partnership).
[91] *Burden v UK* hudoc (2006); 44 EHRR 1023 para 60 (Chamber judgment). See also *Stec v UK* (hudoc) 2006; 43 EHRR 1017 para 52 GC (differential regime between men and women for industrial injuries social security benefits).
[92] A 87 (1984); 7 EHRR 371 para 41. See Helfer, 65 NYULR 1044 at 1075–100 (1990). On discrimination in contesting paternity and the need for proportionality see also *Paulik v Slovakia* hudoc (2006); 46 EHRR 142.
[93] See also *Petrovic v Austria* 1998-II; 33 EHRR 307.

Often, however, the situation in issue will be peculiar to that state and the search for European standards will be fruitless, so resort is made to the general proportionality test whereby the more limited in scope the alleged differential treatment is the easier it is for it to be outweighed by 'lighter' public interest considerations. In the *Belgian Linguistic* case, with a single exception,[94] the Court found that the policies adopted by Belgium for promoting the language regions could be justified and did not impinge excessively on the rights of individuals. In the *National Union of Belgian Police* case,[95] the denial of consultation rights to a trade union (made on the basis of its small size compared to unions given consultation rights) was justified as striking a reasonable balance between the right of the union and the interests of the employers in ensuring a 'coherent and balanced staff policy'. In *Sidabras and Dziautas v Lithuania*[96] a law operated so as to deny the applicants' employment prospects in the private sector as they were former KGB officers. The Court found this to be disproportionate, amongst other things drawing a distinction between public and private sector employment. In *Cha'are Shalom ve Tsedek v France*,[97] the applicant association submitted that by refusing it the approval necessary for it to authorize its own ritual slaughters, in accordance with the religious prescriptions of its members, and by granting such approval to another organization alone, the French authorities had infringed in a discriminatory way its right to manifest its religion through observance of the rites of the Jewish religion. The Grand Chamber first found there to be no violation of Article 9 and then addressed that Article with Article 14. Rejecting this claim too, the Court asserted that the interference with Article 9 was of 'limited effect' and that the difference of treatment was therefore 'limited in scope'.[98] *Chapman v UK*[99] concerned planning restrictions on the use of land owned by gypsies, the Grand Chamber finding no violation of Article 8 as the interference was proportionate to the legitimate aim of preservation of the environment. It briefly dismissed the claim under Article 8 in conjunction with Article 14 by referring to the finding under Article 8 alone and concluding that there had been no discrimination.[100]

One factor in assessing proportionality is the possibility of alternative means for achieving the same end. However, remembering that the Court frequently asserts that it is not its function to substitute itself for the national decision-maker, if an applicant can identify an alternative this will not be decisive evidence that the state has acted excessively. According to the Court in the *Rasmussen*[101] case, a state's margin of appreciation extends to choosing between alternatives. The fact that some schemes will have even a marked disparity in their impact on separate individuals will not be conclusive that the arrangements are disproportionate if the overall effect is achieved with reasonable tolerance. In *James v UK*,[102] a scheme of leasehold enfranchisement aimed at protecting disadvantaged leaseholders in general produced windfall benefits for some tenants and

---

[94] The Court held that there was no objective and reasonable justification for allowing Dutch-speaking children resident in the French language region to have access to Dutch language schools in the bilingual zone while French-speaking children resident in the Dutch language area were denied access to French language schools in the same zone: *Belgian Linguistic* case A 6 (1968); 1 EHRR 252 PC.

[95] A 19 (1975); 1 EHRR 578 para 48 PC.   [96] 2004-VIII; 42 EHRR 104 paras 58–62.

[97] 2000-VII GC.

[98] Id, para 87. See, however, the strong criticism within the joint dissenting opinion of Judges Bratza, Fischbach, Thomassen, Tsatsa-nikolovska, Pantîru, Levits, and Traja.

[99] 2001-I; 33 EHRR 399 GC.

[100] Id, para 129. See the similar approach to Article 14 taken by the Court in *Rekvényi v Hungary* 1999-III; 30 EHRR 519 GC (restrictions on freedom of expression and association for police officers) and also at admissibility in *McGuinness v UK* 1999-V (alleged discrimination regarding the oath requirement before taking a seat in the House of Commons).

[101] A 87 (1984); 7 EHRR 371 para 41.   [102] A 98 (1986); 8 EHRR 123 para 77 PC.

large losses for some landlords but these exceptional cases were not sufficient for the Court to condemn the whole deal. If much of a margin of appreciation is granted to the state (whether expressly or otherwise,)[103] the impression can be gained that Strasbourg does not much more than endorse the state's own conclusion in Article 14 case law.[104] However, it needs to be remembered that in some cases the respondent government may not be able to establish that there is a proper legitimate aim in the first place and the differential treatment may be condemned on this ground under Article 14.[105] Furthermore, as shall now be observed, the Court treats some forms of discrimination particularly seriously.

6. INTENSIVE SCRUTINY OF DIFFERENTIAL TREATMENT FOR 'SUSPECT CATEGORIES'

The notion of proportionality implies that the more serious the difference of treatment is deemed to be then the greater the reasons required from the state to justify it must be. Where (potentially) serious discrimination is at stake, usually the margin of appreciation owing to a state will be narrower and the disproportionality of the state's chosen means more easily condemned by evidence of practical alternatives.

The Court has identified differential treatment on the basis of certain badges as particularly serious, making them equivalent to 'suspect categories' in United States constitutional law.[106] In fact, the European Court has never used these words but it has stated that certain types of differences of treatment can only to be justified if 'very weighty reasons' have been put forward. This statement has been made in connection with differential treatment based on sex, on nationality, on sexual orientation, and with respect to cases based on discrimination due to the illegitimate (birth) status of an individual.[107] Precisely the same language has not been used in relation to differential treatment based on race (or ethnical origin) and religion, but the Court has indicated that it will treat these as serious too.

It will be appreciated that these categories generally relate to those specifically set out in the text of Article 14 and to what might be broadly termed the 'right to respect for the individuality of a human being'.[108] They are issues that go to the core of the notion of equal treatment and so may be distinguished from other grounds when this last quality is not in evidence, as with for example, differentiation based on residence in a country or abroad[109] and where considerations of general social policy may have a greater role in justifying what may appear to be differential treatment.

---

[103] In recent years the Court has shown some inconsistency here.

[104] Eg, *Gillow v UK* A 109 (1986); 11 EHRR 335 (concerning housing policy on a small island) and *National and Provincial Building Society and Others v UK* 1997-VII; 25 EHRR 127 (wide margin of appreciation for taxation policy).

[105] *Larkos v Cyprus* 1999-I; 30 EHRR 597, also *Pine Valley Developments Ltd v Ireland* A 222 (1992); 14 EHRR 319.

[106] Ely, *Democarcy and Distrust: A Theory of Judicial Review*, 1980, pp 145–70.

[107] See also *Sahin v Germany*, p 599 below, regarding certain fathers' access to their children.

[108] Lord Hoffmann in *R v Secretary of State for Work and Pensions, ex p Carson* [2005] UKHL 37 at para 17. As the Commission's Report in the *Abdulaziz* case suggested, the existence of international treaties covering the particular form of discrimination may be highly influential in identifying the existence of 'suspect categories'.

[109] Cf, *R v Secretary of State for Work and Pensions, ex p Carson* [2005] UKHL 37.

One might compare the 'suspect category' under Article 14 with the special weight given to interests (eg privacy in sexual matters) falling within the sphere of a protected Convention right.[110] Certainly the thrust of the function of the identification of these 'suspect categories' is to put a heavy burden on the state to justify differential treatment when identified. However, as we will see it is not automatically the case that, just because the applicant can identify himself as coming within a so-called suspect category, his Article 14 claim will succeed. Even for suspect categories, there are some cases when the margin of appreciation doctrine has provided protection for the state, especially when no European consensus can be found or when 'general measures of economic or social strategy' are concerned. This once again reflects the reality that the national authorities' 'direct knowledge of their society and its needs, [entails that they]…are in principle better placed than the international judge to appreciate what is in the public interest on social or economic grounds'. Here the Court will 'generally respect the legislature's policy choice', unless it is 'manifestly without reasonable foundation'.[111]

I. RACE (OR ETHNIC ORIGIN)

As early as 1973, the Commission expressed the view that publicly to single out a group of persons for differential treatment on the basis of race might, in certain circumstances,[112] constitute a special affront to human dignity amounting to degrading treatment in violation of Article 3.[113] Consistent with this the Strasbourg jurisprudence indicates that a special importance should be attached to discrimination based on race[114] (or ethnic or national origin)[115] which the Court describes as, 'a particularly invidious kind of discrimination…[that], in view of its perilous consequences, requires from the authorities special vigilance and a vigorous reaction'.[116] For this reason, the Court states, 'the authorities must use all available means to combat racism, thereby reinforcing democracy's vision of a society in which diversity is not perceived as a threat but as a source of enrichment'.[117]

Where a difference in treatment concerning the enjoyment of a Convention right is based on 'race, colour or ethnic origin', the Grand Chamber has stated that 'the notion of objective and reasonable justification must be interpreted as strictly as possible'.[118] In a case that concerned a difference in treatment between persons of Chechen and non-Chechen ethnic origin as regards the enjoyment of their right to liberty of movement, the Court expressed the view that 'no difference in treatment which is based exclusively or to a decisive extent on a person's ethnic origin is capable of being objectively justified in a contemporary democratic society built on the principles of pluralism and respect for different cultures'.[119]

---

[110] See p 370 above.

[111] *Stec v UK* (hudoc) 2006; 43 EHRR 1017 para 52 GC (citing *James v UK* A 98 (1986); 8 EHRR 123 para 46 PC).

[112] An indication of the general circumstances was given in *Abdulaziz, Cabales and Balkandali v UK* A 94 (1985); 7 EHRR 163 PC. In that case the immigration rules did not lead to a violation of Article 3 as '… the difference in treatment…did not denote any contempt or lack of respect for the personality of the applicants…it was not designed to, and did not, humiliate or debase them', para 91.

[113] See p 101.

[114] As regards race discrimination in Europe generally, see Goldston, 5 EHRLR 462 (1999). Details of the Council of Europe's 'European Commission against Racism and Intolerance' can be found at <http://www.coe.int/DefaultEN.asp>.

[115] For the Court's understanding of these terms see *Timishev v Russia* hudoc (2005); 44 EHRR776 para 55.

[116] *DH v Czech Republic* hudoc (2007) para 176 GC.   [117] *Ibid.*   [118] Id, para 196.

[119] *Timishev v Russia* hudoc (2005); 44 EHRR 776 para 58. See also *DH v Czech Republic* hudoc (2007) GC; *Moldovan and Others v Romania (No 2)* hudoc (2005); 44 EHRR 302; *Cisse v France No 51346/99*, 2001-I DA

II. NATIONALITY

As regards discrimination based on national origin, in *Gaygusuz v Austria*[120] the Court made reference to a state's margin of appreciation but added:

> However, very weighty reasons would have to be put forward before the Court could regard a difference of treatment based exclusively on the ground of nationality as compatible with the Convention.[121]

As is noted below,[122] there have been some important judgments regarding Article 14 with Articles 2 and 3 and concerning death and serious ill-treatment allegedly motivated by racial prejudice. The race context has also been important for key case law concerning indirect discrimination, for example in the field of education.[123]

III. SEX

The Court established that discrimination based on 'sex' is a 'suspect category' in the *Abdulaziz* case.[124] It said that:

> the advancement of the equality of the sexes is today a major goal in the member states of the Council of Europe. This means that very weighty reasons would have to be advanced before a difference of treatment on the ground of sex could be regarded as compatible with the Convention.

The Commission in *Abdulaziz*[125] stated that:

> the elimination of all forms of discrimination against women is an accepted general principle in the member states of the Council of Europe, confirmed in domestic legislation, and regional and international treaties.

In *Ünal Tekeli v Turkey*[126] the Court noted the emergence of a consensus among the contracting states of the Council of Europe in favour of allowing a spouse to choose whether her family name should remain her maiden name or be changed to that of her new husband. There had been a violation of Article 14 read with Article 8 in this case insofar as under Turkish law a woman could not bear her maiden name alone after marriage whereas married men could. The Court stated that the objective of reflecting family

---

(whether a system of identity checks in which only dark-skinned occupants are stopped and subsequently detained, may raise issues under Article 5 in conjunction with Article 14); *Gregory v UK* 1997-I; 25 EHRR 577 (alleged racial bias in the context of the right to a fair trial); *Reid v UK No 32350/96* hudoc (1997) DA (allegedly racist summing up remarks of judge in civil action—inadmissible); and *Conka v Belgium No 51564/99* hudoc (2001) DA (Court rejected allegations of racial discrimination in the context of collective expulsion (Article 4 of the Fourth Protocol with Article 14).

[120] 1996-IV; 23 EHRR 364 para 42 (refusal to grant emergency social security assistance to non-national). See also *Koua Poirrez v France* 2003-X; 40 EHRR 2.

[121] However, note Article 16 of the Convention and its implications. Of course, virtually all states make certain distinctions based on nationality concerning certain rights or entitlements to benefits in the immigration context, etc and the Court will frequently find that applications growing out of these scenarios will not pass the analogous situation test: *Moustaqium v Belgium* A 193 (1991); 13 EHRR 802 para 49 (Belgian juveniles could not legally be deported whilst the Moroccan juvenile applicant could); cf, *C v Belgium* 1996-III; 32 EHRR 19 para 38 (preferential treatment of EC nationals compared to non-EC nationals deemed objective and reasonable for purposes of Article 14).

[122] See pp 603–6.   [123] See below, p 607.

[124] *Abdulaziz, Cabales, and Balkandali v UK* A 94 (1985); 7 EHRR 163 para 78 PC.

[125] B 77 (1983) para 102 Com Rep.   [126] Hudoc (2004); 42 EHRR 1185 para 61.

unity through a joint family name could not provide a justification for the gender-based difference in treatment complained of on the facts before it.

That the Court has found discrimination on the ground of 'sex' against women[127] and men[128] is illustrated by case law concerning lack of equality regarding financial benefits where Article 1 of the First Protocol usually has been in issue.[129] Here the Court reassures states that they have a margin of appreciation but the principle is that exemptions or benefits should be applied even-handedly to both men and women unless 'compelling reasons' are adduced to justify a difference of treatment.[130] In *Stec v UK*[131] the difference in state pensionable age between men and women in the UK which was at the root of the applicants' claims concerning differences in the entitlement for men and women to certain industrial social security benefits, did not entail a violation of Article 1 of the First Protocol when read with Article 14. The difference of treatment was reasonably and objectively justified in that it was intended to correct the disadvantaged economic position of women. Also, whilst measures were being taken to remove the difference in treatment the state concerned benefited from a wide margin of appreciation given that, amongst other things, general measures of economic or social strategy were concerned and in many European states there remained a difference in the ages at which men and women become eligible for the state retirement pension.[132]

Petrovic v Austria[133] arguably illustrates the potential problems that could be associated with an insistence on even-handedness in all circumstances. It concerned parental leave allowances which were paid only to mothers, not fathers. The Court stressed that the margin of appreciation was broad in this case, such that there was no violation of Article 14 read with Article 8, given the absence at the material time of a 'common standard in this field, as the majority of Contracting states did not provide for parental leave allowances to be paid to fathers'[134] (indeed there was 'a very great disparity between the legal systems of the Contracting states in this field').[135] It was noted by the Court that '[o]nly gradually, as society has moved towards a more equal sharing between men and women of responsibilities for the bringing up of their children, have the Contracting states introduced measures extending to fathers, like entitlement to parental leave',[136] let alone parental leave allowance. In other words, the 'very weighty reasons' that were in principle required

[127] Eg, *Wessels-Bergervoet v Netherlands* 2002-IV; 38 EHRR 793 (differential treatment of married women under pension legislation).
[128] Eg, *Schmidt v Germany* A 291-B (1994); 18 EHRR 523; *Burghartz v Switzerland* A 280-B (1994); 18 EHRR 101 paras 25–30; and *Zarb Adami v Malta* hudoc (2006); 44 EHRR 49. Note also *Spöttl v Austria No 22956/93* hudoc (1996); 22 EHRR 88 DA.
[129] Eg, *Van Raalte v Netherlands* 1997-I; 24 EHRR 503. There have been many UK-originated complaints both before the domestic courts (post the Human Rights Act 1998) and before Strasbourg regarding discrimination and social security provision, see eg, *Willis v UK* 2002-IV; 35 EHRR 547 (sex discrimination in connection with claim for Widow's Payment Allowance). An application alleging sex discrimination given the differing retirement ages of men and women in the UK was declared inadmissible for lack of victim status on the basis that the applicant received the same amount in state benefits as would a woman of the same age in his position: *Bland v UK No 52301/99* hudoc (2002) DA. A friendly settlement was reached in a case when sex discrimination had been alleged because the applicant had been denied an elderly person's bus permit when aged sixty-four even though a women could obtain the same at sixty, *Matthews v UK No 40302/98* hudoc (2002) (F Sett).
[130] *Van Raalte v Netherlands* 1997-I; 24 EHRR 503 para 42.
[131] *Stec v UK* hudoc (2006); 43 EHRR 1017 GC.   [132] Id, paras 61–5.
[133] 1998-II; 33 EHRR 307. *Spöttl v Austria No 22956/93* hudoc (1996); 22 EHRR 88 DA, concerning military service being confined to men only (Article 4 with Article 14), was another case of 'valid' sex discrimination, here justified by national traditions, public opinion, and the public interest in maintaining an effective national defence system (wide margin of appreciation afforded to the Contracting states in relation to the organization of their national defence and given lack of European consensus on the specific issue of alleged discrimination).
[134] Id, para 39.   [135] Id, para 42.   [136] Id, para 40.

here to justify the different treatment based on sex were subsumed by the application of the generous margin of appreciation that itself flowed from lack of European consensus. The Court stated that it was 'difficult to criticise the Austrian legislature for having introduced in a gradual manner, reflecting the evolution of society in that sphere, legislation which is, all things considered, very progressive in Europe'.[137] Judges Bernhardt and Spielman dissented in *Petrovic* agreeing with the Commission, which had noted the lack of European consensus but considered that this should not absolve those states which had adopted a special scheme of parental leave allowances from granting benefits without discrimination.

IV. BIRTH

Another suspect category is discrimination based on birth status, in particular 'illegitimacy'. Here, with respect to succession matters in particular, the principle that children should be treated equally regardless of their descent has been firmly established in the Strasbourg jurisprudence. In the *Marckx* case the Court found that the reasons for treating the 'illegitimate' mother and child differently from the legitimate mother and child were not sufficiently supported in fact or, even if generally true, imposed too big a burden on those 'illegitimate' mothers and children which did not fit the state's stereotype. In relation to the different processes by which legitimate and 'illegitimate' mothers had to establish the affiliation of their children, the government said, *inter alia*, that they were justified because legitimate mothers were more likely to accept the responsibilities of motherhood than 'illegitimate' mothers. The Court found this unsustainable. The government had provided no evidence to support its general assertions and it clearly was not true that all 'illegitimate' mothers were susceptible to abandoning their children.[138] Later, in 1987, in *Inze v Austria*,[139] the Court stated that:

> [t]he question of equality between children born in and children born out of wedlock as regards their civil rights is today given importance in the member states of the Council of Europe[140] ... Very weighty reasons would accordingly have to be advanced before a difference of treatment on the ground of birth out of wedlock could be regarded as compatible with the Convention.

The leading cases on illegitimacy and succession remain the 'old court' judgments in *Inze* and, before that, *Marckx v Belgium*,[141] but even in the new millennium the Court has still been addressing cases of discrimination under this head from longstanding Convention member states.[142] *Pla and Puncernau v Andorra*[143] is notable as the violation of Article 14 stemmed not from domestic legislation but the domestic court's interpretation of a will

---

[137] Id, para 41. On the facts of a case the Court may be prepared to give states some leeway as regards the timing of equality reforms, see *Runkee and White v UK* hudoc (2007) para 41 (widows' pension reform).

[138] *Marckx v Belgium* A 31 (1979); 2 EHRR 330 paras 38–9 PC. See also the later case of *Vermeire v Belgium* A 214-C (1991); 15 EHRR 313. As regards the exclusion of an adopted child from inheritance, see *Pla and Puncernau v Andorra* 2004-VIII; 42 EHRR 522.

[139] A 126 (1987); 10 EHRR 394 para 41.

[140] Reference was then made to the 1975 European Convention on the Legal Status of Children born out of Wedlock. ETS 85; UKTS 43 (1981), Cmnd 8287.

[141] A 31 (1979); 2 EHRR 330 PC.

[142] See *Mazurek v France* 2000-II; 42 EHRR 170; *Merger and Cros v France* hudoc (2004); 43 EHRR 1103 and *Camp and Bourimi v Netherlands* 2000-X; 34 EHRR 1446. Cf, *Haas v Netherlands* hudoc (2004); 39 EHRR 897.

[143] 2004-VIII; 42 EHRR 522.

dating from 1939. This had stipulated that the estate was to pass to a son or grandson of lawful and canonical marriage. The domestic courts had assessed the intention of the testatrix and interpreted the clause in question so as to exclude application to the applicant, who was an adopted child. The Court, emphasizing the Convention's character as a living instrument and the importance attached to eradicating discrimination based on birth out of wedlock, found a violation of Article 14. In dissent Judges Bratza and Garlicki noted that this was not a case of direct interference by the state, arguing that the domestic court's ruling had, on the facts, not been arbitrary or manifestly erroneous or unreasonable, and that, again on the facts, the state should not be held liable for giving effect to the will in accordance with the testatrix's wishes.

V. RELIGION

Hoffman v Austria[144] concerned parental rights with respect to children, the Court stating that '[n]otwithstanding any possible arguments to the contrary, a distinction based essentially on a difference in religion alone is not acceptable'. As noted above,[145] this case had concerned alleged discrimination against the applicant who was a Jehovah's Witness. The right to freedom of religion is protected by Article 9 of the Convention and there is of course a potential distinction to be made between discrimination with respect to the enjoyment of a Convention right based on religion[146] and discrimination regarding the enjoyment of the right to freedom of religion itself.[147] As regards the latter, the establishment of delicate relations between the Church and state may bring a margin of appreciation into play.[148]

VI. SEXUAL ORIENTATION

In 2000 a Parliamentary Assembly opinion[149] proposed that 'sexual orientation' be added to the list of prohibited grounds of discrimination for Protocol Twelve. Although the proposal was not taken up[150] it recognized the advances in attitudes that there has been toward discrimination in this particular field. These advances have been reflected in the Strasbourg jurisprudence, which has undergone a significant evolution over the last

---

[144] A 255-C (1993); 14 EHRR 437 para 36 (the Court was split five to four in this judgment and several dissenting opinions were attached). See also *Palau-Martinez v France* 2003-XII; 41 EHRR 136 and *Ismailova v Russia* hudoc (2007).

[145] See p 582.   [146] Eg, *Canea Catholic Church v Greece* 1997-VIII; 25 EHRR 521.

[147] The need to identify a claim as one of genuine discrimination regarding enjoyment of Article 9 can be important, as is illustrated by *Dahlab v Switzerland* 2001-V, discussed above at n 38. See also *Stedman v UK No 29107/95* hudoc (1997); 23 EHRR CD 168 in which an applicant complained that she was dismissed for refusing to work on a Sunday but the Commission took the view that the dismissal was not based on her religious convictions as such, but on the fact she refused to sign a contract which contained terms (working on a Sunday), with which she disagreed (inadmissible). Further, the limited scope of Article 9 and the fact that an applicant is not actually treated any differently from others may be fatal to Article 9 discrimination applications. Hence, Article 9 does not cover the right to take certain days off work in order to worship for religious reasons and this has meant that certain applications have failed at admissibility: eg, *Ahmad v UK No 8160/78*, 22 DR 27 (1981); 4 EHRR 126 and *Konttinen v Finland No 24949/94*, 87-A DR 68 (1996). If the state were to grant time off for one religion but not others then Article 9 in conjunction with Article 14 could come into play. But provided all are treated the same there is no discrimination.

[148] See eg, *Cha'are Shalom ve Tsedek v France* 2000-VII GC, see n 589 above.

[149] Opinion No 216 (2000), *Draft Protocol No 12 to the European Convention on Human Rights*, para 6. On Protocol Twelve see below p 611.

[150] See p 612 below.

decade or so.[151] *Smith and Grady v UK*,[152] the so-called 'gays in the military' case, where the Court found a violation of Article 8, arguably marked the start of a fresh approach, even though the Court did not address Article 14 issues in that case. It did however state that it 'would not exclude that treatment which is grounded upon a predisposed bias on the part of a heterosexual majority against a homosexual minority of the nature [occurring in that case]...could, in principle, fall within the scope of Article 3'.[153]

It is perhaps surprising that it was not until 1999 and the case of *Salgueiro da Silva Mouta v Portugal*[154] that the Court found a violation of Article 14 in conjunction with another Article (Article 8) in a case concerning sexual orientation. The applicant's homosexuality was a decisive factor in the domestic court's decision to award parental responsibility for his daughter to his ex-wife rather than to himself, a distinction which the Court stated was 'not acceptable under the Convention'.[155] Before this, in 1997, the Convention's quality as 'a living instrument' was cited when the Commission for the first time condemned differences in the criminal law as regards the age of consent to enter sexual relations for homosexuals as opposed to heterosexuals.[156] The Court showed its approval of this authority in *L and V v Austria*[157] in 2003 when it stated that '[j]ust like differences based on sex...differences based on sexual orientation require particularly serious reasons by way of justification'[158] for the purposes of Article 14. It warned that if the laws permitting differing age of consent 'embodied a predisposed bias on the part of a heterosexual majority against a homosexual minority, these negative attitudes cannot of themselves be considered by [the Court] to amount to sufficient justification for the differential treatment any more than similar negative attitudes towards those of a different race, origin or colour'.[159]

Karner v Austria,[160] which concerned the housing rights of same-sex partnerships, was also delivered in 2003.[161] The domestic courts had denied the homosexual applicant the status of 'life companion' with respect to his late partner thereby preventing him from succeeding to his tenancy. The Court accepted that protection of the family in the traditional sense was, in principle, a weighty and legitimate reason which might justify a difference in treatment. However, after citing information from third party interveners to the effect that there was an emerging European consensus in favour of the applicant on the point in issue, when the Court came to the proportionality test it stated:

> The aim of protecting the family in the traditional sense is rather abstract and a broad variety of concrete measures may be used to implement it. In cases in which the margin of appreciation afforded to member states is narrow, as the position where there is a

[151] See Helfer 95 AJIL 422 (2001). It is clear that 'sexual orientation' is covered by Article 14, though not whether it is always to be so through the label of 'sex' (cf, the UN Human Rights Committee, in *Toonen v Australia* decision of 4 April 1994) or 'other status' (as employed by European Commission of Human Rights, *Sutherland v UK* hudoc (1997) para 51 Com Rep).

[152] 1999-VI; 29 EHRR 493, see p 370.

[153] Id, para 121. Other leading judgments concerning human rights and homosexuality, when Article 14 has not necessarily been addressed by the Court, include *Dudgeon v UK* A 45 (1981); 4 EHRR 149 PC; *Norris v Ireland* A 142; 13 EHRR 186 PC; *Modinos v Cyprus* A 259; 16 EHRR 485; *Laskey, Jaggard and Brown v UK* 1997-I; 24 EHRR 39; and *ADT v UK* 2000-IX; 31 EHRR 803.

[154] *Salgueiro da Silva Mouta v Portugal* 1999-IX; 31 EHRR 1055.   [155] Id, para 36.

[156] *Sutherland v UK* hudoc (1997) Com Rep, and judgment (striking off list) hudoc (2001). (Cf, *BB v UK* hudoc (2004); 39 EHRR 635.)

[157] 2003-I; 36 EHRR 1022. The Court noted that it was not contested that there was 'an ever growing European consensus to apply equal ages of consent for heterosexual, lesbian and homosexual relations', para 50.

[158] Id, para 45.   [159] Id, para 52, citing *Smith and Grady v UK* 1999-VI; 29 EHRR 493 para 97.

[160] 2003-IX; 38 EHRR 528. See also *PB and JS v Austria No 18984/02* hudoc 2008 DA (judgment pending) (allegations of discrimination as homosexual partner excluded from insurance cover for 'dependants').

[161] Cf, *Mendoza v Ghaidan* [2004] UKHL 30.

difference in treatment based on sex or sexual orientation, the principle of proportionality does not merely require that the measure chosen is in principle suited for realising the aim sought. It must also be shown that it was necessary to exclude persons living in a homosexual relationship from the scope of application of Section 14 of the Rent Act in order to achieve that aim.[162]

The Court concluded that insufficient reasons had been advanced by the respondent state and found a violation of Article 8 in conjunction with Article 14.

The recent Grand Chamber's ruling in *EB v France*[163] is probably the most significant case yet in the field of Article 14 and sexual orientation. The applicant, who was in a lesbian relationship, had been refused authorization to adopt as a single person; she claimed she had been discriminated against on grounds of her sexuality. Crucially French law permitted adoption by single persons, so the case fell within the ambit of Article 8 for the purposes of an Article 14 claim.[164] As sexual orientation was 'in issue' in this context the Court called for 'particularly convincing and weighty reasons to justify a difference in treatment regarding rights falling within Article 8'.[165] Citing the Convention's character as a living instrument[166] it stated that there would be discrimination if the reasons advanced for a difference in treatment 'were based solely on considerations regarding the applicant's sexual orientation'.[167] The Court proceeded to hold that the applicant's sexuality had indeed been 'a decisive factor leading to the decision to refuse her authorization to adopt',[168] and, by ten votes to seven, found a violation of Article 8 read with Article 14. The division concerned the bold stance taken by the majority in scrutinizing, indeed reassessing, the negative decisions taken by the domestic authorities and concluding that they were indeed decisively influenced by the applicant's sexuality.[169] However there appeared to be unanimous acceptance of the general principles noted above, in particular the conclusion that a person must not be prevented from adopting a child merely on the basis on his or her sexuality.[170] *EB* therefore overturned *Fretté v France*,[171] which had been decided by a Chamber of the Court just five years earlier. In that judgment the Court had found (albeit by four votes to three) that there had been a difference of treatment based on sexuality in the (single) applicant's application for adoption but that it pursued a legitimate aim (protecting the health and rights of children who could be involved in an adoption procedure).[172] Further the difference of treatment was, according to the Chamber, proportionate on the facts, given, amongst other things, the margin of appreciation owed to the respondent state.[173]

Finally, *Baczkowski v Poland*[174] provides another example of the Court's progressive approach to Article 14 and sexual orientation in an altogether different context. The applicants claimed they had been refused permission to organize an assembly on a commemorative date important to them in Warsaw, the aim of which was to draw attention to discrimination against various minorities, including homosexuals. Their point was

---

162 *Karner v Austria* 2003-IX; 38 EHRR 528 para 41.　　163 Hudoc (2008) GC.
164 See *EB v France* hudoc (2008) para 49 GC.
165 Id, para 91.　　166 Id, para 92.
167 Id, para 93 (citing *Salgueiro da Silva Mouta*, n 154 above at para 36).　　168 Id, para 89.
169 See the four dissenting opinions attached to the judgment.
170 Note, however, the text accompanying n 164 above (the ambit test).
171 2002-I; 38 EHRR 438. The Court in *EB* sought to distinsguish the two cases, however, in separate opinions several judges acknowlegded that *Fretté* had been overturned.
172 Id, para 38.
173 Sir Nicolas Bratza and Judges Fuhrmann and Tulkens argued that there had been a violation on the facts.
174 Hudoc (2007).

that a number of other groups, for example one against homosexual adoption, had been permitted to protest on the same day. The decisions in this regard had all been taken at the same time by administrative authorities who acted in the name of the mayor. There was nothing in the texts of the decision refusing the applicants permission to indicate discrimination, but at the relevant time the mayor had publicly expressed strong personal opinions against homosexuality. A striking feature of the judgment was that the Court was of the view that 'it may be reasonably surmised that [the mayor's] opinions could have affected the decision-making process in the present case and, as a result, impinged on the applicants' right to freedom of assembly in a discriminatory manner'.[175] The Court found a violation of Article 14 with Article 11, but it did not refer to a particular 'badge' of discrimination.

EB and *Baczkowski* therefore demonstrate the Court's heightened awareness of the unacceptability of discrimination on grounds of sexual orientation and its greater readiness to scrutinize cases coming before it in this regard. *EB* is especially significant for the Grand Chamber's endorsement of the principle that distinctions based solely or decisively on sexual orientation are unacceptable under the Convention. Having said this, Article 14's inherent limitations as a parasitic provision entail that its impact and potential in this field should not be exaggerated. EB's claim would have failed if French law had not allowed single persons to adopt.[176] Furthermore, in *Karner* the Court addressed Article 8 in conjunction with Article 14 through the specific (and more discrete) notion of respect for 'home',[177] not the broader notion of right to respect for 'private' or 'family life'. Indeed the Commission's case law whereby long-term homosexual relationships do not fall within the scope of the right to respect for 'family life'[178] remains in place, inevitably limiting the role Article 14 may have.[179] Furthermore, even when Article 8 family life issues are relevant an Article 14 claim is not bound to succeed. In a case concerning parental authority over a child the Commission found that a homosexual couple cannot be equated to a man and a woman living together.[180] Similarly *Estevez v Spain*[181] demonstrated the Court's willingness to make distinctions based on the special status of the institution of marriage. It accepted differences of treatment regarding eligibility for a survivor's pension between *de facto* homosexual partners (who were not allowed the pension) and married couples (who were), or even unmarried heterosexual couples (who also were in certain circumstances). The applicant and his deceased partner had been together ten years, but the former was denied a survivor's pension even though, as the Court noted, had they been of the opposite sex the claim might well have succeeded. The Court accepted that Article 8 applied with respect to the refusal to grant the survivor's pension as 'the applicant's emotional and sexual relationship related to his private life'.

---

[175] *Bączkowski v Poland* hudoc (2007) para 100 (see also paras 97–9 for the Court's comments on the importance attached by it to the notion that elected politicians exercise their powers of freedom of expression responsibly).

[176] See discussion of the 'ambit' test at p 581 above.   [177] 2003–IX; 38 EHRR 24 para 33.

[178] See *X and Y v UK* No 9369/81 32 DR 220 (1983); *Simpson v UK* No 11716/85, 47 DR 274 (1986); and *Kerkhoven, Hinke and Hinke v Netherlands* No 15666/89 hudoc (1992) DA. Cf, Commission decisions concerning Article 8 'family life' which have held that no discrimination exists contrary to Article 14 where the Immigration Rules give priority and better guarantees to established couples living in a family relationship as opposed to other established relationships such as lesbian or homosexual relationships, *C and LM v UK* No 14753/89 hudoc (1989) DA.

[179] *Salgueiro da Silva Mouta*, n 154 above, concerned the family life relationship between a biological parent and child.

[180] *Kerhoven and Hinke v Netherlands* No 15666/89 hudoc (1992) DA. See also *Parry v UK* No 42971/05 hudoc (2006) DA (dismissal of transsexual's claim of discrimination with respect to right to marry).

[181] No 56501/00 hudoc (2001) DA.

However, marriage constituted an essential precondition for eligibility for a survivor's pension and Spain did not permit marriage between persons of the same sex. Moreover, the legislation was found to have a legitimate aim, which was the protection of the family based on marriage bonds. The Court then summarily refused the application on the basis that that difference in treatment 'can be considered to fall within the state's margin of appreciation' although the decision did not fully explain why this was so.

VII. UNMARRIED FATHERS' ACCESS TO CHILDREN AND ISSUES RELATING TO MARITAL STATUS

As a general rule unmarried fathers who have established family life with their children can claim equal rights of contact and custody with married fathers. In *Sahin v Germany*[182] domestic law gave divorced fathers a legal right of access to their child whereas unmarried fathers had no such automatic right. The Grand Chamber stated that 'very weighty reasons' will be required to justify a 'difference in the treatment of the father of a child born of a relationship *where the parties were living together out of wedlock* as compared with the father of a child born of a marriage-based relationship'[183] (emphasis added). The emphasized words in this passage are clearly important.

More generally, however, the Court has found that differences in treatment on the basis of marital status can have objective and reasonable justification.[184] Furthermore unmarried partners are not generally considered by the Court to be in an analogous position to spouses for the purpose of Article 14, 'marriage continu[ing] to be characterised by a corpus of rights and obligations that differentiate it markedly from the situation of a man and woman who cohabit'.[185] This statement was made in *Nylund v Finland*,[186] which is one example of several applications that have been declared inadmissible on this basis.[187] The applicant claimed to be the father of a child and had lived with its mother, but he was unable to obtain a paternity test because the mother blocked the application for this. She had given birth after marrying another man and domestic law then presumed the husband to be the father. The applicant complained of preferential treatment for the mother compared to him as she could block the paternity claim now she was married. The Court questioned whether the analogous situation test was passed but took the view that in any case the domestic law pursued the legitimate aim of 'securing or reconciling the rights of the child and its family' and was not disproportionate.

The Court is therefore prepared to allow some differential treatment on the basis of the promotion of marriage which, in its words, 'remains an institution that is widely accepted as conferring a particular status on those who enter it and, indeed, . . . is singled out for

---

[182] 2003-VIII; 44 EHRR 99 GC. See also *PM v UK* hudoc (2005); 42 EHRR 1015 para 28 (different tax regime for maintenance payments applicable for unmarried and married fathers subsequently divorced and separated violated Article 14).

[183] Id, para 94. See also *Elsholz v Germany* 2000-VIII; 34 EHRR 1412 GC.

[184] See *McMichael v UK* A 307-B (1995); 20 EHRR 205. This concerned legislation which did not grant automatic parental responsibility to unmarried fathers since they varied in their commitment to and interest in, or even knowledge of, their children. There was no violation of Article 14 with Article 8 as the relevant legislation pursued a legitimate aim—identifying meritorious fathers—and the conditions imposed upon the applicant were proportionate.

[185] *Nylund v Finland No 27110/95*, 1999-VI DA. See also *Burden v UK* hudoc (2008) at para 63 GC ('marriage remains an institution which is widely accepted as conferring a particular status on those who enter it').

[186] *Ibid*.

[187] Eg, *Lindsay v UK No 11089/84*, 49 DR 181 (1986); 9 EHRR 555 (different tax rules for married and unmarried couples) and *Shackell v UK No 45851/99* hudoc (2000) DA (widow different to unmarried partner upon death of husband/partner for purpose of entitlement to social security benefits).

special treatment under Article 12 of the Convention'.[188] *Saucedo Gómez v Spain*[189] demonstrates this. It concerned a former cohabiter who complained about the legal arrangements regarding property entitlement put in place following her relationship break up, claiming that there had been discrimination based on her status as a non-married woman as compared to a married one. Declaring the application inadmissible,[190] the Chamber indicated that it had doubts whether this was a case of discrimination at all. But it made it clear that, even if there had been differential treatment, it was justifiable (protection of the traditional family) and not disproportionate (especially as the applicant had been able to marry her former partner but had declined to do so). This was an area, the Court stated, where a margin of appreciation applied and it was not for it to dictate or indicate to states the measures that they should take with regard to the existence of stable, non-married, relationships between men and women.

Accordingly, even when the Court has been prepared to accept that in a case concerning unmarried applicants it is faced with an analogous situation to married couples, it has recognized that states 'may be allowed a certain margin of appreciation to treat differently married and unmarried couples in the fields of, for instance, taxation, social security or social policy'.[191] There are, however, limits to this. Article 8 read with Article 14 was violated in a case[192] concerning contact telephone calls for individuals held in custody. The law allowed married partners to call each other in such circumstances but not unmarried partners even when they had established family life in the sense required by Article 8. The disparate treatment was unjustified.

VIII. DISABILITY?

It might be thought that the European Court would require 'very weighty reasons' to be put forward before it regarded a difference of treatment based exclusively on the ground of disability as compatible with the Convention. In fact, no statements to this effect can be found in the jurisprudence and there is little Article 14 case law directly addressing the rights of disabled people.[193] This may be a reflection, above all, of the weakness of that Article as a parasitic right and the Court's approach to interpreting Article 8 in relevant case law.[194]

7. ARTICLE 14, THE BURDEN OF PROOF AND THE PROTECTION OF MINORITIES

I. BURDEN OF PROOF AND STATISTICS

In many of the cases discussed above, the applicant will be able to point to a particular law, rule, or decision and describe its impact on him or her in order to establish the necessary

[188] *Shackell v UK No 45851/99* hudoc (2000) DA.

[189] *Saucedo Gómez v Spain No 37784/97* hudoc (1999) DA.   [190] This was a majority decision.

[191] *Petrov v Bulgaria* hudoc (2008) para 55 (citing *Shackell* and *Lindsay*, above n 187; *McMichael v UK* A 307-B (1995); 20 EHRR 205 and *Sahin v Germany* 2003-VIII; 44 EHRR 99 GC).

[192] *Petrov v Bulgaria* hudoc (2008).

[193] Although this is not to say that the Convention does not have relevance in this field: see eg, *Price v UK* 2001-VII; 34 EHRR 1285. See generally Clements, *Disabled People and European Human Rights*, 2003. See also Article 26 of the Charter of Fundamental Rights of the European Union, available at <http://www.europarl.eu.int/charter/default_en.htm>.

[194] The most notable cases have been *Botta v Italy* 1998-I; 26 EHRR 241 (no violation of Article 8 with Article 14) and *Zehnalová and Zehnal v Czech Republic No 38621/97* hudoc (2002) DA—inadmissible. See also *Malone v UK No 25290/94* hudoc (1996) DA—inadmissible.

prima facie evidence of discrimination required for Article 14. It will then fall to the state to discharge the burden placed upon it and justify the difference of treatment. However, even when discrimination is rife it may be very difficult for an applicant to establish a *prima facie* case of this on the facts of his or her case. The law or regulation in issue may not be explicitly racist or sexist, but in practice it may be applied by public officials in discriminatory ways. This may be particularly so if there is so-called 'institutional' discrimination.

As regards what constitutes *prima facie* evidence capable of placing a burden of proof on the respondent state for Article 14, the Grand Chamber has stated:

> there are no procedural barriers to the admissibility of evidence or pre-determined formulae for its assessment. The Court adopts the conclusions that are, in its view, supported by the free evaluation of all evidence, including such inferences as may flow from the facts and the parties' submissions. According to its established case-law, proof may follow from the coexistence of sufficiently strong, clear and concordant inferences or of similar unrebutted presumptions of fact. Moreover, the level of persuasion necessary for reaching a particular conclusion and, in this connection, the distribution of the burden of proof are intrinsically linked to the specificity of the facts, the nature of the allegation made and the Convention right at stake.[195]

The last sentence is particularly relevant to the examples detailed below concerning indirect discrimination and allegations of violence motivated by discrimination, ie situations where it may be practically difficult for applicants to establish a *prima facie* case of discrimination. In these cases it has been put to the Court that where credible statistics are overwhelming in the disproportionate (and discriminatory) impact they reveal, then they should shift the burden of proof to the respondent state so as to require it to rebut a finding of discrimination.[196] Initially this argument was rejected,[197] however the Court's case law evolved in 2006[198] and in the highly significant Grand Chamber judgment in *DH v Czech Republic*[199] the Court confirmed that it had modified its position with respect to indirect discrimination (a concept which is discussed further below).[200] The Court stated that 'less strict evidential rules' should apply to this field of discrimination in order to guarantee those concerned 'the effective protection of their rights'.[201] The Grand Chamber cited an earlier admissibility decision[202] which had placed a burden on the state to account for statistics which apparently evidenced discrimination. It also cited relevant EC law[203] concerning the burden of proof and referred generally to the equivalent practice of domestic courts as well as the supervisory bodies of UN human rights treaties before concluding

---

[195] *DH v Czech Republic* (hudoc) 2007 para 178 GC. See also para 179.

[196] See Third Party Intervention of Interights and Human Rights Watch in *DH v Czech Republic*, id, para 36.

[197] See *Hugh Jordan v UK* 2001-III; 37 EHRR 52 where the Court rejected arguments that statistics concerning civilian deaths in Northern Ireland exhibited discrimination against the Catholic community. See also *Ireland v UK* A 25 (1978); 2 EHRR 225 paras 224–9 PC. See further *DH v Czech Republic* hudoc (2006); 43 EHRR 923 para 46 (this Chamber ruling was reversed by the GC: *DH v Czech Republic*, id) and *Zarb Adami v Malta* hudoc (2006); 44 EHRR 49 para 76.

[198] See *Zarb Adami*, id, paras 78 and 82–3 (violation of Article 14 as civic obligation of jury service fell predominantly on males not females, and respondent state could not justify the difference in treatment; the Court accepted that statistics revealed a difference of treatment between two groups in a relevantly similar situation).

[199] See n 195 above.

[200] P 607 below.   [201] N 195 above, para 186. See also para 189.

[202] Id, para 180, citing *Hoogendijk v Netherlands No 58641/00* hudoc (2005) DA.

[203] Id, para 187 and paras 81–91. The European Union's Race Directive (Directive 2000/43/EC implementing the principle of equal treatment between persons irrespective of racial or ethnic origin), which applies to limited fields including education, training, and employment, provides for the reversal of the burden of proof, see Article 8. As regards sex discrimination, see Directive 97/80/EC (Article 4(1)). See also Directive 2000/78/EC.

that, 'when it comes to assessing the impact of a measure or practice on an individual or group, statistics which appear on critical examination to be reliable and significant will be sufficient to constitute the *prima facie* evidence the applicant is required to produce [to place the burden on the respondent state to justify a difference of treatment]'.[204] It remains to be seen if the new stance taken on statistics has a more general relevance for Article 14, ie beyond indirect discrimination, and, of course, what the Court regards as 'reliable and significant' statistics.

As shall be seen below, the issue of the burden of proof and the use that may be made of statistical evidence has been highly relevant to cases concerning racism against Roma. The European Commissioner on Human Rights has acknowledged that there is a serious problem in many Council of Europe states regarding widespread and deep-rooted racial discrimination against Roma.[205]

II. THE CONVENTION AND THE PROTECTION OF MINORITIES

At first sight it would seem that there is little role for Article 14 here. Many minorities' concerns fall outside the Convention altogether, so neither as individual rights nor as an aspect of Article 14 protection do they fall within the competence of the Strasbourg authorities.[206] Article 14 cites 'association with a national minority' as a specific 'badge' of forbidden discrimination, but the Convention provides only partial and indirect obligations in favour of minorities.[207] States may insist, indeed may have a duty to insist, that minorities respect the rights of others guaranteed by the Convention.[208] The thrust of the Convention is the securing of individual rather than group rights,[209] so generally speaking minority organizations may assert rights of their own only if they are, *mutatis mutandis*, like individual rights. Of key importance will be rights such as the right of a political party to a free and fair election, plus the rights of freedom of expression, assembly, association, and religion. Some compensation may be found in the development of positive obligations for states so that individual members of a minority may enjoy their rights effectively, for instance in matters of religion, education, or right to respect for Article 8 rights.[210] However, it is difficult to demonstrate the existence of such obligations and relatively easy for a state to show that it has satisfied them[211]—hence the importance of the burden of proof in such cases.

[204] Id, para 188 GC (it added, '[t]his does not, however, mean that indirect discrimination cannot be proved without statistical evidence').

[205] See especially Council of Europe Human Rights Commissioner, *Final report on the human rights situation of the Roma, Sinti and Travellers in Europe*, CommDH(2006)1. For Council of Europe documentation relevant to the situation of 'Roma and Travellers' see <http://www.coe.int/T/DG3/RomaTravellers/Default_en.asp>. The Court has adopted some important statements of principle regarding the need to afford particular protection to Roma/gypsies, see *Chapman v UK* 2001-I; 33 EHRR 399 para 96 GC; *Connors v UK* hudoc (2004); 40 EHRR 189 para 84; and *DH v Czech Republic* hudoc (2007) para 181 GC.

[206] This includes economic and social rights, where the prospects of oblique protection relying on *Airey v Ireland* A 32 (1980); 2 EHRR 305, are not encouraging. See eg, *X v UK No 8160/78*, 22 DR 27 (1981).

[207] Gilbert, 23 NYIL 57 at 81–93 (1992) and 24 HRQ 736 (2002).

[208] Poulter, 36 ICLQ 589 at 614–15 (1987). Although making a strong plea for tolerance and pluralism, the author accepts the limits imposed by international human rights obligations.

[209] See *48 Kalderas Gipsies v FRG and Netherlands Nos 7823/77 and 7824/77*, 11 DR 221 (1977) (the applicants were *individual* gypsies).

[210] In this connection, see the joint dissenting opinion of Judges Pastor Ridruejo *et al* in *Chapman v UK* 2001-I; 33 EHRR 399 GC and *Connors v UK* hudoc (2004); 40 EHRR 189 para 84.

[211] As demonstrated by the almost complete lack of success of the applicants in *Belgian Linguistic* case A 6 (1968); 1 EHRR 252 PC.

Past plans to create a new Protocol to the Convention addressing minorities' protection have not progressed to completion.[212] However the Council of Europe has adopted a number of measures in this field,[213] the most notable of which is the Framework Convention for the Protection of National Minorities,[214] the first ever legally binding multilateral instrument devoted to the protection of *national* minorities in general. This has been in force since 1998 and has been ratified by thirty-nine member states to the Council of Europe, and signed by a further four.

8. ARTICLE 14 AND VIOLENCE MOTIVATED BY DISCRIMINATION

I. *NACHOVA V BULGARIA*: ARTICLE 14 AND RACIAL VIOLENCE IN THE CONTEXT OF POLICING AND CRIMINAL JUSTICE

The Court's abhorrence of racial discrimination generally is clear.[215] As regards racial violence, the Grand Chamber has stated that this:

> is a particular affront to human dignity and, in view of its perilous consequences, requires from the authorities special vigilance and a vigorous reaction. It is for this reason that the authorities must use all available means to combat racism and racist violence, thereby reinforcing democracy's vision of a society in which diversity is not perceived as a threat but as a source of its enrichment.[216]

The Court has nonetheless acknowledged that 'proving racial motivation [for Article 14 claims] will often be extremely difficult'[217] on the facts of a case. Indeed the Court has been strongly criticized[218] as it has repeatedly found violations of Articles 2 and 3 in cases of violence against Roma, but has apparently been very reluctant to find that such violence was inflicted for racial reasons so as to contravene Article 14. The leading case here is *Nachova v Bulgaria*,[219] which was heard by both the Chamber and the Grand Chamber. Two unarmed Roma conscripts were shot dead by the police who, it was claimed, had acted in a racially motivated way (there was excessive use of force and witness evidence of racist verbal abuse by one officer who shot the deceased). It was further claimed that the investigation that followed failed to properly pursue and unmask this racial abuse, so apparently reflecting a culture of impunity as regards this issue. Violations of Article 2 were found under two heads—unlawful death and the failure to effectively investigate

---

[212] As to the proposals see Malinverni, 12 HRLJ 265 (1992).

[213] See Council of Europe ((DH-MIN), Activities of the Council of Europe in the Field of the Protection of National Minorities, DH-MIN(2005)003; see also generally, <http://www.coe.int/T/E/human_rights/minorities/>.

[214] ETS 157. On this Convention, see Wheatley, 6 EHRLR 583 (1996); Keller, 18 OJLS 29 (1998) and Weller, *The Rights of Minorities: A Commentary on the European Framework Convention for the Protection of National Minorities* 2006. For general information and reports consult <http://www.coe.int/T/E/human_rights/minorities/>.

[215] See p 591 above.   [216] *Nachova v Bulgaria* 2005-VII; 42 EHRR 933 para 145 GC.

[217] *Nachova v Bulgaria* hudoc (2004); 39 EHRR 793 para 159 (Chamber judgment). The violations of Article 14 found in *Moldovan and Others v Romania* 2005-VII; 44 EHRR 302 and *Timishev v Russia* hudoc (2005); 44 EHRR 776 were exceptional for their factual circumstances in that the racial discrimination occurring was blatant.

[218] See Goldston, 5 EHRLR 462 (1999) and the separate opinions of Judge Bonello in *Anguelova v Bulgaria* 2002-IV; 38 EHRR 659 and *Nachova v Bulgaria, ibid.* (Chamber judgment).

[219] *Ibid* and above, n 216.

the same—and it was claimed that there were corresponding violations of Article 14 too. The case proceeded against the backdrop of substantial *general* evidence of the existence of widespread discrimination against Roma in Bulgaria, reference being made in the judgment to previous case law reaching the Court raising similar issues and a body of germane reports and opinions authored by institutions within the Council of Europe and the UN, some of which had not been contested by the Bulgarian authorities.[220]

a. Article 14 and state responsibility for racial violence committed by the authorities (the substantive question)

As regards Article 14, the most controversial issue in *Nachova* was whether the individuals had been killed as a result of racism. Given the evidential difficulty of proving at Strasbourg that this was so, a critical issue was the approach taken by the Court to Article 14, in particular whether, given the general circumstances of the case and the background reports of discrimination against Roma, the onus should be placed on the authorities to disprove the applicant's claim of racially motivated killing.

The Grand Chamber departed from the novel approach set by the Chamber[221] and followed the Court's standard approach to the substantive question relevant to Articles 2 and 14. That is the Court undertakes a free assessment of all the evidence before it,[222] and will conclude that Article 2 or 3 ill-treatment has been racially motivated (in violation of Article 14) if it is established beyond reasonable doubt that racist attitudes played a role in the applicants' treatment by the police.[223] This approach had been adopted in earlier cases concerning police violence against Roma in Bulgaria[224] when no violation of Article 14 read with Article 2 was found and in *Nachova* it was concluded once again that, on the facts, there was no violation under this head.[225] In reaching its conclusion the Grand Chamber acknowledged to some extent the general situation of Roma in Bulgaria—'a number of organisations, including intergovernmental bodies, have expressed concern about the occurrence of such incidents [of racial violence]'—but it emphasized that 'its sole concern [was] to ascertain whether in the case at hand the killing of [the deceased] was motivated by racism'.[226] *Interights* had argued that the beyond reasonable doubt standard of proof was 'inappropriate in a human rights context and provides too great an evidentiary obstacle for applicants'.[227] However the Grand Chamber was not persuaded that it should reverse the burden of proof. It stated that it would not 'exclude the possibility that in certain cases of alleged discrimination it may require the respondent Government to disprove an arguable allegation of discrimination and—if they fail to do so—find a violation of Article 14 of the Convention on that basis'.[228] But it then highlighted the evidentiary

---

[220] Id, paras 173- 4 (Chamber judgment).

[221] The Chamber came close to suggesting that the burden of proof could be reversed if there was evidence of a culture of impunity as regards treatment of the racial issue in the ensuing police investigation and by general background circumstances, id, paras 168–9.

[222] See the Court's elaboration at *Nachova v Bulgaria* 2005-VII; 42 EHRR 933 para 155 GC. See also *DH v Czech Republic* hudoc (2007) para 178 GC (text accompanying n 195 above).

[223] See also *Bekos and Koutropoulos v Greece* hudoc (2005); 43 EHRR 22 paras 47 and 67 (allegations of Article 3 ill-treatment motivated by racial prejudices) and *Moldovan and Others v Romania* 2005-VII; 44 EHRR 302 (racist attitudes clearly influencing enjoyment of Article 6 and Article 8 rights).

[224] See *Velikova v Bulgaria* 2000-VII and *Anguelova v Bulgaria* 2002-IV; 38 EHRR 659.

[225] *Nachova v Bulgaria* 2005-VII; 42 EHRR 933 para 155 GC. See also *Ognyanova and Choban v Bulgaria* hudoc (2006); 44 EHRR 169.

[226] Id, para 155.   [227] Third Party Intervention of Interights in *Nachova v Bulgaria*, para 27.

[228] *Nachova v Bulgaria* 2005-VII; 42 EHRR 933 para 157 GC, cf, the comments made by the Chamber at para 165. See the concurring opinion of Judge Bratza who provided examples of when reversal of the burden would be appropriate in his view.

difficulties that would face a respondent state in discharging a burden placed upon it in cases where there were allegations that individual police officers used lethal force in a racially motivated way. To reverse the burden for violent acts motivated by racial prejudice, the Court stated, 'would amount to requiring the respondent Government to prove the absence of a particular subjective attitude on the part of the person concerned'.[229]

For the reasons just identified the Grand Chamber therefore indicated its reluctance to require that a state disprove that acts contrary to Article 2 or 3 were racially motivated. It nevertheless held open the possibility of doing so, and indeed, in a recent ruling, *Stoica v Romania*,[230] a Chamber did just this. The case concerned a serious assault on the applicant which occurred in the context of a day of racist confrontations between the police and members of a Roma village. From the general facts, including various statements made by the police on the day (eg, assaulting an individual after having asked him whether he was 'Gypsy or Romanian'), the Court concluded that there was 'clear'[231] evidence that individuals such as the applicant had been deliberately targeted on the basis of their ethnic origin. The burden was therefore placed on the respondent government to establish that the particular attack on the applicant, which violated Article 3 on its own, was not racially motivated. The Court found a violation of Article 3 read with Article 14.

b. Article 14 and effective domestic investigations into racial violence (the procedural question)

As to the (less controversial) procedural aspect of Article 14, the Grand Chamber in *Nachova* took into account general indications of a culture of impunity as regards racial violence. It held that Article 14 with Article 2 had been violated with respect to the positive obligation to investigate allegations of racially-motivated violence. In particular, the authorities had failed to carry out a thorough examination of the wider circumstances of the deaths in order to uncover possible racist motives. They should have done so as they had 'plausible information'[232] before them in the form of witness evidence of racist verbal abuse by the shooting officer; furthermore that had to be 'seen against the background of the many published accounts of the existence in Bulgaria of prejudice and hostility against Roma'.[233] This finding was accompanied by some strong statements regarding the extent of the procedural obligation imposed on states under Article 14 when read with Article 2. The Court insisted that where 'there is suspicion that racial attitudes induced a violent act it is particularly important that the official investigation is pursued with vigour and impartiality, having regard to the need to reassert continuously society's condemnation of racism and ethnic hatred and to maintain the confidence of minorities in the ability of the authorities to protect them from the threat of racist violence'.[234] The duty to investigate under Article 2 had to be conducted without discrimination and the domestic legal system had to 'demonstrate its capacity to enforce [the] criminal law against those who unlawfully took the life of another, irrespective of the victim's racial or ethnic origin'.[235] Investigations into violent incidents and, in particular, deaths at the hands of state agents, the Court stated, placed the state authorities under an additional duty to take 'all reasonable steps to unmask any racist motive and to establish whether or not ethnic hatred or prejudice may have played a role in the events', failing

---

[229] Id, para 157.   [230] Hudoc (2008).   [231] Id, para 131 (see generally paras 117–33).
[232] Id, para 166.   [233] Id, para 163.
[234] *Nachova v Bulgaria* hudoc (2004); 39 EHRR 793 para 157 (Chamber judgment), endorsed by the GC at para 160. The Chamber also emphasized that acts motivated by ethnic hatred and that lead to deprivation of life undermine the foundations of democratic society, para 155.
[235] Id, para 157 (Chamber judgment), endorsed by the GC at para 160.

which a breach of Article 14 with Article 2 might ensue. In order to maintain 'public confidence in their law enforcement machinery', states had to ensure that in the investigation of incidents involving the use of force 'a distinction is made both in their legal systems and in practice between cases of excessive use of force and of racist killing'.[236] The authorities had to do 'what is reasonable in the circumstances to collect and secure the evidence, explore all practical means of discovering the truth and deliver fully reasoned, impartial and objective decisions, without omitting suspicious facts that may be indicative of a racially induced violence'.[237] Hence the obligation was not absolute, but 'to use best endeavours'.[238]

It follows that by Article 14 taken together with Article 2[239] a duty may be imposed on a state to take considerable steps to investigate whether or not racial discrimination influenced a loss of life committed by the authorities. This will be triggered by a concrete element in the facts of the case which suggest that the death or ill-treatment was actually the result of racial prejudice. On the facts of some cases it may be enough that there is general recognition in published accounts of a pattern of prejudice and hostility against the minority concerned in the respondent state, and which the authorities are aware of.[240] Equivalent standards apply to Article 3 ill-treatment purportedly inspired by racism.[241] The special investigative duties upon the state that have just been described will also apply when the actual treatment contrary to Article 3 or 2 of the Convention was inflicted by private individuals.[242]

In summary, the Court will no doubt remain open to criticism as regards the issue of the burden of proof in connection with 'the substantive question' (see above). However, as regards 'the procedural question' there is a clear message in the jurisprudence which should encourage states acting in good faith to put procedures in place which start to end impunity in the field of racial violence.

II. STATE TOLERATION OF VIOLENCE MOTIVATED BY DISCRIMINATION

The Court found a violation of Article 14 with Article 9 (as well, in fact, of Article 3) in the case of *97 Members of the Gldani Congregation of Jehovah's Witnesses and 4 Others v Georgia*.[243] The case concerned an extremely violent physical attack on a congregation of Jehovah's Witnesses by an extremist Orthodox religious group, the applicants' complaint being that the authorities' comments and attitudes upon being notified of the same evidenced official toleration of what had occurred. The Court accepted that the authorities had refused to intervene to stop the continuation of the attack and had shown indifference toward the perpetrators' prosecution to an extent that was incompatible 'with the

---

[236] Id, para 158 (Chamber judgment), endorsed by the GC at para 160. See also *Stoica v Romania* hudoc (2008) para 119.

[237] Id, para 159 (Chamber judgment), endorsed by the GC at para 160.

[238] Ibid. Cf, *Stoica v Romania* hudoc (2008) para 124 ('authorities did not do everything in their power to investigate the possible racist motives').

[239] For an explanation as to the relationship between the two Articles, see *Nachova*, para 161 GC.

[240] See *Cobzaru v Romania* hudoc (2007) para 97 (although the violation found there apparently owed much to the tendentious remarks made by the prosecutor, see paras 98–101); see also *Ognyanova and Choban v Bulgaria* hudoc (2006); 44 EHRR 7 para 148 (authorities not sufficiently on notice by virtue of general reports of racism).

[241] See *Bekos and Koutropoulos v Greece* hudoc (2005); 43 EHRR 22 para 73.

[242] See eg, *Šečić v Croatia* hudoc (2007) para 67.

[243] *97 Members of the Gldani Congregation of Jehovah's Witnesses v Georgia* hudoc (2007); 46 EHRR 613 para 140.

principle of equality of every person before the law'[244] and even raised objective doubts as to whether the authorities could be regarded as complicit.[245] The applicants were 'victims of a violation of Article 14 in conjunction with Articles 3 and 9 of the Convention'.[246]

9. INDIRECT DISCRIMINATION

Indirect discrimination results from a rule or practice that in itself does not involve impermissible discrimination but that disproportionately and adversely affects members of a particular group. An obvious example would be a rule that required all motorcyclists to wear a crash helmet, which would have a disproportionate effect upon Sikhs. Such a requirement would be unacceptable as indirect discrimination because of its effects unless it could be shown to be justified on public safety or other recognized public interest grounds.[247] There does not necessarily have to be discriminatory intent for indirect discrimination.

Article 14 potentially covers indirect discrimination, the Court stating that 'a difference in treatment may take the form of disproportionately prejudicial effects of a general policy or measure which, though couched in neutral terms, discriminates against a group'.[248] It has accepted that discrimination contrary to the Convention may arise not only from the direct actions of the state, but also from 'a *de facto* situation'.[249] However, the burden that is in practice upon the applicant to establish that indirect discrimination exists can be severe and so the Court's approach to statistical evidence of discrimination and the burden of proof in this context is very important.

In *DH v Czech Republic*,[250] the eighteen applicants claimed that they had been victims of indirect discrimination with respect to the right to education. They were all members of the Roma community and pointed to the significantly disproportionate numbers of Roma children living in their area of the Czech Republic who were educated in ordinary schools. As in the case of the applicants, Roma children tended to be placed in 'special schools' for intellectually less able children, and so received an inferior education with inevitable consequences for their life chances thereafter. Amongst other things the applicants produced a survey which revealed that in their region 1.8 per cent of non-Roma children were placed in special schools compared to 50.3 per cent of Roma children.[251] Their claim was not that the regime governing school selection and allocation was explicitly and deliberately discriminatory in terms of requiring, in effect, separate schooling arrangements. However, they insisted that the way the system worked entailed that habitually a

---

[244] Id, para 141. [245] Id, para 142. [246] Id, para 143.

[247] The legal origin of this idea is *Griggs v Duke Power Co* 401 US 424 (1971). The EU's Race Directive, n 203 above, states 'indirect discrimination shall be taken to occur where an apparently neutral provision, criterion or practice would put persons of a racial or ethnic origin at a particular disadvantage compared with other persons, unless that provision, criterion or practice is objectively justified by a legitimate aim and the means of achieving that aim are appropriate and necessary', Article 2(1)(b).

[248] *DH v Czech Republic* hudoc (2007) para 184 GC (citing, *inter alia*, *Hugh Jordan v UK* hudoc (2001); 37 EHRR 52 para 154, plus relevant Community law (Council Directives 97/80/EC and 2000/43/EC) and documentation authored by the European Commission against Racism and Intolerance). The case of *Thlimmenos v Greece* 2000-IV; 31 EHRR 411 GC, discussed above, p 584, might also be considered one of indirect discrimination.

[249] *Zarb Adami v Malta* hudoc (2006); 44 EHRR 49 para 76, where the civic obligation of jury service fell predominantly on men not women, this not as a result of the wording of domestic provisions as such but established working practices by those responsible for creating jury lists and through the practical working of the criteria for exemption for jury service.

[250] *DH v Czech Republic* hudoc (2007) GC. [251] Id, para 190.

disproportionate number of Roma children—including themselves—had been placed in special schools without justification, this being due to the manner in which the relevant legislation was applied in practice. As a consequence of their inferior schooling the applicants claimed that they had been placed at a significant disadvantage.

The Court upheld the applicants' claim. Critical to this outcome was the stance it took on statistics and the burden of proof, which was discussed above.[252] Relying on statistics found in documentation[253] authored by Council of Europe bodies and the (UN) Committee on the Elimination of Racial Discrimination, the Grand Chamber concluded that the relevant statutory education provisions in the Czech Republic had 'had considerably more impact in practice on Roma children than on non-Roma children and resulted in statistically disproportionate numbers of placements of the former in special schools'.[254] With the burden of proof placed upon it, the Czech government was not able to persuade the Court that there was an objective and reasonable justification for this situation. The Court refused to accept that the educational tests employed to decide on schooling were not unbiased in their impact on Roma children.[255] It also rejected the argument that each parent had consented to their child's placement in a special school, taking the view that there could be no waiver of the right in question and that the parents themselves were ill-equipped to make an informed and responsible decision on the matter.[256]

The Court's conclusion, by thirteen votes to four, that there had been a violation of Article 14 read with the right to education was prefaced by several paragraphs further highlighting the importance of this judgment. The Grand Chamber was clear that it did not need to examine the individual applicants' cases.[257] It saw no need to do so as it regarded it as established that 'the relevant legislation as applied in practice at the material time had a disproportionately prejudicial effect *on the Roma community*'[258] (emphasis added), which the applicants formed part of. The Court acknowledged that the Czech authorities had a margin of appreciation in the field under consideration, ie education provision and curriculum design etc. However they had failed to institute schooling arrangements for Roma children that were attended by 'safeguards...that would ensure that...the state took into account their special needs as members of a disadvantaged class'.[259] It was therefore the state's fault that the applicant children had 'received an education which compounded their difficulties and compromised their subsequent personal development instead of tackling their real problems or helping them to integrate into the ordinary schools and develop the skills that would facilitate life among the majority population'.[260]

In terms of the law of the ECHR, the stance taken by the Grand Chamber in *DH* on statistics and burden of proof potentially makes Article 14 a much more effective tool against indirect discrimination since applicants no longer have to prove discriminatory intent on the part of the relevant authorities. How far the Court will go in applying these new tests[261] and what statistical evidence it requires to establish the rebuttable presumption will have to await further case law. Of course, the potential reach of Article 14 remains limited owing to the parasitic nature of this provision. However, it is presumed that Protocol Twelve covers indirect discrimination.

---

[252] See text accompanying n 199 above.   [253] Hudoc (2007) para 192 GC.   [254] Id, para 193.
[255] Id, paras 200–1 and 204.
[256] Id, para 203, cf, the dissenting opinion of Judge Borrego Borrego at paras 14–16.   [257] Id, para 209.
[258] *Ibid.*   [259] Id, para 207, cf, para 181.   [260] *Ibid.*
[261] Cf, para 194. See *Sampanis v Greece* hudoc (2008) (evidence giving rise to presumption of discrimination in case concerning education of Roma applicants).

The Court's ruing in *DH* must also be seen in a wider political context, namely the human rights of Roma in Europe.[262] The case was sponsored by the European Roma Rights Centre and it is striking that nine non-governmental organizations were involved in submitting third party interventions to the Court. Indeed, the situation identified as a violation of Article 14 in *DH* is apparently not uncommon in Europe. In a general report concerning the human rights of Roma in Europe, the Council of Europe's Commissioner of Human Rights raised a 'particular concern' relating to 'segregation in education, which, in one form or another, is a common feature in many Council of Europe member states'.[263] He referred to the fact that there are '[i]n some countries...segregated schools in segregated settlements'. The Grand Chamber ruling in *DH* therefore evidenced that the Court was not afraid to deliver a judgment with major political ramifications. However, one dissenter insisted that it was obvious that the Court had been brought into play 'for ulterior purposes, which [had] little to do with the special education of Roma children in the Czech Republic', declaring that '[t]he future will show what specific purpose this precedent will serve'.[264] Another dissenting judge, Judge Borrego Borrego, warned that the approach taken by the Court entailed that it risked departing from its 'judicial role' and that this would 'lead it into a state of confusion...that can only have negative consequences for Europe'.[265] Amongst other things, he pointed out that the Chamber ruling, which had found no violation of Article 14, had cautioned that the Court's role was not to 'assess the overall social context' forming the background to the case, rather it was to examine the individual applications alone to see if the reason for the applicants' placement in the special schools was their ethnic or racial origin.[266] In Judge Borrego Borrego's view the Grand Chamber had done 'the exact opposite'.[267] This may have been true, but the majority also recognized that Article 14 risked being ineffective if the approach taken to statistics, which necessarily entailed looking at the general picture, was not adopted.[268] It is also notable that the approach taken by the Grand Chamber was in line with EU law.[269] The majority recognized that a number of Convention states faced difficulties in providing appropriate schooling for Roma children and that the Czech Republic deserved praise for the efforts made in this field and given the challenges faced.[270] Indeed, one dissenting judge argued that it was inappropriate to condemn the Czech Republic since it had made a good faith effort to deal with the issue of segregated education, unlike a number of other states.[271]

---

[262] Cf, text accompanying n 205 above [CoE Commissioner Report]. See also the background material presented in *DH* at paras 39–45.

[263] See above, n 205, para 46.

[264] Dissenting opinion of Judge Zupančič.

[265] Dissenting opinion of Judge Borrego Borrego at para 18.

[266] *DH v Czech Republic* hudoc (2006); 43 EHRR 41 para 45. The Chamber (six votes to one) did not find so: it accepted that the relevant school tests were carried out professionally and objectively and that parents generally consented to enrolment in special schools and had opportunities to challenge the placement decisions. It was noted too that the special schools did not cater solely for children of Roma origin.

[267] Dissenting opinion of Judge Borrego Borrego at para 5.

[268] Hudoc (2007) para 186 GC. See also para 189.   [269] Id, paras 81–91. See also n 203 above.

[270] Id, para 205. See also para 208 (the Court noting that new Czech legislation had abolished special schools and provided for children with special educational needs, including socially disadvantaged children, to be educated in ordinary schools).

[271] Dissenting opinion of Judge Jungwiert. He also took issue with the statistical analysis accepted by the Court.

10. POSITIVE OBLIGATIONS TO PROTECT AGAINST DISCRIMINATION AND REVERSE DISCRIMINATION

I. POSITIVE OBLIGATION TO PROTECT AGAINST PRIVATE DISCRIMINATION

According to Article 14, the enjoyment of the rights and freedoms in the Convention 'shall be secured' without discrimination. This replicates the language of the guarantee in Article 1[272] and emphasizes that states may have positive obligations under Article 14 as well as the negative obligation not to discriminate in their official acts.[273] There is no express positive obligation under Article 14 so any obligation of this kind must be implied.

The obligation of the state to take action to protect against private acts of discrimination which affect the enjoyment of Convention rights could embrace matters like membership of private associations or the right to be freed from privately imposed discriminatory fetters, like restrictive covenants on property rights. The inference to be drawn from *Young, James and Webster v UK*[274] and *Sigurjonsson v Iceland*[275] is that a state does have a duty to prevent private action which compels a person to be a member of an association. On the other hand, there cannot, in general, be a duty to compel a private club to accept a member because that would violate the freedom of association of the club. Yet, if the reason for the exclusion were discriminatory, it is arguable that the state should have a positive duty to disallow it. Like other positive obligations, that duty will be qualified. The egregiousness of the badge of differentiation, the 'closeness' of the society, the impact of the decision on the individual (membership of a trade union might be more important than participation in a social club), and the rationality of the exclusion (restricting political associations to supporters, churches to believers) will all weigh in assessing the compliance with a positive duty with respect to private action once one is established. It has been considered already that a state might justify as having an objective and reasonable justification action taken against some kinds of expression or some kinds of association (without necessarily relying on Article 14 or Article 17).[276] The Convention may impose some positive obligations on states to take action against expression which gratuitously insults religious feelings.[277] It remains to be seen whether a like obligation can be found in other substantive articles to restrain racially inflammatory speech or associations.[278] As a strong European consensus about the unacceptability of such opinions or activities develops, it cannot be ruled out that the Court would imply into Article 14 a positive obligation on the state to take action against private speech or action to ensure the effective enjoyment of other Convention rights of those against whom the sentiments were directed.[279]

As was noted above, the state may be under specific positive obligations to investigate racial elements to violent crime[280] and cases of indirect discrimination may imply a corresponding positive obligation upon states under Article 14 as when the state fails to introduce appropriate exceptions to the rule barring persons convicted of a serious crime

---

[272] On this Article, see p 804 below.   [273] See *Belgian Linguistic* case B 3 (1965) para 400.
[274] A 44 (1981); 4 EHRR 38 para 57 PC.   [275] A 264 (1993); 16 EHRR 462 para 37.
[276] On Article 17, see Ch 17.
[277] *Otto-Preminger-Institut v Austria* A 295-A (1994); 19 EHRR 34 para 49.
[278] Cf, Article 20(1), ICCPR and Article 4, Racial Discrimination Convention.
[279] Such other Convention rights include the rights in Articles 10 and 11.   [280] See p 605 above.

from the profession of chartered accountant.[281] One may also keep in mind the operation of Article 8 insofar as it may impact on the position of minorities such as gypsies.

Finally, although it will concededly be a rare example, the Commission has envisaged that there may be circumstances where there is a positive obligation on the state to secure access to private facilities, ie a positive obligation to impose and enforce a positive duty on private individuals. An example is the suggestion that, while there was in general no right of access under Article 10 for private persons to broadcasting facilities, there might be in connection with Article 14, 'if one party was excluded from broadcasting facilities at election time while other parties were given broadcasting time'.[282]

II. REVERSE DISCRIMINATION

Reverse discrimination involves 'programmes designed to favour or promote the interests of disadvantaged groups'.[283] A state may engage in reverse discrimination within the ambit of Convention rights without being in breach of Article 14. The Court acknowledged this in the *Belgian Linguistic* case[284] when it noted generally that not all instances of differential treatment are unacceptable and that 'certain legal inequalities tend only to correct factual inequalities'. Thus a protected quota of university student places for members of a particular racial group would be discrimination within the ambit of a Convention right (the right to education, Article 2 of the First Protocol), but would not be in breach of Article 14 if it had the 'objective and reasonable justification' of increasing the disproportionately low percentage of members of that disadvantaged group in the university student population.[285] However, given the parasitic nature of Article 14, there can be no *legal obligation* on the part of states derived from that Article to engage in a policy or act of reverse discrimination; any such obligation would stem from a positive obligation in another Article guaranteeing a Convention right. As noted above, in the *Airey* case the Court held that the applicant was entitled to legal aid on the basis of Article 6 and did not examine her Article 14 claim. If there was an Article 14 claim on the facts of that case, it stemmed from the positive obligation in Article 6 to provide a 'fair hearing' coupled with Article 14, not from any reverse discrimination claim based upon Article 14 by itself.

11. PROTOCOL TWELVE

Article 1—General prohibition of discrimination

1. The enjoyment of any right set forth by law shall be secured without discrimination on any ground such as sex, race, colour, language, religion, political or other opinion,

---

[281] *Thlimmenos v Greece* 2000-IV; 31 EHRR 411 para 48. See also the separate opinion of Judge Greve in *Price v UK* 2001-VII; 35 EHRR 1285. On indirect discrimination see p 607 above.

[282] Cf, *X and Assn Z v UK No 4515/70*, 38 CD 86 at 88 (1971). In this application, the access envisaged was to public broadcasting. What is considered here is access to private stations.

[283] Parekh, in Hepple and Szyszczak, eds, *Discrimination: The Limits of Law*, 1992, Ch 15, p 261.

[284] A 6 (1968); 1 EHRR 252 para 10 PC. See also *Stec v UK* (hudoc) 2006; 43 EHRR 1017 para 51.

[285] Cf, *DG and DW Lindsay v UK No 11089/84*, 49 DR 181 at 190–1 (1986); 9 EHRR CD 555 at 559 (a tax advantage for married women, which fell within the ambit of the right to property, Article 1, First Protocol, had 'an objective and reasonable justification in the aim of providing positive discrimination' to encourage married women back to work).

national or social origin, association with a national minority, property, birth or other status.

2. No one shall be discriminated against by any public authority on any ground such as those mentioned in paragraph 1.

Protocol Twelve[286] was drafted in recognition of the deficiencies of Article 14, but it is a weaker text than Article 26 ICCPR.[287] It was opened for signature on 4 November 2000 and entered into force on 1 April 2005, but, as of 1 July 2008, has been ratified by just seventeen states (although a further twenty have signed it). Some states have been reluctant to ratify the Protocol as they consider that it contains too many uncertainties and that its application is potentially too wide. The British government, for example, has stated that it will 'wait and see' how the Court interprets and applies Protocol Twelve before ratifying it.[288] As yet there is no jurisprudence under this Protocol to allay the concerns of such states. However the Explanatory Report provides some detailed (if non-binding) comments on the Protocol's expected application.

The Protocol does not prevent all differential treatment. The notion of 'discrimination' is to be understood in the same way as that already existing under Article 14 such that distinctions or differences of treatment are possible. Positive discrimination that can be justified by objective and reasonable grounds should be compatible with Protocol Twelve.[289] Also the list of non-discrimination grounds remains the same as for Article 14, it being understood that it was not necessary to add new badges of discrimination to the list given its non-exhaustive nature, the Court's capacity to do this in any case and for fear that the inclusion of any particular additional ground might give rise to unwarranted *a contrario* interpretations as regards discrimination based on grounds not so included.[290]

The advance offered by the Protocol is that the narrow field to which Article 14 currently restricts non-discrimination standards is extended to 'any right set forth by law'. However the essential question is, what does this terminology potentially cover? For example, do the words relate to existing domestic law or do they extend to international law? Some governments apparently fear that if the scope of Protocol Twelve is extended to the latter then significant new commitments could be introduced into domestic law.[291] According to the Explanatory Report, the additional scope of protection under Article 1 concerns cases where a person is discriminated against: '(i) in the enjoyment of any right specifically granted to an individual under national law; (ii) in the enjoyment of a right which may be inferred from a clear obligation of a public authority under national law, that is, where a public authority is under an obligation under national law to behave in a particular manner; (iii) by a public authority in the exercise of discretionary power

---

[286] ETS 177. See Explanatory Report to Protocol No 12 ('Explanatory Report'), available at <http://conventions. coe.int/>; Grief, 27 (HR Supp) ELR 3 (2002); Khaliq, 2001 PL 458; Council of Europe, *Non-Discrimination: a Human Right*, 2005; Danish Institute for Human Rights in Lagoutte, ed, *Prohibition of Discrimination in the Nordic Countries: The Complicated Fate of Protocol No 12 to the European Convention on Human Rights*, 2005.

[287] All Convention states are parties to the ICCPR and almost all (though not the UK) have accepted the Optional Protocol to that instrument allowing individuals to bring complaints before the Human Rights Committee.

[288] See Kissane, in Council of Europe, *Non-Discrimination: a Human Right*, 2005, p 87 and Grief, 27 (HR Supp) ELR 3 (2002).

[289] Explanatory Report para 16. See also the Preamble to the Protocol.   [290] Id, para 20.

[291] For discussion see Grief, 27 (HR Supp) ELR 3 (2002) and Khaliq, 2001 PL 458. The Protocol is not to be construed as limiting or derogating from domestic or treaty provisions which provide further protection from discrimination, such as those found under the Convention on Elimination of All Forms of Racial Discrimination and the Convention on the Elimination of All Forms of Discrimination against Women.

(for example, granting certain subsidies); and (iv) by any other act or omission by a public authority (for example, the behaviour of law enforcement officers when controlling a riot)'.[292]

The extent to which the Protocol might place positive obligations upon the state to prevent discrimination, even between private individuals, is also debateable. The Explanatory Report states that 'the prime objective of Article 1 is to embody a negative obligation for the Parties: the obligation not to discriminate against individuals'.[293] In this respect the Protocol is 'not intended to impose a general positive obligation on the Parties to take measures to prevent or remedy all instances of discrimination in relations between private persons'. This is because '[a]n additional protocol to the Convention, which typically contains justiciable individual rights formulated in concise provisions, would not be a suitable instrument for defining the various elements of such a wide-ranging obligation of a programmatic character'.[294] However the Explanatory Report suggests that positive obligations could arise if there is a clear lacuna in domestic law protection from discrimination. In particular, as regards private persons, 'a failure to provide protection from discrimination in such relations might be so clear-cut and grave that it might engage clearly the responsibility of the state and then Article 1 of the Protocol could come into play' in accordance with the stance taken by the Court in *X and Y v Netherlands*.[295] The Explanatory Report specifically states that:

> any positive obligation in the area of relations between private persons would concern, at the most, relations in the public sphere normally regulated by law, for which the state has a certain responsibility (for example, arbitrary denial of access to work, access to restaurants, or to services which private persons may make available to the public such as medical care or utilities such as water and electricity, etc). The precise form of the response which the state should take will vary according to the circumstances. It is understood that purely private matters would not be affected. Regulation of such matters would also be likely to interfere with the individual's right to respect for his private and family life, his home and his correspondence, as guaranteed by Article 8 of the Convention.[296]

That Protocol Twelve concerns primarily negative obligations is consistent with the general understanding that it does not create new rights but that it is principally aimed at non-discrimination with respect to existing rights.

12. CONCLUSION

By envisaging very early on in its career that there could be a violation of Article 14 when read with a main Convention right, even though that main right had not itself been violated on its own, the Court ensured that the Convention's non-discrimination provision would not remain the dead letter that it might otherwise have been. However, through the 1970s and into the 1990s, the Court often opted not to resolve Article 14 questions in some apparently key cases and it is certainly striking that, for example, only in 1999 did it find a violation of Article 14 in conjunction with another Article in respect of a 'homosexual' case.[297] It is open to debate whether the apparent early reluctance to address Article 14 properly reflected the parasitic nature of that provision or was evidence that

---

[292] Explanatory Report para 22.   [293] Id, para 24.   [294] Id, para 25.
[295] A 91 (1985); 8 EHRR 235 paras 23–4, 27, and 30.   [296] Explanatory Report para 28.
[297] *Salgueiro da Silva Mouta v Portugal* 1999-IX; 31 EHRR 1055.

the Court was not taking Article 14 as seriously as it should have. Either way, since the late 1990s, cases such as *EB v France, DH v Czech Republic*, and *Thlimmenos v Greece* illustrate a positive approach to Article 14 and more discrimination cases have been addressed by the Court. Areas of Convention jurisprudence such as discrimination based on 'birth' have been re-applied to new contexts, and there is now in place a richer jurisprudence on discrimination in the field of, for example, 'sex' and 'sexual orientation'. One explanation as to why there is a lack of key judgments on important areas such as differences in treatment on the basis of marital status is that to date these cases have not often survived the admissibility stage of proceedings.

It will be appreciated that advances in Convention jurisprudence with respect to the main substantive rights have served to heighten the potential impact that Article 14 may have. For example, the Grand Chamber's admissibility decision in *Stec v UK*, which determined that Article 1 of the First Protocol applied to individuals who have 'an assertable right under domestic law to a welfare benefit',[298] has entailed that, in effect, Article 14 will apply to a great proportion of social security provision in the member states. It is interesting to observe that the Court's judgment was criticized by one member of the Court who argued that the way Article 1, Protocol 1 had been construed in this case implied the 'entry into force of Protocol No 12 in a very important sphere (social-security benefits), in respect of a Contracting Party [the UK] which has not even signed Protocol No 12'.[299] It remains to be seen how the Court will interpret and apply Protocol Twelve, how this will strengthen the effectiveness of the Convention in the field of anti-discrimination and if this will have an impact on the application of Article 14 itself. The Protocol should establish a much more robust anti-discrimination basis for the Convention, allowing it, to some extent at least, to catch up with EU law in this field. It may therefore be especially significant for non-EU states.

It is certainly fair comment to say that the application of Article 14 can be very technical and, in certain respects, rather unclear. The 'analogous situation' and 'within the ambit' tests can be rather ambiguous and recent case law on indirect discrimination and the use of statistical evidence would benefit from clarification by the Grand Chamber. The Court's judgments have been also criticized, at least in the past, for being too favourable to states.[300] If, as seems to be the case, Article 14 has not played as prominent a part in furthering the protection of Convention rights as might have been expected one might be wary of blaming the Court too quickly. National non-discrimination law is often more elaborate than the brief language of Article 14. The list of 'suspect categories' is necessarily short and even when one of them is in issue in a case the margin of appreciation may have a proper place at several stages in the process of deciding whether Article 14 has been violated. When reading cases such as *Stec* and *Petrovic* it is necessary to keep in mind that it is not for the Strasbourg Court to seek to impose equality standards on the (now forty-seven) sovereign member states to the Convention. Sight should not be lost of the Court's position as 'subsidiary' to the national legal system and it should be remembered that its task is to interpret and apply the text of Article 14, which is of limited scope.

Finally, case law from several of the member states that ratified the Convention in the 1990s and concerning allegations of severe discrimination against Roma has presented

---

[298] *Stec v UK* Nos 65731/01 and 65900/01 hudoc (2005); 41 EHRR SE 295 para 34 GC.

[299] See the concurring opinion of Judge Borrego Borrego in *Stec v UK* (hudoc) 2006; 43 EHRR 1017. Cf, the concurring opinion of Judge Costa in *Fretté v France* 2002-I; 38 EHRR 438.

[300] For a more sympathetic view of the Court's jurisprudence, see Merrills, *The Development of International Law by the European Court of Human Rights*, 2nd edn, 1993, pp 169–75.

major new challenges for the Court. It has made some strong comments condemning racism and ethnic hatred, and set new standards for Article 14 as regards, for example, the procedural obligation to investigate police violence motivated by race. The Grand Chamber ruling in *DH v Czech Republic* is arguably the most important Article 14 case ever. It remains to be seen what contribution Article 14, and indeed Protocol Twelve, will make to the plight of minorities such as the Roma in the future.

16

ARTICLE 15: DEROGATION IN TIME OF WAR OR OTHER PUBLIC EMERGENCY THREATENING THE LIFE OF THE NATION

Article 15

1. In time of war or other public emergency threatening the life of the nation any High Contracting Party may take measures derogating from its obligations under this Convention to the extent strictly required by the exigencies of the situation, provided that such measures are not inconsistent with its other obligations under international law.

2. No derogation from Article 2, except in respect of deaths resulting from lawful acts of war, or from Articles 3, 4 (paragraph 1) and 7 shall be made under this provision.

3. Any High Contracting Party availing itself of this right of derogation shall keep the Secretary General of the Council of Europe fully informed of the measures which it has taken and the reasons therefor. It shall also inform the Secretary General of the Council of Europe when such measures have ceased to operate and the provisions of the Convention are again being fully executed.

1. INTRODUCTION[1]

Article 15 enables a state to unilaterally derogate from some of its substantive Convention obligations in certain exceptional circumstances. The provision is therefore of great importance to the Convention's general integrity and, in practice, the protection of human rights in situations where individuals may be especially vulnerable to the authoritarian actions of the state. Accordingly, Article 15 subjects the measure of derogation to a specific regime of safeguards that may be monitored by the Court, though only in applications reaching it.

---

[1] The literature on emergency derogations is extensive. The principal items focusing on the ECHR include Ergec, *Les Droits de l'homme à l'épreuve des circonstances exceptionnelles: Etude sur l'article 15 de la Convention Européenne des droits de l'homme*, 1987; Chowdhury, *Rule of Law in State of Emergency: The Paris Minimum Standards of Human Rights Norms in a State of Emergency*, 1989; Oraa, *Human Rights in States of Emergency in International Law*, 1992; Fitzpatrick, *Human Rights in Conflict: the International System for Protecting Human Rights during States of Emergency*, 1994; Svensson-McCarthy, *The International Law of Human Rights and States of Exception*, 1998.

National constitutions usually contain equivalent provisions to Article 15. Where they do not, some doctrine of necessity is relied on as an alternative legal basis for taking extraordinary action.[2] At the international level, instruments for the general protection of civil and political rights usually[3] have a derogation clause. They are very similar in their terms, and the practice of international institutions under other international human rights treaties[4] is potentially more useful in the interpretation of Article 15 than anywhere else in the European Convention. The dilemma posed by derogation clauses is as easy to state as it is hard to resolve. Once the necessity for derogation is conceded, it becomes difficult to control abusive recourse to the power of suspending rights that the provision permits. In many cases, the effective use of the power will require expedition. The evidence on which recourse to the power is based may be extensive but at the same time sensitive. The determination of the propriety of particular measures of derogation, once the existence of an emergency has been established or conceded is a matter of practical judgment rather than refined analysis. Any review, especially by an international court, is inevitably open to the criticism that fraught decisions made at a time of crisis are being subjected to considered re-evaluation with the comfort of hindsight. It has been suggested that the value of judicial intervention in the exercise of what is essentially a political power is limited—and that the more narrowly the power of derogation is confined, that is to say, the more serious the circumstances must be before it may be relied upon, the less the room for judicial review.[5] However, the experience of abusive recourse to the derogation power is extensive enough for an abstentionist approach to be highly undesirable. In the nature of things, the national judicial means of redress will often have been undermined, so the responsibility of international institutions is the more compelling.

The Strasbourg authorities have rejected the claims of states that questions arising under Article 15 are beyond their competence altogether but they have approached cases before them rather cautiously, some say too cautiously. Happily, the number of occasions when states have relied on Article 15 has been small. Details of the notices of derogation submitted by member states can be found in the respective editions of the Yearbook of the European Convention.[6] The great majority of states have never derogated from the Convention at any time. As of 1 July 2008, no state had entered a notice of derogation. However, only in March 2005 did the UK withdraw a derogation made soon after the events of September 11.[7]

Examples of derogations that have been addressed by the Strasbourg organs in the context of cases reaching them include: the British derogation in the second half of the 1950s concerning the governance of Cyprus (*Greece v UK*);[8] the derogation entered

---

[2] For the United States, see *Korematsu v US* 323 US 81 (1943).

[3] The African Charter of Human and Peoples' Rights does not have an express emergency clause.

[4] See Oraa and Svensson-McCarthy, *op cit* at n 1. The equivalent Article under the International Covenant on Civil and Political Rights is Article 4 which has been the subject of a General Comment by the Human Rights Committee: General Comment No 29 CCPR/C/21/Rev.1/Add.11, 31 August 2001. For commentary see Joseph, 2 HRLR 81 (2002).

[5] Alexander, 5 HRLJ 1 (1984).   [6] See also < http://conventions.coe.int>.

[7] See below n 20. Russia has not derogated with respect to the situation in Chechnya, see *Isayeva v Russia* hudoc (2005); 41 EHRR 791 paras 133 and 191. Albania entered a derogation, referring to a constitutional and public order crisis, covering the period 10 March 1997 until 24 July 1997. Armenia appears to have briefly derogated from the Convention in March 2008, concerning 'the state of emergency in the city of Yerevan'. Georgia entered a derogation for a thirteen-day period in March 2006 aimed at preventing the further spread of bird flu. For details consult <http://conventions.coe.int>.

[8] *No 176/56*, 2 YB 176 (1958) Com Rep, fully reported at 18 HRLJ 348 (1997); CM Res (59) 12. See especially Simpson, *Human Rights and the End of Empire*, 2001.

by Ireland in 1957 following terrorist violence connected to Northern Ireland (*Lawless v Ireland*);[9] the derogation submitted by the Greek government in 1967 connected to the *coup d'état* occurring in that country (the *Greek* case);[10] the derogation entered by the United Kingdom in respect of its rule in Northern Ireland in the early 1970s (*Ireland v UK*)[11] and which was renewed on a number of occasions; a further derogation submitted by the United Kingdom in 1989 in respect of Northern Ireland (*Brannigan and McBride v UK*);[12] and derogations made by the Turkish government in respect of south-east Turkey and which have been examined in various cases (including *Aksoy v Turkey*).[13] It is worth noticing that most of these authorities are now many years old.

It should also be noted that the House of Lords ruled on the derogation submitted by the United Kingdom in 2001 (soon after September 11) in *A and others v Secretary of State for the Home Department*.[14] The domestic judgment in *A* is an important precedent for the application of Article 15 and so it is mentioned in this chapter, albeit briefly. A number of issues growing out of this case have been raised before the Grand Chamber in *A and Others v UK*.[15] At the time of writing judgment is awaited. It is not known then whether the Court will rule on certain Article 15(1) issues which were pleaded by the UK government as one of its defences to the claim that there had been a breach of Article 5(1)(f).

2. THE NEED TO RESORT TO ARTICLE 15 (SOME COMMENTS ON THE COURT'S GENERAL APPROACH TO 'TERRORISM CASES')[16]

The Strasbourg jurisprudence reveals that states have some leeway within the Convention itself before having to contemplate invoking Article 15 in the context of there being a 'public emergency threatening the life of the nation'. Hence it has been suggested that part of the explanation why states other than the UK did not derogate from the Convention given the apparent threat of terrorism[17] after September 11 was that such states had 'found quite enough flexibility in the Convention standards to accommodate any special

---

[9] A 3 (1961); 1 EHRR 15. See Doolan, *Lawless v Ireland (1957–1961): The First Case Before the European Court of Human Rights*, 2001.

[10] 12 YB (the *Greek* case) 1 (1969) CM Res (70) DH 1 and 17 YB 618 (1974); CM Res (74) DH 2. See Coleman, 2 IYHR 121 (1972).

[11] A 25 (1978); 2 EHRR 25 PC. See O'Boyle, 71 AJIL 674 (1977).

[12] A 258-B (1993); 17 EHRR 539 PC. See Marks, 15 OJLS 69 (1995).   [13] 1996-VI; 23 EHRR 553.

[14] *A and Others v Secretary of State for the Home Department* [2004] UKHL 56. See Tomkins, 2005 PL 259 and Arden, 121 LQR 604 (2005).

[15] *A and Others v UK No 3455/05*. See European Court of Human Rights, Press Release, 21 May 2008.

[16] On the European response to terrorism and protection of human rights see Warbrick, 15 EJIL 989 (2004) and 3 EHRLR 287 (2002), plus Hedigan, 28 Fordham 2005 Int'l L J 392. The Council of Europe has elaborated *The Guidelines of the Committee of Ministers of the Council of Europe on human rights and the fight against terrorism* ('CoE Terrorism Guidelines'), which were adopted by the Committee of Ministers on 11 July 2002 (available at <http://www.coe.int>). These are designed to serve as a guide for anti-terrorist policies, legislation, and operations which are both effective and respectful of human rights. See also *the International Commission of Jurists Declaration on Upholding Human Rights and the Rule of Law in Combating Terrorism* ('The Berlin Declaration' adopted 28 August 2004).

[17] 'Terrorist' and 'terrorism' are used for convenience and because they are used by the Court (which has never defined the word 'terrorism'). They are not legal terms of art and are unhelpful in some circumstances, eg, in considering the application of international humanitarian law. On the definition of terrorism by Council of Europe bodies see Parliamentary Assembly Recommendation 1426 (1999), *European Democracies Facing Up to Terrorism* (23 September 1999), para 5. See also *CoE Terrorism Guidelines* at 16–17.

provisions for counter-terrorist purposes'.[18] The following paragraphs briefly comment on the relatively flexible approach adopted by the Court to cases involving terrorism when Article 15 has not been relied upon.

In general, states will wish to avoid relying on Article 15, especially in cases of internal disorder, where there is a risk that the government's opponents will use the emergency derogation as evidence of the effectiveness of their campaign against the authorities. Article 15(2) makes it clear that some measures of derogation are impermissible whatever the emergency, so some options that the state might wish to take advantage of are absolutely forbidden to it. Article 3, for example, is an absolute non-derogable right, so it provides for no exceptions, even if they are purportedly justified by the fight against terrorism and organized crime.[19] The British government was therefore unable to derogate from Article 3 in December 2001, so as to permit it to expel certain suspected international terrorists in circumstances that might otherwise have breached that provision.[20]

The majority of the Articles of the Convention have express limitation clauses in them that allow restriction on rights in most of the circumstances that fall within a 'public emergency'. So it may be 'necessary in a democratic society' for a state to interfere with, say, freedom of expression to preserve public order to a greater extent in time of emergency than it would be in more settled conditions.[21] A similar comment may be made, for example, as regards certain potential restrictions on the right to respect for private life when there is an identifiable need to conduct secret surveillance of terrorist suspects.[22] As early as 1978 the Court stated that:

> some compromise between the requirements for defending democratic society and individual rights is inherent in the system of the Convention... As the Preamble to the Convention states, 'Fundamental Freedoms ... are best maintained on the one hand by an effective political democracy and on the other by a common understanding and observance of the Human Rights upon which (the Contracting States) depend'. In the context of Article 8, this means that a balance must be sought between the exercise by the individual of the right guaranteed to him under paragraph 1 and the necessity under paragraph 2 to impose secret surveillance for the protection of the democratic society as a whole.[23]

It follows that, in practice, the measures of derogation most likely to be implemented under the authority of Article 15 will be ones that involve derogation from those Articles

---

[18] Warbrick, 3 EHRLR 287 (2002) at p 311.

[19] *Chahal v UK* 1996-V; 23 EHRR 413 paras 78–80. In *Saadi v Italy* hudoc (2008) GC a Grand Chamber upheld *Chahal* unanimously.

[20] It derogated from Article 5(1)(f) instead, see <http://conventions.coe.int>. It was claimed by the British government that this derogation allowed the UK to detain without trial, and on a potentially indefinite basis, suspected international terrorists (as defined by domestic legislation and certified by the Home Secretary) who it was unable to expel and who would otherwise be protected by the legal precedent in *Chahal v UK* 1996-V; 23 EHRR 413 paras 112–13 (detention only permissible under Article 5(1)(f) if deportation proceedings are prosecuted with due diligence and duration of such proceedings should not be excessive). In *A and Others v Secretary of State for the Home Department* [2004] UKHL 56, the House of Lords ruled that the domestic legal arrangements providing for such detention were incompatible with Articles 5 and 14 as they were disproportionate and permitted the detention of suspected international terrorists in a way that discriminated on the ground of nationality or immigration status.

[21] Eg, *Brind v UK* No18714/91, 77-A DR 42 (1994); 18 EHRR CD 76. Cf, *Çetin v Turkey* 2003-III.

[22] Eg, *Klass v FRG* A 28 (1978); 2 EHRR 214 PC and *Erdem v Germany* 2001-VII; 35 EHRR 383 (monitoring of prison correspondence).

[23] *Klass*, id, para 59.

which are not qualified in the same way as, for example, Articles 8–11. Here states have argued that special regimes to meet emergency circumstances, while deviating from the ordinary standards of domestic law, do not violate the Convention because the ordinary rules are above the minimum standards of Articles 5 and 6 and the exceptional measures do not fall below these levels.[24]

In 1990, in the context of a case concerning arrest and detention under criminal legislation enacted to deal with acts of terrorism connected with the affairs of Northern Ireland, the Court explained that its 'general approach' was to take into account 'the need, inherent in the Convention system, for a proper balance between the defence of the institutions of democracy in the common interest and the protection of individual rights'. It would therefore 'take into account the special nature of terrorist crime and the exigencies of dealing with it, as far as is compatible with the applicable provisions of the Convention in the light of their particular wording and its overall object and purpose'.[25] Accordingly, when a state has not derogated under Article 15 the Court will proceed on the basis that the Articles of the Convention in respect of which complaints have been made are fully applicable.[26] However, this does preclude proper account being taken of the background circumstances[27] of the case, ie 'problems linked to the prevention of terrorism',[28] and the balancing exercise referred to above is undertaken in that context. Nevertheless, there are limits as the Article 5 and 6 jurisprudence demonstrates.

As will be seen from the cases noted in this chapter, typically emergency legislation is directed to extending the powers of the executive to arrest and detain persons suspected of engagement in forbidden activities, who would normally rely on Articles 5 and 6 to protect them. A number of applications involving these Articles against the backdrop of terrorist situations have reached the Court's attention when the particular right in issue has not been derogated from. Several of these cases reveal that, even in the context of terrorism and defence of national security, certain interpretations of Articles 5 and 6 cannot be accepted. Hence, in *Lawless v Ireland*,[29] the Court declined to interpret Article 5(1)(c) in a manner wide enough to embrace the measures of preventative detention used in Ireland at the time. In *Incal v Turkey*,[30] the Court found that a National Security Court, which included a military legal officer as one of its three judges, did not satisfy standards of independence and objective impartiality for the purposes of Article 6.

Other cases indicate that whilst the Court is prepared to take into account the terrorism or national security context, consistent with the fact that the state has not derogated, it will not allow the very essence of the safeguard in issue to be impaired. For example,

---

[24] This was the argument in *Klass*. See also Diplock, *Report of the Commission to Consider Legal Procedures to Deal with Terrorist Activities in Northern Ireland*, Cmnd 5185 para 16.

[25] *Fox, Campbell and Hartley v UK* A 182 (1990); 13 EHRR 157 para 28.

[26] See *Isayeva v Russia* hudoc (2005); 41 EHRR 791 para 191 (no derogation so operation in question had to be 'judged against a normal legal background').

[27] *Brogan v UK* A 145-B (1988); 11 EHRR 117 para 48 PC. See also the statement made by the Commission in *McVeigh, O'Neill and Evans v UK* Nos 8022/77, 8025/77 and 8027/77, 25 DR 15 at 39 (1981); 5 EHRR 71 para 157.

[28] *Incal v Turkey* 1998-IV; 29 EHRR 449 para 58. Amongst many other authorities see also *Ireland v UK* A 25 (1978); 2 EHRR 25 PC; *Aksoy v Turkey* 1996-VI; 23 EHRR 553 paras 70 and 84; *Zana v Turkey* 1997-VII; 27 EHRR 667 paras 59–60; *United Communist Party of Turkey and Others v Turkey* 1998-I; 26 EHRR 121 para 59. See also the Court's comments on 'international terrorism' and its relevance to Article 5(3) (length of pre-trial detention) as articulated in *Chraidi v Germany* 2006-XII; 47 EHRR 47 para 37.

[29] A 3 (1961); 1 EHRR 15 para 15 (in fact this case did concern a derogation from the Convention).

[30] 1998-IV; 29 EHRR 449.

the Court evidently did take notice of the background of terrorism in *Fox, Campbell and Hartley v UK*,[31] when it said:

> Certainly Article 5(1)(c) of the Convention should not be applied in such a manner as to put disproportionate difficulties in the way of the police authorities of the Contracting States in taking effective measures to counter organised terrorism…

Nonetheless, *some* evidence of 'reasonable suspicion' to justify an arrest has to be produced to satisfy Article 5(1)(c). In the *Fox* case, the Court held that there had been a breach because no evidence had been produced. In contrast, in *Murray v UK*[32] and *O'Hara v UK*[33] there was sufficient evidence from national court proceedings to satisfy the Court's discounted 'reasonable suspicion' test in terrorist cases. As the Court has acknowledged on several occasions 'the investigation of terrorist offences undoubtedly presents the authorities with special problems',[34] but this does not mean 'that the investigating authorities have *carte blanche* under Article 5 to arrest suspects for questioning, free from effective control by the domestic courts and, ultimately, by the Convention supervisory institutions, whenever they choose to assert that terrorism is involved'.[35]

A similar approach was evident in *Chahal v UK*.[36] On the one hand, the Court refused to accept arguments regarding legitimate security concerns about the nature and sources of information identifying the applicant as a security threat as a justification for denying the individual a substantial measure of procedural justice under Article 5(4). On the other hand, given the national security context, the Court indicated that it might be satisfied with an approach which did not necessarily afford full procedural justice but struck a better balance between that aim and national security concerns.[37] Again in *Brogan v UK*,[38] a majority of the Court was not persuaded that the background of terrorism justified, on the facts before them, the extended periods of post-arrest detention in the absence of judicial supervision under Article 5(3). However, the Court did accept that 'subject to the existence of adequate safeguards, the context of terrorism in Northern Ireland has the effect of prolonging the period during which the authorities may, without violating Article 5 para 3, keep a person suspected of serious terrorist offences in custody before bringing him before a judge or other judicial officer'.[39]

It will be observed, therefore, that the Court has acknowledged the relevance of exceptional circumstances of disorder to the interpretation of Articles 5 and 6, although it

---

[31] A 182 (1990); 13 EHRR 157 para 34. See also para 32 ('terrorist crime falls into a special category' and 'the "reasonableness" of the suspicion justifying such arrests [of suspected terrorists] cannot always be judged according to the same standards as are applied in dealing with conventional crime').

[32] A 300-A (1994); 19 EHRR 191 paras 47 and 63 GC (by thirteen votes to five).

[33] 2001-X; 34 EHRR 812. See, however, Judge Loucaides' dissent.

[34] See *Murray v UK* A 300-A (1994); 19 EHRR 193 para 58; *Aksoy v Turkey* 1996-VI; 23 EHRR 553 para 78; *Sakık v Turkey* 1997-VII; 26 EHRR 662 para 44; *Demir v Turkey* 1998-VI; 33 EHHR1056 para 41; *Dikme v Turkey* 2000-VII para 64.

[35] *Murray*, id, para 58.

[36] 1996-V; 23 EHRR 413 GC. See also *Al-Nashif v Bulgaria* hudoc (2002); 36 EHRR 655 para 94, the Court insisting that '[n]ational authorities cannot do away with effective control of lawfulness of detention by the domestic courts whenever they choose to assert that national security and terrorism are involved'.

[37] Id, para 131.

[38] A 145-B (1988); 11 EHRR 117 paras 55–62 PC. The judgment was by twelve votes to seven.

[39] Id, para 61. Judge Evans, dissenting in *Brogan*, pointed out that, despite the admitted intensity of the threat to public order in Northern Ireland, the majority was not prepared to countenance as compatible with the Convention periods of detention hardly greater than those accepted as satisfying Article 5(3) in ordinary times. There was no support for Judge Martens's dissenting opinion, which sought to establish a wider margin of appreciation for states faced with terrorist campaigns. Although not expressly, his opinion seeks to introduce the *Klass* principle into the interpretation of Article 5.

has been generally reluctant to give decisive weight to them given the importance of the (non-derogated from) right at stake. The jurisprudence is in keeping with the general principle that '[w]hen a measure restricts human rights, restrictions must be defined as precisely as possible and be necessary and proportionate to the aim pursued'.[40]

Arguably, therefore, some of the judgments noted above go some way towards sparing a state from having to make an Article 15 declaration in the face of a terrorist campaign.[41] It must be made clear, however, that the fight against terrorism alone is not enough to justify derogation from the Convention. A state may only legally take this highly significant step when the fight against terrorism takes place in the context of 'a public emergency threatening the life of the nation' and then the other qualifying requirements set out by Article 15 must be satisfied too.

3. THE GENERAL PATTERN OF ARTICLE 15

The language of Article 15 seeks to balance the formidable power given to states by subjecting its exercise to various kinds of limitation. The first are textual limitations, confining the power to 'time of war or other public emergency threatening the life of the nation' and allowing states to take only such action as is 'strictly required by the exigencies of the situation'. Next, the power to derogate is subject to substantive restrictions: no derogation is permitted in the case of the specific Articles of the Convention referred to in Article 15(2),[42] nor those covered by the Sixth[43] and Thirteenth[44] Protocols, and the derogating state must not contravene other international law obligations (Article 15(1)). It has been argued that there are other Articles of the Convention which operate as substantive restrictions on the power of derogation.[45] Finally, there are procedural conditions in Article 15(3) which attend recourse to the derogation power and which have the important consequence of drawing attention to these special situations and which are also a source of information which will be useful in the pursuit of any applications in Strasbourg.

4. 'IN TIME OF WAR OR OTHER PUBLIC EMERGENCY THREATENING THE LIFE OF THE NATION'

It is for the Court to interpret each element in Article 15, including what can constitute a 'public emergency'.[46] The Court's capacity to undertake this task was disputed by the Irish government in the *Lawless* case, yet the former Commission and Court have nevertheless done so on several occasions. It will be appreciated nonetheless that there is probably no more delicate task for the European Court than when it is asked to assess whether a respondent was correct in identifying the existence of a 'public emergency' under Article 15. Hence the case law is strongly associated with the granting to the respondent

---

[40] *CoE Terrorism Guidelines* III (2).

[41] See Vercher, *Terrorism in Europe: an International Comparative Legal Analysis*, 1994, pp 342–50.

[42] These are 'Article 2, except in respect of deaths resulting from lawful acts of war,...Articles 3, 4 (paragraph 1), and 7'.

[43] Article 3, Sixth Protocol.   [44] Article 2, Thirteenth Protocol.   [45] See below, p 639.

[46] *Greece v UK No 176/56*, 2 YB 176 (1958) Com Rep, fully reported at 18 HRLJ 348 (1997); CM Res (59) 12 and *Lawless v Ireland* A 3 (1961); 1 EHRR 15 para 28.

state of a generous margin of appreciation[47] which has led some to question the effectiveness of Strasbourg review in this important context.[48] Only in one instance, the *Greek* case, has a Strasbourg institution (in fact, the Commission—the case did not reach the Court) disagreed with a respondent state as to the very existence of a 'public emergency'. In that case it was strongly arguable that the derogation was made in bad faith by the military Greek government and the Commission refused to extend to the respondent state any margin of appreciation.

I. INTERPRETATION OF ARTICLE 15(1): CIRCUMSTANCES REPRESENTING 'A PUBLIC EMERGENCY THREATENING THE LIFE OF THE NATION'

It has been suggested that 'the question whether a threat to the life of a nation exists is capable of objective answer',[49] but precisely what is meant by 'threat to the life of the nation' and, in particular, the severity of the violence, harm or threat required to trigger Article 15(1) is unclear from the jurisprudence. Indeed in all cases reaching the Court for judgment on the merits since *Lawless* the existence of a 'public emergency' has not been the subject of great dispute between the parties. The jurisprudence on precisely what is covered by the notion of 'public emergency threatening the life of the nation', notably in terms of the severity of the situation concerned, and how 'imminent' a potential emergency must be, is therefore lacking detail.

In *Lawless v Ireland*[50] the Court adopted the language of the Commission in holding that:

> in the general context of Article 15 of the Convention, the natural and customary meaning of the words 'other public emergency threatening the life of the nation' is sufficiently clear;[51] ... they refer to an exceptional situation of crisis or emergency which affects the whole population and constitutes a threat to the organised life of the community of which the State is composed.

In the *Greek* case[52] the Commission noted that the French text of the *Lawless* judgment was authentic and that it had additionally referred to the notion that an emergency may be not just actual but also 'imminent'. It described the qualifying features of such an emergency as follows:

(1) It must be actual or imminent.

(2) Its effects must involve the whole nation.

(3) The continuance of the organised life of the community must be threatened.

(4) The crisis or danger must be exceptional, in that the normal measures or restrictions, permitted by the Convention for the maintenance of public safety, health and order, are plainly inadequate.[53]

---

[47] On the evolution of this doctrine in the Article 15 context see O'Boyle, 19 HRLJ 23 (1998) and Arai-Takahashi, *The Margin of Appreciation Doctrine and the Principle of Proportionality in the Jurisprudence of the ECHR*, 2002, Ch 10. For a highly critical appraisal see Gross and Ní Aoláin, 23 HRQ 625 (2001).

[48] Van Dijk and Van Hoof at 1059 and 1071–5.

[49] 48 BYIL 281 at 299 (1976–77). See also Oraa, n 1, above, p 32.

[50] A3 (1961); 1 EHRR 15 para 28.

[51] The Court did not, therefore, consult the *Travaux Préparatoires* to the Convention.

[52] 12 YB (the *Greek* case) 1 (1969) Com Rep; CM Res (70) DH 1.   [53] Id, para 153.

There has been no case before the Strasbourg organs when a respondent state has claimed that it has derogated from the Convention on the basis that a state of war exists. Although it has been argued that 'war' should be both read narrowly and serve so as to limit the kinds of 'other' public emergencies that are envisaged by Article 15, the practice of the former Commission and the Court has established that such a restricted understanding is not a proper one. They have not limited 'other' public emergencies to 'war'-like situations, ie those where there is an external threat to the state[54] or other kinds of undisputed crises such as economic dislocation or natural disaster.[55] Even if 'war' were to be confined to its international legal meaning, 'other public emergency' covers other incidents of serious violence. Civil war and insurrection are the main categories.

The requirements that the consequences of the emergency be plenary in their effects and, what is more, be 'exceptional' (*Lawless* judgment), so as to 'threaten the life of the nation' (Article 15) should be significant blocks against too wide a reading of Article 15(1).[56] However, the threshold for reliance on Article 15(1) has been set by the Strasbourg Court at a considerably lower level than a strict reading of the text might require. In this connection it may be noted that the Convention was drafted in 1950 and many of the cases that have reached the Commission and Court's attention have concerned the phenomenon of terrorist violence—something that the drafters of the Convention almost certainly did not have specifically in mind in 1949–50. In *Lawless* the Court found the existence of the emergency to be 'reasonably deduced' from a combination of three factors: the violent operations of a secret army (the IRA), the fact that its cross-border activities threatened Ireland's relations with the UK, and the escalation of terrorist activities during the period under review, culminating in a particularly serious incident which triggered the introduction of emergency legislation. The Court's acceptance that there was a public emergency seemed to be owed as much to the very existence of the IRA and the fact that its cross-border raids could seriously jeopardize relations between Ireland and the UK, as to the actual level of the violence occurring and anticipated at the time the emergency was declared. It is certainly arguable that *Lawless* appears to set the threshold for the application of Article 15 at a rather low level given the critical nature of the provision in question. The case is nearly fifty years old and was the first ever judgment on the merits delivered by the Court, so it is strongly arguable that the Court would take a stricter approach to Article 15(1) today.

The case law reveals that Article 15 potentially allows a state to derogate from its Convention obligations in the face of relatively low-intensity, irregular terrorist violence stretching over a number of years. This may involve some reconsideration of the derogation power as a temporary expedient.[57] Article 15(1) has been read flexibly in other ways too. In *Lawless*, the Court referred to 'an exceptional situation of crisis or emergency *which affects the whole population*' (emphasis added) but, in practice, this standard has been relaxed or, put another way, it has been accepted that the whole population may be affected by events in only part of a state and that the derogation may be restricted to that

[54] *Lawless v Ireland* A3 (1961); 1 EHRR 15.   [55] Oraa, n 1, above, p 31.

[56] See Lord Hoffmann, dissenting, in *A and Others v Secretary of State for the Home Department* [2004] UKHL 56. He argued 'fanatical groups of terrorists' could kill and destroy, but they did not 'threaten our institutions of government or our existence as a civil community', para 96.

[57] Oraa, *loc cit*, n 1, p 30, notes, 'The Institution of states of emergency is by its very nature temporary...' but that does not necessarily mean brief'. On public emergencies as a temporary phenomenon, amongst many authorities see Human Rights Committee General Comment No 29, *op cit*, paras 1 and 2; *CoE Terrorism Guidelines* XV(1) and (3). Note also Judge Makarczyk, dissenting in *Brannigan and McBride v UK* A 258-B (1993); 17 EHRR 539 PC (derogation should only ever be 'a strictly temporary measure'). For criticism of the Strasbourg jurisprudence from this perspective see Gross, 23 Yale JIL 437 (1998).

part. Hence, derogation notices submitted by Turkey have, in the past, confined the territorial applicability of the notice to the south-east region of that country and the Court has
not questioned the validity of the notice on this ground.[58] The Court will, however, construe such territorial limitations strictly. In *Sakik v Turkey*,[59] the applicant was arrested
in Ankara (an area not specified as being covered by the derogation). The respondent
government argued that the terrorist threat concerned was not confined to any particular
part of Turkish territory and that the applicant's detention had to be seen in the context
of the prolongation of a terrorist campaign being conducted from inside the area where
the state of emergency had been proclaimed. However, the Court did not accept this. It
noted the requirement under Article 15(1) that derogations be confined 'to the extent
strictly required by the exigencies of the situation'. It stated that the very object and purpose of Article 15 would be undermined if a respondent government were able to extend
the effects of derogation to an area not explicitly named in the notice.[60]

II. APPLYING ARTICLE 15(1): EXISTENCE OF PUBLIC
EMERGENCY AND MARGIN OF APPRECIATION

For the Court to assess whether there existed at the relevant time an Article 15 'public emergency', it is required to undertake a qualitative evaluation of the factual situation existing in the derogating state at the time of the derogation. But what standard
of review should the European Court employ here? The Court stated in *Brannigan and
McBride v UK*:[61]

> The Court recalls that it falls to each Contracting State, with its responsibility for 'the life
> of [its] nation', to determine whether that life is threatened by a 'public emergency' and,
> if so, how far it is necessary to go in attempting to overcome the emergency. By reason of
> their direct and continuous contact with the pressing needs of the moment, the national
> authorities are in principle in a better position than the international judge to decide both
> on the presence of such an emergency and on the nature and scope of derogations neces-
> sary to avert it. Accordingly, in this matter a wide margin of appreciation should be left to
> the national authorities...
>
> Nevertheless, Contracting Parties do not enjoy an unlimited power of appreciation.
> It is for the Court to rule on whether *inter alia* the States have gone beyond the 'extent
> strictly required by the exigencies' of the crisis. The domestic margin of appreciation is
> thus accompanied by a European supervision...At the same time, in exercising its super-
> vision the Court must give appropriate weight to such relevant factors as the nature of the
> rights affected by the derogation, the circumstances leading to, and the duration of, the
> emergency situation.

It was a matter of dispute amongst the members of the Commission as to whether any
margin of appreciation at all was owing to the respondent government in the *Greek* case.[62]
The Greek government argued that there had been a decline in public order for a number
of months bringing the country to the brink of anarchy, such that the government had
had to take action (including emergency derogations) to pre-empt an armed Communist
takeover in Greece. The Commission said that its task was 'to examine on the evidence
before it' whether there was a situation of such scope and intensity that it constituted an

---

⁵⁸ Eg, *Aksoy v Turkey* 1996-VI; 23 EHRR 553.   ⁵⁹ 1997-VII; 26 EHRR 662.
⁶⁰ Id, para 39.   ⁶¹ A 258-B (1993); 17 EHRR 539 para 43 PC.
⁶² 12 YB (the *Greek* case) 1 (1969); CM Res DH (70) 1.

actual or imminent threat to the life of the Greek nation.[63] The Commission concluded that there was no evidence of such a situation, the only case in which one of the Strasbourg authorities had not endorsed the government's claim that there was an emergency.[64] Three dissenting opinions differed from this conclusion. They relied on the 'margin of appreciation' available to the authorities, an idea introduced in the first *Cyprus* case when the Commission said (in a slightly different context):

> the government should be able to exercise a certain measure of discretion in assessing the extent strictly required by the exigencies of the situation.[65]

The views of the dissenting Commissioners in the *Greek* case, though different in emphasis, gave weight to the difficulty, close to impossibility, of a review of the evidence and the assessment of its significance by the Commission.[66] Deference to the government's calculations was, therefore, practically a matter of necessity. There is little sign of any deference in the decision of the majority, whose conclusion was simply different to the government's.[67] The Commission's report went on to express the view that there had been a catalogue of very serious human rights violations and, furthermore, shortly after the report was produced, Greece denounced its membership of the Council of Europe.

Arguably, therefore, the robust stance of the majority of the Commission in the *Greek* case as regards Article 15 is best viewed in the light of the fact that it appears that the respondent government in that case, which was a revolutionary (military) government, resorted to Article 15 in highly questionable, bad faith, circumstances. Elsewhere, the application of a margin of appreciation to respondent states has been pivotal,[68] although in the leading judgments the existence of a public emergency was not hotly disputed. In *Ireland v UK*,[69] the Irish government accepted that conditions in the province were sufficiently exceptional for Article 15 to apply. The period involved was from 1970 to 1976, which included the most violent period in the continuing disturbances from Northern Ireland. From August 1971 to March 1972, more than 200 people were killed and nearly 30,000 injured in over 3,000 bombing and shooting incidents.[70] Even so, it has been questioned whether the Court was correct to endorse the applicant government's assessment that there was a public emergency without making its own inquiries and assessment. That there ought to be this obligation on the Court is explained by the nature of the rights in the Convention: since they are the rights of individuals, they ought not to be capable of being diminished by the unilateral act of a state.

While it is not suggested that an independent inquiry by the Court would have resulted in a different outcome in *Ireland v UK*, the possibility of unjustifiable reliance on Article 15 increases as the level of violence diminishes. In *Brannigan and McBride v UK*,[71] the applicants accepted that there was a public emergency in Northern Ireland but the Commission said that it had to make its own assessment of the situation, 'albeit [a] limited [one]'. It was very limited, the Commission concluding on the basis of cumulative government statistics[72] that the situation remained 'very serious'.[73] The brief of one of the intervening parties, the NGO 'Liberty', argued that there was not an emergency of

---

[63] Id, para 157.   [64] Id, paras 159–65.

[65] *Greece v UK No 176/56*, 2 YB 176 (1958) Com Rep, fully reported at 18 HRLJ 348 (1997); CM Res (59) 12.

[66] 12 YB (the *Greek* case) 1 at 76–93 (1969).   [67] Id, 71–6.

[68] In fact, the Court did not refer to a margin of appreciation in the *Lawless* case (A 3 (1961); 1 EHRR 15 para 28), though as noted above, it agreed that the existence of an emergency had been 'reasonably deduced' by the Irish government.

[69] A 25 (1978); 1 EHRR 15 paras 20–77 PC.   [70] Id, para 48.

[71] A 258-B (1993); 17 EHRR 539 PC.   [72] Id, paras 26–7.   [73] Id, para 49.

sufficient seriousness for Article 15 to be relied upon.[74] The Court briefly endorsed the Commission's conclusion:

> ...making its own assessment, in the light of all the material before it as to the extent and impact of terrorist violence in Northern Ireland and elsewhere in the United Kingdom..., the Court considers there can be no doubt that such a public emergency existed at the relevant time.[75]

This degree of scrutiny is hardly different from accepting the parties' own view of the situation. Similar comments may be made regarding the assessment of the existence of a public emergency in the case of *Aksoy v Turkey*. In that judgment the Court simply stated that it considered that 'in the light of all the material before it, that the particular extent and impact of PKK terrorist activity in south-east Turkey has undoubtedly created, in the region concerned' a 'public emergency'.[76]

The extension of a '*wide* margin of appreciation' (emphasis added) to the state as regards the assessment of the existence of an emergency was confirmed by the Court in *Brannigan and McBride v UK* although this was the focus of criticism from commentators[77] and was the subject of controversy within the Court at the time. Judge Martens in that case stated that:

> [t]he first question is whether there is an objective ground for derogating which meets the requirements laid down in the opening words of Article 15. Inevitably, in this context, a certain margin of appreciation should be left to the national authorities. There is, however, no justification for leaving them a wide margin of appreciation because the Court, being the 'last-resort' protector of the fundamental rights and freedoms guaranteed under the Convention, is called upon to strictly scrutinise every derogation by a High Contracting Party from its obligations.

For Judge Martens, there was no need to follow the precedent of *Ireland v UK* and make the margin a 'wide' one. At the time of the last-mentioned case (1978), he argued, the judges might have been influenced by 'the view that the majority of the then member states of the Council of Europe might be assumed to be societies which...had been democracies for a long time and, as such, were fully aware both of the importance of the individual right to liberty and of the inherent danger of giving too wide a power of detention to the executive'. However, '[s]ince the accession of eastern and central European States that assumption has lost its pertinence'. Also in *Brannigan and McBride*, Judge Makarczyk argued:

> A derogation made by any State affects not only the position of that State, but also the integrity of the Convention system of protection as a whole. It is relevant for other member States—old and new—and even for States aspiring to become Parties which are in the process of adapting their legal systems to the standards of the Convention. For the new Contracting Parties, the fact of being admitted, often after long periods of preparation and negotiation, means not only the acceptance of Convention obligations, but also recognition by the community of European States of their equal standing as regards the democratic system and the rule of law. In other words, what is considered by the old democracies as a natural state of affairs, is seen as a privilege by the newcomers which is not to be disposed of lightly. A derogation made by a new Contracting Party from eastern and central Europe would call into question this new legitimacy and is, in my opinion, quite

---

[74] A 258-B (1993); 17 EHRR 539 para 45 PC.   [75] Id, para 47.   [76] 1996-VI; 23 EHRR 553 para 70.
[77] See below, n 90.

improbable. Any decision of the Court concerning Article 15 should encourage and confirm this philosophy.

The Court may allow for some flexibility on the state's part as regards the timing of the decision to derogate and when to withdraw the derogation. In the *Lawless* case the President of the Commission put it to the Court that it may be consistent with the goal of Article 15 to allow a state acting in good faith to derogate from the Convention before a 'public emergency' fully erupts and in order to 'nip trouble in the bud'.[78] Clearly there are dangers to guard against if this is so.

Marshall v UK[79] suggests that, against the backdrop of a prolonged terrorist campaign satisfying Article 15(1), the Strasbourg Court is prepared to afford a state a considerable benefit of doubt as regards when to *withdraw* a derogation. This is so if there is reason to believe that there is a genuine risk of a return to serious violence of an Article 15(1) order in contrast to the relative calm that may exist when an application is made. *Marshall*, which was decided in 2001, was one of a series of cases concerning the public emergency declared in relation to terrorism connected with the affairs of Northern Ireland, the relevant derogation subsisting from December 1988[80] until withdrawal in February 2001 (it was renewed annually at the domestic level). The derogation from Article 5(3) was originally made in 1988 in reaction to the Court's judgment in *Brogan*, and it was in issue in *Brannigan and McBride* when the Court accepted its legality and the proportionality of the measures taken pursuant to it. Through the derogation the UK government sought to curtail the full application of Article 5(3) by enabling an individual terrorist suspect to be detained on the authority of the state (ie without the judicial intervention required by Article 5(3)) for up to seven days. The existence of a public emergency had not been fully contested by the applicants in *Brannigan and McBride*, which related to events taking place in 1989, a time of heightened terrorist activity in Northern Ireland. However, after the major paramilitary groups declared a ceasefire in 1994, the derogation remained in place because of ongoing terrorist activity and the threat posed by dissident groups that was confirmed by annual, independent reviews. The applicant in *Marshall* questioned the continuing validity of the derogation, having been detained in 1998 in circumstances which, but for derogation, would normally infringe Article 5(3). He argued that by this stage there was no longer a genuine 'public emergency' for the purposes of Article 15(1) given the significant improvement in the security situation in Northern Ireland at the time. Given the paucity of the Strasbourg jurisprudence on the conditions for reliance on Article 15(1) and the significance of the issues involved, it is disappointing that the application was refused at the admissibility stage by a Chamber of the Court. It stated that it was required to address 'with special vigilance the fact that almost nine years separate the prolonged administrative detention of the applicants in *Brannigan and McBride* from that of the applicant in the case before it'. Although the decision referred in some detail to the factual situation existing in Northern Ireland at the relevant time, as regards the question of the existence of a 'public emergency' the Court stated that it:

> [did] not agree with the applicant's submission that the security situation in Northern Ireland at the time of his detention had improved to the point where it was no longer justified to refer to it as a public emergency 'threatening the life of the nation'. It notes that the

---

[78] See O'Boyle, 19 HRLJ 23 (1998) at 26; cf, the Court's statement in *Refah Partisi (The Welfare Party) v Turkey* 2003-II; 37 EHRR 1 paras 98–9 GC regarding the timing for the dissolution of a political party with an anti-democratic agenda.

[79] *Marshall v UK No 41571/98* hudoc (2001) DA.

[80] Derogations had applied to the territory before 1984 too.

authorities continued to be confronted with the threat of terrorist violence notwithstanding a reduction in its incidence. It cannot but note that the weeks preceding the applicant's detention were characterised by an outbreak of deadly violence. This of itself confirms that there had been no return to normality since the date of the *Brannigan and McBride* judgment such as to lead the Court to controvert the authorities' assessment of the situation in the province in terms of the threats which organised violence posed for the life of the community and the search for a peaceful settlement. It recalls in this connection that by reason of their direct and continuous contact with the pressing needs of the moment, the national authorities are in principle better placed than the international judge to decide both on the presence of such an emergency and on the nature and scope of the derogation necessary to avoid it.

The Court also refused to accept submissions to the effect that the authorities had failed to conduct meaningful reviews of the continuing necessity for the derogation to Article 5(3). It was satisfied that the matter had been addressed with sufficient frequency given the annual renewal debate that took place in Parliament. More generally it was stated that 'the authorities have approached the operation of the 1989 Act with an eye to developments in the political and security situation in Northern Ireland'. It seems that a significant benefit of doubt was granted to the state on the facts of this case and, as the peace process progressed, the Court was unwilling to intrude into what undoubtedly was a very delicate state of affairs. Perhaps the Court was comforted by the fact that by the time it delivered its admissibility decision, in 2001, the UK had in fact withdrawn the derogation in issue.

III. THE HOUSE OF LORDS' RULING IN *A AND OTHERS*

The UK case of *A and Others* to some extent exposed the lack of clarity in the Strasbourg case law as regards what is encompassed by the notion of 'public emergency threatening the life of the nation'.[81] Did Article 15(1) apply to the uncertainty of a situation apparently represented by the purported *threat* posed to the UK by a highly organized and secretive terrorist organization supposedly capable and willing to perpetrate events such as those witnessed on September 11? In *A and Others*, eight[82] of the nine Law Lords accepted that Article 15(1) applied. The majority applied what they saw as the generally rather low threshold for reliance on Article 15(1) found in the Strasbourg jurisprudence (as displayed in the *Lawless* case) and in doing so showed considerable deference to the executive in its capacity to take what was regarded as a primarily 'political' decision that verged on being 'non-justiciable'.[83] This approach comes close to the 'wide margin of appreciation' employed by the Strasbourg Court in the past, reflecting what Lord Bingham described as an 'unintrusive' stance.[84] Nonetheless Lord Bingham noted that his conclusion that Article 15(1) applied was not without some 'misgiving',[85] Lord Rodger also acknowledged his own 'hesitation'[86] on the matter, whilst Lord Scott had 'very grave doubt whether the "public emergency" [was] one that justif[ied] the description of "threatening he life of the nation"'.[87] Lords Bingham

---

[81] See Bates, 76 BYIL 245 (2005).

[82] *A and Others v Secretary of State for the Home Department* [2004] UKHL 56, Lord Hoffmann disagreed on this point. See also the judgment of Lord Scott at para 154.

[83] See eg, the judgment of Lord Bingham at para 29.

[84] Id, Lord Bingham para 29. See also Lord Hope at para 112.

[85] Id, Lord Bingham para 26. See, however, Lord Hope who considered that there was 'ample evidence' as to a 'public emergency', para 118 judgment.

[86] Id, Lord Rodger para 165.   [87] Id, Lord Scott para 154.

and Rodger expressed some sympathy with Lord Hoffmann's view that there was in fact no public emergency in the sense required by Article 15(1) for whilst 'fanatical groups of terrorists' could kill and destroy, they did not 'threaten our institutions of government or our existence as a civil community'.[88]

IV. SUMMARY

Cases such as *Marshall*, plus the Court's apparent general reliance in the Article 15 juris-prudence on cumulative figures relating to deaths, casualties and property destruction, which necessarily do not give an accurate picture of the seriousness of the circumstances at a particular time, provide an indication that the Strasbourg authorities accept a view of some emergencies as 'campaigns' or continuing events. Where there is an organized campaign of violence resulting in deaths at a relatively low level among the security forces and civilians it remains hard to see how the Court could avoid confirming a state's claim that there is a public emergency within Article 15 assuming there is no evidence of bad faith on the latter's part. The case law indicates that derogations will not be condemned by the Court simply because of their prolonged effect. It is not necessarily the case, there-fore, that the notion of 'emergency' implies a requirement of temporariness as regards the derogation. However, the longer the derogation subsists then the greater the need is for the Court to effectively address whether there are sufficient and effective safeguards in place domestically to ensure that the public emergency is not perpetuated indefinitely.[89] Throughout the measures must be 'strictly required by the exigencies of the situation'.

5. 'MEASURES... TO THE EXTENT STRICTLY REQUIRED BY THE EXIGENCIES OF THE SITUATION...'

Even when a state validly declares there to be a public emergency threatening the life of the nation, it does not have *carte blanche* as to what measures it might take. In the first place, as is noted above, certain rights protected by the Convention are non-derogable (Article 15(2)). As regards derogable rights, the extent to which their normal operation may be curtailed must be proportionate to the nature of the emergency existing: the measures taken must be 'to the extent strictly required by the exigencies of the situ-ation...'. Essentially, the issue here is whether the actual measures resorted to, and which in normal circumstances would infringe the Convention, are proportional to the actual crisis facing the governing authorities at the time. Here the Court asserts a right of review and states must carefully justify their actions but this is again an area where a margin of appreciation will be available to them.[90] In this connection we are once more reminded of the relatively limited role that is feasible for an international court in the conduct of such a

---

[88] Id, Lord Hoffman para 96.

[89] *CoE Terrorism Guidelines* state 'The circumstances which led to the adoption of such derogations need to be reassessed on a regular basis with the purpose of lifting these derogations as soon as these circumstances no longer exist', XV(3). In *Brannigan and McBride* the interveners, *Liberty, Interights* and the *Committee of the Administration of Justice* had argued that the margin of appreciation available to a state should become narrower the more permanent the emergency becomes, A 258-B (1993), 17 EHRR 539 para 42 PC.

[90] See the extract from *Brannigan and McBride v UK* cited in text accompanying n 61 above and at para 66 (judgment). For criticism of the Court's approach see Marks, 15 OJLS (1995) 85; Gross, 23 YJIL (1998) 437; Gross and Ní Aoláin, 23(1) HRQ (2001); and Campbell, 54 ICLQ 321 (2005).

review. As was noted in the *Marshall*[91] case, it is not the Court's role to 'substitute its view as to what measures were most appropriate or expedient at the relevant time in dealing with an emergency situation for that of the Government which have direct responsibility for establishing the balance between the taking of effective measures to combat terrorism on the one hand, and respecting individual rights on the other'. The Court has stated that 'in exercising its supervision [it] must give appropriate weight to such relevant factors as the nature of the rights affected by the derogation, the circumstances leading to, and the duration of, the emergency situation'.[92] It has also stressed the great importance of the existence of safeguards against abuse of power that may serve to reduce the chance that an individual will be the subject of serious human rights violations whilst the emergency situation and modified legal regime associated with it subsists.

I. 'STRICTLY REQUIRED...'

As to the interpretation of 'strictly required', the language of Article 15(1) suggests a test more demanding than 'necessary' in, for example, Article 10(2), which requires that the state show a 'pressing social need' for its measures of limitation. The Court has worked out a series of factors to be taken into account to determine whether measures are strictly required. The first inquiry is into the necessity for the measures at all by examining why the ordinary law or action otherwise compatible with the Convention is not adequate to meet the emergency and why the exceptional measures are. In *Lawless v Ireland*,[93] the Court accepted that neither ordinary nor special courts in Ireland were able to meet the dangers to public order occasioned by the secret, terrorist character of the IRA, in particular the near impossibility of obtaining evidence necessary to convict suspects by judicial proceedings. Internment or detention without trial did have the effect of meeting this problem. In *Ireland v UK*,[94] the Court held that 'the British government was reasonably entitled to consider' that the ordinary criminal procedure was inadequate to meet the 'far-reaching and acute danger' presented by the 'massive wave of violence and intimidation', characterizing the IRA's activities in Northern Ireland. Extrajudicial deprivation of liberty, even for the purposes of interrogating witnesses—otherwise contrary to Article 5(1)—and the removal of procedural guarantees to regulate deprivation of liberty—otherwise in violation of Article 5(4)—were necessary to meet the emergency situation.[95] In *Brannigan and McBride v UK*,[96] the Court acceded to the government's argument that, in a common law system, it was not feasible to introduce a judicial element into the detention process at an early stage. It accepted also that extended detention was necessary to investigate successfully terrorist crimes when some of the suspects would have been given training in resisting interrogation and where extensive forensic checks might be required.[97] The Court therefore held that the UK government had not exceeded its margin of appreciation by derogating from obligations under Article 5(3) of the Convention to the extent that individuals suspected of terrorist offences were allowed to be held for up to seven days without judicial control. In reaching this conclusion it is important to note that the Court expressed the view that it was satisfied that there were

---

[91] *Marshall v UK No 41571/98* hudoc (2001) p 12 DA.
[92] *Brannigan and McBride v UK* A 258-B (1993); 17 EHRR 539 para 43 PC.
[93] A 3 (1961); 1 EHRR 15 para 36.   [94] A 25 (1978); 2 EHRR 25 para 212 PC.
[95] Id, paras 214—20.   [96] A 258-B (1993), 17 EHRR 539 PC.
[97] The Court found that the government's position had been supported by the various independent inquiries into the situation in Northern Ireland, but there was little analysis of the evidence or assessment of its worth in the judgment. For comment, see Marks, 15 OJLS 69 (1995).

effective safeguards in operation in Northern Ireland which, in the Court's view, provided a significant measure of protection against the dangers of arbitrary behaviour and *incommunicado* detention. Such basic safeguards included the fact that the actual arrest remained challengeable by *habeas corpus* in the ordinary courts. Also there was a right to see a solicitor after forty-eight hours of detention and a detainee was entitled to have other persons informed about his detention and have access to a doctor.

The continuing presence of such safeguards appears to have been an important factor in the dismissal of the application in *Marshall v UK* where the applicant disputed the effectiveness of *habeas corpus* as an effective remedy but did not claim an actual violation of Article 5(4). It is arguable that the suspension of habeas corpus could never be justified given the fundamental nature of the guarantee in a democracy and the importance the Court attaches to the provision of safeguards against abuse of exceptional powers.[98]

The judgment in the *Brannigan* case was open to the criticism that it did not answer sufficiently the concerns of Amnesty International in its intervention that, in particular circumstances, safeguards were necessary not only to protect against unnecessarily prolonged detentions but also to protect detainees who might be detained *incommunicado* during the first forty-eight hours detention. The evidence of worldwide abuse of persons detained without supervision during interrogation is strong[99] and in *Aksoy v Turkey*,[100] the first case in which the Court found a state to have tortured an individual, it stressed the fact that prompt judicial intervention may lead to the detection and prevention of serious ill-treatment. In *Aksoy* laws were in place that potentially permitted detention of an individual without being brought before a judge or other officer (Article 5(3)) for up to thirty days. The government sought to justify this by reference to the particular demands of police investigations in a geographically vast area and as it was faced with a terrorist organization receiving outside support (although generally the Court criticized the fact that the government had not adduced any detailed reasons before it as to why the fight against terrorism in south-east Turkey rendered judicial intervention impracticable). The applicant was in fact detained in the way identified for at least fourteen days, a period described by the Court as 'exceptionally long'[101] and which gave rise to a situation which 'left the applicant vulnerable not only to arbitrary interference with his right to liberty but also to torture'. The Court went on the condemn the insufficient nature of the safeguards available to the applicant: 'the denial of access to a lawyer, doctor, relative or friend and the absence of any realistic possibility of being brought before a court to test the legality of the detention' meant that he was left completely at the mercy of those holding him'.[102] On the one hand, the Court was prepared to take account of 'the unquestionably serious problem of terrorism in south-east Turkey and the difficulties faced by the State in taking effective measures against it'.[103] On the other hand, it was 'not persuaded that the exigencies of the situation necessitated the holding of the applicant on suspicion of involvement in terrorist offences for fourteen days or more in *incommunicado* detention without access to a judge or other judicial officer'. The Court therefore held that there had been a violation of Article 5(3), the first time that it had concluded that measures taken by a state pursuant to a 'public emergency' were not 'strictly required by the exigencies of the situation'. In

---

[98] Cf, *Habeas Corpus in Emergency Situations* (Articles 27(2), 25(1), ACHR), I-A Ct HRts Rep, Series A 8 (1987); 9 HRLJ 94 (1988) advisory opinion.

[99] See Amnesty International in *Brannigan and McBride v UK* A 258-B (1993), 17 EHRR 539 para 61 PC. See also Judge Pettiti dissenting, id; *Ireland v UK* A 25 (1978); 2 EHRR 25 paras 165–8 PC; *Tomasi v France* A241-A (1993); 15 EHRR 1 paras 114–15 (1992) and id, paras 99–100 Com Rep. See further, *Report of the European Committee for the Prevention of Torture: Northern Ireland*, 1994, para 110.

[100] 1996-VI; 23 EHRR 553.   [101] Id, para 78.   [102] Id, para 83.   [103] Id, para 84.

subsequent judgments[104] the Court has indicated that in cases of prolonged extra-judicial detention under Article 5(3) it will expect to be furnished with 'precise reasons relating to the actual facts'[105] of the case before it which demonstrate that 'judicial scrutiny of the applicants' detention [would] have prejudiced the progress of the investigation' in process. It will not be sufficient for the respondent state 'to refer in a general way to the difficulties caused by terrorism and the number of people involved in the inquiries'.[106]

As indicated above, in practice the emergency situations that have reached the Court's attention have involved continuing campaigns of irregular, terrorist violence. Inevitably the question arises whether a state can justify the continuance of measures, which may be a proper response to the most intense periods of violence and disorder, during periods of relative calm, albeit possibly temporary ones. The exact point has not been fully addressed on the merits by the Court, but the admissibility decision in *Marshall v UK* [107] throws some light on this. The decision suggests that at a later, less violent stage of a public emergency it may be difficult to persuade the Court to condemn measures which it has accepted as justified at the beginning of that emergency, provided that the state can muster evidence to the effect that its belief that the campaign was at least dormant (with real potential to revive) was not an unreasonable one. In *Marshall* the Court accepted that the UK authorities had not 'overstepp[ed] their margin of appreciation' by maintaining the extended period of pre-trial detention that had been in issue in *Brannigan and McBride*. The justifications provided by the UK for such measures in *Marshall* were the same as those in *Brannigan and McBride* and the Court accepted that they remained 'relevant and sufficient'. Although the peace process was well underway the Court pointed out that, as of 1998, 'the threat of terrorist outrage was still real and...the paramilitary groups in Northern Ireland retained the organisational capacity to kill and maim on a wide scale'.[108] The applicant had argued that, in fact, the level of violence in Northern Ireland in 1998 was little different to that which had existed at other times in other parts of the UK but where there had been no recourse to derogation under Article 5(3). To this the Court stated that it 'consider[ed] that the applicant's reasoning does not take sufficient account of the specific nature of the violence which has beset Northern Ireland, less so the political and historical considerations which form the backdrop to the emergency situation'.

In *Ireland v UK*,[109] the Irish government maintained that the measures adopted by the authorities in Northern Ireland had manifestly failed in their purpose because the period during which they had been in operation had seen an increase in terrorist violence and, eventually, the British government had abandoned administrative detention. In principle, the argument about effectiveness has much to recommend it: how can an interference with human rights which does not contribute to some other good end be 'strictly required'? Indeed, one might go further and argue that, because of what is at stake, the government should be called upon to demonstrate the effectiveness of the measures it has introduced. However the difficulty is not of principle and desirability but of practicability and justiciability. Hence the Court refused to accept the Irish government's

---

[104] The Turkish government has been found in breach of Article 15 in subsequent cases raising the same issue, including a case in which the Court stated that a period of eleven days' *incommunicado* detention could not be justified, see *Nuray Şen v Turkey* hudoc (2003).

[105] *Demir v Turkey* 1998-VI; 33 EHRR 1056 para 52.

[106] *Ibid*. The subsequent conviction of the detainee for a 'terrorist' offence is not a relevant factor for the purpose of Article 5(3), para 53.

[107] *Marshall v UK No 41571/98* hudoc (2001) DA.   [108] Id, para 12.

[109] A 25 (1978); 2 EHRR 25 para 214 PC. See also Judge Makarczyk, dissenting, in *Brannigan and McBride v UK* A 258-B (1993); 17 EHRR 539 PC.

argument as noted immediately above, emphasizing that its function was confined not to assessing what was the most prudent or most expedient policy to combat terrorism, rather it had to do no more than review the lawfulness, under the Convention, of the measures adopted. In this the margin of appreciation applied and the Court had to look to the conditions and circumstances reigning when the measures were originally taken and subsequently applied, and so avoid 'a purely retrospective examination of the efficacy of those measures'.[110] It follows that the simple fact that a government modifies and mitigates the measures on which it relies under Article 15 during the course of a campaign against the authorities is not, of itself, evidence that the measures were not 'strictly required' at some earlier stage.[111] The interpretation of Article 15 'must leave a place for progressive adaptations'[112] and '[w]hen a State is struggling against a public emergency threatening the life of the nation, it would be rendered defenceless if it were required to accomplish everything at once, to furnish from the outset each of its chosen means of action with each of the safeguards reconcilable with the priority requirements for the proper functioning of the authorities and for restoring peace within the community'.[113]

It remains the case, of course, that establishing the necessity for having some emergency measures will not always be sufficient to demonstrate that the particular measures employed are 'strictly required'. The Strasbourg authorities may go on to inquire into the proportionality between the need and the response.[114] The greater the need—eg, the 'very exceptional situation' in Northern Ireland, acknowledged by the Court in *Ireland v UK*[115]—the greater the permissible derogation—eg, detention of a person not suspected of an offence for the purposes of the investigation. Proportionality does not imply some arithmetic calibration. Instead, the Court takes into account whether the measure is less draconian than others which might have been contemplated. In the *Lawless* case,[116] the Court considered that one alternative—sealing the border between Ireland and Northern Ireland as a means of combating cross-border raids—would have gone beyond the exigencies of the emergency in Ireland, thus reinforcing the proportionality of the government's lesser reaction. Many of the contested measures of derogation have involved the removal of safeguards against abuse of powers of arrest or detention, usually the removal of the judicial element. In establishing the proportionality of the response, the Court also looks at the alternative mechanisms of supervision introduced by the state. Thus the system of administrative detention examined in the *Lawless* case was accompanied by detailed and continuous supervision by Parliament and a detainee could make representations to a tribunal, the 'Detention Commission'.[117] In *Ireland v UK*,[118] the judicial control of detention was replaced by non-judicial advisory committees and there remained a residuary and, in the view of the Court, not a wholly illusory possibility of access to the courts. In *Brannigan and McBride v UK*,[119] as well as *Marshall v UK*,[120] though not in *Aksoy v Turkey*, the respondent government succeeded in rebutting the claim that there were no effective safeguards against abuse of the extended period of pre-trial detention in issue.

In *Brannigan and McBride v UK*[121] the applicants argued that the extended period of pre-trial detention could not be strictly required because the government had previously withdrawn its derogation notice. That was because, the government responded, it

[110] *Ibid.*   [111] Id, para 213.   [112] Id, para 220.   [113] *Ibid.*
[114] *De Becker v Belgium* B 4 (1962) ; 1 EHRR 43 para 271 Com Rep.
[115] A 25 (1978); 2 EHRR 25 para 212 PC.   [116] A 3 (1961); 1 EHRR 15 para 36.   [117] Id, para 67.
[118] A 25 (1978); 2 EHRR 25 paras 218–19 PC.   [119] A 258-B (1993); 17 EHRR 539 paras 61–5 PC.
[120] *No 41571/98* hudoc (2001) DA (Court remained satisfied that the safeguards employed in *Brannigan and McBride* continued to 'provide an important measure of protection against arbitrary behaviour and incommunicado detention', at p 13).
[121] A 258-B (1993); 17 EHRR 539 paras 47 and 51 PC.

had taken the view that the detention power was compatible with Article 5 and that no derogation was necessary. The withdrawal of the notice did not show that there was no emergency, nor that it was not one for which the power was strictly required. The Court agreed. It rejected by a majority the arguments that because there had been no increase in the intensity of the emergency in the time between the withdrawal of the notice and the judgment in *Brogan* there was no power to rely on Article 15, and so the real purpose of the British government had been to avoid the effect of the *Brogan* judgment.[122] The British government's claim was that the *power* of extended detention had always been necessary and that the dispute hinged only on the appropriate legal basis for it.

II. MARGIN OF APPRECIATION

The Court accepts that the state has a margin of appreciation in assessing whether the measures which it has taken were 'strictly required'. In *Brannigan and McBride v UK*,[123] the Court stated that the respondent state would benefit from a '*wide* margin of appreciation', however the emphasized word was not used in the *Marshall v UK*[124] decision. Either way the practical effect is that the decision about what measures to adopt, whether to modify them, whether to continue or discontinue them, so long as they otherwise satisfy Article 15, is principally for the state. Matters of prudence or expediency are not for the Court.[125] While the Court did not refer explicitly to the margin of appreciation in the *Lawless* case, it did rely on the idea in *Ireland v UK*,[126] when it said, in somewhat curious language, that internment could 'reasonably have been considered strictly required' by the emergency. The words used in *Brannigan and McBride v UK*,[127] couched in the negative, further underline the primacy of the state's assessment of what is strictly required. At one stage, the Court noted that, 'The Commission was of the opinion that the government had *not overstepped* their margin of appreciation ...' and it said that, 'it *cannot be said* that the government *have exceeded* their margin of appreciation ...'[128] and again, 'the Court takes the view that the government have *not exceeded* their margin of appreciation ...'.[129] This essentially negative review, which takes into account matters of evidence, necessity, proportionality, adequacy of safeguards, individually and together, does not amount to a particularly intrusive form of review, despite the strong words of Article 15(1).[130] What it does do is force the state into a public justification for its actions but there are some doubts whether this is enough.[131] Too generous an employment of a margin of appreciation avoids a rigorous review by the Court of alternative, less authoritarian, methods that might have been employed by the respondent state. This would not accord with the notion of real and effective protection, a principle that has been at the heart of so much Strasbourg jurisprudence.

---

[122] Van Dijk and Van Hoof, at p 1073, maintain that the events demonstrated the bad faith of the British government.

[123] A 258-B (1993); 17 EHRR 539 paras 57 and 43 PC, emphasis added.

[124] *No 41571/98* hudoc (2001) DA.

[125] *Ireland v UK* A 25 (1978); 2 EHRR 25 paras 207 and 214 PC.   [126] Id, para 213.

[127] A 258-B (1993); 17 EHRR 539 para 57 PC, emphasis added.   [128] Id, para 60, emphasis added.

[129] Id, para 66, emphasis added. Cf, *Marshall v UK No 41571/98* hudoc (2001) DA, on the facts the authorities had not 'overstepp[ed] ... the margin of appreciation which is accorded to the authorities in determining their response to the threat to the community', at p 12.

[130] The Court's approach is endorsed by Merrills, *The Development of International Law by the European Court of Human Rights*, 2nd edn, 1993, pp 139–40.

[131] *Brannigan and McBride v UK* A 258-B (1993); 17 EHRR 539 PC, Judge Martens, concurring, Judges Pettiti and Walsh dissenting. See also Marks, 15 OJLS 69, 84–95 (1995).

The Council of Europe's Commissioner for Human Rights has argued that national authorities enjoy a large margin of appreciation in respect of derogations 'precisely because the Convention presupposes domestic controls in the form of a preventive parliamentary scrutiny and posterior judicial review'.[132] In the *A and Others* case the House of Lords refused to follow the Strasbourg jurisprudence to the extent that the government was not afforded the equivalent of a 'wide' or 'large' margin of appreciation on the issue of whether the measures taken by the state in response to the derogation made were 'strictly required'. Given the importance of the right at stake several or the Law Lords emphasized the duty of a national court, in distinction to an international one, to scrutinize the actions of the executive with close attention. In particular it was more appropriate for a domestic court, rather than an international one,[133] to assess the relative effectiveness of competing alternative measures that might be less harmful to the rights of the individuals concerned so as to establish the disproportionate nature of the existing measures. By eight votes to one, the Law Lords held that the special detention regime was, *inter alia*, disproportional (and, in fact, discriminatory) for a combination of reasons. These included the fact that the Secretary of State had not established that the special detention arrangements were 'strictly required' by the public emergency in that he had not shown that monitoring arrangements or movement restrictions less severe than incarceration in prison would have sufficed.

6. OTHER INTERNATIONAL LAW OBLIGATIONS

Even if measures of derogation can be justified under Article 15, a state is precluded from relying on them if their introduction would breach other international law obligations of the state.[134] This specific provision reinforces the general principle of Article 53.[135] The obvious sources of treaty obligations are the ICCPR[136] and the Geneva Red Cross Conventions.[137] It is conceivable that the European Union treaties could contain obligations which would be relevant to emergency measures, especially if the emergency were economic or industrial in character. While the terms of Article 15(1) do not preclude obligations under customary international law, these are unlikely to raise any questions in practice because of the wide participation of the European states in the Covenant and the Conventions. In all these cases, it will be necessary for the European Court to interpret the other treaty to identify the state's obligation. In practice, this provision has been of little significance. In *Lawless v Ireland*[138] and *Ireland v UK*,[139] the Court decided that the measures of derogation did not conflict with the defendant state's obligations, if any, under international law. In *Brannigan and McBride v UK*,[140] it was argued that

---

[132] *Opinion of the Commissioner for Human Rights, Mr Alvaro Gil-Robes on certain aspects of the UK 2001 derogation from Article 5 par. 1 of the European Convention on Human Rights*, CommDH (2002)7/28 August 2002 (hereafter '*Opinion of the Commissioner for Human Rights*') para 9.

[133] See eg, Lord Rodger at para 176 and Lord Hope, para 114 and paras 108, 130–1 (citing the *Opinion of the Commissioner for Human Rights*) see also Lord Bingham at para 40.

[134] See Allain, 5 EHRLR (2005) 480.

[135] Article 53: 'Nothing in this Convention shall be construed as limiting or derogating from any of the human rights and fundamental freedoms which may be ensured under the laws of any High Contracting Party or *under any other agreement to which it is a Party*' (emphasis added).

[136] All the Convention member states are parties to the ICCPR.

[137] The great majority of Convention member states are parties to the 1949 Geneva Conventions.

[138] A 3 (1961); 1 EHRR 15 para 41. The Court undertook this inquiry *proprio motu*.

[139] A 25 (1978); 2 EHRR 25 para 222 PC (Geneva Conventions).

[140] A 258-B (1993); 17 EHRR 539 para 68 PC.

the more stringent provisions of Article 4 of the ICCPR—that the existence of the emergency be 'officially proclaimed'—had not been satisfied. There was a dispute between the applicants and the government about what Article 4 required. The Court disclaimed any responsibility to resolve it authoritatively but was satisfied that parliamentary statements by a British minister were sufficient in terms of their certainty and publicity to comply with Article 4.[141] The Court said that it was obliged to examine the applicants' argument but it found it was without 'any plausible basis'.[142] The Court in *Marshall* was quick to dismiss the ICCPR's Human Rights Committee's adverse comments regarding the measures taken pursuant to the emergency situation in Northern Ireland in 1996.

According to Article 4(1) ICCPR one of the conditions for the justifiability of any derogation from the Covenant is that the measures taken do not involve discrimination solely on the ground of race, colour, sex, language, religion, or social origin.[143] Article 4 contains a longer list of non-derogable provisions than Article 15(2). It is a convincing argument that a state which is a party to the Convention and the ICCPR is precluded from derogating under the Convention from those rights listed in Article 4 that are not in Article 15(2), *viz* the right not be imprisoned for the non-fulfilment of a contractual obligation, the right to be recognized as a person before the law, and the right to freedom of thought, etc.[144]

One of the arguments put to the Commission by the applicant government in *Cyprus v Turkey*[145] was that Turkey was not entitled to avail itself of Article 15 because its military action in Cyprus was an aggressive war in breach of its obligations under the UN Charter. The Commission found that Turkey was not entitled to rely on Article 15 in any event because there was no declaration of derogation with respect to northern Cyprus[146] and did not address the 'aggressive war' claim. This was perhaps as well. Such matters are for the UN Security Council and the consideration of them by the Strasbourg authorities would raise enormously complicated problems of fact-finding and intricate legal questions. If the Security Council had determined that a state was the aggressor, then perhaps the Strasbourg authorities could draw legal conclusions from this finding, which, on an *ex turpi causa* basis, might include denying the government the right to take advantage of Article 15.

7. ARTICLE 15(2): THE NON-DEROGABLE PROVISIONS

Whatever the seriousness of the emergency and however convincing the case a state might make that a derogation was strictly required, in no circumstances may a state depart from its obligations under Articles 2, 3, 4(1), and 7. These limitations are not the absolute prohibitions they might at first appear. Article 15(2) itself makes an exception for deaths

---

[141] Id, paras 73–4.   [142] Id, para 72.

[143] In the *A and Others* case Lord Bingham ruled that the measures applied by the British government had been discriminatory in violation of Article 14 of the Convention and also Article 26 of the ICCPR which he argued applied by virtue of the 'other obligations under international law' clause of Article 15, *A and Others v Secretary of State for the Home Department* [2004] UKHL 56, Lord Bingham para 68.

[144] Van Dijk and Van Hoof, at p 1067. In 2001 the Human Rights Committee produced a detailed General Comment regarding the operation of Article 4 ICCPR. In this it pointed out that in addition to those rights specifically listed under Article 4, in its view, there were certain other obligations under the ICCPR (and, in fact, international law generally) that were non-derogable. Human Rights Committee *General Comment No 29, op cit,* see especially para 13 and also para 16 relevant to *habeas corpus* and core aspects of the right to a fair trial.

[145] *Cyprus v Turkey* 4 EHRR 482 at 552 (1976) Com Rep; CM Res DH (79) 1.   [146] Id, 556.

resulting from lawful acts of war and Article 2 contains exceptions, some of which, such as the right to use force resulting in death to suppress an insurrection, are clearly relevant to some kinds of emergency.[147] Article 7(2) of the Convention provides an exception to the proscription against retrospective criminal penalties, which may be applicable in some emergency situations, notably international armed conflicts. There are no limitations in Articles 3 and 4(1) and these, it has been pointed out, are the only true absolute obligations in the Convention.[148]

Although there is no specific reference to them in Article 15, there are other provisions of the Convention which may have an impact on the legality of measures of derogation. One example is Article 14.[149] In *Ireland v UK*,[150] the Court examined the Irish government's complaint that internment had been applied discriminatorily to republican/nationalist suspects in conjunction with Article 5. It held that there were objective and reasonable differences between republican/nationalist and loyalist/unionist violence, notably the much greater extent of the former. Furthermore, the authorities had found it easier to proceed in the ordinary courts against loyalist/unionist defendants. There was, accordingly, no breach of Article 14 combined with Article 5 and, thus, no need to consider the matter separately under Article 15. Judge Matscher, who dissented on this matter, raised but did not answer the question whether a breach of Article 14 could be strictly necessary within the terms of Article 15(1). He alluded to this again in *Brannigan and McBride v UK*.[151] In the *A and Others*[152] case, a majority of the House of Lords held that even in the context of the subsisting public emergency there had been a violation of Article 14 read with Article 5 given the discriminatory treatment existing (on grounds of nationality) between suspected international terrorists and UK nationals who were also suspected of terrorism.

The American Convention on Human Rights prohibits the suspension of a list of numerated substantive rights and also 'the judicial guarantees essential for the protection of such rights' (Article 27(2)).[153] Relying on these words, the Inter-American Court has advised that states may not suspend the rights to a judicial remedy to test the lawfulness of detention (Article 7(6)) and the general right of judicial protection (Article 25). The Inter-American Court recognized that the right of emergency derogation was not unlimited and that, both in the scope and application of emergency measures, national courts had a role to play in guaranteeing that the emergency powers were not exceeded.[154] While this argument cannot be made in precisely the same terms, given the language of Article 15 of the European Convention, it does enhance the position taken by the Court that the proportionality of derogation measures will ordinarily require a process for their supervision to prevent or reduce the possibility of abuse.

---

[147] Cases involving the use of force which has resulted in death in Northern Ireland have been argued under Article 2, see Ch 2. Derogation under Article 15 from the Sixth Protocol—which abolishes the death penalty—is prohibited (Article 3, Sixth Protocol), but Article 2 of that Protocol allows states to make provision for the death penalty for acts committed in time of or under imminent threat of war, another exception which would be applicable in certain kinds of emergency. Protocol 13, however, abolishes the death penalty in all circumstances.

[148] Higgins, 48 BYIL 281 (1976–77) p 306.

[149] There is also conceivably room for the application of Articles 17 and 18 as limitations on a state's powers under Article 15.

[150] A 25 (1978); 2 EHRR 25 paras 225–32 PC.   [151] A 258-B (1993); 17 EHRR 539 PC.

[152] [2004] UKHL 56.

[153] See Fitzpatrick, in Harris and Livingstone, eds, *The Inter-American System of Human Rights*, 1998.

[154] See n 98 above.

8. ARTICLE 15(3):
THE PROCEDURAL REQUIREMENTS

The Convention does not expressly require an effective domestic parliamentary scrutiny of the decision to enter a derogation under Article 15, and the Court has not addressed this issue.[155] The specific requirement of Article 15(3) is that a state relying on the right of derogation shall keep the Secretary General fully informed of the measures it has taken and the reasons for doing so. The importance of this safeguard is that the Secretary General informs the other parties to the Convention about the notice of derogation.[156] If the idea that the Convention contains a collective guarantee is to mean anything at all, it surely ought to apply when exceptional measures of interference with human rights are introduced. The other parties to the Convention are thus put on notice that there is a situation which demands their consideration. As mentioned already, Article 4 of the ICCPR requires a public proclamation of the emergency. In *Cyprus v Turkey*,[157] the Commission said that some formal and public declaration of the state of emergency (unless special circumstances prevented it) was a precondition for reliance on Article 15(1).

The obligation under Article 15(3) is not necessarily one of prior notification, that is to say, prior to the date from which the state wishes to execute the measures of derogation, at least if the state can give reasons why this should be so. In *Ireland v UK*,[158] the British government explained that its notifications (communicated on 20 August 1971) had been delayed until after the implementation of internment (9 August 1971) so that no persons whom it was desired to detain might have notice and escape. In accepting the adequacy of this justification,[159] the Court relied on the *Lawless* case,[160] where a twelve-day delay in notification was accepted as having been made 'without delay'. In the *Greek* case,[161] the Commission concluded that Greece had 'not fully met the requirements of Article 15(3)'. In particular, while the Commission did not find that Article 15(3) required the state to identify the provisions from which it was derogating, the respondent government had failed to communicate to the Secretary General the texts of some of its emergency legislation and had not provided full information on the administrative measures taken, especially measures for the detention of persons without a court order; the provision of information to the Commission in the course of the proceedings in the application brought against the state was not a substitute for its obligation to communicate the required information to the Secretary General. In addition, it had not informed the Secretary General of the reasons for the measures of derogation for more than four months after they had been taken. Since the *Greek* case, notices of derogation have generally appeared adequate for the purpose of Article 15(3) and to have been delivered without delay.[162] The exception has been Turkey's unwillingness to accept responsibility under the Convention for the acts of its forces in northern Cyprus, which has led it not to make any formal declaration applicable there.[163] Turkey maintained that it had no jurisdiction

---

[155] See, however, text accompanying n 132 above.

[156] The Secretary General circulates notices of derogation to other member states: CM Res (56) 16. See also the *Greek* case, 12 YB (the *Greek* case) 1 at 42 (1969).

[157] *Cyprus v Turkey* 4 EHRR 482 (1976) para 527 Com Rep; CM Res DH (79)1. But note the dissent of Mr Sperduti in *Cyprus v Turkey* and the judgment of the Court in *Lawless v Ireland* A 3 (1961); 1 EHRR 15 para 47.

[158] A 25 (1978); 2 EHRR 25 para 80 PC.   [159] Id, para 223.   [160] A 3 (1961); 1 EHRR 15 para 47.

[161] 12 YB (the *Greek* case) 1 at 41–2 (1969); CM Res DH (70) 1.   [162] Oraa, *loc cit*, n 1, above, p 85.

[163] *Cyprus v Turkey* 4 EHRR (1976) 482 at 555–556; CM Res DH (79) 1 and id, *No 8007/77*, para 67, 72 DR 5 at 24 (1992).

over any part of Cyprus, which was exercised in the northern part of the island by the Turkish Cypriot authorities.[164] The Commission took the view that Turkey is responsible under the Convention for acts which can be attributed to its armed forces, wherever they may be.[165]

Because the Commission found that there was no emergency in the *Greek* case, it had no need to consider what were the legal consequences of a violation of Article 15(3). While it might be salutary if the Strasbourg authorities regarded a deficiency in notification as rendering the declaration a nullity, the seriousness of what is at stake if the state demonstrates the existence of an emergency at the appropriate time may equally make it appear too draconian a sanction and one which is likely to be of little efficacy. Higgins[166] suggests that failure to notify in reasonable time might be evidence of bad faith which would be a matter to be taken into account in deciding whether Article 15(1) was satisfied.

Article 15(3) requires that the Secretary General be notified when the derogation measures have been terminated. The Court has said that Article 15(3) implies an obligation to keep the need for emergency measures under permanent review, an obligation implicit in the proportionality of any measures of derogation.[167] Action taken under measures justified only by the emergency may not be continued after the emergency has ended.[168]

9. PROPOSALS FOR REFORM AND THE ROLE OF THE COMMISSIONER FOR HUMAN RIGHTS OF THE COUNCIL OF EUROPE

Judge MacDonald, a former Judge on the 'old' Court, has stated '[a]n emergency or crisis situation challenging a state Party is also a test for Convention system as a whole... If the Convention system can function only when times are good, but fails to respond to a real emergency, then its authority and legitimacy in all situations is undermined.'[169] Some strong arguments have been made for the case that the institutions of the Council of Europe should have a more proactive role in the supervision of derogations made under Article 15 (as opposed to the merely reactive role performed by the European Court after an application reaches it).[170] Although these do not specifically relate to how Article 15 should be interpreted and applied by the Court, they are referred to here briefly as they highlight the general weaknesses of the supervision regime available under that Article and the consequential need for monitoring by other bodies within the Council of Europe.

It is a major weakness of Article 15 that once a derogation has been entered it is necessary for an individual or inter-state application to be made before the Court can address

---

[164] *Cyprus v Turkey Nos 6780/74 and 6950/74*, 2 DR 125 at 130 (1975). See Necatigil, *The Cyprus Question and the Turkish Position in International Law*, 1989, pp 94–100.

[165] *Cyprus v Turkey* 4 EHRR 482 at 509 (1982); CM Res DH (79) 1 and id, *No 8077/77*, 72 DR 5 at 23 (1992). The Commission declined also to accept Turkey's argument that its Article 15 declaration for parts of its national territory could be taken into account with respect to its treatment of Greek Cypriots taken to Turkey. See now *Loizidou v Turkey* A 310 (1995); 20 EHRR 99 GC and *Cyprus v Turkey* 2001-IV; 35 EHRR 731 GC.

[166] *Loc cit*, n 148 above, p 291. See also Van Dijk and Van Hoof at pp 1069–71.

[167] *Brannigan and McBride v UK* A 258-B (1993); 17 EHRR 539 para 54 PC.

[168] *De Becker v Belgium*, B 4 (1962); 1 EHRR 43 para 271 Com Rep.

[169] Macdonald, in *Ryssdal Melanges* p 817.   [170] See especially, Macdonald, *ibid*.

the derogation's validity and the proportionality of the measures taken in accordance with it. As has been the case in the past, even when such an application has been made the ensuing judgment from the Court is delivered a number of years after the declaration of the emergency. This entails the real risk that the existence of the emergency and the measures taken pursuant to it remain wholly unsupervised for a considerable period of time, and perhaps at the very time when supervision, guidance and, quite possibly, condemnation are required. In this connection it has been proposed that the powers of the Secretary General of the Council of Europe under Articles 15(3) and 52 be widened so as to enable requests for further information on derogations as and when necessary and assuming that the initial information provision (required by Article 15(3)) is regarded as inadequate. More effective would be the implementation of a requirement for states to submit periodic reports to the Secretary General regarding the ongoing existence of the emergency and the proportionality of the measures taken. Similarly, the Committee of Ministers might be given some sort of monitoring role once a derogation notice has been submitted to the Secretary General. A role for this institution might be regarded as particularly appropriate in some instances given the political attributes of that body and the power it has to impose sanctions such as expulsion from the Council of Europe.

It is part of the mandate of the Commissioner for Human Rights of the Council of Europe[171] to 'identify possible shortcomings in the law and practice of member states concerning the compliance with human rights as embodied in the instruments of the Council of Europe'.[172] He may 'issue recommendations, opinions and reports',[173] though he must not take up individual complaints and must 'respect the competence of, and perform functions other than those fulfilled by, the supervisory bodies set up under the European Convention of Human Rights'.[174] There is some scope therefore for the monitoring of derogations and it is noteworthy that in 2002 the Commissioner for Human Rights issued an opinion on certain aspects of the United Kingdom's 2001 derogation from Article 5(1) of the European Convention on Human Rights.[175] Amongst other things this was critical of the adequacy of the UK procedure with respect to derogations in terms of whether there existed sufficient initial parliamentary scrutiny of the decision to derogate. It also commented on the regime in place according to domestic law for review and renewal of the derogation, and was critical of whether the measures taken by the British government were fully justified.

10. RESERVATIONS TO ARTICLE 15

When France ratified the Convention, it made the following reservation to Article 15(1):

Firstly, that the circumstances specified in Article 16 of the Constitution regarding the implementation of that Article, in section 1 of the Act of 3 April 1878 and the Act of 9 August 1849 regarding proclamation of a state of siege, and in section 1 of Act No 55–385 of 3 April 1955 regarding proclamation of a state of emergency, and in which it is permissible to apply the provisions of those texts, must be understood as complying with the purpose of Article 15 of the Convention and that, secondly, for the interpretation and application of

---

[171] See <http://www.coe.int/t/commissioner/default_EN.asp>.

[172] Articles 3(e) of Resolution (99) 50 of the Committee of Ministers on the Commissioner for Human Rights.

[173] Id, Article 8(1).   [174] Id, Article 1(2).

[175] *Opinion of the Commissioner for Human Rights, op cit* n 132.

Article 16 of the Constitution of the Republic, the terms 'to the extent strictly required by the exigencies of the situation' shall not restrict the power of the President of the Republic to take 'the measures required by the circumstances'.[176]

The validity of the reservation has never been an issue in any application.[177] It surely could not be maintained that, if the French government found it necessary to resort to treatment which violated Article 2 or Article 3 to meet an emergency, the effect of the reservation would be to preclude consideration of a case challenging the action. In *France, Norway, Denmark, Sweden and Netherlands v Turkey*,[178] Turkey argued that that in line with the principle of reciprocity, the terms of the reservation precluded France contesting emergency measures taken by Turkey under Article 15(1). The Commission rejected this, relying on the objective nature of the obligation under the Convention.

11. CONCLUSION

Article 15 occupies a very important position in the Convention. It might be intolerable for a state faced by an extraordinary crisis not to be able to derogate from certain of the international obligations the Convention provides for. One justification for suspension of full enjoyment of derogable rights in the circumstances covered by Article 15 is that without such drastic measures it could transpire that there would be an even greater threat to the liberty and freedom of a population, and perhaps even the existence of the state itself. In other words, derogations can be justified upon the basis of preserving democracy and maintaining the fabric of the state.

Derogation from the Convention is and has been an exceptional event. It must be anticipated that a democratic state will usually think hard before resort to Article 15 because of the political consequences of acknowledging there to be a 'public emergency'. However, although it is notable how few states have resorted to Article 15 in the past, one wonders what message the Article 15 jurisprudence might communicate to them for the future. The *Aksoy* judgment revealed that the Court has indicated that there are limits beyond which a state may not proceed even during an emergency. In the more borderline cases, the Court has been content to employ a wide margin of appreciation so as to favour the state when it finds the reassurance provided by safeguards against abuse (*Brannigan and McBride*). Does this jurisprudence, in particular the reliance on a wide margin of appreciation, convey the message that Strasbourg scrutiny of Article 15 issues will not be particularly rigorous?

With respect to Article 15 in particular one sees a real tension between the status of the Court as an international institution and as a human rights tribunal interpreting a Convention, which, as it has stated on many occasions, is designed to protect rights that are not theoretical and illusory but which are real and effective.

On the one hand, it may observed that the Strasbourg Court is an international Court and the Convention system as a whole is founded on the principle of subsidiarity. From *that* perspective in assessing the fair balance to be struck between the rights of individuals

---

[176] 17 YB 4 (1974). See also the Andorran reservation to Article 15, the text of which is available at <http://conventions.coe.int>.

[177] It has been argued that the French reservation 'conflicts with the Convention', Van Dijk and Van Hoof, at p 1110. On the status of France's equivalent reservation to the International Covenant on Civil and Political Rights, see McGoldrick, *The Human Rights Committee*, 1991, pp 304–5.

[178] *Nos 9940–9944/82*, 35 DR 143 at 168–9 (1983) Com Rep; 44 DR 31 (1985) F Sett.

and the general interest of the community a respondent government that has derogated in good faith and is seen to be democratic should surely be given a significant benefit of doubt assuming there has been proper domestic review of the emergency and its associated measures. If this entails a risk that in practice the absolute minimum interference with rights does not occur this might be accepted for several reasons. First, restricting rights to the absolute minimum required by the circumstances in emergency scenarios is not an exact science. Furthermore, an international institution of control should be reluctant to second-guess governmental actions growing out of Article 15. Indeed, the Court risks being accused of adjudicating too much with the luxury of hindsight, perhaps meddling too deeply in affairs about which it has little practical expertise, detached from the true realities and politics of a highly complex situation, and precisely at a time of great sensitivity for the respondent state concerned. This would appear to be the rationale for the application of a margin of appreciation by the Court in the case law although, as has been noted,[179] apart from the statements made in *Ireland v UK* the Court itself has provided little explanation of its rationale generally here.

On the other hand, it may be observed that practice has demonstrated that it is precisely during emergency situations that some of the greatest threats to the human rights of individuals arise. Arguably, therefore, it is inappropriate for the Court's power of review to be confined in effect to assessing essentially not much more than the general good faith nature of declarations of public emergency and the measures taken in connection with it, especially when that 'emergency' has existed for some time. From this perspective the Court has been sharply criticized for being too deferential in its approach to Article 15, especially its examination of whether the measures taken in accordance with a derogation are 'strictly required'.[180] It has been argued that the deference employed 'inject[s] a strong subjective element into the interpretation of the European Convention, weakening the Court's authoritative position vis-à-vis national Governments', which may 'in turn, undermine any hope of effective regional supervision and enforcement of rights protected by the European Convention'.[181] In particular it has been said that the Court has wrongly condoned entrenched public emergencies.[182]

It may be argued that the use of a wide margin of appreciation as regards the existence of a 'public emergency' may be compensated for by a more stringent examination by the Court under the second limb of Article 15(1), 'exigencies of the situation'. However, if the Court wishes to dispel the perception that it has been simply too slack in its application of Article 15 and that there is, for example, almost ritual incantation of the margin of appreciation in such case law, it might, as one commentator has requested, provide 'a more principled approach' to the application of that doctrine in the context of Article 15.[183] To the extent that the Court has apparently granted a wide margin of appreciation in individual cases on the basis that it believes that there are sufficient safeguards against abuse, the Court would serve European public law well if it could explain more clearly why this was so and why, for example, it is convinced that less stringent alternative measures were not more appropriate. Is it correct, as the Council of Europe's European Commissioner for Human Rights has suggested, that it is 'precisely because the Convention presupposes domestic controls in the form of a preventive parliamentary scrutiny and posterior judicial review that national authorities enjoy a large margin of appreciation in respect

---

[179]   O'Boyle, 19 HRLJ 23 (1998) at 25.
[180]   Marks, 15 OJLS (1995) 85; Gross and Ní Aoláin, 23(1) HRQ (2001); Gross, 23 YJIL (1998) 437; and Campbell, 54 ICLQ (2005) 321.
[181]   Gross and Ní Aoláin, id, pp 628–9.
[182]   Gross, 23 Yale JIL 437 (1998) and Marks, 15 OJLS (1995) 85.
[183]   O'Boyle, 19 HRLJ 23 (1998) at 29.

of derogations'?[184] If so, what is encompassed by 'preventive parliamentary scrutiny and posterior judicial review'? Article 15 judgments are perhaps the ultimate test for the Court in deciding 'those cases brought before [it] but [also], more generally, [its role in] elucidat[ing], safeguard[ing] and develop[ing] the rules instituted by the Convention, thereby contributing to the observance by the states of the engagements undertaken by them as Contracting Parties'.[185]

---

[184] *Opinion of the Commissioner for Human Rights,* op cit n 132, para 9.
[185] *Ireland v UK* A 25 (1978); 2 EHRR 25 para 154 PC

17

ARTICLES 16–18: OTHER RESTRICTIONS UPON THE RIGHTS PROTECTED

1. ARTICLE 16: RESTRICTIONS ON THE POLITICAL RIGHTS OF ALIENS

Article 16

Nothing in Articles 10, 11 and 14 shall be regarded as preventing the High Contracting Parties from imposing restrictions on the political activities of aliens.

Article 16 allows potentially wide-ranging interference with the political rights of aliens. It runs counter to the basic principle of Article 1 that rights in the Convention are to be enjoyed by 'everyone within [the state's] jurisdiction'.[1] It applies specifically to Articles 10 and 11 but there is no indication that the reference to Article 14 is confined to restrictions imposed on aliens' rights under those articles. Rather, it appears that the state may take advantage of Article 16 with respect to discriminatory rules within the ambit of any of the Convention's provisions. This includes rights under Article 3 of the First Protocol involving the right to vote.[2] Draconian though such a power would be, it must not be forgotten that a state has the ultimate remedy of deportation against an alien to whose activities it objects and the Convention provides no direct protection[3] against the use of that power, even if it is because of the political activities of the person expelled.[4] The right to vote in national law is frequently confined to citizens. Article 25 of the International Covenant on Civil and Political Rights also protects the right to vote expressly for citizens only and the United Nations Declaration on the Human Rights of Individuals who are not Nationals of the Country in which They Live[5] does not afford any protection for the political rights of aliens.

Piermont v France[6] was the first case in which the Court had to give serious consideration to Article 16. The applicant was an environmental activist who was a member of the European Parliament, elected in Germany, and had been invited to French overseas territories in the South Pacific by groups opposed to the French government's nuclear testing policy. She went to French Polynesia and took part in peaceful demonstrations

---

[1] Distinctions are drawn between nationals and aliens with respect to freedom of movement, see Articles 3 and 4 of the Fourth Protocol, Ch 21, and, formally at least, there is different protection for national and alien-owned property under Article 1 of the First Protocol: see below, Ch 18.

[2] *Mathieu-Mohin v Belgium* A 113 (1987); 10 EHRR 1 para 54 PC.

[3] Indirect protection may be provided by Article 3 (likely treatment in destination state, see below, pp 79–90) or Article 8 (family ties in expelling state).

[4] See *Agee v UK No 7729/76*, 7 DR 164 (1976).   [5] GA Res 40/53.

[6] A 314 (1995); 20 EHRR 301.

against the government, but was formally expelled from the territory and forbidden to re-enter. One of her claims was that the action violated her rights of expression under Article 10, either alone or in conjunction with Article 14. For its part, the respondent government argued that the interference, if not otherwise justified under the Convention, could be excused by relying on Article 16. However, the Court refused to accept this, the majority maintaining that Article 16 could not be raised against Mrs Piermont to restrict her Article 10 rights as she was a national of an EU state and a member of the European Parliament, and this 'especially as the people of the [Overseas Territories] take part in the European Parliament elections'.[7] The case was, therefore considered under Article 10 alone, with a narrow majority of the Court finding that the interference with the applicant's rights was disproportionate to the protection of any interest under Article 10(2).

The Court in *Piermont* refused to accept the applicant's argument that Article 16 did not apply on the simple basis that she was a European citizen, since 'the Community treaties did not at the time [of the facts] recognise any such citizenship'.[8] If, as seems to be the implication, today European Union citizens are not considered to be 'aliens' for the purposes of Article 16,[9] this will be an important re-reading of the text. There has been no ruling or decision on the point.

Even if Article 16 does have relevance to a case this would not necessarily mean that the host state has an unfettered right to restrict the exercise of Articles 10 and 11 by an 'alien', as the joint partly dissenting opinion of four judges[10] in *Piermont* noted. Referring to 'the increased internationalisation of politics in modern circumstances' they took the view that the principles embodied in Article 16 could be taken into account in the context of the restrictions found under the second paragraphs of Articles 10 and 11.

Finally, it should be stressed that Article 16 only expressly applies to the 'political activities' of aliens. The Court might be persuaded to interpret these words narrowly to include only matters directly part of the political process: the setting up and the operation of political parties; expression in connection with the programmes and campaigns of these parties; and participation in elections which fall within Article 3 of the First Protocol. Even so, there remains the possibility that a state could take advantage of Article 16 to inhibit the political activities of expatriate groups, the opportunities for which increase as European states become more cosmopolitan communities. The Parliamentary Assembly has called for the deletion of Article 16.[11]

2. ARTICLE 17: RESTRICTIONS ON ACTIVITIES SUBVERSIVE OF CONVENTION RIGHTS

Article 17

Nothing in this Convention may be interpreted as implying for any state, group or person any right to engage in any activity or perform any act aimed at the destruction of any of

---

[7] Id, para 64. See, however, the joint partly dissenting opinion of Judges Ryssdal, Matscher, Sir John Freeland, and Jungwiert at paras 4–5.

[8] *Ibid.*

[9] Cf, European Union citizenship now recognized under EC Treaty Articles 17–18(1).

[10] *Piermont*, id, joint partly dissenting opinion of Judges Ryssdal, Matscher, Sir John Freeland, and Jungwiert.

[11] Recommendation 799 (1977) on the Political Rights and Position of Aliens, CE Parl Ass, 28th Ord sess, 3rd Pt, Texts Adopted.

the rights and freedoms set forth herein or at their limitation to a greater extent than is provided for in the Convention.

I. INTRODUCTION

The function of Article 17 is 'to protect the rights enshrined in the Convention by safeguarding the free functioning of democratic institutions....'[12] One of its main objectives is 'to prevent totalitarian or extremist groups from justifying their activities by referring to the Convention',[13] for example by relying on Article 10 to advocate violent racist programmes. Article 17 is to be seen in the context of the emphasis placed by the Court on the protection of democracy, in particular Strasbourg jurisprudence expounding the notion of 'a democracy capable of defending itself'.[14] The notion that the Convention's provisions may not be relied upon to weaken or destroy the ideals and values of a democratic society has been at the heart of key judgments such as *Refah Partisi (The Welfare Party) v Turkey*.[15]

Cases involving Article 17 have usually involved applicants with controversial racist, religious, or political agendas claiming that their freedom of expression or freedom of association rights have been breached by the state. In such cases the state will often claim that censorship of some sort or, as the case may be, the banning of a political party is a necessary measure as the ambition of the applicant is to destroy the rights of others. It will maintain that Article 17 applies such that the applicant will not be able to rely on a Convention right.

It has been suggested that for Article 17 to apply 'the aim of the offending actions must be to spread violence or hatred, to resort to illegal or undemocratic methods, to encourage the use of violence, to undermine the nation's democratic and pluralist political system, or to pursue objectives that are racist or likely to destroy the rights and freedoms of others'.[16] However, it is important to appreciate that Article 17 only comes into play when the applicant actually seeks to rely on the Convention to destroy the rights it protects, not other interests. Hence, the Court refused the Turkish government's argument that Article 17 applied to a series of cases concerning political parties which had been banned for reasons such as acting contrary to the unity of the Turkish nation[17] (ie an interest that the Convention did not directly protect).

Article 17 allows action to be taken against an individual where he seeks to use his Convention rights in a subversive way, but this does not mean that such a person is deprived of all Convention rights. The Article covers 'essentially [only] those rights which, if invoked, will facilitate the attempt to derive therefrom a right to engage personally in activities aimed at the destruction of any of the rights and freedoms set forth in the Convention'.[18] So, in *Lawless v Ireland*,[19] the Court held that, even if the applicant,

---

[12] *KPD v FRG No 250/57*, 1 YB 222 at 223 (1957).

[13] *Zdanoka v Latvia* hudoc (2004); 41 EHRR 659 para 109 (Chamber judgment).

[14] See *Zdanoka v Latvia* hudoc (2006); 45 EHRR 478 paras 98–101 GC.

[15] 2003-II; 37 EHRR 1 paras 98–9 GC.

[16] *Lehideux and Isorni v France* 1998-VII; 30 EHRR 665, concurring opinion of Judge Jambrek para 2, citing observations made by the delegate of the Commission before the Court in the *United Communist Party* case, see *United Communist Party of Turkey v Turkey* 1998-I; 26 EHRR 121 para 23 GC.

[17] See eg, *United Communist Party* case, id, para 60. Cf, *WP v Poland No 42264/98* hudoc (2004) DA where the Court applied Article 17 in an application concerning a banned association as its memorandum of association included statements that could revive anti-Semitism (inadmissible).

[18] *WP v Poland, ibid.*

[19] A 3 (1961); 1 EHRR 15 para 7. In *Open Door and Well Women v Ireland* A 246 (1992); 15 EHRR 244 paras 78–9 PC, the Court rejected an argument by the government based on Article 17 and Article 60 that Article 10

who was interned under an accusation of being a member of a terrorist organization, could have been deprived of some of his rights under the Convention, the state was not, by that reason alone, entitled to deprive him of his rights under Articles 5 and 6. After all, Lawless was not seeking to take advantage of his rights under Articles 5 and 6 in order to subvert the rights of others. The result is that Article 17, whether in conjunction with Article 14 or otherwise, is most likely to be called in aid by a state when it acts to restrict rights under Articles 8, 10, and 11 and under Article 3 of the First Protocol.[20]

The Commission and Court have approached the actual application of Article 17 in various ways in the past.[21] An important issue is whether Article 17 is addressed by the Court at the merits stage of its examination of an application, or at the admissibility stage. Article 17 may concern some controversial cases and the effect of its application is very significant, for it potentially negates the exercise of a particular right(s) by a group or individual. It is important therefore that Article 17 is strictly scrutinized by the Court. So, unless it is clear from the facts that an application is manifestly ill-founded under Article 17, the best approach is for the Court to examine the case on the merits,[22] or at least ensure that dismissal at the admissibility stage is by a Chamber rather than a committee of three.

II. ARTICLE 17 PLEADED BY THE STATE

When relied upon by a state, Article 17 is intended as a safeguard against the threat of totalitarianism, especially in circumstances where the threat has not reached such proportions that the state could rely on Article 15 and where there might be difficulties in showing that an interference with an individual's rights was otherwise justified under the Convention.

The original threat to which Article 17 was directed was communist manipulation of political rights. Hence, in a very early decision,[23] the Commission held that an order banning the German Communist Party could be founded on Article 17 because the programme of the party inevitably envisaged a period of dictatorship by the proletariat in which rights under the Convention would be destroyed.

In recent years the focus of Article 17 has switched to racist and xenophobic groups,[24] and questions concerning this provision have arisen in the context of hate speech and Holocaust denial cases.

In *Norwood v UK*,[25] the applicant was a regional organizer of the British National Party (in the words of the Court, 'an extreme right wing political party') and, following complaints, had had a poster removed by the police from his window, the display of which

---

should not be interpreted to limit the right to life. The Court said that it was Irish law which made any limitation of the right to life possible (by allowing women to travel abroad to obtain abortions) not the interpretation of Article 10.

[20] There was a suggestion in *Retimag SA v FRG No 712/60*, 4 YB 384 (1961), that Article 17 could apply to interferences with the right to property under First Protocol, Article 1 but the question was not determined.

[21] See *Van Dijk and Van Hoof* pp 1085–6.   [22] Cf, Van Dijk and Van Hoof, at pp 1086–7.

[23] *KPD v FRG No 250/57*, 1 YB 222 (1957.).

[24] See *Kühnen v FRG No 12194/86*, 56 DR 205 (1988).

[25] *No 23131/03* hudoc (2004); 40 EHRR SE 111, cf, *Jersild v Denmark* A 298 (1994); 19 EHRR 1 para 35. See also *Glimmerveen and Hagenback v Netherlands Nos 8348/78 and 8406/78*, 18 DR 187 (1979); 4 EHRR 260 (1982) (inadmissible: applicants convicted for distributing racist pamphlets and excluded from participating in an election on a racist platform; the Commission relied on Article 17 to justify interference with Article 10 and Article 3 of the First Protocol); *WP v Poland No 42264/98* hudoc (2004) DA; *Schimanek v Austria No 32307/96* hudoc (2000) DA (inadmissible: 'National Socialism is a totalitarian doctrine incompatible with democracy and human rights and its adherents undoubtedly pursue aims of the kind referred to in Article 17 of the Convention').

led to a conviction. As described by the Court, the poster 'contained a photograph of the Twin Towers in flame, the words "Islam out of Britain—Protect the British People" and a symbol of a crescent and star in a prohibition sign'. A chamber of the Court rejected the applicant's complaint of a violation of Article 10, refusing the application as incompatible *ratione materiae* with the Convention for the display of the poster was an 'act' within the meaning of Article 17 which was not protected by Article 10 or Article 14. The Court stated that it agreed with the domestic courts' assessment of the poster as 'a public expression of attack on all Muslims' in the UK. It was clear that '[s]uch a general, vehement attack against a religious group, linking the group as a whole with a grave act of terrorism, [was] incompatible with the values proclaimed and guaranteed by the Convention, notably tolerance, social peace and non-discrimination'.

Two cases concerning issues relating to Holocaust denial are *Garaudy v France*[26] and *Lehideux and Isorni v France*.[27] In *Lehideux and Isorni* the Court indicated that Holocaust deniers could not rely on Article 10, referring to categories of certain 'clearly established historical facts—such as the Holocaust—whose negation or revision would be removed from the protection of Article 10 by Article 17'.[28] The Court was nevertheless clear that Article 17 would not be employed to suppress genuine historical debate, and that the facts of the case before it fell into this category. It examined the case under Article 10, found a violation of this provision and then stated that it considered that it was inappropriate to apply Article 17 on the facts.[29]

In *Garaudy*, by contrast, the Court applied Article 17 in a case concerning a book which resulted in the applicant's criminal conviction for Holocaust denial. The Court agreed that the book's 'real purpose [was] to rehabilitate the National-Socialist regime and [so] accuse the victims themselves of falsifying history'. It was not deserving of protection as a serious historical analysis of matters such as the Holocaust and the Nuremberg Trials. Denying crimes against humanity was 'one of the most serious forms of racial defamation of Jews and of incitement to hatred of them'. Negationist speech, such as Holocaust denial, was unacceptable and racist: it was a denial of or an attempt to rewrite 'historical fact', so it 'undermine[d] the values on which the fight against racism and anti-Semitism are based and constitute[d] a serious threat to public order'. Such acts were 'incompatible with democracy and human rights because they infringe the rights of others'.

It is conceivable that terrorist groups and their supporters could find their rights limited by reliance by the state on Article 17. However, in many cases, the necessity for a state to act could be assessed elsewhere under the Convention as, in principle, it ought to be, so that Article 17 becomes an instrument of last resort. Even where reliance on Article 17 is appropriate, the state's power must be exercised, 'to an extent strictly proportionate to the seriousness and duration of [the threat to the democratic system] ....'.[30]

III. ARTICLE 17 PLEADED AGAINST THE STATE

Article 17 is unusual in the Convention in that it may be invoked both by an individual against a state and by a state to justify its interference with the rights of an individual. The

---

[26] *No 65831/01* hudoc (2003) DA .

[27] 1998-VII; 30 EHRR 665 (conviction as applicants had procured an advert in a national newspaper which, it was claimed, showed their support for Nazi collaborators during the war (in particular, Philippe Pétain)).

[28] Id, para 47.

[29] Cf, *Purcell v Ireland No 15404/89*, 70 DR 262 at 278 (1991). The Commission used Article 17 in the *Purcell* case and in the *Kühnen* case, *loc cit* at n 24, above, to reinforce its conclusion that an interference with freedom of expression is justified under Article 10(2).

[30] *De Becker v Belgium* B 2 (1960) para 279 Com Rep.

Article serves to control the powers of the state, as well as to enhance them in the manner just discussed. The nature of the complaint by an applicant will be that the state has used its powers to interfere with rights for a purpose or in a manner beyond those permitted by the Convention. It is essentially an allegation of bad faith against the state because it is hardly conceivable that a limitation of a right which, on its face, could otherwise be justified under the Convention, would be excluded by Article 17.[31] Thus, when relied on by an individual, the applicant frequently couples his complaint that Article 17 has been violated with an allegation that there has been a breach of Article 18 also. Bad faith to one side—and there are always the greatest difficulties in demonstrating this—Article 17 thus becomes subsidiary to the determination that interferences with Convention rights by the state are, in any event, not compatible with the Convention. It explains why, even in the relatively few cases in which it has been called upon to consider Article 17 as applied against a state, the Court has found no need to deal with the question.

In the *Greek* case,[32] the applicant states argued that the government of Greece could not under Article 17 limit the exercise of individual rights in order to consolidate its hold on power. They said that Article 17 was directed against 'totalitarian conspiracies' and that the Greek government was one of these. The majority of the Commission found no need to decide this question because it had already decided that the government could not base its actions on Article 15, there being no emergency. Mr Ermacora found the derogation to be impermissible under Article 17, accepting the applicants' argument and pointing out that the government had shown no inclination to comply with its obligation to hold free and fair elections.[33] Mr Busuttil allowed that there might be circumstances when a revolutionary government might have to rely on Article 17 while it set about restoring democracy; it was entitled to a 'reasonable period' to prove that this was its objective, an obligation manifestly not met by the Greek regime.[34]

Allegations that Article 17 should be applied to state activities have been rare and, even where the Commission was prepared to look at them, the Court has managed to avoid reaching a decision.[35] Article 17 confers a power on states to act,[36] not a positive duty.[37] On the one hand, in what will be a narrow range of circumstances, Article 17 legitimates action by a state which, as a matter of routine, cannot be brought within any of the ordinary exceptions of the Convention when circumstances sufficient to give a wider power to derogate under Article 15 have not arisen. On the other hand, it provides some protection against states, where the individual shows that the state is interfering with his rights other than for the good (in Convention terms) reason it claims.

3. ARTICLE 18: PROHIBITION OF THE USE OF RESTRICTIONS FOR AN IMPROPER PURPOSE

Article 18

The restrictions permitted under this Convention to the said rights and freedoms shall not be applied for any purpose other than those for which they have been prescribed.

---

[31] See *Engel v Netherlands* A 22 (1976); 1 EHRR 647 para 108 PC and *Lithgow v UK* A 102 (1986) para 448 Com Rep (the Article 17 point was not argued before the Court).

[32] 12 YB (the *Greek* case) 1 at 111–12 (1969); CM Res DH (70) 1.   [33] Id, pp 102–3.   [34] Id, p 119.

[35] Eg, *Sporrong and Lönnroth v Sweden* A 52 (1982); 5 EHRR 35 para 76 PC. For the Commission, see id, B 46 (1980) paras 122–3 Com Rep.   [36] Warbrick, 32 ICLQ 82 at 91–3 (1983).

[37] But see Fawcett, pp 275–6, suggesting that in some circumstances there may be a positive obligation to discriminate against a group whose activities are covered by Article 17.

Article 18 gives protection against misuse of powers or breaches of the principle of good faith. As the Court has said:

> Article 18...does not have an autonomous role. It can only be applied in conjunction with other Articles of the Convention. There may, however, be a violation of Article 18 in connection with another Article, although there is no violation of that Article taken alone. It further follows from the terms of Article 18 that a violation can only arise where the right or freedom concerned is subject to restrictions permitted under the Convention.[38]

There was a violation of Article 18 taken with Article 5(1)(c) in *Gusinskiy v Russia*.[39] The applicant was a businessman involved in a commercial dispute with 'Gazprom', a company controlled by the state. He was arrested and detained for several weeks in connection with a completely separate matter relating to his media business. So, on the face of it there was a valid basis for detention: Article 5(1)(c) in connection with the media business investigations. Indeed the Court held that this provision was not breached. However, during the detention period a deal had been struck. The applicant agreed to sell certain interests to Gazprom at a favourable rate and in return the investigation against him was dropped. A state minister signed the agreement off. The Court concluded that the applicant's prosecution was used to intimidate him, insisting, 'it is not the purpose of such public-law matters as criminal proceedings and detention on remand to be used as part of commercial bargaining strategies'.[40] The restriction of the applicant's liberty permitted under Article 5(1)(c) was applied 'not only for the purpose of bringing him before the competent legal authority on reasonable suspicion of having committed an offence, but also for other reasons'.[41] There was a violation of Article 5(1)(c) read with Article 18.

In *De Becker v Belgium*,[42] the Commission said that Article 18 was a bar to relying on derogations legitimately made under Article 15 once the emergency had passed, a matter conceded by the government. The concession was not without importance because allegations of breaches of Article 18 will impugn the good faith of the state or cast serious doubts on the efficiency of its administration and the system of its democratic remedies for dealing with them. In *Bozano v France*,[43] the Commission was not prepared to accept an allegation of unlawful collusion between the police authorities of France and Switzerland which had been considered and found to be without foundation by a Swiss court. However, it did accept that there had been an abuse of power by the French police, prior to the applicant's expulsion from France, on the basis of a judgment to that effect by a French court.[44] Indeed, the evidential barrier is often the greatest obstacle to sustaining claims of violations of Article 18. In the *Kamma* case,[45] the applicant could show no more than that, while he was properly detained on suspicion of committing one offence, the police questioned him about his involvement in another. While there was an ambiguity about the ground on which he was being held, the Commission held that this did not demonstrate a breach of Article 18 and that, since one of the grounds on which he was detained could be justified, he had not been held contrary to the Convention.[46] In *Engel v Netherlands*,[47] the applicants were not able to prove the motive of the authorities, nor in *Handyside v UK*[48] could the applicant show that his books were seized for political

---

[38] *Gusinskiy v Russia* 2004-IV; 41 EHRR 281 para 73.

[39] *Ibid.*   [40] Id, para 76.   [41] Id, para 77.

[42] B 2 (1960) para 271 Com Rep.   [43] *No 9990/82*, 39 DR 119 at 142 (1984).   [44] Id, p 141.

[45] *Kamma v Netherlands No 4771/71*, 1 DR 4 (1974) Com Rep at, pp 11–12.

[46] Cf, *Gusinskiy v Russia*, loc cit paras 75–7, the Court intimating that the facts left it with no alternative but to conclude that there had been bad faith.

[47] A 22 (1976); 1 EHRR 647 PC.

[48] B 22 (1976) para 175 Com Rep. See also *X v FRG No 6038/73*, 44 CD 115 at 119 (1973) and *McFeeley v UK No 8317/78*, 20 DR 44 at 102 (1980); 3 EHRR 161 para 131.

reasons rather than for 'the protection of morals' of a child audience. Some claims have failed where the applicant has not demonstrated an abuse of the power, even on his version of the facts.[49] The Strasbourg authorities should be alive to the possibility of the rationalization of the reasons for interfering with an individual's rights, presented only when the state is required to explain itself in Strasbourg. A legitimate reason for so acting must have been *the* reason for acting.[50] However, unless there is something of a shift in the burden of proof, an applicant is unlikely to be able to prove that this is not the case in only the most exceptional case.

Where the institutions have found a violation by reason of a failure to comply with the specific limits of a restriction provision, the Court has been unwilling to go on to decide whether Article 18 has been breached also.[51] If this turns out to be invariably the case, Article 18 will serve little purpose.

[49] *Bozano v Switzerland No 9909/80*, 39 DR 58 at 70 (1984) (state obliged to extradite, no matter how the person came in to its territory) and *Bozano v Italy No 9991/82*, 39 DR 147 at 157 (1984). Both cases might be reconsidered in the light of developments in situations where an accused is brought unlawfully to a state's territory: see *Stocke v Germany* A 199 (1991); 13 EHRR 839 (where the claim failed on the facts).

[50] *Quinn v France No 18580/91* hudoc (1993); 16 EHRR CD 23.

[51] *Sporrong and Lönnroth v Sweden* A 52 (1982); 5 EHRR 35 para 56 PC and *Bozano v France* A 111 (1986); 9 EHRR 297 para 61. On the reluctance of the Court to proceed under Article 18, see Sudre, 91 RGDIP 533 at 580-3 (1987).

18

ARTICLE 1, FIRST PROTOCOL: THE RIGHT TO PROPERTY

Article 1, First Protocol

Every natural or legal person is entitled to the peaceful enjoyment of his possessions. No one shall be deprived of his possessions except in the public interest and subject to the conditions provided for by law and by the general principles of international law.

The preceding provisions shall not, however, in any way impair the right of a state to enforce such laws as it deems necessary to control the use of property in accordance with the general interest or to secure the payment of taxes or other contributions or penalties.

1. INTRODUCTION

It proved exceedingly difficult to reach agreement on a formulation of the right to property when the European Convention was being drafted.[1] Eventually, it was one of the provisions left over until the First Protocol. Even then, the differences between states were considerable and the provision finally adopted guarantees only a much qualified right, allowing the state a wide power to interfere with property.[2] The United Kingdom and Sweden in particular were concerned that no substantial fetter be placed on the power of states to implement programmes of nationalization of industries for political and social purposes.[3] In its final form, Article 1 of the First Protocol contains no express reference to a right to compensation at any level in the event of interference with property, save any that might be found in the reference to 'the general principles of international law'. The Court has made frequent reference to the drafting history of Article 1 of the First Protocol and its influence has been substantial in confirming the wide latitude states have in interfering with the right.

The right of '[e]very natural or legal person' is protected, wording which provides specific recognition of the general position that corporate bodies have rights under the Convention. It is necessary that the applicant be the real 'victim', ie the corporation if its rights are affected, the shareholder if his rights have been interfered with.[4]

---

[1] See Robertson, 28 BYIL 359 (1951); Peukert, 2 HRLJ 37 at 38–42 (1981) and Allen, *Property and the Human Rights Act 1998,* 2005 (hereafter 'Allen, *Property*'), pp 17–33. On Article 1 generally, see Sermet, *La Convention européenne des droits de l'homme et le droit de propriété*, Dossiers sur les droits de l'homme, 1998; Van Der Broek, LIEI 52 (1986); Frowein, *European System*, Ch 20; Windisdoerffer, 19 HRLR 18 (1998); Çoban, *Protection of Property Rights within the European Convention on Human Rights*, 2004; and Allen, *Property*.

[2] For the main items in the preparatory work, see 3 TP 92–6, 106–8 (Consultative Assembly) and 134–6 (Secretary General's Memorandum). The text was eventually approved by the Consultative Assembly: 8 TP 168.

[3] 6 TP 140, 200.

[4] *Olczak v Poland No 30417/96* 2002-X DA. A company's legal personality will be disregarded only in 'exceptional circumstances': eg, *Pine Valley Developments v Ireland* A 222 (1991); 14 EHRR 319 (managing director

I. POSSESSIONS

The English language text uses the word 'possessions' to describe the protected interest but any suggestions that it should be read narrowly is refuted by the word '*biens*' in the French text which indicates that a wide range of proprietorial interests were intended to be protected. It embraces immoveable and moveable property[5] and corporal and incorporeal interests, such as company shares[6] and intellectual property.[7] A cause of action that has unconditionally vested may qualify as an 'asset' constituting a 'possession'.[8] Contractual rights,[9] including leases,[10] and judgment debts[11] are possessions. The essential

and sole shareholder 'victim' of interference with company land as company was a 'vehicle' for applicant); *Ankarcrona v Sweden No 35178/97*, 2000-VI DA (sole shareholder 'victim' as company injured was his 'vehicle'); *Eugenia Michaelidou Developments Ltd and Michael Tymvios v Turkey* hudoc (2003) (sole director and substantial majority shareholder 'victim' when company and applicant 'so closely identified with each other'); and *Khamidov v Russia* hudoc (2007) (co-owner of family company issued with general power of attorney by other owner a 'victim' of interference with company's property). Cf, *Agrotexim v Greece* A 330-A (1995); 21 EHRR 250 (bare majority shareholders not 'victims' by reason of damage to company which depreciated the value of their shares where it is not established that it is impossible for company to apply under Convention); *Lebedev v Russia No 4493/04* hudoc (2004) DA (applicant receiving income from holding company owning majority shares not a 'victim'); *TW Computeranimation GmbH v Austria No 53818/00* hudoc (2005) DA (former 50% shareholder with continuing pecuniary interest in company not a 'victim'); *Bayramov v Azerbaijan No 23055/03* hudoc (2006) DA (executive director not a 'victim' of interference with company's property); and *Družstevni Záložna Pria v Czech Republic* hudoc (2008) (members of a credit union not 'victims' of interference with credit union's property). See Emberland, *The Human Rights of Companies—Exploring the Structure of ECHR Protection*, 2006, pp 65–109, for an analysis of the Court's approach to corporate personality.

 5 *Wiggins v UK No 7456/76*, 13 DR 40 (1978).

 6 *Bramelid and Malmström v Sweden Nos 8588/79 and 8589/79*, 29 DR 64 (1982); 5 EHRR 249 and *Sovtransavto Holding v Ukraine* 2002-VII; 34 EHRR 44. Including the corresponding rights that the holder of a share in a company possesses, see *Olczak v Poland No 30417/96*, 2002-X DA. Whether influence and power as a majority shareholder, as such, constitutes a 'possession' remains an open question: *Türk Ticaret Bankasi Munzam Sosyal Güvenlik Emekli Ve Yardim Sandiği Vakfi v Turkey Nos 48925/99 and 36109/04* hudoc (2006) DA.

 7 *Anheuser-Busch Inc v Portugal* hudoc (2007); 45 EHRR 830 GC. Eg, *Smith Kline and French Laboratories v Netherlands No 12633/87*, 66 DR 70 (1990) (patent); *Lenzing AG v UK No 38817/97* hudoc (1998) DA (patent); *Anheuser-Busch Inc v Portugal* hudoc (2007); 45 EHRR 830 GC (application for registration of trade mark); *Aral, Tekin and Aral v Turkey No 24563/94* hudoc (1998) DA (copyright); and *Melnychuk v Ukraine No 28743/03* 2005-IX DA (copyright). See Helfer, 49 HILJ 1 (2008).

 8 *Kopecký v Slovakia* 2004-XI; 41 EHRR 944 GC (no 'asset' where claim for restitution did not vest because a statutory condition for recovery not met. Judge Strážnická dissenting argues a 'formalistic and strict interpretation (of national provisions by national authorities) cannot be compatible with the principles of the Convention'). A claim is conditional when it depends upon a future uncertain event: *Gavella v Croatia No 33244/02* hudoc (2006) DA (right of pre-emption not an 'asset'). See also *Draon v France* hudoc (2005); 42 EHRR 807 GC and *Maurice v France* hudoc (2005); 42 EHRR 885 GC (pending negligence claim for special damages an 'asset'); *Pressos Compania Naviera SA v Belgium* A 332 (1995); 21 EHRR 301 (negligence claim arising when damage occurred an 'asset'). Regarding the stage of proceedings that the claim must reach in order to constitute a 'possession', see *Stran Greek Refineries and Stratis Andreadis v Greece* A 301-B (1994); 19 EHRR 293 (final judgment); *Smokovitis v Greece* hudoc (2002) (first instance decision); and *SA Dangeville v France* 2002-III; 38 EHRR 699 (first instance decision in line with authority). Cf, *Arvanitaki-Robati v Greece* hudoc (2006) (no 'possession' where claim not established by final court decision).

 9 *A, B and Company AS v FRG No 7742/76*, 14 DR 146 (1978); *Association of General Practitioners v Denmark No 12947/87*, 62 DR 226 (1989); and *Gasus Dosier und Fordertechnik GmbH v Netherlands* A 306-B (1995); 20 EHRR 403.

 10 *Mellacher v Austria* A 169 (1989); 12 EHRR 391 PC. Cf, *JLS v Spain No 41917/98*, 1999-V DA (occupier of premises under an arrangement with authorities). Claims for rent are not 'possessions': *Xenodochiaki SA v Greece No 49213/99* hudoc (2001) DA.

 11 *Stran Greek Refineries and Stratis Andreadis v Greece* A 301-B (1994); 19 EHRR 293 (arbitral award) and *Burdov v Russia* 2002-III; 38 EHRR 639 (final and binding court judgment). See also *Nosov v Russia No 30877/02* hudoc (2005) DA (assignment of a debt).

characteristic is the acquired economic value of the individual interest.[12] Expectations do not generally have the degree of concreteness to bring them within the idea of 'possessions', although 'legitimate expectations' may be relevant in establishing that there are rights to be protected by Article 1 of the First Protocol. For example, in *Pressos Compania Naviera SA v Belgium*[13] the applicants argued that Article 1 of the First Protocol was breached when their pending claims against the state for negligence in the provision of piloting services to the applicants' ships were extinguished by legislation that took effect retrospectively. The government contended that the applicants' claims did not constitute 'possessions' as none of the claims had been recognized and determined by a judicial decision having final effect. The Court found that the claims constituted an 'asset' for the purposes of Article 1 of the First Protocol because under the national law of negligence the claims for compensation came into existence as soon as the damage occurred. Further, the Court said the applicants had a 'legitimate expectation' that their claims would be determined in accordance with the general law of tort in which the highest national court following early case law had recognized the liability of public authorities in negligence. The Court concluded that the applicants' claims therefore constituted 'possessions'.[14] In *Kopecký v Slovakia* the Grand Chamber explained the role of legitimate expectations in establishing a 'possession' in the *Pressos* case as follows:

> The Court (in *Pressos*) did not expressly state that the 'legitimate expectation' was a component of, or attached to, a property right.... It was however implicit that no such expectation could come into play in the absence of an 'asset' falling within the ambit of Article 1 of Protocol 1, in this instance the claim in tort. The 'legitimate expectation' identified in *Pressos Compania Naviera SA* was not in itself constitutive of a proprietary interest; it related to the way in which the claim qualifying as an 'asset' would be treated under domestic law and in particular to reliance on the fact that the established case-law of the national courts would continue to be applied in respect of damage which had already occurred.[15]

On this reasoning there must first be an 'asset' that can qualify as a 'possession' under Article 1 of the First Protocol. The 'legitimate expectation' relates to the merits of the

---

[12] See eg, *De La Cierva Osorio de Moscovo v Spain* Nos 41127/98 et al 1999-VII DA (peerage not a 'possession' where title has no economic value); *Anheuser-Busch Inc v Portugal* hudoc (2007); 45 EHRR 830 GC (application for registration of trade mark); and *Paeffgen GmbH v Germany* Nos 25379/04, 21688/05, 21722/05 and 21770/05 hudoc (2007) DA (exclusive right to use internet domain names). Cf, *Chassagnou v France* 1999-III; 29 EHRR 615 GC.

[13] A 332 (1995); 21 EHRR 301. See also, where there is a claim, *Draon v France* hudoc (2005); 42 EHRR 807 GC and *Maurice v France* hudoc (2005); 42 EHRR 885 GC ('possession' where legitimate expectation generated by an enforceable claim reasonably established under domestic law); *Smokovitis v Greece* hudoc (2002) ('possession' where legitimate expectation based on national case law indicating claims had strong likelihood of success); *SA Dangeville v France* 2002-III; 38 EHRR 699 ('possession' where legitimate expectation generated by European Community Directive); and *National & Provincial Building Society, Leeds Permanent Building Society and Yorkshire Building Society v UK* 1997-VII; 25 EHRR 127 (no 'possession' where no legitimate expectation pending claim would succeed owing to foreshadowed legislative intervention). Where a public authority has acted beyond its powers, see eg, *Pine Valley Developments Ltd v Ireland* A 222 (1992); 14 EHRR 319 (reliance on planning permission granted in excess of powers) and *Stretch v UK* hudoc (2003); 38 EHRR 196 (local authority acting in excess of powers, by granting an option to renew a lease, created legitimate expectation that the applicant could exercise the option). See also *The Former King of Greece v Greece* 2000-XII; 33 EHRR 516 GC (royal family's 'assets' held to constitute possessions as the authorities allowed the family to deal with them in their private capacity) and *Öneryildiz v Turkey* 2004-XII; 41 EHRR 325 GC (authorities' conduct gave rise to legitimate expectation).

[14] A 332 (1995); 21 EHRR 301 para 31.

[15] 2004-XI; 41 EHRR 944 para 48 GC. For the facts of *Kopecký's* case, see below p 661.

'asset', which in *Pressos* referred to the claim's prospect of success under domestic law.[16] Thus, where an applicant's submission on the correct interpretation and application of domestic law has been rejected by the national courts no 'legitimate expectation' arises.[17]

Initially, the ascription and identification of property rights is for the national legal system[18] and it is incumbent on an applicant to establish the precise nature of the right in the national law and his entitlement to enjoy it.[19] However, the mere fact that the national law does not acknowledge as a legal right a particular interest or does so in terms which do not result in it being recognized as a property right does not conclusively determine that the interest is not a 'possession' for the purposes of Article 1 of the First Protocol. The concept of 'possession' is autonomous.[20] When deciding whether Article 1 of the First Protocol applies to a complaint the Court will examine 'whether the circumstances of the case, considered as a whole, conferred on the applicant title to a substantive interest protected by Article 1 of the First Protocol.' For example, when concluding that an application for registration of a trade mark came within the meaning of Article 1 of the First Protocol, the Grand Chamber in *Anheuser-Busch Inc v Portugal*[21] took into account the 'bundle of financial rights and interests', which are at least capable of possessing 'a substantial financial value', and the legal rights that both arise upon an application for registration of a trade mark. The fact that the rights attached to the application were conditional upon the trade mark being registered made no difference. The Grand Chamber reasoned:

> when it filed its application for registration, the applicant company was entitled to expect that it would be examined under the applicable legislation if it satisfied the other relevant substantive and procedural conditions. The applicant company therefore owned a set of proprietary rights—linked to its application for the registration of a trade mark—that were recognised under Portugese law, even though they could be revoked under certain conditions.[22]

The demonstration of an established economic interest by an applicant may be sufficient to establish a right protected by the Convention. Thus in *Tre Traktörer Aktiebolag v Sweden*,[23] the Court rejected the government's argument that because a liquor licence conferred no rights in national law, it could not be a 'possession' for the purposes of

---

[16] The role of 'legitimate expectations' under Article 1 of the First Protocol is far from settled, see generally Allen, *Property*, pp 46–57 and Popelier, 10 EHRLR 10 at 12–20 (2006).

[17] *Kopecký v Slovakia* 2004-XI; 41 EHRR 944 para 50 GC and *Anheuser-Busch Inc v Portugal* hudoc (2007); 45 EHRR 830 para 65 GC.

[18] Eg, there are few restrictions upon what a state may regard as capable of being owned—perhaps only individuals because of freedom from slavery in Article 4. But the fact that something is capable of being owned in one legal system (eg human blood or organs) is not a reason why it must be capable of being owned in another.

[19] *Agneessens v Belgium No 12164/86*, 58 DR 63 (1988) (claims to a debt rejected by court not a 'possession'); *JLS v Spain No 41917/98* hudoc (1999) DA (occupation of property without legal right not a 'possession'); *Kopecký v Slovakia* 2004-XI; 41 EHRR 944 GC (claim for restitution of land rejected by court not a 'possession'); and *Jhigalev v Russia* hudoc (2006) (claim to sole ownership of farm not upheld by courts not a 'possession').

[20] Eg, *Gasus Dosier und Fördertechnik GmbH v Netherlands* A 306-B (1995); 20 EHRR 403 and *Broniowski v Poland* 2004-V; 40 EHRR 495 GC. This means formal title to land is not necessarily required, see eg, *Öneryildiz v Turkey* 2004-XII; 41 EHRR 325 GC and *Doğan and Others v Turkey* 2004-VI; 41 EHRR 231.

[21] Hudoc (2007); 45 EHRR 830 para 75 GC.   [22] Id, paras 76–8.

[23] A 159 (1989); 13 EHRR 309. See also *Van Marle v Netherlands* A 101 (1986); 8 EHRR 483 PC and *Iatridis v Greece* 1999-II; 30 EHRR 97 GC (clientele built up by the applicants' efforts an 'asset' (cf, business goodwill) that qualified as a 'possession'); *Buzescu v Romania* hudoc (2005) (legal practice and its goodwill an 'asset' that qualified as a 'possession') and *Megadat.com srl v Moldova* hudoc (2008) (licence to conduct a business a 'possession'), cf, *Bauquel v France No 71120/01* hudoc (2004) DA (no possession where no established professional practice).

Article 1 of the First Protocol. It was essential to the successful conduct of the applicant's restaurant and its withdrawal had adverse effects on the goodwill and value of the business. The Court may also be prepared to undertake a broader examination of the circumstances of a case where property is held in possession contrary to national law or under a contract having no legal effect. For instance, in *Beyeler v Italy*[24] a contract for the purchase of a painting was 'null and void' under national law yet the Court found an interest protected by Article 1 of the First Protocol on the basis that the applicant had been in possession of the property for several years and the authorities had, for some purposes, treated the applicant as having a proprietary interest it.

As indicated in an earlier chapter,[25] the right to a fair trial in Article 6 applies to the determination of 'civil rights and obligations'. This is a term with an autonomous Convention meaning that has been interpreted as including pecuniary rights. The coherence of the Convention as a whole demands that the autonomous concept of 'possessions' in Article 1 of the First Protocol be no less a category than the concept of pecuniary rights for the purposes of Article 6: the reasoning about the essence of the interest measured by its nature and importance to an individual should apply to its formal protection (Article 6(1)) and its substance (Article 1 of the First Protocol) alike.[26] The minimum in each case is that the applicant shows that he is entitled to some real, if yet unattributed, economic benefit. This is relevant to the treatment of welfare benefits as property. While the Court has consistently said that there is no general right to welfare benefits to be derived from Article 1 of the First Protocol, it has allowed that a welfare right under domestic law is a possession for the purposes of Article 1 of the First Protocol. What is required is that the applicant demonstrates that he has a legal right in domestic law to some benefit if he satisfies certain conditions, rather than that he seeks to ensure that a discretion is exercised in his favour.[27] In *Stec v UK*[28] the Grand Chamber said:

> Where an individual has an assertable right under domestic law to a welfare benefit, the importance of that interest should also be reflected by holding Article 1 of Protocol No 1 to be applicable.

In this connection there is no distinction to be drawn between benefits to which the applicant has made contributions and those to which no direct contribution has been made.[29] However, while he may be entitled under Article 6(1) to a fair hearing to determine

---

[24] 2000-I; 33 EHRR 1225 GC. See also *Matos e Silva, Lda v Portugal* 1996-IV; 24 EHRR 573; *The Synod College of the Evangelical Reformed Church of Lithuania v Lithuania No 44548/98* hudoc (2002); 36 EHRR CD 94; and *Öneryildiz v Turkey* 2004-XII; 41 EHRR 325 GC (Judges Mularoni and Türmen dissenting). Cf, *Kötterl and Schittily v Austria No 32957/96* hudoc (2003); 37 EHRR CD 205, in which the Court based its assessment of the facts on the determination of the national courts that the contract was void.

[25] See above, pp 210–25. See eg, *Beaumartin v France* A 296-B (1994); 19 EHRR 485, discussed above, p 286 (compensation agreement negotiated by France for its nationals concerned the applicant's pecuniary rights so that Article 6 applied even though no legal right in French law; right to compensation was likewise treated as a 'possession' under Article 1 of the First Protocol).

[26] *Feldbrugge v Netherlands* A 99 (1986); 8 EHRR 425 PC; *Salesi v Italy* A 257-E (1993); 26 EHRR 187; and *Stec v UK* hudoc (2005), 41 EHRR SE 295 GC (welfare rights cases). To similar effect, see Rosas, in Rosas and Helgesen, eds, *The Strength of Diversity: Human Rights and Pluralist Democracy*, 1992, pp 150–1.

[27] Similarly, Article 6 does not extend to discretionary welfare payments: see above, p 217.

[28] Hudoc (2005), 41 EHRR SE 295 GC, para 51. See also *Gaygusuz v Austria* 1996-IV; 23 EHRR 364. It does not follow that under Article 1 of the First Protocol there is a right to a benefit of a particular amount: *Kjartan Ásmundsson v Iceland* 2004-IX; 41 EHRR 927. See Allen, 28 MJIL 287 at 310–1 (2007).

[29] The Court sought to adopt an interpretation of the concept of 'possessions' that promoted consistency with the concept of pecuniary rights under Article 6(1), reflected 'the variety of funding methods and the interlocking nature of benefits under most welfare systems' within member states and recognized the social function of welfare benefits: id, para 50.

whether any conditions for their payment are satisfied, if they are not, the applicant will have no right to the benefit and the state will not be put to justifying why the benefit does not accrue except where the conditions comprise a discriminatory ground under Article 14, in which case there will be a breach of Article 1 of the First Protocol and Article 14 taken together: a right to receive the benefit will exist notwithstanding a failure to fulfil the conditions.[30]

The Convention protects an applicant's existing possessions and assets against interference. It is not a right to be put into the possession of things one does not already have, however strong the individual's interest in this happening may be.[31] In *Marckx v Belgium*,[32] the Court said that Article 1 of the First Protocol 'does not guarantee the right to acquire possessions whether on intestacy or through voluntary dispositions'. There is no right to have food or to have shelter, whatever one's destitution, under this provision.[33] This confirms that the protection offered by Article 1 of the First Protocol is much closer to the origins of property rights as civil rights than to modern ideas of economic rights, even though it is now to the defence of economic interests that the provision is directed.[34] However, the affiliation with civil rights need not severely circumscribe the reach of Article 1 of the First Protocol for, as the Grand Chamber in *Stec v UK*[35] observed in the context of welfare rights, there is no 'water-tight division' separating the sphere of economic and social rights from that of civil and political rights set forth in the Convention.

Property rights constituting possessions may cease to do so if they have 'long been impossible to exercise effectively'.[36] The principle appears in cases dealing with the restoration of property rights in the aftermath of the Second World War and upon the fall of the former communist governments in Central and Eastern Europe. In this context the Court has granted states wide latitude in the determination of claims for restitution and compensation.[37] One situation is where property has been expropriated by the state under domestic law. In *Malhous v Czech Republic*[38] a right of ownership in land held by the applicant's father was extinguished when the land was expropriated, without compensation, under legislation enacted in 1948 by the communist regime. While legislation

---

[30] *Stec v UK* hudoc (2006); 43 EHRR 1017 GC (eligibility for reduced earnings allowance based on difference in UK pensionable ages between men and women not a violation of Article 14 with Article 1 of the First Protocol; cf, Judge Loucaides dissenting). See also *Runkee and White v UK* hudoc (2007) (non-payment of widow's pension to male widowers not a violation of Article 14 with Article 1 of the First Protocol). Cf, *Gaygusuz v Austria* 1996-IV; 23 EHRR 364 (eligibility for work-related welfare benefits based on nationality a violation of Article 14 with Article 1 of the First Protocol) and *Luczak v Poland* hudoc (2007) (eligibility for farmers' social-security scheme based on nationality a violation of Article 14 with Article 1 of the First Protocol).

[31] *Kopecký v Slovakia* 2004-XI; 41 EHRR 944 para 35 GC. Eg, future income not a possession until it has 'been earned or an enforceable claim to it exists': *Denimark Ltd v UK No 37660/97* hudoc (2000); 30 EHRR CD 144 (value of commercial business); *Xenodochiaki SA v Greece No 49213/99* hudoc (2001) DA (rent); *Ambruosi v Italy* hudoc (2000); 35 EHRR 125 (legal fees); and *Levänen v Finland No 34600/03* hudoc (2006) DA (possible loss of future income and value of business assets, inadmissible).

[32] A 31 (1979); 2 EHRR 330 PC. Cf, *Inze v Austria* A 126 (1987); 10 EHRR 394.

[33] See eg, *Slivenko v Latvia* 2003-XI; 39 EHRR 490 GC (housing); *Sardin v Russia No 69582/01*, 2004-II DA (medical and other social benefits); and *Kutepov and Anikeyenko v Russia* hudoc (2005) (ownership and control over resources necessary for basic subsistence). Cf, Cassese, 1 EJIL 141 (1991) with discussion of *Van Volsem v Belgium No 14641/89* (1990), unreported. Insufficient state provision may raise an issue under Article 3: *Larioshina v Russia No 56869/00* hudoc (2002) DA. See above, p 103, n 322.

[34] *Van der Mussele v Belgium* A 70 (1983); 6 EHRR 163 PC and *Linde v Sweden No 11628/85*, 47 DR 270 (1986).

[35] Hudoc (2005); 41 EHRR SE 295 para 52 GC.

[36] *Mayer v Germany Nos 18890/91, 19048/91 and 19549/92*, 85 DR 5 (1996) Com Rep and *Von Maltzan v Germany* 2005-V; 42 EHRR SE 93 para 74 GC. See Allen, 13 CJEL 1 at 17–22 (2006–7).

[37] *Von Maltzan*, id, para 74.   [38] *No 33071/96*, 2000-XII GC.

passed after the collapse of the communist government provided for restitution of land taken under the 1948 legislation, this entitlement was expressed to exclude land that had been transferred under the 1948 legislation to natural persons, as had the applicant's land. In the case of *Von Maltzan v Germany*[39] the political framework established for the reunification of the communist German Democratic Republic with the democratic Federal Republic of Germany expressly excluded the right to restitution of land, such as the applicants' land, expropriated between 1945 and 1949 in the Soviet occupied zone in Germany. In neither case did the applicant's interest in property survive in a form that was recognized as a possession: the 'mere hope of restitution' lacked a sufficient basis in law to qualify for protection under Article 1 of the First Protocol.[40] The position will differ where rights not able to be exercised have nevertheless had 'a continuing legal basis in domestic law'. Such a case is *Broniowski v Poland*[41] where the applicants held 'a right to credit'[42] under Polish law in lieu of restitution of real property lost as a result of repatriation from territories 'across the Bug River' when those territories ceased to be in Poland after the Second World War. Acknowledgement of the right in domestic law during the communist era and afterwards provided a basis for the Polish courts to define the right as a 'debt chargeable to the State Treasury which had a pecuniary and inheritable character', a right sufficiently concrete to constitute a 'possession' for the purposes of Article 1 of the First Protocol.

Another situation in which property rights may be lost is where a claim has been made conditional upon the fulfilment of statutory criteria such as time limits,[43] place of residence,[44] nationality,[45] or proof of location of the property.[46] In *Kopecký v Slovakia*[47] the Grand Chamber confirmed the principle that a conditional claim which lapses as a result of non-fulfilment of the condition does not constitute a possession for the purposes of Article 1 of the First Protocol. The nature of the condition is irrelevant to the determination.[48] In cases where property has been confiscated as a result of a criminal conviction, the Court has also rejected the idea that the right of ownership revives where the conviction and confiscation order are quashed with retrospective effect.[49] Nor will a claim for restitution constitute an 'asset' if the statutory requirements for restitution cannot be met, for there is no proprietary interest established in law to which a legitimate expectation may attach.[50] This was the situation in *Kopecký*[51] where the applicant claimed the return of coins taken in 1959 from his father by the authorities following a conviction. In 1992 the conviction and confiscation were quashed by judicial rehabilitation legislation. The legislation further provided that the state would restore movable property that had been

[39] 2005-V; 42 EHRR SE 11 GC.

[40] *Malhous v Czech Republic No 33071/96*, 2000-XII GC and *Von Maltzan v Germany* 2005-V; 42 EHRR SE 93 para 112 GC. See also *Myšáková v Czech Republic No 30021/03* hudoc (2006).

[41] 2004-V; 43 EHRR 1 para 130. Cf, *Loizidou v Turkey* 1996-VI; 23 EHRR 513 GC.

[42] By this the value of the property was offset against the cost of buying land or a house from the state.

[43] *De Napoles Pacheco v Belgium No 7775/77*, 15 DR 143 (1979) Com Rep (reimbursement of proceeds of sale of shares).

[44] *Jantner v Slovakia No 39050/97* hudoc (2003) DA.

[45] *Gratzinger and Gratzingerova v Czech Republic No 39794/98*, 2002-VII; 35 EHRR CD 202 GC and *Polacek and Polackova v Czech Republic No 38645/97* hudoc (2002) GC.

[46] *Kopecký v Slovakia* 2004-XI; 41 EHRR 944 GC.

[47] Id, para 35. See also *Malhous v Czech Republic No 33071/96*, 2000-XII GC.

[48] Accordingly, a further complaint in relation to a statutory condition based on Article 14 in conjunction with Article 1 of the First Protocol will also fail: *Gratzinger and Gratzingerova v Czech Republic No 39794/98*, 2002-VII; 35 EHRR CD 202 GC. Cf, the welfare benefits cases above pp 659–60. See further Allen, *Property*, pp 61–2 and Allen, 13 CJEL 1 at 23–4 (2006–7).

[49] *Polacek and Polackova v Czech Republic No 38645/97* hudoc (2002) GC.

[50] *Kopecký v Slovakia* 2004-XI; 41 EHRR 944 GC.

[51] Id. See also *Glaser v Czech Republic* hudoc (2008).

confiscated on receiving a written request showing the location of the property. However, the applicant could not say where the coins were (nor could the authorities), and the domestic court found that he had not complied with the statutory requirements for restitution of the coins. The Grand Chamber held that in these circumstances the applicant's claim for restitution was not 'sufficiently established' to qualify as an 'asset'.[52] Thus, there was no longer a 'possession' for the purposes of Article 1 of the First Protocol.

II. PEACEFUL ENJOYMENT

The specific right protected by Article 1 of the First Protocol is the right to the 'peaceful enjoyment' of possessions: the right to have, to use, to repair, to dispose of, to pledge, to lend, even to destroy one's possessions. Moreover, it includes the possibility to exercise those rights.[53] As the Court said in the *Marckx* case, 'Article 1 is in substance guaranteeing the right of property'.[54] Enjoyment is protected principally against interference by the state.[55] Interference may be in the forms specifically referred to in Article 1 of the First Protocol—deprivation or control of use—but it is a wider category. So in *Sporrong and Lönnroth v Sweden*,[56] where there was a long delay between an initial decision indicating that property was likely to be expropriated and its execution, the Court held that there had been an interference with the applicants' right to the enjoyment of their possessions even though the interference was neither a seizure nor a measure of control. So also the imposition of financial liability that is not concerned with securing the payment of taxes constitutes an interference with enjoyment of possessions.[57] The state will be responsible under Article 1 of the First Protocol for interferences which affect the economic value of property.[58] Accordingly, claims about interferences with the aesthetic or environmental qualities of possessions are protected, if they be protected at all, elsewhere in the Convention.[59] In *S v France*[60] the Commission looked at the effects on the value of property as a result of noise pollution but did not consider, as the French court also had not considered, amenity loss of the rural aspect from the property, resulting from industrial development nearby. Nevertheless, demonstration of economic loss sufficient to establish an interference with possessions may not always be necessary. In *Chassagnou v France*[61] there was an interference with property because of the personal

---

[52] Id, para 58.

[53] *Sporrong and Lönnroth v Sweden* A 52 (1982); 5 EHRR 35 PC and *Loizidou v Turkey* 1996-VI; 23 EHRR 513 GC, see below, p 663.

[54] A 31 (1979); 2 EHRR 330 para 63.

[55] No distinction has been made between interferences with property rights by public and private entities: eg, *Bramelid and Malmström v Sweden Nos 8588/79 and 8589/79*, 29 DR 64 (1982); 5 EHRR 249. As to private interferences, see below p 665.

[56] A 52 (1982); 5 EHRR 35 PC. See also *Erkner and Hofauer v Austria* A 117 (1987); 9 EHRR 464 and *Poiss v Austria* A 117 (1987); 10 EHRR 231. In *Akkuş v Turkey* 1997-IV; 30 EHRR 533, delay in payment of compensation for the expropriation of property constituted an interference with the enjoyment of property.

[57] Eg, *X v Netherlands* 14 YB 224 (1971) (social security contributions).

[58] See eg, *Krickl v Austria No 21752/93* hudoc (1997) DA; *Pitkänen v Finland No 30508/96* hudoc (2003) DA and *Ashworth v UK No 39561/98* hudoc (2004) DA. Cf, the position of shareholders where an interference with a possession held by the company results in a reduction in the value of their shares: *Agrotexim v Greece* A 330-A (1995); 21 EHRR 250.

[59] Eg, *López Ostra v Spain* A 303-C (1994); 20 EHRR 277 (Article 8) and *Hatton v UK* 2003-VIII; 37 EHRR 611 (Article 8).

[60] *No 13728/88*, 65 DR 250 (1990) and *Rayner v UK No 9310/81*, 47 DR 5 (1986) (Article 1 of the First Protocol 'does not, in principle, guarantee a right to the peaceful enjoyment of possessions in a pleasant environment').

[61] 1999-III; 29 EHRR 615 GC.

impact of French laws allowing public entry onto the applicants' lands in order to pursue an activity—hunting—to which they held strong ethical objections.

III. ACCESS TO PROPERTY

In *Loizidou v Turkey*,[62] the Court had to deal with what it characterized as an issue of access to property in order that the property owner could exercise her rights. The facts of the case are complicated by the political background to the application, which concerns the Turkish occupation of northern Cyprus.[63] The applicant claimed that the defendant state had interfered with her rights under Article 1 of the First Protocol because, directly or indirectly, it had responsibility for her, a Greek Cypriot, being denied access to her real property in northern Cyprus. A majority of the Commission held that the complaint was really about the applicant's freedom of movement, the denial of which had the effect of preventing her physical access to the land. It said that 'the right of peaceful enjoyment of one's possessions' does not include, as a corollary, the right of freedom of movement'.[64] In two separate dissenting opinions, Messrs Rozakis and Pellonpää took a much wider view of the content of the right to enjoy one's possessions.[65] The Court, finding resonance in the Commission's minority view, rejected the majority characterization of the applicant's complaint.[66] It noted that her complaint was not limited to the denial of physical access to her property; it was that the refusal of access 'has gradually, over the last 16 years affected the right of the applicant as a property owner'.[67] The Court considered that the applicant 'effectively lost all control over, as well as all possibilities to use and enjoy, her property. The continuous denial of access must therefore be regarded as an interference with her rights under Article 1 of the First Protocol'.[68] There is force in this argument: alien property owners may have no right of entry to a state to visit their property but the rights they have in respect of their property which do not require their presence should not be interfered with. Nor should they be deprived of their property by reason of their absence alone.

The finding of a violation Article 1 of the First Protocol on the basis of a denial of access to property has significant implications for the right of return for internally displaced persons. It was later applied in *Doğan and Others v Turkey*[69] where the authorities cited terrorist-related incidents in the local area as the ground for the decision to refuse Turkish nationals access to their villages. The Court found that the measures 'deprived the applicants of all resources from which they derived their living' and 'affected the very substance of ownership' of the properties.[70] In the exercise of its powers to order 'just

---

[62] 1996-VI; 23 EHRR 513 GC.

[63] See *Chrysostomos, Papachrysostomou and Loizidou v Turkey Nos 15299/89, 15300/89 and 15318/89*, 68 DR 216 (1991).

[64] *Loizidou v Turkey* A 310 (1995); 20 EHRR 99 para 98 Com Rep. Apart from the very particular circumstances of this application, the position of the majority might be explained by the way the case was pleaded, because matters of freedom of movement as aspects of the applicant's right to liberty featured prominently in her claims.

[65] In Mr Rozakis's words, it includes 'the possibility to repair an immoveable good; or the possibility usefully to exploit the possession; or the possibility to exchange a possession through the free acquisition of another one, etc...'.

[66] *Loizidou v Turkey* 1996-VI; 23 EHRR 513 GC.   [67] Id, para 60.

[68] Id, paras 60, 61, and 63. See also *Cyprus v Turkey* 2001-IV; 35 EHRR 731 GC; *Eugenia Michaelidou Developments Ltd and Michael Tymvios v Turkey* hudoc (2003); and *Xenides-Arestis v Turkey* hudoc (2005); 44 EHRR SE 185.

[69] 2004-VI; 41 EHRR 231, where, unlike the applicant in the *Loizidou* case, the applicants did not hold formal title, but derived economic benefit from the land.

[70] Id, para 143.

satisfaction' the Court stated that the most appropriate remedy for denial of access cases was for the national authorities to facilitate return of the applicants to their villages and pay compensation for the period during which they were denied access. In the *Doğan* case, 'just satisfaction' was an award of compensation only because the applicants no longer wished to return to their villages.[71]

IV. POSITIVE OBLIGATIONS

Positive obligations on the state to protect the enjoyment of possessions are implied in Article 1 of the First Protocol. In *Öneryildiz v Turkey*[72] the Grand Chamber said of the protection afforded by Article 1 of the First Protocol:

> Genuine, effective exercise of the right protected by that provision does not depend merely on the state's duty not to interfere, but may require positive measures of protection, particularly where there is a direct link between the measures which an applicant may legitimately expect from the authorities and his effective enjoyment of his possessions.

The case concerned a methane explosion in a municipal rubbish tip, which resulted in thirty-nine deaths and the destruction of ten homes in a surrounding illegal settlement. Two years before the explosion, the local council responsible for the tip and relevant government departments received an experts' report advising that the tip did not comply with health and safety regulations. Specifically, the report warned of the danger of a methane explosion to neighbouring dwellings due to the absence of a ventilation system to allow for the controlled release of accumulated gases. The applicant contended that the failure to inform the settlement's inhabitants of the danger posed by the tip together with the failure to install ventilation shafts violated Article 1 of the First Protocol. The Court held that the obligation to protect property required the authorities to 'take practical steps' to avoid the destruction of the applicant's house: an effective measure would have been 'the timely installation of a gas-extraction system' at the tip since this would have complied with the relevant regulations and general practice in the area. Without a practical response of this kind the mere provision of information to nearby residents enabling them to assess the risks they might run as a result of their choice to live near the tip would not have absolved the state of its responsibilities.[73] The Court majority concluded that, as there was clearly a causal link between the state's 'negligence' and the destruction of the applicant's house, there was a breach of a positive obligation to protect property, which a mere award of compensation on generous terms could not remedy.[74] In *Öneryildiz* the authorities had actual knowledge of the risk of damage to property if the state failed to act and of the measures required to obviate the risk.

In other cases it has been held that positive obligations may also include obligations to provide compensation and expeditious processes,[75] and, where interference leads to the determination of a civil right, a process that fully satisfies Article 6(1).[76] Further, the obligation to protect property includes an obligation to prevent private interferences. State

---

[71] *Doğan and Others v Turkey* hudoc (2006) (just satisfaction).

[72] 2004-XII; 41 EHRR 325 para GC.   [73] Id, paras 101, 107–8 and 136.

[74] Id, paras 135 and 137. Judge Mularoni opined that no positive obligation to protect a right of property should extend to buildings erected in breach of town planning regulations. Judge Türmen confined his dissent to the issue of whether there was a 'possession'.

[75] *Almeida Garrett, Mascarenhas Falcão v Portugal* 2000-I; 34 EHRR 642. See also *Păduraru v Romania* 2005-XII (failure by state to take 'timely and consistent action' to address the restitution of property unlawfully taken under a previous regime).

[76] See below, pp 675–6.

responsibility will be engaged when the private interference with property is an outcome of the exercise of governmental authority[77] or a failure to exercise governmental authority that is required by law to uphold private law rights.[78] In *Gustafsson v Sweden*[79] the state had no legal obligation to act to protect the applicant's business from industrial action, which interfered with the delivery of supplies, as under Swedish law the authorities had no legal role to play in upholding the relations between the applicant and his suppliers. The Court considered that the matter 'concerned exclusively relationships of a contractual nature between private individuals'.[80] This is to be contrasted with the situation in the public law sphere where the state may be required to 'provide adequate protection' to individuals against interference with the enjoyment of their property whatever the requirements of domestic law.[81]

It is clear that the state is not obliged to act to prevent loss of value as a result of market factors.[82] Further, the scope of the positive obligation has not extended to protecting identifiable persons from economic loss that has been knowingly caused by the state in the reform of the economic sector. This is illustrated in *Gayduk v Ukraine*[83] where the state implemented a programme of monetary reform that, combined with high inflation, resulted in severe depreciation of the value of money deposited in savings accounts. In order to rectify the hardship caused to account holders, laws were passed that established an 'indexation-of-deposits' scheme to compensate savers for financial loss following devaluation and to maintain the real value of deposits. Payments under the scheme were subject to funds being made available in the state Treasury, but, as matters transpired, the funds were never provided. The applicants contended that in establishing the scheme the state had assumed an obligation to pay the indexed amounts. The Court, however, applied a general principle regardless of the particular circumstances contended by the applicant: it held that Article 1 of the First Protocol was not applicable because it 'does not impose any general obligation on states to maintain the purchasing power of sums deposited through the systematic indexation of savings'.[84]

In practice, whether an obligation is considered as a positive or negative obligation, the analysis will be the same. In *Broniowski v Poland*[85] the Grand Chamber explained the approach to be taken:

> In both contexts regard must be had to the fair balance to be struck between the competing interests of the individual and the community as a whole. It also holds true that the

---

[77] Eg, *James v UK* A 98 (1986); 8 EHRR 123 PC (enactment of legislation enabling long lease tenants to purchase the freehold interest in privately rented property).

[78] Eg, *Immobiliare Saffi v Italy* 1999-V; 30 EHRR 756 GC, see further below p 689, and *Prodan v Moldova* 2004-III (authorities failed to provide the means required by law to execute judgments for eviction of tenants and restitution of apartments). The judicial determination of private law disputes will not necessarily engage the state's responsibility: in *Törmälä v Finland* No 41258/98 hudoc (2004) DA, the Court said 'domestic court regulation of property disputes according to domestic law does not, by itself, raise an issue under Article 1 of the First Protocol'. See also *Anheuser-Busch Inc v Portugal* hudoc (2007); 45 EHRR 830 para 83 GC.

[79] 1996-II; 22 EHRR 409.   [80] Id, para 60.

[81] *Whiteside v UK* No 20357/92, 76-A DR 80 (1994) (Article 1 of the First Protocol applied where the applicant was persistently harassed in her home by a former boyfriend) and *Novoseletskiy v Ukraine* No 47148/99 hudoc (2003) (complaint of failure of authorities to investigate theft admissible).

[82] Nor to protect against the effects of inflation, *X v FRG* No 8724/79, 20 DR 226 (1980). Cf, *Akkuş v Turkey* 1997-IV; 30 EHRR 533 (inflation may be relevant in determining the fair balance where there is delay by the state in the payment of a judgment debt) and *Solodyuk v Russia* hudoc (2005) (inflation relevant to the fair balance where there is delay in payment of pensions).

[83] *Nos 45526/99 et al* 2002-VI DA.   [84] *Ibid.*   [85] 2004-V; 40 EHRR 495 para 144 GC.

aims mentioned in that provision may be of some relevance in assessing whether a balance between the demands of the public interest involved and the applicant's fundamental right of property has been struck. In both contexts the State enjoys a certain margin of appreciation in determining the steps to be taken to ensure compliance with the Convention...

It was the close inter-relation of the alleged omissions and acts that led the Court to decline to examine the facts under the head of positive obligations or negative duties in the *Broniowski* case. Instead it simply proceeded to determine whether the conduct of the state had struck a fair balance after having decided Article 1 of the First Protocol applied.

2. THE STRUCTURE OF ARTICLE 1, FIRST PROTOCOL AND THE INTER-RELATIONSHIP OF ITS PROVISIONS

I. THE THREE RULES

The Court has broken down Article 1 of the First Protocol into its component parts and has gradually established the relationship between them. Its language has become familiar by frequent repetition. In *Sporrong and Lönnroth v Sweden*,[86] the Court stated:

[This provision] comprises three distinct rules. The first rule, which is of a general nature enounces the principle of peaceful enjoyment of property; it is set out in the first sentence of the first paragraph. The second rule covers deprivation of possessions and subjects it to certain conditions; it appears in the second sentence of the same paragraph. The third rule recognises that the [contracting] states are entitled, amongst other things, to control the use of property in accordance with the general interest, by enforcing such laws as they deem necessary for the purpose; it is contained in the second paragraph.

In *James v UK*,[87] the Court explained the relationship between the three sentences:

The three rules are not 'distinct' in the sense of being unconnected: the second and third rules are concerned with particular instances of interference with the right to peaceful enjoyment of property and should therefore be construed in the light of the general principle enunciated in the first rule.

The three sentences in Article 1 of the First Protocol will henceforth be referred to as Article 1/1/1, Article 1/1/2, and Article 1/2.

It follows from the above passage that Article 1/1/1 is not only a statement of principle. It also provides a third, separate basis for regulating interferences with the 'peaceful enjoyment of possessions' that do not qualify as a deprivation of a person's possessions subject to Article 1/1/2 or a control of the use of property subject to Article 1/2.[88] For example, in the *Sporrong and Lönnroth* case itself, the Court found that the grant of

---

[86] A 52 (1982); 5 EHRR 35 para 61 PC. Cf, *James v UK* A 98 (1986); 8 EHRR 123 para 37 PC.

[87] A 98 (1986); 8 EHRR 123 para 37 PC. See also eg, *Anheuser-Busch Inc v Portugal* hudoc (2007); 45 EHRR 830 para 62 GC.

[88] Regarding the rationale for developing a residual category of interferences, see Allen, *Property*, pp 103–4; and Pellonpää, in Mahoney, Matscher, Petzold, and Wildhaber, eds, *Protecting Human Rights: The European Perspective*, 2000, pp 1088–92.

expropriation permits, which did not fall within Article 1/1/2 or 1/2, was subject to control under Article 1/1/1 as an interference with the peaceful enjoyment of the houses concerned. The Court said that an analysis of the nature of an interference requires a consideration of the first sentence only after it is determined that the second and third sentences do not apply.[89]

When considering whether Article 1/1/1 has been complied with, the Court applies a 'fair balance' test. In the *Sporrong and Lönnroth* case,[90] the Court stated:

> For the purposes of [Article 1/1/1] ... the Court must determine whether a fair balance was struck between the demands of the general interest of the community and the requirements of the protection of the individual's fundamental rights. The search for this balance is inherent in the whole of the Convention and is also reflected in the structure of Article 1.

On the facts of the *Sporrong and Lönnroth* case[91] the Court found that there had been a breach of Article 1/1/1 because the grant of the expropriation permits, which adversely affected the property rights of the applicants, did not involve a 'fair balance' between the public and the private interests concerned.[92] In terms of the structure of Article 1, what is important to note is that, as the passage from the judgment quoted in the preceding paragraph suggests, the Court has since applied its 'fair balance' test—which was devised particularly to provide a criterion by which to assess compliance with Article 1/1/1—when deciding cases under Articles 1/1/2 and 1/2 also. Indeed, although cases may still be dealt with by reference to Article 1/1/2 or Article 1/2 separately, and may focus upon the particular language of these sentences when this is done, there is a tendency for the Court to decide cases simply by reference to its 'fair balance' test whatever sentence, if any, it identifies as being the one within which the case might technically fall.

When applying the 'fair balance' test, the Court generally leaves it to the state to identify the community interest; claims made by the state will seldom be reviewed.[93] The balancing process thereafter may be complex and will always involve acts of judgment of a political (or policy) kind. It is hardly surprising that the Court has conceded a wide margin of appreciation to a state in reaching its decision that the community interest outweighs the individual's claims. This is true whether the case falls within Article 1/1/1 or Article 1/1/2 or Article 1/2, although the language of these last two sentences indicates a little further what factors the state ought to take into account. To that extent, an applicant may enjoy a certain advantage if he is able to persuade the Court to consider the matter under these provisions rather than under the general principle, but the benefits will be marginal only. For instance, under Article 1/1/2, a foreign owner of property could always be assured of the minimum protection of general international law, even if a state were able to persuade the Court that the fair balance did not import equivalent protection for national owners. The language of Article 1/2 has also afforded states particularly wide latitude in respect of interferences that amount to a control of the use of property.[94]

As will be apparent, it may be very difficult to determine within which sentence of Article 1 a particular case falls. It is perhaps for this reason that the Court does not always indicate under which sentence a case is being decided. This may be illustrated

---

[89] A 52 (1982); 5 EHRR 35 para 61 PC. [90] Id, para 69. [91] See further, below, p 672.
[92] See further, below, p 674, on the *Sporrong and Lönnroth* case. [93] See below, p 668.
[94] See further, below, pp 686–94.

by reference to the treatment in *Papamichalopoulos v Greece*[95] of the question whether there was a *de facto* deprivation of property that brought Article 1/1/2 into play. The applicants' land in Greece had been occupied by a public body for public purposes but without legal sanction. The Greek courts had upheld the applicants' title to the land but it, or land of equivalent value, had not been returned to them. The applicants had been denied access to the land and were effectively precluded from dealing with it in any way; even though they remained formally the owners, that situation had not been remedied.[96] What is remarkable, however, is that the Court did not identify the particular sentence within which the case fell. Although it concluded that the *de facto* interference was serious enough to amount to an expropriation of the property, which would suggest that technically Article 1/1/2 was the relevant sentence, the Court does not mention any particular sentence, merely deciding that there had been a breach of Article 1.[97] The Court's recent disinclination in a number of cases[98] to specify the relevant sentence into which an interference falls to be considered, and use of earlier decisions to determine the fair balance regardless of the sentence under which they were decided, also suggests that the identification of the type of interference is less important to the outcome of a case than is the process involved in the application of the 'fair balance' test.

II. A LEGITIMATE AIM

For an interference with the right to property to comply with Article 1 of the First Protocol, it must have a legitimate aim. This requirement has been read into Article 1/1/1,[99] and is expressly stated 'in the public interest' and 'in the general interest or to secure the payment of taxes and other contributions or penalties' requirements in Articles 1/1/2 and 1/2 respectively. There is no distinction to be made between the 'public interest' and the 'general interest'. Absence of a legitimate aim will entail a violation of Article 1 of the First Protocol without more.[100] The identification of the objective of an interference with property and its characterization as being for a legitimate aim is primarily for the state. Measures taken in compliance with European Community law pursue a legitimate aim.[101] Where the interference involves the implementation of social and economic policies by legislative action it will be presumed that the interference has a legitimate aim, and the burden will rest with the applicant to demonstrate that the state's judgment is 'manifestly without reasonable foundation'.[102] It is difficult to imagine circumstances in which the Court would dispute the purpose alleged by the government[103] or contest its assertion

---

[95] A 260-B (1993); 16 EHRR 440 Com Rep. On *de facto* deprivation, see further below, p 678.

[96] Id, para 45.

[97] It is argued that in light of the treatment of the *Papamichalopoulos* case in *Matose e Silva, Lda v Portugal* 1996-IV; 24 EHRR 573, the *de facto* expropriation should be regarded as governed by Article1/1/1: Pellonpää, *Protecting Human Rights*, p 1100.

[98] Eg, *Öneryildiz v Turkey* 2004-XII; 41 EHRR 325 GC; *Stretch v UK* hudoc (2003); 38 EHRR 196; *SA Dangeville v France* 2002-III; 38 EHRR 699; and *Solodyuk v Russia* hudoc (2005).

[99] *Beyeler v Italy* 2000-I; 33 EHRR 1225 GC.   [100] *Burdov v Russia* 2002-III; 38 EHRR 639.

[101] *SA Dangeville v France* 2002-III; 38 EHRR 699 and *Bosphorus Airways v Ireland* hudoc (2005); 42 EHRR 1 GC.

[102] *Broniowski v Poland* 2004-V; 43 EHRR 1 para 149 GC. See also *James v UK* A 98 (1986); 8 EHRR 123 para 46 PC; *Pressos Compania Naviera SA v Belgium* A 332 (1996); 21 EHRR 301 para 37; *Zvolský and Zvolská v Czech Republic* 2002-IX para 67; *Jahn v Germany* 2005-VI; 42 EHRR 1084 para 91 GC; and *JA Pye Ltd and JA Pye (Oxford) Land Ltd v UK* hudoc (2007); 46 EHRR 1083 para 71 GC.

[103] The standard of proof is low: see eg, *Ambruosi v Italy* hudoc (2001); 35 EHRR 125 para 28, where the state failed to indicate the purpose but the Court gleaned it from the 'elements of the case'. See also *Phocas v France* 1996-II; 32 EHRR 221.

that the measure had a legitimate aim.[104] In *Lithgow v UK*,[105] the Court said that the 'public interest' factor in Article 1/1/2 'relates to the justification and motives for the actual taking'. In that case, the applicants strongly, but unsuccessfully, contested the desirability of measures for the nationalisation of the ship-building industry. In *James v UK*,[106] they challenged the characterization as being in the public interest of a legislative programme designed to transfer property rights from one individual to another for the purpose of enfranchising long lease-holders. The applicants relied on the French text—'*pour cause d'utilité publique*'—and the practice of some European states to narrow the notion of public interest to 'community interest'. The Court rejected this claim, maintaining that the object and purpose of Article 1 of the First Protocol was to protect against '*arbitrary confiscation of property*'. Accordingly:

> The taking of property in pursuance of a policy calculated to enhance social justice within the community can properly be described as being 'in the public interest'.[107]

The Court's preparedness to describe the aim of an interference at a high level of abstraction means that even penal confiscations might be explained as being legitimate. In such a case, the most an applicant would be able to establish would be a lack of due process if the interference were decided to be in the determination of a criminal charge against him and the fair hearing obligation in Article 6 was not satisfied. In many cases, deprivations of property will be under acts of legislation by Parliament. Any 'civil' right that the applicant may have had will have been removed by the legislation and there will be no place for Article 6(1).[108] If, therefore, the expropriation is to be attacked successfully, it must be on the conditions that attach to it rather than for the reason for which it was done.

III. THE PRINCIPLE OF LAWFULNESS

Article 1 of the First Protocol requires that the interference in question satisfy the requirement of lawfulness.[109] The condition derives from the 'rule of law, one of the fundamental principles of a democratic society, inherent in all the Articles of the Convention'.[110] A finding that the requirement of lawfulness has been offended is conclusive of a violation

---

[104] In *Hentrich v France* A 296-A (1994); 18 EHRR 440 para 39, the Court accepted the first (the prevention of tax evasion) of two reasons the state had given for interfering with the applicant's property and then found no need to consider the other (regulation of the property market). See also *The Former King of Greece v Greece* 2000-XII; 33 EHRR 516 GC and *Chassagnou v France* 1999-III; 29 EHRR 615 GC. The Court has found it sufficient to establish the legitimacy of the interference that the state 'considered it necessary to resolve this problem': *Zvolský and Zvolská v Czech Republic* 2002-IX para 68. The Court may, however, take international law into account: *Beyeler v Italy* 2000-I; 33 EHRR 1225 GC, and the practice of other member states: *Bäck v Finland* 2004-VIII; 40 EHRR 1184. There is no test of strict necessity for the interference: *James v UK* A 98 (1986); 8 EHRR 123 PC and *Bäck v Finland*, ibid; cf, *Allard v Sweden* 2003-VII; 39 EHRR 321. See generally Arai, *The Margin of Appreciation Doctrine and the Principle of Proportionality in the Jurisprudence of the ECHR*, 2002, pp 154–6.

[105] A 102 (1986); 8 EHRR 329 PC and *Rosenweig and Bonded Warehouses Ltd v Poland* hudoc (2005); 43 EHRR 955.

[106] A 98 (1986); 8 EHRR 123 PC. See also *Holy Monasteries v Greece* A 301-A (1994); 20 EHRR 1 para 76 Com Rep. In most cases under Article 1/1/2, the public interest will be, in a wide sense, a planning objective. On the redistribution of property to private persons, see *Bramelid and Malmström v Sweden* Nos 8588/79 and 8589/79, 29 DR 64 (1982); 5 EHRR 249 and *Prötsch v Austria* 1996-V; 32 EHRR 255.

[107] *James v UK* A 98 (1986); 8 EHRR 123 para 49 PC. See also *Holy Monasteries v Greece* A 301-A (1994); 20 EHRR 1 paras 67–9.

[108] *Holy Monasteries v Greece* A 301-A (1994); 20 EHRR 1 para 80.

[109] Expressly stated in Article 1/1/2 ('provided by law') and Article 1/2 ('such laws'); implied in Article 1/1/1: see *Iatridis v Greece* 1999-II; 30 EHRR 97 para 58 GC.

[110] *Ibid.*

of Article 1 of the First Protocol; the Court need not then proceed to determine the fair balance.[111] In the context of the Convention, the requirement of lawfulness means the state must have a basis in national law for its interference[112] and that the law concerned must be accessible, precise, and foreseeable.[113] The identification of the legal basis of interferences and the satisfaction of the criteria of accessibility and certainty have seldom posed difficulties for the Strasbourg authorities.[114] An applicant's awareness of the way in which laws are publicized and an ability to seek information about the law will be relevant in determining whether laws are accessible and foreseeable. Where the applicant is a company, the Court has indicated that it will expect the company to obtain specialist advice on the requirements of domestic law.[115]

The Court is unlikely to review the interpretation or the application of national law by national authorities unless it has been applied 'manifestly erroneously or so as to reach arbitrary conclusions'.[116] Decisions of courts and tribunals affecting property rights should therefore adequately state the reasons on which they are based.[117] In *Baklanov v Russia*[118] the Court held that the law was not formulated with sufficient precision to 'enable the applicant to foresee, to a degree that is reasonable in the circumstances, the consequences of his actions' because of the national courts' lack of reference in their decisions to any legal provision as a basis for the interference and the apparent inconsistencies between the case law applied by the national court compared to the relevant legislation.

The compatibility of the interpretation and application of domestic law with the principle of lawfulness was also in issue in *Carbonara and Ventura v Italy*.[119] In that case the local authorities took possession of the applicants' land and built a school without following the procedures for expropriation of land set down in legislation. At the time of the works there was a substantial divergence in the decisions of the Italian Court of Cassation as to the effect on the landowners' title where public works had been completed upon land unlawfully taken into possession by the authorities. Eleven years after completion of the works in *Carbonara*, the Court of Cassation developed a doctrine of 'constructive expropriation' whereby a landowner unlawfully dispossessed of land by the authorities in order to construct public works, automatically lost ownership when the works were completed. Nine years after the Court of Cassation's decision it was determined that

---

[111] *Iatridis v Greece* 1999-II; 30 EHRR 97 para 58 GC. Cf, *Hentrich v France* A 296-A (1994); 18 EHRR 440. However, in *Doğan and Others v Turkey* 2004-VI; 41 EHRR 231, the Court expressly declined to determine the lawfulness of the refusal to allow access to homes, proceeding directly to determine the fair balance. See also *Brumărescu v Romania* 1999-VII; 33 EHRR 862 GC.

[112] A concept referring to both statutory law and case law: *Špaček, sro v Czech Republic* hudoc (1999); 30 EHRR 1010. European Community law will provide sufficient basis in national law where the interference results from compliance with its legal obligations: *Bosphorus Airways v Ireland* hudoc (2005); 42 EHRR 1 GC. Eg, *Iatridis v Greece* 1999-I; 30 EHRR 97 para 62 GC (refusal of the national authorities to reinstate the applicant in a cinema which he was licensed to operate, after the Athens High Court had quashed the order evicting him from the premises, was 'manifestly in breach of Greek law').

[113] *Carbonara and Ventura v Italy* 2000-VI paras 91 and 107 and *Beyeler v Italy* 2000-I; 33 EHRR 1225 para 88 GC.

[114] *Papamichalopoulos v Greece* A 260-B (1993); 16 EHRR 440 might be explained on the basis that there was no law authorizing the taking of the property.

[115] *Špaček, sro v Czech Republic* hudoc (1999); 30 EHRR 1010 para 59.

[116] *Beyeler v Italy* 2000-I; 33 EHRR 1225 para 108 GC; cf, *Špaček, sro v Czech Republic* hudoc (1999); 30 EHRR 1010. In a case confined to the conduct of administrative authorities in the application of national law, the Court may prefer to consider the conduct when applying the fair balance test, where the conduct is not determinative of the complaint: see *Broniowski v Poland* 2004-V; 43 EHRR 1 para 154 GC (fair balance not struck where conduct had a basis in statutory law but failed to comply with judgments of the Polish courts declaring the provisions unconstitutional).

[117] *Kushoglu v Bulgaria* hudoc (2007) para 52.   [118] Hudoc (2005) para 46.

[119] 2000-VI. See also *Belvedere Alberghiera srl v Italy* 2000-VI.

the five-year limitation period for compensation claims commenced running from the date of completion of the works, whereas at the time of the works on the applicants' land the Court of Cassation had held that no limitation period applied. In a case brought by the applicant, the Court of Cassation held that the constructive expropriation rule and the limitation period applied retrospectively to the applicants' situation, effectively barring any claim to compensation for the expropriation, while the state derived a benefit from taking unlawful possession of the land. The European Court considered that the outcome for the applicants 'could not be regarded as "foreseeable" as it was only in the final decision, the judgment of the Court of Cassation, that the constructive expropriation rule could be regarded as being effectively applied'. The unpredictable nature of the evolution of the Court of Cassation's jurisprudence, taken with the state's evidence that the Italian courts are not bound to apply a case law rule, and the denial of any possibility for the applicants to obtain damages led the Court to conclude that the effect of the application of the case law to the applicants' situation 'could only be described as arbitrary'.[120] The case highlights the value of uniformity in the interpretation and application of law by the highest domestic appeal court, but underlying the Court's findings is doubt about the lawfulness of a legal doctrine 'which, generally, enables the authorities to benefit from an unlawful situation in which the landowner is presented with a *fait accompli*'.[121]

The conferral under statute of wide powers to take exceptional measures may be lawful.[122] However, the Court in the *Hentrich* case[123] found that a right to take property by way of pre-emption, vested in the tax authorities but exercised by them according to an unexplicated policy, did not satisfy the requirement of foreseeability. Furthermore, there were no procedural safeguards to prevent the unfair use of the power.[124] The Court proceeded to find that the level of compensation awarded was inadequate.[125] While in *Družstevní Záložna Pri v Czech Republic*[126] the Court found that the exercise of a statutory power to place a credit union in receivership was not lawful for the purpose of Article 1 of the First Protocol solely because of the absence of procedural safeguards accompanying the interference. What was required was a reasonable opportunity for the applicant credit union to present its case with a view to effectively challenging the decision to place it in receivership.[127] This entailed access by the credit union to its business documents and the availability of judicial review by an independent tribunal of any denial to grant access. The safeguards against arbitrariness are implied conditions on the power of the state to interfere with the right to property.

The principle of legal certainty may altogether release the state from the requirement of lawfulness in situations involving either the continuing application of a law that has been held to be an unconstitutional 'for a limited, purely transitional, period of time' until a new law has been enacted, or the correction of legislative defects with only prospective effect, in order to avoid a 'substantial legal lacuna'.[128] Further, at times uncertainty in the law that is not sufficient to offend the lawfulness principle may be relevant in determining

---

[120] Id, paras 69 and 71–2.   [121] Id, para 66.

[122] Eg, *Air Canada v UK* A 316-A (1995); 20 EHRR 150 para 41 (forfeiture of aircraft).

[123] A 296-A (1994); 18 EHRR 440 para 42.

[124] The applicant was not given the opportunity in domestic proceedings to make submissions on the underestimation of the price or the tax authorities' position. See further below, at n 682. Cf, *Air Canada v UK* A 316-A (1995); 20 EHRR 150, where judicial review proceedings were available. See also *Fredin v Sweden (No 1)* A 192 (1991); 13 EHRR 784 para 50, in which the Court said that the absence of judicial review proceedings will not, in itself, constitute a violation of Article 1 of the First Protocol, although an issue under Article 6 may arise.

[125] *Hentrich v France* A 296-A (1994); 18 EHRR 440 para 48.

[126] Hudoc (2008). The Court distinguished *Fredin v Sweden (No 1)* A 192 (1991); 13 EHRR 784.

[127] Id, para 89.   [128] *Roshka v Russia* No 63343/00 hudoc (2003) DA (tax legislation).

whether the fair balance has been upset. This is illustrated in *Beyeler v Italy*[129] in relation to the lack of clarity in the statutory time limits for the exercise of a right of pre-emption over cultural works and the considerable latitude the Court afforded the authorities in the exercise of that right.

3. ARTICLE 1/1/1: INTERFERENCE WITH THE PEACEFUL ENJOYMENT OF POSSESSIONS

As noted, the origin of the Court's opinion that Article 1/1/1 provides a ground for regulating interferences with a person's peaceful enjoyment of his possessions[130] that is separate from and additional to those in Articles 1/1/2 and 1/2 is the judgment in *Sporrong and Lönnroth v Sweden*.[131] There the applicants' properties had been affected by expropriation permits granted to the City of Stockholm for the purposes of redevelopment of the city centre. The expropriations had not been executed but, while the permits were in force, the owners were prohibited from construction on the sites and were subject to planning blight. The permits and prohibition orders remained in place in one case for twenty-three and twenty-five years and in the other for eight and twelve years. The prohibitions on construction were clearly measures of control of use within Article 1/2. However, the Court decided that neither the expropriation permits as a matter of form nor the consequential prohibitions on construction as a matter of substance amounted to a deprivation within Article 1/1/2.[132] It was their purpose as an initial step towards deprivation of property that precluded their consideration as deprivations.[133] Instead, there had been an 'interference' with the applicants' enjoyment of their possessions under Article 1/1/1.

Since the *Sporrong and Lönnroth* case there have been others involving an interference with the peaceful enjoyment of possessions against which Article 1/1/1 provides protection where there is neither a deprivation nor a control of property. Consequently, distinct types of Article 1/1/1 interferences have developed although the jurisprudence does not establish a principle by which an interference within the first sentence may be discerned. In some cases the Court provides no reason for classifying a particular case under Article 1/1/1,[134] but in most a general approach by which such a classification may be arrived is indicated.[135] The Court uses a sequential analysis of an interference, by which it considers the application of the first sentence only after eliminating the applicability of the particular instances contained in the second and third sentences,[136] which enables it to maintain a clear definition of the ambit of Article 1/1/2 and Article 1/2 while allowing the types of Article 1/1/1 interferences to otherwise remain open. For instance, cases involving measures taken with a view to the expropriation of property, as in the *Sporrong and Lönnroth* case, will fall within Article 1/1/1 for the reasons stated above.[137] For the

---

[129] 2000-I; 33 EHRR 1225 GC.   [130] See further above, p 666.   [131] A 52 (1982); 5 EHRR 35 PC.
[132] Id, paras 62–5.
[133] See also *JA Pye (Oxford) Ltd and JA Pye (Oxford) Land Ltd v UK* hudoc (2007); 46 EHRR 1083 GC, where the purpose, rather than effect, of the interference was decisive in the determination that the measure was a 'control of use' of land not a 'deprivation of possessions'.
[134] Eg, cases involving the delayed payment of compensation or inadequate compensation for the expropriation of land: see *Akkuş v Turkey* 1997-IV; 30 EHRR 365 para 27 and *Platakou v Greece* 2001-I para 54.
[135] Allen, *Property*, pp 108–10, argues for one conception of Article 1/1/1 that 'is concerned with the appropriation of resources for public use, where such appropriation is not in the form of a taking of a full ownership interest' although noting some important cases in which the Court has not adopted this approach.
[136] See below, p 675.
[137] See also *Erkner and Hofauer v Austria* A 117 (1987); 9 EHRR 464; *Poiss v Austria* A 117 (1987); 10 EHRR 231; *Prötsch v Austria* 1996-V; 32 EHRR 255 (transfers pending the completion of land consolidation schemes);

same reasons, where the state denies access to property this will amount to an interference with the peaceful enjoyment of possessions.[138]

The Court has found Article 1/1/1 applicable in various other situations. In *Iatridis v Greece*[139] the Court indicated that an interference with a leasehold interest by the state that could amount to neither a deprivation, as the applicant held less than an ownership interest in the premises, nor a control on use of property, nonetheless fell within Article 1/1/1. In *Bramelid and Malmström v Sweden*[140] the Commission further circumscribed Article 1/1/2 when it considered that Article 1/1/1 was applicable to legislation permitting majority shareholders to buy out shares held by a minority on the basis that Article 1/1/2 should apply only to acquisitions by a public body. Extinction of a judgment debt by legislation may also fall within Article 1/1/1. In *Stran Greek Refineries and Stratis Andreadis v Greece*,[141] the Court (somewhat surprisingly) decided that the making null and unenforceable by legislation of an arbitration award in the applicants' favour was an 'interference' within Article 1/1/1 rather than (as contended by the applicants) a *de facto* deprivation, or even a *de iure* deprivation within Article 1/1/2.[142]

The Court has also relied upon Article 1/1/1 in the case where the 'complexity of the factual and legal position prevents it being classified in a precise legal category'.[143] In *Beyeler v Italy*[144] the classification under Article 1/1/1 of an exercise of a right of pre-emption, over an art work purchased under a contract that was held to be void by the national authorities, released the Court from inquiring into the correctness of the decision of the national courts and the nature of the applicant's property interest under national law, which would have been required for a classification under Article 1/1/2 or Article 1/2. While in *Jokela v Finland*[145] the 'interconnected factual and legal elements' of the case, involving a comparison between the valuation methods for the expropriation of land and the levying of tax with respect to it, led the Court to examine the nature of each interference and the effects of the interferences separately: the expropriation of the land, which clearly fell within Article 1/1/2, and the inheritance tax imposed on the land, within Article 1/2, were found to be proportionate and not in breach of Article 1; however, their combined effects, considered under Article 1/1/1, were excessive.

Pialopoulos v Greece hudoc (2001); 33 EHRR 977; *Phocas v France* 1996-II; 32 EHRR 221; and *Matos e Silva, Lda v Portugal* 1996-IV; 24 EHRR 573 (interferences with development of land pending expropriation).

[138] See *Loizidou v Turkey* 1996-VI; 23 EHRR 513 GC; *Cyprus v Turkey* 2001-IV; 35 EHRR 30 GC; and *Xenides-Arestis v Turkey* hudoc (2005); 44 EHRR SE 185. See also *Doğan and Others v Turkey* 2004-VI; 41 EHRR 231. See further above, pp 663–4.

[139] 1999-II; 30 EHRR 97 GC. See also *Bruncrona v Finland* hudoc (2004); 41 EHRR 592.

[140] Nos 8588/79 and 8589/79, 29 DR 64 (1982); 5 EHRR 249. See also, *Bäck v Finland* No 37598/97 hudoc (2002) DA (debt adjustment legislation). Cf, *James v UK* A 98 (1986); 8 EHRR 123 PC, where legislation providing for the purchase of property by private persons was classified under Article 1/1/2.

[141] A 301-B (1994); 19 EHRR 293 para 67. See Sermet, *The European Court on Human Rights and Property Rights*, 1998, p 29. See also *Smokovitis v Greece* hudoc (2002) (retrospective legislation extinguishing judgment debts) and *Mykhaylenky v Ukraine* 2004-XII (failure to enforce court order for three to seven years).

[142] Regarding the extinction of civil claims by legislation, see eg, *Pressos Compania Naviera SA v Belgium* A 332 (1995); 21 EHRR 301 (extinction of civil claim a 'deprivation' within Article 1/1/2); *Draon v France* hudoc (2005); 42 EHRR 807 GC; and *Maurice v France* hudoc (2005); 42 EHRR 885 GC (head of damage extinguished a 'deprivation' within Article 1/1/2); and *National & Provincial Building Society, Leeds Permanent Building Society and Yorkshire Building Society v UK* 1997-VII; 25 EHRR 127 (extinction of civil claims for the recovery of monies paid as taxes a control on the use of property to secure the payment of taxes within Article 1/2).

[143] *Beyeler v Italy* 2000-I; 33 EHRR 1225 para 106 GC. This is relevant where positive obligations are engaged: *Broniowski v Poland* 2004-V; 43 EHRR 1 para 136 GC; *Öneryildiz v Turkey* 2004-XII; 41 EHRR 325 para 133 GC; and *Prodan v Moldova* 2004-III para 60.

[144] Id. Cf, *Hentrich v France* A 296-A (1996); 18 EHRR 440. For criticism of the classification of the interference in *Beyeler* under Article 1/1/1 rather than Article 1/1/2, see Rudolf, 94 AJIL 736 at 739–40 (2000).

[145] 2002-IV; 37 EHRR 581 paras 55, 60, and 65.

Where there has been an interference with the peaceful enjoyment of possessions in the sense of Article 1/1/1, the Court must consider whether the interference complies with the principle of lawfulness.[146] Only once the legality of the interference is established does the question of whether there has been a fair balance between 'the demands of the general interest of the community and the requirements of the protection of the individual's fundamental rights' arise for determination.[147]

As to the application of the 'fair balance' test under Article 1/1/1, even though the Court in *Sporrong and Lönnroth* was prepared to concede a wide margin to the state in 'complex and difficult' matters of city centre planning, when deciding whether a 'fair balance' had been struck, it did not find acceptable the 'inflexibility' of the Swedish arrangements which left the property owners in a state of great uncertainty over an extensive period, without any effective remedy for their concerns. The applicants, the Court said, had borne:

> an individual and excessive burden which could have been rendered legitimate only if they had the possibility of seeking a reduction of the time-limits or of claiming compensation.[148]

What is interesting about this approach is the suggestion that the *way* in which the national authorities strike the balance may be a factor in deciding whether in *substance* they have struck the balance compatibly with the Convention's requirements.[149] Further, the provision of compensation as an element in striking the right balance can arise other than in cases of outright deprivation which would fall within Article 1/1/2.[150] Similar considerations motivated the Court in finding that the administration of a scheme for the consolidation of agricultural holdings in the interest of their economic exploitation was in violation of Article 1/1/1.[151] The scheme had not been brought to a conclusion sixteen years after it had been implemented against the applicants' land and there was no means of redress for their interim losses up to the time it was implemented.

The 'fair balance' principle or test laid down in the *Sporrong and Lönnroth* case finds its authority in two complementary sources. The first is the general balance which the Court holds to be pervasive throughout the Convention between the enjoyment of individual rights and the protection of the public interest.[152] The second is in the substantive content of 'law' as understood by the Strasbourg authorities to include protection against the arbitrary and disproportionate effects of an otherwise formally valid national law.[153] The first provides the elements for the balancing equation. The second gives more precise guidance as to how the weight of the factors in the balance are to be assessed. One important

---

[146] *Iatridis v Greece* 1999-II; 30 EHRR 97 GC, where the Court unanimously decided that it was not necessary to determine whether a fair balance had been struck because the interference was unlawful. See further, above p 670.

[147] *Stran Greek Refineries and Stratis Andreadis v Greece* A 301-B (1994); 19 EHRR 293 para 69.

[148] Id, para 73. The Court found no need to go on to consider the question of the construction prohibitions. See also *Matos e Silva, Lda v Portugal* 1996-IV; 24 EHRR 573 (measures taken preliminary to expropriation in place for thirteen years with the detriment to the applicant aggravated by uncertainty as to the fate of the property and compensation) and *Terazzi srl v Italy* hudoc (2002) DA.

[149] See also *Bäck v Finland* 2004-VIII; 40 EHRR 1184, where the excessiveness of a court ordered irrevocable extinction of a creditor's debt depended on the procedure applied.

[150] A 52 (1982); 5 EHRR 35 PC.

[151] *Erkner and Hofauer v Austria* A 117 (1987); 9 EHRR 464 and *Poiss v Austria* A 117 (1987); 10 EHRR 231. The cases are examples in which the Court did consider the facts in terms of each of the three particular sentences in Article 1. After concluding that the cases did not fall within either Article 1/1/2 or 1/2, it decided that there was a breach of Article 1/1/1.

[152] *Belgian Linguistic* case A 6 p 32 (1968); 9 EHRR 252. [153] See above, pp 344–8.

aspect of the insistence that interferences with possessions be found in an identified legal source in the national legal system is that the law will generally provide an indication of the factors motivating the measures of interference and the application of the law will be evidence of how the state has assessed the competing interests. While the state's conclusions are not the last word, since the European Court claims the ultimate power of review,[154] they nonetheless carry great weight because the language of Article 1 suggests a wide measure of discretion for the state and because many factors have to be taken into account, some of which are not amenable to objective assessment.

The clear tendency in the jurisprudence has, as suggested, been to assimilate the assessment of all interferences with the peaceful enjoyment of possessions under the single principle of fair balance set out in the *Sporrong and Lönnroth* case, this despite the language of Article 1 of the First Protocol suggesting distinct standards for measures which deprive a person of his property and measures which seek to control property. There are two reasons for this. The first is, as already indicated, that the Court has isolated a third head of interference with the peaceful enjoyment of possessions in the *Sporrong and Lönnroth* case, a category which has assumed greater importance because of the reluctance of the Court to expand the notion of 'deprivation' to cover *de facto* deprivations of property beyond all but the most clear cases. The Court has subsumed other, extensive but less absolute measures affecting property under the *Sporrong and Lönnroth* head. The second reason is that the Court has had to spell out the conditions upon which an interference in the sense of Article 1/1/1 could be properly exercised. These conditions are both substantive and procedural and are elaborated in such a way that has proved useful with respect to the express powers of interference in the second and third sentences of Article 1 of the First Protocol. The applicants succeeded in the *Sporrong and Lönnroth* case because there was no procedure by which they could challenge the long-continued application of the expropriation permits which were blighting their property nor were they entitled to any compensation for the loss that this situation had brought about.[155] These matters are of general importance because neither of the express grounds of interference, deprivation or control of use, is expressly accompanied by either procedural conditions or compensatory obligations (save as may be required by 'the general principles of international law') for its use.[156] The Court has relied on the *Sporrong and Lönnroth* principle to import similar considerations into cases falling under Article 1/1/2 or Article 1/2.[157] This is not to say that the detailed application of the 'fair balance' test will be the same in all circumstances[158] but that it provides the framework for resolving issues whatever the characterization of the interference.[159] The protection the 'fair balance' test gives is that the burden of promoting a community interest should not fall excessively on a property owner. This was relevant,

---

[154] *Sporrong and Lönnroth v Sweden* A 52 (1982); 5 EHRR 35 PC and *Broniowski v Poland* 2004-V; 43 EHRR 1 GC.

[155] See also *Bruncrona v Finland* hudoc (2004); 41 EHRR 592. One of the factors which counted against the applicants in *Katte Klitsche de la Grange v Italy* A 293-B (1994); 19 EHRR 368 and *Phocas v France* 1996-II; 32 EHRR 221 was that they had not used a procedure available to them to remedy the interference.

[156] See below, pp 679–80, on 'the general principles of international law'.

[157] Eg, deprivation of property (*Tre Traktörer Aktiebolag v Sweden* A 159 (1989); 13 EHRR 551 and *Hentrich v France* A 296-A (1994); 18 EHRR 440) and control of use of property (*Allan Jacobsson v Sweden (No 1)* A 163 (1989); 12 EHRR 56; *Immobillaire Saffi v Italy* 1999-V; 30 EHRR 756 GC; and *Megadat.com srl v Moldova* hudoc (2008)).

[158] Eg, in *Gillow v UK* A 109 (1986); 11 EHRR 355 para 148 Com Rep, the Commission suggested that the application of the proportionality principle is different in cases involving deprivation and cases involving control of use.

[159] Eg, *Stretch v UK* hudoc (2003); 38 EHRR 196.

for example, in *Kjartan Asmundsson v Iceland*[160] where the Court found a violation of Article 1 of the First Protocol because of the harsh impact on the individual of changes made to pension rules and the availability of an alternative method of securing the public interest. Property owners should also have some process to challenge whether this is the case, a process which can take into account not just the balance of advantage but which can consider whether the public good pursued could otherwise have been achieved than by trespassing on the individual rights of the property owner.[161] In the *Stran Greek Refineries* case,[162] the Court made reference to the position in public international law (even though it had no formal relevance because the case involved the government of Greece and two Greek nationals) as one element in deciding whether the state had struck a 'fair balance' between the rights of the applicants and the interests of the community.

Delay, unpredictability, and inconsistency in the exercise of the state's power to interfere with property rights are all evidence that the measures adopted by the state and their implementation have led to a disproportionate interference with property rights. The obligation to safeguard these rights in a 'practical and effective' way requires the state to ensure that these features are not present when the power is exercised. In *Broniowski v Poland*[163] the Grand Chamber said:

> [I]t should be stressed that uncertainty—be it legislative, administrative or arising from practices applied by the authorities—is a factor to be taken into account in assessing the state's conduct. Indeed, where an issue in the general interest is at stake, it is incumbent on the public authorities to act in good time, in an appropriate and consistent manner.

Moreover, in *Broniowski* the contradiction between national law and legislative promises establishing rights of property on the one hand and legislation and administrative practices obstructing the exercise of those rights on the other was a matter of such general interest within the community that its continuation was considered to have undermined the principle of the rule of law underlying the Convention. The Grand Chamber[164] reasoned:

> [T]he imperative of maintaining citizen's legitimate confidence in the state and the law made by it, inherent in the rule of law, required the authorities to eliminate the dysfunctional provisions from the legal system and to rectify the extra-legal practices.

Uncertainty surrounding property rights that is generated by state action or inaction has been an influential factor in the decision that a fair balance has been upset in cases characterized under Article 1/1/2[165] and Article 1/2[166] as well, articulating a broader concern

---

[160] 2004-IX; 41 EHRR 927, where the Court considered a reduction, instead of a total deprivation, of entitlement would have amounted to an interference justified by legitimate community interests.

[161] Many interferences with the enjoyment of possessions will involve the 'determination of a civil right' and therefore the individual will be entitled to an Article 6(1) procedure: *Sporrong and Lönnroth v Sweden* A 52 (1982); 5 EHRR 35 PC. See eg, *Katsoulis v Greece* hudoc (2004). However, this will not always be the case, eg for taxation.

[162] *Stran Greek Refineries and Stratis Andreadis v Greece* A 301-B (1994); 19 EHRR 293 para 72.

[163] 2004-V; 43 EHRR 1 paras 151 and 184 GC. See also *Beyeler v Italy* 2000-I; 33 EHRR 1225 paras 114 and 120 GC. In *Erkner and Hofauer v Austria* A 117 (1987); 9 EHRR 464 para 76, the Court noted that the passing of time for the purposes of the balance in Article 1/1/1 was independent of the 'reasonable time' required by Article 6(1).

[164] Id, para 184.

[165] Eg, *Hentrich v France* A 296-A (1994); 18 EHRR 440 para 47 (power of pre-emption over land was exercised 'rarely and scarcely foreseeably').

[166] Eg, the series of eviction cases against Italy, eg *Immobiliare Saffi v Italy* 1999-V; 30 EHRR 756 para 54 GC (inefficient enforcement of court orders); *Stere v Romania* hudoc (2006); 45 EHRR 191 para 53; *Hutten-Czapska v Poland* 2006-VIII; 45 EHRR 52 para 168 GC; and *Megadat.com slr v Moldova* hudoc (2008) para 71, a case decided as a 'control on use' under Article 1/2. See below, pp 689–90.

with the effects of the manner of exercise by national authorities of their powers of interference that goes beyond a consideration of the impact of the interference on the individual to an examination of the nature of the impact on the community.[167]

A 'fair balance' will sometimes require the payment of compensation for the interference with property rights under Article 1/1/1.[168] The *Sporrong and Lönnroth* case does not
establish clearly the nature and extent of this obligation. While we know the extent of the
'just satisfaction' ordered by the Court, the judgment, typically, does not enunciate the
principles upon which the award was made.[169] The identification and assessment of the loss
endured by the applicants was difficult. Because a central element of their claim was that
there had been no national process to make even a tentative evaluation of it, the Court was
without any guidance from the national authorities, still less decisions, to which it could
defer. It is not possible to discern whether the measures of 'just satisfaction' represent a
different valuation of the loss suffered by the applicants or a proportion of the loss, the
proportion required to satisfy the balance between the public interest in urban planning
and the burden that should fall on any property owner. If the state had decided the question of compensation differently from that awarded by the Court by way of satisfaction,
it does not follow that the Court would have found a violation of Article 1/1/1, given the
wide margin conceded to the state to fix the fair balance. The measure of compensation
required by the fair balance test has been considered in cases concerning deprivations
under Article 1/1/2 and measures of control under Article 1/2.[170]

4. ARTICLE 1/1/2: DEPRIVATION OF PROPERTY

I. WHAT IS A DEPRIVATION?

For there to have been a deprivation of property, the applicant must, of course, demonstrate that he or she had title to it.[171] In principle, there will be a deprivation of property
only where all the legal rights of the owner are extinguished by operation of law[172] or
by the exercise of a legal power to the same effect.[173] However, not all such incidents are
deprivations. The Court has treated some seizures of property as an aspect of the control
of property.[174] If ownership is seen as a bundle of rights, the fact that an owner has been
deprived of one right will not usually be sufficient to say that he has been deprived of
ownership: rather it is a control of the use of property.[175] In the *Holy Monasteries* case,[176]

---

[167] See generally Allen, *Property*, pp 155–62.   [168] See generally Allen, 28 MJIL 287 (2007).
[169] *Sporrong and Lönnroth v Sweden* A 88 (1984); 7 EHRR 293 (just satisfaction). In *Erkner and Hofauer v
Austria* A 124-D (1987); 13 EHRR 413 and *Poiss v Austria* A 124-E (1987); 13 EHRR 414, the Court approved
friendly settlements which involved elements of compensation. There is much more detail in *Pine Valley
Developments v Ireland* A 246-B (1993); 16 EHRR 379.
[170] See further below, pp 680–6 and 688.   [171] In *Holy Monasteries v Greece* A 301-A (1995); 20 EHRR 1.
[172] Eg, *Pressos Compania Naviera SA v Belgium* A 332 (1995); 21 EHRR 301.
[173] Eg, *Lithgow v UK* A 102 (1986); 8 EHRR 329 PC. Acts in accordance with the condition upon which property is held are not interferences and, *a fortiori*, not deprivations of property: *Fredin v Sweden* A 192 (1991); 13
EHRR 784.
[174] The purpose, rather than the effect, of an interference will be important: eg *Allegemeine Gold-und
Silberscheideanstalt [AGOSI] v UK* A 108 (1986); 9 EHRR 1 and *Air Canada v UK* A 316-A (1995); 20 EHRR 150.
See further below, pp 690–1.
[175] *Banér v Sweden No 11763/85*, 60 DR 128 at 140 (1989) and *Hutten-Czapska v Poland* 2006-VIII; 45 EHRR
52 para 160 GC. See Pellonpää, *Protecting Human Rights*, pp 1096–7. Eg, where the operation of law transfers the
beneficial ownership in registered land the interference is a 'control on the use' of property: see *JA Pye (Oxford)
Ltd and JA Pye (Oxford) Land Ltd v UK* hudoc (2007); 46 EHRR 1083 GC.
[176] A 301-A (1995); 20 EHRR 1 para 66.

the government argued that the creation of a presumption in favour of state ownership of disputed land was merely a procedural device to allow the settlement of such disputes and not an interference with established titles. In any event, no steps had been taken to implement the provisions of any law which might have transferred title from the applicants. The Court found that the presumption effectively vested an unchallengeable title in the state because the monasteries were not in a position to prove their own superior title, relying as they did on ancient, adverse possession. The Greek law was, the Court said, a substantive provision, the effect of which was to transfer ownership to the state. The fact that the law had not yet been implemented was no guarantee that it would not be. Taking both matters together, there had been a deprivation of the applicants' property.

In the absence of a formal extinction of the owner's rights, the Court has been very cautious about accepting that a *de facto* deprivation of property qualifies as a 'deprivation' for the purpose of Article 1/2.[177] *De facto* takings are generally understood to occur when the authorities interfere substantially with the enjoyment of possessions without formally divesting the owner of his title. In the *Sporrong and Lönnroth* case the Court held that the facts did not amount to a *de facto* deprivation of property so that Article 1/1/2 did not apply.[178] It was in the *Papamichalopoulos* case[179] that the Court first conceded that the physical occupation of land was so extensive and the possibility of dealing with it in any way so remote that there was a *de facto* expropriation, though even here the Court did not say expressly that there had been a 'deprivation'. In *Hentrich v France*,[180] the applicant claimed that there had been a *de facto* expropriation, even though the effect of the national decision was to transfer ownership from the individual to the state. The act of interference complained of in the *Hentrich* case was the exercise of a right of pre-emption by the tax authorities over property bought by the applicant at a price the tax authorities considered to be below its market value. No allegation of fraud was necessary to trigger the right. An independent procedure to recover any lost tax revenue was available. If the right of pre-emption were exercised, the purchaser was paid his purchase price plus 10 per cent.[181] The Court did not explicitly endorse the applicant's claim that there had been a *de facto* taking, although it did agree that there had been a deprivation of property. Its treatment of the lawfulness of the deprivation entirely in terms of the substantive qualities of the French law indicates that the Court regarded the taking as *de iure*. Real instances of *de facto* takings will be rare and will be in breach of the Convention because they will not have been 'provided for by law'.[182] There has been little support so far for Professor Pellonpää's suggestion that the test should be whether the interference amounts to a taking under international law.[183]

---

[177] Eg, *Stran Greek Refineries and Stratis Andreadis v Greece* A 301-B (1994); 19 EHRR 293 and *Hutten-Czapska v Poland* 2006-VIII; 45 EHRR 52 GC. The Court noted without comment that the treatment of the applicant was not regarded by the national law as a *de facto* expropriation (and that, therefore, he was not entitled to compensation) in *Katte Klitsche de la Grange v Italy* A 293-B (1994); 19 EHRR 368 para 47.

[178] Id, paras 62–3. For criticism of the judgment, see Higgins, 176 *Hague Recueil* 260 at 343–57 and 367–8 (1982). The judgment was by ten votes to nine, but the dissenting judges did not regard this as a case of *de facto* deprivation of property either. See also *Saliba v Malta* hudoc (2005) and *Matos e Silva, Lda v Portugal* 1996-IV; 24 EHRR 573 para 85, where, in deciding there was no deprivation within Article 1/1/1, the Court emphasized the reversible nature of the situation.

[179] A 260-B (1993); 16 EHRR 440. See above, p 668. The Court suggested in *Matos e Silva, Lda v Portugal* 1996-IV; 24 EHRR 573, that the *de facto* expropriation in *Papamichalopoulos* was governed by Article 1/1/2.

[180] A 296-A (1994); 18 EHRR 440. Cf, *Beyeler v Italy* 2000-I; 33 EHRR 1225 GC (exercise of a right of pre-emption considered under Article 1/1/1).   [181] Id, paras 20–1.

[182] Eg, *Loizidou v Turkey* 1996-VI; 23 EHRR 513 GC; *Vasilescu v Romania* 1998-III; 28 EHRR 241; and *Carbonara and Ventura v Italy* 2000-VI (case law was arbitrary). See also *Brumărescu v Romania* 1999-VII; 33 EHRR 862 GC (the lawfulness of the interference was not decided).

[183] Concurring in *Papamichalopoulos v Greece* A 260-B (1993); 16 EHRR 440 Com Rep.

It may be formally necessary to determine whether an interference is a deprivation of property or an extensive control of the use of property because, in principle, they are governed by different provisions. But in practice the classification is not so important (and the Court sometimes does not make the distinction) because of the overriding importance and general and common application of the 'fair balance' test.[184]

II. THE GENERAL PRINCIPLES OF INTERNATIONAL LAW

It is necessary first to consider the reference in Article 1/1/2 to the 'general principles of international law'. General international law protects *alien* property against arbitrary expropriation without compensation.[185] Both the compensation standard[186] for and the methods of valuation of property[187] taken are controversial and, arguably, they have changed considerably since the Convention was drafted.[188] The content of the 'general principles' to one side, reference to them in Article 1/1/2 allows two possible interpretations of their effect. The first is that the reference benefits only alien property holders, since they are, if only indirectly, the only beneficiaries under international law.[189] On this interpretation, what the Convention does is give such persons a tribunal where they, as individuals or legal persons, may bring claims against an expropriating state without the intervention of their governments.[190] The alternative is that the Convention incorporates the *standards* of general international law in this particular case for the benefit of all persons protected by the Convention, thereby establishing a right to compensation for all persons deprived of their property with the compensation payable being defined by the 'general principles of international law'.[191] In *James v UK*,[192] relying on the *travaux*, the Court opted for the former interpretation, stating that it was not the intention of the drafting states to extend the protection of general international law to nationals. In fact, practically all cases arising under Article 1 of the First Protocol, have involved the property of nationals.

Whether reference to 'general principles of international law' will ever be given much effect for the compensation of aliens is doubtful if the view of the Commission in the *Gasus* case prevails.[193] A German company was deprived of its property which had been in the possession of a Dutch company, sold by the former to the latter under a reservation of title agreement by which title was not to pass to the purchaser until the final purchase

---

[184] Regarding the 'fair balance' test, see further above, pp 667 and 675.

[185] Jennings and Watts, eds, *Oppenheim's International Law*, Vol I, 9th edn, pp 911–27.

[186] Western states insist on prompt, adequate, and effective compensation; developing states argue for a standard that is more favourable to the state. Portugal made the following reservation (now withdrawn) on becoming a party to the Convention (21 YB 16–17 (1978)): 'expropriation of large landowners, big property owners and entrepreneurs or shareholders may be subject to no compensation under conditions to be laid down by the law', to which France, Germany, and the UK responded: 'The general principles of international law require the payment of prompt, adequate and effective compensation in respect of the expropriation of foreign property' 22 YB 16–20 (1979).

[187] See Jennings and Watts, *op cit*, pp 921–2.

[188] Christie, 38 BYIL 307 (1962); Aldrich, 88 AJIL 585 (1994); and *ELSI* case (*US v Italy*) (1989) ICJ Rep 15 at 67–71.

[189] See *Beaumartin v France* A 296-B (1994); 19 EHRR 485.

[190] *James v UK* A 98 (1986); 8 EHRR 123 para 62 PC.

[191] Id, para 61. In the European context, these would probably mean 'prompt, adequate and effective compensation'.

[192] Id, paras 58–66. The Court made extensive reference to the preparatory work, para 64. The judgment confirms the long-established position of the Commission: see *Gudmundsson v Iceland No 511/59*, YB 394 (1960). See also *Lithgow v UK* A 102 (1986); 8 EHRR 239 paras 111–19 PC.

[193] *Gasus Dosier-und Fördertechnik v Netherlands* A 306-B (1995); 20 EHRR 403.

price had been paid in full. On the bankruptcy of the Dutch company, the property had been seized by the Dutch authorities for the settlement of the company's tax debts. The Commission found no violation of Article 1/1/2, the seizure being in the public interest, according to Dutch law, and not disproportionate to the purpose of protecting creditors. This was a case where the nationality of the property owner might have been of consequence. However, the Commission said only:

> the deprivation of property which occurred cannot be compared to these measures of confiscation, nationalisation or expropriation in regard to which international law provides special protection to foreign citizens and companies.[194]

Whether this really represents the condition of international law is open to doubt. Lump sum settlements commonly include isolated items of foreign property taken or destroyed by a state as well as those seized under nationalization programmes.[195] Still, if the former Commission's position prevails, even more attention will be focused on the 'fair balance' test, applying to the deprivation of some alien possessions as well as all national possessions, to establish the incidence and content of the obligation to provide compensation in the event of a deprivation of property.[196] In the *Gasus* case, the Court did not need to address this question because it found the case to be governed by Article 1/2 (to secure the payment of taxes) rather than Article 1/1/2.[197]

III. COMPENSATION

While it is clearly established under the Convention that nationals may not take advantage of the substance of 'the general principles of international law' to protect them against the consequences of deprivations of their property by their own state, the Court has not left such people bereft of protection. What it has said is that the need for a 'fair balance' between the public and the private interest that runs through Article 1 of the First Protocol requires, in all but the exceptional case,[198] *some* compensation.[199] Even interferences in protection of strong public interests may require some compensation. In the *Stran Greek Refineries* case,[200] the Court was unanimously of the view that the cancellation of an arbitration award by legislation, rendering it unenforceable, in pursuit of the policy of rectifying distorted arrangements entered into by the former military dictatorship in Greece, was a disproportionate interference with the applicants' rights. The effect of the national law was that they had lost the entire award, which was an assessment of

[194] Id, para 63. The finding of no violation was only on the casting vote of the President but the dissenting opinions place practically no importance on the nationality of the applicant.

[195] Eg, *Yeager v Iran*, Iran-US Claims Tribunal, 17 Iran-US CTR92 (1987).

[196] A further reason why this is desirable is that it provides a proper standard of protection under the Convention for aliens, even if the development of the rules of general international law diminishes their entitlement: Frowein, at p 655, n 1, above, p 522.

[197] See below, pp 692-3. See also *Beyeler v Italy* 2000-I; 33 EHRR 1225 GC. For criticism of the application of Article 1/1/1 to the exercise of a right of pre-emption in *Beyeler* as an attempt to circumvent the compensation standards applicable to aliens under the general principles of international law, see Rudolf, 91 AJIL 736 at 739 (2000).

[198] See further below, pp 684-5.

[199] *Lithgow v UK* A 102 (1986); 8 EHRR 329 para 120 PC. The state will be vulnerable where there is *no* right to *any* compensation in national law: *Papastavrou v Greece* 2003-IV; 40 EHRR 361. Moreover, compensation must be paid within a reasonable time: *Guillemin v France* 1997-I; 25 EHRR 435 and *Jucys v Lithuania* No 5457/03 hudoc (2008) (a case decided under Article 1/2). This compensation requirement under the fair balance test will apply to non-nationals as well as nationals.

[200] A 301-B (1994); 19 EHRR 293.

the compensation due to the applicants as a result of the termination of their contractual rights. The Court effectively deferred to the arbitration tribunal's judgment that this was the proportionate level of compensation by ordering the state to pay the full amount of the award plus interest as just satisfaction. The compensation requirement was also infringed in the *Holy Monasteries* case where there were strong public interest considerations as well.[201] The law which the Court found deprived the monasteries of their lands effectively made no provision for compensation, providing only a discretionary power for use by a public body if a monastery were left with insufficient land to support its monks. The law as a whole failed to provide a fair balance between the rights of the applicants and the public interest.

The level of compensation must be 'reasonably related' to the 'value' of the property taken.[202] The general measure of compensation for an expropriation is stated in *Pincová and Pinc v Czech Republic*[203] as one that is 'reasonably related to its "market" value, as determined at the time of the expropriation'.[204] However, Article 1/1/2 requires neither full compensation[205] nor the same level of compensation for every category of deprivation.[206] In *James v UK*,[207] the Court said that where the state was pursuing economic reform or social justice, less reimbursement was due to the dispossessed owners than full market value. The state enjoys a wide margin in assessing the appropriate level of compensation and, indeed, in estimating the value of the property in the first place. Where the amounts are fixed by reference to objective standards, with the possibility of representation for those deprived of property in the process, intervention by the Court is unlikely.

The importance of valuation methods is demonstrated in a series of Greek cases in which the Court held that a standardized system of assessing compensation for land expropriated for the construction of roads imposed on the applicants 'an individual and excessive burden'. Greek legislation deemed that all land adjoining a major road derived a benefit from any road improvements, and provided for this presumed increase in value

---

[201] A 301-A (1994); 20 EHRR 1. The Court approved a friendly settlement. See also *Draon v France* hudoc (2005); 42 EHRR 807 GC and *Maurice v France* hudoc (2005); 42 EHRR 885 GC, where ethical considerations, equitable treatment, and the proper organization of the health service did not justify extinguishing pending claims without compensation.

[202] Eg, *Draon v France* hudoc (2005); 42 EHRR 807 GC and *Maurice v France* hudoc (2005); 42 EHRR 885 GC; and *Papachelas v Greece* 1999-II; 30 EHRR 923 para 48 GC. See also *Lallement v France* hudoc (2002) (the applicant's attachment to his family home was taken into account in deciding the adequacy of market value compensation paid for the expropriation of another portion of the applicant's farm) and *Kozacioğlu v Turkey* hudoc (2008) (failure to take into account the historical value of an expropriated building when calculating compensation or during proceedings to increase the award was a violation; judgment upheld by the Grand Chamber (2009)).

[203] 2002-VIII.

[204] Id, para 53. See also *Papamichalopoulos v Greece* A 330-B (1995) para 39 (just satisfaction) and *Hentrich v France* A 296-A (1994); 18 EHRR 440 para 71 ('current market value').

[205] See *Papachelas v Greece* 1999-II; 30 EHRR 923 GC and *JA Pye (Oxford) Ltd and JA Pye (Oxford) Land Ltd v UK* hudoc (2001); 46 EHRR 1083 para 54 GC. Contrast Frowein, at p 655, n 1, above, p 525, who states, '[I]t would seem that under normal circumstances for the expropriation of private property the full value must be paid to assure fair compensation.' Pellonpää argues that compensation in deprivation cases should generally correspond to the full value of the property where the violation is not merely in a failure to pay compensation, *Protecting Human Rights*, p 1089.

[206] *Lithgow v UK* A 102 (1986); 8 EHRR 329 PC, rejecting the applicants' claim that the measure of compensation in nationalization cases should be the same (ie market value) as for compulsory purchase of land. See also *Papamichalopoulos v Greece* A 330-B (1995), stating that the criteria for determining reparation for an unlawful deprivation of property will differ from that used for a lawful one.

[207] A 98 (1986); 8 EHRR 123 PC. In *The Former King of Greece v Greece* hudoc (2002); 36 EHRR CD 43 para 78 GC, it was accepted that less than full compensation may also be called for where the expropriation is with a view to achieving 'such fundamental changes of a country's constitutional system as the transition from monarchy to republic'. The onus is on the state to justify a departure from the market value standard: *Scordino v Italy (No 1)* hudoc (2006); 45 EHRR 207 GC.

to be deducted from the compensation payable for the land expropriated to construct the road. While the Court considered it legitimate to take into account the benefit derived from the works by owners of expropriated land who retained ownership of land adjoining the road, it rejected the method of assessing compensation as 'too inflexible' so as to be 'manifestly without reasonable foundation' because the presumption of benefit could not be rebutted. What was required in order to respect the fair balance was a system that gave landowners an opportunity to make representation in the valuation proceedings[208] that the work had no, or less, benefit or caused varying degrees of loss.[209]

However, the Court has accepted that nationalization may require the application of a general scheme for assessing compensation. In *Lithgow v UK*,[210] the legislation established alternative methods for valuing the ship building companies nationalized under the Aircraft and Shipbuilding Industries Act 1977, depending on the position of the companies to be nationalized. One method relied on the market value of the shares in quoted companies; the other, for shares in unquoted companies, was based on an assumed 'base value'. The value of all shares was assessed during a 'reference period' before the election after which the legislation was enacted, on the assumption that this was a period when the value would be influenced by market factors alone and not by political considerations, like the prospect of nationalization. Other methods of valuation, claimed by the applicants to be more appropriate, were nominated by them but the Court held that those adopted by the government were not inconsistent with Article 1/1/2. The Court held to this conclusion even though the effects of the scheme in the legislation, both generally and in relation to individual firms, resulted in levels of compensation quite different from those claimed by the firms. Once the Court had accepted the rationality of the method itself, it was in no case persuaded that assessments were inconsistent with Article 1/1/2 by reason of the application of the general scheme.[211] Because the disparities between the companies' own valuations and the amounts of compensation awarded under the Act and approved by the Court were so great—for instance, one company received 1.8 million GBP in compensation when its cash assets alone totalled 2.2 million GBP—it would be a rare case for the Court to find a breach of Article 1 of the First Protocol by reason of the level of compensation alone.

In *Hentrich v France*,[212] the government's interference took the form of the exercise of a right of pre-emption over the applicant's land. The Court measured the proportionality of the government's action against its objective: the prevention of tax evasion. *One element* in the equation was the level of compensation. The Court found that the action was arbitrary in that the right of pre-emption was not exercised systematically, that there were other methods available for dealing with tax evasion which were not so burdensome on the individual *and* the level of compensation was inadequate. It was 'all these factors' which resulted in the conclusion that the applicant bore an 'individual and excessive burden'. While the judgment suggested that the matter might have been put right by procedural changes, it did not suggest that enhanced compensation would have done the same in the absence of procedural changes.[213] However, in *Beyeler v Italy*,[214] where

---

[208] *Efstathiou and Michailidis and Co Motel Amerika v Greece* 2003-IX; 43 EHRR 490.

[209] *Katikaridis v Greece* 1996-V; 32 EHRR 113 para 49 and *Papachelas v Greece* 1999-II; 30 EHRR 923 para 53 GC.

[210] A 102 (1986); 8 EHRR 329 paras 125–36 PC.

[211] Id, paras 137–51. For extensive comment, see Mendelson, 58 BYIL 33 at 52–63 (1987).

[212] A 296-A (1994); 18 EHRR 440 paras 47–9.

[213] Id, para 49. Given the nature of the violation, the Court considered, at para 71, that return of the land was the best form of redress, failing which there must be compensation paid for pecuniary damage assessed on the 'current market value of the land'. See also *Papamichalopoulos v Greece* A 330-B (1995) (just satisfaction).

[214] 2000-I; 33 EHRR 1225 GC, a case characterized as an Article 1/1/1 interference.

the issue focused on delay, enhanced compensation might have ensured that the exercise of a right of pre-emption over a work of art struck a fair balance. Central to the Court's judgment was its finding that the state had 'derived an unjust enrichment' by delaying for six years the exercise of the pre-emption right and then basing compensation on the price the buyer earlier paid for the painting, effectively ensuring it acquired the property 'well below its market value'.[215]

A combination of the level of compensation and concerns about consistency in the conduct of the state led a unanimous Grand Chamber in *Broniowski v Poland*[216] to find a breach of Article 1 of the First Protocol. In that case, the state had provided compensation for property owners for real property lost by them following the redrawing of territorial boundaries after the Second World War.[217] For economic reasons, the compensation was capped at 15 per cent of the market value, with no entitlement to compensation even at this level where some compensation had been paid earlier under other arrangements. As the applicant fell within the exception, he received only the 2 per cent of the value of his expropriated property that he had been paid earlier. The Court affirmed the approach taken in *James* and *Lithgow* in allowing that gains and losses to particular persons may be an inevitable consequence of measures taken in the complex and wide-reaching reform of the state, justifying a wide margin of appreciation in the assessment of compensation.[218] Nevertheless, this margin was not without its limits: ascertaining the fair balance requires 'an overall assessment of the various interests in issue'.[219] In *Broniowski* this involved an assessment of the compensation terms and also the conduct of the parties. In deciding whether the amount of compensation was reasonably related to the value of the property taken, the Court once more examined the method for determining levels of compensation. By contrast with *James* and *Lithgow*, however, it rejected the rationality of the method adopted by the state, finding 'no cogent reason why such an insignificant amount should *per se* deprive the applicant of the possibility of at least a portion of his entitlement on an equal basis with other Bug River claimants'.[220] Nor had the authorities acted in a foreseeable and consistent manner as required by the rule of law: administrative practices made the exercise of the applicant's legal entitlement unenforceable and legal provisions imposed continuing limitations on the applicant's assertion of his entitlement.[221]

In *Pincová and Pinc v Czech Republic* the level of compensation was central to the Court finding a breach of Article 1/1/2. In this case the Court focused on the impact on the individual of the method of assessing compensation. The unanimous view of the Court was that the applicants bore an 'excessive burden' as compensation payable under legislation, that restored property wrongfully taken during the previous regime, was based on the purchase price of the property paid by the applicants thirty years earlier. This amount did not enable the applicants to buy another home and, therefore, failed to take account of the applicants' consequent 'uncertain, and indeed difficult, social situation.'[222]

---

[215] Id, para 121. Compensation ordered on an 'equitable basis' also took into account the uncertainty and precariousness endured during the delay: hudoc (2002) para 2 GC (just satisfaction).

[216] 2004-V; 43 EHRR 1 GC, where the interference is characterized under Article 1/1/1.

[217] For the facts, see further above, p 661.   [218] Id, para 182.   [219] Id, para 151.

[220] Id, para 186. This reasoning suggests that 15% of the market value of the property would have sufficed to establish the fair balance, at least where other claimants were also receiving that level of compensation.

[221] Id, paras 184–5.

[222] 2002-VIII paras 61–2. Also relevant was the fact that the applicants had obtained the property in 'good faith' (para 59) and that costs reasonably incurred in the upkeep of the property, and required by law to be reimbursed, remained outstanding after seven years (para 63). See also *Velikovi v Bulgaria* hudoc (2007). See Allen, 13 CJEL 1 at 38–41 (2006–7).

An exceptional circumstance justifying no payment of compensation may arise as a result of the manner in which property has been acquired. In *Jahn v Germany*[223] the Grand Chamber considered the issue in a case involving a deprivation of property acquired during a transition period between two regimes. By land reform in the old German Democratic Republic (GDR), land was re-allocated to 'new farmers'. Their heirs could inherit the 'new farmers' rights to the land, which fell short of ownership under the communist GDR system, on condition that they kept the land in agricultural use; otherwise the land reverted to the state. The applicants in the *Jahn* case were heirs who did not meet this condition, but who, unlike other heirs in the same position, did not lose possession of their land owing to an administrative oversight. As a part of the process of transition to a system of private ownership of land in a capitalist system when the GDR became part of the new Germany, the GDR parliament enacted the 1990 Modrow law giving 'new farmers' and their heirs full ownership of their land (so that no limitation as to agricultural use applied), seemingly (their position was not mentioned) including persons such as the applicants who had benefited inadvertently. Following reunification, the German Parliament legislated in 1992 placing all heirs in the position they would have been in had the GDR land reform been properly applied, so that the applicants lost their land, without any compensation. It did so 'for reasons of fairness and social justice', seeking to prevent heirs who had met the agricultural use condition having an 'unfair advantage' over others to whom the Modrow law properly applied.[224] The Grand Chamber[225] held that the deprivation of property without payment of compensation did not upset the fair balance to be struck between protection of property and the public interest. Three factors were decisive: the uncertainty of the applicants' legal position under the Modrow law, the fact that the German legislature intervened 'within a reasonable time' after reunification to correct the defect in the Modrow law, and the social justice objective of the legislation.[226] The Court considered that the fact that the interference with property rights was implemented without compensation did not render it disproportionate 'given the "windfall" from which the applicants undeniably benefited as a result of the Modrow Law'.[227]

The majority view in *Jahn's* case does find support elsewhere in the Court's jurisprudence. In *National & Provincial Building Society, Leeds Permanent Building Society and Yorkshire Building Society v UK*[228] a similar approach towards applicants who exploit a situation of legal change to secure a property interest is evident. In *National & Provincial* the applicants claimed reimbursement of tax paid in the period mistakenly not covered by the relevant tax legislation between the end of a voluntary tax payment scheme and the commencement of a legally binding scheme for the payment of taxes, which applied retroactively. The Court unanimously decided that retrospective legislation extinguishing the applicants' claims to restitution of the unlawfully imposed tax without payment of compensation did not upset the fair balance. The 'windfall' feature of the case was relevant to both the strength of the public interest and the effect of the measure. The Court weighed 'the obvious and compelling public interest' to ensure private entities do not enjoy windfalls during transitional tax arrangements, particularly when they clearly understand it was Parliament's intention to include that period, against the fact that the applicants would have been obliged to pay the tax under the previous system of

---

[223] 2005-VI; 42 EHRR 1084 GC. See Allen, 13 CJEL 1 at 33–7 (2006–7).   [224] Id, paras 107–8.
[225] By eleven votes to six, reversing the unanimous judgment of the Chamber.
[226] Id, para 116. For a critique of the majority reasoning, see McCarthy, 3 EHRLR 295 at 300–2 (2007).
[227] *Ibid*.
[228] 1997-VII; 25 EHRR 127, a case considered under Article 1/2, see further below, p 693. Although expressly relied on by the majority of the Grand Chamber, the dissenting judges did not address the case.

taxation.[229] More fundamentally, the Court viewed the case against the background of the public interest in creating legal certainty in the lawfulness of revenue collected and the applicant's 'attempts to frustrate by all legal means those efforts'.[230] However, the *National & Provincial* case differs materially from *Jahn* on the manner of acquisition of the property insofar as at the time the property right was acquired it was clear to the applicants that it was the legislature's intent that no property should be acquired; whereas in *Jahn* the legislative intent at the point of acquisition (under the Modrow law) did not address the applicants' situation.

In *Zvolský and Zvolská v Czech Republic*,[231] the Court said that 'the manner in which land was generally acquired' by individuals under a former communist regime—in violation of property rights—will constitute an exceptional circumstance justifying the lack of compensation for a lawful expropriation carried out to redress such an infringement. However, the fair balance between protection of private property and the demands of the general interest may dictate that there be a mechanism by which the special circumstances of individual cases can be reviewed before government power to interfere with property rights is exercised. In *Zvolský and Zvolská* the applicants bore a 'disproportionate burden' when Czech legislation obliged them to return to previous owners, without compensation, land they had acquired in good faith under a deed that was freely entered into for good consideration during the communist era.[232]

The manner of acquisition of the property taken by the state may relate not only to conduct of the applicant but also to the source of the funding for the property. In *The Former King of Greece v Greece*[233] the state argued that there was no entitlement to compensation for the expropriation of property belonging to the deposed Greek royal family because the property benefited from considerable tax exemptions and other benefits that had been donated to the king acting in his public capacity. The Grand Chamber rejected the state's submission for three reasons. First, as a finding of fact, at least part of the property was paid for out of the Royal Family's private funds. Secondly, compensation had been paid when the property was previously expropriated, giving rise to a 'legitimate expectation to be compensated by the Greek legislation for the taking of their estates'. Thirdly, it was inappropriate that the state set off financial benefits granted against compensation, as benefits 'have no direct relevance to the issue of proportionality' of the interference.[234] This reasoning leaves open the question of the proper approach to be taken towards the payment of compensation where the property has been acquired or maintained by public funds. The first ground suggests that fairness requires the payment of compensation and counters the state's argument, as it is a rare case in which the state would have paid for the entire interest without contribution by the applicant. However, the second ground suggests that past practice establishing an expectation of compensation may qualify the operation of the principle contended and thus arguably upholds the principle's essential validity; while the third ground deals with the argument by an examination of the facts without determining the correctness of the principle asserted. In its just satisfaction judgment, the Court said that 'the manner of acquisition of the properties cannot deprive the first applicant of his right to compensation; it may, though, be taken into account for the determination of the level of compensation'.[235] While the Court was not prepared to

---

[229] Id, para 81.

[230] Id, para 82. See also *OGIS-Institut Stanislas, Ogec St Pie X and Blanche de Castille v France* hudoc (2004).

[231] 2002-IX para 72. See also *Pincová and Pinc v Czech Republic* 2002-VIII and Allen, 13 CJEL 1 at 38–41 (2006–7).

[232] Id, para 74.   [233] 2000-XII; 33 EHRR 516 GC.   [234] Id, para 98.

[235] Hudoc (2002); 36 EHRR CD 43 para 83 GC.

take into account the benefits accruing from state financial support when determining whether the failure to pay compensation was disproportionate, it was prepared to reduce the amount of pecuniary damages by a substantial amount 'in view of the privileges and other benefits awarded in the past to the properties.[236]

To summarize, in general the guiding principle remains the 'fair balance', reliance upon which is necessary to establish *any* right to compensation for nationals. It is also a principle that leaves a wide, though not unlimited, margin of appreciation to the state to determine what the level of compensation should be.

5. ARTICLE 1/2: CONTROL OF USE

I. CONTROL IN THE GENERAL INTEREST

If the provisions of Article 1/1 do not appear in practice to impose a substantial fetter on interference with property rights, the language of Article 1/2 is even more favourable to the state. Articles 1/1 and 1/1/1 are said 'not ... in any way to impair' the right of a state to *control the use* of property. Instead, any protection for an individual must be found in the 'in accordance with the general interest' limitation in the text of Article 1/2.[237] That the limitation upon state authority that flows from this wording will be narrow is confirmed by the phrase 'as it [the state] deems necessary', which suggests an unfettered discretion.[238] However, the Court has moved to the position that Article 1/2 is merely one of the three, not unconnected, rules in Article 1, all of which must be read in the light of the general principle of 'fair balance'.[239] Given the narrow reading ascribed to 'deprivation' of property in Article 1/1/2, the notion of 'control' of property in Article 1/2 is a correspondingly wider one[240] but, as the *Sporrong and Lönnroth* case shows, not every interference short of deprivation will be an act of controlling the use of property.[241]

The power of the state to intervene in cases of control that fall within Article 1/2 is a wide one. The Court has been notably unsympathetic to those who have taken development risks and who have failed to make any gains as a result of action or inaction by the state.[242]

---

[236] Id, paras 96 and 98. The impact of this approach to the assessment of compensation was significant as the Court awarded a sum for pecuniary damage at €13.2 million, far below the state's estimate of the properties' value of approximately €70.6 million.

[237] There is no significant difference between the way the Court regards 'general interest' in Article 1/2 and 'public interest' in Articles 1/1/1 and 1/1/2, see above, p 668.

[238] *Handyside v UK* A 24 (1976); 1 EHRR 737 PC and *Gasus Dosier und Fördertechnik GmbH v Netherlands* A 306-B (1995); 20 EHRR 403 (states as the 'sole judges' of necessity; Court to supervise the lawfulness and purposes of the restriction). The power of review extends also to proportionality of the measures taken to their purpose: *Chassagnou v France* 1999-III; 29 EHRR 615 GC and Peukert, above, p 665, n 1, p 64.

[239] Eg, *Allan Jacobsson v Sweden* A 163 (1989); 12 EHRR 56; *Hutten-Czapska v Poland* 2006-VIII; 45 EHRR 52 GC; and *JA Pye (Oxford) Ltd and JA Pye (Oxford) Land Ltd v UK* hudoc (2007); 46 EHRR 1083 GC.

[240] Eg, *Pine Valley Developments v Ireland* A 222 (1991); 14 EHRR 319, where the Court held that the failure to re-validate a planning permission nullified by the courts, resulting in very substantial reduction in the value of land, was not a *de facto* deprivation but a control of use. See also *Housing Association of War Disabled and Victims of War of Attica v Greece No 35859/02* hudoc (2006) DA (prohibitions on construction on land). Moreover, 'control' refers not only to use of property, but also to the right to dispose of property: see *Marckx v Belgium* A 31 (1979); 2 EHRR 330 PC, and the right to possess property: see *Hutten-Czapska v Poland* 2006-VIII; 45 EHRR 52 GC.

[241] A 52 (1982); 5 EHRR 35 PC. See also *Katte Klitsche de la Grange v Italy* A 293-B (1994); 19 EHRR 368, where a prohibition on construction imposed by a land use plan was characterized as an interference under Article 1/1/1.

[242] *Allan Jacobsson v Sweden* A 163 (1989); 12 EHRR 56; *Pine Valley Developments v Ireland* A 222 (1991); 14 EHRR 319; and *Håkansson and Sturesson v Sweden* A 171 (1990); 13 EHRR 1.

Given that the power of control of the state under Article 1/2 is so wide, an applicant may be driven to seeking protection of his property elsewhere in the Convention. Thus the powers of control under Article 1/2 may not be used discriminatorily,[243] and there may be specific guarantees that benefit some kinds of property, such as the guarantees of one's private life or home[244] or of the means of artistic communication.[245] There may also be procedural requirements under Article 6(1) or Article 13, which should accompany the exercise of Article 1/2 powers.[246]

A state may effect 'control' by requiring positive action by individuals or legal persons,[247] as well as by imposing restrictions upon their activities. Such restrictions might result from planning controls,[248] environmental orders,[249] rent control,[250] import and export laws,[251] forfeiture[252] and confiscation orders,[253] economic regulation of professions,[254] the seizure of property for legal proceedings,[255] inheritance laws,[256] regulation of vehicle registration,[257] limitation periods for actions for recovery of land,[258] regulation of the use of materials in the course of business,[259] protection of trademarks,[260] sanctions regimes,[261] business licences,[262] or regulation of hunting.[263]

While the state must indicate what 'general interest' is being served by the interference, it is unlikely to have its claim that the measure is necessary to secure it successfully challenged.[264] But because Article 1/2 has been brought under the 'fair balance' umbrella, the Court may go on to investigate the lawfulness and the proportionality of the controlling measure. Apart from the lawfulness in national law of the measures of control, the state must show that the fair balance is satisfied, ie that, in the light of the public good

[243] *Pine Valley Developments Ltd v Ireland* A 222 (1991); 14 EHRR 319 (Article 14).

[244] *Niemietz v Germany* A 251-B (1992); 16 EHRR 97 and *Gillow v UK* A 109 (1986); 11 EHRR 335 (Article 8).

[245] Cf, *Müller v Switzerland* A 133 (1988); 13 EHRR 212, where the Article 1 of the First Protocol argument was not even put to the Court (although, in the end, the Article 10 claim failed).

[246] In *Allan Jacobsson v Sweden* A 163 (1989); 12 EHRR 56 and *Webb v UK No 56054/00* hudoc (2004) DA, the Court found that there were adequate procedural avenues through which the applicants could have raised their complaints.

[247] *Denev v Sweden No 12570/86*, 59 DR 127 (1989) (obligation on landowner to plant trees in interests of environmental protection).

[248] Eg, *Allan Jacobsson v Sweden* A 163 (1989); 12 EHRR 56; *Pine Valley Developments v Ireland* A 222 (1991); 14 EHRR 319; *Haider v Austria No 63413/00* hudoc (2004) DA; *Papastavrou v Greece* 2003-IV; 40 EHRR 361; and *Saliba v Malta* hudoc (2005).

[249] Eg, *Fredin v Sweden* A 192 (1991); 13 EHRR 784.

[250] Eg, *Mellacher v Austria* A 169 (1989); 12 EHRR 391 PC and *Hutten-Czapska v Poland* 2006-VIII; 45 EHRR 52 GC.

[251] Eg, *AGOSI v UK* A 108 (1986); 9 EHRR 1.

[252] Eg, *Air Canada v UK* A 316 (1995); 20 EHRR 150 and *Butler v UK* 2002-VI.

[253] Eg, *Yildirim v Italy* 2003-IV. This will including restraint orders while criminal investigations and proceedings are in progress with a view to confiscation: eg, *Andrews v UK No 49584/99* hudoc (2002) DA.

[254] Eg, *Karni v Sweden No 11540/85*, 55 DR 157 (1988).

[255] Eg, *G, S and M v Austria No 9614/81*, 34 DR 119 (1983).

[256] Eg, *Inze v Austria* A 126 (1987); 10 EHRR 394.

[257] Eg, *Yaroslavtsev v Russia* hudoc (2004) and *Sildedzis v Poland* hudoc (2005); 44 EHRR 263.

[258] Eg, *JA Pye (Oxford) Ltd and JA Pye (Oxford) Land Ltd v UK* hudoc (2007); 46 EHRR 1083 GC.

[259] Eg, *Pinnacle Meat Processors Company v UK No 33298/96* hudoc (1998); 27 EHRR CD 217 and *Denimark Ltd v UK No 37660/97* hudoc (2000); 30 EHRR CD 144.

[260] *Paeffgen GmbH v Germany Nos 25379/04, 21688/05, 21722/05 and 21770/05* hudoc (2007) DA.

[261] *Bosphorus Airways v Ireland* hudoc (2005); 42 EHRR 1 GC.

[262] *Megadat.com srl v Moldova* hudoc (2008).

[263] Eg, *Posti and Rahko v Finland* hudoc (2002); 37 EHRR 158 and *Alatulkkila v Finland No 33538/96* hudoc (2005) DA (fishing rights).

[264] See above, pp 668–9.

underlying the control, the burden which falls on the individual is not excessive[265] and that the measures are not disproportionate.

JA Pye (Oxford) Ltd and JA Pye (Oxford) Land Ltd v UK[266] illustrates the wide scope of the margin of appreciation that may be enjoyed by the state when regulating the use of property. In *Pye's* case the Court considered the claim that the system of adverse possession as it applied to registered land in the United Kingdom was a disproportionate interference with the registered owners' property rights under Article 1 of the First Protocol. Under the UK legislation then in force, an action by a landowner for recovery of possession of registered land was prohibited after the land had been in adverse possession for a period of twelve years,[267] and the registered proprietor would be deemed to hold title to the land for the benefit of the adverse possessor, who therefore became the beneficial owner of the land.[268] The applicants in *Pye* were land development companies who, as the successive registered proprietors of agricultural land, entered into a grazing agreement with the Grahams, who were the owners of adjacent farmland. It was a term of the agreement that the Grahams were required to vacate the land when the agreement expired in 1983; however, the Grahams continued to use it for grazing even after their request for a further grazing agreement was refused and no response to their inquiries about their continued use of the land was received. In 1997 the Grahams registered cautions at the Land Registry Office indicating that they had obtained title to the land on the ground of adverse possession. In proceedings before the British courts, the applicants unsuccessfully sought to recover possession of the land by arguing that the Grahams had not been in 'adverse possession' as defined by domestic law. The applicants then took their complaints to the European Court where they argued, *inter alia*, that the absence of compensation for the loss of their right to ownership of the registered land upset the fair balance required by Article 1 of the First Protocol. The Grand Chamber disagreed: it held that there was no requirement to pay compensation for a loss resulting from the applicants' failure to observe a limitation period as this would undermine the aim of legal certainty, ie to prevent landowners from pursuing legal actions after the passing of a certain period of time.[269] Moreover, the Grand Chamber observed that there is no entitlement to compensation for lost possessions where the interference is a 'control of use' of property. There is no suggestion in the case that the size of the economic loss could have a bearing on the question of the payment of compensation for an interference categorized under Article 1/2. Nor was the legislation disproportionate on the ground that the applicants' economic loss was substantial.[270] The Grand Chamber attributed importance to the purpose of statutory limitation periods, which it reasoned must apply regardless of size of the value of the land. Regarding the 'windfall profit' to the adverse possessor, the Grand Chamber stated:

> [T]he registered land regime in the United Kingdom is a reflection of a long established system in which a term of years' possession gave sufficient title to sell. Such arrangements

---

[265] Compensation may be less likely to be required for a fair balance under Article 1/2 than under Article 1/1/2: *Banér v Sweden No 11763/85*, 60 DR 128 (1989) and *JA Pye Ltd and JA Pye (Oxford) Land Ltd v UK* hudoc (2007); 46 EHRR 1083 para 79 GC. However, it may be a relevant factor in assessing proportionality: *Immobiliare Saffi v Italy* 1999-V; 30 EHRR 756; *Housing Association of War Disabled and Victims of War of Attica v Greece* hudoc (2006); *Islamic Republic of Iran Shipping Lines v Turkey* hudoc (2007), at least where the control is not in the nature of a penalty: *AGOSI v UK* A 108 (1986); 9 EHRR 1 and *Air Canada v UK* A 316-A (1995); 20 EHRR 150, or a limitation provision: *JA Pye Ltd and JA Pye (Oxford) Land Ltd v UK* hudoc (2007); 46 EHRR 1083 GC. Regarding compensation, see further above, pp 680–6.

[266] Hudoc (2007); 46 EHRR 1083 GC.   [267] Section 15(1) of the Limitation Act 1980 (UK).

[268] Section 75(1) of the Land Registration Act 1920 (UK).

[269] Five of the dissentient judges agreed on this point. The Chamber had found the absence of compensation violated Article 1 of the First Protocol, but had categorized the interference under Article 1/1/2.

[270] The government valued the land in 2002 at £2.5 million.

fall within the State's margin of appreciation, unless they give rise to results which are so anomalous as to render the legislation unacceptable.[271]

In this situation there was no anomaly as the acquisition of rights by the adverse possessor corresponded with the loss of property rights for the former owner. Any 'moral entitlement' to ownership of the land fell within the state's margin of appreciation in assessing what the fair balance required in a longstanding area of law that regulates private law matters between individuals. The Grand Chamber also rejected the applicants' argument that there were no adequate procedural safeguards for the registered proprietor.[272] The opportunity to take court action for repossession of the land within the twelve-year period would have stopped the limitation period from operating and, as they had done, it was open to the applicants to dispute before the domestic courts that there had been an adverse possession. The Grand Chamber concluded that the fair balance required by Article 1/2 was not upset by the operation of limitation periods in the land registration system in the United Kingdom.[273]

In a series of eviction cases brought against Italy, the Court initially considered that a fair balance had been struck in the administration of a temporary system for staggering the enforcement of court orders for the repossession of housing, given the strong community interest in protecting tenants on low incomes and avoiding the risk of prejudice to public order in a time of chronic housing shortage.[274] This was so despite the severe limitations placed on the landlords' disposition and use of the property by the resulting lengthy delays in repossession. It was only when the Court was presented with repeated petitions, evidencing the existence of a structural failure in the execution of court orders, that the need was identified for a national process capable of challenging the decision to delay enforcement action and to order compensation, to ensure that the impact of an otherwise acceptable system on the property owner is 'neither arbitrary nor unforeseeable'.[275]

The fact that a generally satisfactory scheme of control may impose greater costs on some individuals than others will not be an objection to it unless those suffering the greater burden can demonstrate a 'inappropriate or disproportionate' interference with the enjoyment of their possessions.[276] A scheme will not be satisfactory if it involves imposing a disproportionate and excessive shared social and financial burden on one particular group of individuals. This is illustrated in *Hutten-Czapska v Poland*,[277] which concerned a rent-control scheme that had operated for eleven years with the aim of radically reforming the Polish housing sector at the end of the communist regime. On several occasions the Polish Constitutional Court had declared the rent-control legislation to be

---

[271] Hudoc (2007); 46 EHRR 1083 para 83 GC.

[272] Judges Rozakis, Bratza, Tsatsa-Nikolovska, Gyulumyan, and Šikuta dissented on the adequacy of the procedural safeguards against the loss of beneficial ownership of the land.

[273] By ten votes to seven, reversing the judgment of the Chamber, which was a slim majority of four votes to three.

[274] Characterizing the interference under Article 1/2, see *Spadea and Scalabrino v Italy* A 315-B (1995); 21 EHRR 482. Cf, *Scollo v Italy* A 315-C (1995); 22 EHRR 514.

[275] Eg, *Immobiliare Saffi v Italy* 1999-V; 30 EHRR 756 para 54 GC. See also Committee of Ministers, Interim Resolution ResDH (2004) 72, listing 156 other cases in which a violation of Article 1 of the First Protocol was found on the same facts. When the state continued to fail to rectify the situation the Court became more prescriptive holding that delays of over four years and one month constitute a violation; see eg, *Sorrentino Prota v Italy* hudoc (2004). See also *Prodan v Moldova* 2004-III, where the Court rejected the state's argument that lack of funds and alternative accommodation could justify the delay of four years in the execution of court orders for repossession of housing.

[276] *Mellacher v Austria* A 169 (1989); 12 EHRR 391 para 55 PC.

[277] 2006-VIII; 45 EHRR 262 GC. See also *Ghigo v Malta* hudoc (2006). Cf, *Spadea and Scalabrino v Italy* A 315-B (1995); 21 EHRR 482 and *Mellacher v Austria* A 169 (1989); 12 EHRR 391 PC.

incompatible with the constitutional principles of the right to property, the rule of law and social justice.[278] Before the Grand Chamber the issue was analyzed in terms of the scheme's suitability for achieving the public good pursued. Notwithstanding the wide margin of appreciation granted to states in the choice of measures for securing the housing needs of the community, a unanimous Court found a violation of Article 1 of the First Protocol based on the harsh impact of the scheme on landlords alone as a result of the combined effect of severe restrictions on their various entitlements: the right to derive income from their property,[279] and the right to use and to possess it. Striking a fair balance required securing the protection of the landlords' property rights and respecting the social rights of tenants. Material to the outcome of the case was the absence of a procedure that would reduce the economic impact of the scheme on landlords and thereby achieve a 'fair distribution' of the cost of the reform of housing throughout the community.[280]

The impact of a control may not be confined to economic loss when determining whether the fair balance has been upset. This is shown in *Chassagnou v France*[281] where the impact of legislation requiring landowners to allow hunting on their property was assessed with reference to the personal beliefs of the landowners. While the last word remains with the Court, evidence that the substance of the 'fair balance' test has been applied by a national body will be helpful to a state in demonstrating that it has remained within the wide margin of appreciation conceded to it.[282] Moreover, measures taken in compliance with legal obligations arising from membership of an international organization are presumed to be justified as long as the organization provides 'equivalent protection' to that afforded human rights under the Convention.[283]

An important sub-set of measures which the Court has regarded as being for the control of property under Article 1/2 are forfeiture provisions for the enforcement of laws relating to the use or possession of property.[284] In *Handyside v UK*,[285] the Court said that the destruction of books after a finding of obscenity had been made was justified under Article 1/2. In *AGOSI v UK*,[286] gold Krugerrands (bullion coins) belonging to the applicants were confiscated by UK customs after third parties had tried unlawfully to import them into the country. The Court characterized the prohibition against importation as a control of the use of property and the forfeiture order as 'a constituent element of the procedure for the control of the use' of the Krugerrands, to be dealt with under Article 1/2 rather than as a deprivation of property within Article 1/1/2. The Court resorted again to the 'fair balance' test, the particular issue here being whether confiscation was justified as a measure of enforcement against an innocent owner. The 'fault' or otherwise of the

---

[278] The Court rejected the government's argument that the findings of the Constitutional Court regarding the general adequacy of the scheme could not be decisive in the individual applicant's case: id, para 201.

[279] The right to derive income from property includes profit, cf, Judge Zupančič dissenting.

[280] Id, para 225. It was on this basis that *Mellacher v Austria* A 169 (1989); 12 EHRR 391 PC was distinguished: id, at para 202.

[281] 1999-III; 29 EHRR 615 (non-pecuniary damages of 30,000 Francs was awarded). Cf, *Piippo v Sweden No 70518/01* hudoc (2006) DA (objection to hunting over landowner's property based on practical personal reasons).

[282] Eg, *ISKCON v UK No 20490/92*, 76-A DR 90 (1994); 18 EHRR CD 133. See also *Megadat.com srl v Moldova* hudoc (2008).

[283] *Bosphorus Airways v Ireland* hudoc (2005); 42 HRLR 1 GC, rebuttable in the case of 'manifest deficiency'. See Costello, 6 HRLR 87 (2006).

[284] But see *Allard v Sweden* 2003-VII; 39 EHRR 321 (destruction of the applicant's house in the enforcement of private law rules on joint ownership was held to be a deprivation of property under Article 1/1/2 with the agreement of the parties). For a discussion of the forfeiture and confiscation of property under Article 1 of the First Protocol, see Allen, *Property*, Ch 9.

[285] A 24 (1976); 1 EHRR 737 PC.   [286] A 108 (1986); 9 EHRR 1.

owner was only one of the factors to be taken into account in reaching the fair balance, according to the Court. One other factor was the existence of a procedure by means of which the owner could put his case before seizure of his goods was confirmed. In UK law, the procedure was an administrative one before the Commissioners of Customs and Excise, whose decisions were subject to judicial review. These processes were sufficient. AGOSI had not established that reasonable account had not been taken of its behaviour in reaching the decision to order the forfeiture of its property.[287] The *AGOSI* case is further confirmation of the importance of procedural avenues to aggrieved parties in establishing the fair balance. Procedures must not only be effective to test an applicant's claims[288] but must be expeditious,[289] so that there is no unacceptable collateral impact on the enjoyment of his property while the exercise of the control measures takes place.[290]

In *AGOSI* the Court held that the forfeiture served the legitimate aim of prohibiting the importation of gold coins into the United Kingdom. If the general interest is strong enough, preventative seizures and confiscation may be even more readily justified. In *Yildirum v Italy*[291] the applicant's bus was seized and destroyed as it had been used for the criminal offence of transporting 'clandestine' immigrants. The drivers of the bus had been convicted and, although no criminal prosecution against the owner was brought, the court in the confiscation proceedings expressed some doubt about his participation in the offence. Consequently, the 'vehicle's availability constituted a danger' to the general interest in preventing clandestine immigration and human trafficking. Before the European Court the applicant contended that he could not be held responsible for the offences for which the drivers had been convicted and, therefore, the domestic court's refusal to order the return of the vehicle violated his right to peaceful enjoyment of property under Article 1 of the First Protocol. The Court accepted that the confiscation served the legitimate aim of crime prevention and said that in this area states enjoy a wide margin of appreciation in choosing the means of enforcement and in ascertaining whether the consequences of enforcement are justified in the general interest. In determining the balance between the general interest and the individual's right the Court confirmed its approach in *AGOSI*, that the property owner's behaviour is a relevant factor, and was satisfied in the applicant's case that the authorities 'had regard for the applicant's degree of fault or care' in a fair judicial procedure. Given the nature of the general interest and the state's wide margin of appreciation, the confiscation was not a disproportionate interference with the applicant's right to peaceful enjoyment of his possessions. In *Raimondo v Italy*[292] confiscation orders were made against land and vehicles owned by the applicant at the same time as criminal proceedings were brought against him on suspicion of belonging to a 'mafia-type' group. The confiscation was ordered on the statutory ground that the property formed the proceeds from unlawful activities and was based on evidence of a discrepancy between his lifestyle and his declared income. The Court agreed with the government that the order served the general interest in ensuring that the property acquired by 'unlawful activities' did not procure 'advantages to the detriment of the

---

[287] See also *Air Canada v UK* A 316-A (1995); 20 EHRR 150 (after a series of incidents involving the importation of prohibited drugs using Air Canada aircraft, forfeiture of a 'jumbo jet' bringing drugs into UK in its cargo was ordered, later returned to it on payment of £50,000 fine; held by a narrow majority of five votes to four, neither the seizure nor the fine were disproportionate; dissentient Judges Walsh, Martens, Russo, and Pekkanen, emphasized the relevance to the fair balance of the applicant's 'innocence' about the use of the aircraft).

[288] *M v Italy* No 12386/86, 70 DR 59 (1991).

[289] Preventative measures must be brought rapidly to an end when the need for them has ceased: *Raimondo v Italy* A 281-A (1994); 18 EHRR 237 and *Vendittelli v Italy* A 293-A (1994); 19 EHRR 464.

[290] *Allan Jacobsson v Sweden* A 163 (1989); 12 EHRR 56.   [291] *No 38602/02*, 2003-IV DA.

[292] A 281-A (1994); 18 EHRR 237.

community' for the applicant or the criminal organization.[293] In concluding that the confiscation was proportionate to this aim, the Court considered the efficiency of the measure in securing the legitimate aim and the way in which organized crime operated by reinvesting proceeds of crime in the real property sector in the respondent state. It concluded that '[c]onfiscation, which is designed to block these movements of suspect capital, is an effective and necessary weapon in the combat against this cancer'.[294] Moreover, the preventative purpose of confiscation justified its immediate application before any appeal was determined. In *Arcuri v Italy*[295] confiscation orders were made against the property of a number of members of the Arcuri family on the basis of the 'lifestyle discrepancy' of the first applicant. Unlike *Raimondo* there were no criminal proceedings directly related to the confiscation order. The presumption that the family's fortune had been created by the proceeds of criminal offences committed by the first applicant was supported by the first applicant's long criminal history, which also indicated his involvement with organized crime. The Court found that the function of the confiscation order was to 'prevent the unlawful use, in a way dangerous to society, of possessions whose lawful origin has not been established'. As a crime prevention policy the Court accorded the state a 'wide margin of appreciation' in its implementation. In assessing the proportionality of the confiscation the Court considered the rationale for the measure was sound taking into account the serious nature of organized crime and the threat it posed to the 'rule of law' in the state.[296] Further, the applicants' right to peaceful enjoyment of their possessions had not been infringed as the Italian courts had provided them with a 'reasonable opportunity of putting their case to the responsible authorities'.[297] In *Butler v UK*[298] the Court allowed the state even greater latitude when ordering a preventative forfeiture. In *Butler* the applicant complained under Article 1 of the First Protocol of the forfeiture of £240,000, which he had asked a friend to take abroad. After being seized by a Customs and Excise Officer, the domestic courts had ordered the forfeiture under the Drug Trafficking Act 1994 (UK) to prevent the money being used by an unidentified third party for the serious crime of drug trafficking. However, a criminal proceeding had not been brought against the applicant or anyone else; nor was there a finding that the applicant, or his friend, would be responsible for its use in drug trafficking. Further, unlike *Acuri's* case, the applicant did not have a serious criminal history. Nonetheless, in declaring the application inadmissible the Court considered that the problems faced by states in combating the problem of drug trafficking justified the wide margin of appreciation accorded to them in this area and was satisfied that the applicant had had been given a fair hearing in his appeal challenging the forfeiture order.

II. PAYMENT OF TAXES, CONTRIBUTIONS, OR PENALTIES

Finally, Article 1/2 concedes a practically unlimited power to a state 'to enforce such laws as it deems necessary ... to secure the payment of taxes or other contributions or penalties'. Because the powers of the state under this provision are very wide, it is a matter of significance whether an interference with the enjoyment of possessions falls within it or not. For example, in *Gasus Dosier-und Fördertechnik v Netherlands*,[299] the Court decided that the seizure by the tax authorities of property in the possession of a tax debtor in which title had been retained by the vendor was not a deprivation of the latter's possessions to

---

[293] Id, para 30.   [294] *Ibid.*
[295] No 52024/99, 2001-VII DA. See also *Riela v Italy No 52439/99* hudoc (2001) DA.
[296] *Ibid.*   [297] *Ibid.*   [298] No 41661/98, 2002-VI DA.   [299] A 306-B (1995); 20 EHRR 403.

be assessed under Article 1/1/2 but a measure for securing the payment of taxes falling within Article 1/2.

The power to secure the payment of taxes is not a separate matter but a specific aspect of the state's right to control the use of property. The 'fair balance' will require procedural guarantees to establish the applicant's liability to make the payments but the state is largely unconstrained about the levels of taxation, the means of assessment, and the manner of exaction to fulfil those liabilities. Nevertheless, the formal power of the state to raise taxes is not totally unlimited. The Commission said that a taxation scheme may 'adversely affect the guarantee of ownership if it places an excessive burden on the taxpayer or fundamentally interferes with his financial position'.[300] However, the state's power of appreciation is wide and it would be an exceptional case indeed where the institutions would declare a tax programme contrary to the Convention.[301] As far as the enforcement of the resulting tax obligations is concerned, the Court said in the *Gasus* case[302] that it 'will respect the legislature's assessment in such matters unless it is devoid of reasonable foundation'. In determining that the Dutch law was not beyond this considerable margin, the Court deferred to the legislature's position that security rights of the kind preserved by reservation of title clauses were not 'true' ownership. In the circumstances of this case, the applicant could not have expected otherwise than that the question would have been governed by this Dutch law and that, appreciating that there was some risk (hence the reservation of title clause), the applicant should have appreciated the risk of seizure of the property by the tax authorities and taken measures to protect itself against this eventuality. There had, then, been no failure of proportionality in the measures taken by the Netherlands to secure the payment of the tax debtor's obligations.[303]

In *National & Provincial Building Society, Leeds Permanent Building Society, and Yorkshire Building Society v UK*[304] the Court said that there is a compelling public interest in the enactment of legislation imposing liability to pay tax with retrospective effect and without compensation where it is to ensure that private entities do not 'enjoy the benefit of a windfall in a changeover to a new tax-payment regime'. The fact that legislation had the incidental effect of extinguishing claims in restitution for taxes unlawfully imposed during the transition period did not create an excessive burden because the claims had arisen from a defect in the transitional law: the applicants had only paid that which would have been required of them to be paid under the old tax-payment regime.[305]

The state will be constrained by Article 6 insofar as it seeks to use the criminal process to enforce tax obligations.[306] The *Hentrich* case[307] shows that Article 1 of the First Protocol itself imposes some limitations upon the methods a state may use to enforce its tax policies, and they arise under this part of Article 1/2[308] as well as under Article 1/1/1 and 1/1/2.

---

[300] *Svenska Managementgruppen v Sweden No 11036/84*, 45 DR 211 (1985) and *Wasa Liv Omsesidigt v Sweden No 13013/87*, 58 DR 163 (1988).

[301] Eg, *Travers v Italy No 15117/89*, 80 DR 5 (1995) (system of advance deduction of tax). Cf, *Darby v Sweden* A 187 (1990); 13 EHRR 774, where the violation was of Article 14 in connection with Article 1 of the First Protocol, and *Schmidt v Germany* A 291-B (1994); 18 EHRR 513, although the Court considered that case under Article 4(3)(d) rather than Article 1 of the First Protocol.

[302] A 306-B (1995); 20 EHRR 403 para 60.   [303] Id, paras 65–74.

[304] 1997-VII; 25 EHRR 127 para 81 GC. For the facts, see further above, p 684.

[305] Cf, *SA Dangeville v France* 2002-III; 38 EHRR 699 and *Stere v Romania* hudoc (2006); 45 EHRR 191 (retrospective legislation quashing final court order for repayment of taxes).

[306] See *Funke v France* A 256-A (1993); 16 EHRR 297. Liability for tax does not constitute a civil right or obligation for the purposes of Article 6(1): *Ferrazzini v Italy* 2001-VII; 14 EHRR 45 GC.

[307] A 296-A; 18 EHRR 440.   [308] Eg, *Jokela v Finland* 2002-IV; 37 EHRR 581.

An order for the confiscation of property following a conviction for a criminal offence may constitute a 'penalty' for the purpose of the Convention.[309] In this case the order will fall within Article 1/2 to control the use of property to secure the payment of penalties. For example, in *Phillips v UK*[310] the Court considered the compliance with Article 1 of the First Protocol of the UK statutory regime for the confiscation of property under the Drug Trafficking Act 1994. Under section 4(2) and (3) of the Act the court hearing the confiscation proceedings following the conviction of a defendant for a drug-trafficking offence was required to assume that any property held by the defendant six years prior to the date of the criminal proceedings, or since the conviction, was received in connection with drug trafficking unless the defendant established on the balance of probability that the property had been acquired by other means or there was a serious risk of injustice. In *Phillips* the applicant was ordered to pay 91,400 GBP or be imprisoned for two years. In establishing whether the confiscation order was a 'penalty' what was significant was that the purpose of the confiscation procedure was not to convict or acquit the individual for any offence, but rather to assess the amount payable, if any, after the conviction. In finding that the confiscation regime was proportionate to the general interest in combating drug trafficking the Court had regard to the function of the confiscation order and the procedural guarantees that operated to determine the defendant's liability. The Court construed the Act as having both a punitive function, in that it aimed to punish the offender against whom the order was made, and preventative functions, in that it aimed to deter others from engaging in crime and reduced the funds available for future drug-trafficking.

6. CONCLUSION

Article 1 of the First Protocol both establishes the right to the peaceful enjoyment of one's possessions and expressly allows a state a wide power to interfere with the right in the public interest. Since the late 1990s the scope of Article 1 of the First Protocol has generally been enhanced to embrace a greater variety of interests with the strengthening of the autonomous concept of possessions[311] and the development of positive obligations, as elsewhere under the Convention. The increasing awareness of the broad protection potentially afforded to property by Article 1 of the First Protocol may, in part, account for the high rise in numbers of complaints received by the Court under this Article. However, the requirement that there be some recognition of a pecuniary right in national law or practice in order for there to be a 'possession' has placed limits on the application of Article 1 of the First Protocol, with the result that many of the numerous restitution cases, from Central and Eastern Europe that refer back to the communist era, have failed.

Although there is specific language to regulate the deprivation and control of the use of property under Articles 1/1/2 and 1/2 respectively, these are not the only occasions when interference by the state may be justified. Nor does the different language of these two sentences indicate much substantial difference in the way the Court approaches claims

---

[309] *Welch v UK* A 307-A.   [310] 2001-VII.

[311] Eg, *Beyeler v Italy* 2001-I; 33 EHRR 1225 GC (null and void contract under national law); *Anheuser-Busch Inc v Portugal* hudoc (2007); 45 EHRR 830 GC (application for trade mark); and *Stec v UK* hudoc (2005), 41 EHRR SE 295 GC (non-contributory welfare benefits).

that Article 1 has been violated. The 'fair balance' between the public interest identi-fied by the state and the burden on the individual applicants affected by the interference set out in the *Sporrong and Lönnroth* case is pervasive throughout Article 1 of the First Protocol cases. It is noticeable how more recent cases proceed straight to the application of the fair balance test, while earlier ones dissected the language of Article 1 of the First Protocol in some detail.[312] When applying that test the Court also makes reference to earlier cases decided by it under this Article regardless of the particular issue before it and the issue considered in the other cases.[313]

The reference to a general 'fair balance' standard of protection against interference under Article 1/1/1 in the *Sporrong and Lönnroth* case avoids the need to break down and classify complex combinations of fact and laws which have had an impact on an applicant's enjoyment of his possessions. While there are factors that are to be taken into account in striking a fair balance—such as timeliness, predictability, and certainty in the exercise of state power; the impact of the interference on the individual; proced-ural safeguards; the payment of compensation; and alternative avenues of securing the legitimate aim—their justiciability is problematic and the Court has deferred extensively to the decisions of national bodies. This is seen in the lack of specificity in the Court's approach to compensation. The language of review here is not that of 'pressing social need' or 'strict necessity' but whether the applicant has shown that the state measures impose an 'individual and excessive burden' or are 'disproportionate'. In cases where the state has addressed the issues, either in establishing the legal basis for interference, which is always required to comply with Article 1 of the First Protocol, or in applying a general legislative scheme, the Court has generally confirmed that the state was acting within its powers under Article 1 of the First Protocol. Nevertheless, the Court has shown that it will be prepared to adopt a stricter approach in applying the fair balance test where there is evidence of systematic breach of the right to property by the state[314] or where the law is 'manifestly without reasonable foundation'.[315]

The recognition in *James v UK* that states have a wide power to interfere with prop-erty rights in the general social and economic interest,[316] even where the benefits fall to the advantage of particular individuals,[317] has been of lasting significance. *Pye's* case[318] demonstrates that this is particularly so where the national law is a long-established and complex one which regulates private law between individuals. The breadth of the margin of appreciation also readily justifies the use of forfeiture and confiscation measures by states to control proscribed activity, such as terrorism, smuggling, drug trafficking, and crime generally.

---

[312] Cf, *James v UK* A 98 (1986); 8 EHRR 123 PC and *Tre Traktörer Aktiebolag v Sweden* A 159 (1989); 13 EHRR 309. See further above, p 668.

[313] Eg, *Pine Valley Development v Ireland* A 222 (1991); 14 EHRR 319 para 59, where the Court relied on *Håkansson and Suresson v Sweden* A 171 (1990) 13 EHRR 1, an Article 1/1/2 case, and *Fredin v Sweden* A 192 (1991); 13 EHRR 784, an Article 1/2 case, for the same point.

[314] Eg, the long series of Italian eviction cases and *Hutten-Czapska v Poland* 2006-VIII; 45 EHRR 262 GC, regarding Polish rent control legislation, see above pp 689–90.

[315] Eg, the series of Greek cases on the standardized system of assessing compensation for land expropriated to construct roads, see above pp 681–2.

[316] A 98 (1986); 8 EHRR 123 PC. See also *National & Provincial Building Society, Leeds Permanent Building Society and Yorkshire Building Society v UK* 1997-VII; 25 EHRR 127 and *Jahn v Germany* 2005-VI; 42 EHRR 1084 GC.

[317] See also *JA Pye Ltd and JA Pye (Oxford) Land Ltd v UK* hudoc (2007); 46 EHRR 1083 GC.

[318] Id, para.

Where the Court does find that a state has exceeded its powers under Article 1 of the First Protocol, the financial consequences can be severe. In the *Beyeler* case, the defendant state was ordered to pay approximately €1.3 million in compensation; in the *Housing Association of War Disabled and Victims of the War in Attica* case it was €5 million; in *The Former King of Greece* it was €13.2 million; in the *Pine Valley* case, it was approximately £1.25 million; and in *Stran Greek Refineries*, the order was for approximately £15 million plus £9 million interest.

19

ARTICLE 2, FIRST PROTOCOL: THE RIGHT TO EDUCATION

Article 2, First Protocol

No person shall be denied the right to education. In the exercise of any functions which it assumes in relation to education and teaching, the state shall respect the right of parents to ensure such education and teaching in conformity with their own religious and philosophical convictions.

1. INTRODUCTION[1]

The right to education had a 'stormy genesis'[2] in the drafting of the Convention. It was possible to reach an agreed text only in the First Protocol[3]—not in the original text—and, even then, an unusually large number of states have appended reservations to Article 2 in their ratifications of the Protocol.[4] The Court has made reference to the preparatory work in its judgments. The text was transmuted from its original form—'every person has the right to education'—to its present one—'No person shall be denied the right to education'—to avoid what some states anticipated might be excessively burdensome, positive obligations.[5]

The result is that there is no obligation upon states parties to have a state system of education or to subsidize private schools or universities or other higher education institutions (hereafter universities). These are matters left to their discretion, with the prohibition of the denial of the right to education only extending to such educational institutions as states choose to provide or allow. Thus in the *Belgian Linguistic* case (No 2),[6] interpreting the first sentence of Article 2, the Court stated:

> The negative formulation indicates, as confirmed by the preparatory work, that the contracting parties do not recognise such a right of education as would require them to establish at their own expense, or to subsidise, education of any particular type or at

---

[1] On Article 2, see Opsahl, in Robertson, ed, *Privacy and Human Rights*, 1973, pp 220–43, and Wildhaber, *European System*, Ch 21.

[2] Opsahl, n 1 above, p 221.   [3] Robertson, 28 BYIL 359 at 362–4 (1951).

[4] For the texts, see <http://conventions.coe.int>. For a summary, see Wildhaber, *loc cit* at n 1 above, p 551. See also *Angeleni v Sweden No 10491/83*, 51 DR 41 at 46–47 (1986) (Swedish reservation valid). In *SP v UK No 28915/95* hudoc (1997) DA, the validity of the UK reservation was left undecided following the *Belilos* case, above, p 21; the Court had not questioned it in the *Campbell and Cosans* case (pre-*Belilos*), below, p 703.

[5] Robertson, *loc cit* at n 3 above, p 362, and Clarke, 22 Ir Jur 28 at 34–41 (1987).

[6] A 6 (1968), p 31; 1 EHRR 252, 280–1 PC. Italics added.

any particular level.... The first sentence...guarantees...a right of access to educational institutions *existing at a given time*....

Article 2 extends to all forms of education provided or permitted by the state-primary, secondary, and higher education. Whereas there is jurisprudence suggesting that Article 2 concerns 'mainly elementary education',[7] there are many cases demonstrating that it applies to secondary education and in *Leyla Sahin v Turkey*[8] the Court confirmed that it extends also to higher education. But individual rights with respect to one level of education may not be the same for another;[9] while a state, if it chooses to establish a state schooling system, may be obliged to provide *universal* primary and secondary education, it is permitted to restrict access to higher education to those with the ability to benefit from whatever it provides,[10] so that it is not strictly correct to speak about a *right* to higher education. Article 2 does not apply to vocational training[11] or retraining programmes for prisoners.[12]

Article 2 extends to private schools and universities.[13] It does so in two senses. First, it guarantees a right to start and run a school (or university) in the private sector. Although the text of the first sentence of Article 2 does not make this clear, the Commission adopted this interpretation in the *Jordebo* case.[14] In doing so, it relied upon the Court's judgment in *Kjeldsen, Busk Madsen and Pedersen v Denmark*,[15] although that judgment refers to a 'freedom' to establish private schools, not a right. If there is not such a right, the requirements of the second sentence of Article 2, that the state respect the religious or philosophical convictions of parents, probably creates a practical imperative to permit the operation of *some* private schools.[16] If there is such a right, so that states must permit private schools to be established, then the corresponding right holder would appear to be the person seeking to establish the school.[17] In any event, the first and second sentences of Article 2 apply to 'existing' private schools whether they exist as of right under the Convention or not. Accordingly, the state has an obligation to regulate them to ensure the Convention is complied with; it cannot delegate this responsibility away to the private sector.[18] But in its regulation of private schools the state cannot take away the essence of the right to education.[19] While a state is not obliged to fund or subsidize private schools,[20] any financial assistance that it gives must not discriminate between different schools in breach of Article 14.[21]

---

[7] See eg, *Valasinas v Lithuania No 44558/98* hudoc (2000) DA and *Yanasik v Turkey No 14524/89*, 74 DR 14 (1993).

[8] 2005-XI; 41 EHRR 109 GC.   [9] *Ibid.*

[10] *Lucach v Russia No 48041/99* hudoc (1999) DA (admission requirements may be set).

[11] *X v UK No 8844/80*, 23 DR 228 (1980).

[12] *Valasinas v Lithuania No 44558/98* hudoc (2000) DA.

[13] *Leyla Sahin v Turkey* 2005-XI; 41 EHRR 109 para 153 GC (Article 2 applies 'equally to pupils in state and independent schools without distinction').

[14] *Ingrid Jordebo Foundation of Christian Schools and Ingrid Jordebo v Sweden No 11533/85*, 51 DR 125 at 128 (1987).

[15] A 23 (1976); 1 EHRR 711 para 50.   [16] Cf, *Opsahl*, n 1 above, p 230.

[17] But see the *Jordebo* case, in which, on the particular facts, the foundation that ran the school was held not to be a 'victim' (the parent was). See also *Bachmann, Hofreiter and Gulyn v Austria No 19315/92* hudoc (1995) DA.

[18] *Kjeldsen, Busk Madsen and Pedersen v Denmark* A 23 (1976); 1 EHRR 711 and *Costello-Roberts v UK* A 247-C (1993); 19 EHRR 112.

[19] *Leyla Sahin v Turkey* 2005-XI; 41 EHRR 109 paras 153-4 GC.

[20] *Belgian Linguistic* case (No 2) A 6 (1968), p. 31; 1 EHRR 252, 281 PC, and *W and KL v Sweden No 10476/83*, 45 DR 143 at 148-9 (1985).

[21] *Bachmann, Hofreiter and Gulyn v Austria No 19315/92* hudoc (1995) DA.

The right to education consists of a variety of rights and freedoms for children and parents. These mostly belong to the pupil or student.[22] When the pupil is young, his or her right may have to be exercised by the parents[23] but, as the child grows up, he or she will develop the capacity to act independently.[24] For higher education, the appropriate right holder will be the student. But under Article 2 parents do have certain rights of their own about the way in which their child is educated.[25]

'Education' and 'teaching' are differentiated in the text of Article 2. On this distinction the Court has said 'the education of children is the whole process whereby, in any society, adults endeavour to transmit their beliefs, culture and other values to the young, whereas teaching or instruction refers in particular to the transmission of knowledge and to intellectual development'.[26] The implication of drawing the distinction this way appears to be that the state may not step between a child or student and a private provider of 'education' outside the school system, such as religious bodies or cultural institutions, lest otherwise a person be 'denied the right to education' in this wide sense. If it wished to intervene, the state would have to rely on its implied power to regulate educational activities. There is nothing in the Convention to identify any particular substantive objectives of education comparable, for instance, to Article 26(2) of the Universal Declaration of Human Rights which reads:

> Education shall be directed to the full development of the human personality and to the strengthening of respect for human rights and fundamental freedoms. It shall promote understanding, tolerance and friendship among all nations, racial or religious groups, and shall partner the activities of the United Nations for the maintenance of peace.[27]

The right to education in Article 2 is not to be interpreted restrictively. To do so would be inconsistent with its purpose given that in 'a democratic society, the right to education, which is indispensable to the furtherance of human rights, plays such a fundamental role'.[28] The right to education benefits from rules that govern the interpretation of the Convention generally, *viz* that Convention rights must be interpreted so as to render them 'practical and effective' and that the Convention is a 'living instrument which must be interpreted in the light of present day conditions'.[29] Since the provisions of the Convention must be read as a whole, 'the two sentences of Article 2 must be read not only in the light of each other but also, in particular, of Articles 8, 9 and 10', on private and family life, religion, and expression respectively.[30]

---

[22] See *Campbell and Cosans v UK* A 48 (1982); 4 EHRR 293 para 40 (right not to be denied education is 'the right of the child').

[23] Or grandparents: *Lee v UK* hudoc (2001); 33 EHRR 677 GC.

[24] See eg, *Simpson v UK No 14688/89*, 64 DR 188 (1989). See also Mr Kellberg, in *Kjeldsen, Busk Madsen and Pedersen v Denmark* B 21 (1975), p 50.

[25] A claim under the second sentence of Article 2 must normally be brought by the parent, as victim, not the child: *Simpson v UK, ibid.*

[26] *Campbell and Cosans v UK* A 48 (1982); 4 EHRR 293 para 33. See Robertson, *loc cit* at n 3 above, p 363, drawing attention to the French text of Article 2.

[27] In the absence of a positive statement of this kind, it is not easy to see how *excluding* a topic from the curriculum would raise an issue under Article 2. On the meaning of education in other international instruments, see Pentti Arajärvi, in Eide *et al*, eds, *The Universal Declaration of Human Rights: A Commentary*, 1992, pp 405–28.

[28] *Leyla Sahin v Turkey* 2005-XI; 41 EHRR 109 para 137 GC.   [29] Id, para 136.

[30] *Kjeldsen, Busk Madsen and Pedersen v Denmark* A 23 (1976); 1 EHRR 711 para 52.

2. NO DENIAL OF THE RIGHT TO EDUCATION

The first sentence of Article 2 states: 'No person shall be denied the right to education'. As the Court stated in the *Belgian Linguistic* case (No 2),[31] despite its negative formulation, this wording 'does enshrine a right', *viz* the right to education, albeit one that is limited in scope. Even in its limited form, it is not an absolute right. It may be regulated by the state, but while the state may take into account 'the needs and resources of the community and of individuals' any restriction must 'never injure the substance of the right to education nor conflict with other rights enshrined in the Convention'.[32] The regulation of educational institutions 'may vary in time and place, inter alia, according to the needs and resources of the community and the distinctive features of different levels of education'; accordingly, states enjoy a 'certain margin of appreciation' when regulating them.[33] When deciding whether restrictions are permissible, the Court will consider whether 'they are foreseeable for those concerned and pursue a legitimate aim' and whether the means employed to realize the intended aim are reasonably proportionate to its attainment.[34]

I. ACCESS TO EXISTING INSTITUTIONS OR EXCLUSION FROM THEM

As noted, the first sentence of Article 2 only guarantees 'a right of access to educational institutions existing at a given time'.[35] This guarantee applies fully to such state institutions as are in being; it also imposes an obligation upon states to regulate private institutions in some respects, for example, so as to prevent arbitrary admission or exclusion policies or practices,[36] although this is not an area in which the Strasbourg jurisprudence is well developed.

The Court has accepted several restrictions upon access to schools or universities, or exclusion from them, as not infringing Article 2. Thus it is permissible for a state to insist upon education occurring in school, whether state or private, instead of at home as the parents might wish[37] and to exclude a disruptive child from school.[38] And the choice of state school for a child to attend will normally be one for the state, not the child or the parents.[39] Neither the fact that a prisoner cannot continue his education while in prison[40] nor that the deportation of a parent will terminate the attendance at school of a child who leaves the country with the parent will infringe Article 2.[41] The issue of school

---

[31] A 6 (1968), p 31; 1 EHRR 252, 280 PC.

[32] Id, p 32; 1 EHRR 252, 282.

[33] *Leyla Sahin v Turkey* 2005-XI; 41 EHRR 109 para 154 GC.   [34] *Ibid.*

[35] *Belgian Linguistic* case (No 2), above, p 697.   [36] *Ibid.*

[37] *Konrad v Germany* No 35504/03 hudoc (2006) DA (no consensus among contracting parties on compulsory attendance at primary schools). Necessary measures to enforce compulsory schooling permissible: *Leuffen v FRG* No 19844/92 hudoc (1992) DA and *BN and SN v Sweden* No 17678/91 hudoc (1993) DA. The permissibility of home education may be relevant to compliance with the second sentence of Article 2. If it allows home education, the state has both a right and a duty (to the child) to ensure that it is effective: see *Family H v UK* No 10233/83, 37 DR 105 (1984).

[38] *Kramelius v Sweden* No 21062/92 hudoc (1996) DA (lessons required at home). See also *Whitman v UK* No 13477/87 hudoc (1989) DA.

[39] *Cohen v UK* No 25959/94 hudoc (1996) DA. On single sex and selective schools see *W & DM and M & HI v UK* Nos 10228/82 and 10229/82, 37 DR 96 (1984); *Rosengren v Sweden* No 9411/81, 29 DR 224 (1982); and further cases in Wildhaber, *loc cit* at n 1 above, p 535, f 19.

[40] *Arslan v Turkey* No 31320/02 hudoc (2006) DA.   [41] *Ebibomi v UK* No 26922/95 hudoc (1995) DA.

uniform requirements has not been ruled upon, but it is predictable that the Court will not normally intervene under Article 2.[42]

As to universities, in *Leyla Sahin v Turkey*[43] the exclusion of the applicant from her state university lectures and examinations for wearing the Islamic headscarf was held not to infringe Article 2. Applying the approach it had followed when ruling that the same facts did not amount to a breach of the applicant's right to religion in Article 9,[44] the Grand Chamber held that the restriction had the legitimate aims of protecting the rights and freedoms of others and maintaining public order, having as its purpose the preservation of the secular character of educational institutions. It was also a proportionate restriction, since it did not hinder the applicant in performing the habitual duties of religious observance and was both imposed following an appropriate decision-making process and subject to various safeguards, including judicial review. By sixteen votes to one, the Grand Chamber held that the restriction did not impair the very essence of the right to education. On a separate matter, in *Sulak v Turkey*[45] it was held that a state university student could be expelled as a disciplinary measure for persistent cheating in examinations. As stated by the Court in the *Sahin* case,[46] the right to education 'does not exclude recourse to disciplinary measures, including suspension or expulsion from an educational institution in order to ensure compliance with its internal rules'.

In some cases, the Court has held a restriction upon access to school or university to be contrary to Article 2. Thus a restriction excluding a child from school because her parent had forcibly surrendered his migrant card validating his residence was clearly a breach of Article 2 because it had no basis in national law.[47] The refusal to admit to a state university a student who had passed the entrance examination in the belief that his good results could not be explained was held to be a breach of Article 2 because it had no basis in national law and, in the absence of proof, was arbitrary.[48]

A number of cases have involved disagreement between the school authorities and parents on the allocation of children with special educational needs to mainstream schools or to suitable special schools. Recognizing the financial and staffing demands involved, the Court has allowed states 'a wide measure of discretion' in decision-making on this matter in order to make the 'best use possible of the resources available to them in the interests of disabled children generally'.[49] In a different kind of case, in *DH v Czech Republic*,[50] the Grand Chamber held that the allocation of the applicant Roma children to special primary schools that were for children with special needs was contrary to the Convention. It did so on the basis that the allocation was indirect racial discrimination in breach of Article 2 of the First Protocol and Article 14 of the Convention.

Other cases have concerned the language of instruction in schools. In the *Belgian Linguistic* case (No 2),[51] the issue of access by children to schools in which they would be instructed in their own language was resolved under Articles 2 of the First Protocol and Article 14 of the Convention, on the basis of discrimination on grounds of language, not under Article 2 by itself. In *Cyprus v Turkey*[52] a somewhat similar issue was resolved

---

[42] See *Stevens v UK No 116754/85* hudoc (1986) DA.   [43] 2005-XI; 41 EHRR 109 GC.

[44] See above, p 437.   [45] *No 24515/94* hudoc (1996) DA.

[46] 2005-XI; 41 EHRR 109 para 156 GC. Cf, *Campbell and Cosans v UK* A 48 (1982); 4 EHRR 293 (suspension not justified).

[47] *Timishev v Russia* 2005-XII; 44 EHRR 776.

[48] *Mursel Eren v Turkey* hudoc (2006); 44 EHRR 619. See also *Lukach v Russia No 48041/99* hudoc (1999) DA.

[49] *SP v UK No 28915/95* hudoc (1997) DA. Cf, *Simpson v UK No 14688/89*, 64 DR 188 (1989); *Klerks v Netherlands No 25215/94* hudoc (1995) DA; *Ford v UK No 28374/95* hudoc (1996) DA; and *McIntyre v UK No 29046/95* hudoc (1998) DA. See also the cases at n 64 below.

[50] Hudoc (2007) GC. On the *DH* case, see above, p 607.   [51] 2001-IV; 35 EHRR 731 GC.

[52] 2001-IV; 35 EHRR 731 para 278 GC.

just under Article 2. In that case, schooling in northern Cyprus had been provided with Greek as the language of instruction at the primary school level for Greek minority children, but secondary schooling was only provided for them in Turkish. The Court held that, 'having assumed responsibility for the provision of Greek-language primary education, the failure of the "TRNC" authorities to make continuing provision for it at the secondary school level must be considered in effect to be a denial of the substance of the right at issue.' Access to Greek language schooling in the south was not sufficient because of its impact on family life, as children who went to the south were not allowed by the TRNC to return north as adults.

II. THE EFFECTIVENESS OF THE EDUCATION PROVIDED

In the *Belgian Linguistic* case (No 2),[53] the Court stated that the right to education had to be 'effective'. It was on this basis that the Court held in that case that the right to education in Article 2 required that 'the individual who is the beneficiary should have the possibility of drawing profit from the education received, that is to say, the right to obtain, in conformity with the rules in force in each state, and in one form or another, official recognition of the studies that he has completed'. Where the challenge to the effectiveness of education depends upon resources or the organization and pattern of the system set up by the state, the negative formulation of the right to education in the first sentence of Article 2 and the intended consequences of this, which were accepted by the Court in the *Belgian Linguistic* case (No 2),[54] mean that a claim based upon such matters as the need for further funding, organizational or managerial change, the role of parents, school starting and leaving ages, the kind and choice of schools, and student loans at university are unlikely to succeed in the absence of clearly arbitrary action or the lack of a legal base.[55] Similarly, the 'setting and planning of the curriculum fall in principle within the competence of the contracting states', and involves 'questions of expediency on which it is not for the Court to rule and whose solution may vary according to the country and the era',[56] so that a challenge is unlikely to succeed outside of the application of the second sentence in Article 2 concerning the obligation to respect the convictions of parents.

3. RESPECT FOR PARENTS' RELIGIOUS AND PHILOSOPHICAL CONVICTIONS[57]

The second sentence in Article 2 must be read together with the first sentence; it is to the fundamental right to education that the right of parents[58] for respect for their religious and philosophical convictions is attached.[59] This right applies to both state and

---

[53] A 6 (1968) p. 31; 1 EHRR 252, 281 PC. Cf, *Leyla Sahin v Turkey* 2005-XI; 41 EHRR 109 GC ('practical and effective').

[54] See above at n 697. Cf, more recently *Leyla Sahin v Turkey,* id, para 154.

[55] See eg, the special needs cases listed at n 49 above where a wide margin of appreciation was allowed.

[56] *Kjeldsen, Busk Madsen and Pedersen v Denmark* A 23 (1976); 1 EHRR 711 para 53. Insistence upon a qualification to take a course is permitted: *Ciftci v Turkey No 71860/01* hudoc (2004) DA. On the recognition of studies abroad, see *Karus v Italy* hudoc (1998) DA.   [57] See Evans, 8 HRLR 449 (2008).

[58] The parent's right continues when the child is in care (*Aminoff v Sweden No 10554/83,* 43 DR 120 at 144 (1985)), but it will cease if the child is adopted (*X v UK No 7626/76,* 11 DR 160 (1977)). If the child is in the custody of one parent, it will cease for the other: *X v Sweden No 7911/77,* 12 DR 192 (1977). The right is that of parents; no mention is made of the convictions of the child, of whatever age.

[59] *Kjeldsen, Busk Madsen and Pedersen v Denmark* A 23 (1976); 1 EHRR 711 para 56.

private systems of education. The state must 'respect' the parents' conviction in such state schools as it provides and it has a positive obligation to ensure that private schools do likewise. This obligation extends to all the functions exercised in connection with education, whether academic or administrative.[60] It is principally a protection against indoctrination by the state[61] and teachers[62] in school but it covers administrative matters as well, such as the manner of maintaining discipline, insofar as they are capable of conflicting with parents' convictions.

If the parents' objection is sufficiently well founded on a religious or philosophical conviction, the state's duty is to 'respect' their right. There is a difference here between the qualified connotation of 'respect' and any stronger right that the parents might claim 'to ensure' appropriate teaching. The qualified nature of the duty 'to respect' has prevailed. It is far from providing an absolute guarantee that children must be educated in accordance with their parents' convictions: parents cannot require that a state provide an alternative course to one that is inconsistent with those convictions.[63] This is a conclusion reinforced by the limited nature of the duty in the first sentence upon which the second sentence is grafted: it is the state which determines and finances the provision of education.[64]

There are two further protections for the state against this potentially wide-ranging right of parental influence in the education system. These are, first, that the convictions which are to be taken into account are limited to religious and philosophical conviction and the burden on the parents to demonstrate their relevance to their stand is heavy. As to the meaning of 'convictions', in *Campbell and Cosans v UK*[65] the Court stated that it was not synonymous with the words 'opinions' and 'ideas' in Article 10 (freedom of expression), but was more akin to the term 'beliefs' in Article 9 of the Convention (freedom of thought, conscience, and religion) and 'denoted views that attain a certain level of cogency, seriousness, cohesion and importance.' It is relatively easy to identify what is a 'religious' conviction.[66] In *Zengin v Turkey*,[67] it was held that the Alevi faith, which is an Islamic faith distinct from the Sunni faith, is a 'religious conviction': in the Court's words, it is 'certainly neither a sect nor a 'belief' which does not attain the level of cogency', etc, required by *Campbell and Cosans*.[68] It is not so simple to set the limits of 'philosophical' convictions.[69] About the latter, the Court said in *Campbell and Cosans* that they comprehend 'such convictions as are worthy of respect in a "democratic society" and are not incompatible with human dignity; in addition, they must not conflict with the fundamental right of the child to education'.[70] As to the burden upon parents, they must show the basis for and the content of the belief;[71] that it is a belief they hold; that holding

[60] *Campbell and Cosans v UK* A 48 (1982); 4 EHRR 293 paras 33–6.

[61] *Kjeldsen, Busk Madsen and Pedersen v Denmark* A 23 (1976); 1 EHRR 711 para 53.

[62] Implied by *X v UK No 8010/77*, 16 DR 101 at 102 (1979).

[63] *Bulski v Poland Nos 46254/99 and 31888/02* hudoc (2004) DA. Cf, *Family H v UK No 10233/83*, 37 DR 105 (1984).

[64] *W & DM and M & HI v UK Nos 10228/82 and 10229/82*, 37 DR 96 (1984). For cases on respect for the convictions of parents of handicapped children, see *L v UK No 14136/88* hudoc (1989) DA; *PD and LD v UK No 14135/88*, 62 DR 292 (1989); *Leuffen v FRG No 19844/92* hudoc (1992) DA; and *Graeme v UK No 13887/88*, 64 DR 158 (1990). And see the cases above, n 49.

[65] A 48 (1982); 4 EHRR 293 para 36.   [66] On the meaning of 'religion', see above, p 426.

[67] 2007-XX. Jehovah's Witnesses are a 'known' religion: *Valsamis v Greece* 1996-VI; 24 EHRR 294 para 26.

[68] Id, para 66. As the Alevi faith is commonly referred to as a sect, the wording quoted from the judgment is understood not as excluding all sects, just sects (or beliefs) that do not satisfy *Campbell and Cosans*.

[69] They do not include convictions as to the language of instruction: *Belgium Linguistic* case (No 2) A 6 (1968) p 35; 1 EHRR 252, 285 PC. See also Robertson, *loc cit* at n 1 above, p 362.

[70] *Campbell and Cosans v UK* A 48 (1982); 4 EHRR 293 para 36.   [71] Id., B 42 (1980) Com Rep para 93.

it is the reason for their objection to what the state is doing;[72] and that they have brought
the reason for their objection to the attention of the authorities. The Court may reject
an objection as not, in its view, offending the parents' convictions. Thus in *Valsamis
v Greece*[73] parents objected to their daughter's participation, on pain of one day's suspension, in a school parade as part of a national day commemorating the outbreak of
war with Fascist Italy in which there was also a military parade. The Court held that the
purpose and arrangements for the parade, together with the limited suspensive sanction, could not be seen as so offending the applicants' pacifist convictions as Jehovah's
Witnesses as to amount to a violation of Article 2.

Should the applicant be able to satisfy the above requirement, the second measure of
protection for the state is that mere incidental treatment in lessons of matters about which
religious and philosophical convictions may be held will not raise an issue under the
second sentence of Article 2. As the Court said in *Kjeldsen, Busk Madsen and Pedersen
v Denmark*,[74] this provision does not permit a parent to object to the integrated teaching
of religious or philosophical information or knowledge, a right that would have disruptive consequences for the organization of teaching. All the parent is entitled to is that this
information or knowledge, like any other, be conveyed 'in an objective, critical and pluralistic manner': the Convention, that is, demands only a negative quality, that students
be not subjected to the indoctrination of a single point of view.[75] But in this connection,
the Court pointed out, 'abuses can occur as to the manner that in which the provisions
in force are applied by a given school or teacher and the competent authorities have a
duty to take the utmost care to see to it that parent's religious and philosophical convictions are not disregarded at this level by carelessness, lack of judgment or misplaced
proselytism'.[76]

As the *Kjeldsen* case showed, these are injunctions which are easier to articulate than
to apply.[77] There, Danish law required the teaching of sex education as an integral part of
the curriculum for nine to eleven-year-olds. Children at state schools were not excused
from the lessons. A claim by parents that this was a violation of their right to have their
religious and philosophical convictions respected was rejected by six votes to one by the
Court. For the majority, the crucial point was that the teaching programme was principally a matter of conveying information. There was no attempt to indoctrinate a particular moral attitude towards sexual activities, especially concerning contraception. Judge
Verdross's dissent conceded that the teaching was not indoctrination but argued that the
proper distinction to be drawn was between the biological science of reproduction and
'sexual practices'. Parents could, for reasons of religious conviction, properly object to
information about the latter being given to their children, even in an objective manner.
Another factor that would appear to have influenced the Court in its decision was that
the government provided 'substantial assistance to private schools' in which the parents
could have their children educated in accordance with their beliefs; although recourse to
such schools involved parents in 'sacrifices', the alternative solution that they provided

[72] *Warwick v UK No 9471/81*, 60 DR 5 at 18 (1986).

[73] 1996-VI; 24 EHRR 294.

[74] A 23 (1976); 1 EHRR 711 para 53.

[75] The state will have the power under Article 17 to prohibit education in values which fall within its scope:
Opsahl, at n 1 above, pp 235–7.

[76] A 23 (1976); 1 EHRR 711 para 54.

[77] For a case going the other way under the International Covenant on Civil and Political Rights where
atheistic parents successfully complained about religious education in state schools, see *Hartikainen v Finland*
(40/1975), A/36/40 p 147.

was not to be 'disregarded in this case'.[78] The emphasis here appears to be on the provision of state subsidy. The Court would not appear to go as far as to say that a state can comply with Article 2 by allowing unsubsidized private schooling (or home education), with no need for it to modify the provision of education in its state schools so as to 'respect' the parents' convictions. The Court's more recent decision in *Jimenez and Jimenez Merino v Spain*[79] can be read as going this far, but private education in Spain is also heavily state subsidized and, although this is not mentioned, it may have been taken into account. The approach in the *Kjeldsen* case as regards subsidy is open to criticism; the better view is that Article 2 requires that if a state engages in schooling it should 'respect' the convictions of the parents, whatever subsidy it provides for private schools.

The Court has also applied its requirement that information or knowledge be conveyed in an 'objective, critical and pluralistic' way to courses in subjects such as religion, ethics, etc, that bear directly upon a parent's religious or philosophical convictions. In the leading case of *Folgerø v Norway*,[80] the applicant parents were humanists who objected to state primary and lower secondary school lessons for their children in the compulsory subject 'Christianity, Religion and Philosophy'. Although the course focused on knowledge about Christianity to a greater extent than knowledge of other religions and philosophies, this was in itself not inconsistent with the requirements of objectivity and pluralism: in view of the place occupied by Christianity in the national history of the respondent state, which has a Lutheran established church, this choice fell within its margin of appreciation. However, the Court considered that the object of the course, which was to give pupils a Christian upbringing, and the *extent* of its focus was upon Christianity were together so great as to make the difference in treatment a qualitative as well as a quantitative one, to the point where the objectivity and pluralism requirement was not met.

If the requirement is not met, the state will nonetheless have met its obligation to respect the parents' right if it allows the children to be exempted from the offending lessons.[81] But the exemption must be a sufficient one, which was not the case in the *Folgerø* case. Pupils could be granted a partial exemption, which meant that exemption would be granted only after the parents had given written reasons that were found to be reasonable. The Grand Chamber held, by just nine votes to eight, that this was not sufficient to remedy the situation. This was mainly because parents could have difficulty in discovering the details of the subject as actually taught and might feel compelled to give reasons that would impinge upon their right to privacy or engage them in controversy. In a collective dissent, the minority disagreed with the majority's finding of imbalance in the context of the course and concerns about requiring the parents to give reasons.

In reaching its decision in the *Folgerø* case, the Grand Chamber summarized and generally re-affirmed its earlier approach to the interpretation of Article 2 in the *Kjeldsen* and other cases. It is noticeable, however, that the Grand Chamber both accepted that the requirements of objectivity and plurality do not prohibit a limited measure of imbalance

---

[78] A 23 (1976); 1 EHRR 711 para 50. Similarly, the permissibility of home education may be taken into account.

[79] *No 51188/99* hudoc (2000) DA (sex education). The UK also subsidizes some private schools: see below.

[80] 2007 GC. The course syllabus in issue in this case was an amended version of one that the UN Human Rights Committee had ruled infringed the Article 18 ICCPR guarantee of freedom of religion: *Leirvag v Norway 2004* 15 IHRR 909 (2008).

[81] *Kjeldsen, Busk Madsen, and Pedersen v Denmark* A 23 (1976); 1 EHRR 711. In the *Campbell and Cosans* case, above, p 703, the Court suggested that a system of exemptions from corporal punishment might satisfy Article 2; the defendant government had argued that such differential treatment of pupils on matters of discipline would not be acceptable.

in the content of a course that reflects a state's national traditions and also demonstrated a willingness to examine and evaluate more closely the details of the content of a challenged course than it had done before.

The approach in the *Folgerø* case was followed in *Zengin v Turkey*.[82] In that case primary and lower secondary children in state schools were given compulsory classes in 'religious culture and ethics'. Although aimed at transmitting knowledge of all of the major religions, the classes focused very largely upon the Sunni understanding of Islam. Whereas it was acceptable in principle under Article 2 to emphasize Islam, as the majority religion in the respondent state, the Court accepted the applicants' argument that the emphasis upon Sunni Islam to the exclusion of the Alevi faith within Islam, of which there were many adherents, including the applicants, in the respondent state did not meet the requirements of objectivity and pluralism. Nor was the situation remedied by a government decision providing for partial exemptions. The decision gave automatic exemptions from the course for children who were Christians and Jews, but made no provision for exemptions by Muslims of any kind, although, the government stated, applications for exemption by the adherents of other religions would be considered. The Court objected to the requirement that individuals disclose their religion as problematic under Article 9 of the Convention, and found that the discretionary and non-legislative basis for possible exemptions for non-Christians and Jews did not comply with Article 2.

If the above cases shows the difficulty of deciding the acceptable limits of the parents' concern on the content of the curriculum, *Campbell and Cosans v UK*[83] raised the same problem about administrative matters, here school discipline maintained by corporal punishment over the parents' objections in breach of Article 2. The Court decided that the parents' objections were 'philosophical' because they attained the required 'level of cogency, seriousness, cohesion and importance'. It was surely not without significance that the practice complained about raised a serious question of the violation of a fundamental Convention provision—Article 3—even if on the facts the Court held that Article 3 had not been breached.[84] It is less likely that the Court would reach the same conclusion about, say, obligations to wear school uniform[85] or the fixing of the school starting and leaving ages, however strongly parents might feel about such things, unless another Convention right were implicated.

Another dimension to the protection of minority education arose in *DH v Czech Republic*, in which the respondent state was found to be in breach of Articles 2 and 14 for a situation in which Roma children were allocated without justification and to their disadvantage to special schools for their education. The Grand Chamber's important judgment in this case is argued entirely in terms of discrimination contrary to Article 14 and is considered above under that Article.[86]

4. DISCRIMINATION AND MINORITY RIGHTS

On the face of it, a state is well protected with defences to claims that it is in violation of Article 2 so long as it runs and finances an efficient system of education which is in some way sensitive to the most heart-felt concerns of parents. Many of their wishes can be met

---

[82] 2007-XX.

[83] A 48 (1982); 4 EHRR 293 para 36. Judge Evans, dissenting, relied on the *travaux* to establish that the parents' convictions protected by Article 2, First Protocol extended only to the subject matter of what was taught and not to how the school was administered.

[84] On school corporal punishment under Article 3, see above, pp 105–6.

[85] See above, p 701.   [86] See above, p 607.

by tolerating a system of private education. However, while the general provision of education by European states may be sound, some individuals or groups of individuals may find themselves at particular disadvantages compared with the majority of parents and children. With this in mind, in the *Folgerø* case[87] the Court cautioned that 'democracy does not simply mean that the views of a majority must always prevail: a balance must be achieved which ensures the fair and proper treatment of minorities and avoids any abuse of a dominant position'. At the international level, discrimination with respect to educational provision has long been a matter of concern and claims for special treatment for minority education are familiar.[88] The *Belgian Linguistic* case[89] remains a core authority on Article 2 of the First Protocol, but it also addressed concerns of the applicants under Article 14. The parents of French-speaking children alleged that several of the schooling arrangements differentiated between their children and Dutch-speaking children and that, because there was no reasonable and objective justification for the differences, they constituted discrimination in breach of the Convention. The Court condemned only one, relatively minor, practice as contravening Article 14, where Dutch-speaking children in a particular area were allowed to be educated in Dutch-speaking schools in a bilingual district outside the neighbourhood, whereas French-speaking children in an equivalent Flemish area could not attend the French-speaking schools in the same bilingual district but were compelled to attend their local Dutch-language schools. The narrow effect the Court gave to Article 14 was in part because it endorsed as a legitimate policy the Belgian state's objective of securing unilingual regions in the bulk of the country. That this policy disadvantaged members of linguistic minorities was not discrimination and the children's rights had not been violated. Nor, because language, rather than religious or philosophical convictions, was the badge of distinction could the parents find any protection in the second sentence of Article 2.[90]

The Court's approach to the Article 14 issue in the case has not escaped criticism.[91] The tolerance the judgment shows for assimilative policies, albeit in discrete regions, is out of line with its insistence on pluralism on other matters. The state, it is thought, may neither discriminate in the access to the educational system it provides nor establish segregated educational systems, although it may have to tolerate separate schools if that is necessary to respect the religious and philosophical convictions of parents.[92] To this extent, parents who are members of religious or philosophical minorities have the right to establish their own schools. Article 14 may then have a role where the state grants subsidies to *some* private schools established in respect of parents' religious and philosophical convictions. There may first be a question as to whether a state should be subsidizing denominational education at all. Since, in fact, several European states do so, here it may be argued that under Article 14 it may do so but that it may not discriminate between such groups by subsidizing some schools for some groups but not others. In the United Kingdom, until recently the power to support grant-maintained schools was exercised only in favour of Christian and Jewish schools; the government rejected applications from Muslim schools.[93] In the absence of a reasonable and objective justification for the decision, this

---

[87] Hudoc (2007) GC para 84.

[88] See Cullen, IJFL 143 at 146–51 (1993). See also the UNESCO Convention against Discrimination in Education 1960, 429 UNTS 93.

[89] A 6 (1968); 1 EHRR 252 PC.   [90] *Ibid.* See also *Skender v FYRM No 62059/00* hudoc (2001) DA.

[91] See Cullen, *loc cit* at n 88, above, pp 171–2 (1993).

[92] *Kjeldsen, Busk Madsen and Pedersen v Denmark* A 23 (1976) para 53 and *Karnell and Hardt v Sweden No 4733/71*, 14 YB 664 (1971). The *Karnell and Hardt* case was settled: *Council of Europe, Stock-Taking 1954–1984*, pp 149–50.

[93] See Cumper, 139 NLJ 1067 (1989). Islamic schools are now supported.

would appear to be incompatible with Article 14, subject to the United Kingdom reservation. In a case from Northern Ireland,[94] the Commission held manifestly unfounded a claim by a parent that differential funding between state schools and 'maintained' schools in which private bodies could exercise a degree of control over the school violated Article 14 in conjunction with Article 2 of the First Protocol. The different treatment was justified because the amount of state subsidy to maintained schools was large (85 per cent of capital costs and 100 per cent of running costs) and the advantages to the private trusts were considerable (a controlling interest in the governors and the vesting of the school property in them).

Even if the obligation to support minority schools goes as far as has been argued, it applies only to those catering for religious or philosophical minorities. Linguistic minorities are certainly excluded and it would appear that groups claiming minority school support rights on cultural, ethnic, or regional grounds would also fall beyond the scope of Article 2.[95] The Council of Europe's 1994 Framework Convention for the Protection of National Minorities[96] sets obligations on states to take measures in the field of education to foster understanding of minority (and majority) culture, to recognize the rights of persons belonging to national minorities to set up and manage their own education departments (though this involves no right to state financial support), and to recognize the right of persons belonging to national minorities to learn their national language and, in minority areas, to endeavour to provide instruction in the minority language.

5. CONCLUSION

Article 2 of the First Protocol is far from the full guarantee of the right to education provided in some international human rights treaties protecting economic, social, and cultural rights.[97] There is no obligation upon the state to provide a state system of education, let alone to fund it appropriately or have it meet European standards as to such matters as course content or management. Its obligation is the more limited one of guaranteeing access to those state and private schools that the state chooses to provide or allow, coupled with a modest duty to secure their effective functioning in certain basic regards and to respect the religious and philosophical conviction of a child's parents in teaching and administration. The significance of the absence of an obligation to provide a state system of education is not so great as might appear for the reason that European states do in fact provide comprehensive systems of state education that are subject to Article 2, which extends to 'existing' institutions. At the same time, claims concerning 'existing' institutions in respect of such matters as the choice of school, the role of parents, school management generally, the curriculum and, above all, the funding of schools and universities are unlikely to succeed in the absence of clearly arbitrary or nationally illegal acts. The largely negative obligation that Article 2 contains leaves beyond its scope the proper funding and management of schools and universities, which is critical to the quality of the education which they provide.

[94] *X v UK No 7782/77*, 14 DR 179 (1978).

[95] Note, however, that in the *Sahin* case, above, p 701, para 152, the Court stated that 'the principle of equality of treatment in the exercise of their right to education' was implicit in Article 2, so that there might no need for an Article 14 claim.

[96] ETS 157, Articles 12–14.

[97] See particularly Articles 13–14, International Covenant on Economic, Social and Cultural Rights 1966, 993 UNTS 3; Article 28, Convention on the Rights of the Child 1989, 28 ILM 1448; and Article 17(2), Revised European Social Charter 1996, ETS 63.

While this situation accurately reflects the drafting history of Article 2, it would be open the Court to adopt a more demanding interpretation of Article 2 by regarding the failure of the state to provide in its state schools or universities the requisite quality of education in a particular case (eg, special needs schooling)[98] as a 'denial' of the right to an effective education contrary to the first sentence of Article 2. This would be consistent with the Convention's character as a 'living instrument'[99] and would fill what is otherwise is a gap in the protection afforded by the Convention to the right to education, which the Court has recognized as playing a 'fundamental role' in a democratic society.[100] It might even be argued that the obligation not to deny education in the first sentence of Article 2 should be read, contrary to the ruling in the *Belgian Linguistic* case,[101] as imposing an obligation to provide a state education system. In *Kjeldsen, Busk Madsen and Pedersen v Denmark*,[102] the Court acknowledged that, given 'the power of the modern state, it is above all through state teaching' that the aim of safeguarding pluralism in education in the second sentence of Article 2 must be realized. The same might be said of the obligation not to deny an effective education in the first sentence of the same Article.

---

[98] See *International Association Autism-Europe v France*, European Committee of Social Rights, Complaint No 13/2002 (2004) (insufficient educational provision made for autistic persons).

[99] *Leyla Sahin v Turkey* 2005-XI; 41 EHRR 109 para 136 GC.

[100] Id, para 137. Such an interpretation would make the UK reservation accepting Article 2 particularly relevant. The reservation reads: 'in view of certain provisions of the Education Acts in the United Kingdom, the principle affirmed in the second sentence of Article 2 is accepted by the United Kingdom only so far as it is compatible with the provision of efficient instruction and training, and the avoidance of unreasonable public expenditure. As to its validity, see above, n 4.

[101] For this ruling, see above, p 697.

[102] A 23 (1976); 1 EHRR 711 para 50. Cf, *Konrad v Germany No 35504/03* hudoc (2006) DA.

20

ARTICLE 3, FIRST PROTOCOL: THE RIGHT TO FREE ELECTIONS

The High Contracting Parties undertake to hold free elections at reasonable intervals by secret ballot, under conditions which will ensure the free expression of the opinion of the people in the choice of the legislature.

1. INTRODUCTION

The right to free elections protected by Article 3 of the First Protocol[1] has been a relatively late addition to the list of individual liberties to receive the regular attention of the Court. The first judgment on this important Article was not delivered until 1987, in *Mathieu-Mohin and Clerfayt v Belgium*.[2] However, since then judgments have been delivered in over forty cases concerning the right to free elections, out of which the Court derives individual rights, such as the right to vote and to stand for elections. The case law has developed over the last few years in particular with significant Grand Chamber judgments being delivered in *Hirst v UK (No 2)*[3] (concerning the disenfranchisement of prisoners), *Zdanoka v Latvia*[4] (concerning the prohibition placed upon former leading communists from standing in elections), and *Yumak and Sadak v Turkey*[5] (concerning whether a requirement to obtain at least 10 per cent of the national vote complied with Article 3).

Today, therefore, the Strasbourg jurisprudence is much richer than it was just a few years ago. Article 3 provides an extensive, yet basic guarantee in respect of the rights of voters, candidates, and representatives. The standards set by the Court are open to criticism in a number of respects. However, it is worth stressing at the outset that any assessment of the Court's jurisprudence should have regard to two important points. First, the peculiar drafting of Article 3. It does not refer to specific rights; instead it imposes a general obligation on the states to maintain 'free elections' in respect of the 'legislature'[6] and sets out certain conditions in this regard. Secondly, the balance the Court must strike between, on the one hand, a commitment to the promotion of the practice of individual rights in this vital sphere yet, on the other, its traditional reluctance as an international court to become involved in policing matters as delicate as the electoral arrangements of the states parties.

---

[1] There are also a number of relevant 'soft law' instruments produced by Council of Europe organs. See eg, the Venice Commission documentation available at <http://www.venice.coe.int/site/main/Elections_ Referendums_E.asp>.

[2] A 113 (1987); 10 EHRR 1 PC.   [3] 2005-IX; 42 EHRR 849 GC.   [4] 2006-IV; 45 EHRR 478 GC.

[5] Hudoc (2008) GC. Chamber judgment: hudoc (2007).   [6] See below, p 730.

2. THE NATURE AND BASIS OF THE RIGHTS PROTECTED BY ARTICLE 3

I. PROTECTION OF INDIVIDUAL RIGHTS AND THE DEMOCRATIC CONTEXT

The guarantee of free elections was displaced from the main text of the treaty into the First Protocol because of a lack of consensus about the form and content of the proposed provision. There was disagreement between the states about the propriety of framing a human right to free elections, some states believing that this went 'outside the traditional domain of human rights'.[7] A contrary view equated the proposed right to free elections with the familiar freedoms of opinion, speech, assembly, and association.[8] Further difficulties surrounded drafting. Various draft versions of Article 3 were rejected because of, for example, concerns that their wording might imply a commitment to some form of proportional representation.[9]

The *travaux préparatoires* are unclear as to whether the states intended to create an enforceable right to free elections or rather to stipulate a general—if unenforceable—obligation upon the states to maintain democratic structures. The Court, however, is clear that Article 3 protects individual rights.[10] Referring generally to the preparatory work on Article 3, the special way the Article is drafted,[11] and the interpretation of the provision in the context of the Convention as a whole, the Court has determined that Article 3 guarantees rights such as the right to vote and to stand for election. It maintains that the Article's 'unique phrasing was intended to give greater solemnity to the Contracting States' commitment and to emphasise that this was an area where they were required to take positive measures as opposed to merely refraining from interference'.[12]

Article 3 does not actually mention 'democracy', rather reference is made to 'the free expression of the opinion of the people in the choice of the legislature'. So what would happen if the will of the people were to elect an anti-democratic, authoritarian party? It seems clear that the Court would support *proportionate* action taken at the domestic level to prevent this from happening, by finding that an interference with Article 3 was justified,[13] or perhaps accepting that Article 17 of the Convention was applicable.[14] The Court is clear that '[d]emocracy constitutes a fundamental element of the "European public order"'[15] and that it 'is the only political model contemplated by the Convention

---

[7] 4 TP 140.   [8] 7 TP 156.

[9] 7 TP 128–30; 8 TP 150–1. The earlier drafts are reproduced in 5 TP 184–6; 7 TP 130, 150–2; 8 TP 12–14.

[10] Cf, early Commission decisions which held that Article 3 did not confer rights on individuals: *X v FRG* No 530/59, 3 YB184 at 190 (1960); see also *X v Belgium* No1065/61, 4 YB 260 at 268 (1961): '...the right to vote is not, as such, guaranteed by Article 3'; *X v Belgium No 1028/61*, 4 YB 324 at 338 (1961): Article 3 'does not guarantee the right to vote, to stand for election or to be elected'.

[11] *Hirst v UK (No 2)* 2005-IX; 42 EHRR 849 para 56–7 GC (citing *Mathieu-Mohin and Clerfayt v Belgium* A 113 (1987); 10 EHRR 1 paras 46–51 PC). See also the dissenting opinion of Judge Rozakis in *Zdanoka v Latvia* 2006-IV; 45 EHRR 478 GC.

[12] *Hirst v UK (No 2)* 2005-IX; 42 EHRR 849 para 57 GC (citing *Mathieu-Mohin and Clerfayt v Belgium* A 113 (1987); 10 EHRR 1 para 50 PC). So, unlike the case law on positive obligations, with Article 3 the Court has derived an individual right from a text which refers explicitly only to a positive obligation on the part of the states to provide a collective good.

[13] See *Zdanoka v Latvia* 2006-IV; 45 EHRR 478, discussed below at p 723.

[14] See Ch 17.

[15] *Zdanoka v Latvia* 2006-IV; 45 EHRR 478 para 98 GC.

and, accordingly, the only one compatible with it'.[16] This last point has been repeatedly made in Article 11 judgments concerning the banning of political parties,[17] the most prominent example being *Refah Partisi (The Welfare Party) v Turkey*.[18]

The democratic ideal permeates Convention jurisprudence and the connection between the right to free elections and 'effective political democracy' is often alluded to by the Court to stress the direct contribution which the right has to make to this goal.[19] The sometimes limited contribution that Article 3 makes via the right for candidates to stand in elections, and the right to vote, should therefore be seen alongside the intense scrutiny given to the political dimension of the rights to freedom of association (notably Article 11 case law on freedom of political parties) and freedom of expression (and so Article 10 case law on political debate in particular),[20] plus the Court's general vision of the state's role as the 'ultimate guarantor of pluralism'.[21] The inter-relationship between these aspects of Convention jurisprudence was recently noted by a Grand Chamber when it stated:

> [e]xpression of the opinion of the people [under Article 3] is inconceivable without the assistance of a plurality of political parties representing the currents of opinion flowing through a country's population. By reflecting those currents, not only within political institutions but also, thanks to the media, at all levels of life in society, they make an irreplaceable contribution to the political debate which is at the very core of the concept of a democratic society.[22]

II. RESTRICTIONS ON INDIVIDUAL RIGHTS

No grounds of restriction are mentioned in Article 3.[23] However, 'the rights in question are not absolute';[24] they are subject to implied limitations.

In the absence of a specific list of legitimate aims justifying restriction, such as those stated in Articles 8–11, a Grand Chamber has held that the states are free to rely upon an aim not contained in the lists enumerated in Articles 8–11 to justify a restriction, 'provided that the compatibility of that aim with the principle of the rule of law and the general objectives of the Convention is proved in the particular circumstances of a

---

[16] *Ibid* para 98 GC (citing *United Communist Party of Turkey v Turkey* 1998-I; 26 EHRR 121 para 45 GC; *Refah Partisi (The Welfare Party) v Turkey* 2003-II; 37 EHRR 1 GC; and *Gorzelik v Poland* 2004-I; 40 EHRR 76 para 89 GC).

[17] See Ch 12.

[18] 2003-II; 37 EHRR 1 GC, see p 529 above. The political party concerned had a real chance of obtaining power in a forthcoming election, but it was adjudged to be espousing undemocratic ideals and banned by the Constitutional Court. The European Court accepted that there were convincing and compelling reasons to justify the interference with Article 11, and that a state could 'reasonably forestall the execution of such [an undemocratic] policy, which is incompatible with the Convention's provisions, before an attempt is made to implement it through concrete steps that might prejudice civil peace and the country's democratic regime', at para 102.

[19] See especially *Zdanoka*, above n 15, para 98; *Sadak and Others v Turkey (No 2)* 2002-IV; 36 EHRR 396 para 32; *Melnychenko v Ukraine* 2004-X; 42 EHRR 784 para 53; and *Hirst v UK (No 2)* 2005-IX; 42 EHRR 849 GC, 'the rights guaranteed under Article 3 . . . are crucial to establishing and maintaining the foundations of an effective and meaningful democracy governed by the rule of law', para 58 (citation omitted).

[20] See Ch 11.   [21] *Yumak and Sadak* hudoc (2008) para 106 GC.

[22] Id, para 107 (citing *Lingens v Austria* A 103 (1986); 8 EHRR 407 para 42 PC; *Castells v Spain* A 236 (1992); 14 EHRR 445 para 43; and *United Communist Party of Turkey v Turkey* 1998-I; 26 EHRR 121 para 44). See also *Zdanoka v Latvia* 2006-IV; 45 EHRR 478 para 115(a) GC.

[23] Article 16 permits restrictions on the exercise of political activity by aliens, see Ch 17.

[24] *Mathieu-Mohin and Clerfayt v Belgium* A 113 (1987); 10 EHRR 1 para 52 PC.

case'.[25] Accordingly the familiar Articles 8–11 tests of 'necessity' or 'pressing social need' are not employed in the analysis of restrictions on the electoral rights,[26] and it is recognized too that, '[t]he standards to be applied for establishing compliance with Article 3 must…be considered to be less stringent than those applied under Articles 8–11 of the Convention'.[27]

The test applied by the Court in assessing whether Article 3 has been violated remains that originally set out in *Mathieu-Mohin and Clerfayt v Belgium*:[28]

> [The Court] has to satisfy itself that the conditions do not curtail the rights in question to such an extent as to impair their very essence and deprive them of their effectiveness; that they are imposed in pursuit of a legitimate aim; and that the means employed are not disproportionate. In particular, such conditions must not thwart the free expression of the opinion of the people in the choice of the legislature.

The Court has repeated this statement many times adding that any restrictions on electoral rights 'must reflect, or not run counter to, the concern to maintain the integrity and effectiveness of an electoral procedure aimed at identifying the will of the people through universal suffrage'.[29] In practice this means that the Court looks for arbitrariness or a lack of proportionality in the matter put before it.[30] The Grand Chamber has also endorsed the former Commission's more general observation that elections must not be conducted 'under any form of pressure in the choice of one or more candidates, and that in this choice the elector must not be unduly induced to vote for one party or another'.[31] So there must be no compulsion on voters as regards candidate choice or parties: 'the different political parties must be ensured a reasonable opportunity to present their candidates at elections'.[32]

Understandably the Court is conscious of the heightened political sensitivity of questions surrounding the design and implementation of electoral systems. At the general level and in principle, therefore, it affords the states a wide margin of appreciation within which to manage their electoral affairs.[33] It acknowledges the consequent latitude granted to each state to fashion an electoral system reflecting its own constitutional traditions.[34] Article 3 jurisprudence thus demands flexibility: 'legislation must be assessed in the light of the political evolution of the country concerned, with the result that features unacceptable in the context of one system may be justified in the context of another'.[35] This is because 'there are numerous ways of organising and running electoral systems and a wealth of differences, *inter alia*, in historical development, cultural diversity and political thought within Europe which it is for each Contracting State to mould into their own democratic vision'.[36]

The Court's argument appears to be that, because the right to free elections is drawn from a text which emphasizes the responsibilities of the state rather than the rights of voters, those rights may be more heavily burdened than other political rights in order to

---

[25] *Zdanoka v Latvia* 2006-IV; 45 EHRR 478 para 115(b) GC. See also *Yumak and Sadak v Turkey* hudoc (2008) para 109(iii) GC.

[26] Id, para 115(c).   [27] Id, para 115(a).

[28] A 113 (1987); 10 EHRR 1 para 52 PC.

[29] *Hirst v UK (No 2)*, 2005-IX; 42 EHRR 849 para 62 GC; *Lykourezos v Greece* 2006-VIII; 46 EHRR 74 para 52.

[30] *Yumak and Sadak v Turkey* hudoc (2008) para 109(iii) GC.

[31] Id, para 108 (citing *X v UK No 7140/75*, 7 DR 96 (1976)).

[32] *Ibid* (citing *X v Iceland No 8941/80*, 27 DR 156 (1981)).

[33] See eg, *Matheiu-Mohin and Clerfayt v Belgium* A 113 (1987); 10 EHRR 1 para 52 PC; *Hirst v UK (No 2)* 2005-IX; 42 EHRR 849 para 61 GC; *Podkolzina v Latvia* 2002-II para 33; *Yumak and Sadak v Turkey* hudoc (2008) para 109(ii) GC.   [34] See eg, *Hirst v UK (No 2)* 2005-IX; 42 EHRR 849 para 61 GC.

[35] *Zdanoka v Latvia* 2006-IV; 45 EHRR 478 para 115 GC.   [36] *Hirst v UK (No 2)*, id, para 61.

grant the states latitude to create the collective good which an electoral system represents. It could be said that this reasoning reflects a rather partial commitment to the creation of a strong voting rights doctrine.[37] It might also be argued that it ignores the constitutional principle which recognizes that the right to free elections warrants even stronger protection than the other civil and political rights precisely because it is required to found the possibility of a democracy within which those other rights may be freely enjoyed.

3. ACTIVE AND PASSIVE ELECTORAL RIGHTS

The Court makes a distinction in its doctrine between 'active' and 'passive' electoral rights.[38] This language is intended to differentiate between the right to participate actively as a voter and the rights to offer oneself passively for election as a candidate, and to be a representative if elected. Both sets of rights are protected, and extend across a broad range of electoral activities. The Court has, however, declared that the so-called passive electoral rights are entitled to less protection than the active voting rights.[39] This doctrine derives from the Court's concern to respect the marked diversity of state laws governing candidature and the qualifications of representatives, and to acknowledge the special sensitivity surrounding the composition of national legislatures which is determined by those laws. State laws governing candidature and the membership of legislatures tend not to display the same approximate consensus about the relevant democratic principles as do laws governing the franchise and other aspects of 'active' voting rights, which the Court consequently reviews more strictly.

4. THE RIGHT TO VOTE

The right to vote is routinely recognized by constitutional regimes as the most fundamental political right precisely because it is the 'preservative of all other rights'.[40] According to the Court, '[t]he common principles of the European constitutional heritage, which form the basis of any genuinely democratic society, frame the right to vote in terms of the possibility to cast a vote in universal, equal, free, secret and direct elections held at regular intervals'.[41] The notion of 'free' voting here comprises both the freedom to form an opinion on who to vote for and freedom to express that opinion in the vote itself.[42]

---

[37] See the dissenting opinion of Judge Rozakis in *Zdanoka*, criticising the Court's 'obscure generalisation' about the nature of the rights created by Article 3.

[38] See eg, *Melnychenko v Ukraine* 2004-X; 42 EHRR 784 para 57 and *Zdanoka v Latvia* 2006-IV; 45 EHRR 478 paras 105–6 GC. On the relationship between the active and passive aspect more generally, see *Tănase and Chirtoacă v Moldova* hudoc (2008) para 113.

[39] See eg, *Zdanoka*, id, para 105.

[40] This is the formulation of the United States Supreme Court, first used in *Yick Wo v Hopkins* 118 US 356 at 370 (1886).

[41] *Russian Conservative Party of Entrepreneurs v Russia* hudoc (2007); 46 EHRR 863 para 70 (citing Resolution 1320 (2003) of the Parliamentary Assembly on the Code of Good Practice in Electoral Matters; the Declaration by the Committee of Ministers on the Code of Good Practice in Electoral Matters; and the Code of Good Practice in Electoral Matters adopted by the Venice Commission).

[42] Id, paras 71–3. However, the right to vote is only exercisable with respect to those candidates or parties appearing on the ballot paper. It does not encompass the right to vote for a party of the applicant's choosing, for a party or candidate may have been disqualified from standing (see also text accompanying n 54 below). If so, issues may arise under the right to stand, see id, paras 75–9, and below pp 719–25.

Judgments on the individual's[43] right to vote endorse the principle of universal suffrage.[44] As the Court has put it, any departure from this principle, 'risks undermining the democratic validity of the legislature thus elected and the laws it promulgates. Exclusion of any groups or categories of the general population must accordingly be reconcilable with the underlying purposes of Article 3'.[45] In *Hirst v UK (No 2)*,[46] which concerned the disenfranchisement of prisoners, the Grand Chamber insisted that its starting point was that 'the right to vote is not a privilege'. It added, 'the presumption in a democratic State must be in favour of inclusion', universal suffrage having 'become the basic principle'. It acknowledged, however, that Article 3 rights were not absolute, but subject to implied limitations, and the state had a margin of appreciation in this regard.[47]

The core principle articulated in Strasbourg judgments is that a state may not create 'clusters' of disenfranchised persons by excluding groups or categories of the general population in a manner which is irreconcilable with the 'underlying purposes of Article 3'.[48] Thus laws denying the vote to sub-populations within the electorate must be justified with reference to ideas of voter equality, free access to and exercise of the right to vote by individuals, and to the protection of the free expression of the opinion of the people as a whole. In *Matthews v UK*[49] the Court ruled that the denial of voting rights in European Parliament[50] elections to residents of Gibraltar flouted Article 3 by creating a cluster of disenfranchised persons whose loss of political rights could not be justified. Similarly, in *Aziz v Cyprus*[51] the denial of voting rights to a Turkish-Cypriot resident in the non-occupied territory of Cyprus violated Article 3 because it amounted to a straightforward fencing-out of such persons from the democratic process. No accommodation was made for Turkish-Cypriot residents whose opportunities for segregated electoral participation had been lost owing to political events. The Court noted that this situation had endured for nearly thirty years and that there had been no legal reform over this period.[52] There was a violation of Article 3: the states must not 'exclude some persons or group of persons from participating in the political life of the country'.[53]

The claim by an individual that he or she has not been able to vote for his or her preferred candidate is not capable of forming the sole basis of a violation of the right to vote.[54] This is partly because of evidential problems: an intention to vote in a particular way 'is essentially a thought confined to the *forum internum* of an individual'.[55] And proof of how an elector did vote may not reflect accurately the person's prior voting intentions, which may have changed at the point of voting. Another problem the Court identifies concerns the risk that to admit such claims might lead a 'virtually unlimited number of individuals to claim that their right to vote had been interfered with solely because they had not voted in accordance with their initial voting intention'.[56] It is difficult to see how this could be so, as an applicant would have to demonstrate the presence of a legal

---

[43] All the cases that follow concern interferences with individual voter rights. It may be noted, however, that in the *Greek* case the former Commission concluded that Article 3 had been violated in that 'the Greek people were... prevented from expressing their political opinion by choosing a legislature...', this due to the dissolution of Parliament and the postponement of new elections, 12 YB (the *Greek* case) 1 at 179–80 (1969) Com Rep.

[44] See *Russian Conservative Party of Entrepreneurs v Russia* hudoc (2007); 46 EHRR 863 para 70: 'Freedom of suffrage is the cornerstone of the protection afforded by Article 3 of Protocol No 1' (para 71).

[45] *Hirst v UK (No 2)* 2005-IX; 42 EHRR 849 para 62 GC (citing *Aziz v Cyprus* 2004-V; 41 EHRR 164 para 28).

[46] Id, para 59.   [47] Id, para 60.   [48] *Zdanoka v Latvia* 2006-IV; 45 EHRR 478 para 105.

[49] 1999-I; 28 EHRR 361.   [50] On this important aspect of the case, see below at p 731.

[51] 2004-V; 41 EHRR 164.   [52] Id, para 30.   [53] Id, para 28.

[54] *Russian Conservative Party of Entrepreneurs v Russia* hudoc (2007); 46 EHRR 863, para 76.

[55] *Ibid.*   [56] Id, para 78.

obstacle, rather than merely a psychological barrier preventing her from casting her vote as originally intended. The Court's approach also overlooks the possible application of the principle of legitimate expectation to voting rights, although it has acknowledged the role of that principle in the protection of the passive rights of representatives.[57]

I. GENERAL RESTRICTIONS ON THE RIGHT TO VOTE

Subject to the considerations just noted, traditional voter qualifications based upon age, residence, and citizenship may comply with Article 3.[58] A Grand Chamber[59] has pointed out that a minimum voting age and residence conditions might be justifiable, the former to ensure 'the maturity of those participating in the electoral process', the latter 'to identify those with sufficiently continuous or close links to, or a stake in, the country concerned'.

II. DISENFRANCHISEMENT

Disenfranchisements attendant on bankruptcy have been held to serve no purpose but to belittle the persons in question and in consequence are in violation of Article 3 owing to their reliance on this illegitimate aim to single out this sub-group.[60] Disenfranchisement of those with known criminal (Mafia) associations have also been declared to violate Article 3 owing to the disproportionate nature of the restrictions, although, as with *Hirst* (see immediately below), the state is free to devise more proportionate laws conditioning electoral rights upon the absence of criminal contacts or convictions.[61]

In *Hirst v UK (No 2)*[62] the Strasbourg Court in effect examined whether the disenfranchisement of the UK prison population violated Article 3. Hirst had been convicted of manslaughter so, like 48,000 UK prisoners, he was disenfranchised pursuant to legislation which automatically removed the vote from all those convicted and serving a custodial sentence. In a controversial ruling, the Court found a violation of Article 3 (twelve votes to five). The Court was insistent that the right to vote be addressed from the perspective of democratic principles and standards such as tolerance and broadmindedness.[63] Accordingly *automatic* disenfranchisement of prisoners simply to please public opinion was contrary to the Convention.[64] Nonetheless the Court recognized that democratic societies were entitled to take steps to protect themselves 'against activities intended to destroy the rights or freedoms set forth in the Convention'.[65] So, Article 3 permitted restrictions on the right to vote for individuals who had, for example, 'seriously abused a public position or whose conduct threatened to undermine the rule of law or democratic foundations'.[66] The essence of the judgment was that disenfranchisement was a 'severe

---

[57] *Lykourezos v Greece* 2006-VIII; 46 EHRR 74, p 720 below.

[58] *X v Netherlands No 6573/74*, 1 DR 87 (1975); *X v UK No 7566/76*, 9 DR 121 (1976); *Luksch v Germany No 27614/95*, 89-B DR 175 (1997); *Hilbe v Lichtenstein No 31981/96*, 1999-IV; *Py v France* 2005-I; 42 EHRR 548; *Sevinger and Eman v Netherlands Nos 17173/07 and 17180/07* hudoc (2007) DA; *Makuc v Slovenia No 26828/06* hudoc (2007) paras 205–8 DA; *Doyle v UK No 30158/06* hudoc (2006) DA.

[59] *Hirst v UK (No 2)* 2005-IX; 42 EHRR 849 para 62 GC (citing *Hilbe v Liechtenstein No 31981/96*, 1999-IV DA and *Melnychenko v Ukraine* 2004-X; 42 EHRR 784 para 56). See also *Doyle v UK No 30158/06* hudoc (2006) DA.

[60] See eg, *Vicenzo Taiani v Italy* hudoc (2006); *Chiumiento v Italy* hudoc (2006); *La Frazia v Italy* hudoc (2006); *Vertucci v Italy* hudoc (2006).

[61] *Labita v Italy* 2000-IV; 46 EHRR 1228 GC; *Vito Sante Santoro v Italy* 2004-VI.

[62] *Hirst v UK (No 2)* 2005-IX; 42 EHRR 849 GC. See Lewis, 2006 PL 209 and Easton, 69 MLR 443 (2006).

[63] Id, para 70.   [64] Id, para 70. See generally paras 63–71.   [65] Id, para 71.

[66] Id, para 71 (citing *X v Netherlands No 6573/74*, 1 DR 87 (1974) and *Glimmerveen and Hagenbeek v Netherlands Nos 8348/78 and 8406/78*, 18 DR 187 (1979)). See also text accompanying n 47 above.

measure' not to be resorted to lightly and that 'the principle of proportionality require[d] a discernible and sufficient link between the sanction and the conduct and circumstances of the individual concerned'.[67] Article 3 was violated as the UK legislation applied in a blanket way since disenfranchisement was automatic for the category of persons affected (those convicted and in prison). There was no 'direct link' between the facts of individual cases and removal of the right to vote.[68]

The Court's willingness to adopt this proportionality approach in *Hirst (No 2)* was striking and illustrated a new, more robust approach to Article 3. The importance attached to the right to vote was in keeping with judgments from the Canadian Supreme and South African Constitutional Courts, which the Court set out in its judgment.[69] The UK government had argued[70] that a wide margin of appreciation should apply as it did generally for Article 3, especially as the domestic legislature and courts had considered the matter and as there was no clear consensus amongst contracting states on the entitlement of prisoners to vote. However, whilst the Court accepted that the applicable margin of appreciation was 'wide', it insisted that it could not be 'all-embracing' for such a 'vitally important Convention right'.[71] It dismissed the significance of the domestic courts' treatment of the case (applying Convention principles under the Human Rights Act) on the basis that it had been overly deferential to Parliament on the key issue. Remarkably[72] it evaluated the way that legislative arrangements for prisoner disenfranchisements had been effected and concluded that there had not been 'any substantive [Parliamentary] debate...on the continued justification in light of modern-day penal policy and of current human rights standards for maintaining such a general restriction on the right of prisoners to vote'.[73] As to the issue of a European consensus, the Court acknowledged that the UK was not alone in disenfranchising convicted prisoners whilst they were detained and indeed that laws elsewhere were more extreme. But it maintained that such states were in a 'minority'[74] and that in any case the lack of a common European approach could not itself be determinative of the issue.[75]

Hirst clearly allows member states to maintain some restrictions on the rights of prisoners to vote. As regards what restrictions are permissible, when pleading before the Grand Chamber the British government referred to the lack of guidance on this point provided in the Chamber judgment. The Grand Chamber nevertheless pointed out that it fell to each member state to decide this issue, subject to Strasbourg supervision.[76] The references made to the a lack of recent parliamentary debate on the issue of prisoner voting is perhaps best seen in this light.

There was a strong dissenting opinion attached to the *Hirst* judgment by Judges Wildhaber, Costa, Lorenzen, Kovler, and Jebens. They were highly critical of the majority on a number of general grounds. Amongst other things, they implied that the Court had 'assume[d] legislative functions'. Reference was made to the fact that prisoner

---

[67] Id, para 71.

[68] Id, para 77. See also the concurring opinion of Judge Caflisch, arguing that disenfranchisement should only be restricted to major crimes, be imposed by a judge, and only then for the punitive phase of detention (where applicable).

[69] Id, paras 35–9.   [70] Id, para 78.   [71] Id, para 82.

[72] Cf, the joint concurring opinion of Judges Tulkens and Zagrebelsky and joint dissenting opinion of Judges Wildhaber, Costa, Lorenzen, Kovler, and Jebens (it was 'obviously compatible with the guarantee of the right to vote to let the legislature decide [on the disenfranchisement of prisoners] in the abstract').

[73] Id, para 79, see also the Chamber judgment at para 17. Cf, the opinion of the dissenters (*ibid*): 'it is not for the Court to prescribe the way in which national legislatures carry out their legislative functions. It must be assumed that [the legal situation] reflects political, social and cultural values in the United Kingdom'.

[74] Id, para 81. The Court noted that, according to the UK, thirteen states banned prisoners from voting.

[75] Id, para 81.   [76] Id, paras 83–4.

disenfranchisement/restrictions on the right to vote for prisoners had a constitutional basis in eight member states. The joint dissent concluded:

> [t]aking into account the sensitive political character of this issue, the diversity of the legal systems within the Contracting States and the lack of a sufficiently clear basis for such a right in Article 3 of Protocol 1, we are not able to accept that it is for the Court to impose on national legal systems an obligation either to abolish disenfranchisement for prisoners or to allow it only to a very limited extent.[77]

5. THE RIGHT TO STAND FOR ELECTION

I. GENERAL APPROACH

The 'passive' electoral rights protect the right to stand as a candidate and, once elected, to sit as a member of parliament.[78] The approach taken here is less strict than for the right to vote and the general comments made above[79] regarding the margin of appreciation and the Court's willingness to look at each system as unique and 'in the light of the political evolution of the country concerned' apply with particular force. Each state has an 'incontestably legitimate' interest in ensuring 'the normal functioning of its own institutional system', especially its national parliament 'which is vested with legislative power and plays a primordial role in a democratic State'.[80] The Court does not want to be seen to meddle in this domain without very good reason. Hence it repeatedly emphasizes that:

> Contracting States enjoy considerable latitude in establishing constitutional rules on the status of members of parliament, including criteria governing eligibility to stand for election.[81] Although they have a common origin in the need to ensure both the independence of elected representatives and the freedom of choice of electors, these criteria vary in accordance with the historical and political factors specific to each State. The multiplicity of situations provided for in the constitutions and electoral legislation of numerous member States of the Council of Europe shows the diversity of possible approaches in this area.[82]

Many of the Court's judgments concerning the passive rights involve the new democracies of Eastern Europe; the Court's challenge is to police these emerging electoral structures without intruding unduly into the freedom of the states to devise distinctive and appropriate political arrangements. To that end, the Court confines its review to 'a check on the absence of arbitrariness in the domestic procedures leading to disqualification of an individual from standing as a candidate'.[83] Applying this principle, what appear at the general level to have been reasonable technical restrictions (in some cases at least) have been found to violate Article 3 on the facts of individual cases. So the deferential approach taken by the Court here does not mean that states have been immune from criticism.

The Court intervened to find a violation of Article 3 in *Sadak and Others v Turkey (No 2)*.[84] In that case the Democratic Party (DEP) was dissolved following the

---

77 Joint dissenting opinion of Judges Wildhaber, Costa, Lorenzen, Kovler, and Jebens at para 9.
78 See *Sadak and Others v Turkey (No 2)* 2002-IV; 36 EHRR 396 para 33.   79 See above, pp 713–14.
80 *Russian Conservative Party of Entrepreneurs v Russia* hudoc (2007); 46 EHRR 863 para 62.
81 See also *Podkolzina v Latvia* 2002-II para 33 and *Gitonas v Greece* 1997-IV; 26 EHRR 691 para 39.
82 *Zdanoka v Latvia* 2006-IV; 45 EHRR 478 para 106 GC (citing *Mathieu-Mohin and Clerfayt v Belgium* A 113 (1987); 10 EHRR 1 para 54 PC and *Podkolzina v Latvia, ibid*).
83 Id, para 115; *Melnychenko v Ukraine* 2004-X; 42 EHRR 784 para 59.   84 2002-IV; 36 EHRR 396.

unconstitutional conduct of some party members, but as a result *all* the party representatives were ejected from parliament. This constituted a disproportionate interference with the electoral rights of the representatives and was 'incompatible with the very substance of the applicants' right to be elected and sit in parliament…and infringed the sovereign power of the electorate who elected them as members of parliament'.[85] Similarly in *Lykourezos v Greece*[86] the Court denounced the application of a disqualification law to a sitting representative who was properly elected before this law took effect. His expulsion from parliament was a breach of the principle of legitimate expectation, a doctrine introduced into Article 3 jurisprudence by this judgment. Both the representative and his electors had acted in the legitimate belief that he would represent them for a full parliamentary term.

Turning to cases which involve the election process itself, in *Russian Conservative Party of Entrepreneurs v Russia*[87] a voter, a candidate, and a political party together challenged a law which stipulated that in the event of any of the top three candidates being rejected, the entire party list was to be withdrawn. In consequence, all the candidates for the Russian Conservative Party were denied a place on the ballot because of false information given by the candidate who held the second place on their party list. In the Court's view, 'legal provisions reinforcing the bond between the top candidates and the entire party list are…instrumental for promoting the emergence of a coherent political will, which is also a legitimate aim under Article 3 of Protocol No 1'.[88] Nonetheless, the denial of passive rights to the candidate and the party was disproportionate to this aim. Interestingly, the argument of the voter, deprived of the opportunity to vote for the party in question, was unsuccessful.

II. TECHNICAL RESTRICTIONS ON STANDING

There have been a series of cases concerning the compatibility with Article 3 of technical restrictions on the right to stand, for example, the need for and proportionality of electoral deposits, and conditions such as language proficiency.

The Court has accepted that certain categories of holders of public office could be barred from standing for election in any constituency where they have performed their duties for more than three months in the three years preceding the election. Such a restriction was well recognized in Europe; it ensured that 'candidates of different political persuasions enjoy equal means of influence (since holders of public office may on occasion have an unfair advantage over other candidates) and protect[ed] the electorate from pressure from such officials who, because of their position, are called upon to take many—and

---

[85] Id, para 40; See also *Kavakci v Turkey* hudoc (2007); *Silay v Turkey* hudoc (2007); *Ilicak v Turkey* hudoc (2007).

[86] *Lykourezos v Greece* 2006-VIII; 46 EHRR 74. See also *Paschalidis, Koutmeridis and Zaharakis v Greece* hudoc (2008) where there was a violation of Article 3 as elected parliamentarians lost their seats following a legal challenge to the status of 'blank' ballot papers which culminated in an unforeseeable departure in the law regarding the method for calculating the electoral quotient. A bar placed on an applicant's access to the facilities available in Parliament on account of his refusal to take the prescribed oath of office did not violate Article 3, see *McGuinness v UK No 39511/98* hudoc (1999) DA. Issues could potentially arise, however, under Article 9, see *Buscarini v San Marino* 1999-I; 30 EHRR 208 GC.

[87] Hudoc (2007); 46 EHRR 863. A political party may bring a claim under Article 3 when electoral laws restrict an individual candidate's right to stand via party list arrangements, see *ibid*, paras 53–67 and *The Georgian Labour Party v Georgia* hudoc (2008) para 72. Claims by political parties are more likely to arise under Article 11, see Ch 12.

[88] Id, para 63. See also *Gorizdra v Moldova No 53180/99* hudoc (2002) DA.

sometimes important—decisions and enjoy substantial prestige in the eyes of the ordinary citizen, whose choice of candidate might be influenced'.[89]

In *Sukhovetskyy v Ukraine*[90] a Chamber adjudged (unanimously) that an election law requiring candidates to pledge a deposit of UAH 1,041, forfeited if the candidate did not win a seat, did not breach Article 3. The applicant's annual income was UAH 960, although the government maintained that the country average was UAH 2,445.9 (for 2001). The deposit, the Court noted, served a legitimate aim: 'guaranteeing the right to effective, streamlined representation by enhancing the responsibility of those standing for election and confining elections to serious candidates, while avoiding the unreasonable outlay of public funds'.[91] As to proportionality, the Court stated that the issue of the deposit and its level had been the subject of detailed and careful parliamentary and judicial scrutiny in Ukraine in recent years. Those institutions had sought to strike a delicate balance between 'deterring frivolous candidates whatever their social standing, and ... allowing the registration of serious candidates including those who happen to be economically disadvantaged'.[92] The Court did not find the sum involved to be unreasonable when compared to other member states, and was of the view that in practice it was not 'excessive or such as to constitute an impenetrable administrative or financial barrier for a determined candidate wishing to enter the electoral race'.[93] The standard set appears to be extremely low, therefore, with no concerns being expressed about the state's comment that the applicant 'could have taken out a bank loan or mortgaged an apartment that he owned to raise the required amount, if he had any faith in being elected'.[94] It is regrettable that this case was not heard by the Grand Chamber. A large deposit places a wealth or property-based restriction on the right to stand which is arguably out of place in modern democracies, and it is unfortunate that the Court did not at least tighten the margin offered to states in this sphere.

In *Krasnov and Skuratov v Russia*[95] the Court considered a law which required prospective candidates to submit accurate information regarding their employment and party membership. Krasnov and Skuratov were both disqualified as candidates because of purported inaccuracies in the information they provided. The Court regarded the law as serving a legitimate purpose: '[it] serves to enable voters to make an informed choice with regard to the candidate's professional and political background'. The requirement that the information be true further protected voters against being misled by false representations. In this context, the application of the law to Krasnov was not disproportionate: his disqualification arose owing to his submission of false details. Suratov, however, had suffered disproportionately by the application of the rules, which had been used to disqualify him for merely omitting to add the description 'professor' to his statement of his employment as acting head of a university department.

Podkolzina v Latvia[96] concerned a law which required prospective parliamentary candidates from Latvia's Russian-speaking minority to demonstrate proficiency in the Latvian language. This was deemed to serve the 'incontestably' legitimate aim of ensuring that the legislature could function properly. More generally the matter of the national

---

[89] *Gitonas v Greece* 1997-IV; 26 EHRR 691 para 40. See also *Ahmed v UK* 1998-VI; 29 EHRR 1 (no violation of Article 3 that local authority officers had to resign before standing in an election), and the Court's comment in *Lykourezos v Greece* 2006-VIII; 46 EHRR 74 that a blanket prohibition on practising any profession in order to stand was something which was 'rarely encountered in other European States', para 53.

[90] 2006-VI; 44 EHRR 1185.

[91] Id, para 62. See also the former Commission's decisions in *Tete v France No 11123/84,* 54 DR 52 (1987) and *Desmeules v France No 12897/87,* 67 DR 166 (1990).

[92] Id, para 67.   [93] Id, para 73.   [94] 2006-VI; 44 EHRR 1185 para 48.   [95] Hudoc (2007).

[96] 2002-II.

parliament's working language was 'in principle one which the State alone has the power to make' since this was 'determined by historical and political considerations specific to each country'.[97] Nonetheless the candidate's passive right had been breached by the unfair manner in which the law had been applied to her.[98] The authorities' assessment of her qualifications and language skills had not complied with principles of procedural fairness and legal certainty. In particular, full responsibility for assessing the applicant's linguistic knowledge rested on a single civil servant. It was telling that the interview conducted in that regard, and which effectively resulted in the applicant being denied the right to stand, mainly concerned the reasons for the applicant's political orientation.[99] In this case the Court highlighted the importance of proper processes being in place to ensure that removal of the right to stand was not arbitrary. In that regard the finding:

> must be reached by a body which can provide a minimum of guarantees of its impartiality. Similarly, the discretion enjoyed by the body concerned must not be exorbitantly wide; it must be circumscribed, with sufficient precision, by the provisions of domestic law. Lastly, the procedure for ruling a candidate ineligible must be such as to guarantee a fair and objective decision and prevent any abuse of power on the part of the relevant authority.[100]

Melnychenko v Ukraine[101] was a similar case. It exhibited the general latitude that the Court granted to the state, here concerning legislation establishing a minimum residence requirement[102] of five years as a condition on the right to stand, but also the requirement that any regime contain sufficient safeguards to ensure that arbitrary—perhaps even bad faith—decisions are not taken. The Court accepted that the residence requirement might be 'appropriate to enable candidates to acquire sufficient knowledge of the issues associated with the national parliament's tasks'.[103] This is a rather surprising assessment: it seems certain that any reasonably politically aware resident could acquire such knowledge in a much shorter time. The applicant had maintained a place of residence within Ukraine during the specified period, but had been absent owing to fear of persecution, which had resulted in his being granted political asylum in the United States.[104] Acknowledging the difficulty of his position, the Court observed that 'if he had stayed in Ukraine his personal safety or physical integrity may have been seriously endangered, rendering the exercise of any political rights impossible, whereas, in leaving the country, he was also prevented from exercising such rights'.[105] In such circumstances, insistence upon continuous residence in Ukraine amounted to an arbitrary application of the law; Article 3 had been breached.[106]

---

[97] Id, para 34.   [98] Id, para 36.   [99] *Ibid.*   [100] Id, para 35.

[101] 2004-X; 42 EHRR 784.

[102] On the broad acceptability of this see id, para 56. See also *Tănase and Chirtoacă v Moldova* hudoc (2008) in which a new law banning individuals holding dual nationality from sitting as an MP was held to be a disproportionate interference with Article 3. The Court had in mind 'the political evolution of Moldova and the historical and political factors specific to it', para 114 (see, generally, paras 7–17) and that a very large proportion of the population of Moldova held or aspired to hold Romanian nationality such that the impact of the law was profound (para 112). Further, only a very small number of states had such a ban, other ways of ensuring MPs held allegiance to the state existed (eg, taking an oath), the law had been criticised by Council of Europe bodies, and the Court expressed concern about the fact that it had been introduced shortly before general elections were held (paras 108–115). Each applicant was a Vice-President of an opposition party.

[103] Id, para 57.

[104] Melnychenko had worked in the office of the President of Ukraine, and was alleged to have tape-recordings of conversations between the President and third parties concerning the disappearance of a political journalist whose decapitated body was found a few weeks before Melnychenko fled Ukraine.

[105] Id, para 65.

[106] Judge Loucaides, dissenting, did not think it was arbitrary, and was critical of the weight given by the Court's to the political circumstances.

III. PREVIOUS BEHAVIOUR AS A BAR TO STANDING

There is an obvious interference with Article 3 rights when an individual is barred from standing in an election owing to his or her past behaviour or political activity. This was so in the important Grand Chamber judgment in *Zdanoka v Latvia*,[107] which concerned whether a former leading member of the communist party could stand in parliamentary elections.

The case was coloured by Latvia's struggle for democracy after the history of occupation by soviet Russia, the failed coup in Latvia in 1991, and the Communist Party of Latvia's (CPL) support for the failed coup in Moscow later that year. Based on the fact that she had been actively involved in the CPL in 1991, the applicant had been prevented from standing as a candidate for election to the Latvian parliament in successive elections occurring years later, in 1998 and 2002. She had nevertheless been elected to Riga City Council and subsequently as an MEP after Latvia joined the EU. The bar in the domestic parliamentary elections was a result of 1995 legislation which prevented those who had 'actively participated' in the CPL after 1991 from standing. A judicial decision concluded that the legislation applied to Zdanoka.

The Court accepted that the restrictions on standing were legitimate in principle. The legislation was not intended to punish; it was passed to 'protect the integrity of the democratic process by excluding from participation in the work of a democratic legislature those individuals who had taken an active and leading role in a party which was directly linked to the attempted violent overthrow of the newly-established democratic regime'.[108] The critical issue therefore was how closely the Court would scrutinize the decision to bar Zdanoka from standing. According to the Grand Chamber, Article 3 did not require 'supervision by the domestic judicial authorities of the proportionality of the impugned statutory restriction in view of the specific features of each and every case'.[109] In other words, the domestic authorities did not have to assess whether the ban against Zdanoka was actually individually justified; it was satisfactory that the domestic courts merely had to establish 'whether a particular individual belongs to the impugned statutory category or group'. Having said this, there needed to be safeguards in the judicial process and the Court also required that 'the statutory distinction itself [was] proportionate and not discriminatory as regards the whole category or group specified in the legislation'.[110]

Applying these general tests the Court noted that the ban applied only to those who had 'actively participated' in the CPL, so the class in question was not formulated too broadly.[111] Further, the ban was reasonably applied to the applicant who clearly fell within this category and there had been a level of judicial review which was accompanied by adequate safeguards against arbitrariness.[112] In summary, 'the impugned legislation was clear and precise as to the definition of the category of persons affected by it, and it was also sufficiently flexible to allow the domestic courts to examine whether or not a particular person belonged to that category'.[113] The Grand Chamber therefore accepted that the restrictions imposed were acceptable under Article 3 and even that they warranted Zdanoka's disqualification from standing 'today', ie when the judgment

---

[107] 2006-IV; 45 EHRR 478 GC. See also *Ādamsons v Latvia* hudoc (2008).

[108] Id, para 122.

[109] Id, para 114. See also paras 115(d) and 125. The general principle was that, 'as long as the statutory distinction itself is proportionate and not discriminatory as regards the whole category or group specified in the legislation, the task of the domestic courts may be limited to establishing whether a particular individual belongs to the impugned statutory category or group', para 114. There was no requirement, then, of 'individualization', for the right to stand under Article 3, at least in this case, see the text accompanying n 110. See, by contrast, *Ādamsons v Latvia* hudoc (2008), discussed below, text accompanying n 129, concerning the ineligibility for election of a former member of a military unit affiliated to the KGB.

[110] Id, para 144.   [111] Id, para 126.
[112] Id, para 127.   [113] Id, para 128.

was delivered (2006), some fifteen years on from the events of 1991.[114] Extraordinarily, however, the Court's judgment was couched in terms that left no doubt as to its view that the impugned Latvian law was unsatisfactory and needed reform. The laws that had been applied to Zdanoka, the Court made clear, would have been unacceptable for 'a country which has an established framework of democratic institutions going back many decades or centuries'.[115] Latvia had been treated specially given the country's 'very special historico-political context',[116] above all the events of the early 1990s and the 'threat to the new democratic order posed by the resurgence of ideas which, if allowed to gain ground, might appear capable of restoring the former regime'.[117] The Court therefore conceded that the Latvian legislative and judicial authorities were 'better placed to assess the difficulties faced in establishing and safeguarding the democratic order' and were entitled to 'sufficient latitude to assess the needs of their society in building confidence in the new democratic institutions, including the national Parliament, and to answer the question whether the impugned measure is still needed for these purposes, provided that the Court has found nothing arbitrary or disproportionate in such an assessment'.[118] Nonetheless, noting the 'greater stability which Latvia now enjoys, *inter alia*, by reason of its full European integration [ie membership of the EU]',[119] the Court issued a warning to the Latvian Parliament: it 'must keep the statutory restriction under constant review, with a view to bringing it to an early end'; failure to 'take active steps in this connection [could] result in a different finding by the Court' in the future.[120]

The Court has, of course, addressed restrictions on rights justified on the basis of demonstrated connections with the communist party before.[121] However, the Grand Chamber in *Zdanoka*, overturning the Chamber's judgment, gave very considerable leeway to Latvia. Undoubtedly this was a reflection of the highly sensitive nature of the 'communist' issue for that country.[122] The majority was prepared, at least for the time-being, to accept the general solution reached albeit with the highly unusual proviso just referred to. However, this was not enough to placate four dissenting judges[123] who all considered, in effect, that the point had come to condemn the restrictions imposed on Zdanoka as Latvia had now moved beyond the difficult times associated with the events of the early 1990s. Their argument, which had much in common with that of the majority in the Chamber judgment, was that, in effect, the measure had become permanent and as such it was disproportionate as it had not been established that the restriction as applied to the applicant was necessary

---

[114] The Court added, 'the applicant's current or recent conduct is not a material consideration, given the statutory restriction in question relates only to her political stance during the crucial period of Latvia's struggle for 'democracy through independence' in 1991', para 132.

[115] Id, para 133.   [116] Id, para 121. See generally paras 119–21.   [117] Id, para 133.

[118] Id, para 134. The Court also emphasized that its deferential approach had been encouraged as both Parliament and the Constitutional Court had reviewed the legislation in issue relatively recently.

[119] Id, para 135.

[120] Id, para 135 (citing *Sheffield and Horsham v UK* 1998-V; 27 EHRR 163 para 60 GC and the follow-up judgment to that case, *Goodwin (Christine) v UK* 2002-VI; 35 EHRR 447 paras 71–93 GC).

[121] Eg, *Vogt v Germany* A 323; 21 EHRR 205 (employment restrictions raising issues under Article 10, see Ch 11) and *Sidabras and Džiautas v Lithuania* 2004-VIII; 42 EHRR 104 (restrictions on former KGB members from accessing spheres of employment in the private sector). See also *Rekvényi v Hungary* 1999-III; 30 EHRR 519 GC (restriction on political activities of members of police, armed forces, and security services).

[122] See 2006-IV; 45 EHRR 478 paras 11–29 GC. In his dissenting opinion attached to the Chamber judgment (where a violation was found) Judge Levits (the Latvian judge) argued that what was at stake was 'a genuine political question, which is important for the society of a new democracy, and which should be decided in the democratic political process within the country', para 50.

[123] See the individual dissenting opinions of Judge Rozakis, and of Judge Zupančič (arguing strongly that the case was really about the Latvian majority's intolerance of a Russian-speaking minority) and the joint dissenting opinion of Judges Mijović and Gyulumyan. *Podkolzina v Latvia* 2002-II, n 721 above, concerned a Russian-speaking Latvian.

on the facts. Could this be the approach taken by the Court if, some time in the future, it revisits the (unreformed) Latvian electoral law on this point?

Assuming the type of special circumstances prevalent in Latvia do not apply, there remains the more general question of what behaviour or background may justify a bar on a particular candidate standing. Jurisprudence from the former Commission indicates that war crimes and treasonous behaviour could justify a permanent bar.[124] It is a well-established feature of the Strasbourg jurisprudence that individuals should not be able to rely on Convention rights to destroy or weaken the ideals and values of the Convention, above all the notion of the democratic society.[125] Furthermore, the Court accepts the concept of a 'democracy capable of defending itself',[126] which requires it to ensure that an appropriate balance is struck between the requirements of defending democratic society and defending individual rights.[127] Questions remain, however, as to what approach should be taken in assessing that balance in the context of Article 3, especially if the bar on standing is the supposed subversive (future) behaviour of the proposed candidate, and there has been no criminal conviction. Should the bar only be imposed justifiably when the democratic order itself is threatened?[128] If so, at what stage can it be imposed? The recent case of *Ādamsons v Latvia*[129] indicates that there are limits to the margin of appreciation extended to a state which prohibits individuals from standing given their connections with a former communist regime. It concerned a law which disqualified former KGB officers from being elected to office and which was applied to the applicant who was barred from standing as a parliamentary candidate even though by then he had held public offices and had been an MP for several years previously. Distinguishing the case from *Zdanoka*, the Court held that at the general level the prohibition may have been justifiable in principle on the basis of defending the democratic order. However, the prohibited group ('former KGB officers') was very generally defined. Accordingly, restrictions on the electoral rights of the members of that group needed a case-by-case approach which addressed the actual conduct of the person concerned. Indeed, the need for such an individualistic approach grew over time as the period when the impugned acts were supposed to have taken place grew more distant in the past. On the facts the Court held that the restrictions as applied to the applicant breached Article 3. In particular, no facts had been adduced indicating that he opposed or expressed hostility to the recovery of Latvia's independence and democratic order or that he had been directly or indirectly involved in the misdeeds of the communist totalitarian regime. In fact, when the restriction was imposed on him he had already held important public offices and embarked on a parliamentary career in 'post-communist' Latvia.

---

[124] See the comments made in *Zdanoka* at paras 109–10 and see eg, *Glimmerveen and Hagenbeek v Netherlands* Nos 8348/78 and 8406/78, 18 DR 187 (1979). The applicants were leaders of a proscribed organization with racist and xenophobic traits and so had been denied the right to stand. The Commission declared the application inadmissible, reference being made to Article 17: the applicants 'intended to participate in these elections and to avail themselves of the right [concerned] for a purpose which the Commission [had] found to be unacceptable under Article 17'.

[125] See eg, case law on Article 17 (Ch 17) and related case law such as *Refah Partisi (The Welfare Party) v Turkey* 2003-II; 37 EHRR 1 para 86 GC. See also *Zdanoka v Latvia* 2006-IV; 45 EHRR 478 para 99 GC.

[126] *Vogt v Germany* A 323 (1995); 21 EHRR 205 GC. See *Zdanoka*, id, para 99.

[127] *Zdanoka*, id, para 100 (with references to *Vogt, ibid; Refah Partisi (The Welfare Party) v Turkey* 2003-II; 37 EHRR 1 GC; and *United Communist Party of Turkey v Turkey* 1998-I; 26 EHRR 121).

[128] See the dissenting opinion of Judge Rozakis in *Zdanoka* [GC] and the references made to *Refah Partisi (The Welfare Party) v Turkey* 2003-II; 37 EHRR 1 GC. Could restrictions be imposed if it is accepted that the candidate's standing poses a threat to 'the authority, the image and the credibility of democracy'? Cf, the dissenting opinion of Judge Bonello attached to the Chamber judgment in *Zdanoka* (hudoc (2004); 41 EHRR 31).

[129] Hudoc (2008).

6. ELECTORAL SYSTEMS AND ADMINISTRATION

The above cases addressed the right to vote and the right to stand, that is individual aspects of the election process. However, as the following sections demonstrate, it is possible to use Article 3 to mount a more general challenge to an election system or the general administration of elections.[130]

I. ELECTORAL ADMINISTRATION

Aspects of the administration of an election may raise issues under Article 3 as with *Bompard v France*[131] where the applicant claimed a violation as the state had failed to review constituency boundaries prior to an election. The Court declared the application inadmissible citing the wide margin of appreciation owed to states in this regard and accepting a plea that it was proper that boundary reviews should not be rushed but must follow comprehensive studies and consultations. In *Purcell v Ireland*,[132] the former Commission said that the rights of individual voters protected by Article 3 did not include the right that all political parties be granted equal coverage by the broadcasting media or, indeed, any coverage at all.[133]

The case of *The Georgian Labour Party v Georgia*[134] raised fundamental issues going to the practical organization and running of the re-election held in that country in 2004, in the aftermath the 'Rose revolution' of 2003, which saw President Shevardnadze's resignation following allegations of widespread electoral fraud. Issues were raised regarding (i) voter registration; (ii) the composition of the electoral commissions which, in effect, oversaw the election process; and (iii) the fact that there was no vote in two major districts, resulting in approximately 60,000 registered voters (2.5 per cent of the national electorate) being disenfranchised.

On the first issue, the Court emphasized the importance of proper management of electoral rolls as a precondition to free and fair elections, and so the proper enjoyment of not only the right to vote but also the right to stand.[135] The Court refused to find a violation of Article 3 following the applicant party's complaint that, just one month before the re-election, the system of voter registration was changed by placing the onus on citizens to register to vote. For the unanimous Court, the system put in place had similarities to that used by some other West European states,[136] though it was recognized that as a matter of policy electoral rules, such as those concerning voter registration, should not be changed in the lead-up to an election.[137] Overall the system was not perfect and reports disclosed shortcomings, nevertheless it and the late introduction of the changes was acceptable bearing in mind the circumstances of the re-election, ie its convening at relatively short notice following the failed election of 2003 and the 'post-revolutionary' political situation.[138]

The claim regarding the electoral commissions was one of political bias since at all levels they were composed of a near majority of presidential appointees. Here the Court emphasized the importance of electoral administration functioning in a transparent

---

[130] See also the Commission's conclusion on Article 3 in the *Greek* case, referred to in n 43 above.

[131] *No 44081/02* hudoc (2006) DA.

[132] *No 15404/89*, 70 DR 262 (1991).

[133] See also *Bowman v UK* 1998-I; 26 EHRR 1, an Article 10 case which raised issues regarding the amount that pressure groups may spend to inform the electorate about candidates standing for election.

[134] *The Georgian Labour Party v Georgia* hudoc (2008).

[135] Id, paras 82–3.   [136] Id, para 91.   [137] Id, para 88.   [138] See paras 89–93.

manner that maintained independence and impartiality,[139] and the text of the judgment leaves no doubt as to the judges' view that the system in place was highly questionable.[140] However, in the absence of proof put to it regarding actual electoral fraud committed by the commissions, the Court explained that it would not find a violation of Article 3.[141]

A violation of Article 3 was nevertheless found on the third issue in *The Georgian Labour Party* case. The Court approached the matter from the principle that 'exclusion of any groups or categories of the general population must be reconcilable with the underlying principles of Article 3 of Protocol 1, including that of universal suffrage' and the notion that 'the democratic validity of the legislature' should not be undermined.[142] The applicant party did not have to prove that disenfranchised voters would have made a difference to its fortunes, for it was clear that the loss of the votes could have an impact of the effectiveness of the right to stand.[143] The essence of the government's defence to what was a clear interference with Article 3 was that the *de facto* disenfranchisement followed extreme circumstances. The first ballot had been voided because of electoral fraud and after this it was not possible to hold a subsequent vote within an appropriate timeframe given the need, after all the political turmoil the country had been through, to institute Parliament and bring closure to the nationwide election. This was especially so as violence erupted in the districts in question, which were located in the Ajarian Autonomous Republic where the central government found it difficult to impose its authority. However, the Court rejected each argument in turn and proceeded to find a technical violation of Article 3. It refused to absolve the respondent government of its responsibility to hold fresh elections in the districts.[144] There was a basic violation of Article 3 on the facts as the two districts in question were excluded from the national vote following hasty decision-making processes that were essentially arbitrary and offensive to the rule of law.[145] The government's argument that the election needed to be brought to a close as quickly as it was, and so without the input of the two disenfranchised districts, was not accepted on the facts.

II. ELECTORAL SYSTEMS

As we have seen, the Court's constant position is that states have a wide latitude to design their own electoral systems to suit their own circumstances and given their own history and traditions.[146] Unsurprisingly then it approaches any assessment of an electoral system overall with caution, also recognizing that: 'electoral systems seek to fulfil objectives which are sometimes scarcely compatible with each other: on the one hand to reflect fairly faithfully the opinions of the people, and on the other, to channel currents of thought so as to promote the emergence of a sufficiently clear and coherent political will'.[147]

In the *Liberal Party* case,[148] the complaint was that the United Kingdom's 'first past the post' electoral system inevitably leads to a dissonance between the proportion of votes

---

[139] Id, paras 100–1. See also para 103 regarding lack of uniform European standards in this area.

[140] Id, paras 106–8. The commissions 'lacked sufficient checks and balances against the President's power' and 'could hardly [have] enjoy[ed] independence from... outside political pressure', at para 110.

[141] The finding was by five votes to two; see the dissenting opinion of Judge Mularoni (subscribed to by Judge Popovic) arguing that independent election monitor reports provided ample evidence of a violation of Article 3.

[142] Id, para 119. See also para 123.   [143] Id, paras 120–1.

[144] See paras 131–6. Regarding the plea of armed clashes with the Ajarian authorities, the Court noted that there had been no derogation from the Convention, see para 131. More generally the Court applied the precedent in *Assanidze v Georgia* 2004-II; 39 EHRR 32 GC.

[145] Id, para 141 (the commission which annulled the election in the controversial districts did so without proper analysis and investigation and exceeded its legal authority in doing so, see para 129).

[146] See above, p 714.   [147] *Yumak and Sadak v Turkey* hudoc (2008) para 112 GC.

[148] *Liberal Party, R and P v UK* No 8765/79, 21 DR 211 at 225 (1980).

cast for a small national party and the proportion of seats it obtained in the legislature. The former Commission said that the United Kingdom system was overall an acceptable system for elections to the legislature and it did not become unfair by reason of the results obtained under it.[149]

It is clear then that Article 3 does not demand that states implement proportional representation.[150] It does not, indeed cannot, ensure complete equality of votes or chances of success for every candidate. Wasted votes have to be tolerated to some extent.[151] The key principle is that everyone is given an equal chance to cast a ballot under the electoral system.[152] So laws requiring political parties to achieve a certain proportion of the total vote before becoming entitled to any seats in the legislature may be compatible with Article 3. A number of such 'threshold' cases have reached the former Commission[153] and Court[154] in the past and none have involved a violation of Article 3. However, it is evident from *Yumak and Sadak v Turkey*[155] that high thresholds can breach Article 3. The case saw a challenge to a law which required a political party to obtain 10 per cent of the *national* vote before it could obtain parliamentary seats. This had a devastating effect on the applicants in 2002 when they stood for election for a party known for its interest in and commitment to the so-called 'Kurdish question'. Even though they had obtained almost 46 per cent of the total vote in their (south-eastern) province,[156] nationally their party's share of the vote was just 6.22 per cent. Accordingly they were barred from taking positions in the National Assembly.

In a detailed and complex judgment, the Grand Chamber rejected the argument that the 10 per cent threshold interfered *excessively* with the free expression of the people for the purposes of Article 3. Thresholds like the one in question were acceptable in principle since they served a legitimate aim: they were 'intended in the main to promote the emergence of sufficiently representative currents of thought within the country'; they avoided 'excessive and debilitating parliamentary fragmentation' and so 'strengthen[ed] governmental stability'.[157] Article 3 nevertheless delineated certain boundaries. On the one hand, it did not go so far as to oblige contracting states to adopt a system whereby parties with an essentially regional base were guaranteed parliamentary representation irrespective of the national vote.[158] On the other hand, issues could arise if the system 'tended to deprive such *parties* of parliamentary representation'.[159] So it was not in itself

---

[149] Id, pp 224–5.

[150] *Yumak and Sadak v Turkey* hudoc (2008) para 110 GC; *Matheiu-Mohin and Clerfayt v Belgium* A 113 (1987); 10 EHRR 1 para 54 PC; *X v Iceland No 8941/80*, 27 DR 145 (1981); nor is proportional representation incompatible with Article 3: *Lindsay v UK No 8364/78*, 4 EHRR 106 (1982).

[151] *Yumak and Sadak, ibid*, para 112 GC (citing *Mathieu-Mohin & Clerfayt v Belgium* A 113 (1987); 10 EHRR 1 PC).

[152] *Bompard v France No 44081/02* hudoc (2006) DA.

[153] *Silvius Magnago and Südtiroler Volkspartei v Italy No 25035/94*, 85-A DR 116 (1996) (4% threshold required for the election of the remaining 25% of the members of the Chamber of Deputies; no violation as covered by wide margin of appreciation left to states in the matter). See also *Etienne Tête v France No 11123/84*, 54 DR 68 (1987).

[154] *Federación nacionalista Canaria v Spain No 56618/00*, 2001-VI DA (proportional representation in the Canary Islands) and *Partija 'Jaunie Demokrati' and Partija 'Musu Zeme' v Latvia Nos 10547/07 and 34049/07* hudoc (2007) DA (5% threshold for parliamentary elections accepted as it encouraged sufficiently representative currents of thought and made it possible to avoid an excessive fragmentation of parliament).

[155] Hudoc (2008) GC. Chamber judgment: hudoc (2007).

[156] In fact, that year as a result of the threshold approximately 45% of people who voted nationally were not represented in Parliament, see para 19.

[157] Id, para 125 citations omitted. In this connection the Court noted that 'the Turkish electoral system, like that of many member states, is predicated on the context of a unitary State', see para 124.

[158] Id, para 124.   [159] *Ibid* (emphasis added).

'decisive' that a high threshold deprived 'part of the electorate of representation'.[160] The Court's task was:

> to determine whether the effect of the rules governing parliamentary elections is to exclude some persons or groups of persons from participating in the political life of the country...and whether the discrepancies created by a particular electoral system can be considered arbitrary or abusive or whether the system tends to favour one political party or candidate by giving them an electoral advantage at the expense of others.[161]

The Court's finding, by thirteen votes to four, that there was no breach of Article 3 reflected this very base level of protection. It would seem too that it was a result of a diplomatic choice from a Grand Chamber prepared to see the best in the Turkish electoral system whilst indicating to the respondent state that it raised serious concerns such that reform would be welcomed. Indeed the Court labelled the 10 per cent threshold as 'excessive'[162] and concurred with the Parliamentary Assembly's view that the 'exceptionally high level...[should] be lowered'.[163] However, each electoral system, the Court insisted, had to be viewed in its country context,[164] so reducing the significance of the fact that the Turkish threshold was the highest in Europe, where a 5 per cent threshold was typical.[165] In the majority's view, an election system that was otherwise dubious under Article 3 was saved as the political parties that were affected by the threshold had managed in practice to 'develop strategies whereby they can attenuate some of its effects'.[166] That is, there existed 'correctives' and 'other safeguards' associated with the electoral system that made it tolerable from the perspective of Article 3. Above all, the applicants could have stood as independent candidates (freeing themselves from the threshold requirement) and formed a parliamentary group once elected, as had happened to the successor of their political party in the 2007 elections. Likewise there was the ability for small parties to form electoral alliances, a tactic that was employed with an element of success in the 2007 election. Thus in that election the proportion of votes nationally cast for candidates who failed to secure a seat had dropped to 13.1 per cent. It may be noticed therefore that the Grand Chamber assessed the Turkish system put before it not only on the facts of the 2002 election, which had provoked the applicants' complaint to Strasbourg, but also the subsequent 2007 election. As to the 2002 election, it was admitted that the outcome (over 45 per cent wasted votes) was 'hardly consistent with the crucial role played in a representative democracy by parliament, which is the main instrument of democratic control and political responsibility, and must reflect as faithfully as possible the desire for a truly democratic political regime'.[167] However, in effect the Court dismissed the 2002 results on the basis that it was generally accepted that they were something of a one-off, the result of a 'crisis climate with many different causes'.[168] Finally, the

---

[160] As the Court explained, such a threshold could 'work as a necessary corrective adjustment to the proportional system, which has always been accepted as allowing for the free expression of the opinion of the people even though it may operate to the detriment of small parties when accompanied by a high threshold', para 122 (citing *Liberal Party, Mrs R and Mr P v UK* No 8765/79, 21 DR 225 (1980)).

[161] Id, para 121 (citing *Aziz v Cyprus* 2004-V; 41 EHRR 164 para 28 and *X v Iceland* No 8941/80, 27 DR 156).

[162] Id, para 147.

[163] *Ibid*, see also para 130. The Chamber, also finding no violation (five votes to two), accepted that the Turkish system did not hinder the emergence of political alternatives (para 74), but it noted that it would be desirable for the 10% threshold to be lowered 'and/or for corrective counterbalances to be introduced to ensure optimal representation of the various political tendencies without sacrificing the objective sought (stable parliamentary majorities)' (para 77). However, the Court refused to find a violation stating that it was important 'to leave sufficient latitude to the national decision-makers' (para 77) and going on to note that civic and political processes were already pressing for this change.

[164] See paras 131–2.   [165] See para 129.

[166] Id, para 143. The Chamber judgment had rejected such arguments, see paras 70–3.

[167] Id, para 140.   [168] Id, para 141.

Court emphasized the safeguard role played by the Turkish Constitutional Court, which had ruled upon the threshold question in 1995: it had proven its ability to exercise 'vigilance to prevent any excessive effects of the impugned electoral threshold by seeking the point of equilibrium between the principles of fair representation and governmental stability' and it provided 'a guarantee calculated to stop the threshold concerned impairing the essence of the right enshrined in Article 3 of Protocol No 1'.

It is not difficult to imagine how controversial the Court's judgment would have been if it had found a violation of Article 3 in *Yumak and Sadak v Turkey*. The Court's reasoning in failing to find a violation is certainly open to strong criticism, as was demonstrated by the joint dissenting opinion of Judges Tulkens, Vajić, Jaeger, and Šikuta who made some very powerful points.[169] It is hard to disagree with their observation that the very essence of Article 3 was impaired in that the threshold deprived 'a large proportion of the population of the possibility of being represented in parliament', and that it had a profoundly negative effect on the fortunes of political parties with a regional focus, something which was hard to reconcile with the need for pluralism in a democratic society, which the Court frequently emphasizes in its Article 11 case law.[170] They also took issue with the validity of the so-called correctives. At the general level they questioned how an improperly functioning system could be saved by what was in effect 'stratagems' used by smaller parties, especially as this was dependent on the vagaries of politics, they had no guaranteed place in the system and relied on the candidates to circumvent the existing electoral rules. More specifically they thought it dubious that smaller parties had to find political allies or disappear (in the sense that individual members had to stand as independents) to achieve a parliamentary presence. As they pointed out, all this went against the grain of Article 11 case law on the importance of political pluralism and the role of parties.

7. THE SCOPE OF PROTOCOL 1, ARTICLE 3 ('THE CHOICE OF THE LEGISLATURE')

The right to vote is limited to guaranteeing the 'free expression of the opinion of the people in the choice of the legislature', so it does not extend to the full range of elections which form part of modern democracies. The Court has stressed the 'primordial role [of the legislature] in a democratic state',[171] but acknowledges also that 'the word "legislature" in Article 3 of Protocol No 1 does not necessarily mean the national parliament: the word has to be interpreted in light of the constitutional structure of the state in question'.[172] So, in *Santoro v Italy*[173] the Court accepted that regional councils formed part of 'the legislature' because they were 'competent to enact, within the territory of the region to which they belong, laws in a number of pivotal areas in a democratic society, such as administrative planning, local policy, public health care, education, town planning and agriculture'. It follows that, for example, the Scottish Parliament would certainly qualify

---

[169] See also, in the Chamber judgment, the joint dissenting opinion of Judges Cabral Barreto and Mularoni, arguing that the 10% rule did exceed the margin of appreciation permitted to Turkey.

[170] See Ch 11 and p 713 above.   [171] *Podkolzina v Latvia* 2002-II para 34.

[172] *Matthews v UK* 1999-I; 28 EHRR 361 para 40 GC.

[173] 2004-VI; 42 EHRR 771 para 53. The Court's first decision on Article 3, *Mathieu-Mohin and Clerfayt v Belgium* A 113 (1987); 10 EHRR 1 PC accepted that the Flemish Council constituted part of the Belgian legislature by virtue of the range of its competence and powers. See also *X v Austria* No 7008/75, 6 DR 120 (1976); *X, Y and Z v FRG* No 6850/74, 5 DR 90 (1976) (Austrian and German *Lander* formed part of 'legislature') and *Py v France* 2005-I; 42 EHRR 548 (New Caledonian Congress was 'sufficiently involved' in the legislative process to count for Article 3).

as a part of the legislature of the United Kingdom, owing to its broad authority to legislate in devolved areas within that territory.[174]

The Court's most significant decision on this aspect of Article 3 concerns the European Parliament, which was declared to be a part of the 'legislature' of Gibraltar in *Matthews v UK*.[175] Overturning the decision of the former Commission, the Grand Chamber concluded that Article 3 could be applicable to the European Parliament, even though it was an international organ,[176] and that in practice it had the characteristics of a 'legislature' for the people of Gibraltar. On the latter point the Court had regard 'not solely to the strictly legislative powers which a body has, but also to that body's role in the overall legislative process'.[177] This landmark decision acknowledged the significant evolution of the European Parliament and its increased role in law-making.[178] Observing that the European Parliament lacked a power to initiate legislation, the Court expressed its view, 'that the European Parliament represents the principal form of democratic, political accountability in the Community system'. The Court then added that, 'whatever its limitations, the European Parliament, which derives democratic legitimation from the direct elections by universal suffrage, must be seen as that part of the European Community structure which best reflects concerns as to "effective political democracy"'.[179]

Given the relatively weak role played by the European Parliament in the legislative process, the Court's willingness to categorize it as a 'legislature' is striking. It seems doubtful, however, that *Matthews* sets a broader precedent. The Court was careful to state that in determining what counted for the purposes of Article 3 it had to 'bear in mind the *sui generis* nature of the European Community, which does not follow in every respect the pattern common in many States of a more or less strict division of powers between the executive and the legislature'.[180]

Article 3 does not apply to elections which have no—or only a very minimal—legislative aspect. The Court has never held, for example, that Article 3 applies to presidential elections,[181] although, rather surprisingly given Article 3's clear text, it has not ruled out the possibility of so holding.[182] Nor does Article 3's scope extend to elections to local governments which lack sufficient legislative authority—either in terms of the scope or strength of their powers—to be deemed to be performing a role as part of the legislature.[183] Referendums are excluded for the same reason,[184] even though in certain

---

[174] Its status as a legislature was assumed for the purposes of Article 3 analysis by the Scottish court and the parties in *Smith v Scott* 2007 SLT 137.

[175] 1999-I; 28 EHRR 361 GC. See Myulle, 6 European Public Law 243 (2000).

[176] Id, para 39. See also paras 40–4. Cf, the dissenting opinion of Judges Freeland and Jungwiert.

[177] Id, para 49.

[178] It was no longer merely 'advisory and supervisory' but had 'moved towards being a body with a decisive role to play in the legislative process of the European Community' (para 50) and in practice there were 'significant areas where Community activity has a direct impact in Gibraltar' (para 53).

[179] Id, paras 51–2. It is difficult not to read this comment in the light of repeated criticisms made of the EC/EU's 'democratic deficit'.   [180] Id, para 48.

[181] *Boskoski v FYRM No11676/04*, 2004-VI DA; *Guliyev v Azerbaijan No35584/02* hudoc (2004) DA; *Baskauskaite v Lithuania No 41090/98* hudoc (1998); 27 EHRR CD 341; *Habsburg-Lothringen v Austria No 15344/89*, 64 DR 210 (1990).

[182] See the rather cautious statement made in *The Georgian Labour Party v Georgia No 9103/04* hudoc (2007) DA. Cf, the criticism offered by Van Dijk and Van Hoof, p 930.

[183] *X v UK No 5155/71*, 6 DR 13 (1976); *Booth-Clibborn v UK No 11391/85*, 43 DR 236 (1985); *Gorizdra v Moldova No 53180/99* hudoc (2002) DA; *Cherepkov v Russia No 51501/99* hudoc (2000) DA; *Salleras Llinares v Spain No 52226/99* hudoc (2000) DA. Local elections may be regarded as feeding into an effective political democracy owing to the function of local government in supporting the legislative role of the national parliament by implementing relevant enactments at the local level. See also Van Dijk and Van Hoof, p 932.

[184] *X v UK No 7096/75*, 3 DR 165 at 166 (1975); *Nurminen v Finland No 27881/95* hudoc (1997) DA; *Castelli v Italy Nos 35790/97 & 38438/97*, 94 DR 102 (1998).

circumstances they may play a significant, if indirect role in determining the subsequent character and role of the legislature (the 1999 referendum on Scottish devolution, for example). It could also be said that elections for heads of state are regarded as central to the maintenance of 'effective political democracy'—which the Court stresses so often it its jurisprudence—even in systems in which the legislative role of the president is minimal. Yet, as we have just seen, Article 3 does not apply here either. The point here is that these restrictions on Article's 3 scope flow directly from its text, which expressly refers to 'the legislature'. It is of course open to member states to amend Article 3 or produce a new Protocol to the Convention on this point.

8. NON-APPLICABILITY OF ARTICLE 6

Article 3 rights are regarded in the Court's classification of rights as 'political' not 'civil'.[185] The guarantees of Article 6 do not therefore extend to them: there is thus no requirement that a state grant an individual a hearing prior to disenfranchisement[186] or disqualification as a candidate or representative. Nor does Article 6 require that states which empower courts to make such determinations prescribe minimum standards to be observed by the judiciary in this task. This is an unfortunate doctrine, aptly criticized in the dissenting opinion of Judge De Meyer in *Pierre-Bloch v France*[187] who observed—accurately—that 'in reality, "political" rights are a special category of "civil" rights. Indeed they are more "civil" than others in that they are more directly inherent in citizenship and, furthermore, are normally exclusive to citizens'. The limitations implied by the Court's contrary doctrine may be offset to some extent by its recent discovery of a principle of legitimate expectation within its Article 3 jurisprudence.[188] This principle works to ensure that existing disqualification laws and procedures are properly applied but does not demand re-design of election laws which make no provision for hearings before denial of electoral rights occurs.

9. CONCLUSION

The Court's approach to the interpretation of the right to free elections is cautious. This is evidenced by the wide margin of appreciation granted to the states and the weaker form of scrutiny adopted compared to the rights protected by Articles 8 to 11. The critic of jurisprudence on the electoral rights of individuals might say that Court judgments are dominated by proportionality review which allows it to evade two basic questions upon which the future effectiveness of the right depends: what are the 'fundamental purposes' of Article 3? How do the asserted aims of challenged laws relate to those purposes? It might be said that it is not sufficient for the Court merely to assume or to assert the legitimacy of such aims in the absence of a deeper consideration of the relevant democratic context. After all, the Court acknowledges repeatedly the fundamental importance of the right to free elections to individuals and to the Convention scheme as a whole.

---

[185] *Pierre-Bloch v France* 1997-VI; 26 EHRR 202. The Court has endorsed this ruling repeatedly in recent years: see eg, *Krasnov and Skuratov v Russia* hudoc (2007); *Boskoski v FYRM No 11676/04* 2004-VI DA; *Guliyev v Azerbaijan No 35584/02* hudoc (2004) DA; *Gorizdra v Moldova No 53180/99* hudoc (2002) DA.
[186] Though see the text accompanying n 68 above.
[187] 1997-VI; 26 EHRR 202.   [188] *Lykourezos v Greece* 2006-VIII; 46 EHRR 74.

Reflecting on the Court's judgments under Article 3 it may be said that *Hirst v UK (No 2)* is emblematic of the seriousness with which the Court treats the issue of disenfranchisement. It places the emphasis on member states to justify the loss of the vote, even if the judgment can be criticized for a lack of clarity in its reasoning. By contrast, Article 3 sets only very basic standards regarding the individual's right to stand. It may still be said, however, that it conveys important messages to states regarding the need for good faith and accountability when decision-making processes curtail that right. The importance of the standards set here has been demonstrated in several cases in recent years.

Zdanoka v Latvia and *Yumak and Sadak v Turkey* are easy targets for those who would argue that the standards set by the Court under Article 3 are simply too low. However, they are certainly the types of cases which Judges Levits[189] had in mind when he observed that the Court faces a 'dilemma' when examining applications under Article 3: 'on the one hand ... it is the Court's task to protect the electoral rights of individuals; but, on the other hand, it should not overstep the limits of its explicit and implicit legitimacy and try to rule instead of the people on the constitutional order which this people creates for itself'. He argued that the dilemma was acute for Article 3 since the rights it protects have a 'double legal character as human rights and an important element of national constitutional order'. It may be recalled that in both *Zdanoka* and also *Yumak and Sadak* the finding that there had been no breach of Article 3 came with clearly expressed reservations about the general acceptability of the laws in question and the Court signalled that ideally there should be legal reform.

Although the Court's Article 3 judgments can be criticized for failing to portray and articulate a stronger vision of what democracy is in the context of free elections, a greater appreciation of those judgments may be gleaned from a recent speech by the Court's President. He stated that it is not for the Court to redesign each state's unique democratic system—a matter that is essentially for the member states alone—rather it is to 'serve the interests of each State's democratic system by maintaining its openness, integrity and effectiveness'.[190] On this understanding of the Court's mission Article 3 will only ever have a limited role, but, as Judge Costa pointed out, the Court will take a 'strict, protective approach to the essential political rights of freedom of expression, freedom of assembly and association'. In this way the Court 'serves the quality of democratic life in the Member States of the Council of Europe, and makes their systems more transparent and pluralist, and their institutions more accountable'.

---

[189] See his dissenting opinion in *Zdanoka* (Chamber judgment) para 17.

[190] Speech by Judge Costa, 'The links between democracy and human rights under the case-law of the European Court of Human Rights', Helsinki 5, June 2008, available at <http://www.echr.coe.int/echr/>.

21

RIGHTS PROTECTED BY THE FOURTH, SIXTH, SEVENTH, AND THIRTEENTH PROTOCOLS TO THE CONVENTION[1]

Compared to the main Convention text, there has been relatively little jurisprudence on the rights covered by the Protocols mentioned in the title to this chapter. However, the great majority of Convention states have ratified most of these Protocols and their growing significance is indicated by the fact that there have been several important cases concerning them in recent years.

Protocols 4 and 7 protect a selection of civil and political rights which are not covered by the main Convention text and which in part[2] make up for the substantive deficiencies of the Convention when compared to the International Covenant on Civil and Political Rights. Protocol 4 entered into force in 1968 and has been ratified by forty-two states (1 July 2008).[3] It addresses a prohibition of imprisonment for debt, the right to freedom of movement, a prohibition of expulsion of nationals, and a prohibition of collective expulsion of aliens.

Protocol 7 entered into force in 1988 and has been ratified by forty-one states (1 July 2008).[4] The rights protected by this instrument are certain procedural safeguards relating to expulsion of aliens, a right to appeal in criminal matters, a right to compensation for wrongful conviction, a right not to be tried or punished twice, and rights relating to equality between spouses.

Protocols 6 (forty-six ratifications)[5] and 13 (forty ratifications)[6] are both concerned with the abolition of the death penalty.

1. ARTICLE 1, FOURTH PROTOCOL: FREEDOM FROM IMPRISONMENT FOR NON-FULFILMENT OF A CONTRACTUAL OBLIGATION

Article 1 of the Fourth Protocol reads:

> No one shall be deprived of his liberty merely on the ground of inability to fulfil a contractual obligation.

---

[1] On Protocol 12, see Ch 15 above.

[2] For examples of the (still more) extensive coverage provided by the ICCPR compared to the Convention and its Protocols, see Articles 10, 14(3)(g), 24–5 and 27 ICCPR.

[3] Spain, Turkey, and UK have signed but not ratified; Greece and Switzerland have never signed the instrument.

[4] Belgium (11 May 2005), Germany, Netherlands, Spain, and Turkey have signed but not ratified; the UK has never signed.   [5] All Convention states except Russia, which signed the instrument in 1997.

[6] The following have signed but not ratified: Armenia, Italy, Latvia, Poland, and Spain. Azerbaijan, and Russia have not signed.

It extends to a failure to fulfil a contractual obligation of any kind. It may thus include non-delivery, non-performance, and non-forbearance, as well as the non-payment of debts.[7] Article 1 is limited in its application by the words 'merely on the ground of inability to fulfil' an obligation. So it 'prohibits imprisonment for debt solely when the debt arises under a contractual obligation'.[8] That is, deprivation of liberty is not forbidden if there is some other factor present, as where the detention is because the debtor acts fraudulently or negligently or for some other reason refuses to honour an obligation that he is able to comply with. Thus, where a person was detained on the request of a creditor for refusing to make an affidavit in respect of his property, Article 1 of the Fourth Protocol did not apply.[9] Other examples given in the Explanatory Report to the Protocol[10] are where a person, knowing that he does not have the money to pay, orders food in a restaurant; through negligence, fails to supply goods under contract; or is preparing to leave the country in order to avoid his contractual obligations.

The term 'deprivation of liberty' is that found in Article 5 of the Convention and can be taken to have the meaning that it has there.[11] Under Article 5(1)(b) of the Convention, a person may be deprived of his liberty for 'non-compliance with a lawful order of a court'. This could include a court order that results from the failure to fulfil a contractual obligation. The effect of Article 1 is that, for parties to the Fourth Protocol, the detention of a person for failure to comply with such a court order merely because that person is unable to comply with the contractual obligation concerned is prohibited.[12]

2. ARTICLE 2, FOURTH PROTOCOL: FREEDOM OF MOVEMENT WITHIN A STATE AND FREEDOM TO LEAVE ITS TERRITORY

Article 2 of the Fourth Protocol reads:

1. Everyone lawfully within the territory of a state shall, within that territory, have the right to liberty of movement and freedom to choose his residence.

2. Everyone shall be free to leave any country, including his own.

3. No restrictions shall be placed on the exercise of these rights other than such as are in accordance with law and are necessary in a democratic society in the interests of national security or public safety, for the maintenance of *ordre public*, for the prevention of crime, for the protection of health or morals, or for the protection of the rights and freedoms of others.

4. The rights set forth in paragraph 1 may also be subject, in particular areas, to restrictions imposed in accordance with law and justified by the public interest in a democratic society.

---

[7] Explanatory Report to Protocol 4 ('Explanatory Report to P4') available at <http://conventions.coe.int/> para 3. Explanatory Reports or Memoranda accompanying Council of Europe treaties provide guidance as to their meaning but are not an authoritative source of interpretation.

[8] *Göktan v France* 2002-V; 37 EHRR 320 para 51 (Article 1 not applicable to French imprisonment in default system as such, but Court expressed reservations about the same: 'an archaic custodial measure available only to the Treasury').

[9] *X v FRG No 5025/71*, 14 YB 692 (1971).   [10] Explanatory Report to P4 para 6.

[11] See above, p 123.

[12] For the view that Article 5(1)(b) does not in any event permit detention in the circumstances covered by Article 1 of the Fourth Protocol, thereby rendering the latter superfluous, see Trechsel, *European System*, p 278.

For the purposes of Article 2 as a whole, a territory to which the Fourth Protocol is extended by declaration upon ratification is a separate territory from a state's metropolitan territory, so that freedom of movement, etc applies only within the non-metropolitan territory concerned (Article 5(1), Fourth Protocol).[13] A state's embassy abroad is not a part of its territory for the purposes of the Fourth Protocol generally.[14]

I. FREEDOM OF MOVEMENT WITHIN A STATE'S TERRITORY

Article 2(1) of the Fourth Protocol provides that 'everyone lawfully within the territory of a state shall, within that territory, have the right to liberty of movement and freedom to choose his residence'. 'Everyone' includes aliens, ie nationals of other states and stateless persons,[15] although, as is well established, 'the Convention does not guarantee the right of an alien to enter or to reside in a particular country and...Contracting States have the right, as a matter of well-established international law and subject to their treaty obligations including the Convention, to control the entry, residence and expulsion of aliens'.[16] Moreover, the term 'lawfully' was inserted to take into account the sovereign power of states to control the entry of aliens.[17] Article 2 does not apply to an illegal entrant, whilst an alien who infringes the conditions attaching to his entry into a state's territory is not 'lawfully' within it,[18] and an individual will no longer be 'lawfully' present once an effective expulsion order has been served.[19] *Piermont v France*[20] established that an applicant is not necessarily 'lawfully' present simply because they have passed passport control at an airport. In that case the applicant was detained by the authorities before leaving the airport perimeter and served with an effective exclusion order. Article 2 of the Fourth Protocol did not apply.

   A person's right to 'liberty of movement' within a state's territory as protected by Article 2(1) of the Fourth Protocol has to be distinguished from the right not to be 'deprived of his liberty', which is protected by Article 5, Convention. The latter involves a severe form of restriction on freedom of movement.[21] The distinction can be critical as Article 5(1) provides for an exhaustive list of circumstances potentially justifying a deprivation of liberty whilst restrictions on the right to freedom of movement are subject to the (much more) general qualifications found within Article 2(3)–(4) (Fourth Protocol). Article 5, for example, does not permit detention purely on the basis of preventing future criminal offences. However, restrictions on freedom of movement may be potentially justified for this reason. Indeed the Court is clear that 'special supervision accompanied by an order for compulsory residence in a specified district does not of itself come within Article 5'.[22]

---

[13] See *Piermont v France* A 314 (1995); 20 EHRR 301 (French Polynesia considered by the Court as a separate territory to metropolitan France).

[14] *WM v Denmark No 17392/90* hudoc *(1992)*; 15 EHRR CD 28.   [15] See Explanatory Report, p 4.

[16] *Sisojeva v Latvia* hudoc (2005); 43 EHRR 694 para 99. See also *Chahal v UK* 1996-V; 23 EHRR 413 para 73.

[17] Explanatory Report to P4 para 8.

[18] *Paramanathan v FRG No 12068/86*, 51 DR 237 (1986); 10 EHRR CD 157. See also *Omwenyeke v Germany No 44294/04* hudoc (2007) DA.

[19] *Piermont v France* A 314 (1995); 20 EHRR 301 para 44. On the 'lawful' requirement see also *Tatishvili v Russia* hudoc (2007); 45 EHRR 1246.

[20] Id, para 49. The case concerned an MEP who claimed, *inter alia*, that her expulsion from the Republic of French Polynesia, which she had entered lawfully, for speaking out against nuclear tests there, restricted her freedom of movement between Tahiti and another island within the Republic where she was to address another meeting. Although the Court found no violation of Article 1 of the Fourth Protocol, it did find a violation of Article 10 of the Convention.   [21] See above, p 124.

[22] *Guzzardi v Italy* A 39 (1980); 3 EHRR 333 para 94 PC. See also *Raimondo v Italy* A 281-A (1994); 18 EHRR 237 para 39, and *Labita v Italy* 2000-IV; 46 EHRR 1228 GC.

Furthermore, Article 5 has not applied to cases concerning preventive regimes whereby an individual has been subjected to curfews periods of ten to twelve hours stretching over long periods.[23] Individuals subject to such regimes, which clearly represent a profound interference with their freedom, will have to argue (if they can)[24] that they have been the subject of an unjustified interference with their right to freedom of movement.[25]

Preventing someone from leaving their house and/or stopping them from leaving a certain area are clear examples of interferences with freedom of movement. What counts is the fact that an individual needs to seek permission to leave, so it is irrelevant if he or she is consistently granted such permission.[26] The Court has also found Article 2 applicable when individuals are required to report to the police every time they change their place of residence or visit family and friends.[27] An interference with the right to freedom of movement can also occur when an individual is excluded from a specified public area, for example a city centre district.[28] Article 2 can also apply to what the Court has referred to as 'restrictions on [an individual's] movements', as in a Cypriot case where the authorities closely monitored the applicants' movements between the northern part of the island and the south, and within the south. They were not allowed to move freely in the south and had to report to the police every time they wanted to go to the north to visit their families or friends or upon their entry into the south.[29]

As to the freedom to choose one's place of 'residence', the restrictions upon the applicants' residence in their home in *Gillow v UK*,[30] which would appear to raise an issue under Article 2, were not considered by the Court because the Fourth Protocol had not been ratified by the defendant state.

As noted above, the rights protected by Article 2(1) of the Fourth Protocol are not absolute; they are curtailed by the restrictions contained in Articles 2(3) and (4), the structure and content of which are similar to that of Articles 8–11, Convention. Article 2(3) requires that a restriction be 'necessary in a democratic society' for one or more of the following reasons: for 'national security or public safety, for the maintenance of *ordre public*, for the prevention of crime, for the protection of health or morals, or for the protection of the rights and freedoms of others'. These grounds for restriction can be taken to have the meaning that they have been given under Articles 8–11, Convention.[31] Article 2(4) adds to them a further ground for restriction that is not found in Articles 8–11, *viz* 'public interest'.[32]

---

[23]   See *Raimondo* and *Labita ibid* (Mafia suspects subjected to ten-hour curfews living at home (inviolable) and subject to reporting restrictions). Also see *Trijonis v Lithuania No2333/02* hudoc (2005) DA (twelve-hour curfew for weekdays and all weekend; Article 5 not engaged as applicant was 'allowed to spend time at work as well as at home' during the (almost) sixteen-month period applicable).

[24]   See n 3 above (not all states have ratified Protocol 4).

[25]   The point at which Article 5 applies is of great relevance to (non-derogating) anti-terrorism control orders in the UK, which is not a state party to the Fourth Protocol.

[26]   See *Ivanov v Ukraine* hudoc (2006) para 85.

[27]   *Denizci v Cyprus* 2001-V; and *Bolat v Russia* hudoc (2006).

[28]   *Olivieira v Netherlands* 2002-IV 1990; 37 EHRR 693.

[29]   *Denizci v Cyprus* 2001-V para 404. It may also have been relevant that they were expelled to the northern part of the island. See also *Bolat v Russia* hudoc (2006).

[30]   A 109 (1986); 11 EHRR 335 para 42. There was a breach of the Article 8, Convention right to respect for the applicants' 'home' in that case. As to whether an order withdrawing a liquor licence that affects a person's place of residence is an interference with the right of residence, see the facts of *X v Belgium No 8901/80*, 23 DR 237 (1980). See also *Lacko v Slovakia No 47237/99* hudoc (2002) DA (allegations of discrimination regarding ability of Slovak nationals of Roma origin to settle in a place where they had been granted permanent residence).

[31]   See above, Ch 8.

[32]   Note also that Article 2(4) requires that a restriction be 'justified', but not 'necessary' in a democratic society, which is the standard and seemingly stricter formula in Article 2(3). The proportionality test still applies for both paragraphs of the Article.

The purpose of Article 2(4) would appear to be to allow the state a broader basis upon which to justify interference with the rights protected by Article 2(1) when the case is confined to 'particular areas'. The precise significance of this phrase has not been the subject of any detailed judicial analysis.[33] The Explanatory Report[34] indicates that paragraph (4) was included because the majority of the committee drafting the Protocol was against including under paragraph (3) a restriction permitting restrictions on the ground of economic welfare. Paragraph (4) was therefore inserted because of the possibility that *in particular areas* it might be necessary, for legitimate reasons, and solely in the 'public interest in a democratic society' (Article 2(4)), to impose restrictions (such as those based on economic welfare) which it might not always be possible to bring within the concept of *'ordre public'*.[35] The intention was not to limit the 'particular area' to any definite geographical or administrative area; any 'well defined area' would qualify.

Both Articles 2(3) and (4) require that a restriction be 'in accordance with law'. This wording can be taken to have the autonomous Convention meaning that it has been given in other provisions.[36] The requirement was infringed in *Raimondo v Italy*[37] when a person who was suspected of Mafia activities was made the subject of a court supervision order by which, *inter alia*, he was required not to leave his home without informing the police. The Court found that the case fell within Article 2 of the Fourth Protocol—not Article 5 of the Convention—and that the restriction upon the applicant's freedom of movement could be justified under Article 2(3) as being necessary 'for the maintenance of *"ordre public"*' and for the 'prevention of crime'. However, the applicant was not informed of the judicial revocation of the order for eighteen days, during which time he continued to be restricted in his movements. The Court held that during this period the restrictions had not been 'in accordance with law'.[38]

The case law illustrates what might be a legitimate basis upon which to restrict the right to freedom of movement. Restrictions upon freedom of movement may be imposed upon an accused person released on bail[39] or a person suspected of Mafia activities on the ground of 'prevention of crime',[40] or for national security reasons if it is feared an individual will disclose state secrets.[41] The withdrawal of a liquor licence (following a person's conviction for running a disorderly house) that affects his place of residence can be justified as being both 'for the prevention of crime' and 'protection of health or morals'.[42] The *'ordre public'* restriction has also been used to justify the removal of families from one mobile site to another.[43]

The restrictions permitted by Articles 2(3) and (4) are subject to the principle of proportionality developed under Articles 8–11 and the 'margin of appreciation' doctrine. The importance of this has become evident in recent case law, as the following paragraphs illustrate.

---

[33] Though it was relevant to *Olivieira v Netherlands* 2002-IV; 37 EHRR 693.

[34] Explanatory Report to P4 para 15.

[35] The notion of *'ordre public'* is to be understood in the broad sense in general use in continental countries.

[36] See above, p 344.

[37] A281 (1994); 18 EHRR 237 paras 39–40. See also *Tatishvili v Russia* hudoc (2007); 45 EHRR 1246 (authorities' refusal to register applicant as resident at her home address).

[38] See also *Vito Sante Santoro v Italy* 2004-VI; *Timishev v Russia* hudoc (2005); 44 EHRR 776; and *Bolat v Russia* hudoc (2006). See also *Olivieira v Netherlands* 2002-IV; 37 EHRR 693 (municipal order prohibiting drug addict from entering specified area for fourteen days; Court divided by four votes to three on the 'in accordance with the law' test).

[39] *Schmid v Austria No 10670/83*, 44 DR 195 (1985). See also *Rosengren v Romania* hudoc (2008) para 33.

[40] *Raimondo v Italy* A 281-A (1994); 18 EHRR 237 and *Ciancimino v Italy No12541/86*, 70 DR 103 (1991).

[41] *Bartik v Russia* hudoc (2007) para 43.   [42] *X v Belgium No 8901/80*, 23 DR 237 (1980).

[43] *Van de Vin v Netherlands No 13628/88* hudoc (1992) DA.

Labita v Italy[44] concerned a very severe restriction on freedom of movement. The applicant was suspected of being a member of the Mafia and subjected to a preventive regime supposedly directed at impeding his involvement in serious criminal activity. For three years he was under daily ten-hour curfews plus he had inform the Police on leaving home and on Sunday mornings. He could not associate with others subject to similar preventative measures or with criminal records, nor visit bars, nor attend public meetings. The grounds relied on by the domestic courts for imposing this regime were informer evidence and because the applicant's deceased brother-in-law was in the Mafia. In the Court's view this was insufficient. Whilst it acknowledged the 'threat posed by the Mafia',[45] it refused to accept the serious interference with Article 2(1) that had occurred was necessary in the absence of 'concrete evidence to show that there was a real risk that [Labita] would offend'.[46] The Court did maintain, nevertheless, that it considered it legitimate for preventive measures, including special supervision, to be taken against persons suspected of being members of the Mafia, 'even prior to conviction, as they are intended to prevent crimes being committed'.[47] Furthermore, restriction of freedom of movement might conceivably be justified even if there was an acquittal as 'concrete evidence gathered at trial, though insufficient to secure a conviction, may nonetheless justify reasonable fears that the person concerned may in the future commit criminal offences'.[48]

More moderate restrictions on freedom of movement than those just described may violate Article 2, especially when imposed for long periods. In *Rosengren v Romania*[49] the applicant was required to remain in Bucharest as he was the subject of a fraud investigation. It dragged on for over five years (when it became time-barred), though even then the restriction remained in place for another eighteen months. The Court suggested that the duration of the restriction alone (six years and three months) was capable of constituting a violation of Article 2,[50] but also referred to the delay in cancelling the order once the criminal prosecution was dropped and the domestic courts' failure to properly justify the measures when the applicant contested them.[51]

An 'automatic' travel ban imposed for debt or unpaid tax may be initially justifiable under the Convention, but risks falling foul of the proportionality principle, especially if it is in place for a significant period.[52] The Court insisted that the restriction should not become 'a *de facto* punishment for inability to pay', but had to exist for the genuine purpose of recovering the debt.[53] Thus, the 'authorities [were] not entitled to maintain over lengthy periods restrictions on the individual's freedom of movement without periodic reassessment of their justification in the light of factors such as whether or not the fiscal authorities had made reasonable efforts to collect the debt through other means and the likelihood that the debtor's leaving the country might undermine the chances to collect the money'.[54]

As the last-mentioned case demonstrates, restrictions imposed under Article 2 must be justified and proportionate throughout their duration. Hence national authorities should

---

[44] 2000-IV; 46 EHRR 1228 GC.   [45] Id, para 197.

[46] Id, para 196. Cf, the early Commission decision in *M v France No 10078/82*, 41 DR 103 at 121–2 (1984), when the latter refused to question the measure imposed as it was purportedly justified on national security grounds.

[47] Id, para 195.   [48] *Ibid*.   [49] Hudoc (2008).

[50] Id, para 38. See also *Ivanov v Ukraine* hudoc (2006) (violation: eleven-year order (nine years of which was in Court's jurisdiction)); *Fedorov and Fedorova v Russia* hudoc (2005); 43 EHRR 943; and *Antonenkov v Ukraine* hudoc (2006).

[51] Id, para 39.

[52] See *Riener v Bulgaria* hudoc (2006); 45 EHRR 723 and *Földes and Földesné Hajlik v Hungary* hudoc (2007); 47 EHRR 316.

[53] Id, paras 122–3.   [54] Id, para 124.

be alive to the reality that the actual need for restriction on movement may diminish with the passage of time. If the restriction exists for a long period the individual circumstances of the applicant must be reviewed regularly so as to ensure its continued need.[55] So a condition that a bankrupt should not absent himself from the district without prior authorization can be acceptable as a legitimate aim on the grounds of *'ordre public'* and the protection of the rights and freedoms of others (ie creditors). Nevertheless a point may be reached where the length of the bankruptcy proceedings, and so the restrictions on movement, result in the imposition of an excessive burden on the applicant given the balance to be maintained between the general interest in payment of a bankrupt's creditors and the applicant's individual interest in freedom of movement.[56]

The proportionality principle will be highly relevant to instances when an individual is excluded from a public area. It was not breached in *Olivieira v Netherlands*,[57] where the area concerned was an 'emergency' zone in Amsterdam blighted by trafficking in and abuse of hard drugs. The applicant had been convicted for breaching a fourteen-day order prohibiting his entry into this area, given his own consistent (and proven) record of drug-related misdemeanours within it. Accepting the proportionality of the measures imposed, the Court acknowledged the margin of appreciation allowed to the domestic court and took into account the fact that the applicant had already been issued with several eight-hour prohibition orders (flouting them by returning and openly using hard drugs in the area), and had been warned that a fourteen-day prohibition order might ensue. It also noted that he did not live or work in the area in question and did not have a post office box there for collection of mail.[58] In the similar case of *Landvreugd v Netherlands*,[59] the Court noted that provision had been made for the applicant to enter the area with impunity for the purpose of collecting his social-security benefits and his mail. On the facts the suggestion that he could be arrested *en route* to these locations was dismissed as hypothetical and unsubstantiated. In both these cases the Court accepted in principle that the authorities might have to take special measures to overcome an emergency situation related to drugs in the areas concerned at the relevant time. This implies that, on the facts of an individual case, the Court could exercise some power of review on the issue of whether it was necessary to establish the emergency restriction area in the first place.[60]

---

[55] See *Bartik v Russia* hudoc (2007) (violation in case of lengthy and absolute foreign travel ban for person with past access to 'state secrets').

[56] See *Luordo v Italy* 2003-IX; 41 EHRR 547 and *Bottaro v Italy* hudoc (2003). A breach was found even though in neither case did the files show that the applicants had wished to leave their place of residence, or that they had been refused permission to do so. The bankruptcy proceedings and associated order lasted approximately fourteen and twelve years respectively and so the very duration of the order made the restriction disproportionate. See also *Goffi v Italy* hudoc (2005) and *Bassani v Italy* hudoc (2003). Cf, *Fedorov and Fedorova v Russia* hudoc (2006); 43 EHRR 943 where the Court viewed the context (criminal proceedings) and duration ('significantly shorter', para 43) as a basis to distinguish the case from *Luordo* such that it was necessary to ascertain 'whether the applicants actually sought to leave the area of their residence and, if so, whether permission to do so was refused', para 44.

[57] 2002-IV; 37 EHRR 693.   [58] Id, para 65.

[59] Hudoc (2002); 36 EHRR 1039. See also *Van den Dungen v Netherlands No 22838/93*, hudoc (1995); 80 DR 147 (anti-abortion protester prohibited from the immediate vicinity of abortion clinic for six months; application declared manifestly ill-founded as restrictions deemed proportionate).

[60] *Olivieira v Netherlands* 2002-IV; 37 EHRR 693 para. 64. The existence of the 'emergency' in the case had been verified by the national courts, though some years previously. In *Landvreugd* the applicant had argued, unsuccessfully, that in practice the emergency areas were not necessary either for crime prevention or other policy reasons, para 69.

II. FREEDOM TO LEAVE A STATE'S TERRITORY

Article 2(2) states that 'everyone shall be free to leave any country, including his own'. Freedom to leave a country is a personal right which does not imply a right to transfer one's possessions out of it.[61] The freedom extends to nationals and aliens. The freedom is subject to the same 'in accordance with law' requirement and the same restrictions in Article 2(3) as apply to the guarantee of freedom of movement within a state's territory in Article 2(1). These limitations are discussed above under Article 2(1) and the same considerations apply under Article 2(2) as apply there. Thus, as far as Article 2(3) restrictions are concerned, an accused may be detained in prison[62] or refused a passport[63] in connection with pending criminal proceedings on grounds of 'ordre public' or 'the prevention of crime'.

The Court has indicated its willingness to view Articles 2(1) and (2) as part of one general right. Both Articles imply 'a right to leave for such country of the person's choice to which he may be admitted'.[64] There will be an interference with the exercise of liberty of movement in terms of Article 2(2) if an individual is dispossessed of an identity document such as, for example, a passport.[65] Such a measure must be proportionate on the facts,[66] as must a refusal to issue a passport, for example as a measure to ensure performance of military service.[67] In *Riener v Bulgaria*[68] the applicant, whose family was in Austria, had been banned from leaving Bulgaria for nine years owing to unpaid taxes. In principle this was a valid reason to prevent exit from the country, but the Court determined that the principle of proportionality demanded that the aim of securing the unpaid debt could only be justified whilst it served its aim. The initial restriction on travel may have been justified, but it had been automatically renewed over the years with little or no reference to the specific facts of the case, including whether the fiscal authorities were still trying to obtain the outstanding money, whether the prospects of obtaining the money would have been reduced if the applicant had left the country, and the fact that the applicants' family was abroad. On the facts, there was a violation of the Article 2(2) of the Fourth Protocol as the reality was that the travel ban was an automatic measure of indefinite duration that had no regard to the individual circumstances of the case.[69]

When the inability to leave a country stems from the applicant's insistence upon remaining in an airport transit area (refusing to enter its territory to complete reasonable administrative documentation and checks) this may be an obstacle preventing enjoyment of the right in question that is not imputable to the respondent state.[70] An order temporarily prohibiting a spouse from taking her children with her when travelling abroad (and

---

[61] *S v Sweden No 10653/83*, 42 DR 224 (1985).

[62] *X v FRG No 7680/76*, 9 DR 190 (1977). See also *X v FRG No 3962/69*, 13 YB 688 (1984).

[63] See *Schmid v Austria No 10670/83*, 44 DR 195 (1985) and *M v FRG No 10307/83*, 37 DR 113 (1984).

[64] *Baumann v France* 2001-V; 34 EHRR 1041 para 61. See also *Peltonen v Finland No 19583/92*, 80-A DR 38, para 31.

[65] Id, para 62. See also *M v Germany No 10307/83*, 37 DR 113. The same applies to an arbitrary entry in a passport that prohibits the individual leaving, *Sissanis v Romania* hudoc (2007).

[66] *Napijalo v Croatia* hudoc (2003); 40 EHRR 735 para 82. See also *Baumann v France* 2001-V; 34 EHRR 1041 where three judges dissented on the basis that there was no actual causal link between the seizure of the applicant's passport and his freedom of movement in practice.

[67] *Peltonen v Finland No 19583/92*, 80-A DR 38 (Commission, accepting that contracting states are entitled to a wide margin of appreciation in the organization of their national defence, rejecting applicant's argument that passport refusal was disproportionate to the offence of draft evasion).

[68] Hudoc (2006); 45 EHRR 723.   [69] Id, paras 127–8.

[70] *Mogos v Romania No 20420/02* hudoc (2004) DA.

aimed at preventing removal of the children from her estranged husband) interferes with Article 2(2), but can be justified under Article 2(3).[71]

3. ARTICLE 3, FOURTH PROTOCOL: THE RIGHT OF A NATIONAL NOT TO BE EXPELLED FROM AND TO ENTER A STATE'S TERRITORY

Article 3 of the Fourth Protocol reads:

1. No one shall be expelled, by means either of an individual or of a collective measure, from the territory of the state of which he is a national.

2. No one shall be deprived of the right to enter the territory of the state of which he is a national.

An expulsion occurs when a person is 'obliged permanently to leave the territory[72] of a state of which he is a national without being left the possibility of returning later'.[73] Extradition of nationals is outside the scope of Article 3, Fourth Protocol.[74] Thus, a request from the East German authorities for the extradition of a West German national from West Germany was not covered by Article 3, Fourth Protocol.[75] Article 3 only protects nationals of the expelling state.[76] The fact that a person has an application for the nationality of the expelling state under consideration by its authorities is not sufficient for Article 3 to apply; if he is granted nationality later, he will be able to return as a national.[77]

Article 3 of the Fourth Protocol secures an absolute and unconditional freedom from expulsion[78] of 'a national', so the meaning and scope of that term can be crucial. It is not explored in the Explanatory Report to the Protocol but was highly relevant to *Slivenko v Latvia*,[79] a case of considerable political significance which concerned a Russian soldier, his wife, and child. All had been resident in Latvia many years but were removed to Russia following Latvian independence in 1991 and a 1994 Russo-Latvian agreement regarding the withdrawal of Russian troops. The wife and child had never been 'nationals' of independent Latvia, but until 1991 they had been nationals of the Latvian SSR and stated that they had not lived in or had citizenship of another country. They, and the Russian government as third party interveners, argued that they should be regarded as Latvian 'nationals' given the autonomous Convention meaning of that term within Article 3 of the Fourth Protocol, and that their removal from Latvia breached that provision. However, in a Grand Chamber admissibility decision, the Court rejected this

---

[71] *Roldan Texeira v Italy No 40655/98* hudoc (2000) DA.

[72] A person who is required to leave his national state's embassy abroad is not expelled from its 'territory', as an embassy is not territory for the purposes of the Fourth Protocol, *V v Denmark No 17392/90* hudoc (1992); 15 EHRR CD 28.

[73] *X v Austria and FRG No 6189/73*, 46 CD 214 (1974). As with Article 2 (see above), a non-metropolitan territory to which the Fourth Protocol is extended is a separate unit for the purposes of Article 3 (Article 5(1), Fourth Protocol).

[74] See, however, the views of Ovey and White, p 343.

[75] *Brückmann v FRG No 6242/73*, 17 YB 458 (1974). As to extradition under Article 3 of the Convention, see above, p 79.

[76] See eg, *X v Sweden No 3916/69*, 32 CD 51 (1969).

[77] *L v FRG No 10564/83*, 40 DR 262 (1984). See also *X v FRG No 3745/68*, 31 CD 107 (1969).

[78] Cf, the qualified nature of Article 8, which may have relevance in expulsion proceedings when the rights protected in para 8(1) are interfered with.

[79] 2003-X; 39 EHRR 490 GC.

argument. It stated that '"nationality" must be determined, in principle, by reference to the national law,'[80] and noted that a 'right to nationality' similar to that in Article 15 of the Universal Declaration of Human Rights was not guaranteed by the Convention or its Protocols. The Court accepted that an arbitrary denial of nationality could under certain circumstances amount to an interference with the rights under Article 8 of the Convention.[81] In determining what is 'arbitrary' it is suggested that the Court would at least take into account the limited controls general international law subjects states to when granting or withdrawing nationality.[82] The Court ultimately determined that as the mother and child in *Slivenko* had not been nationals of Latvia since it had ratified the Convention in 1997, and, as it appeared that neither had been arbitrarily denied Latvian citizenship, then their complaints were manifestly ill-founded.[83]

Article 3(2) provides that 'no one shall be deprived of the right to enter the territory of the state of which he is a national'. As was noted by Mr Fawcett in his separate opinion in the *East African Asians* cases,[84] the right of entry guaranteed for nationals by it does not exclude the possibility that the failure to admit nationals may be a breach of Article 3, Convention, on the basis that publicly to single out a group of persons for differential treatment on the basis of race might, in certain circumstances, constitute a special affront to human dignity amounting to 'degrading treatment' within the meaning of Article 3.[85] The relevance of this point is brought out by the fact that not all states have ratified Protocol 4, including the United Kingdom where many resident in Commonwealth countries have British nationality by birth.

4. ARTICLE 4, FOURTH PROTOCOL: FREEDOM OF ALIENS FROM COLLECTIVE EXPULSION

Article 4 of the Fourth Protocol reads:

Collective expulsion of aliens is prohibited.

This provision applies regardless of whether the individual has entered the state concerned lawfully or remains a lawful entrant.[86] Aliens are understood to include stateless persons.[87] 'Expulsion' can be taken to have the same meaning as it has under Article 3, Fourth Protocol (above). Article 4 does not prohibit individual cases of expulsion; this is a matter dealt with by Article 1 of the Seventh Protocol instead (below).

The Court has stated that 'collective expulsion' is to be understood as 'any measure compelling aliens, as a group, to leave a country, except where such a measure is taken on the basis of a reasonable and objective examination of the particular case of each individual alien of the group'.[88] It has also stated that 'the fact that a number of aliens receive similar decisions does not lead to the conclusion that there is a collective expulsion when each

[80] *No 48321/99* hudoc (2002) para 77 GC.

[81] *Ibid.* See also *Karassev and Family v Finland No 31414/96*, 1999-II DA.

[82] According to the Explanatory Report, it was thought 'inadvisable' for Article 3 'to touch on the delicate question' of the legitimacy of measures depriving individuals of nationality. The drafting committee nevertheless approved in principle the notion that a state should not be allowed to deprive a national of his nationality for the purpose of expelling him (Explanatory Report to P4 paras 21–3) and this would appear to be supported by both case law (*X v FRG No 3745/68*, 31 CD 107 (1970)) and a reading of Article 3 according to the principle of effective protection.

[83] *Slivenko v Latvia* 2003-X; 39 EHRR 490 paras 78–9 GC.

[84] 3 EHRR 76 (1973) Com Rep para 242; CM Res DH (77) 2.   [85] See p 101 above.

[86] Cf, Article 2 applies to those 'lawfully' within a territory.   [87] Explanatory Report to P4 para 32.

[88] *Andric v Sweden No 45917/99* hudoc (1999) DA.

person concerned has been given the opportunity to put arguments against his expulsion to the competent authorities on an individual basis'.[89] In its judgment in *Conka v Belgium*,[90] the Court expressly approved the first sentence just quoted, but did not cite the second. This should not be taken to suggest that Article 4 of the Fourth Protocol only prevents repatriation of individuals as a group provided the first condition is met[91] and *Conka*, where the Court found a violation of Article 4 by four votes to three, may best be viewed on its individual facts. In that case some Slovakian nationals of Romany origin had exhausted legal channels regarding their asylum requests—in which the Court duly recognized that each individual's circumstances were addressed—and had been properly served with orders requiring them to leave Belgium. Those orders were ignored. A short period of time after this the unsuspecting applicants were tricked into attending a police station along with around seventy other individuals of the same status and nationality. They received a notice informing them that their presence was required in order to proceed with further aspects of their asylum claim. On arrival they were detained[92] and then deported after having been served with 'fresh' expulsion orders which identified them as illegal immigrants and which did not indicate that they had been formulated with regard to individual personal circumstances. The Court's division stemmed from the influence these background circumstances had on the Article 4 claim. The majority of four, finding a violation, cited the deficiency associated with the fresh expulsion order and appear to have been influenced by the nature of what was evidently a pre-planned operation to execute group repatriation. They could not 'eliminate all doubt that the expulsion might have been collective'[93] and criticized the fact that the personal circumstances of each applicant had not been 'genuinely and individually' taken into account in the period following when they were encouraged to attend the police station via the misleading notice.[94] The minority of three took a less formalistic approach to the 'fresh' expulsion order given the completeness of the legal procedures that had been concluded before, albeit some time before, the applicants went to the police station. They emphasized the freedom for a state to repatriate as a group (after a reasonable and objective examination of the particular case of each individual alien of the group),[95] an option the national authorities were free to choose for reasons of efficiency and economy, and one which clearly could not take place without prior preparation.

Finally, Article 3 of the main Convention may be relevant to collective expulsion in certain circumstances.[96]

5. THE SIXTH AND THIRTEENTH PROTOCOLS: THE DEATH PENALTY

In the 1990s abolition of the death penalty became a precondition for membership of the Council of Europe and today the Sixth and Thirteenth Protocols have been ratified by the great majority of Convention states.[97] No execution has taken place in the Council of

---

[89] *Ibid*; see also *A v Netherlands No 14209/88*, 59 DR 274 (1988) and *Becker v Denmark No 7011/75*, 4 DR 215 at 235 (1975).   [90] 2002-I; 34 EHRR 1298. See also *Sultani v France* hudoc (2007).

[91] In *Andric v Sweden No 45917/99* hudoc (1999) DA the applicant was an asylum seeker from Croatia who was returned to that country soon after the Swedish authorities had listed it as generally 'safe' for the purposes of asylum claims. Even so his case had still been individually considered domestically by the Swedish authorities and so the expulsion was not therefore 'collective' in the sense of Article 4.

[92] Which was also a violation of Article 5(1)(f), see p 163 above.

[93] *Conka v Belgium* 2002-I; 34 EHRR 1298 para 61. See also the reasoning at para 62.

[94] Id, para 63.   [95] On group repatriation see also *Sulejmanovic v Italy* hudoc (2002) F Sett.

[96] See Ch 3 above.   [97] See nn 5 and 6 above.

Europe's member states since 1997,[98] and it has been claimed that Europe has become a 'death penalty free area', since all Convention states have either abolished this sentence or at least have instituted a moratorium on executions.

Article 1 of the Sixth Protocol states '[t]he death penalty shall be abolished. No-one shall be condemned to such penalty or executed', but Article 2 allowed use of the death penalty in time of war. This exception was removed by the Thirteenth Protocol through which ratifying states express their resolve to 'take the final step in order to abolish the death penalty in all circumstances' (Preamble to Thirteenth Protocol).[99] Parties to the Protocols must abolish the death penalty, if it still exists in its law, and must not reintroduce it. The Protocols create a 'subjective right', ie one that a person is able to enforce in the national courts.[100] No reservations are allowed to either Protocol, nor may either instrument be the subject of a derogation.

In its Chamber judgment in *Öcalan v Turkey*[101] in 2003 the Court suggested that Article 2 of the main Convention text might have been amended by state practice. It had regard to the Convention states' practice as regards abolition of the death penalty and the near universal ratification of the Sixth Protocol to conclude that capital punishment *in peacetime* had 'come to be regarded as an unacceptable, if not inhuman, form of punishment which is no longer permissible under Article 2'.[102] Both the Chamber and Grand Chamber avoided a firm conclusion as to whether the death penalty was incompatible *per se* with Article 3 of the Convention. The Chamber stated that state practice regarding Sixth and Thirteenth Protocols entailed that 'it can also be argued that *the implementation of the death penalty* can be regarded as inhuman and degrading treatment contrary to Article 3' (emphasis added);[103] the Grand Chamber was more cautious, implying that it was probably not possible to say that the death penalty was contrary to Article 3 *per se* until all states had ratified the Thirteenth Protocol, though it would not commit itself to a definitive statement on the point.[104] In *Öcalan* the applicant had had his death sentence commuted to life imprisonment. The Court nevertheless concluded that imposition of the death sentence on the applicant following an unfair trial amounted to inhuman treatment in violation of Article 3.[105]

It is possible that a contracting state's responsibility might be engaged under Article 2 of the Convention or Article 1 of Sixth Protocol, 'where an alien is deported to a country where he or she is seriously at risk of being executed, as a result of the imposition of the death penalty'.[106] In such situations, in order for the removal to proceed it will be

---

[98]   For further information consult <http://www.coe.int/T/E/Com/Files/Themes/Death-penalty>.

[99]   Article 2(2) of the EU Charter of Fundamental Rights states: 'No one shall be condemned to the death penalty, or executed'. There are no qualifications.

[100]   Explanatory Report to the Sixth Protocol, CE Doc H (83) 3, p 6.

[101]   Hudoc (2003); 37 EHRR 238 (Chamber judgment); see also *Öcalan v Turkey* 2005-IV; 41 EHRR 985 GC.

[102]   Id, paras 196 and 198. The Grand Chamber stated that it agreed with the relevant passages of the judgment expressed by the Chamber, id, para 163. Cf, the statement in the (Chamber) judgment in *Shamayev v Georgia and Russia* 2005-III para 333.

[103]   Id, para 198. See however the dissenting judgment of Judge Türmen. Cf, *Soering v UK* A 161 (1989); 11 EHRR 439 para 103 PC.

[104]   *Öcalan v Turkey* 2005-IV; 41 EHRR 985 GC para 165. In *GB v Bulgaria* hudoc (2004) para 72 the Court cited European state practice and stated that 'capital punishment, . . . is no longer seen as having any legitimate place in democratic society'.

[105]   The imposition of the death penalty in certain other circumstances can violate Article 3, see *Shamayev v Georgia and Russia* 2005-III para 333 and *Ilaşcu v Moldova and Russia* 2004-VII; 40 EHRR 1030 paras 431 and 440 GC.

[106]   *Bader v Sweden* hudoc (2006); 46 EHRR 197 para 42, citing *SR v Sweden No 62806/00* hudoc (2002) DA; *Ismaili v Germany No 58128/00* hudoc (2001) DA. Article 19(2) of the EU Charter of Fundamental Rights states '2. No one may be removed, expelled or extradited to a state where there is a serious risk that he or she would be subjected to the death penalty . . .'.

necessary to obtain sufficient guarantees from the receiving state that the death penalty would not be sought or imposed.[107] As regards return to a country where the death penalty has been suspended by a moratorium, the mere allegation, otherwise unsubstantiated, that the said moratorium could be revoked at any time does not suffice to bring an expulsion measure within the ambit of Article 1 of the Sixth Protocol.[108]

6. ARTICLE 1, SEVENTH PROTOCOL: FREEDOM FROM EXPLUSION OF INDIVIDUAL ALIENS

Article 1 of the Seventh Protocol reads:

1. An alien lawfully resident in the territory of a state shall not be expelled therefrom except in pursuance of a decision reached in accordance with law and shall be allowed:
    a. to submit reasons against his expulsion,
    b. to have his case reviewed, and
    c. to be represented for these purposes before the competent authority or a person or persons designated by that authority.
2. An alien may be expelled before the exercise of his rights under paragraph 1, a, b and c of this Article, when such expulsion is necessary in the interests of public order or is grounded on reasons of national security.

This guarantees that an alien 'lawfully resident in the territory of a state shall not be expelled except in pursuance of a decision reached in accordance with law' and only, in most cases, after specified procedural rights have been respected.[109] In contrast with Article 4 of the Fourth Protocol, it concerns cases of individual, rather than collective, expulsion. However, unlike Article 4, it requires only that the rule of law be complied with; it is not a prohibition on expulsion.

Article 1 applies only to aliens who are 'lawfully resident' in a state's territory, so it does not apply to illegal entrants. It does not protect aliens who have not passed through immigration, those in transit, those admitted for a non-residential purpose, those awaiting a decision on residence,[110] or those whose visa or residence permit has expired.[111] A person will not be lawfully resident if he has gained admission illegally or has infringed other conditions of his permit.[112] The term 'lawful' refers to national law, which must therefore be followed.[113] 'Expulsion' is an autonomous concept[114] and can be taken *mutatis mutandis* to have the meaning that it has under Article 3 of the Fourth Protocol,[115] so that, *inter alia*, it does not include extradition. The requirement that the expulsion be 'in accordance with law' can likewise be taken to have the autonomous meaning that it has in other Convention provisions,[116] that is it addresses matters such as the quality of the law.[117]

---

[107] Cf, *Einhorn v France No 71555/01* hudoc (2001) DA.
[108] *Muhadri v Austria No 31007/96* hudoc (1997) DA.
[109] Expulsion cases may also raise issues under Articles 3, 8, and 13 of the Convention.
[110] Explanatory Report on the Seventh Protocol ('Explanatory Report P7'), CE Doc H (83) 3, para 9. An alien in this context can be taken to include a stateless person.
[111] *Bolat v Russia* hudoc (2006) para 76 (citing *Voulfovitch and Oulianova v Sweden No 19373/92* hudoc (1993) DA.
[112] *Ibid.* [113] It was not in *Bolat v Russia* hudoc (2006). [114] Id, para 79.
[115] See above, p 743. [116] See above, p 344.
[117] See *Lupsa v Romania* hudoc (2006); 46 EHRR 810 para 55 and *CG v Bulgaria* hudoc (2008).

Where Article 1 applies, the applicant must be allowed '(a) to submit reasons against his expulsion, (b) to have his case reviewed, and (c) to be represented for these purposes before the competent authority or a person or persons designated by that authority' (Article 1(1)). Exceptionally, an alien may be expelled before he has exercised these procedural rights where the expulsion is 'necessary in the interests of public order or is grounded on reasons of national security' (Article 1(2)).[118] If so these exceptions should be applied taking into account the principle of proportionality[119] plus the rights set out in Article 1(1) should be available after expulsion.[120]

According to the Explanatory Report for Protocol Seven, an alien's right to submit reasons against his expulsion applies 'even before being able to have his case reviewed'.[121] As to the right to have the expulsion decision 'reviewed', this 'does not necessarily require a two-stage procedure before different authorities'; it would be sufficient for the 'competent authority' that took the decision to consider the matter again.[122] The 'competent authority' does not have to give the alien or his representative an oral hearing; a written procedure would suffice. Nor does it have to have a power of decision; it is enough that it may make a recommendation to the body that does take the final decision. Clearly, the 'competent authority' does not itself have to be a judicial body that complies with Article 6, Convention.[123] Although, therefore, Article 1 offers an alien at least the possibility of having his arguments against expulsion taken into account by the executive, it offers only a modest guarantee of procedural due process. Having said this, as regards the nature of the review process itself the Court has referred to the principle of effectiveness and found a violation of this provision when the review itself was a pure formality such that 'the applicant was not genuinely able to have his case examined in the light of reasons militating against his deportation'.[124]

Finally, it will be appreciated that various of the other rights protected by the Convention may potentially be relevant to an alien facing deportation: these include Articles 3, 5(1)(f), 8, and Article 4 of the Fourth Protocol.

7. ARTICLE 2, SEVENTH PROTOCOL: THE RIGHT TO REVIEW IN CRIMINAL CASES

Article 2 of the Seventh Protocol reads:

1. Everyone convicted of a criminal offence by a tribunal shall have the right to have his conviction or sentence reviewed by a higher tribunal. The exercise of this right, including the grounds on which it may be exercised, shall be governed by law.

2. This right may be subject to exceptions in regard to offences of a minor character, as prescribed by law, or in cases in which the person concerned was tried in the first instance by the highest tribunal or was convicted following an appeal against acquittal.

[118]   See eg, *Al-Dabbagh v Sweden No 36765/97* hudoc (1997) DA.
[119]   *CG v Bulgaria* hudoc (2008) paras 77–8 (Court concluded that expedited expulsion was not necessary on national security grounds or otherwise proportionate).
[120]   *Lupsa v Romania* hudoc (2006); 46 EHRR 810 para 53.
[121]   Explanatory Report, p 7.   [122]   *Ibid.*
[123]   *Maaouia v France* 2000-X; 33 EHRR 1037 para 37 GC (by 'adopting Article 1 of Protocol 7 containing guarantees specifically concerning proceedings for the expulsion of aliens the states clearly intimated their intention not to include such proceedings within the scope of Article 6(1) of the Convention').
[124]   *Lupsa v Romania* hudoc (2006); 46 EHRR 810 para 60 (expulsion for 'national security' reasons). See also *CG v Bulgaria* hudoc (2008) para 74.

Article 2 of the Seventh Protocol guarantees a right to 'review' for a conviction or sentence by a higher tribunal. It does not provide for a right to appeal on the 'merits' of a judgment, and this is not protected by Article 6 of the main Convention either, although that provision has been interpreted as controlling any right of appeal in criminal cases that a state in its discretion may provide under its law.[125]

In *Krombach v France*[126] the Court stated that the contracting states had a 'wide margin of appreciation' to determine how the right secured by Article 2 of the Seventh Protocol was to be exercised. It acknowledged (as is confirmed in the Explanatory Report) that the review by a higher court of a conviction or sentence may concern both points of fact and points of law or be confined solely to points of law. Procedural limitations, such as the requirement to seek leave to appeal, are compatible with Article 2, but the right to review must be directly available to those concerned and 'independent of any discretionary action by the authorities'.[127] Restrictions on the right to a review have to pursue a legitimate aim and not infringe the very essence of the right.[128] This is analogous with the right of access to a court embodied in Article 6(1) of the Convention[129] and consistent with the exception authorized by paragraph 2 of Article 2.

The term 'tribunal' within Article 2(1) is capable of an autonomous interpretation and has the same meaning as 'tribunal' within Article 6(1) of the main Convention text.[130] Still, the condition that Article 2(1) only applies to offences tried by a 'tribunal' is restrictive, Hence, someone who is the subject of a disciplinary offence which qualifies as a 'criminal offence' for the purposes of Article 2 has no right to review of that decision under Article 2 if it was not made by a 'tribunal'.[131] It is submitted that the fair trial requirements in Article 6 of the Convention, as they apply to appeal proceedings,[132] must be respected by the 'higher tribunal' when it conducts its review of the tribunal decision for Article 2 to be complied with.

The guarantee in Article 2(1) of the Seventh Protocol is in certain respects limited in its impact by Article 2(2). This provides that the right of appeal 'may be subject to exceptions in regard to offences of a minor character, as prescribed by law, or in cases in which the person concerned was tried in the first instance by the highest tribunal or was convicted following an appeal against acquittal'. As to the meaning of 'minor' offences, the Explanatory Report[133] suggests that 'an important criterion is whether the offence is punishable by imprisonment or not'. The Report[134] also suggests that where a person pleads guilty at his trial, his right of review is limited to his sentence. The same Report also states that the same right is satisfied by leave to appeal proceedings where leave is not given[135] and, as the Commission confirmed,[136] that it is not necessary for the appeal to be on points of fact and law; the state concerned may decide to limit it to one or the other.

---

[125] As to the effect of Article 2 of the Seventh Protocol, on the interpretation of Article 6 of the Convention, see above, p 298, n 908.

[126] 2001-II para 96 (French law denied a right of appeal on points of law to an applicant convicted in his absence). See also *Papon v France* 2002-VII; 39 EHRR 217; *Pesti and Frodl v Austria Nos 27618–27619/95*, 2000-I DA; *Zaicevs v Latvia* hudoc 2007; and *Galstylan v Armenia* hudoc (2007).

[127] *Gurepka v Ukraine* hudoc (2005); 43 EHRR 1004 paras 59–60.

[128] *Krombach v France* 2001-II para 96.   [129] See above p 235.

[130] *Didier v France No 58188/00*, 2002-VII DA. See also Explanatory Report P7 para 17.

[131] Of course, if the offence is a 'criminal' one in the sense of Article 6, that provision requires at least an appeal to an Article 6 tribunal. In that case, Article 2 of the Seventh Protocol requires a right of review of the second, Article 6 tribunal, decision. See further Van Dijk and Van Hoof, p 972.

[132] For the application of Article 6 to appeal proceedings, see above, p 298.

[133] Explanatory Report P7 para 21.   [134] *Ibid.*   [135] *Ibid.*

[136] *NW v Luxembourg No 19715/92* hudoc (1992); 15 EHRR CD 107.

8.   ARTICLE 3, SEVENTH PROTOCOL:
RIGHT TO COMPENSATION FOR
MISCARRIAGES OF JUSTICE

Article 3 of the Seventh Protocol reads:

> When a person has by a final decision been convicted of a criminal offence and when
> subsequently his conviction has been reversed, or he has been pardoned, on the ground
> that a new or newly discovered fact shows conclusively that there has been a miscarriage
> of justice, the person who has suffered punishment as a result of such conviction shall be
> compensated according to the law or the practice of the state concerned, unless it proved
> that the non-disclosure of the unknown fact in time is wholly or partly attributable
> to him.

Article 3 provides for a right to compensation for miscarriages of justice in the circumstances and subject to the conditions that are set out. The person must have been convicted of a criminal offence by a final decision and suffered consequential punishment.
A decision will be final when it is *res judicata*. The Explanatory Report states that this will
be the case where it 'is irrevocable, that is to say when no further ordinary remedies are
available or when the parties have exhausted such remedies or have permitted the time-
limit to expire without availing themselves of them'.[137] Article 3 does not apply where
a charge has been dismissed or an accused person is acquitted by the trial court or by a
higher court on appeal.[138] The conviction must have been overturned or a pardon granted
because new or newly discovered facts show conclusively that there has been a miscarriage of justice, by which is meant 'some serious failure in the judicial process involving
grave prejudice to the convicted person'.[139]

The Explanatory Report states that the procedure to be followed to establish a miscarriage of justice is a matter for national law.[140] Article 3 provides that there is no right
to compensation if the non-disclosure of the unknown fact in time is wholly or partly
attributable to the person convicted. It is for the state concerned to determine the compensation to be paid in accordance with its law and practice, although presumably the
Strasbourg authorities are competent to ensure that it is not totally insufficient.

The Explanatory Report indicates that Article 3 should oblige states to compensate persons 'only in clear cases of miscarriage of justice, in the sense that there would
be acknowledgement that the person concerned was clearly innocent'. Thus only if all the
conditions mentioned in Article 3 are satisfied should compensation be paid. So there
would be no automatic violation of this provision where no compensation is awarded
after an appellate court had quashed a conviction because it had discovered some fact
which introduced a reasonable doubt as to the guilt of the accused which had been over-
looked by the trial judge.[141]

Article 3 of Protocol 7 is a derogable right. As regards the right to compensation for
illegal detention under Article 5, reference should be made to Article 5(5).[142]

---

[137] Explanatory Report P7 para 22. The Report is quoting the Explanatory Report of the European Convention
on the International Validity of Criminal Judgments 1970, p 22.

[138] It clearly does not apply when an applicant is detained on remand, *Nakov v FYROM No 68286/01* hudoc
(2002) DA.

[139] Explanatory Report P7 para 23.   [140] *Ibid.*   [141] Id, para 25.   [142] See above p 197.

9. ARTICLE 4, SEVENTH PROTOCOL:
NE BIS IN IDEM

Article 4 of the Seventh Protocol reads:

1. No one shall be liable to be tried or punished again in criminal proceedings under the jurisdiction of the same state for an offence for which he has already been finally acquitted or convicted in accordance with the law and penal procedure of that state.

2. The provisions of the preceding paragraph shall not prevent the re-opening of the case in accordance with the law and penal procedure of the state concerned, if there is evidence of new or newly discovered facts, or if there has been a fundamental defect in the previous proceedings, which could affect the outcome of the case.

Article 4 of the Seventh Protocol incorporates the principle *ne bis in idem*. In other terms it protects freedom from double jeopardy. The protection against duplication of criminal proceedings is one of the specific safeguards associated with the general guarantee of a fair hearing in criminal proceedings. Nevertheless, in the Convention system in principle *ne bis in idem* is protected under Article 4 of the Seventh Protocol and not Article 6 of the main Convention. Accordingly, if the respondent state concerned has not ratified the Protocol, those parts of applications raising a *ne bis in idem* claim will be rejected at the admissibility stage.[143]

The *ne bis in idem* principle applies to the fact that proceedings are brought again, so it does not matter for the purpose of Article 4 whether the person was convicted or not in a first set of proceedings.[144] However some caveats may be added. Article 4(2) does allow a re-trial in certain circumstances. Moreover, the words 'under the jurisdiction of the same state' limit the application of the Article to the national level only. That is, the principle *ne bis in idem* does not apply to where a person has been or will be tried or punished by the courts of different states.[145] The Article only applies to trial and conviction of a person in criminal proceedings. So it does not prevent an individual being subject to criminal proceedings and then, for the same act, to action of a different character (for example, disciplinary action in the case of an official).[146]

The notion of 'criminal' is however an autonomous one.[147] So, when the Court is satisfied that the first decision before it is 'final', it must also address whether it was 'criminal' for the purposes of Article 4. Here it looks to the 'general principles concerning the corresponding words "criminal charge" and "penalty" respectively in Articles 6 and 7 of the

[143] *Blokker v Netherlands No 45282/99* hudoc (2000) DA.

[144] In the absence of any damage proved by the applicant, only new proceedings brought in the knowledge that the defendant has already been tried in previous proceedings contravene Article 4, see *Zigarella v Italy No 48154/99* 2002-IX DA (Italian authorities brought prosecution in ignorance of earlier proceedings and immediately closed them when their mistake was realized).

[145] *Amrollahi v Denmark No 56811/00* hudoc (2001) DA. Cf, Article 50 of the EU Charter of Fundamental Rights which reads 'No one shall be liable to be tried or punished again in criminal proceedings for an offence for which he or she has already been finally acquitted or convicted *within the Union* in accordance with the law' (emphasis added).

[146] See *RT v Switzerland No 31982/96* hudoc (2000) DA and Explanatory Report P7 para 32.

[147] See *Storbråten v Norway No 12277/04* hudoc (2007) DA; 44 EHRR SE 289 (citing authorities including *Rosenquist v Sweden No 60619/00* hudoc (2004) DA; 40 EHRR SE 222; *Manasson v Sweden No 41265/98* (2003) DA; and *Göktan v France* 2002-V; 37 EHRR 320 para 48).

Convention'. It has regard to such factors as 'the legal classification of the *offence* under national law; the nature of the offence; the national legal characterisation of the *measure*; its purpose, nature and degree of severity; whether the measure was imposed following conviction for a criminal offence and the procedures involved in the making and implementation of the measure'.[148] As the Court has noted,[149] this range of criteria is wider than that used in *Engel* for Article 6 of the Convention.

It may be the case that what the applicant alleges is a new set of proceedings is not viewed that way by the Court. For example, one application declared inadmissible concerned an individual convicted for drink driving and who, as a result of a subsequent administrative decision, had his licence taken away. The Court agreed that the latter penalty was 'criminal' for the purposes of Article 4; however, there was 'a sufficiently close connection...in substance and in time' between the conviction and penalty such that the withdrawal was viewed as part of the sanctions under domestic law for the offences in issue.[150]

The aim of Article 4 is to prohibit the repetition of criminal proceedings that have been concluded by a 'final decision' acquitting the individual.[151] So that provision does not apply before new proceedings have been opened.[152] According to the Explanatory Report to the Seventh Protocol, which itself referred back to the European Convention on the International Validity of Criminal Judgments, a 'decision is final "if, according to the traditional expression, it has acquired the force of *res judicata*. This is the case when it is irrevocable, that is to say when no further ordinary remedies are available or when the parties have exhausted such remedies or have permitted the time-limit to expire without availing themselves of them." '[153] Prosecution rights of appeal are compatible with Article 4. A procedure of supervisory review allowing certain officials to challenge a judgment which has entered into force, but which was an integral part of the ordinary procedure and itself provided a 'final decision', will not come within the scope of Article 4 because all the decisions concerned relate to the same, single set of proceedings.[154]

Article 4 is not confined to the right not to be punished twice; it concerns the right not to be *tried* twice.[155] It is clear that, subject to Article 4(2), Article 4(1) prohibits a further prosecution for exactly the same offence. However, a matter that has troubled the Court is how Article 4 might be relevant to a single criminal act which is capable of being separated out into more than one criminal 'offence', for example a driving offence which may be caught by various statutory definitions. In principle Article 4 does not preclude separate offences being tried by the same[156] or even different courts[157] if they were part of a single criminal act. But whilst in some cases identifying what are separate offences will be a straightforward exercise,[158] in others the issue is very complicated.[159]

---

[148] *Ibid. (Storbråten).* See also *Sergey Zolotukhin v Russia* hudoc (2007) para 29 (referred to the Grand Chamber).
[149] *Ibid.*   [150] *Nilsson v Sweden No 73661/01* hudoc (2005) DA.
[151] What follows will need to be read in the light of the important Grand Chamber judgment (pending at the time of writing) in *Sergey Zolotukhin, ibid.*
[152] *Gradinger v Austria* A 328-C (1995) para 53. Note, however, that Article 4(1) refers to an individual 'liable' to be tried again, see *Nikitin v Russia* 2004-VIII; 41 EHRR 149 paras 42–3.
[153] Explanatory Report P7 para 22.
[154] *Nikitin v Russia* 2004-VIII; 41 EHRR 149 (supervisory review was not an attempt at re-trial, para 47).
[155] *Franz Fischer v Austria* hudoc (2001) para 29. See also *Sergey Zolotukhin v Russia*, n 148 above, para 34.
[156] *Goktan v France* 2002-V; 37 EHRR 320 (dealing in illegally imported drugs as an offence under the general criminal law and as a customs offence resulting in a fine which when not paid resulted in further imprisonment; no violation of Article 4).   [157] *Oliveira v Switzerland* 1998-V; 28 EHRR 289.
[158] Convictions for speeding eight times in the course of one journey will not attract the applicability of Article 4 when the offences are treated as separate events involving different speed limit zones, *Kantner v Austria No 29990/96* hudoc (1999) DA. See also *Aşçi v Austria No 4483/02* hudoc (2006) DA.
[159] Applications rejected at the admissibility stage of proceedings because separate offences were in issue include: *Ponsetti and Chesnel v France No 36855/97* and *No 41731/98*, 1999-VI DA (criminal as well as

In *Gradinger v Austria*,[160] the Court found Article 4 of the Seventh Protocol violated as the applicant had been punished twice, by two different courts, on formally different accusations though both for causing death by negligence while driving under the influence of alcohol. It was critical that 'both impugned [domestic court] decisions were *based on the same conduct*'.[161] By contrast, in *Oliveira v Switzerland*,[162] the Court, distinguishing the case from *Gradinger*, found that there had been a single act constituting multiple offences (*concours idéal d'infractions*) and held that there had been no violation of Article 4. That Article, the Court stressed, 'prohibits people being tried twice for the same offence whereas in cases concerning a single act constituting various offences (*concours idéal d'infractions*) one criminal act constitutes two separate offences [which could be tried by different courts]'.[163] *Oliveira* concerned one driving event leading to two separate criminal convictions based on (i) the failure to control a vehicle; and (ii) the negligent causing of physical injury (as a consequence of (i)). The conclusion that Article 4 had not been violated was reinforced, the Court noted, by the fact that the penalties in the two sets of proceedings were *not* 'cumulative' as the lesser was absorbed by the greater.[164] This last point has been emphasized in later case law.[165]

In *Franz Fischer v Austria*,[166] the Court acknowledged that the approaches adopted in *Oliveira* and *Gradinger* were 'somewhat contradictory' and set out a new approach to Article 4. Following one event, the applicant was first convicted by an administrative authority for drunken driving then convicted by a domestic court of causing death by negligence. The Court held that there was a violation of Article 4(1) as the two offences did not differ 'in their essential elements'.[167] Elucidating its approach to Article 4, the Court noted that 'there are cases where one act, at first sight, appears to constitute more than one offence, whereas a closer examination shows that only one offence should be prosecuted because it encompasses all the wrongs contained in the others... An obvious example would be an act which constitutes two offences, one of which contains precisely the same elements as the other plus an additional one'.[168] It emphasized that the key issue for *ne bis in idem* under Article 4 was whether there had in reality been a trial or punishment 'again' (Article 4(1), the Court pointed out, uses this word, not the expression 'the same offence')[169] for an offence for which the applicant had already been finally acquitted or convicted. Where different offences based on one act are prosecuted consecutively, one after the final decision of the other, the Court, therefore, has 'to examine whether or not such offences have the same essential elements'.[170]

It must be said that the Court's case law in this area is in need of clarification.[171] The position as it stands appears to be as follows. It does not automatically follow that there will be a violation of Article 4 of the Seventh Protocol if one act constitutes more than one offence and these are prosecuted on different occasions, perhaps in different courts. But if there are consecutive prosecutions for apparently different offences based on one act (one after the final decision of the other) the key test is whether such offences have '*the same essential elements*'[172] (emphasis added). If they do Article 4(1) will be violated for,

administrative penalties imposed for failure to complete tax declarations) and *Isaksen v Norway No 13596/02* hudoc (2003) DA (conviction for tax fraud and imposition of a tax surcharge were two distinct legal entities).

[160] A 328-C (1995).   [161] Id, para 55 (emphasis added).   [162] 1998-V; 28 EHRR 289 para 26.
[163] *Ibid*.

[164] Id, para 27. See however the strong dissenting opinion of Judge Repik who rejected the Court's attempt to distinguish between *Oliveira* and *Gradinger*. He argued that the essence of Article 4 was legal certainty and to ensure that the individual 'is not exposed more than once to the constraints of criminal proceedings or convicted and sentenced in respect of the same incident'.

[165] *Nikitin v Russia* 2004-VIII; 41 EHRR 149 para 35.   [166] Hudoc (2001) para 23.
[167] Id, para 29.   [168] *Ibid*.   [169] Id, para 25.   [170] *Ibid*.   [171] See above, n 151.

[172] *Franz Fischer v Austria* hudoc (2001) para 25. Cf, the emphasis on 'same conduct' in the *Gradinger* case, n 160 above. Of course, if it is clear that there has in fact been two criminal acts in one event then no Article 4

as the Court has subsequently put it, Article 4(1) is aimed at preventing duplication of what is essentially the same criminal proceedings, it being 'the repetitive aspect of trial or punishment [which] is central to the legal problem' in issue.[173]

Article 4(2) specifically envisages the resumption of a trial ('re-opening of the case', Article 4(2)), perhaps involving prosecution on exactly the same counts, in relatively exceptional circumstances. Such resumption must be 'in accordance with the law and penal procedure of the state concerned', a qualification that evidently prevents arbitrary decisions to re-try individuals. Moreover, the re-opening of the case may only occur, 'if there is evidence of new or newly discovered facts, or if there has been a fundamental defect in the previous proceedings'. Article 4(2) requires that the new facts or defect be significant enough that they 'could affect the outcome of the case', suggesting a significant level of caution is required from the authorities before re-opening a case lest this provision be breached (as does the word 'fundamental', as in 'fundamental defect'). According to the Explanatory Report the words 'new or newly discovered facts' can encompass new means of proof relating to previously existing facts.[174] Precisely what is meant by this is not clear, but it will presumably be particularly relevant given scientific advances for example in the field of DNA analysis. The Explanatory Report to the Seventh Protocol states that Article 4(2) 'does not prevent a reopening of the proceedings in favour of the convicted person and any other changing of the judgment to the benefit of the convicted person'.[175]

Article 4 may not be derogated from under Article 15 of the Convention in time of war or other public emergency threatening the life of the nation.

10. ARTICLE 5, SEVENTH PROTOCOL:
EQUALITY OF RIGHTS OF SPOUSES

Article 5 of the Seventh Protocol reads:

> Spouses shall enjoy equality of rights and responsibilities of a private law character between them, and in their relations with their children, as to marriage, during marriage, and in the event of its dissolution. This Article shall not prevent states from taking such measures as are necessary in the interests of the children.

This provision relates to the rights and responsibilities of spouses under private law only. The Explanatory Report[176] states that it 'does not apply to other fields of law, such as administrative, fiscal, criminal, social, ecclesiastical or labour law'. Accordingly, the state's obligation under Article 5 involves essentially a positive obligation to provide a satisfactory framework of law by which spouses have equal rights and obligations concerning such matters as property rights and their relations with their children.[177] Article 5 does not protect the partners to any relationship outside marriage,[178] and specifically excludes the period preceding marriage. Article 5 does not concern the 'conditions of capacity to enter into marriage provided by national law'; the words 'as to marriage' relate instead to

---

issue will arise, see *Aşci v Austria No 4483/02* hudoc (2006) DA (separate convictions for violence against two police officers committed one after another and differing in their degree of seriousness).

[173] *Nikitin v Russia* 2004-VIII; 41 EHRR 149 para 35.   [174] Explanatory Report P7 para 31.
[175] *Ibid.*
[176] *Ibid*, para 35. See also *Klöpper v Switzerland No 25053/94* hudoc (1996) DA.
[177] See *Iosub Caras v Romania* hudoc (2006) para 56 and *Purtonen v Finland No 32700/96* hudoc (1998) DA.
[178] See *Kaijalainen v Finland No 24671/94* (1996) DA.

the 'legal effects connected with the conclusion of marriage'.[179] Although Article 5 refers
to the 'dissolution of marriage', the Explanatory Report states that this does not 'imply
any obligation on a state to provide for dissolution of marriage'.[180] The Report also suggests that Article 5 does not prevent the national authorities 'from taking due account
of all relevant factors when reaching decisions with regard to the division of property in
the event of dissolution of marriage'.[181] The final sentence of Article 5 enters the caveat
that Article 5 does not prevent state legislative or administrative action that results in the
spouses not having equal private law rights and responsibilities in their relations with
their children where this is necessary in the 'interests of the children'.

The case law indicates an understandable reluctance on the part of the Court to question a final domestic judgment based on the interests of the child unless it is manifestly
unreasonable. Such decisions are likely to be in the margin of appreciation of the national
authorities.[182] At the general level, Article 5 of the Seventh Protocol is not violated by a
law which excludes the possibility of joint custody after divorce whilst providing access
and information rights to the parent not having custody.[183] Although this would be an
interference with one of the former spouse's right to equality, it would not be disproportionate to the aim of protecting the children by providing a clear solution for custody and
would fall within the respondent state's margin of appreciation.[184]

As the Explanatory Report[185] notes, the need to take the interests of the children into
account is already reflected in the Strasbourg jurisprudence under Articles 8 and 14, as
is the basic principle of equality of treatment between spouses. Citing this aspect of the
Explanatory Report the Court has stated that the necessity clause contained in Article 5
should be interpreted in the same way as the necessity clauses contained in other provisions of the Convention.[186]

---

[179] Explanatory Report P7 para 37. As to the capacity to marry, see Article 12, Convention, above, Ch 13.
[180] Id, para 37.
[181] Id, para 38. In *EP v Slovak Republic No 33706/96* hudoc (1998) DA, the Commission exercised a power of
review over the decision of the domestic court but found that decision 'neither unfair nor arbitrary'.
[182] See *Purtonen v Finland No 32700/96* hudoc (1998) DA and *Heckl v Austria No 32012/96* hudoc (1999) DA.
[183] See *Cernecki v Austria No 31061/96* hudoc (2000) DA.   [184] *Ibid.*
[185] Explanatory Report P7 para 36.   [186] See *Cernecki v Austria No 31061/96* hudoc (2000) DA.

22

ADMISSIBILITY OF
APPLICATIONS

Over the years, the Court (and before it the Commission) has established an impressive body of case law interpreting and applying the various conditions of admissibility set out in Articles 34 and 35 and selecting from the large volume of registered cases those that deserve closer examination on the merits. The Court's case law, for example, on exhaustion of domestic remedies has made an important contribution to international law where the rule is of general application. Most of the admissibility requirements are procedural in nature such as the six-month and exhaustion of domestic remedies rules; but some of the criteria, such as those of 'manifestly ill-founded' and 'incompatibility', require the Court to assess the merits of the case at this preliminary phase. Undoubtedly many cases which were rejected on these grounds twenty years ago would, in the light of the developing jurisprudence, be admissible cases today. In today's practice, the Court will reject as manifestly ill-founded, applications that repeat complaints previously rejected as inadmissible or where no violation has been found. As will be seen below, this process has involved the examination of many thousands of cases, most of which have been rejected as inadmissible. Finally in recent years the Court has made wider use of Article 29 §3 of the Convention which allows it to examine the admissibility and merits of a case at the same time. This joint procedure has become the standard practice of the Court in most cases.[1]

1. THE GENERAL APPROACH TO ADMISSIBILITY

The Court has frequently stated that the rules on admissibility must be applied with some degree of flexibility and without excessive formalism.[2] In addition, it has stated that account also has to be taken of their object and purpose[3] and of those of the Convention in general which, as a human rights treaty, must be interpreted and applied so as to make its safeguards practical and effective.[4] It has relied on those precepts to give a more favourable interpretation to rules such as the six-month rule and the obligation to exhaust domestic remedies for the benefit of applicants. Similarly, those precepts have been relied on to reject objections by governments to the admissibility of applications which are not raised at the earliest possible stage of proceedings.

---

[1] While separate statistics on the different heads of admissibility are not available, in 2006 the Court in its various decision bodies declared inadmissible or struck off 28,160 applications (26,116 of these in committees) whilst the number of judgments delivered was 1,498. In 2005, 27,611 applications were declared inadmissible or struck off against 952 judgments. See Court's Annual Survey of Activities 2006 at pp 37 and 50 and those of 2007/08—see below p 812, n3. These are available at: <http://www.echr.coe.int>.

[2] *Ilhan v Turkey* 2000-VII; 34 EHRR 869 at para 51 GC; *Cardot v France* A 200 (1991); 13 EHRR 853.

[3] *Worm v Austria* 1997-V; 25 EHRR 454.   [4] *Yaşa v Turkey* 1998-VI; 28 EHRR 408.

In terms of the Court's procedures for applying the admissibility criteria, two phases must be distinguished. Before an application is communicated to the respondent government for its observations, the Court may of its own motion declare the application inadmissible on the basis of the criteria set out in Articles 34 and 35 of the Convention. After an application has been communicated, the Court will general only examine admissibility questions if the respondent government raises any admissibility objections.[5] The exception to this rule is that the Court can, at any time in the proceedings, consider questions relating to incompatibility *ratione loci, personae,* and *temporis* on its own motion.[6] The justification for this is that these go to the heart of the Court's jurisdiction to hear complaints under the Convention. The six-month rule is also one that the Court can always apply of its own motion for this reason.[7] After communication, the Court will not examine questions relating to non-exhaustion of domestic remedies unless explicitly raised by the government.[8] Where cases are referred to the Grand Chamber under Article 43 of the Convention, the Grand Chamber may also reconsider admissibility objections raised by the government where these have already been addressed by the Chamber and thus it is entitled to come to different conclusion to the Chamber.[9] However, subject to the above, a government will be estopped from raising admissibility objections in proceedings before the Grand Chamber if it has not already raised them before the Chamber[10] or if the Chamber considered the same admissibility question on its own motion.[11]

As for the order it which the admissibility criteria will be applied by the Court, it will not address admissibility objections raised by the respondent government if it appears that the application (or part of it) may be dismissed on other, more straightforward grounds. For example, the Court will frequently find that it is unnecessary for it to rule on preliminary objections as to the non-exhaustion of domestic remedies when it may be more expeditious to find that the complaint in question is clearly incompatible *ratione materiae.*

While the Rules of Court are silent on the question, in the most exceptional circumstances the Court will allow a request for revision of an admissibility decision but will only do so where there has been a clear error which has affected its original decision.

---

[5] See Rule 55 of the Rules of Court. A doctrine of estoppel will normally also apply to government admissibility objections: while the Court may declare an application inadmissible at any stage of the proceedings in accordance with Article 35(4), this does not signify that a respondent state is able to raise an admissibility question at any stage of the proceedings if that question could have been raised earlier. See *Velikova v Bulgaria* 2000-VI para 57; *NC v Italy* 2002-X paras 42–7 GC.

[6] *Blecic v Croatia* 2006-III paras 63–9 GC.

[7] See *Assanidze v Georgia* 2004-II; 39 EHRR 653 para 160 GC; *Belaousof and Others v Greece* hudoc (2004); *Kadikis v Latvia (No 2) No 62393/00* hudoc (2003) p 22 DA; *Soto Sanchez v Spain No 66990/01* hudoc (2003) DA. Nor can the rule be waived, regardless of whether the respondent government objects: *Walker v UK No 34979/97* hudoc (2000) DA.

[8] See *K and T v Finland* 2001-VII; 36 EHRR 255 para 145 GC; *NC v Italy* 2002-X para 44 GC; *Sejdovic v Italy* 2006-II paras 40–1 GC; and *Citizens of Louvain v Belgium No 1994/63,* 7 YB 253 at 261 (1964). This same principle has been applied where the respondent government has not submitted any observations at all. See *Ergi v Turkey No 23818/94,* 80 DR 157 at 160 (1995) and the judgment in the same case: 1998-IV paras 65–7; *Dobrev v Bulgaria* hudoc (2006) para 112.

[9] *Odièvre v France* 2003-III; 38 EHRR 871 para 22 GC; *Azinas v Cyprus* 2004-III; 40 EHRR 166 paras 32, 37 GC.

[10] See *mutatis mutandis Nikolova v Bulgaria* 1999-II; 31EHRR 64 paras 41–4 GC; *Hasan and Chaush v Bulgaria* 2000-XI; 34 EHRR 1339 para 56 GC, (in both cases the government having failed to raise the question in proceedings before the old Commission meaning it was estopped from raising it before the Grand Chamber of the new Court).

[11] *Mutatis mutandis Freedom and Democracy (Özdep) v Turkey* 1999-VIII; 31 EHRR 674 para 23 GC (the Commission had considered the admissibility question on its own motion being sufficient to allow the government to raise it before the Grand Chamber).

Thus in *Ölmez and Ölmez v Turkey*[12] where the application had been rejected under the six-month rule, the Court found that the erroneous calculation of the date of the final domestic decision and the fact that it had not properly verified the relevant date meant that it would be counter to the interests of justice to refuse the applicants' request for re-examination of their application. The power to do so was found to be part of the Court's inherent jurisdiction.

2. APPLICATION OF ADMISSIBILITY REQUIREMENTS TO INTER-STATE CASES

It is clear from the terms of paragraphs (2) and (3) of Article 35 that apart from conditions *ratione materiae, personae, loci*, and *temporis*, the only admissibility requirements applicable to inter-state cases, which are brought under Article 33, are those set out in Article 35(1), namely the requirement to exhaust domestic remedies and the six-month rule.[13] In the third *Cyprus v Turkey* case[14] the Commission explicitly refused to reject the application on the basis that it was 'substantially the same as a matter which has already been examined by the Commission' and contains 'no relevant new information' on the grounds that Article 35(2)(b) (at the time Article 27(1)(b)) was not applicable to an inter-state case and that rejection would imply a preliminary examination of the merits of the case—an examination which in Article 33 cases is entirely reserved for the post-admissibility stage.

The Commission also used consistently refused to assess the merits of an inter-state case at the admissibility stage. Thus an Article 33 application cannot be rejected under Article 35(3) as manifestly ill-founded. In *France, Norway, Denmark, Sweden and Netherlands v Turkey*,[15] for example, the Turkish government submitted that the applicant states had failed to adduce *prima facie* evidence of their allegations of multiple breaches of the Convention. They supported their argument with reference to the rules and practice on questions of admissibility of the International Court of Justice and the Inter-American Commission of Human Rights. The European Commission noted that the text of Article 33[16] ('may refer to...any alleged breach'), in particular the French text '*qu'elle croira*', made it clear that the applicant state can submit 'allegations' for examination. It was thus not the Commission's role to 'carry out' a preliminary examination of the merits.[17] The Court reaffirmed this in *Denmark v Turkey*[18] stating that the manifestly ill-founded criterion applied only to individual applications under Article 34. Consequently, any examination of the merits of Denmark's allegations of torture of one of its nationals in Turkey had to be reserved for the post-admissibility stage. At the same time the Commission stated that an application submitted under Article 33 could be declared inadmissible 'if it is clear, from the outset, that it is wholly unsubstantiated, or otherwise lacking the requirements of a genuine allegation in the sense of [that] Article...'.[19] Thus, apart from this unlikely situation, the merits of an inter-state case escape scrutiny at the

---

[12] *No 39464/98* hudoc (2005) (re-opening decision) at p 5 (see also references therein) and *Edwards v UK No 13071/87* hudoc (1991) DA.

[13] See *Denmark v Turkey No 34382/97* hudoc (1999) p 33 DA. See also Prebensen, in Alfredsson *et al*, eds, *International Human Rights Monitoring Mechanisms*, 2001, pp 533–59.

[14] *No 8007/77*, 13 DR 85 at 154–5 (1978) Com Rep; CM Res DH (92) 12. See also *Ireland v UK* B 23-I at 670 Com Rep.

[15] *Nos 9940–9944/82*, 35 DR 143 at 160–2 (1983).   [16] Formerly Article 24, Convention.

[17] Id, p 161.   [18] *No 34382/97* hudoc (1999) DA.

[19] *France, Norway, Denmark, Sweden and Netherlands v Turkey Nos 9940–9944/82*, 35 DR 143 at 162 (1983).

admissibility phase. The application of this principle means, therefore, that in Article 33 cases the defence of derogation from the Convention under Article 15 will only be examined at the merits stage.[20]

It has also been argued in various inter-state cases that the application should be rejected as 'abusive' on the grounds that it was politically inspired or that it consisted of accusations of a political nature designed to further a propaganda campaign. In *Denmark, Norway, Sweden and Netherlands v Greece*[21] the Commission found that even if the allegations had a political element it was not such as to render them 'abusive' in the general sense of the term. In both this case and the third *Cyprus v Turkey* case[22] the Commission held that the 'abuse of the right of petition' ground of inadmissibility was restricted under Article 35(3) to cases brought by individuals. It left open, however, the issue as to whether an Article 33 application could be rejected on the basis of a general principle of international law that proceedings before an international tribunal must not be abused.

The sole condition for the Court's competence *ratione personae* to hear an inter-state case is that both the applicant and respondent states have ratified the Convention, ie by Article 33 the capacity to sue—as well as the liability to be sued—is limited to those states which have become contracting parties to the Convention. This is natural in view of the fact that the machinery of protection set up under the Convention is grounded in the concept of a collective enforcement by like-minded states of the guaranteed rights. An applicant state, unlike an individual applicant, does not have to claim to be a 'victim' in any way of the alleged breach. Article 33 is therefore wider than Article 34 in that the applicant state does not have to justify a special interest in the subject matter of the complaint; in particular, it is not a condition that the matter complained of should have affected or prejudiced one of its nationals.[23] As the Commission explained in the case of *Austria v Italy*,[24] the enforcement mechanism provided in Article 33 reflects the objective character of the engagements assumed by the contracting parties under the Convention:

> the obligations undertaken by the High Contracting Parties in the Convention are essentially of an objective character, being designed rather to protect the fundamental rights of the individual human being from infringement by any of the High Contracting Parties than to create subjective and reciprocal rights for the High Contracting Parties themselves;...it follows that a High Contracting Party, when it refers an alleged breach of the Convention to the Commission under Article 24 [now Article 33], is not to be regarded as exercising a right of action for the purpose of enforcing its own rights, but rather as bringing before the Commission an alleged violation of the public order of Europe....[25]

Accordingly, as a matter of law, inter-state proceedings are taken in the common interest of all the contracting parties and have the objective and purpose of securing observance of common standards of conduct in the field of human rights. Hence a state may take proceedings under Article 33 not only in support of the rights of its own nationals but

---

[20] Id, p 170.   [21] 11 YB 764 (1968).   [22] *No 8007/77*, 13 DR 85 at 156 (1978).
[23] *Ireland v UK* A 25 (1978); 2 EHRR 25 para 239 PC.   [24] *No 788/60*, 4 YB 140 (1961) (*Pfunders* case).
[25] The relationship between the Convention system and the public order of Europe has been a leitmotif of the Court and illustrates the wider importance it attaches to the Convention. In *Loizidou v Turkey* A 310 (1992); 20 EHRR 99 GC, concerning northern Cyprus, the Court struck down Turkey's declarations made in relation to the then optional clauses on the right of individual petition and the compulsory jurisdiction of the Court which declared that these only extended to acts performed within the boundaries of the national territory of the Republic of Turkey. The Court held (at para 75) that to permit such qualifications would 'not only seriously weaken the role of the Commission and Court in the discharge of their functions but would also diminish the effectiveness of the Convention as a constitutional instrument of European public order (ordre public)'. See also the *Bosphorus Airways* case, below, p 789.

also on behalf of the nationals of the respondent state and indeed on behalf of any person, regardless of nationality and regardless of whether the alleged breach particularly affects its own national interests. In addition, the application may concern not only a specific case but the broader allegation of an administrative practice.[26]

It follows from this conception of the inter-state case and the objective character of the Convention that the principle of reciprocity does not apply to inter-state cases. Thus in *France, Norway, Denmark, Sweden and Netherlands v Turkey*[27] the Commission concluded that France was not barred from bringing a case against Turkey which concerned issues that might be covered by the French reservation under Article 15 had the case been brought against France. In addition, the non-recognition of the applicant government by the respondent government cannot remove the right to bring a case under Article 33. As the Commission held in the third *Cyprus v Turkey* case,[28] 'to accept that governments may avoid "collective enforcement" of the Convention under [former] Article 24, by asserting that they do not recognise the government of the applicant state, would defeat the purpose of the Convention'. At the same time, in deciding whether Cyprus had *locus standi* to bring the case against Turkey, the Commission based its approach on international practice, particularly of the Council of Europe, as regards the status of the government. It observed that:

> the applicant government have been, and continue to be, recognised internationally as the government of the Republic of Cyprus and that their representation and acts are accepted accordingly in a number of contexts of diplomatic and treaty relations and of the working of international organisations.

Reference to international practice was also relied upon to rebut the argument that the applicant government had acted unconstitutionally in bringing the application.[29] These rulings were affirmed by the Court in the fourth *Cyprus v Turkey*[30] case, where, in reference to the 'Turkish Republic of Northern Cyprus' (TRNC), the Court reiterated its conclusion in *Loizidou v Turkey*[31] that the Republic of Cyprus remained the sole legitimate government of Cyprus and on that account its *locus standi* was beyond doubt.

The absence of a 'victim' requirement means that a contracting party may, unlike an individual applicant, challenge a law or practice *in abstracto*, without having to adduce evidence as to actual prejudice of the application of the law or practice. The Court stated in *Ireland v UK*[32] that such a complaint would be possible where the alleged breach 'results from the mere existence of a law which introduces, directs or authorises measures incompatible with the rights and freedoms guaranteed'. The judgment, however, added a proviso:

> Nevertheless, the institutions established by the Convention may find a breach of this kind only if the law challenged pursuant to [former] Article 24 is couched in terms sufficiently clear and precise to make the breach immediately apparent; otherwise, the decision of

---

[26] See *Denmark v Turkey No 34382/07* hudoc (1999) DA.

[27] *Nos 9940–9944/82*, 35 DR 143 at 168–9 (1983).   [28] *No 8007/77*, 13 DR 85 at 146–7 (1978).

[29] Id at p 146. It was argued that the applicant government was not the government of Cyprus but only the leaders of the Greek Cypriot community who, in 1963, had assumed control of the state in violation of the London and Zurich Agreements of 1959, the Treaty of Guarantee of 1960, and the Constitution of Cyprus of 1960. This argument had been previously rejected in the first and second *Cyprus v Turkey* cases—*Nos 6780/74 and 6950/75*, 2 DR 125 at 135–6 (1975); Com Rep; CM Res DH (79). It was also argued that, in lodging the case with the Commission, the government had acted unconstitutionally since the decision had not been taken by the competent organ under Article 54 of the Constitution of Cyprus of 1960: 13 DR 85 at 148 (1978).

[30] 2001-IV; 35 EHRR 731 paras 59–62 GC.   [31] 1996-VI; 23 EHRR 513.

[32] A 25 (1978); 2 EHRR 25 para 240 PC.

the Convention institutions must be arrived at by reference to the manner in which the respondent state interprets and applies *in concreto* the impugned text or texts.

In principle, the exhaustion rule applies in inter-state cases. In *Austria v Italy*[33] the Commission rejected the Austrian argument that former Article 26 did not apply since there was no injury to the state itself and since, by initiating proceedings, it was merely enforcing the collective guarantee embodied in the Convention system. In *Greece v UK*[34] the Commission found that the requirement was not satisfied in respect of various allegations of torture where the identity of the accused was known. However, it held that the court remedies were ineffective in cases where the identity of the interrogators had been withheld. Further, in *Ireland v UK*[35] the Commission rejected complaints concerning the killing by the army of twenty-two persons in Northern Ireland on the basis that domestic remedies had not been exhausted. It also found that the Irish government had not offered 'substantial evidence' of an administrative practice in breach of Article 2 so as to waive the exhaustion requirement. In the first and second *Cyprus v Turkey* inter-state cases,[36] the respondent government had complained that the alleged victim had made no use of remedies before the courts in Turkey or before the courts in 'the Turkish Federated State of Cyprus'. The Commission considered that any remedies before domestic courts in Turkey could not be regarded, in respect of complaints concerning the violation of human rights of Greek Cypriots in Cyprus, as 'both practicable and normally functioning in such cases'. The same view was expressed in respect of remedies in the northern part of Cyprus which Greek Cypriots were not permitted to enter. However, in the fourth *Cyprus v Turkey* inter-state case,[37] the Court concluded that remedies available within the 'TRNC' may in principle be regarded as domestic remedies, noting in particular that the alleged illegality of the 'TRNC' courts seemed to contradict the assertion made by the Cypriot government that Turkey was responsible for the violations alleged in the northern part of Cyprus. It appeared difficult to admit that a state was responsible for acts occurring in a territory it occupied and to deny that state the opportunity to try to avoid such responsibility by correcting the wrongs imputable to it in its courts. However, while in principle 'TRNC' remedies could be regarded as domestic remedies, the question of the effectiveness of those remedies had to be considered in the specific circumstances.[38]

It is settled case law that the local remedies rule does not apply to inter-state complaints concerning legislative measures or where 'substantial evidence' is provided of an administrative practice in breach of the Convention.[39] The dispensation as regards legislative measures 'must be seen as a consequence of the absence, in many countries, of legal

[33] *No 788/60*, 4 YB 116 (1961).   [34] *No 299/57*, 2 YB 186 (1957).

[35] A 25 (1978); 2 EHRR 25 para 240 PC.

[36] *Nos 6780/74 and 6950/75*; 2 DR 125 (1975). See also the third *Cyprus v Turkey* case, *No 8007/77*, 13 DR 85 at 150–3 (1978).

[37] 2001-IV; 35 EHRR 731 paras 101–2 GC.

[38] In fact, the Court went on to find two separate violations of Article 13 in respect of the ineffectiveness of 'TRNC' remedies in relation to the property rights of Greek Cypriots not living in northern Cyprus and the rights under Articles 3, 8, 9, and 10 of the Convention and Articles 1 and 2 of Protocol 1 of Greek Cypriots living in northern Cyprus (paras 194 and 324 of the judgment). It did though find no violation of Article 13 in respect of interferences by private persons with the rights of Greek Cypriots living in northern Cyprus (para 324) and no violation of Article 13 in respect of an alleged administrative practice of failing to secure effective remedies to Turkish Cypriots living in northern Cyprus (para 383). The Commission in its report had reached identical conclusions on these four findings.

[39] *Greece v UK No 299/57*, 2 YB 186 at 192 (1957); the *Greek* case 11 YB-II 690 at 726 (1968); *Second Greek* case *No 4448/70*, 13 YB 109 at 134 (1970); *Ireland v UK Nos 5310/71 and 5451/72*, 41 CD 3 at 84 (1972); *Cyprus v Turkey No 8007/77 (Third Application)*, 13 DR 85 at 151–2 (1978); *France, Norway, Denmark, Sweden and Netherlands v Turkey Nos 9940–9944/82*, 35 DR 143 at 162 (1983).

remedies against legislation'.[40] It must also be seen as the corollary of the state's right under the Convention to complain of an incompatibility of legislation with Convention standards without being required to show that it is adversely affected or to point to particular victims. In *France, Norway, Denmark, Sweden and Netherlands v Turkey*,[41] the Turkish government contended that the applicant states had not furnished substantial evidence of an administrative practice of torture or ill-treatment of prisoners. In particular, they referred to cases where those responsible for ill-treating prisoners had been successfully prosecuted. The issue to be decided thus concerned the level of proof of a practice that must be offered by the complaining state.

The concept of administrative practice, which applies to individual cases in the same way as to inter-state applications, involves: (i) a repetition of acts; and (ii) official tolerance.[42] The Court in *Ireland v UK*[43] described the first criterion as 'an accumulation of identical or analogous breaches which are sufficiently numerous and inter-connected to amount not merely to isolated incidents or exceptions but to a pattern or system'. Official tolerance means that superiors, though cognisant of acts of ill-treatment, refuse to take action to punish those responsible or to prevent their repetition; or that a higher authority manifests indifference by refusing any adequate investigation of their truth or falsity; or that in judicial proceedings a fair hearing of such complaints is denied. In this regard the conduct of the higher authority must be on a scale which is sufficient to put an end to the repetition of acts or to interrupt the pattern or system.[44]

The significance of the concept of administrative practice as far as domestic remedies are concerned was highlighted by the Commission in the *Greek* case:

> Where...there is a practice of non-observance of certain Convention provisions, the remedies prescribed will of necessity be side-stepped or rendered inadequate. Thus, if there was an administrative practice of torture or ill-treatment, judicial remedies prescribed would tend to be rendered ineffective by the difficulty of securing probative evidence, and administrative inquiries would either be not instituted, or, if they were, would be likely to be half-hearted and incomplete...[45]

In *France, Norway, Denmark, Sweden and Netherlands v Turkey*[46] the Commission was confronted with the paradox that, while at the admissibility stage there is no requirement on the state to make out a *prima facie* case of its allegation of violations of the Convention, the 'substantial' evidence test as regards an administrative practice appeared to suggest a degree of proof appropriate only to the merits stage of the examination. It resolved this difficulty by holding that at the admissibility stage only *prima facie* evidence of a practice was required. It went on to find this standard of proof to have been satisfied as regards both a repetition of acts and official tolerance. In particular it held that the efforts of the authorities to prevent violations of Article 3 on a considerable scale were not sufficient judging by the large number of complaints lodged with the competent national bodies which indicated a degree of tolerance at the level of direct superiors of those immediately responsible. The rule on exhaustion of domestic remedies thus did not apply. Similarly in *Denmark v Turkey*[47] the Court noted that part of Denmark's application related to an alleged widespread practice of torture and ill-treatment in policy custody in Turkey. The Court found that in principle the rule did not apply where the applicant state complained of a practice as such with the aim of preventing its continuation or recurrence. Since

---

[40] *France, Norway, Denmark, Sweden and Netherlands v Turkey*, id, p 163.   [41] Id, pp 162–8.

[42] *Donnelly v UK Nos 5577–83/72*, 4 DR 64 (1975).   [43] A 25 (1978); 2 EHRR 25 para 159.

[44] 12 YB (the *Greek* case) at 196 (1969) (report of the Commission).   [45] Id, p 194.

[46] 35 DR 143 at 162–8 (1983).   [47] *No 34387/97* hudoc (1999).

Denmark's complaint in this respect was of a general nature and was not 'wholly unsub-stantiated' it followed that the rule as to the exhaustion of domestic remedies did not apply to this part of its application. The Court further noted that the six-month rule will apply equally to inter-state cases in this respect: if the administrative practices or situa-tions ended six months before the date of the application they will fall outside the scope of the Court's examination.

3. EXHAUSTION OF DOMESTIC REMEDIES

I. THE GENERAL REQUIREMENTS OF THE RULE

Article 35(1) provides that:

> The Court may only deal with the matter after all domestic remedies have been exhausted, according to the generally recognised rules of international law...

The purpose of Article 35(1) is to afford the contracting states the opportunity of prevent-ing or putting right the violations alleged against them before those allegations are sub-mitted to the Court.[48] Consequently, states are dispensed from answering for their acts before an international body before they have had an opportunity to put matters right through their own legal system.[49] The Court has also stated that the rule is based on 'the assumption, reflected in Article 13 of the Convention—with which it has close affinity—that there is an effective remedy available in respect of the alleged breach in the domestic system. In this way, it is an important aspect of the principle that the machinery of pro-tection established by the Convention is subsidiary to the national systems safeguarding human rights.'[50] As noted, the local remedies rule applies to both inter-state and indi-vidual applications.

The crux of the rule on exhaustion is that the complaint intended to be made subse-quently to the Court must first have been made—at least in substance—to the appro-priate domestic body, and in compliance with the formal requirements and time limits laid down in domestic law.[51] These basic requirements—in substance, to the appropri-ate domestic body and in compliance with the formal requirements and time limits in domestic law—will be considered in this section. The questions of the burden of proof and what remedies are considered adequate and effective will be considered in the fol-lowing two sections.

As concerns the requirement that the complaint be made in substance, it is settled case law that this does not mean expressly invoking an Article of the Convention. In *Fressoz and Roire v France*[52] the applicants were journalists who had been convicted of handling stolen goods, notably documents relating to the tax assessments of a third party which had formed the basis of an article they had written. The government had argued that the applicants had failed to exhaust domestic remedies since they had confined themselves to denying the charge that had been brought against them and had not argued before

---

[48] *Selmouni v France* 1999-V; 29 EHRR 403 para 74 GC; *Hentrich v France* A 296-A (1994) para 33; and *Remli v France* 1996-II; 22 EHRR 253 para 33.

[49] Thus the rule is founded on the principle of international law that states must first have the opportunity to redress the wrong alleged in their own legal system. See, *inter alia, Van Oosterwijck v Belgium* A 40 (1980); 3 EHRR 557 para 34 PC.

[50] *Selmouni v France, loc cit* at n 48 above. See also *Akdivar v Turkey* 1996-IV; 23 EHRR 143 para 65.

[51] See *Cardot v France* A 200 (1991); 13 EHRR 853 para 34.

[52] 1999-I; 31 EHRR 28 paras 33–7 GC.

the trial court that there was a contradiction between that charge and their freedom of expression. The Court rejected that submission. In their cassation appeal, the applicants had made explicit reference to the domestic Freedom of the Press Act. They had also argued that they had improperly been charged with a general offence of handling stolen goods and that this had been done in order to circumvent the special provisions of French law governing the media. In the Court's view, by ruling on this point, the Court of Cassation had also ruled indirectly on the scope of the right of journalists to information. On that basis, the Strasbourg Court held that freedom of expression was in issue, if only impliedly, in the proceedings before the Court of Cassation such that an Article 10 complaint was raised at least in substance before that court.[53]

However, in *Azinas v Cyprus*[54] the Grand Chamber took a rather stricter approach. In a dispute over loss of pension rights, the applicant had withdrawn that part of his appeal to the Supreme Court that asserted that the loss of pension rights was contrary to his right to property. In finding that the applicant had not exhausted domestic remedies, the Grand Chamber stated that it was not sufficient that the applicant might have unsuccessfully exercised another remedy which could have overturned the impugned decision on other grounds not connected with the complaint of a violation of a Convention right. The Convention complaint had to have been aired at national level for there to have been exhaustion. Further justification for this strict approach came from the fact that the Convention was an integral part of the Cypriot legal system and Article 1 of Protocol 1 was directly applicable.[55]

Whether a particular court is an appropriate domestic body may however depend more on the right in question than on the court itself. For example in Spanish cases, given the overlap between the Convention and the rights guaranteed by the Spanish constitution, applicants will normally be required to lodge *amparo* appeals with the Constitutional Court.[56] However, in *de Parias Merry v Spain*,[57] a case concerning property rights, the applicant had lodged such an *amparo* appeal with the Constitutional Court. This was dismissed on the ground that the right of property was not among those in respect of which such an appeal could be made. The inappropriateness of an *amparo* appeal to the Constitutional Court as regards this right therefore meant that the rejection by the Constitutional Court was not the final domestic decision in the applicant's case. Since the final domestic decision was therefore the earlier Administrative Court decision and since this was given more than six months prior to the lodging of the application in Strasbourg,

[53] See also *Castells v Spain* A 236 (1992); 14 EHRR 445 paras 24–32. Cf, *Cardot v France* A 200 (1991); 13 EHRR 853 paras 32–5 where the Court held that the applicant had failed to raise his complaint in substance before the French courts. The applicant had alleged a violation of Article 6(3)(d) since he had been convicted of drugs charges on the basis of evidence given by former co-defendants in proceedings to which he had not been a party and that he had not had an opportunity, either at his trial or on appeal, to challenge their testimony. The Court rejected the case on the grounds that before the trial court he had not expressed any wish to hear evidence from the co-defendants or made an application to the Court of Appeal for such evidence to be heard. Moreover, his pleadings to the Court of Cassation were too vague to draw that court's attention to his real complaint under Article 6(3)(d).

[54] 2004-III; 40 EHRR 166.

[55] But see the joint dissenting opinion of Judges Costa and Garlicki to the effect that this ruling was unduly strict and formalistic, relying *inter alia* on the Court's ruling in *Fressoz and Roire*.

[56] *Castells v Spain* A 236 (1992); 14 EHRR 445. This rule that overlap between Convention rights and rights guaranteed by national constitutions (and thus requiring that prospective applicants go first to constitutional courts charged with protecting those constitutional rights) is of general application: see *mutatis mutandis Grisankova and Grisankovs v Latvia No 36117/02* hudoc (2003) DA. This will of course depend on the constitutional court in question being an effective remedy for individual complainants: see *Apostol v Georgia* in the following section and discussion thereof.

[57] *No 40177/98* hudoc (1999) DA.

the application was declared inadmissible. The case is illustrative therefore of the care than should be taken in exhausting the appropriate domestic remedy for any given right and lodging an application promptly thereafter.[58]

Article 35(1) also operates with some deference to national procedural law, in that it normally requires compliance with the formal requirements and time limits laid down in domestic law for exhausting remedies. In one sense, this has the same justification as the Court's own six-month time limit in fostering legal certainty. Thus in ordinary legal proceedings where there are no special circumstances justifying a failure to abide by national procedures, the Court will frequently reject cases for non-exhaustion where the applicant had clearly sought to exhaust a remedy but through his own negligence failed to observe the requirements of domestic law.[59] This is most common in cases where there is a clear failure to lodge an appeal in time and will apply even where the appeal, if it had been properly lodged, would have had a reasonable prospect of success.[60] However, it will also be applicable to other procedural requirements such as paying the applicable court fees.[61] One possible area of flexibility in this regard may be when the applicant seeks to make reference to new case law of the Strasbourg Court in domestic proceedings when the relevant decision or judgment is delivered after the deadline for submissions in the domestic proceedings. New case law of the Court is a factor beyond the control of prospective applicants when they are still engaged in domestic proceedings.[62]

Finally, the assessment of whether domestic remedies have been exhausted is normally carried out with reference to the date on which the application was lodged with the Court.[63] However, this rule is subject to exceptions.[64] Notably, if a new domestic remedy in respect of length of proceedings becomes available to the applicant after the introduction of the application but before the Court is called upon to decide on its admissibility, the applicant must exhaust this new domestic remedy.[65] As concerns repetitive cases, if the government creates a new remedy, the Court will examine whether that remedy is effective in a leading case. If the remedy is found to be effective, the Court will hold that applicants in pending applications in similar cases are required to exhaust the new remedy, provided they are not time-barred from doing so. It will thus declare these applications inadmissible under Article 35(1), even when they were lodged before the creation of the new remedy.[66]

---

[58] Though this decision should be read in the light of the later decision in *Fernandez-Molina Gonzalez and 370 other applications v Spain No 64359/01 et al* hudoc (2002) DA where the applicants had taken an *amparo* appeal to the Constitutional Court *inter alia* on the basis of Article 24 of the Constitution guaranteeing the principle of non-discrimination. In Strasbourg they complained, *inter alia*, of a breach of Article 1 of Protocol 1 taken together with Article 14 of the Convention. The Court took the view that it would be too formalistic to require the applicants to apply to the Court on two different dates in order for the Article 1 of Protocol 1 complaint and the Article 14 complaint to be compatible with the six-month rule.

[59] *Agbovi v Germany No 71759/01* hudoc (2006) DA with further references therein.

[60] *Ugilt Hansen v Denmark No 11968/04* hudoc (2006) DA; *Ben Salah Adraqui and Dhaime v Spain No 45023/98* DA hudoc (2000) *Cardot v France* A 200 (1991); 13 EHRR 853 para 34.

[61] *Reuther v Germany No 74789/01* 2003-IX DA.

[62] *Merger and Cros v France No 68864/01* hudoc (2004) DA.

[63] *Csikos v Hungary* 2006-XIV para 17 and references therein.

[64] *Icyer v Turkey No 18888/02* hudoc (2006) para 72 DA and references therein.

[65] *Predil Anstalt v Italy No 31993/96* hudoc (2002) DA; *Bottaro v Italy No 56298/00* hudoc (2002) DA; *Andrasik and Others v Slovakia No 57984/00* hudoc (2002) DA; *Nogolica v Croatia No 77784/01* hudoc (2002); *Fell v UK No 7878/77*, 23 DR 102 (1981).

[66] *Icyer v Turkey* hudoc (2006) paras 74 *et seq* DA; *Scordino v Italy (No 1)* 2006-V; 45 EHRR 207 paras 140–9 GC; *Michalak v Poland No 24549/03* hudoc (2005) DA; *Charzynski v Poland No 15212/03* hudoc (2005) DA.

II. BURDEN OF PROOF

The Court has also stated that Article 35 provides for a distribution of the burden of proof.[67] In practice, the burden of proof operates as follows. Prior to the communication of an application to the respondent state for observations, the applicant must provide information to show that the requirements of Article 35 have been satisfied (Rule 47(f) of the Rules of Court). The Court will examine the matter on its own motion at this stage and will reject for non-exhaustion if it appears that an appropriate remedy has not been availed of. Where the case is formally communicated for observations, the burden is then on the respondent government. It is then incumbent on a government claiming non-exhaustion to satisfy the Court that the remedy was an effective one available in theory and in practice at the relevant time, that is to say, that it was accessible, was one which was capable of providing redress in respect of the applicant's complaints, and offered reasonable prospects of success.[68] However, once this burden of proof has been satisfied it falls to the applicant to establish that the remedy advanced by the government was in fact exhausted or was for some reason inadequate and ineffective in the particular circumstances of the case or that there existed special circumstances absolving him or her from the requirement.[69] After communication, the respondent government may, of course, expressly waive the right to rely on the rule.[70]

Though the normal course is for it simply to state that the respondent government has not shown with a sufficient degree of certainty the existence of an available and effective remedy, the Court has occasionally explicitly stated that the respondent government has failed to discharge the burden of proof. For example in *Apostol v Georgia*,[71] the government had sought to argue that the right to enforcement of a judicial decision was a right guaranteed by the constitutional right of access to court. The Court noted that the government had not referred to any decisions or judgments of the Georgian Constitutional Court interpreting the right of access in this way.

III. ADEQUACY AND EFFECTIVENESS OF REMEDIES

The only remedies which Article 35 of the Convention requires to be exhausted are those that relate to the breaches alleged and at the same time are available and sufficient.[72] These remedies must be sufficiently certain not only in theory but also in practice, failing which they will lack the requisite accessibility and effectiveness. It falls to the respondent government to establish that these various conditions are satisfied. It is then for the Court in any case where a plea of non-exhaustion is made by the government to appreciate whether any given remedy is, in the light of its particular attributes and the applicant's

---

[67] *Selmouni v France*, 1999-V; 29 EHRR 403 GC para 76.

[68] This will also require a degree of precision from the government. In the case of *Deweer v Belgium* A 35 (1980); 2 EHRR 439 para 26, the government had, *inter alia*, relied on 'other remedies' which the applicant could have availed of without specifying their nature. The Court took the view that it would be straying outside its role were it to set about identifying the remedies the government had in mind. See also *Foti v Italy* A 56 (1982) 5 EHRR 313 para 48: vague assertions as to the existence of remedies.

[69] On special circumstances see the *Akdivar* judgment, below, p 774, para 68 and the following section of this chapter on special circumstances.

[70] *Urbanczyk v Poland* No 33777/96 hudoc (2002) DA; *Van der Mussele v Belgium* No 8919/80, 23 DR 244 (1981); and *57 Inhabitants of Louvain v Belgium* No 1994/63, 7 YB 252 (1964). The Court has on one occasion applied the rule on its own motion after communication to the respondent government (in *Laidin v France* No 43191/98 hudoc (2002)). However, this ruling has not been followed and it is to be queried whether the case is still good law.

[71] 2006-XIV para 39. [72] *Selmouni v France* 1999-V; 29 EHRR 403 para 75.

particular circumstances, adequate and effective.[73] Although in the relevant case law a certain overlap exists between the notions of the 'adequacy' and 'effectiveness' of a given remedy, appropriate distinctions between the two concepts can be drawn. For example, a remedy may be adequate in the sense that it would in theory address the grievances but not be effective if it took too long or if the applicant was prevented from having recourse to it.[74] Thus in *Bertuzzi v France*[75] the applicant had been granted legal aid to sue a lawyer. After the withdrawal of three lawyers appointed by the president of the bar to represent him, his legal aid entitlement lapsed. Among the remedies suggested by the government, there was the possibility of a disciplinary appeal against the president of the bar to the Prosecutor General at the Court of Appeal. The Court rejected this remedy on the ground that it was not an available remedy: the applicant could not be expected, unassisted by a lawyer, to know all the arcane judicial or disciplinary remedies against the president of the bar.

The availability as opposed to the effectiveness of a remedy will of course depend on the circumstances of the applicant's case and can often depend on when a remedy appears. In *Giumarra and Others v France*[76] the applicants' complaints related to the length of criminal proceedings which they had joined as a civil party. Some months before the applicants introduced their application, a landmark judgment (*l'arrêt Gautier*) of the Paris Court of Appeal in January 1999 created a remedy for length of proceedings based on Article L 781–1 of the Judicial Code. The Court noted that the judgment had been followed by a number of other Appeal Courts and that the person who had obtained the judgment had not applied to the Strasbourg Court within six months of it. This meant it acquired a sufficient degree of certainty such that it could and should be considered a remedy for the purposes of Article 35(1) by the time the applicants introduced their application in August 2000.

More generally, the remedies available under national law to which recourse must be had will of course depend on the nature of the breach alleged. For example, if an applicant complained of police brutality he would be required to bring civil proceedings for damages against the police or, in some jurisdictions (eg, France), criminal proceedings to which he could be joined as a civil party. The lodging of a criminal complaint in such jurisdictions is regarded as an effective and sufficient remedy. Where there is no follow-up to the complaint, the victim is not required to bring additional civil proceedings for compensation or to challenge the decision not to pursue the complaint.[77] Similarly, a complainant alleging that he will be subjected to ill-treatment contrary to Article 3 if, for example, he is to be deported from the United Kingdom, will normally be required to appeal against the decision to make a deportation order to the Asylum and Immigration Tribunal. If the determination of the AIT is unfavourable to him, he must apply for reconsideration of the determination to the Senior Immigration Judge and from there apply to the High Court for permission for leave to apply for statutory or judicial review. Since he will not be deported pending these proceedings or in the event of a decision in his favour, these will normally be effective remedies.[78] On the other hand,

---

[73] *Civet v France* 1999-VI; 31 EHRR 871 para 41.   [74] *Mikheyev v Russia* hudoc (2006) para 86.

[75] *No 36378/97* hudoc (2002).

[76] *No 61166/00* hudoc (2001). See by contrast, *Zannouti v France No 42211/98* hudoc (2000) DA, where the same remedy had not been demonstrated as effective for length of pre-trial detention complaints and the relevant domestic judgments referred to by the government post-dated the lodging of the application to the Court.

[77] *Assenov and Others v Bulgaria* 1998-VIII; 28 EHRR 652 para 86.

[78] This will also be the case in countries where it is open to applicants to seek interim injunctions whilst they are pursuing remedies. If they do not pursue such remedies when interim injunctions are available, this may result in a finding of non-exhaustion: *Bahaddar v Netherlands* 1998-I; 26 EHRR 278 paras 47 and 48.

if equivalent proceedings in other jurisdictions do not have suspensive effect, they would not be seen as providing an effective remedy.[79]

In general therefore, procedures that involve the vindication of a right must be tried. Normally, but not necessarily, these will be judicial procedures. In certain situations, they may also be administrative procedures. Thus, for example, complaints by prisoners in the United Kingdom that the Prison Rules are not being observed should first be raised by means of a complaint to the prison authorities and if necessary by judicial review of their decision.[80] An applicant is only required to have recourse to remedies which are capable of providing an effective and sufficient means of redressing the alleged wrong. Extraordinary remedies such as petitions for a re-opening of proceedings or for supervisory review are not regarded as effective and sufficient remedies.[81] Submitting to a re-trial in order to have a first, *in absentia* trial set aside will not constitute a normal remedy that an applicant can be expected to pursue, especially if his complaint relates in part to the fairness of that first trial.[82] The same principle will apply to discretionary remedies or actions to obtain a 'favour' such as, in the United Kingdom, a petition to the Queen or applications to the Criminal Cases Review Commission.[83]

Also for the United Kingdom and in accordance with the Court's ruling in *Hobbs v UK*,[84] at present an application for a declaration of incompatibility under the Human Rights Act 1998 will not be an effective remedy since the declaration will only provide the appropriate minister with the power and not the duty to amend the offending legislation. However in the later case of *Burden and Burden*[85] the Court took note of the fact that while there was no legal obligation on the minister to amend a legislative provision which had been found by a court to be incompatible with the Convention, such amendments had occurred in ten out of the thirteen cases where a declaration had been finally issued by the courts, and in the remaining three, reforms were pending or under consideration. It observed that it was possible that at some future date evidence of a longstanding practice of ministers giving effect to the courts' declarations of incompatibility might be sufficient to persuade it of the effectiveness of the procedure

Complaints to ombudsmen or other organs which supervise the administration are also, in principle, inadequate[86] as are administrative remedies which betray a lack of independence such as internal police complaints procedures.[87] However, in light of the growing powers awarded to national ombudsmen and a strong custom of national authorities abiding by the decisions of ombudsmen in future case law it may be that the Court will have occasion to allow exceptions to this general principle.

In light of this case law and as stated above, the remedies to be exhausted will normally be judicial procedures. There, in principle, the complainant must appeal to the

---

[79] *Jabari v Turkey No 40035/98* hudoc (1999) DA.   [80] See eg, *Young v UK* hudoc 2007; 45 EHRR 689.

[81] *Cinar v Turkey No 28602/95* hudoc (2003) DA; *Kutcherenko v Ukraine No 41974/98* hudoc (1999) DA; *Tumilovich v Russia No 47033/99* hudoc (1999) DA.

[82] *Krombach v France* 2001-II.

[83] Though see *Reilly v UK No 53731/00* hudoc (2003) DA. There the Court reiterated that did not generally regard an application to the CCRC as part of the normal process of exhaustion of domestic remedies as its procedure offered an exceptional and non-judicial review of purported miscarriages of justice albeit with the possibility of subsequent referral to the Court of Appeal. However, the Court considered the failure to make such an application to be of some relevance in that case, where the applicant had not taken the step of appealing against his sentence after his trial, since a CCRC application was one means of having his case referred to the Court of Appeal.

[84] *No 63684/00* hudoc (2002) DA.   [85] Hudoc (2008) GC.

[86] *Lehtinen v Finland* 1999-VII; *Jasar v FYRM No 69908/01* hudoc (2006) DA; *Montion v France No 11192/84*, 52 DR 227 (1987); *Leander v Sweden* A 116 (1987) paras 80–4.

[87] *Khan v UK* 2000-V; 31 EHRR 1016; *Jasar v FRYM, ibid.*

highest court of appeal against an unfavourable decision at first or second instance.[88] Mere doubts as to the prospects of success of national proceedings do not absolve the applicant from the obligation to exhaust.[89] While this is a somewhat strict rule, it can occasionally work to the benefit of applicants where there is a question of inadmissibility under the six-months rule for pursuing ineffective remedies—and produce surprising results in the process. For example, in *Roseiro Bento v Portugal*[90] the applicant had been the losing party in a defamation action and had to pay compensation. Under a new law, an appeal was only admissible if the amount of compensation exceeded a certain amount, which it did not in the applicant's case. He appealed arguing that the new law was unconstitutional. The day before he lodged his appeal, the Constitutional Court ruled that the new law was constitutional, its judgment being published one month later. His constitutional complaint was dismissed in application of this precedent. Clearly, if the Constitutional Court remedy had no prospect of success then it could not be taken to be the final domestic decision in the case and the application risked being inadmissible under the six-month rule. However, the Court found it reasonable to conclude that the applicant did not know of the Constitutional Court's ruling when he filed his own complaint. The appeal to the Constitutional Court was also understandable as at that point the Constitutional Court's case law consisted of a single decision. The Court therefore found the final domestic decision was the Constitutional Court's decision in the applicant's case. This decision is perhaps difficult to reconcile with the Court's findings in other cases where a single adverse precedent of a higher court was found to be enough to absolve applicants of the obligation to appeal to that court.[91]

In this respect, traditionally, the Court has found that applicants are not obliged to make use of remedies which, according to 'settled legal opinion' existing at the relevant time, do not provide redress for their complaints.[92] A well-reasoned opinion from counsel which sets out the position under national law has in the past provided evidence of 'settled legal opinion'.[93] However, in the United Kingdom at least, after the Human Rights Act 1998, it is highly unlikely that the Court will accept this given the remedies available under the Act. Indeed, even before the Human Rights Act the former Commission had held that in a common law system it was incumbent on an aggrieved individual to allow the domestic courts the opportunity to develop existing rights by way of interpretation.[94] This was recently reaffirmed in *D v Ireland*,[95] concerning the exceptional circumstances

---

[88] *Vorobyeva v Ukraine No 27517/02* hudoc (2002) DA.

[89] *Pellegriti v Italy No 77363/01* hudoc (2005) DA; *MPP Golub v Ukraine No 6778/05* hudoc (2005) DA; *Milosevic v Netherlands No 77631/01* hudoc (2002) DA.

[90] *No 29288/02,* 2004-XII DA.   [91] See pp 771–2 below.

[92] *De Wilde, Ooms and Versyp v Belgium* (the *Vagrancy* cases) A 12 (1971) p 33; 1 EHRR 373, 401 PC.

[93] In *McFeeley v UK No 8317/98,* 20 DR 44 (1980) the applicants were able to show with reference to counsel's opinion that no remedy existed under Northern Ireland law in respect of their complaints concerning the continuous imposition of disciplinary punishments by the prison governor as well as their general prison conditions and treatment by the prison authorities. However, even this case was rather exceptional on its facts and cf, *K, F and P v UK No 10789/84,* 40 DR 298 (1984) where, despite counsel's opinion to the contrary, the Commission rejected for non-exhaustion a UK case where the applicants had not sought to appeal to the House of Lords against an unfavourable Court of Appeal decision. The Court of Appeal had refused leave to appeal and the applicants were advised that petitioning the House of Lords directly for leave would be to no avail. The Commission was not satisfied that the state of the law on the issue in question was clear and observed that, in a subsequent case on similar facts, leave to appeal to the House of Lords had in fact been granted by the Court of Appeal.

[94] See *Whiteside v UK No 20357/92,* 76-A DR 80 (1994); *Leech v UK No 20075/92* hudoc (1994) DA (failure to appeal to the House of Lords from a decision of the Court of Session in Scotland); and *Veenstra v UK No 20946/92* hudoc (1994) DA.

[95] *No 26499/02* hudoc (2006) DA.

in which abortion was legally available in Ireland and whether, given the obvious time factors involved as well as a desire for anonymity in any legal proceedings, a woman would be obliged to exhaust domestic remedies before travelling abroad for the abortion. The Court found that there had been a failure to exhaust domestic remedies. There was a constitutional remedy in principle available and, although there was some uncertainty arising from the novelty of the substantive issue and the procedural imperatives in the case, the potential and importance of the constitutional remedy in a common law system meant the applicant could reasonably have been expected to take certain preliminary steps towards resolving these uncertainties. This approach is not just confined to common law systems. For example, in *Augusto v France*[96] the Court recently reaffirmed that a cassation appeal is in principle among the remedies which require to be exhausted.

As a general rule, it is still clear from the Court's jurisprudence that an applicant will be considered to have exhausted domestic remedies if he can demonstrate with reference to relevant domestic case law that an appeal would be doomed to failure.[97] This will normally be where there is a recent precedent of the appeal court that clearly applies to the applicant's case and where there is no likelihood of the appeal court reversing its own recent precedent.[98] However, following *Augusto*, even settled domestic case law may not prevent the lodging of such an appeal being required in order to comply with domestic remedies. This will be especially so if the applicant himself believes there is the possibility of the court in question reversing that case law in his case or in subsequent case law the court in question does in fact do so.[99] Where analysis of the national case law reveals a dispute in the domestic courts as to what the relevant legal rules are, the situation may be different. In such a situation, an applicant will still be required to bring proceedings in order to assert his version of the appropriate rule.[100]

In this context, some dispute has arisen over the question of the effectiveness of appeals in that an appeals process which is limited to questions of lawfulness may be inadequate where the complaint concerns the facts or the law itself.[101] However, in *Civet v France*,[102] concerning a complaint of excessive length of detention on remand, the Grand Chamber rejected the applicant's plea that he was not required to submit an appeal to the Court of Cassation since this was of a factual nature whereas the Court of Cassation's jurisdiction only covered points of law. For the Grand Chamber 'facts' and the 'law' could not be conceived of as two radically separate fields. While the Court of Cassation's jurisdiction was limited to examining grounds of 'law', the Court of Cassation nonetheless had the task of checking that the facts found by the tribunals of fact support the conclusions reached by

---

[96] Hudoc (2007) paras 37–46. See also *Hamaidi v France No 39291/98* hudoc (2001) DA.

[97] *Kleyn v Netherlands* 2003-VI; 38 EHRR 239 para 156 GC. See also *Johnston v Ireland* A 112 (1986); 9 EHRR 203 para 44 PC; *Open Door and Dublin Well Woman v Ireland* A 246 (1992); 15 EHRR 44 para 47 PC; and *Keegan v Ireland* A 290 (1994); 18 EHRR 342 para 39.

[98] See eg, *Salah Sheekh v Netherlands* hudoc (2007); 45 EHRR 1158 paras 121–3 on the proposed expulsion of the applicant, a member of a minority clan, to a 'relatively safe' area of Somalia, where the Court held that although the Administrative Jurisdiction Division of the Dutch Council of State would in theory have been capable of reversing the decision of the Regional Court against the applicant, in practice a further appeal to the former court would have had 'virtually no prospect of success'. It referred in particular to a decision the Administrative Jurisdiction Division had given on Article 3 of the Convention in relation to the appropriate test for expulsion of those belonging to minority groups as evidence that the Administrative Jurisdiction Division would not have come to a different conclusion in the applicant's case.

[99] *Augusto v France* hudoc para 42. However, where an applicant's request for legal aid has been refused on the absence of grounds for pursuing the appeal, an application will not be inadmissible for failure to pursue the appeal to the Court of Cassation: *LL v France* 2006-XI.

[100] *Van Oosterwijck v Belgium* A 40 (1980); 3 EHRR 557 paras 30–41 PC.

[101] *S v UK No 10741/84*, 41 DR 226 (1984) (Lands Tribunal in Northern Ireland).

[102] 1999-VI; 31 EHRR 871 para 43 GC.

them on the basis of those findings. It had the ability to check whether the lower court had given adequate reasons for its decision to prolong pre-trial detention and if not, it would quash the lower court's decision. Failure to appeal to the Court of Cassation therefore amounted to a failure to exhaust domestic remedies.

In legal systems with a written constitution and a constitutional bill of rights, the highest court of appeal will normally be the constitutional court, so that a constitutional action must be taken to challenge the law or administrative practice alleged to be in breach of the Convention. Thus in the Czech Republic, Germany, Poland, and Spain, complaints must, where possible, be pursued to the constitutional court.[103] Similarly, in Ireland the constitutionality of the law or practice must be challenged before the courts.[104] However, this will depend on the nature of the constitutional remedy in each contracting state. For example, in Italy where individuals cannot bring cases directly before the Constitutional Court but rely on lower courts to refer the case, this will not constitute a remedy that requires exhaustion.[105] Equally, in Hungary the Hungarian Constitutional Court will be an ineffective remedy since it is only entitled to control the general constitutionality of laws and cannot quash or modify specific measures taken against an individual by the state.[106] Finally, in *Apostol v Georgia*,[107] the Court held that in Georgia the Constitutional Court is an ineffective remedy since it cannot set aside decisions of public authorities or courts and a finding of unconstitutionality of an act will not lead to the quashing of judicial decisions taken on the basis of that act. From the *Apostol* judgment, where the Court surveyed its case law on a number of constitutional courts, it would appear that the key factor is whether a constitutional complaint makes it possible to remedy violations of rights committed by public authorities or forbid authorities from continuing to infringe on the right in question. As concerns judicial decisions, the constitutional complaint must make it possible, where a law is found to be unconstitutional, to annul all final decisions made on the basis of the law and provide direct and speedy redress to the complainant.

Finally, where numerous remedies exist which are likely to be adequate and effective it is enough that the applicant has had recourse to one of them. Thus in *TW v Malta*,[108] where there were a number of remedies to challenge detention on remand, the Court stated that an applicant who has exhausted a remedy that is apparently effective and sufficient

---

[103] *Hartman v Czech Republic* 2003-VIII; 42 EHRR 587 (though finding that since the Constitutional Court could not take practical steps to expedite proceedings in lower courts, it was not a remedy that need be exhausted in length of proceedings cases); *Allaoui and Others v Germany No 44911/98* hudoc (1999) DA; *Mogos and Krifka v Germany No 78084/01* hudoc (2003) DA; *Paslawski v Poland No 38678/97* hudoc (2002) DA; and *Castells v Spain* A 236 (1992); 14 EHRR 445.

[104] Recently re-affirmed in *D v Ireland No 26499/02* hudoc (2006) DA. See also *Holland v Ireland No 24827/94* hudoc (1998) DA.

[105] *Immobiliare Saffi v Italy* 1999-V; 30 EHRR 756 para 42 GC; *De Jorio v Italy No 73936/01* hudoc (2003) DA; *Brozicek v Italy* A 167 (1989); 12 EHRR 371 para 34 PC. See also *Miconi v Italy No 66432/01* hudoc (2004) discussed at p 778.

[106] *Ven v Hungary No 21495/93* hudoc (1993) DA; *Csikos v Hungary* 2006-XIV paras 18–19. See also *Sergey Smirnov v Russia No 14085/04* hudoc (2006) concerning a failure to apply to the Russian Constitutional Court. The Court found that while the Constitutional Court was competent to examine individual complaints challenging the constitutionality of a law, it could not be an effective remedy if the alleged violation resulted only from erroneous application or interpretation of a statutory provision which was not unconstitutional. Since the applicant was not contesting the constitutionality of a statutory provision but the way domestic courts had interpreted it, an application to the Constitutional Court would have had no prospect of success and the applicant had exhausted domestic remedies.

[107] 2006-XIV.

[108] Hudoc (1999); 29 EHRR 185 para 34 GC; *Iatridis v Greece* 1999-II; 30 EHRR 97 para 47 GC; *Jasar v FRYM, ibid* n 86 and references therein.

cannot be required also to have tried others that were available but probably no more likely to be successful. In *Moreira Barbosa v Portugal*,[109] the applicant's complaint related to the length of criminal proceedings which he had begun against a third party. He had applied unsuccessfully to have the proceedings expedited. The government had argued that, in addition to this, he ought to have begun an action to establish non-contractual liability on the part of the state. The Court found that applicants must have made normal use of those domestic remedies which are likely to be effective and sufficient; when a remedy has been attempted, use of another remedy which has essentially the same objective is not required. The question has become more complex when there is a range of possible remedies in domestic law and the Convention can be argued directly before the domestic authorities. In *Salah v Netherlands* and *Baybasin v Netherlands*,[110] the applicants were detainees in a maximum security prison and complained about the regime in place there. After lodging his application, Baybasin had brought civil proceedings in tort against the state seeking compensation for non-pecuniary damage suffered in the prison, Dutch courts having previously awarded compensation to former Strasbourg applicants beyond what those applicants had received as compensation in Strasbourg. The applicant in *Salah* later joined those proceedings which were still pending at the time of the Strasbourg Court's examination of both applications. The Court noted that the normal remedy for challenging the decision relating to the maximum security prison regime was an appeal to the relevant appeal body for criminal justice ('the Appeal Board') and the applicants had done this. The Court then went on to state that it had found no indication that a civil action had ever been entertained by a domestic civil court on the basis that the remedy before the Appeal Board was flawed. The applicants were thus not required to turn to the civil courts after their appeals to the Appeal Board were dismissed. Controversially perhaps it went on to state that it could not allow proceedings before it and proceedings in domestic courts to be pursued in parallel but considered this under the rubric of Articles 41 and 46 rather than Article 35(1) and found that the matter should be reserved pending a final domestic decision in the matter.[111]

It is also settled case law that for serious human rights violations concerning Articles 2 and 3 applicants will not be required to exhaust both civil and administrative remedies on the one hand and criminal remedies on the other in order to comply with Article 35(1). The justification for this is that the extent of the state's obligations under the procedural heads of both Articles will require that the state undertake its own investigations into the events surrounding the alleged violations and if necessary prosecute those responsible. Furthermore, these obligations cannot be satisfied merely by awarding damages.[112] A possible exception to this rule exists insofar as it is possible to appeal against the decision of prosecutors not to prosecute those responsible. Thus in *Epözdemir v Turkey*,[113] where the applicant had not appealed to an Assize Court, which had the power to direct that a prosecution or further investigative measures take place, the substantive complaint under Article 2 had to be declared inadmissible. Similarly, where criminal proceedings are brought against those responsible and where the applicant has the possibility of joining the proceedings as a third party and claiming compensation, he or she will have failed to exhaust domestic remedies if this is not done so.[114] Finally, where the applicants do not allege that the death or ill-treatment was caused deliberately but merely as a result of the

---

[109] *No 65681/01*, 2004-V DA.   [110] Hudoc (2006); 44 EHRR 1131 and hudoc (2006).

[111] See extensive discussion in *Baybasin* at paras 67–84.

[112] See *Hugh Jordan v UK* 2001-III; 37 EHRR 52 paras 102–15; *Ogur v Turkey* 1999-III; 31 EHRR 912 para 66 GC; *Senses v Turkey No 24991/94* hudoc (2000) DA; *Jasar v FRYM* hudoc (2007) pp 11–12; *Pantea v Romania No 33343/96* hudoc (2001) DA; *Koksal v Netherlands No 31725/96* hudoc (2000) DA.

[113] *No 57039/00* hudoc (2002) DA.   [114] *Putun v Turkey No 31734/96* hudoc (2004) DA.

negligence of state agents, a civil action for compensation will be an effective remedy that applicants will not be at fault for pursuing.[115]

IV. SPECIAL CIRCUMSTANCES AND EXEMPTION FROM OBLIGATION TO EXHAUST

It has been recognized by the Strasbourg organs that according to the 'generally recognised principles of international law', there may be special circumstances where an applicant is absolved from the requirement to exhaust even adequate and effective domestic remedies.[116] This flows from the understanding of the rule as one that must be applied 'with some degree of flexibility and without excessive formalism'.[117]

As noted above, where an applicant alleges that there exists an administrative practice and is able to show that there is official tolerance at the highest level of the state, he will be absolved from exhausting remedies since there will be an assumption that they will be ineffective in practice. Where the administrative practice involves official tolerance at the middle or lower levels of command it will be a question of fact to be resolved in each case whether the remedies are still effective and sufficient.[118]

In *Akdivar and Others v Turkey*[119] the Court was called upon to examine the destruction of the applicants' homes during security operations in south-east Turkey during a time of serious disturbance when most of the region was subject to emergency rule. The Turkish government had argued that, despite this, there was a range of civil, administrative, and criminal remedies available to the applicants. In rejecting this submission, the Court held, in determining whether special circumstances existed, that it had to take 'realistic account not only of the existence of formal remedies in the legal system of the Contracting Party concerned but also of the general legal and political context in which they operate'. The general context prevailing in south-east Turkey at the time was such there were obstacles to the proper functioning of the system of the administration of justice such as the difficulties in securing probative evidence. Similarly, the severe civil strife in the region meant the prospects of success of civil proceedings based on allegations against the security forces had to be considered to be negligible in the absence of any official inquiry into their allegations, even assuming that the applicants would have been able to secure the services of lawyers willing to press their claims before the courts.[120] Despite the possible breadth of the Court's ruling in *Akdivar*, it would appear that the circumstances in this case were indeed exceptional and the Court in later cases has not been prepared to find the existence of special circumstances due to local conditions. In *Siddik Aslan and others*,[121] the applicants had alleged that their relatives had been unlawfully killed by security forces and that there had been a failure to investigate on the part of the authorities. While there had been attempts to recover the bodies, it appears that

[115] *Scavuzzo-Hager v Switzerland No 41773/98* hudoc (2004) DA.
[116] See *Van Oosterwijck v Belgium* A 40 (1980); 3 EHRR 557 paras 36–40 PC and *Selmouni v France* 1999-V; 29 EHRR 403 paras 76–7.
[117] *Selmouni v France*, id, para 77; *Cardot v France* A 200 (1991); 13 EHRR 853 para 34.
[118] *Donnelly v UK Nos 5577–5583/72*, 4 DR 4 (1975). [119] 1996-IV; 23 EHRR 143 para 69.
[120] See also *Aksoy v Turkey* 1996-VI; 23 EHRR 553 paras 41–57 and *Aydin and Others v Turkey Nos 28293/95, 29494/95 and 30219/96*, 2000-III DA, the latter with references to other Turkish cases where the *Akdivar* ruling has been applied. In *Aksoy* (and subsequently in *Aydin*) the Court extended its ruling in *Akdivar* to allegations of torture on the part of the authorities. It found that after the public prosecutor, who had seen the injuries to the applicant, had taken no action, it was understandable if the applicant formed the belief that he could not hope to secure concern and satisfaction through national legal channels and this amounted to special circumstances absolving him of the need to exhaust domestic remedies (paras 56–7).
[121] Hudoc (2005).

the applicants themselves had buried them without informing the authorities for fear of reprisals. The Court was not convinced that their fears were well-founded. Equally in *Kanlibas v Turkey*[122] the applicant had alleged that his brother had been killed by security forces and the body mutilated. He had a medical report by a British forensic pathologist to this effect which he alleged he did not submit to the Turkish authorities for fear of reprisals. The Court again found no verifiable evidence to support or corroborate that argument and found that the complaints made under Articles 2 and 3 in their substantive aspects to be inadmissible.

The Court has had occasion to apply its ruling in *Akdivar* in the first Chechen cases to come before it. In *Isayeva, Yusupova and Bazayeva v Russia*[123] the applicants complained about the deaths of their relatives and their own injuries as a result of the bombing of Grozny in October 1999. The government had argued that both civil and criminal remedies remained open to the applicants. The Court noted that while these remedies were in principle available under Russian law, in respect of civil actions, Russian courts were unable to consider properly the merits of a claim relating to alleged serious criminal actions in the absence of any results from a criminal investigation. It further noted the practical difficulties cited by the applicants in bringing such an action and the fact that the law-enforcement bodies were not functioning properly in Chechnya at the time. It therefore found that special circumstances existed which affected the applicants' obligation to exhaust remedies. In respect of the possibility of criminal remedies, the Court considered that this limb of the government's preliminary objection on non-exhaustion raised issues concerning the effectiveness of the criminal investigation. Indeed it went on to find a violation of the procedural limb of Article 2 in this respect.

In a more peaceful general context, however, the plea of 'special circumstances' has been rarely accepted. The old Commission refused to absolve the applicant, for example, on the grounds that he or she was a mental patient or had lack of legal knowledge[124] or because he or she had doubts as to the prospects of success[125] or had no legal aid[126] or was old and sick or depressive.[127] In one case where the Commission did find special circumstances, namely the imminent expulsion of the applicant which absolved him from filing an appeal, the Court overruled it, finding instead that the applicant's lawyer could have requested an extension of the time limit for filing the appeal.[128] Of some controversy in this respect is when legal aid is not available to bring costly national proceedings such as a constitutional action. It may be questioned, as noted above, whether the remedy is an effective one in practice and whether the limited means of the applicant amounts to special circumstances requiring the non-exhaustion rule to be waived. The case law, however, suggests that the rule is to be applied strictly even in such circumstances: lack of financial means does not absolve an applicant from making some attempt to take legal proceedings.[129]

---

[122] *No 32444/96* hudoc (2005) DA.

[123] Hudoc (2005); 41 EHRR 847. See also *Khashiyev and Akayeva v Russia* hudoc (2005) and *Isayeva v Russia* hudoc (2005); 41 EHRR 791, judgments of the same date.

[124] *X v UK No 6840/74*, 10 DR 5 (1977).

[125] *Garcia v Switzerland No 10148/82*, 42 DR 98 (1985) and *McDonnell v Ireland No 15141/89*, 64 DR 203 (1990).

[126] *Van Oosterwijck v Belgium* A 40 (1980); 3 EHRR 557 para 38 PC (although he had not made an application for legal aid).

[127] *No 289/57*, 1 YB 148 (1957). See also *B v Belgium No 16301/90*, 68 DR 290 (1991) (depressive state did not exempt the applicant from applying to the Belgium Conseil d'Etat to have an expulsion order quashed).

[128] *Bahaddar v Netherlands* 1998-I; 26 EHRR 278.

[129] *Cyprus v Turkey* (fourth inter-state case) 2001-IV; 35 EHRR 731 para 352 and *D v Ireland*, para 100.

However the Court has had occasion to find the existence of special circumstances. *AB v Netherlands*[130] concerned the applicant's conditions of detention in the Netherlands Antilles, the authorities' interference with his correspondence, and the question of a lack of an effective remedy in respect of these complaints. The government had argued that the applicant could have pursued a civil claim in tort through summary proceedings where he could also have sought necessary interim measures. The Court found that in assessing this remedy it had to take account of its existence in the legal system of the Netherlands Antilles and, on the basis of *Akdivar* ruling, the general legal and political context in which it operated as well as the personal circumstances of the applicant. It referred to similar proceedings taken by six detainees of the same prison. It appeared that the authorities had remained totally passive for more than a year in complying with six injunctions granted by the court hearing that case. The absence of convincing explanations from the government as to the failure to remedy the situation and observe these injunctions meant there were special circumstances dispensing the applicant from the obligation to exhaust the remedy suggested by the government. In *Öcalan v Turkey*,[131] the Chamber and Grand Chamber concurred in finding that the manner of the applicant's detention was a special circumstance absolving him from taking proceedings by which the lawfulness of it could be challenged. He had been kept in total isolation, possessed no legal training, and had no possibility of consulting a lawyer while in police custody. An additional factor was the unusual manner of the applicant's arrest (he had been arrested by security forces in Kenya after leaving the Greek embassy *en route* to Nairobi airport), which meant he was the principal source of direct information on his arrest. Finally, the movement of his lawyers had been obstructed by the police.

These rulings would seem to indicate that the threshold for a 'special circumstances' dispensation is an extremely high one. Special circumstances will only exist when it can be demonstrated that pursuing a remedy would have been dangerous or impossible rather than simply difficult or particular onerous for the applicant in question. So far, the Court's remarks in *Cardot v France*[132] and *Akdivar v Turkey* that the rule should be applied with some degree of flexibility and without excessive formalism have not always been given a generous interpretation in the day-to-day application of the rule.

4. THE SIX-MONTH RULE

Article 35(1) further provides that the Court 'may only deal with the matter...within a period of six months from the date on which the final decision was taken'. The *ratio legis* of the rule is the desire of contracting parties to prevent past decisions being constantly called into question.[133] It marks out the temporal limits of supervision carried out by the Court and signals to both individuals and state authorities the period beyond which such supervision is no longer possible.[134] The Court stated in *Alzery v Sweden*[135] that the rule

---

[130] Hudoc (2002); 37 EHRR 928 at para 63–74.
[131] Hudoc (2003) paras 66–76; 37 EHRR 238 and 2005-IV; 41 EHRR 985 paras 62–71 GC.
[132] A 200 (1991); 13 EHRR 853 para 34.   [133] *X v France No 9587/81*, 29 DR 228 (1982).
[134] *K v Ireland No 10416/83*, 38 DR 158 (1984).
[135] *No 10786/04* hudoc (2004). There the Court rejected an application filed on behalf of an Egyptian national who had been expelled from Sweden on 18 December 2001. An incomplete application form was submitted by his lawyer on 16 June 2002 with no authority form. While the lawyer and applicant met in Egypt in January 2004, a signed authority form was not submitted until 19 March 2004 and a fully completed application was sent only on 21 May 2004. Not persuaded by the reasons offered by the applicant's lawyer for the delay, the Court considered the date of introduction to be 19 March 2004 and thus out of time.

ought also to prevent the authorities and other persons concerned from being kept in a state of uncertainty for a long period of time. Finally as it also stated in *Alzery* it should facilitate the establishment of the facts of the case; otherwise, with the passage of time, this would become more and more difficult, and a fair examination of the issue raised under the Convention would thus become problematic. As stated above, it applies to both inter-state and individual applications.[136] Given the importance of the provision in enabling the Court to avoid the examination of 'historic' complaints, it is not surprising that it has held that the state cannot waive the application of the rule on its own authority.[137]

Rule 47(5) of the Rules of Court states that as a general rule the date of introduction of the application will be considered to be the date of the first communication from the applicant setting out, even summarily, the object of the application.[138] Normally this will prove uncontroversial and the date for these purposes will normally be taken as the postmark or the date the letter was written rather than the date of registration at the Court's Registry. Where there is a significant interval between the date on which the letter was written and the postmark, in the absence of explanations by the applicant, the Court will take the date of the postmark as the date of introduction.[139] The Court is frequently faced with the problem of applications being registered following substantial periods of inaction on the part of applicants. Such applications may be rejected on the basis of the six-month rule. In such cases, the Court will examine the particular circumstances of the case to determine what date should be regarded as the date of introduction.[140] The Court will normally require the applicant's representatives to maintain regular contact with it and to provide explanations for periods of inactivity.[141] The applicant or his representative will be required to give 'duly justified reasons connected to the subject matter of the application or the applicant personally'.[142]

As a general rule, delays in pursuing an application on the ground that the applicant is in the process of exhausting further domestic remedies will not be acceptable. Hover, one pragmatic exception to this rule is when the applicant wishes to pursue further or new domestic remedies and has reasonable doubts as to their effectiveness. An example from the United Kingdom might be seeking a declaration of incompatibility. In such a case, the applicant may run the risk on the one hand that his application will be rejected under the six-month rule (ineffective remedies not interrupting the six-month period) and on the other that the application will be rejected for non-exhaustion if the Court considers that the further or new domestic remedies are indeed effective and required to be exhausted. In such a case, the applicant should introduce an application before embarking on the further or new remedy but in the introductory letter should set out in detail the remedy to be pursued. The Registry would then register the application subject to the condition that the applicant or his representative keep it regularly informed of the status of the domestic proceedings. This is part of a general duty applicants and their lawyers have towards the Court. In assessing whether domestic remedies have been exhausted, it

---

[136] Eg, *Cyprus v Turkey* (fourth inter-state case) 2001-IV; 35 EHRR 731.

[137] See the *Walker* case, above, n 7. See also *X v France No 9587/81*, 29 DR 228 (1982); *K v Ireland*, *ibid*, n 134; *Bozano v France No 9990/82*, 39 DR 119 (1984).

[138] As to what information the Court requires for a valid application, see Rule 47 of the Rules of Court. The applicant must now complete the application form within 8 weeks—see Court's website for further details.

[139] *Arslan v Turkey No 36747/02* 2002-X DA.   [140] *PM v UK No 6638/03* hudoc (2004) DA.

[141] *Nee v Ireland No 52787/99* hudoc (2003) DA; *Chalkley v UK No 63831/00* hudoc (2002) DA; *Gaillard v France No 47337/99* hudoc (2000) DA; *Kirk v UK No 26299/95* hudoc (1996) DA.

[142] See *Quaresma Afonso Palma v Portugal No 72496/01* hudoc (2003) DA.

will be a factor which weighs against applicants if they fail to inform the Court of domestic remedies which they are pursuing or are involved in.[143]

The 'final decision' for purposes of Article 35 will normally be the final domestic decision rejecting the applicant's claim.[144] The time limit only starts to run from the final decision resulting from the exhaustion of remedies which are adequate and effective to provide redress in respect of the matter complained of. The six-month rule and the exhaustion requirement are thus intertwined in this respect. It follows that the time limit will not run from the date of decisions resulting from extraordinary remedies such as requests for a pardon or applications to re-open the proceedings,[145] inappropriate appeals to higher courts,[146] or waiting on other parties such as prosecutors to lodge appeals.[147] Where no adequate and effective remedy is available, the 'final decision' will be the act or decision complained of and thus the six-month rule will apply strictly from this date.[148] In *Miconi v Italy*,[149] the alleged violation of the Convention (preventing full legal costs being awarded in a certain class of litigation involving pension rights) was held to be the automatic effect of the entry into force of two laws regulating the matter. There was no remedy through the courts against the laws in question since the courts were bound by them and had no discretion in their implementation. In addition, although the Constitutional Court ruled on the compatibility of the laws with the constitution after their entry into force, since individuals were not entitled to apply directly to that court it was not a remedy that required to be exhausted.[150] The six-month period was held to run from the entry into force of the relevant laws. However, the Court has also stated that special considerations could apply in exceptional cases where applicants first avail themselves of a domestic remedy and only at a later stage become aware, or should have become aware, of the circumstances which make that remedy ineffective. In such a situation, the six-month period might be calculated from the time when the applicant becomes aware, or should have become aware, of these circumstances.[151] Equally, in *Veznedaroglu v Turkey*,[152] the applicant alleged that she had been forced to sign a confession under duress in violation of Article 3. She had then been tried by a Security Court and acquitted. While there were no remedies against the Article 3 complaint, the relevant date could be taken as the date of her acquittal: it was not unreasonable for her to wait for the court's verdict since she had raised the complaint before the court and expected an investigation would be opened on the basis of it.

---

[143] *Aytekin v Turkey* 1998-VII; 32 EHRR 501 para 80.

[144] *Paul and Audrey Edwards v UK No 46477/99* hudoc (2001) DA.

[145] See *Withey v UK* No 59493/00, 2003-X DA and *Kadikis v Latvia* udoc (2006); *X v Ireland No 9136/80*, 26 DR 242 at 244 (1981). The remedy concerned an application to the Attorney General for a certificate to appeal to the Supreme Court on a point of law of exceptional importance. Since, *inter alia*, the remedy could be sought at any time subsequent to a criminal conviction it was not considered effective. See also *X and Church of Scientology v Sweden No 7805/77*, 16 DR 68 (1979) and *R v Denmark No 10326/83*, 35 DR 218 (1983).

[146] See *de Parias Merry v Spain* hudoc (1999).

[147] *Moyo Alaverez No 44677/98* hudoc (1999) DA.

[148] *Bayram and Yildirim v Turkey No 38587/97*, 2002-III DA; *Veznedaroglu v Turkey No 32357/96* hudoc (1999). *Sardin v Russia No 69582/01* hudoc (2004) DA; and *Sitokhova v Russia No 55609/00* hudoc (2004) DA (the quashing of a final judgment in supervisory review proceedings being the final domestic decision).

[149] *No 66432/01* hudoc (2004) DA. See also *X v UK No 7379/76*, 8 DR 211 (1976) where the applicant complained that the British Railways Act 1968 had deprived him of certain property he would have obtained following the closure of a railway line. The Commission found that since the Act could not be challenged in court, the date of the entry into force of the Act should be considered as the 'final decision'.

[150] See above at n 105.

[151] *Aydin, Aydin and Aydin No 28293/95* hudoc (2000) DA. See also *Bayram and Yildirim v Turkey*, ibid, n 148.

[152] *No 32357/96* hudoc (1999).

There have been a number of problems with the application of the six-month rule in situations where the final domestic decision is not in dispute but the parties disagree as to what date to take for the purposes of the rule. This arises from different national practices in delivering judgments. Two situations must be distinguished. First, where a judgment is not pronounced in open court and the applicant is entitled to be served with a written copy of it, the time limit will be calculated from the date on which the judgment is actually served.[153] If the judgment is served on the applicant's lawyer then the six-month period will run from this date, even if the applicant only became aware of the judgment later.[154] In this respect, an applicant's negligence in maintaining contact with a former lawyer may be a factor to be taken into account.[155] It is for the state that invokes the six-month rule, however, to establish the date on which the applicant learned of the final decision.[156] Secondly, where the judgment is not served on the parties because domestic law does not provide for such service, the date taken will be the date on which the judgment is finalized, certified, and signed. This will be the date on which the parties are definitively able to find out the content of the judgment and obtain copies.[157] In legal systems where it is established practice that appeal judgments are not served or notified but deposited with the lower court's registry, applicants will be taken to be aware of this practice and thus under a duty to follow the appeal proceedings with due diligence.[158]

The six-month rule does not apply to continuing situations where the alleged violation takes the form of a state of affairs as opposed to a specific act or decision.[159] The rule will not apply where the alleged violation stems from a legislative provision or public policy which constantly impinges on or restricts particular activities. Thus in *De Becker v Belgium*[160] the Commission did not consider that the rule applied to the continuing restrictions on De Becker in the exercise of his profession as a journalist which flowed from a criminal conviction for collaborating with the enemy. In *Ülke v Turkey*,[161] the applicant was a conscientious objector who was called up for military service. He was repeatedly convicted and imprisoned for refusing to wear uniform or deserting. Each time he was released he was sent back to his unit, refused again to wear uniform, and was convicted again. This series of prosecutions and convictions was found to amount to an 'ongoing state of affairs' against which he had no remedy in domestic law. Nor will the rule apply where there is a refusal of the executive to comply with a specific decision.

---

[153] *Worm v Austria* 1997-V; 25 EHRR 454; *Sarıbek v Turkey No 41055/98* hudoc (2004) DA. In *Baghli v France* 1999-VIII; 33 EHRR 32 paras 29–31 an application concerning a deportation order imposed on a settled immigrant, the applicant had never been served with the full text of the final judgment dismissing his appeal against the deportation order. The Court rejected the government's preliminary objection to the effect that it would have been straightforward for the applicant or his lawyer to have established the tenor of the judgment against him. The Court held that the six-month period cannot start to run until the applicant has effective and sufficient knowledge of the final domestic decision.

[154] *Andorka and Vavra v Hungary Nos 25694/03 and 28338/03* hudoc (2006) DA.

[155] *Celik v Turkey No 52991/99* hudoc (2004) DA.

[156] *X v France No 9908/82*, 32 DR 266 (1983). See also *Ali Sahmo v Turkey No 37415/97* hudoc (2003) DA and *Gama Da Costa v Portugal No 12659/87*, 65 DR 136 (1990).

[157] *Haralambidis and Others v Greece* hudoc (2001); *Papachelas v Greece* 1999-II; 30 EHRR 923 GC.

[158] *Tahsin Ipek v Turkey No 39706/98* hudoc (2000) DA; *Yavuz and Others v Turkey No 48064/99* hudoc (2005) DA.

[159] In states which have only recently ratified the Convention, this overlaps considerably with questions of compatibility *ratione temporis* considered below. See also Loucaides, *The Concept of a Continuing Human Rights Violation* in *Ryssdal Mélanges*, pp 803–13.

[160] *No 214/56*, 2 YB 214 at 230–4 (1958). See also: *Tete v France No 11123/84*, 54 DR 52 (1987) (provisions of French electoral law concerning election to the European Parliament).

[161] *No 39437/98* hudoc (2004). See also *McFeeley v UK No 8317/78*, 20 DR 44 (1980): repeated disciplinary punishments for persistent refusal to obey the prison rules was considered to amount to a continuing situation.

In *Iatridis v Greece*[162] the applicant had obtained a decision of the Athens Court of First Instance in his favour, quashing an eviction order against him concerning an open-air cinema which he had operated. The Minister of Finance had refused to comply with that decision. The Court found that this refusal meant that the six-month period did not run from the decision of the Athens Court of First Instance.

In criminal matters, the possibility of pending investigations or charges can give rise to problems in determining whether there is a continuing situation. In *Withey v UK*,[163] the Court considered the practice of leaving charges on the file, ie not proceeding with the case but leaving the possibility of the charges being resurrected in the event of a repetition of the alleged acts. The issue for the Court was whether the charges could be said to be still pending. Since the prosecution would have had to apply to the court to resurrect the proceedings and the applicant could oppose this, even if there was no undertaking by the prosecution not to pursue the charges, the order of the court leaving the charges on the file was taken to be the date for ending the criminal proceedings. The application, being submitted six months after this date, was out of time.

The rule will start to apply, however, if the continuing situation comes to an end. This is a common ground for rejecting complaints relating to detention, a continuing situation, which are filed six months after the date of release from detention.[164] However, if proceedings challenging a deprivation of liberty commence after the detention has finished, the six-month period will run from the end of the proceedings not the end of the detention.[165] In the same vein, trial proceedings leading to imprisonment are not regarded as leading to a continuing deprivation of liberty in respect of a complaint concerning the fairness of proceedings. Acts of expropriation depriving a person of his property are not usually seen as involving a continuing situation of lack of property.[166]

Finally, the running of the period may be interrupted by 'special circumstances' which absolve the applicant from the strict application of the rule. The burden of establishing such circumstances falls on the applicant. In *K v Ireland*[167] the applicant maintained that his mental state rendered him incapable of lodging a complaint within the time limit. The Commission rejected the claim notwithstanding the fact that the government did not contest the existence of special circumstances. It noted laconically that his state of mind did not appear to hinder the pursuit of numerous appeals before the Irish courts and, further, that Ireland could not waive the requirement in this way. While preventing a prisoner from writing to the Court would undoubtedly constitute a special circumstance, error or ignorance of the law would not.[168]

Cases frequently arise when applicants seek to amend or amplify their application to the Court. Such amendments may be rejected for non-compliance with the six-month rule, even if the initial application is introduced within the time limit. Thus while the date of introduction is taken as the date on which the applicant sets out even summarily, the object of the application, this should not be taken as a licence to introduce entirely new complaints that are not mentioned in the original application. For example the Court has found that the mere fact that the original application invoked Article 6 of the Convention

---

[162] 1999-II; 30 EHRR 97.   [163] *No 59493/00* hudoc (2003).

[164] For example, *Ječius v Lithuania* 2000-IX; 35 EHRR 400 para 44; *Ege v Turkey No 47117/99* hudoc (2004) DA.

[165] *O'Hara v UK No 37555/97* hudoc (2000) DA.

[166] *X v UK No 7379/76*, 8 DR 211 (1976). Cf, *Malhous v Czech Republic No 33071/96*, 2000-XII GC; *Kopecký v Slovakia* 2004-IX; 41 EHRR 944 para 35 GC; and *Chrysostomos v Turkey Nos 15299/89, 15300/89 and 15318/89*, 68 DR 216 (1991).

[167] *No 10416/83*, 38 DR 158 (1984). See also *X v Austria No 6317/73*, 2 DR 87 (1975).

[168] *Bozano v France* A 111 (1987); 9 EHRR 297.

is not sufficient to constitute introduction of all subsequent complaints made under that provision,[169] nor will it be sufficient to simply send documents from domestic proceedings and subsequently introduce complaints based on those proceedings.[170] Complaints raised after the end of the six months' period will not be examined unless they touch upon particular aspects of complaints initially raised within the period. However, it will be sufficient if the complaints are raised in substance or arise from the facts as submitted within the period.[171]

5. OTHER GROUNDS OF INADMISSIBILITY

Article 35(2) and (3) provide:

2. The Court shall not deal with any application submitted under Article 34 that:
   (a) is anonymous; or
   (b) is substantially the same as a matter which has already been examined by the Court or has already been submitted to another procedure of international investigation or settlement and if it contains no relevant new information.

3. The Court shall declare inadmissible any individual application submitted under Article 34 which it considers incompatible with the provisions of the Convention or the protocols thereto, manifestly ill-founded, or an abuse of the right of application.

Unlike the non-exhaustion and six-month rule these requirements, as is clear from the wording of Article 35, do not apply to inter-state cases. The Court has, however, left it open that an inter-state complaint could be rejected as abusive in the light of general principles of international law.[172] The question of inadmissibility on the ground that the application is 'incompatible with the provisions of the Convention' (Article 35(3)) is considered separately below.[173]

I. ANONYMITY (ARTICLE 35(2)(A))

In practice this is not an important ground of inadmissibility since applicants are required to disclose their identity when completing the application form. The Court's Registry will not register an anonymous application.[174] However, *in Shamayev v Georgia and Russia*,[175] the Court, in exceptional circumstances, accepted applications registered under pseudonyms where the applicants felt that they would have been at risk of serious ill-treatment if they had furnished their full names. The Court accepted the reasons for initially furnishing pseudonyms and accepted that the applicants were real and identifiable persons. It is, however, open to applicants to request that their identity not be made public but they are required to submit a statement of the reasons justifying this request. If this request is granted by the President of the Chamber,[176] anonymity will be ensured in any eventual

---

[169] *Allan v UK No 48539/99* hudoc (2004) DA.

[170] *Bozinovksi v FYRM No 68368/01* hudoc (2005) DA.

[171] See *Paroisse Gréco-Catholique Sambata Bihor v Romania No 48107/99* hudoc (2004) pp 14–16 DA and references therein.

[172] *Loizidou v Turkey (Preliminary Objections)* A 310 (1995); 20 EHRR 99. As did the Commission in *Cyprus v Turkey (first and second applications)*, 2 DR 125 at 138 (1975).

[173] See p 787.   [174] See Rule 55 of the Rules of Court.

[175] *No 36378/02* hudoc (2003) pp 36–8 DA.

[176] Rule 47 of the Rules of Court gives the president of the chamber the power to authorize anonymity in 'exceptional and duly justified cases'.

judgment or decision in their case. However, the identity of the applicant is not concealed from the respondent government. The application and all documents relating to it are copied in full and sent to the representative of the government concerned.

In an application brought by a Church, a political party, or other non-governmental organization concerning an infringement of its rights, it is not necessary to reveal the identity of members, though Rule 45 of the Rules of Court requires that the application be signed by those persons competent to represent the organization. However, the Commission and Court have also held that a Church or other religious organization is capable of possessing and exercising Article 9 rights in its own capacity in addition to acting as a representative of its members.[177]

II. SUBSTANTIALLY THE SAME (ARTICLE 35(2)(B))

The Court will reject an application under this head if the factual basis of the new application is the same as that of an application that has previously been rejected by it[178] or has been the subject of a friendly settlement between the parties.[179] It makes no difference if the second application contains new legal arguments.[180] However, if the applicant has previously made an application to the Court but has not pursued it or if no formal decision has been taken by the Court then the rule will not apply.[181] The situation is also different where new information is provided which alters the factual basis of the complaint. For example, an application which has been rejected for non-exhaustion of domestic remedies may be re-examined after the applicant has had recourse to the remedy.[182] Similarly it is open to applicants complaining of length of proceedings or of the length of detention on remand to bring a second application if the proceedings have still not terminated or if the detention continues.[183] In such cases, although the Convention complaint remains the same, the facts have evolved.[184]

Occasionally numerous applications are brought concerning the same matter; for example social security legislation affecting large numbers of people or property disputes affecting entire regions of a country. While often these applications result from the same piece of legislation or administrative decision, they would not normally be rejected under this head where they are brought by different applicants. The Court will normally select one case which will act as a lead or pilot case for the other applications. While the Court is examining this pilot case, the other applications will be adjourned. If the Court finds the pilot case inadmissible or that there is no violation then the follow up cases will be rejected as manifestly ill-founded rather than substantially the same.

The purpose of the second limb of Article 35(2)(b) is to prevent a duplication of examination by different international bodies.[185] The term 'international investigation or

---

[177] *X and Church of Scientology v Sweden No 7805/77*, 16 DR 68 (1979); *Omkarananda and Divine Light Zentrum v Switzerland No 8118/77*, 25 DR 105 (1981); *Metropolitan Church of Bessarabia and Others v Moldova* 2001-XII para 105; *Church of Scientology Moscow v Russia* hudoc (2007); 46 EHRR 304; *The Moscow Branch of the Salvation Army v Russia* 2006-XI; 44 EHRR 912; and, concerning a mosque, *El Jajjaoui and Stichting Touba Moskee v Netherlands No 25525/03* hudoc (2006) DA.

[178] See eg, *Ekholm v Finland No 5952/03* hudoc (2006) DA.

[179] *Kezer and Others v Turkey No 58058/00* hudoc (2004) DA.

[180] *Lutz v France No 49531/99* hudoc (2002) DA; *IJL v UK No 39029/97* hudoc (1999) DA.

[181] *Surmeli v Germany No 75529/01* hudoc (2004) DA.

[182] *AD v Netherlands No 21962/93*, 76 DR 157 (1994).

[183] *Delgado v France No 38437/97* hudoc (1998) DA; *W v FRG No 10785/84*, 48 DR 102 (1986); and *Vallon v Italy No 9621/81*, 33 DR 217 (1983).

[184] See *CG and Others v Bulgaria No 1365/07* hudoc (2007) DA.

[185] *Smirnova and Smirnova v Russia Nos 46133/99 and 48183/99* hudoc (2002) DA.

settlement' is rather vague in two respects: what is considered an *international* procedure and precisely what kind of procedure the Article contemplates. In respect of the former, in *Jelicic v Bosnia and Herzegovina*[186] the Court was called upon to decide whether the Human Rights Chamber for Bosnia and Herzegovina was a domestic or an international body. It examined various aspects of the Chamber—the body's composition, its competence, its place (if any) in the legal system of Bosnia and Herzegovina, and its funding. While the Chamber had been set up pursuant to an international agreement, had a mixed composition of national and foreign members, and depended on international organizations for both part of its funding and the supervision of the execution of its decisions, many of these factors were related to the particular post-war context of its establishment and were of a transitional nature. The mandate of the Chamber was to assist only Bosnia and Herzegovina in honouring its own obligations under the Convention and other human rights treaties and was finally terminated by Bosnia and Herzegovina and its entities in 2003 without the involvement of any other state. The Court was therefore able to conclude that the Chamber was part of the legal system of Bosnia and Herzegovina and of an essentially domestic character.

When the procedure in question is of an international nature then it is clear from the case-law that the term refers to refers to judicial or quasi-judicial proceedings similar to those set up by the Convention. In this respect, the procedures contemplated by the rule are procedures in which a matter is submitted by way of a petition lodged by an applicant. For example, in *Varnava and Others v Turkey*[187] the United Nations Committee on Missing Persons in Cyprus did not constitute another international investigation or settlement since it could not receive petitions, could not attribute responsibility for the deaths of any missing persons and had limited investigative capacity.

Equally, the fact that the problem of foreign currency savings in the various successor states of the Socialist Federal Republic of Yugoslavia had been the subject of failed arbitration by the International Monetary Fund and failed mediation by the Bank for International Settlements was not a bar to the affected individuals filing an application with the Strasbourg Court.[188] The parties to the arbitration and mediation proceedings were different from those before the Court and indeed the IMF and BIS proceedings appear to have been entirely inter-governmental.

The term 'international investigation or settlement' refers to institutions and procedures set up by states and excludes non-governmental bodies. Thus in *Lukanov v Bulgaria*[189] the Human Rights Committee of the Inter-Parliamentary Union, a non-governmental organization, was not considered to fall within the scope of the Article. The term has been interpreted as encompassing organs such as the United Nations Human Rights Committee and other enforcement agencies set up within the UN system (such as International Labour Organization bodies). In the *GCHQ* case[190] the government had drawn the Commission's attention to the fact that an identical complaint had been examined by ILO organs. The Commission did not consider that the applicant was substantially the same since the ILO complaint had been brought by the Trades Union Congress on its own behalf whereas the *GCHQ* case had been brought by the Council of Civil Service Unions and six individual applicants. It is implicit in the Commission's decision, however, that the rule would have been applied had the applicant been the TUC. In a subsequent case, *Martin and 22*

---

[186] *No 41183/02* hudoc (2005) DA.   [187] *Nos 16064–66/90 and 16068–73/90*, 93-A DR 5 (1998).
[188] *Kovacic and Others v Slovenia Nos 44574/98, 45133/98 and 48316/9* 2004, DA.
[189] *No 21915/93*, 80-A DR 180 (1995).
[190] *Council of Civil Service Unions v UK No 11603/85*, 50 DR 228 (1987).

Others v Spain[191] the Commission rejected an Article 11 complaint that the applicants had been dismissed because of trade union activities on the basis that the same complaint had been made and examined by the Committee of Freedom of Association provided for under ILO Convention No 87. Although the ILO complaint had been brought by a major trade union body, it had been joined by the union branches representing the applicants. In the Commission's view, the European Convention complaint had been brought by essentially the same applicants.

Complaints that have been lodged with the United Nations Human Rights Committee have also been rejected on this basis even where the applicant had filed his Convention complaint first and had sought an adjournment of the United Nations procedure. What counts is the situation which exists at the moment of examination of admissibility. The fact that an identical case is pending before the Human Rights Committee and has not been withdrawn is enough for the rule to apply.[192] However, if the application before the Court is significantly wider than the application before the Human Rights Committee then the rule will not apply. Thus in *Smirnova and Smirnova v Russia*[193] the first applicant had lodged a petition before the Human Rights Committee concerning her arrest and detention on fraud charges. Further proceedings and arrests took place involving her and the second applicant, her sister. The first applicant's internal passport was also withdrawn. The Strasbourg application was brought by both sisters and covered various aspects of the proceedings since the first arrest as well as the circumstances surrounding the withdrawal of the internal passport. The Court noted that the petition before the Human Rights Committee concerned only the first applicant and its effects could not be extended to the second applicant. While the scope of the factual basis for the first applicant's application to the Court went back to the first arrest it was significantly wider than that. Therefore the application was not substantially the same. Equally, the rule will not apply unless the complainants before the two institutions are identical. In *Folgerø and others v Norway*[194] a group of parents and their children had unsuccessfully taken proceedings in Norway challenging the absence of an exemption from a religious education course in public schools. Some of the parents filed an application in Strasbourg, while four other sets of parents lodged a communication in Geneva.[195] Even though the applicants before the Court and the authors of the communication before the Human Rights Committee were complaining about the same question, if the complainants before the two institutions were not identical then the application to the Court was not substantially the same and could not be rejected.[196]

---

[191] No 16358/90, 73 DR 120 (1992).

[192] *Calcerrada Fornieles v Spain No 17512/90*, 73 DR 214 (1992).   [193] See n 185 above, at pp 10–11.

[194] No 15472/02 hudoc (2006) DA. It is worth noting that unsuccessful applicants to Strasbourg are not prevented from then taking their cases to the Human Rights Committee in Geneva since the similar provision in the Optional Protocol to the ICCPR (Article 5(2)(a)) only provides that a communication will be inadmissible if it is *being examined* under another procedure of international investigation or settlement. One example of this is *Correia de Matos v Portugal No 48188/99* 2001-XII DA which before the Human Rights Committee became Communication No 1123/2002, 28 March 2006; 13 IHRR 948 (2006). The applicant, a lawyer, claimed unsuccessfully in Strasbourg that the requirement that he be represented in criminal proceedings was a violation of his right to fair trial under Articles 6(1) and 3(c) of the Convention. After his application had been rejected as manifestly ill-founded, the applicant successfully argued the same point before the Human Rights Committee on the basis of the almost identical wording of Article 14(3)(d) of the Covenant. See O'Boyle, in *Liber Amicorum Luzius Wildhaber* and Phong, 7 HRLR 385 (2007).

[195] *Leirvag v Norway*, decision of 23 November 2004; 4 IHRR 909.

[196] The Norwegian government had argued the same point before the Human Rights Committee under Article 5(2)(a) of the Optional Protocol (see previous note), arguing that the Committee could not examine the communication because it was being examined in Strasbourg. The Committee rejected that argument on the

III. MANIFESTLY ILL-FOUNDED (ARTICLE 35(3))

This provision requires the Court to make a preliminary examination of the merits of an application and decide whether it deserves further examination at the merits stage. The term has been broadly interpreted as encompassing cases which have no merit, because the applicant has failed to substantiate his allegations, to cases where the Court considers that no *prima facie* violation of the Convention has been made out.[197] This spectrum of standards, ranging from totally unmeritorious to no *prima facie* breach, means in effect that the qualification 'manifestly' may not always be applied and that cases will be rejected on the grounds that the Court considers them to be 'ill-founded'. In its practice the Court has departed from the literal and ordinary meaning of the words employed in this provision. Occasionally, the practice of the Court in this regard has given rise to criticism on the grounds that there is an excessive tendency to reject cases that might not survive scrutiny but which are perhaps deserving of full examination on the merits. The question is asked how a case can be rejected as *manifestly* ill-founded after extensive legal argument, often involving an oral hearing, and a lengthy fully reasoned decision of the Court with which not all the judges agree?[198] It is true that there is a general European interest in having important issues of interpretation of the Convention examined at the highest level. However, given the extraordinary numbers of cases pending before the Court, this practice has become an important technique in the selection process that is essential to the Court's survival. Finally, it should be noted that admissibility decisions being final, there is no possibility of the applicant requesting referral of the decision to the Grand Chamber under Article 43 of the Convention. As already noted, an inter-state case cannot be rejected on this basis.

IV. ABUSE OF THE RIGHT OF PETITION (ARTICLE 35(3))

Dismissal on this ground is a rare occurrence and is mostly reserved for applicants who file multiple complaints which have no foundation. Since the introduction of the Committee system under Protocol 11, which enables the Court to dispose summarily of groundless complaints, rejection on this ground has become unnecessary. Nevertheless the Court has from time to time asserted the right to police the petition system by considering applications to be abusive. In particular it has stressed that it is not its task to examine a succession of ill-founded and querulous complaints which create unnecessary work and hinders it in fulfilling its real function.[199] The persistent use of insulting, provocative, and threatening language may also be considered abusive, particularly where the applicant has been warned of the possible consequences.[200] Serious defamatory

---

same grounds as the Court later rejected it, holding that 'the same matter' had to be understood as 'referring to one and the same claim concerning the same individual, as submitted by that individual'.

[197] The Court frequently uses this ground for dismissing *de plano* applications which make numerous unsupported or worthless complaints. Such cases will be rejected by Committees using the so-called 'global formula' which reads: 'An examination of this case by the Court as it has been submitted does not disclose any appearance of a violation of the rights and freedoms set out in the Convention.'

[198] Recent examples might include *Garaudy v France No 65831/01*, 2003-IX DA (various proceedings against applicant for Holocaust denial); *Weber and Saravia v Germany No 54934/00* hudoc (2006) DA (strategic monitoring system for telecommunications); *Eskinazi and Chelouche v Turkey No 14600/05* hudoc (2005) DA (compatibility of obligations under the Hague Convention on the Civil Aspects of International Child Abduction with Article 8 of the Convention).

[199] *M v UK No 13284/87*, 54 DR 214 (1987).

[200] *Duringer and Grunge v France Nos 61164/00 and 18589/02*, 2003-II DA; *Stamoulakatos v UK No 27567/95* hudoc (1997) DA; *LR v Austria No 2424/65*, 20 CD 54 (1966); *X v Germany No 2724/66*, 22 CD 89 (1967); and

statements about the Court and Registry made in repeated applications will, if they exceed the normal bounds of criticism and amount to contempt of court, similarly be rejected as abusive.[201]

Misleading the Court deliberately or failing to reply to requests for information have also been construed as abusive.[202] In *Popov v Moldova*[203] the Court was prepared to consider the possibility that disclosing the terms of friendly settlement negotiations (which are confidential) could amount to an abuse of the right of petition but, perhaps given that the applicant had alleged improper coercion on the part of the respondent government to agree to a friendly settlement, the Court declined to declare the application inadmissible on this basis. The Court in *Popov* also confirmed that an application will not normally be rejected as abusive on the basis that it was offensive or defamatory unless it was knowingly based on untrue facts.

An application is also not considered abusive merely by the fact that it is motivated by the desire for publicity or propaganda unless the allegations are groundless or outside the purview of the Convention. The Commission so held in the case of *McFeeley v UK*[204] which had been brought by convicted IRA members engaged in an acrimonious protest at the requirement that they wear prison uniform. In another case, however, it stressed that it might be otherwise if the primary object of the case was to exert pressure or engage in political propaganda, alien to the purpose and spirit of the Convention.[205]

An application will not now be rejected under this head by an applicant who has fled from domestic law enforcement.[206] In *Van Der Tang v Spain*,[207] the applicant, a Dutch national, had been charged with drugs offences in Spain. He was detained on remand for over three years and then released on bail. While on bail he fled to the Netherlands. The Court found that the alleged violation of the Convention which the applicant complained of, his length of detention on remand, occurred before he absconded. His subsequent act of flight, albeit wrongful, did not render illegitimate his interest in obtaining a ruling from the Convention institutions. Similarly in *Averill v UK*,[208] the applicant had absconded after introducing his application. The Court again found that this did not render illegitimate his interest in obtaining a ruling on his complaint relating to the fairness of his trial. Finally, the fact that the applicant was a convicted spy who had escaped from prison in the United Kingdom and fled to the Soviet Union was not a bar to his subsequently bringing an application against the United Kingdom in relation to the length of civil proceedings brought to prevent him profiting from publishing in the United Kingdom.[209]

X and Y v Germany No 2625/65, 28 CD 26 (1968). However, when the language used is merely irrelevant, polemic, or excessively emotional this will not amount to an abuse (*Chernitsyn v Russia No 5964/02* hudoc (2004) DA; *Kolosovskiy v Latvia No 50183/99* hudoc (2004) DA).

[201] *Rehak v Czech Republic No 67208/01* hudoc (2004) DA.

[202] *Akdivar and Others v Turkey* 1996-IV; 23 EHRR 553 GC; *Varbanov v Bulgaria* 2000-X; *Keretchachvili v Georgia No 5667/02* hudoc (2006) DA; *Jian v Romania No 46640/99* hudoc (2004) DA; *Assenov and Others v Bulgaria*, 86-B DR 54 (1996).

[203] Hudoc (2005).

[204] *No 8317/78*, 20 DR 44 (1980). See also *McQuiston v UK No 11208/84*, 46 DR 182 (1986).

[205] *Foti Lentini and Cenerini v Italy Nos 7604/76, 7719/76 and 7781/77*, 14 DR 133 (1978).

[206] The Commission had rejected one case under this heading where the applicant, who had gone into hiding, complained about the length of extradition proceedings: *X v Ireland No 9742/82*, 32 DR 251 at 254 (1983).

[207] A 321 (1995); 22 EHRR 363.

[208] *No 36408/97* hudoc (1999) DA. See also the reports of the Commission in *Lala v Netherlands* A 297-A (1994); 18 EHRR 586 and *Pelladoah v Netherlands* A 297-B (1994); 19 EHRR 81.

[209] *Blake v UK No 68890/01* 2005-XII (decision), and hudoc (2006) (judgment).

6. INCOMPATIBILTY AND THE COMPETENCE OF THE COURT

This head of admissibility concerns the competence of the Court to examine individual or inter-state complaints. It is the practice of the Court to examine questions of competence as issues of admissibility under Article 35(3). However, it should be noted that, in contrast to the other admissibility criteria which are of a more procedural nature, questions of competence are essentially concerned with the limits of the Court's jurisdiction. As such, they must be examined by the Court on its own motion even when the respondent government fails to raise them.[210] They concern questions such as who is competent to bring a case and against whom (*ratione personae*), the subject matter of the application (*ratione materiae*), and the time and place of the alleged violation (*ratione temporis* and *ratione loci*).

I. COMPETENCE *RATIONE PERSONAE*

Competence *ratione personae* has two components: the application must be brought *against* a contracting state and *by* a legal or physical person with standing before the Court, in accordance with the terms of Article 34.

a. The respondent state

Competence or compatibility *ratione personae* requires the alleged violation of the Convention to have been committed by a contracting state or to be in some way imputable to it.[211] Individual complaints against states which have not ratified the Convention (or its Protocols) will therefore be rejected on this ground. If the complaint involves a Protocol which the respondent state has not ratified, this will also be considered incompatible *ratione personae*.[212]

Complaints can only be brought against the state concerning actions of the state itself or of state bodies such as the courts, the security forces, or local government. An individual cannot complain of the actions of a private person or body such as a lawyer or newspaper.[213] Acts by private individuals or bodies may, however, give rise to state responsibility in certain circumstances. The Court has repeatedly stated that the state cannot absolve itself from responsibility *ratione personae* by delegating its obligations to private bodies or individuals. Thus in *Costello-Roberts v UK*[214] the United Kingdom was found responsible for the use of corporal punishment in private schools alleged to be in breach of Article 3.

Moreover, the state may have a positive obligation to secure particular Convention rights against possible violations of those rights by private individuals. It is impossible to set out precisely the extent of states' positive obligations under the Convention since they

---

[210] *Blecic v Croatia* 2006-III para 67.

[211] *Gentilhomme, Schaff-Benhadji and Zerouki v France* hudoc (2002).

[212] *Rabus v Germany No 43371/02* hudoc (2006) DA; *Kaya v Turkey No 43517/02* hudoc (2005) DA; *Ay-Akguel v Switzerland No 48628/99* hudoc (2001) DA; *Partington v UK No 58853/00* hudoc (2003) DA; *Horsham v UK No 23390/94* hudoc (1995) DA.

[213] *X v UK No 6956/75*, 8 DR 103 (1976); *Durini v Italy No 19217/91*, 76-B DR 76 (1994). A lawyer, even if officially appointed, does not incur the liability of the state under the Convention: *W v Switzerland No 9022/80*, 33 DR 21 (1983).

[214] A 247-C (1993); 19 EHRR 112 para 27.

cannot be divorced from an examination of the substance of the rights guaranteed.[215] Nor can those positive obligations ever be clearly distinguished from the primarily negative nature of states' obligations under the Convention ie their obligation to refrain from committing any act which will violate an individual's Convention rights. Indeed the Court has often stated that the boundaries between states' negative and positive obligations do not always lend themselves to precise definition.[216]

In *Paul and Audrey Edwards v UK*,[217] the applicant's son, Christopher Edwards, had been placed in a prison cell with a violent, mentally ill prisoner, where he was beaten to death. The Court found a violation of Article 2 holding that the failure of the domestic authorities to properly process information on the risk posed by this other prisoner and the decision to place the two men in a cell together meant that the United Kingdom had failed in its positive obligation to protect the life of Christopher Edwards. The Court's task in this case was made easier by the fact that the domestic authorities had a substantial degree of control over the private parties involved and had (or should have had) sufficient information at their disposal in order to determine the risks involved in placing them in the same cell. Where the state does not have the same proximity to the circumstances leading to the violation of an individual's Convention rights by another private party, then the Court may be more reluctant to impose positive obligations on the state or find that it has breached those positive obligations. In *Osman v UK*,[218] the Court held that Article 2 imposed a positive obligation to take preventative operational measures to protect an individual whose life is at risk from another private person, but attached conditions to it, which were not met on the facts. The Court took a slightly different approach in *Siliadin v France*[219] where it held that that contemporary norms and trends in this field meant that states were under a positive obligation to criminalize and ensure the effective prosecution of acts of forced labour.

The development of the positive obligations doctrine has somewhat solved the difficult questions of state responsibility under the Convention which may or may not arise in respect of the acts of public corporations or other public bodies. The old Commission, for example, preferred to leave open the question whether the United Kingdom was responsible for the acts of the BBC or whether the actions of British Rail were imputable to the state.[220] What will appear decisive for the Court now is not the degree of autonomy a body has from the state or whether it is even a public body at all rather whether the act complained of is regulated by domestic law. Thus in *Vgt Verein Gegen Tierfabriken v Switzerland*,[221] where the applicant complained of the refusal of a private commercial television station to show its advertisement, the Court observed that this refusal was based on a law prohibiting political advertising and the responsibility of Switzerland was engaged on this basis.

Complaints under the Convention can only be brought by a 'person, non-governmental organisation or group of individuals claiming to be the victim of a violation' of a Convention right (Article 34). While 'non-governmental organizations' and 'groups of

---

[215] Though for an Article-by-Article analysis of the doctrine of positive obligations, see Mowbray, *The Development of Positive Obligations Under the European Convention on Human Rights by the European Court of Human Rights*, 2004.

[216] *X, Y and Z v UK* 1997-II; 24 EHRR 143 para 41.   [217] 2002-II.   [218] See above, p 43.

[219] See above, p 113.

[220] *Hilton v UK No 12015/86*, 57 DR 108 at 117–18 (1988): question of the state's responsibility under Article 8 for an act of the BBC in carrying out a security check left open; *Young, James and Webster v UK* A 44 (1981); 4 EHRR 38 paras 48–9, and B 39 Com Rep para 169 (1979). See also *X v UK No 8295/78*, 15 DR 242 (1978)—where the Commission also left open the question of state responsibility for an organ of the English Bar.

[221] 2001-VI; 34 EHRR 159.

individuals' are broad categories, they do not cover, for example, municipalities, other local government organizations, or semi-state bodies.[222] However, state broadcasters may be non-governmental organizations. Since they clearly do not exercise governmental powers but are, to an extent, public bodies, the Court will look to operational matters such as how the broadcaster is financed, its management and how it is regulated, and the competitive environment in which it operates. In applying this test to the Austrian broadcasting corporation, it found that it was a non-governmental organization capable of lodging an application.[223]

Complaints against the European Union as an international organization or which concern the acts of the Union will also be rejected as incompatible *ratione personae* until such time as the Union adheres to the Convention.[224] In *CFDT v European Communities*,[225] the Commission rejected the applicants' complaint (i) against the Communities; and (ii) against the member states jointly and severally. It considered that the member states, by taking part in a decision of the Council of the European Communities, had not exercised their 'jurisdiction' within the meaning of Article 1 of the Convention. Insofar as the complaint was directed against the states jointly, it was rejected on the basis that it was essentially a complaint against the Council of the European Communities. Insofar as the complaint was directed against the states severally, the complaint against France was held to be incompatible *ratione personae* since France had not yet accepted the right of individual petition. The remaining eight member states, by voting in the community institutions, were considered to have been acting outside the purview of their 'jurisdiction' for purposes of the Convention. Similarly in *Matthews v UK*[226] concerning the failure of the United Kingdom to extend elections for the European Parliament to Gibraltar, the Court was quite clear that acts of the EC as such could not be challenged before the Court because the EC (as it then was) was not a contracting party. However, the Court in *Matthews* was also quite clear that the United Kingdom, together with all the other parties to the (then) Maastricht Treaty, was responsible *ratione materiae* under Article 1 of the Convention for the consequences of that Treaty. In the particular circumstances of the case, the United Kingdom's responsibility derived from it having entered into treaty commitments after extending the applicability of Article 3 of Protocol No 1 to Gibraltar. In *Bosphorus Airways v Ireland*[227] the Court was more careful to distinguish jurisdiction from responsibility. The applicant had complained about the impounding of its leased aircraft by Ireland pursuant to an EC Regulation which in turn implemented a United Nations Security Council Resolution. It was not disputed that the impoundment of the aircraft was implemented by Ireland on its territory. In such circumstances the applicant company, as the addressee of the impugned act, fell within the 'jurisdiction' of Ireland, with the consequence that the complaint about that act was compatible *ratione loci*, *personae*, and *materiae* with the provisions of the Convention. The question of the scope Ireland's responsibility (in question given that the impoundment was in furtherance of

---

[222] *Municipal Section of Antilly v France No 45129/98*, 1999-VIII DA; *Rothenthurm Commune v Switzerland No 13252/87*, 59 DR 251 (1988); and *Ayuntamiento de M v Spain No 15090/89*, 68 DR 209 (1991). The same logic would appear to apply to local government officials to the extent that they may share responsibility for the acts complained of (*Pasa and Erkan Erol v Turkey* hudoc (2006) paras 19–22).

[223] *Osterreichischer Rundfunk v Austria* hudoc (2006) paras 46–54.

[224] See above, pp 28–30. Applications against other international organizations have strangely been inadmissible as incompatible *ratione materiae*: *Heinz v Contracting Parties who are also Parties to the European Patent Convention No 12090/92*, 74-A DR 125 (1994).

[225] *No 8030/77*, 13 DR 231 (1978).   [226] 1999-I; 28 EHRR 361 para 32 GC.

[227] *Bosphorus Hava Yollari Turizm ve Ticaret Anonim Sirketi (Bosphorus Airways) v Ireland* 2005-VI; 42 EHRR 1-para 137 GC.

its EC obligations) went to the merits of the complaint under Article 1 of Protocol 1. On the merits of the case, the Court held contracting states could not be absolved of their Convention responsibility by the transfer of sovereignty to an international organization. However, if equivalent protection of human rights was provided for in that international organization then the presumption would be that a state had not departed from the requirements of the Convention when it did no more than implement legal obligations flowing from its membership of the organization. The Court then stated that any such presumption could be rebutted if it is considered that the protection of Convention rights was manifestly deficient. In such cases it held that 'the interest of international co-operation would be outweighed by the Convention's role as a "constitutional instrument of European public order" in the field of human rights'.[228]

In *Behrami and Behrami v France* and *Saramati v France, Germany and Norway*[229] the Court was not prepared to go as far as to analyze the question of equivalence protection for human rights by subsidiary bodies of the United Nations Security Council, in particular KFOR and UNMIK in Kosovo.[230] In *Behrami* the first applicant complained about the death of his son as a result of a mine, which he alleged French troops serving with KFOR had negligently failed to clear. The second applicant complained about his injuries from the same mine. In *Saramati*, the applicant's complaint related to his detention by KFOR. The Court agreed that Saramati's detention fell within the mandate of KFOR but that in *Behrami*, the supervision of de-mining fell within the mandate of UNMIK. In any event, in both cases the Court found the impugned actions to be attributable to the United Nations. The Court, having regard to the extensive coercive measures available under Chapter VII of the United Nations Charter, found that it was not competent *ratione personae* to review acts of respondent states carried out on behalf of the United Nations. According to the Court, such acts, while not obligations flowing from membership of the United Nations, 'remained crucial to the effective fulfilment by the UNSC [United Nations Security Council] of its Chapter VII mandate and, consequently, by the UN of its imperative peace and security aim'.[231] This was essentially different from the *Bosphorus* case because there the impugned act had been carried out by the respondent state authorities on its territory. Thus in *Behrami* and *Saramati*, the question of presumption of Convention compliance did not arise.

b. Victim status

Article 34 requires that the applicant claim to be a victim of a violation of one of the rights in the Convention. 'Victim' is an autonomous concept that the Court will interpret independently of any domestic law concepts such as the capacity to take part in or bring proceedings.[232] The essence of the rule is that the applicant claims to be directly affected in some way by the matter complained of.[233]

---

228 Id, para 156.   229 *Nos 71412/01 and 78166/01* hudoc (2007) GC.

230 KFOR is the Kosovo Force, the international security presence in Kosovo established under United Nations Security Council Res 1244. UNMIK is the United Nations Interim Administration in Kosovo.

231 Id, para 149.

232 *Norris v Ireland* A 142 (1988); 13 EHRR 186 para 31 PC; *Scozzari and Giunta v Italy* 2000 VIII; 35 EHRR 243 para 139 GC.

233 However, it is not necessary to show damage: this is more a question for just satisfaction under Article 41 and there is no *de minimis* principle (*Eckle v Germany* A 51 (1982); 5 EHRR 1). In this respect, see following case law on potential victims, though if any damage has in fact been repaired by the state then the applicant may no longer be a victim; see the following section.

This provision has been characterized by the Court in *Klass v Germany*[234] as one of the keystones in the machinery of enforcement and at times it has been interpreted quite broadly by the Strasbourg organs. For example, in that case, the Court held that an individual may, under certain conditions, claim to be the victim of a violation occasioned by the mere existence of secret measures or of legislation permitting secret measures, without having to allege that such measures were in fact applied to him. Since all users or potential users of the postal and telecommunication services in the state were directly affected by legislation which provided for secret surveillance, they fell into the category of victim.[235] In subsequent cases, however, the Strasbourg organs have narrowed the breadth of this ruling and in such situations the Court will now ask applicants to provide evidence sufficient to establish a 'reasonable likelihood' of such interference.[236]

Even beyond such instances of secret or undeterminable interferences, the category of persons affected by a particular issue may be very broad. Thus in *Open Door and Dublin Well Woman v Ireland*,[237] which concerned a Supreme Court injunction against the provision of information by the applicant companies concerning abortion facilities outside Ireland, the Commission and Court considered that women of child-bearing age could claim to be victims since they belonged to a class of women who may have been adversely affected by the restriction. In other areas the Court has been more circumspect. In *Russian Conservative Party of Entrepreneurs v Russia*,[238] in which an application was brought by a prohibited political party and some of its supporters, the Court refused to entertain the argument that not allowing the party to stand in elections had forced its supporters to change their voting preference or not to cast their vote at all. Accepting this argument would, in the Court's words, 'confer standing on a virtually unlimited number of individuals to claim that their right to vote had been interfered with'.

The position is more problematic in respect of applicants who complain as 'potential victims', normally where they argue there is a threat or risk of them being directly affected by a particular measure. Following the ruling in *Open Door*, this is in principle possible but the Strasbourg organs have been careful to draw a distinction between such applicants and those who simply seek to challenge domestic laws. An application of the latter kind, often referred to in the case law as an *actio popularis*, will be declared inadmissible as incompatible *ratione personae*. As to the former, the Court will accept applications from persons who complain that there will be an interference with a Convention right if the state has already decided to take certain steps against them and the interference only requires the execution or implementation of that decision. The most common example of this is when an extradition or deportation order has been made but the applicant is waiting for the removal directions which will fix the date and time of his removal from the state.[239] Such an approach is linked to the imperative of seeking to protect an applicant from harm that may be irremediable. However, in such cases a final expulsion order will be required before the applicant will acquire victim status.[240] Beyond immigration

[234] A 28 (1978); 2 EHRR 214 para 34 PC.
[235] Even though in the hearing before the Court, the agent of the government stated that none of the applicants had been subject to the surveillance measures in question: id, para 37.
[236] *Halford v UK* 1997-III; 24 EHRR 523 paras 47–8; *N v UK No 12327/86*, 58 DR 85 (1988); *Hilton v UK No 12015/86*, 57 DR 108 (1988).
[237] A 246 (1992); 15 EHRR 44 para 41 PC.
[238] Hudoc (2007); 46 EHRR 863 para 78. See also *Georgian Labour Party v Georgia (No 2) No 9103/04* hudoc (2006) DA and (2007) DA. The same logic has been applied to readers of a newspaper seized by security forces complaining that this violated their right to receive information: *Tanrikulu, Cetin, Kaya and Others v Turkey Nos 40150/98, 40153/98 and 40160/98* hudoc (2001) DA.
[239] *Soering v UK* A 161 (1989); 11 EHRR 439 PC, see also para 199 Com Rep.
[240] *Vijayanathan and Pusparajah v France* A 241-B (1992); 15 EHRR 62.

matters, there are numerous other examples of potential victims in the Court's case law. In *Johnston v Ireland*[241] and *Marckx v Belgium*[242] the applicants risked being directly affected by provisions of succession legislation concerning children born out of wedlock. In *Campbell and Cosans v UK*[243] the Commission accepted that the applicants' children had a direct and immediate personal interest in complaining about corporal punishment by virtue of attending a school where it was practised even though they had not actually been punished. In *Dudgeon v UK* and *Norris v Ireland*[244] the Court considered that the very existence of legislation prohibiting private homosexual acts continuously and directly affected the applicants' private life—either they respected the law and refrained from the prohibited behaviour or they engaged in such acts and became liable to criminal prosecution. The Court has recently gone slightly further. In *SL v Austria*,[245] the applicant, aged seventeen when he introduced his application, complained about a provision of the Criminal Code prohibiting homosexual acts between an adult male and a minor between fourteen and eighteen. The applicant was directly affected by the legislation, even though there had been no prosecutions and, according to the Code, only his adult partner would have been prosecuted. It was sufficient that the applicant risked being involved in criminal investigations and having to testify on his sex life for him to be directly affected.

However, the Court has also said that it is for the applicant to produce reasonable and convincing evidence of the likelihood that a violation affecting him personally will occur; mere suspicion or conjecture is insufficient in this respect.[246] For example, *Association Ekin v France*[247] concerned the banning of a foreign language book in France on the grounds that it encouraged separatism and violence. In the domestic proceedings, the applicant association had challenged both the relevant law, on grounds of incompatibility with Articles 10 and 14 of the Convention, and the application of the law in its case. The *Conseil d'Etat* found in the applicant's favour but did not rule on the former question, the compatibility of the law with the Convention. The fact that the law therefore remained in force meant the risk that it would be applied again to the applicants was not hypothetical but real and effective and was sufficient to maintain its victim status. More recently in *Burden and Burden v UK*,[248] two elderly sisters complained about the discriminatory nature of inheritance tax. One of the sisters would have to pay the tax upon the death of the other. The government raised a preliminary objection as to the sisters' victim status on the ground that their complaint was prospective and hypothetical. The Court dismissed the objection holding that it was virtually certain that one of the sisters would be required to pay the tax on the property inherited from the other sister. In contrast, in *Christian Federation of Jehovah's Witnesses in France v France*[249] the applicant organization complained that two parliamentary commissions had produced reports which were critical of them and which also recommended a series of general measures to be taken against sects. The Court took the view that the reports produced had no legal effect and could not serve as a basis for future proceedings against Jehovah's Witnesses or the

---

[241] A 112 (1986); 9 EHRR 203 para 42 PC.   [242] A 31 (1979); 2 EHRR 330 para 27 PC.

[243] A 48 (1982); 4 EHRR 293 paras 116–17 Com Rep.

[244] A 45 (1981) para 41 PC and A 142 (1988) paras 28–34 PC. In both cases there had been no prosecution; but there was no stated policy *not* to enforce the law. There was thus a risk of prosecution. A similar approach was followed by the Court in *Modinos v Cyprus* A 259 (1993) paras 17–24, as regards the question whether there was an interference with the applicant's rights under Article 8 where the law had been described as a 'dead letter' because of its incompatibility with constitutional provisions. See also the dissenting opinion of Judge Pikis in the *Modinos* case.

[245] *No 45330/99* hudoc (2001) DA.

[246] *Halford v UK* 1997-III; 24 EHRR 523; *Ocic v Croatia No 46306/99* hudoc (1999) DA; *Noël Narvii Tauira and 18 Others v France*, 83 DR 112 (1995).

[247] 2001-VIII; 35 EHRR 1207.   [248] Hudoc (2006).   [249] *No 53430/99*, 2001-IX DA.

applicant organization, so it was not a victim. By the same token, in *Rosca Stanescu and Ardeleanu v Romania*,[250] where the two journalists complained that provisions of the criminal code outlawing defamation of public servants put them at risk of conviction, the Court found that the domestic court had expressly found that the relevant provision did not apply to the press so the applicants were no longer at risk.

In *Segi and Gestora Pro-Amnistia and Others v Austria and fourteen other States*,[251] the applicant organizations and their spokesperson challenged the European Union's Common Foreign and Security Policy common positions on combating terrorism. According to those common positions and an annexed list of organizations to whom they applied, the organizations were not subject to the provisions concerning the freezing of funds (Articles 2 and 3 of Common Position 2001/931/CFSP) but were subject to Article 4 which required member states, through police and judicial co-operation, to assist each other with respect to enquiries and proceedings conducted against the listed organizations. The Court distinguished between Articles 2 and 3 and Article 4, finding that the latter did not create any new powers which could be exercised against the applicants. Article 4 was only an obligation for member states to afford each other co-operation and, as such, was not directed at individuals and did not affect them directly. No particular measures had been taken against the applicants pursuant to the common position and the mere fact of being on the list was too tenuous to justify application of the Convention.

As stated above, where the applicant cannot demonstrate that he or she is directly affected, the Court may reiterate its time-honoured position that the Convention does not provide for applications in the form of an *actio popularis* nor may it form the basis of a claim made *in abstracto* that a particular law contravenes the Convention. The rule that the conditions governing individual applications under Article 34 are not necessarily the same as national criteria relating to *locus standi* may be relevant here: national law (and even national constitutions) may provide for abstract judicial review of legislative or executive acts but the Convention does not.[252] Thus it is not open to a citizen to complain in general of the provisions of abortion legislation or a general prohibition on assisted suicide unless he or she can show that they are in some way affected.[253] At the same time, an individual can complain of an administrative practice in breach of the Convention. However, it is not sufficient merely to allege the existence of an administrative practice; this must be shown by substantial evidence, namely evidence *prima facie* substantiating its existence.[254]

An applicant will be deprived of his status of 'victim' where the national authorities have acknowledged, either expressly or in substance, the breach of the Convention and then afforded appropriate redress for it.[255] A decision or measure that is merely favourable to the applicant is not in principle sufficient. This approach was confirmed in *Amuur v France*[256] where the applicants had come to France seeking refugee status and had been detained in the international transit zone at Orly airport. A domestic court had ruled that holding them in the international transit zone was unlawful but this was twenty-two

---

[250] *No 35441/97*, 2002-III DA.   [251] *Nos 6422/02 and 9916/02*, 2002-V DA.

[252] *Hoffman Karlskov v Denmark No 62560/00* hudoc (2003) DA where the applicant complained about a closed shop agreement in a sector that she did not work in (cf, *Jensen and Rasmussen v Denmark No 52620/99* hudoc (2003) DA where the applicants did work in the same sector as the closed shop agreement and were thus directly affected by it).

[253] *Sanles Sanles v Spain No 48335/99* 2000-XI DA (assisted suicide); *X v Austria No 7045/75*, 7 DR 87 (1976) (abortion).

[254] *Caraher v UK No 2452/94*, 2000-I DA and *Akdivar v Turkey*, 1996-IV; 23 EHRR 143 DA, where applicants' complaints to this effect were dismissed for lack of sufficient evidence.

[255] *Rotaru v Romania* 2000-V paras 33–8 GC.   [256] 1996-III; 2 EHRR 533.

days after they had been detained and, more importantly, two days after they had been deported. Similarly in *Mehemi v France (No 2)*,[257] the applicant, an Algerian national, had been made the subject of a permanent exclusion *order* from France after a criminal conviction. He had filed an application with the Court (*Mehemi v France (No 1)*)[258] alleging that this violated Article 8 of the Convention. This had resulted in a finding of a violation by the Court, after which the permanent exclusion order was commuted to a ten-year order. Once this expired, he was given a series of six-month residence permits. In response to Mr Mehemi's second application, the government argued that the residence permits meant he was no longer a victim. This argument was rejected since there had still been periods after the Court's first judgment where the applicant could not return to France and the temporary residence permits with their accompanying limitations were not comparable to the status he had previously enjoyed in France.

This issue more commonly arises in criminal proceedings where compensation for possible violations of the Convention is made by a reduction in the applicant's sentence. For example, in the earlier case of *Lüdi v Switzerland*[259] the applicant's sentence had been reduced to what his lawyer had suggested at the trial. He had complained, *inter alia* under Article 8, of the activities of an undercover agent whose evidence had led to his conviction on drug charges. The Court rejected the argument that he was no longer a victim since the authorities, far from acknowledging a violation, had expressly decided that the actions of the undercover agent were in fact compatible with the Convention. By contrast, in *Morby v Luxembourg*,[260] the applicant was guilty of corruption, the maximum sentence being one year's imprisonment and a sizeable fine. He successfully argued before the trial court that the proceedings had exceeded the reasonable time provided for in Article 6(1). The trial court considered it appropriate to impose a suspended sentence of nine months and a much-reduced fine. The Court considered that the trial court had expressly recognized and then made reparation for the alleged violation of Article 6(1) such that the applicant could not claim to be a victim. In the same manner, an acquitted defendant or a person against whom criminal proceedings have been discontinued cannot claim to be a victim of violations of the Convention which allegedly took place in the course of the proceedings.[261] However, this will only apply when the applicant is no longer affected at all by the proceedings in question. In *Correira de Matos v Portugal*[262] the applicant had been charged with insulting a judge and had been denied the right to represent himself. He had later benefited from a general amnesty law but still had to pay damages to the judge in question. This was enough to maintain his victim status.

The question has also arisen of whether the payment of compensation satisfies the double criteria of a recognition, express or in substance, on the one hand and the need for adequate redress on the other. It may be argued that compensation on its own, even if a substantial amount, only satisfies the latter criterion. Even so, in *Rechachi and Abdulhafid v UK*[263] the applicants had complained of unlawful detention (the legal basis

[257] No 53470/99 hudoc (2002) DA, followed in *Sayoud v France No 70456/01* hudoc (2006) DA.
[258] 1997-VI; 30 EHRR 739.
[259] A 238 (1992); 15 EHRR 173 para 34. See also *Constantinescu v Romania* 2000-VIII; 33 EHRR 817; *Guisset v France* 2000;-IX; 34 EHRR 1100; *Wejrup v Denmark No 49126/99* hudoc (2002) DA; *Jensen v Denmark No 48470/99* hudoc (2001) DA.
[260] No 27156/02 hudoc (2003) DA. See also *Beck v Norway* hudoc (2001).
[261] *Osmanov and Husseinov v Bulgaria No 54178/00* hudoc (2003) DA; *Eğinlioğlu v Turkey No 31312/96* hudoc (1998) DA.
[262] No 48188/99, 2001-XII DA.
[263] No 55554/00 hudoc (2003) DA. See also *Powell v UK No 45305/99*, 2000-V DA; *Hay v UK No 41894/98*, 2000-XI DA.

for the offences with which they were charged had lapsed) and had received sizeable compensation from an *ex gratia* scheme under which there was no acknowledgement of the alleged breach. However, the Metropolitan Police Commissioner had expressly acknowledged the unlawfulness of their detention and the Home Secretary had announced the problem of the lapse of the offences in Parliament. The applicants were therefore no longer victims.

Professional associations and non-governmental organizations, to be regarded as victims, must show that they are in some way affected by the measure complained of. Normally, organizations will not be able to claim to be a victim of measures which affect the rights of their members; so for example in *Norris,* discussed above, the Commission did not regard the National Gay Federation as a victim of the law prohibiting homosexual acts.[264] Similarly, in *Maupas and Others v France*[265] the issue was the expropriation of property in order to build a motorway. The applicants were two home owners and a community association set up to defend the rights of those affected by the motorway building scheme. The Court rejected that part of the application brought by the association. In contrast, where an association set up to defend the rights of a group of people is party to domestic proceedings while its individual members are not, then both the association and the individual members can be victims of any violations arising from those domestic proceedings. The Court, in so finding in *Gorraiz Lizarriga and Others v Spain,*[266] observed that when citizens are confronted with particularly complex administrative decisions, recourse to collective bodies such as associations is sometimes the only means whereby they can defend their interests properly.

Churches, newspapers, political parties, and trade unions may of course be directly affected in their own right in relation to the freedom of religion, expression, and association.[267] Companies can also claim to be victims of violations of, for example, property rights or the right to have proceedings heard within a reasonable time.[268] However, not all the rights in the Convention are of relevance to them.[269] In *Pine Valley v Ireland*[270]

---

[264] *No 10581/83,* 44 DR 132 (1985).

[265] Hudoc (2006). See also *Association de défense des intérêts du sport v France No 36178/03* hudoc (2007) DA; *L'association et la ligue pour la protection des acheteurs d'automobiles, Abid and 646 others v Romania No 34746/97* hudoc (2001) DA; *Conka, la Ligue des droits de l'homme and others v Belgium No 51564/99* hudoc (2001) DA; *L'association des amis de Saint-Raphaël et de Frejus and others v France No 45053/98* hudoc (2000) DA; *Le comité des médecins à diplômes étrangers v France No 39527/98* hudoc (1999) DA; *Purcell v Ireland No 15404/89,* 70 DR 262 (1991).   [266] 2004-III para 38.

[267] For churches and other religious organizations, see above Ch 10 and references therein. For newspapers, from many authorities, see *Sunday Times v UK* A 30 (1979); 2 EHRR 254 PC and more recently *Tanrikulu, Cetin, Kaya and others* (n 238 above) and references therein. For trade unions see most recently *Associated Society of Locomotive Engineers and Firemen (ASLEF) v UK* hudoc (2007); 45 EHRR 793. However, the Court has also found that *ad hoc* strike committees have no standing in this respect: *Manole v Moldova No 13936/02* hudoc (2004) and (2006). For political parties see *Refah Partisi (the Welfare Party) and Others v Turkey* 2003 II GC.

[268] *Comingersoll SA v Portugal* 2000-IV; 31 EHRR 722 GC.

[269] Eg, a company could not claim to be a victim of a violation of, *inter alia,* Article 2 (right to life) or Article 3 (freedom from torture, inhuman, or degrading treatment) or Article 5 (unlawful detention). In *Open Door and Dublin Well Woman and Others v Ireland* A 246 (1992); 15 EHRR 44 PC the Commission found that the Open Door clinic could not make a privacy complaint on behalf of its clients (pp 60–1). The issue was left open by the Court (paras 81–3). The question also arises as to whether a company or other association can receive pecuniary compensation for non-pecuniary damage. This will very much depend on the nature of the violation found: see *Comingersoll,* id, para 32. In that case, the Grand Chamber was prepared to make an award of 1,500,000 escudos for non-pecuniary damage for a violation of Article 6 on account of length of proceedings and the 'considerable inconvenience and prolonged uncertainty' that these proceedings would have caused the company, its directors, and shareholders. For a survey of the applicability of the Convention to companies see Austin, 11 Commercial Law Practitioner 223 (2004).

[270] A 222 (1991) paras 40–3.

the Court upheld the status of victim of the two applicant companies even though one had been struck off the register of companies and a receiver had been appointed for the other. The Court considered that the companies were no more than vehicles through which the third applicant (Mr Healy) had sought to implement a property development for which outline planning permission had been granted. To draw a distinction between the applicants was thus regarded as artificial. In addition the company that had been dissolved had initiated the national proceedings and obtained the planning permission. This was considered sufficient to permit a claim to be made on its behalf. Insolvency was also considered immaterial to the Article 34 issue. It is now established that the share-holders of a company including the majority shareholders cannot claim to be victims of an alleged violation of the company's rights under the Convention.[271] An exception will only be made when it is clearly established that it is impossible for the company to apply to the Court through the organs set up under its articles of incorporation or, in the event of liquidation, through its liquidators.[272] The same principle will apply when the application is brought on behalf of a company in administration by a former president of the board or majority shareholder. In *Credit and Industrial Bank v Czech Republic*,[273] the essence of the complaint was the denial of effective access to court to oppose or appeal against the appointment of a compulsory administrator. The Court there stated that to hold that the administrator alone was authorized to represent the bank in lodging an application would be to render the right of individual petition theoretical and illusory.

c. The loss of victim status after the lodging of an application

If the basis of the applicant's complaint is remedied while proceedings are pending before the Court, then the Court will frequently find that he or she can no longer claim to be a victim and it will strike the case out of the list. Early case law seemed to indicate that an applicant could cease to be a victim if a remedy was provided in the course of proceed-ings before the Court without an express recognition of a violation of the Convention by the contracting state.[274] This was problematic given that in such cases the applicant was deprived of a ruling on a complaint which raised important Convention issues of general interest. However, the Court's recent case law clearly indicates that recognition of a viola-tion, either expressly or in substance, is required together with adequate redress.[275] As with measures taken before an application is filed (*Amuur, Lüdi* above), partial redress is not enough.[276] This is very much an individual assessment based on the particular facts of the case but the general test applied by the Court is first whether the circumstances com-plained of by the applicant still obtain and secondly where the effects of a possible viola-tion of the Convention on account of those circumstances have also been redressed.[277]

---

[271] *Pokis v Latvia No 528/02* hudoc (2006) DA; *Terem Ltd Chechetkin; and Olius v Ukraine* hudoc (2005) para 28; *Vesela and Loyka v Slovakia No 54811/00* hudoc (2005) DA; *F Santos Lda and Fachadas v Portugal* 2000-X; and *Agrotexim and Others v Greece* A 330-A (1995) paras 59–72.

[272] See *Agrotexim* and *Vesela and Loyka ibid*; *CDI Holding and Others v Slovakia No 37398/97* hudoc (2001) DA; *Camberrow MM5 AD v Bulgaria No 50357/99* hudoc (2004) DA and *GJ v Luxembourg* hudoc (2000); 36 EHRR 710 paras 22–5.

[273] 2003-XI; 39 EHRR 860 para 51.

[274] See eg, *X v Denmark No 7658/76*, 15 DR 128 (1978) and *Pitarque v Spain No 13420/87*, 62 DR 258 (1989).

[275] *Dalban v Romania* 1999-VI; 31 EHRR 893 paras 41–5 GC; and *Burdov v Russia* 2002-III; 38 EHRR 639 paras 27–32.

[276] *Chevrol v France* 2003-III paras 30–43.

[277] *Ohlen v Denmark* hudoc (2005) para 26. See also *Freimanis and Lidums v Lithuania* hudoc (2006) paras 66–74 and references therein.

For example in *Koç and Tambaş v Turkey*[278] the applicants had been convicted by a state security court, in apparent violation of Article 6(1) of the Convention. However, the sentences handed down by the Court had not been executed and, after changes to the Criminal Code, their criminal records had been erased. This meant that all the harmful consequences of the impartiality and independence of the state security court had been redressed and they could no longer be considered victims under Article 34.

Compensation or settlement of domestic claims will also be relevant to continued victim status. In *Caraher v UK*,[279] the applicant had accepted damages for the lethal shooting of her husband by security forces. Two soldiers were acquitted of all charges brought in connection with the shooting. After lodging the application, the applicant started civil proceedings before the High Court to obtain compensation. A settlement was reached in which she received £50,000 compensation. The Court looked to the adequacy and context of the settlement and found that such a sum was substantial. Furthermore, it rejected her contention that she was effectively forced to accept the settlement owing to the risk of being held liable to pay costs, observing that when cases are settled the parties are influenced by a number of considerations which affect the amount of compensation, in particular, the saving of time and further expense and the uncertainty of the final result.

In this connection, the Court has faced a number of difficulties in recent years where domestic remedies have been created specifically to redress systemic violations of the Convention but the compensation awarded by the domestic courts under these new remedies has been substantially less than the Court itself would have awarded. While the Court may tolerate a situation in which the level of compensation awarded by the domestic authorities may be lower than that awarded by the Court, if it is significantly lower the applicant can still be said to be a victim. Conversely, it is difficult to draw conclusions from these cases as to what percentage of compensation the Court will accept as a reasonable amount. In the leading cases on the question, nine Grand Chamber judgments against Italy,[280] the amount of compensation given under the Italian remedy, the Pinto Law, was very small, as little as 10 per cent in one case, justifying the continuation of the applicants' victim status. The Court did make it clear that in general it will look to the nature of the remedy or remedies on offer. If the remedy only awards compensation then the percentage will need to be higher than a remedy which awards compensation and also expedites pending proceedings. In such circumstances, lower compensation than the Court normally awards will be acceptable on the condition that the remedies are 'speedy, reasoned and executed very quickly'.[281]

d. Indirect victims

The Strasbourg organs have rendered Convention proceedings more effective by permitting applications not only by the person immediately affected (the direct victim) but also by an indirect victim. For example, in respect of alleged violations of the right to life (Article 2) close relatives such as spouses or parents will be regarded as indirectly

---

[278] No 46947/99 hudoc (2005) DA. Cf, *Achour v France No 67335/01* hudoc (2004) DA and *Senator Lines GmbH v 15 Member States No 56672/00*, 2004-IV GC.

[279] No 2452/94, 2001-I DA. See most recently *Murillo Saldias v Spain No 76973/01* hudoc (2006) (accepting compensation for flooding in which the applicant's family died meaning he was no longer a victim).

[280] See the leading judgment of *Scordino v Italy (No 1)* 2006-V; 45 EHRR 207 paras 214 and 215 GC. The other judgments are *Giuseppina and Orestina Procaccini v Italy* hudoc (2006) GC; *Ernestina Zullo v Italy* hudoc (2006) GC; *Cocchiarella v Italy* hudoc (2006) GC; *Musci v Italy* hudoc (2006) GC; *Apicella v Italy* hudoc (2006) GC; *Giuseppe Mostacciuolo v Italy (No 1)* hudoc (2006) GC; *Giuseppe Mostacciuolo v Italy (No 2)* hudoc (2006) GC; *Riccardi Pizzati v Italy* hudoc (2006) GC.

[281] See eg, *Cocchiarella*, id, para 97.

affected and able to bring applications.[282] Whether the person bringing the application is the deceased's legal heir in domestic law is irrelevant: what matters is the closeness of the ties between the applicant and the deceased.[283] Similarly for the purposes of Article 2 and complaints concerning the effectiveness of domestic investigations, it will be irrelevant if one close relative files a criminal complaint with the authorities but another relative brings the application to Strasbourg.[284]

Family members of those who have been detained or relatives of physically or mentally incapable victims such as young children, hospital patients, and persons of unsound mind—may also be seen as indirect victims.[285] Broadly speaking the concept of indirect victims encompasses those who are also prejudiced by the violation, as well as those who may have a valid personal interest in having the violation established such as parents or persons *in loco parentis*. In applications challenging decisions to take children into care, the parents will have standing to bring the application on their own behalf and on behalf of their children since the nature of their complaint is precisely the fact that they have been deprived of the parental rights in domestic law.[286]

A person may also be able to claim that he or she is directly affected as a consequence of a violation of the rights of someone else (eg, spouse or parents of a person liable to be deported, a wife complaining that damage to her husband's property also affected her own property, or someone suffering and anguish in violation of Article 3 on account of the disappearance of a close relative).[287] It is a quite different matter when the original victims die before they can bring an application and a relative or heir seeks to bring an application on their behalf. The victim status of the relative or heirs will depend on whether the complaints in question can be considered to be transferable or whether the right concerned is so eminently personal that it cannot be transferred. In *Sanles Sanles v Spain*[288] the applicant was the sister-in-law and legal heir of a man who had sought the right to assisted suicide in domestic courts. After his death, she brought an application before the Court complaining that the failure to recognize that right in domestic law was unjustified. The Court found that even supposing such a right was available in domestic law, it was in any event of an 'eminently personal and non-transferable nature'. Similarly, in *Fairfield and Others v UK*,[289] a case brought after the death of the victim, the applicants were the daughters and executors of a man who had been convicted of causing public disorder in the course of a demonstration he had conducted. The applicants claimed unsuccessfully that this was in violation of his rights under Articles 9 and 10. The Court

---

[282] *McCann v UK* A 324 (1995); 21 EHRR 97 GC.   [283] *AV v Bulgaria No 41488/98* hudoc (1999) DA.

[284] *Celikbilek v Turkey No 27693/95* hudoc (1999) DA (the deceased's wife lodged the criminal complaint; his brother was the applicant in Strasbourg, the Court finding that it would have made no difference if the applicant had lodged the complaint instead).

[285] *Paton v UK No 8416/78*, 19 DR 244 at 248 (1980) (a prospective father alleging a denial of the right to life on behalf of the foetus following the termination of his wife's pregnancy was considered to be so closely affected that he was a 'victim').

[286] *Scozzari and Giunta v Italy* 2000-VIII; 35 EHRR 243 GC paras 135–41; *Covezzi and Morselli v Italy No 52763/99* hudoc (2002) DA.

[287] *Kurt v Turkey* 1998-III; 27 EHRR 373; *X and Y v Belgium No 1478/62*, 6 YB 591 at 618–20 (1964); *Abdulaziz, Cabales, and Balkandali v UK Nos 9214/80, 9473/81 and 9474/81*, 29 DR 176 at 181–12 (1982). See also *Fidan v Turkey No 24209/04* hudoc (2000) DA where the applicant complained of the forced gynaecological examination of his wife, found to be admissible. However, in the case of disappearances involving anguish and suffering on the part of a relative, see also *Cakici v Turkey* 1999-IV; 31 EHRR 133 GC where the Court found no violation of Article 3 in respect of an applicant whose brother had disappeared. The Court distinguished *Kurt* on the grounds that, in that case, the applicant had been present at the time when the security forces took her son whereas in *Cakici* the applicant had been in another town. In addition, the applicant in *Cakici* had not borne the brunt of making enquiries as to the whereabouts of his disappeared brother.

[288] *No 48335/99*, 2000-XI DA.   [289] *No 24790/04*, 2005-VI DA.

emphasized that next of kin could only bring applications in their own right in exceptional circumstances, notably in relation to Article 2, and the applicants therefore lacked the requisite standing.

In *Bic and Others v Turkey*,[290] the application concerned complaints under Article 5 in relation to length of detention and Article 6 in relation to the length and fairness of criminal proceedings. It had been brought by the widow and children of Ihsan Bic. They brought the application three months after his death. The Court declared their application inadmissible since they could not be considered victims. While the Court recognized that under Article 2 individuals who are the next of kin of persons who have died in circumstances giving rise to issues under that Article may apply as applicants in their own right, it found that this was a particular situation governed by the nature of the violation alleged and considerations of the effective implementation of one of the most fundamental provisions in the Convention system. However complaints brought under Articles 5 and 6 of the Convention did not fall within this category. The Court noted in this regard that the case was to be distinguished from the applications which were introduced by the applicants themselves and only continued by their relatives after their subsequent death. Similarly in the case of *Georgia Makri and Others v Greece*,[291] the Court also held that relatives of a deceased person could not be considered as victims for complaints concerning the length of proceedings (Article 6) and lack of effective of remedies (Article 13).

However, two other decisions have cast doubt on this approach. In *Marie-Louise Loyen and Bruneel v France*,[292] the applicants were the late wife and daughter of a René Loyen who had brought proceedings in domestic courts relating to his detention in a hospital. They complained under Articles 6(1) and 13 as regards the length and fairness of those proceedings as well as under Article 5(5). The Court found that their status as close relatives and the fact that they had brought the application only two months after the death of Mr Loyen gave them a legitimate interest in bringing a case on his behalf. Again in *Ressegatti v Switzerland*[293] the application concerned complaints brought under Article 6 related to the unfairness of civil proceedings over a property dispute. It was filed by the husband and children of Alice Ressegatti-Müller who had died three months before. The Court considered the applicants were victims since the alleged violation had a direct effect on their property rights as heirs of Mrs Ressegatti-Müller. While in *Ressegatti* the difference with *Bic* is clear given the direct effect on the property rights of the heirs in *Ressegatti*, the difference between *Loyen* and *Bic* is perhaps less obvious given that in both *Loyen* and *Bic* there was an Article 5 element to the applicants' complaints.

e. Death of the applicant

Conceptually, the indirect victim is to be distinguished from the representation of a direct victim by a third party or the continuation of Convention proceedings by an heir or personal representative.[294] In this connection, the death of the original applicant does not automatically mean that the Court will strike out the case under Article 37. The Court's case law is rather generous in this regard. In *Ječius v Lithuania*,[295] the applicant died after the case had been declared admissible. Both the Court and the Commission decided that the applicant's widow had a legitimate interest in pursuing the application in his place

---

[290] Hudoc (2006); 44 EHRR 793 in particular paras 22–3, followed in *Direkci v Turkey No 47826/99* hudoc (2006) DA. See also *Anja and Anne Lönnholtz and the estate of Martta Lönnholtz v Denmark No 60790/00* hudoc (2006) DA.

[291] *No 5977/03* hudoc (2005) DA.   [292] Hudoc (2005).   [293] Hudoc (2006).

[294] See above, p 798.

[295] 2000-IX; 35 EHRR IX. See also *Hibbert v Netherlands No 38087/97* hudoc (1999) DA (the deceased's mother being able to continue the application).

and continued with the examination of the case on the merits. However, in *Thévenon v France*[296] the Court held that the applicant's sole legatee ('*légataire universel*') could not pursue the applicant's complaints after his death since she was neither his close relative nor, under French law, an heir.

In *Malhous v Czech Republic*,[297] the person wishing to continue the application was the nephew of the original applicant. The original complaint had related to attempts to recover nationalized property from the state and, at the time of the Court's examination of the case, the nephew was in the middle of an inheritance dispute with the original applicant's children. In finding that the nephew could continue the original application, the Court did not attach decisive importance to the fact that he was not the original applicant's next of kin and had not been confirmed as the applicant's heir according to the provisions of the national law. What was essential was that he could claim a legitimate interest in having the proceedings in the applicant's case being pursued before the Court. It was sufficient that the original applicant has designated him as his heir and that there were prospects of his eventually being recognized as such, in which case at least part of the applicant's estate including the property claims in issue in the case would accrue to him. It added that human rights cases before the Court generally also have a moral dimension and persons near to an applicant may thus have a legitimate interest in seeing to it that justice is done even after the applicant's death. This was all the more true if the leading issue raised by the case transcended the person and the interests of the applicant and his heirs and could affect other persons.[298]

If there is a general interest at stake in the case then the Court may in exceptional circumstances continue to examine the case even where no heir can be found to continue the application. In *Karner v Austria*,[299] the original applicant had complained of his inability to succeed to the tenancy of his homosexual partner when a heterosexual partner would be able to. After the original applicant's death, his heir waived her right to succeed to his estate. The Court chose not to strike the application out of its list. It recalled that its judgments served not only to decide those cases before it but, more generally, to elucidate, safeguard, and develop the rules instituted by the Convention. Furthermore, although the primary purpose of the Convention system was to provide individual relief, its mission was also to determine issues on public-policy grounds in the common interest, thereby raising the general standards of protection of human rights and extending human rights jurisprudence throughout the community of Convention states. It noted that the issue in the case was of general importance for Austria and other states and thus respect for human rights required that it continue to examine the case.[300] It must be emphasized that this case is somewhat unusual and it has been far more common for the Court to strike out a case where no heirs have presented themselves.[301]

II. COMPETENCE *RATIONE MATERIAE*

The competence of the Court only extends to examining complaints concerning the rights and freedoms contained in the Convention and its Protocols. Complaints concerning

---

[296] *No 2476/02* hudoc (2006) DA.   [297] *No 33071/96*, 2000-XII GC.

[298] See also *Dalban v Romania* 1999-VI; 31 EHRR 893 where the applicant's widow was found to have a legitimate interest in obtaining a ruling that her late husband's conviction for libel constituted a breach of the right to freedom of expression.

[299] 2003-IX; 32 EHRR 528. See also *Leger v France* (pending before the Grand Chamber).

[300] Id, paras 20–8. The Court did go on to find a violation and ordered that the awards made as just satisfaction be paid to the applicant's estate.

[301] *Direkci v Turkey No 47826/99* hudoc (2005) DA; *Keser and Others v Turkey* hudoc (2006).

rights not covered by the Convention are dismissed as incompatible *ratione materiae*. Thus, for example, the Convention does not guarantee, as such, socio-economic rights,[302] a right to asylum,[303] the right of an alien to enter or to reside in a particular country,[304] the right to be detained in a particular prison,[305] the right to diplomatic protection,[306] the right to work,[307] or the right to institute criminal proceedings against a third party.[308] Nor does it guarantee a right to divorce[309] or social security[310] where these are not provided in domestic law.

This list is far from exhaustive. However, the fact that a particular right is not contained in the Convention does not necessarily mean that all Convention protection is excluded. For example, while the right to asylum is not guaranteed, expulsion or extradition to a country where there are substantial reasons to fear that the person may be subjected to inhuman and degrading treatment may amount to a breach of Article 3 by the sending state.[311] Similarly, while the Convention does not guarantee a right of appeal in criminal cases, the national authorities must respect the rights contained in Article 6 where an appeal is in fact possible.[312] The Court has also stated that it cannot examine errors of law or fact that may have been committed by national courts; in this sense it is not a tribunal of fourth instance.[313] It does, however, have competence under Article 6 to examine whether the national proceedings complied with the requirements of a fair trial.

It is now well-established in the Court's case law that individuals can complain of violations of rights set out in Section II of the Convention. In particular the Court has found violations of Article 34 (the undertaking not to hinder the right of individual petition)[314] and Article 38(1)(a) (the obligation to furnish all necessary facilities to enable the Court to examine the case).[315] As regards Article 34, this is possible even where the Court finds no violation of the substantive rights that formed the subject of the original application.[316]

Complaints concerning rights in respect of which the state has filed a reservation under Article 57 will also be rejected as incompatible *ratione materiae*.[317] The Court is, however, competent to examine whether the reservation is in conformity with Article 57.[318]

III. COMPETENCE *RATIONE TEMPORIS*

In consonance with the general principle of non-retroactivity of treaties, the Court has no competence to examine complaints concerning matters which took place before the entry into force of the Convention or the date of ratification by the respondent state.

---

[302] *Pančenko v Latvia No 40772/98* hudoc (1999) DA.

[303] *Chahal v UK* 1996-I; 23 EHRR 413 paras 73–4 GC.

[304] From many authorities see *Üner v Netherlands* 2006-XII; 45 EHRR 421 at para 54 GC with references.

[305] *McQuiston v UK No 11208/84*, 46 DR 182 (1986).

[306] *Bertrand Russell Peace Foundation Ltd v UK No 7597/76*, 14 DR 117 (1978) and *Kaplan v UK No 12822/87*, 54 DR 201 (1987).

[307] *Chen v Netherlands No 37075/06* hudoc (2007) DA; *Coorplan-Jenni GmbH and Elvir Hascic v Austria No 10523/02* hudoc (2005) DA.

[308] *Rampogna and Murgia v Italy No 40753/98* hudoc (1999).

[309] *Johnston v Ireland*, A 112 (1986); 9 EHRR 203 PC.

[310] *Stec and Others v UK Nos 65731/01 and 65900/01*, 2005-X para 54 GC.

[311] See above, pp 77 *et seq*.   [312] See above, p 210.

[313] *Garcia Ruiz v Spain* 1999-I; 31 EHRR 589 para 28.

[314] For example, *Ilaşcu and Others v Moldova and Russia* 2004-VII; 40 EHRR 1030 GC; *Mamatkulov and Askarov v Turkey* 2005-I; 41 EHRR 494 GC.

[315] *Imakayeva v Russia* 2006-VIII; *Tepe v Turkey* hudoc (2003); 39 EHRR 584.

[316] *Aoulmi v France* 2006-I; 46 EHRR 1.

[317] See eg, *Shestjorkin v Estonia No 49450/99* hudoc (2000) DA; *MC v Finland No 28460/95* hudoc (2001) DA.

[318] See above, pp 21–3.

This will be obviously of decreasing importance but cases frequently arise under this heading, especially from newer member states. The general principle of compatibility *ratione temporis* is that the Convention imposes no specific obligation on the contracting states to provide redress for wrongs or damage caused prior to the date of ratification.[319] Determining the date of ratification itself will not pose any problem but cases have arisen as regards the declarations made by states at the time of ratification. Before Protocol 11 introduced the compulsory jurisdiction of the Court, the right of individual petition required states to make declarations allowing it. The Court accepted these declarations as limiting the scope of its jurisdiction to facts arising after the date specified in the declaration in question.[320] If no date was specified in the declaration then the Court's competence began at the date of ratification of Convention.[321]

The question still arises whether the facts giving rise to the application occurred before or after the relevant date. Clearly if the facts were instantaneous and were prior to the relevant date then the application is incompatible *ratione temporis*. However, many of the more difficult cases arise when the first act was prior to the relevant date but the applicant still suffered adverse effects of that act or commenced proceedings to challenge it after that date. In *Stamoulakatos v Greece (No 1)*[322] the applicant was convicted *in absentia* of three separate criminal offences in proceedings prior to Greece's acceptance of the right of individual petition on 19 November 1985. In 1986 he appealed against the judgment effectively seeking a re-hearing of the charges against him. He had argued before the Convention institutions that the appeals could give rise to a violation of Article 6 in their own right. The Court considered that, although the appeals were lodged after the 'critical' date of 19 November 1985, they were closely bound up with the proceedings that led to his conviction. In the appeal proceedings he had attacked the unlawfulness of the summonses and of the service of the judgments given *in absentia*. In the Court's judgment, to divorce the appeals from the events which gave rise to them would be 'tantamount to rendering Greece's declaration nugatory'. However, in *Zana v Turkey*,[323] where the applicant was convicted by a state security court after the relevant date for acts committed before that date, the Court found that the principal fact was the date of conviction by the security court and thus rejected the government's plea of incompatibility *ratione temporis*.

Where legal proceedings begin before the relevant date and continue after it, the Court's jurisdiction has to be determined in relation to the exact time of the alleged interference. In assessing this, the Court will consider both the facts of which the applicant complains and the scope of the Convention right alleged to have been violated. The Court has provided some degree of clarification of how this will be assessed in *Blecic v Croatia*,[324] where the applicant had taken legal proceedings to recover property before the relevant date but had appealed unsuccessfully to the Constitutional Court after it. The Court found that the interference with the applicant's property rights occurred with the Supreme Court's judgment before the relevant date. It was this judgment that was a definitive act which was by itself capable of violating the applicant's rights. The subsequent Constitutional Court decision only resulted in allowing the interference allegedly caused by that Supreme Court's judgment to subsist. While an application to the Croatian Constitutional Court was an effective remedy it did not amount to a new or independent

---

[319] *Kopecký v Slovakia* 2004-IX; 41 EHRR 944 para 38 GC.
[320] *Stamoulakatos v Greece (No 1)* A 271 (1993); 17 EHRR 479.
[321] *X v France No 9587/81*, 29 DR 228 (1982).   [322] A 271 (1993); 17 EHRR 479.
[323] 1997-VII; 27 EHRR 667.   [324] 2006-III para 82 GC.

interference. The key issue appeared to be whether the act identified as constituting a violation of the Convention is before or after the relevant date.

In this connection, the notion of a continuing violation is of great importance to complaints brought under Article 1 of Protocol 1, especially from former communist countries. In cases of deprivation of property under communist regimes, the Court has distinguished nationalization and its continuing effects from the subsequent proceedings for restitution initiated after ratification of the Convention. For the former, deprivation of ownership or of another right *in rem* is in principle an instantaneous act and does not produce a continuing situation: thus applications complaining solely of nationalization by communist regimes are incompatible *ratione temporis*.[325] For the latter, the question of compatibility is less straightforward. The Court has been prepared to countenance the possibility that once a contracting state, having ratified the Convention including Protocol 1, enacts legislation providing for the full or partial restoration of property confiscated under a previous regime, such legislation may be regarded as generating a new property right protected by Article 1 of Protocol 1 for persons satisfying the requirements for entitlement. The same may apply in respect of arrangements for restitution or compensation established under pre-ratification legislation, if such legislation remained in force after the contracting state's ratification of Protocol 1.[326] In *Broniowski v Poland*, the applicant belonged to a large category of persons who had been deprived of their property on the other side of the Bug River after the Second World War. Poland had taken on the obligation to compensate those owners in an international agreement concluded in 1944. This obligation had subsisted in Polish law after the transition and still existed at the time of Poland's ratification of the Convention. In its admissibility decision in the case,[327] the Grand Chamber of the Court noted that the applicant did not complain of the original deprivation of property or a single specific decision taken before or after the date of ratification. The factual basis for his application was the failure to satisfy an entitlement to compensation which was vested in him under Polish law at the time of the ratification and existed at the time of the Grand Chamber's decision. Since the application was directed at Poland's omission to fulfil this entitlement, the application was compatible *ratione temporis*.[328]

Where the complaints concern the length of proceedings which started before the ratification but continue after that date, the period to be taken into consideration starts from the date of ratification. However, the Court will take into account the state of proceedings at that date.[329] The same applies to complaints involving the length of detention on remand where the Court will consider the entire period of detention (before and after the relevant date) in forming an assessment of the reasonableness of the length.[330] Finally, it is not clear whether there is a requirement to carry out effective investigations for the purposes of Articles 2 and 3 of the Convention where the events giving rise to the substantive violation occurred before the date of ratification.[331]

[325] From the many authorities see *Malhous v Czech Republic No 33071/96*, 2000-XII DA.
[326] *Maltzan and Others v Germany Nos 71916/01, 71917/01 and 10260/02* hudoc (2005) DA.
[327] *Broniowski v Poland No 31443/96*, 2002 X GC.
[328] The same principle was applied in *Hutten-Czapska v Poland No 35014/97* hudoc (2003) DA, where the complaint related to rent controls based on legislation passed before the date of ratification, the Court noting that it was common ground that the laws were still in force (at p 17). See also the Grand Chamber's judgment, hudoc (2006); 45 EHRR 52.
[329] *Styranowski v Poland* 1998-VIII; *Proszak v Poland* 1997-VIII; *Foti and Others v Italy* A 56 (1982).
[330] Eg, *Klyakhin v Russia* hudoc (2004).
[331] *Moldovan and Others and Rostas and Others v Romania Nos 41138/98 and 64320/01* hudoc (2001) DA; but see *Silih v Slovenia* (pending before the Grand Chamber).

IV. COMPETENCE *RATIONE LOCI*

a. The concept of 'jurisdiction' in Article 1

The concept of jurisdiction has been the subject of a long evolution in the case law of the Strasbourg organs, though the clearest expression of the concept has come in the cases they have heard involving northern Cyprus.[332] In the first two inter-state cases brought by Cyprus against Turkey in relation to acts allegedly committed in northern Cyprus,[333] Turkey's contention was that the Commission did not have jurisdiction *ratione loci* to examine the applications and that under Article 1 its competence was limited to acts committed in the national territory of the High Contracting Party concerned. In response, the Commission held that the term 'within their jurisdiction' ('*relevant de leur juridiction*') was not equivalent to or limited to the national territory of the High Contracting Party. It stated that:

> the High Contracting Parties are bound to secure the said rights and freedoms to all persons under their actual authority and responsibility, whether that authority is exercised within their own territory or abroad. Authorised agents of a State, including diplomatic or consular agents and armed forces, not only remain under its jurisdiction when abroad but bring any other persons or property 'within the jurisdiction' of that State, to the extent that they exercise authority over such persons or property.[334]

It found as a matter of fact that such 'authority' was exercised by the armed forces of Turkey operating in northern Cyprus.[335]

The Court has developed its approach as follows. In *Loizidou v Turkey (Preliminary Objections)*,[336] which also concerned northern Cyprus, the Court agreed with the Commission that the concept of 'jurisdiction' in Article 1 was 'not restricted to the national territory' of the contracting parties. In addition, the Court stated, 'the responsibility of Contracting Parties can be involved because of acts of their authorities, whether performed within or outside national boundaries, which produce effects outside their own territory[337] ... Bearing in mind the object and purpose of the Convention, the responsibility of a Contracting party may also arise when as a consequence of military action—whether lawful or unlawful—it *exercises effective control of an area outside its national territory.*'[338]

---

[332] For two earlier cases see *X v FRG No 1611/62* hudoc (1965) DA (where the Commission was prepared to countenance extraterritorial jurisdiction as a result of diplomatic or consular activities abroad) and *Hess v UK No 6231/73,* 2 DR 72 (1975) DA (concerning the detention of the applicant in the Allied Military Prison in Berlin-Spandau where the Court concluded that the administration of the prison was not within the jurisdiction of the United Kingdom).

[333] *Cyprus v Turkey (First and Second Applications) Nos 6780/74 and 6950/75,* 2 DR 125 (1975).

[334] Id, para 8.

[335] Id, para 10. The Commission reiterated this position in the third inter-state case between Cyprus and Turkey, *No 8007/77,* 13 DR 85 (1978), with a slight modification allowing for the establishment of the (then) 'Turkish Federated State of Cyprus'. It found that the 'TFSC' could not be regarded as an entity which exercised jurisdiction within the meaning of Article 1 (para 24). The presence of Turkish armed forces in the north of Cyprus, which prevented the exercise of jurisdiction by the Republic of Cyprus, could not be excluded on the ground that the jurisdiction was allegedly exercised by the TFSC. The Court has also held that the Republic of Cyprus is not responsible for acts that occur in the northern part of the island (*An and others v Cyprus No 18270/91* hudoc (1991) DA) and that Turkey is not responsible for acts that occur in the southern part of the island (*Aziz v Cyprus, Greece, Turkey and the UK No 69949/01* hudoc (2002) para 5 DA).

[336] A 310 (1995); 20 EHRR 99 para 62.

[337] *Drozd and Janousek v France and Spain* A 240 (1992); 14 EHRR 745 Ed. The Court referred, *inter alia*, to the Commission cases cited above, n 333.

[338] Italics added. The Court repeated the 'effective control' test formulated in the above passage in *Loizidou v Turkey* 1996-VI; 23 EHRR 513 para 56, this time making explicit reference to the now 'Turkish Republic of Northern Cyprus'. It stated that it was not necessary to rule on the question of whether Turkey exercised detailed control over

The next significant case on jurisdiction is the rather different case of *Bankovic and Others v Belgium and 16 other Contracting States*.[339] The applicants were the relatives of those killed during the NATO bombing of a radio and television station during the Kosovo war and their application was brought against all the High Contracting Parties to the Convention who were also members of NATO, a total of seventeen states. The applicants argued, *inter alia*, that their application was compatible *ratione loci* with the Convention; that their relatives had been brought within the jurisdiction of the respondent state by the bombing. They proposed adapting the 'effective control' test outlined by the Court in *Loizidou* such that the extent of the positive obligations imposed by Article 1 would be proportionate to the level of control exercised by the state or states in question. The Court found that the real connection between the applicants and the respondent states was the bombing, an extraterritorial act. Therefore the 'essential question was whether the applicants and their deceased relatives were, as a result of that extraterritorial act, capable of falling within the jurisdiction of the respondent States'.[340] It went on to state that Article 1 must be considered to reflect the ordinary and essentially territorial notion of jurisdiction in public international law; other bases of jurisdiction were exceptions that required special justification. The Court then turned to the question of the relevant test for jurisdiction that it has set out in the northern Cyprus cases. It stated that:

> In sum, the case-law of the Court demonstrates that its recognition of the exercise of extra-territorial jurisdiction by a Contracting State is exceptional: it has done so when the respondent State, through the effective control of the relevant territory and its inhabitants abroad as a consequence of military occupation or through the consent, invitation or acquiescence of the Government of that territory, exercises all or some of the public powers normally to be exercised by that Government.[341]

Applying this test, the Court decided that it lacked jurisdiction *ratione loci* and declared the application inadmissible.

The Court was prepared to conclude that there had been an extra-territorial exercise of jurisdiction to which Article 1 applied in the later case of *Öcalan v Turkey*.[342] In that case, it was accepted by the Court that the Convention applied to the arrest and detention of the applicant by members of the Turkish security forces inside the international zone of Nairobi airport. The Court noted that it was 'common ground that, directly after being handed over to the Turkish officials by the Kenyan officials, the applicant was effectively under Turkish authority and therefore within the "jurisdiction" of that state for the purposes of Article 1 of the Convention, even though in this instance Turkey exercised its authority outside its territory'. *Bankovic* was distinguished on the grounds the applicant was physically forced to return to Turkey by Turkish officials and was subject to their authority and control following his arrest and return to Turkey.[343]

---

the policies and actions of the authorities of the 'TRNC' since it was: 'obvious from the large number of troops engaged in active duties in northern Cyprus that her army exercises effective overall control over that part of the island'. Such control entailed Turkey's responsibility for the policies and actions of the 'TRNC' and those affected by such policies or actions therefore came within the 'jurisdiction' of Turkey for the purposes of Article 1 of the Convention. See finally the fourth *Cyprus v Turkey* inter-state application, 2001-IV; 35 EHRR 731 GC para 78, where the Court reiterated its previous rulings on the responsibility of Turkey and added that any other finding would 'result in a regrettable vacuum in the system of human rights protection in the territory in question'.

[339] 2001-XII; 44 EHRR SE 5GC. The case has generated a great deal of academic writing. In English, see in particular both Lawson and O'Boyle, in Coomans and Kamminga, eds, *Extraterritorial Application of Human Rights Treaties*, 2004. See also Markovic, 8 HRLR 411 (2008).

[340] Id, para 54.   [341] Id, para 71.   [342] 2005-IV; 41 EHRR 985 para 91 GC.

[343] Grand Chamber judgment at para 91; Chamber judgment at para 93. For differing interpretations of this case see the literature cited at n 339 above.

The 'effective control' basis for jurisdiction was developed again in *Ilascu and Others v Moldova and Russia*,[344] concerning the separatist regime in the east of Moldova called Transdniestria (also referred to in the Court's judgment as the 'Moldavian Republic of Transdniestria' ('the MRT')). The applicants were opponents of the Transdniestrian regime. In 1992, they were arrested in Transdniestria. They alleged, and the Court agreed, that some of those who arrested them were from the former USSR's Fourteenth Army. They complained about their arrest, trial, and subsequent detention. In their complaint against Moldova, they argued that the Moldovan authorities' responsibility lay in the fact that they had not taken adequate measures to put a stop to their detention and the other human rights violations they complained of. They argued that Moldova's positive obligations under the Convention applied throughout its territory even in the absence of effective control of part of it. As against Russia, they argued that it shared responsibility as the territory of Transdniestria was under its *de facto* control because of the troops and military equipment it had there as well as the economic and financial support it gave to the Transdniestrian authorities. As regards Russia, the Court found as a matter of fact that during the conflict in 1991–92, forces of the former Fourteenth Army were stationed in Transdniestria. It also found that during the fighting between Moldova and the separatist authorities of Transdniestria the Fourteenth Army had fought with and on behalf of the Transdniestrian separatist forces. The Court further held that the 'MRT' remained under the effective authority, or at the very least under 'the decisive influence', of Russia, and in any event that it survived by virtue of the support that Russia gave it.[345] The applicants therefore came within the 'jurisdiction' of Russia. This finding closely follows from the test of 'effective overall control' set out in the northern Cyprus cases. The case is more problematic as regards the jurisdiction of Moldova, especially given the divisions among the Grand Chamber judges on this point. By eleven votes to six, the Court found the applicants to come within the jurisdiction of Moldova. The majority considered that the Moldovan government, which it found to be the only legitimate government of Moldova under international law, did not exercise authority over Transdniestria. However, it found that, in such a situation, a state did not cease to have 'jurisdiction' within the meaning of Article 1 of the Convention over that part of its territory. Instead the scope of that jurisdiction was reduced such that 'the undertaking given by the State under Article 1 must be considered by the Court *only in the light of the Contracting State's positive obligations towards persons within its territory*'.[346] This enabled the Court to also say that whilst it considered that Moldova did not exercise authority over Transdniestria, it still had a positive obligation to take the diplomatic, economic, judicial, or other measures that are in its power to take to secure to the applicants the rights guaranteed by the Convention.

Issa v Turkey[347] concerned the alleged killing of Iraqi shepherds by Turkish military forces in the course of military operations carried out in the north of Iraq in the spring of 1995. The Court was not satisfied that those killed were within the jurisdiction of Turkey. The significance of the case lies in two points in the judgment. First, the Court reiterated that a state could be held accountable for violation of the Convention rights and freedoms of persons who are in the territory of another state. This would be when the persons concerned were 'found to be under the former State's *authority and control* through its agents operating—whether lawfully or unlawfully—in the latter State', the reason being that states could not be allowed to perpetrate violations of the Convention on the territory of another state, which it could not perpetrate on its own territory.[348] Secondly, the

---

344 2004-VII; 40 EHRR 1030 GC.   345 Id, paras 382 and 392.   346 Id, para 333. Emphasis added.
347 Hudoc (2004); 41 EHRR 567.
348 Id, para 71 (references omitted).

Court did not exclude the possibility that as a consequence of extra-territorial military action a state could *temporarily* have effective overall control of an area outside its own borders.[349] Were that established on the facts, which was not done to the satisfaction of the Court in the *Issa* case, those within that area would be within the jurisdiction of the state, even if, like the north of Iraq, that area were normally outside the legal space of the contracting parties.

Also concerning Iraq, in *Saddam Hussein v Albania and 20 other States*,[350] the applicant, the former President of Iraq, complained of various aspects of his arrest, detention, handover, trial (ongoing at the time of the decision), and possible execution at the trial's conclusion. He brought the complaint against all those Convention contracting parties that had participated in the invasion of Iraq, arguing that they continued to hold *de facto* power in Iraq. The application was found to be inadmissible because of the applicant's failure to demonstrate any jurisdictional link between himself and the respondent states. The Court observed that the applicant had only referred to the coalition partners acting together as the basis for the responsibility of the contracting parties. The Court found that he could not fall within the jurisdiction of those states on the sole basis that those states formed part of a coalition with the United States when the acts of which he complained were carried out by the United States in its 'zone' of Iraq and when the United States was in overall command of the coalition.

b. Article 56 (former Article 63)

Article 56(1), commonly referred to as the 'colonial clause', provides that a state may declare that 'the present Convention shall extend to all or any of the territories of whose international relations it is responsible'.[351] Article 56(3) provides: 'The provisions of this Convention shall be applied in such territories with due regard... to local requirements'. In a 1961 case brought against Belgium, it was argued that since, at the time of the events complained of, the Belgian Congo formed an integral part of the national territory, Article 56 was inapplicable. The Commission held that, whatever the exact status of the Congo, it clearly came within the category of territories referred to in Article 56. In the absence of a special declaration, the Commission thus lacked competence *ratione loci*.[352] However, it should not be inferred from this case that a declaration is required under Article 56 for the Convention to apply to an overseas territory, whatever its status, if it is situated outside the European continent. The determining factor is the status given to the territory under domestic law: as a dependent territory of the kind intended to be covered by Article 56 or as an integral part of the national territory. France, for example, has chosen to treat a number of overseas territories, the '*départements d'outre mer*' (DOM),[353] on the same footing as metropolitan '*départements*' and not at all as dependent territories. The Court should arguably respect that choice and regard those overseas '*départements*' as coming within the ordinary jurisdiction of France and not as being covered by Article 56. France would seem to have opted for a different solution with regard to its '*térritoires d'outre mer*',[354] which have a slightly different status leaving a greater degree of autonomy to the local authorities.[355]

---

[349] Id, para 74.   [350] *No 23276/04* hudoc (2006) DA.

[351] On the background and history of Article 56, see Simpson, *op cit*, Ch 16, n 8 above.

[352] *X v Belgium No 1065/61*, 4 YB 260 at 264–8 (1961).

[353] Guadeloupe, Guyana, Martinique, and Réunion.

[354] Antarctic territories, New Caledonia, Pacific territories, Saint Pierre, and Miquelon. See also *Piermont v France* A 314 (1995); 20 EHRR 301. See eg, *Py v France* hudoc (2005).

[355] In the French instrument of ratification of 3 May 1974 it was stated: 'The government of the Republic further declares that the Convention shall apply to the whole territory of the Republic, having due regard, where the

On the other side of the coin, Article 56 has been recognized as applying to dependent territories situated in Europe and having no special cultural or development differences in comparison with the metropolitan territory of the contracting state concerned. Such recognition has been given by the Court in cases against the United Kingdom concerning the Isle of Man and Guernsey.[356] Here again decisive importance was attached to the intention of the respondent state. In the *Gillow* case,[357] the Court relied on a statement issued in 1950 by the United Kingdom government to the effect that Guernsey was to be regarded as a territory for the international relations of which the United Kingdom is responsible, in order to hold that an express declaration of extension under Article 4 of the First Protocol (the equivalent of Article 56 of the Convention) was necessary for the application of the Protocol to the island. It must be questioned whether the Isle of Man and Guernsey, given the closeness of their links to the metropolitan territory and the fact that they are situated in Europe, ought to require a special declaration of a type intended for the colonial territories. However, it should also be noted in this respect that the United Kingdom declaration accepting the territorial extension of the Convention to the Isle of Man states that this is on a permanent basis.[358] Even where a declaration is made under Article 56 extending the Convention to a particular territory, a separate declaration is required in order for the First Protocol to apply. In *Quark Fishing Ltd v UK*[359] the United Kingdom had made declaration under Article 56 extending the Convention to the South Georgia and the South Sandwich Islands but had not made a similar declaration under Article 4 of the First Protocol such that it would also apply there. The Court was clear that an express declaration was required for the Protocol to apply and stressed that there was no obligation under the Convention for a contracting state to ratify any particular protocol or give reasons for their decisions. The question has arisen whether responsibility under the Convention could arise through the exercise of 'jurisdiction' in respect of a territory which has not been the subject of an Article 56 declaration. In *Yonghong v Portugal*,[360] concerning the then Portuguese territory of Macao, the Court found this was not possible. It acknowledged that 'jurisdiction' is not limited to the national territory of the contracting state and that their responsibility can be involved because of acts of their authorities producing effects outside their own territory. It observed, however, that Article 1 of the Convention had to be read in the light of Article 56. In the absence of a Portuguese declaration the Court found it had no jurisdiction *ratione loci* to examine the application.[361]

The 'local requirements' referred to in paragraph 3 of Article 56 may permit a lower standard of compliance with the Convention's requirements in dependent territories. There are, however, limits. Thus, the Court held in the *Tyrer* case that no requirement relative to the maintenance of law and order would entitle any contracting state, under

overseas territories are concerned, to local requirements as mentioned in Article 63 [now Article 56]'. Available from the Council of Europe Treaty Office, online at: <http://conventions.coe.int>.

[356] *Tyrer v UK* A 26 (1978); 2 EHRR 1 and *Gillow v UK* A 109 (1986); 11 EHRR 335 paras 60–2.

[357] *Ibid.* The United Kingdom had originally argued the case before the Commission and Court on the mistaken assumption that the Protocol applied to Guernsey. The mistake was discovered eight months after the oral hearing before the Court.

[358] The current UK declaration under Article 56 makes two classes of acceptance: territorial extension renewed for a period of five years (for Anguilla, Bermuda, Montserrat, St Helena, St Helena Dependencies, Turks and Caicos Islands) and territorial extension on a permanent basis (Bailiwick of Jersey, Bailiwick of Guernsey, Cayman Islands, Isle of Man, Sovereign Base Areas of Akrotiri and Dhekelia in Cyprus, Falkland Islands, Gibraltar, South Georgia, and South Sandwich Islands).

[359] *No 15305/06* hudoc (2006) DA.   [360] *No 50887/99*, 1999-IX DA.

[361] Id, pp 391–2. See also *Bui Van Thanh v UK No 16137/90*, 65 DR 330 (1990) (detention of Vietnamese 'boat people' in Hong Kong), the Commission declining competence to examine the application. Nor does the principle of effective control replace the system of declarations: see *Quark Fishing* at pp 4–5.

Article 56, to make use of an 'inhuman or degrading punishment' (Article 3) in any territory, whatever its state of development. It is also difficult to see how a European self-governing territory such as the Isle of Man could have any 'local requirements' allowing for a different application of the Convention from the rest of Europe. In addition, there must be proof of 'local requirements'; beliefs and local public opinion do not on their own constitute such proof.[362] The Court did accept 'local requirements' in *Py v France*,[363] concerning the restriction of voting rights to individuals in New Caledonia. The Court found those restrictions to be appropriately linked to a series of transitional measures aimed at alleviating the bloody conflict there and reflecting the territory's transition to the acquisition of full sovereignty.

The clear purpose of Article 56 was facilitative: to allow for contracting states with overseas territories to arrange for the application of the Convention to those territories as they saw fit. However, the provisions of the Article have also been considered in a negative sense, where states have sought to argue that its provision can operate to exclude liability for certain territories for which they may otherwise be responsible. Also relevant is Article 57(1) which allows for a state, when signing or depositing its instrument of ratification, to make a reservation in respect of any particular provision of the Convention to the extent that forbids any reservations of a general character. Three states, Azerbaijan, Georgia, and Moldova, currently have entered open-ended declarations to the Convention in relation to areas which nominally fall within their national territory but would appear to be outside their *de facto* control. In the case of Moldova, the declaration states:

> The Republic of Moldova declares that it will be unable to guarantee compliance with the provisions of the Convention in respect of omissions and acts committed by the organs of the self-proclaimed Trans-Dniester republic within the territory actually controlled by such organs, until the conflict in the region is finally settled.[364]

At the admissibility stage of the *Ilascu* case[365] which concerned illegal detention in the separatist territory of Transdniestria (discussed in detail above), the Moldovan government argued that Articles 56 and 57 applied together. While it conceded that the purpose of Article 56 was to enable a state to extend the application of the Convention, it argued for a broader interpretation of Article 56 to cover also the novel situation where a state has

---

[362] *Ibid.* In *Piermont v France* Series A 314 (1995); 20 EHRR 301, the Court did not consider a 'tense local political' atmosphere in French Polynesia during an election campaign to be 'local requirements' justifying an interference with Article 10 rights. These were thought to be 'circumstances and conditions' rather than 'requirements' (see paras 55–9).

[363] 2005-I; 42 EHRR 548.

[364] The Azeri declaration is in the fashion of the Moldovan declaration: 'The Republic of Azerbaijan declares that it is unable to guarantee the application of the provisions of the Convention in the territories occupied by the Republic of Armenia until these territories are liberated from that occupation (the schematic map of the occupied territories of the Republic of Azerbaijan is enclosed).' The Georgian declaration (contained in the instrument of ratification of Protocol 1 but also applying to the Convention) provides as follows: 'Georgia declares, that due to the existing situation in Abkhazia and Tskhinvali region, Georgian authorities are unable to undertake commitments concerning the respect and protection of the provisions of the Convention and its Additional Protocols on these territories. Georgia therefore declines its responsibility for violations of the provisions of the Protocol by the organs of self-proclaimed illegal forces on the territories of Abkhazia and Tskhinvali region until the possibility of realization of the full jurisdiction of Georgia is restored over these territories.' The Cyprus declaration was a little different stating: 'the competence of the Commission by virtue of Article 25 of the Convention [the right of individual petition under the old system] is not to extend to petitions concerning acts or omissions...if the acts or omissions relate to measures taken by the Government of the Republic of Cyprus to meet the needs resulting from the situation created by the continuing invasion and military occupation of part of the territory of the Republic of Cyprus by Turkey.'

[365] *No 48787/99* hudoc (2001), p 20.

agreed to be bound by the Convention although *de facto* part of its territory is not under
its control. The Court rejected this reasoning saying that neither the spirit nor the terms
of Article 56 could permit a negative interpretation. In respect of Article 57, it went on
to hold that this declaration did not amount to a reservation within the meaning of the
Convention since it was of a general character. Its effect was 'unlimited as to the provisions of the Convention but limited in space and time, whose effect would be that persons
on that "territory" would be wholly deprived of the protection of the Convention for an
indefinite period'.[366]

The issue also arose in relation to northern Cyprus, in the opposite sense, as it were, in
relation to Turkey's attempt to evade responsibility for territory outside its national territory but under its control. In *Loizidou v Turkey*[367] the Court struck down Turkey's declarations made in relation to the then optional clauses on the right of individual petition and
the compulsory jurisdiction of the Court which declared that these only extended to acts
performed within the boundaries of the national territory of the Republic of Turkey.[368]
The Court stated:

> If, as contended by the respondent Government, substantive or territorial restrictions
> were permissible under these provisions, Contracting Parties would be free to subscribe
> to separate regimes of enforcement of Convention obligations depending on the scope of
> their acceptances. Such a system, which would enable States to qualify their consent under
> the optional clauses, would not only seriously weaken the role of the Commission and
> Court in the discharge of their functions but would also diminish the effectiveness of the
> Convention as a constitutional instrument of European public order (*ordre public*).

366 *Ibid.*   367 A 310 (1995); 20 EHRR 99 GC.   368 Id, paras 18 and 25–7.

23

THE EUROPEAN COURT OF HUMAN RIGHTS: ORGANIZATION, PRACTICE, AND PROCEDURE

1. THE ORGANIZATION OF THE COURT

I. THE SETTING UP OF THE NEW COURT

The European Court of Human Rights is a unique body in the history of international law. More than 800 million people have direct access to the Court to complain of violations of their fundamental rights. The Court is at the centre of a system of human rights protection which radiates its influence to the democratic legal orders of virtually all European states. It has established standards which permeate the legal order of the contracting parties and has made a major contribution to the shaping of domestic law and practice in almost every area of law—the administration of criminal justice, civil and criminal law, family law, and the law of property, to name but a few. This is a notable achievement for an international tribunal that was set up in 1959 with the role of providing an early warning system against the decline of democratic standards and the growth of dictatorships. This essentially political mandate was to be achieved through the operation of law, in particular through the exercise of the right of individual petition.

The present permanent Court, which started its work on 1 November 1998 on the entry into force of Protocol 11, is the product of the fusion of two separate, part-time enforcement bodies, the now defunct European Commission of Human Rights and the former European Court of Human Rights.[1] The adoption of Protocol 11 was prompted by a series of factors: the increasing workload of the Commission and Court, the length of time taken to dispose of cases, and a desire to eliminate the duplication in the procedure whereby both the Commission and Court undertook an examination of the merits of admissible cases. Under Protocol 11, the existing Commission and Court were replaced by a single full-time institution composed of one judge in respect of each contracting party to the Convention. Judges would be permanently based in Strasbourg and would not be permitted to engage in any activity incompatible with the demands of a full-time office. Protocol 11 also formally abolished the requirement that the contracting parties recognize the jurisdiction of the Court before it could examine individual cases. Moreover the role of the Committee of Ministers was reduced to that of supervising the execution of Court judgments and was no longer called on to decide the merits of cases not referred

---

[1] For the operation of the former Commission and Court of Human Rights—see Chs 22 and 24 of the first edition of this book. On the Commission's role, see above, p 5, n 35.

to the Court. Accordingly the present Court's role goes far beyond that of ruling on the substantive issues raised by a case. It is an all-purpose Court which has inherited from the Commission the essential tasks of filtering applications, fact-finding, determining admissibility, and negotiating friendly settlement in addition to providing binding rulings in admissible cases.[2]

The constant growth in the number of cases being brought to the Court since 1998 has required it to change continuously its working methods to find ways of rejecting obviously inadmissible cases with an economy of procedure.[3] It was soon realized that Protocol 11 was not sufficient and that further structural change was needed (the reform of the reform) to enable the Court to operate effectively. This led to the drafting of Protocol 14 which has so far been ratified by forty-six of the contracting parties but not yet by Russia.[4] It was also recognized that the continuous growth of cases by 12 per cent every year was steadily asphyxiating the Court and undermining its authority. In 2005 the Committee of Ministers set up a group of Wise Persons to examine the future of the Court and to set out a blueprint for its future long-term development. The Group reported in November 2006 and made a number of far-reaching proposals.[5] However it was clear that the Group's thinking was predicated on the assumption that the changes brought about by Protocol 14 would be in place soon and that the future discussion on their proposals would be enriched by information as to the operation of the changes brought about by that Protocol. The process of reform has thus stalled, hopefully temporarily, pending a final decision by Russia as to whether it will ratify the Protocol.

II. COMPOSITION OF THE COURT[6]

Section II of the Convention governs the operation of the Court and its procedures. Article 30 provides that the number of judges shall equal the number of contracting parties; currently therefore there are forty-seven judges.[7] The judges are elected for a six-year term and may be re-elected, though under Protocol 14, after a transitional period, this

---

[2] On reform of the Court generally see Wildhaber, *The European Court of Human Rights 1998–2006: History, Achievements, Reform*, 2006; also Benoît-Rohmer, 73 RTDH 3 (2008) and also Reform of the European Human Rights System: Proceedings of the High-level Seminar, Oslo, 2004, Directorate General of Human Rights, Strasbourg: Council of Europe, 2004.

[3] In January 2008 there were 79,400 cases pending before a decision body and 103,850 applications pending altogether. Thus 24,450 cases were in a pre-judicial phase. Five countries gave rise to 58% of all applications: Russia (23.6%), Romania (11.7%), Turkey (9.8%), Ukraine (8.2%), Poland (5.3%). For statistical information see *Survey of Activities 2008*, Registry of the European Court of Human Rights (2009). In the early years of the Convention, the number of applications lodged with the Commission was comparatively small, and the number of cases decided by the Court was much lower again. This changed in the 1980s, by which time the steady growth in the number of cases brought before the Convention institutions made it increasingly difficult to keep the length of proceedings within acceptable limits. Adding to the problem was the rapid increase in the number of Contracting States from 1990 onwards, rising from twenty-two to the current total of forty-seven. The number of applications registered annually with the Commission increased from 404 in 1981 to 4,750 in 1997, the last full year of operation of the original supervisory mechanism. By that same date, the number of unregistered or provisional files opened each year in the Commission had risen to over 12,000. Although on a much lower scale, the former Court's statistics reflected a similar story, with the number of cases referred annually rising from 7 in 1981 to 119 in 1997.

[4] For a description of Protocol 14, see below pp 863–7.

[5] Final Report of the Group of Wise Persons to the Committee of Ministers, Council of Europe, November 2006 (available at <http://www.echr.coe.int>). See also Future Developments of the European Court of Human Rights in the Light of the Wise Persons Report: proceedings of the colloquy, San Marino, 22–23 March, Council of Europe, 2007.

[6] For details of the current composition of the Court, see the Court's website <http://www.echr.coe.int>.

[7] At the time of writing (April 2008) seventeen judges are women.

would be replaced by a single, non-renewable term of nine years in order to reinforce judicial independence. Judges' terms of office expire when they reach seventy years of age and contracting parties are asked not to nominate anyone who will be unable to serve a full six-year term because of this rule.[8] However, when read with the following provision in Article 23(7) ('judges shall hold office until replaced') a certain ambiguity appears. The practice has been that judges over the age of seventy have continued to sit until replaced.[9]

Questions may be raised as to the desirability of a single judicial body of this size and the Wise Persons Report presented to the Committee of Ministers in November 2006 suggested reducing the number of judges, though this would require an amendment to Article 20 and any reformed system would require persuading the contracting parties to agree to some equitable arrangement for nominating less judges than contracting parties.[10]

The criteria for office are set out in Article 21 of the Convention, which specifies that judges shall be of 'high moral character' and must possess the qualifications required for appointment to high judicial office or be jurisconsults of recognized competence. The latter term, taken to mean 'experts in law', considerably expands the pool of eligible candidates. The result is a Strasbourg judiciary of diverse professional backgrounds: the current Court includes former supreme and constitutional court judges, academics, former diplomats, prosecutors, and those recruited from the practising bar in contracting parties.[11]

In keeping with the nature of any full-time court, Article 21(3) requires that judges shall not engage in activity which is incompatible with their independence or impartiality or the demands of a full-time office. Rule 4 of the Rules of Court supplements this by making it clear that they shall not engage in any political or administrative activity which is incompatible with their independence or impartiality. Judges are expected to work full time in Strasbourg. All new judges are informed of this by the President of the Court and it is further reinforced both by the oath they swear upon taking up office[12] and the election procedures of the Parliamentary Assembly of the Council of Europe (PACE) considered in the following section. Rule 4 also provides that judges must declare any additional activity to the President and that in the event of a disagreement between the President and the judge concerned, any question arising shall be decided by the plenary Court.

Article 51 of the Convention entitles judges to privileges and immunities in the exercise of their functions, thus reinforcing the independence of the Court. These are today governed by the 1996 Sixth Protocol to the General Agreement on Privileges and Immunities

---

[8] Article 23(6) of the Convention. There is no provision or procedure for the impeachment of sitting judges. The matter is instead regulated by Article 24 of the Convention and Rule 7 of the Rules of Court which allow for dismissal by a two-thirds majority of the plenary Court.

[9] On this point and the election of judges in general, see Hedigan, in Kohen, ed, *Liber Amicorum Lucius Caflisch*, 2007, pp 235–53. See further, Krüger, 1996 RUDH, 113; Valticos, in *Liber Amicorum M-A Eissen*, 1995; Carrillo-Salcedo, 1997 RUDH 1; and 'Judicial Independence: The Law and Practice of Appointments to the European Court of Human Rights' Interights, May 2003, available at: <http://www.interights.org/jud-ind-en/index.html>.

[10] This will always be a contentious issue since the states are attached to the principle of 'one State, one judge'. There is no requirement that a judge be a national of the state in respect of which he or she is elected (eg, Judge MacDonald (Canadian national) sat in respect of Liechtenstein, 1980–98) although the Court has emphasized the utility of a national judge with a knowledge of national law and procedures—see the Advisory Opinion of 12 Feburary 2008, below, p 815, para 52.

[11] See the Court's website for the judges' curricula vitae.

[12] The text of which is set out in Rule 3 of the Rules of Court.

of the Council of Europe,[13] ratified by nearly all of the contracting parties. This entitles judges to the privileges and immunities accorded to diplomatic envoys and guarantees them immunity from legal process in respect of words or acts done in the discharge of their duties. It also guarantees the inviolability of their papers and correspondence as well as that of the Court and the Registry. By Article 4 of the Protocol, immunity can only be waived by the plenary Court.

The President of the Court is assisted by two Vice-Presidents who are also Presidents of Sections and three further Section (or Chamber) Presidents, all of whom are elected by the plenary Court for a three-year term which may be renewed once.[14] The Convention itself is silent on many of the duties now assumed by the President save for stating that he or she (with the Vice-Presidents and Presidents of the Chambers) will automatically be a member of the Grand Chamber, and even then in practice this duty may be delegated.

Rule 9 of the Rules of Court elucidates the President's role in greater detail.[15] The first paragraph specifies that the President shall direct the work and administration of the Court and represent it, with particular responsibility for its relations with the authorities of the Council of Europe. He or she also has power to issue practice directions (Article 32). These are wide-ranging duties and will include managing the Court's relationship with its Registry, establishing and maintaining relations with national courts and governments (including protocol matters such as receiving delegations to the Court), and relations with the Committee of Ministers and the Secretariat of the Council of Europe, including, most importantly, budgetary matters. The proper relationship between the Court and other parts of the Council of Europe can be a difficult one, not least because the President must ensure that the Court is fully independent in judicial matters whilst also accepting that, at least administratively, the Court and its Registry are an autonomous part of the wider Council of Europe system. For the judicial functions of the President, Rule 9(2) makes explicit what the Convention assumes: he or she will preside at plenary meetings of the Court, meetings of the Grand Chamber, and meetings of the panel of five judges which considers requests for referral to the Grand Chamber. At stated above, in practice these presiding roles can be delegated to either of the two Vice-Presidents and will always be so delegated in any case against the contracting party in respect of which the President has been elected.[16]

III. THE ELECTION OF JUDGES

Article 22 entrusts election of judges to the Parliamentary Assembly of the Council of Europe from a list of three candidates nominated by the contracting party. The lists submitted by contracting parties have at times proved controversial. While the election is a matter for PACE, it is not clear what, if any, conditions it may impose on candidates. Pursuant to its Resolutions 1366 (2004) and 1436 (2005), the Parliamentary Assembly's

---

[13] ETS 162; available from the Treaty Office online at: <http://conventions.coe.int/>. In force 1998. Azerbaijan, Bosnia and Herzegovina, Montenegro, Portugal, and San Marino have not yet ratified the Protocol.

[14] By Article 26 of the Convention. Though that Article simply provides that they may be re-elected, Rule 8(3) of the Rules of Court limits this to one re-election. Rule 8(5) sets out elaborate procedures for their election.

[15] Note also the role of the Bureau which assists the President in directing the work and administration of the Court. It is composed of the President, the Vice-Presidents, the three Section Presidents, the Registrar, and the Deputy Registrar—Rule 9 A of the Rules of Court.

[16] For reasons of workload, Rule 9(3) provides that the President will not take part in the consideration of Chamber cases unless he or she is national judge in the case concerned. It is common practice that the President will try during his term of office to sit in a variety of Sections in order to follow, but not participate in, the judicial work of the Sections.

practice is that it will not vote on a list until it is satisfied that certain conditions are met, such as all three nominees being qualified to serve as judges, demonstrating sufficient independence from the nominating state, being capable of working in at least one of the Court's official languages, being willing to take up permanent residence in Strasbourg, and, in the interests of gender balance of the Court, that the list contain at least one man and one woman.[17] Lists which have not met these criteria have been regularly rejected as have lists which are not considered to offer the Assembly a real choice because of wide disparities in the qualifications and experience of the candidates. However, in such circumstances the contracting party retains the right to nominate candidates. Therefore if a state were to insist on submitting the same list as has previously been rejected by the Parliamentary Assembly then an impasse would develop, the resolution of which is not provided for by the Convention.

Such a stand-off occurred in relation to the Maltese list, which was rejected by the Parliamentary Assembly because there were no female candidates on it. The Maltese government then made representations to the Parliamentary Assembly arguing that a transparent and public selection process had taken place in Malta but no suitably qualified female candidates had come forward and that it was improper for the Parliamentary Assembly to impose such a rigid rule without due regard for the difficulties of smaller states in finding suitably qualified candidates of both sexes. In the ensuing impasse, Malta prevailed upon the Committee of Ministers to ask the Court for an advisory opinion on two questions: first, whether a list which satisfied the criteria listed in Article 21 (see above) could be rejected on gender grounds and second, whether the relevant resolutions of the Parliamentary Assembly adopting the requirement of both genders being represented on a list were in breach of the Assembly's responsibilities under Article 22. The Court in its advisory opinion of 12 February 2008[18] found it not necessary to answer the second question and answered the first by stating that while there was no implicit link between the criteria laid down in Article 21 and insistence on mixed sex lists, a gender equality policy could, in principle, constitute grounds for rejection of a list by the Assembly. However there were boundaries that the Assembly could not overstep in its pursuit of that policy. In particular it should not have the effect of making it more difficult for contracting parties to put forward candidates who satisfied all the requirements of Article 21. Accordingly provision had to be made for some exceptions to enable states to choose national candidates who satisfied the requirements of Article 21, especially for states where the legal profession was small. The practice of the Parliamentary Assembly in not allowing such exceptions was thus considered incompatible with the Convention.

The Assembly has also made some efforts to reform the way in which states produce their lists of candidates. For example, its Recommendation 1429 (1999) urges states to issue open calls for candidatures through the specialized press, to consult national parliaments when drawing up lists, and to submit the lists in alphabetical order so as not to betray preferences for candidates. These efforts have had mixed success. A number of states, such as the United Kingdom and Ireland, have advertised for candidatures. In the United Kingdom, at the last election, an independent selection board was set up which included a representative of the Equal Opportunities Commission, a judge of the Court of Appeal of England and Wales, and the Lord President of the Court of Session,[19] though

---

[17] See also the report of the Assembly's Committee on Legal Affairs and Human Rights on Resolution 1366 (Doc 9963 of 7 October 2003) which further outlines the general qualities it will look for in a candidate.

[18] *Advisory Opinion on Certain Legal Questions Concerning the Lists of Candidates for the Election of Judges to the European Court of Human Rights* hudoc (2008). See Mowbray, 8 HRLR 549 (2008).

[19] See working documents for the 873rd Meeting of the Committee of Ministers, 18 February 2004: CM(2004)25 Addendum.

other countries have been slower to implement that part of the recommendation and the alphabetical listing requirement seems to have been honoured only in the breach.[20]

IV. INELIGIBILITY TO SIT AND WITHDRAWAL

As noted above, Article 21(3) states that the judges shall not engage in any activity which is incompatible with their independence, impartiality, or with the demands of a full-time office. Occasionally judges have had to withdraw from hearing individual cases because of inevitable conflicts of interest, most commonly when the judge, who may previously have held high judicial office in his or her home state, has already heard a case at the national level or been involved in a case as an advocate. In the early years of the new Court, judges who had previously been members of the Commission frequently had to withdraw because they had previously heard the case at the Commission. Similarly, judges who have previously been agents of their government or ambassadors involved, even remotely, in dealing with cases before the Court will not be able to hear cases which were communicated to the government when they acted in these capacities. Rule 28(2) sets out situations where the judge may not take part in the consideration of any case including having a personal interest in the case or where the judge has expressed opinions publicly concerning the case that 'are objectively capable of adversely affecting his or her impartiality'. The mere fact that a judge has written an academic article concerning the interpretation of a provision of the Convention and has expressed a general opinion on the case law, unrelated to the facts of the case being considered, would not normally disqualify him or her from sitting. But, as with any court, difficult questions of judgment can arise in this context. Normally, the judge himself will simply notify the President that he cannot sit and Rule 28(1) places the burden on the judge to notify the relevant President if he is prevented from sitting. If there is any doubt on the part of the judge or the President as to the existence of any grounds for ineligibility to sit, then, by Rule 28(4), the issue is decided by the Chamber (or, as appropriate, the Grand Chamber) without the presence of the judge concerned but after the judge has had an opportunity to express his views on the matter.

V. *AD HOC* AND COMMON INTEREST JUDGES

In the event that a judge withdraws from a case, if it is not a case in which he or she is the national judge, then his or her place will simply be taken by one of the substitute judges in the Chamber or Grand Chamber. If he or she is the national judge then this necessitates the appointment of another judge since Article 28 requires the presence of the national judge. In accordance with an arrangement that was introduced to facilitate the Court's work and accepted by the government agents, the President will invite the respondent government to decide whether to appoint another elected judge to sit in the case or an *ad hoc* judge.[21] Where the Chamber seeks to reject a case *de limine* without communicating it to the government for observations, the Chamber will not ask for an *ad hoc* judge to be appointed. The Convention itself does not regulate the appointment of *ad hoc* judges, apart from providing in Article 27(2) that for Chambers and Grand Chambers the judge elected in respect of the state party concerned shall sit *ex officio* and, if there is none or

---

[20] The Parliamentary Assembly will alphabetize any list not submitted in that form for the purposes of its own procedures but, of course, by then any state preference will be apparent. Following the *Advisory Opinions*, the Assembly changed its rules to permit exceptions to the gender requirement—Resolution 1627 (2008).

[21] See eg, the appointment of the judge elected in respect of San Marino to replace the judge elected in respect of Italy in *Labita v Italy* 2000-IV; 46 EHRR 1228 para 4 GC.

he or she is unable to sit, a person of its choice shall sit in the capacity of judge. This is fleshed out by Rule 29 of the Rules of Court. The respondent government has thirty days within which to nominate either another elected judge or an *ad hoc* judge failing which it is deemed to have waived its right of appointment. Rule 29(1) makes it clear that *ad hoc* judges should possess the qualifications required by Article 21(1) and must not be ineligible to sit on any of the grounds set out in Rule 28 (see above).[22] This is a matter for the Chamber or Grand Chamber to decide and Rule 29(2) makes it clear that the government will be presumed to have waived its right of appointment if it twice appoints persons who do not satisfy the requirements for appointment. There is no reference to Article 23(6) and thus no requirement that the *ad hoc* judge be under seventy years of age. This has been a felicitous omission since it has allowed the appointment as *ad hoc* judge of experienced former judges of the Court.

Neither the Convention nor the Rules of Court provide for the possibility of challenging a judge or *ad hoc* judge although it is open to either an applicant, a contracting party, or a third party intervener to request a judge's withdrawal to the President of the Chamber, setting out the reasons for any objection. It would then be a matter for the President to decide after having consulted the Chamber. Moreover, since the Rules do not provide for any consultation of the applicant before the appointment of an *ad hoc* judge, no right of veto can be inferred and thus the matter is wholly at the discretion of the Chamber.[23]

Protocol 14 would change the rules concerning the nomination of *ad hoc* judges. Each contracting party would be required to draw up a reserve list of *ad hoc* judges from which the President of the Court would choose when the need arises to make an appointment. The Explanatory Report to the Protocol explains that the reform is a response to criticism of the current system, expressed in particular by the Parliamentary Assembly, on the grounds that it allows a contracting state to choose an *ad hoc* judge after the beginning of proceedings.[24] The precise details of how the new system would work, for example, concerning the number of people on the reserve list and the extent of the obligation to sit if chosen, are to be left to the Court to specify in the Rules of Court.

Finally when two or more applicant or respondent contracting states have a common interest in a particular case, for example when the application is brought against more than one contracting state, it is possible for the states to nominate a common interest judge. This occurred, for example, in the case of *Behrami and Saramati v France, Germany and Norway*,[25] concerning the actions of UNMIK in Kosovo, where the three respondent governments agreed to the appointment of Judge Costa, the judge elected in respect of France and currently President of the Court, as common interest judge.

---

[22] They must also be in a position to meet the demands of availability and attendance—Rule 29(1)(c) and (5).

[23] The matter arose in the fourth *Cyprus v Turkey* inter-state case 2001-IV; 35 EHRR 731 para 8 GC, where both the respondent and applicant governments objected to a series of *ad hoc* judges appointed by the others after the judge elected in respect of Turkey withdrew from sitting on the case and the Turkish government objected to the judge elected in respect of Cyprus. It appears that, in each case, the decision on whether the national or *ad hoc* judges were eligible to sit was finally decided by the Grand Chamber in accordance with Rule 28(4). While not expressly provided for by the Convention or Rules of Court, a third party could also object to an *ad hoc* judge, particularly if it is a state exercising its right to intervene.

[24] Id, para 64. Available at: <http://conventions.coe.int/Treaty/EN/Reports/html/194.htm>.

[25] *Behrami and Behrami v France and Saramati v France, Germany and Norway* Nos 71412/01 and 78166/01 hudoc (2007) DA. See also *Banković and Others v Belgium and 16 Other Contracting States* No 52207/99, 2001-XII GC and *Senator Lines GmbH v Austria and 14 Other Contracting States* No 56672/00, 2004-IV GC.

VI. COURT'S FORMATIONS: PLENARY, SECTIONS, GRAND CHAMBER, CHAMBERS, AND COMMITTEES

The administrative and judicial work of the Court takes place in a number of formations. For administrative work, the most significant decisions are taken by the plenary Court, composed of all of the Court judges. Article 26 provides that it is the plenary Court that elects the President and Vice-Presidents of the Court as well as the Presidents of the Chambers.[26] It also sets up the Chambers, adopts the rules of court, and elects the Court's Registrar and Deputy Registrar.

For judicial work, the Court is divided into Sections, currently five, of nine or ten judges. The Sections are changed every three years to ensure a rotation of judges across the Sections, a time-frame that will correspond with the election or re-election of the President, Vice-Presidents, and Section Presidents. The composition of each Section is geographically and gender-balanced and is designed to reflect the different legal systems among the contracting parties.[27] Decisions as to admissibility are taken by Chambers of seven judges or, in clearly inadmissible cases, Committees of three judges. Decisions on the merits of admitted cases are taken by Chambers or the Grand Chamber. Normally, any given Chamber or Committee formation is composed from judges within the same Section. The Grand Chamber of seventeen judges is drawn by lot from across the Sections.

The procedures followed by Committees, Chambers, and the Grand Chamber are set out separately in the later sections of this chapter but in essence the formation that will make the final decision or judgment on an application will depend entirely on the case's relative merit and importance.

VII. THE COURT'S REGISTRY

Article 25 of the Convention provides: 'The Court shall have a registry, the functions and organisation of which shall be laid down in the Rules of Court. The Court shall be assisted by legal secretaries.' The task of the Registry is to provide legal and administrative support to the Court in the exercise of its judicial functions. It is therefore composed of lawyers, administrative, and technical staff and translators.[28] The Court elects its Registrar and Deputy Registrar—the head and deputy head of the Registry respectively.[29] Each of the Court's five judicial Sections is assisted by a Section Registrar and a Deputy Section Registrar. The principal function of the Registry is to process and prepare

---

[26] While Article 26 speaks of electing Presidents of Chambers, in practice the plenary Court elects Presidents of Sections, who will in most cases (except when they are the national judge) preside in the chambers of seven judges which are drawn from that Section.

[27] See Rule 25(2). Each section itself elects its Vice-President who presides when the President cannot. For example a President will not preside when a case against his or her state is being considered.

[28] There are currently more than 620 staff in the Registry including 250 lawyers and support staff. Registry employees are staff members of the Council of Europe, the Court's parent organization, and are subject to the Council of Europe's Staff Regulations concerning conditions of work and pension entitlement. Approximately half the Registry is employed on contracts of unlimited duration and may be expected to pursue a career in the Registry or in other parts of the Council of Europe. They are recruited on the basis of open competitions. All members of the Registry are required to adhere to strict conditions as to their independence and impartiality and are answerable in practice to the President of the Court rather than to the Secretary General of the Council of Europe.

[29] Article 26(e) of the Convention and Rules 15 and 16 of the Rules of Court.

for adjudication applications lodged by individuals and states with the Court.[30] The lawyers prepare files and analytical notes for the judge rapporteurs. They are also responsible for drafting decisions and judgments under the supervision of the judge rapporteur, responding to inquiries and investigating issues of national or international law relevant to the Court's work. Their legal work is subject to different layers of review: first within the Registry itself by Heads of Division and Section Registrars and then by the judge rapporteur (in Chamber or Grand Chamber cases) and ultimately by the Court itself. They also correspond with the parties on procedural matters.[31] The Registry is recruited by the Council of Europe but is necessarily autonomous in the performance of its functions in order to preserve the independence of the Court and ultimately answerable only to the President of the Court. As a matter of convention, this autonomy has been more or less respected in practice by successive Secretaries General of the Council of Europe.

2. PROCEDURE BEFORE THE COURT (I): FROM THE INITIAL APPLICATION TO JUDGMENT

I. INDIVIDUAL COMPLAINTS

As the statistics of individual complaints indicate, it is almost entirely through the exercise of the right of individual petition (Article 34) that the Court functions.[32] It is considered by the Court as 'a key component of the machinery' for the protection of human rights.[33] In accordance with Protocol 11, contracting states are no longer required to accept the competence of the Court to hear individual complaints. It is now compulsory. While the sheer volume of cases imposes substantial pressure on the Court to deal with cases within a reasonable time, there have been calls to dismantle the right of individual petition and to confer on the Court a much wider power to choose the cases that it wishes to examine (the so-called 'pick and choose' solution). However, the Group of Wise Persons, while recognizing that the sheer mass of cases poses a serious threat to the effectiveness of the right of petition, has placed the emphasis on the creation of a judicial filtering body which would be part of the Court itself and would be entrusted with the task of determining admissibility and dealing with repetitive cases.[34]

---

[30] The Registry's lawyers are divided into thirty-one case-processing divisions, each of which is assisted by an administrative team. Cases are assigned to the different divisions on the basis of knowledge of the language and legal system concerned. The documents prepared by the Registry for the Court are all drafted in one of its two official languages (English and French).

[31] In addition to its case-processing divisions, the Registry has divisions dealing with the following sectors of activity: information technology; case law information and publications; research and the library; just satisfaction; press and public relations; and internal administration. It also has a central office, which handles mail, files, and archives. The Court also has a Jurisconsult who heads the Research Division and keeps the consistency of the case law of the Sections under review. There are two language divisions, whose main work is translating the Court's judgments into the second official language.

[32] See n 3 above.

[33] See *Mamatkulov and Askarov v Turkey* 2005-I; 41 EHRR 494 paras 100 and 122 GC. Individual complaints can be brought by any natural person or legal entity, regardless of nationality, place of residence, civil status, or capacity to possess rights and to be bound by obligations—*Scozzari and Giunta v Italy* 2000-VIII; 35 EHRR 243 para 138 GC. See further above, pp 790–800.

[34] Report of the Group of Wise Persons to the Committee of Ministers (Council of Europe, November 2006) paras 51–65.

II. HINDERING THE EFFECTIVE EXERCISE OF THE RIGHT OF INDIVIDUAL PETITION

Article 34 last sentence indicates that the contracting parties must not 'hinder in any way the effective exercise of this right'. The Court has emphasized, in its case law on the scope of this obligation, that it is of the utmost importance for the effective operation of the system of individual petition that applicants or potential applicants are able to communicate freely with the Court without being subjected to any form of pressure from the authorities to withdraw or modify their complaints. The right is an absolute one and admits of no hindrance. The word 'pressure' is understood as covering not only direct coercion and flagrant acts of intimidation of applicants or their families or legal representatives but also other improper indirect acts or contacts designed to dissuade or discourage them from pursuing a Convention remedy.[35] In making its assessment of whether improper pressure has been imposed on an applicant the circumstances of each case will be examined and the Court will have particular regard to the vulnerability of the complainant and his or her susceptibility to influence exerted by the authorities.[36] Interference with an applicant's letters to a lawyer or to the Court concerning the filing of an application or the carrying out of reprisals on an applicant would also give rise to an issue under Article 34.[37] In *McShane v UK*[38] the Court found a violation under this head after the lawyer was reported by the police to the Law Society for beaching confidentiality by disclosing documents to the applicant for purposes of the application before the Court. Although no action was taken against him by the Law Society, the Court found a violation on the basis that the initiation of disciplinary proceedings could have a 'chilling effect' on the exercise of the right of individual petition by both lawyers and applicants. The context in which alleged interference takes place is also of importance. Putting pressure on villagers from south-east Turkey who feared reprisals to withdraw their applications and filming an interview by state authorities with them about their application was considered improper behaviour.[39] So was questioning by the very gendarmes whose behaviour was the subject of the application in Strasbourg.[40] The Court has also stressed that it is unacceptable to question an applicant where doubts have arisen concerning the authenticity of the power of attorney of the person acting for him; where a government believes that the right of petition is being abused, the correct course of action is to inform the Court and not bring the applicant in for questioning.[41] Not all questioning by the authorities, though frowned upon by the Court, leads to a finding of a breach of this

[35] See *Fedotova v Russia* hudoc (2006) (police questioning of the applicant's lawyer and translator concerning the claim for just satisfaction); *Oferta Plus SRL v Moldova* hudoc (2006) (failure to respect the confidentiality of lawyer-applicant discussions in a meeting room); *Petra v Romania* 1998-VII; 33 EHRR 105 (threats by the prison authorities); *Nurmagomedov v Russia* hudoc (2007) (refusal by the prison authorities to forward an application to the Court on the grounds that the applicant was not considered to have exhausted his domestic remedies); *Boicenko v Moldova* hudoc (2006) (preventing a lawyer from having access to a client's medical file which was considered to be essential for the purposes of the application).
[36] *Sisojeva and Others v Latvia* hudoc (2007); 45 EHRR 753 para 116 GC—and the many authorities cited therein.
[37] *Maksym v Poland* hudoc (2006) (delaying the posting of a prisoner's letter to lawyer); *Drozdowski v Poland* hudoc (2005) (opening letters to a prisoner sent by the ECtHR); also *Peers v Greece* 2001-III; 33 EHRR 1192. See, in this connection, the European Agreement relating to persons participating in proceedings of the European Court of Human Rights, ETS 161.
[38] Hudoc (2002); 35 EHRR 593 para 151.
[39] *Akdivar and Others v Turkey* 1996-IV; 23 EHRR 143 paras 104–5.
[40] *Bilgin v Turkey* hudoc (2000); 36 EHRR 879 paras 132–6.
[41] *Tanrıkulu v Turkey* 1999-IV; 30 EHRR 950 paras 129–32 GC.

provision. In *Sisojeva v Latvia*,[42] in an immigration context, the applicant was questioned by the security police about her application. However the Court, while sceptical about the supposed reasons for the interrogation, emphasized that there was no evidence of pressure or intimidation, and that there were no legal consequences when she refused to answer the questions. Refusing to comply with the Court's interim measures is also considered as a hindrance in breach of this provision.[43] In addition, account should be taken of specific requirements on the parties to co-operate fully in the conduct of proceedings, to comply with orders of the Court, and to provide all information requested by the Court.[44] A failure to comply with these provisions is a relevant factor in determining compliance with this elementary but crucial obligation.

III. INTER-STATE COMPLAINTS[45]

Article 33 (formerly Article 24) provides that any contracting party may refer to the Court any alleged breach of the Convention and the Protocols thereto by another contracting party. The right to bring a case flows directly from the ratification of the Convention and is not subject to any other conditions. In bringing an application the state is fulfilling its role as one of the collective guarantors of Convention rights. As the former Commission indicated in *Austria v Italy*,[46] Convention obligations are essentially of an objective character being designed to protect 'the fundamental rights of individual human beings from infringement by any of the High Contracting Parties rather than to create subjective and reciprocal rights for themselves'. From this characterization of the nature of the Convention, the former Commission deduced that a contracting party could refer to the Commission any alleged breach of the Convention, regardless of whether the victims were its nationals or whether its own interests were at stake. It is not exercising a right of action for the purpose of enforcing its own rights but rather to bring before the Commission an alleged violation of the public order of Europe.[47] The complaint under Article 33 forms part of the collective enforcement of human rights referred to in the Preamble.[48] It follows from this notion of the collective guarantee of the Convention that the principle of reciprocity is subordinated to the states' right to take enforcement action. Thus in *Austria v Italy* the Commission accepted that Austria could file a complaint against Italy concerning matters arising before Austria became a party to the Convention. It appears to follow that an applicant state would not be prevented from complaining under Article 33 because it had entered a reservation to the provision allegedly violated by the respondent state or because the right concerned is protected by a Protocol which the applicant state has not ratified.[49] Nor is it relevant that the applicant government has not been recognized by the

---

[42] Hudoc (2007); 45 EHRR 753 paras 121–4 GC—the Court attached weight to the 'wider context' of the interrogation when compared to the very different and more intimidatory contexts examined in the Turkish cases.

[43] See the section on interim measures below, pp 842–6.   [44] Rules 44 A–C of the Rules of Court.

[45] See Rogge, in Hartig, ed, *Études à la mémoire de Wolfgang Strasser*, 2007; and Prebensen, in Gudmundur Alfredsson *et al*, eds, *International human rights monitoring mechanisms: essays in honour of Jakob Th Möller*, 2001, pp 533–59; Greer, *European Convention*, pp 24–8; Kamminga, 12 NQHR 153 (1994).

[46] *No 788/60*, 4 YB 112, 140 (1961).

[47] *Ibid*. See also *Ireland v UK* A 25 (1978) pp 90–1; 2 EHRR 25 at 104 PC and *Cyprus v Turkey No 8007/77 (Third Application)*, 13 DR 85 (1978).

[48] *Ireland v UK*, id, para 239.

[49] These specific issues have not yet arisen in an inter-state case. However in *France, Norway, Denmark, Sweden and Netherlands v Turkey Nos 9940–9944/82*, 35 DR 143 at 168–9 (1983) the Commission found, with reference to the objective character of the Convention system, that France was not barred from bringing a case against Turkey which gave rise to a consideration of issues under Article 15 to which France has entered a reservation.

respondent government.[50] Inter-state complaints under Article 33 differ from individual complaints in the following respects.

(i)   Under Article 33, states may refer 'any alleged breach' of the Convention to the Court while individual applicants can only complain under Article 34 of a violation of the rights and freedoms in the Convention. Thus allegations can be made of breaches of procedural as well as substantive provisions of the Convention. However the significance of this difference has been diminished by the Court's recognition that the individual can complain of breaches of Articles 35 §1 (*in fine*) and 38(1)(a) (see below pp 844 and 848).

(ii)   The state can challenge a legislative measure *in abstracto* where the law is couched in terms sufficiently clear and precise to make the breach apparent or with reference to the manner in which it is interpreted and applied *in concreto*.[51] In contrast, the individual must show that he is a 'victim' of the measure complained of.

(iii) The only formal admissibility requirements are the local remedies and six-month rule (Article 35). The requirements contained in Article 35(2) and (3) apply to individual complaints only.

(iv)   An inter-state application is automatically communicated to the respondent government for observations on admissibility. The Court has no discretion in this respect. Moreover, unlike the procedure in individual cases, there are separate proceedings on questions of admissibility and the merits (Rules 48 and 58 of the Rules of Procedure).

In practice there have been few inter-state complaints.[52] In many of the cases that have been brought, the applicant state has had a political interest to assert in the

[50] *Cyprus v Turkey No 8007/77 (Third Application)*, 13 DR 85 (1978). The constitutional propriety of the state's right to bring the complaint was discussed in the first two *Cyprus v Turkey* cases, *Nos 6780/74 and 6950/75*, 2 DR 125 (1975). The Commission, in finding that the applicant state had *locus standi*, based itself on the fact that the government was and continued to be internationally recognized by States and international organizations as the government of the Republic of Cyprus.

[51] *Ireland v UK* A 25 (1978); 2 EHRR 25 paras 239–40 PC and *Denmark, Norway, Sweden and Netherlands v Greece*, 12 YB (the *Greek* case) 134 (1969).

[52] So far, twenty-one inter-state applications (referred to below by application number) (relating to eight separate disputes) have been brought—many of them before the former Commission and three before the new Court: *Greece v UK Nos 176/56 and 299/57*, 2 YB 186 (1958) Com Rep; CM Res (59) 12 and (59) 32 (two applications relating to the United Kingdom. It was alleged that various emergency laws and regulations were not compatible with the Convention and that there had been torture—the cases were settled after the Zurich agreement on Cypriot independence); *Austria v Italy No 788/60*, 4 YB 113 (1961) Com Rep; CM Res (63) DH 3 (Articles 6 and 14—criminal trial connected with the prosecution of members of the German-speaking minority in South Tyrol); *Denmark, Norway, Sweden and Netherlands v Greece Nos 3321–3/67, 3344/67*, 11 YB-II 691 (1968) and 12 YB (the *Greek* case) (1969) Com Rep; CM Res DH (70) 1 (wide-scale violations of human rights under the Greek dictatorship and abolition of democratic institutions); *Denmark, Norway, Sweden v Greece No 4448/70*, 13 YB 109 (1970) (*Second Greek* case: trial of thirty-four persons before a court-martial in Athens; withdrawn after Greece re-entered the Council of Europe); *Ireland v UK No 5451/72*, 41 CD 82 (1972) (allegations of violation of Article 7 withdrawn after UK undertaking); *Ireland v UK* A 25 (1978); 2 EHRR 25 PC (interrogation techniques involving alleged use of torture and detention of suspects under emergency powers in Northern Ireland; the first inter-state case to have been referred to the Court); *Cyprus v Turkey Nos 6780/74 and 6950/75 (First and Second Applications)*, 2 DR 125 (1975); 4 EHRR 482 (1976); Com Rep; CM Res DH (79) 1 (consequences of the Turkish military intervention in northern Cyprus in 1974); *Cyprus v Turkey No 8007/77 (Third Application)*, 13 DR 85 (1978); 13 HRLJ 154 (1992) Com Rep; CM Res (92) 12 (facts as above); *No 25781/94 (Fourth Application—referred to the Court)*, Com Rep, 4 June 1999; 2001-V; 35 EHRR 731 GC; *France, Norway, Denmark, Sweden and Netherlands v Turkey Nos 9940–9944/82*, 35 DR 143 (1983) and 44 DR 31 (1985) friendly settlement (the *Turkish* case; consequences of the military takeover in Turkey in 1980 with allegations of wide-scale violations of human rights and abolition of democratic institutions); *Denmark v Turkey* 2000-IV (alleged ill-treatment of a Danish

proceedings.[53] Often they have concerned allegations of violations of human rights on a large scale involving no national interest but evoking a concern for the 'public order of Europe'. The reality is that states will be reluctant to have recourse to legal action under the Convention to resolve their disputes. In the close-knit community of like-minded states in the Council of Europe, contracting states will be reluctant to jeopardize their good diplomatic relationships with other states and undoubtedly prefer negotiation to a legal process which may be lengthy, counterproductive, and ultimately ineffective.[54]

While the Court has jurisdiction to hear inter-state cases and, under more restricted conditions, to give advisory opinions, the vast majority of its work is based on individual applications lodged under Article 34.[55] The Convention itself does not provide for any different procedures to be followed for inter-state cases though Rule 58 of the Rules of Court provides for automatic notification to the respondent government and separation of the admissibility and merits phases of the procedure. There is, for example, no express requirement that such a case be heard by the Grand Chamber, though such cases are potential candidates for Grand Chamber examination following relinquishment if no friendly settlement takes place before the Chamber.[56]

IV. THE APPLICATION[57]

An application to the Court will always begin with initial contact from an individual or their legal representative. While the Court receives many letters from concerned parties who wish to draw the Court's attention to a particular problem affecting others, the Court will take no action on such representations. Nor will it solicit applications from possible applicants.

The official languages of the Court are English and French but an application may be sent in the language of any of the contracting parties. However if the case is communicated

national—case ended in a friendly settlement); *Georgia v Russia No 13255/07*, press release of 27 March 2007 (allegations of harassment of the Georgian immigrant population in the Russian Federation—alleged violations, *inter alia*, of Articles 3, 5, 8, 13, 14, and 18). See also Press release of 12 August 2008.

[53] Rogge, n 45 above, places nine of the cases in this category: *Greece v UK, Austria v Italy, Ireland v UK, Cyprus v Turkey*; to which can be added *Georgia v Russia*.

[54] Consider for example the *Cyprus v Turkey* dispute. The Commission's report in the first two applications was forwarded to the Committee of Ministers in 1976. The Committee took formal note of the report as well as a memorial of the Turkish government, urged the parties to resume inter-communal talks, and 'found that events which occurred in Cyprus constitute violations of the Convention' without attaching direct responsibility. It took until 31 August 1979 for the case documentation (including the Commission's report) to be declassified (Resolution DH (79) 1 of 20 January 1979). In the third case the Commission's report of 4 October 1983 remained pending before the Committee of Ministers until 2 April 1992 when it was decided to publish it. The Committee of Ministers resolved that the decision to publish completed its consideration of the case under Article 32 (Resolution DH (92) 12).

[55] The conditions set out in Article 34 are considered in Ch 22.

[56] This is a requirement for any advisory opinion (see Article 31(b)). The procedure governing advisory opinions is considered separately below, p 838. *Denmark v Turkey* was the subject of a settlement adopted by a Chamber—n 52 above.

[57] See, generally, the Practice Direction on the Institution of Proceedings, annexed to the Rules of Court (1 November 2003). Applicants should be diligent in conducting correspondence with the Registry. Files will be destroyed if an applicant does not return a completed application form within a year or has not answered any letter sent by the Registry—id, paras 9–11. Failure to return a completed application form within six months may result in rejection under the six-month rule—see Ch 22. In response to proposals made by Lord Woolf, the Court has recently lowered to eight weeks the time period for the submission of a completed application form following receipt of the first letter interrupting the running of the six-month period. See the 'Woolf Report'—Review of the Working Methods of the European Court of Human Rights, December 2005, at pp 19–22. Available at <http://www.echr.coe.int/ECHR/EN/Header/Reports+and+Statistics/Reports/Other+reports/>.

for observations, all communications (including oral and written submissions) shall be in one of the official languages unless a special exemption is granted by the President. When a case is communicated accompanying Annexes to the observations need not be translated into the official languages and can be sent in the language in which they were lodged.[58]

Save in exceptional circumstances (such as an imminent expulsion or deportation), the Registry will take no immediate action on a simple letter setting out the complaints of the applicant. The application will be registered provisionally and prospective applicants will be sent an application form which they will be asked to complete. If no response is received within six months, the file will be destroyed.

Rule 47 of the Rules of Court sets out what the application form should contain, as of course does the form itself.[59] It is not necessary to fill out the actual form: an appropriately drafted document which closely follows the headings and fields contained in the form and complies with Rule 47 will suffice. Failure to comply with the requirements of Rule 47 may result in the application not being examined by the Court and applicants will be warned if they do not.[60]

V. ASSIGNMENT OF CASES

After an application is received and registered, the procedure thereafter will very much depend on the merit and importance of the complaints. As stated above, the Committee procedure is reserved for applications which are clearly inadmissible. The procedure will involve the Court's Registry preparing a case for consideration. Once the case is considered by the Registry to be ready for decision and placed before a decision body (ie a complete application form with the necessary supporting documents has been received), it will be assigned to the appropriate Section of the Court. Applications are usually assigned to Sections on the basis of what contracting party they are brought against. Normally, applications brought against a particular state will be assigned to the Section in which the judge elected in respect of that state sits although with high case-count countries such as Russia, Turkey, or Ukraine there may be a certain cross-Section distribution. After this assignment, a provisional decision to assign an application to a Committee or Chamber case is taken.

VI. THE COMMITTEE PROCEDURE

In accordance with Article 28, applications which are clearly inadmissible are considered by a Committee of three judges.[61] These play an important role in enabling the Court to reject large numbers of inadmissible cases with an economy of procedure. They are used not only to reject cases which are obviously hopeless but also cases which can be rejected as inadmissible *de plano* on the grounds that they give rise to no Convention issue, judged from the standpoint of the Court's established case law, even though they may sometimes concern important questions and are supported by detailed written argument. Committees are thus an important part of the Court's armoury in coping with the relentless rise in applications. Each Section constitutes a number of Committees for a period of

---

[58] Rule 34 regulates the use of languages in the procedure before the Court.
[59] Details such as personal identification information; a brief statement of facts and complaints; an explanation as to compliance with the six months rule and the rule of exhaustion of domestic remedies; the object of the application and all supporting documents especially national court decisions.
[60] Rule 47(4) of the Rules of Court.
[61] See Rule 27 of the Rules of Court which regulates Committees.

twelve months and each Section generally has three Committees at any one time. Their only power is to declare a case inadmissible, failing which it will be referred to a Chamber for examination. They must be unanimous. If one or more judges do not consider the application to be *prima facie* inadmissible then it is referred to the relevant Chamber for its decision. If, on the other hand, the three judges agree the case is inadmissible, their decision is final. Although national judges do not necessarily sit in the Committee dealing with cases concerning their countries, they will be provided with the copies of draft decisions concerning them and can make their views known.

Where a Committee declares an application inadmissible, the applicant will receive a letter informing him of this decision which states the names of the judges who considered the application and includes a brief statement of the reasons for the decision. The reasons given will only mention which of the admissibility criteria the application failed to meet (six months, non-exhaustion, etc). As a general rule, no further correspondence is entered into having regard to the final character of the decision. However in very exceptional cases where the Court itself has made a factual or legal mistake in the course of its examination—such as the date of the final decision for purposes of the six-month rule—it has an inherent power to re-open the case and restore it to the list.[62] This power would not, however, be used to correct errors made by lawyers in the presentation of the case.

VII. CHAMBER PROCEDURE: COMMUNICATION AND THE JOINT PROCEDURE

Cases which are not clearly inadmissible or which raise a *prima facie* issue will initially be assigned to a Chamber of seven judges which can take a number of steps from declaring the application inadmissible to declaring it admissible and subsequently adopting a judgment on the merits of it. If an application is assigned to a Chamber, a judge rapporteur will be nominated by the President of the Section. He or she has the task of presenting the application to the Chamber and formally proposing the various procedural steps that the Chamber may take. The principal decision, which may be by a majority, is whether the application warrants communication to the respondent government for their observations on admissibility and merits. If it does not, then the Chamber may immediately adopt an inadmissibility decision, which is published on the website,[63] though this too is final and not subject to appeal. If the application is communicated to the respondent government, this will involve sending a copy of the application to the government with all relevant documents, a statement of facts prepared by the Registry and a question or series of questions that their observations should address.[64] Once the observations are received, the applicant will be given an opportunity to submit observations in reply with any claims for just satisfaction under Article 41 of the Convention. The government will be given a final opportunity to make further submissions in reply, after which the case is considered by the Chamber.[65] If any further observations are received at this stage they will be considered as unsolicited and, unless the President of the Chamber decides otherwise, they will be returned to the party and not admitted to the file.

---

[62] *Ölmez and Ölmez v Turkey No 39464/98* hudoc (2005) (re-opening decision) and the authorities cited therein; also *Edwards v UK* A 247-B; 35 EHRR 487 para 26. See also p 759.

[63] If the decision is deemed sufficiently important it may be published in the official reports. This follows a decision by the Court's Publications Committee.

[64] Both the statement of facts and the questions are now available online on the Court's website (Hudoc, statement of facts collection).

[65] The Chamber can however ask for further observations, clarifications, and factual information from either party as it sees fit.

It has become the rule in recent years, due to the large number of pending cases, for the Court, by expressly invoking Article 29(3) of the Convention, to examine jointly the admissibility and merits of the application.[66] The reason for this is economy of process. If the admissibility and merits of an application are examined separately then this would require a separate decision and two rounds of observations. In many cases there are no substantial questions of admissibility. Thus questions of admissibility, if indeed there are any, are considered in the judgment on the merits. The parties can object to the application of Article 29(3), though, unlike objection to relinquishment, an objection can be overridden by the Court if it considers that no significant admissibility issues arise that would warrant a separate admissibility decision. They will be asked to submit their observations, including submissions concerning just satisfaction and any proposals for a friendly settlement. For applicants and government agents who object to the use of the joint procedure it should be noted that an admissibility decision is final and cannot be referred to the Grand Chamber whereas a judgment which considers admissibility and merits together can be so referred.[67]

VIII. THE GRAND CHAMBER

While the vast majority of the Court's work takes place in Committees and Chambers, the Grand Chamber is the constitutional formation of the Court. It consists of seventeen judges and has the task of hearing and giving judgment on the most important cases.[68] It has the central task of ensuring overall coherence and consistency of the Court's case law. Cases arrive before the Grand Chamber by two means: relinquishment by a Chamber before it renders its judgment (Article 30) and, after a Chamber gives judgment, if one of the parties requests referral (Article 43). In the former case, the simple decision to relinquish is enough to seize the Grand Chamber of the case provided one of the parties does not object.[69] In the latter case, the Convention provides for a panel of five judges of the Grand Chamber which decides whether to accept or reject the party's request. In 2007, seventeen new cases were referred to the Grand Chamber, of which eight resulted from the relinquishment of jurisdiction by a Chamber and nine followed referral after a Chamber judgment.

Strangely, the criteria as to when a Chamber should relinquish and when the panel should accept a referral request are slightly different. Article 30 provides as follows:

> Where a case pending before a Chamber raises a serious question affecting the interpretation of the Convention or the protocols thereto, or where the resolution of a question before the Chamber might have a result inconsistent with a judgment previously delivered

---

[66] See also Rule 54 A on the joint examination of admissibility and merits.   [67] See below, p 827.

[68] See Rule 24 for the regime governing the composition of the Grand Chamber. The President, Vice-Presidents, and Presidents of Sections sit as *ex officio* members of the Grand Chamber. In a referral case under Article 43 the remaining members are drawn by lot by the President. The members of the Chamber which gave the original judgment are not eligible apart from the President of the Section and the national judge. It often happens in a referral case that the President of the Section (unless he is also the national judge) will not exercise his right to sit in the Grand Chamber for reasons of conscience; having already given judgment in the case, it may be considered inappropriate form the standpoint of 'appearances' to sit a second time. In a relinquishment case (Article 30) the full members of the relinquishing Chamber are automatically members of the Grand Chamber. The modalities for drawing lots to complete the formations have been worked out 'with due regard to the need for a geographically balanced composition reflecting the different legal systems among the Contracting Parties' (Rule 24(3)).

[69] The parties have a month following notification of the intention to relinquish to file a 'duly reasoned objection'—Rule 72(2). Cf, Article 30 of the Convention.

by the Court, the Chamber may, at any time before it has rendered its judgement, relinquish jurisdiction in favour of the Grand Chamber, unless one of the parties to the case objects.

Article 43(2), on the other hand, states that the panel shall accept a referral request if the case 'raises a serious question affecting the interpretation or application of the Convention or the protocols thereto, or a serious issue of general importance'. It is not clear why the serious question contemplated in Article 43(2) refers to the interpretation or application of the Convention whereas Article 30 refers only to the interpretation of the Convention. Likewise, it is not clear why the drafters of the two Articles sought fit include 'a serious issue of general importance' as a criterion for referral but not a criterion for relinquishment. The drafting history of Protocol 11 does not shed any light on the difference of wording.[70]

In relation to Article 30, the normal procedure is for the Chamber in question to notify the parties of its intention to relinquish and to give them one month to object. If no objection is received (and silence is taken as tacit consent to relinquishment) then the Chamber will formally relinquish. Rule 72(1) indicates that reasons need not be given for the decision to relinquish. However the objection to relinquishment by one of the parties must be 'duly reasoned'. In practice it is sufficient for one of the parties to indicate that it wishes to have the case examined by a Chamber with the possibility of re-examination by the Grand Chamber. It has occurred that a state objects to relinquishment under Article 43(2) and then subsequently seeks to refer the case to the Grand Chamber once the Chamber judgment has been handed down. In the practice of the panel this is not seen as a reason for refusing a referral if there are important issues of law raised in the case.[71] No principle of estoppel is applied. It is not always clear why a party would object to relinquishment since in the event of the objecting party obtaining a favourable result before the Chamber it remains open to the other party to request referral under Article 43(2) and the same reasons why the Chamber contemplated relinquishment may also lead the panel to accept the referral request. An interest in delaying the proceedings may be one reason. Another may be the conviction, based on the drafting history of Protocol 11 and the famous historic compromise between states that were in favour of a two-tier system and those that were not, that the state has a right to an examination of the case by two instances.[72]

The composition of the panel that considers requests for referral under Article 43(2) is not provided for in the Convention (though the matter is governed by Rule 24(5) of the Rules of Court)[73] and requesting parties are not told the names of the judges who considered their request. Nor are they given reasons for the decision to accept or reject their request. All parts of the judgment can be grounds for referral including the level or means

---

[70] The difference in wording suggests that relinquishment should be limited to cases raising difficult issues of interpretation only. However, this has not been the practice of the Court to date. The Explanatory Report states that the wording was taken from the Rules of Court of the former Court (para 79) but gives no further explanation for the different wording. Relinquishment cases are described as 'cases with specified serious implications' (para 46)—a wording which is not limitative.

[71] See eg, *Mamatkulov and Askarov v Turkey* 2005-I; 41 EHRR 494 para 6 GC, where the government requested referral to the Grand Chamber and *Mamatkulov and Abdurasulovic v Turkey* hudoc (2003) (the Chamber judgment in the same case where they objected to relinquishment). The same happened in *Öcalan v Turkey* 2005-IV; 41 EHRR 985 GC and *Öcalan v Turkey* hudoc (2003); 37 EHRR 238 para 6.

[72] See Ch 26 of the first edition of this book for the drafting history of Protocol 11.

[73] Which Rule provides that it shall be composed of the President of the Court, two Presidents of Sections designated by rotation, two other judges designated by rotation from the remaining sections, and two further substitute judges, save that it will not include any judge who took part in the consideration of the admissibility and merits of the case and any judge who is elected in respect of or who is a national of the contracting party concerned.

of calculating just satisfaction under Article 41.[74] It therefore sometimes occurs that both parties request referral.[75] The request for referral must be received by the Registry within three months of the date of the judgment, failing which the panel will not examine the request, even though it may have been posted within the three-month period. This is different from the application of the six-month rule in respect of new applications where the date will normally be taken as the postmark or the date the letter was written rather than the date of registration at the Court's Registry.[76] The difference with referral requests is that judgments automatically become final three months after their delivery, unless the parties request referral, so there is a greater interest in legal certainty. The Court and the outside world have a stronger interest in knowing when its judgments acquire the status of *res judicata*. In most cases, faxing a copy of the request within the three-month period will prevent any problems arising. The panel accepts very few requests for referral and the fact that the Chamber may have been divided is not necessarily an indication that the case will be accepted. While Article 43 does not explicitly mention departure from previous case law as a ground on which the panel of five judges may accept a case, a 'serious issue affecting the interpretation' of the Convention could arise if a Chamber gave a judgment which significantly develops the case law. This would be an indication that an issue of consistency was involved which might require an authoritative interpretation by the Grand Chamber.[77] New issues on which there is no established case law are also likely candidates for acceptance.[78]

In cases where there is more than one applicant, a request for referral by one applicant can be taken as a request on behalf of all applicants. In *Cumpănă and Mazăre v Romania*[79] two applicants brought a single application. Following an adverse finding by the Chamber, the first applicant lodged and signed a referral request on behalf of both applicants. A Panel of the Grand Chamber accepted that request. The respondent government, in its observations in the Grand Chamber, submitted that the scope of the Grand Chamber's jurisdiction was limited to the first applicant's complaints and requested the Grand Chamber not to examine the second applicant's complaints. The Grand Chamber rejected that submission, holding that the 'case' referred to the Grand Chamber necessarily embraces all aspects of the application previously examined by the Chamber in its judgment, there being no basis for a merely partial referral.[80]

It is not open to the parties to contest the decision of the panel on the question of referral to the Grand Chamber.[81] When a case is referred by the panel, the scope of the case before the Grand Chamber is not limited to the grounds set out in the referral request: instead it embraces all aspects of the application considered by the Chamber. The Grand Chamber may also reconsider admissibility objections raised by the government where these have already been addressed by the Chamber and thus it is entitled to come to a different conclusion from that of the Chamber.[82] However, subject to the above, a government will be estopped from raising admissibility objections in proceedings before the

[74] See *Arvanitaki-Roboti and Others v Greece* hudoc (2006) and hudoc (2008) GC.
[75] *Öcalan v Turkey* 2005-IV; 41 EHRR 985 para 9 GC.   [76] See above, p 777.
[77] See eg, *Stec and Others v UK* 2006-VI GC (whether a non contributory social security benefits came within Article 1 of Protocol 1) and *Kopecký v Slovakia* 2004-IX; 41 EHRR 944 GC concerning the meaning of legitimate expectation in the area of property rights).
[78] See eg, *Pretty v UK* 2002-III; 35 EHRR 1 (concerning refusal of euthanasia to a seriously ill person) and *Evans v UK* hudoc (2007); 46 EHRR 728 (concerning the implantation of embryos and the issue of consent).
[79] 2004-XI; 41 EHRR 200 paras 62–9 GC.   [80] Id, para 66 and references therein.
[81] *Pisano v Italy* hudoc (2002) paras 24–9 GC.
[82] *Odièvre v France* 2003-III; 38 EHRR 871 para 22 GC; *Azinas v Cyprus* 2004-III; 40 EHRR 166 paras 32, 37 GC.

Grand Chamber if it has not already raised them before the Chamber[83] or the Chamber considered the same admissibility question on its own motion.[84]

In *Pisano v Italy*, the Grand Chamber stated that once a case is referred, it may 'employ the full range of judicial powers conferred on the Court'.[85] Hence it may approve friendly settlements, strike out cases, and form its own assessment of the facts of the case even where the original Chamber has already addressed such issues. Equally, after it accepts a referral request it remains open to the Grand Chamber to limit the scope of its examination of a case at any stage in the proceedings and to adopt a judgment on a preliminary issue of admissibility.[86] Finally, after it accepts a referral request, the Grand Chamber may also strike out part of a case and at the same time give judgment on the merits of other complaints.[87]

IX. INTERNAL MECHANISMS FOR ENSURING CONSISTENCY OF CASE LAW[88]

The Court is aware that with five Sections operating on a weekly basis and each Section adopting hundreds of judgments every year there is a risk of divergent approaches or inconsistent application of the case law to the facts of new cases. Apart from the decisions of the Grand Chamber panel, the Court has responded to this risk by creating a variety of structures to address the problem at an earlier stage in the procedure. The first stage is the scrutiny of the draft judgments and decisions as soon as the file is distributed to judges. This is done by a group of registry lawyers under the authority of the Jurisconsult collectively known as the CLCP—Case Law Conflict Prevention unit. Such scrutiny is of a continuous nature and must be completed within a tight deadline since there is usually only one week between distribution of the files and the meetings of the Sections. Where a potential conflict is noted, the CLCP will draw it to the attention of the relevant President and Section Registrar. If the matter is not resolved in this manner the issue may be referred to the Conflict Resolution Board (CRB). This may be done by the Section Presidents themselves or by the Jurisconsult. The CRB is an informal body composed of the Court's President and Section Presidents, assisted by senior officials of the registry. Since its creation in 2005, it has met two or three times a year. It will generally issue conclusions and recommendations to guide the Sections in their handling of those issues where divergent practice has been observed. It should be stressed that the role of the CRB is advisory only. It is not its function to direct the Sections which retain full responsibility to adjudicate on the cases allocated to them.

X. FRIENDLY SETTLEMENT

Article 38 of the Convention provides that once the Court declares an application admissible, in addition to continuing its examination of the case, it shall place itself at the

---

[83] See *mutatis mutandis Nikolova v Bulgaria* 1999-II; 31 EHRR 64 paras 41–4 GC; *Hasan and Chaush v Bulgaria* 2000-XI; 34 EHRR 1339 para 56 GC (in both cases the government having failed to raise the question in proceedings before the old Commission meaning it was estopped from raising it before the Grand Chamber of the new Court).

[84] *Mutatis mutandis Freedom and Democracy (ÖZDEP) v Turkey* 1999-VII; 31 EHRR 674 para 23 GC (the old Commission have considered the admissibility question on its own motion being sufficient to allow the government to raise it before the Grand Chamber).

[85] Hudoc (2002) GC.   [86] *Tahsin Acar v Turkey* ECHR 2003-VI paras 63–4 GC.

[87] *Sisojeva and Others v Latvia* hudoc (2007); 45 EHRR 753 GC.

[88] See the speech by the President of the Court, J-P Costa, to Leiden University on 30 May 2008 obtainable on the Court's website <http://www.echr.coe.int>.

disposal of the parties concerned with a view to securing a friendly settlement. While not stated in Article 39, the parties may, at any stage of the procedure, make proposals for the friendly settlement of the case. Indeed they are invited to make any proposals when they submit their observations. A friendly settlement proposal will generally involve the offer of a sum of money by the respondent government to the applicant which the applicant may choose to accept. Occasionally, other terms will also appear, such as in *Köksal v Netherlands*[89] (which concerned a death in police custody) where, in addition to the *ex gratia* payment of a sum of money, the Dutch government expressed its 'deepest regret' at the death. Another common term of a friendly settlement in immigration cases is for the applicant to be given a residence permit or for the state to give some equivalent undertaking not to deport the applicant.[90]

States may also promise to make legislative or policy changes. For example, in *Sutherland v UK*,[91] a challenge to the difference between the heterosexual and homosexual age of consent, the application was struck out after the government abolished the difference in new legislation. In *Ali Erol v Turkey*[92] a newspaper editor had been convicted of incitement to hatred and hostility on the basis of race or religion. The Court accepted a friendly settlement by which Turkey undertook urgently to bring its laws into conformity with Article 10 of the Convention and abide by the terms of Committee of Ministers resolution on the same matter.

The inter-state case of *Denmark v Turkey*[93] was one of the most constructive settlements before the Court in this respect. It concerned the ill-treatment of a single Danish national in police custody in Turkey and Denmark's request that the Commission examine whether the interrogation techniques applied to him were applied in Turkey as a widespread practice. By the terms of the settlement, Turkey recognized there was a problem and set out the measures that had been taken since the filing of the application while undertaking to make further improvements. Denmark undertook to finance several projects, including a bilateral project with Turkey, which aimed to eradicate torture by training police officers in human rights. The two parties finally agreed an action plan on the development of bilateral relations in which they committed themselves to continuous political dialogue in the framework of which general and specific issues of concern could be raised.[94]

Even in the context of individual applications, states can undertake to implement general measures as part of a friendly settlement. The most prominent example to date is the friendly settlement of *Broniowski v Poland*[95] where Poland undertook a series of general measures, as demanded by the Court in its initial judgment on the merits.[96] The Court noted that in the context of such a 'pilot' judgment, the criterion for accepting a friendly settlement on a basis of 'respect of human rights as defined in the Convention and the Protocols thereto' necessarily extended beyond the sole interests of the individual applicant and required the Court to examine the case also from the point of view of 'relevant

---

[89] Hudoc (2001) para 14.   [90] *Ahmed v Sweden* hudoc (2007).   [91] Hudoc (2001) GC.

[92] Hudoc (2002).   [93] 2000-IV para 2.

[94] See also the friendly settlement of *France, Norway, Denmark, Sweden and Netherlands v Turkey Nos 9940–44/82*, 44 DR 31 (1985) outlining the terms of a settlement whereby Turkey agreed to submit a series of reports on its implementation of Article 3 which would form the basis for a series of dialogues between Turkey and the Commission, to a final non-public report, and to a progressive reduction in the scope of its Article 15 derogations.

[95] 2005-IX; 43 EHRR 1 GC.

[96] 2004 V; 40 EHRR 495 GC. Cf, the settlement in *Hutten-Czapska v Poland* 2006-VIII; 45 EHRR 52 GC—see the section on pilot judgments below, pp 851–3.

general measures'.[97] The Court, in accepting the terms of the settlement in respect of both individual and general measures, attached particular weight to the general measures already taken (and to be taken) by Poland including legislation that had been passed between the initial judgment and the friendly settlement judgment, which was intended to remedy the structural problem underlying the case.

The Court 'placing itself at the disposal of the parties' in practice means that the Registry acts as a conduit for such proposals and can also suggest appropriate terms of settlement based on comparable previous settlements. In the practice of the old Commission, there were frequent friendly settlement meetings organized by the Secretary. While there has been a substantial increase in the number of friendly settlements in the new Court,[98] repetitive cases account for the majority of these and friendly settlement negotiations between the parties are not so frequent any longer, a casualty of the increased workload and time pressures upon the Registry. Where a settlement is reached, the parties will inform the Court of the terms of the settlement through the Registry. The Court will decide whether the matter has been resolved such that the case can be struck off its list. The criterion for doing so is set out in Article 37(1)(b) of the Convention, namely if the Court is satisfied that the matter has been resolved and that the settlement has been reached on the basis of respect for human rights as defined in the Convention and its Protocols. When it is so satisfied, under Article 39 the Court is empowered to strike the case out of its list by means of a decision. The same Article states that this shall be confined to a brief statement of the facts and of the solution reached. When the Court is not satisfied that the matter has been resolved it can refuse to accept the terms of the settlement and, if special circumstances regarding respect for human rights as defined in the Convention and its Protocols require the examination of the application to be continued, it will do so. Such instances are extremely rare, and will either be when the Court is concerned about the manner in which a settlement has been reached or if the terms of the settlement are not commensurate to the seriousness of the alleged violation. For example, in *Paladi v Moldova*,[99] the applicant and government agreed to settle the case for 596 Euros but the applicant later asked the Court to continue its examination of the case. The Court agreed to do so on the ground that the amount of compensation bore no reasonable relationship to the alleged violations of the Convention and had been agreed by the applicant while in a poor state of health and without the benefit of legal advice. In contrast, applicants who have simply changed their minds about accepting a settlement in the hope of further compensation will be given short shrift by the Court.[100]

While the terms of the settlement are usually set out in the judgment striking the case out of the list, under Article 38(2), the negotiations leading up to such a settlement are strictly confidential whether successful or unsuccessful. The Rules of Court are also strict on this point. Under Rule 33(1), friendly settlement documents are also not accessible to the public and by Rule 62(2) no offer or concession made during negotiations may be referred to in the contentious proceedings. Pleadings in the contentious proceedings

---

[97] *Broniowski v Poland* 2005-IX; 43 EHRR 1 para 36 GC. F Sett judgment.

[98] Precise numbers of friendly settlements are not possible because many friendly settlements are struck out by way of decision and the Court's statistics do not distinguish between decisions striking cases out the list because of friendly settlements and decisions which strike out cases on other grounds such as the failure to pursue an application. In 2007 the Court handed down sixty friendly settlement judgments (out of 1,503 judgments in total) and a total of 764 decisions striking out cases, of which it is estimated half were due to friendly settlements being reached. Taken from the Court's Annual Report 2007—available at: <http://www.echr.coe.int>.

[99] Hudoc (2007), see below, p 844, n 158.

[100] See eg, *Sukhorukikh v Russia No 37548/04* hudoc (2006); *Paritchi v Moldova No 54396/00* (2005); and *Podbolotova v Russia No 26091/02* hudoc (2005).

which do so will be sent back to the relevant party. Finally in *Hadrabova and Others v Czech Republic*,[101] the Court found disclosing the terms of these negotiations in ancillary domestic proceedings amounted to an abuse of the right of petition, leading to the application being declared inadmissible.

When the parties have been unable to agree a friendly settlement, or when the applicant has unreasonably refused a settlement offer, it is still open to the Court to strike a case out when the government submits a unilateral declaration acknowledging liability and undertaking to pay compensation *ex gratia* even though the applicant wishes the Court to continue to examine the case.[102] It would appear that this practice has developed because the Court considers that it should not necessarily be for the applicant to determine whether it is to carry out an examination of the merits of the case. As such, it is a consideration which touches on the notion of the proper administration of justice. However there are limits to the readiness of the Court to accept such declarations. In *Tahsin Acar v Turkey*[103] the Grand Chamber sought to define when such a unilateral declaration would be acceptable. A non-exhaustive list of factors to be taken into account included the nature of the complaints made, whether the issues raised were comparable to issues already determined by the Court in previous cases, and the nature and scope of any measures taken by the respondent government in the context of the execution of judgments delivered by the Court in any such previous cases. It would also be material whether the facts were in dispute between the parties. Other relevant factors included whether the unilateral declaration made any admission in relation to the alleged violations of the Convention and, if so, the scope of such admissions and the manner in which they intended to provide redress to the applicant. As to the latter, in cases in which it was possible to eliminate the effects of an alleged violation, the intended redress was more likely to be regarded as appropriate for the purposes of striking out the application. Finally, the Court emphasized that in this assessment it always retained the power to restore the application to its list.[104] In the *Tahsin Acar* case, involving an alleged disappearance at the hands of the security forces, the declaration did not contain any admission of liability. The Court accepted that a full admission of liability could not be regarded as a condition *sine qua non* for striking an application out on the basis of a unilateral declaration by a respondent government but since the declaration contained neither an admission of liability nor an undertaking to conduct an investigation into the disappearance, it fell short of what was required and respect for human rights required the continued examination of the case.[105]

---

[101] *Nos 42165/02 and 466/03* hudoc (2007).

[102] See eg, *Akman v Turkey* 2001-VI—the first unilateral declaration adopted by the Court. The government had *inter alia* admitted liability in respect of a killing by the security forces and offered to pay £85,000 in compensation. The Court took into account not only the admissions and undertakings made by the government but also the fact that it had previously specified in numerous cases the nature and extent of the obligations which arise for states concerning killings by the security forces. Criticism has focused on the fact that the compensation was paid *ex gratia* (notwithstanding the admission) and that no proper investigation had been carried out by the authorities. For critical comment on such decisions see Sardaro, 2003 EHRLR 601.

[103] 2003-VI para 76 GC. See also the dissenting opinion of Judge Loucaides in the Chamber judgment in this case—judgment of 9 April 2002 for criticism of unilateral declarations in disappearance cases.

[104] As provided in Article 37(2) of the Convention and Rule 44(5) of the Rules of Court.

[105] The Court eventually gave judgment in the case finding no substantive violation of Article 2 but a procedural violation of that Article: *Tahsin Acar v Turkey* 2004-III GC. Other cases struck out on this basis include *Haran v Turkey* hudoc (2002); *Meriakri v Moldova* hudoc (2005); and *Van Houten v Netherlands* 2005-IX. For further discussion see Rozakis, in Kohen, ed, *Promoting Justice, Human Rights and Conflict Resolution through International Law: Liber Amicorum Lucius Caflisch*, 2007. Also Myjer, in Caflisch *et al*, eds, *Liber Amicorum Luzius Wildhaber*, 2007 pp 309–27.

Protocol 14 would change the friendly settlement procedure under the Convention in three ways.[106] First, it would allow the Court to pursue friendly settlements at any stage of the proceedings and not only after the Court has declared a case admissible, though, as noted by the Woolf Report, this would not be a radical change since the current wording does not inhibit the Registry from discussing friendly settlement proposals in advance of an admissibility decision.[107] Secondly, Protocol 14 would provide that the Committee of Ministers would supervise the execution of friendly settlement decisions, as it already does for judgments.

Finally it is envisaged in Protocol 14 that the Court would strike cases off the list by way of a decision and not a judgment, as has often been the case—thus the importance of Committee of Ministers' supervision. It has been explained in the Explanatory Report to Protocol 14 that a judgment might be seen as having negative connotations for respondent governments and make it harder to secure settlements. While this may be true as regards certain governments, the fact that a settlement can be adopted by way of a judgment can also be an incentive for applicants to settle on the basis that a judgment is more likely to attract media interest.

XI. STRIKING OUT CASES

In addition to cases where the government has submitted a unilateral declaration, the Court enjoys the power, granted under Article 37, to strike out cases from its list at any stage of the proceedings. This is to all intents and purposes an unfettered power. It will normally only be used in cases which have been formally registered as applications and thus are actually on the Court's list of cases requiring a decision or judgment. 'Any stage of the proceedings' has been given a wide meaning and may even be applied after the parties' observations have been received and even by the Grand Chamber when a Chamber has already given judgment on the matter.[108] The Court (Chamber or Grand Chamber) can also strike out part of an application whilst in the same judgment examining the applicant's remaining complaints on their merits.[109]

There are three conditions for striking out applications in Article 37(1): when the applicant does not intend to pursue his application; when the matter has been resolved; or, for any other reason established by the Court, it is no longer justified to continue the examination of the application (sub-paragraphs (a)–(c) of the Article). For the first, a clear indication that the applicant intends to pursue the application will render the provision inapplicable but the applicant's consent is not required for the other two conditions.[110] For the second, in assessing whether the matter has been resolved, the Court will ask two questions: first, whether the circumstances complained of directly by the applicants still obtain and, second, whether the effects of a possible violation of the Convention on account of those circumstances have also been redressed.[111] The first is plainly a factual

---

[106] See new Article 39.   [107] Id, p 44. Available at: <http://www.echr.coe.int>.

[108] See eg, *Sisojeva and Others v Latvia* hudoc (2007); 45 EHRR 753 GC; also *Shevanova v Latvia* hudoc (2007) GC and *Kaftailova v Latvia* hudoc (2007) GC where the Grand Chamber, taking a different view from the Chamber, found that the applicants, long-term immigrants who did not benefit from residents status in Latvia, could avail themselves of options outlined by the Latvian authorities to regularize their status, thus considering the matter to be 'resolved' within the meaning of Article 37(1)(b).

[109] See *Sisojeva,* id, paras 104 and 105 *et seq* (striking out the application insofar as it related to Article 8 and continuing its examination in relation to the Article 34 complaint).

[110] See *Akman v Turkey* 2001-VI; *Pisano v Italy* hudoc (2002) para 41; and *Ohlen v Denmark* hudoc (2005) para 25.

[111] *El Majjaoui and Stichting Touba Moskee v Netherlands* hudoc (2007) para 30 GC.

assessment that will turn on the circumstances of each case. The second, is similar to the Court's assessment of whether the applicant is still a victim at the time of its examination of the case,[112] namely whether there has been recognition of a violation, either expressly or in substance and whether adequate redress has been provided.[113]

The Court will attempt to focus on what the 'matter' of the case actually is, ie the question in dispute which brings the applicant and respondent state before it. Thus in *Association SOS Attentats and De Boëry v France*,[114] concerning the refusal of France to allow the victims of an explosion on board a passenger plane to sue the Libyan head of state Colonel Gaddafi and the applicants' complaint that this violated their right of access to court under Article 6 of the Convention, it was irrelevant to the matter in dispute that an agreement to compensate the victims of the attack had been reached between Libya and the applicants. This agreement did not enable the applicants to sue Colonel Gaddafi and thus a key aspect of the applicants' direct complaint persisted, which sufficed to conclude that Article 37(1)(b) did not apply.

The Grand Chamber in *SOS Attentats* also exhaustively considered the application of Article 37(1)(c). It identified broadly five reasons for striking out an application this way: on the basis of a unilateral declaration by the government (see above); when the applicants had reached a settlement with domestic authorities which largely satisfied their demands under the Convention and they had thus lost their victim status; when the applicant had died in the course of the proceedings before the Court and no heir had come forward (or one had but had no legitimate interest); a lack of diligence by the applicant or his lawyer; and a failure to abide by the Rules of Court (such as failing to appoint a lawyer). This was not considered to be an exhaustive list since the Grand Chamber emphasized that the Court 'enjoys a wide discretion in identifying grounds capable of being relied upon in striking out an application on this basis'.[115] On the facts of that particular application, the Grand Chamber concluded that the agreement reached between the applicants and Libya and brokered by France, was sufficient to warrant striking out the application. Material perhaps in that conclusion was that the agreement contained a waiver that the victims would not bring any civil or criminal proceedings before any French or international court based on the explosion. Some applicants had signed the waiver and others had indicated that they might do so depending on the outcome of the application in Strasbourg. France's role in brokering the agreement and managing the payment of compensation under it, the fact that the agreement appeared to be in line with the victims' interests, the apparent contradiction in accepting a waiver and simultaneously complaining of the impossibility of bringing proceedings and the fact that a judgment *in absentia* had been obtained against those responsible for the explosion, were all factors in the Court's conclusion that continued examination of the application was unjustified.

Article 37 provides the caveat that even where one of the above three conditions has been satisfied, the Court shall continue the examination of the application if respect for human rights as defined in the Convention and protocols thereto so requires. This is a rare occurrence and the Court risks accusations of judicial activism if it continues to examine an application and finds a violation of the Convention where there is no longer a live dispute between the parties. Nonetheless, there have been instances where this has

---

[112] See above, pp 793–6.

[113] *Dalban v Romania* 1999-VI; 31 EHRR 39 paras 41–5 GC; *Burdov v Russia* 2002-III paras 27–32; *Ohlen v Denmark* hudoc (2005) para 26. See also *Freimanis and Lidums v Lithuania* hudoc (2006) paras 66–74 and references therein. However the requirement of a recognition of a violation is not a requirement in deportation cases—see *Sisojeva and Others v Latvia* hudoc (2007); 45 EHRR 753 para 93 GC.

[114] 2006-XIV GC.   [115] Id, para 37 and the extensive authorities cited therein.

occurred. In *Karner v Austria*,[116] the original applicant had complained of his inability to succeed to the tenancy of his homosexual partner when a heterosexual partner would be able to do so. After the original applicant's death, his heir (the applicant's mother) waived her right to succeed to his estate. The Court chose not to strike the application out of its list. It recalled that its judgments served not only to decide those cases before it but, more generally, to elucidate, safeguard, and develop the rules instituted by the Convention.[117]

XII. DELIVERY OF JUDGMENT

Once the parties' observations have been received, the Court will deliberate and adopt its judgment. The parties are notified that the judgment will be delivered and delivery usually takes place three weeks after the judgment is adopted. They are sent a certified copy of the judgment and the same day an electronic copy is posted on the Court's website accompanied by a press release summarizing the facts of the case and the Court's reasoning. The Court's judgments are highly structured: the procedural history of the case is summarized as are the facts as submitted by the parties or established by the Court and any relevant domestic law and practice. Any relevant European, international, and comparative law may also be included. This is followed by a summary of the applicant's complaints and the parties' submissions. In the Court's reasoning it is common to find a statement of the general principles of law before an application of those principles to the facts of the case. The main text of the judgment concludes with an 'operative' part of judgment which states the Court's separate findings on admissibility (if Article 29(3) applies), the merits of the case, and any just satisfaction awarded and records the votes of judges for and against each of these findings. Any separate, concurring, partly concurring, partly dissenting, and dissenting opinions of judges are appended to the judgment in that order.[118] Grand Chamber judgments follow a similar pattern save in Article 43 cases where, since a Chamber will already have given judgment, it is common to see portions of the Chamber judgment reproduced if only so that the Grand Chamber may state its approval or disapproval of the Chamber's reasoning.

One recent development concerns the inclusion of consequential measures in the Court's judgments and, a stage further, in the operative part of those judgments. Traditionally, the view had been that the Court was only capable of finding either a violation or non-violation of the Convention on the basis of the applicant's complaints and of awarding just satisfaction accordingly. In recent years, the Court has gone on to consider what general or individual measures the respondent government should take to rectify any violation found in the context of Article 46 of the Convention. Such measures have, on occasion, been replicated in the operative part of the judgment and are considered further below.[119]

---

[116] 2003-IX; 38 EHRR 528.   [117] See the discussion of the *Karner* case, above, p 810.

[118] The full list of information that a judgment must contain is set out in Rule 74 of the Rules of Court. On separate opinions see Villiger, in Caflisch *et al*, eds, *Liber Amicorum Luzius Wildhaber*, 2007; Spielmann, 126 Journal des tribunaux 310 (2007); Bratza and O'Boyle, eds, *Free trade of ideas: the separate opinions of Judge Vanni Bonello*, 2006.

[119] The first such instance was in *Assanidze v Georgia* 2004-II; 39 EHRR 653 GC where the Court, having found the applicant's detention to be illegal, held that Georgia had to secure his release at the earliest possible date (point 14(a) of the operative part). The same finding was made in *Ilascu and Others v Moldova and Russia* 2004-VII; 40 EHRR 1030 GC at point 22. The Court went further in *Broniowski v Poland* 2004-V; 40 EHRR 495 GC, about Poland's failure to live up to its commitment to provide adequate compensation for those who had been repatriated in the course of a re-drawing of Poland's borders during the Second World War (so-called 'Bug River claimants'). The Court noted that the violation was a result of 'a malfunctioning of Polish legislation and administrative practice' affecting a large but identifiable class of citizens (para 189 of the judgment) and that

XIII. REQUESTS FOR RECTIFICATION, INTERPRETATION, AND REVISION

Article 44 directs that Grand Chamber judgments shall be final. According to the same provision, Chamber judgments become final either (i) when the parties declare that they will not seek referral to the Grand Chamber; or (ii) three months after the date of the judgment when neither party seeks referral; or (iii) when the panel of the Grand Chamber rejects any request for referral. However, even when judgments do become final, while not provided for in the Convention, the Rules of Court allow for three types of requests for reconsideration of judgments: requests for interpretation (Rule 79), requests for revision (Rule 80), and requests for rectification of errors (Rule 81). These Rules reflect the Court's inherent jurisdiction to review the judgment in certain circumstances. Protocol 14 also provides the possibility of a request for interpretation of a judgment being made by the Committee of Ministers. The Explanatory Report stresses that it is not the intention of this new provision to ask the Court to give an opinion on the compatibility of proposed amendments to national law introduced pursuant to the judgment.[120]

Rule 81 is straightforward and allows the Court, of its own motion or at the request of a party made within one month of the delivery of a decision or judgment, to rectify clerical errors, errors in calculation, or obvious mistakes. The errors, however, must be patent mistakes. The Court will not accept proposals to alter the text of a judgment with a view to rephrasing or to striking out an argument. It will correct obvious mistakes, for example, as regards the text of legislative provisions or the professional qualifications of those appearing before it. However nothing that might affect the substance of the decision reached could be dealt with under this head. The Court need not wait for such a request and can correct such basic mistakes itself by way of its editorial revision of judgments. This possibility is noted in the preface to all Court judgments.

Rule 79 allows either party to request interpretation within a period of one year following the delivery of the judgment. The request must state the point or points in the operative provisions of the judgment on which interpretation is required. The Chamber may of its own motion refuse the request. If it does not do so, the request is communicated to the other party or parties who have the opportunity to submit comments. An oral hearing can also be held before the Chamber gives its decision by way of a judgment. Requests for interpretation of judgments have been rare and have related to issues concerning the payment of compensation. In the first such request the Court held in *Ringeisen v Austria*[121] that damages awarded under the head of non-pecuniary damage in respect of a violation of Article 5(3) were to be paid directly to the applicant, who was then living in Germany, free from attachment. The Commission had explicitly requested this in view of the applicant's needy circumstances. The Austrian authorities had paid the money into court since it had been claimed by various creditors. The government had challenged the Court's jurisdiction to examine the issue on the basis that the Convention did not provide for requests for interpretation and that the matter was only governed by a Rule of Court. The Court held that it was a matter of its inherent jurisdiction and that such proceedings did

---

general measures were called for at the national level. It accordingly included in the operative part of the judgment the holding that Poland 'must, through appropriate measures and administrative practices, secure the implementation of the property right in question in respect of the remaining Bug River claimants' (point 4). Similar general measures were indicated in *Hutten-Czapska v Poland* 2006-VIII; 45 EHRR 52 GC at point 4 (concerning a system of rent control found to be in violation of Article 1 of Protocol 1); *Lukenda v Slovenia* 2005-X at point 5 (length of proceedings); *Xenides-Arestis v Turkey* hudoc (2005) at point 5 (property claims in relation to Northern Cyprus).

[120] See below, p 866.   [121] A 16 (1973).

not involve an appeal against the original judgment. The Court's role was limited to clarifying the meaning and scope which it intended to give to a previous decision. The Court has stressed in subsequent cases that the clarification of a judgment does not involve modification in respect of issues which the Court has already decided with binding force. Thus in *Allenet de Ribemont*,[122] where the Court had awarded a global sum to the applicant without making any distinction between pecuniary and non-pecuniary damage, the Court pointed out that it had not provided in its judgment that the sums awarded to the applicant were to be free from attachment as requested by the applicant and the matter had been left to the national authorities in accordance with national law. Nor was it prepared to rule, as requested by the Commission, that awards in respect of compensation were to be free from attachment since it did not have jurisdiction under Article 50 (now Article 41) to issue orders to a contracting party.[123] In a similar vein, in the case of *Hentrich v France*,[124] the Court rejected a request for interpretation that the state should pay default interest in respect of delay in payments. This was not considered to be a matter of interpretation as such. The requirement to pay default interest was later introduced by the Court in January 1996.

The procedure is similar under Rule 80 as regards requests for revision of a judgment. This Rule provides for revision of the judgment when a party discovers 'a fact which might by its nature have a decisive influence and which, when a judgment was delivered, was unknown to the Court and could not reasonably have been known to that party'. The party has six months from when it acquired knowledge of the fact to make the request. As under Rule 79, the Chamber may of its own motion refuse the request. If it does not, the request is communicated to the other party or parties who have the opportunity to submit comments. An oral hearing can also be held before the Chamber gives its decision by way of a judgment.

The Court has shown that it is willing to accept revision of a judgment as regards issues relating to Article 41, for example, when information is submitted after the delivery of judgment that the applicant has died beforehand and the Court has been unaware of this fact. Thus in *Resul Sadak and Others v Turkey*[125] where one of the applicants had died before judgment was given, the Court was prepared to revise the judgment to provide that the applicant's heirs should be awarded the amounts awarded to the deceased under Article 41. The applicant had been one of twelve applicants and it appears that no blame could be attached to either the lawyer who was unaware of the death or the heirs who may not have been aware of the proceedings. However in *Gabay v Turkey*,[126] the Court revised the judgment to strike the case (length of proceedings) out of the list when the government brought to its attention that the applicant had in fact died and the relatives had not informed the Court of this or indicated a wish to continue the proceedings. In *Sabri Taş v Turkey*[127] the Court had previously rejected claims for just satisfaction on the basis that the Court's request for claims to be submitted had not been complied with. The applicant's lawyer demonstrated to the Court's satisfaction that in fact he had not been so requested and the Court revised its judgment to make an award to the applicant. In *EP v Italy*[128] the Court revised its judgment at the government's request to provide that no monies were to be awarded under the head of non-pecuniary damage since the Court had not been informed of the names of those to whom the monies could legitimately paid.

---

[122] 1996-III; 20 EHRR 557.
[123] Attachment is discussed further in the following section on Article 41.
[124] 1997-IV; 18 EHRR 440.
[125] Hudoc (2008). In the same vein—see *Bajrami v Albania* hudoc (2007) where judgment was revised for the same reason but at the government's request since it could not execute the judgment.
[126] Hudoc (2006).   [127] Hudoc (2006).   [128] Hudoc (2001).

No award of costs and expenses was made to the lawyer who had not informed the Court of the applicant's death. The case of *Stoicescu v Romania*[129] was subsequently declared inadmissible on revision when the Court learned that the applicant in an expropriation case had previously lost his status of heir to the property in question following court proceedings in Romania and had not drawn the Court's attention to this crucial fact which had removed his victim status. The government could not have been aware of this development owing to the absence of a database of pending cases at the relevant time.

While these cases demonstrate a relatively liberal practice on matters concerning Article 41, the Court has shown itself extremely reticent to revise its determination of whether or not there has been a violation of the Convention—apart from circumstances where vital facts have been withheld from it as in *Stoicescu*. The Court's approach is one of strict scrutiny coupled with a clear reluctance to re-open a final judgment on the merits. A heavy burden thus rests with lawyers seeking to overturn the Court's original judgment. In *McGinley and Egan v UK*[130] it observed:

> The Court notes the embodiment of the principle of the finality of judgments in the present Article 44 of the Convention and recalls that, insofar as it calls into question the final character of judgments of the Court, the possibility of revision is considered to be an exceptional procedure. Requests for revision of judgments are therefore to be subjected to strict scrutiny.

In that case, new information was brought to the Court's attention following the original judgment concerning the existence of correspondence which had not been submitted to the Court and which cast doubt on the reasoning leading to the finding of no violation of Articles 6 and 8. In reaching its conclusion the Court had relied on a statement by the government that, when an applicant sought access to documents concerning his military service in connection with a pension application, it was not necessary to point to any specific document but rather to refer in general terms to the category of documents sought. The Court, in rejecting the revision request, held that the applicant's lawyer was aware that there had been significant correspondence on this matter in another case and that the new facts now relied on 'could reasonably have been known' to him prior to the original judgment. It left open the question whether or not the new material might have had a decisive influence on the outcome of the case. In the earlier case of *Pardo v France*[131] the applicant had complained under Article 6(1) that he had not been given an oral hearing in his case despite a promise to this effect by the President of the Court of Appeal. The claim had been rejected in the original judgment for non-substantiation. When new documents subsequently came to light substantiating his claim the revision request was held to be admissible, by five votes to four, on the grounds that it could not be excluded that the new facts could have led to a different finding by the Court. The matter was sent back to the Chamber that gave the original judgment. It, however, dismissed the request on its merits on the basis that the new facts did not cast doubt on the Court's original findings of no violation.

XIV. ADVISORY OPINIONS

Under Article 47, the Committee of Ministers may request an advisory opinion concerning the interpretation of the Convention and its protocols.[132] This is subject to two

---

[129] Hudoc (2004).
[130] 2000-I para 36; see also the dissenting opinions of Judges Casadevall and Maruste.
[131] 1996-III and 1997-III; 22 EHRR 563.
[132] By Article 31, such requests are considered by the Grand Chamber.

important and constraining caveats: by paragraph two of the same article such opinions may not deal with the content and scope of the rights or freedoms defined in Section I of the Convention and the Protocols or any other question the Court or Committee of Ministers may have to consider in consequence of any such proceedings as could be instituted in accordance with the Convention. Given the limited scope for advisory opinions under this provision it is not surprising that there have only been two of them. In the first, the Committee of Ministers sought an opinion on whether the Commonwealth of Independent States (CIS) Convention was another procedure of international investigation or settlement in the sense of Article 35(2)(b) of the ECHR.[133] The Court ruled that it was not competent to give an advisory opinion.[134] One of the issues arising from the request related to the question of whether any complaint submitted to the CIS Convention enforcement mechanism which was subsequently submitted to Strasbourg would be inadmissible as a result of Article 35(2)(b) of the ECHR.[135] Since this was a question the Court might have had to consider in contentious proceedings it held, with reference to the second caveat in Article 47(2), that it could not give an opinion.

The Court gave its first advisory opinion on the merits on 12 February 2008.[136] As stated earlier, in electing judges of the Court, the Parliamentary Assembly will not vote on a list of judges submitted unless the list is gender-balanced. In its advisory opinion, the Court noted that its jurisdiction under Article 47 is confined to 'legal questions'. It had been decided by the drafters of Protocol 2 to the Convention (the source of Article 47) to maintain the adjective 'legal' in order to rule out jurisdiction on matters of policy. It had been argued by the Austrian and Spanish governments in the advisory opinion proceedings that the Court should refrain from giving an opinion since the matter was essentially political in nature. The French government had argued that it should not examine the issue because the Court had no jurisdiction to assess the compatibility of Parliamentary Assembly resolutions with the Convention. The Court considered that that it was confronted with a proper 'legal' question that did not result from any 'contentious proceedings', namely whether it was lawful for the Parliamentary Assembly to reject a list on the grounds that it was not gender-balanced. The question, whatever its implications, therefore concerned the rights and obligations of the Parliamentary Assembly in the procedure for electing judges, as derived from Article 22 in particular and from the Convention system in general. The Court examined a further criterion—not explicitly stated in Article 47—namely whether it would be expedient for the Court to give an opinion. It held that it was appropriate to give a ruling on this question in the interests of the proper functioning of the Convention system, as there was a need to ensure that the situation which gave rise to the request for the opinion—that is, the disagreement between the Committee of Ministers and the Parliamentary Assembly on this issue—did not cause a blockage in the system. By opting to examine this issue the Court has signalled that it will be master of the 'legal issues' that it chooses to examine in an advisory opinion and that there could well be issues in the future which it judges inappropriate to examine—for example where the issue is over-broad, vague, or hypothetical. As stated above, the Court

[133] The Court's 'reasoned' decision can be found at: <http://www.echr.coe.int>.

[134] Article 48 provides that is for the Court to decide whether a request for an advisory opinion is within its competence as defined in Article 47. Rules 87, 88, and 89 Court refer to the concept of a 'reasoned decision' for decisions taken pursuant to Article 48 on whether a request for an advisory opinion is within the Court's competence. This was the first such decision.

[135] On Article 35(2)(b), see above, pp 782–3.

[136] *Advisory Opinion on Certain Legal Questions Concerning the Lists of Candidates for the Election of Judges to the European Court of Human Rights* hudoc (2008). See above, p 815.

found on the merits that the policy of the Parliamentary Assembly was not sufficiently flexible and summoned it to draft an exception clause.[137]

Article 49 of the Convention provides that advisory opinions shall be reasoned, that judges are entitled to deliver separate opinions and that the opinion shall be communicated to the Committee of Ministers. Chapter IX of the Rules of Court regulates the Court's procedure in dealing with advisory opinions. In particular, all requests for an opinion shall be considered by the Grand Chamber of the Court. In addition, under Rule 84(2), contracting parties are given the right to submit written comments which, under Rule 86, may be developed at a oral hearing if the President decides to hold one.[138]

3. PROCEDURE BEFORE THE COURT (II): ADDITIONAL PROCEDURAL MATTERS

Regardless of the judicial formation which finally gives a decision or judgment in a particular case, there are a variety of procedural issues that may arise in a case and which are considered in the following sections.

I. PUBLICITY

The name of an applicant is public unless the President of the Chamber grants anonymity for good cause shown.[139] Anonymity would usually be granted in cases concerning issues of private health, custody, or sex abuse or divorce issues and it is open to the President to grant anonymity in such cases even though it may not be asked for by the applicant. A mere desire to avoid publicity is not in itself a sufficient reason for anonymity.

II. LEGAL REPRESENTATION

If the application is introduced by a legal representative, he or she will be required to submit a power of attorney. The Court's website provides a suitable authority form which requires the signatures of both the applicant and his or her designated representative. It is, of course, possible for the applicant later to revoke that authority and appoint different representatives. There is some flexibility in the initial stages of proceedings as to who can actually be a representative. A legal qualification is not required at the outset of proceedings but only after an application is communicated to the respondent government. Rule 36(2) requires the applicant to be represented by an 'advocate' authorized to practise

---

[137] See above, p 815.

[138] No oral hearing has yet been held. The opinion of 12 February 2008 involved a written procedure in which each contracting party, as well as PACE, were given an opportunity to file written observations. It does not appear that the Convention makes any provision for third party interventions by NGOs in advisory opinion proceedings. Article 36 of the Convention covering such interventions speaks only of 'cases' and so appears only to contemplate inter-state cases and individual applications. However, support for the right to seek leave to intervene may be found in Rule 82 which allows the Court to apply other provisions of the Rules of Court to the extent it considers this to be appropriate and this may allow for such interventions in application of Rule 44, which regulates them for cases.

[139] Rule 33. In keeping with the philosophy of transparency underlying Protocol 11 setting up the new Court, all documents will also be accessible unless the President decides otherwise for good cause—Rule 33(2). Arrangements can be made at the Registry for the public or journalists to inspect such documents—see the Court's website for details. It is the Court's policy that documents must be consulted at the seat of the Court. It will not normally send them by post to interested parties for reasons of cost.

in any of the contracting parties and resident in the territory of one of them, or any other person approved by the President of the Chamber.[140] For the United Kingdom and Ireland, this can be a solicitor or a barrister/advocate. A number of NGOs have sought and obtained the President's leave to represent applicants where they have qualified lawyers on their staff who may not have fulfilled all the formalities for private legal practice. Lawyers may be refused permission to act in Court proceedings if the President of the Chamber considers that their behaviour warrants such a decision.[141] It is open to a lawyer practising in a non-contracting party, such as an American attorney or Canadian barrister/avocat, to seek leave to appear.[142] Permission may be given by the President of the Chamber to allow an applicant to represent himself. However the Court would normally insist on the applicant being legally represented or assisted by an advocate if there was to be an oral hearing.[143] An applicant who represents himself would only be reimbursed expenses and would not be eligible to receive legal aid.

III. LEGAL AID

Legal aid is available to applicants when it is necessary for the proper conduct of the case and the applicant has insufficient means to meet all or part of the costs entailed,[144] but only after an application has been communicated to the government and only at the request of the applicant or his representatives.[145] For any request received before communication, the representative will be informed by the Registry that the request is premature, although if legal aid is subsequently granted the offer will cover the initial preparatory phase of an application. On communication the applicant is requested to submit a declaration of means. It must be certified by the appropriate domestic authority. It is no longer the rule that governments will be asked to comment on the declaration of means although the President of the Chamber may request comments if necessary.[146] Offers of legal aid will be sent at each stage of the procedure: communication, oral hearings before the Chamber and Grand Chamber, and participation in friendly settlement discussions.[147] The amounts offered are small in comparison to legal costs in many western legal systems but more reasonable when compared with costs in Central and East European countries. They are seen as a contribution to legal costs and it is open to the applicant to recoup the real cost of legal representation under Article 41 if he wins his case.

IV. ORAL HEARINGS

The parties can request an oral hearing at any stage of the proceedings, though it is for the Court to decide if a hearing is necessary. It might decide to do so if some novel point of law is involved. The Court can also on its own motion decide to have a hearing, which will usually take place in public.[148] Since 2007, hearings are usually webcast

---

[140] See generally, Rule 36(1)–(5).

[141] Rule 36(4)(b). For a decision to refuse a lawyer permission to appear, see *Manoussos v Czech Republic and Germany No 46468/99* hudoc (2002).

[142] See eg, *Open Door and Dublin Well Woman v Ireland* A 246-A (1992); 15 EHRR 44 PC and *Kamasinski v Austria* A 168 (1989); 13 EHRR 36.

[143] Rule 36(3).   [144] Rule 92.

[145] National legal aid schemes rarely offer legal aid for Strasbourg proceedings. The Danish Legal Aid Act (1999) is an exception—see *Vasileva v Denmark* hudoc (2003); 40 EHRR 681 para 50.

[146] Rule 93(2).   [147] The payment of legal aid is regulated by Chapter X of the Rules of Court.

[148] Rule 63. The public may be excluded 'in the interests of morals, public order or national security in a democratic society, where the interest of juveniles or the protection of the private life of the parties so require';

a few hours after the hearing unless the Chamber decides otherwise.[149] It is not open to the parties to object if the Court schedules a hearing. When an oral hearing is set, the parties will be sent a list of questions to be addressed which reflect what the Court considers to be the main questions in the case. These may cover both factual and legal issues. At the end of the hearing the parties may be given an opportunity to submit supplementary information within a prescribed time limit. Normally hearings are the exception at Section level. Most Grand Chamber cases will involve a hearing but each of the five Sections of the Court will only hold two or three hearings each per year.[150] Apart from the bilingual nature of the proceedings, oral procedure does not differ significantly from similar hearings at the appellate level in national courts, though it may be rather short by comparison. The parties are requested to provide the interpreters with a copy of their submissions at least one day in advance in order to facilitate their work. Each party is given a set time for their intervention (usually half an hour), questions may be put by the judges, and the President may permit a short adjournment to allow the parties to prepare their answers. There follows a brief second round when the parties are given an opportunity to respond to those questions and to the principal arguments of the other side. Non-governmental organizations intervening as third parties will not normally be permitted to make oral submissions. But contracting parties exercising their rights on behalf of a national under Article 36(1) have a right to appear at the hearing. Contracting parties which have intervened for other reasons may also be authorized to make further submissions at a hearing.[151] Under Protocol 14, the Commissioner for Human Rights would be able to appear before the Court as of right if he chose to intervene.

V. INTERIM MEASURES[152]

Rule 39 of the Rules of Court provides as follows:

1. The Chamber or, where appropriate, its President may, at the request of a party or of any other person concerned, or of its own motion, indicate to the parties any interim measure which it considers should be adopted in the interests of the parties or of the proper conduct of the proceedings before it.

2. Notice of these measures shall be given to the Committee of Ministers.

3. The Chamber may request information from the parties on any matter connected with the implementation of any interim measure it has indicated.

Applications before the Court do not have suspensive effect. Consequently it is not normally open to the Court to issue an injunction to restrain a state from enforcing a particular measure. However in some situations, as where life or death may be at stake, most

see Rule 63(2). *In camera* hearings have been rare but have taken place in a number of cases where the rights of children were at stake: *Z v Finland* 1997-I; 25 EHRR 371; before the Chamber in *K and T v Finland* hudoc (2000); 31 EHRR 484 and *L v Finland* hudoc (2000); 31 EHRR 737.

[149] See the Court's website for an archive of oral hearing webcasts. Webcasting of hearings is not live and will take place in the afternoon of the hearing following a favourable decision of the Chamber.

[150] In 2007 the Grand Chamber held sixteen hearings and the five Sections of the Court a total of ten (Annual Activity Reports of the Grand Chamber and the Sections available in the reports section of the Court's website).

[151] Eg, the United Kingdom's oral submissions in *Saadi v Italy* hudoc (2008).

[152] See Caflisch, in Dupuy *et al*, eds, *Common Values in International Law: Essays in Honour of Christian Tomuschat*, 2006, pp 493–515; Garry, 17 EPL 399 (2001); Rozakis, in Pintens *et al*, eds, *Feestbundel voor Hugo Vandenberghe*, 2007; and Vajic in Kohen, ed, *Liber Amicorum Lucius Caflisch*, cited at n 105 above.

commonly in a case of expulsion or extradition to a state where ill-treatment is feared, an injunctive power is necessary if the right of individual petition is to be effective. If this were not the case, the Court could only carry out its examination of the complaint when the feared harm had actually materialized or where the individual had been exposed to the risk of such harm. Accordingly the object of an interim measure is to maintain the *status quo* pending the Court's determination of the compatibility of the impugned decision with the Convention. Most of the cases where an interim measure is requested concern expulsion or extradition from a contracting party.

The number of such requests has increased exponentially in recent years with increased migration to Europe and the development of firm exclusionary policies by many states.[153] As more failed asylum seekers are being sent back to their countries of origin, a last minute application to the Court for a stay against removal is seen as the final bid for asylum. Despite this trend, interim measures are not a new feature of the permanent Court. The old Commission and Court had similar provisions under Rule 36 of their respective rules,[154] although the old Court had famously held the Commission's power to indicate interim measures not to be binding, in part because the Commission had no power to give binding judgments and the Convention lacked a specific interim measures provision.[155] What is distinctive about the new Court's practice on interim measures is that, as a result of the Grand Chamber's judgment in *Mamatkulov and Askarov v Turkey*,[156] they are now considered binding on contracting parties in that failure to abide by them will in most cases (see below) lead to a violation of Article 34 *in fine* which obliges states not to 'hinder the effective exercise of the right of individual petition'. In reaching this conclusion the Court attached weight to developments in other international tribunals such as the International Court of Justice and the Inter-American Court of Human Rights as well as the fact that the Court's judgments, unlike the opinions of the old Commission, are binding by virtue of Article 46.

In *Olaechea Cahuas v Spain*,[157] the government did not comply with the indication made under Rule 39 that it should not remove the applicant (a suspected leader of the Sendero Luminosa) to Peru, having received assurances from the Peruvian authorities that he would not be subjected to torture or other ill-treatment. The risk of ill-treatment, in the event, did not materialize after his return and the Spanish government argued that in such circumstances the Court should not find a breach of its obligations under Article 34. The Court held that a state's decision as to whether to comply with the measure could not be deferred pending the hypothetical confirmation of the existence of a risk. Non-compliance with an interim measure on the basis of the existence of a risk was, in itself, a serious hindrance at that precise point in time of the effective exercise of the right of individual petition. In short, and crucial to the effectiveness of the Court's system of interim measures, the obligation of compliance took effect at the moment the measure was indicated, irrespective of whether the risk which motivated the Rule 39 decision later materialized.

In expulsion/extradition cases, especially in the light of the *Olaeacha Cahuas* judgment, a failure to abide by the interim measure will normally lead to a finding of a violation of Article 34. However in cases not involving expulsion a breach will not automatically

---

[153] See the Court's annual *Survey of Activities* for details of the number of requests for interim measures available at <http://www.echr.coe.int>.

[154] For an early example see the indication of the old Court that extradition be deferred while Strasbourg proceedings were pending in *Soering v UK* A 161 (1989); 11 EHRR 439 PC.

[155] *Cruz Varas and Others v Sweden* A 201 (1991) PC.

[156] 2005-I; 41 EHRR 494 GC. See Tams, 63 ZAORV 681 (2003).   [157] 2006-X.

follow from the failure to comply. In *Paladi v Moldova*,[158] the issue concerned a delay in implementing an interim measure requesting urgent medical treatment for an applicant, a detainee, by means of a transfer to a more appropriate hospital. The Court ultimately found a violation of Article 34, though no irreparable damage to the applicant's health had occurred. It considered that a state's responsibility for failing to comply with its Convention obligations should not depend on unpredictable circumstances such as the non-occurrence of a medical emergency during the period of non-compliance with the interim measure. Actual damage was not required before the Court could find a breach of the obligation to comply with interim measures.

Despite such episodic instances of non-compliance, it must be said that in practice there has always been widespread compliance with interim measures even when they were considered non-binding. Refusals to comply have been very infrequent.[159] This can probably be explained by a certain apprehension that the Court could subsequently find a violation on the merits of the case. However an inherent respect for the rule of law and the proper administration of justice are also factors which arguably weigh heavily with most of the contracting parties in such cases.

Interim measures can be both positive and negative in character. The majority will be negative (asking states to delay removals) but occasionally the Court will indicate positive measures such as asking states to provide urgent or emergency medical treatment to detained persons[160] or requesting hunger strikers to give up their protest to enable the Court to examine their complaints. In *Ilascu and Others v Moldova and Russia*,[161] the President of the Grand Chamber requested the respondent governments, under Rule 39, to take all necessary steps to ensure that one of the applicants who had been on hunger strike since 2003 'was detained in conditions which were consistent with respect for his rights under the Convention'. Several days later the President called on the applicant, under Rule 39, to call off his hunger strike. He complied with the request on the same day.

The object of interim relief is set out in paragraph 108 of the *Mamatkulov* judgment:

> In cases such as the present one where there is plausibly asserted to be a risk of irreparable damage to the enjoyment by the applicant of one of the core rights under the Convention, the object of an interim measure is to maintain the status quo pending the Court's determination of the justification for the measure.

The references to 'irreparable damage' and 'core rights' have appropriately circumscribed the scope of Rule 39. In practice, Rule 39 will only be applied where the complaint relates to

[158] Hudoc (2007). The case is pending before the Grand Chamber. In a partly dissenting opinion, Judge Bratza found no hindrance of the right of petition on the facts of the case, especially in light of the relatively short delay in complying with the measure.

[159] Two prominent examples, in addition to *Mamatkulov*, are *Conka and Others v Belgium* No 51564/99 hudoc (2001) DA (where there was allegedly a breakdown in communication) and *Aoulmi v France* 2006-I; 46 EHRR 1, though it must be added that in each case, the failure to abide by the interim measure took place before the Court's ruling in *Mamatkulov*. See also *Shamayev and Others v Georgia and Russia* 2005-III, concerning the extradition of Chechen applicants from Georgia to Russia. See also the pending case of *Al-Saadoon and Mufdhi v UK* No 61498/08 hudoc concerning two detainees in Basra who were handed over by the UK to Iraqi authorities on 31 December 2008 despite a Rule 39 measure.

[160] As in the *Paladi* case above. The Court took the further step of asking the Turkish authorities to delay the detention of a number of applicants who had Wernicke-Korsakoff syndrome at least until they had been examined by a team of medical experts and a delegation of judges sent by the Court: *Gürbüz v Turkey* hudoc (2005) and *Tekin Yilidiz v Turkey* hudoc (2005). In *Ensslin, Baader, and Raspe v Germany* No 7572/76, 14 DR 91 (1978), the old Commission also invoked Rule 36 (as it then was) to send a delegation prior to admissibility to Stammheim prison, Stuttgart, to investigate the alleged suicides of the applicants. In admissible cases such a step would now be taken pursuant to Article 38 of the Convention—see fact-finding below, p 846.

[161] 2004-VII; 40 EHRR 1030 paras 10 and 11 GC.

Articles 2 and 3 of the Convention although the Court in *Soering* (para 113) has suggested that it could also apply to allegations of a flagrant violation of Article 6. This remains to be confirmed in the case law. Moreover where the complaint concerns expulsion to one of the contracting parties, the Court will operate a presumption that the guarantees of the Convention will be respected. However the Court has on occasion applied Rule 39 in such cases. In *Öcalan v Turkey*,[162] for example, where the applicant risked the death penalty before the State Security Court, the Court requested, *inter alia*, that Turkey ensure that the requirements of Article 6 were complied with and that the applicant was able to exercise the right of individual petition to the Court through lawyers of his own choosing. Subsequently the Court requested the government to take all necessary steps to ensure that the death penalty was not carried out so that it could examine effectively the applicant's complaints under the Convention. Requests for interim measures in respect of other Convention complaints such as interference with property rights are most unlikely to succeed unless, as illustrated by the *Öcalan* case, there are special elements linked to the notion of irreparable harm to life or limb whereas interferences with property rights, will in most cases be capable of being remedied by monetary compensation.

After Articles 2 and 3, the highest number of Rule 39 requests concern Article 8 of the Convention, especially from parents who seek to prevent the adoption or taking into care of their children. Another category is when immigrants are to be deported from a contracting party and allege only that the deportation will violate their private and family life, the rest of the family residing in the contracting party concerned. Rule 39 will only be applied exceptionally in such cases (indeed there would be a presumption that it would not be applied) since it is rare that the 'irreparable damage' test will be met. Rule 39 was applied in *Evans v UK*[163] where the Court indicated that the government should take appropriate measures to preserve frozen embryos belonging to the applicant until it could rule on whether she could use them over the objections of her ex-boyfriend with whom she had created them. The Chamber subsequently indicated in the operative part of its judgment that the Rule 39 measure was to continue until the judgment became final or until 'further order' in order to ensure that the embryos were protected in the event of the case being referred to the Grand Chamber. In the case of *D v UK*,[164] interim measures were granted in the case of a patient who was suffering from full blown AIDS and whose expulsion to St Kitts had been ordered. Similarly, interim measures were directed in the case of *N v UK*,[165] in which the applicant submitted that her expulsion to Uganda, where she would not have access to life-sustaining medicine for AIDS, would be tantamount to the imposition of a death sentence.

Rule 39 requests are dealt with on an urgent basis. Unless there is sufficient time for the case to be considered by a Chamber, it is the President of one of the Sections who will take the decision. Owing to the large numbers of complaints being submitted at the last moment, the President of the Court has issued a Practice Direction on interim measures which sets out the proper procedures to be followed by applicants and their lawyers seeking Rule 39 measures.[166] Applicants are warned, *inter alia*, that a failure to make a request expeditiously or to submit all supporting documents—in particular domestic court decisions—may result in the Court being unable to examine the request properly or in good time. Normally, domestic remedies will have to be exhausted, especially where

---

[162] 2005-IV; 41 EHRR 985 GC. See also pp 79, 205, and 427 (n 57) as regards Articles 6 and 9.

[163] Hudoc (2007); 46 EHRR 728 GC (the relevant British law required the continued consent of both gamete providers for the storage of the embryos (see para 38 of the judgment).

[164] 1997-III; 24 EHRR 423. [165] Hudoc (2008) GC.

[166] Available at <http://www.echr.coe.int/ECHR/EN/Header/Basic+Texts/Basic+Texts/Practice+directions/>.

these have suspensive effect. Where domestic remedies have been exhausted, it is certainly advisable for an application to be brought as soon as possible after an unfavourable decision has been obtained or even earlier where it is apprehended that there may be a risk of immediate removal in the event of an adverse decision on appeal.

It must be emphasized that Rule 39 measures granted by the President are usually limited in time, for example, until the Court has an opportunity to examine the admissibility and merits of the application. If the Court is persuaded that there is a real risk of ill-treatment it may decide to extend the measure for an indefinite period. They are also wholly interim in nature. In contrast to domestic proceedings where interim injunctions can become permanent injunctions, when the matter has finally been determined by the Court, even a judgment favourable to the applicant will not normally be accompanied by similar measures. However, the Court on occasion has ordered specific measures to be taken in accordance with Article 46 of the Convention,[167] though in most cases where interim measures have been granted, provided the state has abided by them, an indication under Article 46 is unlikely to prove necessary.[168]

Finally, it is also possible for the Court to accept certain undertakings by contracting parties in lieu of indicating interim measures, for example, an undertaking not to remove applicants from the territory of a state while their application is pending or, where notice has been given to the government of a request for an interim measure, an undertaking to inform the Court in good time of a proposed removal of the applicant so that the Court can consider whether to apply Rule 39. A failure to comply with such a good faith undertaking is most unlikely. If it did occur it would give rise to the traditional issue under Article 34 whether the state had hindered the effective exercise of the right of individual petition.

VI. INVESTIGATIONS AND FACT-FINDING[169]

In most cases the facts of the case are undisputed and can be determined on the basis of the facts as found by the national courts. The Court will normally accept the facts as established and has indicated that it would require cogent elements to lead it to depart from reasoned findings of fact reached by the national judicial authorities which have had the benefit of seeing and examining the relevant witnesses. Such cogent elements have been found to be present where the fact-finding by the national courts presented serious deficiencies. Thus in a criminal prosecution against Turkish police officers arising out of the killing of five suspects in four separate arrest operations, the Court noted that there were serious deficiencies in the manner in which the national court established the facts. These related to the absence of any effective investigation of the planning of the arrest operations; the absence of any photograph or sketch plans of the scenes of the incidents; the lack of any fingerprint, ballistics, or other forensic evidence; and the lack of contemporary individual statements by the police officers who participated in the operations. In these circumstances the Court held that it must treat the findings of fact by the criminal court with some caution.[170] It went on to find a violation of both the substantive and procedural obligations under Article 2.

---

[167] See the section on Article 46 at p 862 below.

[168] See eg, *Saadi v Italy* hudoc (2008) GC.

[169] See Costa, in *Mélanges en l'honneur de JP Puissochet*, 2008, pp 47–56; Erdal and Bakirci, *Article 3 of the ECHR: A Practitioner's Handbook*, OMCT Handbook Series, 2006, pp 231–59. See also Leach *et al*, Report by the Human Rights and Social Justice Research Institute, London Metropolitan University, on Fact-Finding by the ECHR, 2009.

[170] *Erdoğan v Turkey* hudoc (2006) paras 71–3.

The Court has powers to conduct fact-findings on the spot although these are rather sparingly used because of the amount of resources needed for such missions. Fact-findings by the Court, like those of the former Commission, have concerned many cases against Turkey concerning killings or disappearances or allegations of torture. Other on-the spot missions have also concerned allegations relating to inhuman and degrading prison conditions.[171] In *Ireland v UK*,[172] the Commission heard over 100 witnesses in Strasbourg, Norway, and the United Kingdom. In *Ilaşcu and Others v Moldova and Russia*,[173] a delegation of four judges took evidence from forty-three witnesses in Tiraspol and Chişinău. The witness hearings took place in different locations (a prison, an OSCE office, the headquarters of the Russian army in Transdniestria) and various political figures were heard. The number of fact-findings by the Court has steadily diminished over the years.[174] This is explicable in part by the development of case law of the Court concerning the drawing of adverse presumptions in certain circumstances when the government fails to co-operate as requested as well as a policy of the Sections to determine even Article 2 cases solely on the basis of a detailed case file, particularly if the facts relate to events that occurred many years ago when the usefulness of hearing witnesses may be in doubt.[175]

The Chamber may appoint one or more of its members to carry out an on-site investigation.[176] The applicant and 'any Contracting Party concerned' are required by the Rules of Court to 'assist the Court as necessary'.[177] The relevant contracting party shall extend to the delegation the facilities and co-operation necessary for the proper conduct of the proceedings. These shall include freedom of movement and all adequate security arrangements for the delegation, the applicant, witnesses, and experts.[178] It is provided in the Rules that 'it shall be the responsibility of the Contracting Party—to take steps to ensure that no adverse consequences are suffered by any person or organisation on account of any evidence given, or any assistance provided, to the delegation'. Since investigations may take place in trouble zones, this obligation to protect witnesses from reprisals is primordial. It has happened that applicants and witnesses have been intimidated or harmed and even killed in suspicious circumstances.[179] Both parties are asked to nominate witnesses and the delegation decides in advance of the mission those witnesses it wishes to hear. The head of the delegation may decide to hold a preparatory meeting with the parties prior to any proceedings taking place,[180] which will greatly assist in the organization of the mission. The rules also make provision for the issuing of summonses and the relevant contracting party has the responsibility for servicing any summons sent to it by the Chamber for service. The contracting party is also required 'to take all reasonable steps to ensure the attendance of persons summoned who are under its authority or control'. The hearing of witnesses is *in camera*[181] and is inquisitorial in style with the delegates and the

---

[171] See eg, *Peers v Greece* 2001-III; 33 EHRR 1192 and *Valašinas v Lithuania* 2001-VIII.

[172] A 25 (1978); 2 EHRR 25 PC.   [173] 2004 VII; 40 EHRR 1030.

[174] Since the Convention institutions were set up there have been around 95 fact-finding missions.

[175] See, as regard both points, *Tanlı v Turkey* 2001-III. The Court usually asks for the national investigation file to be forwarded in such cases. See Leach *et al*, cited in n 169.

[176] For the investigation procedure, see the Annex to the Rules (concerning investigations).

[177] Rule A2(1). The President of the Chamber may grant leave to third parties to take part in an investigative measure although this has not yet occurred (Rule A(6)).

[178] Rule A2(2). This rule should be read in conjunction with Rule 44A which imposes a general duty on the parties to co-operate fully with the Court. See also Rules 44B and C.

[179] For a detailed account of such instances see the Report of the Committee on Legal Affairs and Human Rights of the Assembly on *Member States' Duty to Co-operate with the European of Human Rights*, by Mr C Pourgourides, paras 18 *et seq*, 9 February 2007.

[180] Rule A4(2).   [181] Rule A1(5).

representatives of the parties being able to question the witnesses.[182] Questions of procedure and objections to lines of questioning are dealt with by the head of the delegation.[183] Witnesses are normally not admitted to the hearing room before they give evidence so that their testimony is not tainted by what other witnesses have said.[184] Following the hearing, a verbatim record of the proceedings is drawn up and circulated to the parties for corrections.[185] Interpretation is organized by the Registry of the Court and costs of the hearing, including reasonable witness expenses, are paid from the Court's budget.

The weakness of the Court's fact-finding machinery lies in the inability of the Court to compel the attendance of witnesses and the production of documents.[186] The Convention does not explicitly impose these obligations on contracting parties. However the failure to ensure the attendance of witnesses or to produce documentation which is considered important to the case can lead to a finding that the state has violated Article 38(1)(a) which requires that states furnish all necessary facilities for the effective conduct of the investigation. The Court has not been shy to record violations of this provision where the state has failed to co-operate. Equally importantly, the Court has held that in certain instances it is only the government that has access to information capable of corroborating or refuting the applicant's allegations and that a failure to submit such information which is in its hands without a satisfactory explanation may not only give rise to a possible breach of Article 38(1)(a) but may also give rise to the drawing of inferences as to the well-foundedness of the applicant's allegations. The same approach will apply where the state fails to secure the attendance of witnesses at a hearing, thereby making it more difficult to establish the facts. In the case of *Akkum and Others v Turkey*[187] the Court went a step further and, drawing a parallel with the approach employed by the Court in cases concerning injuries inflicted during detention, held that the withholding of vital documents concerning the killings of the applicants' relatives had the effect of shifting the burden of proof to the government to disprove the applicants' allegations:

> It is appropriate, therefore, that in cases such as the present one, where it is the non-disclosure by the Government of crucial documents in their exclusive possession which is preventing the Court from establishing the facts, it is for the Government either to argue conclusively why the documents in question cannot serve to corroborate the allegations made by the applicants, or to provide a satisfactory and convincing explanation of how the events in question occurred, failing which an issue under Article 2 and/or Article 3 of the Convention will arise.

It remains to be seen whether such an approach would be approved by the Grand Chamber.[188]

---

[182] Rule A7(1–5).   [183] Id, (5).   [184] Id, (3).

[185] Rule A8. Corrections may be made by the parties but in no case may such corrections affect the sense and bearing of what was said—Rule A8(3).

[186] See eg, *Tanis and Others v Turkey* 2005-VIII para 160 where the Commanding Officer would not appear to give evidence in a disappearance case before the delegates and the authorities would not submit an unexpurgated version of the investigation file. The Court drew adverse inferences in this case as well as finding a breach of Article 38(1)(a). Cf, *Musayeva and Others v Russia* hudoc (2007) paras 121–4.

[187] 2005-II; 43 EHRR 526 para 211.

[188] In *Nachova and Others v Bulgaria* 2005-VII; 42 EHRR 933 para 157, for example, the Grand Chamber did not follow the Chamber's approach of reversing the burden of proof as regards an allegation of a violation of Article 14 concerning racially motivated killings.

VII. BURDEN AND STANDARD OF PROOF[189]

Evidence is presented to the Court in a variety of forms—the decisions of national courts on issues of fact, affidavit evidence of witnesses, medical reports and testimony, official investigation reports, and other documentary evidence such as video or photographic evidence. In many complaints under Article 3 about prison conditions, the Court has relied on reports of the Committee for the Prevention of Torture to corroborate allegations about prison conditions or facilities.[190] There is no prohibition of hearsay evidence and no fixed rules concerning illegally obtained evidence, privileged documents, or perjury. Such evidential issues will be decided on a case-to-case basis having regard to all the facts established in the case and the nature of the allegations. The proceedings are governed by the principle of the free admission and assessment of evidence.[191] The case law reveals, however, a distinct approach to the burden of proof both as regards admissibility issues and issues of fact.[192]

At the admissibility stage the applicant must present facts which are supportive (albeit not conclusive) of his allegations by way of a 'beginning of proof' (*commencement de preuve*). There should be enough factual elements to enable the Court, at this initial stage, to conclude that the allegations are not completely groundless. As regards issues of domestic remedies, there is a distribution of the burden of proof. The burden is on the state to demonstrate the existence of adequate and effective remedies but then shifts to the applicant to demonstrate that the remedies adduced by the state are, in fact, inadequate and ineffective. It then remains to the state to rebut the arguments submitted by the applicant under this head.[193]

At the merits stage, the approach to the burden of proof is subtle and context dependent. The level of persuasion necessary for reaching a particular conclusion and the distribution of the burden of proof are linked to the specific circumstances of the case, the nature of the allegation made, and the Convention right at stake. The Court may also be attentive to the seriousness that attaches to a ruling that a contracting party has violated fundamental rights.[194] For example, as regards expulsion cases raising Article 3 issues, it is for the applicant to adduce evidence capable of proving that there are substantial grounds for believing that, if removed to the country of destination, he or she would be exposed to a real risk of being subjected to treatment contrary to Article 3. Where such evidence is adduced, it is for the government to dispel any doubts about it.[195] In cases concerning torture or ill-treatment of a detainee, the Court has consistently applied the rule that where a person is detained in good health but is found to be injured on release, it is incumbent on the state to provide a plausible explanation of how the injury occurred.[196]

---

[189] See Erdal, 26 ELR, Human Rights Survey 68 (2001) and Kokott, *The Burden of Proof in Comparative and International Human Rights Law: Civil and Common Law Approaches with Special Reference to the American and German Legal Systems*, 1998.

[190] Eg, *Yakovenko v Ukraine* hudoc (2007) para 83 and *Ostrovar v Moldova* hudoc (2005) para 80.

[191] *Nachova v Bulgaria* 2005-VII; 42 EHRR 933 para 157 GC.

[192] In *Ireland v UK* A 25 (1978); 2 EHRR 25 para 160 PC, the former Court made it clear that it would not rely on the concept that the burden of proof is borne by one of the two governments appearing before it and that its approach was to examine all the material before it including material obtained *proprio motu*. Since under the former system the fact-finding had been carried out by the Commission this approach is understandable. But it was inevitable that the new Court, which must establish the facts for itself, would develop a different approach to the burden of proof.

[193] *Selmouni v France* 1999-V; 29 EHRR 403 para 87 and the authorities cited therein. See also above, p 767.

[194] *Nachova and Others v Bulgaria* 2005-VII; 42 EHRR 933 para 147 GC.

[195] *Saadi v Italy* hudoc (2008) para 129 GC and *N v Finland* hudoc (2005) para 167; 43 EHRR 195.

[196] *Tomasi v France* A 241-A (1992) para 108–11; *Ribitsch v Austria* A 336 (1995) para 34; *Selmouni, loc cit* at n 193 above, para 87. See also above, pp 73–4.

The same principle has been applied to the disappearance of a person who had been in custody.[197] In cases concerning the use of lethal force by the security forces, the case law conveys the impression that it is incumbent on the applicant to establish a violation of Article 2. As pointed out by Judge Bratza in a dissenting opinion, the wording of Article 2 strongly suggests that it falls to the state to demonstrate that the force used was 'no more than absolutely necessary'.[198]

Generally it for the state to demonstrate the 'necessity' of an interference with a Convention right under the second paragraph of Articles 8–11. For example, in freedom of speech cases, it will fall to the state, once an applicant has demonstrated that there has been an interference with his Article 10 rights, to prove the necessity for the interference with reference to reasons that are considered by the Court to be both relevant and sufficient.[199] However, the Court has refused to reverse the burden of proof in a discrimination case under Article 14 where the authorities had not carried out an adequate investigation into the question whether unlawful killings were racially motivated on the basis that such an approach went too far since it would require the authorities to disprove a subjective attitude by the person concerned.[200] Nevertheless, the Court recognizes that discrimination is notoriously difficult to prove and that less strict evidential rules may be justified in certain circumstances. In *DH and Others v Czech Republic*,[201] concerning allegations of discrimination against the Roma community, the Court considered that once the applicants had shown, with reference to statistical information, evidence of indirect discrimination against them as a group, the burden of proof shifted to the respondent government to show that the difference in treatment was not discriminatory. Finally, as noted in the preceding section on fact-finding, there are many instances where the Court will reverse the burden or draw adverse inferences from a state's refusal to co-operate or to provide information in respect of matters within their particular knowledge.

The standard of proof is that of 'beyond reasonable doubt'. This is regularly employed by the Court in allegations of violations of Articles 2 and 3. For the Court, such proof may follow 'from the coexistence of sufficiently strong, clear and concordant inferences or of similar unrebutted presumptions of fact' as well as from the conduct of the parties when evidence is being taken.[202] A reasonable doubt is a doubt for which reasons can be drawn from the facts presented and not a doubt raised on the basis of a mere theoretical possibility or to avoid a disagreeable conclusion.[203] It has been stressed that it has never been the Court's purpose to borrow the approach of the national systems which use that standard and that the Court's role is not to establish criminal or civil liability but to determine the contracting parties' responsibility under the Convention.[204] Thus the fact that police officers may have been acquitted in criminal proceedings of the use of unlawful force cannot be decisive of the issue that arises under the Convention, namely whether the force used has been more than absolutely necessary in the circumstances.[205] Accordingly, the standard does not correspond with the high criminal law standard that is employed in many legal systems though it does nevertheless connote a high standard of proof as regards the facts that are alleged to have occurred. The standard has been criti-

---

[197] *Kurt v Turkey* 1998-III; 27 EHRR 373 para 124 and *Çakıcı v Turkey* 1999-IV; 31 EHRR 133 GC. See also above, p 132.

[198] *Ağdaş v Turkey* hudoc (2004).   [199] See above, p 444.

[200] *Nachova v Bulgaria* 2005-VII; 42 EHRR 933 para 157 GC.

[201] *DH and Others v Czech Republic* hudoc (2007) paras 186–9 GC.

[202] First employed in *Ireland v UK* A 25 (1978) PC; 2 EHRR 25. See also, *inter alia, Salman v Turkey* 2000-VII; 34 EHRR 425 para 100 GC.

[203] *Ireland v UK*, id, para 30.   [204] *Nachova v Bulgaria* 2005-VII; 42 EHRR 933 para 147 GC.

[205] *Erdogan v Turkey* hudoc (2006) para 71.

cized in various dissenting opinions as inadequate, possibly illogical, and unworkable when trying to determine whether a person in custody has been ill-treated.[206]

VIII. PILOT JUDGMENTS[207]

A pilot judgment is the Court's recently developed response to the recurring problem of repetitive or 'clone cases', ie large numbers of cases raising essentially the same issue. In the 1980s the problem was reflected in the large number of cases brought against Italy concerning length of procedure. Since the establishment of the new Court in 1998 a large volume of repetitive cases have been brought against many different countries concerning not only length of civil and criminal proceedings but many other issues including non-enforcement of domestic judgments, delays in payment following expropriation, and access to property in northern Cyprus.

The Court itself proposed the introduction of a 'pilot judgment procedure' in cases which were related to a systemic or structural problem in the country concerned.[208] It was envisaged that the pilot judgment would give rise to an accelerated execution procedure before the Committee of Ministers and would impose on the state an obligation to address the structural problem and thereby provide domestic redress in respect of applications pending in Strasbourg.

The 'pilot judgment procedure' was applied for the first time in the case of *Bronowski v Poland*.[209] In the operative part of the judgment the Court held that the violation of Article 1 of Protocol 1 found in the case originated 'in a systemic problem connected with the malfunctioning of domestic legislation and practice caused by the failure to set up an effective mechanism to implement the "right to credit" of Bug River claimants'. The Court enjoined the state to secure the implementation of the property right in question in respect not only of the applicant but also of the remaining Bug River claimants. In the judgment the Court had noted that some 80,000 people were affected by the systemic problem. Following a friendly settlement concerning the setting-up of a compensation scheme for all those affected, the case was eventually struck off the Court's list. The compensation scheme later set up by the Polish authorities was subsequently accepted by the Court as providing a remedy which satisfied the principal *Broniowski* judgment[210] A further pilot judgment was adopted by the Court in the case of *Hutten-Czapska v Poland*[211] which concerned failure of Polish law to secure a 'decent profit' for landlords. In its judgment on the merits, the Grand Chamber held that 'in order to put an end to the systemic violation identified in the present case, the respondent Government must through appropriate legal and/or other measures, secure in its domestic legal order a mechanism maintaining a fair balance between the interests of landlords and the general interests of the community, in accordance with the standards of protection of property rights under

---

[206] See eg, the dissenting opinion of eight judges in *Labita v Italy* 2000-IV; 46 EHRR 1228 GC and the dissent of Judge Bonnello in *Veznedaroğlu v Turkey* hudoc 2000; 33 EHRR 1412.

[207] See Colendra, 7 HRLR 397 (2007); Garlicki, in Caflisch *et al*, eds, *Liber Amicorum Luzius Wildhaber*, 2007, pp 177–92; Leach, 2005 EHRLR 148. The Human Rights and Social Justice Research Institute at London Metropolitan University are carrying out a research project into the pilot judgment procedure in the course of 2008–09. See also p 885 below.

[208] Position Paper of the European Court of Human Rights on proposals for reform of the ECHR and other measures, CDDH GDR (2003)024, 26 September 2003, paras 43–6.

[209] 2004-V; 40 EHRR 495 GC. See Degener and Mahoney, in Hartig, ed, *Recueil à la mémoire de Wolfgang Strasser*, 2007, pp 173–209.

[210] *Wolkenberg and Others v Poland No 50003/99* hudoc (2007) DA (extracts).

[211] 2006-VIII; 45 EHRR 52 GC.

the Convention'. This case was also struck out following a friendly settlement concerning the general measures adopted by Poland in response to the Court's judgment.[212]

In the case of *Lukenda v Slovenia*[213] the Court noted there were some 500 Slovenian length of proceedings cases pending before it. This was identified as a systemic problem resulting from inadequate legislation and inefficiency in the administration of justice. The Court urged the Slovenian government to amend the existing range of legal remedies in order to secure genuinely effective address for such violations. The introduction of a remedy in Slovenia for length of proceedings subsequently enabled the Court to dispose of large numbers of such cases.

The category of pilot judgments also includes judgments which stop short of requiring the state to introduce corrective measures in the operative part of the judgment but nevertheless relate to structural problems and propose that measures be taken by the state to address them.[214]

The pilot judgment procedure has been endorsed by the Committee of Ministers,[215] the Woolf Report,[216] and the Wise Persons Group.[217] The Court itself has set up a sub-committee to examine how the procedure can best be utilized in the future as well as the types of cases that may be appropriately dealt with by this procedure. They have most significantly concerned specific structural problems arising in the area of property rights. The question arises whether such judgments can also be used to deal with common endemic problems in many contracting parties such as non-enforcement of judgments or cases concerning length of civil and criminal procedure, detention on remand, and prison conditions. Some commentators have suggested that a measure of circumspection in resorting to the procedure may be desirable and that an inflation of pilot judgments would be counter-productive.[218] This is undoubtedly the case since such a judgment requires the state to remedy often deeply-entrenched legal or socio-economic problems in its national system that may not admit of an easy legislative resolution.[219] While the procedure offers a useful tool to bring about such structural change, an excessive recourse to the procedure could lead to judgments that were not complied with. This in turn would undermine the usefulness of the procedure. Nevertheless there has been a general acceptance by governments of the utility of the procedure as a sensible method of dealing with repetitive complaints and only one government so far has actually challenged the legal basis of such a procedure under the Convention.[220]

The pilot judgment procedure reflects the view of the Court that its role should not be to act as a claims commission examining large numbers of repetitive cases and, further, that states must assume their responsibilities to tackle the root problems underlying repetitive complaints. It also evidences the reality that the Court is not capable of dealing with such large numbers of frequently well-founded complaints. The essential challenge facing the Court is to ensure that the root problems are addressed by the state within a reasonable time-frame and that pending cases which have been adjourned pending the outcome of the pilot procedure can be repatriated following the introduction

---

[212] *Hutten-Czapska v Poland* hudoc (2008) GC and the separate opinions of Judges Zagrebelsky, Jaeger, and Ziemele for critical remarks on the settlement.

[213] 2005-X. See also the section pilot judgment of 15 January 2009 in *Burdov v Russia (No 2)* No 33509/04 hudoc (2009) concerning the recurrent problem of non-enforcement of court judgments in Russia.

[214] See eg, *Xenides-Arestis v Turkey* hudoc (2005) and *Scordino v Italy (No 1)* 2006-V; 45 EHRR 207 GC.

[215] Committee of Ministers' Resolution (2004) 3 on Judgments Revealing an Underlying Systemic Problem.

[216] Review of the Working Methods of the European Court of Human Rights, December 2005, pp 37–8.

[217] Report of the Group of Wise Persons to the Committee of Ministers, Council of Europe, November 2006 at paras 100–5.

[218] Garlicki, in *Liber Amicorum Luzius Wildhaber*, p 191.

[219] See, in this context, Judge Zagrebelsky's dissenting opinion in *Lukenda v Slovenia* hudoc (2005).

[220] See the arguments of the Italian government in *Sejdovic v Italy* 2006-II GC.

of satisfactory corrective measures. To date the negotiation of friendly settlements in *Broniowski* and *Hutten-Czapska* whereby agreement is reached on a series of general measures which seek to tackle the structural problems underlying the case have essentially relieved the Committee of Ministers of the thorny problem of implementation. However it may be questioned whether friendly settlement is, in all circumstances, the most appropriate manner of implementing such judgments and whether the Committee should be deprived of the opportunity of expressing a view on the nature of the general measures adopted.[221] Be that as it may, the future of this procedure is ultimately in the hands of the Committee of Ministers since it is the successful enforcement of such judgments that will validate the Court's continued recourse to them.

IX. THIRD PARTY INTERVENTIONS

Article 36 of the Convention makes provision for third parties to intervene in proceedings.[222] Indeed this is a frequent occurrence in the Court's higher profile cases where there may be points of general importance at stake. According to Rule 44 of the Rules of Court requests should be submitted within twelve weeks of the communication of an application to the respondent government.[223] In Article 36, two types of intervention must be distinguished. First, when the application is brought by the national of one state against another contracting party, the state of which the applicant is a national has the right to intervene under Article 36(1), reflecting the traditional right of diplomatic protection.[224] Second, under Article 36(2), the President of the Court may, in the interests of the proper administration of justice, invite any other contracting party or any other person concerned to submit written comments.

In respect of the first, this right also extends to appearing before the Court in oral hearings. Accordingly, states in this category are in a considerably stronger legal position that an NGO seeking leave to intervene. They can, for example, insist on having access to the entire case file. However the Court has decided that they cannot insist on the right to appoint an *ad hoc* judge since they are not parties to the case *stricto sensu*; nor do they have a right to comment on the terms of any friendly settlement that has been reached although they will usually be sent the settlement for information. It must be stressed that this is a right but not a duty and states can and do decline to take part in the proceedings, especially when there is no wider principle at stake or the national link between applicant and state is wholly incidental.[225]

---

[221] Is it appropriate, for example, that the discussion about general measures in friendly settlement meetings take place only between the applicant and the government—without the presence of other interested parties such as NGOs or other groups directly affected by the proposed legislation?

[222] For a survey of third party interventions before the Court see Mahoney and Sicilianos, in Ruiz Fabri and Sorel, eds, *La tiers à l'instance devant les jurisdictions internationales*, 2005.

[223] This is made easier by the Court's decision to publish details of most communicated cases on its website as well as cases accepted for reference to the Grand Chamber by the panel and cases where jurisdiction has been relinquished to the Grand Chamber. See 'Communicated Cases Collection' at <http://www.echr.coe.int/echr/en/hudoc>.

[224] See eg, the Russian government's intervention in *Slivenko v Latvia* 2003-XI; 39 EHRR 490 GC (concerning the rights of Russian-speaking settled immigrants to regular residence status) or the Cypriot government's intervention in *Eugenia Michaelidou Developments Ltd and Michael Tymvios v Turkey* hudoc (2003); 39 EHRR 772 (concerning access to property in northern Cyprus; and the intervention by the government of Serbia and Montenegro (as it then was) in *Markovic v Italy* 2006-XIV; 44 EHRR 1045 GC (concerning the unsuccessful attempts of Serbian nationals to obtain compensation through the Italian courts for an air strike by NATO).

[225] See eg, *GJ v Luxembourg* hudoc (2000); 30 EHRR 710; *Krombach v France* 2001-II; and *Fogarty v UK* 2001-IX; 34 EHRR 302 GC, where, respectively, the Danish, German, and Irish governments declined to intervene.

In relation to the latter type (interventions which require leave from the Court), in the practice of the Court, one can further distinguish three types of interveners. First, interventions by governments other than the respondent government that have a specific interest in the subject matter of the case. Second, persons other than the applicant who are directly implicated in the facts of the case may also intervene with leave.[226] Finally, and most commonly, NGOs with particular experience in the area of law or practice being examined frequently seek (and are granted) leave to intervene.

In respect of the first category, governments asserting an interest will almost always be given leave to intervene.[227] This frequently occurs in cases where a point of general public international law is being considered such as in *Behrami and Saramati*, discussed above, where five states intervened.[228] It has also occurred when the issue under consideration will have implications for their legal system or immigration policy.[229] Equally in *Üner v Netherlands*,[230] concerning the deportation of a settled immigrant with young children with a series of criminal convictions, the German government intervened given the similarity of its policy on deportation to that of the Dutch government. It is extremely unusual for a contracting party whose nationals are not applicants to intervene in support of the finding of a violation, though it has occurred in one case involving the death of a journalist in northern Cyprus.[231]

With regard to the second category, interventions by persons directly concerned or affected by the facts, there are fewer examples. In *T and V v UK*,[232] concerning the right to a fair trial of two boys who had been convicted of murdering a toddler, the parents of the victim were given leave to intervene. In *Perna v Italy*,[233] where the applicant had been convicted of defaming a judge, the judge was also given leave to intervene.

More common is the third category, where an interested party intervenes because of the legal importance of a case in an area where it has special expertise. Non-governmental organizations are frequent interveners on this basis. Thus, to give just a few examples, in

---

[226] The Court has given a wide meaning to the notion of 'any person concerned who is not the applicant' in Rule 44(2). It encompasses not only individuals and NGOs but also government-appointed human rights bodies such as the Northern Ireland Human Rights Commission. The Council of Europe's Venice Commission has also been given leave. Protocol 14 will confer on the Commissioner a right to intervene (Article 13) but it would be open to him to request to intervene under the existing rules. If the Commissioner has not so far sought to intervene it may arguably be explained by a certain tension between his traditional statutory role and any involvement in cases brought against countries on whose co-operation he depends. If and when Protocol 14 comes into force this tension may become even more apparent. It is submitted that a judicious use of the Commissioner's right to intervene under the Protocol will be beneficial to the Court since his specific knowledge of the human rights situation in particular countries nourished by his contacts with national human rights institutions could be of substantial benefit, especially in pilot cases relating to systemic problems giving rise to large numbers of repetitive cases.

[227] The United Kingdom has been a frequent intervener on this ground. See for example, its interventions in *Association SOS Attentats and De Boëry v France* 2006-XIV GC (in support of the contention that heads of state in office enjoyed immunity *ratione personae* from civil and criminal proceedings); *Kyprianou v Cyprus* 2005-XIII; 44 EHRR 565 GC (contempt of court); *Bosphorus Hava Yollari Turizm ve Ticaret Anonim Sirketi (Bosphorus Airways) v Ireland* 2005-VI; 42 EHRR 1 GC (concerning the appropriate level of review to be applied by the Court when the alleged violation results from a state's legal obligations flowing from membership in another international organization, in this case the European Union).

[228] Denmark, Estonia, Poland, Portugal, and the United Kingdom.

[229] *Saadi v Italy* hudoc (2008) GC where the UK government intervened to argue that the Court should overturn its view in *Chahal* that, in expulsion cases under Article 3, considerations relating to national security were not to be taken into account once a substantial risk of ill-treatment was established.

[230] 2006-XII; 45 EHRR 421 GC.

[231] *Adali v Turkey* hudoc (2005). The applicant, the widow of the deceased, was a Turkish national and the Cypriot government intervened in support of her.

[232] 1999-IX; 30 EHRR 121 GC.   [233] 2003-V; 39 EHRR 563 GC.

Nikula v Finland,[234] Interights submitted a comparative law survey concerning restrictions on speech imposed on lawyers. In *Hugh Jordan v UK*,[235] the Northern Ireland Human Rights Commission was given leave to comment on the right to life in international jurisprudence with reference to UN principles and the case law of the Inter-American Court. In *Pretty v UK*,[236] the Voluntary Euthanasia Society submitted a comparative law survey of relevant legal principles concerning euthanasia as well as ethical arguments in support of its position. The Catholic Bishops' Conference of England was also authorized to make written submissions on the moral issues underlying the case.[237] Frequently, such interventions will involve comparative law studies across different states, which may point to a practice in the respondent state that is out of step with that in other contracting parties.

In general, the Court has a liberal policy as regards interventions generally and leave to intervene will normally be granted by the President if the party submits a request outlining the nature of the proposed intervention and the reasons why it will further the proper administration of justice (Rule 44). If the case is subsequently heard by the Grand Chamber it is not necessary to ask for permission a second time. There are, however, limitations attached to any authorization since the intervener is not considered as a party. It is usually stipulated in the letter permitting intervention that it should not address directly the admissibility or merits of the case but provide information based on the expertise or experience of the interveners.[238] Interventions which do not conform to this condition may be refused or only accepted in part (Rule 44(4)). Requests may also be refused when they are submitted out of time or too close to the hearing of the case or where the Court has already granted permission to other organizations. The Court has on occasions requested interveners to group their submissions.[239] On moral or sensitive social issues, the Court is careful to grant permission to organizations on different sides of the issue if requests have been made, as for example in the *Pretty* case discussed above.[240] Finally it should be noted that intervention by organizations is usually limited to written submissions. The Court would not normally grant permission for an intervener to appear before it, although in exceptional situations where the intervener has a direct interest in the outcome of the case this has been authorized (as was the case in *T and V v UK*). The Rules of Court also provide that the President may invite or grant leave to a third party to participate in an investigative measure such as a fact-finding (Rule A1(6) of the Annex to the Rules of Court concerning investigations).[241] The Court is, however, strict about the length of third party interventions normally restricting them to ten pages, excluding appendices. The respondent government and applicant are always given an opportunity to comment on the third party's observations as they may open up new lines of argument to be addressed by the parties.[242]

[234] 2002-II; 38 EHRR 944.   [235] 2001-III; 37 EHRR 52.   [236] 2002-III; 35 EHRR 1.

[237] See further Sicilianos and Mahoney, *loc cit* at n 222 above and Leach, *Taking a Case to the European Court of Human Rights*, 2nd edn, 2005, pp 57–61, for further examples.

[238] There may be occasional exceptions to this approach, for example, where the Court seeks information in an expulsion case about conditions in another country.

[239] Eg, *McCann and Others v UK* A 324 (1995); 21 EHRR 97 para 5 GC.

[240] See also the five interventions in *Tysiac v Poland* hudoc (2007), concerning the inability of a woman to obtain an abortion in circumstances where, it was held, domestic law provided for that possibility.

[241] This has not yet happened.

[242] See eg, the verbatim record of the hearing of 24 November 1992 in *Brannigan and McBride v UK*, p 16 where the government stated as follows: 'The comments lodged by these two sets of organisations appear to us not only to be far wider in ambit than was contemplated by the Court in granting leave, but to be made without any regard to the nature and scope of the claim actually advanced by these applicants and considered by the Commission in its decision on admissibility and in its report. It is our respectful submission that much of what is contained in the comments is wholly inappropriate, coming as it does from organisations which are

Though it is unusual, the Court may also invite interventions of its own motion. This occurred in *Young, James and Webster v UK*[243] where the applicants complained that a 'closed shop agreement' violated their freedom of association under Article 11 and the United Kingdom government confined its observations to stating that there was no violation. The Court of its own motion invited the TUC to submit comments and to appear as a witness on certain factual matters, which it did, albeit in support of the argument that the closed shop was compatible with the Convention.

There is no doubt that the Court has been greatly assisted over the years by third party interventions particularly by NGOs who have been able to provide much relevant information concerning comparative and international law and practice. Such a contribution not only brings to the Court's attention relevant judicial authorities but also greatly assists the Court in determining whether there exists a common ground within the contracting parties on particular issues. The liberal practice that the new Court has developed over the years is thus based on its own desire to have as much relevant information at its disposal as possible when deciding a case. It also reflects an understanding that many NGOs have a wealth of knowledge and expertise at their disposal which can enrich the deliberations in a case. While *Young, James and Webster* was exceptional in its day, the Court can be expected to reach out more frequently of its own accord—a possibility which is open to it under Rule 44—and invite particular interveners to file comments when it has received no requests to intervene and the case is of general importance.

4. ARTICLE 41: JUST SATISFACTION

Article 41 reads:

> If the Court finds that there has been a violation of the Convention or the protocols thereto, and if the internal law of the High Contracting Party concerned allows only partial reparation to be made, the Court shall, if necessary, afford just satisfaction to the injured party.

The case law under Article 41 (which replaces Article 50) is characterized by the lack of a consistently applied law of damages at the level of detail which one would find in national systems and which permit specific calculations to be made on the basis of precedent for injury, loss of life, unlawful imprisonment, and loss of property. The Court applies a series of general principles—as set out below—to the facts of each case when a violation has been found.[244] Given the existence of five Sections and a Grand Chamber all taking decisions on just satisfaction, problems of consistency of awards have inevitably crept in. However the precedential value of awards in Grand Chamber cases and the setting up of an Article 41 Unit with the Registry of the Court to advise the Chambers on the

not parties to the proceedings but have been permitted to lodge comments in what are and remain individual applications.'

[243] A 44 (1981) para 8 PC. The Chamber in *Andrejeva v Latvia No 55707/00* hudoc (2006), (currently pending before the Grand Chamber following relinquishment of jurisdiction) invited the Russian and Ukrainian governments to intervene, the applicant having worked in both countries. The issue concerns a pension dispute. The invitation was not accepted.

[244] For commentaries on the Court's practice, see Shelton, *Remedies in International Human Rights Law*, 2005, pp 294 *et seq*; Bernhardt, *Schachter Collection*, p. 243; Costa, in Fairgrieve *et al*, eds, *Tort Liability of Public Authorities in Comparative Perspective*, 2002; Myjer, in Vandenberghe *et al*, eds, *Property and Human Rights*. 2006; Leach, *Taking a Case to the European Court of Human Rights*, 2nd edn, pp 397ff; and Loucaides, 2 EHRLR 182 (2008). For a highly critical view of the case law on Article 41 see Tavernier, 72 RDH 945 (2007).

appropriate level of awards in similar cases show that attempts are being made within the Court to strive for greater consistency. One particular difficulty is that, unlike a national court, the Court must have regard to the standard of living applicable in the country concerned. Since the contracting parties encompass countries with a very low gross national income to countries with a high GDP awards made in respect of similar violations will vary in consequence.

Despite the wording of Article 41 (that the Court shall afford just satisfaction 'if the internal law of the High Contracting Party concerned allows only partial reparation') the Court does not require an applicant who has won his case to avail of national procedures to secure compensation even if these were available. The Court has indicated that it would not be compatible with the effective protection of human rights to require an applicant who has already exhausted domestic remedies to initiate further proceedings.[245] When it finds one or more violations of the Convention, it will, in the same judgment consider what, if any, just satisfaction to award the applicant under Article 41 of the Convention. The award of just satisfaction is not a right when a violation has been found. It is a matter entirely within the Court's discretion. Part of the explanation for this is that Article 46 requires states to abide by the final judgments of the Court in any case to which they are parties, execution being supervised by the Committee of Ministers. A judgment in which the Court finds a breach imposes on the respondent state a legal obligation not just to pay those concerned the sums awarded by way of just satisfaction, but also to choose, subject to supervision by the Committee of Ministers, the general and/or, if appropriate, individual measures to be adopted in their domestic legal order to put an end to the violation found by the Court and to redress so far as possible its effects.[246] Hence the purpose of awarding sums by way of just satisfaction is to provide reparation solely for damage suffered by those concerned to the extent that such events constitute a consequence of the violation that cannot otherwise be remedied.[247]

Thus the Court may and frequently does decide to hold that the finding of a violation is, in itself, sufficient vindication of the applicant's rights and limits its award to costs and expenses. The Court will not make an award of its own motion where no claim has been made or where a claim is made out of time.[248] In a minority of cases and in accordance with Rule 75 of the Rules of Court, the Court may decide that the question of just satisfaction is not ready for decision and reserve its decision in whole or in part on the question. This occurs most frequently in cases concerning Article 1 of Protocol 1 when the calculation of pecuniary loss may be complex and require further deliberation. When it does so, and when the matter is ready for decision (usually after further observations from the parties) it will render a separate judgment if the parties have not managed to settle the issue themselves. If there is a settlement the Court will verify the 'equitable nature' of the agreement and, if satisfied, strike the case out of its list.[249] It has been the practice of the Court occasionally to reserve Article 41 when it indicates general measures under Article 46.[250]

The Court makes awards under three headings: costs and expenses, awards for pecuniary damage, and awards for non-pecuniary damage. It may also in certain circumstances indicate particular individual or general measures contracting parties must take

---

[245] *Barberà, Messegué and Jabardo v Spain* A 285-C (1994) para 17 PC.

[246] *Papamichalopoulos and Others v Greece* A 330-B (1995) para 34.

[247] *Scozzari and Giunta v Italy* 2000-VIII; 35 EHRR 243 paras 248–50 GC.

[248] Eg, *Nasri v France* A 320-B (1995) para 49.

[249] Rule 75(4). See section on friendly settlement above pp 829–33.

[250] See *Broniowski v Poland* 2004-V; 40 EHRR 495 GC.

in order to remedy the violation found,[251] although in general these stop short of specific consequential measures, for example, that the state is required to take penal or administrative action in regard to the persons responsible for the infringement.[252] In the operative provisions of the judgment the Court will provide that just satisfaction is to be paid within three months failing which default interest is payable at a particular rate.

The process of considering the application of Article 41 will start when the Court sends the government's observations to the applicant's legal representative for comment. At the same time, the representative will be invited to submit his claims for just satisfaction. Where the joint procedure is used under Article 29(3) (ie in most cases) the Article 41 claims must be submitted with the observations in reply on both the admissibility and merits of the application. The representative will be reminded of Rule 60 of the Rules of Court which provides that an applicant who wishes to obtain an award of just satisfaction under Article 41 must make a specific claim to that effect. The same rule states that the applicant must submit itemized particulars of all claims, together with any relevant supporting documents.[253] The claims are then sent to the respondent government for comment.

I. COSTS AND EXPENSES

As regards costs and expenses, the Court is normally strict with representatives and frequently finds that they have either failed to itemize their costs properly or that the number of hours billed is excessive or that the hourly rate is excessive. Time limits for the submission of claims should be respected and the Court will not usually grant extensions of time limits in respect of Article 41 submissions unless good cause is shown for the delay. As it frequently states, an applicant is entitled to reimbursement of his costs and expenses only insofar as it has been shown that these relate to the violation(s) found, have been actually and necessarily incurred, and are reasonable as to quantum.[254] Nonetheless, the costs of a full legal team can be claimed provided each of the representatives' costs are within these bounds and are properly itemized. Thus for a complex case, there will be no bar on claiming the costs of an instructing solicitor and both senior and junior counsel, though this must not involve an unnecessary duplication of work.[255] Additionally, the Court may award a lump sum to the applicant, which may prove problematic when this is a percentage of what is claimed and there are several legal representatives seeking to recover their fees. The Court is not bound by the scale of fees applied in national law but these may be used by the Court as a benchmark for its calculation. Costs will not be awarded where a lawyer has acted free of charge. Expenses will be considered under the same rubric, save for when the applicant obtains leave to represent himself in which case he may claim expenses but not costs for the time he or she has spent working on the case.[256] Expenses incurred in respect of translation costs, photocopies, and the use of

---

[251] See below p 862.

[252] For example in *Dickson v UK* hudoc (2007); 46 EHRR 927 para 88 GC, the Court refused to order the government to provide artificial insemination facilities to a prisoner despite having found that the failure of the UK prison authorities was a breach of his and his wife's Article 8 rights.

[253] Rule 60 is supplemented by a Practice Direction, available at: <http://www.echr.coe.int>.

[254] Eg, in *Sahin v Germany* 2003-VIII para 105 GC. They are also only recoverable insofar as they relate to the violation found: see *Beyeler v Italy* hudoc (2002) GC.

[255] *Associated Society of Locomotive Engineers and Firemen (ASLEF) v UK* hudoc (2007); 45 EHRR 793 para 60.

[256] *Steel and Morris v UK* 2005-II; 41 EHRR 403 para 112 (and references therein) and *Bhandari v UK* hudoc (2007) paras 28–30.

expert testimony may be recoverable if such expenses have been actually and reasonably incurred.[257] It is in principle open to applicants to seek recovery of costs and expenses incurred before the domestic courts; the Court will only make such an award where these proceedings were concerned with preventing or seeking redress for the alleged violation of the Convention.[258] Where the Court finds that there is only a violation as regards part of the case presented, this may result in the Court reducing the amount awarded for costs and expenses. Finally Rule 43(4) provides that an award of costs may be made by the Court in respect of an application that has been struck out. This provision was added to the Rules in recognition of the work done by a legal representative in a case which may be struck out because the proceedings have led to some form of redress being given.[259]

II. PECUNIARY AND NON-PECUNIARY DAMAGE[260]

For an award of pecuniary damage to be made the applicant must demonstrate, to the Court's satisfaction, that there is causal link between the violation and any financial loss alleged. This is seen as a matter of proof rather than speculation. It is easily established when there has been a taking of property but significantly more difficult in other contexts. For example, a finding of a violation of Article 6 in the context of a criminal trial will not allow the applicant to claim lost earnings for any time he has spent in prison. However, the Court has been prepared to compensate for lost earnings in other situations, notably in right to life cases when the applicant is the widow or another dependent of the deceased[261] or where there have been lost earnings flowing from the Convention breach.[262] Claims for pecuniary damage will normally arise in cases involving property under Article 1 of Protocol 1.[263] Where the Court has found a violation, this can often give rise to complex calculations of how much to award, especially when the property in question is of significant value.[264] The amount awarded in these cases is rarely the market value. In the *Former King of Greece* case,[265] the Court found that less than full compensation could be justified where the taking of property had been intended to complete 'such fundamental changes of a country's constitutional system as the transition from monarchy to republic'.[266]

---

[257] Eg, *Salomonsson v Sweden* hudoc (2002); *Fretté v France* 2002-I; 38 EHRR 438 para 56.

[258] *King v UK* hudoc (2004); 41 EHRR 11 para 52; *Associated Society of Locomotive Engineers and Firemen (ASLEF) v UK, loc cit* at n 255 above, para 58; *IJL, GMR and AKP v UK* hudoc (2001).

[259] *Pisano v Italy* hudoc (2002) paras 51–6 GC, although the same rules on submitting specific claims and schedules of costs applies: also *Sisojeva and Others v Latvia* hudoc (2007); 45 EHRR 753 paras 133 and 134 GC. Cf, *Paez v Sweden* 1997-VII, where the former Court struck out an Article 3 case concerning expulsion to Peru after the applicant had been allowed to stay in Sweden and after extensive examination of the case by the Commission which expressed the view that there would be no violation in sending him back. At that time the rules did not allow an award in such circumstances.

[260] See Reid, *A Practitioners Guide to the ECHR,* 3rd edn, 2008, pp 608–62 for detailed tables of awards made by the Court for pecuniary and non-pecuniary loss.

[261] *Imakayeva v Russia* 2006-XIII para 213; *Çakıcı v Turkey* 1999-IV para 127; 31 EHRR 133 GC.

[262] *Lustig-Prean and Beckett v UK* hudoc (2000); 31 EHRR 601; *Young, James and Webster v UK* A 55 (1982) para 11.

[263] For example, *Beyeler v Italy* hudoc (2002) GC; *Brumărescu v Romania* 2001-I; 33 EHRR 36 GC; *Iatridis v Greece* 2000-XI GC; *James and Others v UK* A 98 (1986); 8 EHRR 123 PC; *Lithgow and Others v UK* A 102 (1986); 8 EHRR 329 PC; *Papamichalopoulos and Others v Greece* A 330-B (1995).

[264] Eg, in *Former King of Greece and Others v Greece* hudoc (2002) GC (see also the principal judgment 2000-XII; 33 EHRR 516) about the expropriation of the former king's properties after his deposition, the final award ran to over €13 million.

[265] *Ibid.*   [266] Id, para 87.

In deciding how much to award, the Court will follow a number of steps. First, it will decide whether *restitutio in integrum* is possible. If it is not or if national law only allows partial reparation, the Court will consider making an award.[267] In property cases, it will then consider whether the parties can agree on the value of the property and, if so, whether they can agree to a settlement of the matter. If they cannot agree to either, the Court may place the valuation in the hands of an independent expert and then, basing itself on the expert's report, award pecuniary damages on the usual equitable basis.[268]

The Court will award non-pecuniary damages (or moral damages) on the basis of equitable considerations more readily than it awards pecuniary damages, although there is usually little explanation as to how it reaches the sums awarded. This head of damage covers such matters as pain and suffering, anguish and distress, and loss of opportunity.[269] For the most part, the amount awarded under this head will be in proportion to the seriousness of the violation (or violations) and its effect on the applicant. The highest awards will therefore tend to be made in relation to violations of Articles 2 and 3 of the Convention.[270] However, given that the Court always rules on an equitable basis and that there is some adjustment according to the cost of living in each member state, past awards are not always reliable predictors of future awards. This is especially so when the violation turns on the particular facts of the application as is frequently the case with Articles 8, 9, 10, and 11 of the Convention. Nonetheless, there is greater consistency in such awards as regards most repetitive cases whether they are particular types of applications from one country (such as non-enforcement of court judgments) or the Court's most common type of application, the length of civil or criminal proceedings. For instance, for the latter, the Court will normally make an award based on the number of years the proceedings lasted as against the number of instances (levels of jurisdiction) before which they took place. In this type of case, the Court is guided by a set of tables which have been prepared within the Registry in respect of a number of countries as a tool to ensure consistency. For the time being such tables are not accessible to the public but the Court is considering making them available in order to serve as a guide for national courts in calculating damages.[271]

As to who can claim non-pecuniary damages, this now appears to be virtually commensurate with victim status under Article 34. There were indications that only individuals and not, say, companies or other legal persons, were eligible for non-pecuniary damages. However, in *Comingersoll SA v Portugal*,[272] a length of proceedings case, the Court found that this possibility could not be excluded. The unreasonable length of the

---

[267] *Former King of Greece and Others v Greece* id, para 73; *Beyeler* (just satisfaction) cited above, n 263.
[268] *Pasculli v Italy* hudoc (2007).
[269] The case law for loss of opportunity is not always consistent—eg, *Bönisch v Austria* A 103 (1986); 13 EHRR 409, and *Weeks v UK* A 145-A (1988); 13 EHRR 435 para 13 PC; *H v UK* A 136-B (1988) PC, where awards under this head were made. In other cases the Court has refused to speculate whether there were such losses: see eg, *Perks and Others v UK* hudoc (1999); 30 EHRR 33, where the applicant was unrepresented before a magistrates' court which sentenced him to a prison term.
[270] At the time of writing a typical Article 2 award was around €20,000 per death (cf, *Ramsahai and Others v Netherlands* hudoc (2007); 46 EHRR 983 GC, the death of one family member giving rise to an award of €20,000 and *Bitiyeva and X v Russia* hudoc (2007), the death of four family members giving rise to an award of €85,000). The awards seem unaffected by the number of relatives of the deceased who apply to the Court.
[271] This was recommended by the Woolf Report (the Review of the Working Methods of the European Court of Human Rights, December 2005). See p 41 of the report available at <http://www.echr.coe.int>.
[272] 2000-IV; 31 EHRR 772 paras 32–7 GC. In assessing this issue 'account should be taken of the company's reputation, uncertainty in decision-planning, disruption in the management of the company (for which there is no precise method of calculating the consequences) and lastly, albeit to a lesser degree, the anxiety and inconvenience caused to the members of the management team'. Id, para 35. See also Emberland, 74 BYIL 409 (2003).

proceedings had caused inconvenience and prolonged uncertainty to the company, its directors, and shareholders justifying an award of damages.[273]

It is always open to the Court to hold that the finding of a violation is sufficient just satisfaction.[274] This has happened regularly in the context of the due process rights set out in Articles 5 and 6 of the Convention where the Court has stated that it would not make an award on the speculative basis that the applicant would not have been convicted if he had had the benefit of the guarantees of Article 5 or 6 of the Convention.[275] It will also take this approach when the focus of the application is having one's rights vindicated rather than seeking damages *per se*. For example in *Hirst v UK (No 2)*,[276] in finding a violation stemming from legislation prohibiting prisoners from voting in elections, the Grand Chamber found that the government would be required to secure the right to vote in compliance with its judgment. In the circumstances, it considered that this could be regarded as providing the applicant with just satisfaction.

It is also open to the Court, in the exercise of its discretion, to decline to make an award on public policy grounds. This happens rarely but did occur in *McCann and Others v UK*[277] concerning the shooting of three terrorist suspects in Gibraltar by British special forces. The Court had regard to the fact that the deceased had been intending to plant a bomb in Gibraltar and so stated that it did not consider it appropriate to make an award under this head.

The Court has also had to consider whether the sums of money it awards under Article 41 can be accompanied by orders or directions that the money should be freely enjoyed by the applicant without attachment or other consequences for the applicant's existing financial situation. The matter first arose in *Allenet de Ribemont v France*,[278] where the applicant asked that any sums awarded to him be free from attachment to avoid enforcement of an outstanding French civil judgment. The Court declined this request, holding that it had no jurisdiction to issue such an order to a state. In *Velikova v Bulgaria*,[279] concerning the death of the applicant's husband in police custody the applicant requested the Court to order that there should be no negative consequences for her, such as reduction in social benefits due to her, as a result of the receipt of any non-pecuniary damages. The Court noted that it would be incongruous to award the applicant an amount in compensation for, *inter alia*, deprivation of life constituting a violation of Article 2 of the Convention if the state itself were then allowed to attach this amount. The purpose of compensation for non-pecuniary damage would inevitably be frustrated and the Article 41 system perverted, if such a situation were to be deemed satisfactory. However, the Court again found it had no power to make such an order and left the matter to the discretion of the Bulgarian authorities.[280]

---

[273] Confirmed in *Sovtransavto Holding v Ukraine* hudoc (2003) paras 78–82.

[274] This has come in for robust criticism by some of the judges. Judge Bonello in *Nikolova v Bulgaria* 1999-II; 31 EHRR 64 GC stated: 'I do not share the Court's view. I consider it wholly inadequate and unacceptable that a court of justice should "satisfy" the victim of a breach of fundamental rights with a mere handout of legal idiom. The first time the Court appears to have resorted to this hapless formula was in the Golder case of 1975... Disregarding its own practice that full reasoning should be given for all decisions, the Court failed to suggest one single reason why the finding should also double up as the remedy. Since then, propelled by the irresistible force of inertia, that formula has resurfaced regularly. In few of the many judgments which relied on it did the Court seem eager to upset the rule that it has to give neither reasons nor explanations.'

[275] For Article 5 see eg, *Thompson v UK* hudoc (2004); 40 EHRR 245 para 50. For Article 6, the standard formula is to state that it is impossible speculate as to the outcome of the criminal trial had the violation of Article 6(1) of the Convention not occurred (see eg, *Findlay v UK* 1997-I; 24 EHRR 221 paras 85 and 88).

[276] 2005-IX; 42 EHRR 849 para 60 GC.   [277] A 324 (1995); 21 EHRR 97 Para 219 GC.

[278] *Allenet de Ribemont v France* A 308 (1995) para 65. See above, p 837.   [279] 2000-VI para 96.

[280] See also the earlier case of *Selmouni v France* 1999-V; 29 EHRR 403 paras 132 and 133 GC, where the Court made a similar observation and finding in respect of sums awarded in respect of a violation of Article 3.

5. ARTICLE 46

Article 46(1) provides: 'The High Contracting Parties undertake to abide by the final judgment of the Court in any case where they are parties.' As noted above the Court has traditionally been reluctant to make 'consequential orders' in the form of directions or recommendations to the state to take a particular course of action. Thus, for example, in *Ireland v UK*[281] it refused the request by the Irish government to order that criminal prosecutions be brought against those responsible for ill-treatment in breach of Article 3. On other occasions it has rejected invitations to require the state to undertake that children will not be corporally punished or to take steps to prevent such breaches in the future.[282] This approach was based on the view that the Court only possesses powers to make an award of compensation.

However the Court has gradually become more adventurous in its judgments in giving indications under Article 46 as to the most appropriate individual and general measures needed to provide redress. The most common instance has been in expropriation cases where the Court has given states the choice to return the property or to pay the value of it in compensation to the applicant.[283] Recently more innovative examples have appeared. In *Assandize v Georgia*[284] the Court having found the applicant's detention to be illegal held that Georgia had to secure his release at the earliest possible date. It was considered that the nature of the violation was such as to leave no real choice as to the measures required to remedy it. A similar direction was made in the case of *Illascu and Others v Moldova and Russia*.[285]

The Court has gone even further in various pilot judgments. Thus in *Broniowski v Poland* the Court noted that the violation was a result of 'a malfunctioning of Polish legislation and administrative practice' affecting a large but identifiable class of citizens and that general measures were called for at the national level. In the operative part of the judgment it held that Poland 'must, through appropriate measures and administrative practices, secure the implementation of the property right in question in respect of the remaining Bug River claimants'. Similar general measures were indicated in *Hutten-Czapska v Poland* where the Court had found a system of rent control in Poland to be in violation of Article 1 of Protocol 1.[286]

In *Gurov v Moldova*,[287] the Court found the applicant's Article 6 rights had been violated by the hearing of her civil claim by a tribunal that was not established by law (the term of office of one of the judges having expired). The Court noted the most appropriate form of relief would be to ensure that the applicant was granted in due course a re-hearing of the case by an independent and impartial tribunal. This was aided by the fact that the possibility existed under Moldovan law for the applicant, if she so requested, to obtain a re-hearing of her civil case in the light of the Court's finding that the proceedings did not comply with Article 6 guarantees. It was content therefore to make no award of damages and let the case take this course.[288]

---

[281] Series A25 (1978); 2 EHRR 25 para 187 PC.

[282] *Campbell and Cosans v UK* A 48 (1982) para 16; *McGoff v Sweden* A 83 (1984) para 31; 8 EHRR 246; *Gillow v UK* A 109 (1986) para 9.

[283] See eg, *Former King of Greece and Others v Greece* hudoc (2002) GC para 77; *Brumărescu v Romania* 2001-I; 33 EHRR 36 GC, at points 1 and 2 of the operative part.

[284] 2004-II; 39 EHRR 653.   [285] 2004-VII; 40 EHRR 1030 GC at point 22 of the operative part.

[286] For these cases, see above, pp 851–3.   [287] Hudoc (2006) paras 41–4.

[288] Other examples include *Malahov v Moldova* hudoc (2007) para 47 (that the applicant's appeal should be heard) and *Bujniţa v Moldova* hudoc (2007) para 29 (that the applicant's final acquittal be confirmed by the authorities and his conviction in breach of the Convention to be erased).

The possibility of having domestic proceedings re-opened as a result of a judgment of the Court has led it to indicate that applicants, especially in criminal cases, be given a re-trial if they so request.[289] Where proceedings are still pending, the Court may make indications in respect of them. In *Naime Doğan and Others v Turkey*,[290] after finding a violation of Article 6(1) in respect of the length of civil proceedings that were ongoing, the Court indicated that the subsequent expedition and resolution of those proceedings within the shortest possible period of time offered appropriate redress for the violation.

In *L v Lithuania*,[291] the applicant had started gender reassignment surgery but could not complete the surgery because there was no domestic law enabling him to do so. The Court found a violation of Article 8. Turning to Article 41 (taken without Article 46), the Court considered that the applicant's claim for pecuniary damage would be satisfied by the enactment of the legislation within three months of the judgment becoming final. If that proved impossible, the Court was of the view that the applicant could have the final stages of the necessary surgery performed abroad and financed, at least in part, by the state. Consequently, as an alternative in the absence of any such subsidiary legislation, the Court would award the applicant 40,000 euros in pecuniary damage.

In two recent Albanian judgments the Court simultaneously indicated two sets of measures: individual measures under Article 41 and general measures under Article 46. In *Driza v Albania*,[292] the issue was the repeat non-enforcement of court judgments awarding compensation for the taking of property. The Court considered this to be a systemic problem and stated that its concern was 'to facilitate the rapid and effective suppression of a malfunctioning found in the national system of human-rights protection'.[293] To this end, it considered that Albania had to remove all obstacles to the award of compensation and went on to give examples of what measures it had to take as a matter of urgency. In respect of the individual applicant, under Article 41 it indicated, *inter alia*, that returning one of the plots of land in question and the additional payment of compensation would put the applicant as far as possible in a situation equivalent to the one in which he would have been if there had not been a breach of the Convention. In the second judgment, *Dybeku v Albania*,[294] the Court examined conditions of detention and in particular the detention of the applicant who suffered from paranoid schizophrenia. The Court found a violation of Article 3 and moved to consider Articles 41 and 46. Under the former it awarded 5,000 euros non-pecuniary damage to the applicant but, before doing so, it considered that it was incumbent upon Albania as a matter of urgency to take necessary measures to secure appropriate conditions of detention and adequate medical treatment, in particular, for prisoners, like the applicant, who needed special care owing to their state of health.

6. PROTOCOL 14[295]

Protocol 14 was opened for signature on 13 May 2005 and at the time of writing has been ratified by forty-six of the forty-seven contracting parties to the Convention, but not by Russia. Although many of the Protocol's provisions, such as the single-judge procedure

---

[289] *Krasniki v Czech Republic* hudoc (2006) para 93. For instances where it has been done under Article 46, see *Sejdovic v Italy* 2006-II paras 119 *et seq* GC; *Öcalan v Turkey* 2005-IV; 41 EHRR 985 para 210 GC. Prior to such cases, such indications were only noted under Article 41: *Gençel v Turkey* hudoc (2003) para 27; *Tahir Duran v Turkey* hudoc (2004) para 23; *Somogyi v Italy* 2004-IV para 86.   [290] Hudoc (2007) para 34.
[291] Hudoc (2007) para 74, as well as points 5 and 6 of the operative part of the judgment.
[292] Hudoc (2007).   [293] Id, para 125.   [294] Hudoc (2007).
[295] For the text of the Protocol and Explanatory Report, see 'Guaranteeing the effectiveness of the European Convention on Human Rights—Collected Texts', Council of Europe, 2004. For commentary, see Eaton and Schokkenbroek, 26 HRLJ 1 (2005) and Greer, 2005 PL 83.

and the three-judge Committee procedure, would benefit Russia, which is by far the largest source of cases before the Court,[296] she did not ratify as expected before 30 June 2007 with the consequence that the mandates of more than twenty judges expired in November 2007. Had the Protocol been ratified in time, its transitional provisions provided for an extension of tenure of two years or more.[297] The reasons for non-ratification of this important Protocol have never been explained although the Duma debates suggest a misunderstanding as to the legal effect of some of its provisions and Russian Parliamentary Assembly representatives have criticized the Court for being 'anti-Russian'. The resulting election procedures have proved especially cumbersome with states not presenting their lists in time or presenting lists with only one properly qualified candidate. This has given rise to calls for review of the election procedures.[298] The failure to ratify has given rise to the perhaps premature apprehension that Russia may never ratify and that the Protocol is a dead letter although the Committee of Ministers will examine in 2008 the possibility of salvaging some of the procedural innovations of the Protocol, such as the single judge procedure, in respect of the forty-six states that have expressed, through ratification, their acceptance of these procedures. The Chairman of the Legal Affairs and Human Rights Committee of the Assembly has also called on the Russian Minister of Justice to agree to a provisional application of the Protocol under Article 25 of the Vienna Convention on the Law of Treaties.[299]

The Protocol was the result of more than four years' reflection by the Council of Europe's Steering Committee for Human Rights on the need for urgent measures to be taken to assist the Court to carry out its functions in the light of the ever-increasing number of applications being brought to the Court.[300] It makes provision for important changes to the functioning of the Court to enable it to dispose more rapidly of clearly inadmissible and repetitive cases and to concentrate its resources on more deserving cases.

Three main changes are provided for which would operate retrospectively in the event of the Protocol coming into force.[301] First, a single judge is empowered to declare a case inadmissible or to strike a case out of the list where such a decision can be taken without further examination—ie clear-cut cases whose inadmissibility is 'manifest from the outset'. This would enable the Court to substantially increase its capacity to reject obviously inadmissible cases with an economy of procedure. The single judge, however, would only be able to declare cases inadmissible and would not be able to examine any cases against his own country. If in doubt, he or she could refer the case to a three judge Committee for further examination. In carrying out this function the single judge would be assisted by rapporteurs drawn from the Registry.[302]

Secondly, the three judge Committees would be empowered to declare repetitive cases admissible and at the same time render a judgment on the merits of the case 'if the

---

[296] More than 20,300 in January 2008 out of 79,400 cases pending before a decision body—ie 26% (statistics available on the Court's website).

[297] Article 21 of Protocol 14 provides that the terms of office of judges serving their first term shall be extended up to nine years. The other judges shall complete their term of office which shall be extended by two years.

[298] See O'Boyle, 2008 EHRLR 1.

[299] The Russian Federation made the following declaration, however, when signing the Protocol: 'The Russian Federation declares that, signing the Protocol under the condition of its subsequent ratification, it proceeds from the following: no provision of the Protocol will be applied prior to its entry into force in accordance with Article 19.'

[300] The Explanatory Report, paras 20–33, charts the work on the Protocol from the Rome Ministerial Conference on Human Rights in 2000, which took stock of the Court's growing case-load, until the opening for signature of the Protocol on 13 May 2004.

[301] Article 20 of the Protocol and Explanatory Report, para 105.

[302] Article 27 as amended and Explanatory Report, paras 6–67.

underlying question is already the subject of established case law of the Court'. This simple and accelerated procedure is introduced to enable the Court to deal more efficiently with the large number of repetitive cases that clog up its docket by enabling questions of admissibility, merits and just satisfaction in such cases to be dealt with together by a small group of judges. However the decision must be taken by a unanimous vote. It is also provided that the Committee may at any stage of the proceedings invite the national judge to take the place of one of the members of the Committee. It is open to the state to contest the use of the procedure on the basis that it does not concern an issue that is the subject of established case law but it can never veto the procedure which lies within the Committee's sole competence. The Explanatory Report indicates that the presence of the national judge may be useful to the Committee where the state has contested the procedure because of the judge's familiarity with national law and practice which will enable the Committee to better assess the objection. Where the Committee fails to reach a unanimous decision the case will be sent to a Chamber for decision. It also remains open to the Committee to reject the case as inadmissible, for example, if it considered that domestic remedies have not been exhausted. Although simple and accelerated, the new procedure will 'preserve the adversarial character of proceedings and the principle of judicial and collegial decision-making on the merits'.[303]

Thirdly, the Protocol introduces a new admissibility criterion which would enable the Court to reject a case 'where the applicant has not suffered a significant disadvantage'.[304] This may be the case where, for example, the case concerns a small amount of money or is otherwise trivial in nature. The purpose of this change was to give the Court an additional tool to assist it in its filtering work although it was recognized that it would take the Court several years to build up a case law delineating the types of cases which could be rejected on this basis since even trivial cases may involve important matters of principle. In recognition of this, the Protocol provides that the new criterion shall not be applied by single judges or Committees of three judges for a period of two years.[305] The new provision also contains two important safeguards to ensure that the criterion is exercised cautiously. The case will not be rejected where 'respect for human rights as defined in the Convention and the Protocols' requires an examination of the case on its merits. In addition, the case must have been 'duly considered by a domestic tribunal'. The new criterion has been introduced to give the Court greater flexibility to dismiss unmeritorious cases on the assumption that the other features of the Protocol will not be sufficient to prevent the Convention system from becoming totally paralyzed with the ever-increasing number of cases being brought and incapable of fulfilling its mission. It is seen as a safety measure which the Court will use constructively to prevent the right of individual petition from becoming illusory. The wording of this new provision, with its two tightly-worded safeguards, bears all the hallmarks of a compromise in the Council of Europe's Steering Committee on Human Rights[306] between factions seeking to trammel the right of individual petition by conferring a greater margin of choice on the Court and those keen on limiting the Court's discretion to genuinely undeserving cases. The end result is a complex provision which will require extensive interpretation by the Court in order to define a coherent policy which it will be able to use to stem the flow of unmeritorious cases. It thus has the potential to become an important tool for the

---

[303] Article 28 as amended and Explanatory Report, paras 68–72.
[304] Article 35 as amended and Explanatory Report, paras 77–85.
[305] Article 20 para 2 of the Protocol.
[306] The Committee, comprised of representatives of each of the member states, which negotiated the draft Protocol.

Court to avail itself of in the future but it will be up to the Court ultimately to ensure that a provision which was designed to give it breathing space will not become a cause of time-consuming disagreement.

The Protocol also introduces a number of other significant changes to the Convention. It provides that judges will be elected for a single term of nine years and that they will not be re-elected;[307] that at the request of the plenary Court, the Committee of Ministers may for a fixed period reduce the number of judges in a Chamber to five;[308] that *ad hoc* judges shall be chosen by the President from a list of candidates submitted in advance by the contracting party;[309] that the Court shall, in principle, decide on admissibility decisions and the merits in the same decision (apart from inter-state cases);[310] that the Court may explore the possibility of friendly settlement at any stage of the proceedings and that the resulting agreement shall be in the form of a decision whose execution is to be supervised by the Committee of Ministers.[311] The Protocol also confers a right on the Council of Europe Commissioner for Human Rights to submit written comments and take part in hearings[312] and on the Committee of Ministers to submit a request to the Court for interpretation of a judgment (for the purpose of supervision of execution of judgments) as well as the possibility to initiate infringement proceedings in respect of a contracting party which refuses to abide by a final judgment.[313] Finally the Protocol provides that the European Union may accede to the Convention.[314]

The Committee of Ministers has also adopted a series of recommendations and resolutions concerning *inter alia* the use of pilot judgments, the practice of friendly settlements, the screening of draft laws for compatibility with the Convention, the improvement of domestic remedies and the dissemination of Convention case law in the member states and university education and professional training in the Convention.[315] In the unhappy event of the Protocol not entering into force, this impressive array of soft law will assume even greater importance since it emphasizes the numerous ways in which the states can

---

[307] Article 23(2) as amended.   [308] Article 26(2) as amended.

[309] Article 26(4) as amended. This provision responds to the criticism that under the current system the State is asked to nominate an *ad hoc* judge after the proceedings have commenced in full knowledge of the issues involved—see Explanatory Report, para 64.

[310] Article 29(1) and (2) as amended. In fact the current practice of the Court has evolved in this direction independently with issues of admissibility and the merits being decided jointly in one judgment (except for inter-state cases); see above, pp 825–6.

[311] Article 39 as amended. The present practice of the Court has also evolved in this sense. Friendly settlement proceedings can be pursued at any stage of the procedure and if agreement is reached prior to admissibility the case will be struck out with the solution reached being signalled to the Committee of Ministers. However the provision providing for execution of the terms of the agreement to be supervised by the Committee of Ministers is an important new safeguard—although there have been in practice very few problems connected with the performance of the terms of settlement agreements.

[312] Article 36(3) as amended. The Commissioner already has the possibility to intervene as a third party today. This new provision would give him the right to intervene both in writing and orally and thus confer on him or her the status of a privileged amicus. The Report explains that his experience in certain structural or systemic problems in national law and practice may enlighten the Court (para 88). This may involve the Commissioner in playing a significant role in the Court's pilot judgment procedure (see p 851).

[313] Article 46(3), (4), and (5) as amended. Both procedures require a majority of two-thirds of the representatives entitled to sit on the Committee. The Report makes it clear that the request for interpretation should be used where difficulties arise on issues of interpretation of the judgment and not to examine the measures taken by a state in compliance with the judgment (para 97). It is also clear that infringement proceedings should only be taken in exceptional circumstances (paras 99–100). While it increases the powers available to the Committee where there has been non-compliance, it is doubted that transferring what is essentially a political problem back to the Court will help resolve matters. It may, however, buy time for the political issues to be resolved amicably.

[314] Article 59(2) as amended.

[315] See Explanatory Report, at pp 52–81 for the texts of these instruments.

implement Convention obligations in national law and hopefully reduce the need for individuals to complain to Strasbourg.

7. THE FUTURE OF THE COURT

The new Court has had to confront two main challenges since it was set up in 1998. First, it had the difficult task of ensuring the continuity of the Convention system as it had been developed by the former Commission and Court for more than forty years.

Building on and consolidating the case law of the Convention institutions in such a manner that it retained the confidence of both the international legal community and the contracting parties was a daunting challenge for a newly restructured Court and one that in the main it has lived up to. While the new Court has been adventurous and creative in its approach to reforming the internal procedures of the Court it has also managed at the same time to develop the case law significantly, especially in the areas of freedom of expression and the core priority rights protected by Articles 2 and 3. What is important in this respect is that the new Court has actively sought to preserve the *acquis conventionnel* and has not engaged in a systematic re-evaluation of fundamental principles, including principles of interpretation, except where it considered that these were no longer valid and could be improved upon. Its second challenge—and one that had to be assumed at the same time as the first—was to absorb and integrate into its membership a large number of Central and East European states and, in particular, Russia. This has also been a vast undertaking—and one which is still underway—when one considers the extent to which the right of petition has been extended to millions of potential applicants and to a wide variety of legal cultures. It is a measure of the Court's achievement that a casual perusal of Hudoc—the Court's case law database—will reveal at any given year large numbers of judgments relating to a wide variety of Convention issues against states such as Russia, Romania, Ukraine, Poland, Moldova, and Croatia. However one might criticize the case law of the Court in particular areas, it must be remembered that since the adhesion of these states, Convention principles have not only been received into national law and practice but have also guided the pace and direction of law reform in many areas of law, aided and abetted by national courts and external Council of Europe bodies such as the CPT, ECRI, the European Social Charter, the Venice Commission, and the European Commissioner for Human Rights. By all accounts this is a major, if not astonishing, achievement for the European system of human rights protection in its widest sense and one that will continue for some time as a work in progress. If the first thirty years of the operation of the Convention system concerned the anchoring of the Convention in the legal systems of Western democratic states, the next phase of development has taken place in Turkey, Central and Eastern Europe, and Russia.

The current difficulties of the Court concern primarily the constant growth of its case docket. There is an increase of around between 12 and 15 per cent of new cases every year. The Court's persistent dilemma is that the number of cases decided every month rarely exceeds its monthly intake. The future of the Court is thus inextricably linked in both the long and short term with the finding of viable solutions to deal with this problem. The ideal objective to aim for is a situation where the Court continues to develop its important constitutional role through the adjudication within a reasonable time of the mainstream human rights problems affecting European societies. It is this role, carried out principally by the Grand Chamber of the Court, that has the strongest and most significant impact throughout Europe as many of the Court's leading pronouncements assume in practice the character of judgments *erga omnes*. As the Wise Persons have recognized in their report, this role presupposes that the Court finds an effective and principled method of filtering individual cases within a proper time-frame and makes proper use of such innovations as the pilot judgment to deal with the problem of repetitive complaints based on structural or systemic problems within the states. Such a vision of a reformed Court will not be brought about by the entry into force of Protocol 14 no matter how desirable that may be. For even if the Protocol was in force already the scale of the problems facing the Court today is such that it would merely endow it with a variety of useful (indeed indispensable) tools to dispose of cases more rapidly to ensure its survival in the short term while more fundamental reforms are considered by the states. However it would only be a temporary panacea. It is the long-term future of the Court, involving a reordering of the Court's internal structures as well as the basic philosophy underpinning the entire system, that needs to be addressed as a matter of urgency.[316] The current drama facing the Court and the Council of Europe is that the crucial process of reflection and action on the Wise Persons proposals is blocked by the failure of Protocol 14 to enter into force, since these proposals were to a large extent predicated on the assumption that the manner in which the new provisions assisted the Court in its work would guide consideration of the direction of future reform. Be that as it may it is clear that the future of the Court is linked to two areas: measures taken by the states at national level to give effect to the Convention and reform of the Court's working methods and architecture.

As regards national measures, it must not be forgotten that the remedy before the Court provides a 'long stop' protection of human rights based on the principle of subsidiarity. It is for this reason that concepts such as the exhaustion of remedies rule and the margin of appreciation play such an important role in the examination of cases. There is a direct correlation between the extent to which Convention principles are enforced nationally and the number of cases brought to Strasbourg. As one commentator has observed, 'Not surprisingly, the availability of effective judicial processes for the litigation of Convention rights, coupled with a positive official responsiveness to judicial correction, appear to be amongst the most significant factors in producing low levels of Convention violation'.[317] The paradigm example of this statement can be seen in the daily operation of the Human Rights Act before the courts of the United Kingdom. The judgments of the House of Lords in major human rights cases applying the case law of the Court have not only contributed to the development of human rights law in the United Kingdom but have become a valuable source of inspiration for the European Court in its application of Convention principles. The Court's future is thus bound up with the direct application of the Convention by national courts and other bodies. This in turn presupposes that the Court's essential case law is translated into the official languages of the contracting parties, that national judges are provided with training in how this law is to be applied in practice, and that they seek to do so in cases before them. It also presupposes that the law of the Convention is taught in law schools and professional legal training institutes throughout Europe and that appropriate teaching manuals are made widely available.[318] However effective national steps extend beyond the judicial sphere and also encompass such measures as the screening of legislation for compatibility with Convention principles, the willingness of state authorities to respond effectively to pilot judgments requiring the introduction of often far-reaching corrective measures to staunch the flow of repetitive complaints

---

[316] According to the Wise Persons: 'The exponential increase in the number of individual applications is now seriously threatening the survival of the machinery for the judicial protection of human rights and the Court's ability to cope with its workload. This dramatic development jeopardises the proper functioning of the Convention's control system'—Wise Persons Report, above n 5, para 26.

[317] Greer, *European Convention*, p 322.   [318] Wise Persons Report, paras 66–75.

as well as the creation of effective remedies to provide national redress thereby obviating the need to complain to Strasbourg. If the Court is to function effectively as an international tribunal it is paramount that the forty-seven states that have ratified the Convention take seriously their obligation genuinely to integrate the Convention into national law and practice. The role of national human rights institutions such as ombudsmen and national commissions have a valuable role to play not only in encouraging the states in these endeavours but also in supervising their effectiveness in practice, in cooperation with the office of the European Commissioner for Human Rights. The vision of the Convention as an international treaty to which states adhere in order to ensure a collective enforcement of human rights in Europe must, in accordance with the principle of subsidiarity, give way progressively to the constitutionalization of Convention principles as an inherent part of such collective action.

Increasingly, the Court will be obliged to amend its own working methods to address the problems besetting it since it is clear that the entire process of reform is marked by serious political difficulties and that many years will pass before a new reforming treaty of the type envisaged by the Wise Persons comes into force. This much is evident from the history of Protocol 14. The Court's problem is thereby redefined since it seems clear that important measures must be taken by the Court itself aided by the Council of Europe over the next two to three years pending the negotiation and entry into force of a structural Protocol—a process which could take as long as eight to ten years. The Court will undoubtedly develop its novel pilot judgment procedure as a technique of identifying the structural problems underlying clone cases against many countries and imposing an obligation of the states to address these problems. It will fall to the Committee of Ministers to ensure, in the absence of a 'pilot' friendly settlement, that these general measures are implemented correctly. This may require a more proactive form of supervision providing expert assistance and advice where needed. The Court will also be obliged to re-examine its policies concerning case priority. Since 92 per cent of all applications are rejected as inadmissible, substantial resources are being utilized for cases which do not have any normative significance for the contracting parties. It would make more sense that these resources should be better used in dealing with the Court's clearly admissible cases even if this had the consequence that large numbers of Committee cases were effectively frozen and placed at the back of the queue. It is to be foreseen that the states will question with increased stridency whether the provision of extra budgetary resources for the Court each year as the docket grows is capable of being sustained for a lengthy period. While the Court's budget by the standards of the European Union is modest, there is little indication that the states are prepared to make further substantial investments of the kind that would be needed to deal with the explosion of cases in order to place the Court on a more secure financial footing. Their dilemma is that there is no guarantee that investing in the process of root and branch reform is going to bring the desired return in the form of a universally ratified amending protocol.

The proposals in the Wise Persons Report mark out the agenda of the reform discussions concerning the Convention for the next decade.[319] The vital question is whether the Court will be in a position during this period of change to continue to perform its function in a manner that will not lead to a damaging loss of confidence and credibility as Europe's leading court. This is the measure of the challenge facing it today.

---

[319] See paras 125–46 of the Report for a summary of these proposals—above n 5.

24

THE EXECUTION OF THE COURT'S JUDGMENTS

When the Court has given a judgment in a particular case, if it has found no violation of any of the provisions of the Convention, clearly that is the end of the dispute and no further action is required. However, if the Court finds at least one violation in its judgment, then it is equally self-evident that further steps will be called for. As with any court, whether national, supranational, or international, judgments of the Court are not self-executing. Nor does the Court have the power to enforce its own judgments. While the Court itself has made strides in recent years towards indicating individual and general measures in its judgments,[1] which will aid enforcement at the national level, at least for the time being, such indications lack the full force of consequential orders of national courts. Instead, by virtue of Article 46(2) of the Convention,[2] the task of execution and enforcement of its judgments falls to the Committee of Ministers of the Council of Europe. The role of the Committee of Ministers, its procedures and common features, and recent developments in the execution process will be considered in the following sections of this chapter.

1. THE ROLE OF THE COMMITTEE OF MINISTERS

To the extent that the Statute of the Council of Europe and the Convention provide for a separation of powers, the Committee of Ministers is the executive organ of the Council of Europe, with a role distinct from the Court's judicial role.[3] According to Article 15 of the Statute, the general role of the Committee is to consider the action required to further the Council's aim, including the conclusion of conventions or agreements and the adoption by governments of a common policy with regard to particular matters. It is composed of the Ministers of Foreign Affairs of all member states. In practice, however, it only meets twice a year at ministerial level. Most of the Committee's business is carried out by Ministers' Deputies who are the permanent representatives of member states at the Council of Europe, ie career diplomats and who are thus in permanent session in Strasbourg. The role of the Committee in the Convention system has evolved with the system itself and there has been an overall trend towards less direct involvement in the judicial process. For example, the Committee originally elected members of the old Commission (former Article 21 of the Convention) and had the important

---

[1] See above, pp 862–3.

[2] 'The final judgment of the Court shall be transmitted to the Committee of Ministers, which shall supervise its execution.'

[3] See Mahoney, 24 HRLJ 152 (2003). On execution in general, see also Sundberg, in *Mélanges en hommage au Doyen Gérard Cohen-Jonathan,* Vol II, 2004.

task of deciding whether or not there had been a violation of the Convention in cases which had not been referred to the old Court (former Article 32). Currently, in addition to the supervision of the execution of judgments of the Court (current Article 46(2) of the Convention), the main tasks of the Committee are to receive and forward the lists of candidates for the election of judges to the Parliamentary Assembly, to request advisory opinions of the Court (Article 47), and to set the Court's annual budget.[4]

2. PROCEDURE

In the exercise of its responsibilities for the execution of judgments under Article 46, the Committee of Ministers meets in four three-day sessions each year.[5] The workload is a heavy one (in reflection of the increasing number of judgments delivered by the Court) and, on average, the Committee will examine over 2,500–3,500 cases at each session, though in practice only twenty to forty are actually debated.[6] The examination of such a large number of cases necessarily places a heavy burden on the Secretariat (which comprises officials from the Council of Europe's Directorate General of Human Rights and Legal Affairs) whose task it is to prepare the cases for examination. The Committee has adopted a series of Rules which will guide its procedures, the latest revision having been adopted in May 2006.[7]

The meetings of the Committee take place *in camera*, though greater efforts have been made in recent years to make the process more transparent, if only through more information being made available through the Council of Europe's website. The agenda of each meeting is public (Rule 2) and available in advance of the meeting, though it may only provide the most basic information on what cases will be examined. After each meeting an annotated agenda and all decisions taken will be made public unless the Committee decides otherwise (Rule 8(4)). The individual applicant and his legal representative are excluded from the Committee's deliberations, in stark contrast to the right of the respondent state to play a full part in the proceedings. However, this has been mitigated (if only slightly) by the Committee being entitled to consider any communication from the applicant with regard to the payment of just satisfaction or the taking of individual

---

[4] To the extent that the Committee regulates personnel matters in the Council (including the staff of the Registry), this administrative aspect of its work might also be said to have an indirect impact on the work of the Court. Article 54 of the Convention also provides that 'Nothing in this Convention shall prejudice the powers conferred on the Committee of Ministers by the Statute…', though this has never given rise to any significant issue or conflict.

[5] A change introduced at the end of 2007; the previous practice was to hold six two-day meetings. The change was to allow more time for the Secretariat and states to prepare cases, especially given the high level of bilateral contact between the states and the Secretariat. See the first annual report on the supervision of the execution of the European Court of Human Rights, March 2008, available at <http://www.coe.int>.

[6] See eg, the annotated agenda of the 1020th meeting (DH), 4–6 March 2008, statistics, CM/Del/OJ/DH(2008)1020. In order to avoid having to debate every single case on its agenda at every meeting, the Committee has adopted a series of guidelines (adopted at the Committee's 879th DH meeting (April 2004)), as to when a case will be proposed for debate. A case will be proposed for debate if: the applicant's situation because of the violation warrants special supervision; it marks a new departure in case law by the European Court; it discloses a potential systemic problem which could give rise to similar cases in future; there is a difference of appreciation between the Secretariat and the respondent state concerning the measures to be taken; there is a delay in execution with reference to the timetable; or a government delegation or the Secretariat requests it.

[7] Rules adopted by the Committee of Ministers for the application of Article 46, para 2, of the European Convention on Human Rights, adopted on 10 May 2006 at the 964th meeting of the Ministers' Deputies. The Rules and all other public documents are available from <http://www.coe.int>. They are discussed in Lambert-Abdelgawad, *The Execution of Judgments of the European Court of Human Rights*, 2nd edn, Human Rights File No 19, 2008, Council of Europe Publishing.

measures (Rule 9(1)) and any communication from non-governmental organizations and national human rights institutions (Rule 9(2)).

The Committee acts by means of resolutions. There are two types it may adopt, each by a two-thirds majority of the representatives casting a vote and of a majority of the representatives entitled to sit on the Committee. Final resolutions are adopted when the Committee has established that the state concerned has taken all the necessary measures to abide by the judgment or that the terms of the friendly settlement have been executed (Rule 17). Interim resolutions may be adopted (though need not be) in the course of the Committee's supervision in order to provide information on the state of progress of the execution of a judgment or, where appropriate, to express concern and/or to make suggestions with respect to execution (Rule 16). Interim resolutions may therefore have a useful role to play when the execution process has not been speedily concluded, whether as a result of the complexity of the case or the unwillingness of the state to hasten execution.

As is evident from the terms of these Rules, the Committee has the competence to supervise the execution of both full judgments on the merits and friendly settlements.[8] All judgments and decisions which are transmitted to the Committee are inscribed on its agenda without delay (Rule 3).[9] Priority is to be given to those cases in which the Court has identified a systemic problem (Rule 4(1)) but not to the detriment of those cases where the violation has caused grave consequences for the injured party (Rule 4.2). The examination of a case begins with an invitation from the Committee to the contracting party against which the violation is found to inform it of the measures which it has taken or intends to take in consequence of the judgment (Rule 6(1)). The Committee will then examine the following three steps: whether any just satisfaction awarded under Article 41 has been paid, whether individual measures have been taken and whether general measures have been taken to comply with the judgment.[10]

As part of efforts to improve working methods in recent years, a developing practice has been to initiate an 'initial phase' procedure where, upon a judgment becoming final, the Secretariat will send a letter to the respondent state requesting a preliminary indication of the measures the state intends to take to comply with the judgment or even suggesting what steps the state might take. The state will then aim to submit an 'action plan' to the Committee (via the Secretariat) within six months of the final judgment, which will in turn be presented to the Committee for discussion at the next possible meeting after the expiry of this six-month deadline. The Committee has noted that 'for the time being it appears clear that the "action plans" when initially submitted constitute unilateral declarations of intent on the part of the respondent state, in the context of their "obligation of result" remedying violations established in the Court's judgments' and that the respondent state is free to alter its 'action plan', though such changes should then preferably be made public.[11] This is a nascent practice and it remains to be seen whether it will put on a more formal or even statutory footing.

The various steps towards final execution that a state must take, namely compliance with the obligation to pay just satisfaction and the adoption of individual and general

---

[8] The Rules applicable to friendly settlements (Rules 12–15) mirror those applicable to judgments and thus are not separately enumerated here.

[9] Cases remain on the Committee's agenda until it decides otherwise: Rule 7.   [10] Set out in Rule 5(2).

[11] See Committee of Ministers Information Document, 'Working methods for supervision of the execution of the European Court of Human Rights' judgments', CM/Inf/DH(2006)9 revised 3, 24 November 2006. See also its Information Document 'Human rights working methods—Improved effectiveness of the Committee of Ministers' supervision of execution of judgments', CM/Inf(2004)8 Final 7 April 2004 and 'Reform of the European Human Rights System: Proceedings of the high-level seminar, Oslo, 18 October 2004', Council of Europe Publishing, 2004.

measures, are considered in the following sections. For the later two, the key principle that guides execution is that states have an obligation of result (ensuring the judgment is executed) but they have the freedom to choose the means to reach it. Thus, respect for different national cultures is preserved but the need for collective enforcement and the pan-European application of the same human rights principles is maintained. As will be shown, this is not always an easy task.

I. JUST SATISFACTION

Verifying whether any just satisfaction awarded by the Court under Article 41[12] has been paid will rarely prove problematic since the applicant (or his or her lawyer) will normally only be required to pass his or her bank details to the appropriate agent of the government who will arrange for payment, without waiting for the Committee to begin its examination.[13]

One case of serious delay in payment was *Loizidou v Turkey (Article 50)*,[14] where the Court awarded 300,000 Cypriot pounds pecuniary damage, 20,000 Cypriot pounds for non-pecuniary damage, and 137,084 Cypriot pounds in costs and expenses arising from its finding of a violation of Article 1 of Protocol 1 because the applicant had been denied access to her property in northern Cyprus.[15] The Turkish government took the position that sums awarded by the Court could only be paid to the applicant in the context of a global settlement of all property cases in Cyprus. In a series of strongly worded interim resolutions adopted between October 1999 and November 2003, the Committee rejected this position, stating, *inter alia*, that the refusal of Turkey to execute the judgment of the Court demonstrated 'a manifest disregard for its international obligations, both as a High Contracting Party to the Convention and as a member state of the Council of Europe'.[16] Turkey finally agreed to pay the sums required, prompting the Committee, in Resolution DH(2003)190 of December 2003, to declare that it had 'exercised its functions under Article 46, paragraph 2, of the Convention'. On the same day, it adopted a further resolution, DH(2003)191, where it stated, rather enigmatically, that it had decided 'to resume consideration of the execution of the judgment of 18 December 1996 in due time, taking into consideration proposals to do so at the end of 2005'.[17]

---

[12] On Article 41, see above, p 857.

[13] Though for a very informative overview of some of the practical difficulties the Committee has faced because of absent applicants, applicants who will have difficulty taking receipt of payment, currency problems, and so on, see Committee of Ministers Information Document, 'Monitoring of the payment of sums awarded by way of just satisfaction: an overview of the Committee of Ministers present practice', memorandum prepared by the Department for the Execution of Judgments of the European Court of Human Rights, 11 March 2008, CM/Inf/DH(2008)7 revised. For all such information documents, see <http://www.coe.int>. One problematic case was *Stran Greek Refineries and Stratis Andreadis v Greece* A 301-B (1994); 19 EHRR 293, where the Court awarded sizable sums of just satisfaction. The Greek government, relying on the size of the award and economic problems in Greece, stated that it was unable to make immediate full payment and sought to pay in instalments. The Committee, in Interim Resolution DH (96) 251 of 15 May 1996, rejected this course, concluding that the modalities of payment envisaged by the Greek government could not be considered to be in conformity with the obligations following from the Court's judgment and urged it to pay without delay. When the final sums of over 30 million US dollars were paid, the Committee closed its examination of the case: Final Resolution DH (97) 184 of 20 March 1997.

[14] 1998-IV.   [15] See the principal judgment in the case, 1996-VI; 22 EHRR 513.

[16] Interim resolutions DH (99) 680, DH (2000) 105, DH(2001)80 and DH(2003)174.

[17] Turkey paid the required sums in 2003.

II. INDIVIDUAL MEASURES

The second step taken by the Committee in the execution of a judgment is governed by Rule 6(2)(b) of its Rules. This states that the Committee will take into account the discretion of the contracting state to choose the means necessary to comply with the judgment, but that the Committee should examine whether individual measures have been taken to ensure that the violation has ceased and that the injured party is put, as far as possible, in the same situation as it enjoyed prior to the violation of the Convention. The Rules themselves give examples of what individual measures may be required, including the striking out of an unjustified criminal conviction from the criminal records, the granting of a residence permit (if the Court finds removal of a non-national would breach the Convention), the re-opening of impugned domestic proceedings, or the release of those found to have been held illegally, but of course all kinds of individual measures may be required of states. Clearly, where the Court itself indicates what individual measures should be taken,[18] then the Committee will take its lead from the terms of the Court's judgment.

The Committee's task has also been helped by its own willingness to adopt recommendations to member states on the steps they should take at the national level to facilitate execution. The best example is Recommendation (2000) 2E 'on the re-examination or reopening of certain cases at domestic level following judgments of the European Court of Human Rights'.[19] In this the Committee noted, *inter alia*, that its practice in supervising the execution of the Court's judgments showed that in exceptional circumstances the re-examination of a case or a re-opening of judicial proceedings had proved the most efficient, if not the only, means of achieving *restitutio in integrum*. Accordingly, it invited the contracting parties to ensure adequate possibilities for *restitutio in integrum* existed at the national level and encouraged them to examine their national legal systems with a view to ensuring that the possibility existed for the re-examination of cases decided by the national courts in which the Court had found a violation of the Convention in the judicial proceedings.[20] This step has greatly enhanced the execution process, especially when one considers that unfair proceedings (whether criminal or civil) are one of the largest single categories of cases considered by the Court. At the time of writing, a clear majority of the member states of the Council of Europe now expressly provide for the re-opening of a case after a Court judgment.[21]

By their nature, the individual measures to be taken will vary from case to case. However, there are a number of areas where similar problems occur repeatedly, perhaps because of intrinsic problems of execution of court judgments in certain subject areas. One such problematic area is the sensitive question of parental visiting rights, for instance where one or both parents have been deprived of access to their child, especially when one parent has started another relationship or the child has been taken into care. Understandably, the social services of member states may encounter some difficulties in

---

[18] Under Article 46: see above, p 862.

[19] Adopted on 19 January 2000 at the 694th meeting of the Ministers' Deputies.

[20] It also said this should apply especially where the injured party continues to suffer very serious negative consequences because of the outcome of the domestic decision at issue, which are not adequately remedied by just satisfaction and cannot be rectified except by re-examination or re-opening, and the judgment of the Court leads to the conclusion that (i) the impugned domestic decision is on the merits contrary to the Convention, or (ii) the violation found is based on procedural errors or shortcomings of such gravity that a serious doubt is cast on the outcome of the domestic proceedings complained of.

[21] See 'Reopening of proceedings before domestic courts following findings of violation by the European Court of Human Rights—Draft survey of existing legislation and case-law', DH-PR(2005)2. Available from the Council's execution department's webpage.

876   THE EXECUTION OF THE COURT'S JUDGMENTS

re-establishing visitation rights when that depends on the co-operation of the child and those responsible for his or her care. It may also require that they seek leave from the family law courts, which may be reluctant to revisit the case, and that they act in accordance with any duties they have to give paramount consideration to the welfare of the child. In such cases, however, in order to establish that the required individual measures have been taken, the Committee will continue with its examination of the case to verify closely the steps taken by the domestic authorities towards re-establishing contact between the parent and child. It will note whether those steps have in fact been taken and are going in the right direction.[22] However, this must raise questions as to whether it is appropriate for the highest level of a pan-European organization to devote four sessions a year to matters as individual as ensuring that weekly contact visits between a parent and his or her child are being observed and whether a local body which is closer to the parties (such as a national human rights ombudsman) could be given this task.

A second common group of cases is, as suggested above, where the Court has found that domestic judicial proceedings have been unfair and where the obvious individual measure to be taken is the re-opening of those proceedings but domestic law does not provide for the possibility. The Committee, pursuant to its Recommendation (2000) 2E (above) on the matter, may ask the state to adopt such legislation. Where there is such legislation but it is inapplicable in the instant case, the Committee will explore whether *ad hoc* measures can be taken which will have the same effect of erasing the consequences of the violations found.[23] One case which reflected badly on both the Committee of Ministers and the respondent state, Italy, was the *Dorigo* case. There the applicant was convicted in 1994 for his part in a terrorist attack on a NATO military base and sentenced to over thirteen years' imprisonment. The original complaint was that he had been unable to examine witnesses against him at his trial and the then Commission and Committee of Ministers found a violation of Article 6(1) and (3)(d) of the Convention. It took several interim resolutions of the Committee, two resolutions of the Parliamentary Assembly, a lengthy enquiry into the possibility of a presidential pardon, failed legislation in the Italian parliament, and two separate sets of legal proceedings (one on the initiative of a local prosecutor) before the Italian judiciary finally concluded that the applicant's continued detention was illegal, by virtue of the need to give direct effect to the Convention, and ordered his release in 2006. It was not until 2007, more than eight years after the Commission's finding of a violation and thirteen years after the initial trial, that the Committee of Ministers closed its examination of the case by which point the applicant had served virtually all of his sentence.[24]

[22] At the time of writing, several examples of such cases include the execution of *Görgülü v Germany*, hudoc (2004); *Reigado Ramos v Portugal* hudoc (2005); and *Bove v Italy* hudoc (2005). See the summaries of the state of execution of each case in the consolidated table of cases pending for supervision of execution (available as a Word document from <http://www.coe.int/t/e/human_rights/execution/02_documents>.

[23] See eg, the cases of *Hulki Güneş v Turkey* 2003-VII; 43 EHRR 263, the subject of the Committee's interim resolutions ResDH(2005)113, ResDH(2007)26, and ResDH(2007)150; *Göçmen v Turkey* hudoc (2006); and *Söylemez v Turkey* hudoc (2006). In all three, the Court found violations in respect of the fairness of criminal proceedings at the conclusion of which the applicants were sentenced to lengthy terms of imprisonment. The relevant Turkish legislation on re-opening did not apply to the Court judgments which became final before 4 February 2003 or judgments rendered in applications lodged with the Court after that date. The applicants, having lodged their applications in 1995, 1999, and 2002 respectively, were not covered by the law. In adopting the last-mentioned interim resolution in the *Hulki Güneş* case (ResDH(2007)150) (and taking note of the *Göçmen* and *Söylemez* cases), the Committee found that the continuation of the present situation would amount to a manifest breach of Turkey's obligations and strongly urged the Turkish authorities 'to remove promptly the legal lacuna preventing the reopening of domestic proceedings'.

[24] *Dorigo v Italy*, Final Resolution CM/ResDH(2007)83, 20 June 2007.

A third group of cases where difficulties have arisen (and continue to do so) in different contracting parties concern Article 2 judgments where the Court has found that the state failed to conduct an effective investigation in breach of its positive obligation under that Article. The Committee has taken the position that the authorities of the state have a continuing obligation to carry out an effective investigation and that this is part of their obligation to take appropriate individual measures to execute the Court's judgment. The assessment of whether an effective investigation can be carried out can be a difficult one. First, domestic authorities may have to amend their procedures for investigations if these were found to be at fault in the Court's judgment and second, there are likely to be practical difficulties in performing such an investigation years after the Court's judgment and many more years after the events which gave rise to the need for such an investigation in the first place.[25]

Repetitive groups of case may also pose logistical problems for the Committee's supervision of individual measures, since each case has to be individually examined. One such problem area at present are cases brought against a number of East European states concerning the failure or serious delay of the domestic authorities or state companies to implement final decisions of domestic courts, which can often involve substantial assets.[26] After the Court's judgments in these cases (which can number in the hundreds), the Committee has to begin the process of individually examining each case to see whether any further steps have been taken at the domestic level, such as whether writs of execution have been issued, whether debtor's assets can be found and transferred to successful litigants, and so on. These can be time-consuming processes involving arcane questions of domestic commercial law, which, it is suggested, is not the best use of the Committee's time and which could be avoided by contracting parties taking the necessary steps of their own volition as well as taking appropriate general measures towards ensuring effective implementation of their own domestic courts' decisions and the right to respect for property rights.

Not all the Committee's work on individual measures concerns such repetitive and mundane matters. New human rights problems will bring new problems for execution. Environmental rights, for example, have become more prominent in the Court's case law and the individual measures needed can be of some scale and complexity. They may also be closely related to the general measures the state must take. For example in *Fadeyeva v Russia*[27] and *Ledyayeva and others v Russia*[28] the Court found violations of Article 8 because of the impact of pollution from a steelworks on the applicants' private and family life. The individual measures currently under examination include rehousing the applicants outside the area affected by the pollution, but also, and this is related to the general measures simultaneously under examination, measures that would prevent or minimize

---

[25] The problem has arisen in several contexts. First, in six judgments on the action of security forces in Northern Ireland: *McKerr v UK* 2001-III; 34 EHRR 553, and others, see, *inter alia*, Interim Resolution CM/ResDH(2007)73 and Committee of Ministers Information Document CM/Inf/DH(2008)2, 22 February 2008, 'Cases concerning the action of security forces in Northern Ireland' (a memorandum prepared by the Secretariat). Second, in Bulgaria with the execution of *Velikova v Bulgaria* 2000-VI and ten other cases, see Interim Resolution CM/Res/DH(2007)107. Third, in the Chechen disappearance cases *Khashiyev and Akayeva v Russia* hudoc (2005); 42 EHRR 397 and others, considered in Committee of Ministers Information Document, 'Violations of the ECHR in the Chechen Republic: Russia's compliance with the European Court's judgments', 12 June 2007, CM/Inf/Dh(2006)32 revised 2.

[26] See eg, *Timofeyev v Russia* hudoc (2003); 40 EHRR 901 (and ninety-seven similar cases) and *Zhovner v Ukraine* hudoc (2004) (and 231 similar cases). The problems arising from the execution of both groups of cases are set out in the order of business for the 1020th (DH) meeting of the Committee, 4–6 March 2008, CM/Del/OT/DH(2008)1020 20 February 2008, available at the Committee's website.

[27] 2005-IV; 49 EHRR 295.   [28] Hudoc (2006).

the pollution, which appears to affect the entire town, Cherepovets, where the steelworks are based.[29]

III. GENERAL MEASURES

The third and most important step in execution is that the Committee will examine whether general measures have been adopted, preventing new violations similar to that found or putting an end to continuing violations (Rule 6(2)(b)(ii)). The need for such measures follows from the general public international law requirement that the parties to a treaty, such as the Convention, have an obligation to ensure that their law and practice conforms with it. The Rules themselves again give examples: legislative or regulatory amendments, changes of case law or administrative practice, or publication of the Court's judgment in the language of the respondent state and its dissemination to the authorities concerned. Training of state officials and other awareness-raising measures have also been considered in recent years. The assessment of whether general measures have been taken is often where the greatest part of the Committee's efforts is directed and often the principal reason for a case remaining on its agenda for some time after any just satisfaction has been afforded and individual measures taken. Questions will always remain, however, as to what extent the Committee is qualified, as a political body composed of diplomatic representatives, to assess the legal issue of whether remedial legislation or amendments to administrative practices are sufficient to comply with the terms of the Court's judgment. As Leuprecht has pointed out, the practical application of this aspect of Article 46 places a heavy responsibility on the shoulders of the Directorate General of Human Rights and Legal Affairs whose duty it is to 'assist and advise' the Committee. As he states:

> Indeed, when there is reason to doubt whether the measures taken by the state as a consequence of a Court judgment are pertinent and sufficient, there is little chance of such doubt being expressed by the representatives of other states.... This uncomfortable task is usually left to the Directorate.[30]

In the light of the numerous administrative and legislative changes that are recorded in Article 46 resolutions, it is evident that the quiet influence brought to bear by the Directorate Secretariat has been well directed. As a result, the level of state compliance with judgments of the Court is recognized to be generally good, though there are certainly more problems of enforcement than there used to be when the membership of the Council of Europe was smaller. Despite occasional hiccups which have threatened to bring the enforcement system into disrepute, the system still works and there continues to be a high rate of compliance. However, the Court is still required to give too many repetitive judgments on points of law which are the subject of well-established case law, the clearest examples of which concern the excessive length of civil or criminal proceedings in violation of Article 6(1) of the Convention. Given that such cases continue to reach the Court, one may well question whether the Committee has been sufficiently diligent in ensuring that states take appropriate general measures since one of the purposes of those measures is to prevent new violations similar to that found in a judgment of the Court.

---

[29] For an outline of the case and the measures taken and to be taken, see the Committee of Ministers Information Document CM/Inf/DH(2007)7, 13 February 2007, 'Industrial pollution in breach of the European Convention: Measures required by a European Court judgment' (a memorandum prepared by the Secretariat), available at the execution of judgments website on information documents.

[30] Leuprecht, *European System*, p 798.

Such repetitive cases aside, the greatest problem the Committee faces is in getting states to adopt remedial legislation and inordinate delays can be common. For example, it took the Belgian authorities almost eight years to introduce legislation amending 'various legal provisions relating to affiliation' in response to the *Marckx* judgment.[31] In the meantime a further application based on the previous legislation was lodged with the Commission culminating in the Court's judgment in the case of *Vermeire v Belgium* in which a further violation was found.[32] Important delays also occurred in the enforcement of the *Sporrong and Lönnroth v Sweden* judgment (six years) and that of *Norris v Ireland* (four years).[33] Finally, it took the United Kingdom seven years to execute the *Matthews* judgment, where the Grand Chamber had found a violation of Article 3 of Protocol 1 because Gibraltarians could not vote in elections to the European Parliament, albeit this delay was because of a Spanish veto to the United Kingdom's proposed change to the relevant EC provisions, causing it to remedy the situation by including Gibraltar in a metropolitan constituency in the United Kingdom.[34]

Although these instances of delay are exceptional, they raise several important questions of principle. In the first place, while it must be recognized that the amendment of national legislation may take some time and may be subject to the vagaries of national politics and busy legislative agendas, proper 'supervision' of execution of the Court judgments presupposes that the Committee take firm and resolute action with recalcitrant states. The absence at present of a more effective procedure to cajole states into making speedier legislative casts a shadow over the integrity of the enforcement system.

Taking general measures can be much more problematic for a contracting party when the problem relates to settled domestic case law even in spite of the growing trend towards the direct effect of the Convention in national legal systems. Here there can sometimes be a tension between the unitary nature of the state in international human rights law (where the state is responsible for acts of all its organs) and the difficulty in getting domestic courts to change their case law without interfering with their independence. In such cases, Ministry of Justice circulars informing courts or officials of the Strasbourg Court judgment is unlikely to suffice for the Committee to close its examination; the Committee may prefer to wait until it has clear evidence that the domestic courts have adopted a more Convention-compliant approach. For example, the matter has arisen in the context of the Committee's execution of the Court's judgments on freedom of expression in Turkey, especially convictions by state Security Courts for insulting the state or nation, which until recently were consistently upheld by the Turkish Court of Cassation. In its last examination of these cases, the Committee noted the legislative and constitutional amendments enacted by Turkey but remained concerned about retention of the criminal offence of 'incitement to violence'. While this had been interpreted in conformity with the Convention by the Court of Cassation, Security Courts, and public prosecutors in a number of decisions, there was still insufficient evidence to draw a general conclusion of consistent conformity with the Convention.[35]

The problem of ensuring that general measures are taken is almost inevitably more acute in inter-state cases. Perhaps because of the extent and number of violations the

---

[31] *Marckx v Belgium* A 31 (1979); 2 EHRR 330 PC.

[32] *Vermeire v Belgium* A 214-C (1991); 15 EHRR 488.

[33] *Sporrong and Lönnroth v Sweden* A 52 (1982); 5 EHRR 35 PC and *Norris v Ireland* A 142 (1988); 13 EHRR 186 PC.

[34] *Matthews v UK* 1999-I; 28 EHRR 361 GC; Final Resolution ResDH(2006)57, 2 November 2006.

[35] See Committee of Ministers Information Document, 'Freedom of expression in Turkey: Progress achieved—Outstanding issues', CM/Inf/DH(2008)26, 23 May 2008 at p 5.

Court found in *Cyprus v Turkey*,[36] after seven years and two interim resolutions, a number of issues remain unresolved, in particular the plight of missing persons in northern Cyprus and the home and property of displaced persons. Indeed while progress has been made in some areas[37] it seems unlikely that the Committee will be able to close its examination of the entire case soon, not least because of its legal and factual complexity which go to the roots of the political dispute between the two countries as well as its diplomatic sensitivity. The execution process is undoubtedly also complicated by the fact that the two litigants have equal weight and voice in the Committee's deliberations. Perhaps the final resolution of the human rights dimension to the Cypriot conflict is inextricable from resolution of the conflict itself.

3. THE COURT AND EXECUTION OF ITS JUDGMENTS[38]

It is still an open question whether the Committee of Ministers possesses exclusive competence in the field of enforcement. Is it open, for example, to the applicant to complain that the state is in breach of its obligations under Article 46 to abide by the Court's judgment, and would the Court have competence to examine such a claim in proceedings instituted by an individual? The former Commission made a clear statement that it had no competence as regards the supervision of the Court's judgments. Following *Sunday Times v UK (No 1)*,[39] the Contempt of Court Act 1981 was enacted. The *Sunday Times* newspaper claimed that the new Act and its subsequent interpretation by the House of Lords could not be seen as full implementation of the United Kingdom's obligation arising from the Court's judgment. A request to invite the Committee to review the matter was rejected in December 1982. The Commission rejected a fresh application by finding that it had no competence in the matter and that, after the adoption of its report under Article 31 (as it then was), 'it cannot examine subsequent developments in the case, nor can it assume any function in relation to the supervision of the Court's judgment'.[40]

The issue came before the old Court in *Olsson v Sweden (No 2)*,[41] in which it too declined to become involved in the execution process. The applicants complained that despite the Court's judgment in the first *Olsson* case (where a violation had been found concerning the implementation of a care order), the Swedish authorities had continued to prevent their reunion with their children.[42] The Court considered that no separate issue arose under former Article 53 (now Article 46) since the fresh complaint raised a new issue which had not been determined by the *Olsson* judgment. Writing extra-judicially, Judge Martens forcefully argued that complaints under former Article 53 should not be decided by the Committee of Ministers but by the Court since: (i) the interpretation of its own judgments was better left to the Court than to a gathering of professional diplomats who were not necessarily trained lawyers possessing the qualifications required for judicial

[36] (*Fourth Inter-State case*) 2001-IV; 35 EHRR 731 GC.

[37] The Committee has so far closed its examination of the issues raised in the judgment concerning military courts, the living conditions of Greek Cypriots in northern Cyprus, as regards secondary education, the censorship of schoolbooks, and freedom of religion (see the Order of Business for the 1028th (DH) meeting, 3–5 June 2008 at p 110).

[38] For a general survey of the Court's own role in execution, see Wildhaber, in Dupuy *et al*, eds, *Völkrrecht als Wertordnung/Common Values in International Law: Festschrift für/Essays in Honour of Christian Tomuschat*, 2006.

[39] A 30 (1979); 2 EHRR 245.   [40] *Times Newspapers Ltd v UK No 10243/83*, 41 DR 123 at 129 (1985).
[41] A 250 (1992); 17 EHRR 134.   [42] *Olsson v Sweden (No 1)* A 130 (1988); 11 EHRR 259 PC.

office; and (ii) the Committee could not be regarded as a 'tribunal': its members were under the direct authority of their internal administration; the representative of the state concerned was not excluded from the deliberations and could even vote; the Committee might be unable to reach a decision because of the requirements of a two-thirds majority; it sat in private and applicants were excluded from participation in its proceedings.[43]

Those arguments remain valid under the present system. A further argument in support of Judge Martens' position is that the Convention does not provide for sanctions against a respondent state for non-execution of a judgment. It is thus imperative that the question of non-execution be examined and authoritatively determined. However, the Court's approach *in Olsson (No 2)* has been vigorously defended by Judge Ryssdal:

> The correct approach in Convention logic was to determine, as the Court did in *Olsson (No 2)*, whether the further interference that occurred with the Olssons' family life in the later period was itself justified under Article 8—rather than first investigating whether the later facts complained of were in some way or another a consequence of the execution or non-execution of the first *Olsson* judgment. Indeed I even have some doubts as to whether the statement in *Olsson (No 2)* that no separate issue arises under [former] Article 53 was necessary. Was there any issue at all under [former] Article 53?[44]

The matter arose again in *Verein gegen Tierfabriken Schweiz (VgT) v Switzerland*,[45] which the Court considered the second application of an animal rights group which had been prevented from showing a television commercial. In its first judgment of 28 June 2001,[46] the Court had held that the Swiss authorities' refusal to broadcast the commercial in question was in violation of Article 10 of the Convention. On 1 December 2001, on the basis of that judgment, the applicant association applied to the Federal Court for revision of the final domestic judgment prohibiting the commercial from being broadcast. On 29 April 2002 the Federal Court refused that request. The Committee of Ministers was not informed that the Federal Court had refused the request for revision and had accordingly ended its examination of the first judgment by adopting a resolution in July 2003. However, that resolution noted the possibility of lodging a request for revision with the Federal Court. The applicant association therefore brought a second application in July 2002, complaining about the continued prohibition on broadcasting the television commercial in question. The Swiss government argued that the application was incompatible *ratione materiae* with the Convention since the Federal Court's judgment did not raise any new issue that had not been determined in the Strasbourg Court's judgment and the Committee of Ministers had discharged its duty in adopting its resolution. The Court rejected that argument. It found a respondent state was free to choose the means by which it discharged its obligation under Article 46 of the Convention and the Court could not assume any role in the dialogue between the state and the Committee in this respect. The Convention did not give the Court jurisdiction to direct a state to hold a new trial or to quash a conviction and it thus could not find a state to be in breach of the Convention on account of its failure to take either of those courses of action when faced with the execution of one of its judgments. However, this was not to say that measures taken by a respondent state in the post-judgment phase to afford redress to an applicant for the violation or violations found fell outside the jurisdiction of the Court. There was nothing to prevent it from examining a subsequent application raising a new issue undecided by the judgment. The Federal Court's later judgment was such a new issue that was capable

---

43 Martens, *Schermers Collection*, Vol III, pp 253–92.
44 Ryssdal, *Schermers Symposium Proceedings*, pp 49–69.
45 Hudoc (2007).   46 *Vgt Verein gegen Tierfabriken v Switzerland* 2001-VI; 34 EHRR 159.

of giving rise to a fresh interference. On the merits, it found that the interference was a violation of Article 10.

While it is clear that the second application might have been avoided if the Committee had been informed of the Federal Court's judgment in good time, it may be argued that it was not necessary for the Court to enter into the question of Article 46 in its second judgment.[47] Since the applicant's complaint was under the same Article of the Convention and related to the same commercial, the only matter for the Court was whether the refusal to broadcast the commercial was a continuing violation or whether, subject to the six-month rule, there was a new violation justifying a second application. The outcome may well have been the same but could have been considered under the Court's well-established admissibility case law rather than the decidedly more sensitive area of Article 46. On the other hand, the failure to comply with the Court's first judgment raises starkly the issue of whether there has been a distinct violation of Article 46 and whether it is politic for the Court to identify this issue as the central one in the case. The case has since been referred to the Grand Chamber, which hopefully will provide some guidance on the matter.

In any event, it may well be a different matter when the second application concerns an earlier judgment where the Court itself expressly indicated individual or general measures under Articles 41 and/or 46 of the Convention and the second application is a complaint made under either of those two Articles rather than a re-invocation of the substantive Article that was the subject of the first application. The Court has been called upon to answer this question in *Ivanţoc, Popa and others v Moldova and Russia*,[48] a follow-up application to the Grand Chamber judgment in *Ilaşcu, Ivanţoc, Leşco and Petrov-Popa v Moldova and Russia*.[49] There the Court found a number of violations of the Convention arising from the trial, conviction, and continuing detention of the applicants in Transdniestria, found Moldova and Russia to be responsible and found that they were to take all necessary measures to put an end to the arbitrary detention of the applicants still imprisoned and secure their immediate release. This was not forthcoming and in a series of interim resolutions the Committee of Ministers had deplored the lack of progress made by Russia in securing the release of the applicants whilst commending Moldova on the efforts it had made. The applicants, still in detention, brought a second application alleging that their detention was still unlawful and that the failure of both states to comply with their obligations to secure their release was a breach of Article 46. The application has been communicated to both states and a judgment is expected soon.[50]

Whatever the outcome of this particular case, it remains at least arguable that the Convention system ought to be able to examine and rule on a claim that a contracting party is in violation of its obligations under Article 46 by either failing to give effect to the Court's judgment or introducing corrective measures which are insufficient. This, it is suggested, remains the case, even though Protocol 14 provides for the possibility of the Committee of Ministers referring the question to the Court for precisely such a judgment. It may be argued that the creation of this remedy by the contracting states *ipso iure* means they did not intend there to be any other means of seizing the Court of the question, ie by the applicants themselves referring the matter to the Court through an ordinary application. There is some force in this argument, but in reply it is equally possible to say that the Court has been willing to find violations of other Articles in Section II of the Convention (eg a violation of Article 34 when a state does not abide by a Rule 39

[47] See eg, *Mehemi v France (No 2)* 2003-IV; 38 EHRR 16.
[48] Hudoc (2008).   [49] 2004-VII; 40 EHRR 1030 GC.
[50] The case proceedings to date are summarized in the Court's Information Note no 84 at p 32, available from the Court's website.

indication and a violation of Article 38 when it fails to furnish all necessary facilities to the Court in the context of a fact-finding investigation) when such a possibility was never expressly foreseen or authorized by the contracting states. The same possibility should apply, *mutatis mutandis* to Article 46.

Thus it may be argued that where the breach resides in a clear-cut refusal to comply (eg to introduce individual and/or general measures) it falls, under the scheme of the Convention, to the Committee of Ministers under Article 46 to take cognizance of such refusal. However, the Court's jurisdiction could perhaps be asserted when it has become clear, for example, from a persistent refusal that there has been a *déni de justice*. Nevertheless, where the case concerns a continuing situation (as in access, custody, or other child care cases), where the facts continue to evolve after the Court has given judgment, it may be more appropriate to examine the new situation on its merits. In any event, it is not difficult to imagine cases where Article 46 ought to have a bearing on the level of just satisfaction awarded.

As has been noted above, despite the possibility of a finding of a breach of Article 46, no sanctions against a respondent state for non-execution are specifically provided for under the Convention. But the Statute of the Council of Europe provides that a serious violation of the principles of the rule of law and human rights may lead to a state having its right of representation suspended and being requested by the Committee of Ministers to withdraw from the Council of Europe (Articles 8 and 3 of the Statute).[51] The likelihood, however, of such a severe sanction being employed for non-compliance with a judgment of the Court is remote.

4. PROTOCOL 14

Were Protocol 14 to enter into force, some of the greatest changes to the Convention system would come in field of execution of the Court's judgments. The rationale for introducing these changes is one of the main reasons for the Protocol in the first place: the need to guarantee the long-term effectiveness of the Court, particularly confronting the problem of the excessive case-load. The explanatory report to the Protocol states:

> Rapid and adequate execution has, of course, an effect on the influx of new cases: the more rapidly general measures are taken by states Parties to execute judgments which point to a structural problem, the fewer repetitive applications there will be.[52]

The Protocol takes two concrete steps to this end through the addition of three more paragraphs to Article 46 (paragraphs (3)–(5)). First, the new Article 46(3) would empower the Committee of Ministers to ask the Court to interpret a final judgment, for the purpose of facilitating the supervision of its execution. The justification for this change is, as stated in the explanatory report to the Protocol,[53] that in the Committee of Ministers'

---

[51] The only relevant instance is the case of Greece which, after the military *coup d'état* in 1967, dramatically withdrew from the organization when it was evident that the Committee would vote to expel her. It returned in 1974 after the restoration of civilian rule. See Magliveras, *Exclusion from Participation in International Organisations: the Law and Practice Behind Member States' Expulsion and Suspension of Membership* 1999, pp 79–87.

[52] Explanatory Report (available at <http://conventions.coe.int/Treaty/EN/Reports/Html/194.htm>) at para 16. See above, pp 863–7.

[53] Id, para 96. The decision to refer the matter to the Court would require a majority vote of two-thirds of the representatives entitled to sit on the Committee; this requirement is said by the explanatory report to show that the Committee of Ministers should 'use this possibility sparingly, to avoid over-burdening the Court'.

execution, difficulties are sometimes encountered due to disagreement as to the interpretation of judgments. Any interpretation by the Court would settle 'any argument' concerning a judgment's exact meaning.[54] The explanatory report also makes clear that the aim of the new paragraph 3 would be to enable the Court to give an interpretation of a judgment, not to pronounce on the measures taken by a High Contracting Party to comply with that judgment.[55] The Court would also be free to decide on the manner and form in which it wished to reply to the request.[56] Secondly, the new paragraph 4 of Article 46 would allow the Committee, if it considered that a High Contracting Party had refused to abide by a final judgment, to refer to the Court the question whether that Party had failed to fulfil its obligation under paragraph 1 to abide by the judgment.[57] This is a controversial change, not least because the Court itself, in its comments on the final drafts of the Protocol did not support it; its argument was that significant legal and practical questions were unanswered by the change.[58] Nonetheless, the change was adopted and the explanation for it is that the parties to the Convention have a collective duty to preserve the Court's authority.[59] The 'infringement proceedings' would be heard by the Grand Chamber (the Protocol would add new Article 31(b) of the Convention to effect this) but would not re-open the question of the violation found in the initial judgment or lead to the award of further compensation. The political pressure of such proceedings was thought to suffice and the final sanction remains suspension of voting rights in the Committee or expulsion from the Council under Article 8 of the Statute. In the event that the Court were to find a violation of Article 46(1), it would refer the case to the Committee of Ministers 'for consideration of the measures to be taken', pursuant to Article 46(5). In the event that the Court were to find no violation, it is to refer the case to the Committee of Ministers, 'which shall close its examination of the case' (the same Article).

It is unlikely, but not inconceivable, that the Committee would ever make use of this new power, not least because under new Article 46(4) the decision to do so would require a two-thirds majority in the Committee. However, the instances of lengthy non-compliance set out above make it at least possible that the Committee would consider this option. There are, of course, difficulties with asking the Court to undertake an assessment of whether a judgment has been executed. Clearly, the Court's task would be easier if in the original judgment it had itself indicated under Article 46 what measures (either individual or general) might be required of a state. If it had not indicated such measures, it might nonetheless be easier for it to decide if individual measure had been taken. But the task is more complicated if the Court is asked to assess whether general measures taken by a

[54] *Ibid.*

[55] Nor would there be any time limit for making such a request since the question of interpretation could arise at any time during the Committee of Ministers' examination of the execution of the judgment.

[56] It would normally be for the formation of the Court which delivered the original judgment to rule on the question of interpretation. *Ibid.*

[57] The Committee is required to serve formal notice on the state in question of the intention to make the reference.

[58] The Court stated: 'As regards the legal issues, the status of the procedure is not entirely clear. What would be the procedural rights of the respondent state? What form would the decision finding a violation take? Who would represent the Committee of Ministers before the Court? What would be the basis for making a finding of violation? Would this not raise questions of interpretation of the initial judgment? Would this not confuse the existing clear distinction between the political/executive branch of the Council of Europe and its judicial branch?...In practical terms, there might be difficulties in establishing the relevant facts. In the rare cases of refusal to comply as a matter of principle as opposed to undue delays in the legislative process, would it actually make a difference? Would the necessary two-thirds majority be achievable?' See 'Response of the European Court of Human Rights to the CDDH Interim Activity Report prepared following the 46th Plenary Administrative Session on 2 February 2004', CDDH-GDR (2004)001 at paras 29 and 30.

[59] Id, para 98.

state are sufficient to meet its obligation under Article 46(1) since this is inevitably a more open-ended and prospective analysis, though as Judge Martens pointed out,[60] one which a court is better equipped to take.

If the Protocol were adopted, both interpretation and infringement proceedings could be of crucial importance for pilot judgments where no friendly settlement had taken place. By definition pilot judgments require states to take general measures of a structural nature and in addition, these cases tend to be high profile so the Committee is likely to take a greater interest in ensuring prompt execution. If there is a dispute between the Committee and the state as to the measures that should be adopted in order to remedy any systemic problem the Court has found, then the Committee may be more inclined to refer the question to the Court. It is thought that it is more likely that the Committee would first bring interpretation proceedings but if a state is dilatory in its response, in pilot judgments that could affect hundreds of applicants, infringement proceedings may be a useful tool for the Committee to employ as a way of assisting or encouraging the state to introduce key reforms. Interestingly though, under the current system the nature of a pilot judgment gives the Court a greater stake in the execution process since if there are many follow-up applications already registered when it delivers a pilot judgment, it will only strike out all those follow-up cases when it is satisfied that the state has created a national remedy to address the problem and the follow-up applications can be 'repatriated'.[61]

5. CONCLUSION

The criticisms of the role of the Committee of Ministers under Article 46 have, at times, been strident. Commentators have expressed their dissatisfaction with a system which entrusts an essentially political body with the task of taking quasi-judicial decisions under Article 46. Nevertheless it is reflective of the maturing of the Convention system that the role of the Committee has been progressively limited by successive amending protocols to the Convention. In its favour, the record of the Committee of Ministers under Article 46, judged by the wealth of legal reform that it has presided over, can be seen as more than satisfactory. The fact that its own authority as a political institution is involved in this process may in fact make it well suited to perform such a role. This perhaps provides an important insight into its success. However, further consideration will need to be given to the establishment of procedures which deal with the episodic problem of delay in introducing remedial legislation, as well as the often complex issues concerning the adequacy and sufficiency of such measures when measured against the judgment of the Court that has provoked them. Consideration should also be given to the manner in which the Committee seeks to enforce pilot judgments since the implementation of such far-reaching judgments raises more complex problems concerning necessary reform than ordinary judgments. The use of national human rights institutions or the good offices of the Council's Commissioner for Human Rights or even outside legal experts to engage the state authorities in discussion as to the nature of the legal reforms required are ideas which reflect the important 'execution' dimension of the pilot judgment procedure and which merit further reflection.[62]

[60] See n 43 above.

[61] See *Broniowski v Poland* 2005-IX; 43 EHRR 1 GC and *Hutten-Czapska v Poland* hudoc (2008) GC.

[62] See Fribergh, 'Pilot judgments from the Court's perspective', Colloquy 'Towards stronger implementation of the European Convention on Human Rights at national level' Stockholm, 9–10 June 2008 and O'Boyle, 2008 EHRLR 1.

Equally the handling of the *Cyprus v Turkey* and *Ilascu v Moldova and Russia* cases demonstrate the limits of a system of execution that is, in the final analysis, inter-governmental and thus dependent on the will of sovereign states. There is perhaps also a tendency in such politically sensitive cases to deal with them as political questions and not, as they should be seen, as legal or rule of law questions relating to the execution of a binding court judgment. This is the natural gravitation of a political body and may also be inevitable given the intractable nature of the underlying political problems reflected in some cases. Unfortunately, apart from raising questions concerning compliance with Article 46, it reveals the limits of the concept of collective enforcement under the Convention in disputes concerning allegations of widespread violations, damages the reputation of the Committee, and undermines the integrity of the Convention system as a whole.

INDEX